Lecture Notes in Computer Science

Lecture Notes in Artificial Intelligence 16017
Founding Editor

Jörg Siekmann

Series Editors

Randy Goebel, *University of Alberta, Edmonton, Canada*
Wolfgang Wahlster, *DFKI, Berlin, Germany*
Zhi-Hua Zhou, *Nanjing University, Nanjing, China*

The series Lecture Notes in Artificial Intelligence (LNAI) was established in 1988 as a topical subseries of LNCS devoted to artificial intelligence.

The series publishes state-of-the-art research results at a high level. As with the LNCS mother series, the mission of the series is to serve the international R & D community by providing an invaluable service, mainly focused on the publication of conference and workshop proceedings and postproceedings.

Rita P. Ribeiro · Bernhard Pfahringer ·
Nathalie Japkowicz · Pedro Larrañaga ·
Alípio M. Jorge · Carlos Soares ·
Pedro H. Abreu · João Gama
Editors

Machine Learning and Knowledge Discovery in Databases

Research Track

European Conference, ECML PKDD 2025
Porto, Portugal, September 15–19, 2025
Proceedings, Part V

Editors
Rita P. Ribeiro
University of Porto
Porto, Portugal

Bernhard Pfahringer
University of Waikato
Hamilton, Waikato, New Zealand

Nathalie Japkowicz
American University
Washington, D.C, WA, USA

Pedro Larrañaga
Technical University of Madrid
Boadilla del Monte, Madrid, Spain

Alípio M. Jorge
Departamento de Ciência de Computadores
University of Porto
Porto, Portugal

Carlos Soares
University of Porto
Porto, Portugal

João Gama
University of Porto
Porto, Portugal

Pedro H. Abreu
University of Coimbra
Coimbra, Portugal

ISSN 0302-9743 ISSN 1611-3349 (electronic)
Lecture Notes in Artificial Intelligence
ISBN 978-3-032-06095-2 ISBN 978-3-032-06096-9 (eBook)
https://doi.org/10.1007/978-3-032-06096-9

LNCS Sublibrary: SL7 – Artificial Intelligence

© The Editor(s) (if applicable) and The Author(s), under exclusive license to Springer Nature Switzerland AG 2026

This work is subject to copyright. All rights are solely and exclusively licensed by the Publisher, whether the whole or part of the material is concerned, specifically the rights of translation, reprinting, reuse of illustrations, recitation, broadcasting, reproduction on microfilms or in any other physical way, and transmission or information storage and retrieval, electronic adaptation, computer software, or by similar or dissimilar methodology now known or hereafter developed.
The use of general descriptive names, registered names, trademarks, service marks, etc. in this publication does not imply, even in the absence of a specific statement, that such names are exempt from the relevant protective laws and regulations and therefore free for general use.
The publisher, the authors and the editors are safe to assume that the advice and information in this book are believed to be true and accurate at the date of publication. Neither the publisher nor the authors or the editors give a warranty, expressed or implied, with respect to the material contained herein or for any errors or omissions that may have been made. The publisher remains neutral with regard to jurisdictional claims in published maps and institutional affiliations.

This Springer imprint is published by the registered company Springer Nature Switzerland AG
The registered company address is: Gewerbestrasse 11, 6330 Cham, Switzerland

If disposing of this product, please recycle the paper.

Preface

The 2025 edition of the European Conference on Machine Learning and Principles and Practice of Knowledge Discovery in Databases (ECML PKDD 2025) was held in the vibrant city of Porto, Portugal on September 15–19, 2025. This marks a significant return of the conference to Porto, following successful editions in 2005 and 2015, underscoring the city's enduring appeal as a hub for scientific exchange.

The annual ECML PKDD conference stands as a premier worldwide platform dedicated to showcasing the latest advancements and fostering insightful discussions in the fields of machine learning and knowledge discovery in databases. Held jointly since 2001, ECML PKDD has firmly established its reputation as the leading European conference in these disciplines. It provides researchers and practitioners with an unparalleled opportunity to exchange knowledge, share innovative ideas, and explore the latest technical advancements. Furthermore, the conference deeply values the synergy between foundational theoretical advances and groundbreaking practical data science applications, actively encouraging contributions that demonstrate how Machine Learning and Data Mining are being effectively employed to address complex real-world challenges.

A Hub for Responsible AI and Cutting-Edge Research

As the technological landscape continues to evolve and societal needs shift, the conference remains committed to adapting to and reflecting these dynamic changes. This year's event saw a robust engagement from the global research community with a substantial increase in the number of submissions.

The three main conference days were organised into five distinct tracks:

- The Research Track received an impressive number of 924 submissions, with 226 papers ultimately accepted, reflecting a highly competitive acceptance rate of 24.5%.
- The Applied Data Science Track received a total of 299 submissions, accepting 74 papers, resulting in an acceptance rate of 24.7%.
- The Journal Track continued to bridge the gap between conference and journal publications, accepting 43 papers (27 for the Machine Learning journal and 16 for the Data Mining and Knowledge Discovery journal) out of 297 submissions.
- The Nectar Track, focusing on recent scientific advances at the frontier of machine learning and data mining, received 30 submissions.
- The Demo Track showcased practical applications and prototypes, accepting 15 papers from a total of 30 submissions.

These proceedings cover the papers accepted in the Research and Applied Data Science tracks.

The high quality and diversity of the accepted papers across all tracks underscore the continued vitality and intellectual breadth of the machine learning and data mining communities. We extend our sincere gratitude to all authors for their valuable contributions, to the program committee members and reviewers for their diligent efforts in ensuring the rigorous double-blind review process, and to the organising committee for their tireless work in making ECML PKDD 2025 a resounding success. We believe these proceedings will serve as a valuable resource, inspiring future research and innovation in these rapidly advancing fields.

This year's conference featured seven insightful keynote talks that focused on crucial and emerging areas within Responsible AI, including trustworthy AI, interpretability, and explainability. The keynotes also explored fundamental theoretical issues, covering causality, neural-symbolic systems, large language models (LLMs), and AI for science. We were honoured to host leading experts who shared their valuable perspectives:

- Cynthia Rudin (Duke University) presented on "Many Good Models Lead to ...";
- Elias Bareinboim (Columbia University) discussed "Towards Causal Artificial Intelligence";
- Francisco Herrera (University of Granada) addressed "Not Just a Trend: Institutionalizing XAI for Responsible and Compliant AI Systems";
- Mirella Lapata (University of Edinburgh) explored "Compositional Intelligence: Coordinating Multiple LLMs for Complex Tasks";
- Nuria Oliver (ELLIS Alicante Foundation, Spain) spoke on "Towards a Fairer World: Uncovering and Addressing Human and Algorithmic Biases";
- Pedro Domingos (University of Washington) shared insights on "A Simple Unification of Neural and Symbolic AI"; and
- Sašo Džeroski (Jožef Stefan Institute, Slovenia) presented on "Artificial Intelligence for Science".

Fostering Diversity and Inclusion

Our Diversity and Inclusion initiative proudly awarded 10 scholarship grants of €500 to early-career researchers. These grants enabled individuals from developing countries and communities underrepresented in science and technology to attend the conference, present their work, and become integral members of the ECML PKDD community.

Acknowledging Our Contributors and Supporters

We extend our sincere gratitude to everyone who contributed to making ECML PKDD 2025 such a success. Our heartfelt thanks go to the authors, workshop and tutorial organisers, and all participants for their valuable scientific contributions.

An outstanding conference program would not be possible without the immense dedication and substantial time investment from our area chairs, program committee, and organising committee. The smooth execution of the event was also largely due to the hard work of our many volunteers and session chairs. A special acknowledgement goes to the local organisers for meticulously handling every detail, making the conference a truly memorable experience.

Finally, we are incredibly grateful for the generous financial support from our wonderful sponsors. We also appreciate Springer's ongoing support and Microsoft's provision of their CMT software for conference management, as well as their continued assistance. Our sincere thanks also go to the ECML PKDD Steering Committee for their invaluable advice and guidance over the past two years.

September 2025

João Gama
Pedro H. Abreu
Alípio M. Jorge
Carlos Soares
Rita P. Ribeiro
Pedro Larrañaga
Nathalie Japkowicz
Bernhard Pfahringer
Inês Dutra
Mykola Pechenizkiy
Sepideh Pashami
Paulo Cortez

Organization

Honorary Chair

Pavel Brazdil — University of Porto, Portugal

General Chairs

João Gama — University of Porto, Portugal
Pedro H. Abreu — University of Coimbra, Portugal
Alípio M. Jorge — University of Porto, Portugal
Carlos Soares — University of Porto, Portugal

Research Track Program Chairs

Bernhard Pfahringer — University of Waikato, New Zealand
Nathalie Japkowicz — American University, USA
Pedro Larrañaga — Technical University of Madrid, Spain
Rita P. Ribeiro — University of Porto, Portugal

Applied Data Science Track Program Chairs

Inês Dutra — University of Porto, Portugal
Mykola Pechenisky — TU Eindhoven, The Netherlands
Paulo Cortez — University of Minho, Portugal
Sepideh Pashami — Halmstad University, Sweden

Journal Track Chairs

Ana Carolina Lorena — Instituto Tecnológico de Aeronáutica, Brazil
Arlindo Oliveira — Instituto Superior Técnico, Portugal
Concha Bielza — Technical University of Madrid, Spain
Longbing Cao — Macquarie University, Australia
Tiago Almeida — Federal University of São Carlos, Brazil

Nectar Track Chairs

Ricard Gavaldà   Amalfi Analytics, Spain
Riccardo Guidotti   University of Pisa, Italy

Demo Track Chairs

Arian Pasquali   Faktion, Belgium
Nuno Moniz   University of Notre Dame, USA

Local Chairs

Bruno Veloso   University of Porto, Portugal
Rita Nogueira   INESC TEC, Portugal
Shazia Tabassum   INESC TEC, Portugal

Workshop Chairs

Irena Koprinska   University of Sydney, Australia
João Mendes Moreira   University of Porto, Portugal
Paula Branco   University of Ottawa, Canada

Tutorial Chairs

Alicia Troncoso   Universidad Pablo de Olavide, Spain
Nikolaj Tatti   University of Helsinki, Finland

PhD Forum Chairs

Raquel Sebastião   Polytechnic Institute of Viseu, Portugal
Yun Sing Koh   University of Auckland, New Zealand

Awards Committee Chairs

André Carvalho   University of São Paulo, Brazil
Amparo Alonso-Betanzos   University of A Coruña, Spain
Katharina Morik   TU Dortmund, Germany
Vítor Santos Costa   University of Porto, Portugal

Proceedings Chairs

João Vinagre   European Commission (JRC), Spain
Miriam Santos   University of Porto, Portugal
Shazia Tabassum   INESC TEC, Portugal

Diversity and Inclusion Chairs

Inês Sousa   Fraunhofer, Portugal
Zahraa Abdallah   University of Bristol, UK

Discovery Challenge Chairs

Carlos Ferreira   Polytechnic Institute of Porto, Portugal
Peter van der Putten   Leiden University, The Netherlands
Rui Camacho   University of Porto, Portugal

Panel Chairs

Pedro H. Abreu   University of Coimbra, Portugal
Paula Brito   University of Porto, Portugal

Publicity Chair

Carlos Ferreira   Polytechnic Institute of Porto, Portugal

Sponsorship Chairs

Mariam Berry	BNP Paribas, France
Nuno Moutinho	University of Porto, Portugal
Rui Teles	Accenture, Portugal

Social Media Chairs

Luis Roque	ZAAI.ai, Portugal
Ricardo Pereira	University of Coimbra, Portugal
Dalila Teixeira	Creative Matter, USA

Web Chair

Thiago Andrade	University of Porto, Portugal

Senior Program Committee – Research Track

Adam Jatowt	University of Innsbruck, Austria
Andrea Passerini	University of Trento, Italy
Anthony Bagnall	University of Southampton, UK
Arno Knobbe	Leiden University, Netherlands
Arno Siebes	Universiteit Utrecht, Netherlands
Arto Klami	University of Helsinki, Finland
Bernhard Pfahringer	University of Waikato, New Zealand
Bettina Berendt	TU Berlin, Germany
Celine Robardet	INSA Lyon, France
Celine Vens	KU Leuven, Belgium
Cesar Ferri	Universitat Politècnica Valencia, Spain
Charalampos Tsourakakis	Boston University, USA
Chedy Raissi	Inria, France
Chen Gong	Nanjing University of Science and Technology, China
Danai Koutra	University of Michigan, USA
Dimitrios Gunopulos	University of Athens, Greece
Donato Malerba	Università degli Studi di Bari Aldo Moro, Italy
Dragi Kocev	Jožef Stefan Institute, Slovenia
Dunja Mladenic	Jožef Stefan Institute, Slovenia
Eirini Ntoutsi	Universität der Bundeswehr München, Germany

Emmanuel Müller	TU Dortmund, Germany
Ernestina Menasalvas	Universidad Politécnica de Madrid, Spain
Esther Galbrun	University of Eastern Finland, Finland
Evaggelia Pitoura	University of Ioannina, Greece
Evangelos Papalexakis	University of California, Riverside, USA
Fabio A. Stella	University of Milano-Bicocca, Italy
Fabrizio Costa	Exeter University, UK
Fragkiskos Malliaros	CentraleSupélec, France
Georg Krempl	Utrecht University, Netherlands
Georgiana Ifrim	University College Dublin, Ireland
Gustavo Batista	University of New South Wales, Australia
Heikki Mannila	Aalto University, Finland
Hendrik Blockeel	KU Leuven, Belgium
Henrik Bostrom	KTH Royal Institute of Technology, Sweden
Henry Gouk	University of Edinburgh, UK
Ioannis Katakis	University of Nicosia, Cyprus
Jan N. Van Rijn	LIACS, Leiden University, Netherlands
Jefrey Lijffijt	Ghent University, Belgium
Jerzy Stefanowski	Poznań University of Technology, Poland
Jesse Davis	KU Leuven, Belgium
Jesse Read	Ecole Polytechnique, France
Jessica Lin	George Mason University, USA
Jesus Cerquides	IIIA-CSIC, Spain
Jilles Vreeken	CISPA Helmholtz Center for Information Security, Germany
João Gama	INESC TEC - LIAAD, Portugal
Jörg Wicker	University of Auckland, New Zealand
José Hernández-Orallo	Universitat Politècnica de Valencia, Spain
Junming Shao	University of Electronic Science and Technology of China, China
Kai Puolamaki	University of Helsinki, Finland
Manfred Jaeger	Aalborg University, Denmark
Marius Kloft	TU Kaiserslautern, Germany
Marius Lindauer	Leibniz University Hannover, Germany
Mark Last	Ben-Gurion University of the Negev, Israel
Matthias Renz	University of Kiel, Germany
Matthias Schubert	Ludwig-Maximilians-Universität München, Germany
Michele Lombardi	University of Bologna, Italy
Michèle Sebag	LISN CNRS, France
Nathalie Japkowicz	American University, USA
Paolo Frasconi	Università degli Studi di Firenze, Italy

Parisa Kordjamshidi — Michigan State University, USA
Pasquale Minervini — University of Edinburgh, UK
Pauli Miettinen — University of Eastern Finland, Finland
Pedro Larrañaga — Technical University of Madrid, Spain
Peer Kroger — Christian-Albrechts-Universität Kiel, Germany
Peter Flach — University of Bristol, UK
Ricardo B. Prudencio — Universidade Federal de Pernambuco, Brazil
Rita P. Ribeiro — University of Porto and INESC TEC, Portugal
Salvatore Ruggieri — University of Pisa, Italy
Sebastijan Dumancic — TU Delft, Netherlands
Sibylle Hess — TU Eindhoven, Netherlands
Sicco Verwer — Delft University of Technology, Netherlands
Siegfried Nijssen — Université catholique de Louvain, Belgium
Sophie Fellenz — RPTU Kaiserslautern-Landau, Germany
Stefano Ferilli — University of Bari, Italy
Stratis Ioannidis — Northeastern University, USA
Szymon Jaroszewicz — Polish Academy of Sciences, Poland
Tijl De Bie — Ghent University, Belgium
Ulf Brefeld — Leuphana University of Lüneburg, Germany
Varvara Vetrova — University of Canterbury, New Zealand
Wannes Meert — KU Leuven, Belgium
Wei Ye — Tongji University, China
Wenbin Zhang — Florida International University, USA
Willem Waegeman — Universiteit Gent, Belgium
Wouter Duivesteijn — Technische Universiteit Eindhoven, Netherlands
Xiao Luo — University of California, Los Angeles, USA
Yun Sing Koh — University of Auckland, New Zealand
Zied Bouraoui — CRIL CNRS and Université d'Artois, France

Senior Program Committee – Applied Data Science Track

Albrecht Zimmermann — Université de Caen Normandie, France
Andreas Hotho — University of Würzburg, Germany
Anirban Dasgupta — IIT Gandhinagar, India
Anna Monreale — University of Pisa, Italy
Annalisa Appice — University of Bari Aldo Moro, Italy
Bruno Cremilleux — Université de Caen Normandie, France
Carlotta Domeniconi — George Mason University, USA
Dejing Dou — BCG, USA
Fabio Pinelli — IMT Lucca, Italy
Fuzhen Zhuang — Beihang University, China

Gabor Melli	PredictionWorks, USA
Giuseppe Manco	ICAR-CNR, Italy
Glenn Fung	Independent Researcher, USA
Grzegorz Nalepa	Jagiellonian University, Poland
Hui Xiong	Hong Kong University of Science and Technology (Guangzhou), China
Inês Dutra	University of Porto, Portugal
Ioanna Miliou	Stockholm University, Sweden
Ira Assent	Aarhus University, Denmark
Jiayu Zhou	Michigan State University, USA
Jiliang Tang	Michigan State University, USA
Jingrui He	University of Illinois at Urbana-Champaign, USA
João Gama	INESC TEC - LIAAD, Portugal
Jose A. Gamez	Universidad de Castilla-La Mancha, Spain
Ke Liang	National University of Defense Technology, China
Kurt Driessens	Maastricht University, Netherlands
Lars Kotthoff	University of Wyoming, USA
Liang Sun	Alibaba Group, China
Martin Atzmueller	Osnabrück University and DFKI, Germany
Michael R. Berthold	KNIME, Germany
Michelangelo Ceci	University of Bari, Italy
Min-Ling Zhang	Southeast University, China
Mykola Pechenizkiy	TU Eindhoven, Netherlands
Myra Spiliopoulou	Otto-von-Guericke-Universität Magdeburg, Germany
Niklas Lavesson	Blekinge Institute of Technology, Sweden
Nikolaj Tatti	Helsinki University, Finland
Panagiotis Papapetrou	Stockholm University, Sweden
Paolo Frasconi	Università degli Studi di Firenze, Italy
Paulo Cortez	University of Minho, Portugal
Peggy Cellier	INSA Rennes, IRISA, France
Rayid Ghani	Carnegie Mellon University, USA
Sahar Asadi	King (Microsoft), UK
Sandeep Tata	Google, USA
Sepideh Pashami	Halmstad University, Sweden
Slawomir Nowaczyk	Halmstad University, Sweden
Sriparna Saha	IIT Patna, India
Thomas Liebig	TU Dortmund, Germany
Thomas Seidl	LMU Munich, Germany
Tom Diethe	AstraZeneca, UK
Tony Lindgren	Stockholm University, Sweden

Vincent S. Tseng — National Yang Ming Chiao Tung University, Taiwan
Vítor Santos Costa — Universidade do Porto, Portugal
Xingquan Zhu — Florida Atlantic University, USA
Yi Chang — Jilin University, China
Yinglong Xia — Meta, USA
Yongxin Tong — Beihang University, China
Yun Sing Koh — University of Auckland, New Zealand
Zhaochun Ren — Shandong University, China
Zheng Wang — Alibaba DAMO Academy, China
Zhiwei (Tony) Qin — Lyft, USA

Program Committee – Research Track

Christoph Bergmeir — Monash University, Australia
A. K. M. Mahbubur Rahman — Independent University, Bangladesh
Abdulhakim Qahtan — Utrecht University, Netherlands
Abhishek A. — Fujitsu Research, India
Acar Tamersoy — Microsoft, USA
Ad Feelders — Universiteit Utrecht, Netherlands
Adam Goodge — I2R, A*STAR, Singapore
Adele Jia — China Agricultural University, China
Adem Kikaj — KU Leuven, Belgium
Aditya Mohan — Leibniz Universität Hannover, Germany
Ajay A. Mahimkar — AT&T, USA
Akka Zemmari — Université de Bordeaux, France
Akshay Sethi — MasterCard, USA
Alborz Geramifard — Meta, USA
Alessandro Antonucci — IDSIA, Switzerland
Alessandro Melchiorre — Johannes Kepler University Linz, Austria
Alexander Dockhorn — Leibniz University Hannover, Germany
Alexander Schiendorfer — Technische Hochschule Ingolstadt, Germany
Alexander Schulz — CITEC, Bielefeld University, Germany
Alexandre Termier — Université de Rennes 1, France
Alexandre Verine — Ecole Normale Supérieure - PSL, France
Alexandru C. Mara — Ghent University, Belgium
Ali Ayadi — University of Strasbourg, France
Ali Ismail-Fawaz — IRIMAS, Université de Haute-Alsace, France
Alicja Wieczorkowska — Polish-Japanese Academy of Information Technology, Poland
Alipio M. G. Jorge — INESC TEC/University of Porto, Portugal

Alireza Gharahighehi	KU Leuven, Belgium
Alistair Shilton	Deakin University, Australia
Alneu A. Lopes	University of São Paulo, Brazil
Alper Demir	Izmir University of Economics, Turkey
Alvaro Figueira	CRACS and Universidade do Porto, Portugal
Amal Saadallah	TU Dortmund, Germany
Aman Chadha	Stanford University and Amazon, USA
Amer Krivosija	TU Dortmund, Germany
Amir H. Payberah	KTH Royal Institute of Technology, Sweden
Ammar Shaker	NEC Laboratories Europe, Europe
Ana Rita Nogueira	INESC TEC, Portugal
Anand Paul	Louisiana State University HSC, USA
Anastasios Gounaris	Aristotle University of Thessaloniki, Greece
Andre V. Carreiro	Fraunhofer Portugal AICOS, Portugal
André C. P. L. F. de Carvalho	University of São Paulo, Brazil
Andrea Cossu	University of Pisa, Italy
Andrea Mastropietro	University of Bonn, Germany
Andrea Pugnana	University of Trento, Italy
Andrea Tagarelli	DIMES - UNICAL, Italy
Andreas Bender	LMU Munich, Germany
Andreas Nürnberger	Otto-von-Guericke-Universität Magdeburg, Germany
Andreas Schwung	Fachhochschule Südwestfalen, Germany
Andrei Paleyes	University of Cambridge, UK
Andrzej Skowron	University of Warsaw, Poland
Andy Song	RMIT University, Australia
Angelica Liguori	ICAR-CNR, Italy
Anirban Dasgupta	IIT Gandhinagar, India
Anke Meyer-Baese	Florida State University, USA
Anna Beer	University of Vienna, Austria
Anna Krause	Universität Wurzburg and Chair X Data Science, Germany
Anna Monreale	University of Pisa, Italy
Annelot W. Bosman	Universiteit Leiden, Netherlands
Antoine Caradot	Hubert Curien Laboratory, France
Antonio Bahamonde	University of Oviedo, Spain
Antonio Mastropietro	Università di Pisa, Italy
Antonio Pellicani	Università degli Studi di Bari, Aldo Moro, Italy
Antonis Matakos	Aalto University, Finland
Antti Laaksonen	University of Helsinki, Finland
Aomar Osmani	LIPN-UMR CNRS, France
Aonghus Lawlor	University College Dublin, Ireland

Aparna S. Varde	Montclair State University, USA
Apostolos N. Papadopoulos	Aristotle University of Thessaloniki, Greece
Aritra Konar	KU Leuven, Belgium
Arjun Roy	Freie Universität Berlin, Germany
Arthur Charpentier	UQAM, Canada
Arunas Lipnickas	Kaunas University of Technology, Lithuania
Atsuhiro Takasu	National Institute of Informatics, Japan
Aurora Esteban	University of Cordoba, Spain
Baosheng Zhang	Tsinghua University, China
Barbara Toniella Corradini	University of Florence and University of Siena, Italy
Bardh Prenkaj	Technical University of Munich, Germany
Barry O'Sullivan	University College Cork, Ireland
Beilun Wang	Southeast University, China
Benjamin Halstead	University of Auckland, New Zealand
Benjamin Paassen	Bielefeld University, Germany
Benjamin Quost	Université de Technologie de Compiègne, France
Benoit Frenay	University of Namur, Belgium
Bernardo Moreno Sanchez	University of Helsinki, Finland
Bernhard Pfahringer	University of Waikato, New Zealand
Bertrand Cuissart	University of Caen, France
Bin Liu	Chongqing University of Posts and Telecommunications, China
Bin Shi	Xi'an Jiaotong University, China
Bin Wu	Zhengzhou University, China
Bin Zhou	National University of Defense Technology, China
Bitao Peng	Guangdong University of Foreign Studies, China
Bo Kang	Ghent University, Belgium
Bogdan Cautis	Université Paris-Saclay, France
Bojan Evkoski	Central European University, Hungary
Boshen Shi	Institute of Computing Technology, Chinese Academy of Sciences, China
Boualem Benatallah	Dublin City University, Ireland
Brandon Gower-Winter	Utrecht University, Netherlands
Bunil K. Balabantaray	NIT Meghalaya, India
Carlos Ferreira	INESC TEC, Portugal
Carlos Monserrat-Aranda	Universitat Politècnica de Valencia, Spain
Carson K. Leung	University of Manitoba, Canada
Catarina Silva	University of Coimbra, Portugal
Cecile Capponi	Aix-Marseille University, France
Celine Rouveirol	LIPN Université de Sorbonne Paris Nord, France

Cesar H. G. Andrade	Porto University, Portugal
Chandrajit Bajaj	University of Texas, Austin, USA
Chang Rajani	University of Helsinki, Finland
Charlotte Laclau	Polytechnique Institute, Télécom Paris, France
Charlotte Pelletier	Université de Bretagne du Sud, France
Chen Wang	DATA61, CSIRO, Australia
Cheng Cheng	Carnegie Mellon University, USA
Cheng Xie	Yunnan University, China
Chenglin Wang	East China Normal University, China
Chenwang Wu	University of Science and Technology of China, China
Chiara Pugliese	IIT Institute of National Research Council, Italy
Chien-Liang Liu	National Chiao Tung University, Taiwan
Chihiro Maru	Chuo University, Japan
Chongsheng Zhang	Henan University, China
Christian Beecks	FernUniversität in Hagen, Germany
Christian M. M. Frey	University of Technology Nuremberg, Germany
Christian Hakert	TU Dortmund, Germany
Christine Largeron	LabHC Lyon University, France
Christophe Rigotti	INSA Lyon, France
Christophe Rodrigues	DVRC Pôle universitaire Léonard de Vinci, France
Christos Anagnostopoulos	University of Glasgow, UK
Christos Diou Harokopio	University of Athens, Greece
Chuan Qin	Chinese Academy of Sciences, China
Chunchun Chen	Tongji University, China
Chunyao Song	Nankai University, China
Claire Nedellec	INRAE, MaIAGE, France
Claudio Borile	CENTAI Institute, Italy
Claudio Gallicchio	University of Pisa, Italy
Claudius Zelenka	Kiel University, Germany
Colin Bellinger	NRC and Dalhousie University, Canada
Collin Leiber	Aalto University, Finland
Cong Qi	New Jersey Institute of Technology, USA
Congfeng Cao	University of Amsterdam, Netherlands
Corrado Loglisci	Università degli Studi di Bari, Aldo Moro, Italy
Cuicui Luo	University of Chinese Academy of Sciences, China
Cuneyt G. Akcora	University of Central Florida, USA
Cynthia C. S. Liem	Delft University of Technology, Netherlands
Dalius Matuzevicius	Vilnius Gediminas Technical University, Lithuania

Dan Li	Sun Yat-sen University, China
Danai Koutra	University of Michigan, USA
Dang Nguyen	Deakin University, Australia
Daniel Neider	TU Dortmund, Germany
Daniel Schlor	Universität Würzburg, Germany
Danil Provodin	TU Eindhoven, Netherlands
Danyang Xiao	Sun Yat-sen University, China
Dario Garcia-Gasulla	Barcelona Supercomputing Center (BSC), Spain
Dario Garigliotti	University of Bergen, Norway
Darius Plonis	Vilnius Gediminas Technical University, Lithuania
Dariusz Brzezinski	Poznań University of Technology, Poland
David Gomez	Universidad Politecnica de Madrid, Spain
David Holzmüller	University of Stuttgart, Germany
David Q. Sun	Apple, USA
Davide Evangelista	University of Bologna, Italy
Debo Cheng	University of South Australia, Australia
Deepayan Chakrabarti	University of Texas at Austin, USA
Deng-Bao Wang	Southeast University, China
Denilson Barbosa	University of Alberta, Canada
Denis Huseljic	University of Kassel, Germany
Denis Lukovnikov	Ruhr-Universität Bochum, Germany
Destercke Sebastien	UTC, France
Di Jin	TikTok, USA
Di Wu	Chongqing Institute of Green and Intelligent Technology, Chinese Academy of Sciences, China
Diana Benavides Prado	University of Auckland, New Zealand
Dianhui Wang	Independent Researcher, Australia
Diego Carrera	STMicroelectronics, Switzerland
Diletta Chiaro	Università degli Studi di Napoli Federico II, Italy
Dimitri Staufer	TU Berlin, Germany
Dimitrios Katsaros	University of Thessaly, Greece
Dimitrios Rafailidis	University of Thessaly, France
Dino Ienco	INRAE, France
Dmitry Kobak	University of Tübingen, Germany
Domenico Redavid	University of Bari, Italy
Dominik M. Endres	Philipps-Universität Marburg, Germany
Dominique Gay	Université de La Réunion, France
Dong Li	Baylor University, USA
Duarte Folgado	Fraunhofer Portugal AICOS, Portugal
Duo Xu	Georgia Institute of Technology, USA

Edoardo Serra	Boise State University, USA
Edouard Fouche	Karlsruhe Institute of Technology (KIT), Germany
Eduardo F. Montesuma	Université Paris-Saclay, France
Edward Apeh	Bournemouth University, UK
Edwin Simpson	University of Bristol, UK
Ehsan Aminian	INESC TEC, Portugal
Ekaterina Antonenko	Mines Paris - PSL, France
Eliana Pastor	Politecnico di Torino, Italy
Emanuela Marasco	George Mason University, USA
Emilio Dorigatti	LMU Munich, Germany
Emilio Parrado-Hernandez	Universidad Carlos III de Madrid, Spain
Emmanouil Krasanakis	CERTH, Greece
Emmanouil Panagiotou	Freie Universität Berlin, Germany
Emre Gursoy	Koc University, Turkey
Engelbert Mephu Nguifo	Université Clermont Auvergne, CNRS, LIMOS, France
Eran Treister	Ben-Gurion University of the Negev, Israel
Erasmo Purificato	Otto-von-Guericke Universität Magdeburg, Germany
Erik Novak	Jožef Stefan Institute, Slovenia
Erwan Le Merrer	Inria, France
Esra Akbas	Georgia State University, USA
Esther-Lydia Silva-Ramirez	Universidad de Cadiz, Spain
Evaldas Vaičiukynas	Kaunas University of Technology, Lithuania
Evangelos Kanoulas	University of Amsterdam, Netherlands
Evelin Amorim	INESC TEC, Portugal
Fabian C. Spaeh	Boston University, USA
Fabio Fassetti	Università della Calabria, Italy
Fabio Fumarola	Prometeia, Italy
Fabio Mercorio	University of Milan-Bicocca, Italy
Fabio Vandin	University of Padova, Italy
Fandel Lin	University of Southern California, USA
Federica Granese	Inria, Université Côte d'Azur, France
Federico Baldo	University of Bologna, Italy
Federico Sabbatini	National Institute for Nuclear Physics (INFN), Italy
Feifan Zhang	China Agricultural University, China
Felipe Kenji Nakano	KU Leuven, Belgium
Fernando Martinez-Plumed	Universitat Politècnica de Valencia, Spain
Filipe Rodrigues	Technical University of Denmark (DTU), Denmark

Flavio Giobergia	Politecnico di Torino, Italy
Florent Masseglia	Inria, France
Florian Beck	JKU Linz, Austria
Florian Lemmerich	University of Passau, Germany
Francesca Naretto	University of Pisa, Italy
Francesco Piccialli	University of Naples Federico II, Italy
Francesco Renna	Universidade do Porto, Portugal
Francisco Pereira	DTU, Denmark
Franco Raimondi	Gran Sasso Science Institute, Italy
Frederic Koriche	Université d'Artois, CRIL CNRS, France
Frederic Pennerath	CentraleSupélec - LORIA, France
Furong Peng	Shanxi University, China
Gabriel Marques Tavares	LMU Munich, Germany
Gabriele Sartor	University of Turin, Italy
Gabriele Venturato	KU Leuven, Belgium
Gaetan De Waele	Ghent University, Belgium
Gaia Saveri	University of Trieste, Italy
Gang Li	Deakin University, Australia
Gaoyuan Du	Amazon, USA
Gavin Smith	University of Nottingham, UK
Geming Xia	National University of Defense Technology, China
Geng Zhao	Heidelberg University, Germany
Gennaro Vessio	University of Bari Aldo Moro, Italy
Geoffrey I. Webb	Monash, Australia
Georgia Baltsou	Centre for Research & Technology, Greece
Geraldin Nanfack	Concordia University, Canada
Germain Forestier	University of Haute Alsace, France
Gerrit Grossmann	DFKI, Germany
Gerrit J. J. van den Burg	Alan Turing Institute, UK
Gherardo Varando	Universitat de Valencia, Spain
Giacomo Medda	University of Cagliari, Italy
Gilberto Bernardes	INESC TEC and University of Porto, Portugal
Giorgio Venturin	University of Padova, Italy
Giovanna Castellano	University of Bari Aldo Moro, Italy
Giovanni Ponti	ENEA, Italy
Giovanni Stilo	Università degli Studi dell'Aquila, Italy
Gisele Pappa	UFMG, Brazil
Giuseppe Manco	ICAR-CNR, IT, Italy
Gizem Gezici	Scuola Normale Superiore, Italy
Gjergji Kasneci	TU Munich, Germany
Goreti Marreiros	ISEP/GECAD, Portugal

Graziella De Martino	University of Bari, Aldo Moro, Italy
Grazina Korvel	Vilnius University, Lithuania
Grigorios Tsoumakas	Aristotle University of Thessaloniki, Greece
Guangyin Jin	National University of Defense Technology, China
Guangzhong Sun	University of Science and Technology of China, China
Guanjin Wang	Murdoch University, Australia
Guilherme Weigert	Cassales University of Waikato, New Zealand
Guillaume Derval	UC Louvain - ICTEAM, Belgium
Guorui Quan	University of Manchester, UK
Guoxi Zhang	Beijing Institute of General Artificial Intelligence, China
Gustau Camps-Valls	Universitat de Valencia, Spain
Gustav Sir	Czech Technical University, Czech Republic
Gustavo Batista	University of New South Wales, Australia
Hachem Kadri	Aix-Marseille University, France
Hadi Asghari	Humboldt Institute for Internet and Society, Germany
Haifeng Sun	University of Science and Technology of China, China
Haihui Fan	Institute of Information Engineering, Chinese Academy of Sciences, China
Haizhou Du	Shanghai University of Electric Power, China
Hajer Salem	AUDENSIEL, France
Hakim Hacid	TII, United Arab Emirates
Hamid Bouchachia	Bournemouth University, UK
Han Wang	Xidian University, China
Hang Yu	Shanghai University, China
Hanna Sumita	Institute of Science Tokyo, Japan
Hao Niu	KDDI Research, Japan
Hao Xue	University of New South Wales, Australia
Hao Yan	Carleton University, Canada
Haowen Zhang	Zhejiang Sci-Tech University, China
Harsh Borse	IIT Kharagpur, India
Heitor M. Gomes	Victoria University of Wellington, New Zealand
Helder Oliveira	FCUP and INESC TEC, Portugal
Helge Langseth	Norwegian University of Science and Technology, Norway
Hendrik Blockeel	KU Leuven, Belgium
Henrique O. Marques	University of Southern Denmark, Denmark
Henryk Maciejewski	Wroclaw University of Science and Technology, Poland

Hideaki Ishibashi	Kyushu Institute of Technology, Japan
Hilde J. P. Weerts	Eindhoven University of Technology, Netherlands
Holger Froening	University of Heidelberg, Germany
Holger Karl	HPI, Germany
Hongbo Bo	University of Bristol, UK
Hongyang Chen	Zhejiang Lab, China
Hua Chu	Xidian University, China
Huaiyu Wan	Beijing Jiaotong University, China
Huaming Chen	University of Sydney, Australia
Huandong Wang	Tsinghua University, China
Huanlai Xing	Southwest Jiaotong University, China
Hui Ji	University of Pittsburgh, USA
Hui (Wendy) Wang	Stevens Institute of Technology, USA
Huiping Chen	University of Birmingham, UK
Humberto Bustince	Universidad Publica de Navarra, Spain
Huong Ha	RMIT University, Australia
Idir Benouaret	Epita Research Laboratory, France
Ines Sousa	Fraunhofer AICOS, Portugal
Ingo Thon	Siemens AG, Germany
Inigo Jauregi Unanue	University of Technology Sydney, Australia
Ioannis Sarridis	Centre for Research & Technology, Greece
Issam Falih	Université Clermont Auvergne, CNRS, LIMOS, France
Ivan Vankov	iris.ai, Norway
Ivor Cribben	University of Alberta, Canada
Jaemin Yoo	KAIST, South Korea
Jakir Hossain	University at Buffalo, USA
Jakub Klikowski	Wroclaw University of Science and Technology, Poland
Jalaj Bhandari	Columbia University, USA
Jaleed Khan	University of Oxford, UK
James Goulding	University of Nottingham, UK
Jan Kalina	Czech Academy of Sciences, Czech Republic
Jan P. Mielniczuk	Polish Academy of Sciences, Poland
Jan Ramon	Inria, France
Jan Verwaeren	Ghent University, Belgium
Jannis Brugger	TU Darmstadt, Germany
Jean-Marc Andreoli	Naverlabs Europe, Netherlands
Jedrzej Potoniec	Poznań University of Technology, Poland
Jeronimo Arenas-Garcia	Universidad Carlos III de Madrid, Spain
Jhony H. Giraldo	Télécom Paris, Institut Polytechnique de Paris, France

Jia Cai	Guangdong University of Finance and Economics, China
Jiahui Jin	Southeast University, China
Jiang Zhong	Independent Researcher, China
Jianwu Wang	University of Maryland, Baltimore County, USA
Jiawei Chen	Tianjin University, China
Jiaxin Ding	Shanghai Jiao Tong University, China
Jidong Yuan	Beijing Jiaotong University, China
Jie Song	Zhejiang University, China
Jie Wu	Fudan University, China
Jie Yang	University of Wollongong, China
Jimeng Shi	Florida International University, USA
Jin Chen	Hong Kong University of Science and Technology, China
Jin Liang	South China Normal University, China
Jing Ren	NUDT, China
Jing Wang	Amazon, USA
Jinghui Zhong	South China University of Technology, China
Jingtao Ding	Tsinghua University, China
Jinli Zhang	Beijing University of Technology, China
Jiri Sima	Czech Academy of Sciences, Czech Republic
João Gama	University of Porto, Portugal
Joao Mendes-Moreira	University of Porto, Portugal
Joao Vinagre	European Commission (JRC), Spain
Joaquim Silva	NOVA LINCS, Universidade Nova de Lisboa, Portugal
Jochen De Weerdt	KU Leuven, Belgium
Joe Mellor	University of Edinburgh, UK
Johanne Cohen	LISN-CNRS, France
Johannes Jakubik	IBM Research, USA
John W. Sheppard	Montana State University, USA
Jonata Tyska Carvalho	Federal University of Santa Catarina, Brazil
Jordi Guitart	Barcelona Supercomputing Center (BSC), Spain
Joris Mattheijssens	Ghent University, Belgium
Jose M. Costa Pereira	University of Porto, Portugal
Jose Oramas	University of Antwerp, sqIRL/IDLab, imec, Belgium
Jose Tomas Palma	University of Murcia, Spain
Joydeep Chandra	Indian Institute of Technology, Patna, India
Juan A. Botia	University of Murcia, Spain
Juan Rodriguez	Universidad de Burgos, Spain
Jukka Heikkonen	University of Turku, Finland

Julien Delaunay	Inria, France
Julien Ferry	Polytechnique Montreal, Canada
Julien Perez	EPITA, France
Jun Zhuang	Boise State University, USA
Jun Yu Hou	Nanjing University, China
Junbo Zhang	JD Intelligent Cities Research, USA
Junze Liu	University of California, Irvine, USA
Jurgita Kapočiūtė-Dzikienė	Tilde SIA, University of Latvia and Tilde IT, Vytautas Magnus University, Lithuania
Justina Mandravickaitė	Vytautas Magnus University, Lithuania
Kamil Adamczewski	Max Planck Institute for Intelligent Systems, Germany
Kamil Michal Ksiazek	Jagiellonian University, Poland
Karim Radouane	Université Sorbonne Paris Nord, France
Kary Framing	Umeå University, Sweden
Katerina Taskova	University of Auckland, New Zealand
Katharina Dost	Jožef Stefan Institute, Slovenia
Kaushik Roy	University of South Carolina, USA
Kejia Chen	Nanjing University of Posts and Telecommunications, China
Ken Kobayashi	Tokyo Institute of Technology, Japan
Khaled Mohammed Saifuddin	Northeastern University, USA
Khalid Benabdeslem	Université de Lyon 1, France
Kim Thang Nguyen	LIG, University Grenoble-Alpes, France
Kira Maag	Heinrich-Heine-Universität Düsseldorf, Germany
Koji Maruhashi	Fujitsu Research, Japan
Koyel Mukherjee	Adobe Research, USA
Kristen M. Scott	KU Leuven, Belgium
Krzysztof Ruda	Polish Academy of Sciences, Poland
Krzysztof Slot	Lodz University of Technology, Poland
Kuldeep Singh	Cerence, Germany
Kushankur Ghosh	University of Alberta, Canada
Lamine Diop	EPITA, France
Latifa Oukhellou	IFSTTAR, France
Laurence Park	Western Sydney University, Australia
Laurens Devos	KU Leuven, Belgium
Len Feremans	Universiteit Antwerpen, Belgium
Lena Wiese	Goethe University Frankfurt, Germany
Lenaig Cornanguer	CISPA Helmholtz Center for Information Security, Germany
Lennert De Smet	KU Leuven, Belgium
Lev Reyzin	University of Illinois at Chicago, USA

Li Wang	National University of Defense Technology, China
Liang Du	Shanxi University, China
Lianyong Qi	China University of Petroleum (East China), China
Lijie Hu	King Abdullah University of Science and Technology, Saudi Arabia
Lijing Zhu	Bowling Green State University, USA
Lingling Zhang	Capital Normal University, China
Lingyue Fu	Shanghai Jiao Tong University, China
Linh Le Pham Van	Deakin University, Australia
Livio Bioglio	University of Turin, Italy
Lixing Yu	Yunnan University, China
Liyan Song	Harbin Institute of Technology, China
Longlong Sun	Chang'an University, China
Luca Corbucci	University of Pisa, Italy
Luca Ferragina	University of Calabria, Italy
Luca Romeo	University of Macerata, Italy
Lucas Pereira	LARSyS, Tecnico Lisboa, Portugal
Luciano Caroprese	ICAR-CNR, Italy
Ludovico Boratto	University of Cagliari, Italy
Luis Rei	Jožef Stefan Institute, Slovenia
Mahardhika Pratama	University of South Australia, Australia
Maiju Karjalainen	University of Eastern Finland, Finland
Makoto Onizuka	Osaka University, Japan
Manali Sharma	Samsung, South Korea
Maneet Singh	MasterCard, India
Manuel M. Garcia-Piqueras	Universidad de Castilla La Mancha, Spain
Manuele Bicego	University of Verona, Italy
Mao A. Cheng	University of California, Berkeley, USA
Marc Plantevit	EPITA, France
Marc Tommasi	Lille University, France
Marcel Wever	Leibniz University Hannover, Germany
Marcilio de Souto	LIFO/Université d'Orleans, France
Marco Lippi	University of Florence, Italy
Marco Loog	Radboud University, Netherlands
Marco Mellia	Politecnico di Torino, Italy
Marco Podda	University of Pisa, Italy
Marco Polignano	Università di Bari, Italy
Marco Viviani	Università degli Studi di Milano Bicocca, Italy
Maria Vasconcelos	Fraunhofer Portugal AICOS, Portugal
Maria Sofia Bucarelli	Sapienza University of Rome, Italy

Mariana Oliveira	Universidade do Porto, Portugal
Mariana Vargas Vieyra	MostlyAI, Austria
Marielle Malfante	CEA, France
Marina Litvak	Shamoon College of Engineering, Israel
Mario Antunes	Universidade de Aveiro, Portugal
Mario Andres Munoz	University of Melbourne, Australia
Marius Koppel	Johannes Gutenberg University Mainz, Germany
Mark Junjie Li	Shenzhen University, China
Marko Robnik-Sikonja	University of Ljubljana, Slovenia
Marta Soare	Université d'Orleans, France
Martin Holena	Czech Academy of Sciences, Czech Republic
Martin Pilat	Charles University, Czech Republic
Martino Ciaperoni	Aalto University, Finland
Marwan Hassani	TU Eindhoven, Netherlands
Masahiro Suzuki	University of Tokyo, Japan
Massimo Guarascio	ICAR-CNR, Italy
Matej Mihelcic	University of Zagreb, Croatia
Mathias Verbeke	KU Leuven, Belgium
Mathieu Lefort	Université de Lyon, France
Matteo Francobaldi	University of Bologna, Italy
Matteo Riondato	Amherst College, USA
Matteo Salis	University of Turin, Italy
Matthew B. Middlehurst	University of Southampton, UK
Matthia Sabatelli	University of Groningen, Netherlands
Mattia Cerrato	JGU Mainz, Germany
Mattia Setzu	University of Pisa, Italy
Mattis Hartwig	German Research Center for Artificial Intelligence, Germany
Matyas Bohacek	Stanford University, USA
Maximilian T. Fischer	University of Konstanz, Germany
Maximilian Münch	University of Applied Sciences, Würzburg-Schweinfurt, Germany
Maximilian Stubbemann	University of Hildesheim, Germany
Maximilian Thiessen	TU Wien, Austria
Maximilian von Zastrow	Southern Denmark University, Denmark
Megha Khosla	TU Delft, Netherlands
Meiyun Zuo	Renmin University of China, China
Meng Liu	National University of Defense Technology, China
Mengying Zhu	Zhejiang University, China
Michael Granitzer	University of Passau, Germany
Michael B. Ito	University of Michigan, USA

Michael G. Madden	National University of Ireland, Galway, Ireland
Michal Wozniak	Wroclaw University of Science and Technology, Poland
Michele Fontana	Università di Pisa, Italy
Michiel Stock	Ghent University, Belgium
Miguel Rocha	University of Minho, Portugal
Miguel Silva	INESC TEC, Portugal
Mike Holenderski	Eindhoven University of Technology, Netherlands
Milos Savic	University of Novi Sad, Serbia
Mina Rezaei	LMU Munich, Germany
Minh P. Nguyen	University of Texas, Austin, USA
Minyoung Choe	Korea Advanced Institute of Science and Technology, South Korea
Minyu Chen	Shanghai Jiaotong University, China
Miquel Perello-Nieto	University of Bristol, UK
Mira Kristin Jurgens	Ghent University, Belgium
Miriam Santos	University of Porto, Portugal
Mirko Bunse	TU Dortmund, Germany
Mirko Polato	University of Turin, Italy
Mitra Baratchi	LIACS, University of Leiden, Netherlands
Mohammed Elbamby	Telefonica Scientific Research, Spain
Moises Rocha dos Santos	University of Porto, Portugal
Monowar Bhuyan	Umeå University, Sweden
Morteza Rakhshaninejad	Ghent University, Belgium
Mounim A. El Yacoubi	Télécom SudParis, France
Muhammad Rajabinasab	University of Southern Denmark, Denmark
Muhao Guo	Arizona State University, USA
Mustapha Lebbah	Paris Saclay University-Versailles, France
Nabeel Hussain Syed	Rheinland-Pfälzische Technische Universität, Kaiserslautern-Landau, Germany
Nandyala Hemachandra	Indian Institute of Technology Bombay, India
Nannan Wu	Tianjin University, China
Nanqing Dong	Shanghai Artificial Intelligence Laboratory, China
Naresh Manwani	International Institute of Information Technology, Hyderabad, India
Natan Tourne	Ghent University, Belgium
Nate Veldt	Texas A&M, USA
Nathalie Japkowicz	American University, USA
Natthawut Kertkeidkachorn	Japan Advanced Institute of Science and Technology (JAIST), Japan
Ngoc-Son Vu	ENSEA, France
Nhat-Tan Bui	University of Arkansas, USA

Nian Li	Tsinghua University, China
Nick Lim	University of Waikato, New Zealand
Nico Piatkowski	Fraunhofer IAIS, Germany
Nicolas Roque dos Santos	University of São Paulo, Brazil
Niklas A. Strauss	LMU Munich, Germany
Nikolaj Tatti	Helsinki University, Finland
Nikolaos Nikolaou	University College London, UK
Nikolaos Stylianou	Information Technologies Institute, Greece
Nikos Kanakaris	University of Southern California, USA
Ning Xu	Southeast University, China
Nripsuta Saxena	University of Southern California, USA
Nuwan Gunasekara	Halmstad University, Sweden
Olga Kurasova	Vilnius University, Lithuania
Olga Slizovskaia	AstraZeneca, UK
Olivier Teste	IRIT, University of Toulouse, France
Oswald C.	NIT Trichy, India
Oswaldo Solarte-Pabon	Universidad del Valle, Colombia
Ozge Alacam	University of Bielefeld, Germany
P. S. Sastry	Indian Institute of Science, India
Pablo Olmos	Universidad Carlos III de Madrid, Spain
Panagiotis Karras	University of Copenhagen, Denmark
Panagiotis Symeonidis	University of the Aegean, Greece
Pance Panov	Jožef Stefan Institute, Slovenia
Paolo Bonetti	Politecnico di Milano, Italy
Paolo Merialdo	Università degli Studi Roma Tre, Italy
Paolo Mignone	University of Bari Aldo Moro, Italy
Pascal Welke	TU Wien, Austria
Patrick Y. Wu	American University, USA
Paul Caillon	LAMSADE Université Paris Dauphine - PSL, France
Paul Davidsson	Malmo University, Sweden
Paul Prasse	University of Potsdam, Germany
Paulo J. Azevedo	Universidade do Minho, Portugal
Pawel Teisseyre	Warsaw University of Technology, Poland
Pawel Zyblewski	Wroclaw University of Science and Technology, Poland
Pedro G. Ferreira	University of Porto, Portugal
Pedro Larrañaga	Technical University of Madrid, Spain
Pedro Ribeiro	University of Porto, Portugal
Pedro H. Abreu	CISUC, Portugal
Peijie Sun	Tsinghua University, China
Peng Wu	Shanghai Jiao Tong University, China

Pengpeng Qiao	Institute of Science Tokyo, Japan
Peter Karsmakers	KU Leuven, Belgium
Peter Schneider-Kamp	SDU, Denmark
Peter van der Putten	Leiden University, Netherlands
Petia Georgieva	University of Aveiro, Portugal
Philipp Vaeth	Technical University of Applied Sciences Würzburg-Schweinfurt and Universität Bielefeld, Germany
Philippe Preux	Inria, France
Phung Lai	SUNY-Albany, USA
Pierre Geurts	Montefiore Institute, University of Liège, Belgium
Pierre Monnin	Université Côte d'Azur, Inria, CNRS, I3S, France
Pierre Schaus	UC Louvain, Belgium
Pierre Wolinski	Paris Dauphine University - PSL, France
Pieter Robberechts	KU Leuven, Belgium
Pietro Sabatino	ICAR-CNR, Italy
Pingchuan Ma	HKUST, China
Piotr Habas	Amazon, USA
Piotr Lipinski	University of Wroclaw, Poland
Piotr Porwik	University of Silesia, Katowice, Poland
Prithwish Chakraborty	IBM Corporation, USA
Lucie Flek	Marburg University, Germany
Przemyslaw Biecek	Warsaw University of Technology, Poland
Qiang Sheng	Institute of Computing Technology, Chinese Academy of Sciences, China
Qiang Zhou	Nanjing University of Aeronautics and Astronautics, China
Rafet Sifa	Fraunhofer IAIS, Germany
Raha Moraffah	Arizona State University, USA
Raivydas Simanas	Vilnius University, Lithuania
Rajeev Rastogi	Amazon, USA
Ranya Almohsen	Baylor College of Medicine, USA
Raphael Romero	Ghent University, Belgium
Raquel Sebastiao	ESTGV-IPV & IEETA-UA, Portugal
Ravi Kolla	Sony Research India, India
Raza Ul Mustafa	Loyola University, USA
Remy Cazabet	Université de Lyon 1, France
Renhe Jiang	University of Tokyo, Japan
Reza Akbarinia	Inria, France
Ricardo P. M. Cruz	University of Porto (FEUP), Portugal
Ricardo B. Prudencio	Universidade Federal de Pernambuco, Brazil
Ricardo Rios	Federal University of Bahia, Brazil

Ricardo Santos	Fraunhofer Portugal AICOS, Portugal
Riccardo Guidotti	University of Pisa, Italy
Robertas Damasevicius	Vytautas Magnus University, Lithuania
Roberto Corizzo	American University, USA
Roberto Interdonato	CIRAD, France
Rocio Chongtay	University of Southern Denmark, Denmark
Rohit Babbar	University of Bath, UK and Aalto University, Finland
Romain Tavenard	Université de Rennes, LETG/IRISA, France
Rosana Veroneze	LBiC, Italy
Ruggero G. Pensa	University of Turin, Italy
Rui Meng	BNU-HKBU United International College, USA
Rui Yu	University of Louisville, USA
Ruixuan Liu	Emory University, USA
Runqun Xiong	Southeast University, China
Runxue Bao	University of Pittsburgh, USA
Ruochun Jin	National University of Defense Technology, China
Ruta Juozaitiene	Vytautas Magnus University, Lithuania
Rytis Maskeliunas	PolsI, Poland
Salvatore Ruggieri	University of Pisa, Italy
Sam Verboven	Vrije Universiteit Brussel, Belgium
Sangkyun Lee	Korea University, South Korea
Sara Abdali	University of California, Riverside, USA
Sarah Masud	LCS2, IIIT-D, India
Sarwan Ali	Georgia State University, USA
Satoru Koda	Fujitsu Limited, Japan
Sebastian Buschjager	Lamarr Institute for ML and AI, Germany
Sebastian Jimenez	Ghent University, Belgium
Sebastian Meznar	Jožef Stefan Institute, Ljubljana, Slovenia
Sebastian Ventura Soto	University of Cordoba, Spain
Sebastien Razakarivony	Safran, France
Selpi Selpi	Chalmers University of Technology, Sweden
Sergio Greco	University of Calabria, Italy
Sergio Jesus	Feedzai, Portugal
Sha Lu	University of South Australia, Australia
Shalini Priya	Indian Institute of Technology Patna, India
Shanqing Guo	Shandong University, China
Shaofu Yang	Southeast University, China
Shazia Tabassum	INESCTEC, Portugal
Shengxiang Gao	Kunming University of Science and Technology, China

Shichao Pei	University of Massachusetts, Boston, USA
Shin Matsushima	University of Tokyo, Japan
Shin-ichi Maeda	Preferred Networks, Japan
Shiwen Ni	Chinese Academy of Sciences, China
Shiyou Qian	Shanghai Jiao Tong University, China
Shu Zhao	Anhui University, China
Shuai Li	University of Cambridge, UK and University of Tokyo, Japan, Tsinghua University, China
Shuang Cheng	Institute of Computing Technology, Chinese Academy of Sciences, China
Shubhranshu Shekhar	Brandeis University, USA
Shurui Cao	Carnegie Mellon University, USA
Shuteng Niu	Mayo Clinic, USA
Siamak Ghodsi	Leibniz University of Hannover, Germany
Sihai Zhang	University of Science and Technology of China, China
Silvia Chiusano	Politecnico di Torino, Italy
Silviu Maniu	Université de Grenoble Alpes, France
Simon Gottschalk	L3S Research Center, Leibniz Universität Hannover, Germany
Simona Nistico	University of Calabria, Italy
Simone Angarano	Politecnico di Torino, Italy
Sinong Zhao	Nankai University, China
Siwei Wang	Intelligent Game and Decision Lab, China
Sofoklis Kitharidis	LIACS, Netherlands
Songlin Du	University of Melbourne, Australia
Songlin Du	Southeast University, China
Soumyajit Chatterjee	Nokia Bell Labs, USA
Sourav Dutta	Huawei Research Centre, China
Stefan Duffner	University of Lyon, France
Stefan Heindorf	Paderborn University, Germany
Stefan Kesselheim	Forschungszentrum Jülich, Germany
Stefano Bortoli	Huawei Research Center, China
Stefanos Vrochidis	Information Technologies Institute, CERTH, Greece
Steffen Thoma	FZI Research Center for Information Technology, Germany
Stephan Doerfel	Kiel University of Applied Sciences, Germany
Steven D. Prestwich	University College Cork, Ireland
Suman Banerjee	IIT Jammu, India
Sunil Aryal	Deakin University, Australia
Surabhi Adhikari	Columbia University, USA

Susan McKeever	TU Dublin, Ireland
Swati Swati	Universität der Bundeswehr München, Germany
Szymon Wojciechowski	Wroclaw University of Science and Technology, Poland
Talip Ucar	AstraZeneca, UK
Taro Tezuka	University of Tsukuba, Japan
Tatiana Passali	Aristotle University of Thessaloniki, Greece
Tatiane Nogueira Rios	UFBA, Brazil
Telmo M. Silva Filho	University of Bristol, UK
Teng Lin	Hong Kong University of Technology (Guangzhou), China
Teng Zhang	Huazhong University of Science and Technology, China
Thach Le Nguyen	Insight Centre, Ireland
Thang Duy Dang	Fujitsu Limited, Japan
Thanh-Son Nguyen	A*STAR, Singapore
Theresa Eimer	Leibniz University Hannover, Germany
Thiago Andrade	INESC TEC & University of Porto, Portugal
Thomas Bonald	Telecom Paris, France
Thomas Guyet	Inria, Centre de Lyon, France
Thomas Lampert	University of Strasbourg, France
Thomas L. Lee	University of Edinburgh, UK
Thomas Mortier	Ghent University, Belgium
Tianyi Chen	Boston University, USA
Tie Luo	University of Kentucky, USA
Tiehang Duan	Mayo Clinic, USA
Tijl De Bie	Ghent University, Belgium
Timilehin B. Aderinola	University College Dublin, Ireland
Timo Bertram	Johannes-Kepler Universität, Germany
Timo Ropinski	Ulm University, Germany
Tobias A. Hille	University of Kassel, Germany
Tom Hanika	University of Hildesheim, Germany
Tomas Kliegr	University of Economics, Prague, Czech Republic
Tomasz Michalak	University of Warsaw and Ideas NCBiR, Poland
Tomasz Walkowiak	Wroclaw University of Science and Technology, Poland
Tommaso Zoppi	University of Florence, Italy
Tong Li	Hong Kong University of Technology, China
Tong Mo	Peking University, China
Tongya Zheng	Hangzhou City University, China
Tonio Weidler	Maastricht University, Netherlands
Tony Lindgren	Stockholm University, Sweden

Tsunenori Mine	Kyushu University, Japan
Tuan Le	New Mexico State University, USA
Tuwe Lofstrom	Jönköping University, Sweden
Ulf Johansson	Jönköping University, Sweden
Vadim Ermolayev	Ukrainian Catholic University, Ukraine
Vahan Martirosyan	CentraleSupélec, Belgium
Vana Kalogeraki	Athens University of Economics and Business, Greece
Vanessa Gomez-Verdejo	Universidad Carlos III de Madrid, Spain
Vasileios Iosifidis	SCHUFA Holding, Germany
Vasilis Gkolemis	ATHENA RC, Greece
Victor Charpenay	Mines Saint-Etienne, France
Vincent Derkinderen	KU Leuven, Belgium
Vincent Lemaire	Orange Research, France
Vincenzo Pasquadibisceglie	University of Bari, Aldo Moro, Italy
Virginijus Marcinkevicius	Vilnius University, Lithuania
Vitor Cerqueira	University of Porto, Portugal
Vivek Kumar	Universität der Bundeswehr München, Germany
Vivek Srikumar	University of Utah, USA
Wagner Meira Jr.	UFMG, Brazil
Wei Wu	Ben Gurion University of the Negev, Israel
Weichen Li	RPTU Kaiserslautern-Landau, Germany
Weifeng Xu	Independent Researcher, China
Weike Pan	Shenzhen University, China
Weiwei Jiang	Beijing University of Posts and Telecommunications, China
Weiwei Sun	Carnegie Mellon University, USA
Weiwei Yuan	Nanjing University of Aeronautics and Astronautics, China
Weixiong Rao	Tongji University, China
Wen-Bo Xie	Southwest Petroleum University, China
Wenhao Li	Tongji University, China
Wenhao Zheng	Shopee, Singapore
Wenjie Feng	National University of Singapore, Singapore
Wenjie Xi	George Mason University, USA
Wenshui Luo	Nanjing University of Science and Technology, China
Wentao Yu	Nanjing University of Science and Technology, China
Wenzhe Yi	Wuhan University, China
Wenzhong Li	Nanjing University, China
Wojciech Rejchel	Nicolaus Copernicus University, Torun, Poland

Xi Jiang	Southern University of Science and Technology, China
Xiang Li	East China Normal University, China
Xiang Lian	Kent State University, USA
Xiao Ma	Beijing University of Posts and Telecommunications, China
Xiao Zhang	Shandong University, China
Xiaobing Zhou	Yunnan University, China
Xiaofeng Cao	University of Technology Sydney, Australia
Xiaofeng Gao	Shanghai Jiaotong University, China
Xiaojun Chen	Institute of Information Engineering, Chinese Academy of Sciences, China
Xiao-Jun Zeng	University of Manchester, UK
Xiaoming Zhang	Beihang University, China
Xiaoting Zhao	Etsy, USA
Xiaowei Mao	Beijing Jiaotong University, China
Xiaoyu Shi	Chinese Academy of Sciences, China
Xin Du	University of Edinburgh, UK
Xin Qin	California State University, Long Beach, USA
Xing Tang	Tencent, China
Xing Xing	Tongji University, China
Xinning Zhu	Beijing University of Posts and Telecommunications, China
Xinpeng Lv	National University of Defense Technology, China
Xintao Wu	University of Arkansas, USA
Xinyang Zhang	University of Illinois at Urbana-Champaign, USA
Xinyu Guan	Xi'an Jiaotong University, China
Xixun Lin	Chinese Academy of Sciences, China
Xiyue Zhang	University of Bristol, UK
Xuan-Hong Dang	IBM T.J. Watson Research Center, USA
Xue Li	University of Queensland, Australia
Xue Yan	Institute of Automation, Chinese Academy of Sciences, China
Xuefeng Chen	Chongqing University, China
Xuemin Wang	Guilin University of Electronic Technology, China
Yachuan Zhang	East China University of Science and Technology, China
Yan Zhang	Peking University, China
Yang Li	University of North Carolina at Chapel Hill, USA
Yang Shu	East China Normal University, China
Yang Wei	Nanjing University of Science and Technology, China

Yanhao Wang	East China Normal University, China
Yanmin Zhu	Shanghai Jiao Tong University, China
Yansong Y. L. Li	University of Ottawa, Canada
Yao-Xiang Ding	Nanjing University, China
Yaqi Xie	Carnegie Mellon University, USA
Yasutoshi Ida	NTT, Japan
Yaying Zhang	Tongji University, China
Ye Zhu	Deakin University, Australia
Yeon-Chang Lee	Ulsan National Institute of Science and Technology, South Korea
Yexiang Xue	Purdue University, USA
Yi Wang	Xinjiang Technical Institute of Physics and Chemistry, Chinese Academy of Sciences, China
Yifeng Gao	University of Texas, Rio Grande Valley, USA
Yilun Jin	Hong Kong University of Science and Technology, China
Yin Zhang	University of Electronic Science and Technology of China, China
Ying Chen	RMIT University, Australia
Yinsheng Li	Fudan University, China
Yong Li	Huawei European Research Center, China
Yongyu Wang	JD Logistics, China
Youhei Akimoto	University of Tsukuba/RIKEN AIP, Japan
You-Wei Luo	Sun Yat-sen University and Jiaying University, China
Yuchen Li	Baidu, China
Yuchen Yang	Harbin Institute of Technology, China
Yudi Zhang	Eindhoven University of Technology, Netherlands
Yuhao Li	University of Melbourne, Australia
Yuheng Jia	Southeast University, China
Yujia Zheng	CMU, USA
Yulong Pei	TU Eindhoven, Netherlands
Yuncheng Jiang	South China Normal University, China
Yuntao Shou	Xi'an Jiaotong University, China
Yunyun Wang	Nanjing University of Posts and Telecommunications, China
Yutong Ye	East China Normal University, China
Yuzhou Chen	University of California, Riverside, USA
Zahraa Abdallah	University of Bristol, UK
Zaineb Chelly Dagdia	UVSQ, Paris-Saclay, France
Zehua Cheng	University of Oxford, UK
Zeyu Chen	University of Auckland, New Zealand

Zhaocheng Ge	Huazhong University of Science and Technology, China
Zhe Yang	Soochow University, China
Zhen Liu	Guangdong University of Foreign Studies, China
Zheng Chen	Osaka University, Japan
Zhenghao Liu	Northeastern University, China
Zhenyu Yang	Macquarie University, Australia
Zhi Li	Tsinghua University, China
Zhichao Han	ETHZ, Switzerland
Zhihui Wang	Fudan University, China
Zhilong Shan	South China Normal University, China
Zhipeng Yin	Florida International University, USA
Zhipeng Zou	Nanjing University of Science and Technology, China
Zhiwen Xiao	Southwest Jiaotong University, China
Zhiwen Zhang	LocationMind, Japan
Zhixin Li	Guangxi Normal University, China
Zhiyong Cheng	Shandong Academy of Sciences, China
Zhong Chen	Southern Illinois University, USA
Zhong Li	Leiden University, Netherlands
Zhong Zhang	Tsinghua University, China
Zhongjing Yu	Peking University, China
Zhuang Liu	Dongbei University of Finance and Economics, China
Zhuo Cao	Forschungszentrum Jülich, Germany
Zhuoming Xie	Guangdong University of Technology, China
Zhuoqun Li	Louisiana State University, USA
Zicheng Zhao	Nanjing University of Science and Technology, China
Zichong Wang	Florida International University, USA
Zifeng Ding	University of Cambridge, UK
Ziheng Chen	Walmart, USA
Zijie J. Wang	Georgia Tech, USA
Zirui Zhuang	Beijing University of Posts and Telecommunications, China
Zixing Song	Chinese University of Hong Kong, China
Ziyu Wang	University of Tokyo, Japan
Ziyue Li	University of Cologne, Germany
Zongxia Xie	Tianjin University, China
Zongyue Li	LMU Munich, Germany
Zuojin Tang	Zhejiang University, China

List of Editors

Bernhard Pfahringer	University of Waikato, New Zealand
Nathalie Japkowicz	American University, USA
Pedro Larrañaga	Technical University of Madrid, Spain
Rita P. Ribeiro	University of Porto, Portugal
Alípio M. Jorge	University of Porto, Portugal
Carlos Soares	University of Porto, Portugal
João Gama	University of Porto, Portugal
Pedro H. Abreu	University of Coimbra, Portugal

Program Committee – Applied Data Science Track

Nasrullah Sheikh	IBM Research, USA
Aakarsh Malhotra	MasterCard, USA
Aakash Goel	Amazon, USA
Abdoulaye Sakho	Artefact, France
Abhijeet Pendyala	Ruhr-Universität Bochum, Germany
Abu Shad Ahammed	University of Siegen, Germany
Adi Lin	Didi, China
Aditya Gautam	Meta, USA
Ahmed K. Mohamed	Meta, USA
Akihiro Yoshida	Kyushu University, Japan
Akshay Sethi	MasterCard, USA
Alejandro Kuratomi	Stockholm University, Sweden
Alessandro Gambetti	Nova School of Business and Economics, Portugal
Alessandro Leite	INSA Rouen, Inria, France
Alessio Russo	Politecnico di Milano, Italy
Alex Beeson	University of Warwick, UK
Alexander Galozy	Halmstad University, Sweden
Alexander Karlsson	University of Skovde, Sweden
Alexander Kovalenko	Czech Technical University in Prague, Czech Republic
Alexey Zaytsev	Skoltech, Russia
Alina Bazarova	Forschungszentrum Jülich, Germany
Alix Lheritier	Amadeus SAS, France
Allan Tucker	Brunel University London, UK
Alvaro Figueira	CRACS and Universidade do Porto, Portugal
Aman Gulati	Amazon, USA
Amira Soliman	Halmstad University, Sweden

Ana Gjorgjevikj	Jožef Stefan Institute, Slovenia
Anders Holst	RISE SICS, Sweden
André C. P. L. F. de Carvalho	University of São Paulo, Brazil
Andrea Seveso	University of Milan-Bicocca, Italy
Andreas Bender	LMU Munich, Germany
Andreas Henelius	Independent Researcher, Finland
Andreas Holzinger	University of Natural Resources and Life Sciences, Vienna, Austria
Andrei Shelopugin	Independent Researcher, Brazil
Angelo Impedovo	Niuma, Italy
Aniket Chakrabarti	Amazon, USA
Animesh Prasad	Roku, USA
Anisio Lacerda	UFMG, Brazil
Anli Ji	Georgia State University, USA
Antoine Doucet	La Rochelle Université, France
Anton Borg	Blekinge Institute of Technology, Sweden
Antonio Bevilacqua	Meetecho, Italy
Antonis Klironomos	University of Mannheim, Germany
Aron Henriksson	Stockholm University, Sweden
Artur Chudzik	Polish-Japanese Academy of Information Technology, Poland
Arun Venkitaraman	EPFL, Switzerland
Arunabha Choudhury	ASML, Netherlands
Asem Omari	Higher Colleges of Technology, UAE
Ashman Mehra	Birla Institute of Technology and Science, India
Ashwani Rao	Amazon, USA
Asier Rodriguez	BBVA, Spain
Asma Atamna	Ruhr-Universität Bochum, Germany
Atiye Sadat Hashemi	Halmstad University, Sweden
Atul Anand Gopalakrishnan	SUNY Buffalo, USA
Avani Wildani	Emory University, USA
Aviv Rovshitz	Ben-Gurion University of the Negev, Israel
Axel Brando	Barcelona Supercomputing Center (BSC) and Universitat de Barcelona (UB), Spain
Azadeh Alavi	RMIT University, Australia
Beihong Jin	Institute of Software, China
Benoit Frenay	University of Namur, Belgium
Berkay Aydin	Georgia State University, USA
Bijaya Adhikari	University of Iowa, USA
Bin Li	Alibaba Group, China
Bo Pang	University of Auckland, New Zealand
Bogdan Ruszczak	Opole University of Technology, Poland

Bohao Qu	Agency for Science, China
Bruno Veloso	INESC TEC, FEP-UP, Portugal
Buyue Qian	Xi'an Jiaotong University, China
Camille Kurtz	Université Paris Cité, France
Cangbai Li	Guangdong University of Technology, China
Carlo Metta	ISTI CNR, Italy
Carlos N. Silla	Pontifical Catholic University of Paraná (PUCPR), Brazil
Cecile Bothorel	IMT Atlantique, France
Cesar Ferri	Universitat Politècnica Valencia, Spain
Chang Li	Apple, USA
Chang-Dong Wang	Sun Yat-sen University, China
Chaofan Li	Karlsruhe Institute of Technology, Germany
Chaoyuan Zuo	Nankai University, China
Chen Gao	Tsinghua University, China
Chen Li	Computer Network Information Center, China
Chen Zhao	Baylor University, USA
Chen-Wei Chang	Virginia Tech, USA
Chenxi Xue	Nanjing Normal University, China
Chongke Bi	Tianjin University, China
Christian M. Adriano	Hasso-Plattner Institute, Germany
Christophe Rodrigues	DVRC Pôle universitaire Léonard de Vinci, France
Chuan Li	Sorbonne University, LIPADE, France
Chunhui Zhang	Dartmouth College, USA
Cristina Soguero Ruiz	Rey Juan Carlos University, Spain
Daheng Wang	Amazon, USA
Daifeng Li	Sun Yat-sen University, China
Damien Fay	HPE Labs, Ireland
Dania Herzalla	Technology Innovation Institute, UAE
Daniel Lemire	University of Quebec (TELUQ), Canada
Daniel Trejo Banos	SDSC, USA
Daochen Zha	Rice University, USA
Dawei Cheng	Tongji University, China
Dayne Freitag	SRI International, USA
Di Yao	Institute of Computing Technology, China
Dimitris Nick Dimitriadis	Aristotle University of Thessaloniki, Greece
Diogo F. Soares	Universidade de Lisboa, Portugal
Dirk Pflueger	University of Stuttgart, Germany
Doheon Han	University of Notre Dame, USA
Dongxiang Zhang	Zhejiang University, China
Dongxiao Yu	Shandong University, China

Dugang Liu	Guangdong Laboratory of Artificial Intelligence and Digital Economy (Shenzen), China
Ece Calikus	Uppsala University, Sweden
Edwyn Brient	Thales LAS/Mines Paris PSL, France
Efstathios Stamatatos	University of the Aegean, Greece
Elaine Faria	UFU, Brazil
Elio Masciari	University of Naples, Italy
Emilie Devijver	Université Grenoble Alpes, Inria, CNRS, Grenoble INP, LIG, France
Emmanuelle Claeys	IRIT, France
Enayat Rajabi	Halmstad University, Sweden
Enda Barrett	University of Galway, Ireland
Enyan Dai	Hong Kong University of Science and Technology (Guangzhou), China
Eric Peukert	ScaDS.AI, Germany
Eric Sanjuan	Avignon University, France
Erik Frisk	Linköping University, Sweden
Eui-Hong (Sam) Han	The Washington Post, USA
Eunil Park	Sungkyunkwan University, South Korea
Fabio Carrara	CNR-ISTI, Italy
Fabiola Pereira	Federal University of Uberlandia, Brazil
Fan Yang	Rice University, USA
Fangzhao Wu	MSRA, China
Fangzhou Shi	Didi Chuxing, China
Fathima Nuzla Ismail	State University of New York, USA
Flavio Bertini	University of Parma, Italy
Francesco Dente	EURECOM, France
Francesco Guerra	University of Modena e Reggio Emilia, Italy
Francesco Scala	CNR-ICAR, Italy
Francesco Spinnato	University of Pisa, Italy
Francesco Paolo Nerini	Sapienza University of Rome, Italy
Francisco P. Romero	UCLM, Spain
Franco Maria Nardini	ISTI-CNR, Italy
Francois Schwarzentruber	ENS Lyon, France
Fudong Lin	University of Delaware, USA
Gabriel Augusto Pinheiro	UNIFESP, Brazil
Gan Sun	South China University of Technology, China
Gargi Srivastava	Rajiv Gandhi Institute of Petroleum Technology Jais, India
Giacomo Boracchi	Politecnico di Milano, Italy
Giuseppe Garofalo	DistriNet, KU Leuven, Belgium
Giuseppina Andresini	University of Bari Aldo Moro, Italy

Goran Falkman	University of Skovde, Sweden
Grzegorz Nalepa	Jagiellonian University, Poland
Guanggang Geng	Jinan University, China
Guojun Liang	Halmstad University, Sweden
Haifang Li	Baidu, China
Haina Tang	University of Chinese Academy of Sciences, China
Hancheng Ge	Amazon, USA
Hao Li	National University of Defense Technology, China
Haohui Chen	CSIRO, Australia
Haomin Yu	Aalborg University, Denmark
Haoyi Xiong	Baidu, China
Hiba Najjar	DFKI, Germany
Hillol Kargupta	Agnik, USA
Hong Zhou	Meta, USA
Hongbin Pei	Xi'an Jiao Tong University, China
Hou-Wan Long	Chinese University of Hong Kong, China
Hua Wei	Arizona State University, USA
Huaiyuan Yao	Xi'an Jiaotong University, China
Huan Song	Amazon, USA
Hubert Baniecki	University of Warsaw, Poland
Hyunsung Kim	KAIST, Fitogether, South Korea
Ibtihal El Mimouni	Inria, France
Ildar Baimuratov	L3S Research Center, Germany
Ilir Jusufi	Blekinge Institute of Technology, Sweden
Inaam Ashraf	Bielefeld University, Germany
Ines Sousa	Fraunhofer AICOS, Portugal
Iris Heerlien	Saxion, Netherlands
Isak Samsten	Stockholm University, Sweden
Ishan Verma	TCS Research, India
Ismail Hakki Toroslu	METU, Turkey
Ivan Carrera	EPN, Ecuador
Jaakko Hollmen	Stockholm University, Sweden
Jairo Cugliari	Laboratoire ERIC, France
Jakub Nalepa	Silesian University of Technology, Poland
Jelica Vasiljeivić	Hoffmann-La Roche, Switzerland
Jens Lundstrom	Halmstad University, Sweden
Jesse Davis	KU Leuven, Belgium
Jiahui Bai	Meta, USA
Jiajun Gu	Carnegie Mellon University, USA
Jiali Pan	Department of Information Management, USA

Jian Yu	Auckland University of Technology, New Zealand
Jiangbin Zheng	Westlake University, China
Jianhua Yin	Shandong University, China
Jingbo Zhou	Baidu, China
Jingjing Liu	MD Anderson Cancer Center, USA
Jingwen Shi	Michigan State University, USA
Jingxuan Wei	University of Chinese Academy of Sciences, China
Jinyoung Han	Sungkyunkwan University, South Korea
Jiue-An Yang	City of Hope Beckman Research Institute, USA
Joao R. Campos	University of Coimbra, Portugal
Jochen De Weerdt	KU Leuven, Belgium
Joe Tekli	Lebanese American University, Lebanon
Joel Ky	University of Lorraine, CNRS, Inria, France
John McCall	Robert Gordon University, UK
John Mitros	University College Dublin, Ireland
Jonas Fischer	Ruhr-Universität Bochum, Germany
Jonas Nordqvist	Linnaeus University, Sweden
Joydeep Chandra	Indian Institute of Technology Patna, India
Julian Martin Rodemann	LMU Munich, Germany
Jun Shen	University of Wollongong, Australia
Junichi Tatemura	Google, USA
Junxuan Li	Microsoft, USA
Jyun-Yu Jiang	Amazon Science, USA
Kai Wang	Shanghai Jiao Tong University, China
Kaiping Zheng	National University of Singapore, Singapore
Kaiwen Dong	University of Notre Dame, USA
Katarzyna Bozek	University of Cologne, Germany
Katerina Schindlerova	UniVie, Austria
Katharina Dost	Jožef Stefan Institute, Slovenia
Katsiaryna Mirylenka	Zalando SE, Germany
Keith Burghardt	ISI, Germany
Klaus Brinker	Hamm-Lippstadt University of Applied Sciences, Germany
Koki Kawabata	Osaka University, Japan
Korbinian Randl	Stockholm University, Sweden
Krzysztof Krawiec	Poznań University of Technology, Poland
Krzysztof Kutt	Jagiellonian University, Poland
Kwan Hui Lim	Singapore University of Technology and Design, Singapore
Lamija Lemes	University of Zenica, Bosnia & Herzegovina
Le Nguyen	University of Oulu, Finland

Lei Li	Hong Kong University of Science and Technology (Guangzhou), China
Lei Liu	York University, Canada
Li Liu	Chongqing University, China
Li Zhang	University College London, UK
Liang Tang	Google, USA
Liang Tong	NEC Labs America, USA
Liang Wang	Alibaba Group, China
Lina Yao	University of New South Wales, Australia
Lingxiao Li	Michigan State University, USA
Lingyang Chu	McMaster University, Canada
Lixin Zou	Wuhan University, China
Lluis Garcia-Pueyo	Meta, USA
Lou Salaun	Nokia Bell Labs, USA
Luca Corbucci	University of Pisa, Italy
Luca Pappalardo	ISTI, Italy
Luca Romeo	University of Macerata, Italy
Luis Ferreira	Olympus Medical Products Portugal, Portugal
Luis Miguel Matos	ALGORITMI Centre, Portugal
Lukas Grasmann	TU Wien, Austria
Lukas Pensel	Johannes Gutenberg University Mainz, Germany
Maciej Grzenda	Warsaw University of Technology, Poland
Maciej Piernik	Poznań University of Technology, Poland
Madiraju Srilakshmi	Dream Sports, India
Mads C. Hansen	A.P. Moller-Maersk, Denmark
Mahardhika Pratama	University of South Australia, Australia
Mahmoud Rahat	Halmstad University, Sweden
Man Tianxing	Jilin University, China
Manish Gupta	Microsoft, USA
Manos Papagelis	York University, Canada
Manuel Lopes	Instituto Tecnico Superior, Portugal
Manuel Portela	Universitat Pompeu Fabra, Spain
Marc Tommasi	Lille University, France
Marco Fisichella	Leibniz Universität, Hannover, Germany
Maria Riveiro	Jonkoping University, Sweden
Maria Ulan	RISE Research Institutes of Sweden, Sweden
Marian Scuturici	LIRIS, France
Marianne Clausel	IECL, France
Mario Doller	University of Applied Sciences, Kufstein, Austria
Marius Schwammle	DLR/BT, Germany
Markus Gotz	Karlsruhe Institute of Technology (KIT), Germany

Markus Leyser	Technische Universität Dresden, Germany
Martin Boldt	Blekinge Institute of Technology, Sweden
Martin Mladenov	Google, USA
Martin Vita	Institute of Physics, Czech Academy of Sciences, Czech Republic
Matthias Demant	Fraunhofer ISE, Germany
Matthias Galipaud	SDSC, Switzerland
Matthias Petri	Amazon, USA
Matthieu Latapy	CNRS, France
Maurice Van Keulen	University of Twente, Netherlands
Maxime Cordy	University of Luxembourg, Luxembourg
Maxwell J. Jacobson	Purdue University, USA
Md Nahid Hasan	Miami University, USA
Md Zia Ullah	Edinburgh Napier University, UK
Mehtab Alam Syed	CIRAD, France
Melanie Neubauer	University of Leoben, Austria
Meng Chen	Shandong University, China
Mengxuan Zhang	Australian National University, Australia
Miao Fan	NavInfo, China
Michael Bain	University of New South Wales, Australia
Michele Bernardini	Uni eCampus.It, Italy
Michiel Dhont	EluciDATA Lab of Sirris, Belgium
Mickael Coustaty	L3i Laboratory, France
Miguel Couceiro	LORIA, France
Mihaela Mitici	Utrecht University, Netherlands
Min Lee	Singapore Management University, Singapore
Min Hun Lee	Singapore Management University, Singapore
Mina Rezaei	LMU Munich, Germany
Ming Ma	Inner Mongolia University, China
Minghao Chen	Tencent, China
Mirco Nanni	CNR-ISTI Pisa, Italy
Mirjam Wattenhofer	Google, USA
Mirko Marras	University of Cagliari, Italy
Mitra Heidari	University of Melbourne, Australia
Modesto Castrillon-Santana	Universidad de Las Palmas de Gran Canaria, Spain
Mohammadmehdi Saberioon	German Research Centre for Geosciences, Germany
Mohammed Amer	Fujitsu Research of Europe, Germany
Mohammed Ghaith Altarabichi	Halmstad University, Sweden
Mojgan Kouhounestani	University of Melbourne, Australia
Moonki Hong	Sogang University, South Korea

Munira Syed	Procter & Gamble, USA
Nan Li	Microsoft, USA
Narendhar Gugulothu	TCS Research, India
Nedra Mellouli	LIASD, Portugal
Ngoc Son Le	University of Hildesheim, Germany
Niklas Lavesson	Blekinge Institute of Technology, Sweden
Niraj Kumar	Fujitsu, Japan
Nitish Kumar	MasterCard, USA
Nuno Cruz Garcia	FCUL, Portugal
Nuno R. P. S. Guimaraes	INESC TEC, University of Porto, Portugal
Nuwan Gunasekara	Halmstad University, Sweden
Pablo Picazo-Sanchez	Halmstad University, Sweden
Pablo Torrijos Arenas	Universidad de Castilla-La Mancha, Spain
Pablo Jose Del Moral Pastor	Ekkono.ai, Finland
Pan He	Auburn University, USA
Panagiotis Kanellopoulos	University of Essex, UK
Panagiotis Papadakos	FORTH-ICS, Greece
Pandey Shourya Prasad	International Institute of Information Technology, Bangalore, India
Panpan Xu	Amazon AWS, USA
Paola Velardi	Sapienza University of Rome, Italy
Paolo Cintia	Kode, Italy
Pascal Plettenberg	Intelligent Embedded Systems, Italy
Paul Boniol	Inria, France
Pavel Blinov	Sber AI Lab, Russia
Pawel Parczyk	Wroclaw University of Science and Technology, Poland
Pedro M. Ferreira	University of Lisbon, Portugal
Pedro Seber	MIT, USA
Peng Qiao	NUDT, China
Pengyuan Wang	University of Georgia, USA
Petr Olegovich Sokerin	Skoltech, Russia
Philipp Bach	University of Hamburg, Germany
Philipp Froehlich	TU Darmstadt, Germany
Philipp Schmidt	Amazon Research, USA
Philipp Zech	University of Innsbruck, Austria
Pinar Karagoz	Middle East Technical University (METU), Turkey
Ping Luo	Chinese Academy of Sciences, China
Po Yang	University of Sheffield, UK
Pop Petrica	Technical University of Cluj-Napoca, Romania
Prathap Manohar Joshi R	Zoho Corporation, India

Praveen Borra	Florida Atlantic University, USA
Praveen Paruchuri	IIIT Hyderabad, India
Qian Li	Curtin University, Australia
Qihang Yao	Georgia Institute of Technology, USA
Qiwei Han	Nova School of Business and Economics, Portugal
Quentin Duchemin	Université Gustave Eiffel, France
Radu Tudor Ionescu	University of Bucharest, Romania
Rafal Kucharski	Jagiellonian University, Poland
Rafet Sifa	Fraunhofer IAIS & University of Bonn, Germany
Ramasamy Savitha	I2R A*STAR, Singapore
Ran Yu	DSIS Research Group, Singapore
Ranga Raju Vatsavai	North Carolina State University, USA
Raphael Couturier	University of Bourgogne Franche-Comte (UBFC), France
Renato M. Assuncao	ESRI, USA
Renaud Lambiotte	University of Oxford, UK
Reuben Kshitiz Borrison	ABB, Switzerland
Reza Shirvany	Zalando SE, Germany
Ricardo R. Pereira	Feedzai, Portugal
Riccardo Rosati	Università Politecnica delle Marche, Ancona, Italy
Richard Allmendinger	University of Manchester, UK
Richard Nordsieck	XITASO GmbH IT and Software Solutions, Germany
Richi Nayak	Queensland University of Technology, Australia
Roberto Trasarti	CNR, Italy
Rogerio Luis de C. Costa	Polytechnic of Leiria, Portugal
Romain Ilbert	Huawei Paris Research Center, France
Roy Ka-Wei Lee	Singapore University of Technology and Design, Singapore
Ruilin Wang	University of Aberdeen, UK
Sabrina Gaito	Università degli Studi di Milano, Italy
Sai Karthikeya Vemuri	Computer Vision Group Jena, Italy
Saisubramaniam Gopalakrishnan	Quantiphi, USA
Sajjad Shumaly	Max-Planck-Institut for Polymer Research, Germany
Salvatore Rinzivillo	KDD Lab, ISTI, CNR, Italy
Samaneh Shafee	LASIGE, Portugal
Sandra Wissing	Fachhochschule Münster, Germany
Sarwan Ali	Georgia State University, USA
Sebastian Becker	Fraunhofer ISST, Germany

Sebastian Honel	Linnaeus University, Sweden
Selin Colakhasanoglu	Saxion University of Applied Sciences, Netherlands
Senzhang Wang	Central South University, China
Sepideh Nahali	York University, Canada
Shahrooz Abghari	Blekinge Institute of Technology, Sweden
Shahroz Tariq	CSIRO, Australia
Shang Yanlei	BUPT, China
Shen Liang	Paris Cité University, France
Shengheng Liu	Southeast University, China
Shereen Elsayed	University of Hildesheim, Germany
Shi-ting Wen	NingboTech University, China
Shiv Krishna Jaiswal	Walmart Global Tech, USA
Shoujin Wang	Macquarie University, Australia
Shuai Li	University of Cambridge, UK and University of Tokyo, UK
Shuchu Han	Capital One Financial Group, Japan
Simon F. Weinberger	EssilorLuxottica, France
Siyuan Chen	Guangzhou University, China
Snehanshu Saha	BITS Pilani Goa Campus, India
Souhaib Ben Taieb	University of Mons, Abu Dhabi
Sriparna Saha	IIT Patna, India
Stefan Rueping	Fraunhofer IAIS, Germany
Stephane Chretien	Université Lyon 2, France
Sunil Aryal	Deakin University, Australia
Susana Ladra	University of A Coruña, Spain
Szymon Bobek	Jagiellonian University, Poland
Szymon Jaroszewicz	Institute of Computer Science, Poland
Szymon Wilk	Poznań University of Technology, Poland
Tanel Tammet	Tallinn University of Technology, Estonia
Thanh Thi Nguyen	Monash University, Australia
Thiago Zangato	Université Sorbonne Paris Nord, France
Theodora Tsikrika	Information Technologies Institute, Greece
Thibault Girardin	Université Jean Monnet, France
Thomas Czernichow	Darwinlabs, Portugal
Thorsteinn Rognvaldsson	Halmstad University, Sweden
Tiago Mendes-Neves	FEUP/INESC TEC, Portugal
Tianshu Yu	Chinese University of Hong Kong (Shenzhen), China
Ting Su	Imperial College London, UK
Tingrui Qiao	University of Auckland, New Zealand
Tobias Glasmachers	Ruhr-Universität Bochum, Germany

Tomas Olsson	RISE SICS, Sweden
Tome Eftimov	Jožef Stefan Institute, Slovenia
Topon Paul	Toshiba Corporation, Japan
Tsuyoshi Okita	Kyushu Institute of Technology, Japan
Unmesh Padalkar	Dream Sports, India
Vahid Shahrivari Joghan	Utrecht University, Netherlands
Valerio Bonsignori	Unipisa, Italy
Vanessa Borst	University of Würzburg, Germany
Venkata Sai Prakash Mukkamala	Quantiphi Analytics, USA
Veselka Boeva	Blekinge Institute of Technology, Sweden
Viacheslav Komisarenko	University of Tartu, Estonia
Vikas Gupta	HPCL, India
Vinayak Gupta	University of Washington, Seattle, USA
Vincent Auriau	Artefact Research Center, France
Vincenzo Pasquadibisceglie	University of Bari, Aldo Moro, Italy
Vincenzo Scotti	KASTEL, Germany
Vinothkumar Kolluru	Stevens Institute of Technology, USA
Vladimir Mic	Aarhus University, Denmark
Wang-Zhou Dai	Nanjing University, China
Wee Siong Ng	Institute for Infocomm Research, Singapore
Wei Cheng	NEC Laboratories America, USA
Wei Li	Harbin Engineering University, China
Wei Wang	Tsinghua University, China
Wei-Peng Chen	Fujitsu Research of America, USA
Wentao Wang	Michigan State University, USA
Wentao Wu	Microsoft Research, USA
Wray Buntine	VinUniversity, Vietnam
Xianchao Wu	Nvidia, USA
Xiang Lian	Kent State University, USA
Xianli Zhang	Xi'an Jiaotong University, China
Xiaobo Jin	Xi'an Jiaotong-Liverpool University, China
Xiaofei Zhou	University of Chinese Academy of Sciences, China
Xiaofeng Gao	Shanghai Jiaotong University, China
Xiaolin Han	Northwestern Polytechnical University, China
Xin Huang	Hong Kong Baptist University, China
Xin Liu	East China Normal University, China
Xing Tang	Tencent, China
Xiuqiang He	Tencent, China
Xiuyuan Hu	Tsinghua University, China
Xueping Peng	University of Technology Sydney, Australia
Yanchang Zhao	CSIRO, Australia

Yang Guo	Xidian University Hangzhou Institute of Technology, China
Yang Song	Apple, USA
Yijun Zhao	Fordham University, USA
Yinghui Wu	Case Western Reserve University, USA
Yingzhen Lin	Harbin Institute of Technology (Shenzhen), China
Yintao Yu	University of Illinois at Urbana-Champaign, USA
Yixiang Fang	Chinese University of Hong Kong, China
Yixuan Cao	Institute of Computing Technology, China
Yizheng Huang	York University, Canada
Yongchao Liu	Ant Group, China
Yu Huang	Indiana University, USA
Yu Wang	University of Oregon, USA
Yuantao Fan	Halmstad University, Sweden
Yucheng Zhou	University of Macau, China
Yue Shi	Meta, USA
Yueyuan Zheng	Beihang University, China
Yunchuan Shi	University of Sydney, Australia
Yunjun Gao	Zhejiang University, China
Yuting Ding	Southeast University, China
Yuzhuo Li	University of Auckland, New Zealand
Zahra Kharazian	Stockholm University, Sweden
Zahra Taghiyarrenani	Halmstad University, Sweden
Zahraa Abdallah	University of Bristol, UK
Zeyi Wen	Hong Kong University of Science and Technology (Guangzhou), China
Zeyu Zhu	National University of Defense Technology, China
Zhanyu Liu	Shanghai Jiao Tong University, China
Zhaogeng Liu	Jilin University, China
Zhaohui Liang	National Library of Medicine, USA
Zhen Zhang	Shandong University, China
Zhendong Chu	Squirrel Ai Learning, China
Zheng Zhang	University of California, USA
Zhengze Li	University of Göttingen, Germany
Zhibin Gu	Hebei Normal University, China
Zhuang Liu	Dongbei University of Finance and Economics, China
Ziyu Guan	Xidian University, China
Zoltan Miklos	Université de Rennes, France
Zunlei Feng	Zhejiang University, China

Program Committee – Demo Track

Andrzej Wójtowicz	Adam Mickiewicz University, Poznań, Poland
Anna Sokol	University of Notre Dame, USA
Arian Pasquali	Faktion AI, Belgium
Bruno Veloso	INESC TEC - FEP-UP, Portugal
Chongsheng Zhang	Henan University, China
Christos Doulkeridis	University of Piraeus, Greece
Danqing Zhang	PathOnAI.org, USA
Fátima Rodrigues	INESC TEC, Portugal
Grigorii Khvatskii	University of Notre Dame, USA
Joe Germino	University of Notre Dame, USA
Jungwon Seo	University of Stavanger, Norway
Ke Li	University of Exeter, England
Manfred Jaeger	Aalborg University, Denmark
Marcin Luckner	Warsaw University of Technology, Poland
Mehwish Alam	Institut Polytechnique de Paris, France
Nuno Moniz	University of Notre Dame, USA
Tânia Carvalho	FCUP, Portugal
Vitor Cerqueira	FEUP, Portugal
Wei-Wei Du	National Yang Ming Chiao Tung University, Taiwan

Additional Reviewers

Andrea D'Angelo	Antonia Hain
Patrick Altmeyer	Md Athikul Islam
Guiseppina Adresini	Michael Ito
Vedangi Bengali	Philipp Jahn
Michele Bernardini	Rahul Kumar
Zhi Cao	Bishal Lakha
Louis Carpentier	Yuwen Liu
Alessio Cascione	Jerry Lonlac
Lilia Chebbah	Shijie Luo
Meng Ding	Francesca Naretto
Roberto Esposito	Navid Nobani
Alina Fastowski	Diego Coello de Portugal
Roger Ferrod	Joana Santos
Michele Fontana	Francesco Scala
Chang Gong	Richard Serrano
Michal Grzejdziak-Zdziarski	Nuno Silva
Paul Hahn	Francesco Spinnato

Pedro C. Vieira
Xiao Wang
Yunyun Wang
Qi Wen
Jianye Xie

Huaiyuan Yao
Yutong Ye
Obaidullah Zaland
Efstratios Zaradoukas
Nan Zhang

Sponsors

Diamond

Platinum

liv   Organization

Gold

Silver

Bronze

Other Sponsors

Partners

Keynotes

Many Good Models Leads to ...

Cynthia Rudin

Duke University, USA

Abstract. As it turns out, many good models leads to amazing things! The Rashomon Effect, coined by Leo Breiman, describes the phenomenon that there exist many equally good predictive models for the same dataset.

This phenomenon happens for many real datasets, and when it does it sparks both magic and consternation, but mostly magic. In light of the Rashomon Effect, my collaborators and I propose to reshape the way we think about machine learning, particularly for tabular data problems in the nondeterministic (noisy) setting. I'll address how the Rashomon Effect impacts (1) the existence of simple-yet-accurate models, (2) flexibility to address user preferences, such as fairness and monotonicity, without losing performance, (3) uncertainty in predictions, fairness, and explanations, (4) reliable variable importance, (5) algorithm choice, specifically, providing advanced knowledge of which algorithms might be suitable for a given problem, and (6) public policy. I'll also discuss a theory of when the Rashomon Effect occurs and why: interestingly, noise in data leads to a large Rashomon Effect. My goal is to illustrate how the Rashomon Effect can have a massive impact on the use of machine learning for complex problems in society.

Towards Causal Artificial Intelligence

Elias Bareinboim

Columbia University, USA

Abstract. While a significant portion of AI scientists and engineers believe we are on the verge of achieving highly general forms of AI, I offer a critical appraisal of this view through a causal lens. In particular, building on foundational developments in the field, I will present my perspective on the relationship between intelligence and causality – and the central role of the latter in building intelligent systems and advancing credible data science.

I frame this discussion in terms of five core capabilities that we should expect from an intelligent AI system: performing causal reasoning and articulating explanations; making precise, surgical, and sample-efficient decisions; generalizing across changing conditions and environments; generating and simulating in a causally consistent manner; and learning causal structures and variables.

In this talk, I will elaborate on this perspective and share current progress toward building causally intelligent AI systems. A more detailed discussion of this thesis is provided in my forthcoming textbook, a draft of which is available here: https://causalai-book.net/.

Not Just a Trend: Institutionalizing XAI for Responsible and Compliant AI Systems

Francisco Herrera

Granada University, Spain

Abstract. As artificial intelligence (AI) systems increasingly mediate decisions in high-stakes domains – from healthcare and finance to public policy – the demand for explainable AI (XAI) has grown rapidly. Yet many current XAI approaches remain disconnected from the practical needs of stakeholders and the requirements of emerging regulatory frameworks. This talk argues that XAI must not be treated as a passing trend or optional technical add-on, but as a foundational principle in the design and deployment of AI systems. We critically examine the state of the field, exposing the gap between model-centric explainability and stakeholder-centric accountability. In response, we propose a framework that aligns explainability with legal, ethical, and social responsibilities, emphasizing co-design with affected users, sensitivity to institutional contexts, and governance over opacity. Our goal is to advance XAI from superficial compliance toward deeply integrated transparency that fosters trust, accountability, and responsible innovation.

Compositional Intelligence: Coordinating Multiple LLMs for Complex Tasks

Mirella Lapata

University of Edinburgh, UK

Abstract. Recent years have witnessed the rise of increasingly larger and more sophisticated language models (LMs) capable of performing every task imaginable, sometimes at (super)human level. In this talk, I will argue that in many realistic scenarios, solely relying on a single general-purpose LLM is suboptimal. A single LLM is likely to underrepresent real-world data distributions, heterogeneous skills, and task-specific requirements. Instead, I will discuss multi-LLM collaboration as an alternative to monolithic generative modeling. By orchestrating multiple LLMs, each with distinct roles, perspectives, or competencies, we can achieve more effective problem-solving while being more inclusive and explainable. I will illustrate this approach through two case studies: narrative story generation and visual question answering, showing how a society of agents can collectively tackle complex tasks while pursuing complementary subgoals. Additionally, I will explore how these agent societies leverage reasoning to improve performance.

Towards a Fairer World: Uncovering and Addressing Human and Algorithmic Biases

Nuria Oliver

ELLIS Alicante Foundation, Spain

Abstract. In my talk, I will first briefly present ELLIS Alicante1, the only ELLIS unit that has been created from scratch as a non-profit research foundation devoted to responsible AI for Social Good. Next, I will provide an overview of AI with a focus on the ethical implications and limitations of today's AI systems, including algorithmic discrimination and bias. On this topic, I will present a few examples of our work on uncovering and mitigating both human and algorithmic biases with AI.

On the human front, I will present the body of work that we have carried out in the context of AI-based beauty filters that are so popular on social media. On the algorithmic front, I will explain the main approaches to address algorithmic discrimination and I will present three novel methods to achieve fairer decisions.

Tensor Logic: A Simple Unification of Neural and Symbolic AI

Pedro Domingos

University of Washington, USA

Abstract. Deep learning has achieved remarkable successes in language generation and other tasks, but is extremely opaque and notoriously unreliable. Both of these problems can be overcome by combining it with the sound reasoning and transparent knowledge representation capabilities of symbolic AI. Tensor logic accomplishes this by unifying tensor algebra and logic programming, the formal languages underlying respectively deep learning and symbolic AI. Tensor logic is based on the observation that predicates are compactly represented Boolean tensors, and can be straightforwardly extended to compactly represent numeric ones. The two key constructs in tensor logic are tensor join and project, numeric operations that generalize database join and project. A tensor logic program is a set of tensor equations, each expressing a tensor as a series of tensor joins, a tensor project, and a univariate nonlinearity applied elementwise. Tensor logic programs can succinctly encode most deep architectures and symbolic AI systems, and many new combinations.

In this talk I will describe the foundations and main features of tensor logic, and present efficient inference and learning algorithms for it. A system based on tensor logic achieves state-of-the-art results on a suite of language and reasoning tasks. How tensor logic will fare on trillion-token corpora and associated tasks remains an open question.

Artificial Intelligence for Science

Sašo Džeroski

Jožef Stefan Institute, Slovenia

Abstract. Artificial intelligence is already transforming science, with its future impact expected to be even greater. Realizing this potential requires addressing key scientific challenges, such as ensuring explainability (of models and their predictions), learning effectively from limited data, and integrating data with prior domain knowledge. It also requires the provision of support for open and reproducible science through formalizing and sharing scientific knowledge.

I will present an overview of my research on the development of AI methods suitable for use in science. These include methods for explainable machine learning – including multi-target prediction and relational learning – that deliver accurate yet interpretable models suitable for complex scientific domains. These methods have been applied in environmental science, life science and materials science. Learning from limited data is critical in science. I will discuss two complementary approaches: semi-supervised learning, which leverages unlabeled data directly, together with labeled data, and foundation models, which use representations learned from vast unlabeled data to support downstream tasks with minimal supervision, i.e., limited amounts of labeled data. Both paradigms expand AI's reach into data-scarce scientific problems.

I will then present our work on automated scientific modeling, where we learn interpretable models of dynamical systems – such as process-based models and differential equations – from time series data and domain knowledge. Finally, I will highlight the role of ontologies and semantic technologies in experimental computer science, including machine learning and optimization. In these areas, we have developed ontologies for the representation and annotation of both data and other artefacts produced by science, such as algorithms, models, and results of experiments.

Artificial Intelligence for Science

Contents – Part V

Neuro Symbolic Approaches

Bridging Logic and Learning: Decoding Temporal Logic Embeddings via Transformers 3
    Sara Candussio, Gaia Saveri, Gabriele Sarti, and Luca Bortolussi

Provably Accurate Adaptive Sampling for Collocation Points in Physics-Informed Neural Networks 19
    Antoine Caradot, Rémi Emonet, Amaury Habrard, Abdel-Rahim Mezidi, and Marc Sebban

The Role of Transformer Architecture in the Logic-as-Loss Framework 38
    Mattia Medina Grespan and Vivek Srikumar

Optimization

GBRF: A Novel Framework for Encoding User-Preferences in Imbalanced Data Distributions via Genetic Optimization 59
    Miguel Carvalho, Armando Pinho, and Susana Brás

Sample and Expand: Discovering Low-Rank Submatrices With Quality Guarantees 78
    Martino Ciaperoni, Aristides Gionis, and Heikki Mannila

Active Preference Optimization for Sample Efficient RLHF 96
    Nirjhar Das, Souradip Chakraborty, Aldo Pacchiano, and Sayak Ray Chowdhury

Fast Proximal Gradient Methods with Node Pruning for Tree-Structured Sparse Regularization 113
    Yasutoshi Ida, Sekitoshi Kanai, Atsutoshi Kumagai, Tomoharu Iwata, and Yasuhiro Fujiwara

Hashing for Fast Pattern Set Selection 129
    Maiju Karjalainen and Pauli Miettinen

Optimizing the Optimal Weighted Average: Efficient Distributed Sparse Classification 147
    Fred Lu, Ryan R. Curtin, Edward Raff, Francis Ferraro, and James Holt

Time-Varying Gaussian Process Bandit Optimization with Experts:
No-Regret in Logarithmically-Many Side Queries 164
    Eliabelle Mauduit, Eloïse Berthier, and Andrea Simonetto

Designing Search Space for Unbounded Bayesian Optimization
via Transfer Learning 183
    Quoc-Anh Hoang Nguyen, Hung The Tran, Sunil Gupta, and Dung D. Le

Privacy and Security

TAMIS: Tailored Membership Inference Attacks on Synthetic Data 203
    Paul Andrey, Batiste Le Bars, and Marc Tommasi

Variance-Based Defense Against Blended Backdoor Attacks 221
    Sujeevan Aseervatham, Achraf Kerzazi, and Younès Bennani

Achieving Flexible Local Differential Privacy in Federated Learning
via Influence Functions 240
    Alycia N. Carey and Xintao Wu

P2NIA: Privacy-Preserving Non-iterative Auditing 259
    Jade Garcia Bourrée, Hadrien Lautraite, Sébastien Gambs,
    Gilles Tredan, Erwan Le Merrer, and Benoît Rottembourg

"I Forgot About You": Exploring Multi-Label Unlearning (MLU)
for Responsible Facial Recognition Systems 276
    Prommy Sultana Hossain, Emanuela Marasco, Jessica Lin,
    and Michael King

Bounding-Box Watermarking: Defense Against Model Extraction Attacks
on Object Detectors 295
    Satoru Koda and Ikuya Morikawa

Stealing Data from Active Party in Vertical Split Learning 313
    Yaxin Liu, Xiaoyang Xu, Wenzhe Yi, Yong Zhuang, Juan Wang,
    Mengda Yang, and Ziang Li

DeepCore: Simple Fingerprint Construction for Differentiating
Homologous and Piracy Models 328
    Haifeng Sun, Lan Zhang, and Xiang-Yang Li

Video-DPRP: A Differentially Private Approach for Visual
Privacy-Preserving Video Human Activity Recognition 345
    Allassan Tchangmena A. Nken, Susan McKeever, Peter Corcoran,
    and Ihsan Ullah

Differentially Private Sparse Linear Regression with Heavy-Tailed
Responses 363
  Xizhi Tian, Meng Ding, Touming Tao, Zihang Xiang, and Di Wang

Leveraging Homophily Under Local Differential Privacy for Effective
Graph Neural Networks 380
  *Yule Xie, Jiaxin Ding, Pengyu Xue, Xin Ding, Haochen Han, Luoyi Fu,
  and Xinbin Wang*

MCMC for Bayesian Estimation of Differential Privacy from Membership
Inference Attacks 397
  Ceren Yıldırım, Kamer Kaya, Sinan Yıldırım, and Erkay Savaş

Machine Unlearning for Random Forest via Method of Images 415
  Hang Zhang and Kai Ming Ting

Stimulating Catastrophic Forgetting in Class-Wise Unlearning via UAP 432
  *Wenxing Zhou, Xinwen Cheng, Yingwen Wu, Ruikai Yang,
  and Xiaolin Huang*

Recommender Systems

Towards Unifying Feature Interaction Models for Click-Through Rate
Prediction 451
  *Yu Kang, Junwei Pan, Jipeng Jin, Shudong Huang, Xiaofeng Gao,
  and Lei Xiao*

Fine-Grained Representation Learning and Multi-view Collaborative
Augmentation for Recommendation 468
  Huiting Li, Wenjun Ma, Weishan Cai, and Yuncheng Jiang

Hierarchical Interaction Summarization and Contrastive Prompting
for Explainable Recommendations 485
  Yibin Liu, Ang Li, and Shijian Li

Aggressive Exploration in Offline Reinforcement Learning for Better
Recommendations 502
  Kexin Shi, Wenjia Wang, and Bingyi Jing

CULC-Net: A Recipe for Tailored Creative Selection in Online Advertising 519
  *Baosheng Zhang, Liufang Sang, Haoran Wang, Wei Wang,
  Wenlong Chen, Changping Peng, Zhangang Lin, Jingping Shao,
  Jie He, Haoqian Wang, and Yuchen Guo*

A Dual-Channel Heterogeneous Hypergraph Convolutional Network
for Dual-target Cross-domain Recommendation 536
  Moyu Zhang and Zhe Yang

Author Index 553

Neuro Symbolic Approaches

Bridging Logic and Learning: Decoding Temporal Logic Embeddings via Transformers

Sara Candussio[1](✉) , Gaia Saveri[1] , Gabriele Sarti[2] ,
and Luca Bortolussi[1]

[1] AILab, MIGe, University of Trieste, 34127 Trieste, Italy
{sara.candussio,gaia.saveri}@phd.units.it, lbortolussi@units.it
[2] Center for Language and Cognition (CLCG), University of Groningen, Groningen, The Netherlands
g.sarti@rug.nl

Abstract. Continuous representations of logic formulae allow us to integrate symbolic knowledge into data-driven learning algorithms. If such embeddings are semantically consistent, i.e. if similar specifications are mapped into nearby vectors, they enable continuous learning and optimization directly in the semantic space of formulae. However, to translate the optimal continuous representation into a concrete requirement, such embeddings must be invertible. We tackle this issue by training a Transformer-based decoder-only model to invert semantic embeddings of Signal Temporal Logic (STL) formulae. STL is a powerful formalism that allows us to describe properties of signals varying over time in an expressive yet concise way. By constructing a small vocabulary from STL syntax, we demonstrate that our proposed model is able to generate valid formulae after only 1 epoch and to generalize to the semantics of the logic in about 10 epochs. Additionally, the model is able to decode a given embedding into formulae that are often simpler in terms of length and nesting while remaining semantically close (or equivalent) to gold references. We show the effectiveness of our methodology across various levels of training formulae complexity to assess the impact of training data on the model's ability to effectively capture the semantic information contained in the embeddings and generalize out-of-distribution. Finally, we deploy our model for solving a requirement mining task, i.e. inferring STL specifications that solve a classification task on trajectories, performing the optimization directly in the semantic space.

Keywords: Transformers · Neuro-Symbolic Embeddings · Temporal Logic

1 Introduction

Integrating learning algorithms and symbolic reasoning is an increasingly prominent research direction in modern Artificial Intelligence (AI), towards striking a balance between the high efficiency of black box data-driven Machine Learning (ML) models and the interpretability of logical languages. The cornerstone of such efforts, within the Neuro-Symbolic (NeSy) computing paradigm [36,37], is knowledge representation by means of formal languages rooted on logic. A promising approach to combine logic with machine learning is that of mapping logic formulae into continuous vectors, i.e. embeddings, which can be natively integrated into ML algorithms [7,11,17,28,33].

Having real-valued representation of logic specifications preserving their semantic, i.e. mapping similar formulae to nearby vectors, enables continuous learning and optimization directly in the semantic space of formulae, e.g. for conditioning generative models on producing data compliant to some background knowledge [28] or finding a requirement able to discriminate among regular and anomalous points [27]. However, to translate the devised optimal continuous representation into a concrete requirement, hence promoting interpretability and reliability of the resulting system, such embeddings must be invertible.

In this work we focus on temporal data and on a dialect of Linear Temporal Logic, namely Signal Temporal Logic (STL) [19,23], which is emerging as the defacto standard language for stating specifications of continuous systems varying over time, in various domains such as biological or cyber-physical systems [2]. Indeed, STL is powerful enough to describe many phenomena, yet easily interpretable, as it avoids the vagueness and redundancy of natural language, still being easy to translate in common words [12]. For example, in STL one can state properties like "within the next 10 minutes, the temperature will reach at least 25 degrees, and will stay above 22 degrees for the next hour". Notably, there exists a well-defined procedure for consistently embedding STL specifications in a real vector space, grounded directly in the semantics of the logic via kernel-based methods [5,28]. This embedding, however, is not invertible, essentially due to the fact that semantically equivalent formulae with different syntactic structure are mapped in the same vector.

On the other hand, Language Models (LMs) based on the Transformer architecture [32] have reached astonishingly high performance on a wide range of applications and for different data modalities [35]. Thanks to their effective and efficient self-attention mechanism, LMs have proven to be the most-powerful general-purpose representation learning models, setting new standards on various domain, beyond the traditional Natural Language Processing (NLP). For this reason, we believe that a decoder-only Transformer-based model could prove itself an effective choice for inverting continuous representations of STL formulae. Indeed, we tackle such decoding task as a translation from semantic vectors to strings representing formulae, constructing a small vocabulary from STL syntax.

Our contributions consist in: (i) end-to-end training of a decoder-only Transformer model for the downstream task of reconstructing STL specifications from a continuous representation encoding their semantics (Sect. 5.1); (ii) extensive experimental analysis on the effectiveness of our methodology across various levels of training formulae complexity to assess the impact of training data on the model's ability to effectively capture the semantic information contained in the embeddings and generalize out-of-distribution, as well as comparisons to related approaches (Sect. 5.1); (iii) leveraging the proposed architecture for requirement mining, i.e. inferring formally specified system properties from observed behaviors, by integrating our architecture inside a Bayesian Optimization (BO) loop, proving that the resulting model is able to extract interpretable information form the input data, promoting knowledge discovery about the system (Sect. 5.2). Data, code and trained models presented in this work can be found at can be found at this[1] link.

2 Related Work

The ability of LM to understand formal languages in general, and temporal logic in particular, has been explored in the literature under different perspectives. A number of works exploits Transformed-based architectures to translate informal natural language statements to formal specifications, towards aiding the error-prone and time-consuming process of writing requirements [22]. In this context, either an encoder-decoder LM is trained from scratch as accurate translator from unstructured natural language sentences to STL formulae [12], or off-the-shelf LMs are finetuned on an analogous translation task for first-order logic (FOL) or linear-time temporal logic (LTL) [6,10]. Notably, Transformers are also trained to solve tasks typically pertaining to the formal methods realm: in [9] a LM is trained end-to-end for solving the LTL verification problem of generating a trace satisfying a given formula, showing generalization abilities of the model to the semantics of the logic; taking a dual perspective, in [14] the LTL requirement mining problem is framed as an auto-regressive language modeling task, in which an encoder-decoder LM is trained as a translator having as source language the input trace and as target language LTL.

Finally, performing symbolic regression (SR) using Transformer-based models is gaining momentum in the field as an alternative to genetic programming. SR is indeed the problem of inferring a symbolic mathematical expression of a function of which we have collected some observations in the form of input-output pairs: in [15] a LM is trained to simultaneously predict the skeleton and the numerical constants of the searched expression, possibly augmenting the generation with a planning strategy [29]; in [8] the investigation is pushed even further, as a Transformer is trained to infer multidimensional ordinary differential equations from observations, i.e. to model a dynamical systems from data.

Mining STL specifications from data has seen a surge of interest in the last few years, as reported in [3]. Many of such works decompose the requirement mining task in two steps, i.e. as bi-level optimization problem: they first learn the structure of the specification from data, and then instantiate a concrete formula using parameter inference methods [1,4,20,21,26,31]. Both in [21,27] Bayesian optimization, and in particular GP-UCB, is used towards optimizing the searched specification. In the same spirit of this work, [27] learns simultaneously both the structure and the parameters of the STL requirement, by performing optimization in a continuous space representing the semantics of formulae.

---

[1] https://github.com/gaoithee/transformers/tree/main/src/transformers/models/stldec.

3 Background

Signal Temporal Logic (STL) is a linear-time temporal logic which expresses properties on trajectories over dense time intervals [19]. Signals (or trajectories) are here defined as functions $\xi : I \to D$, where $I \subseteq \mathbb{R}_{\geq 0}$ is the time domain and $D \subseteq \mathbb{R}^k, k \in \mathbb{N}$ is the state space. The syntax of STL is given by:

$$\varphi := tt \mid \pi \mid \neg\varphi \mid \varphi_1 \wedge \varphi_2 \mid \varphi_1 \mathbf{U}_{[a,b]} \varphi_2$$

where tt is the Boolean *true* constant; π is an *atomic predicate*, i.e. a function over variables $\boldsymbol{x} \in \mathbb{R}^n$ of the form $f_\pi(\boldsymbol{x}) \geq 0$; $\neg$ and $\wedge$ are the Boolean *negation* and *conjunction*, respectively (from which the *disjunction* $\vee$ follows by De Morgan's law); $\mathbf{U}_{[a,b]}$, with $a, b \in \mathbb{Q}, a < b$, is the *until* operator, from which *eventually* $\mathbf{F}_{[a,b]}$ and the *always* $\mathbf{G}_{[a,b]}$ temporal operators can be derived. We can intuitively interpret the temporal operators over $[a,b]$ as follows: a property is *eventually* satisfied if it is satisfied at some point inside the temporal interval, while a property is *globally* satisfied if it is true continuously in $[a,b]$; finally the *until* operator captures the relationship between two conditions φ, ψ in which the first condition φ holds until, at some point in $[a,b]$, the second condition ψ becomes true. We call $\mathcal{P}$ the set of well-formed STL formulae. STL is endowed with both a *qualitative* (or Boolean) semantics, giving the classical notion of satisfaction of a property over a trajectory, i.e. $s(\varphi, \xi, t) = 1$ if the trajectory ξ at time t satisfies the STL formula φ, and a *quantitative* semantics, denoted by $\rho(\varphi, \xi, t) \in \mathbb{R}$. The latter, also called *robustness*, is a measure of how robust is the satisfaction of φ w.r.t. perturbations of the signals. Intuitively, robustness measures how far is a signal ξ from violating a specification φ, with the sign indicating the satisfaction status. Indeed, robustness is compatible with satisfaction via the following *soundness* property: if $\rho(\varphi, \xi, t) > 0$ then $s(\varphi, \xi, t) = 1$ and if $\rho(\varphi, \xi, t) < 0$ then $s(\varphi, \xi, t) = 0$. When $\rho(\varphi, \xi, t) = 0$ arbitrary small perturbations of the signal might lead to changes in satisfaction value.

Embeddings of STL formulae are devised with an ad-hoc kernel in [5], which yields representations that have been experimentally proven to be semantic-preserving [28], i.e. STL specifications with similar meaning are mapped to nearby vectors. Indeed, such embeddings are not learned but grounded in the semantics of the logic, moving form the observation that robustness allows formulae to be considered as functionals mapping trajectories into real numbers, i.e. $\rho(\varphi, \cdot) : \mathcal{T} \to \mathbb{R}$ such that $\xi \mapsto \rho(\varphi, \xi)$. Considering these as feature maps, and fixing a probability measure μ_0 on the space of trajectories $\mathcal{T}$, a kernel function capturing similarity among STL formulae on mentioned feature representations can be defined as:

$$k(\varphi, \psi) = \langle \rho(\varphi, \cdot), \rho(\psi, \cdot) \rangle = \int_{\xi \in \mathcal{T}} \rho(\varphi, \xi) \rho(\psi, \xi) d\mu_0(\xi) \quad (1)$$

opening the doors to the use of the scalar product in the Hilbert space L^2 as a kernel for $\mathcal{P}$; at a high level, this results in a kernel having high positive value for formulae that behave similarly on high-probability trajectories (w.r.t. μ_0), and viceversa low negative value for formulae that on those trajectories disagree. Hence, a D-dimensional embedding $k(\varphi) \in \mathbb{R}^D$ of a formula φ is obtained from Eq. 1 by fixing (possibly at random) an *anchor set* of D STL requirements $\psi_1, \ldots, \psi_D$ such that $k(\varphi) = [k(\varphi, \psi_1), \ldots, k(\varphi, \psi_D)]$.

Transformers are a class of deep learning models designed to autoregressively handle sequential data effectively by leveraging self-attention mechanism [32]. Given a sequence of tokens $t = [t_1, \ldots, t_m]$, the model learns the distribution $P(t)$ that can be decomposed as $P(t) = P(t_1) \prod_{i=1}^{m-1} P(t_{i+1}|t_1, \ldots, t_i)$ using the chain rule, so that each conditional can be parameterized using a neural network optimized via Stochastic Gradient Descent (SGD) to maximize the likelihood of a corpus used for training.

Here, we focus on the decoder-only variant of this architecture [25], whose objective is to predict the next token given a context made of the last k already generated tokens. The fundamental learning mechanism in the Transformer decoder is the attention mechanism, that allows the model to contextualize token representation at each layer, dynamically determining the importance of each token in a computationally efficient (i.e. parallelizable) way.

4 Decoding STL Embeddings via Transformers

The main research question addressed with this work is that of checking whether a Transformer-based decoder-only model is able to decode a STL formula starting from a real-valued vector representing its semantics. In this context, we frame this problem as the approximate inversion of STL kernel embeddings computed as described in Sect. 3, i.e. using Eq. 1. A positive answer to this question can be interpreted as an experimental proof of the fact that, in this setting, ad-hoc trained Transformers are able to grasp the semantics of STL.

4.1 Data

In order to train the model, we need to collect a set of pairs $\{(\varphi_i, k(\varphi_i))\}_i$ consisting of STL formulae φ_i and their corresponding kernel embeddings $k(\varphi_i)$ computed as described in Sect. 1. To construct such a set of formulae φ, we can consider a distribution $\mathcal{F}$ over STL formulae, defined by a syntax-tree random recursive growing scheme, which recursively generates the nodes of a formula given the probability p_{leaf} of each node being an atomic predicate, and a uniform distribution over the other operator nodes. Intuitively, the higher p_{leaf}, the smaller (in terms of number of operators and depth of the resulting syntax tree) the generated formula will be.

The work of [24] spots a light on the impact that training data has in making the model learn hierarchical patterns, resulting in different generalization abilities at inference time. While they work on linear and hierarchical rules on

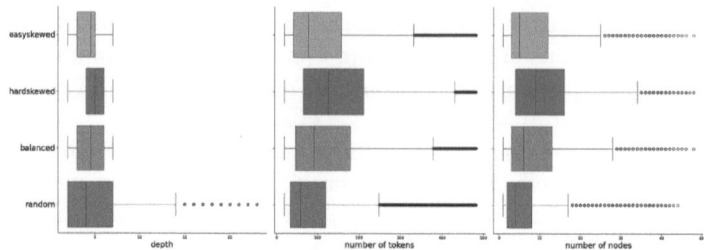

Fig. 1. Distribution of depth, number of tokens and number of nodes of the formulae composing the different training sets used.

natural language syntax trees, our case study is focused on syntactically reasonable representations of semantic vectors. We question whether, also in this different scenario, complexity level of training data (i.e. the composition of these sets in terms of formulae depths) should be reflected in some margin into the model's prediction abilities.

Specifically, we compose 4 different training sets, by sampling from the distribution $\mathcal{F}$ varying the parameter p_{leaf} and possibly filtering the obtained formulae based on the desired depth, each containing 78000 examples as follows:

- easyskewed: 52000 easier formulae (i.e. of depths 2, 3, 4), 26000 harder formulae (i.e. of depths 5, 6, 7);
- hardskewed: 26000 easier formulae (i.e. of depths 2, 3, 4), 52000 harder formulae (i.e. of depths 5, 6, 7);
- balanced: 13000 formulae of each considered depth level (i.e. depths 2, 3, 4, 5, 6, 7);
- random: 78000 formulae randomly sampled from $\mathcal{F}$ with $p_{\text{leaf}} = 0.45$, without filtering on the minimum or maximum depths; the result is a broadly spread distribution, comprising formulae from depth 2 to depth 23.

A glance on the distribution of the depth and number of nodes of the syntax tree of the formulae in the different training sets is shown in Fig. 1.

The idea behind the exploitation of multiple training sets is to test whether the model can effectively learn to reconstruct a formula corresponding to a given embedding, or if the learning process is limited to replicating a superficial pattern observed in the training data [24]. To assess the generalization abilities acquired during the training stage, we test each model on a balanced test set consisting in formulae with various depths (from 2 to 7).

4.2 Model

The model follows a decoder-only architecture consisting in 12 layers (as it was originally proposed by [34]), each of which comprises 16 attention heads, and a feed-forward layer of dimension 4096 with Gaussian Error Linear Unit (GELU) [13] activation function. Each attention layer is followed by a residual connection and a normalization layer to enhance training stability. This is also applied after the feed-forward layer. In order to prevent overfitting, we apply dropout with rate 0.1 before each residual connection and normalization operations.

The vocabulary is customized on the STL syntax, thus is limited to 35 tokens corresponding to the numbers, the (temporal and propositional) operators, the parentheses and the blank space separating the different logical structures. Additionally, the unk (i.e. unknown token), pad (i.e. pad token), bos (i.e. beginning-of-sentence) and eos (i.e. end-of-sentence) special tokens are added to the vocabulary.

The semantic information contained in the embedding of a STL formula is integrated through the cross-attention mechanism into the generating process: during the inference phase, each auto-regressively generated token is conditioned on the information contained in this semantic embedding.

Training. Our experiments aim at assessing the ability of a decoder-only Transformer architecture to reconstruct a plausible formula starting from a semantic embedding. In this direction, we train from scratch the formerly described architecture using different training sets, as detailed in Sect. 4.1 and obtained different models, which we will refer to using the same name of the used training set (namely random, hardskewed, easyskewed, balanced).

Another point of interest in our analysis consists in the impact of the richness of the semantic representations, i.e. the chosen embedding dimension. Indeed, we both train models with hidden dimensions of 512 and 1024 and studied the differences in the generalization abilities of the resulting models. This is achieved by embedding both training and test sets using the STL kernel of Eq. 1, fixing a set of either 1024 or 512 anchor formulae sampled from $\mathcal{F}$. As expected, the training time doubles when the hidden dimension is duplicated. To refer to the model trained with embedding of size 512, we append the suffix small to the name of the model.

We train all the models for 10 epochs (corresponding to ~ 24000 steps) on those training sets, all of size 78000, with a batch size of 32. We further elongate the training stage for the best models (according to the criteria described in Sect. 5.1) for 10 more epochs, in order to test whether or not we could observe a more refined behavior, when allowing for a greater training time. The optimization is performed using the AdamW optimizer [18], which decouples weight decay from gradient updates for improved generalization. A linear learning rate scheduler is applied, starting with a warm-up phase of 5000 steps before gradually decreasing over 50000 total training steps. The initial learning rate is set to $5 \cdot 10^{-5}$, with weight decay of 0.01 to mitigate possible overfitting.

At inference time the semantic embedding of a formula is fed to the trained model along with the bos (begin of sentence) starting token. The model auto-regressively infers the next formula elements starting from this NeSy representation.

5 Experiments

We claim and experimentally prove the effectiveness of our methodology in capturing the semantic information contained in the STL kernel representations in two different settings: (i) approximately inverting embeddings of STL formulae, see Sect. 5.1 and (ii) performing the requirement mining task in several benchmark datasets, as shown in Sect. 5.2.

5.1 Approximately Inverting STL Kernel Embeddings

The goal of this suite of experiments is twofold: verifying that a Transformer-based model is able to effectively grasp the semantics of STL, as encoded by the STL kernel embeddings, and compare it to a related approach based on Information Retrieval (IR) techniques; investigating if and how much the model size and the training set distribution influence such capabilities.

We test these abilities on a set of formulae with balanced depth levels, in order to robustly assess the aforementioned *desiderata*. The depths of the formulae range from 2 to 7, and it is worth noting that depth-4 formulae can already involve up to three different temporal operators, making them quite complex.

As an example, we can consider the sentence "the temperature τ of the room will reach 25° within the next 10 min and will stay above 22° for the successive 60 min", which translates in STL as $F_{[0,10]}(\tau \geq 25 \land G_{[0,60]}\tau \geq 22)$ (i.e. a requirement with depth 4 and 3 logical operators).

Ideally, if we query our model with the embedding $k(\varphi)$ of a known formula φ, then we expect to decode a specification $\hat{\varphi}$ which has the same semantics of φ, with possibly a different syntax. To verify this property, we can consider the robustness vector of a formula, i.e. $\boldsymbol{\rho}(\varphi) = [\rho(\varphi, \xi_i)]_{i=1}^M$ for an arbitrary, but fixed, set of trajectories $\Xi = \{\xi_i\}_{i=1}^M$, and compute the quantity $d(\boldsymbol{\rho}(\varphi), \boldsymbol{\rho}(\hat{\varphi})) = ||\boldsymbol{\rho}(\varphi) - \boldsymbol{\rho}(\hat{\varphi})||_2$: given that two STL formulae are semantically similar if they behave similarly on the same set of signals, a lower value of $d(\boldsymbol{\rho}(\varphi), \boldsymbol{\rho}(\hat{\varphi}))$ indicates a good approximation of the inverse of $k(\varphi)$. Following the same reasoning line, as additional metrics we can consider: (a) the cosine similarity between robustness vectors, namely $\cos(\boldsymbol{\rho}(\varphi), \boldsymbol{\rho}(\hat{\varphi})) = \frac{\boldsymbol{\rho}(\varphi) \cdot \boldsymbol{\rho}(\hat{\varphi})}{||\boldsymbol{\rho}(\varphi)||\,||\boldsymbol{\rho}(\hat{\varphi})||} \in [-1, 1]$, with $\cos(\boldsymbol{\rho}(\varphi), \boldsymbol{\rho}(\hat{\varphi})) = 1$ if the original φ and reconstructed $\hat{\varphi}$ are (un)satisfied on the same set of trajectories of Ξ, possibly with different robustness degrees and (b) average number of signals in which φ and $\hat{\varphi}$ have opposite satisfaction status, i.e. $\text{diff}(\boldsymbol{s}(\varphi), \boldsymbol{s}(\hat{\varphi})) = \frac{\sum_{i=1}^M \mathbb{I}(s(\varphi, \xi_i) \neq s(\hat{\varphi}, \xi_i))}{M}$ being $\mathbb{I}$ the indicator function. When $\text{diff}(\boldsymbol{s}(\varphi), \boldsymbol{s}(\hat{\varphi})) = 0$ the the original φ and reconstructed $\hat{\varphi}$ are (un)satisfied on exactly the same set of trajectories.

Besides comparing all the trained models on the above mentioned metrics, we also analyze their performance w.r.t. the IR-based approach devised in [27], in which a dense vector database (hereafter denoted as DB) containing STL kernel embeddings of millions of formulae is built, so that an approximate inverse $\hat{\varphi}$ of the embedding $k(\varphi)$ of a specification φ is obtained with approximate nearest neighbors by querying the DB with $k(\varphi)$.

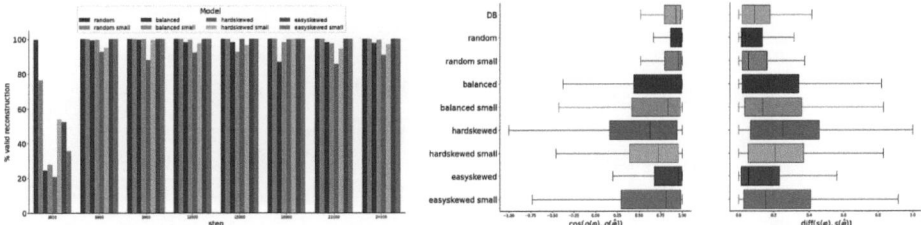

Fig. 2. Considering all the trained models: (left) percentage of syntactically valid formulae generated across the training steps and (right) comparison of results between transformer-based after 24000 steps of training models and semantic vector database.

Table 1. Comparison of results of different checkpoints of the best Transformer-based models and of the DB. On parenthesis the percentile of the distribution of the corresponding metric on a random set of formulae.

Model	$d(\rho(\varphi), \rho(\hat{\varphi}))$				$\cos(\rho(\varphi), \rho(\hat{\varphi}))$				$\mathrm{diff}(s(\varphi), s(\hat{\varphi}))$			
	1quart	median	3quart	99perc	1quart	median	3quart	99perc	1quart	median	3quart	99perc
DB	16.51 (1)	28.13 (4)	43.87 (12)	81.46 (75)	0.795 (91)	0.9262 (98)	0.9802 (99)	0.9995 (100)	0.0225 (1)	0.0908 (4)	0.1797 (11)	0.4831 (47)
random (step 24K)	8.447 (1)	17.63 (2)	36.03 (7)	123.4 (100)	0.8617 (95)	0.9718 (99)	0.9939 (100)	1.000 (100)	0.0159 (1)	0.0423 (2)	0.1354 (7)	0.7571 (85)
random small (step 24K)	11.66 (2)	23.06 (2)	44.51 (12)	113.4 (100)	0.7985 (91)	0.9518 (99)	0.9885 (100)	1.000 (100)	0.0224 (1)	0.0586 (3)	0.1631 (9)	0.7154 (81)
random (step 48K)	6.054 (0)	12.71 (1)	29.89 (4)	110.1 (100)	0.9012 (96)	0.9854 (100)	0.9971 (100)	1.000 (100)	0.0073 (0)	0.0274 (1)	0.1085 (6)	0.6625 (75)
random small (step 48K)	7.462 (1)	16.01 (1)	31.22 (5)	101.1 (100)	0.8944 (96)	0.9774 (99)	0.9952 (100)	1.000 (100)	0.0106 (1)	0.0359 (2)	0.1159 (6)	0.5563 (61)

In Fig. 2 and Table 1 we report the results of tests done on a `balanced` test set of 3000 formulae, i.e. constructed as the one used to train the homonymous model described in Sect. 4.1. From Fig. 2 (left) it is possible to notice that `random` model decodes only syntactically valid formulae after just 3000 steps (~ 1.5 epoch) of training, and that by step 24000 (~ 10 epochs) all architectures reach $\geq 85\%$ of valid generations, highlighting the ability of Transformer-based models to grasp the syntax of STL. Moreover, on Fig. 2 (right) we can check that the two models trained on the `random` training set are outperforming all the others, with the bigger one surpassing also the DB approach on the tested metrics. Indeed, after 24000 steps they achieve a median $\cos(\rho(\varphi), \rho(\hat{\varphi})) \geq 0.95$ and median $\mathrm{diff}(s(\varphi), s(\hat{\varphi})) \leq 0.06$. Pushing further the investigation, we trained these 2 top-performing model for additional 24000 steps (hence for a total of ~ 20 epochs) and showed the results on Table 1. There, we not only report the quantiles of the test distribution of the 3 considered metrics, but also the corresponding percentile of the distribution of the same quantities computed on a set of 10000 random formulae. Hence, we see that the additional training steps bring a relatively small improvement on all the considered metrics, and that the Transformer-based architecture is able to grasp the semantics of STL after ~ 10 epochs of training, reporting a median ~ 0.98 cosine similarity between the vectors of the robustness of the ground truth and retrieved formula, with the two having a different satisfaction status on $\sim 3\%$ of trajectories. The median value of $d(\rho(\varphi), \rho(\hat{\varphi}))$, despite not being interpretable, corresponds to the 1st percentile of the random distribution, hence significantly low, enforcing the observation that the `random` model effectively learns the semantics of STL as encoded by the STL kernel embeddings.

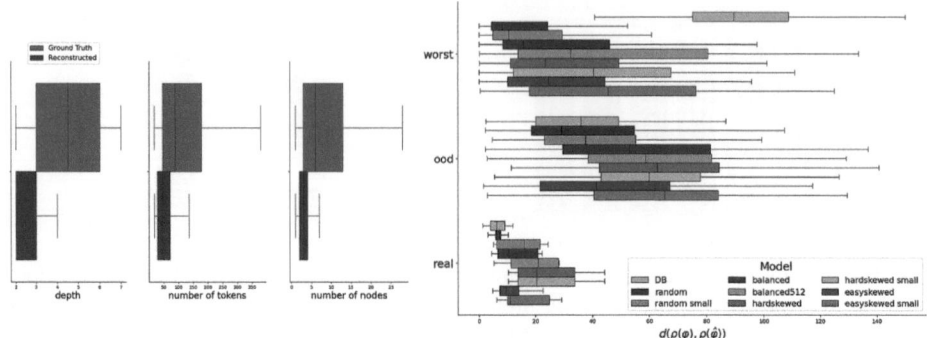

Fig. 3. (left) Distribution of depth, number of tokens and number of nodes of the ground truth and reconstructed formulae (by the `random` architecture) composing the `balanced` test set; (right) comparison of results between transformer-based models and semantic vector database on the test sets `worst`, `ood`, `real`.

Notably, from Fig. 3, we observe that the `random` model tends to decode formulae that are syntactically simpler than those used to generate the test embeddings. We argue that this behavior may stem from the high syntactic variability observed in its training set, as shown in Fig. 1. Since formulae with very different syntactic structures might nonetheless share very similar semantics, it is likely that the `random` training set contains pairs of specifications that are semantically close but very different in their structure, in terms e.g. of depth and number of nodes. However, given that the majority of training requirements are relatively simple, the Transformer is biased toward decoding shorter formulae. This results in a significant advantage for downstream applications in terms of interpretability: we are able to reconstruct a formula with very similar semantic meaning yet syntactically simpler.

Additionally, we tested our model on the following datasets:

- `worst`: a set of 400 formulae sampled from $\mathcal{F}$ using $p_{\text{leaf}} = 0.4$ which we experimentally found to be those on which the DB performs the worst. This set aims at testing whether the transformer-based model is able to generalize to the space of STL kernel embeddings which are scarcely covered by the formulae contained in DB;
- `ood`: a set of 500 STL formulae of depth 8, which are absent from the training sets of the `balanced`, `easyskewed`, and `hardskewed` models, and only present in a very limited amount in that of the `random` models;
- `real`: a small set of 15 formulae taken from [16], to check whether the proposed model is effective on requirements coming form real CPS applications.

The results are shown in Fig. 3 (right), where all models successfully decode only valid formulae. The x-axis represents $d(\boldsymbol{\rho}(\varphi), \boldsymbol{\rho}(\hat{\varphi}))$, the distance between the robustness vectors of the gold and reconstructed formulae, and should be interpreted as *the lower, the better*. While this metric may offer limited interpretability, it allows for a more fine-grained assessment of the relative differences between formulae.

For what concerns the `worst` dataset, all the trained model outperform the DB, confirming that the transformer-based decoder is able to effectively grasp the semantic of STL. Regarding the `ood` set, we notice that the DB is the best performing architecture, with the two models trained on the `random` set showing comparable performance, and the others reporting slightly worst results. This indicates that a greater variability in the structure of formulae over which the models are trained aids in length generalization. Finally, the `random` model is best performing on the `real` dataset, immediately followed by the DB.

5.2 STL Requirement Mining

The objective of the experiments described in this Section is that of checking whether our model can be leveraged for solving the requirement task, i.e. that of inferring a property (in the form of STL formula) characterizing the behavior of an observed system. We follow the approach of [1,4,20,21,26,27] and frame it as a supervised two-class classification problem, where the input consists of a set of trajectories divided in: those classified as regular (or positive) and those identified as anomalous (or negative), denoted as $\mathcal{D}_p$ and $\mathcal{D}_n$, respectively. The output is a (set of) STL formula(e) designed to distinguish between these two subsets. Additionally, we assume that these datasets originate from unknown stochastic processes, denoted as $\boldsymbol{X}_p$ and $\boldsymbol{X}_n$, respectively and adopt the approach of [21] and maximize the following function in order to mine a STL formula φ able to discriminate between positive and negative trajectories:

$$G(\varphi) = \frac{\mathbb{E}_{\mathbf{X_p}}[R_\varphi(\mathbf{X_p})] - \mathbb{E}_{\mathbf{X_n}}[R_\varphi(\mathbf{X_n})]}{\sigma_{\mathbf{X_p}}(R_\varphi(\mathbf{X_p})) + \sigma_{\mathbf{X_n}}(R_\varphi(\mathbf{X_n}))} \qquad (2)$$

denoting as $\mathbb{E}_{\boldsymbol{X}}[R_\varphi(\boldsymbol{X})]$ and $\sigma_{\boldsymbol{X}}[R_\varphi(\boldsymbol{X})]$ respectively the expected value and the standard deviation of the robustness of a formula φ on trajectories sampled from the system $\boldsymbol{X}$. Following [27], we (i) frame the learning problem as the optimization of Eq. 2 in the latent semantic space of formulae, i.e. in the space of embeddings of formulae individuated by the STL kernel of Eq. 1 and (ii) tackle it by means of Bayesian Optimization (BO), and more specifically of the Gaussian Process Upper-Confidence Bound (GP-UCB) algorithm [30]. Hence, the overall iterative methodology follows these steps in each iteration:

1. Optimize the acquisition function based on the current set of pairs $(k(\varphi), G(\varphi))$ of kernel embeddings and corresponding objective function values to obtain new candidate embeddings;
2. Retrieve STL formulae corresponding to such candidate embeddings by inverting the them using the transformer-based decoder model;
3. Evaluate the objective function $G(\varphi)$ on the obtained formulae and record the pair achieving the maximum value.

Table 2. Best mined formula $\hat{\varphi}$, mean and standard deviation of MCR and $Prec$ in the test set across 3 different initialization seeds.

		$\hat{\varphi}$	MCR	$Prec$
Linear	random (step 24K)	$G_{[3,\infty]}(x_0 \geq -11.44)$	0.0200 ± 0.0291	0.9650 ± 0.0489
	random small (step 24K)	$G(x_0 \geq -15.09)$	0.0150 ± 0.0300	0.9714 ± 0.0571
	random (step 48K)	$F(x_0 \geq 0.1918)$	0.0150 ± 0.0300	0.9700 ± 0.0600
	random small (step 48K)	$G(x_0 \geq -5.586)$	0.0150 ± 0.0201	0.9670 ± 0.0485
HAR	random (step 24K)	$G_{[5,\infty]}(x_0 \geq 39.93)$	0.1333 ± 0.2666	0.8666 ± 0.2668
	random small (step 24K)	$G_{[3,8]}(x_0 \geq 29.37)$	0.1368 ± 0.2736	0.8631 ± 0.2736
	random (step 48K)	$G_{[2,\infty]}(x_0 \geq 33.62)$	0.0947 ± 0.1894	0.9052 ± 0.1894
	random small (step 48K)	$G_{[5,9]}(x_0 \geq 32.92)$	0.0736 ± 0.1473	0.9304 ± 0.1392
LP5	random (step 24K)	$G(x_2 \geq -9.272)$	0.0571 ± 0.0534	0.8818 ± 0.0754
	random small (step 24K)	$G(x_2 \geq -12.75)$	0.1713 ± 0.2731	0.9377 ± 0.0509
	random (step 48K)	$G(x_2 \geq -8.142)$	0.0857 ± 0.0534	0.9043 ± 0.0830
	random small (step 48K)	$G(x_2 \geq -5.614)$	0.0857 ± 0.0699	0.8777 ± 0.0976
Train	random (step 24K)	$F_{[18,22]}(G_{[13,16]}(x_0 \leq 4.823))$	0.0468 ± 0.0422	0.9183 ± 0.0716
	random small (step 24K)	$G_{[16,19]}(F_{[12,18]}(x_0 \leq 1.894))$	0.0428 ± 0.0346	0.7979 ± 0.3113
	random (step 48K)	$G_{[13,\infty]}(x_0 \leq 24.64)$	0.0652 ± 0.0717	0.8968 ± 0.1046
	random small (step 48K)	$\neg(F_{[16,\infty]}(x_0 \geq 1.538))$	0.1101 ± 0.1593	0.7929 ± 0.3041

In our experiments, we employ Gaussian Processes with a Matérn kernel, initialized with a batch of 100 points. Due to the high-dimensional STL kernel space (either 1024 or 512, as detailed in Sect. 4.2), we optimize the Upper Confidence Bound (UCB) acquisition function via Stochastic Gradient Descent (SGD).

Following the related literature [20,27], we test the Linear System (`Linear`), Human Activity Recognition (`HAR`), Robot Execution Failure in Motion with Part (`LP5`) and Cruise Control of Train (`Train`) time series classification datasets. Results in terms of Misclassification Rate (MCR) and Precision ($Prec$), are reported in Table 2 for the most promising checkpoints of our model; recall is not shown being always equal to 1. For all datasets the `HAR` the `random` model trained for 24000 steps achieves an accuracy $\geq 90\%$ (which is always achieved by the `random` model trained for 48000 steps). Additionally, in Table 2 we show the best mined formula $\hat{\varphi}$ by each architecture, which we choose as the one obtaining the lowest MCR (namely 0 in all reported cases), using the syntactic simplicity as tiebreaker. Notably, in line with recent related works [20,27], all $\hat{\varphi}$ have at most 3 nodes in their syntax tree, hence are highly interpretable, thus promoting knowledge discovery of the resulting system.

Since our architecture is a learned model, it is highly likely that, when queried with a vector that is out-of-distribution (OOD) with respect to the STL kernel embeddings, it produces an invalid formula. This situation can arise, for example, during the exploration phase of the UCB acquisition function. In such cases, we assign an extremely low value to the objective function in Eq. 2, in order to encourage the GP-UCB to explore more plausible regions of the STL embedding space. On the one hand, this has the positive effect of automatically detecting OOD samples. A possible interpretation of why this occurs is that the embeddings of logical formulae lives in a lower dimensional manifold, hence vectors outside this manifold do not correspond to real requirements, hence embeddings corresponding to such a situation (or belonging to formulae which are semantically very different from the training data) are likely to give rise to invalid outputs. More in detail, the 1024-dimensional architectures take ∼1 s to invert an embedding, while the 512-dimensional roughly 0.5 s. Practically, due to the mentioned issue, we witness an computational time of ∼300 s for the bigger models and ∼120 s for the smaller ones, on the tests reported in Table 2.

6 Conclusion

In this work, we investigate the possibility of using a decoder-only Transformer-based architecture to invert continuous representation of Signal Temporal Logic formulae into valid requirements, which are semantically similar to the ground truth searched formulae. Our experiments prove that such model is able to generate valid formulae after only 1 epoch of training and to generalize to the semantics of the logic in about 10 epochs. Indeed, not only it is able to decode a given embedding into formulae which are semantically close to gold references, but that are often simpler in terms of length and nesting. It is worth noting that, due to the nature of Transformer-based architectures (and neural models in general), deriving meaningful theoretical bounds with practical applicability is extremely challenging. There is an inherent trade-off between speed and accuracy on one hand, and strong theoretical guarantees on the other.

These results leave open the question of whether Transformer-based models can be leveraged in other related Neuro-Symbolic tasks, possibly involving different formal languages, such as first-order logic. We indeed envision that such powerful generative capabilities of Language Models might be leveraged both, as we do here, to decode formulae from a continuous vector representing their semantic and, in an encoder-decoder setting, even to devise invertible by-design continuous semantic-preserving representations, opening the doors to a whole new range of applications. Finally, a further direction that could be explored involves the interpretability of these models; in particular, it could be interesting to study their internals, and check e.g. how the attention heads contribute in the decoding process when provided with the semantic embedding.

Acknowledgments. This study was carried out within the PNRR research activities of the consortium iNEST (Interconnected North-Est Innovation Ecosystem) funded by the European Union Next-GenerationEU (Piano Nazionale di Ripresa e Resilienza (PNRR) – Missione 4 Componente 2, Investimento 1.5 – D.D. 1058 · 23/06/2022, ECS_00000043). This manuscript reflects only the Authors' views and opinions, neither the European Union nor the European Commission can be considered responsible for them. Gabriele Sarti is supported by the Dutch Research Council (NWO) for the project InDeep ('NWA.1292.19.399').

Disclosure of Interests. The authors have no competing interests to declare that are relevant to the content of this article.

References

1. Aydin, S.K., Gol, E.A.: Synthesis of monitoring rules with STL. J. Circ. Syst. Comput. **29**(11), 2050177:1–2050177:26 (2020)
2. Bartocci, E., Deshmukh, J., Donzé, A., Fainekos, G., Maler, O., Ničković, D., Sankaranarayanan, S.: Specification-based monitoring of cyber-physical systems: a survey on theory, tools and Applications. In: Bartocci, E., Falcone, Y. (eds.) Lectures on Runtime Verification. LNCS, vol. 10457, pp. 135–175. Springer, Cham (2018). https://doi.org/10.1007/978-3-319-75632-5_5
3. Bartocci, E., Mateis, C., Nesterini, E., Nickovic, D.: Survey on mining signal temporal logic specifications. Inf. Comput. **289**(Part), 104957 (2022)
4. Bombara, G., Vasile, C.I., Penedo, F., Yasuoka, H., Belta, C.: A decision tree approach to data classification using signal temporal logic. In: Proceedings of the 19th International Conference on Hybrid Systems: Computation and Control, HSCC 2016, pp. 1–10. ACM (2016)
5. Bortolussi, L., Gallo, G.M., Křetínský, J., Nenzi, L.: Learning model checking and the kernel trick for signal temporal logic on stochastic processes. In: TACAS 2022. LNCS, vol. 13243, pp. 281–300. Springer, Cham (2022). https://doi.org/10.1007/978-3-030-99524-9_15
6. Cosler, M., Hahn, C., Mendoza, D., Schmitt, F., Trippel, C.: nl2spec: interactively translating unstructured natural language to temporal logics with large language models. In: Enea, C., Lal, A. (eds.) Computer Aided Verification - 35th International Conference, CAV 2023, Paris, France, 17–22 July 2023, Proceedings, Part II. Lecture Notes in Computer Science, vol. 13965, pp. 383–396. Springer, Heidelberg (2023). https://doi.org/10.1007/978-3-031-37703-7_18
7. Crouse, M., et al.: Improving graph neural network representations of logical formulae with subgraph pooling. CoRR arxiv:1911.06904 (2019)
8. d'Ascoli, S., Becker, S., Schwaller, P., Mathis, A., Kilbertus, N.: Odeformer: symbolic regression of dynamical systems with transformers. In: The Twelfth International Conference on Learning Representations, ICLR 2024, Vienna, Austria, 7–11 May 2024. OpenReview.net (2024)
9. Hahn, C., Schmitt, F., Kreber, J.U., Rabe, M.N., Finkbeiner, B.: Teaching temporal logics to neural networks. In: 9th International Conference on Learning Representations, ICLR 2021, Virtual Event, Austria, 3–7 May 2021. OpenReview.net (2021)
10. Hahn, C., Schmitt, F., Tillman, J.J., Metzger, N., Siber, J., Finkbeiner, B.: Formal specifications from natural language. CoRR arxiv:2206.01962 (2022)
11. Hashimoto, W., Hashimoto, K., Takai, S.: Stl2vec: signal temporal logic embeddings for control synthesis with recurrent neural networks. IEEE Rob. Autom. Lett. **7**(2), 5246–5253 (2022)
12. He, J., Bartocci, E., Nickovic, D., Isakovic, H., Grosu, R.: Deepstl - from english requirements to signal temporal logic. In: 44th IEEE/ACM 44th International Conference on Software Engineering, ICSE 2022, Pittsburgh, PA, USA, 25–27 May 2022, pp. 610–622. ACM (2022)
13. Hendrycks, D., Gimpel, K.: Gaussian error linear units (gelus) (2016). https://api.semanticscholar.org/CorpusID:125617073

14. Isik, I., Gol, E.A., Cinbis, R.G.: Learning to estimate system specifications in linear temporal logic using transformers and mamba. CoRR arxiv:2405.20917 (2024)
15. Kamienny, P., d'Ascoli, S., Lample, G., Charton, F.: End-to-end symbolic regression with transformers. In: Koyejo, S., Mohamed, S., Agarwal, A., Belgrave, D., Cho, K., Oh, A. (eds.) Advances in Neural Information Processing Systems 35: Annual Conference on Neural Information Processing Systems 2022, NeurIPS 2022, New Orleans, LA, USA, 28 November–9 December 2022 (2022)
16. Khandait, T., et al.: Arch-comp 2024 category report: falsification. In: Frehse, G., Althoff, M. (eds.) Proceedings of the 11th International Workshop on Applied Verification for Continuous and Hybrid Systems. EPiC Series in Computing, vol. 103, pp. 122–144. EasyChair (2024). https://doi.org/10.29007/hgfv. https://easychair.org/publications/paper/fKVR
17. Lin, Q., et al.: Contrastive graph representations for logical formulas embedding. IEEE Trans. Knowl. Data Eng. **35**(4), 3563–3574 (2023)
18. Loshchilov, I., Hutter, F.: Decoupled weight decay regularization (2019). https://arxiv.org/abs/1711.05101
19. Maler, O., Nickovic, D.: Monitoring temporal properties of continuous signals. In: Lakhnech, Y., Yovine, S. (eds.) FORMATS/FTRTFT -2004. LNCS, vol. 3253, pp. 152–166. Springer, Heidelberg (2004). https://doi.org/10.1007/978-3-540-30206-3_12
20. Mohammadinejad, S., Deshmukh, J.V., Puranic, A.G., Vazquez-Chanlatte, M., Donzé, A.: Interpretable classification of time-series data using efficient enumerative techniques. In: HSCC '20: 23rd ACM International Conference on Hybrid Systems: Computation and Control, pp. 9:1–9:10. ACM (2020)
21. Nenzi, L., Silvetti, S., Bartocci, E., Bortolussi, L.: A robust genetic algorithm for learning temporal specifications from data. In: McIver, A., Horvath, A. (eds.) QEST 2018. LNCS, vol. 11024, pp. 323–338. Springer, Cham (2018). https://doi.org/10.1007/978-3-319-99154-2_20
22. Norheim, J.J., Rebentisch, E., Xiao, D., Draeger, L., Kerbrat, A., de Weck, O.L.: Challenges in applying large language models to requirements engineering tasks. Des. Sci. **10** (2024)
23. Pnueli, A.: The temporal logic of programs. In: 18th Annual Symposium on Foundations of Computer Science (sfcs 1977), pp. 46–57 (1977)
24. Qin, T., Saphra, N., Alvarez-Melis, D.: Sometimes i am a tree: data drives fragile hierarchical generalization. In: NeurIPS 2024 Workshop on Scientific Methods for Understanding Deep Learning (2024). https://openreview.net/forum?id=AHakCjAPOh
25. Radford, A., Narasimhan, K., Salimans, T., Sutskever, I.: Improving language understanding by generative pre-training. OpenAI Blog (2018). https://cdn.openai.com/research-covers/language-unsupervised/language_understanding_paper.pdf
26. Saglam, I., Gol, E.A.: Cause mining and controller synthesis with STL. In: 58th IEEE Conference on Decision and Control, CDC 2019, pp. 4589–4594. IEEE (2019)
27. Saveri, G., Bortolussi, L.: Retrieval-augmented mining of temporal logic specifications from data. In: Machine Learning and Knowledge Discovery in Databases. Research Track - European Conference, ECML PKDD 2024, Vilnius, Lithuania, 9–13 September 2024, Proceedings, Part VII. Lecture Notes in Computer Science, vol. 14947, pp. 315–331. Springer, Heidelberg (2024). https://doi.org/10.1007/978-3-031-70368-3_19

28. Saveri, G., Nenzi, L., Bortolussi, L., Kretínský, J.: stl2vec: Semantic and interpretable vector representation of temporal logic. In: 27th European Conference on Artificial Intelligence, Santiago de Compostela, Spain, 19–24 October 2024. Frontiers in Artificial Intelligence and Applications, vol. 392, pp. 1381 – 1388. IOS Press (2024)
29. Shojaee, P., Meidani, K., Farimani, A.B., Reddy, C.K.: Transformer-based planning for symbolic regression. In: Oh, A., Naumann, T., Globerson, A., Saenko, K., Hardt, M., Levine, S. (eds.) Advances in Neural Information Processing Systems 36: Annual Conference on Neural Information Processing Systems 2023, NeurIPS 2023, New Orleans, LA, USA, 10–16 December 2023 (2023)
30. Srinivas, N., Krause, A., Kakade, S.M., Seeger, M.W.: Information-theoretic regret bounds for gaussian process optimization in the bandit setting. IEEE Trans. Inf. Theory **58**(5), 3250–3265 (2012)
31. Vaidyanathan, P., et al.: Grid-based temporal logic inference. In: 56th IEEE Annual Conference on Decision and Control, CDC 2017, pp. 5354–5359. IEEE (2017)
32. Vaswani, A., et al.: Attention is all you need. In: Advances in Neural Information Processing Systems 30: Annual Conference on Neural Information Processing Systems, pp. 5998–6008 (2017)
33. Xie, Y., Xu, Z., Meel, K.S., Kankanhalli, M.S., Soh, H.: Embedding symbolic knowledge into deep networks. In: NeurIPS 2019, Vancouver, BC, Canada, 8–14 December 2019, pp. 4235–4245 (2019)
34. Yenduri, G., et al.: Generative pre-trained transformer: a comprehensive review on enabling technologies, potential applications, emerging challenges, and future directions (2023). https://arxiv.org/abs/2305.10435
35. Zhao, W.X., et al.: A survey of large language models. CoRR arxiv:2303.18223 (2025)
36. d'A Garcez, A., Lamb, L.C.: Neurosymbolic AI: the 3rd wave. Artif. Intell. Rev. **56**(11) (2023)
37. Marra, G., Manhaeve, R., Tiddi, I., De Raedt, L.: From statistical relational to neurosymbolic artificial intelligence: a survey. Artif. Intell. **328**, 104062 (2024)

Provably Accurate Adaptive Sampling for Collocation Points in Physics-Informed Neural Networks

Antoine Caradot[✉], Rémi Emonet, Amaury Habrard, Abdel-Rahim Mezidi, and Marc Sebban

Université Jean Monnet Saint-Étienne, CNRS, Institut d'Optique Graduate School, Inria, Laboratoire Hubert Curien UMR 5516, 42023 Saint-Étienne, France
{antoine.caradot,remi.emonet,amaury.habrard,abdel.rahim.mezidi, marc.sebban}@univ-st-etienne.fr

Abstract. Despite considerable scientific advances in numerical simulation, efficiently solving PDEs remains a complex and often expensive problem. Physics-informed Neural Networks (PINN) have emerged as an efficient way to learn surrogate solvers by embedding the PDE in the loss function and minimizing its residuals using automatic differentiation at so-called collocation points. Originally uniformly sampled, the choice of the latter has been the subject of recent advances leading to adaptive sampling refinements for PINNs. In this paper, leveraging a new quadrature method for approximating definite integrals, we introduce a provably accurate sampling method for collocation points based on the Hessian of the PDE residuals. Comparative experiments conducted on a set of 1D and 2D PDEs demonstrate the benefits of our method.

Keywords: PINN · Collocation points · Adaptive sampling · Quadrature method

1 Introduction

Incorporating domain knowledge into machine learning algorithms has become a widespread strategy for managing ill-posed problems, data scarcity and solution consistency. Indeed, ignoring the fundamental principles of the underlying theory may lead to, yet optimal, implausible solutions yielding poor generalization and predictions with a high level of uncertainty. Embedding domain knowledge has been shown to be useful when used at different levels of the learning process for (i) constraining/regularizing the optimization problem, (ii) designing suitable theory-guided loss functions, (iii) initializing models with meaningful parameters, (iv) designing consistent neural network architectures, or (v) building (theory/data)-driven hybrid models. In this context, physics is probably the scientific domain that has benefited the most during the past years from advances in the so-called *Physics-informed Machine Learning* (PiML) field [10] by leveraging physical laws, typically in the form of Partial Differential Equations (PDEs) that govern some underlying dynamical system. This new line of research led to a novel generation of deep-learning architectures, including Neural ODE [2], PINN [17], FNO [12], PINO [13], PDE-Net [14], etc.

In this paper, we specifically focus on Physics-informed Neural Networks (PINNs) that have received much attention from the PiML community and can be used for both forward as well as inverse problems for differential equations. Despite important scientific advances in numerical simulation, solving efficiently PDEs remains complex and often prohibitively costly. By embedding the physical knowledge into the loss function, PINNs appeared as a natural way for learning efficient neural PDE solvers by minimizing the residuals at collocation points typically randomly sampled from the spatio-temporal domain. Despite indisputable progress, PINNs are still at an early stage and it has become crucial to study their theoretical foundations and algorithmic properties to gain a comprehensive grasp of their capabilities and limitation. Indeed, different studies have shown that PINNs may be subject to pathological behaviors, leading to trivial solutions with 0 residuals, thus plausible w.r.t. the physical law, while converging to an incorrect solution [1,7]. Characterizing these "failure modes" [20] has led to an active area of research addressing this task from two main perspectives: a first line of investigation that aims at building theoretical foundations when learning PINNs from a uniform sampling of collocation points (e.g., equispaced uniform grid or uniformly random sampling), resulting in consistency and convergence guarantees in the form of estimation/approximation/optimization bounds (see, e.g., [4,6–8,11]); a second one with the objective of enhancing PINN performance through the lens of the collocation point sampling. Rather than drawing them uniformly, several intuitive strategies have flourished in the literature that suggest guiding the selection during the learning process according to the magnitude (or the gradient) of the PDE residuals. This gave rise to a new family of *adaptive sampling* methods for PINNs (see, e.g., [3,15,16,18,19,21,22]). However, it is worth noting that even though these methods have shown remarkable performances in practice, they share the common feature of not coming with theoretical guarantees of their advantage over a uniform sampling.

The objective of this paper is to bridge the gap by providing two new methodological contributions: (i) Recalling that minimizing an empirical loss in machine learning can be approached from a mathematical perspective as the approximation of the integral of some function f, we propose a new quadrature rule based on a simple trapezoidal interpolation and information about the second-order derivative f''. We derive an upper bound on the approximation error and show its tightness compared to that of issued from an equispaced uniform grid. This theoretical result is supported by several experiments. (ii) This finding prompts us to design a new theoretically founded adaptive sampling method for PINNs where f takes the form of the residual-based loss function. This strategy selects collocation points in the spatio-temporal domain where f'' varies the most. Experiments conducted on 1D and 2D PDEs highlight the interesting properties of our method.

The rest of this paper is organized as follows: in Sect. 2, we introduce the necessary background and related work; Sect. 3 is devoted to the presentation of our refined quadrature method and the upper bound derived on the total approximation error. In Sect. 4, we leverage our quadrature method to propose a new adaptive sampling method for PINNs and test it on 1D and 2D PDEs.

2 Background and Related Work

In this paper, we consider PDEs of the general form: $\frac{\partial u}{\partial t} + \mathcal{N}[u; \phi] = 0$, where $\mathcal{N}[\cdot; \phi]$ is a possibly nonlinear operator parameterized by ϕ and involving partial derivatives in either time or (multidimensional) space and $u(t, \mathbf{x})$ is the latent hidden solution, with $t \in [0, T]$ and $\mathbf{x} \in \Omega$. This equation is typically augmented by appropriate initial and boundary conditions defined respectively as follows:

$$\mathcal{I}[u](0, \mathbf{x}) = 0, \quad \mathbf{x} \in \Omega$$
$$\mathcal{B}[u](t, \mathbf{x}) = 0, \quad \mathbf{x} \in \partial\Omega, t \in [0, T]$$

where $\mathcal{B}$ is a boundary operator that applies to the domain boundary $\partial\Omega$, and $\mathcal{I}$ is an initial operator describing what happens at $t = 0$.

A PINN [17] aims at learning an approximation $u_\theta(t, \mathbf{x})$ of the solution $u(t, \mathbf{x})$ by optimizing the parameters θ of a neural network through the minimization of a loss $\mathcal{L}(\theta)$ composed of the following non-negative PDE residual terms:

$$\mathcal{L}_\mathcal{N}(\theta) = \int_{[0,T] \times \Omega} \left(\frac{\partial u_\theta}{\partial t} + \mathcal{N}[u_\theta; \phi] \right)^2 dt d\mathbf{x}$$

$$\mathcal{L}_\mathcal{I}(\theta) = \int_\Omega (\mathcal{I}[u_\theta](0, \mathbf{x}))^2 d\mathbf{x}$$

$$\mathcal{L}_\mathcal{B}(\theta) = \int_{[0,T] \times \partial\Omega} (\mathcal{B}[u_\theta](t, \mathbf{x}))^2 dt d\mathbf{x}$$

Therefore, a PINN optimization problem takes the following form[1]:

$$\min_\theta \mathcal{L}(\theta) = \min_\theta (\mathcal{L}_\mathcal{N}(\theta) + \lambda_1 \mathcal{L}_\mathcal{I}(\theta) + \lambda_2 \mathcal{L}_\mathcal{B}(\theta) + \lambda_3 R(\theta)), \quad (1)$$

where $\lambda_1, \lambda_2, \lambda_3$ are hyperparameters and $R(\cdot)$ is some regularization term. Since $\mathcal{L}(\theta)$ involves integrals, it cannot be directly minimized. In practice, these three integrals are approximated by finite sums computed over $N_\mathcal{N}$ collocation, $N_\mathcal{I}$ initial and $N_\mathcal{B}$ boundary points respectively.

From a mathematical perspective, one of the underlying problems when solving Eq. (1) involves approximating the integral of some function $f : \Omega \longrightarrow \mathbb{R}$ from N evaluations of the integrand by a suitable *numerical quadrature rule* such that:

$$\sum_{i=1}^N w_i f(\mathbf{x}_i) \approx \int_\Omega f(\mathbf{x}) d\mathbf{x}, \quad (2)$$

---

[1] Note that PINNs can easily incorporate both PDE information and data measurements into the loss function. Our contributions still hold in such hybrid scenario.

where $w_i \geq 0$ are so-called quadrature weights. It is well-known that the accuracy of this approximation depends on the chosen quadrature rule, the regularity of f and the number of quadrature points N. If this remark obviously holds for any machine learning problem minimizing the empirical counterpart of some *true risk* with N training data, it is even truer when it comes to learning surrogate neural solvers of complicated PDEs. This explains why, despite a remarkable effectiveness, PINNs have been shown to face pathological behaviors. In particular, they can be subject to trivial solutions with 0 residuals while converging to an incorrect solution as illustrated, e.g., in [1,7] (characterized as "failure modes" of PINNs, see, e.g., [20]). One way to overcome this pitfall consists in resorting to a suitable regularization term $R(\theta)$ (in Eq. (1)) as done in gPINN [22] that embeds the gradient of the PDE residuals in the loss so as to enforce their derivatives to be zero as well, or in [7], where the authors use a ridge regularization associated with a Sobolev norm to make PINNs both consistent and strongly convergent.

Regularization apart, the location and distribution of the $N = N_{\mathcal{N}} + N_{\mathcal{I}} + N_{\mathcal{B}}$ quadrature points are key and they can have a significant influence on the accuracy and/or the convergence of PINNs. Yet, equispaced uniform grids and uniformly random sampling have been widely used up to now and it is only recently that the placement of these quadrature points has become an active area of research for PINNs leading to several adaptive nonuniform sampling methods (see an extensive comparison study, e.g., in [21]). Beyond being easy to operate, one reason that may justify the still widespread use of uniform sampling stems from the resulting possibility to leverage theoretical frameworks for deriving error estimates for PINNs. For instance, using a midpoint quadrature rule with a regular grid has led to the first approximation error bounds with tanh PINNs (see, e.g., [5,8]). On the other hand, taking advantage of uniformly sampled collocation points and resorting to concentration inequalities, the authors of [7] derived generalization bounds for this new family of networks. Setting theoretical considerations aside, several methods have been designed during the past four years for experimentally improving uniform sampling approaches. Residual-based Adaptive Refinement [15] (a.k.a. RAR) is a greedy adaptive method which consists in adding new collocation points along the learning iterations by selecting the locations where the PDE residuals are the largest. Although RAR has been shown to improve the performance of PINNs, its main limitation (beyond the requirement of a dense set of collocation candidates) lies in the fact that it reduces the opportunity to explore other regions of the space by always picking locations with the largest residuals. Introduced in 2023, RAD [21], for Residual-based Adaptive Distribution, replaces the current collocation points by new ones drawn according to a distribution proportional to the PDE residuals, thus introducing some stochasticity in the sampling process. A hybrid method, called RAR-D, combines RAR and RAD by stacking new points according to the density function. Both RAD and RAR-D (and other adaptive residual-based distribution variants, e.g., [3,16]) have been shown to perform better than non-adaptive uniform sampling [21]. In this category of methods, Retain-Resample-Release sampling (R3) algorithm [3] is the only one that accumulates collocation points in regions of high PDE residuals and which comes with guarantees. Indeed, the authors prove that this algorithm retains points from high residual regions if they persist over iterations and releases points if they have been resolved by PINN training.

While the previous methods leverage the magnitude of the PDE residuals to guide the selection of the locations, some others employ their gradient. This is the case in [22] where the authors combine gPINN and RAR. In the same vein, the authors of [18] present an *Adaptive Sampling for Self-supervision* method that allows a combination of uniformly sampled points and data drawn according to the residuals or their gradient. The first-order derivative has been also recently exploited in PACMANN [19] which leverages gradient information for moving collocation points toward regions of higher residuals using gradient-based optimization. These methods have been shown to further improve the performance of PINNs, especially for PDEs where solutions have steep changes. Drawing inspiration from these derivative-based methods, we define in the next section a new provably accurate quadrature rule for approximating the integral of a function. We prove that this method based on a simple trapezoid-based interpolation and second-order derivative information gives a tighter error bound than an equispaced uniform grid-based quadrature. Leveraging this finding, we present then, as far as we know, the first theoretically founded adaptive sampling method of collocation points for PINNs based on the Hessian of the PDE residuals.

3 Quadrature Rules

Let $a, b \in \mathbb{R}$ and consider a function $f : [a, b] \longrightarrow \mathbb{R}$. We recall that the goal of the quadrature problem is to approximate the integral $\int_a^b f(x)dx$ by an expression of the form $\sum_i w_i f(x_i)$ where the $w_i \in \mathbb{R}$ are the weights of the quadrature points x_i. There are two main strategies of quadrature rules:

1. We take $x_0, \ldots, x_N \in [a, b]$ and the weights $w_0, \ldots, w_N$ are obtained by approximating the function f using polynomials. This is the Newton-Cotes method.
2. We fix a scalar product on the space of polynomials, which provides an orthonormal basis via a Gram-Schmidt procedure. Then the zeros of one element of this basis are the $x_0, \ldots, x_N$, and the weights are found by a matrix inversion.

The second approach, in which the points are a consequence of the chosen scalar product, is very effective and has many variants depending on the interval $[a, b]$, such as Gauss-Legendre for $a, b \in \mathbb{R}$, Gauss-Chebyshev for $[a, b] = [-1, 1]$, and Gauss-Hermite for $[a, b] = [-\infty, \infty]$. However, as our objective is to leverage a quadrature rule for designing a new efficient adaptive sampling method for PINNs, the first approach appears to be much more suitable from a computational perspective because it does not require to compute the orthonormal basis as well as the zeros of one of its elements followed by matrix inversion.

On the other hand, an issue one might encounter using the Newton-Cotes method is that, as it relies on a polynomial approximation of f, the so-called Runge's phenomenon might occur. This problem happens when $\max_{x\in[a,b]} |f^{(n)}(x)|$ is an increasing function of n, where $f^{(n)}$ is the nth-order derivative. Under these circumstances, the interpolation polynomial of f may have sharp oscillating spikes near the edges of the interval, and thus diverging from f as N increases. In order to avoid this pitfall, we suggest controlling the expressiveness of the approximation and focus on a simple trapezoid-based interpolation.

In the following, we first present the quadrature rule when the quadrature points are evenly spaced in the domain and recall a known result on the upper bound on the approximation error in this trapezoid-based setting. Then, we introduced a refined quadrature rule which selects the quadrature points where the second-order derivative of f varies the most. The main result of this section takes the form of a tighter upper bound on the total approximation error.

3.1 Uniform Approach

Let us approximate f on $[z_1, z_2]$, with $z_1, z_2 \in [a, b]$, by the line passing through $(z_1, f(z_1))$ and $(z_2, f(z_2))$. We set $h = z_2 - z_1$. The interpolation $p(x)$ is defined as follows:

$$p(x) = \frac{x - z_1}{h} f(z_2) - \frac{x - z_2}{h} f(z_1). \tag{3}$$

As it is a polynomial of degree 1, the Lagrange remainder form states that there exists $\xi \in [z_1, z_2]$ such that

$$f(x) - p(x) = \frac{f''(\xi)}{2}(x - z_1)(x - z_2).$$

Note that while the existence of ξ is guaranteed, we do not know its position within $[z_1, z_2]$. Moreover, by setting $s = \frac{x-z_1}{h}$, we see that $(x - z_1)(x - z_2) = s(s-1)h^2$. It follows that the error $E_{z_1, z_2} = \int_{z_1}^{z_2} f(x)dx - \int_{z_1}^{z_2} p(x)dx$ on $[z_1, z_2]$ satisfies

$$E_{z_1, z_2} = -\frac{1}{12} h^3 f''(\xi). \tag{4}$$

We will need the following lemma:

Lemma 1. *Let $g(x)$ be a continuous function and let $x_0 < x_1 < \cdots < x_N$ be points within its domain. Set $c_0, \ldots, c_N \geq 0$. Then there exists $\xi \in [x_0, x_N]$ such that*

$$\sum_{i=0}^{N} c_i g(x_i) = g(\xi) \sum_{i=0}^{N} c_i.$$

Proof. cf. [9, Theorem 20.5.1].

Proposition 1. Set $a, b \in \mathbb{R}$, $N \in \mathbb{N}$, and $f : [a,b] \longrightarrow \mathbb{R}$ a function of class C^2, i.e., with continuous second derivative. Then the total error $E_{\text{tot,unif}}$ of the uniform quadrature of the integral of f by N trapezoids is upper bounded by:

$$E_{\text{tot,unif}} \leqslant B_{\text{tot,unif}} = \frac{1}{12} \frac{(b-a)^3}{N^2} \max_{x \in [a,b]} |f''(x)|. \tag{5}$$

Proof. Consider the interval $[a,b]$ and divide it into N subintervals of length $h = \frac{b-a}{N}$. We set $x_0 = a$ and $x_i = x_0 + hi$ for $1 \leqslant i \leqslant N$. We approximate the function f on each $[x_{i-1}, x_i]$ by a trapezoid, and so $p(x)$ is a piecewise linear function given by Eq. (3). Using Eq. (4), for each $1 \leqslant i \leqslant N$, there exists $\xi_i \in [x_{i-1}, x_i]$ such that the total integration error $E_{\text{tot,unif}}$ on $[x_0, x_N] = [a,b]$ is

$$E_{\text{tot,unif}} = \sum_{i=1}^{N} -\frac{1}{12} h^3 f''(\xi_i).$$

By applying the lemma to $E_{\text{tot,unif}}$, there exists $\xi \in [\xi_1, \xi_N]$ such that

$$E_{\text{tot,unif}} = -\frac{1}{12} N h^3 f''(\xi) = -\frac{1}{12}(b-a) h^2 f''(\xi). \tag{6}$$

It follows that for this uniform choice of points $x_0, \ldots, x_N$, the total quadrature error satisfies

$$|E_{\text{tot,unif}}| \leqslant B_{\text{tot,unif}} \tag{7}$$

where $B_{\text{tot,unif}} = \frac{1}{12} \frac{(b-a)^3}{N^2} \max_{x \in [a,b]} |f''(x)|$.

3.2 Second-Order Derivative-Based Quadrature Rule

Rather than defining the quadrature points according to an equispaced uniform grid (as done in the previous section), we suggest here to sample them according to the variations of the second-order derivative of f. Consider $f : [a,b] \longrightarrow \mathbb{R}$ a function of class C^2 and set $k \leqslant N$ integers. We divide $[a,b]$ into k intervals I_j, $1 \leqslant j \leqslant k$, of length $l = \frac{b-a}{k}$. To allow a fair comparison with the uniform method of Sect. 3.1, on each subinterval, we perform a trapezoid interpolation such that the total number of trapezoids is N. Let us split each I_j into n_j subintervals where

$$n_j = \left\lceil N \frac{\sqrt{M_j}}{\sum_{p=1}^{k} \sqrt{M_p}} \right\rceil \tag{8}$$

and where $M_j = \max_{x \in I_j} |f''(x)|$ for each $1 \leqslant j \leqslant k$. It follows that $\sum_{j=1}^{k} n_j \approx \sum_{j=1}^{k} N \frac{\sqrt{M_j}}{\sum_{p=1}^{k} \sqrt{M_p}} = N$ where the difference between the number of trapezoids and N is at most k due to the ceiling function. As a consequence, if $N \gg k$, this difference becomes negligible. For each interval I_j, our refined method consists in doing a piecewise interpolation of $f_{|I_j} : I_j \longrightarrow \mathbb{R}$ with n_j trapezoids and then aggregating the results. We can now present our main theoretical result.

Theorem 1. *Set $a, b, \in \mathbb{R}$, $k, N \in \mathbb{N}$ with $k \leq N$, and $f : [a, b] \longrightarrow \mathbb{R}$ a function of class C^2. Then the upper bound $B_{\text{tot,refined}}$ on the total error $E_{\text{tot,refined}}$ of our refined quadrature of the integral of f is tighter than that of Eq. (5) with the same number N of trapezoids:*

$$E_{\text{tot,refined}} \leq B_{\text{tot,refined}} = \sum_{j=1}^{k} \frac{l^3}{12} \frac{1}{\left(\left\lceil N \frac{\sqrt{M_j}}{\sum_{p=1}^{k} \sqrt{M_p}} \right\rceil\right)^2} |f''(\xi_j)| \leq B_{\text{tot,unif}}.$$

Here, for each $1 \leq j \leq k$, ξ_j is a well-chosen element in I_j. In particular, the more f'' varies the more the inequality on the right-hand side is strict, thus in favor of our refined quadrature rule.

Proof. Set $h_j = \frac{l}{n_j}$ for each $1 \leq j \leq k$. Then, for each $1 \leq j \leq k$, we use Eq. (6) to show that there exists $\xi_j \in I_j$ such that the total error of quadrature satisfies

$$E_{\text{tot,refined}} = \sum_{j=1}^{k} -\frac{1}{12} l h_j^2 f''(\xi_j).$$

It follows that $E_{\text{tot,refined}}$ is upper bounded by

$$B_{\text{tot,refined}} = \sum_{j=1}^{k} \frac{l^3}{12} \frac{1}{\left(\left\lceil N \frac{\sqrt{M_j}}{\sum_{p=1}^{k} \sqrt{M_p}} \right\rceil\right)^2} |f''(\xi_j)|$$

$$\leq \sum_{j=1}^{k} \frac{l^3}{12} \frac{1}{\left(N \frac{\sqrt{M_j}}{\sum_{p=1}^{k} \sqrt{M_p}} \right)^2} |f''(\xi_j)|$$

$$= \frac{l^3}{12N^2} \sum_{j=1}^{k} \left(\sum_{p=1}^{k} \frac{\sqrt{M_p}}{\sqrt{M_j}} \right)^2 |f''(\xi_j)|$$

$$\leq \frac{l^3}{12N^2} \sum_{j=1}^{k} \left(\sum_{p=1}^{k} \frac{\sqrt{M}}{\sqrt{M_j}} \right)^2 |f''(\xi_j)| \text{ (where } M = \max_{1 \leq p \leq k} M_p\text{)}$$

$$= \frac{l^3}{12N^2} \sum_{j=1}^{k} k^2 \frac{M}{M_j} |f''(\xi_j)|$$

$$= \frac{l^3 k^2}{12N^2} \left(\sum_{j=1}^{k} \frac{|f''(\xi_j)|}{M_j} \right) M$$

$$\leq \frac{l^3 k^2}{12N^2} \left(\sum_{j=1}^{k} 1 \right) M \tag{9}$$

$$= \frac{l^3 k^3}{12 N^2} M = B_{\text{tot,unif}}.$$

In particular, note that we get Eq. (9) by using the fact that $|f''(\xi_j)| \leq M_j$, and so the more f'' varies, the more this inequality is strict.

3.3 Experiments

In this section, we illustrate the behavior of our refined quadrature rule on three functions $f : [a, b] \longrightarrow \mathbb{R}$ and integers $k \leq N$. In order to determine M_j for each $1 \leq j \leq k$, we sample $S = 100$ equidistant points $x_{j,s} \in I_j$ and set $M_j = \max_{1 \leq s \leq S} |f''(x_{j,s})|$. We then compute n_j according to Eq. (8). It is worth noting at this step of the paper that the cost for computing M_j (here by selecting the max from S evaluations of f'') does not matter. The goal of this section is to give evidence that selecting $N + 1$ points according to f'' is better in terms of quadrature error than using evenly spaced points. When it comes to taking this idea, implementing it in PINNs, and comparing it with SOTA adaptive sampling methods, the same budget in terms of collocation points will be used in the learning process.

In order to avoid pathological cases, we proceed to the following adjustments:

1. If $n_j = 0$, which theoretically would happen only if $f'' = 0$ on I_j, i.e., f is linear on this interval, then we set $n_j = 1$. This will ensure that every interval contributes to the approximation of the integral of f.
2. As explained in the previous section, due to the ceiling function, the sum $\sum_{j=1}^{k} n_j$ might differ from N by at most k. In order to use exactly the same number N of trapezoids, we use the following rule: while $\sum_{j=1}^{k} n_j \neq N$,
   - if $\sum_{j=1}^{k} n_j > N$, then decrease $\max_{1 \leq j \leq k} n_j$ by 1;
   - else increase $\min_{1 \leq j \leq k} n_j$ by 1.

For the uniform method, we select $N + 1$ equidistant points between a and b included. These are the endpoints of the N trapezoids. If we write $x_i < x_{i+1}$ for the endpoints of such a trapezoid, we approximate the integral of f on $[x_i, x_{i+1}]$ by the area of said trapezoid, i.e., by $(x_{i+1} - x_i) \frac{f(x_{i+1}) + f(x_i)}{2}$. It then remains to sum over all trapezoids. The code of the examples below is available on GitHub.

3.3.1 Example 1

Consider $f(x) = (-1.4 + 3x^2) \sin(16x)$ on $[0, 2]$. For illustration, we choose $N = 25$ and $k = 11$. We report in Fig. 1 the target function f (in red) with the uniform (left) and refined (right) trapezoid approximations (in blue), and the boundary of the intervals (in green). We can see that on the right part of the domain, where there are more variations, our method is able to automatically place more points in this region. On the other hand, it uses a smaller budget where f varies less. This leads to a better approximation of the integral, reflected by a much smaller relative error (5.47%) compared to the uniform method (15.3%).

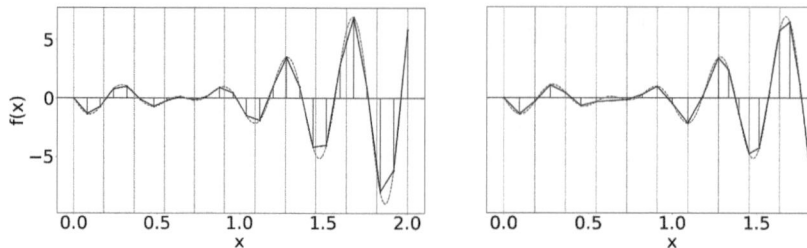

Fig. 1. Plots of $f(x) = (-1.4 + 3x^2)\sin(16x)$ on $[0, 2]$ (in red) and its trapezoid approximations (in blue) with $N = 25$; (left): uniform method; (right): refined method with $k = 11$. The relative errors are respectively 15.3% and 5.47%. (Color figure online)

We also compare in Fig. 2 both methods by varying the number k of intervals (10, 20, 30 and 40). We see that except for some local spikes, our refined method (black line) consistently gives better results than the uniform method (dashed red line, which is independent from k). As expected, the gain is higher as k increases, our method leveraging more precise information about the local variations of the function. Note that the exceptions (i.e., when the black line is above the red one) are mainly due to the use of the ceiling function in Eq. (8) which may lead to $\sum_{j=1}^{k} n_j \neq N$. In this case, we need to resort to the aforementioned manual adjustments that may lead to local overpessimistic approximations.

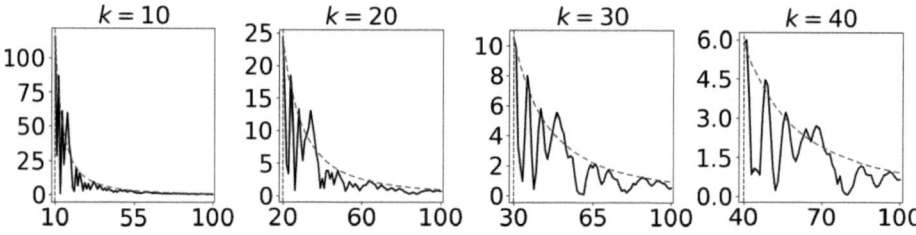

Fig. 2. Relative error for approximating $f(x) = (-1.4+3x^2)\sin(16x)$ on $[0, 2]$ as a function of N for different values of k; (red): uniform method; (black): refined quadrature; (green): $\{N = k\}$. (Color figure online)

3.3.2 Example 2

Consider now the function $f(x) = \sin(\frac{1}{\sqrt{x}})$ on $[0.1, 1]$. We report in Fig. 3 an illustration of the behavior of the two quadrature methods when $N = 25$ and $k = 10$. This example highlights a pathological behavior of the uniform method which is not able with evenly spaced quadrature points to capture the large variations of f (red curve) on some small intervals. On the other hand, our method uses only a little part of the budget (7 points among 25) for approximating the right-

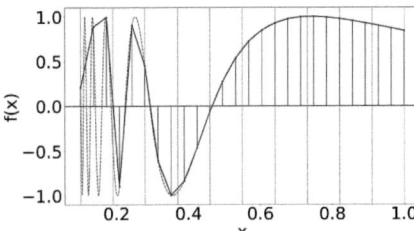 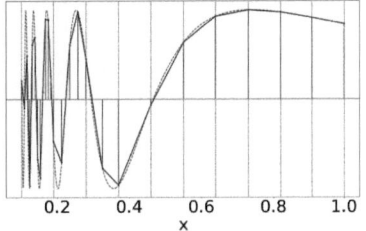

Fig. 3. Plots of $f(x) = \sin(\frac{1}{\sqrt{x}})$ on $[0.1, 1]$ (in red) and its trapezoid approximations (in blue) with $N = 25$; (left): uniform method; (right): refined method with $k = 10$. The relative errors are respectively 16.4% and 1.89%. (Color figure online)

hand part of the function and keeps most of these quadrature points for locations where the function has steep changes.

Figure 4 reports the relative approximation error as k grows from 10 to 40. As already observed in the first example, the relative gain of our refined method increases as k grows by benefiting from finer intervals and thus better capturing the variations of the function.

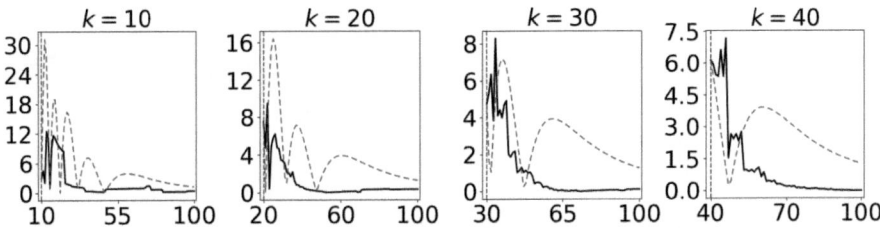

Fig. 4. Relative error for approximating $f(x) = \sin(\frac{1}{\sqrt{x}})$ on $[0.1, 1]$ as a function of N for different k; (red): uniform method; (black): refined; (green): $\{N = k\}$. (Color figure online)

3.3.3 Example 3

The last function considered in these experiments is defined as follows on $[0, 2]$. It describes a sort of shark fin.

$$f(x) = \begin{cases} -0.1 + \sqrt{1.22 - (x - 1.1)^2} & \text{if } 0 \leq x < 1, \\ 1.1 - \sqrt{1.22 - (x - 2.1)^2} & \text{if } 1 \leq x \leq 2. \end{cases} \qquad (10)$$

As illustrated in Fig. 5, this function has been chosen to emphasize the huge difference between the two methods in terms of density of quadrature points along the domain. Whereas our quadrature rule concentrates most of the points

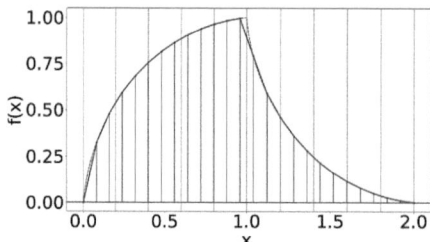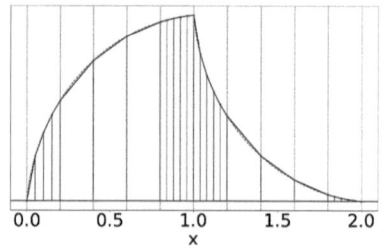

Fig. 5. Plots of function (10) (in red) and its trapezoid approximations (in blue) with $N = 25$; (left): uniform method; (right): refined method with $k = 10$. The relative quadrature errors are respectively 0.59% and 0.049%. (Color figure online)

in regions with steep variations, the uniform method makes no distinction and wastes part of the budget on easily predictable areas at the expense of a higher approximation error in the more complex regions.

Figure 6 confirms the benefit of our method (black line) in terms of relative error for different values of k. In particular, we notice oscillations with the uniform method based on the parity of N. This is because when N is odd, the top vertex of the curve is not a vertex of a trapezoid, so the precision decreases.

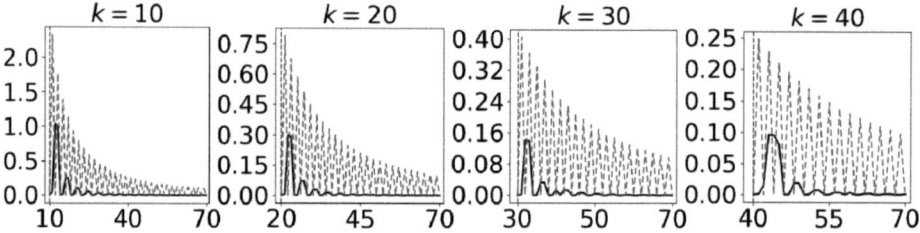

Fig. 6. Relative error for approximating Eq. (10) on $[0, 2]$ as a function of N for different values of k; (red): uniform method; (black): refined; (green): $\{N = k\}$. (Color figure online)

4 Adaptive Sampling Methods for PINNs

The previous theoretical and experimental results highlighted the importance of using the second-order derivative of f in a quadrature rule for better approximating its integral. In the context of PINNs, where f is the integrand of the loss function made of the PDE residuals (i.e., the integrand of $\mathcal{L}(\theta)$), our results state that using information from the Hessian of the residuals for sampling collocation points is better than uniformly sampling them. As mentioned in the related work section, while leveraging the gradient of the residuals has been recently used in a couple of papers (see, e.g., [18,19,22]), as far as we know, resorting

---
Algorithm 1 ★-RAD

1: Set ★ ∈ {"res", "grad", "hessian", "unif"}, τ, c, N and #$epochs$.
2: Sample a set S of initial collocation points randomly.
3: Train a PINN for a certain number of epochs.
4: **while** #$epochs$ not reached **do**
5:     Build distribution $p(\mathbf{x})$ of Eq. (11) given ★ from a set of random points.
6:     $S \leftarrow$ New set of N collocation points sampled according to $p(x)$.
7:     Train a PINN for a certain number of epochs.
8: **end while**
---

to the Hessian has not been investigated yet. Even though we formally proved that using f'' to define quadrature points is better than selecting evenly spaced points, we do not yet know how such a strategy behaves in PINNs when compared to sampling methods that leverage the magnitude or the gradient of the residuals. This is the goal of this section, which aims to gain a comprehensive grasp of the capabilities and limitation of f'' on different PDEs.

4.1 Generic Algorithm STAR-RAD (★-RAD)

To allow a fair comparison, we use a RAD-like framework where the N collocation points are sampled according to a probability density function proportional to *a criterion of interest*. The latter can be the **PDE residuals** as used in RAD [21], the **gradient** of the residuals as in [18], the **Hessian** of the residuals for our method, or a **uniform distribution** as used in a standard PINN [17]. In order to use the same setting for this comparison study, we rely on the RAD algorithm and modify it so as to allow different underlying probability density functions. Let us use the following generic distribution:

$$p(\mathbf{x}) \propto \frac{\gamma(\mathbf{x})^\tau}{\mathbb{E}[\gamma(\mathbf{x})^\tau]} + c, \tag{11}$$

where τ and c are hyperparameters. This formulation is interesting because the SOTA sampling methods can be viewed as special cases of Eq. (11). Let us consider them as instantiations of what we call in the following ★-RAD, where res-RAD, grad-RAD, hessian-RAD, and unif-RAD correspond respectively to the residual-based (i.e., where $\gamma(\mathbf{x}) = f(\mathbf{x})$), gradient-based ($\gamma(\mathbf{x}) = f'(\mathbf{x})$), Hessian-based ($\gamma(\mathbf{x}) = f''(\mathbf{x})$) and uniform-based sampling method (standard PINN obtained with $\tau = 0$ and $c \to \infty$). The pseudo-code of ★-RAD is presented in Algorithm 1.

4.2 Experimental Results

Here we perform experiments for three different PDEs, namely the 1D Newton's law of cooling, 1D Brinkman-Forchheimer equation, and 2D Poisson's equation. The analysis is mainly made in terms of convergence speed of the methods, keeping in mind that faster convergence can also be interpreted as a lower need

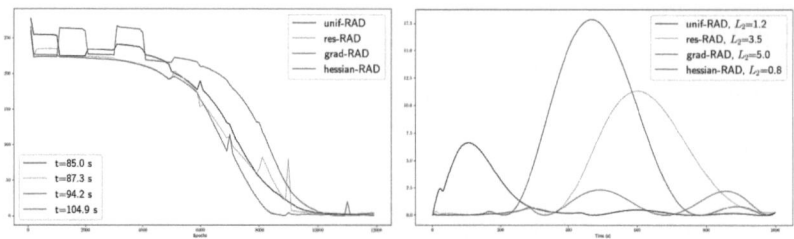

Fig. 7. (Left) L_2-test error along the first 12000 training epochs, as well as the total computational time (after the total 30000 epochs), for various sampling methods on Newton's law of cooling; (Right) Squared prediction errors along the domain $[0, 1000]$ after 12000 epochs as well as the total L_2-error.

for collocation points to achieve the same performance after a certain number of epochs. The experiments[2] have been conducted using ADAM optimizer on a Apple M1 Pro chip with 16Go RAM.

4.2.1 Newton's Law of Cooling Equation

Newton's law of cooling describes the rate of heat loss of a body as follows: $\frac{dT}{dt} = R(T_{env} - T(t))$, with $t \in [0, 1000]$, $T_{env} = 25$, $T(0) = 100$, and $R = 0.005$ (coefficient of heat transfer). The analytical solution given by $T(t) = T_{env} + (T(0) - T_{env})e^{-Rt}$ states that this rate is proportional to the difference in the temperatures between the body and its environment. We learn a PINN with a RELU activation function composed of 4 hidden layers with 100 neurons followed by a fully connected layer. The number of epochs $\#epochs = 30000$, the learning rate $\eta = 10^{-5}$, the number of collocation points $N = 40$ drawn according to $p(x)$ (Eq. (11)) approximated from 4000 candidates, $\tau = 1/2$ and $c = 0$. We resample every 1000 epochs.

Figure 7 (left) reports the L_2-test error (i.e., $(T(x) - u_\theta(x))^2$) computed along the first 12000 training epochs (i.e., until convergence is reached for all methods) from an equispaced uniform grid composed of 1000 test points. We can see that even though the four competing methods successfully learn the neural solver, benefiting from the second-order derivative (green curve) allows to converge faster. To illustrate the gain in terms of prediction errors over the entire domain, Fig. 7 (right) describes the error suffered by $u_\theta(x)$ after 12000 epochs (the behaviors of the 4 methods do not change afterwards). We can see that our hessian-RAD gives a better approximation of the solution without suffering from a too large computational burden.

---

[2] The code is available in our GitHub repository.

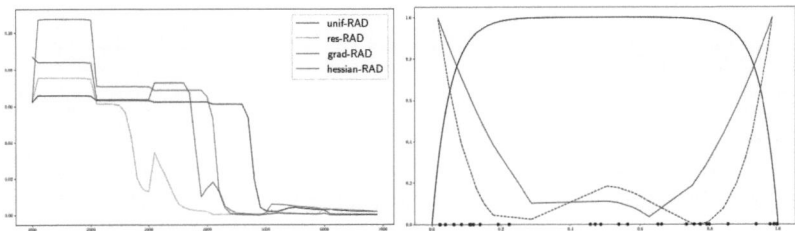

Fig. 8. (Left) Comparison of the L_2-test errors between iterations 1000 and 7000 on Brinkman-Forchheimer; (Right): Analytical solution of the PDE (black), normalized loss (purple dashed) and $|f''|$ (green) after 3000 epochs, and collocation points (in blue) generated by hessian-RAD after 3000 epochs. (Color figure online)

4.2.2 Brinkman-Forchheimer

The Brinkman-Forchheimer model is an extended Darcy's law and is used to describe wall-bounded porous media flows:

$$-\frac{\nu_e}{\epsilon}\frac{d^2 u}{d\mathbf{x}^2} + \frac{\nu}{K}u(\mathbf{x}) = g,$$

with $\mathbf{x} \in [0, H]$, $\nu_e = \nu = 10^{-3}$, $\epsilon = 0.4$, $K = 10^{-3}$, $g = 1$, and $H = 1$. The analytical solution is $u(x) = \frac{gK}{\nu}\left(1 - \frac{\cosh(r(x - \frac{H}{2}))}{\cosh(\frac{rH}{2})}\right)$ with $r = \sqrt{\frac{\nu\epsilon}{\nu_e K}}$ and is depicted in Fig. 8 (right, black curve). u represents the fluid velocity, g denotes the external force, ν is the kinetic viscosity of the fluid, ϵ is the porosity of the porous medium, and K is the permeability. The effective viscosity ν_e is related to the pore structure. A no-slip boundary condition is imposed, i.e., $u(0) = u(1) = 0$. We learn a PINN with the tanh activation function composed of 3 hidden layers with 20 neurons followed by a fully connected layer. We used the following parameters: #epochs = 30000, $\eta = 10^{-3}$, $N = 30$, $\tau = 1/2$ and $c = 0$. We resample every 1000 epochs.

Figure 8 (left) reports the L_2-test error computed along the first 7000 training epochs before convergence of the 4 competing methods. If we can observe that the three adaptive methods (using f, f' and f'') are better than a standard uniform sampling-based PINN (blue line), this figure also states that the convergence of derivative-based methods (both f' and f'') is a bit slower than a residual-based sampling. The reason for this phenomenon comes from the shape of the function which, apart the initial and final steep changes, presents a large plateau. To analyze the impact of the latter, we plot on Fig. 8 (right) the residuals (dashed purple line) as well as $|f''|$ (green line) after 3000 epochs (illustrating a situation where f is much better than f''). As expected, as f'' does not vary much between 0.3 and 0.6, hessian-RAD places only a few collocation points along this interval, keeping most of the budget where it varies the most. Consequently, the resulting PINN makes errors in this region that do not affect the empirical loss too much, but leading to a poor behavior at test time. The same interpretation can be

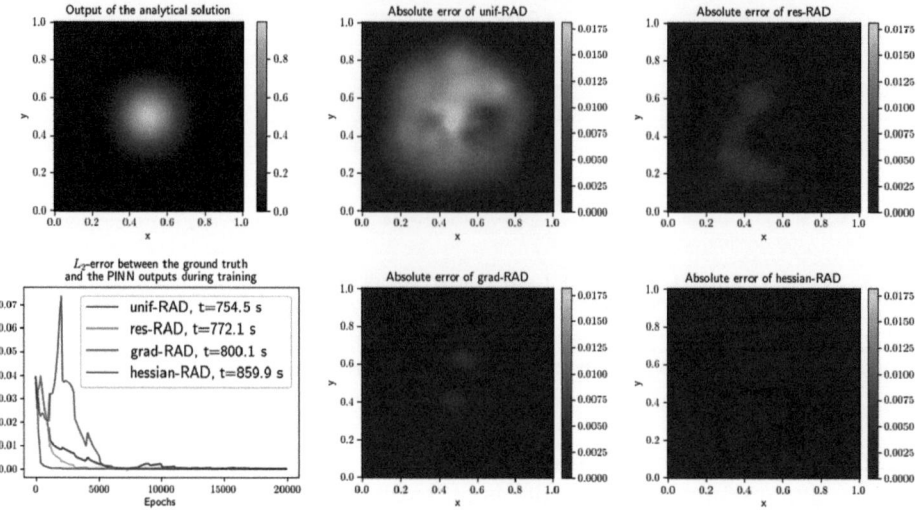

Fig. 9. (Top left) Analytical solution of Poisson's PDE; (Bottom Left) L_2-test error along the first 20000 training epochs, with computational time; (Right) Heatmaps of errors of the 4 sampling methods after 20000 epochs.

provided for grad-RAD, both methods requiring more iterations to converge. Nevertheless, note that hessian-RAD reaches eventually the best prediction.

4.2.3 2D Poisson's PDE

Poisson's equation is an elliptic PDE used in theoretical physics. It involves second derivatives of $u(x, y)$ and is given by $\Delta u = F(x, y)$, where $(x, y) \in [0, 1]^2$. We take F such that $u(x, y) = 2^{4a} x^a (1-x)^a y^a (1-y)^a$ with $a = 10$ is the analytical solution (depicted in Fig. 9 (top left)). We learn a PINN with the tanh activation function composed of 3 hidden layers with 20 neurons followed by a fully connected layer. We used the following parameters: $\#epochs = 20000$, $\eta = 10^{-3}$, $N = 400$ drawn according to $p(x)$ approximated from 40000 candidates, $\tau = 1/2$ and $c = 0$. We resample every 1000 epochs. The most striking comment we can make from Fig. 9 (bottom left) is that hessian-RAD fully takes advantage of the abrupt variations of the Poisson solution to converge much faster than the others. About 1000 epochs are sufficient for learning the problem while the competing strategies require much more iterations to stabilize. Interestingly, even after 20000 epochs when the methods seem to have converged to an exact solution, the gap in terms of prediction error in favor of our method is important, as illustrated with the four heat maps of Fig. 9 (right part). Again, even though computing the Hessian is more costly, the additional burden is reasonable and compensated by a better prediction.

5 Conclusion and Perspectives

We have presented a provably accurate quadrature method based on second-order derivatives, which performs very well for estimating the integral of a function f. Exploiting the Hessian of the residuals shows also promising results when used in a sampling method for PINNs. The observations made from the Brinkman-Forchheimer PDE give raise to a future possible direction consisting in sampling the collocation points according to different distributions. This has already been done in [18], but only by combining uniformly sampled points with others drawn according to residual information (magnitude or gradient). The results obtained on this PDE rather suggest that a combination of f with f' and/or f'' in complicated regions would be relevant. Identifying automatically these challenging parts of the domain is an open question. One could consider a hybrid approach in which the zones where the derivative is below some threshold are decomposed into grids. The size of such a grid could be proportional to the size of the zone and the total number of collocation points. Elsewhere, the sampling would follow the values of the derivative. This would ensure that such areas are not left out during the training process and the L_2-test error might go down more rapidly. On the other hand, while using the Hessian has been shown to be beneficial in a PINN training, it can become costly in high dimensions. A first mitigation attempt would be a simple stochastic approach, where at each resampling iteration, the entries of the Hessian to be computed are sampled. Another approach is to build on the fact that methods like gPINN are beneficial and already do a big part of the computations necessary for the Hessian, and thus these can be combined almost for free. Indeed, these methods compute the gradient (w.r.t. the parameters) of the gradient (w.r.t. spatio-temporal dimensions). In a deep network, this gradient of gradient already needs to back-propagate almost back to the input and thus computing the Hessian is almost free in such a case. This would also allow having a resampling step that is executed more often, possibly at every iteration, by computing the empirical max of f'' (using the current collocation points) in cells and resampling points using this information. Finally, note that the reasoning in Sect. 3.1 is based on the Lagrange remainder theorem, which itself uses the fact that $p(x)$ is a polynomial in x of degree at most 1, hence $p''(x) = 0$. Consider $f(x, y)$ of two variables in a square $[x_1, x_2] \times [y_1, y_2]$. The natural analogue of p would be a function $P(x, y) = a_0 + a_1 x + a_2 y + a_3 xy$ linear in both x and y such that $f = P$ on the corners of the square. But if $a_3 \neq 0$, then $P(x, y)$ has non-zero second order terms, so the reasoning cannot be extended. Moreover, if one were to push the computations further, the error term becomes too complicated to manipulate like in the proof of Theorem 1. Another approach is hence needed in order to generalize to higher dimensions.

Acknowledgments. This work has been funded by a public grant from the French National Research Agency under the "France 2030" investment plan, which has the reference EUR MANUTECH SLEIGHT - ANR-17-EURE-0026.

Disclosure of Interests. The authors have no competing interests to declare that are relevant to the content of this article.

References

1. Bajaj, C., McLennan, L., Andeen, T., Roy, A.: Recipes for when physics fails: recovering robust learning of physics informed neural networks. Mach. Learn. Sci. Technol. **4**(1) (2023)
2. Chen, R.T.Q., Rubanova, Y., Bettencourt, J., Duvenaud, D.: Neural ordinary differential equations. In: NeurIPS (2018)
3. Daw, A., Bu, J., Wang, S., Perdikaris, P., Karpatne, A.: Mitigating propagation failures in physics-informed neural networks using retain-resample-release (R3) sampling. Proc. Mach. Learn. Res. **202** (2023)
4. De Ryck, T., Jagtap, A.D., Mishra, S.: Error estimates for physics informed neural networks approximating the Navier-Stokes equations. IMA J. Numer. Anal. **44**(1), 83–119 (2024)
5. De Ryck, T., Lanthaler, S., Mishra, S.: On the approximation of functions by tanh neural networks. Neural Netw. **143**, 732–750 (2021)
6. De Ryck, T, Mishra, S.: Generic bounds on the approximation error for physics-informed (and) operator learning. In: NeurIPS (2022)
7. Doumèche, N., Biau, G., Boyer, C.: Convergence and error analysis of PINNs. arXiv:2305.01240 (2023)
8. Girault, B., Emonet, R., Habrard, A., Patracone, J., Sebban, M.: Approximation error of Sobolev regular functions with tanh neural networks: theoretical impact on PINNs. In: ECML (2024)
9. Hamming, R.W.: Numerical methods for scientists and engineers, 2nd ed. International Series in Pure and Applied Mathematics (1973)
10. Karniadakis, G.E., Kevrekidis, I.G., Lu, L., Perdikaris, P., Wang, S., Yang, L.: Physics-informed machine learning. Nat. Rev. Phys. **3**(6), 422–440 (2021)
11. Lanthaler, S., Mishra, S., Karniadakis, G.E.: Error estimates for DeepONets: a deep learning framework in infinite dimensions. Trans. Math. Appl. **6**(1) (2022)
12. Li, Z., et al.: Fourier neural operator for parametric partial differential equations. In: ICLR 2021, Austria, 3–7 May 2021. OpenReview.net (2021)
13. Li, Z., et al.: Physics-informed neural operator for learning partial differential equations. arXiv:2111.03794 (2021)
14. Long, Z., Lu, Y., Ma, X., Dong, B.: PDE-Net: learning PDEs from data. In: Proceedings of the 35th International Conference on Machine Learning (2018)
15. Lu, L., Meng, X., Mao, Z., Karniadakis, G.E.: Deepxde: a deep learning library for solving differential equations. SIAM Rev. **63**(1), 208–228 (2021)
16. Peng, W., Zhou, W., Zhang, X., Yao, W., Liu, Z.: RANG: a residual-based adaptive node generation method for physics-informed neural networks. arXiv:2205.01051 (2022)
17. Raissi, M., Perdikaris, P., Karniadakis, G.E.: Physics-informed neural networks: a deep learning framework for solving forward and inverse problems involving nonlinear partial differential equations. J. Comput. Phys. (2019)
18. Subramanian, S., Kirby, R.M., Mahoney, M.W., Gholami, A.: Adaptive self-supervision algorithms for physics-informed neural networks. In: ECAI (2023)
19. Visser, C., Heinlein, A., Giovanardi, B.: PACMANN: point adaptive collocation method for artificial neural networks. arXiv:2411.19632 (2024)

20. Wang, S., Yu, X., Perdikaris, P.: When and why PINNs fail to train: a neural tangent kernel perspective. J. Comput. Phys. **449** (2022)
21. Wu, C., Zhu, M., Tan, Q., Kartha, Y., Lu, L.: A comprehensive study of non-adaptive and residual-based adaptive sampling for physics-informed neural networks. Comput. Methods Appl. Mech. Eng. **403** (2023)
22. Yu, J., Lu, L., Meng, X., Karniadakis, G.E.: Gradient-enhanced physics-informed neural networks for forward and inverse PDE problems. Comput. Methods Appl. Mech. Eng. **393** (2022)

The Role of Transformer Architecture in the Logic-as-Loss Framework

Mattia Medina Grespan and Vivek Srikumar(✉)

Kahlert School of Computing, University of Utah, Salt Lake City, UT 84112, USA
{mattiamg,svivek}@cs.utah.edu

Abstract. The logic-as-loss framework has enabled transformer models to incorporate domain knowledge by encoding logical constraints as differentiable objectives, allowing neural networks to learn from explicit rules. Despite its effectiveness across diverse tasks, the relationship between neural architecture and rule internalization remains poorly understood. This study systematically investigates how transformer encoder configurations influence the ingestion of logical rules, beyond simply scaling up model capacity. We aim to identify the architectural factors that enable successful rule internalization and the inherent limitations of this process. Empirical analysis on controlled reasoning tasks reveals a capacity threshold: transformers perform poorly at rule adherence below a critical parameter count, while performance plateaus above it. A key finding is that embedding dimensionality drives rule ingestion efficacy, while increased network depth mitigates spurious solutions that satisfy rules without improving task performance. Our work highlights the role of architectural design choices for effective neuro-symbolic learning.

Keywords: Neuro-symbolic models · Logic-as-loss · Knowledge-driven learning

1 Introduction

Integrating domain knowledge into deep learning models using logic rules is an effective strategy to address data inefficiencies [9]. One successful approach calls for encoding data and task-specific rules declaratively in predicate logic, which is then compiled to define loss functions [10,13,17,22,30]. The models trained with these losses not only fit observed data but also tend to adhere to domain constraints. We will call this the *logic-as-loss* framework, which includes two broad technical strategies: using model-counting based approaches (e.g., the semantic loss [30]), or using t-norm logic relaxations [13]. Both transform logical formulas into sub-differentiable loss functions, and have shown success across a diverse set of tasks [4,17]. In this work, we focus on the t-norm logic relaxations.

Despite empirical successes across multiple tasks, especially those involving the transformer architecture, the factors that lead to this effectiveness are relatively underexplored. In particular, while previous work compares different

---

Supplementary Information The online version contains supplementary material available at https://doi.org/10.1007/978-3-032-06096-9_3.

t-norm relaxations [7,10,24], the interplay between the neural network architectural choices and the success of the logic-as-loss agenda remains unexamined.

By training neural networks to produce only logically consistent outputs, we expect model parameters to encode the rules. *How do the architectural choices, and consequently the expressive capacity, of a model influence its ability to ingest and enforce logical constraints?* Although transformer models [26] are ubiquitous across many domains [6,20], there is no systematic analysis of how their configurations — layer depth, embedding dimensionality, or number of attention heads — affect the ability to ingest rules for multi-hop logical reasoning.

In this paper, we investigate the impact of transformer architectural choices on the logic-as-loss approach. We ask: (1) How large must a model be (i.e., how many parameters are needed) to learn complex logical constraints? (2) How do architectural factors (beyond sheer parameter count) influence this process? We employ controlled reasoning tasks to study these questions: collinearity in the plane and two Latin square based puzzles, Futoshiki and Sudoku. For each task, we examine the impact of transformer architectural parameters — embedding dimensionality, number of encoder layers, attention heads, and feed-forward dimensionality — on the ability to ingest rules via losses.

Across these experiments, we find a capacity threshold below which the model struggles to learn logical constraints; once the threshold is crossed, performance stabilizes. Embedding dimensionality emerges as an especially critical design choice, while increased depth helps mitigate vacuous rule satisfaction. In certain settings, smaller models even outperform larger ones, suggesting that scaling alone does not guarantee better logic ingestion. Together, these observations underscore the importance of tailoring architectural choices — particularly embedding size and depth — to reap the benefits of the logic-as-loss approach.

Our contributions are threefold. First, we design a focused set of controlled tasks to help study the ability of neural models to learn from rules. Second, we systematically explore the influence of transformer architecture in the logic-as-loss framework, revealing how model capacity, depth, and embedding size shape performance. Finally, we discuss key insights on balancing depth versus width and present guidelines for designing models that effectively integrate domain knowledge through logical constraints.[1]

2 Logic-As-Loss Approach: Background

The logic-as-loss approach views machine learning tasks as declarative contracts for a neural network to satisfy. Models are required not only to produce correct labels for supervised examples, but also to satisfy logical constraints drawn from domain knowledge. This section gives a brief overview of the framework.

2.1 Declarative Specification with Predicate Logic

Predicate logic is the specification language in the logic-as-loss framework. Let $\mathcal{X}$ be the input domain and $\mathcal{Y}$ the finite set of task labels. A labeled dataset is

---
[1] The code and data for replicating our results, along with the appendix document, are archived at https://github.com/utahnlp/logic_as_loss_with_transformers/.

a set $D \subset \mathcal{X} \times \mathcal{Y}$ of pairs (x,y), while $U \subset \mathcal{X}$ denotes additional inputs drawn from the same distribution but without ground-truth labels.

Atomic Predicates and Rules. For every label $y \in \mathcal{Y}$ we introduce the atomic predicate
$$\text{y}(x) : \text{"the instance } x \text{ has the label } y\text{"}.$$
Task-specific axioms or expert knowledge are expressed by rules $C(x)$ that may apply to any instance $x \in D \cup U$. Because every unlabeled input will ultimately be mapped to some $y \in \mathcal{Y}$ by the model, the atomic predicates $\text{y}(x)$ and the constraints $C(x)$ are well-defined for all inputs in $D \cup U$.

Logic-as-Loss Objective. The labeled examples require the model to match ground-truth labels, while the rules propagate domain knowledge to all inputs. Learning amounts to ensuring the following logical expression holds:

$$\left(\bigwedge_{(x,y) \in D} \text{y}(x) \right) \wedge \left(\bigwedge_{(x \in U)} C(x) \right). \qquad (1)$$

2.2 Loss Relaxation with T-Norm Logics

A common strategy to construct losses from the specification above employs t-norms [12] that generalize the logical connectives into the real domain. Each element in the declarative loss is relaxed by translating the connectives with their corresponding relaxation definition, enabling standard gradient-based optimization. There are infinitely many t-norms; Table 1 in Appendix A presents the three canonical t-norms typically used.

Neural models predict the probabilities for the atomic predicates. The goal of learning is to find model parameters that maximize a real-valued relaxation of the specification (1). Logic directly yields a differentiable loss function, making it possible to learn the predicate models by optimizing the total loss derived from the labeled data D and the constraints C applied to unlabeled examples:

$$L = L_D + \lambda L_C. \qquad (2)$$

Here, λ is a non-negative hyper-parameter for the knowledge constraints.

T-norm losses have been successfully used in recent literature across multiple tasks [13,17,27]. While the underlying framework is agnostic to the choice of the neural network, these applications use language models that rely on the transformer family of models.

2.3 General Learning Setting for the Logic-as-Loss Framework

Let $O = \{o_1, o_2, \ldots, o_m\}$ denote a set of objects (e.g., sentences, one cell in a Sudoku game). An instance x may consist of one or more objects from the set O (e.g., $x = o_1$ or $x = (o_1, o_2, o_3)$) and represents a collection of objects (e.g., a document, or an entire Sudoku with multiple cells). Let $Y = \{y_1, y_2, \ldots, y_n\}$ be the set of possible task labels that are attached to objects in instances. We associate each label y_i with a predicate y_i defined over objects in the set O. A single labeled observation (o, y) corresponds to the predicate $y(o)$. Together, we have the labeled dataset D in (1). Additionally, logical rules specify how these predicates labels interact within an instance (e.g., $y_1(o_1) \rightarrow \neg y_2(o_2)$). Aggregated across instances, we get the constraints C in (1).

We can identify two learning settings that differ in how many labeled observations are available.

Setting 1: Learning with Supervision or the "Generalization" Setting. An instance x may contain both labeled objects (observations) and unlabeled ones. The observations and task rules constitute the sets D and C in (1) respectively. The constraints C indirectly supervise the unlabeled objects through their relationships with labeled objects. In this setting, we evaluate the model by its accuracy on objects whose labels were entirely withheld during training—revealed only at test time—together with the degree to which its predictions satisfy the specified logical rules.

Setting 2: Rule-Only or the "Solving" Setting. A second scenario involves no direct supervision (i.e., $D = \emptyset$). The truth value of every predicate is determined solely by instance-level logical constraints. This is akin to solving a puzzle with internally consistent labels. Here, the training process adapts the model parameters to satisfy all the rules for a single instance. Because there is no labeled data and no constraints crossing instances, we can disentangle the instances from each other. In other words, there is no notion of generalizing beyond a given instance. This scenario resembles a classical constraint satisfaction problem, rather than a standard predictive task.

These two settings illustrate how logic-as-loss can flexibly accommodate different availability of labeled data and types of domain knowledge, ranging from partially supervised tasks to purely rule-defined puzzles.

3 Investigating Logic-Aware Transformers

The logic-as-loss framework requires neural networks to produce logically consistent outputs after training. This drives the network's parameters to capture the task-specific rules introduced during training. A natural question then arises: *how do the size and complexity of a model impact its ability to learn from rules?*

We focus on transformer networks. They are not only the de facto choice for a broad range of tasks, but have also been successfully used in logic-as-loss pipelines as noted in §2. Yet, little is known about the impact of architectural design decisions on their ability to internalize and enforce logical constraints. To probe this, we use three controlled tasks. We introduce a new **collinearity** task in §3.1, which requires inferring whether a set of points on a plane are collinear. We examine two Latin square reasoning puzzles—specifically, **Sudoku** and **Futoshiki**—in §3.2. Due to their structural complexity, these have been used in recent literature to study model reasoning capabilities [5,18,21].

By varying transformer size and architectural configurations in these tasks, we aim to uncover when and why logic-as-loss succeeds (or fails), and how model design contributes to logically consistent behavior.

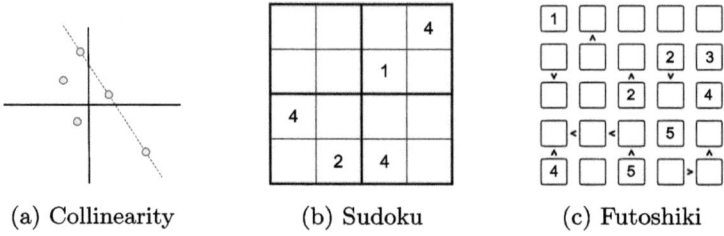

Fig. 1. Controlled reasoning tasks used for evaluation. (a) **Collinearity**: determine whether a given set of points in the plane lies on a common straight line. (b) **Sudoku** (4 × 4 variant): complete the grid so that each row, column, and 2 × 2 block contains all digits exactly once. (c) **Futoshiki** (5 × 5 variant): fill the grid such that each row and column contains all digits exactly once, while also satisfying the specified inequality constraints between adjacent cells; note that no sub-block constraints apply.

3.1 Collinearity in the Real Plane

We introduce a new task of detecting collinearity among points in the real plane. Each instance is a finite *set* of points $\{p_1, p_2, \ldots\} \subset \mathbb{R}^2$ (Fig. 1a). We define multiple collinearity-related predicates, detailed below.

At the core of the collinearity task is the predicate $\texttt{Collinear3}(p_1, p_2, p_3)$, which is *true* if, and only if, three points p_1, p_2, p_3 lie on the same straight line. This predicate serves as the primary source of supervision: we have a labeled dataset of triplets indicating whether they are collinear or not.

Building on $\texttt{Collinear3}$, we define three more predicates by logical formulas that tie back to $\texttt{Collinear3}$.

1. **Collinearity of four points:** A group of four points is collinear if *every triplet* within that group is collinear.

$$\texttt{Collinear4}(p_1, p_2, p_3, p_4) \leftrightarrow \bigwedge_{1 \leq i < j < k \leq 4} \texttt{Collinear3}(p_i, p_j, p_k). \quad (3)$$

2. **Presence of 3-point collinearity:** A set S *has three collinear points* if it contains at least one collinear triplet.

$$\texttt{HasCollinear3}(S) \leftrightarrow \exists p_1, p_2, p_3 \in S : \texttt{Collinear3}(p_1, p_2, p_3). \quad (4)$$

3. **Presence of 4-point collinearity:** A set S has *four collinear points* if it contains at least one collinear subset with four points.

$$\texttt{HasCollinear4}(S) \leftrightarrow \exists p_1, p_2, p_3, p_4 \in S : \texttt{Collinear4}(p_1, p_2, p_3, p_4). \quad (5)$$

Note that *only* Collinear3 is supervised directly from data. The rest — Collinear4, HasCollinear3, and HasCollinear4 — receive no direct labels and instead derive their semantics through their definitions.

Joint Training via Logic-as-Loss. We use a common transformer network to embed an instance (a point set), and define separate classification heads for each predicate. Using logic-as-loss, we can derive the t-norm losses corresponding to labeled examples and each of the constraints. (Due to space constraints, we do not show the relaxations here. They can be obtained systematically as detailed in §2 and Appendix A.) The loss penalizes the network whenever Collinear3 deviates from its labeled ground truth *or* any of the derived formulas are violated. That is, the training objective enforces: (a) correct classification of labeled triplets for Collinear3, and (b) consistency with logical rules (3)–(5).

This task exemplifies the setting 1 of partially supervised logic-as-loss in §2.3. By minimizing logical violations, the model learns to propagate collinearity knowledge from the supervised triplets to the more complex unlabeled predicates relying solely on rules.

3.2 Sudoku and Futoshiki

Beyond geometric reasoning, we consider two logic puzzles: *Sudoku* and *Futoshiki*. Both are defined over an $n \times n$ grid, where some cells are *given* (pre-filled) and the rest must be *predicted*.

A standard Sudoku grid is governed by three *fixed* constraints that apply to every instance: (i) each row must contain the digits $1, \ldots, n$ exactly once, (ii) each column must contain the digits $1, \ldots, n$ exactly once, and (iii) each $\sqrt{n} \times \sqrt{n}$ sub-grid (or "block") must also contain each digit exactly once (Fig. 1b).

Futoshiki[2] is a Latin square puzzle variant that always enforces the row and column uniqueness constraints (i)–(ii). Unlike Sudoku, it lacks block constraints. Instead, each instance includes a set of $<$ or $>$ relations between adjacent cells (Fig. 1c). These inequality constraints are dynamic: both their number and placement vary across puzzles.

The label space for these tasks comprises all possible digit assignments for each cell, formalized as predicates $\texttt{Cell}(r, c, d)$: the cell in row r and column c contains digit d. Puzzle-specific rules (e.g., "each digit must appear exactly once in every row, column, and sub-grid" for Sudoku, or Futoshiki inequalities) form the logical constraints.

For example, consider the rule that each digit must appear exactly once in every row. First, each digit must appear on each row: for each digit d and row

---

[2] From the Japanese word for "inequality." The standard grid size is $n = 5$, though larger sizes are common.

r, some column c contains the digit d. Second, no digit can appear more than once in each row. This is, for a digit d, a row r, and two columns c, c', the cells (r, c) and (r, c') cannot both contain the digit d. That is, we have

$$\forall d, r \,\exists c : \texttt{Cell}(r, c, d). \tag{6}$$

$$\forall d, r, c, c' \neq c : \neg[\texttt{Cell}(r, c, d) \land \texttt{Cell}(r, c', d)]. \tag{7}$$

Puzzle-Solving Setting. Each puzzle is an independent instance. So, given a puzzle, we can train a model to solve *only that puzzle*. The system trivially learns the given cells (as they are fully known) and relies on puzzle rules to fill in the remaining cells. Since there is no labeled supervision for the hidden cells, the model must derive their values exclusively from the logical constraints. This instantiates the purely rule-defined learning scenario, i.e., setting 2 from §2.3.

Generalization Setting. In this setting, we train on a collection of distinct Sudoku or Futoshiki instances—each defined by its own set of given cells and, in the case of Futoshiki, a unique pattern of cell-to-cell inequalities. We evaluate on a disjoint test set comprising puzzle configurations that were never seen during training. Thus, each test example is an *unseen puzzle*, differing both in its initial given values and, for Futoshiki, in its inequality layout.

1. **Given-Cells Only**: Only the puzzle's given cells are available, forcing the model to *copy* them into the solution and use the *rules* for the other cells.
2. **Full Solutions**: Each puzzle's complete solution is labeled, offering direct supervision for every cell in addition to the puzzle constraints.

By training over multiple puzzles, we seek to learn a *general procedure* for solving new puzzles in a single forward pass. This setting is considerably more challenging as it incentivizes network parameters to internalize rules and patterns across various puzzle configurations.

4 Experimental Setup

Our experiments share a common framework built around the transformer architecture. Given input sequences (e.g., points in the real plane or puzzle cells), we first apply an embedding layer and a positional encoding module, then process them with a transformer encoder. The encoder output is mapped to a set of linear classifier heads, each corresponding to an atomic predicate in the declarative objective. Following [10], we use the R-product t-norm relaxations of logic to obtain loss functions. Appendix A provides additional details.

Training proceeds in two stages. First, we optimize predicates whose ground-truth labels are available, monitoring performance on a development set for early stopping. We then introduce knowledge rules into the objective and continue training with the combined loss. Final model selection is guided by both labeled predicates performance on the development set and the degree of rule consistency over unlabeled instances. We optimize our system with AdamW with weight decay [16] and learning rate scheduling with warmup and linear decay. Both, optimizer and scheduler are reset before the second stage of training with rules. We applied gradient clipping to stabilize training.

We explore various configurations of the standard transformer encoder architecture by modifying the input embedding dimension, number of encoder layers, attention heads, and feedforward dimensionalities. For each configuration, we further tune learning rates, batch sizes, layer normalization position, and rule coefficients in the declarative loss. We run experiments with three random seeds and report the mean performance in a hold-out test set unless otherwise stated. The best values for these hyperparameters and architectural settings differ across tasks. We describe these, and the datasets and experimental protocols in subsequent sections. Appendix B also gives more details for experiment replication.

Statistical Analysis of Architectural Parameters. To assess the impact of architectural parameters on performance, we group model results by each parameter individually (e.g., embedding dimensionality, number of layers, attention heads, and feedforward dimensionality). Within each parameter, models with identical settings form a distinct group, and we examine performance differences among these groups. Our preliminary analysis revealed that scores for the metrics evaluated across groups are similarly distributed but typically not normally distributed, as confirmed by the Shapiro–Wilk test ($p \leq 0.05$). Therefore, we apply the non-parametric Kruskal–Wallis test to identify significant overall differences in median performance across groups. If a significant difference emerges ($p \leq 0.05$), we perform pairwise comparisons using Dunn's post-hoc test with Bonferroni correction. Significant differences between adjacent parameter sizes are denoted in our results as: * ($p \leq 0.05$), ** ($p \leq 0.01$), and *** ($p \leq 0.001$).

5 Collinearity Experiments

Data Generation. We have four predicates, each representing a different collinearity concept, and we collect a separate dataset for each. We sample points on the real plane uniformly from the square $[-1, 1] \times [-1, 1]$ to construct four datasets: (a) *Collinear3*: Triplets of points, (b) *Collinear4*: Sets of four points, (c) *HasCollinear3*: Sets of five points, and, (d) *HasCollinear4*: sets of five points. Every dataset is split into 20K training examples, 4K development examples, and 4K test examples, balanced with positive and negative labels.

Model and Training. We use the experimental setup described in §4. The first stage of training focuses on `Collinear3` for 100 epochs (with early stopping based on development-set F1). *Stage 2* incorporates rule-based terms for `Collinear4`, `HasCollinear3`, and `HasCollinear4`, continuing training for 30 epochs (with reinitialized learning scheduler and optimizer) under early stopping. The best rule-constrained model is selected using the average between `Collinear3` F1 performance and the proportions of examples satisfying the rules (3), (4), and (5) in §3.1. Importantly, only `Collinear3` has direct supervision.

We conduct a grid search over batch sizes $\{16, 32, 64\}$, learning rates $\{10^{-3}, 10^{-4}, 10^{-5}\}$, and rule-loss coefficients $\{5, 1, 0.1, 0.01, 0.001\}$ for each transformer configuration. We study the following architectural variations:

- **Embedding Dimensions**: $\{4, 16, 32, 64, 128\}$,
- **Encoder Layers**: $\{1, 2, 4, 6, 8\}$,
- **Attention Heads**: $\{2, 4, 8, 16\}$,
- **Feedforward Dimensionality**: $\frac{1}{2}\times$, $1\times$, or $2\times$ the embedding size.

This results in 270 distinct configurations. Further details on implementation and batching are in the Appendix C.

Evaluation. We evaluate the jointly trained model on the held-out test sets by reporting the **F1** score for each predicate classifier: `Collinear3`, `Collinear4`, `HasCollinear3`, and `HasCollinear4`. Predictions are generated by applying the corresponding linear head to each point tuple. Since only `Collinear3` is directly supervised, performance on the remaining predicates reflects the model's grasp of the rule-based definitions acquired during training.

Results. Figure 2 reports median F1 scores for each predicate across the transformer architectures (see §4). We observe a significant improvement in performance when embedding dimensionality increases from 4 to 16 across all predicates, after which performance does not improve with larger embedding dimensions (Fig. 2a). Similarly, models with two or more encoder layers significantly outperform single-layer models (Fig. 2b). This indicates that the system requires a minimum input dimensionality and encoders to achieve optimal performance; increasing above this threshold does not help.

Configurations with the maximum number of attention heads (16) outperform those with fewer heads, but only slightly so (Fig. 2c). Varying feedforward dimensionality do not exhibit statistically significant differences (Fig. 2d).

We found that the median baseline F1 for `Collinear3` is 97.1%, based on ground-truth supervision before introducing logical constraints. However, after constrained training, models with limited capacity (embedding dimension 4 and depth 1, Figs. 2a and 2b) perform worse than direct supervision. Yet, such models exhibit perfect rule satisfaction, suggesting they converge to spurious solutions that trivially satisfy the constraints.

Figure 3 shows F1 scores for the `HasCollinear3` predicate against model capacity (total parameter count). We observe a performance jump when models reach approximately 16 embedding dimensions and 6 encoder layers. Below this threshold, models struggle to use logical rules effectively. However, once the minimum parameter requirement is met (darker green points), performance stabilizes, with little to no improvement for larger models. Past this threshold, narrow and deep architectures outperform wide and shallow architectures, consistent with previous studies [23, 29]. Furthermore, wider and shallower models with higher number of parameters are more susceptible to degenerate solutions, but increased depth mitigates this issue.

We find similar trends for the unsupervised `Collinear4` and `HasCollinear4` predicates. Due to space constraints, the details are in Appendix C.

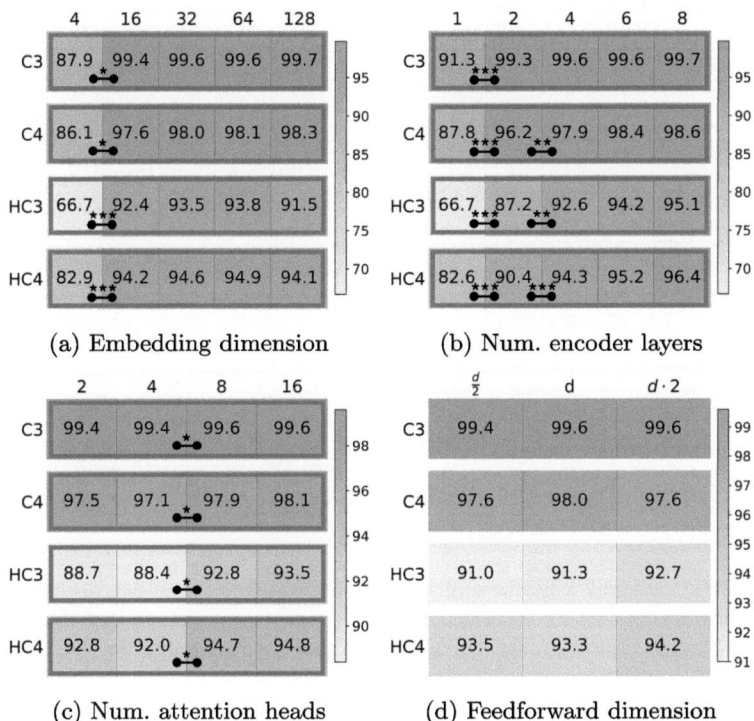

Fig. 2. Median F1 score for each architectural parameter value for the predicates `Collinear3` (C3), `Collinear4` (C4), `HasCollinear3` (HC3), and `HasCollinear4` (HC4). Groups of values statistically different are enclosed in green rectangles, and post-hoc significant adjacent pairs are connected by black segments. (Color figure online)

6 Puzzle Tasks

Sudoku and Futoshiki Datasets. For both puzzle tasks, we construct datasets for two learning settings: a *solving* setting, where the model learns to solve a single instance solely through rule interactions; and a *generalization* setting, where the model is trained on a set of puzzles with rule-based supervision and evaluated on its ability to solve unseen instances.

For Sudoku, we use the *4×4 sudoku* Kaggle dataset.[3] We extract 288 puzzles with unique solutions[4] and different difficulty levels: 96 easy puzzles (6–7 hidden cells), 96 medium puzzles (8–9 hidden cells), and 96 hard puzzles (10–12 hidden cells). From this set, we sample 100 puzzles (33 easy, 34 medium, 33 hard) for the solving setting. For the generalization setting, the 288 puzzles are split into training (70%), development (15%), and test (15%) sets, stratified by difficulty.

---

[3] https://www.kaggle.com/datasets/redraiment/complete-13-million-4x4-sudoku-puzzles.
[4] The total number of distinct 4x4 Sudoku solutions is 288.

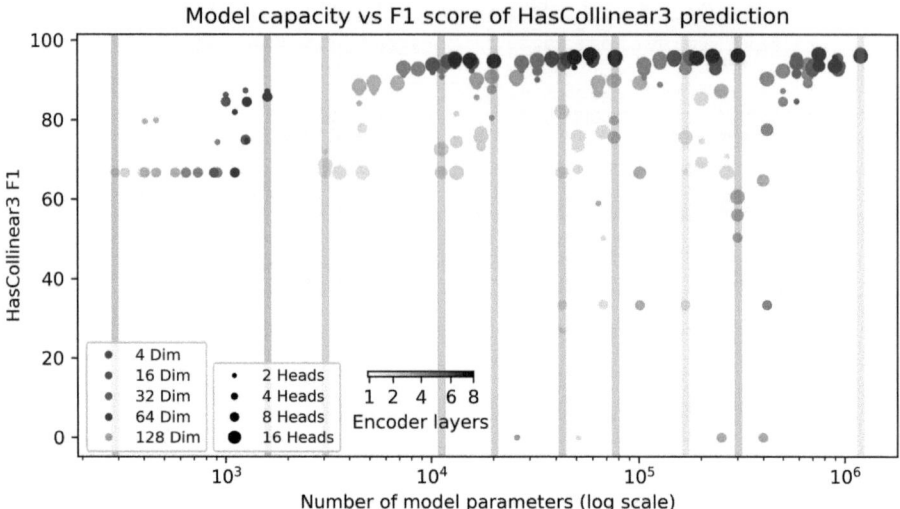

Fig. 3. `HasCollinear3` F1 performance (avg. of three runs) against the total number of model parameters (log scale). Each point represents a different transformer configuration, with color denoting the embedding dimensionality, color intensity indicating the number of encoder layers, dot size reflecting the number of attention heads, and feedforward dimensionality increasing from left to right within each color group. The maximum and average standard deviation across runs are 10.9 and 0.8 respectively. (Color figure online)

For Futoshiki, we use 5×5 puzzles with unique solutions and 10 inequalities introduced in [19]. We sample 1000 boards spanning different difficulty levels: 345 easy (7–10 hidden cells), 402 medium (11–13 hidden cells), and 253 hard (14–17 hidden cells). For the solving setting, we subsample 100 puzzles (33 easy, 34 medium, 33 hard). As with Sudoku, for the generalization setting, we use a 70/15/15 stratified train/dev/test split.

Each puzzle and its corresponding solution are encoded as a sequence of one-hot vectors corresponding to a digit or an empty cell.

Solving Setting Encoding. Here, we solve a single puzzle instance. The input thus encodes only the given digits and empty cells. All Sudoku constraints and Futoshiki inequalities are enforced via the loss, so no explicit rule encoding is required in the input.

Generalization Setting Encoding. At test time the network receives a new (unseen) puzzle without any external rule module; we expect the solving procedure to be internalized in the model weights. For Sudoku, the input encoding remains the same, containing only digits and empty cells. For Futoshiki, since inequalities vary across puzzles, we augment the one-hot input with an additional binary encoding marking the positions and orientations of each inequality sign ("<" or ">"). This extra information enables the model to adjust its reasoning according to puzzle-specific inequality constraints. Further implementation details are provided in Appendix E.

Model and Training. Each input puzzle is represented as a sequence of one-hot encoded vectors. These vectors pass through an embedding layer and we use a 2D sinusoidal positional encoding layer [28]. The resulting sequence is fed into a transformer encoder. Each position in the puzzle grid is assigned a dedicated predicate classifier head that produces the probability distribution of the cell having any of the possible digits in the puzzle (i.e., for Sudoku 4×4 each classifier head produces a probability distribution of four elements modeling the score of the corresponding cell taking values 1–4).

During training, we use puzzles one at a time (batch size 1) to compute the loss with respect to the rule constraints. In the first stage of training, the system learns to "copy" the given cells without constraints. We continue training introducing the rules of the game in the second stage (for 400 and 100 epochs, for solving and generalization settings resp.). We perform a grid search over learning rates $\{10^{-5}, 10^{-4}, 10^{-3}, 10^{-2}\}$ and rule-loss coefficients $\{10^{-5}, 10^{-4}, 10^{-3}, 10^{-2}, 10^{-1}, 1, 5\}$. We explore the following architectural variations:

- **Embedding Dimensions**: $\{16, 64, 256, 1024\}$,
- **Encoder Layers**: $\{1, 2, 6, 12\}$,
- **Attention Heads**: $\{4, 8, 16\}$,
- **Feedforward Dimensionality**: $\frac{1}{2}\times$, $1\times$, or $2\times$ the embedding size.

This results in 144 distinct configurations. Further details on implementation and batching are in Appendix D.

Evaluation. We evaluate each architecture configuration under both *solving* and *generalization* experiments. For the former, we train a model to solve each puzzle and measure the fraction of puzzles fully solved and the proportion of rule components satisfied across all puzzles. For the latter, we train models on puzzles from the train set and evaluate on unseen puzzles in the test set, considering two regimes (cf. §3.2): given-cells only and full-solution supervision. We report the ratio of correctly predicted hidden cells and fully solved puzzles from the test set for both settings, averaged over three random seeds.

6.1 Solving Setting Results

Figure 4 shows that both tasks require a minimum embedding dimensionality to reach near peak performance: 256 for Futoshiki and 64 for Sudoku. Smaller embeddings struggle to fully solve puzzles, but surpassing the threshold triggers a sharp increase in completion rates — a "phase shift" effect. Additional dimensionality yields only limited gains.

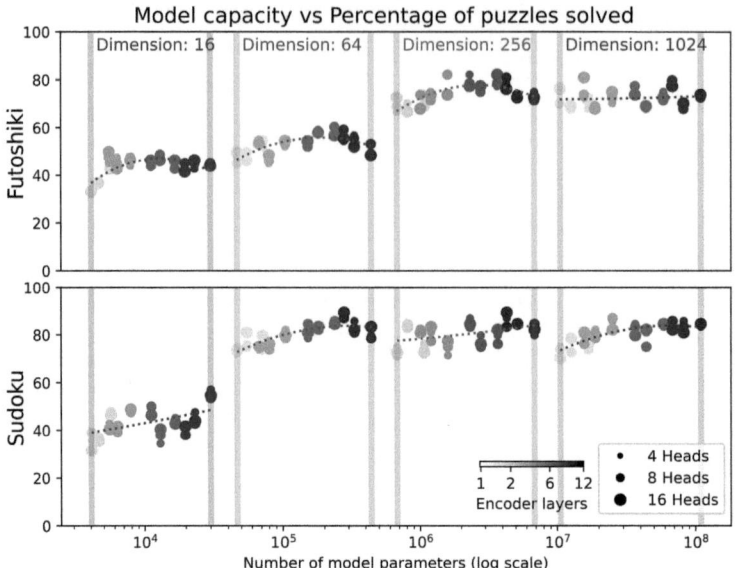

Fig. 4. Solved Futoshiki (top) and Sudoku (bottom) puzzles (three-run average) against number of model parameters (log scale). The visual encoding is as in Fig. 3. The maximum and average standard deviation across runs are 7.5 and 9.0 and 3.1 and 4.5 for Futoshiki and Sudoku runs respectively. (Color figure online)

Figure 5 reports the medians of solved puzzle rates for each architectural parameter value. Below their respective dimensionality thresholds (16 and 64), the performance for Futoshiki and Sudoku models is significantly worse than at or above the threshold, and higher embedding dimensions offer no significant improvements (Fig. 5a). No statistically significant differences exist for the other architectural choices (Figures. 5b–5d).

Appendix D presents additional analyses demonstrating that this trend persists when evaluating performance in terms of hidden-cell prediction accuracy. Furthermore, when performance is analyzed separately across different puzzle difficulty levels (easy, medium, and hard), the results consistently indicate that embedding dimensionality remains the most critical architectural parameter.

6.2 Generalization Setting Results

Given-cells-only Supervision. Figure 6 shows the median fraction of correctly predicted hidden cells. For both puzzles, smaller embedding dimensionalities yield the best results. For Futoshiki, increasing dimensionality from 16 to 64 provides a statistically significant improvement of 8.2% (Fig. 6a), and network depth also significantly impacts performance: architectures with 12 layers outperform (10%) those with 1 or 2 layers (Fig. 6b). For Sudoku, embedding dimensionalities

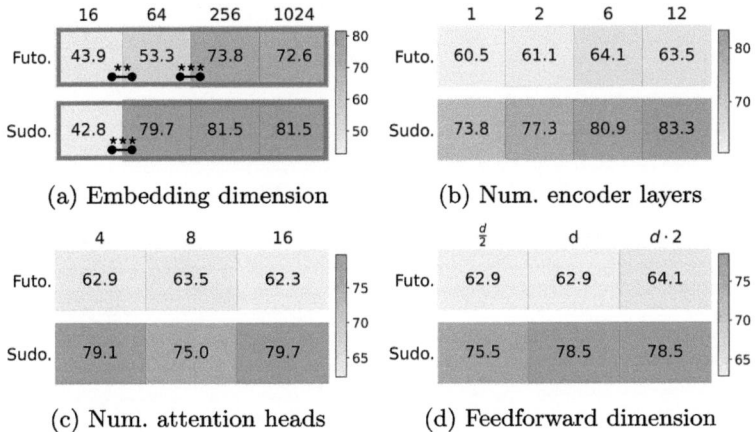

Fig. 5. Solving setting: Median percentage of puzzles solved for each architectural parameter value–Futoshiki (Futo.) above, Sudoku (Sudo.) below. Groups of values statistically different are enclosed in green rectangles, and post-hoc significant contiguous pairs are connected by black segments. (Color figure online)

of 16 and 64 outperform the others. Network depth, number of attention heads, and feedforward dimensionality show no significant effects.

Curiously, models with larger embedding dimensionalities are significantly worse. Evaluating them on the training sets reveals clear overfitting. We conjecture that smaller networks more readily lock onto puzzle constraints, leading to faster convergence to consistent solutions. In contrast, larger networks likely have more complex optimization landscapes, are more sensitive to hyperparameter choices, and more prone to convergence to local minima. While our experiments focus on architectural factors, we note that the degree of overfitting may also be influenced by optimization choices such as learning rate, regularization, and stopping criteria—variables we did not systematically ablate in this study.

Figure 7 shows hidden-cell prediction performance as a function of total model parameters. Futoshiki models fare better than the Sudoku, despite the former's reputation as being more difficult. We conjecture that this is the case due to our richer input encoding for Futoshiki puzzles, which incorporates inequality positions. Importantly, these models do not see any labeled data during training, and rely only on the logical rules in the loss function to generalize to unseen puzzles. Yet, some architectural configurations can fully solve up to 75% of Futoshikis and 12% of Sudokus from the test set. Appendix E has more details.

Full-Solution Supervision. For the fully-supervised (full-solution) setting, results follow analogous trends, but exhibit consistently higher performance due to the additional explicit supervision. Here, rules function as auxiliary guidance on top of direct puzzle solutions. Comparing performance before (stage one) and after rule incorporation (stage two), we observe consistent improvements due to rules,

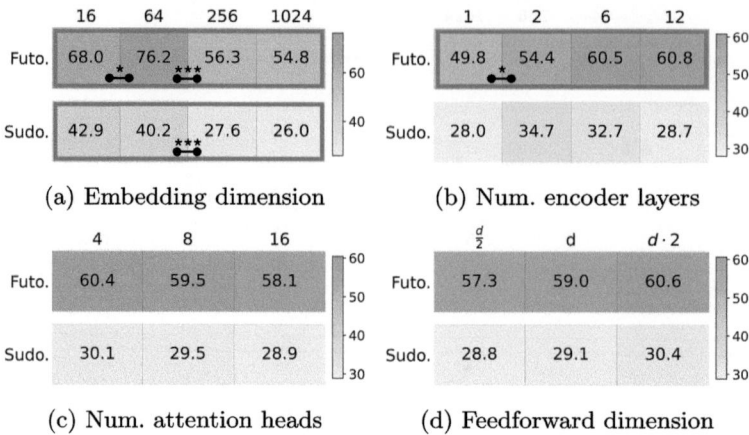

Fig. 6. Given-cells-only setting: Median percent of correctly predicted hidden cell for each architectural parameter value–Futoshiki (Futo.) above, Sudoku (Sudo.) below. Groups of values statistically different are enclosed in green rectangles, and post-hoc significant contiguous pairs are connected by black segments. (Color figure online)

especially pronounced in deeper networks. Due to space constraints, detailed figures and additional analyses are provided in Appendix E.

7 Discussion

Unlike other work on neuro-symbolic models that seek to improve reasoning performance [1,15,19,31], we do not introduce a model or a framework that surpasses state-of-the-art results. Rather, our goal is to analyze the role and impact of transformer architectural choices when these architectures serve as the underlying neural component in logic-as-loss frameworks.

In this study, we design rule-governed synthetic tasks—such as planar collinearity and Latin square puzzles—where each instance is fully defined by a known set of logical constraints. Success in these tasks depends entirely on the model's ability to adhere to the rules, providing a noise-free setting to analyze how Transformer design choices interact with the *logic-as-loss* objective. While this controlled setup limits direct real-world applicability, it offers a clear lens for studying rule internalization. Extending this analysis to more naturalistic domains, where constraints are only partially known, is an important direction for future work. Additionally, exploring how architectural factors interact with specific classes of logical rules (e.g., monotonic vs. non-monotonic) is an interesting avenue for further research.

Our empirical findings consistently highlight the input embedding dimensionality as a critical architectural parameter, significantly impacting model performance across all tasks (green squares in Figs. 2a, 6a, 5a). Specifically, in the collinearity task and puzzle-solving scenarios, we identify a clear threshold or

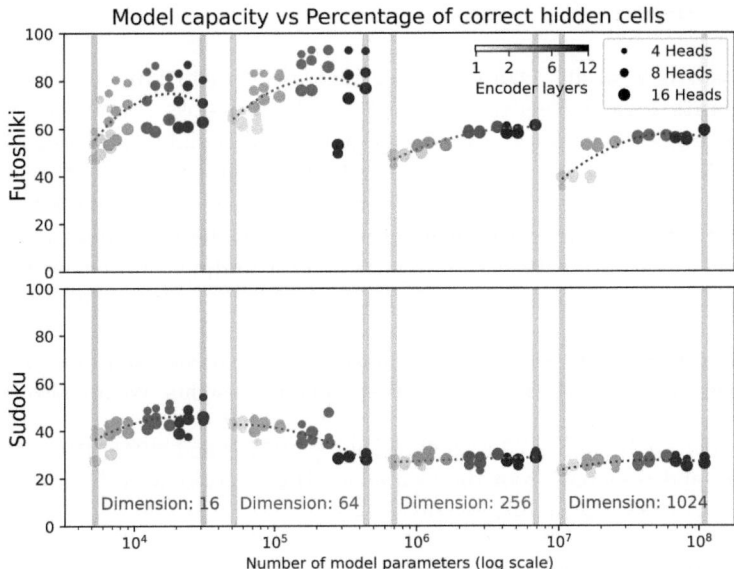

Fig. 7. Given-cells-only setting: Average percent (over three runs) of correctly predicted hidden cells for Futoshiki (top) and Sudoku (bottom), plotted against the total number of model parameters (log scale). The visual encoding is as in Fig. 3. The maximum and average standard deviation across runs are 8.1 and 10.0 and 1.1 and 1.5 for Futoshiki and Sudoku experiments respectively. (Color figure online)

"phase shift" effect: performance significantly improves once embedding dimensionality exceeds a critical value, beyond which additional capacity yields no substantial gains. This observation suggests that increasing embedding size beyond a necessary threshold is computationally inefficient without performance benefits. For generalization scenarios, smaller-capacity models appeared to incorporate the training rules more efficiently, often outperforming larger networks, which exhibited higher susceptibility to overfitting and greater sensitivity to hyperparameter tuning.

We further observe that network depth can positively impact performance within fixed embedding dimensions. Particularly, in the collinearity task, deeper networks were less prone to degenerate, trivial solutions. This result motivates further exploration of network depth alongside other strategies from the literature aimed at mitigating spurious or degenerate solutions [11,14].

While our analysis focused specifically on logic-as-loss using t-norm relaxations, prior studies have observed similar learning behaviors in probabilistic logic-relaxation techniques [2,3,8]. Moreover, theoretical results indicate fundamental similarities between model-counting approaches such as semantic loss and t-norm based methods within the logic-as-loss framework [24,25]. Thus, we anticipate that our architectural insights may generalize broadly across various logic-relaxation methods, although empirical validation remains necessary.

8 Conclusion

We analyzed how architectural choices in transformers influence their ability to incorporate logical constraints using the logic-as-loss framework. We used controlled reasoning tasks—collinearity detection, Sudoku, and Futoshiki—to identify a clear pattern: above a certain embedding dimensionality threshold, further capacity increments provided limited performance improvements. Additionally, deeper networks mitigated degenerate solutions, highlighting the advantage of depth over width for robust rule ingestion. Our findings emphasize the critical role of architectural design in transformer-based logic-as-loss applications.

Acknowledgments. We thank Ana Marasović, Kyle Richardson, Jeff M. Phillips, and members of the UtahNLP group for their valuable insights. We are also grateful to the reviewers for their helpful comments, corrections, and suggestions for related work. This work was partly supported by NSF grants #2217154 and #2411319. Additionally, the support and resources from the Center for High Performance Computing at the University of Utah are gratefully acknowledged.

Disclosure of Interests. The authors have no competing interests to declare that are relevant to the content of this article.

References

1. Ahmed, K., Chang, K.W., Van den Broeck, G.: A pseudo-semantic loss for autoregressive models with logical constraints. In: NeurIPS (2023)
2. Ahmed, K., Chang, K.W., Van den Broeck, G.: Semantic strengthening of neuro-symbolic learning. In: AISTATS (2023)
3. Ahmed, K., Teso, S., Chang, K.W., Van den Broeck, G., Vergari, A.: Semantic probabilistic layers for neuro-symbolic learning. In: Proceedings of the 36th International Conference on Neural Information Processing Systems (2022)
4. Cătălina Stoian, M., Giunchiglia, E., Lukasiewicz, T.: Exploiting T-norms for deep learning in autonomous driving. arXiv (2024)
5. Defresne, M., Barbe, S., Schiex, T.: Scalable coupling of deep learning with logical reasoning. In: IJCAI (2023)
6. Dosovitskiy, A., et al.: An image is worth 16x16 words: transformers for image recognition at scale. In: ICLR (2021)
7. Flinkow, T., Pearlmutter, B.A., Monahan, R.: Comparing differentiable logics for learning with logical constraints. Sci. Comput. Program. **244**, 103280 (2025)
8. Flügel, S., Glauer, M., Mossakowski, T., Neuhaus, F.: A fuzzy loss for ontology classification. In: Besold, T.R., d'Avila Garcez, A., Jimenez-Ruiz, E., Confalonieri, R., Madhyastha, P., Wagner, B. (eds.) Neural-Symbolic Learning and Reasoning: 18th International Conference, NeSy 2024, Barcelona, Spain, September 9–12, 2024, Proceedings, Part I. Springer, Cham (2024). https://doi.org/10.1007/978-3-031-71167-1_6
9. Giunchiglia, E., Stoian, M.C., Lukasiewicz, T.: Deep learning with logical constraints. In: IJCAI (2022)
10. Grespan, M.M., Gupta, A., Srikumar, V.: Evaluating relaxations of logic for neural networks: a comprehensive study. In: IJCAI (2021)

11. He, H.Y., Dai, W.Z., Li, M.: Reduced implication-bias logic loss for neuro-symbolic learning. Machine Learning (2024)
12. Klement, E.P., Mesiar, R., Pap, E.: Triangular Norms, vol. 8. Springer Science & Business Media (2013). https://doi.org/10.1007/978-94-015-9540-7
13. Li, T., Gupta, V., Mehta, M., Srikumar, V.: A logic-driven framework for consistency of neural models. In: EMNLP-IJCNLP (2019)
14. Li, Z., et al.: Learning with logical constraints but without shortcut satisfaction. In: ICLR (2023)
15. Li, Z., Guo, J., Jiang, Y., Si, X.: Learning reliable logical rules with satnet. In: NeurIPS (2023)
16. Loshchilov, I., Hutter, F.: Decoupled weight decay regularization. In: ICLR (2019)
17. Medina Grespan, M., et al.: Logic-driven indirect supervision: an application to crisis counseling. In: ACL (2023)
18. Nam, A.J., Abdool, M., Maxfield, T., McClelland, J.L.: Achieving and understanding out-of-distribution generalization in systematic reasoning in small-scale transformers. arXiv (2022)
19. Nandwani, Y., Jain, V., Mausam, Singla, P.: Neural models for output-space invariance in combinatorial problems. In: ICLR (2022)
20. OpenAI: GPT-4 technical report. Tech. rep., OpenAI (2023)
21. Palm, R.B., Paquet, U., Winther, O.: Recurrent relational networks. In: NeurIPS, pp. 3368–3378 (2018)
22. Richardson, K., Srikumar, V., Sabharwal, A.: Understanding the logic of direct preference alignment through logic. In: ICML (2025)
23. Tay, Y., et al.: Scale efficiently: insights from pretraining and finetuning transformers. In: ICLR (2022)
24. van Krieken, E., Acar, E., van Harmelen, F.: Analyzing differentiable fuzzy logic operators. Artif. Intell. **302**, 103602 (2022)
25. Van Krieken, E., Minervini, P., Ponti, E.M., Vergari, A.: On the independence assumption in neurosymbolic learning. In: Proceedings of the 41st International Conference on Machine Learning (2024)
26. Vaswani, A., et al.: Attention is all you need. In: NeurIPS (2017)
27. Wang, H., Chen, M., Zhang, H., Roth, D.: Joint constrained learning for event-event relation extraction. In: EMNLP (2020)
28. Wang, Z., Liu, J.-C.: Translating math formula images to LaTeX sequences using deep neural networks with sequence-level training. Int. J. Document Anal. Recognit. (IJDAR) **24**(1), 63–75 (2020). https://doi.org/10.1007/s10032-020-00360-2
29. Warner, B., et al.: Smarter, better, faster, longer: a modern bidirectional encoder for fast, memory efficient, and long context finetuning and inference. arXiv (2024)
30. Xu, J., Zhang, Z., Friedman, T., Liang, Y., Van den Broeck, G.: A semantic loss function for deep learning with symbolic knowledge. In: ICML (2018)
31. Yang, Z., Ishay, A., Lee, J.: Learning to solve constraint satisfaction problems with recurrent transformer. In: ICLR (2023)

Optimization

GBRF: A Novel Framework for Encoding User-Preferences in Imbalanced Data Distributions via Genetic Optimization

Miguel Carvalho^(✉), Armando Pinho, and Susana Brás

IEETA, DETI, LASI, University of Aveiro, 3810-193 Aveiro, Portugal
{miguelacarvalho,ap,susana.bras}@ua.pt

Abstract. Resampling techniques are widely used by researchers and practitioners to address class imbalance due to their adaptability across diverse classification tasks. However, they inherently lack the ability to enforce user-defined preferences regarding model behavior after training, a feature typically exclusive to cost-sensitive learning frameworks or prediction post-processing techniques. This limitation is particularly critical in high-stakes applications, such as in the medical domain, where maximizing minority class accuracy while minimizing false negatives is essential. To overcome this constraint, we introduce the Genetic Beta Resampling Framework (GBRF), a novel, customizable and computationally efficient resampling framework that integrates user preferences into the process of synthetic data generation. GBRF leverages Genetic Algorithms to optimize two probability mass functions (PMFs) that govern the sampling probabilities of different instance groups, enabling synthetic data generation and/or instance removal. Consequently, GBRF can function as a hybrid sampling, oversampling or undersampling technique. User preferences are encoded through a parameter, β, which controls the trade-off between precision and recall. Comprehensive experiments on 60 OpenML datasets demonstrate that GBRF effectively embeds user preferences into data distributions, thus shaping model behavior accordingly. It consistently outperforms state-of-the-art resampling techniques, such as SMOTE-IPF and ProWSyn, as well as cost-sensitive classifiers, even when integrated with various classification models. Furthermore, by employing a non-instance-wise genetic optimization approach, GBRF significantly reduces the search space, achieving faster convergence to optimal solutions. Finally, since synthetic data generation is governed by two PMFs, GBRF provides an intuitive and transparent mechanism for understanding how data is generated. Code available at: https://github.com/MiguelCarvalhoPhD/GBRF.

Keywords: Class Imbalance · Genetic Optimization · Resampling

---

Supplementary Information The online version contains supplementary material available at https://doi.org/10.1007/978-3-032-06096-9_4.

1 Introduction

Class imbalance refers to the unequal distribution of the target variable in supervised learning tasks, where the underrepresented class, often termed the minority class in binary classification problems, typically experiences reduced predictive performance [4]. This skewed data distribution has far-reaching consequences in applications where correctly classifying the minority class holds critical importance, such as fraud detection, rare medical condition diagnosis, forecasting natural disasters, and fields including chemical and biochemical engineering, IT security, agriculture, and emergency management [21]. This problem arises from the assumption embedded in most learning algorithms that all data points are equally important, leading to accuracy-oriented optimization strategies with uniform misclassification penalties across all classes [17]. Consequently, classifiers often prioritize majority class performance, as correctly classifying majority instances while disproportionately misclassifying minority samples typically incurs lower training loss [17]. However, it is essential to recognize that class imbalance alone does not affect model performance [20]. Note that in cases where the classes are easily linearly separable with large margins, optimal training loss can still be achieved without the need to bias the decision boundary in favor of the majority class [20]. As such, class imbalance becomes truly problematic when combined with other existing data adverse characteristics (also referred to as data irregularities), such as class overlap, existence of small disjuncts, high dimensionality, and noise [20].

Given the widespread incidence of class imbalance across diverse sectors and its significant impact on model performance, a wide range of methods has been developed to address this issue, which can be broadly divided into data-level and algorithmic-level approaches [4,10]. Data-level approaches involve modifying the data distribution to magnify the relative importance of the minority class during model training, typically by generating synthetic minority samples (oversampling) or extracting majority samples (undersampling) until identical class frequencies are attained. Contrarily, algorithmic level approaches focus on altering existing learning algorithms to mitigate the bias towards the majority class, without altering the training data [7,19]. Strategies encompass adjusting the decision threshold, training class-specific classifiers, weighting-based approaches, among others [7]. Data-level approaches are more widely utilized by researchers and practitioners given their ability to be utilized alongside any other learning algorithm or classification context, contrasting with algorithmic-level approaches which are constrained to models capable of being adapted to imbalanced domains and often rely on expert knowledge for fine-tuning [4,16,19]. However, a key limitation of resampling methods is their inability to directly encode user-specific objectives for model behavior. As Branco et al. highlighted in [4], determining the optimal degree of undersampling based on user preferences remains an open research problem. This issue is mainly addressed through cost-sensitive classifiers, which provide a structured framework for incorporating class-specific costs into the learning process [4].

To overcome this fundamental limitation of resampling approaches, we propose an explainable, customizable, and computationally efficient framework for synthetic dataset generation. This framework, designated Genetic Beta Resampling Framework (GBRF), ensures that models trained on the generated artificial data adhere to predefined user preferences, which are encoded in a parameter, β. This parameter regulates the trade-off between recall and precision: higher β values prioritize recall, favoring synthetic datasets that reduce false negatives at the expense of false positives, and vice versa. In practice, penalizing false negatives more heavily encourages synthetic sample generation within the decision boundary, effectively expanding underrepresented regions and reducing minority class misclassifications. However, selecting an optimal resampling approach is not solely dependent on user preferences but is also influenced by the aforementioned intrinsic dataset characteristics. As suggested by the No Free Lunch Theorem, no universally optimal resampling strategy exists [22], and the connection between data irregularities and effective resampling protocols remains an open research question [20]. To provide an adaptive solution, our framework employs Genetic Algorithms to optimize two probability mass functions (PMF) that govern the sampling probability of different instance groups, determining whether samples are synthesized or eliminated.

The main contributions of this work are manifold:

- We present a mathematical analysis, leveraging Bayes' Theorem, to demonstrate how selectively resampling minority class instances with different class-conditional densities can alter the decision boundary and subsequently influence model behavior. This analysis substantiates the validity of our resampling strategy.
- We propose a novel resampling framework designed to determine optimal resampling strategies for a wide range of datasets and user-specified preferences—an objective that, until now, has been achievable only through algorithmic changes of existing models. The framework's efficacy is empirically demonstrated across 60 OpenML benchmarks and further supported by a visual inspection of the generated synthetic datasets. The proposed framework is also fully customizable, enabling users to specify custom functions for sample grouping and generation, which are then optimized by GBRF.
- By deviating from conventional instance-wise optimization in genetic resampling, we ensure that the search space of the genetic algorithm scales with the number of generated sample groups rather than increasing exponentially with dataset size, enabling faster convergence to high-quality solutions.

2 Related Work

Resampling Tabular Datasets to Address Class Imbalance. The majority of recent research on resampling in tabular data has focused on addressing the limitations of the Synthetic Minority Oversampling TEchnique (SMOTE) to develop more robust oversampling methods [9]. SMOTE is an interpolation-based data generation technique that operates as follows [6]: Given a training dataset $D = \{(\mathbf{x}_i, y_i)\}_{i=1}^n$, where $\text{NN}_j(\mathbf{x}_i)$ denotes the j-th minority-class nearest neighbor of $\mathbf{x}_i$, the generation of a synthetic instance, $\mathbf{x}_{\text{new}}$, is formalized as:

$$x_{new} = x_i + \alpha(x_i - NN_j(x_i)), \quad \alpha \sim \mathcal{U}(0,1) \tag{1}$$

with $\mathcal{U}(0,1)$ denoting a uniform random variable from the interval $[0,1]$ This procedure is repeated until the desired class ratio is achieved. Importantly, SMOTE applies uniform sampling probabilities across all minority class instances, which introduces three major issues: (i) it fails to address within-class imbalance, as low-density regions remain underrepresented post-oversampling, (ii) it may oversample outliers, potentially propagating existing noise and degradating classifier performance, and (iii) it does not consider the structure of the majority class, which can lead to class overlap. To overcome these limitations, numerous SMOTE variants have been developed, each introducing specific modifications to the original algorithm [16]. As categorized in [9], these variations include (1) initial selection of samples for oversampling, (2) adaptive generation of synthetic instances, (3) integration with undersampling, among others. While these approaches introduce distinct methodological refinements, they typically share a commom principle: they aim to identify and quantify existing data irregularities and adapt the resampling process accordingly. However, fully characterizing these data irregularities remains an unresolved research challenge, particularly given the intricate and multifaceted nature of class overlap (see [20] for a detailed discussion). This limitation imposes fundamental constraints on conventional resampling methods, which rely on predefined metrics to adjust different aspects of the resampling algorithm. This is major factor dictating why we adopt a metaheuristic framework capable of optimizing resampling protocols dynamically, eliminating the dependence on handcrafted dataset characterization metrics and enabling a more adaptable and generalizable solution.

Genetic Algorithms in Resampling Genetic Algorithms. Genetic Algorithms are population based search algorithms that model complex systems by constructing a simulated environment that mimics natural evolution, allowing them to solve problems that do not have a well-defined efficient solution [5]. The fundamental components of a GA include chromosome encoding, genetic operators (selection, mutation, and crossover), and a fitness function that quantifies the suitability of each candidate solution. GA typically begins with a randomly initialized population, where each chromosome encodes a candidate solution. Fitness evaluation determines solution quality, guiding selection and crossover processes that generate offspring by combining traits of the fittest individuals [5]. Mutation introduces genetic diversity by altering genes, preventing premature convergence to local optima and enhancing exploration of the search space. Selection mechanisms determine which individuals advance to the next generation, and this iterative process continues until a stopping criterion or predefined number of generations is met [1].

In resampling applications, Genetic Algorithms are primarily used for undersampling [8,13,15]. Typically, each majority-class sample is represented by a boolean gene indicating its inclusion or exclusion from the final dataset. Such representations lead to exponentially expanding search spaces as dataset size increases, making large-scale applications computationally demanding and reducing convergence speed to high-quality solutions. Common fitness functions include AUC, G-Mean, and AUC-ROC, evaluated on the training set [14,15]. However, assessing performance on the same dataset used for training often leads to unreliable generalization estimates. In [11], the authors propose stratified partitioning to create a validation dataset, though this approach risks overfitting to that specific partition.

3 Proposed Method

3.1 Overview

The proposed algorithm follows a four-stage process: (1) Framework instantiation, where sample grouping and sample generation algorithms are defined, a β parameter is introduced to control the trade-off between precision and recall according to user-defined preferences, and each PMF is assigned the function of either generating or removing samples (2) Genetic algorithm initialization encodes PMFs as chromosomal structures and generates all the required synthetic samples for subsequent optimization. (3) Genetic optimization identifies the optimal PMFs, the ratio of samples generated/removed by each PMF and the extent of outlier removal to be conducted, ensuring an adaptive resampling strategy. (4) Synthetic dataset generation constructs the final resampled dataset using the fittest solution identified through genetic optimization.

As the core premise of this resampling approach is the selective generation and removal of samples in specific regions of the feature space to encode user-defined preferences on the data distribution, it is essential to first demonstrate theoretically that this mechanism can meaningfully shift a model's decision boundary.

3.2 Theoretical Considerations on Encoding User-Preferences in the Data Distribution

Setup and Notation. Let D be a one-dimensional dataset with two classes, $y \in \{-,+\}$, with a high imbalance degree, that is, $n_+ \gg n_-$, with n_+ and n_- representing the number of majority and minority samples, respectively. Let the minority samples follow $N(\mu_-, \sigma)$ and majority samples follow $N(\mu_+, \sigma)$, where $\mu_- < \mu_+$. Let the class priors be $\pi_- = p(y = -)$ and $\pi_+ = p(y = +)$ such that $\pi_- + \pi_+ = 1$ and $\pi_- \ll \pi_+$. The optimal Bayes decision boundary, denoted by k, is defined as the unique solution to:

$$p(x \mid y = -)\pi_- = p(x \mid y = +)\pi_+. \tag{2}$$

where $p(x \mid y = +)$ and $p(x \mid y = -)$ represent the class-conditional densities for the majority and minority class, respectively. The uniqueness of k follows from the fact that the likelihood ratio $\lambda(x) = \frac{p(x|y=-)}{p(x|y=+)}$ is strictly monotonic in x for these Gaussian densities.

Resampling the Minority Class. Let us define a nonnegative, measurable weighting function $w(x)$ that emphasizes regions of interest. For instance, one may choose $w(x)$ such that it is large for $x > \mu_-$, thereby upweighting the tail of the minority class. We assume that $0 < \int_{-\infty}^{\infty} p(t \mid y = -) w(t) \, dt < \infty$. The normalized re-weighted minority density is:

$$\tilde{p}(x \mid y = -) = \frac{p(x \mid y = -) w(x)}{\int_{-\infty}^{\infty} p(t \mid y = -) w(t) \, dt} \quad (3)$$

This mimics the effect of adding synthetic samples to the region $x > \mu_-$. Moreover, assume that re-sampling adjusts the minority class prior to $\tilde{\pi}_-$, matching the class prior of the majority class, that is, $\tilde{\pi}_- = \tilde{\pi}_+$. Thus, the joint densities after re-sampling become:

$$\tilde{p}(x, y = -) = \tilde{p}(x \mid y = -) \tilde{\pi}_- \quad (4)$$

$$\tilde{p}(x, y = +) = p(x \mid y = +) \tilde{\pi}_+ \quad (5)$$

New Decision Boundary. A classifier trained on the re-sampled data will have its decision boundary $\tilde{k}$ defined by $\tilde{p}(\tilde{k} \mid y = -) \tilde{\pi}_- = p(\tilde{k} \mid y = +) \tilde{\pi}_+$. Substitute the expression for $\tilde{p}(x \mid y = -)$:

$$\tilde{\pi}_- \frac{p(\tilde{k} \mid y = -) w(\tilde{k})}{Z} = p(\tilde{k} \mid y = +) \tilde{\pi}_+ \quad (6)$$

with $Z = \int_{-\infty}^{\infty} p(t \mid y = -) w(t) \, dt$. Rearranging gives:

$$\frac{p(\tilde{k} \mid y = -)}{p(\tilde{k} \mid y = +)} = \frac{Z \tilde{\pi}_+}{w(\tilde{k}) \tilde{\pi}_-} \quad (7)$$

Because the likelihood ratio $\lambda(x) = \frac{p(x \mid y = -)}{p(x \mid y = +)}$ is strictly monotonic, Eq. 7 admits a unique solution for $\tilde{k}$. Notice that if $w(\tilde{k})$ increases (as is the case when $\tilde{k}$ lies in a region where $w(x)$ is large), then the right-hand side decreases. To restore the equality, $\tilde{k}$ must shift to a region where $\lambda(x)$ is naturally lower. For the Gaussian densities under consideration (with $\mu_- < \mu_+$), $\lambda(x)$ is decreasing in x, so the new decision boundary $\tilde{k}$ shifts rightward relative to the original boundary k. This reasoning highlights how, depending on the applied $w(x)$, different shifts of the decision boundary will take place.

Impact on the False-Positive Probability. To finalize this analysis, let us consider the impact on the behavior of the resulting classifier. The false-positive probability under the original (true) distribution for class $y = +$ is:

$$\tilde{P}(\text{FP}) = \int_{-\infty}^{\tilde{k}} p(x \mid y = +) \pi_+ \, dx \quad (8)$$

Since upweighting the tail causes k to shift to a higher value, $\tilde{k}$, the integration region $[-\infty, \tilde{k})$ becomes bigger. Therefore, more true "+" points fall into the region where the classifier predicts "−", and the false-positive probability of class $y = +$ increases. The same line of reasoning can be applied to the probability of false negatives, demonstrating how selectively resampling regions of the minority class can encode preferences on the data distribution.

3.3 GBRF: Algorithm Instantiation

As outlined in Sect. 3.1, initializing the algorithm requires specifying several parameters, notably: (i) functions that construct sample groups with similar characteristics (ii) functions that govern the synthetic sample generation process, and (iii) the β parameter dictating user-preferences. Lastly, it is important to discuss how synthetic dataset generation is mediated by the two distinct probability mass functions.

Sample Grouping Functions. Prior to introducing the two sample grouping functions tested in this work, let us formally describe them. Let $X \subset \mathbb{R}^d$ be the feature space and $Y = \{0, 1\}$ the class labels. A sample grouping function

$$g : X_{min} \to G, \quad G = \{G_1, \ldots, G_k\} \tag{9}$$

partitions X_{min}, with $X_{min} = \{x \in X : y(x) = 1\}$, into disjoint sets, i.e., $X_{min} = \bigcup_{i=1}^{k} G_i$ with $G_i \cap G_j = \emptyset$ for $i \neq j$. The first utilized sample grouping function, g_1, partitions samples by analyzing their local neighborhood, specifically by counting the number of majority-class samples among their five nearest neighbors, denoted by $N_5(x)$, thereby forming at most six distinct sample groups: $g_1(x) = G_{m_5(x)+1}$, where $m_5(x) = |\{x_j \in N_5(x) \mid y_j = 0\}|$. Note that, by Cover and Hart's theorem (1967), k-NN classification error is upper bounded by twice the error of a Bayes classifier, making nearest-neighbor analysis a reliable non-parametric estimate of class-conditional density [18]. As such, samples heavily surrounded by majority class samples tend to lie near the decision boundary, providing avenues from which user-preferences can be encoded in the distribution as suggested in Sect. 3.2.

For the second sample grouping function, g_2, we adopt the ProWsyn methodology, which partitions the minority class based on its global structure relative to the majority class, as opposed to the more localized analysis provided by g_1 [3]. The process iteratively constructs N_{sets} disjoint subsets of minority samples. Initialization starts with an empty set G_1, which is populated with all minority samples appearing among the five nearest neighbors of any majority-class sample. These selected samples are then removed from the dataset, and the process repeats for N_{sets} iterations [3]. Furthermore, it is important to highlight that algorithm instantiation requires specifying whether sample grouping functions are intended for instance removal or synthetic generation. When configured for removal, the method is applied to the majority class instead of the minority class, wherein majority samples are grouped into distinct subsets, enabling subsequent instance elimination.

Sample Generation Functions. We implement two procedures for sample generation. First, the standard SMOTE procedure is implemented, which is denoted by $f_{\text{SMOTE}}(G_k)$, where $f_{\text{SMOTE}}: G_k \to X^*$, with X^* representing the synthetic data space [6]. Here, a minority sample is randomly selected from an existing group, G_k, from which one of its five nearest minority-class neighbors is utilized for interpolation, as described in Eq. 1 [6]. Secondly, the ProWsyn-based procedure is employed, which is represented as $f_{ProWsyn}(G_k)$ [3]. Instead of restricting the selection to the five nearest neighbors, all elements of the grouping set G_k are considered for interpolation. This broader neighborhood yields greater synthetic sample diversity and increases the framework's degrees of freedom to impose user-preferences. In summary, our implementation couples the grouping function g_1 with the SMOTE-based generation function f_{SMOTE} and the grouping function g_2 with the ProWsyn-based generation function f_{ProWsyn}. Note that, as previously outlined, if either of the sample grouping functions is designated for sample removal, the sample generation procedure is not conducted and random samples are removed from the generated groups, allowing the framework to act as an oversampling, hybrid sampling and undersampling method depending on the chosen configuration. Lastly, we stress the fact that, since sample generation functions are dependent on sample groups, g_1 can be applied in conjunction with $f_{ProWsyn}$ and g_2 with f_{SMOTE}, illustrating the framework's flexibility to incorporate any of the vast resampling methodologies described in the literature [9]. However, it should be noted that most SMOTE variants assign sample-wise instance sampling probabilities, as opposed to group-wise sampling probabilities [9], but this can be easily addressed by discretizing the sampling distribution.

Dual PMF-Based Synthetic Dataset Generation. Within the proposed framework, we define two probability mass functions, p_1 and p_2, each mapping the set of sample groups G to the interval $[0, 1]$. That is, for each function $p_i: G \to [0, 1]$ (with $G = \{G_1, G_2, \ldots, G_k\}$ obtained via g_1 and g_2), we have

$$\forall j, \quad p_i(G_j) \geq 0 \quad \text{and} \quad \sum_j p_i(G_j) = 1 \tag{10}$$

These functions govern the sampling probabilities for each group. Within each group, samples are then randomly selected for either generation—using the corresponding sample generation function—or removal, based on predetermined parameters. Note that, p_1 is used alongside g_1 and f_{SMOTE}, whereas p_2 is utilized in conjunction with g_2 and $f_{ProWSyn}$.

Defining User-Preferences. The encoding of user-preferences is conducted through the trade-off between precision, P, and recall, R, and is inspired by [2], which states that the relative importance a user attaches to precision and recall is the R/P ratio at which $\frac{dE}{dR} = \frac{dE}{dP}$, with E being a measure of effectiveness based on precision and recall, that is, $E = E(P, R)$. Practically, this premise leads to the $F\beta$-score formulation:

$$F\beta - \text{score} = \frac{(1+\beta^2)PR}{(\beta^2 P)+R} \tag{11}$$

where β times more importance is attached to recall than precision. Naturally, by assigning β values higher than 1, higher importance is given to recall, which then means that minimizing false negatives will be prioritized as opposed to false positives, and vice-versa. This preference is then embedded into the genetic algorithm through the fitness function. Specifically, the fitness function, which directs the optimization process, is formulated as the average $F\beta$-score obtained via 5-fold cross-validation, where resampled data is used for training and a partition of the original data is reserved for testing. This approach is deliberately adopted to avoid evaluation bias associated with the inclusion of synthetic data in the test set, as is prevalent in many current methods [14,15].

3.4 Genetic Optimization

Upon establishing the synthetic data generation mechanisms and the corresponding fitness function, the next step is to determine how the PMFs (i.e. p_1 and p_2) are encoded as chromosomes to enable genetic optimization, along with the selection of the appropriate genetic operators.

PMF Genetic Encoding. Within each chromosome, one gene is allocated for each sample group per probability mass function, in addition to a gene that specifies the proportion of samples generated by each PMF and an optional gene regulating the percentage of outlier removal. Collectively, these genes provide all the necessary information for synthetic data generation. For instance, if g_1 generates six groups in a dataset and the first six genes are assigned equal values, all minority samples will have an equal probability of being selected for oversampling, thereby replicating the baseline SMOTE approach. Conversely, if the last two of these six genes assume significantly higher values than the others, the resulting behavior will resemble that of ADASYN [12]. Note that, this example implies both p_1 and p_2 are set for sample generation.

Genetic Operators. All the adopted genetic operators and corresponding parametrization are inspired in existing literature regarding genetic resampling [8,11,13–15]. In the proposed framework, a fixed population size of 24 chromosomes is maintained. At each generation, tournament selection ($k=4$) is applied with replacement to select parent pairs for reproduction. Single-point crossover is applied with a probability of 0.75, followed by random mutation with a probability of 0.25. A total of 20 offspring are generated per generation, and the top 4 individuals from the current population are preserved via elitism. The algorithm terminates either when the average $F\beta$-score reaches 1 or upon completion of 300 iterations.

Pre-optimization Sample Generation. Prior to initializing the genetic optimization process, all required samples are pre-generated. Specifically, N samples, with N being the total number of samples required to achieve the desired class ratio (typically 1:1), are produced for each sample group and for each PMF, ensuring that every potential convergence solution is fully supported by the necessary data. This design choice is based on experimental testing, which demonstrated that dynamically generating samples during optimization significantly degrades algorithm runtime. Moreover, using a consistent set of samples throughout the optimization enhances convergence speed by obviating the stochastic component of interpolation-based sample generation (as outlined in Eq. 1).

3.5 Genetic Optimization and Synthetic Data Generation

After establishing all necessary functions and parameters, the genetic optimization process begins by initializing all genes with one of 20 equally spaced values between zero and one. This approach restricts gene space complexity, promotes rapid convergence, and mitigates overfitting. As a result, the proposed method has a substantially reduced search space, which depends only on the number of sample groups generated by g_1 and g_2. Each candidate solution is then normalized to ensure that the probability mass function properties are satisfied (Eq. 10). Subsequently, samples are retrieved from the pre-generated data matrices and concatenated to form the synthetic dataset. This process is conducted for 5 train/test splits, where a model is trained on the resampled train data partition and fitness is computed by assessing model performance on the test partition. Finally, when the genetic optimization process terminates, the final dataset is generated based on the fittest solution using the same procedure.

4 Experiments

To comprehensively evaluate the effectiveness of our framework, GBRF, we address the following research questions:

- **RQ1**: Is GBRF capable of encoding user preferences in data distributions while achieving superior performance compared to state-of-the-art methods? Furthermore, can GBRF be used effectively alongside different classifiers, as is the case with standard resampling techniques?
- **RQ2**: Do the optimal probability mass functions obtained by GBRF conform to theoretical expectations?
- **RQ3**: What is the impact of the group-wise genetic optimization approach on the convergence speed of the genetic algorithm, and how does this translate into improvements in overall performance?

4.1 Experimental Setup

Datasets. We randomly selected 60 datasets from OpenML, all with an imbalance ratio above 3. The set includes 30 binary datasets and 30 obtained through binary decomposition of imbalanced multiclass datasets (via One-vs-All). The binarization of multiclass datasets was intentionally employed to amplify the existing class imbalance. Table 1 presents the primary statistical characteristics of the datasets analyzed in this study. The datasets exhibit considerable heterogeneity in class imbalance, sample sizes, and feature dimensionality, thereby encompassing a broad spectrum of classification problems. This diversity facilitates a rigorous assessment of GBRF's efficacy.

Table 1. Mean, standard deviation, median and range for the utilized 60 benchmark datasets of OpenML.

Metric	Mean ± Std	Median	Range
Imbalance Ratio	54.2 ± 117.5	9.0	[3.0, 695.2]
Number of Samples	2433.5 ± 1965.1	2407.0	[31, 5473]
Number of Features	18.2 ± 41.9	8.0	[1, 299]

The names and IDs of the utilized OpenML datasets are the following: **Binary**: sick (38), hepatitis (55), oil_spill (311), scene (312), yeast_ml8 (316), SPECT (336), SyskillWebertSheep (376), various analcatdata datasets (450, 463, 465, 479, 728, 747, 757, 760, 764, 765, 767, 852, 865, 867, 875), backache (463), balloon (914), socmob (934), water-treatment (940), various arsenic datasets (947, 949, 950, 951), spectrometer (954), braziltourism (957), segment (958), mfeatmorphological (962); **Multiclass**: page-blocks (30.0–30.4), abalone (183.1–183.10, 183.12–183.15, 183.21–183.27). IDs with "." refer to different binary decompositions of multiclass datasets, all of which exhibit different sample sizes and imbalance ratios.

Preprocessing involved mode imputation and ordinal encoding for categorical features, while missing numerical values were imputed using $k-$nearest neighbors (with $k = 5$).

Compared Baselines. Our method was compared against four resampling techniques: the widely used SMOTE and ADASYN, along with SMOTE-IPF and ProWSyn, two of the best-performing methods identified in a comprehensive study of 85 SMOTE variants [16]. Since resampling methods cannot encode user preferences in data generation, we also compared our approach with cost-sensitive classifiers, including cost-sensitive Random Forest, SVM, Extra Trees, and AdaBoost with cost-sensitive Decision Trees as the base classifier.

Evaluation Metrics. We assess user preferences using the $F\beta - score$ via 5-fold cross-validation, ensuring resampling is only applied to the training set. To compare performance across datasets, methods are ranked by their average $F\beta$-score per dataset (1 to 9, lower is better), and the mean rank is reported. We also compute the median percentage difference in $F\beta$-score between competing approaches and our method to quantify relative performance increase/decrease (positive values indicate an increase of performance versus competing method and vice-versa). Various β values are tested to evaluate the method's ability to achieve specific trade-offs between precision and recall. Note that, to incorporate the same objective in cost-sensitive classifiers as in GBRF, for each tested β, the missclassification penalty of the minority class is set to β^2, whereas the misslcassification penalty of the majority class is always kept at 1, as stipulated by Eq. 11.

Implementation Hyperparameters and Settings. $\textbf{GBRF}_{hybrid}$ refers to the use of g_1 and f_{SMOTE} for sample generation, guided by p_1, while g_2 is employed to form sample groups from which instances are removed based on p_2. In this configuration, outlier removal is disabled. In contrast, $\textbf{GBRF}_{over}$ denotes the use of both p_1 and p_2 for sample generation, with outlier removal enabled. When either of the framework variants is applied with a classifier, the same type of classifier is used within the fitness function.

4.2 Performance Comparisons (RQ1)

Tables 2 and 3 present the average rankings for the $\textbf{GBRF}_{over}$ and $\textbf{GBRF}_{hybrid}$ variants of the proposed framework, respectively, applied with the Naïve Bayes and Random Forest classifiers.

In Table 2, $\textbf{GBRF}_{over}$ exhibits higher performance across all β values, except for $\beta = 10$, for both classifiers. In addition, the method's average performance is notably superior to all other approaches. This demonstrates its ability to maximize either recall or precision based on predefined user preferences by selectively resampling specific regions of the feature space. Notably, when paired with Gaussian Naïve Bayes—a typically less effective classifier due to its assumption of feature independence and normal distributed data—$\textbf{GBRF}_{over}$ outperforms cost-sensitive ensemble methods, which are often the strongest performers for tabular data. This result underscores both the robustness of the proposed method and the limitations of cost-sensitive approaches. The latter impose a fixed β^2 misclassification penalty on the minority class, which effectively mimics replicating (i.e. oversampling) each sample β^2 times. In practice, this rigid penalization often results in highly nonlinear and overfitted decision boundaries that fail to generalize well (or at all), similar to the shortcomings of random oversampling [4]. This effect was particularly evident in more challenging datasets, where cost-sensitive methods showed substantial declines in performance compared to resampling-based techniques, thus justifying the large observed differences in median performance. In contrast, resampling-based methods can more effectively expand the minority class distribution through interpolation-based sample generation, which is less susceptible to overfitting when tailored to the dataset characteristics and aligned with user preferences. Furthermore, it is evident that conventional resampling methods lack the ability to incorporate user preferences into the data distribution, as evidenced by their reduced performance at extreme β values.

Table 2. Average rank obtained over the $F\beta$-scores across all datasets for different β values with **GRFB$_{\text{over}}$**, excluding ties. Tests are conducted with Naives Bayes (top) and Random Forest (bottom). Average median % performance difference of GBRF relative to the competing methods is also presented. Best result per β is **bolded**.

Approach	Methods | β values	0.1	0.2	0.5	1	2	5	10	Average
Resampling + Gaussian NB	GRFB$_{\text{over}}$ (Ours)	**3.91**	**3.96**	**4.08**	**3.77**	**3.88**	4.12	4.00	**3.96 (0.00%)**
	SMOTE-IPF	5.11	4.96	4.71	4.59	4.36	4.35	4.45	4.65 (1.55%)
	ProWSyn	4.90	4.75	4.20	4.40	4.38	4.49	4.75	4.55 (1.56%)
	SMOTE	4.79	4.84	4.76	4.62	4.70	4.49	4.80	4.71 (1.19%)
	ADASYN	5.00	4.97	5.19	4.92	4.61	4.29	4.58	4.79 (1.17%)
Cost-sensitive Classifiers	CS Random Forest	4.55	4.89	5.44	5.50	6.11	6.23	6.33	5.58 (25.36%)
	CS SVM	7.67	7.55	7.14	6.44	5.74	4.63	**3.68**	6.12 (58.64%)
	CS ExtraTrees	4.85	4.92	5.32	5.79	6.25	6.76	6.77	5.81 (28.46%)
	CS AdaBoost	4.22	4.15	4.15	4.96	4.98	5.64	5.64	4.82 (18.96%)
Resampling + Random Forest	GRFB$_{\text{over}}$ (Ours)	**3.37**	**3.30**	**3.85**	**3.97**	**3.53**	**3.57**	3.80	**3.63 (0.00%)**
	SMOTE-IPF	4.79	4.81	4.09	4.20	4.79	4.99	5.08	4.68 (2.63%)
	ProWSyn	3.92	4.16	4.51	4.44	4.33	4.12	4.51	4.28 (0.70%)
	SMOTE	4.41	4.23	4.09	4.36	4.36	4.92	5.15	4.50 (2.24%)
	ADASYN	4.74	4.51	4.40	4.05	4.47	4.74	4.73	4.52 (2.03%)
Cost-sensitive Classifiers	CS Random Forest	5.15	5.41	5.65	5.68	6.34	6.21	6.22	5.81 (19.18%)
	CS SVM	8.01	7.99	7.67	6.72	5.38	4.19	**3.48**	6.21 (53.75%)
	CS ExtraTrees	5.35	5.60	6.12	6.15	6.50	6.70	6.55	6.14 (17.82%)
	CS AdaBoost	5.27	4.99	4.61	5.42	5.29	5.54	5.48	5.23 (7.20%)

CS: Cost sensitive; NB: Naive Bayes;

Regarding **GBRF$_{hybrid}$**, it demonstrates even greater effectiveness than **GBRF$_{over}$**, achieving up to 8% improvement in $F\beta$-score compared to all other resampling approaches. By introducing the ability to remove majority-class samples, the framework can refine the decision boundary by modifying both class distributions, thereby providing additional flexibility in achieving the desired trade-off between precision and recall. Notably, this improvement is particularly observed for $\beta = 1$ with the Random Forrest, highlighting GBRF's ability to outperform traditional resampling methods even at their designed precision-recall operating region. This is made possible by the method's ability to adapt its resampling strategy to the dataset's specific characteristics. Additionally, the framework performs optimally with multiple classifiers, maintaining a model-agnostic property similar to conventional resampling techniques (with results from additional classifiers available in Appendix A). To further validate the proposed framework's ability to encode user preferences in the data distribution, we present a graphical analysis of the differences in resampled datasets and their corresponding probability mass functions using **GBRF$_{hybrid}$** with varying β values. The contrast between $\beta = 0.1$ and $\beta = 10$ is immediately evident: at $\beta = 0.1$, sample generation occurs primarily in regions densely populated by minority class samples, thereby reducing false positives. In contrast, $\beta = 10$ results in a substantial removal of majority class samples, as indicated by the high values of

p_2 in several sample groups, to ensure correct classification of all minority samples and minimize false negatives. This showcases how GBRF shapes sampling distributions to achieve the desired model behavior. Moreover, GBRF enhances transparency by providing explicit information on how the resampling was conducted, which is typically lacking in existing resampling techniques.

Table 3. Average rank obtained over the $F\beta$-scores across all datasets for different β values with **GRFB$_{hybrid}$**, excluding ties. Tests are conducted with Naives Bayes (top) and Random Forest (bottom). Average median % performance of GBRF difference relative to the competing method is also presented. Best result per β is **bolded**.

Approach	Methods | β values	0.1	0.2	0.5	1	2	5	10	Average
Resampling + Gaussian NB	GRFB$_{hybrid}$ (Ours)	**4.12**	**4.32**	**3.77**	**3.76**	**3.61**	**3.62**	3.77	**3.85 (0.00%)**
	SMOTE-IPF	5.08	5.08	5.01	4.62	4.57	4.81	4.64	4.83 (2.47%)
	ProWSyn	4.65	4.72	4.27	4.32	4.30	4.47	4.53	4.47 (1.84%)
	SMOTE	4.99	4.85	4.77	4.73	4.62	4.58	4.59	4.73 (1.96%)
	ADASYN	4.99	5.12	5.28	4.90	4.66	4.51	4.74	4.89 (2.60%)
Cost-sensitive Classifiers	CS Random Forest	4.45	4.51	5.13	5.59	6.18	6.29	6.58	5.53 (27.73%)
	CS SVM	7.65	7.59	7.17	6.50	5.74	4.65	**3.74**	6.15 (59.57%)
	CS ExtraTrees	4.73	4.74	5.50	5.83	6.22	6.70	6.74	5.78 (28.44%)
	CS AdaBoost	4.33	4.09	4.10	4.76	5.11	5.38	5.67	4.77 (17.27%)
Resampling + Random Forest	GRFB$_{hybrid}$ (Ours)	**3.49**	**3.30**	**3.69**	**2.98**	**2.96**	**2.90**	**3.16**	**3.21 (0.00%)**
	SMOTE-IPF	4.64	4.81	4.30	4.23	4.49	5.01	5.14	4.66 (7.57%)
	ProWSyn	4.43	4.16	4.29	4.80	4.57	4.71	4.76	4.53 (4.94%)
	SMOTE	4.47	4.23	4.02	4.48	4.73	5.18	4.94	4.58 (7.96%)
	ADASYN	4.23	4.51	4.54	4.20	4.42	5.16	5.24	4.61 (7.69%)
Cost-sensitive Classifiers	CS Random Forest	5.44	5.41	5.87	5.87	6.37	5.92	6.16	5.86 (29.07%)
	CS SVM	7.85	7.99	7.60	6.82	5.61	4.20	3.53	6.23 (59.23%)
	CS ExtraTrees	5.10	5.60	6.06	6.40	6.55	6.63	6.48	6.12 (24.74%)
	CS AdaBoost	5.35	4.99	4.63	5.22	5.30	5.29	5.60	5.20 (15.62%)

CS: Cost sensitive; NB: Naive Bayes;

4.3 Probability Mass Function Analysis (RQ2)

Figure 2 presents the average probability mass functions (PMFs) obtained for datasets with five sample groups for both g_1 and g_2, thus simplifying the analysis. Initially, it is evident that for g_1, β values greater than one tend to acquire significantly higher sampling probabilities in regions of low minority density, aggressively promoting the expansion of the majority class by generating samples in such areas. Conversely, β values lower than one preferentially generate samples in high minority density regions, reinforcing existing clusters in a more controlled manner. Moreover, in the case of g_2, since sample generation is based on a broader neighborhood, thus facilitating the expansion of the majority class, higher probabilities are assigned to these sample groups for larger β values, and vice-versa. These findings align with the theoretical discussion in Sect. 3.2, where sampling in regions of lower minority class likelihood is shown to shift the decision boundary towards the majority class, and vice-versa (Fig. 1).

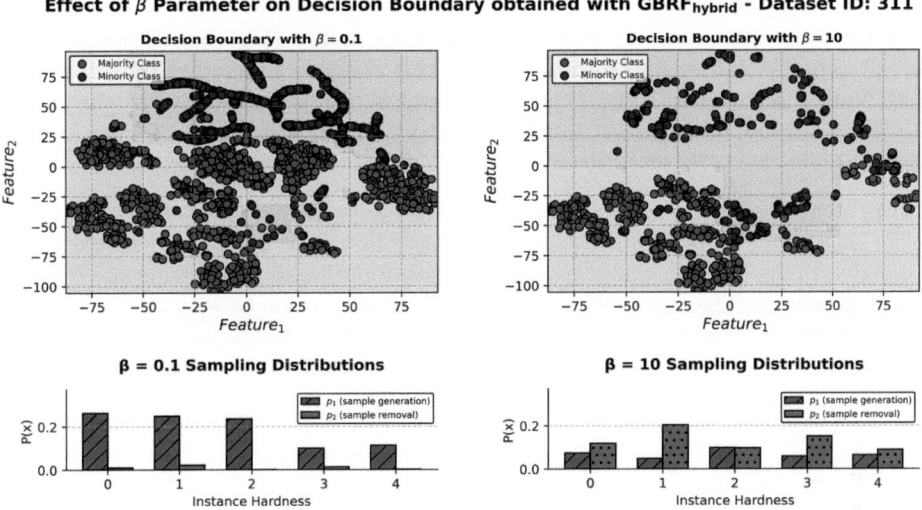

Fig. 1. Synthetic dataset obtained after applying **GBRF**$_{hybrid}$ on Dataset ID 311 (randomly selected) from the OpenML repository with $\beta = 0.1$ (left) and $\beta = 10$ (right). The optimal PMF for both scenarios is shown below, where the x-axis represents the number of majority samples within the neighborhood of minority samples for g_1 and the proximity to the decision boundary for g_2, thereby reflecting instance hardness.

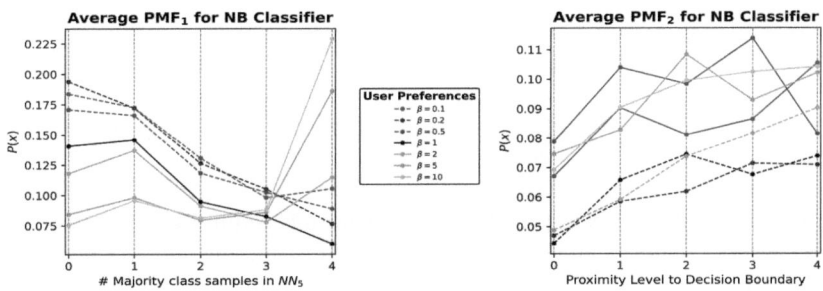

Fig. 2. Optimal average PMFs obtained for p_1 (left) and p_2 (right) with **GBRF**$_{overs}$ on a set of 88 train splits (generated via 5-fold cross validation of the 60 OpenML datasets), where the same amount of sample groups were generated per PMF. These averages are computed for each β value individually, with $\beta \geq 1$ represented with a solid line, whereas $\beta < 1$ are represented with a dotted line.

4.4 Impact of Architectural Choices on Computational Efficiency (RQ3)

To evaluate the effect of expanding the search space on the method's ability to attain high-quality solutions, we compared the average ranks of **GRFB$_{over}$** under two conditions: one where each $g_1(G_k)$ and $g_2(G_k)$ is restricted to 20 equally spaced values and another where this range is expanded by a factor of 100. Note that, even a 100× expansion remains negligible relative to the search spaces routinely encountered in instance-wise genetic resampling approaches.

Table 4. Average ranks for the **GRFB$_{over}$** methodology with Naives Bayes Classifier, when considering a 100-fold increase in possible values of p_1 and p_2 per sample group, compared to the baseline search space. Median runtime across all datasets and β values is also presented. The experiments were conducted on a machine with an AMD Ryzen 7 5800H and GeForce RTX 3070 Mobile/Max-Q running Ubuntu 22.04.4 LTS without any background processes running simultaneously. Best results are **bolded**.

Methodology | β values	0.1	0.2	0.5	1	2	5	10	Average
100x search space **GRFB$_{over}$** (Median Runtime: 9.696 s)	4.74	4.99	4.84	5.20	5.03	4.51	4.72	4.86
Baseline **GRFB$_{over}$** (Median Runtime: **5.294 s**)	**3.91**	**3.96**	**4.08**	**3.77**	**3.88**	**4.12**	**4.00**	**3.96**

Analysis of Table 4 reveals that a larger parameter grid incurs a significant drop in performance alongside increased runtime, thereby highlighting the advantage of the proposed architectural design. Our fixed-size, group-wise mechanism offsets the combinatorial explosion of search space in standard genetic-resampling methods, producing superior solutions. This framework also expedites convergence via more frequent activation of the early stopping criteria, as noted by the reduced runtime under identical genetic hyperparametrizations (except search space). A median runtime of approximately 5 s was recorded, which is notably efficient for a genetic-based algorithm. Still, the predominant contributor to total runtime is the model training required for fitness estimation. These bottlenecks may be alleviated by optimizing key parameters dictating runtime (e.g., population size, generation count), exploiting in-context learning for tabular data to bypass the need for model training, or initializing the evolutionary search with a low time complexity classifier, as models trained with equivalent objectives (β parameters) generally converge to analogous data distributions.

5 Conclusion

The widespread adoption of resampling methods for addressing class imbalance originates from their compatibility with diverse learning algorithms. However, their inability to explicitly encode user preferences in the resulting models has driven the development of this work. We introduce GBRF, a novel framework that integrates user-defined preferences into the data distribution, shaping model behavior through a tunable parameter, β, which governs the precision-recall trade-off. GBRF leverages genetic algorithms to optimize two probability mass functions that control the generation and removal of samples, effectively functioning as an oversampling, undersampling, or hybrid resampling method. By employing an evolutionary strategy, we ensure that resampling is conducted to account for both user-preferences and dataset characteristics. Theoretical analysis and empirical validation across 60 benchmark datasets confirm that GBRF effectively encodes user preferences, consistently surpassing eight state-of-the-art resampling and cost-sensitive approaches, particularly in hybrid settings. Additionally, the learned probability mass functions provide accurate and interpretable insights into the resampling process, offering a structured approach to understanding the inter-dependencies between data characteristics, user preferences, and resampling strategies. Future research will focus on extending this methodology to multiclass scenarios and improving scalability.

Acknowledgments. This work was supported by FCT - Fundação para a Ciência e Tecnologia, I.P. by project reference PRT/BD/154859/2023 and DOI identifier https://doi.org/10.54499/PRT/BD/154859/2023. Additionally, this work was also funded by FCT under unit 00127-IEETA.

Disclosure of Interests. The authors have no competing interests to declare that are relevant to the content of this article.

References

1. Alam, T., Qamar, S., Dixit, A., Benaida, M.: Genetic algorithm: reviews, implementations, and applications (2020). https://arxiv.org/abs/2007.12673
2. Alimohammadi, D., Bolin, M.: Mathematics for classical information retrieval: roots and applications (2010)
3. Barua, S., Islam, M.M., Murase, K.: ProWSyn: proximity weighted synthetic oversampling technique for imbalanced data set learning. In: Pei, J., Tseng, V.S., Cao, L., Motoda, H., Xu, G. (eds.) PAKDD 2013. LNCS (LNAI), vol. 7819, pp. 317–328. Springer, Heidelberg (2013). https://doi.org/10.1007/978-3-642-37456-2_27
4. Branco, P., Torgo, L., Ribeiro, R.P.: A survey of predictive modeling on imbalanced domains. ACM Comput. Surv. **49**(2) (2016). https://doi.org/10.1145/2907070
5. Katoch, S., Chauhan, S.S., Kumar, V.: A review on genetic algorithm: past, present, and future. Multimedia Tools Appl. **80**(5), 8091–8126 (2020). https://doi.org/10.1007/s11042-020-10139-6
6. Chawla, N.V., Bowyer, K.W., Hall, L.O., Kegelmeyer, W.P.: Smote: synthetic minority over-sampling technique. J. Artif. Intell. Res. **16**, 321–357 (2002). https://doi.org/10.1613/jair.953

7. Douzas, G., Bação, F., Last, F.: Improving imbalanced learning through a heuristic oversampling method based on k-means and smote. Inf. Sci. **465** (2018). https://doi.org/10.1016/j.ins.2018.06.056
8. Drown, D., Khoshgoftaar, T., Seliya, N.: Evolutionary sampling and software quality modeling of high-assurance systems. IEEE Trans. Syst. Man Cybern. Part A **39**, 1097–1107 (2009). https://doi.org/10.1109/TSMCA.2009.2020804
9. Fernández, A., Garcia, S., Herrera, F., Chawla, N.: Smote for learning from imbalanced data: progress and challenges, marking the 15-year anniversary. J. Artif. Intell. Res. **61**, 863–905 (2018). https://doi.org/10.1613/jair.1.11192
10. Fernández, A., García, S., Galar, M., Prati, R., Krawczyk, B., Herrera, F.: Learning from Imbalanced Data Sets (2018). https://doi.org/10.1007/978-3-319-98074-4
11. Ha, J., Lee, J.S.: A new under-sampling method using genetic algorithm for imbalanced data classification. In: Proceedings of the 10th International Conference on Ubiquitous Information Management and Communication. IMCOM '16. Association for Computing Machinery, New York (2016). https://doi.org/10.1145/2857546.2857643
12. He, H., Bai, Y., Garcia, E.A., Li, S.: Adasyn: adaptive synthetic sampling approach for imbalanced learning. In: 2008 IEEE International Joint Conference on Neural Networks (IEEE World Congress on Computational Intelligence), pp. 1322–1328 (2008). https://doi.org/10.1109/IJCNN.2008.4633969
13. Jain, A., Ratnoo, S., Kumar, D.: Addressing class imbalance problem in medical diagnosis: a genetic algorithm approach, pp. 1–8 (2017). https://doi.org/10.1109/ICOMICON.2017.8279150
14. Jiang, K., Lu, J., Xia, K.: A novel algorithm for imbalance data classification based on genetic algorithm improved SMOTE. Arab. J. Sci. Eng. **41**(8), 3255–3266 (2016). https://doi.org/10.1007/s13369-016-2179-2
15. Kim, H.J., Jo, N.O., Shin, K.S.: Optimization of cluster-based evolutionary undersampling for the artificial neural networks in corporate bankruptcy prediction. Expert Syst. Appl. **59**(C), 226–234 (2016). https://doi.org/10.1016/j.eswa.2016.04.027
16. Kovács, G.: An empirical comparison and evaluation of minority oversampling techniques on a large number of imbalanced datasets. Appl. Soft Comput. (2019). https://doi.org/10.1016/j.asoc.2019.105662
17. Kulkarni, A., Chong, D., Batarseh, F.A.: 5 - foundations of data imbalance and solutions for a data democracy. In: Batarseh, F.A., Yang, R. (eds.) Data Democracy, pp. 83–106. Academic Press (2020). https://doi.org/10.1016/B978-0-12-818366-3.00005-8. https://www.sciencedirect.com/science/article/pii/B9780128183663000058
18. Lu, Y., Cheung, Y.M., Tang, Y.Y.: Bayes imbalance impact index: a measure of class imbalanced dataset for classification problem (2019). https://arxiv.org/abs/1901.10173
19. Onan, A., García-Díaz, V.: Consensus clustering-based undersampling approach to imbalanced learning. Sci. Program. **2019** (2019). https://doi.org/10.1155/2019/5901087
20. Santos, M.S., Abreu, P.H., Japkowicz, N., Fernández, A., Santos, J.: A unifying view of class overlap and imbalance: key concepts, multi-view panorama, and open avenues for research. Inf. Fusion **89**, 228–253 (2023). https://doi.org/10.1016/j.inffus.2022.08.017. https://www.sciencedirect.com/science/article/pii/S1566253522001099

21. Werner nbsp;den nbsp;Vargas, V., Schneider nbsp;Aranda, J.A., dos Santos nbsp;Costa, R., da Silva nbsp;Pereira, P.R., Victória nbsp;Barbosa, J.L.: Imbalanced data preprocessing techniques for machine learning: a systematic mapping study. Knowl. Inf. Syst. **65**(1), 31–57 (2022). https://doi.org/10.1007/s10115-022-01772-8
22. Wolpert, D., Macready, W.: No free lunch theorems for optimization. IEEE Trans. Evol. Comput. **1**(1), 67–82 (1997). https://doi.org/10.1109/4235.585893

Sample and Expand: Discovering Low-Rank Submatrices With Quality Guarantees

Martino Ciaperoni[1]([✉]), Aristides Gionis[2], and Heikki Mannila[3]

[1] Scuola Normale Superiore, Pisa, Italy
martino.ciaperoni@sns.it
[2] KTH Royal Institute of Technology, Stockholm, Sweden
argioni@kth.se
[3] Aalto University, Espoo, Finland
heikki.mannila@aalto.fi

Abstract. The problem of approximating a matrix by a low-rank one has been extensively studied. This problem assumes, however, that the whole matrix has a low-rank structure. This assumption is often false for real-world matrices. We consider the problem of discovering submatrices from the given matrix with bounded deviations from their low-rank approximations. We introduce an effective two-phase method for this task: first, we use sampling to discover small nearly low-rank submatrices, and then they are expanded while preserving proximity to a low-rank approximation. An extensive experimental evaluation confirms that the method we introduce compares favorably to existing approaches.

Keywords: Low-rank approximation · submatrix detection

1 Introduction

Low-rank approximation has emerged as a fundamental task in many data-analysis applications, including machine-learning pipelines [26], large language models [14], recommender systems [16], image compression and denoising [12]. The goal of low-rank approximation is to represent an input matrix as accurately as possible using a small number of row and column vectors.

For decades, the *singular value decomposition* (SVD), with the closely related principal component analysis (PCA), has remained the gold standard for low-rank approximation [11]. Despite its success, SVD has certain limitations. Among others, when applying SVD we aim to find a low-rank approximation for the entire input matrix. This assumption can be rather restrictive, as in real-world data it might be that only certain submatrices are well approximated by low-rank structures. For instance, in ratings data originating in movie recommender systems, low-rank submatrices occur because subsets of users may share a similar taste only for a subset of movies. Similar local patterns could be observed in data coming from other domains, such as market-basket analysis,

---

M. Ciaperoni—The work was done while the author was at Aalto University.

© The Author(s), under exclusive license to Springer Nature Switzerland AG 2026
R. P. Ribeiro et al. (Eds.): ECML PKDD 2025, LNAI 16017, pp. 78–95, 2026.
https://doi.org/10.1007/978-3-032-06096-9_5

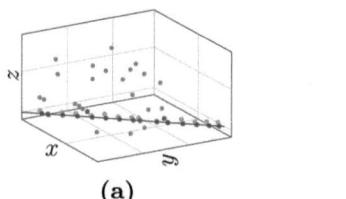 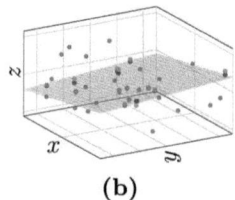

(a) (b)

Fig. 1. Example. A subset of data points (in orange) in the 3-dimensional space are close to their projection (in red) onto a line in the xy-plane (a) or to a plane in the 3-dimensional space (b), while other points (in blue) can be further away.

image processing, and biology [6]. The SVD can fail to identify local low-rank submatrices.

Existing Approaches to Find Local Low-rank Submatrices. The task of identifying submatrices that are well described by low-rank structures has been largely overlooked until recently [6]. Existing work in this direction is based primarily on the SVD, and does not provide any guarantee on the quality of the approximation for the identified submatrices.

Our Approach. In this work, we adopt a different perspective on discovering local low-rank patterns, and we address the problem of identifying submatrices that are guaranteed to be close to a low-rank approximation. Our quality guarantees hold with respect to an approximation that can be easily interpreted in terms of the original data, which can be particularly valuable for applications in different domains. For example, near-rank-1 submatrices can be accurately approximated by each row in the submatrix being colinear with a single row. Unlike previous work, our work does not directly rely on the SVD. Nearly-low-rank submatrices correspond to subsets of points (matrix rows) that approximately lie on a low-dimensional subspace, for a subset of dimensions (matrix columns). For rank equal to 1, which is a particularly interesting case, the points approximately lie on a line through the origin, and for rank equal to 2 the points are close to a plane through the origin, as in the example of Fig. 1, which shows data points identifying a 15×2 near-rank-1 submatrix and a 15×3 near-rank-2 submatrix.

While SVD may fail to reveal dense lines in the data, it is possible to find such structures by sampling. A naïve approach would be to sample subsets of points and dimensions until a large set of nearly-collinear points is found. However, this procedure quickly becomes inefficient. Instead, to identify points approximately distributed along a line, we introduce a method that only relies on sampling in an initialization phase to find a minimal structure that can exhibit this property, i.e., two points in two-dimensions. In a subsequent phase, the 2×2 submatrix is expanded deterministically to obtain the entire subset of points and dimensions associated with the target line. Based on such a two-phase method, we discover arbitrary submatrices that admit low-rank approximations that can be easily interpreted in terms of the original submatrix rows or columns, and are supported by quality guarantees. A real-world example is given in Fig. 2.

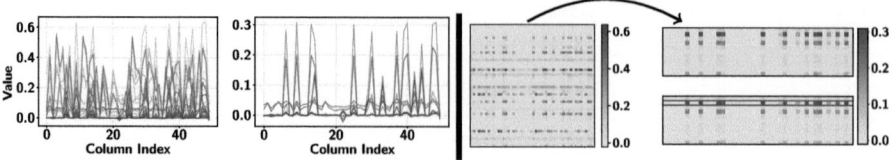

Fig. 2. HYPERSPECTRAL dataset. On the left, we show the values of the rows in a 50×50 matrix and the nearly-proportional values of the rows in a near-rank-1 11×44 submatrix discovered by our method. On the right we show the matrix and, next to it, the discovered submatrix (top) and its accurate approximation expressing each row as collinear with the row highlighted in red (bottom).

Our Contributions. Our main contributions can be summarized as follows.

- We formalize the problem of finding submatrices that are provably close to a low-rank approximation.
- We introduce an effective method for finding submatrices that are provably close to rank 1. Then, we generalize this method to the rank-k case.
- We analyze the theoretical properties of the method we introduce.
- We demonstrate the advantages of our method over previous work.

Roadmap. The rest of the paper is organized as follows. In Sect. 2 we discuss related work. Section 3 introduces the notation used throughout the paper as well as key preliminary concepts. In Sect. 4 we present the problem we study and in Sect. 5 we illustrate our method to address it. In Sect. 6 we analyze the properties of the method, and in Sect. 7 we assess its empirical performance. Finally, Sect. 8 provides conclusions.

2 Related Work

Low-rank Matrix Approximation. Low-rank approximation techniques are widely used to decompose a matrix into simpler components, capturing essential patterns while reducing noise and dimensionality. The SVD and the related PCA are among the most popular techniques [11]. Nonnegative matrix factorization techniques [9] have become popular in applications where the goal is to decompose data in nonnegative components. Boolean matrix decomposition relies on boolean algebra instead of linear algebra [21]. Column subset selection [3] and the CUR decomposition [19] have emerged as more interpretable alternatives to the SVD. In 2019, Gillis and Shitov [10] studied the problem of low-rank approximation to minimize the maximum entry-wise deviation. More recently, an approach to low-rank approximation that accounts for multiplicative effects was introduced [4].

Local Low-rank Matrix Approximation. Relatively less research has been conducted for finding decompositions that do not assume a *global* low-rank structure, which is the focus of our paper. The goal here is to find submatrices that are *locally* well-approximated by a low-rank structure. A simple heuristic to local low-rank approximation is obtained by imposing a sparsity constraint on matrix decomposition, and sparse PCA [20] is a prominent example of such methods.

Doan and Vavasis proposed the problem of recovering near-rank-1 submatrices by framing it as a convex-optimization problem [8]. Lee et al. [16] introduced the LLORMA method to address matrix-completion tasks while relaxing the assumption that the entire matrix has low rank. LLORMA approximates the entire input matrix, and thus, it is fundamentally different from our work, which focuses on detecting local low-rank patterns. On the other hand, the problem we study finds application in matrix completion, as shown by the work of Ruchansky et al. [22], which introduces the SVP method to quickly detect low-rank submatrices with the ultimate goal of improving the accuracy in matrix completion. While SVP cannot discover arbitrary low-rank submatrices, Dang et al. [6] introduced the RPSP method, which addresses this lack of generality. The core idea behind RPSP is to sample submatrices and count the number of times that each entry belongs to a low-rank submatrix. Like RPSP, our method targets arbitrary near-low-rank submatrices. Unlike previous methods, our method can in principle identify submatrices that are close to a specific target rank.

Co-clustering, Projective Clustering, and Subspace Clustering. Co-clustering algorithms [7] simultaneously cluster the rows and columns of a matrix. Although co-clustering algorithms can be used for detecting low-rank submatrices, they cannot generally discover such structures, except in specific cases where the values of the low-rank submatrices deviate significantly from the background. Projective clustering and subspace clustering are also related problems. In projective clustering [1], the goal is to partition the data into subsets such that the points in each subset are close to each other in some subspace. In subspace clustering [25] the goal is to find a representation of the input data as a union of different subspaces. In general, clustering problems are fundamentally different from the problem we study, as they seek a partitioning of the entire data matrix.

3 Preliminaries

Notation and basic definitions. Matrices are denoted by upper-case boldface letters, and we use $\mathbf{D}$ to denote the input data matrix. $\mathbf{D}_{i,j}$ indicates the entry of $\mathbf{D}$ in row i and column j, while the i-th row and j-th column of $\mathbf{D}$ are denoted by $\mathbf{D}_{i,:}$ and $\mathbf{D}_{:,j}$, respectively. Sets are denoted by upper-case letters and scalars by lower-case letters. Vectors are denoted by lower-case boldface letters, e.g., $\mathbf{x} = (x_1, \ldots, x_d)$. We denote the L_2 (or Euclidean) norm of a vector $\mathbf{x}$ as $\|\mathbf{x}\|_2$ and the inner product between two vectors $\mathbf{x}$ and $\mathbf{y}$ as $\mathbf{x}^T \mathbf{y}$. We consider different matrix norms: the Frobenius norm $\|\mathbf{D}\|_F = (\sum_{i,j} |\mathbf{D}_{i,j}|^2)^{1/2}$, the spectral norm $\|\mathbf{D}\|_2 = \sup_{\|\mathbf{x}\|_2 \leq 1} \|\mathbf{D}\mathbf{x}\|_2$, and the max norm $\|\mathbf{D}\|_{\max} = \max_{i,j} |\mathbf{D}_{i,j}|$. We use $\|\mathbf{D}\|_*$ with $* = \{2, F, \max\}$ to indicate the above norms. We refer to the total number of entries of a (sub)matrix $\mathbf{D}$ as its *size*, which is also simply denoted by $|\mathbf{D}|$, if there is no risk of confusion with the entry-wise absolute value. For a matrix $\mathbf{X}$, we denote by $\hat{\mathbf{X}}$ a low-rank approximation of $\mathbf{X}$ and by $\mathbf{E}_{\mathbf{X},\hat{\mathbf{X}}}$ the difference $\mathbf{E}_{\mathbf{X},\hat{\mathbf{X}}} = \mathbf{X} - \hat{\mathbf{X}}$.

Orthogonal Projections. Given a nonzero vector $\mathbf{x}$ and a vector $\mathbf{y}$, the *orthogonal projection* of $\mathbf{y}$ onto $\mathbf{x}$ is given by $\operatorname{Proj}_{\mathbf{x}} \mathbf{y} = (\mathbf{y}^T \mathbf{x})/(\mathbf{x}^T \mathbf{x}) \mathbf{x}$. Similarly, given a matrix $\mathbf{B}$ and a matrix $\mathbf{A}$ with linearly independent columns, the orthogonal projection of $\mathbf{B}$ onto the column space of $\mathbf{A}$ is given by $\operatorname{Proj}_{\mathbf{A}} \mathbf{B} = \mathbf{A} \mathbf{A}^+ \mathbf{B}$, where $\mathbf{A}^+ = (\mathbf{A}^T \mathbf{A})^{-1} \mathbf{A}^T$ is the *Moore-Penrose pseudoinverse* of $\mathbf{A}$.

Low-rank Approximation and SVD. The *singular value decomposition* (SVD) of a matrix $\mathbf{D} \in \mathbb{R}^{n \times m}$ is given by $\mathbf{D} = \mathbf{U} \boldsymbol{\Sigma} \mathbf{V}^T$, where $\mathbf{U} \in \mathbb{R}^{n \times n}$ and $\mathbf{V} \in \mathbb{R}^{m \times m}$ are unitary matrices, and $\boldsymbol{\Sigma} \in \mathbb{R}^{n \times m}$ is a diagonal matrix with singular values $\{\sigma_1, \sigma_2 \ldots \sigma_{\min\{n,m\}}\}$ as diagonal entries, conventionally sorted in decreasing order. If the matrix is not clear from the context, we denote as $\sigma_i(\mathbf{X})$ the i-th singular value of $\mathbf{X}$. It is known that the optimal rank-k approximation of $\mathbf{D}$ for the Frobenius and the spectral norm (but not for the max norm) is obtained from the SVD by retaining the first k singular values, along with the associated k columns of $\mathbf{U}$ and rows of $\mathbf{V}^T$. The largest singular value of a matrix equals its spectral norm, and the number of non-zero singular values indicates the rank.

As real-world data are often noisy, the singular values are seldom exactly zero. Accordingly, to measure the proximity of a matrix to rank 1, in this work, we use the *low-rankness score* [6], which is given by $\ell r(\mathbf{X}) = \frac{\sigma_1(\mathbf{X})^2}{\sum_{i=1}^{\min(n,m)} \sigma_i(\mathbf{X})^2}$. A matrix whose singular values after the k-th one are close to zero can be accurately approximated by a rank-k matrix, and is loosely referred to as *near-rank-k* matrix.

4 Problem Formulation

Next, we formalize the problems we study in this paper. To provide better insight, we first present a special case, and then introduce the more general problems.

Searching for a Near-Rank-1 Subset of Rows or Columns. As a warm-up, we first introduce a simple problem that fixes the matrix columns or rows.

Problem 1 (Largest near-rank-1 subset of rows (LNROSR)). Given a matrix $\mathbf{D} \in \mathbb{R}^{n \times m}$ with set of rows $\mathcal{R}$ and a threshold $\epsilon \in \mathbb{R}^+$, find the largest subset of rows $\mathcal{R}' \subseteq \mathcal{R}$ such that there exist a rank-1 matrix $\hat{\mathbf{X}} \propto \mathbf{x} \mathbf{y}^T$, where $\mathbf{y}^T \in \mathbb{R}^m$ is a row of $\mathbf{D}$, satisfying

$$\|\mathbf{D}_{i,:} - \hat{\mathbf{X}}_{i,:}\|_2 \leq \epsilon, \quad \text{for all } i \in \mathcal{R}'. \tag{1}$$

Problem 1 asks to find the largest near-rank-1 submatrix defined over a subset of rows of $\mathbf{D}$ and all columns. This problem is computationally tractable.

Proposition 1. *The LNROSR problem can be solved in polynomial time.*

The proof, via a simple algorithm, is presented in Appendix A of the extended version of the paper [5].

While Problem 1 asks for a subset of rows, the symmetric problem asking for a subset of columns can be solved by considering $\mathbf{D}^T$ in place of $\mathbf{D}$.

Searching for a Near-Rank-1 Submatrix. Next, we discuss the more challenging problem of finding a near-rank-1 submatrix, without fixing neither the rows nor the columns of the input matrix.

Problem 2 (Largest near-rank-1 submatrix (LNROS)). Given a matrix $\mathbf{D} \in \mathbb{R}^{n \times m}$ and a threshold $\epsilon \in \mathbb{R}^+$, find a submatrix $\mathbf{X} \in \mathbb{R}^{n' \times m'}$ of maximum size such that there exist a rank-1 matrix $\hat{\mathbf{X}}$ satisfying

$$\|\mathbf{E}_{\mathbf{X},\hat{\mathbf{X}}}\|_* = \|\mathbf{X} - \hat{\mathbf{X}}\|_* \leq \epsilon, \text{ where } * \text{ can be any of the norms } \{F, 2, \max\}. \quad (2)$$

Unfortunately, due to the interaction between rows and columns, the LNROS problem is computationally intractable.

Proposition 2. *The LNROS problem is* **NP**-*hard.*

The **NP**-hardness of LNROS follows from that of the largest rank-1 submatrix problem [8] by setting $\epsilon = 0$, and highlights the connection with the *maximum-edge biclique* problem [18], which is made evident in Sect. 5.

Searching for a Near-Rank-k Submatrix. We generalize the LNROS problem to the case of near-rank-k submatrices.

Problem 3 (Largest near-rank-k submatrix (LNRkS)). Given a matrix $\mathbf{D} \in \mathbb{R}^{n \times m}$ and a threshold $\epsilon \in \mathbb{R}^+$, find a submatrix $\mathbf{X} \in \mathbb{R}^{n' \times m'}$ of maximum size such that there exist a rank-k matrix $\hat{\mathbf{X}}$ satisfying

$$\|\mathbf{X} - \hat{\mathbf{X}}\|_* \leq \epsilon, \text{ where } * \text{ can be any of the norms } \{F, 2, \max\}. \quad (3)$$

As LNRkS is a generalization of LNROS, the LNRkS problem is also **NP**-hard.

Extensions. The problem formulations presented above focus on extracting a single submatrix. In practice, one may wish to find a representation of the input matrix as a sum of N local low-rank patterns. Such a problem is a generalization of both LNROS and LNRkS, and hence, inherits their hardness.

Additionally, it may be of interest to identify submatrices that define affine subspaces. Extending our problem formulations and method to the case of affine subspaces (or near-low-rank submatrices up to a particular translation) is straightforward. The details are deferred to an extended version of this work.

5 Algorithms

In this section, we present SAMPLEANDEXPAND, our method for discovering near-low-rank submatrices. We first give an overview of the method, and then we present the algorithms to detect near-rank-1 and near-rank-k submatrices.

5.1 High-level Overview of the Method

SAMPLEANDEXPAND is based on a simple two-phase procedure. The first phase *samples* small seed submatrices, and the second phase *expands* those seed submatrices into larger near-low-rank submatrices.

Algorithm 1. Overview of SAMPLEANDEXPAND.

1: **Input:** Matrix **D**, target rank k, number of initializations N_{init}, initial tolerance δ_{init}, tolerance δ.
2: **Output:** Near-rank-k submatrix $\mathbf{X}^*$.
3: $\mathbf{X}^* \leftarrow \mathbf{0}$
4: **for** $i = 1$ to N_{init} **do**
5:     $\mathbf{P} \leftarrow$ **Initialization**($\mathbf{D}$, k, δ_{init})   // first phase: initialization (sampling)
6:     $\mathbf{X} \leftarrow$ **Expansion**($\mathbf{P}$, k, δ)   // second phase: expansion
7:     **if** $f(\mathbf{X}) \geq f(\mathbf{X}^*)$ **then**
8:        $\mathbf{X}^* \leftarrow \mathbf{X}$ // select the best submatrix across different initializations
9:     **end if**
10: **end for**
11: **Return** $\mathbf{X}^*$

The main idea relies on the simple principle that any submatrix of a rank-k matrix must also have rank at most k. Thereby, a near-rank-1 submatrix **X** of size $n' \times m'$ contains a large number of 2×2 near-rank-1 submatrices. Thus, if we are looking for a rank-1 submatrix, in the first phase (initialization phase) we identify a *seed*, which is a 2×2 submatrix that can be expanded into a larger near-rank-1 submatrix. The goal of the second phase (expansion phase) is to expand the seed into a large near-rank-1 submatrix. Similarly, if we are looking for a near-rank-k submatrix, in the first phase we identify a seed submatrix of minimal size that is close to rank k, and then we expand it as much as possible.

The two-phase procedure is repeated N_{init} times, to explore different random initializations. Each repetition outputs a nearly low-rank submatrix **X**. SAMPLE-ANDEXPAND accepts a parameter δ that controls the trade-off between proximity to the target rank and size of the output matrices. Higher values of δ tend to yield submatrices that are larger but deviate more from their low-rank approximation.

After the last repetition, we return the submatrix **X** that maximizes the objective function $f(\mathbf{X}) = |\mathbf{X}| - \frac{\lambda}{|\mathbf{X}|} \|\mathbf{E}_{\mathbf{X},\hat{\mathbf{X}}}\|_F^2$. By default, in the absence of prior information, we standardize the error term and the size, and set $\lambda = 1$. However, SAMPLEANDEXPAND is flexible and supports any objective function.

The pseudocode of the high-level SAMPLEANDEXPAND method is given in Algorithm 1. The details of the sampling and expansion phase of the method for the rank-1 case and for the general rank-k case are described later.

Approximating the Discovered Submatrices. The discovered submatrices can be approximated via SVD. Further, SAMPLEANDEXPAND also naturally leads to a low-rank approximation that is more interpretable than the SVD since it is based on the rows (or columns) of **X**. For the rank-1 case, this approximation is given by $\hat{\mathbf{X}} = \mathbf{x}\mathbf{y}^T$, where, either $\mathbf{y}^T$ is a row or $\mathbf{x}$ a column of **X**. If, e.g., $\mathbf{y}^T$ is a row of **X**, **x** can be chosen to minimize $\|\mathbf{X} - \mathbf{x}\mathbf{y}^T\|_F^2$. The resulting optimal **x** is the vector of coefficients that describe the orthogonal projections of the rows of **X** onto $\mathbf{y}^T$. An analogous argument also applies to the columns. As discussed in Sect. 6, this approximation is supported by approximation guarantees.

Although the rank-1 SVD may be more accurate than the interpretable alternative, if a matrix is sufficiently close to rank 1, the difference is often negligible. To gain some intuition for this claim, note that a matrix that has exactly rank 1 can be represented with no error not only by the discussed interpretable approximation, but also by the rescaled outer product $\alpha \mathbf{X}_{:,j}\mathbf{X}_{i,:}^T$ of any of its rows and columns, for some $\alpha \in \mathbb{R}$. If instead the matrix deviates significantly from rank 1, the rank-k interpretable approximation based on orthogonal projections is often not as accurate as the rank-k SVD.

Discovering Multiple Submatrices. In practice, we may wish to discover multiple submatrices within a single matrix $\mathbf{D}$ and eventually obtain an approximation $\hat{\mathbf{D}}$ of the matrix as sum of local low-rank patterns. To achieve this, we run SAMPLEANDEXPAND iteratively. In each iteration, the method finds a single near-rank-k submatrix, and then updates $\hat{\mathbf{D}}$ and the input matrix. This simple procedure is summarized in Algorithm 2 of the extended version of the paper [5].

5.2 Recovering a Near-Rank-1 SubMatrix

Here, we present the initialization (sampling) and expansion phases of the algorithm to discover near-rank-1 submatrices. Algorithm 3 in the extended version of the paper [5] presents the pseudocode.

Initialization. To find the initial 2×2 near-rank-1 submatrix $\mathbf{P}$, we sample two distinct row indices $\{i_1, i_2\}$ and column indices $\{j_1, j_2\}$ of the input matrix $\mathbf{D}$, and then we compute the determinant of the associated 2×2 submatrix $\mathbf{P}'$:

$$\det(\mathbf{P}') = \mathbf{D}_{i_1,j_1}\mathbf{D}_{i_2,j_2} - \mathbf{D}_{i_1,j_2}\mathbf{D}_{i_2,j_1}.$$

If $|\det(\mathbf{P}')| \leq \delta_{init}$, for some input $\delta_{init} \in \mathbb{R}^+$, $\mathbf{P}'$ is close to rank 1, and hence it may be contained into a larger near-rank-1 submatrix. Therefore, $\mathbf{P}'$ is the seed $\mathbf{P}$ that will be expanded. If instead $|\det(\mathbf{P}')| > \delta_{init}$, we sample different 2×2 submatrices $\mathbf{P}'$ until we find a seed to expand. In practice, δ_{init} is initialized to a small value (10^{-11} by default) and progressively increased until the seed is found.

Expansion. To extend $\mathbf{P}$ into a larger submatrix, we consider one of the entries (i_a, j_a) in $\mathbf{P}$, which we call *anchor*. Then, we divide all rows in $\mathbf{D}$ by the i_a-th row, obtaining the row-wise ratio matrix $\mathbf{R}^r$ and all columns by the j_a-th column, obtaining the column-wise ratio matrix $\mathbf{R}^c$. If an entry in the i_a-th row or j_a-th column of $\mathbf{D}$ is zero, we add a small positive constant to prevent division by zero.

The ratios indicate which entries may belong to a near-rank-1 submatrix with the anchor. As illustrated in Fig. 3, if the matrix $\mathbf{D}$ contains a submatrix $\mathbf{X}$ of rank 1, the entries corresponding to $\mathbf{X}$ in $\mathbf{R}^r$ and $\mathbf{R}^c$ will be row-wise and column-wise constant, respectively. More generally, as we explain in Sect. 6, bounding the variation across rows of row-wise and columns of column-wise ratios in a submatrix leads to quality guarantees for its rank-1 approximation. Thus, the goal of the expansion stage is to identify a submatrix of maximum size with bounded variation in the rows of the row-wise ratios and in the columns of the column-wise ratios. To this end, our algorithm examines the rows of $\mathbf{R}^r$ to find subsets of near-constant entries including column j_a and the columns of

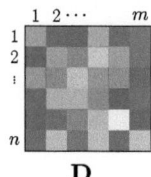 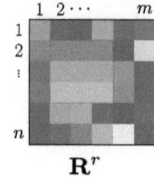 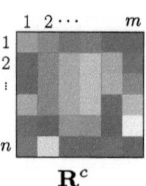

Fig. 3. Example of row-wise ($\mathbf{R}^r$) and column-wise ($\mathbf{R}^c$) ratio matrices associated with an input matrix ($\mathbf{D}$) containing a rank-1 submatrix (highlighted in red). Within this rank-1 submatrix, the entries of $\mathbf{R}^r$ are constant across rows, and the entries of $\mathbf{R}^c$ are constant across columns.

$\mathbf{R}^c$ to find subset of near-constant entries including row i_a. More specifically, for an input parameter $\delta \in \mathbb{R}^+$, we select, for each row of $\mathbf{R}^r$, the j_a-th entry and all other entries such that the maximum variation is less than δ in absolute value. Similarly, for each column of $\mathbf{R}^c$, we select the i_a-th entry and all other entries such that the maximum variation is less than δ in absolute value. Subsets within each row can be efficiently retrieved by sorting the row elements by their absolute deviation from the j-th element and similarly for the columns.

Given the identified subsets, we construct two indicator matrices: $\mathbf{I}^r \in \{0,1\}^{n \times m}$, where the entries with value 1 correspond to subsets of near-constant row-wise ratios; and $\mathbf{I}^c \in \{0,1\}^{n \times m}$, where the entries with value 1 correspond to subsets of near-constant column-wise ratios. We can then compute the intersection of the two matrices $\mathbf{I}^r$ and $\mathbf{I}^c$ to obtain the intersection indicator matrix $\mathbf{I}$ of the same dimension. The problem of extracting a submatrix of maximum size with all row-wise and column-wise ratios with bounded deviations can then be framed as the problem of finding the largest possible all-ones submatrix within $\mathbf{I}$. This problem is equivalent to the extraction of a maximum-edge biclique [18] from the bipartite graph $\mathcal{G}_\mathbf{I}$ that has $\mathbf{I}$ as adjacency matrix. Although this is an **NP**-hard problem [18], so that it cannot be solved in polynomial time, we can leverage recent algorithmic advances that solve the problem quickly in considerably dense and large bipartite graphs [18]. In addition, to avoid possible scalability issues that may still arise, we also rely on effective heuristics, as discussed in Sect. 5.4.

5.3 Recovering a Near-Rank-k SubMatrix

Next, we illustrate the adaptation of the initialization and expansion phases of SAMPLEANDEXPAND to the general case of recovery of near-rank-k submatrices. The pseudocode is given as Algorithm 4 in the extended version of the paper [5].

Initialization. The goal of the initialization phase is to identify a seed, i.e., a minimal near-rank-k submatrix to be expanded at a later time. To find the seed, we sample matrices $\mathbf{P}'$ with $k+1$ rows and columns until we find a seed matrix $\mathbf{P}$ that is close to rank k or lower. In order to determine whether a $k+1 \times k+1$ matrix $\mathbf{P}'$ has rank k or lower, we check whether $|\det(\mathbf{P}')| \leq \delta_{init}$, for a small $\delta_{init} \in \mathbb{R}^+$, which, as for the algorithm tailored to near-rank-1 submatrices, is first initialized to a to a small value, and then increased until the seed is found.

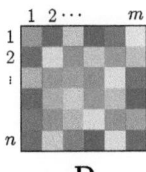 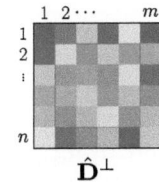 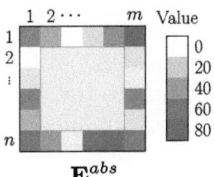

Fig. 4. Example of matrices of orthogonal projections ($\hat{\mathbf{D}}^\perp$) and absolute errors ($\mathbf{E}^{abs}$) associated with an input matrix ($\mathbf{D}$) containing a rank-k submatrix (highlighted in red). Within this rank-k submatrix, the entries of $\hat{\mathbf{D}}^\perp$ are equal to those of $\mathbf{D}$, and the entries of $\mathbf{E}^{abs}$ are therefore all identically zero.

Expansion. Given the seed matrix $\mathbf{P} \in \mathbb{R}^{k+1 \times k+1}$, of rank $k' \leq k$, we sample k' anchor rows from the rows of $\mathbf{P}$. Let $\mathcal{C}_\mathbf{P}$ denote the set of the $k+1$ indices of the columns in $\mathbf{P}$. Considering only the columns in $\mathcal{C}_\mathbf{P}$, we compute the coefficients of the orthogonal projection of each row of $\mathbf{D}$ onto the subspace spanned by the k' anchor rows. We then compute the orthogonal projections $\hat{\mathbf{D}}^\perp \in \mathbb{R}^{n \times m}$ expressing each row as a linear combination of the anchor rows with weights given by the orthogonal-projection coefficients. The coefficients are obtained by considering only the columns in $\mathcal{C}_\mathbf{P}$ identified in the initialization phase. Nevertheless, the matrix $\hat{\mathbf{D}}^\perp \in \mathbb{R}^{n \times m}$, similarly to the ratio matrices in the rank-1 case, indicates which additional columns and rows are close to a rank-k approximation. More specifically, all entries $\mathbf{D}_{i,j}$ that are closely approximated by $\hat{\mathbf{D}}^\perp_{i,j}$ lie close to the k-dimensional subspace identified in the initialization phase.

Therefore, to find a near-k submatrix of maximum size, which is the goal of the expansion phase, we need to identify the largest submatrix of $\hat{\mathbf{D}}^\perp_{i,j}$ where all entries nearly match the corresponding entries of $\mathbf{D}$. To obtain such a submatrix, we calculate the matrix of absolute errors $\mathbf{E}^{abs} = |\mathbf{D} - \hat{\mathbf{D}}^\perp|$, and from it, the indicator matrix $\mathbf{I}^r$, which takes value 1 for entry (i,j) if $\mathbf{E}^{abs}_{i,j} \leq \delta$ and 0 otherwise, for some input $\delta \in \mathbb{R}^+$. Figure 4 presents an example of matrices $\hat{\mathbf{D}}^\perp$ and $\mathbf{E}^{abs}$.

The same procedure followed to determine $\mathbf{I}^r$, but on input $\mathbf{D}^T$ and $\mathbf{P}^T$ yields $\mathbf{I}^c$. The intersection of $\mathbf{I}^r$ and $\mathbf{I}^c$ gives the matrix $\mathbf{I}$ and the associated bipartite graph $\mathcal{G}_\mathbf{I}$. As for the case of near-rank-1 submatrix discovery, the desired output near-rank-k submatrix is then given by a submatrix of $\mathbf{I}$ consisting of all ones, or, equivalently, by a maximum-edge biclique of $\mathcal{G}_\mathbf{I}$.

5.4 Scalability Considerations

One limitation of SAMPLEANDEXPAND is its reliance on solving the maximum-edge biclique problem, which is **NP**-hard. While the algorithm we use to extract these bicliques is often efficient in practice [18], scalability issues may still arise. To address such issues, the algorithm for finding maximum-edge bicliques can be replaced with a more scalable heuristic. Among many possible different heuristic approaches, by default, we rely on spectral biclustering [15], which is empirically found to be particularly effective in quickly identifying a dense submatrix of $\mathbf{I}$. Even more efficient and scalable approaches include algorithms to extract dense bipartite subgraphs, a greedy algorithm removing rows and columns from $\mathbf{I}$, e.g., based on the amount of ones, or a randomized algorithm sampling submatrices from $\mathbf{I}$ according to the amount of ones they contain [2]. A comprehensive evaluation of the performance of various heuristics for approximating maximum-edge bicliques in SAMPLEANDEXPAND is left to future work.

6 Analysis

In this section, we explain how the proposed methods yield submatrices with bounded approximation error. We also provide a brief discussion on the probabilistic aspects and on the computational complexity of the methods.

6.1 Approximation Error Guarantees

In global low-rank approximation, the presence of outliers in the data may lead to situations where the whole matrix cannot be approximated with a low-rank structure without compromising the overall approximation quality. However, as our problem definition lifts the requirement that the whole matrix must be approximated, it is interesting to control the *entry-wise* maximum approximation error in the discovered submatrices. We thus provide approximation-error guarantees in terms of the max norm. A bound on the max norm yields bounds on the Frobenius and spectral norms, albeit loose. In the case of near-rank-1 submatrix discovery, we also provide interesting bounds on the spectral and Frobenius norms that are not a direct consequence of the bound on the max norm.

Near-Rank-1 Submatrices. As mentioned in Sect. 5.1, $n' \times m'$ near-rank-1 submatrices contain many near-rank-1 2×2 submatrices. Building on this intuition, SAMPLEANDEXPAND starts by locating a 2×2 submatrix $\mathbf{P}$ with bounded determinant, and hence close to rank 1. Then, it computes row-wise and column-wise ratios dividing all rows (columns) by a single anchor row (column) with index sampled from those of $\mathbf{P}$, and finds submatrices with rows (columns) of nearly-constant ratios. Nearly-constant ratios correspond to bounded 2×2 determinants. For instance, if $\left| \frac{\mathbf{D}_{i,j_1}}{x^r_{j_1}} - \frac{\mathbf{D}_{i,j_2}}{x^r_{j_2}} \right| \leq \delta$, then $|\mathbf{D}_{i,j_1} x^r_{j_2} - \mathbf{D}_{i,j_2} x^r_{j_1}| \leq \delta |x^r_{j_1}||x^r_{j_2}|$ where the left-hand side is a 2×2 determinant. Bounding the variation of all ratios within each row and column, and thus the corresponding 2×2 determinants, SAMPLEANDEXPAND yields submatrices composed of 2×2 near-rank-1 submatrices, which, as formalized in Theorem 1, results in approximation guarantees.

Theorem 1. *Let* $\mathbf{X} \in \mathbb{R}^{n' \times m'}$ *be a near-rank-1 submatrix output by* SAMPLE-ANDEXPAND *with anchor row* $\mathbf{x}^r$, *anchor column* $\mathbf{x}^c$ *and input tolerance* δ. *There exists a rank-1 approximation* $\hat{\mathbf{X}}$ *of* $\mathbf{X}$ *such that for* $\mathbf{E}_{\mathbf{X},\hat{\mathbf{X}}} = \mathbf{X} - \hat{\mathbf{X}}$ *it holds:*

$$\|\mathbf{E}_{\mathbf{X},\hat{\mathbf{X}}}\|_{\max} \leq \min\{\delta g_{\max}(\mathbf{x}^r), \delta g_{\max}(\mathbf{x}^c)\}, \tag{4}$$

and

$$\|\mathbf{E}_{\mathbf{X},\hat{\mathbf{X}}}\|_2 \leq \|\mathbf{E}_{\mathbf{X},\hat{\mathbf{X}}}\|_F \leq \min\left\{\delta\sqrt{(n-1)g_F(\mathbf{x}^r)}, \delta\sqrt{(m-1)g_F(\mathbf{x}^c)}\right\}, \tag{5}$$

where $g_{\max}(\mathbf{x}) = \frac{\max_i |x_i|^3}{2 \min_i x_i^2}$ *and* $g_F(\mathbf{x}) = \frac{\sum_{i<j} x_i^2 x_j^2}{\|\mathbf{x}\|_2^2}$.

Theorem 1 suggests that the low-rank-approximation error incurred by the near-rank-1 submatrices discovered by SAMPLEANDEXPAND can be bounded by a function of the input parameter δ and of the scale of $\mathbf{x}^r$ or $\mathbf{x}^c$. Therefore, given the anchor row and column, one can set the value of δ to guarantee that the maximum or the total approximation error is bounded by a user-specified threshold $\epsilon \in \mathbb{R}^+$, as requested by Problem 2. However, the approximation-error guarantees given in Theorem 1 only hold if SAMPLEANDEXPAND extracts a biclique in the last step. Alternative heuristic approaches that do not extract a biclique can be effective in practice, but they are not supported by approximation-error guarantees.

Notably, the approximation-error guarantees are achieved by the interpretable rank-1 approximation discussed in Sect. 5.1. In addition, for the rank-1 SVD approximation $\hat{\mathbf{X}}$, Theorem 2 in Appendix B of the extended version of the paper [5] bounds the spectral norm of the error $\mathbf{E}_{\mathbf{X},\hat{\mathbf{X}}} = \mathbf{X} - \hat{\mathbf{X}}$.

Near-Rank-k Submatrices. The algorithm for the more general task of identifying near-rank-k submatrices does not admit the same analysis as the algorithm for identifying near-rank-1 submatrices. However, the algorithm for the rank-k case, by design, discovers submatrices $\mathbf{X}$ such that $\mathbf{E}_{\mathbf{X},\hat{\mathbf{X}}} = \mathbf{X} - \hat{\mathbf{X}}$ satisfies $\|\mathbf{E}_{\mathbf{X},\hat{\mathbf{X}}}\|_{\max} \leq \delta$. As mentioned, the bound on the max norm leads to a straightforward bound on the Frobenius and spectral norms, namely $\|\mathbf{E}_{\mathbf{X},\hat{\mathbf{X}}}\|_2 \leq \|\mathbf{E}_{\mathbf{X},\hat{\mathbf{X}}}\|_F \leq \delta\sqrt{(n-k)(m-k)}$, which can also be used to set the value of δ based on user-specified error threshold ϵ on the Frobenius or spectral norm.

6.2 Probabilistic Analysis

In this section, we discuss simple probabilistic aspects of our method.

Probability of discovering a Near-Rank-1 Submatrix. Let $\mathbf{X}$ be a target near-rank-1 submatrix of size $|\mathbf{X}|$ within $\mathbf{D} \in \mathbb{R}^{n \times m}$. The probability that SAMPLEANDEXPAND discovers $\mathbf{X}$ by one sample is $p = \frac{|\mathbf{X}|}{nm} \frac{|\mathbf{X}|-1}{nm-1}$. Hence, the probability of discovering $\mathbf{X}$ in N_{init} iterations is $1 - (1-p)^{N_{init}}$, and therefore the number of iterations required to discover $\mathbf{X}$ with probability at least α_p is $N_{init} \geq \frac{\ln(1-\alpha_p)}{\ln(1-p)}$. For instance, if $p = 0.1$ and $\alpha_p = 0.9$, we need $N_{init} > \frac{\ln(1-0.9)}{\ln(1-0.1)} \approx 22$ iterations.

Basic probability theory implies that, in expectation, the number of iterations necessary to discover $\mathbf{X}$ is $\frac{1}{p}$, and we discover it pN_{init} times in N_{init} iterations.

Probability of Discovering a Near-Rank-k Submatrix. The simple probabilistic analysis presented above for near-rank-1 submatrices also applies to near-rank-k submatrices. The only difference is that, in this case, we have $p = \frac{|\mathbf{X}|}{nm} \frac{|\mathbf{X}|-1}{nm} \cdots \frac{|\mathbf{X}|-k}{nm-k}$, which can become small as k grows. Yet, larger values of k tend to be associated with larger values of $|\mathbf{X}|$ and, in practice, we are interested in small values of k.

Probability of Occurrence of a 2 × 2 near-rank-1 matrix. We conclude the section by investigating the probability with which SAMPLEANDEXPAND identifies a seed 2 × 2 submatrix with near-zero determinant in random matrices. Let $\mathbf{D}$ be a random matrix with i.i.d. entries distributed according to $\mathcal{Z}$, and let $E(\mathcal{Z}) = \mu$ and $Var(\mathcal{Z}) = \sigma^2$ be the expectation and variance of $\mathcal{Z}$. To study the probability of occurrence of 2 × 2 submatrices with near-zero determinant, we consider the random variable $\mathcal{W} = x_1 y_2 - x_2 y_1$, where x_1, x_2, y_1 and y_2 are the entries of a 2 × 2 submatrix.

By independence, $E(x_1 y_2) = E(x_1) E(y_2)$ and $Var(x_1 y_2) = Var(x_1) Var(y_2) + E(y_2)^2 Var(x_1) + E(x_1)^2 Var(y_2) = \sigma^4 + 2\mu^2 \sigma^2$, and similarly for $x_2 y_1$. Further, since $x_2 y_1$ and $x_2 y_1$ are independent,

$$E(x_1 y_2 - x_2 y_1) = E(x_1 y_2) - E(x_2 y_1) = 0 \text{ and}$$
$$Var(x_1 y_2 - x_2 y_1) = Var(x_1 y_2) + Var(x_2 y_1) = 2\sigma^4 + 4\mu^2 \sigma^2.$$

Chebyshev's inequality [23] then implies that:

$$P(|\mathcal{W}| \geq \delta_{init}) \leq \frac{2\sigma^4 + 4\mu^2 \sigma^2}{\delta_{init}^2},$$

giving a bound on the probability that a 2 × 2-submatrix deviates significantly from rank 1. The preliminary experiments presented in Appendix E of the extended version of the paper [5] additionally provide an empirical investigation of this probability. Assumptions on $\mathcal{Z}$ may lead to tighter bounds, a question that we leave open for future work.

6.3 Computational Complexity

Finally, we discuss the computational complexity of SAMPLEANDEXPAND.

Consider a single iteration of the method. The runtime bottleneck is due to finding a maximum-edge biclique, which, in the worst case can take exponential time. However, the algorithm introduced by Lyu et al. [18] prunes large portions of the search space and can be very efficient in practice. As discussed in Sect. 5, to improve scalability, we can use a more scalable heuristic for finding an approximate maximum-edge biclique. The spectral biclustering algorithm, which is the heuristic we rely on by default, has computational complexity determined by the computation of the (truncated) SVD, which is $\mathcal{O}\left(\min(n^2 m, m^2 n)\right)$. If an even more scalable heuristic is leveraged, such as a basic linear-time algorithm removing rows and columns of $\mathbf{I}$ with less than a given proportion of ones, SAMPLEANDEXPAND for the rank-1 case and for the general rank-k case incurs computational complexity $\mathcal{O}(n + m)$ and $\mathcal{O}(nkm)$, respectively.

As SAMPLEANDEXPAND generally explores different initializations, if τ is the complexity of a single iteration, then $\mathcal{O}(N_{init} \tau)$ is the overall complexity.

7 Experiments

In this section, we evaluate the performance of SAMPLEANDEXPAND against existing approaches. We consider both synthetic data and real-world data. More

Table 1. Summary characteristics for real-world datasets. We report the number of rows, columns, the low-rankness score, the entry-wise maximum squared deviation from the rank-1 SVD (Max rank-1 deviation) and a reference.

Dataset	# Rows	# Columns	Low-rankness score	Max rank-1 deviation	Reference
HYPERSPECTRAL	5 554	2 151	0.89	0.23	[17]
MOVIELENS	943	1682	0.30	1.00	[13]
CAMERAMAN	256	256	0.86	0.56	[24]

details on the experimental setup and additional experimental results are presented in the extended version of the paper [5].

7.1 Experimental Setup

Datasets. We conduct experiments on both synthetic and real-world datasets.

The synthetic data are generated by planting near-rank-1 submatrices into larger matrices. To make the discovery task as challenging as possible, the entries of the planted submatrices and of the background are generated from the same distributions. We consider 6 different distributions. The details of the synthetic datasets are in Appendix D of the extended version of the paper [5].

Additionally, we consider 15 real-world matrices from different applications, including user ratings, images, and gene expression. We report summary characteristics for three datasets in Table 1, while the same information for the other datasets is provided in the extended version of the paper [5].

Baselines. We compare SAMPLEANDEXPAND against baselines discussed in Sect. 2. Specifically, we consider a method (CVX) based on convex optimization [8], PCA with sparsity constraints (SPARSEPCA) [20], SVP [22], and RPSP [6]. In the experiments with real data, we restrict the comparison to the most recently introduced methods, SVP and RPSP, which specifically aim at discovering (possibly multiple) near-low-rank submatrices.

Metrics. In experiments with synthetic data, all methods output matrices $\hat{D}$ that contain low-rank approximations of the identified submatrices and zero entries for all indices that are not part of such submatrices. To measure the ability of a method in recovering the indices of the planted ground-truth submatrices, we report the F_1 score. Based on the same output, we also report the error (squared Frobenius norm averaged over the entries) incurred in approximating the ground-truth submatrices. SAMPLEANDEXPAND approximates submatrices through the interpretable approach discussed in Sect. 5.1 for $k = 1$ and via SVD for $k > 1$. All baselines approximate submatrices via SVD.

In real-world datasets, where no ground truth is available, we report the size and low-rankness score (introduced in Sect. 3) of the returned submatrices.

In all cases, we measure runtimes in seconds.

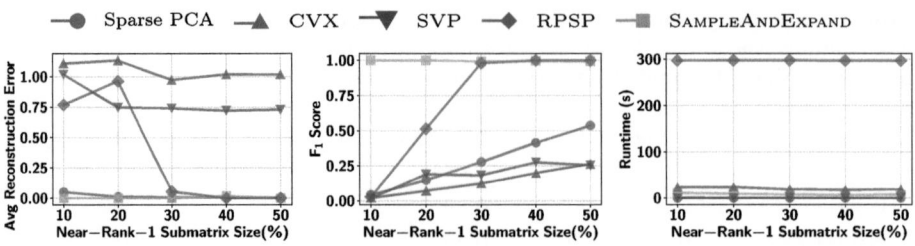

Fig. 5. Full-rank synthetic 250×250 matrices generated from a standard normal distribution with a planted near-rank-1 submatrix. Performance of different methods in the task of near-rank-1 submatrix discovery. We show the average (per-entry) reconstruction error (left), the F_1 score (center) and the runtime (right) of different methods as a function of planted submatrix size.

Parameters. The important parameter to set for our method is the tolerance δ controlling the trade-off between low-rankness and size. As explained in Sect. 6, one can set δ to match an input bound ϵ on the allowed low-rank-approximation error. In our experiments, however, we explore few fixed values of δ. Specifically, for experiments with synthetic data, we set δ to 0.05 and the number of initializations N_{init} to 25. For experiments with real-world data, we let δ vary in $\{10^{-1}, 10^{-2}, 10^{-3}, 10^{-4}\}$, and we consider $N_{init} = 25$ initializations for each value of δ. Finally, the initialization parameter δ_{init} is set to 10^{-11} and is increased by 10 every 10000 samples that do not result in a submatrix to expand.

Implementation. Our Python implementation and datasets are available online[1]. Experiments are performed on a computer with 2×10 core Xeon E5 processor and 256 GB memory. All reported results are averages over 10 runs.

7.2 Experiment Results

We first present results for synthetic datasets and then for real-world datasets.

Results on Synthetic Data. Fig. 5 presents results for the task of near-rank-1-submatrix discovery in 250×250 matrices of entries generated from the standard normal distribution. Figure 5 in the extended version of the paper [5] provides analogous results for other 5 distributions. The results show that our method, unlike the baselines, consistently recovers the ground truth (as indicated by F_1 score close to 1 and reconstruction error close to 0). More specifically, RPSP tends to recover the ground-truth submatrix as its size increases, but it is also considerably slower than the other methods. SPARSEPCA and SVP are the fastest algorithms, but, like CVX, they often fail in detecting the ground truth.

Figure 6 shows, for data matrices with entries generated from a standard normal distribution, the same metrics as in Fig. 5, but in the setting where multiple, possibly overlapping, near-rank-1 submatrices are planted and discovered. Figure 6 in the extended version of the paper [5] shows the same results for

---

[1] https://github.com/maciap/SaE.

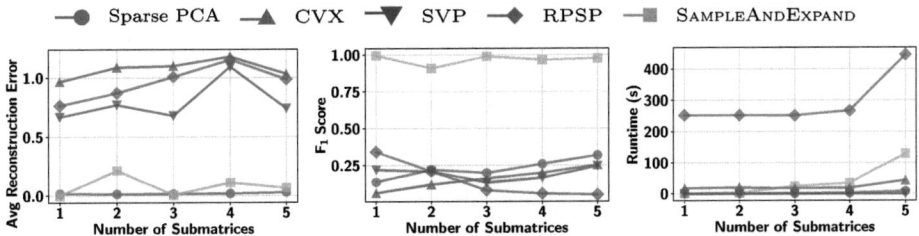

Fig. 6. Full-rank synthetic 250 × 250 matrices generated from a standard normal distribution with multiple (possibly overlapping) planted near-rank-1 submatrices. Performance of different methods in discovering planted submatrices. We show the average (per-entry) reconstruction error (left), the F_1 score (center) and the runtime (right) as a function of the number of planted submatrices.

matrices generated from other 5 distributions. The results in this more challenging setting highlight that SAMPLEANDEXPAND is the only method that consistently retrieves the ground-truth submatrices. Among the baselines, SPARSE-PCA stands out for its accurate reconstruction. However, the estimate $\hat{D}$ of the input matrix it generates quickly becomes very dense as more submatrices are discovered, and hence this approach fails to identify the locations of the ground-truth submatrices.

Finally, Fig. 10 in the extended version of the paper [5] (Appendix E) demonstrates the robustness of our method to the presence of noise.

Results on Real-World Data. Table 2 reports low-rankness score and size averaged over the top-5 submatrices retrieved by our method, SVP and RPSP for three datasets. Similar results for the other 12 datasets considered in our experiments are given in the extended version of the paper [5]. To determine the top-5 submatrices returned by each method, we select those that maximize the minimum between the low-rankness score and the size. Moreover, to offer a more complete picture, in the extended version of the paper [5] (Fig. 11), we additionally display the low-rankness and size of the individual top-5 patterns.

Finding submatrices with high low-rankness is not an easy task. SVP returns large submatrices. However, those submatrices usually have smaller low-rankness compared to those discovered by our method or RPSP, and, in several cases, compared to the input matrix. SAMPLEANDEXPAND and RPSP are more likely than SVP to return submatrices with large low-rankness. Further, SAMPLE-ANDEXPAND tends to discover submatrices that strike a more desirable balance between low-rankness and size compared to RPSP. As concerns runtime, SAMPLEANDEXPAND is drastically faster than RPSP in smaller datasets, but it can become slower in larger datasets. Nonetheless, the runtime of our method could be significantly reduced by leveraging a more efficient approach to maximum-edge-biclique extraction and by reducing the number of iterations, which, however, could deteriorate the quality of the results. As mentioned in Sect. 5.4, future work will consider efficient heuristic approaches to maximum-edge-biclique extraction.

Table 2. Performance in real-world data. For the top 5 local low-rank patterns identified by the methods, we show the average relative percentage increase (L-R) with respect to the low-rankness score of the input matrix, the size (in percentage of entries of the input matrix) and the runtime (in seconds) to obtain them.

Dataset	SVP			RPSP			SAMPLEANDEXPAND		
	L-R	Size	Runtime	L-R	Size	Runtime	L-R	Size	Runtime
HYPERSPECTRAL	4.05	2.88	47.0	9.84	2.10	590	11.09	21.43	1 697
MOVIELENS	49.61	8.59	1.0	46.69	2.88	373	116.42	1.06	152
CAMERAMAN	1.69	3.64	0.3	5.67	3.44	102	14.44	24.83	18

Finally, for our method, we also explore the trade-off between size and low-rankness by varying the value of δ; the results are presented in Appendix E of the extended version of the paper [5].

8 Conclusion

Low-rank approximation finds applications in many data-analysis tasks. Typically, methods assume that the entire matrix exhibits low-rank structure, while in real-world data this is often true only for certain submatrices. In this work, we study the problem of finding submatrices that are provably close to a rank-k approximation. We introduce a novel method that finds such submatrices, study the properties of the method, and, with a thorough experimental evaluation, we show that our method outperforms strong baselines.

There are several directions for future work. For instance, future work could study a more robust initialization strategy, develop more efficient and scalable alternative algorithms, and optimize the selection of the anchor rows and columns. It would also be valuable to investigate more the probabilistic aspects of our method. From a practical perspective, it would be interesting to explore further the benefits of our approach in different applications.

Acknowledgments. Martino Ciaperoni is supported by the European Union through the ERC-2018-ADG GA 834756 ("XAI: Science and Technology for the Explanation of AI Decision-Making") and the Partnership Extended PE00000013 ("FAIR: Future Artificial Intelligence Research"), Spoke 1: "Human-Centered AI". Aristides Gionis is supported by the ERC Advanced Grant REBOUND (834862), EC H2020 RIA project SoBigData++ (871042), and the Wallenberg AI, Autonomous Systems and Software Program (WASP) funded by the Knut and Alice Wallenberg Foundation. Heikki Mannila is supported by the Technology Industries of Finland Centennial Foundation.

References

1. Agarwal, P.K., Procopiuc, C.M.: Approximation algorithms for projective clustering. J. Algorithms **46**(2), 115–139 (2003)

2. Boley, M., Lucchese, C., Paurat, D., Gärtner, T.: Direct local pattern sampling by efficient two-step random procedures. In: ACM SIGKDD, pp. 582–590 (2011)
3. Boutsidis, C., Mahoney, M.W., Drineas, P.: An improved approximation algorithm for the column subset selection problem. In: SODA pp. 968–977 (2009)
4. Ciaperoni, M., Gionis, A., Mannila, H.: The Hadamard decomposition problem. In: Data Mining and Knowledge Discovery, pp. 1–42 (2024)
5. Ciaperoni, M., Gionis, A., Mannila, H.: Sample and expand: discovering low-rank submatrices with quality guarantees (2025). https://arxiv.org/abs/2506.06456
6. Dang, P., et al.: Generalized matrix local low rank representation by random projection and submatrix propagation. In: ACM SIGKDD, pp. 390–401 (2023)
7. Dhillon, I.S.: Co-clustering documents and words using bipartite spectral graph partitioning. In: ACM SIGKDD, pp. 269–274 (2001)
8. Doan, X.V., Vavasis, S.: Finding approximately rank-one submatrices with the nuclear norm and l_1-norm. SIAM J. Optim. **23**(4), 2502–2540 (2013)
9. Gillis, N., Glineur, F.: Using underapproximations for sparse nonnegative matrix factorization. Pattern Recogn. **43**(4), 1676–1687 (2010)
10. Gillis, N., Shitov, Y.: Low-rank matrix approximation in the infinity norm. Linear Algebra Appl. **581**, 367–382 (2019)
11. Golub, G.H., Van Loan, C.F.: Matrix Computations. JHU press (2013)
12. Guo, Q., Zhang, C., Zhang, Y., Liu, H.: An efficient SVD-based method for image denoising. IEEE Trans. Circuits Syst. Video Technol. **26**(5), 868–880 (2015)
13. Harper, F.M., Konstan, J.A.: The MovieLens datasets: history and context. ACM Trans. Interact. Intell. Systems (TIIS) **5**(4), 1–19 (2015)
14. Hu, E.J., et al.: LoRA: low-rank adaptation of large language models. ICLR **1**(2), 3 (2022)
15. Kluger, Y., Basri, R., Chang, J.T., Gerstein, M.: Spectral biclustering of microarray data: coclustering genes and conditions. Genome Res. **13**(4), 703–716 (2003)
16. Lee, J., Kim, S., Lebanon, G., Singer, Y., Bengio, S.: LLORMA: local low-rank matrix approximation. J. Mach. Learn. Res. **17**(15), 1–24 (2016)
17. Leone, G., et al.: Hyperspectral reflectance dataset of pristine, weathered and biofouled plastics. Earth Syst. Sci. Data Discuss. **2022**, 1–24 (2022)
18. Lyu, B., Qin, L., Lin, X., Zhang, Y., Qian, Z., Zhou, J.: Maximum biclique search at billion scale. In: Proceedings of the VLDB Endowment (2020)
19. Mahoney, M.W., Drineas, P.: Cur matrix decompositions for improved data analysis. Proc. Natl. Acad. Sci. **106**(3), 697–702 (2009)
20. Mairal, J., Bach, F., Ponce, J., Sapiro, G.: Online dictionary learning for sparse coding. In: ICML, pp. 689–696 (2009)
21. Miettinen, P., Neumann, S.: Recent developments in Boolean matrix factorization. In: IJCAI (2021)
22. Ruchansky, N., Crovella, M., Terzi, E.: Targeted matrix completion. In: SIAM SDM, pp. 255–263 (2017)
23. Saw, J.G., Yang, M.C., Mo, T.C.: Chebyshev inequality with estimated mean and variance. Am. Stat. **38**(2), 130–132 (1984)
24. University of Southern California: Signal and Image Processing Institute: USC-SIPI image database (2024). https://sipi.usc.edu/database/
25. Vidal, R.: Subspace clustering. IEEE Sig. Process. **28**(2), 52–68 (2011)
26. Wang, Y., Zhu, L.: Research and implementation of SVD in machine learning. In: ICIS, pp. 471–475 (2017)

Active Preference Optimization for Sample Efficient RLHF

Nirjhar Das[1(✉)], Souradip Chakraborty[2], Aldo Pacchiano[3], and Sayak Ray Chowdhury[4]

[1] Indian Institute of Science, Bangalore, India
`nirjhardas@iisc.ac.in`
[2] University of Maryland, College Park, USA
`schakra3@umd.edu`
[3] Boston University, Boston, USA
`pacchian@bu.edu`
[4] Indian Institute of Technology Kanpur, Kanpur, India
`sayakrc@cse.iitk.ac.in`

Abstract. Large Language Models (LLMs) aligned using Reinforcement Learning from Human Feedback (RLHF) have shown remarkable generation abilities in numerous tasks. However, collecting high-quality human preferences creates costly bottlenecks in practical deployments, and hence, training data are often budgeted. In these scenarios, it is crucial to collect training data (e.g., contexts, a pair of generations for each context, and a preference indicating which generation is better) carefully, yet most of the existing methods sample contexts uniformly at random from a given collection. Given this, under the Bradley-Terry-Luce preference model and with a small budget of training data, we show that uniform sampling of contexts could lead to a policy (i.e., an aligned model) that suffers a constant sub-optimality gap from the optimal policy. This highlights the need for an adaptive context sampling strategy for effective alignment under a small sample budget. To address this, we reformulate RLHF within the contextual preference bandit framework, treating generations as actions, and give a nearly complete characterization of the sub-optimality gap in terms of both lower and upper bounds. First, when the action set is a d-dimensional hypercube and the number of samples is T, we show an $\Omega(d/\sqrt{T})$ lower bound. Next, we propose an algorithm, *Active Preference Optimization* (`APO`), that iteratively collects preferences for the most uncertain contexts. We show that the sub-optimality gap of the policy learned via `APO` matches the lower bound up to a log factor and a non-linearity constant. Finally, we perform experiments on practical datasets to validate `APO`'s efficacy over existing methods, establishing it as a sample-efficient and cost-effective solution for LLM alignment.

Supplementary Information The online version contains supplementary material available at https://doi.org/10.1007/978-3-032-06096-9_6.

1 Introduction

Reinforcement Learning from Human Feedback (RLHF) has proven highly effective in aligning Large Language Models (LLMs) with human preferences [6,8,20]. This approach involves collecting extensive data, each comprising a context (e.g., a movie review), a pair of generations (e.g., completions of the review), and a preference indicating which generation is better than the other. First, a reward model is trained to classify preferred generations, and subsequently, a language model policy is trained using RL (e.g., Proximal Policy Optimization [28]) to output high-reward generations while minimizing divergence from a reference policy. Given the practical success, recent theoretical advances have been made in training reward models as well as aligning policies from pairwise comparisons [5,26,32]. In these settings, the learner doesn't have any control over selecting the contexts, and the aim is to minimize cumulative loss or regret due to not knowing the ground-truth reward or the optimal policy in advance. However, in the case of aligning LLMs using RLHF, the learner has control over both the contexts and actions, i.e., the contexts and generations for which preference data needs to be collected, yet most of the existing RLHF algorithms pick contexts uniformly at random from a given pool [20,29]. This is followed by first generating a pair of responses for each sampled prompt based on a supervised fine-tuned (SFT) policy and then sending all the pairs to a human labeler to collect preferences.

The success of RLHF hinges on the quality of human preferences. This could create costly bottlenecks in practical deployments since high-quality preferences are expensive to collect as this demands a certain level of expertise from labelers. Hence, there is often a budget on the number of contexts and associated generation pairs that could be sent to expert labelers for comparison. While uniform sampling of contexts as a simple approach has been proven effective for aligning LLMs so far, one is bound to ask whether this is a good enough strategy, especially given a fixed budget for labeling. Or do we need potentially more involved sampling strategies to deliver better model alignment under budget constraints? Such algorithms need to be sample efficient as high-quality samples are expensive to obtain, while they should not compromise on the performance of the aligned policy. This work takes a step in developing theory and algorithms for RLHF under a small sample budget.

1.1 Overview of Main Results

We first show that the naive way of collecting preferences by choosing contexts uniformly at random can lead to wastage of samples under the Bradley-Terry-Luce (BTL) preference model characterized by a finite dimensional parameter [3, 15].

Result 1 (Constant sub-optimality under uniform context sampling). *There exists an instance of the alignment problem for which an algorithm that (i) collects preferences by sampling contexts uniformly at random, (ii) learns a* reward model by maximizing likelihood of the preferred generations, and (iii) trains a greedy policy w.r.t. the learnt reward model suffers an $\Omega(1)$ sub-optimality gap[1] with high probability when the sample budget is smaller than number of contexts.

To the best of our knowledge, this is the first provable negative result for the alignment performance of RLHF algorithms that sample contexts uniformly under a small sample budget. This necessitates designing of RLHF algorithms that adaptively sample contexts, with an aim to improve alignment of the learned policy with human preferences. Our next result benchmarks the alignment performance of any RLHF algorithm under the BTL preference model when there is no restriction on how contexts can be sampled.

Result 2 (Lower bound on sub-optimality for any sampling strategy). *For any RLHF algorithm there exists an instance of the alignment problem for which the policy that the algorithm outputs after collecting T samples (contexts, generations and preferences) would suffer a sub-optimality gap $\Omega(d/\sqrt{T})$, where d is the dimension of the parameter characterizing the BTL model.*

This is the first theoretical lower bound on the alignment performance of RLHF algorithms, which has been crucially missing in the literature. This result effectively eliminates the possibility of achieving better than sub-linear convergence under a finite sample budget. Next, we propose an algorithm – *Active Preference Optimization* (APO) – that achieves this sub-optimality gap by iteratively sampling the most uncertain contexts and collecting preferences for their generation pairs.

Result 3 (Upper bound on sub-optimality for APO). *The sub-optimality gap of the policy learned via APO after collecting T samples scales as $\tilde{O}(d\sqrt{\kappa/T})$ with high probability, where d is the parameter dimension and κ is a problem-dependent nonlinearity constant.*

Next, we generalize our result from parameterized BTL model to non-parametric preference models with function approximation. We propose an analogue of APO albeit with non-trivial modifications, namely APO-Gen, that achieves a similar sub-optimality gap (see Subsect. 4.2 and Appendix D). This is the first known upper bound on the alignment performance of an active context selection strategy under generic preference models, which recovers the result for the parameterized BTL model as a special case.

Result 4 (Upper bound on sub-optimality under general preferences). *The sub-optimality gap of the policy learned via APO-Gen after collecting T samples scales as $\tilde{O}(\sqrt{d_{\mathcal{E}}\log(\mathcal{N}T)/T})$ with high probability, where $\mathcal{N}$ and $d_{\mathcal{E}}$ measure the complexity of the underlying preference model.*

---

[1] Measured by the maximum difference between latent rewards of the optimal policy and the trained policy over the context set.

Empirical Evidence. For practical purposes, we propose a batch version of APO to make it computationally more efficient (see Sect. 5). We experiment with GPT-2 on IMDb sentiment dataset [16] and demonstrate significant improvement in LLM alignment over uniform context sampling and prior baselines [18,19]. We show similar improvement in the performance of the aligned policy on Anthropic-HH dataset [2] with Gemma-2b. Our work contributes towards a sample-efficient and practical solution to preference data collection for RLHF.

1.2 Comparison with Prior Work

Active learning in the context of Preference-based Reinforcement Learning (PbRL) [5,26], which is used as a theoretical framework for RLHF, has received some attention recently. In PbRL literature, the problem of learning the reward function by actively querying the human labeller has been considered in [4,10,14,24,31]. The work [14] provides variance and entropy-based heuristics for learning the optimal policy without providing any provable guarantee. On the other hand, in [24], the authors design an algorithm for learning the reward function by actively synthesizing trajectories via a volume removal scheme over the distribution of the unknown parameter. They show that under certain strong assumptions, their algorithm makes progress in reducing the uncertainty over the parameter distribution. Similarly, [4] also aims at actively learning the reward function using model epistemic uncertainty as well as the entropy estimate of acquiring a data point but does not provide any provable guarantee. Hence, both of these are orthogonal to our work since they consider learning the reward function, whereas we focus on learning a policy - while learning a good reward function is sufficient for learning a good policy, it is not at all necessary.

In [31], the authors propose a pure exploration strategy for the PbRL problem that finds an ε-optimal policy with $O(\kappa^2 d^2/\varepsilon^2)$ queries to the human labeler.

Instead of modeling RLHF as a PbRL problem, we model it as a contextual dueling bandit problem, where contexts model prompts and actions model generations of an LLM. This necessitates a strategy for not only actively selecting actions but also selecting contexts actively. This is a major point of departure from most active-learning based PbRL works and from pure exploration in dueling bandits literature [7,17]. It is unclear apriori what should be the optimal strategy to select the context, towards which we show that a design-matrix-based exploration bonus is sufficient (see Sect. 4). Moreover, a direct comparison shows that our result (Theorem 3) is tighter in terms of κ. In [10], the authors consider an active learning-based approach to regret minimization in the contextual dueling bandits. Again, [10] does not address the question of context selection but rather allows contexts to be adversarially presented to the learner, who only chooses action given the context and whether to observe the labeler feedback.

Existing works closest to ours are [18,19], which also investigate the problem of actively selecting prompts and generations for RLHF in LLMs. [19] proposes an algorithm that actively selects contexts using a heuristic based on generation uncertainty, but they do not give any theoretical guarantee for the proposed method. [18] proves a sub-optimality gap bound for an active context selection strategy that goes down sub-linearly with the number of samples. However, they assume a strong restrictive condition on the preference model, which *doesn't hold in general* for the BTL model. We remove this restrictive assumption and provide an improved guarantee (see Remark 2 for a detailed comparison).

2 Problem Setup

We have a set of contexts $\mathcal{X}$ and a set of possible actions per context $\mathcal{A}$. To learn using preference feedback, the agent selects $x \in \mathcal{X}$ and $a, a' \in \mathcal{A}$ to present to a human labeller, who then reveals a binary preference y that takes value 1 if a wins over a' and 0 otherwise. We assume that given (x, a, a'), y is sampled from the Bradley-Terry-Luce (BTL) preference model [3,15] with r^* as the latent (unknown) reward function, i.e.,

$$\mathbb{P}[y=1|x,a,a';r^*] = \frac{\exp(r^*(x,a))}{\exp(r^*(x,a)) + \exp(r^*(x,a'))},$$

The goal of the agent is to first learn r^* over T rounds of sequential interaction with the labeller, collecting dataset $\mathcal{D} = (x_s, a_s, a'_s, y_s)_{s=1}^T$, and then employ the learned reward to train a policy $\pi : \mathcal{X} \to \mathcal{A}$, which will eventually fetch high latent rewards $r^*(x, \pi(x))$.

In this work, we consider linear latent rewards $r^*(x,a) = \phi(x,a)^\top \theta^*$, where $\theta^* \in \mathbb{R}^d$ is the unknown reward parameter, and $\phi : \mathcal{X} \times \mathcal{A} \to \mathbb{R}^d$ is some known and fixed feature map. For instance, such a ϕ can be constructed by removing the last layer of a pre-trained language model, and in that case, θ^* corresponds to the weights of the last layer. With this model, for any $\theta \in \mathbb{R}^d$, one can equivalently write the probability of sampling $y_s = 1$ given (x_s, a_s, a'_s) as

$$\mathbb{P}[y_s=1|x_s,a_s,a'_s;\theta] = \sigma\big((\phi(x_s,a_s)-\phi(x_s,a'_s))^\top \theta\big) = \sigma(z_s^\top \theta),$$

where $\sigma(w) = \frac{1}{1+e^{-w}}$ is the sigmoid function and $z_s = \phi(x_s, a_s) - \phi(x_s, a'_s)$ is the feature difference of actions a_s and a'_s for context x_s.

With this, the latent reward parameter θ^* is typically estimated by minimizing the binary cross entropy loss (log-loss) [20], which is equivalent to *maximum likelihood estimation* (MLE). Specifically, At round t, the MLE of θ^* is computed as $\widehat{\theta}_t = \arg\min_{\theta \in \Theta} \mathcal{L}_t(\theta)$ using the preference dataset $\{(x_s, a_s, a'_s, y_s)\}_{s=1}^{t-1}$, where log-loss $\mathcal{L}_t(\theta)$ is given by

$$\mathcal{L}_t(\theta) = -\sum_{s=1}^{t-1} y_s \log(\sigma(z_s^\top \theta)) + (1-y_s)\log(1 - \sigma(z_s^\top \theta)). \quad (1)$$

The above optimization problem is convex if we let the constraint set $\Theta \subset \mathbb{R}^d$ to be convex, and hence can be solved using standard algorithms [9].

Performance Measure. Our goal is to learn a policy over the collected data $\mathcal{D}$, which has high rewards or, equivalently, low sub-optimality. Formally, the sub-optimality gap of a policy π_T trained on the dataset $\mathcal{D}$ is defined as

$$R(T) = \max_{x \in \mathcal{X}} \max_{a \in \mathcal{A}} \{r^*(x,a) - r^*(x, \pi_T(x))\}. \quad (2)$$

Here, our policy π_T competes with the *Condorcet* winner for a given context – an action that fetches a higher reward than all other actions. The sub-optimality gap is the worst possible difference in rewards over the set of contexts. Prior work [18] competes against the *Borda* winner – an action that fetches a higher reward on average than another randomly chosen action – a weaker competitor (the *Condorcet* winner is also the *Borda* winner but not the other way around).

Remark 1. To the best of our knowledge, common practical implementations of the RLHF pipeline use the following method: (i) remove the top layer of the LLM and convert it into an encoder, (ii) append a new linear layer on top of it, and (iii) output the logit score. Hence, the linear reward assumption is not restrictive in the sense that we only train the linear layer, keeping the encoder fixed. In practice, however, one needs to train the encoder, and hence, a more general function class needs to be considered. To this end, we generalize this setup to preference models with bounded class complexities, removing the need for explicit linear reward models (see Sect. 4 and Appendix D for details).

3 Lower Bounds

We first illustrate the pitfall of a learner who samples contexts uniformly. We characterize such a learner in preference-based learning/RLHF and then show that such a learner can suffer a constant sub-optimality gap under budget constraints.

Definition 1 (Uniform Learner) *Say an algorithm Alg samples T contexts uniformly at random from a set $\mathcal{X}$ and for each context x_t, picks two actions a_t, a'_t from a set $\mathcal{A}$. For each chosen triplet (x_t, a_t, a'_t), Alg queries the preference model parameterized by θ^* and observes a stochastic preference $y_t \in \{0, 1\}$ between the actions. Alg then solves an MLE on this data to obtain $\widehat{\theta}$, and learns a greedy policy with respect to $\widehat{\theta}$. We call such an algorithm Alg a Uniform Learner.*

Theorem 1 (Lower bound for uniform context sampling). *There exists a problem instance $(\mathcal{X}, \mathcal{A}, \theta^*)$ for which the policy learnt by a Uniform Learner Alg under the budget $T \ll |\mathcal{X}|$ suffers $\Omega(1)$ sub-optimality gap with high probability.*

Proof (Sketch). We show the result for $d = 2$ for simplicity. The main idea is to divide the set of contexts into two groups—*good* and *bad*. Further, every context has only two actions, a and a'. The *good* group has a large number of contexts, so the uniform learner mostly samples contexts from this group. For all context x in the *good* group, the feature difference $\phi(x, a) - \phi(x, a') = z_g$ is the same. For *bad* contexts, this feature difference is z_b, such that $\langle z_b, z_g \rangle < 0$. Finally, θ^* is taken as the angle-bisector of z_g and z_b.

From this construction (Fig. 2 in Appendix A), we have that a gets a higher reward for every context. Then, we show that the uniform learner only samples context-actions corresponding to z_g when the sample budget T is much smaller than the number of contexts. Under this scenario, the MLE estimate of the uniform learner correctly classifies the reward of a to be higher than that of a' for all the *good* contexts, but it wrongly classifies the rewards for the *bad* contexts. Thus, for *bad* contexts, the uniform learner suffers a constant suboptimality gap. Details are in Appendix A. □

Theorem 1 effectively shows that the uniform learner cannot make efficient use of the sampling budget because its performance may not increase with an increasing budget. Now, it is essential to characterize the limits of learning in this setting. To this end, we prove a lower bound on the sub-optimality gap of any algorithm with no restriction on how contexts and action pairs can be sampled. Note that standard regret lower bounds for dueling [25] and logistic bandits [1] are not applicable here because we bound the sub-optimality gap and not regret.

Theorem 2 (Lower Bound for any sampling strategy). *Let $\mathcal{X}$ be a finite set of contexts, $\Theta = \{-\frac{1}{\sqrt{T}}, \frac{1}{\sqrt{T}}\}^d$, $\mathcal{A} = \{-\frac{1}{2}, \frac{1}{2}\}^d$. Then, for any algorithm, there exists a parameter $\theta^* \in \Theta$ such that sub-optimality gap of a policy learnt by the algorithm after collecting T samples satisfies[2]*

$$\mathbb{E}_{\theta^*}[R(T)] \geq \Omega\left(d/\sqrt{T}\right).$$

Proof (Sketch). Without loss of generality, choose any $x \in \mathcal{X}$. Let $\pi_T(x)$ denote the action chosen by the policy learnt using T samples. Define the event $\mathcal{E}_{\theta,i} = \{\text{sign}(\pi_{T,i}(x)) \neq \text{sign}(\theta_i)\}$, for all $i \in [d]$, where $\pi_{T,i}(x)$ and θ_i are the i-th coordinates of $\pi_T(x)$ and the parameter $\theta \in \Theta$, respectively. Note that under the event $\mathcal{E}_{\theta,i}$, the algorithm suffers a sub-optimality of $\frac{1}{\sqrt{T}}$ for the i-th coordinate. We need to lower bound the probability of this event. To this end, let $\theta' \in \Theta$ be such that $\theta'_i = -\theta_i$ and $\theta'_j = \theta_j$ for $j \neq i$. Note that $\mathcal{E}^c_{\theta,i} = \mathcal{E}_{\theta',i}$. Therefore, from Lemma 3 (Appendix B), we have, $\mathbb{P}_\theta[\mathcal{E}_{\theta,i}] + \mathbb{P}_{\theta'}[\mathcal{E}_{\theta',i}] \geq \frac{1}{2} \exp(-D_{KL}(\mathbb{P}_\theta, \mathbb{P}_{\theta'}))$.
Next, we need an upper bound on $D_{KL}(\mathbb{P}_\theta, \mathbb{P}_{\theta'})$. Using [12, Lemma 15.1] and Taylor expansion of log-sigmoid, we obtain $D_{KL}(\mathbb{P}_\theta, \mathbb{P}_{\theta'}) \leq \frac{1}{8}\mathbb{E}_\theta\left[\sum_{t=1}^T \langle z_t, \theta - \theta'\rangle^2\right]$, where $z_t = a_t - a'_t$. Since $z_t \in [-1,1]^d$, and θ, θ' are equal in every coordinate except the i-th one, we have, $D_{KL}(\mathbb{P}_\theta, \mathbb{P}_{\theta'}) \leq \frac{1}{8}\sum_{t=1}^T \mathbb{E}_\theta[(2z_{t,i}\theta_i)^2] \leq \frac{1}{2}$. Hence,

$$\frac{1}{|\Theta|}\sum_{\theta \in \Theta}\sum_{i=1}^d \mathbb{P}_\theta[\mathcal{E}_{\theta,i}] \geq \frac{d}{4}\exp(-\frac{1}{2}).$$

Therefore, there exists a $\theta^* \in \Theta$ such that $\sum_{i=1}^d \mathbb{P}_{\theta^*}[\mathcal{E}_{\theta^*,i}] \geq \frac{d}{4}\exp(-\frac{1}{2})$. Finally, it is easy to see that the expected sub-optimality gap is lower bounded by the expected gap for context x. Hence, we have the following chain of inequalities:

$$\mathbb{E}_{\theta^*}[R(T)] \geq \mathbb{E}_{\theta^*}\left[\sum_{i=1}^d \mathbb{1}[\mathcal{E}_{\theta^*,i}] \cdot 2|\theta_i^*|\right] = \frac{2}{\sqrt{T}}\sum_{i=1}^d \mathbb{P}_{\theta^*}[\mathcal{E}_{\theta^*,i}] \geq \frac{d\exp(-1/2)}{2\sqrt{T}}$$

which completes the proof. Details are in Appendix B. □

---
[2] Expectation is over the randomness of $(x_1, a_1, a'_1, y_1, \ldots, y_T)$ under hypothesis θ^*.

To the best of our knowledge, Theorem 2 gives the first lower bound for general active-learning algorithms, which was missing in prior work [18,19]. Now, the immediate question is whether one can design an algorithm that learns a policy whose sub-optimality gap matches this lower bound. In the next section, we present an algorithm *Active Preference Optimization* (APO) that achieves this up to log factors and an instance-dependent non-linear factor.

Algorithm 1. APO: Active Preference Optimization

Require: Context set $\mathcal{X}$, action set $\mathcal{A}$, feature map $\phi : \mathcal{X} \times \mathcal{A} \to \mathbb{R}^d$, regularization $\lambda > 0$, and failure probability $\delta \in (0, 1]$. Initialize $\widehat{\theta}_1 = 0$.
1: **for** $t = 1, \ldots, T$ **do**
2: Choose the triplet (x_t, a_t, a'_t) using (3) and (5).
3: Observe preference feedback $y_t \sim \text{Ber}(\sigma(z_t^\top \theta^*))$, where $z_t = \phi(x_t, a_t) - \phi(x_t, a'_t)$.
4: Compute reward estimate $\widehat{\theta}_{t+1}$ that minimizes the constrained log-loss (1).
5: Compute (scaled) design matrix $H_{t+1}(\widehat{\theta}_{t+1})$ via (4).
6: Compute final policy $\pi_T(x)$ using (6).

---

4 Our Approach: Active Preference Optimization

At each round t, APO (Algorithm 1) proceeds by computing the MLE estimate $\widehat{\theta}_t$ based on the data obtained in the past $t - 1$ steps (1). Based on $\widehat{\theta}_t$, our goal is to maximize exploration. To do this, for a context $x \in \mathcal{X}$, we compute the uncertainty $b_t(x, a, a')$ for each action (a, a') available for that context and choose the one which maximizes this, i.e., we choose the pair

$$(a_t(x), a'_t(x)) = \operatorname{argmax}_{(a,a') \in \mathcal{A} \times \mathcal{A}} b_t(x, a, a'), \qquad (3)$$

where $b_t(x, a, a') = \|\phi(x, a) - \phi(x, a')\|_{H_t^{-1}(\widehat{\theta}_t)}$ and $H_t(\widehat{\theta}_t)$ is a matrix that describes a confidence ellipsoid around the unknown reward parameter θ^* after $t - 1$ steps of data collection. For any $\theta \in \Theta$, this is defined as

$$H_t(\theta) = \nabla^2 \mathcal{L}_t(\theta) + \lambda \mathbf{I}_d = \sum_{s=1}^{t-1} \dot{\sigma}(z_s^\top \theta) z_s z_s^\top + \lambda \mathbf{I}_d , \qquad (4)$$

where $z_s = \phi(x_s, a_s) - \phi(x_s, a'_s)$ is the feature difference for the triplet (x_s, a_s, a'_s). Intuitively, the confidence ellipsoid keeps shrinking along whichever direction (in $\mathbb{R}^d$) we decide to explore. Thus, for a given context x, choosing the pair $(a_t(x), a'_t(x))$ maximally reduces the uncertainty among all other possible action duels. However, our algorithm picks not only the action pair that maximizes uncertainty but also the context that increases it the most, i.e.,

$$x_t = \operatorname{argmax}_{x \in \mathcal{X}} b_t(x, a_t(x), a'_t(x)) . \qquad (5)$$

This is a crucial step in our approach that ensures that the uncertainty of the reward function over all contexts decreases at a fast rate, which in turn ensures a low sub-optimality gap. After T rounds, we define $\theta_T = \frac{1}{T}\sum_{s=1}^{T} \widehat{\theta}_t$ as the average of all the past parameter estimates. Our final policy π_T for any context $x \in \mathcal{X}$ is to play the action that maximizes the reward parameterized by θ_T, i.e.,

$$\pi_T(x) = \mathrm{argmax}_{a \in \mathcal{A}(x)}\, \widehat{r}_T(x,a) = \mathrm{argmax}_{a \in \mathcal{A}(x)}\, \phi(x,a)^\top \theta_T\,. \tag{6}$$

4.1 Suboptimality Gap of APO

We make the following assumption, which is standard in the literature [23,32].

Assumption 1 (Boundedness). *(a) θ^* lies in the set $\Theta = \{\theta \in \mathbb{R}^d | \langle \mathbf{1}, \theta \rangle = 0, \|\theta\| \leq S\}$. (b) Features are bounded, i.e., $\|\phi(x,a)\| \leq 1,\ \forall\ (x,a) \in \mathcal{X} \times \mathcal{A}$.*

The condition $\langle \mathbf{1}, \theta \rangle = 0$ ensures identifiability of θ^*. Now, we define a key quantity that captures learning complexity under the BTL preference model:

$$\kappa = \max_{x \in \mathcal{X}}\ \max_{a,a' \in \mathcal{A}}\ \max_{\theta \in \Theta}\ \frac{1}{\dot{\sigma}(\phi(x,a)^\top \theta - \phi(x,a')^\top \theta)}\,. \tag{7}$$

This parameter κ specifies difficulty in learning via the worst-case non-linearity in preference feedback. Note that we don't need the knowledge of κ beforehand. Next, we present the guarantee that our algorithm enjoys.

Theorem 3 (Sub-optimality gap of APO). *Let $\delta \in (0,1]$. Under Assumption 1, setting $\lambda = \frac{1}{4S^2(2+2S)^2}$ and $\gamma = O\left(S\sqrt{d\log(ST/d) + \log(T/\delta)}\right)$, the policy π_T returned by APO, with probability at least $1 - \delta$, enjoys the suboptimality gap*

$$R(T) \leq O\left(\gamma \sqrt{S \log\left(1 + (T/\lambda \kappa d)\right) \kappa d / T}\right)\,.$$

Comparison with lower bound and dependence on κ. Theorem 3 implies an $\widetilde{O}(d\sqrt{\kappa/T})$ upper bound on the sub-optimality gap of APO policy. This matches the lower bound of Theorem 2 in parameter dimension d and number of samples T, implying optimal scaling w.r.t. these two terms (up to a log factor). There remains a gap in characterizing the optimal dependence on the non-linearity parameter κ, which, in the worst-case, can be exponential in the parameter norm S. In the logistic bandit literature, the state-of-the-art regret guarantee is (almost) κ-independent - the dependence is only in terms independent of T [13,27]. We believe the $\sqrt{\kappa}$ dependence is unavoidable in the RLHF setting as the sub-optimality gap is w.r.t. real-valued rewards $r^*(x,a) = \phi(x,a)^\top \theta^*$ instead of the sigmoid rewards $\sigma(\phi(x,a)^\top \theta^*)$ in logistic bandits. Given this, we conjecture that it could be possible to improve the lower bound of Theorem 2 to $\Omega(d\sqrt{\kappa/T})$. We keep this as an interesting future direction.

Proof (Sketch). First, we quantify the error in estimating θ^* in the following lemma. This is obtained by using a novel inequality derived from the self-concordance property of the sigmoid function (i.e., $|\ddot{\sigma}| \leq \dot{\sigma}$) and adapting the arguments from [13]. Proof of this lemma is deferred to Appendix C.

Lemma 1 (Estimation error at round t). *Let $\delta \in (0, 1]$. Under the hypothesis of Theorem 3, with probability $\geq 1 - \delta$, for some universal constant $C > 0$,*

$$\|\theta^* - \widehat{\theta}_t\|_{H_t(\widehat{\theta}_t)} \leq C S^{3/2} \sqrt{d \log(St/d) + \log(t/\delta)},$$

where $\widehat{\theta}_t$ is the estimated reward parameter that minimizes the constrained log-loss (1) and $H_t(\widehat{\theta}_t)$ is the (scaled) design matrix (4) at round t.

The proof of Theorem 3 proceeds by upper bounding the sub-optimality gap for every context with the error in parameter estimation times an arm-dependent quantity. Specifically, for context x, let $z_T(x) = \phi(x, a^*(x)) - \phi(x, \pi_T(x))$ denotes the feature difference for the triplet $(x, a^*(x), \pi_T(x))$, where $a^*(x)$ is the optimal action at context x. Then, from (2), the sub-optimality gap for context x can be bounded as $z_T(x)^\top \theta^* \leq z_T(x)^\top \theta^* - z_T(x)^\top \theta_T = \frac{1}{T}\sum_{t=1}^T z_T(x)^\top (\theta^* - \widehat{\theta}_t)$. Here, the first inequality is because $\phi(x, \pi_T(x))^\top \theta_T \geq \phi(x, a^*(x))^\top \theta_T$, which follows from definition of π_T, and so $z_T(x)^\top \theta_T \leq 0$. Then, by Cauchy-Schwarz inequality, we get $z_T(x)^\top \theta^* \leq \frac{1}{T} \sum_{t=1}^T \|z_T(x)\|_{H_t(\widehat{\theta}_t)^{-1}} \|\theta^* - \widehat{\theta}_t\|_{H_t(\widehat{\theta}_t)}$.

Now, we apply Lemma 1 to upper bound $\|\theta^* - \widehat{\theta}_t\|_{H_t(\widehat{\theta}_t)}$. Next, we note that $\|z_T(x)\|_{H_t(\widehat{\theta}_t)^{-1}} \leq \|z_t\|_{H_t(\widehat{\theta}_t)^{-1}}$ by the design of our algorithm. To bound this, consider the regularized sample covariance matrix of feature differences, defined as $V_t = \sum_{s=1}^{t-1} z_s z_s^\top + \kappa \lambda \mathbf{I}_d$. Compare this with $H_t(\theta)$, which scales each rank-one component inside the sum by its variance given that the parameter is θ (see Eq. 4). A key relation between these two matrices is that $H_t(\theta) \succcurlyeq V_t/\kappa$. Using this, we upper bound $\|z_t\|_{H_t(\widehat{\theta}_t)^{-1}}$ by $\sqrt{\kappa} \|z_t\|_{V_t^{-1}}$. Finally, applying Elliptic Potential Lemma (Lemma 10) finishes the proof. Details are in Appendix C. □

Remark 2. To the best of our knowledge, [18] is the only work similar to ours with theoretical guarantees. Therefore, we highlight in detail the major differences. First, the algorithm design is entirely different as we choose both the actions for any context by maximizing the exploration bonus $b_t(x, a, a')$, while [18] chooses one action uniformly at random. This can be wasteful in practice as the choice of the second action is equally crucial in preference-based learning. Further, the context selection rule is entirely different. While we pick the context with the highest exploration bonus (Eq. 5), [18] uses an uncertainty estimate calculated via upper and lower confidence bounds of the rewards. Moreover, their suboptimality gap scales linearly with κ, while our guarantee only scales as $\sqrt{\kappa}$.

Next, [18] competes against the *Borda* winner, while we do so against the (stronger) *Condorcet* winner. Moreover, [18] assumes that the Borda function $g^*(x, a) = \mathbb{E}_{a' \sim \text{Unif}(\mathcal{A})}[\sigma(r^*(x, a) - r^*(x, a'))]$ lie in the same function space as the reward function $r^*(x, a) = \langle \theta^*, \phi(x, a) \rangle$. This assumption doesn't hold in general due to the non-linearity in σ and hence restricts the preference probabilities. The assumption holds trivially if each $\phi(x,a)$ is a one-hot vector $\mathbf{e}_{x,a}$, but it pushes θ^* to $|\mathcal{X}| \cdot |\mathcal{A}|$ dimensions and blows up the suboptimality gap significantly. We remove this restriction and provide the guarantee in dimension $d \ll |\mathcal{X}| \cdot |\mathcal{A}|$, by crucially exploiting properties of the sigmoid function.

Remark 3 (Extension to Direct Preference Optimization (DPO)). Another popular alignment algorithm DPO [22] does not train a reward model separately, rather it uses the log-probability $r_\theta(x,a) = \log \pi_\theta(a|x) - \log \pi_{\text{ref}}(a|x)$ as the reward, where $\theta \in \mathbb{R}^d$ parameterizes the policy to be learnt. For example, Softmax policies take the form $\pi_\theta(a|x) \propto \exp(f_\theta(x,a))$, where f_θ is a differentiable function. Now if we assume f_θ to be linear, then π_θ becomes a log-linear policy, i.e., $\log \pi_\theta(a|x) \propto \langle \theta, \phi(x,a) \rangle$, which eventually makes r_θ a (shifted) linear function. Hence, one would be able to apply our proposed approach to learn the policy parameter θ directly from the preference dataset $\mathcal{D}$.

4.2 Generalization Beyond BTL Model

In this section, we remove the assumption of the BTL preference model and assume access to a non-parametric function class

$$\mathcal{F} = \{f : \mathcal{X} \times \mathcal{A} \times \mathcal{A} \to [0,1] : f(x,a,a') + f(x,a',a) = 1\},$$

where $f(x,a,a')$ denotes the probability that action a wins over action a' (denoted by $a \succcurlyeq a'$) given context x when the preference function is f, i.e., $f(x,a,a') = \mathbb{P}[a \succcurlyeq a'|x, f]$. Note that in this case, there is no latent reward model, and hence, this is a strict generalization of the BTL model. Now, we assume that there is a realizable $f^* \in \mathcal{F}$ from which preferences are observed at each round t, i.e. $y_t \sim \text{Ber}(f^*(x_t, a_t, a'_t))$. Further, we assume a *Condorcet winner* at each context $x \in \mathcal{X}$ w.r.t. f^*, i.e. there is an action $a^*(x) \in \mathcal{A}$ such that $f^*(x, a^*(x), a) \geq 1/2$ for all $a \in \mathcal{A}$. Accordingly, the sub-optimality gap of policy π_T is defined as

$$R(T) = \max_{x \in \mathcal{X}} f^*(x, a^*(x), \pi_T(x)) - 1/2.$$

In this setting, we propose a generalization of APO, namely, APO-Gen (Algorithm 3 in Appendix D). Similar to APO, it selects a context and a pair of actions at each round by maximizing an uncertainty score that depends on the complexity of the function class $\mathcal{F}$. However, unlike APO, (a) at each round, it prunes out sub-optimal actions for every context, and (b) after T rounds, the final policy is to sample an action uniformly from the remaining near-optimal actions for each context. APO-Gen enjoys the following guarantee (details, proof in Appendix D).

Theorem 4. (Suboptimality Gap of APO-Gen). *Let $\delta \in (0,1)$, and $\mathcal{N}(\mathcal{F})$ and $d_\mathcal{E}(\mathcal{F})$ be the covering number and Eluder dimension of $\mathcal{F}$ respectively. Then, with probability $\geq 1 - \delta$, the policy returned by APO-Gen enjoys sub-optimality gap*

$$R(T) \leq \tilde{O}\left(\sqrt{\log(\mathcal{N}(\mathcal{F})T/\delta) d_\mathcal{E}(\mathcal{F})/T}\right),$$

For the BTL preference model, we have $\log \mathcal{N}(\mathcal{F}) = O(d \log T)$ and $d_{\mathcal{E}}(\mathcal{F}) = O(\kappa^2 d \log T)$. Hence, we get an $\tilde{O}(\kappa d/\sqrt{T})$ sub-optimality gap for APO-Gen, which is $\sqrt{\kappa}$ factor loose than Theorem 3. This is because we crucially use self-concordance of the sigmoid function in Theorem 3 to shave this extra $\sqrt{\kappa}$ factor. Nevertheless, this result is general enough to subsume other preference models (e.g., Thurstone) beyond the BTL model.

5 Experiments

We first present a practical version of APO, which largely follows the former with minor changes adapted for the computationally efficient implementation required in large-scale experiments. Next, we present experimental results that demonstrate the efficacy of APO over random sampling (hereafter denoted by Random) and baselines [18,19]. Hyperparameter details are given in Appendix F. The experiment code can be found here.

Algorithm 2. APO (Practical version)

Require: Context-generation pairs $\mathcal{M} = \{(x, a, a')\}$, sample budget T, encoder ϕ, SFT policy π_{SFT}, log-loss $\mathcal{L}$, batch size B, uncertainty regularizer $\lambda > 0$, KL regularizer $\beta > 0$, learning rate $\eta > 0$. Initialize $V_1 = \lambda I, \widehat{\theta}_1 = 0, \mathcal{D} = \emptyset$.
1: **for** batch $t = 1, \ldots, \lfloor T/B \rfloor$ **do**
2:     Set $b_t(x, a, a') = \|\phi(x, a) - \phi(x, a')\|_{V_t^{-1}}$ for each $(x, a, a') \in \mathcal{M}$. Set $\mathcal{M}_t = \emptyset$.
3:     **for** $j = 1, \ldots, B$ **do**
4:         Pick $(x_{t,j}, a_{t,j}, a'_{t,j}) = \underset{(x,a,a') \in \mathcal{M} \setminus \mathcal{M}_t}{\arg\max} b_t(x, a, a')$; Observe preference $y_{t,j}$.
5:         Update $\mathcal{M}_t \leftarrow \mathcal{M}_t \cup \{(x_{t,j}, a_{t,j}, a'_{t,j})\}$ and $\mathcal{D} \leftarrow \mathcal{D} \cup \{(x_{t,j}, a_{t,j}, a'_{t,j}, y_{t,j})\}$.
6:     Update $\widehat{\theta}_{t+1} \leftarrow \texttt{Gradient-step}(\mathcal{L}, \widehat{\theta}_t, \mathcal{D}, \eta)$.
7:     Update $V_{t+1} \leftarrow V_t + \sum_{j=1}^{B} z_{t,j} z_{t,j}^{\top}$, where $z_{t,j} = \phi(x_{t,j}, a_{t,j}) - \phi(x_{t,j}, a'_{t,j})$.
8: Set reward $\widehat{r}_T(x, a) = \phi(x, a)^{\top} \widehat{\theta}_{\lfloor T/B \rfloor + 1} \forall (x, a)$ and policy $\pi_T \leftarrow \texttt{PPO}(\pi_{\text{SFT}}, \widehat{r}_T, \beta)$.

5.1 Practical Version of APO for RLHF

In this practical version of APO (Algorithm 2), we access preference data in batches instead of being fully online. At the start of each batch t, we first compute the uncertainty $b_t(x, a, a')$ of each triplet (x, a, a') (Step 2). This is similar to Algorithm 1 except that here we compute the norm w.r.t. the inverted sample covariance matrix of feature differences V_t^{-1} instead of $H_t(\widehat{\theta}_t)^{-1}$ (Step 7). We do so since it is both compute and memory efficient for large scale experiments. To maximize exploration, only those B triplets (x, a, a') are sent for labeling in a batch that have the highest uncertainty $b_t(x, a, a')$, and those are stored in a buffer $\mathcal{D}$. At the end of each batch t, we update the parameter estimate $\widehat{\theta}_t$ via a black-box gradient-descend-based algorithm (e.g. Adam [11]) on the log-loss (1) over the dataset $\mathcal{D}$. Finally, after the budget T is exhausted, we first learn an estimate $\widehat{r}_T$ of the latent reward model r^*, and then align the policy via proximal policy optimization (PPO) [28], which takes as input the SFT policy π_{SFT}, the learnt reward model $\widehat{r}_T$ and a KL-regularizer β, and returns π_T.

5.2 Results on Controlled Sentiment Generation Task

In this experiment, we consider a user group that prefers positive sentiment completions for movie reviews in the IMDb dataset [16]. The goal is to output generations a that exhibit positive sentiment, catering to the user group's preferences for a given context x. For controlled evaluation, we generate preference pairs (a, a') utilizing a pre-trained sentiment classifier where $\mathbb{P}(\text{positive-sentiment} \mid x, a) > \mathbb{P}(\text{positive-sentiment} \mid x, a')$. We generate a total of 10000 preference samples (x, a, a') and use 4:1 train-test split. For the SFT policy, we fine-tune GPT-2 [21] on preferred reviews from the train set (8000 samples) and use this GPT-2 backbone for both reward learning and policy alignment.

For reward training, we adaptively select context and generation pairs from the train set. We use the feature representation $\phi(x, a)$, and estimate the uncertainty $b_t(x, a, a')$ for each (x, a, a') in the train set and select top-B samples

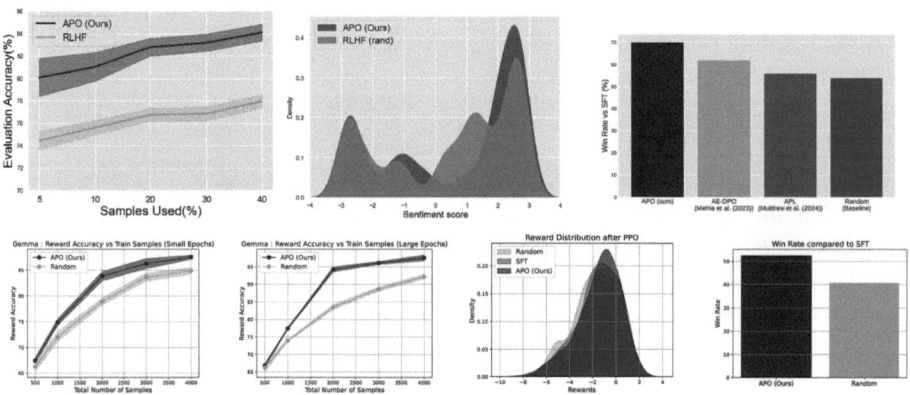

Fig. 1. Top Row: Controlled Sentiment Generation Task: Left: Evaluation accuracy of trained reward model vs. no. of samples (in %) comparing APO with Random. **Middle:** Sentiment score distribution of aligned policies trained on reward model learned with APO and on Random's highest accuracy reward model. Generations by APO-trained reward is more shifted towards positive, showing better alignment than Random. **Right:** Win rates of APO, AE-DPO [18] and APL [19] and Random against SFT policy. APO outperforms AE-DPO, APL and Random by 72 : 62 : 56 : 54 win rate. **Bottom Row: Single-turn Dialogue Task: Left and 2nd Left:** Evaluation accuracy of trained reward model vs. no. of samples comparing APO with Random, when the number of epochs is 5 (**Left**) and 20 (**2nd Left**). Evaluation accuracy of APO is higher than the Random in both cases. **2nd Right:** Reward distribution of APO-aligned, SFT and Random-aligned policies for generations on prompts in the test dataset. Clearly, APO's alignment is better than Random. **Right:** Win rates of APO and Random aligned policies against SFT policy. APO outperforms Random by 55 : 40 win rate.

to update the reward model. We repeat this process K times and return the final trained reward model. We evaluate the performance of the trained reward model against Random (where we select B samples randomly at every batch) on the test set of 2000 samples. Figure 1 (**Top Left**) shows the result: evaluation accuracy of the reward model learned by APO is much higher than the one learned via Random even when APO's sample budget is only 5% of the data and Random's is 40%.

For policy alignment, we align the SFT policy with respective trained reward models (via APO and Random) using PPO (step 8). To demonstrate the effectiveness of adaptive sampling, we use the reward model trained on a sample budget of only 10% for APO, while we use the highest accuracy reward model (corresponding to 40% samples) for Random. Similar to [22], the generations of aligned policies are evaluated against the ground truth reward r^* for positive sentiment, which is provided by the pre-trained sentiment classifier. From Fig. 1 (**Top Middle**), it can be seen that the reward distribution of the generations of APO -aligned policy achieves a higher density of positive sentiment compared to that aligned by Random. Moreover, from Fig. 1 (**Top Right**) it is evident that APO outperforms APL [19], AE-DPO [18] and Random in terms of win-rate against the SFT policy demonstrating the efficiency of the proposed method.

5.3 Results on Single-Turn Dialogue Task

In this experiment, we use Anthropic-HH [2] preference dataset and instruction-tuned Gemma-2b [30] language model. We collect all the contexts with single-turn dialogues and split these into two sets in a 4:1 ratio. We put samples from the larger collection into three buckets based on reward difference between *chosen* and *rejected* responses using Mistral-7b reward model as latent reward r^*. These buckets contain data points that are progressively easier to classify: (B1) reward difference between -1 to 1, (B2) reward difference between 1 to 3 and (B3) reward difference of more than 3. Out of these three buckets, we take 4500 samples from (B1), 2500 from (B2), and 1000 from (B3) to carefully curate a collection of 8000 training samples. Such a collection (more samples taken from the buckets with a smaller reward difference and fewer samples from the bucket with a larger reward difference) highlights the importance of selecting prompts carefully to obtain useful information during reward training – randomly sampling contexts to collect feedback is more likely to hurt the performance in such a setting. For the test set, we sample 2000 data points from the smaller collection set aside.

Reward Evaluation. We compare the reward models learnt by APO and Random by computing the % of samples in the test set for which the models assign higher reward to the *chosen* responses than to the *rejected* responses. We study how this accuracy changes with the number of batches or epochs, keeping the sample budget the same (Fig. 1 (**Bottom Left**) for 5 epochs and Fig. 1 (**Bottom 2nd Left**) for 20 epochs). We observe that APO always outperforms Random. We also see that the reward accuracy increases with an increasing number of epochs for a given sample budget. We show results by varying training samples till 4000 as we want to demonstrate the effectiveness of APO under budget constraint.

Win Rate. Based on reward models learnt by APO and Random, we fine tune the SFT policy with PPO to obtain APO-policy and Random-policy respectively. Then we generate responses for contexts in the test set using APO, Random, and SFT policies, and get them evaluated by the Mistral-7b reward model. The reward distributions of these three policies are shown in Fig. 1 (**Bottom 2nd right**). It can be seen that APO has a higher density of positive rewards. Win rate of APO-policy and Random-policy against SFT policy is shown in Fig. 1 (**Bottom Right**), which shows that APO outperforms Random by a 55 : 40 win rate.

6 Conclusion

In this work, we studied whether sampling prompts uniformly at random from a dataset to solicit feedback is sample efficient. We first showed that this method can suffer a constant suboptimality gap when aligning a language model policy with human preferences. Next, we characterized the sub-optimality gap lower bound for any active-learning algorithm with sample budget T and problem dimension d, showing it to be $\Omega(d/\sqrt{T})$. Then, we proposed an algorithm APO, which actively samples prompts to achieve an $\tilde{O}(d/\sqrt{T})$ sub-optimality gap. We also extended the results of APO to general function approximation to better capture modern-day RLHF training. Finally, we showed its efficacy over the random-sampling baseline on practical datasets. Although APO's sub-optimality gap is minimax optimal in d and T, the optimal dependence on κ is unknown and seems to be an interesting future work.

References

1. Abeille, M., Faury, L., Calauzènes, C.: Instance-wise minimax-optimal algorithms for logistic bandits. In: International Conference on Artificial Intelligence and Statistics, pp. 3691–3699. PMLR (2021)
2. Bai, Y., et al.: Training a helpful and harmless assistant with reinforcement learning from human feedback (2022)
3. Bradley, R.A., Terry, M.E.: Rank analysis of incomplete block designs: I. The method of paired comparisons. Biometrika **39**(3/4), 324–345 (1952)
4. Carvalho Melo, L., Tigas, P., Abate, A., Gal, Y.: Deep Bayesian active learning for preference modeling in large language models. Adv. Neural. Inf. Process. Syst. **37**, 118052–118085 (2024)
5. Chen, X., Zhong, H., Yang, Z., Wang, Z., Wang, L.: Human-in-the-loop: provably efficient preference-based reinforcement learning with general function approximation. In: International Conference on Machine Learning, pp. 3773–3793 (2022)
6. Christiano, P.F., Leike, J., Brown, T., Martic, M., Legg, S., Amodei, D.: Deep reinforcement learning from human preferences. In: Advances in Neural Information Processing Systems, vol. 30 (2017)
7. Even-Dar, E., Mannor, S., Mansour, Y.: Action elimination and stopping conditions for the multi-armed bandit and reinforcement learning problems. J. Mach. Learn. Res. **7**(39), 1079–1105 (2006)

8. Glaese, A., et al.: Improving alignment of dialogue agents via targeted human judgements. arXiv preprint arXiv:2209.14375 (2022)
9. Hazan, E., et al.: Introduction to online convex optimization. Found. Trends® Optim. **2**(3-4), 157–325 (2016)
10. Ji, K., He, J., Gu, Q.: Reinforcement learning from human feedback with active queries. arXiv preprint arXiv:2402.09401 (2024)
11. Kingma, D., Ba, J.: Adam: a method for stochastic optimization. In: International Conference on Learning Representations (ICLR). San Diego, CA, USA (2015)
12. Lattimore, T., Szepesvári, C.: Bandit Algorithms. Cambridge University Press (2020)
13. Lee, J., Yun, S.Y., Jun, K.S.: Improved regret bounds of (multinomial) logistic bandits via regret-to-confidence-set conversion. In: International Conference on Artificial Intelligence and Statistics, pp. 4474–4482. PMLR (2024)
14. Lee, K., Smith, L.M., Abbeel, P.: Pebble: Feedback-efficient interactive reinforcement learning via relabeling experience and unsupervised pre-training. In: Proceedings of the 38th International Conference on Machine Learning. Proceedings of Machine Learning Research, vol. 139, pp. 6152–6163. PMLR (2021)
15. Luce, R.D.: Individual Choice Behavior. Wiley (1959)
16. Maas, A.L., Daly, R.E., Pham, P.T., Huang, D., Ng, A.Y., Potts, C.: Learning word vectors for sentiment analysis. In: Proceedings of the 49th Annual Meeting of the Association for Computational Linguistics: human Language Technologies, pp. 142–150. Association for Computational Linguistics (2011)
17. Maiti, A., Boczar, R., Jamieson, K., Ratliff, L.: Near-optimal pure exploration in matrix games: a generalization of stochastic bandits and dueling bandits. In: Proceedings of The 27th International Conference on Artificial Intelligence and Statistics, pp. 2602–2610 (2024)
18. Mehta, V., et al.: Sample efficient reinforcement learning from human feedback via active exploration. arXiv preprint arXiv:2312.00267 (2023)
19. Muldrew, W., Hayes, P., Zhang, M., Barber, D.: Active preference learning for large language models. In: Proceedings of the 41st International Conference on Machine Learning, pp. 36577–36590. PMLR (2024)
20. Ouyang, L., et al.: Training language models to follow instructions with human feedback. In: Advances in Neural Information Processing Systems (2022)
21. Radford, A., Wu, J., Child, R., Luan, D., Amodei, D., Sutskever, I.: Language models are unsupervised multitask learners (2019)
22. Rafailov, R., Sharma, A., Mitchell, E., Manning, C.D., Ermon, S., Finn, C.: Direct preference optimization: your language model is secretly a reward model. In: Thirty-seventh Conference on Neural Information Processing Systems (2023)
23. Ray Chowdhury, S., Kini, A., Natarajan, N.: Provably robust DPO: aligning language models with noisy feedback. In: Proceedings of the 41st International Conference on Machine Learning, pp. 42258–42274. PMLR (2024)
24. Sadigh, D., Dragan, A.D., Sastry, S.S., Seshia, S.A.: Active preference-based learning of reward functions. In: Robotics: Science and Systems (2017)
25. Saha, A.: Optimal algorithms for stochastic contextual preference bandits. Adv. Neural. Inf. Process. Syst. **34**, 30050–30062 (2021)
26. Saha, A., Pacchiano, A., Lee, J.: Dueling RL: reinforcement learning with trajectory preferences. In: Proceedings of The 26th International Conference on Artificial Intelligence and Statistics, pp. 6263–6289. PMLR (2023)
27. Sawarni, A., Das, N., Barman, S., Sinha, G.: Generalized linear bandits with limited adaptivity. In: Advances in Neural Information Processing Systems (2024)

28. Schulman, J., Wolski, F., Dhariwal, P., Radford, A., Klimov, O.: Proximal policy optimization algorithms. arXiv preprint arXiv:1707.06347 (2017)
29. Stiennon, N., et al.: Learning to summarize with human feedback. Adv. Neural. Inf. Process. Syst. **33**, 3008–3021 (2020)
30. Team, G., et al.: Gemma: open models based on Gemini research and technology. arXiv preprint arXiv:2403.08295 (2024)
31. Zhan, W., Uehara, M., Sun, W., Lee, J.D.: How to query human feedback efficiently in RL? ArXiv abs/2305.18505 (2023)
32. Zhu, B., Jordan, M., Jiao, J.: Principled reinforcement learning with human feedback from pairwise or k-wise comparisons. In: Proceedings of the 40th International Conference on Machine Learning, pp. 43037–43067. PMLR (2023)

Fast Proximal Gradient Methods with Node Pruning for Tree-Structured Sparse Regularization

Yasutoshi Ida[1](✉)[iD], Sekitoshi Kanai[1], Atsutoshi Kumagai[1], Tomoharu Iwata[2], and Yasuhiro Fujiwara[2]

[1] NTT Computer and Data Science Laboratories, Tokyo, Japan
yasutoshi.ida@ieee.org, {sekitoshi.kanai,atsutoshi.kumagai}@ntt.com
[2] NTT Communication Science Laboratories, Tokyo, Japan
{tomoharu.iwata,yasuhiro.fujiwara}@ntt.com

Abstract. Sparse learning with structural information is a fundamental framework for feature selection. Among the various structures, the tree is a basic one that appears in feature vectors, and tree-structured regularization has been utilized to incorporate trees into objective functions. Although proximal gradient methods (PGMs) are usually used for optimization, they incur high computation costs for deep tree structures or large datasets. We propose a fast PGM for tree-structured regularization. Our method safely skips parameter updates of PGMs for pruning unnecessary leaf nodes in the tree. In addition, it prunes unnecessary computations for internal nodes in a hierarchical manner. Our method guarantees the same optimization results and convergence rate as the original method. Furthermore, it can be applied to various PGMs for tree-structured regularization. Experiments show that our method reduces the processing time by up to 56% from the original method without degrading accuracy.

Keywords: Sparse learning · Feature selection · Pruning method

1 Introduction

Feature selection using sparsity-inducing regularization, as in Lasso [7,27], is a fundamental technique of data analysis. In many applications, as shown in Fig. 1, a tree structure naturally appears in the feature vector wherein the features and groups of features correspond to leaf nodes and internal nodes, respectively [14, 21,22]. Tree-structured regularization [16,21] effectively handles such structural information by solving a regularized optimization problem. It is based on a linear regression model whose parameter vector has the same tree structure as

---

Supplementary Information The online version contains supplementary material available at https://doi.org/10.1007/978-3-032-06096-9_7.

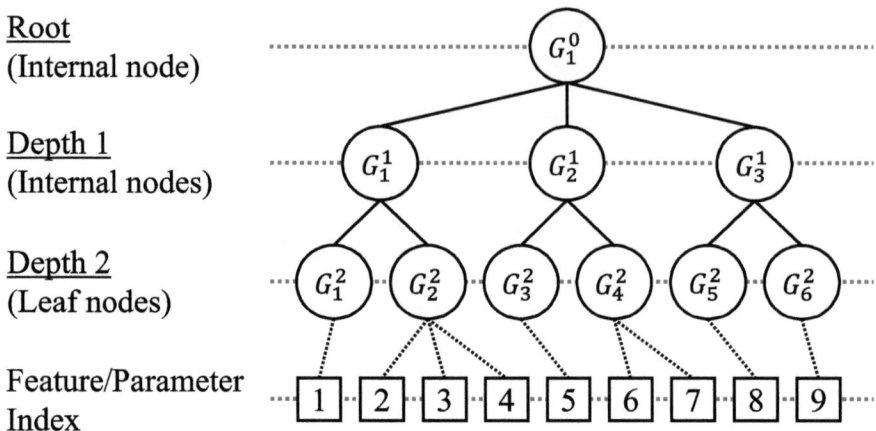

Fig. 1. Example tree structure of features.

that of the feature vector. By inducing sparsity at each node of the tree, it selects important features from all the features. Owing to its effectiveness, tree-structured regularization has been used for many applications, including multi-task learning where multiple tasks are related through a tree structure [19], multi-scale mining of fMRI data where each parent node contains a series of child nodes that enjoy spatial locality [14], and traffic-sign recognition where the sign categories are tree-structured [22].

Although solving the optimization problem seems difficult because of its tree-structured regularization, [16,21] derived a proximal operator in a closed form and applied a proximal gradient method (PGM), called the iterative shrinkage thresholding algorithm (ISTA), to the problem. Specifically, the PGM updates the parameters and applies the proximal operator in each iteration of a gradient method. The proximal operator applies a soft-thresholding function to parameters corresponding to each node of the tree in bottom-up breadth-first order. Intuitively, this function shrinks the parameters to zero if the ℓ_2 norm of the passed parameters is less than or equal to a threshold. As a result, the entire parameter vector becomes sparse and its nonzero parameters correspond to important features.

From the perspective of computation cost, the proximal operator for tree-structured regularization requires high computation cost when the number of features p or the depth of the tree d is large. Specifically, it is $\mathcal{O}(pd)$ time for each iteration of the PGM [21]. This is because it repeatedly applies a soft-thresholding function to each node in the tree. In addition to the proximal operator, we have to take the gradient with respect to each of the parameters before the proximal operator is applied. Since the gradient computation requires $\mathcal{O}(p^2)$ or $\mathcal{O}(np)$ time, where n is the number of data points, it also incurs high computation costs on large datasets.

This paper proposes a fast proximal gradient descent for tree-structured regularization. The method is based on two ideas as follows:

Pruning leaf Nodes to Reduce the Cost of Gradient Computations.
The first idea is to prune unnecessary parameter updates, including gradient computations which require $\mathcal{O}(p^2)$ or $\mathcal{O}(np)$ time. Specifically, we prune updates for parameters that turn to be zeros during optimization. Since a leaf node in the tree corresponds to a set of parameters as shown in Fig. 1, this idea corresponds to pruning unnecessary computations for leaf nodes. We utilize an upper bound of the ℓ_2 norm of the parameters passed to the soft-thresholding function for pruning. Specifically, if this upper bound is less than or equal to the threshold, we prune the computation of the leaf node.

Pruning Internal Nodes to Reduce the Cost of the Proximal Operator.
The second idea is to prune unnecessary computations for internal nodes to reduce the computation cost of the proximal operator which requires $\mathcal{O}(pd)$ time. The key is that an upper bound of a parent node can be computed by summing the upper bounds of its child nodes. It enables us to efficiently compute upper bounds for the internal nodes and prune unnecessary computations in the same way as the first idea. Because our upper bound requires $\mathcal{O}(1)$ time for one node, our method requires only $\mathcal{O}(p)$ time for computing the upper bounds of the entire tree.

Since our method only changes the computation of the proximal operator, it can be used with various PGMs, such as ISTA, fast ISTA (FISTA) [3], optimized ISTA (OISTA) [18], and modified FISTA (FISTA-Mod) [20]. In addition, it guarantees the same optimization results and convergence rate as the original methods because we can safely prune unnecessary computations for zero parameters. Experiments show that our method reduces the processing time by up to 56% from the original PGM while achieving the same objective values.

2 Preliminary

2.1 Tree-Structured Regularization

Let $X \in \mathbb{R}^{n \times p}$ be a matrix of features, where n is the number of data points and each data point is represented by a p-dimensional feature vector. $y \in \mathbb{R}^n$ is a set of continuous responses. We consider the following optimization problem with sparsity-inducing regularization:

$$\min_{\beta \in \mathbb{R}^p} \tfrac{1}{2}\|y - X\beta\|_2^2 + \lambda \phi(\beta), \tag{1}$$

where $\|\cdot\|_2$ is the ℓ_2 norm, $\beta \in \mathbb{R}^p$ is the parameter vector, $\lambda > 0$ is the regularization constant, and $\phi(\beta)$ is the sparsity-inducing regularization term for β. Here, we will let $f(\beta) = \tfrac{1}{2}\|y - X\beta\|_2^2$ for simplicity. Owing to $\phi(\beta)$, β will be sparse after optimization and we can select important features for predicting y from among all the features. To utilize the tree structure of the features, [21] incorporate structural information into $\phi(\beta)$. The structure is defined using the following index tree:

Algorithm 1. FISTA

1: **Input:** A Lipschitz constant L of ∇f
2: **Initialization:** $\beta_0 \in \mathbb{R}^p$, $\hat{\beta}_0 = \beta_0$, $s_0 = 1$, $t = 0$, $\eta = 1/L$
3: **repeat**
4: $\quad \beta_{t+1} = \text{prox}_{\lambda\eta}^\phi(\hat{\beta}_t - \eta \nabla f(\hat{\beta}_t))$
5: $\quad s_{t+1} = \frac{1+\sqrt{1+4s_t^2}}{2}$
6: $\quad \hat{\beta}_{t+1} = \beta_{t+1} + (\frac{s_t - 1}{s_{t+1}})(\beta_{t+1} - \beta_t)$
7: $\quad t = t+1$
8: **until** convergence

Definition 1 (Index Tree [21]). *For an index tree $\mathbb{T}$ of depth d, let $\mathbb{T}_i = \{G_1^i, G_2^i, ..., G_{n_i}^i\}$ contain all the nodes corresponding to depth i, where $n_0 = 1$, $G_1^0 = \{1, 2, ..., p\}$ and $n_i \geq 1$, $i = 1, 2, ..., d$. Each node G_j^i corresponds to a subset of $\{1, 2, ..., p\}$. The nodes satisfy the following conditions: 1) the nodes from the same depth level have non-overlapping indices, i.e., $G_j^i \cap G_k^i = \emptyset$, $\forall i = 1, ..., d$, $j \neq k$, $1 \leq j, k \leq n_i$; and 2) $G_j^i \subseteq G_{j0}^{i-1}$, where G_{j0}^{i-1} is the parent node of a non-root node G_j^i.*

Figure 1 shows an example of the index tree. Tree-structured regularization is defined using the index tree as follows:

$$\phi(\beta) = \sum_{i=0}^{d} \sum_{j=1}^{n_i} w_j^i \|\beta[G_j^i]\|_2, \quad (2)$$

where $w_j^i \geq 0$ ($i = 0, 1, ..., d$, $j = 1, 2, ..., n_i$) is a pre-defined weight for node G_j^i, and $\beta[G_j^i]$ is a vector composed of the entries of β whose indices are in G_j^i. For instance, if $G_j^i = \{1, 3, 5\}$, $\beta[G_j^i]$ consists of the first, third and fifth elements of β. Intuitively, $\beta[G_j^i]$ tends to have zeros after optimization because $\phi(\beta)$ consists of the l_2 norms of the parameters, the same as group Lasso [10, 30].

2.2 Proximal Gradient Method

Problem (1) can be solved by using PGMs such as ISTA and FISTA [3, 21]. As a representative example, we describe FISTA, the pseudocode of which is in Algorithm 1. FISTA consists of a parameter update (line 4) and a linear combination of parameters (lines 5–6). Note that ISTA, FISTA, OISTA, and FISTA-Mod share part of this parameter update (line 4). The parameter vector $\hat{\beta}_t$ is updated as $\hat{\beta}_t - \eta \nabla f(\hat{\beta}_t)$, where the gradient $\nabla f(\hat{\beta}_t)$ is computed as follows:

$$\nabla f(\hat{\beta}_t) = X^\top X \hat{\beta}_t - X^\top y. \quad (3)$$

Then, the updated parameter vector is passed to the proximal operator, $\text{prox}_{\lambda\eta}^\phi(\cdot)$, which yields β_{t+1} (line 4). We will describe the specific procedure of the proximal operator later. Lines 5–6 compute a linear combination of β_{t+1} and β_t on the basis of Nesterov's acceleration method [24].

Algorithm 2. $\text{prox}^{\phi}_{\lambda\eta}(v)$

1: **Initialization:** $u^{d+1} = v$
2: **for** $i = d, ..., 0$ **do**
3:    **for** $j = 1, ..., n_i$ **do**
4:       $\lambda^i_j = \lambda w^i_j \eta$
5:       **if** $\|u^{i+1}[G^i_j]\|_2 \leq \lambda^i_j$ **then**
6:          $u^i[G^i_j] = \mathbf{0}$
7:       **else**
8:          $u^i[G^i_j] = \frac{\|u^{i+1}[G^i_j]\|_2 - \lambda^i_j}{\|u^{i+1}[G^i_j]\|_2} u^{i+1}[G^i_j]$
9: **return** u^0

The proximal operator on line 4 is defined as

$$\text{prox}^{\phi}_{\lambda\eta}(v) = \underset{u \in \mathbb{R}^p}{\arg\min}\, \lambda \phi(u) + \frac{1}{2\eta}\|v - u\|^2_2, \tag{4}$$

where $v \in \mathbb{R}^p$. Although $\phi(\cdot)$ has the tree structure shown in Equation (2), [21] found an analytical solution for Equation (4) via the Moreau-Yosida regularization (Moreau envelope) [25,29] of $\phi(\cdot)$. The procedure is described in Algorithm 2. First, u^{d+1}, which is the target of the proximal operator, is initialized (line 1). Next, u^{d+1} is updated by traversing the index tree T in bottom-up breadth-first order (lines 2–8). Then, λ^i_j is computed as a threshold of the soft-thresholding function (line 4). After that, $u^i[G^i_j]$ is updated at each traversed node G^i_j (lines 5–8). If $\|u^{i+1}[G^i_j]\|_2 \leq \lambda^i_j$, $u^i[G^i_j]$ is updated to a zero vector (lines 5–6). If not, $u^i[G^i_j]$ is shrunk by multiplying $(\|u^{i+1}[G^i_j]\|_2 - \lambda^i_j)/\|u^{i+1}[G^i_j]\|_2$ (lines 7–8). This procedure can be regarded as being the same as the soft-thresholding function of group Lasso [30]. As a result, the parameter vector is expected to be sparse during optimization.

Although we can compute the gradient and the proximal operator by Eqs. (3) and (4), the computation cost corresponding to line 4 of Algorithm 1 clearly dominates the other costs. Specifically, computing the proximal operator requires $\mathcal{O}(pd)$ time for Algorithm 2 in every iteration of Algorithm 1 [21]. If the tree is a perfect binary tree, it requires $\mathcal{O}(p \log p)$ time because of $d = \mathcal{O}(\log p)$. In addition, line 4 of Algorithm 1 computes $\hat{\beta}_t - \eta \nabla f(\hat{\beta}_t)$ including the gradient computation before Algorithm 2 is called. The gradient computation requires $\mathcal{O}(p^2)$ or $\mathcal{O}(np)$ time in every iteration because of Eq. (3). As a result, executing line 4 of Algorithm 1 takes $\mathcal{O}(p^2 + pd)$ or $\mathcal{O}(pn + pd)$ time. Namely, the cost of Algorithm 1 is high when the depth of the tree or the dataset is large.

3 Proposed Approach

This section describes ideas of the proposed method. For the sake of simplicity, the discussion of the algorithm and the time complexity will assume the tree structure to be a perfect binary tree, although our method is applicable to any

3.1 Overview of the Ideas

The bottleneck of the PGMs is line 4 of Algorithm 1. It can be decomposed into two problems wherein 1) the existing method computes $\hat{\beta}_t - \eta \nabla f(\hat{\beta}_t)$ at $\mathcal{O}(p^2)$ or $\mathcal{O}(np)$ time and 2) the proximal operator requires $\mathcal{O}(p \log p)$ time. These computation costs are incurred at every iteration until convergence. We tackle these two problems with the two ideas.

The first idea is to prune unnecessary computations of $\hat{\beta}_t - \eta \nabla f(\hat{\beta}_t)$ corresponding to parameters that turn out to be zero. Specifically, our method checks whether each parameter is zero or not before computing $\hat{\beta}_t - \eta \nabla f(\hat{\beta}_t)$. If a parameter is determined to be zero, we prune the corresponding computation of $\hat{\beta}_t - \eta \nabla f(\hat{\beta}_t)$. To identify parameters that turn out to be zero, we introduce an upper bound of $\|u^{d+1}[G_j^d]\|_2$ at line 5 of Algorithm 2. If this upper bound is less than or equal to λ_j^i, the corresponding parameter is zero. The upper bound can be efficiently computed because it only requires $\mathcal{O}(p)$ time for all the parameters. This pruning corresponds to pruning computations for leaf nodes because $u^{d+1} = v = \hat{\beta}_t - \eta \nabla f(\hat{\beta}_t)$ holds, from line 1 in Algorithm 2. We describe the details of this procedure in Sect. 3.2.

The second idea is to prune internal nodes in the tree on the basis of upper bounds. Although this idea appears to be similar to the first one, the computation of the upper bounds is different. Specifically, the upper bounds of internal nodes are computed by summing the upper bounds of their child nodes, as we will describe in Sect. 3.3. This method allows us to efficiently compute upper bounds for all the internal nodes in bottom-up breadth-first order at $\mathcal{O}(p)$ time. As a result, although original methods require $\mathcal{O}(p \log p)$ time to compute the proximal operator, we can efficiently prune unnecessary computations of the proximal operator by using the upper bounds.

3.2 Pruning Leaf Nodes

As described in Sect. 3.1, pruning unnecessary computations of $\hat{\beta}_t - \eta \nabla f(\hat{\beta}_t)$ corresponds to pruning leaf nodes because $u^{d+1} = v = \hat{\beta}_t - \eta \nabla f(\hat{\beta}_t)$ holds from line 1 in Algorithm 2. Specifically, u_t^{d+1}, which is u^{d+1} at the t-th iteration of Algorithm 1, is computed from Eq. (3) as follows:

$$u_t^{d+1} = \hat{\beta}_t - \eta(X^\top X \hat{\beta}_t - X^\top y) = M\hat{\beta}_t + \eta X^\top y, \tag{5}$$

where

$$M = I - \eta X^\top X. \tag{6}$$

Then, to prune unnecessary computations for leaf nodes, we introduce $\overline{u}_t^{d+1}[G_j^d]$ as follows:

Definition 2. Let t' be $0 \leq t' < t$ in Algorithm 1; $\overline{u}_t^{d+1}[G_j^d]$ is computed as

$$\overline{u}_t^{d+1}[G_j^d] = \|u_{t'}^{d+1}[G_j^d]\|_2 + \|M[G_j^d]\|_F \|\Delta\hat{\beta}_t\|_2, \tag{7}$$

where $\|M[G_j^d]\|_F$ represents the Frobenius norm of the submatrix of M containing only G_j^d rows and $\Delta\hat{\beta}_t = \hat{\beta}_t - \hat{\beta}_{t'}$.

$\|M[G_j^d]\|_F$ is computed only once before the optimization because it does not depend on any parameters. $\|u_{t'}^{d+1}[G_j^d]\|_2$ is computed at regular iteration intervals in the PGM, as described in Sect. 3.4. The following lemma shows that $\overline{u}_t^{d+1}[G_j^d]$ is an upper bound of $\|u_t^{d+1}[G_j^d]\|_2$:

Lemma 1 (Upper Bound for Leaf Nodes). We have $\overline{u}_t^{d+1}[G_j^d] \geq \|u_t^{d+1}[G_j^d]\|_2$ when $\overline{u}_t^{d+1}[G_j^d]$ is computed by using Eq. (7).

The following lemma shows that the upper bound enables us to prune unnecessary leaf nodes:

Lemma 2. If $\overline{u}_t^{d+1}[G_j^d] \leq \lambda_j^d$ holds, we have $u_t^d[G_j^d] = \mathbf{0}$.

From Eq. (7), the total computation cost of the upper bounds for all the leaf nodes is as follows:

Lemma 3. The total computation cost of Eq. (7) for the leaf nodes $j \in \{1, ..., n_d\}$ is $\mathcal{O}(p)$ time given precomputed $u_{t'}^{d+1}[G_j^d]$ and $\|M[G_j^d]\|_F$ for $j \in \{1, ..., n_d\}$.

According to Lemmas 2 and 3, we can identify the indices G_j^d of the unnecessary leaf nodes in $\mathcal{O}(p)$ time by using the upper bound $\overline{u}_t^{d+1}[G_j^d]$ instead of $\|u_t^{d+1}[G_j^d]\|_2$ at line 5 in Algorithm 2. Since the total computation cost of $\|u_t^{d+1}[G_j^d]\|_2$ for all the leaf nodes is $\mathcal{O}(p^2)$ or $\mathcal{O}(np)$ time as a result of computing $u_t^{d+1} = \hat{\beta}_t - \eta \nabla f(\hat{\beta}_t)$, our upper bounds efficiently identify unnecessary leaf nodes.

We should note that $\overline{u}_t^{d+1}[G_j^d]$ is an approximation of $\|u_t^{d+1}[G_j^d]\|_2$. We have the following error bound for this approximation:

Lemma 4. Let ϵ be $2\|M[G_j^d]\|_F \|\Delta\hat{\beta}_t\|_2$. Then, it satisfies $|\overline{u}_t^{d+1}[G_j^d] - \|u_t^{d+1}[G_j^d]\|_2| \leq \epsilon$.

This section introduced the upper bound for leaf nodes that are the cases of $i = d$ in Algorithm 2. In the gradient computation, we can use the above upper bound for the leaf nodes. However, the bound cannot be used for the internal nodes. In the next section therefore, we derive another upper bound for internal nodes that are the cases of $i \neq d$.

3.3 Pruning Internal Nodes

First, let us introduce $\overline{u}_t^{i+1}[G_j^i]$, where $i \neq d$:

Algorithm 3. Fast Proximal Operator for Tree

1: **for** $i = d, ..., 0$ **do**
2:     **for** $j = 1, ..., n_i$ **do**
3:         $\lambda_j^i = \lambda w_j^i \eta$
4:         **if** $i = d$ **then**
5:             compute $\overline{u}_t^{i+1}[G_j^i]$ by Eq. (7)
6:         **else**
7:             compute $\overline{u}_t^{i+1}[G_j^i]$ by Eq. (8)
8:         **if** $\overline{u}_t^{i+1}[G_j^i] \leq \lambda_j^i$ **then**
9:             $u^i[G_j^i] = \mathbf{0}$
10:        **else**
11:           **if** $i = d$ **then**
12:               compute $u_t^{i+1}[G_j^i]$ by Eq. (5)
13:             $u^i[G_j^i] = \max\left(0, \frac{\|u^{i+1}[G_j^i]\|_2 - \lambda_j^i}{\|u^{i+1}[G_j^i]\|_2}\right) u^{i+1}[G_j^i]$
14: **return** u^0

Definition 3. *Suppose that $\overline{u}_t^{d+1}[G_j^d]$ is computed by Eq. (7) for an index tree T. Then, $\overline{u}_t^{i+1}[G_j^i]$, where $i = d-1, ..., 0$, is computed in the bottom-up breadth-first order as follows:*

$$\overline{u}_t^{i+1}[G_j^i] = \sum_{k \in \mathbb{D}_j^i} \max(0, \overline{u}_t^{i+2}[G_k^{i+1}] - \lambda_k^{i+1}), \tag{8}$$

where $\mathbb{D}_j^i$ is a set of indices k such that $G_k^{i+1} \subseteq G_j^i$.

Equation (8) indicates that $\overline{u}_t^{i+1}[G_j^i]$ of node G_j^i is computed by using the upper bounds of its child nodes $G_k^{i+1} \subseteq G_j^i$. $\overline{u}_t^{i+1}[G_j^i]$ has the following property:

Lemma 5 (Upper Bound for Internal Nodes). *For $i = d-1, ..., 0$, we have $\overline{u}_t^{i+1}[G_j^i] \geq \|u_t^{i+1}[G_j^i]\|_2$ when $\overline{u}_t^{i+1}[G_j^i]$ is computed using Eq. (8).*

By using the upper bound, we can identify unnecessary internal nodes as follows:

Lemma 6. *If $\overline{u}_t^{i+1}[G_j^i] \leq \lambda_j^i$ holds for $i \in \{d-1, ..., 0\}$, we have $u_t^i[G_j^i] = \mathbf{0}$.*

The cost of computing the upper bounds of all the internal nodes is as follows:

Lemma 7. *The computation cost of Eq. (8) for all the internal nodes is $\mathcal{O}(p)$ time.*

3.4 Algorithm

Algorithm 3 presents the pseudocode of our method for computing the gradient and the proximal operator based on the discussion in Sects. 3.2 and 3.3. It computes upper bounds (lines 4–7) and decides whether to prune the nodes (lines 8–13). The computation is performed in bottom-up breadth-first order (lines 1–2). In particular, it computes the upper bound by using Eq. (7) (lines 4–5) when the node is a leaf node and Eq. (8) (lines 6–7) when the node is an internal node.

Algorithm 4. Pruned FISTA with Algorithm 3
___
1: **Input:** A Lipschitz constant L of ∇f, $r > 1$
2: **Initialization:** $\beta_0 = \hat{\beta}_0$, $s_0 = 1$, $t = 0$, $\eta = 1/L$
3: **for** $j = 1, ..., n_d$ **do**
4: $\quad$ compute $\|M[G_j^d]\|_F$
5: **repeat**
6: $\quad \hat{\beta}_{t'} = \hat{\beta}_t$
7: $\quad$ **for** $j = 1, ..., n_d$ **do**
8: $\quad\quad$ compute $\|u_{t'}^{d+1}[G_j^d]\|_2$ by Eq. (5)
9: $\quad$ **for** $m = 1, ..., r$ **do**
10: $\quad\quad$ compute β_{t+1} by Algorithm 3
11: $\quad\quad s_{t+1} = \frac{1+\sqrt{1+4s_t^2}}{2}$
12: $\quad\quad \hat{\beta}_{t+1} = \beta_{t+1} + (\frac{s_t-1}{s_{t+1}})(\beta_{t+1} - \beta_t)$
13: $\quad\quad t = t + 1$
14: **until** convergence
___

If the upper bound is less than or equal to the threshold $\lambda_j^i = \lambda w_j^i \eta$, the node is pruned (lines 8–9). If not, the exact value is computed (lines 10–13). In this case, if the node is a leaf node, the value is computed with Eq. (5) only for the dimension corresponding to G_j^i. (lines 11–12).

Algorithm 4 is the pseudocode of FISTA with Algorithm 3. First, it precomputes $\|M[G_j^d]\|_F$, which is used for computing the upper bounds (lines 3–4). The main loop of the algorithm is lines 5–14. To compute the upper bounds for the leaf nodes (Eq. (7)), the algorithm computes $\hat{\beta}_{t'}$ and $\|u_{t'}^{d+1}[G_j^d]\|_2$ (lines 6–8). It computes these values at regular iteration intervals $r > 1$ (line 9). Note that, $r = 2$ in this study. The performance variation with r is shown in Sect. 5.1. Lines 10–13 are the same procedure as in the original FISTA (Algorithm 1) except for the computation of the proximal operator. Specifically, the proximal operator is computed using Algorithm 3.

Although Algorithm 4 is based on FISTA, our method can be also used with other PGMs such as ISTA, OISTA [18], and FISTA-Mod [20] as shown in the Appendix. This is because our approach only changes the computation of the proximal operator in these methods.

3.5 Theoretical Analysis

Algorithm 4 has the following property:

Theorem 1 (Optimization Result). *Suppose that Algorithm 4 has the same hyperparameters and initial parameter vector as those of Algorithm 1. Then, Algorithm 4 converges to the same objective value and solution as Algorithm 1.*

This theorem suggests that our method returns the same results as the original method. This property also holds for ISTA, OISTA, and FISTA-Mod when they use our method. From Theorem 1 and its proof, our method has the following property regarding the convergence rate:

Corollary 1. *Algorithm 4 achieves the same convergence rate as Algorithm 1.*

Since the computation results of Algorithm 4 for the gradient and the proximal operator are the same as those of Algorithm 1 in every iteration, the proof is the same as in [3] and the above corollary clearly holds. Since Algorithm 4 is based on FISTA (Algorithm 1), it runs in $\mathcal{O}(1/t^2)$.

The computation cost of Algorithm 4 is as follows:

Theorem 2 (Computation Cost). *Let n_u be the total number of dimensions of vectors corresponding to un-pruned internal nodes and let n_l be that for un-pruned leaf nodes. If T is the total number of loops of lines 9–13, the computation cost of Algorithm 4 is $\mathcal{O}(p^2(n + \frac{T}{r}) + p(n + T + n_l) + n_u)$ time.*

This theorem suggests that if n_u and n_l are small, the processing time will be reduced by using Algorithm 4. Since the cost of the original FISTA with the tree-structured regularization (Algorithm 1) is $\mathcal{O}(p^2(n + T) + p(n + Td))$ time, our method also reduces the coefficient of p^2 in its cost.

The error bound of the upper bound for Algorithm 4 has the following property:

Theorem 3 (Convergence of Error Bound) *We have $\epsilon = 0$ when $\hat{\beta}_t$ in Algorithm 4 converges.*

The above theorem suggests that $\overline{u}_t^{d+1}[G_j^d]$ matches $\|u_t^{d+1}[G_j^d]\|_2$ if $\hat{\beta}_t$ converges. Namely, the upper bounds can accurately identify unnecessary leaf nodes when $\hat{\beta}_t$ converges.

4 Related Work

Several algorithms have been proposed to solve optimization problems with tree-structured regularizers [16]. [31,32] used a boosting-like technique based on BLasso [33]. Since it utilizes a path-following strategy, it can obtain regularization paths although it has difficulty computing them in parallel for each regularization constant. [19] used a reweighted least-squares scheme based on a variational formulation [1]. However, it cannot yield sparse parameters [16].

PGMs for tree-structured regularizers overcome the above drawbacks [15,21]. Together with the PGM, an acceleration technique with momentum can be utilized to reduce the processing time. A popular one is FISTA [3], which leverages Nesterov's acceleration method [24]. It decreases the function value at the rate $\mathcal{O}(1/t^2)$. FISTA is the most widely used accelerated PGM, and numerous improvements to it have been proposed. A typical example is Monotone FISTA (MFISTA), which does not increase the function value during optimization by introducing an extra computation of the objective function in each iteration [2,34]. Another example is OISTA, which improves on the convergence of FISTA on the basis of a performance estimation problem (PEP) [5,8,18,26]. FISTA-Mod incorporates hyperparameters to control s_{t+1}, which leads to enhanced convergence speed and improved stability [20]. [4] proposed smoothing proximal gradient (SPG) to deal with structured sparsity-inducing regularization. Although it can be also used with FISTA, the dimension of the gradient vector increases if there are a lot of overlapping groups such as the tree structure of Definition 1. Specifically, the space complexity is $\mathcal{O}(pd)$ space while the approach in this paper requires $\mathcal{O}(p)$ space [15,21].

5 Experiment

We evaluated the processing times and the objective values of our method. FISTA [3], OISTA [18], and FISTA-Mod [20] were chosen as baselines for comparison. Note that ISTA was removed from the comparison because it had not finished executing within a month. Since our approach is applicable to FISTA, OISTA, and FISTA-Mod, we also evaluated their combinations, i.e., pruned FISTA (pFISTA), pruned OISTA (pOISTA), and pruned FISTA-Mod (pFISTA-Mod). We tried $\lambda w_j^i = \{\lambda_{\max}/10, \lambda_{\max}/10^2, \lambda_{\max}/10^3\}$ after consulting previous papers [6,12]. $\lambda_{\max}$ is the smallest regularization constant for which all the parameters are zero at the optimal solutions [28]. We stopped each algorithm when the relative tolerance of the parameter vector dropped below 10^{-5} [9,11,13]. For additional hyperpameters of FISTA-Mod, we used the same values as those in the experiment of the original paper [20]. We used the climate dataset from NCEP/NCAR Reanalysis 1 [17,23]. It contains the means of climate data measurements spread across the globe in a grid of $2.5° \times 2.5°$ resolution for each month from 1948/1/1 to 2022/6/1. Each grid point has a group of seven variables: air temperature, precipitable water, relative humidity, pressure, sea level pressure, horizontal wind speed, and vertical wind speed. The size of the data matrix was 894×57344. This dataset has spatial locality in the features of adjacent grid points and a hierarchical structure of areas due to the spatial data. To exploit this property, we constructed a perfect binary tree with adjacent coordinates in grids. Since we could handle the seven variables as a group, each leaf node corresponded to a group and the depth of the tree was 13. As targeted responses, we used air temperatures in neighborhoods of Beijing, Canberra, Dakar, Paris, Tokyo, and Washington. Therefore, our experiments consisted of six regression tasks. All the experiments were conducted with one CPU core and 264 GB of main memory on a 2.20 GHz Intel Xeon server running Linux.

5.1 Processing Time

Figures. 2(a)–(c) show the wall clock times of the six regression tasks for each hyperparameter. Our methods, pFISTA, pOISTA, and pFISTA-Mod, were faster than FISTA, OISTA, and FISTA-Mod, respectively. The efficiency of our methods increased as we set larger hyperparameters. Specifically, since the hyperparameter setting in Fig. 2(a) strengthens the regularization, many parameters turned out to be zero. In this case, our method pruned unnecessary computations relatively easily; it reduced the processing time by up to 56% form the existing

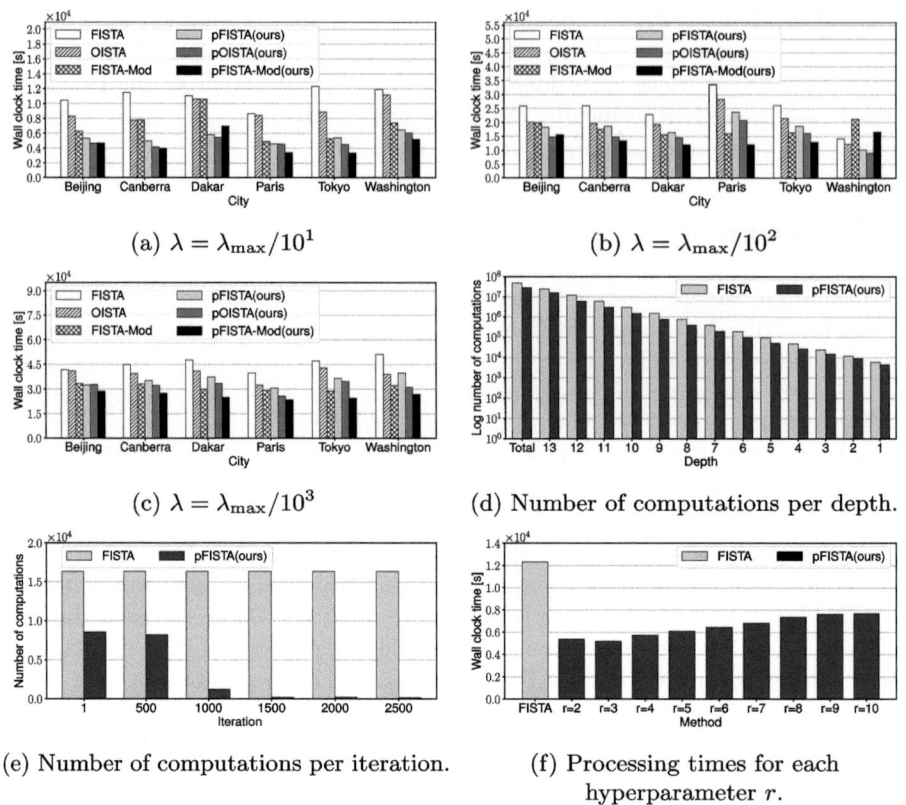

Fig. 2. (a)–(c): Processing times for each hyperparameter λ. (d)–(e): Numbers of computations at nodes per depth and iteration. (f): Processing times for each hyperparameter r.

methods. For all cases, our methods uniformly accelerated FISTA, OISTA, and FISTA-Mod, demonstrating the generality of method.

Number of Computations at Nodes per Depth. The main idea of our method is to prune unnecessary computations at nodes in the tree. Therefore, we compared the numbers of computations at nodes of the original method with those of our method. Figure 2(d) shows the number of computations per depth and their total. As a representative example, we compared FISTA and pFISTA (ours) for predicting the air temperature in Tokyo when $\lambda w_j^i = \lambda_{\max}/10$. Note that the trend was almost the same for other cities and methods. Our method reduced the number of the total computations to 58.35% compared with the original method. Specifically, regarding the first idea of pruning leaf nodes, the number was reduced to 66.37% as shown at depth 13 in the figure. Regarding the second idea of pruning internal nodes, the number was reduced to 50.32%

Table 1. Comparison of objective values for FISTA and pFISTA (ours).

City	λ	FISTA	pFISTA(ours)
Canberra	$\lambda_{\max}/10^1$	1311×10^{-1}	1311×10^{-1}
	$\lambda_{\max}/10^2$	9824×10^{-3}	9824×10^{-3}
	$\lambda_{\max}/10^3$	1494×10^{-3}	1494×10^{-3}
Paris	$\lambda_{\max}/10^1$	9934×10^{-2}	9934×10^{-2}
	$\lambda_{\max}/10^2$	5389×10^{-3}	5389×10^{-3}
	$\lambda_{\max}/10^3$	9595×10^{-4}	9595×10^{-4}
Washington	$\lambda_{\max}/10^1$	1301×10^{-1}	1301×10^{-1}
	$\lambda_{\max}/10^2$	6620×10^{-3}	6620×10^{-3}
	$\lambda_{\max}/10^3$	1355×10^{-3}	1355×10^{-3}

from the sum of computations for depths 1 to 12. The result reveals that our ideas effectively pruned unnecessary computations.

Number of Computations at Nodes per Iteration. We also investigated the number of computations at nodes for each iteration under the experimental settings described above. Specifically, we counted the numbers at the 1st, 500-th, 1000-th, 1500-th, 2000-th, 2500-th iteration. The algorithms were stopped at the 2984-th iteration. Figure 2(e) shows the results, which suggest that our method pruned half of the computations even at the beginning of optimization. Our method further reduced the number of computations as it converged. This is because $\|\Delta\hat{\beta}_t\|_2$ in Eq. (7) turned out to be small as the optimization progressed and the error bound of Lemma 4 became small. In addition, the upper bounds accurately identify unnecessary leaf nodes in the tree when the parameter vector converges as shown in Theorem 3. As a result, our approach could more accurately identify and prune unnecessary computations later in the optimization.

Impact of Hyperparameter r. Our method has a hyperparameter $r > 1$ that is the interval in which to obtain $\hat{\beta}_{t'}$ and $\|u_{t'}^{d+1}[G_j^d]\|_2$ in Eq. (7) (line 9 in Algorithm 4). We investigated the effect on processing time by changing r between 2 to 10 under the same experimental settings described above. Figure 2(f) shows the results. Our method reduced the processing time at small values of r, but the processing time increased as the value increased. This increase is because $\|\Delta\hat{\beta}_t\|_2$ in Eq. (7) becomes large when the value of r is large. In this case, the error bound of Lemma 4 turned out to be large and it became difficult to prune unnecessary computations by using the upper bounds. Given these results, we recommend setting a small value for r in practice, e.g., $r = 2$.

Limitation. The reduction ratios of pFISTA-Mod (ours) relative to FISTA-Mod for the dense parameter vectors are moderate as shown in Figs. 2(c). This is because our method is based on the pruning method and cannot prune the computations due to the dense parameter vector. However, since a goal of sparse

5.2 Value of Objective Function

Table 1 shows the final objective values of Canberra, Paris and Washington for FISTA and pFISTA. The full results are shown in the Appendix. Our methods achieved the same values of the objectives as those of the original methods. The indices of the selected features also matched those of the original methods though the results are omitted. This result supports Theorem 1: our method returned the same optimization results as the original method because it safely pruned unnecessary computations.

6 Conclusion

We proposed fast proximal gradient methods (PGMs) for tree-structured regularization. The bottlenecks of the original method are parameter updates including gradient computation and computation of the proximal operator with a hierarchical structure. We tackled the first bottleneck by pruning computations for leaf nodes of the tree: our method safely skips updates by identifying the parameters that must be zero on the basis of an upper bound. The second bottleneck was conquered by pruning computations for internal nodes: they are hierarchically pruned by summing the upper bounds of the child nodes. Our method provably guarantees the same optimization results and convergence rate as those of the original methods. In addition, since our method only changes the computation of the proximal operator, it can be used with various PGMs. Experiments showed that our method reduced the processing time by up to 56% from the original methods without any loss of accuracy.

References

1. Argyriou, A., Evgeniou, T., Pontil, M.: Convex multi-task feature learning. Mach. Learn. **73**(3), 243–272 (2008)
2. Beck, A., Teboulle, M.: Fast gradient-based algorithms for constrained total variation image denoising and deblurring problems. Trans. Imging. Proc. **18**(11), 2419–2434 (2009)
3. Beck, A., Teboulle, M.: A fast iterative shrinkage-thresholding algorithm for linear inverse problems. SIAM J. Imaging. Sci. **2**(1), 183–202 (2009)
4. Chen, X., Lin, Q., Kim, S., Carbonell, J.G., Xing, E.P.: Smoothing proximal gradient method for general structured sparse regression. Ann. Appl. Stat. **6**(2), 719–752 (2012)
5. Drori, Y., Teboulle, M.: Performance of first-order methods for smooth convex minimization: a novel approach. Math. Program. **145**(1–2), 451–482 (2014)
6. Fujiwara, Y., Ida, Y., Arai, J., Nishimura, M., Iwamura, S.: Fast algorithm for the lasso based L1-graph construction. Proc. VLDB Endow. **10**(3), 229–240 (2016)

7. Fujiwara, Y., Ida, Y., Shiokawa, H., Iwamura, S.: Fast lasso algorithm via selective coordinate descent. In: Proceedings of the AAAI Conference on Artificial Intelligence (AAAI), pp. 1561–1567 (2016)
8. Helou, E.S., Zibetti, M.V.W., Herman, G.T.: Fast proximal gradient methods for nonsmooth convex optimization for tomographic image reconstruction. Sens. Imaging **21**(1), 1–31 (2020). https://doi.org/10.1007/s11220-020-00309-z
9. Ida, Y., Fujiwara, Y., Kashima, H.: Fast sparse group lasso. In: Advances in Neural Information Processing Systems (NeurIPS), pp. 1702–1710 (2019)
10. Ida, Y., Kanai, S., Adachi, K., Kumagai, A., Fujiwara, Y.: Fast regularized discrete optimal transport with group-sparse regularizers. In: Proceedings of the AAAI Conference on Artificial Intelligence (AAAI), pp. 7980–7987 (2023)
11. Ida, Y., Kanai, S., Fujiwara, Y., Iwata, T., Takeuchi, K., Kashima, H.: Fast deterministic CUR matrix decomposition with accuracy assurance. In: Proceedings of International Conference on Machine Learning (ICML), pp. 4594–4603 (2020)
12. Ida, Y., Kanai, S., Kumagai, A.: Fast block coordinate descent for non-convex group regularizations. In: International Conference on Artificial Intelligence and Statistics (AISTATS), pp. 2481–2493 (2023)
13. Ida, Y., Kanai, S., Kumagai, A., Iwata, T., Fujiwara, Y.: Fast iterative hard thresholding methods with pruning gradient computations. In: Advances in Neural Information Processing Systems (NeurIPS), pp. 52836–52857 (2024)
14. Gramfort, A., et al.: Multiscale mining of fMRI data with hierarchical structured sparsity. SIAM J. Imaging. Sci. **5**(3), 835–856 (2012)
15. Jenatton, R., Mairal, J., Obozinski, G., Bach, F.: Proximal methods for sparse hierarchical dictionary learning. In: International Conference on Machine Learning (ICML), pp. 487–494 (2010)
16. Jenatton, R., Mairal, J., Obozinski, G., Bach, F.: Proximal methods for hierarchical sparse coding. J. Mach. Learn. Res. (JMLR) **12**(67), 2297–2334 (2011)
17. Kalnay, E., et al.: The NCEP/NCAR 40-year reanalysis project. Bull. Am. Meteor. Soc. **77**(3), 437–472 (1996)
18. Kim, D., Fessler, J.A.: An optimized first-order method for image restoration. In: IEEE International Conference on Image Processing (ICIP), pp. 3675–3679 (2015)
19. Kim, S., Xing, E.P.: Tree-guided group lasso for multi-task regression with structured sparsity. In: International Conference on Machine Learning (ICML), pp. 543–550 (2010)
20. Liang, J., Luo, T., Schönlieb, C.B.: Improving "fast iterative shrinkage-thresholding algorithm": faster, smarter, and greedier. SIAM J. Sci. Comput. **44**(3), A1069–A1091 (2022)
21. Liu, J., Ye, J.: Moreau-Yosida Regularization for Grouped Tree Structure Learning. In: Advances in Neural Information Processing Systems (NeurIPS), pp. 1459–1467 (2010)
22. Lu, X., Wang, Y., Zhou, X., Zhang, Z., Ling, Z.: Traffic sign recognition via multi-modal tree-structure embedded multi-task learning. IEEE Trans. Intell. Transp. Syst. **18**(4), 960–972 (2017)
23. Ndiaye, E., Fercoq, O., Gramfort, A., Salmon, J.: Gap safe screening rules for sparsity enforcing penalties. J. Mach. Learn. Res. (JMLR) **18**(1), 4671–4703 (2017)
24. Nesterov, Y.: A method for solving the convex programming problem with convergence rate $\mathcal{O}(1/k^2)$. Proc. USSR Acad. Sci. **269**, 543–547 (1983)
25. Parikh, N., Boyd, S.: Proximal algorithms. Found. Trends Optim. **1**(3), 127–239 (2014)

26. Taylor, A.B., Hendrickx, J.M., Glineur, F.: Exact worst-case performance of first-order methods for composite convex optimization. SIAM J. Optim. **27**(3), 1283–1313 (2017)
27. Tibshirani, R.: Regression shrinkage and selection via the lasso. J. Roy. Stat. Soc. **58**, 267–288 (1996)
28. Tibshirani, R., et al.: Strong rules for discarding predictors in lasso-type problems. J. Roy. Stat. Soc. B **74**(2), 245–266 (2012)
29. Yosida, K.: Functional Analysis. CM, vol. 123. Springer, Heidelberg (1995). https://doi.org/10.1007/978-3-642-61859-8
30. Yuan, M., Lin, Y.: Model selection and estimation in regression with grouped variables. J. Roy. Stat. Soc. **68**(1), 49–67 (2006)
31. Zhao, P., Rocha, G., Yu, B.: Grouped and hierarchical model selection through composite absolute penalties. Department of Statistics, UC Berkeley, Tech. Rep., vol. 37 (2006)
32. Zhao, P., Rocha, G., Yu, B.: The composite absolute penalties family for grouped and hierarchical variable selection. Ann. Stat. **37**(6A), 3468–3497 (2009)
33. Zhao, P., Yu, B.: Boosted Lasso. Statistics Department, University of California, Berkeley, Tech. rep. (2004)
34. Zibetti, M.V.W., Helou, E.S., Regatte, R.R., Herman, G.T.: Monotone FISTA with variable acceleration for compressed sensing magnetic resonance imaging. IEEE Trans. Comput. Imaging **5**, 109–119 (2019)

Hashing for Fast Pattern Set Selection

Maiju Karjalainen[(✉)] and Pauli Miettinen

University of Eastern Finland, Kuopio, Finland
{maiju.karjalainen,pauli.miettinen}@uef.fi

Abstract. Pattern set mining, which is the task of finding a good set of patterns instead of all patterns, is a fundamental problem in data mining. Many different definitions of what constitutes a good set have been proposed in recent years. In this paper, we consider the reconstruction error as a proxy measure for the goodness of the set, and concentrate on the adjacent problem of how to find a good set efficiently. We propose a method based on bottom-k hashing for efficiently selecting the set and extend the method for the common case where the patterns might only appear in approximate form in the data. Our approach has applications in tiling databases, Boolean matrix factorization, and redescription mining, among others. We show that our hashing-based approach is significantly faster than the standard greedy algorithm while obtaining almost equally good results in both synthetic and real-world data sets.

Keywords: Hashing · Pattern Set Mining · BMF · Redescription Mining

1 Introduction

The goal of data mining is to find surprising, new information about the data. A common problem with many methods that find local patterns from the data is that they find *too many* of those patterns—so-called pattern explosion problem. The popular solution to the pattern explosion problem is to switch to *pattern set mining*; that is, to the task of finding a good set of patterns instead of all patterns.

The definition of what is a good set is a topic of active study, and approaches such as MDL [26] or subjective interestingness [5] have been proposed for that. In this paper we approach the problem from a different perspective. We take the reconstruction error as the means of defining a good set, and ask the question: how fast can we find the set of patterns that minimizes the reconstruction error?

The motivation for our approach is twofold: For one, we argue that the reconstruction error is often a good proxy for the more sophisticated pattern set selection methods. Indeed, they all ask the question: how much yet unexplained data this new pattern explains, the main difference being how the "how much" part is defined. Of these, the "plain" reconstruction error is also the fastest to compute, which is why we prefer it.

For two, we argue that selecting the set of patterns is typically slow. This can be shadowed by the fact that *generating* the patterns can be slower and hence speeding up the task of selecting the patterns does not feel important. But this is often not so straightforward. In many cases, each pattern is independent of the others, and they can be generated efficiently in parallel. With modern multi-core CPUs and GPUs the pattern generation, even for a huge number of patterns, can be very effective. *Selecting* the patterns in the set, however, is inherently sequential process: in a good pattern set every selected pattern depends on the others. The selection of the patterns can easily become the slower part of the process.

To obtain our fast pattern set selection algorithm, we utilize the bottom-k hashing idea [3,4,25] using the efficient computation proposed in [23]. While [23] studies, in some sense, the quality of a pattern set, our approach will build the set, and furthermore, we propose a way to handle inexact patterns, that is, patterns that do not appear as such in the data.

In the next section we will formally define our problems and analyze their computational complexity. We will also discuss how our problems model different pattern set mining problems, although we postpone the other related work to Sect. 5. We will end Sect. 2 with a brief analysis of the standard greedy algorithm before introducing our algorithm in Sect. 3. The experiments are presented in Sect. 4.

2 Notation, Problems, and Theoretical Analysis

In this paper, we study the problem of selecting a good subset of patterns to explain the data. There are two variants: in *exact patterns* the patterns are exact subsets of the data; in *inexact patterns* the patterns can cover things that are not in the data. We formalise the problems using binary matrices. For that, we need the following concepts. We denote a matrix (Boolean or otherwise) with a bold-face upper-case letter, such as $\mathbf{M}$. Vectors are denoted with bold-face lower-case letters, such as $\mathbf{v}$. All vectors are considered to be column vectors. The (i,j) element of matrix $\mathbf{M}$ is m_{ij} and the ith element of vector $\mathbf{v}$ is v_i. We say that a binary matrix $\mathbf{S} \in \{0,1\}^{m \times n}$ is *dominated by* a binary matrix $\mathbf{D} \in \{0,1\}^{m \times n}$ if $s_{ij} \leq d_{ij}$ for all i and j. We denote that by $\mathbf{S} \leq \mathbf{D}$. Given a collection of binary matrices $\mathcal{C} = \{\mathbf{S}_i : i = 1, \ldots, \ell, \mathbf{S}_i \in \{0,1\}^{m \times n}\}$, we define $\bigvee_{\mathbf{S} \in \mathcal{C}} \mathbf{S} = \mathbf{C}$ as the element-wise logical *or* over matrices $\mathbf{S}$, that is, $c_{ij} = \bigvee_{\mathbf{S} \in \mathcal{C}} s_{ij}$. Matrix $\mathbf{M}$, of size m-by-n, is *rank-1* if it can be expressed as an outer product of two vectors, $\mathbf{M} = \mathbf{u}\mathbf{v}^T$. Matrix $\mathbf{M} \in \{0,1\}^{m \times n}$ is *Boolean rank-1* if $\mathbf{M} = \mathbf{u}\mathbf{v}^T$ where $\mathbf{u} \in \{0,1\}^m$ and $\mathbf{v} \in \{0,1\}^n$. Finally, we use $|\cdot|$ to denote the number of non-zero entries in a matrix or a vector, that is, $|\mathbf{M}| = |\{(i,j) : m_{ij} \neq 0\}|$, where the latter $|\cdot|$ is the usual set cardinality operator.

2.1 Problem Statement

We give the exact definitions of our problems below. For an explanation of how these definitions relate to pattern set mining tasks, see Sect. 2.3.

Problem 1 (Exact Patterns). Given a binary data matrix $\mathbf{D} \in \{0,1\}^{m \times n}$, a collection of (rank-1) binary matrices of the same size, $\mathcal{S} = \{\mathbf{S}_1, \mathbf{S}_2, \ldots, \mathbf{S}_\ell : \mathbf{S}_i \in \{0,1\}^{m \times n}, \mathbf{S}_i \leq \mathbf{D}\}$, and an integer k, find a subcollection $\mathcal{C} \subseteq \mathcal{S}$ of size k that minimizes

$$\left| \mathbf{D} - \bigvee_{\mathbf{S} \in \mathcal{C}} \mathbf{S} \right|. \tag{1}$$

Alternatively, the size of collection $\mathcal{C}$ can be unlimited and (1) can be replaced with a requirement that

$$\bigvee_{\mathbf{S} \in \mathcal{C}} \mathbf{S} = \mathbf{D}, \tag{2}$$

where we now assume that $\cup \mathcal{S} = \bigcup_{\mathbf{S} \in \mathcal{S}} \mathbf{S} = \mathbf{D}$. Notice that as $\mathbf{S}$ are dominated by $\mathbf{D}$, the union can never have 1s in locations where $\mathbf{D}$ does not have them. Consequently, the subtraction in (1) cannot produce negative entries. We say that $\cup \mathcal{S}$ does not *cover* any 0s of $\mathbf{D}$.

When the pattern matrices are not dominated by the data, the problem definition is as follows.

Problem 2 (Inexact Patterns). Given a binary data matrix $\mathbf{D} \in \{0,1\}^{m \times n}$ and a collection of (rank-1) binary matrices of the same size, $\mathcal{S} = \{\mathbf{S}_1, \mathbf{S}_2, \ldots, \mathbf{S}_\ell : \mathbf{S}_i \in \{0,1\}^{m \times n}\}$, find a subcollection $\mathcal{C} \subseteq \mathcal{S}$ that minimizes

$$\left| \mathbf{D} - \bigvee_{\mathbf{S} \in \mathcal{C}} \mathbf{S} \right|. \tag{3}$$

Contrary to (1), in (3) the matrices $\mathbf{S}$ are not necessarily dominated by $\mathbf{D}$ and hence the subtraction can yield negative values. Similarly to Problem 1, it is also possible to limit the size of $\mathcal{C}$ in Problem 2 by some user-defined constant k.

In the above definitions, we have limited the patterns to be rank-1 binary matrices. As we shall see below, this still allows us to represent many different kinds of patterns commonly encountered in data mining. Our algorithm will utilize the rank-1 structure for efficiency; however, we can still handle arbitrary binary matrices as patterns, with a cost in the running time of the algorithm (see Sect. 3.1). We will use terms *pattern*, *tile*, and *rank-1 matrix* interchangeably in this paper.

2.2 Computational Complexity

Both problems (and their variants) are NP-hard. The Max k-Cover problem can be reduced to Problem 1, and the Set Cover problem to the variant of Problem 1 with unlimeted cover size (see, e.g. [11]). The simplest form of this reduction is to consider a case where $\mathbf{D}$ has only one m-dimensional column full of 1s. Each $\mathbf{S}$ is also an m-dimensional column vector and they correspond to incidence vectors of the sets in Set Cover or Max k-Cover. It is trivial to see that solutions that maximize (1) or (2) maximize Max k-Cover or Set Cover, respectively.

In the Positive–Negative Partial Set Cover [18], the input consists of positive and negative elements and a collection of sets of those elements and the goal is to select a subcollection of the sets that minimizes the sum of covered negative elements plus the sum of uncovered positive elements. Consider again a case where **D** is m-dimensional vector. Each entry d_i of the input vector corresponds to an element in the input; $d_i = 1$ if the element is positive and $d_i = 0$ otherwise. The matrices **S** are again incidence vectors of the sets. It is straightforward to see that minimizing (3) is the same as minimizing the sum of uncovered 1s plus the sum of covered 0s.

Furthermore, these reductions are approximation-preserving as the values of cost functions (number of used matrices/sets or number of uncovered 1s plus covered 0s/uncovered positive and covered negative elements) are exactly the same after the reductions. Hence, Problem 1 with optimization goal (1) cannot be approximated better than $\Omega(1-1/e)$. With optimization goal (2) the approximation lower bound is $\Omega(\ln(m))$ [8]. For Problem 2, the approximation lower bound is much higher $\Omega(2^{\log^{1-\varepsilon} \ell^4})$, where ℓ is the number of sets in $\mathcal{S}$ [18]. The intuition behind the vast difference in inapproximability lower bounds is that in the case of exact patterns, we should aim to select maximally disjoint patterns, whereas in the case of inexact patterns, we should aim to select patterns that cover maximally disjoint set of 1s but maximally similar set of 0s, as we only "pay" the cost of covering a 0 once. This latter problem is clearly much harder.

2.3 Connections to Other Forms of Pattern Set Mining

While we described our problems in the terms of binary matrices, it is relatively easy to see that the description applies to many different pattern set mining tasks. Here we describe three such tasks: tiling databases, Boolean matrix factorization, and redescription mining.

Tiling databases [11] is the task of selecting a subset of (frequent or closed) itemsets to cover all the items in a transaction database. In our setting, the transaction database is the data matrix **D** with items as columns and transactions as rows, and each rank-1 matrix is one itemset: the columns with 1s correspond to the items in the itemset and the rows with 1s correspond to the transactions that contain the itemset. As every item of the itemset must appear in a transaction for the transaction to contain the itemset, the patterns are dominated and we have the exact patterns of Problem 1.

Equation (1) is a natural optimization goal for tiling. Equation (2) requires that every item in every transaction is included in some pattern; this is achieved most easily by including the singleton itemsets for each item in the set $\mathcal{S}$. Such exact cover is also required when one uses alternative means of selecting the pattern set, such as MDL [26] (see also Sect. 5).

Boolean matrix factorization [19] is the task of (approximately) expressing a given binary matrix as a Boolean product of two binary factor matrices. Equivalently, it is the task of expressing the input as a element-wise Boolean *or* of rank-1 binary matrices. With this definition, the connection to our problem is clear. As Boolean factorization can be approximated both by not covering some 1s and by

$$q_L = ([a \leq 0.4] \wedge [b \geq 0.6]) \vee [d = 1.0] \qquad q_R = [x = 1] \vee [y = 1]$$

$$\mathbf{D}_L = \begin{array}{c} \\ 1 \\ 2 \\ 3 \\ 4 \end{array}\begin{array}{c} a\ b\ c\ d \\ \left(\begin{array}{cccc} 0.3 & 0.7 & 0.2 & 0.9 \\ 0.5 & 0.4 & 0.6 & 0.8 \\ 0.4 & 0.6 & 0.3 & 0.9 \\ 0.3 & 0.5 & 0.3 & 1.0 \end{array}\right) \end{array} \qquad \mathbf{D}_R = \begin{array}{c} \\ 1 \\ 2 \\ 3 \\ 4 \end{array}\begin{array}{c} x\ y \\ \left(\begin{array}{cc} 1 & 1 \\ 1 & 0 \\ 0 & 0 \\ 0 & 1 \end{array}\right)\end{array} \qquad \mathbf{S} = \begin{array}{c} \\ 1 \\ 2 \\ 3 \\ 4 \end{array}\begin{array}{c} a\ b\ c\ d\ x\ y \\ \left(\begin{array}{cccccc} 1 & 1 & 0 & 1 & 1 & 1 \\ 0 & 0 & 0 & 0 & 0 & 0 \\ 0 & 0 & 0 & 0 & 0 & 0 \\ 1 & 1 & 0 & 1 & 1 & 1 \end{array}\right)\end{array}$$

Fig. 1. Example of how redescriptions can be expressed in the framework of Problem 1. **Top:** A pair of queries, forming a redescripition. **Bottom left and middle:** Original data matrices $\mathbf{D}_L$ and $\mathbf{D}_R$ for redescription mining. Cells shaded in gray will be 1 in $\mathbf{u}_L\mathbf{v}_L^T$ and $\mathbf{u}_R\mathbf{v}_R^T$. **Bottom right:** The final matrix $\mathbf{S} = (\mathbf{u}_L \wedge \mathbf{u}_R)[\mathbf{v}_L^T, \mathbf{v}_R^T]$.

covering some 0s, the appropriate formulation is typically that of Problem 2. For computing the smallest exact Boolean factorization (so-called *Boolean rank* [21]), however, Problem 1 with optimization goal (2) is the appropriate formulation.

Redescription mining [10,22] is a data analysis method that, unlike the aforementioned ones, can, and often does, use numerical data. The goal of redescription mining is to mine *redescriptions*, that is, pairs of queries (q_L, q_R) over two sets of data, $\mathbf{D}_L$ and $\mathbf{D}_R$, that provide two different views to the same entities. A classical example of redescription mining is species presence–absence data and climate data. These provide different "views" to the same geographical locations and a good redescription on such data would describe a query (or a rule) over the species (i.e. the presence or absence of certain species) and a query over the climate variables (e.g. temperature or precipitation) such that the two queries hold in approximately same geographic areas. The quality of a redescription is often measured using the Jaccard coefficient between the sets of entities where the individual queries hold.

While the data in redescription mining can be numerical, every individual query can be seen as a rank-1 binary matrix. The 1s in the columns correspond to the attributes that appear in the query; the 1s in the rows correspond to the entities where the query holds. For a pair of queries, we can concatenate these two matrices next to each other (note that they must have the same number of rows) and consider only those rows where both matrices have a 1. That is, if $\mathbf{u}_L\mathbf{v}_L^T$ is the rank-1 matrix corresponding to q_L and $\mathbf{u}_R\mathbf{v}_R^T$ is that for q_R, the rank-1 matrix corresponding to pair (q_L, q_R) is $(\mathbf{u}_L \wedge \mathbf{u}_R)[\mathbf{v}_L^T, \mathbf{v}_R^T]$, where $\wedge$ is the element-wise *and* and the right-hand vectors are concatenated. Figure 1 shows an example of one pair of queries over numerical and Boolean data and the resulting pattern matrix $\mathbf{S}$.

2.4 The Greedy Algorithm

By far the most common algorithm to do the pattern set selection for minimum error case is the greedy algorithm. This algorithm takes first the pattern that minimizes the error the most, then the pattern from the remaining ones that minimizes the error the most given the already selected pattern, and so on and so forth until it has either selected a predefined number of patterns or no further pattern reduces the error. This approach is used in tiling [11], in BMF [19], and in redescription mining[1] [10] for selecting a set of patterns. For the exact case, the greedy algorithm has approximation ratio of $O(1-1/e)$ (for (1)) or $O(\ln(m))$ (for (2)), matching the lower bounds. For inexact patterns, however, the greedy algorithm can be arbitrarily bad, although it seems to work well in practice [19].

The time complexity of the greedy algorithm is $\tilde{O}(mn\ell^2)$ for data matrix of size m-by-n and $|\mathcal{S}| = \ell$: after selecting every new pattern, the algorithm must re-compute how good the remaining patterns are. We use $\tilde{O}(\cdot)$ to denote the time complexity that ignores the logarithmic factors (that are needed to find the best pattern after the updates). For sparse patterns, tighter analysis can be obtained, as updating each pattern takes at most as much time as the number of 1s in the pattern.

3 The Algorithm

Our algorithm, called HaPSi (Hashing for Pattern Selection), is based on using hash values to estimate the sizes of rank-1 matrices and their combinations. The main idea, presented in [1,23], is to calculate hash values uniformly distributed in $[0, 1]$ for all 1s in a rank-1 matrix, and to use the kth smallest hash value v to estimate the number of 1s in the rank-1 matrix as k/v. This can be used as an estimate, because, if there are z values uniformly distributed in $[0, 1]$, the expected value of the kth smallest value is $k/(z+1)$. This method is used by [23] to estimate the product of two Boolean matrices, by iterating efficiently over the rank-1 matrices and keeping track of the k smallest hash values seen at each point.[2] Next we will explain a technique for estimating sizes of overlapping tiles before explaining the algorithm in Sect. 3.2. We analyse the time complexity in Sect. 3.3.

3.1 Estimating Overlapping Tile Size

This section describes a hashing-based technique of estimating the number of 1s in a single tile and in a collection of overlapping tiles. It is based on [23], although with some changes to make the approach suitable for our application.

The hash value $h(x, y)$ for a point (x, y) in a rank-1 matrix is computed based on two pairwise independent hash functions $h_1, h_2 \colon U \to [0, 1]$ which map the row and column indices to $[0, 1]$. The hash value for the point is then defined as $h(x, y) = (h_1(x) - h_2(y)) \mod 1$.

To find the k smallest hash values of a rank-1 matrix $\mathbf{u}\mathbf{v}^T$, $h(x, y)$ are arranged into a matrix of size $|\mathbf{u}|$-by-$|\mathbf{v}|$. The rows are ordered by increasing values of h_1 and the columns by increasing values of h_2. Going down a column the values of $h(x, y)$ will increase, except at one point where the value drops to

---

[1] In redescription mining the approaches in literature have some technical differences to the approach outlined above.
[2] Notice that this k is different to the number of selected tiles in problem definitions.

the minimum value of that column. Similarly on the rows, the values decrease going to the right, except for one increase to the maximum value of that row.

The algorithm is given a value p which serves as an initial maximum hash value to be stored. The values of the hash matrix are visited starting from the top of the left-most column, first finding the smallest value of the column. After that, going through the column, all values that are smaller than p are stored. After all such values have been found, the next column is searched, this time starting one row below the row where the previous column had its smallest value. When k values have been found, if the kth value is smaller than p, p is updated to this new smallest value.

The idea of using the kth smallest hash value as a size estimate can be applied to a matrix of any rank, but the efficiency of this algorithm comes from iterating over the row and column indices which only works on rank-1 matrices. Hence, if we want to use non-rank-1 patterns, we have to give up on this optimization.

3.2 The Algorithm for the Exact Patterns

The first step of our algorithm is to compute the hash values for each tile. This is done as explained above. For pairwise independent hash functions, we use random affine transformations in $\mathbb{Z}/p$, where $p \in \mathbb{N}$ is a prime number larger than largest dimension of the matrix. That is, each hash function is of form $h(x) = (ax + b \mod p)/p$ for some random a and b. Unlike [23], we store the k smallest hash values separately for each tile instead of maintaining a single collection of size k over all tiles.

The pseudocode for HaPSi is given in Algorithm 1. The algorithm starts by choosing the largest tile. Then, it goes through rest of the tiles, trying to find the one that increases the number of ones covered the most. For each tile that has not been chosen yet, we concatenate its hash values and those of the already-chosen tiles' in line 9. The combined hash values are sorted and we use the kth smallest value to get the estimated size of these tiles together. In our preliminary experiments we noticed that this method gives generally very accurate estimates, but sometimes gives an exceptionally large or small result. This is why we get the final size estimate as the median over several ($|\mathcal{H}|$, typically 10 in our experiments) estimates (line 12).

When we have the estimated sizes for all tiles, we sort the tiles in a descending order according to the estimate. Then, in line 16, we go through a limited number m (typically 30) of top candidates, and calculate the actual reconstruction error (or the number of 1s in the resulting matrix in the exact case) we would get when adding that tile to the already chosen ones. Once we find a tile that lowers the reconstruction error, we stop the search and add that tile to the collection. The process is repeated until the error no longer improves, or the maximum number of tiles is met (constraint set by the user).

Handling Inexact Tiles. In the case where the tiles can cover zeros, the first tile chosen is the one with the smallest reconstruction error, meaning it has the least amount of uncovered ones and the least amount of covered zeros. In addition

Algorithm 1. Exact Patterns (Problem 1)

Input: Data matrix $\mathbf{D}$, tiles $\mathcal{T}$, collection of vectors of hashvalues for each tile $\mathcal{H}$, maximum number of tiles returned $t_{\max}$, k for bottom-k hashing, and maximum number of tiles searched in each iteration m
Output: A set of tiles $\mathcal{Q}$

```
 1: function HaPSi(T, H, t)
 2:     Q ← tile t₀ with the smallest reconstruction error
 3:     T ← T \ t₀
 4:     while len(Q) < t_max do
 5:         C ← ∅
 6:         for t ∈ T do
 7:             E ← ∅
 8:             for h ∈ H[t] do
 9:                 h ← Sort(H[Q] ∪ h)[: k]
10:                 E ← E ∪ {k/h[k]}
11:             end for
12:             v ← median(E)
13:             C ← C ∪ {(v, t)}
14:         end for
15:         C ← Sort(C) in descending order by v
16:         for (v, c) ∈ C[: m] do
17:             if error(Q ∪ {c}) < error(Q) then
18:                 Q ← Q ∪ {c}
19:                 break
20:             else
21:                 return Q
22:             end if
23:         end for
24:     end while
25:     return Q
26: end function
```

to estimating the combined size with the already chosen tiles, we subtract the number of zeros covered by the tile from the joined size estimate. This means that the line 12 changes to $\text{median}(\mathcal{E}) - \mathcal{Z}_t$, where $\mathcal{Z}_t$ is the number of zeros the tile t covers.

We note that by subtracting every 0 from every tile that covers it, we are probably over-penalizing the tiles; if an already-chosen tile covers some of the same 0s as this tile, using this tile does not increase the cost for those 0s. While this approach might seem naïve, the inapproximability of the inexact case indicates that much better algorithms are unlikely to exist.

3.3 Time Complexity

For an input matrix of size m-by-n and number of tiles ℓ, the time complexity of HaPSi is $\tilde{O}((n+m)\ell + \ell^2 + mn\ell)$. Computing the hash values for one tile $\mathbf{uv}^T$ takes amortized time $O(|\mathbf{u}| + |\mathbf{v}|)$ [23], where $|\mathbf{u}|$ is the number of non-zeros in $\mathbf{u}$.

This explains the first term. After each tile has been chosen, we need update how well the others do given the chose tile (the second term), and to choose the tile, we need to compute its exact error (the final term). We could omit calculating the actual error, but we would then be susceptible to cascading errors in size estimates.

4 Experiments

We evaluate the performance of our algorithm on both synthetic and real-world data. The aim of the synthetic data experiments is to assess how different data features affect the algorithm; experiments with real-word data then validate these results.

4.1 Experimental Setup

We generate the synthetic data as follows. First, we make 100 random rank-1 matrices (aka tiles or patterns) of size m-by-n by sampling vectors $\mathbf{u}_i \in \{0,1\}^m$ and $\mathbf{v}_i \in \{0,1\}^n$ from m- and n-dimensional Bernoulli distributions with parameter $p \in (0,1)$. Each "original" tile is $\mathbf{u}_i\mathbf{v}_i^T$. We make 5 copies of each of these tiles, and for each copy $\mathbf{u}_i'\mathbf{v}_i'^T$, we move a fraction d of the 1s from $\mathbf{u}_i'$ and $\mathbf{v}_i'$ to other locations. This gives us 100 mostly non-overlapping rank-1 matrices, each of which have 5 copies that have a given amount overlap with the original and each other.

Then, we have two ways of creating a data matrix out of these 600 patterns, either by multiplying the original 100 patterns, or by multiplying all 600. After this we can add noise to the data matrix by randomly flipping a portion of the elements.

For the exact pattern experiments we only created the data matrix by multiplying all 600 tiles and did not add any noise, to ensure that the tiles are dominated by the data. For the inexact pattern experiments, we used both methods of creating the data matrix and also added noise.

There are four features we test with the synthetic matrices: overlap between the tiles, density of the data matrix and the tiles, size of the matrix, and the added noise. We tested all of these with the inexact patterns, and the first two (overlap and density) also with the exact patterns.

We created the data 5 times for each set of parameters tested, and the results are the average over these five runs. As our own algorithm has some randomness in creating the hash values, we initially tested it with three restarts on the same data. However, since the algorithm uses the median estimate over multiple hash values on a single run, running it more times did not have much variance in the results.

We compared HaPSi to two baselines. Greedy is the standard greedy algorithm for Set Cover (see Sect. 2.4). Naïve is a simpler and faster algorithm that always selects the tile from the unselected tiles that alone covers the most 1s (or reduces the error most, in inexact case), irrespective of what has been selected before. These two algorithms represent two extremes. Greedy, while not being optimal, is the state of the art solution for minimizing the error, while Naïve is about as fast as it can get: it's time complexity is $\tilde{O}(nm\ell)$, that is, it only requires one linear scan over the input data.

For all experiments, we report *relative reconstruction error*, that is, reconstruction error divided by the matrix size. The algorithms were implemented on Python and are freely available.[3] The experiments were conducted on a machine with 2 AMD EPYC 7702 processors with 64 cores each. All experiments were run single-threaded.

4.2 Setting the Hyperparameters for HaPSi

We evaluated the effect of the hyperparameters of HaPSi on the reconstruction error and the running time. The following hyperparameters were tested: number of hash values used in bottom-k hashing, k; number of times the hashing is repeated for the data, $|\mathcal{H}|$; and the maximum number of tiles for which the reconstruction error is computed before stopping, m. The other parameter for Algorithm 1 is the maximum number of tiles returned, $t_{\max}$, but it was not tested here since it only affects the final error and running time.

The default values used for the experiments were $m = 30$, $k = 30$, $|\mathcal{H}| = 10$. The tests were ran on a synthetic data of size 1000-by-1200 with data density 0.06; fraction of rows and columns changed in copied tiles by 0.1 and noise added to the data matrix was 10 %. Each hyperparameter was varied separately, while keeping others constant.

The results of the tests are shown in Fig. 2. The results show that two of the parameters had a noticeable effect on the reconstruction error: $|\mathcal{H}|$, the number of times the hashing was repeated, and the k for the bottom-k hashing method (Fig. 2(a) and (c)). Naturally as the hash values are computed several times, the final estimate (calculated as the median over all of the estimates) will be more accurate. A larger value here also significantly affects the running time. The choice of optimal value of k is explained in detail in [23], and our results show that a larger value improves the error at least to some point. However, we chose not to use a large value of k in our experiments, as in real-world applications the rank-1 matrices can have varying densities; in particular, rank-1 matrices with less than k 1s would be automatically discarded. Another approach for choosing the value of k would be to choose it after all of the rank-1 matrices have had their hash values calculated, and their sizes are known, but testing this is left for future work.

4.3 Results on Synthetic Data

In each test, all other data generation parameters except the one being tested for were kept constant. The default values used in the data generation were as follows. Data size: 1000-by-1200; data density: 0.3; fraction of rows and columns

---
[3] https://doi.org/10.5281/zenodo.15629578.

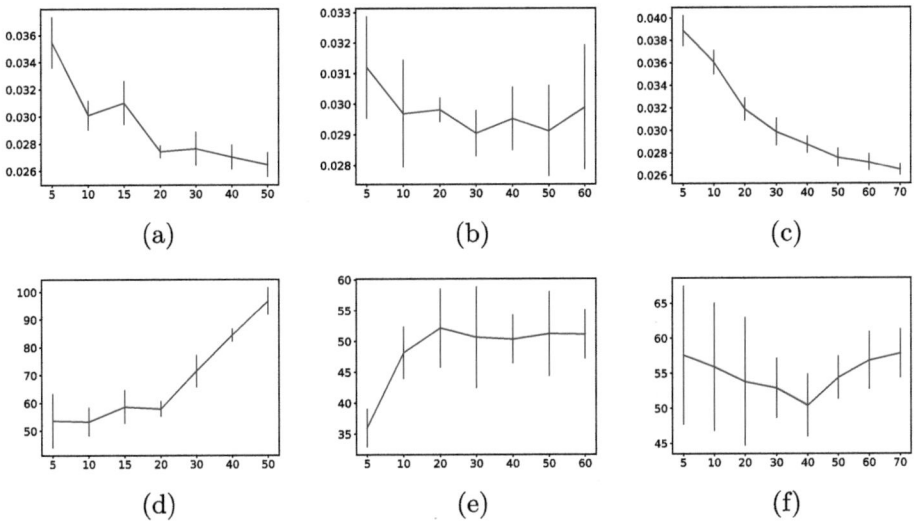

Fig. 2. Reconstruction errors and running times from the hyperparameter tests. **Top row:** x-axis: (a) $|\mathcal{H}|$, number of times the hashing is repeated; (b) m, maximum number of tiles for which the reconstruction error is computed; (c) k, number of hash values. Relative reconstruction error on y-axis. **Bottom row:** Running time in seconds on y-axis. (d)–(f) as (a)–(c).

changed in copied tiles: 0.1; noise added to the data matrix: 10 %. Each algorithm searched for a maximum of 200 tiles unless otherwise specified.

Overlap Between the Tiles. We created the data as explained above. In the step where the 100 tiles are copied, we vary the fraction of rows and columns that are changed. The fractions we used were 0.05, 0.1, 0.25, and 0.5.

Reconstruction errors for these experiments are shown in Fig. 3(a)–(c). There the overlap *decreases* as y-axis increases. Naïve can include tiles that increase the error. With 100 tiles, we also show the best result it obtained. This is depicted as a dashed line in Fig. 3(a).

With 600 tiles, the results show that the error increases as the overlap reduces. This is most likely due to the fact that there are more 1s to be covered as each tile is more disjoint. In case of 100 tiles, situation is different. Now, there are basically 100 "correct" tiles and 500 "incorrect" tiles to select, with increasing non-overlap making the incorrectness worse. Here we see that Greedy always selects the correct tiles. HaPSi selects good tiles initially, but starts deteriorating as the tiles get more disjoint. Naïve is always the worst eventually, but its best result is actually better than HaPSi with least overlap.

Data Density. We considered data with density 0.06, 0.1, 0.15, 0.2, 0.25, 0.3, and 0.4. The tile density was adjusted depending whether 100 or 600 tiles were used, so that the data matrix has the desired density. The results are depicted

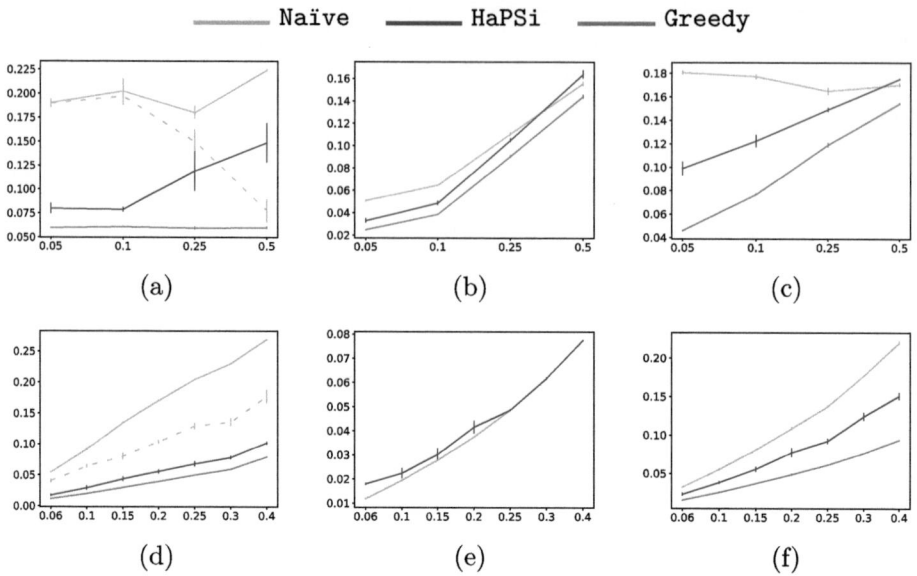

Fig. 3. Relative reconstruction error on y-axis. **Top row:** The amount d of changed 1s on x-axis. (a) Inexact case with 100 tiles. (b) Inexact case with 600 tiles. (c) Exact case with 600 tiles. In (a), the dashed line indicates the best error Naïve obtained. **Bottom row:** Data density on x-axis. (d)–(f) as (a)–(c).

in Fig. 3(d)–(f). All algorithms perform worse as density increases with HaPSi being close to Greedy in all cases and Naïve being clearly worse in Fig. 3(d) and (f), even when considering its best result in (d).

Added Noise. We added 5 %, 10 %, 20 %, and 30 % noise to the data matrix. Results are shown in Fig. 4(a)–(b). Again, as noise increases all methods get worse, and the order is clear: Naïve (worst), HaPSi, and Greedy, with HaPSi being relatively close to Greedy.

Data Size. Finally we tested data size by generating matrices of size x-by-$(x + 200)$ for x values of 1000, 2000, 3000, and 4000. The reconstruction errors are depicted in Fig. 4(d)–(e), showing that HaPSi performs very similarly to Greedy in terms of reconstruction error.

Running Time. Running times of the algorithms with respect to number of tiles and size of the data are shown in Fig. 4(c) and (f), respectively. These plots show clearly that Greedy is significantly slower that HaPSi, which in turn is very close to Naïve, showing that HaPSi reaches a good balance between result quality and running time.

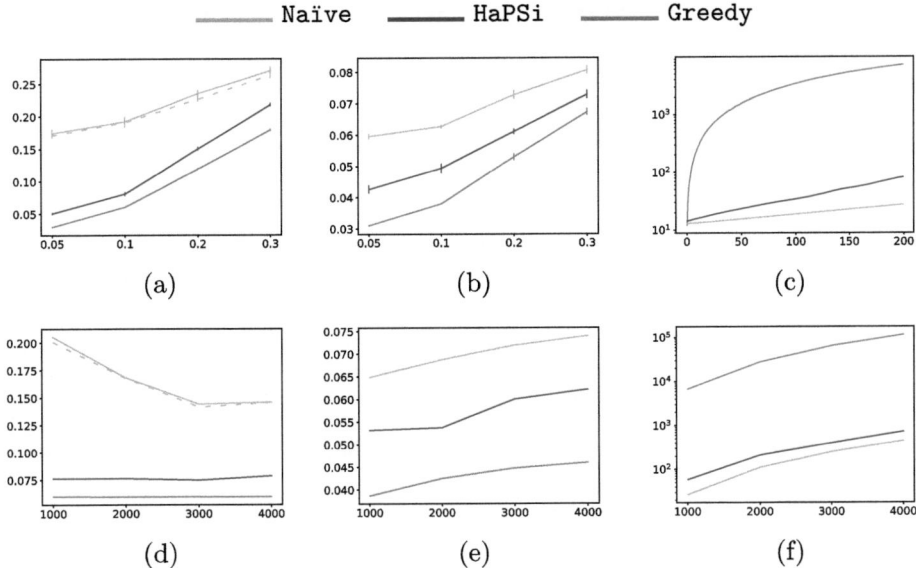

Fig. 4. Top row, (a)–(b): The amount of noise on x-axis, relative reconstruction error on y-axis. (a) Inexact, 100 tiles. (b) Inexact, 600 tiles. In (a), the dashed line indicates the best error Naïve obtained. **Top row, (c):** Running time (seconds, logarithmic scale) as number of selected patterns increases. **Bottom row, (d)–(e):** Number of rows in data on x-axis, relative reconstruction error on y-axis. (d)–(e) as (a)–(b). **Bottom row, (f):** Running time (seconds, logarithmic scale) as matrix size increases.

4.4 Results on Real-World Data

Data Sets. We used four real-world data sets in our experiments. Some statistics about them are presented in Table 1. The Mammals dataset contains information about which mammal species inhabit which areas of the world on one side, and climate information on the other side [12]. The Dialect data contains features of spoken dialects of Finnish over different geographical regions [6,7]. The 20Newsgroups data[4] is a corpus of 1000 posts from 20 different newsgroups, stemmed and with rare terms removed. The Abstracts data[5] is another corpus, this time of project abstracts. Terms are stemmed and rare ones are removed.

Redescription Mining. We used redescriptions mined using the fast redescription mining algorithm Fier [14]. These results contained 161 redescriptions, some of them very similar to each other. The results are shown in Fig. 5(a) and (d). The results show that HaPSi is able to find very fast a good set of approximately 50 redescriptions. It should be noted that this data can be fully covered using all

---

[4] https://archive.ics.uci.edu/dataset/113/twenty+newsgroups.
[5] https://archive.ics.uci.edu/dataset/134/nsf+research+award+abstracts+1990+2003.

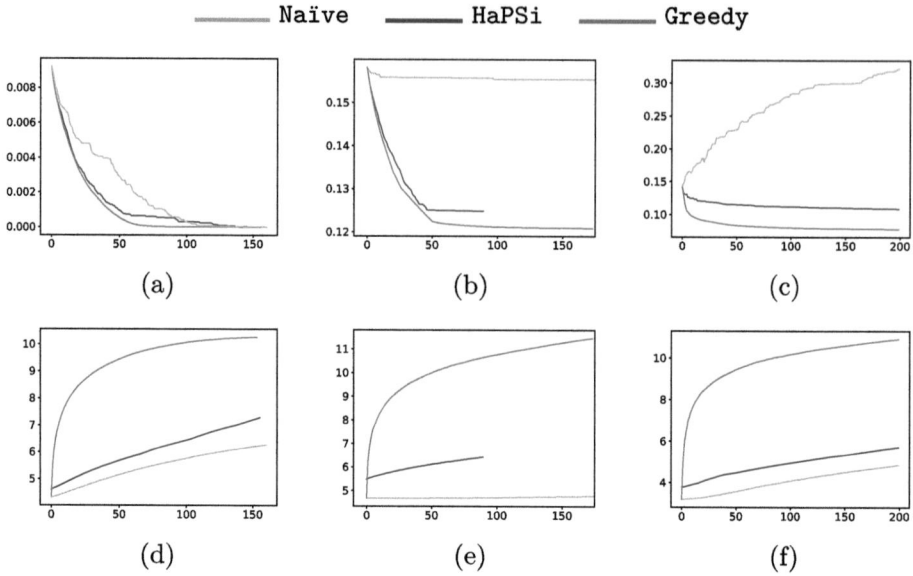

Fig. 5. Top row: Relative reconstruction error on the y-axis and number of tiles on the x-axis. (a) Tiles are redescriptions from the Mammals data. (b) Tiles are frequent itemsets from the Dialect data. (c) Tiles are rank-1 Boolean matrices for BMF from the Dialect data. **Bottom row:** Time (in seconds) on y-axis and number of tiles on x axis. (d)–(f) as (a)–(c).

Table 1. Properties of real-world data sets

Data	Rows	Columns	Density (%)	Note
Mammals	54013	4802	—	Numerical data
Dialect	1334	506	16.14	
20Newsgroups	5163	19997	0.89	
Abstracts	4894	12841	0.90	

161 tiles, so all methods converge towards the end. Notice also that Greedy is very slow.

Tiling Databases. We mine frequent itemsets from the Dialect dataset with minimum frequency of 15 %. This gave us 28 535 frequent itemsets. We used all of these as tiles, and searched for a set of maximum 1000 tiles. The results are in Fig. 5(b) and (e). We see that HaPSi is again very good up to about 50 itemsets, after which it has converged. It is again significantly faster than Greedy and significantly better than Naïve.

Boolean Matrix Factorization. We created the rank-1 Boolean matrices using the association matrix technique used by the Asso algorithm and the restarted random walks technique [19]. These rank-1 matrices can cover 0s in the data, unlike in the previous cases. The results using the Dialect data are shown in Fig. 5(c) and (f). The results are similar to the other real-world use cases, except that in this case the Naïve algorithm increases its error consistently. But again HaPSi is competitive with Greedy, especially when we consider the significant advance it has on running time.

We also ran experiments with tiles found only by the association matrix technique using the two large corpus matrices. This created approximately 5000 tiles for 20Newsgroups and 12000 for Abstracts. HaPSi took 850 s for Abstracts, while Greedy took 101 h. For 20Newsgroups HaPSi took 665 s and Greedy 74 h. This shows that HaPSi can find results efficiently with input sizes where Greedy is unable to produce the results in a reasonable amount of time.

5 Related Work

Tiling databases was first studied in [11], where also the use of the greedy algorithm was proposed. The problem was later independently studied in [27]. The tiling was later extended to hierarchical representations (where tiles contain other tiles) [24], data streams [15], and ranked data [16], among others.

Boolean matrix factorization (BMF) can be seen as a variant of tiling. It has been originally studied in combinatorics (see [21] and references therein), but it has also seen significant research interest in data mining (see [19] and references therein). An exact Boolean matrix factorization is the same as exact tiling, and [2] propose an algorithm for exact BMF based on greedy Set Cover algorithm.

The aforementioned methods use reconstruction error as the primary means of deciding which tiles or rank-1 matrices to use. Minimum Description Length (MDL) principle is another popular method for selecting the pattern set (see, e.g. [17,20,26]). In MDL, the idea is to select those tiles that compress the data the best.

Another method for selecting the set of patterns was proposed by De Bie [5]. His proposal is based on modelling the data with a maximum-entropy distribution, and selecting the tiles that are the most surprising (i.e. least likely) under this distribution. After each selected tile, the distribution is updated by constraining it with the selected tile such that the new distribution has the maximum entropy over all those distributions where the found tiles appear. Later, [13] extended that approach to selecting a set of redescriptions.

Redescription mining [10] was proposed in [22] and has seen various algorithms and applications proposed since (see [10]). The first redescription set mining approach was proposed in [9] and later [13] proposed a version based on subjective interestingness.

The idea of using bottom-k hashing for size estimation was first proposed in [1], while [23] extended it to the size of Boolean matrix product and explained the efficient algorithm we use as the basis of HaPSi.

6 Conclusions

Bottom-k hashing can provide significant speedups for selecting a good set of patterns with minimal effects on the quality of patterns selected. We showed how our algorithm can be applied to tiling, Boolean matrix factorization, and redescription set mining, but we believe that there are other pattern set mining problems where our approach can be useful, as well.

The hashing techniques presented in this paper are limited to reconstruction error. Algorithms like `HaPSi` are not directly good for selecting itemsets based on measures like MDL, as they pay no attention to the "cost" of the selected patterns. Indeed, we can see in Fig. 5 that `HaPSi` sometimes selects patterns that improve the error very little if at all; such patterns are very unsuitable for optimizing MDL, say. In principle, the description length could be taken into account when selecting the patterns, but it is not clear if the bottom-k hashing would ever find patterns that are good in MDL-sense. Developing these algorithms is an interesting topic for a future work.

Being able to select the pattern set faster can also facilitate novel algorithms that build sets of pattern sets. Such algorithms can provide a hierarchical view to the data, supporting exploration with few high-level pattern-sets-as-patterns, each of which can be "zoomed in" to see the actual patterns.

Our method does not allow novel unethical uses of data mining techniques although the vast speed improvements do allow existing potentially unethical uses to be scaled to much larger data sets.

Disclosure of Interests. The authors have no competing interests to declare that are relevant to the content of this article.

References

1. Bar-Yossef, Z., Jayram, T.S., Kumar, R., Sivakumar, D., Trevisan, L.: Counting distinct elements in a data stream. In: Rolim, J.D.P., Vadhan, S. (eds.) RANDOM 2002. LNCS, vol. 2483, pp. 1–10. Springer, Heidelberg (2002). https://doi.org/10.1007/3-540-45726-7_1
2. Bělohlávek, R., Vychodil, V.: Discovery of optimal factors in binary data via a novel method of matrix decomposition. J. Comput. Syst. Sci. **76**(1), 3–20 (2010). https://doi.org/10.1016/j.jcss.2009.05.002
3. Cohen, E.: Size-estimation framework with applications to transitive closure and reachability. J. Comput. Syst. Sci. **55**(3), 441–453 (1997). https://doi.org/10.1006/jcss.1997.1534, https://www.sciencedirect.com/science/article/pii/S0022000097915348
4. Cohen, E., Kaplan, H.: Summarizing data using bottom-k sketches. In: Proceedings of the Twenty-Sixth Annual ACM Symposium on Principles of Distributed Computing, pp. 225–234. PODC 2007, Association for Computing Machinery, New York, NY, USA (2007). https://doi.org/10.1145/1281100.1281133
5. De Bie, T.: Maximum entropy models and subjective interestingness: an application to tiles in binary databases. Data Min. Knowl. Disc. **23**(3), 407–446 (2011). https://doi.org/10.1007/s10618-010-0209-3

6. Embleton, S.M., Wheeler, E.S.: Finnish dialect atlas for quantitative studies. J. Quant. Linguist. **4**(1–3), 99–102 (1997). https://doi.org/10.1080/09296179708590082
7. Embleton, S.M., Wheeler, E.S.: Computerized dialect atlas of Finnish: dealing with ambiguity. J. Quant. Linguist. **7**(3), 227–231 (2000). https://doi.org/10.1076/jqul.7.3.227.4109
8. Feige, U.: A threshold of $\ln n$ for approximating set cover. J. ACM **45**(4), 634–652 (1998). https://doi.org/10.1145/285055.285059
9. Galbrun, E., Miettinen, P.: Mining redescriptions with siren. ACM Trans. Knowl. Discov. Data **12**(1), 1–30 (2018). https://doi.org/10.1145/3007212
10. Galbrun, E., Miettinen, P.: Redescription Mining. Springer, Cham (2018). https://doi.org/10.1007/978-3-319-72889-6
11. Geerts, F., Goethals, B., Mielikäinen, T.: Tiling databases. In: Suzuki, E., Arikawa, S. (eds.) DS 2004. LNCS (LNAI), vol. 3245, pp. 278–289. Springer, Heidelberg (2004). https://doi.org/10.1007/978-3-540-30214-8_22
12. Hijmans, R.J., Cameron, S.E., Parra, J.L., Jones, P.G., Jarvis, A.: Very high resolution interpolated climate surfaces for global land areas. Int. J. Climatol. **25**(15), 1965–1978 (2005). https://doi.org/10.1002/joc.1276
13. Kalofolias, J., Galbrun, E., Miettinen, P.: From sets of good redescriptions to good sets of redescriptions. Knowl. Inf. Syst. **57**(1), 21–54 (2018). https://doi.org/10.1007/s10115-017-1149-7
14. Karjalainen, M., Galbrun, E., Miettinen, P.: Fast redescription mining using locality-sensitive hashing. In: Proceedings of the European Conference on Machine Learning and Knowledge Discovery in Databases (ECML PKDD), pp. 124–142. Springer, Cham (2024). https://doi.org/10.1007/978-3-031-70368-3_8
15. Lam, H.T., Pei, W., Prado, A., Jeudy, B., Fromont, É.: Mining top-k largest tiles in a data stream. In: Calders, T., Esposito, F., Hüllermeier, E., Meo, R. (eds.) ECML PKDD 2014. LNCS (LNAI), vol. 8725, pp. 82–97. Springer, Heidelberg (2014). https://doi.org/10.1007/978-3-662-44851-9_6
16. Le Van, T., van Leeuwen, M., Nijssen, S., Fierro, A.C., Marchal, K., De Raedt, L.: Ranked tiling. In: Calders, T., Esposito, F., Hüllermeier, E., Meo, R. (eds.) ECML PKDD 2014. LNCS (LNAI), vol. 8725, pp. 98–113. Springer, Heidelberg (2014). https://doi.org/10.1007/978-3-662-44851-9_7
17. Mampaey, M., Tatti, N., Vreeken, J.: Tell me what i need to know: succinctly summarizing data with itemsets. In: Proceedings 20th ACM SIGKDD International Conference on Knowledge Discovery and Data Mining (KDD), pp. 573–581 (2011). https://doi.org/10.1145/2020408.2020499
18. Miettinen, P.: On the positive-negative partial set cover problem. Inf. Process. Lett. **108**(4), 219–221 (2008). https://doi.org/10.1016/j.ipl.2008.05.007
19. Miettinen, P., Neumann, S.: Recent developments in Boolean matrix factorization. In: Proceedings of the 29th International Joint Conference on Artificial Intelligence (IJCAI), pp. 4922–4928 (2020). https://doi.org/10.24963/ijcai.2020/685
20. Miettinen, P., Vreeken, J.: MDL4BMF: minimum description length for boolean matrix factorization. ACM Trans. Knowl. Discov. Data **8**(4) (2014). https://doi.org/10.1145/2601437
21. Monson, S.D., Pullman, N.J., Rees, R.: A survey of clique and biclique coverings and factorizations of (0,1)-matrices. Bull. ICA **14**, 17–86 (1995)
22. Ramakrishnan, N., Kumar, D., Mishra, B., Potts, M., Helm, R.F.: Turning CARTwheels: an alternating algorithm for mining redescriptions. In: Proceedings of the 10th ACM SIGKDD International Conference on Knowledge Discovery

and Data Mining (KDD), pp. 266–275 (2004). https://doi.org/10.1145/1014052.1014083
23. Amossen, R.R., Campagna, A., Pagh, R.: Better size estimation for sparse matrix products. Algorithmica **69**(3), 741–757 (2013). https://doi.org/10.1007/s00453-012-9692-9
24. Tatti, N., Vreeken, J.: Discovering descriptive tile trees. In: Flach, P.A., De Bie, T., Cristianini, N. (eds.) ECML PKDD 2012. LNCS (LNAI), vol. 7523, pp. 9–24. Springer, Heidelberg (2012). https://doi.org/10.1007/978-3-642-33460-3_6
25. Thorup, M.: Bottom-k and priority sampling, set similarity and subset sums with minimal independence. In: Proceedings of the forty-fifth annual ACM symposium on Theory of Computing (STOC), pp. 371–380 (2013). https://doi.org/10.1145/2488608.2488655
26. Vreeken, J., van Leeuwen, M., Siebes, A.: KRIMP: mining itemsets that compress. Data Min. Knowl. Disc. **23**(1), 169–214 (2011). https://doi.org/10.1007/s10618-010-0202-x
27. Xiang, Y., Jin, R., Fuhry, D., Dragan, F.F.: Summarizing transactional databases with overlapped hyperrectangles. Data Min. Knowl. Disc. **23**(2), 215–251 (2010). https://doi.org/10.1007/s10618-010-0203-9

Optimizing the Optimal Weighted Average: Efficient Distributed Sparse Classification

Fred Lu[1,2](✉), Ryan R. Curtin[1], Edward Raff[1,2], Francis Ferraro[2], and James Holt[3]

[1] Booz Allen Hamilton, McLean, VA, USA
{Fred_Lu,Curtin_Ryan}@bah.com
[2] University of Maryland, Baltimore, USA
[3] Laboratory for Physical Sciences, College Park, MD, USA

Abstract. While distributed training is often viewed as a solution to optimizing linear models on increasingly large datasets, inter-machine communication costs of popular distributed approaches can dominate as data dimensionality increases. Recent work on non-interactive algorithms shows that approximate solutions for linear models can be obtained efficiently with only a single round of communication among machines. However, this approximation often degenerates as the number of machines increases. In this paper, building on the recent optimal weighted average method, we introduce a new technique, *ACOWA*, that allows an extra round of communication to achieve noticeably better approximation quality with minor runtime increases. Results show that for sparse distributed logistic regression, ACOWA obtains solutions that are more faithful to the empirical risk minimizer and attain substantially higher accuracy than other distributed algorithms. We also introduce isoefficiency analysis to distributed logistic regression and show that ACOWA maintains favorable scaling with respect to data size and processor count relative to prior distributed algorithms.

1 Introduction

Statistical and machine learning research trends have had one important underlying trend for the past few decades: practitioners want to train models on larger and larger datasets [15,22]. Massive-scale datasets present significant computational issues, regardless of the complexity of the models being used. Even training linear models is a challenge when the datasets get large and high-dimensional. As an example, consider a logistic regression model, which may be penalized with either the L_1-regularizer for sparsity, the L_2-regularizer to prevent overfitting,

---

F. Lu and R. R. Curtin—These authors contributed equally to this work.

Supplementary Information The online version contains supplementary material available at https://doi.org/10.1007/978-3-032-06096-9_9.

© The Author(s), under exclusive license to Springer Nature Switzerland AG 2026
R. P. Ribeiro et al. (Eds.): ECML PKDD 2025, LNAI 16017, pp. 147–163, 2026.
https://doi.org/10.1007/978-3-032-06096-9_9

or both (the 'elastic net' [47]). Given a dataset $\mathcal{X}$ with n points in d dimensions, and labels $\mathcal{Y}$ with value -1 or 1, we want to find

$$\hat{w} := \arg\min_{w} \mathcal{L}_w(\mathcal{X}) + \lambda_1 \|w\|_1 + \lambda_2 \|w\|_2^2 \qquad (1)$$

where $\mathcal{L}_w(\mathcal{X})$ is the logistic regression objective:

$$\mathcal{L}_w(\mathcal{X}) := \sum_{(x_i, y_i) \in (\mathcal{X}, \mathcal{Y})} \ln(1 + e^{-y_i w^\top x_i}) \qquad (2)$$

Solving this problem on moderately-sized datasets is fast and easy [7], but on datasets with millions or more of samples or features (or both!), this is computationally challenging. Having observed this, we wish to accelerate the training of linear models on large-scale data. Here we will consider the logistic regression objective, but our approach can be easily adapted for more general models.

Importance of Sparse Linear Modeling. Despite flourishing attention towards complex machine learning models, generalized linear models have real-world impact in both applied and scientific settings to this day. They have attractive properties for downstream inference and are very effective in high-dimensional problems with limited samples [25,42]. Furthermore, research in linear models continues to improve our understanding of machine learning [20,40]. As we will show, our work offers practical and theoretical scalability contributions toward distributed linear modeling.

Sparse linear models have particular value because they encompass methods which simultaneously perform feature selection and model fitting [16], including the Lasso and other L_1-regularized linear models [10]. There are relatively few methods which can do both in a statistically principled manner. Even in more complex models such as neural networks, recent work on sparsity leverages fundamental principles from sparse linear models [23]. Sparse models have significant advantages for explainability and computational efficiency.

Early Singlethreaded Attempts. We are far from the first to consider accelerating the training of logistic regression models. For smaller datasets, the problem has been intensively studied [16]. There is extra difficulty when considering the L_1 penalty ($\lambda_1 > 0$), as this causes $L_w(\mathcal{X})$ to be non-differentiable and thus simple gradient descent techniques cannot be applied. Instead, algorithms such as FISTA and FASTA [12], based on proximal gradient descent, are often used. Proximal Newton techniques, using coordinate descent to solve the inner step, are highly popular, with the *GLMNET* [10] and *newGLMNET* [41] algorithms offering fast convergence. *newGLMNET* is specifically tuned for expensive objective functions such as logistic regression, and through the LIBLINEAR library [9] has become likely the most widely-used solver in practice.

Multithreaded Single-System Approaches. As the number of cores on processors has increased, interest in single-system parallelism has also. In this vein, LIBLINEAR-MP [45] is a modified multi-core newGLMNET implementation.

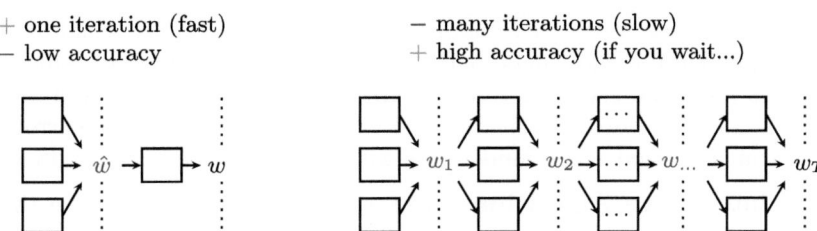

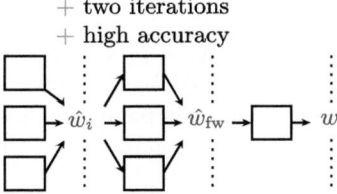

Fig. 1. Vertical dashed lines show synchronization points between threads and boxes indicate different compute nodes. Approaches for many-core and distributed training of models with an L_1 penalty are either one-shot (left), or iterative (right), neither of which produce satisfying solutions of high accuracy in a limited time frame. Our ACOWA strikes a careful balance of sharing information, such that a more accurate solution can be obtained with just two rounds of communication.

Hogwild [31] and the more recent SAUS [29] use lock-free parallelism to prevent conflicts during gradient updates.

Iterative Distributed Approaches. However, even with a multithreaded approach, very large datasets may be larger than the memory of a single system, and thus a distributed approach is required. The use of distributed algorithms to train logistic regression models has been studied extensively [13,26,44]. In typical approaches, the dataset $\mathcal{X}$ is partitioned across p nodes, and then the model is learned iteratively. The simplest approach is to partition by data points; this partitioning strategy has been paired with distributed Newton methods [35,44] and also ADMM [3]. Block coordinate descent methods which split over features have also been shown to work [32,38]. A large disadvantage of these techniques is that they involve significant communication overhead: at every iteration, the gradients from each machine must be sent back to the main node. These communication costs become very painful with increased problem dimensionality.

A number of approaches have been developed to reduce communication costs. The CoCoA [19,36] and ProxCoCoA+ [37] frameworks are two notable examples. ProxCoCoA+ uses the dual of the logistic regression objective function, partitioning the data by dimension instead of points. In each iteration, each worker solves a local quadratic approximation of the objective, communicating its solution back to the main node for aggregation. The DANE and CSL frameworks [35,39] first find single-partition solutions independently, which are averaged as an initial estimator. Global gradients are then collected and combined with local higher-order derivatives on each partition to solve a surrogate likelihood function that has bounded loss with respect to the true likelihood.

Non-interactive Algorithms. Still, even with efforts to reduce the amount of communication, the iterative nature of all the previous algorithms presents a problematic overhead when the number of iterations is large. Hence, there has recently been increased interest in *non-interactive* or *one-shot* algorithms [28,43], which use only a single round of communication. These methods tend to be extremely fast, but produce models with a larger amount of approximation. The recent *optimal weighted average* (OWA) approach is a compelling example of a non-interactive algorithm [18]. In the OWA approach, data is partitioned along samples; each worker trains a model independently on its data partition and returns its trained model weights to the main node; then, the final model is a learned linear combination of each partition's model.

Our Contribution: ACOWA. We have observed the compelling speedups of non-interactive algorithms, but found ourselves disappointed by the approximation quality—especially as the number of partitions p grows large, and as the dataset becomes sparse. Aiming to trade a small amount of speed for a much better approximation, we relax the one-shot requirement, and use two rounds of communication. Starting from OWA [18], we introduce ACOWA with a number of novel improvements:

1. We *augment each partition's data with summary information from other partitions*, reducing the variance of each partition's model.
2. We allow a *second round of weighted distributed learning*. This improves approximation quality by ensuring that ACOWA selects only features that have support across many partitions' models.
3. We introduce the study of *isoefficiency* (a measure of communication efficiency) to distributed logistic regression. We then show that ACOWA has isoefficiency comparable to the original OWA, and thus *retains its favorable scaling properties*.
4. Our experimental results demonstrate the *significant quality increases* that ACOWA yields, on a variety of datasets, with only a modest additional runtime cost. Our ablation studies show that all of our proposed improvements are mutually beneficial.

The differences between ACOWA and other approaches is shown in Fig. 1. A publicly-available implementation of our algorithm can be found online at https://github.com/FutureComputing4AI/Acowa.

2 Problems with OWA

Before describing OWA in detail, we first consider the simplest one-shot approach: *naive averaging*. In both approaches, the dataset $(\mathcal{X}, \mathcal{Y})$ is split into p

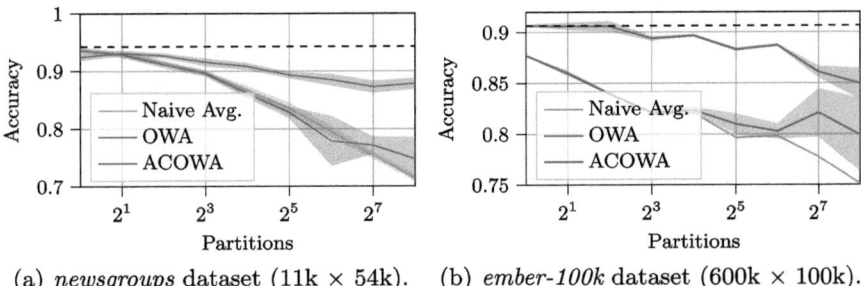

Fig. 2. Accuracy on held-out test sets for different numbers of partitions p, when sparsity is fixed. The quality of the naive averaging and OWA models degrade significantly as p increases. ACOWA improves accuracy across all levels of $p > 1$.

equal-sized partitions $(\mathcal{X}_i, \mathcal{Y}_i)$. For naive averaging, each worker i learns a model $\hat{w}_i$ independently on its partition, and then all models are collected on the main worker and averaged: $\hat{w}_{\mathrm{na}} := (1/p) \sum_{i \in [p]} \hat{w}_i$. Naive averaging is trivial to implement, only involves one round of communication, and gives reasonable approximate solutions to the true $\hat{w}$. While naive averaging has been shown to be asymptotically optimal for nearly unbiased linear models, in high-dimensional models higher-order loss terms cause increasing error [33]. Specifically, naive aggregates show greater error as the number of partitions p grows, likely due to increasing bias of the subsampled estimators.

OWA [18] works similarly to naive averaging, but has an improved merge step that results in an optimal rate of decay for approximation and generalization error of $\mathcal{O}(\sqrt{d/n})$. To reduce the bias of $\hat{w}_{\mathrm{na}}$, OWA instead learns a weighted linear combination of each $\hat{w}_i$: after each $\hat{w}_i$ is computed and returned to the main node, a small subsample $\mathcal{X}_C \subseteq \mathcal{X}$ and $\mathcal{Y}_C \subseteq \mathcal{Y}$ is computed. This sample can be as small as pn/d points, which in most settings is substantially smaller than n. Then, the optimal weighted average is defined as $\hat{w}_{\mathrm{owa}} := \hat{W}\hat{v}$, where $\hat{W} := [\hat{w}_1, \ldots, \hat{w}_p]$. For logistic regression, $\hat{v} \in \mathbb{R}^p$ is the linear combination of models found by solving the optimization

$$\min_{v} \sum_{(x_i, y_i) \in (\mathcal{X}_c, \mathcal{Y}_c)} \ln(1 + e^{-y_i (\hat{W}v)^\top x_i}) + \lambda_{\mathrm{cv}} \|v\|_2^2 \quad (3)$$

Here, the original penalty is replaced with an L_2 penalty for v. This term can be taken as a surrogate for the 'true' penalty term $\lambda_1 \|\hat{W}v\|_1 + \lambda_2 \|\hat{W}v\|_2^2$, and it is suggested that λ_{cv} be set by cross-validation. Because $\mathcal{X}_C$ and $\mathcal{Y}_C$ are small subsets, the cost of cross-validation is generally small as compared to the cost of training each $\hat{w}_i$. Adapting the OWA strategy to other statistical problems just involves reworking the original objective function to learn v instead of $\hat{W}v$.

While the OWA estimator $\hat{w}_{\mathrm{owa}}$ tends to improve over the naive average $\hat{w}_{\mathrm{na}}$, in practice the accuracy of the resulting model also degrades significantly when the number of partitions p becomes large. This may be due to the need for a subsample for the second optimization, which remains biased. In addition, the variance of the OWA estimator increases. Figure 2 shows a representative example.

3 First Improvement: Centroid Augmentation

The increasing variance of OWA as p increases is a result of degradation in each $\hat{w}_i$: the smaller $\mathcal{X}_i$ is, the more likely $\hat{w}_i$ is to be further from the true $\hat{w}$. We now leverage theory on *coresets*: subsamples of data with bounded loss approximation error to the original dataset [27].

As a first line of reasoning, view $\mathcal{X}_i$ as a uniform subsample of $\mathcal{X}$: as $|\mathcal{X}_i|$ shrinks, $\mathcal{X}_i$ behaves as an ϵ-coreset whose bound on the relative error increases quadratically [7]. That is, let $L_w(\mathcal{X})$ be the full objective minimized in Eq. 1, evaluated over $\mathcal{X}$. Then for any w, we have that $|L_w(\mathcal{X}_i) - L_w(\mathcal{X})| \leq \epsilon \cdot L_w(\mathcal{X})$.

Secondly, consider that a coreset of a high-dimensional sparse dataset may contain features that are entirely zero-valued. These 'dead' features are then effectively ignored by any model on that coreset. In either viewpoint, $\mathcal{X}_i$ may not contain enough information to produce an accurate approximation of $\hat{w}$. Thus, consider a scheme where we augment $\mathcal{X}_i$ with centroids of other partitions:

$$\mathcal{X}_i^{(\text{aug})} := \mathcal{X}_i \cup \left(\bigcup_{j \in [p] \setminus \{i\}} \mu_j^+ \cup \mu_j^- \right) \tag{4}$$

with positive and negative centroids μ^+ and μ^- defined as

$$\mu_j^+ := \frac{1}{|\mathcal{X}_j^+|} \sum_{x_k \in \mathcal{X}_j^+} x_k, \quad \mu_j^- := \frac{1}{|\mathcal{X}_j^-|} \sum_{x_k \in \mathcal{X}_j^-} x_k \tag{5}$$

where $\mathcal{X}_j^+$ is the subset of $\mathcal{X}_j$ with positive labels in $\mathcal{Y}_j$, and correspondingly for $\mathcal{X}_j^-$. The weight of any point in $\mathcal{X}_i$ is taken as 1, and the weight of any μ_j^+ or μ_j^- is $|\mathcal{X}_j^+|$ or $|\mathcal{X}_j^-|$, respectively. (This is trivially adaptable to the multiclass case.)

The idea of centroid augmentation is theoretically justifiable; it can be shown that augmenting $\mathcal{X}_i$ with $2p$ centroids is guaranteed to produce a better approximation to $\hat{w}$ than increasing the size of $\mathcal{X}_i$ by sampling $2p$ additional points

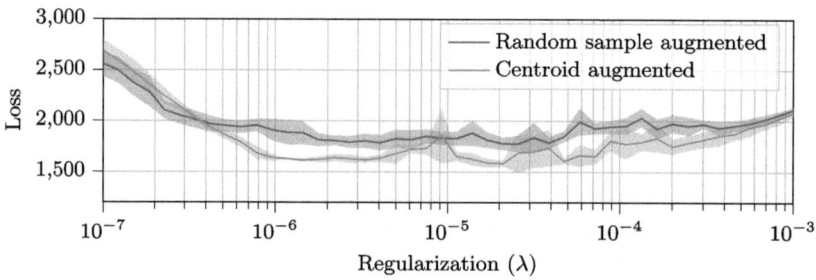

Fig. 3. Model loss values for *newsgroups* dataset with 128 partitions, augmented with centroids of other partitions vs. random samples. Lower loss is better. Centroid augmentation produces models with lower loss as regularization increases. (Too much regularization causes underfitting.)

from $\mathcal{X}$. See the supplementary material for details. To experimentally observe and confirm the theoretical result, we swept λ across a range of values for the newsgroups dataset, comparing the loss of the best models obtained when using partitions of the newsgroups dataset augmented with centroids, and augmented with random samples. The result is shown in Fig. 3, confirming the result holds as regularization increases.

4 Second Improvement: Feature Weighting

When $\mathcal{X}$ is high-dimensional and sparse, not only do we have the problem of 'dead features' as previously discussed, but we also may have the situation where individual features are significantly over- or under-represented in any $\mathcal{X}_i$. This can also cause greater variance in the performance of OWA, as seen in Fig. 2. This phenomenon is amplified because L_1-regularized logistic regression (and elastic net) is not guaranteed to be consistent or possess the oracle property [46]. Even in low dimensions, L_1-regularized LASSO-type procedures are known to be inconsistent in variable selection [11,24]. Thus, if an $\mathcal{X}_i$ over- or under-represents a feature of $\mathcal{X}$, the effects on variable selection can be even worse.

Zou [46] proposed a solution for the consistency of the simple linear regression Lasso estimator with the adaptive Lasso, which makes variable selection consistent by applying weights to each feature. This was then extended to the case of L_1-regularized logistic regression with the 'iterated Lasso' [17], where a first model is trained on the data, and then its weights are used to weight each feature for a second round of learning. The iterated Lasso is selection-consistent and possesses the oracle property under a few general assumptions on the data.

The strategy of the iterated Lasso is straightforward to adapt to the distributed case: we relax the one-round communication constraint and allow an additional round of feature-weighted learning, using weights from the first round of learning. Given first-round models $\hat{w}_i$, we can compute the percentage of models $\hat{w}_i$ that used a particular feature j: $P_j := (1/p) \sum_{i \in [p]} \mathbb{1}(\hat{w}_{ij} \neq 0)$. Then, we can define the weight for feature j as $\alpha_j := 1 + \beta P_j$ where β is a tunable parameter that controls the severity of the feature weighting. Then, separately in each partition, we solve an adaptive feature-weighted second round optimization:

$$\hat{w}^{\text{fw}} := \arg\min_{w \in \mathbb{R}^d} \sum_{i=1}^n \ell(y_i, x_i^\top w) + \lambda_1 \sum_{j \in [d]} \alpha_j^{-1} |w_j| + \lambda_2 \sum_{j \in [d]} (\alpha_j^{-1} w_j)^2. \quad (6)$$

Note that this problem is equivalent to scaling each dimension j of $\mathcal{X}$ by α_j with a rescaled penalty parameter $\lambda_{fw} := \lambda d/(\sum_{i \in [d]} \alpha_i^{-1})$. This use of a weighted second round is another improvement over standard OWA, and in our experiments, it improves stability by acting as a soft feature-selection step. This matches our expectation: the iterated Lasso can be understood as doing the same thing.

Algorithm 1. ACOWA.

1: **Input:** $\mathcal{X} \in \mathbb{R}^{n \times d}$, $\mathcal{Y} \in \{-1, 1\}^n$, regularization penalty λ, p processors, β
2: **Output:** learned model $\hat{w}_{\text{acowa}}$

3: split $(\mathcal{X}, \mathcal{Y})$ into p partitions and distribute to p workers
4: **for** $i \in [p]$ **in parallel do**
5:    compute μ_i^+ and μ_i^- using Eq. 5
6: **end for**
7: distribute all μ_i^+ and μ_i^- to all p workers
8: **for** $i \in [p]$ **in parallel do**
9:    learn $\hat{w}_i$ using local optimizer on $\mathcal{X}_i^{\text{aug}}$ (Eq. 4)
10: **end for**
11: compute α_j for all $j \in [d]$
12: **for** $i \in [p]$ **in parallel do**
13:    learn $\hat{w}_i^{\text{fw}}$ (Eq. 6) using local optimizer on $\mathcal{X}_i^{\text{aug}}$
14: **end for**
15: form $(\mathcal{X}_C, \mathcal{Y}_C)$ as a sample of size $\max(n/p, pn/d)$ from $(\mathcal{X}, \mathcal{Y})$
16: compute $\hat{w}_{\text{acowa}}$ as the solution to Eq. 3 with $\hat{W} = \{\hat{w}_1^{\text{fw}}, \ldots, \hat{w}_p^{\text{fw}}\}$

5 ACOWA

With these two major improvements over OWA, we can now introduce ACOWA, shown in Algorithm 1. ACOWA uses centroid augmentation, described earlier, for the first distributed round of learning, and then computes feature weights as described in the previous section for a second distributed round of learning. Then, the standard OWA merge step (Eq. 3) is applied. We highlight two additional improvements:

Larger Merge Set. OWA's merge step uses a dataset $\mathcal{X}_C$, of size pn/d. For high-dimensional problems, this set can be extremely small, causing high variance in $\hat{w}_{\text{owa}}$. Thus, it makes sense to increase the subsample size. Given that data is already distributed across partitions, we can simply use the main node's partition (with size n/p) as the second round. This significantly reduces the variance of $\hat{w}_{\text{owa}}$ with negligible runtime cost (see supplementary material).

Better Optimizer. Our implementation (described further in the Experiments section) uses *newGLMNET* as provided by LIBLINEAR [9]. We found that relaxing the optimizer by reducing the number of inner coordinate descent iterations to 50 and the number of outer Newton iterations to 20 gives good speedup without loss in accuracy. Since the first round of learning can intuitively be understood as a 'soft' feature selection step, it is not necessary to run the first round of optimization to full convergence.

Extensions. In our exposition, for the sake of simplicity, we have specifically considered the regularized logistic regression problem, and our theoretical results have been restricted to that problem. However, ACOWA is a general algorithm, and as such it is straightforward to substitute any other type of linear model (such as, e.g., the linear SVM). Theoretical results for centroid augmentation still apply, by adapting Lemma 2 in the supplementary material to the objective function of interest. Theoretical scaling results (in the next section) apply so long as the individual solvers for each partition scale similarly to *newGLMNET* (if not, the results can be adapted).

6 Scalability Analysis: Isoefficiency

Background. We next aim to characterize the *computational scalability* of ACOWA. Here, we introduce and discuss a classic parallel performance metric known as *isoefficiency* [14]. Isoefficiency measures how a distributed algorithm scales as the number of processors and the dataset size is increased, while taking into account communication costs, synchronization, and other overheads. To our knowledge, this is the first isoefficiency analysis of distributed logistic regression.

Although isoefficiency is not often studied in a machine learning context, we highlight that it is in fact well suited to analysis of distributed learning algorithms, as it is a principled way to quantify the marginal shrinkage of improvement as the number of processors p is increased. Intuitively, increasing p from 10 to 20 on a task should greatly improve runtime. But while further increasing p to 40 may still reduce runtime, it would likely be to a smaller extent than would be expected by simple mathematical analysis. This is because communication overhead rises with the number of partitions, which outweighs the speedup due to parallelism. A parallel algorithm which is more isoefficient than another will better utilize parallelism with fewer communication costs, and thus will scale better with the number of processors. This will be formalized in the following exposition. Due to space constraints, all proofs are in the supplementary materials.

Suppose we have a parallel computing system with p processors and dataset size z (to be defined later). We let $T_1(z)$ be the serial solve time of logistic regression and $T_p(z)$ be the solve time using p processors. Generally, increasing p causes a boost in relative speed $S_p(z) = T_1(z)/T_p(z)$ compared to serial, but also incurs increasing overhead $T_0(z)$, which is defined as $T_0 := pT_p - T_1$. (We suppress the dependence on z when convenient.) We notice here that by definition, the overhead represents an excess cost invoked by the parallel algorithm compared to serial, which is not limited to work but can also include idle time. In an algorithm and system with no overhead, then $pT_p = T_1$, and $S_p = p$. In reality, for a given z, when p is increased linearly, S_p tends to grow sublinearly: if we define *efficiency* as $E_p(z) = S_p(z)/p$, then E_p decreases as p increases.

However, the more interesting and actionable quantity to a practitioner is the rate at which p must increase to retain the same efficiency E_p as the problem size z increases. This rate is formalized as the *isoefficiency function* and is the target of our analysis. The smaller this isoefficiency function, the more scalable the algorithm. For instance, an isoefficiency function of $z = \Theta(p)$ implies that when p is doubled, the overall runtime and efficiency can be maintained if z is also doubled. Such a fortunate situation cannot generally be expected, though; a linear isoefficiency function implies an embarrassingly parallel problem with no communication overhead, which of course is not going to be the case for any distributed machine learning algorithm.

Computing the Isoefficiency. The next step is to properly define the data size z. In our case, if we define z as the number of nonzero entries in $\mathcal{X}$, the serial newGLMNET solver runs linearly in z, as shown in Lemma 3 in the supplementary material. Conveniently, the linear scaling of the serial solver simplifies the next calculation.

Obtaining the isoefficiency function is equivalent to finding the function f describing $z \propto f(p)$ so that $E_p(z)$ is constant. Solving for E_p, we get

$$E = \frac{S}{p} = \frac{T_1}{pT_p} = \frac{T_1}{T_0 + T_1} = \frac{1}{1 + T_0/T_1} \propto \frac{1}{1 + T_0/z} \qquad (7)$$

since $T_1 \propto z$. From this we see that for E_p to remain constant, we require that $z \propto T_0$. Further substituting in the definition of T_0, we see that the isoefficiency reduces to computing z as a function of p in the equation $z \propto pT_p - T_1$.

Results for Distributed Logistic Regression. Because z can scale in various ways with the underlying dataset dimensions, the relative growth rates of samples n and features d can affect an algorithm's scaling. We keep in mind two regimes: (1) bounded d where $z \propto n$, and (2) $z \propto nd$. (1) implies we get more samples, while in (2) we get more samples and features, with the same underlying sparsity ratio. After distributed training, we define the support set S to be the union of all non-zero features across the partitions, and let $s = |S|$. Our first result concerns naive averaging.

Theorem 1. *Given distributed sparse logistic regression with sparsity level s, naive averaging has isoefficiency function $z = \Theta(sp \log p)$. If we suppose that (1) d is constant, or (2) $d(z) \to D$ for bounded D, then $z = \Theta(p \log p)$. Alternately, if n and d grow at the same rate such that $z \propto nd$, then the isoefficiency function is $z = \Theta(p^2 \log^2 p)$.*

Moving on to consider OWA, we find that the behavior not only depends on growth rates of the dataset, as in naive averaging, but also on certain parameters involved in the algorithm. In particular, the second round on the subsampled set of size n_c can pose a challenge to scalability if n_c grows on par with z, due to the overhead of solving the objective while the other processors are idle. In practice, n_c can be kept small as z grows without loss in accuracy.

Theorem 2. *Consider OWA with subsampled second round dataset $\mathcal{X}_C$ with n_c rows. If the growth rate of n_c is such that $n_c \propto z^\alpha$ for some $0 < \alpha < 1$, then OWA has isoefficiency function $z = \Theta(\max\{p^2, p^{2/(1-\alpha)}\})$. When $n \propto z$, we have $n_c \propto n^\alpha$. When $n \propto \sqrt{z}$, we have $n_c \propto n^{2\alpha}$.*

As a practical example, suppose a user observes a 5× speedup running OWA with p processors on 10^4 data points compared to serial *newGLMNET*. Using $2p$ processors, they would need roughly 10^8 samples to maintain a 5× speedup. We finally show that despite its additional round of computation, ACOWA has the same scalability as OWA.

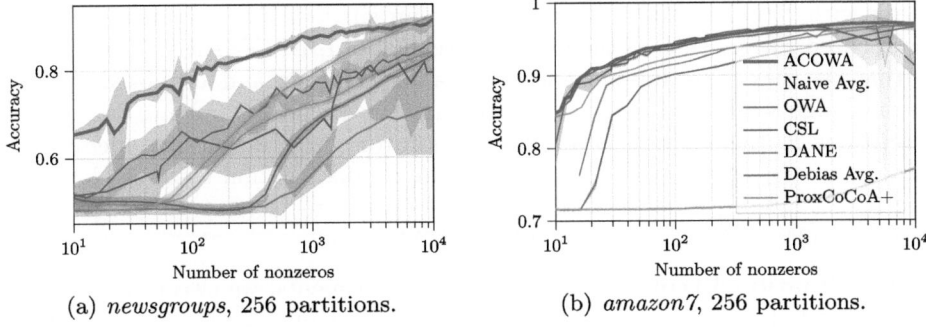

Fig. 4. Number of nonzeros vs. test set accuracy in the single-node parallel setting. ACOWA has consistently better performance than other distributed methods, especially for sparser solutions on *newsgroups*. It generally also performs the best on *amazon7* across a range of sparsities, compared to the second best method (CSL).

Theorem 3. *Consider the ACOWA algorithm with subsampled second round dataset $\mathcal{X}_C$ with n_c rows. If the growth rate of n_c is such that $n_c \propto z^\alpha$ for some $0 < \alpha < 1$, then ACOWA has isoefficiency function $z = \Theta(\max\{p^2, p^{2/(1-\alpha)}\})$.*

7 Experiments

We conducted thorough experiments to compare the performance and runtime of ACOWA with competitive baselines: standard OWA [18], naive averaging, ProxCoCoA+ [37], CSL [21], and DANE [35].

We implemented ACOWA, OWA, naive averaging, and debiased averaging in C++ with OpenMP and MPI using the Armadillo linear algebra library [34], the ensmallen optimization library [5], and adapted parts of the mlpack machine learning library [6]. Our OWA implementation is tuned to allow a higher optimizer tolerance and a larger merge set size (like ACOWA). CSL and DANE were implemented similarly, using $\hat{w}_{\text{owa}}$ as the initial solution and OWL-QN [2] from libLBFGS (see https://github.com/chokkan/liblbfgs) as the per-iteration solver. To keep communication costs similar to OWA and ACOWA, we only ran one iteration of CSL and DANE. (We found further iterations did not improve the model significantly, and caused CSL and DANE to take much longer.) For ProxCoCoA+ we used the Scala implementation from the authors.

For datasets, we used several large-scale real-world datasets with sizes from approximately 10 MB to 250 GB. Our aim was to replicate a variety of real-world usage scenarios. All except EMBER [1] are available on the LIBSVM website [4] or UCI repository [8]. For EMBER, we compute length-8 n-grams [30] and keep the most common 100k and 1M to produce *ember-100k* and *ember-1M*.

We are interested in two settings: *(1)* single-node multicore, and *(2)* fully distributed. The first setting is relevant in modern environments, as modern systems can have very many cores available. In our case, we used a powerful server with 256 cores and 4TB of RAM for our single-node experiments. Simple parallelized solvers such as the OpenMP version of LIBLINEAR struggle in this setting, as they were designed for only a few threads and cannot distribute large enough work chunks to very large numbers of cores. Applying distributed algorithms in this context is an effective strategy; the algorithms operate the same as in the fully distributed setting, but communication costs are lower as no network latency is incurred. For our fully distributed setting, we use a cluster with 16 nodes, with 32 cores and 1TB of RAM each.

Approximation Error. In the first set of experiments, we sweep over a logarithmic grid of λ_1 and compute the model's accuracy on a held-out test set, with λ_2 set to 0. We perform 10 trials with random partitions and random seeds. Because practitioners often try to tune sparse logistic regression to optimize accuracy at a certain level of sparsity, we plot the number of nonzeros in the solution versus accuracy. This gives us a good picture of how each algorithm behaves at different sparsity levels.

Figure 4 shows the results of the sweep on smaller datasets in the single-node multi-core environment. ACOWA (blue) consistently attains higher accuracy, especially as the solution becomes more sparse (our setting of interest). This is also true in the fully distributed setting (Fig. 5). We found that CSL and DANE sometimes struggled to produce sparse solutions; for instance, on the EMBER datasets, the models produced by CSL and DANE only become competitive when they are dense (not our setting of interest).

ACOWA, due to the centroid augmentation and feature reweighting, is able to identify relevant features for the full model. This is especially true for sparser

Table 1. Runtime results for different techniques. *Fail* indicates the method took over two hours or had an out-of-memory issue. Although ACOWA takes longer to converge than naive averaging and OWA, it provides significantly better performance (see Fig. 4). This also generally holds when comparing with CSL and DANE.

(a) single-node parallel

dataset	n	d	nnz	ProxCoCoA+	Naive Avg.	OWA	ACOWA
newsgroups	11k	54k	1.5M	40.129s	0.226s	0.242s	2.154s
amazon7	1.3M	262k	133M	531.778s	2.356s	14.933s	31.675s
criteo	45M	1M	1.78B	Fail	17.085s	218.092s	264.200s
ember-100k	600k	100k	8.48B	Fail	7.811s	13.245s	80.814s

(b) fully distributed

dataset	n	d	nnz	CSL	DANE	Naive Avg.	OWA	ACOWA
ember-100k	600k	100k	8.48B	28.831s	40.318s	0.863s	1.129s	19.147s
ember-1M	600k	1M	38.0B	81.634s	68.975s	6.176s	5.836s	145.051s
criteo	45M	1M	1.78B	36.069s	65.618s	2.349s	25.885s	150.383s

models, where other methods struggle due to the variance of models produced by each partition. In the supplementary material, we perform several additional experiments: an ablation study shows that *both* centroid augmentation and feature reweighting are necessary for the improved approximation that ACOWA gives. Approximation results are similar for $\lambda_2 \neq 0$ (the elastic net); in addition, ACOWA is also robust to the choice of β.

Runtime. In the second set of experiments, we characterize ACOWA's runtime. We expect ACOWA to be slower than other one-shot algorithms, as we chose to increase the amount of communication modestly in exchange for significantly improving model performance. We tune λ_1 to produce approximately 1000 nonzeros in the final model, and take $\lambda_2 = 0$. We record the time taken to learn the model (excluding data loading and unrelated preprocessing).

Results are shown for each dataset in Table 1. These results match expectations: ACOWA is slower than the other one-shot algorithms, because it involves an additional round of communication, plus the initial communication of the centroids. ProxCoCoA+ is unable to complete within two hours for many datasets; we believe this to be a result of high communication overhead. In the distributed setting, the increased complexity of solving the surrogate loss function for CSL (and similar for DANE) causes slowdowns. As mentioned earlier, in our experiments we only use one iteration of CSL and DANE. Were we to run those to convergence, the runtime (and communication costs) would be much higher.

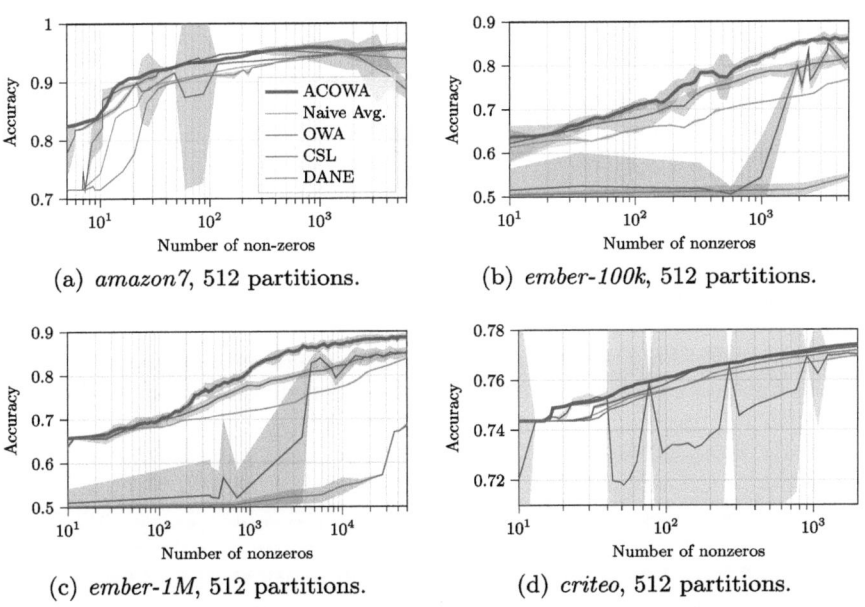

Fig. 5. Number of nonzeros vs. test set accuracy in the multi-node distributed setting. ACOWA outperforms, again especially for sparser solutions. OWA on the criteo dataset exhibited significant variance. We were unable to run ProxCoCoA+ in this setting due to memory usage issues and extremely long runtimes.

Table 2. Runtime breakdown for ACOWA. Each step is associated with lines in Alg 1.

step	ember-100k	ember-1M	criteo
Centroids (4–5)	1.786 s	6.724 s	2.021 s
All-to-all (6)	7.658 s	58.268 s	109.464 s
Round 1 (7–8)	5.284 s	45.376 s	8.855 s
Model gather	0.167 s	1.540 s	1.099 s
Compute α_j (9)	0.134 s	1.443 s	1.319 s
Round 2 (10–11)	4.281 s	29.875 s	7.068 s
Model gather	0.173 s	1.274 s	0.940 s
Round 3 (12–13)	0.310 s	0.551 s	19.617 s
Total	19.793 s	145.051 s	150.383 s

Runtime Breakdown. Next we perform a detailed breakdown of the runtime cost of each step of ACOWA. Again tuning for 1000 nonzeros, we ran ACOWA in the fully distributed setting for 10 trials, collecting the average runtime of each step (specifically splitting out communication costs) in Table 2.

We can see that the communication rounds of ACOWA ('model gather') take a negligible fraction of the overall runtime, and because the communication being performed is only each (sparse) model $\hat{w}_i$, adding more data (but preserving the sparsity of the solution) does not affect the communication cost. Although the centroid computation and communication steps are computationally intensive, they do not scale with the dataset size (only with the number of partitions), and the computational and communication burdens of this step could be significantly alleviated by, e.g., the use of sparse centroids or other approximations. We plan to investigate this improvement in future work. As mentioned by Izbicki and Shelton [18], the last round of learning on the smaller set $(\mathcal{X}_C, \mathcal{Y}_C)$ takes a negligible amount of time compared to the rest of ACOWA.

Additional Studies. Due to space constraints, we are unable to fit all of our experiments in the main paper; some are described in the appendix:

- *Ablation study.* Our results indicate that the combination of both centroid augmentation and a feature reweighted second round are mutually beneficial, and both improvements are necessary to provide the best accuracy.
- *General Objective Functions.* Our general approach can be readily adapted for other loss functions besides L_1 penalized logistic regression. We use ACOWA to solve Elastic Net logistic regression; ACOWA works successfully in this setting too, and can be further applied to any linear modeling problem.
- *Oracle Solution.* We compare more thoroughly with the serial full-data solution provided by LIBLINEAR. We find that ACOWA can often come close to full-data performance, especially for highly sparse models.
- *Effect of β.* We investigate the effects of the parameter β, showing that ACOWA is robust to the choice of β.

8 Conclusion

We presented a minimally interactive method, ACOWA, for distributed logistic regression, which substantially improves on prior one- or few-shot distributed estimators. Our method scales to massive datasets, with better accuracy-to-sparsity ratio and similar runtimes than other methods, across multi-core and multi-node experiments, and has favorable theoretical justification.

References

1. Anderson, H.S., Roth, P.: EMBER: an open dataset for training static PE malware machine learning models. arXiv preprint arXiv:1804.04637 (2018)
2. Andrew, G., Gao, J.: Scalable training of L1-regularized log-linear models. In: 24th International Conference on Machine Learning, pp. 33–40 (2007)
3. Boyd, S., Parikh, N., Chu, E., Peleato, B., Eckstein, J., et al.: Distributed optimization and statistical learning via the alternating direction method of multipliers. Found. Trends® Mach. Learn. **3**(1), 1–122 (2011)
4. Chang, C.C., Lin, C.J.: LIBSVM: a library for support vector machines. ACM Trans. Intell. Syst. Technol. **2**(3), 1–27 (2011)
5. Curtin, R.R., Edel, M., Prabhu, R.G., Basak, S., Lou, Z., Sanderson, C.: The ensmallen library for flexible numerical optimization. JMLR **22**(1), 7552–7557 (2021)
6. Curtin, R.R., et al.: MLPACK 4: a fast, header-only C++ machine learning library. J. Open Source Softw. **8**(82), 1–1 (2023)
7. Curtin, R.R., Im, S., Moseley, B., Pruhs, K., Samadian, A.: Unconditional coresets for regularized loss minimization. In: AISTATS 2020, pp. 482–492 (2020)
8. Dua, D., Graff, C.: UCI ML repository (2017). http://archive.ics.uci.edu/ml
9. Fan, R.E., Chang, K.W., Hsieh, C.J., Wang, X.R., Lin, C.J.: LIBLINEAR: a library for large linear classification. JMLR **9**, 1871–1874 (2008)
10. Friedman, J., Hastie, T., Tibshirani, R.: Regularization paths for generalized linear models via coordinate descent. J. Stat. Softw. **33**(1), 1 (2010)
11. Fu, W., Knight, K.: Asymptotics for lasso-type estimators. Ann. Stat. **28**(5), 1356–1378 (2000)
12. Goldstein, T., Studer, C., Baraniuk, R.: A field guide to forward-backward splitting with a FASTA implementation. arXiv preprint arXiv:1411.3406 (2014)
13. Gopal, S., Yang, Y.: Distributed training of large-scale logistic models. In: ICML, pp. 289–297 (2013)
14. Grama, A.Y., Gupta, A., Kumar, V.: Isoefficiency: measuring the scalability of parallel algorithms and architectures. IEEE Parallel Distrib. Technol. Syst. Appl. **1**(3), 12–21 (1993)
15. Halevy, A., Norvig, P., Pereira, F.: The unreasonable effectiveness of data. IEEE Intell. Syst. **24**(2), 8–12 (2009)
16. Hastie, T., Tibshirani, R., Wainwright, M.: Statistical learning with sparsity: the lasso and generalizations (2015)
17. Huang, J., Ma, S., Zhang, C.H.: The iterated lasso for high-dimensional logistic regression. Univ. Iowa, Dept. Stat. Actuarial Sci. **7**, 1–20 (2008)
18. Izbicki, M., Shelton, C.R.: Distributed learning of non-convex linear models with one round of communication. In: ECML PKDD 2019, pp. 197–212 (2020)

19. Jaggi, M., Smith, V., Takác, M., Terhorst, J., Krishnan, S., Hofmann, T., Jordan, M.I.: Communication-efficient distributed dual coordinate ascent. In: NIPS, vol. 27 (2014)
20. Jin, R., Li, D., Gao, J., Liu, Z., Chen, L., Zhou, Y.: Towards a better understanding of linear models for recommendation. In: KDD 2021, pp. 776–785 (2021)
21. Jordan, M.I., Lee, J.D., Yang, Y.: Communication-efficient distributed statistical inference. J. Am. Stat. Assoc. **114**(526), 668–681 (2018)
22. Jordan, M.I., Mitchell, T.M.: Machine learning: trends, perspectives, and prospects. Science **349**(6245), 255–260 (2015)
23. Kassani, P.H., Lu, F., Le Guen, Y., Belloy, M.E., He, Z.: Deep neural networks with controlled variable selection for the identification of putative causal genetic variants. Nat. Mach. Intell. **4**(9), 761–771 (2022)
24. Leng, C., Lin, Y., Wahba, G.: A note on the lasso and related procedures in model selection. Statistica Sinica **16**, 1273–1284 (2006)
25. Li, R., et al.: Fast lasso method for large-scale and ultrahigh-dimensional cox model with applications to UK biobank. Biostatistics **23**(2), 522–540 (2022)
26. Lin, C.Y., Tsai, C.H., Lee, C.P., Lin, C.J.: Large-scale logistic regression and linear support vector machines using spark. In: BIGDATA 2014, pp. 519–528 (2014)
27. Lu, F., Raff, E., Holt, J.: A coreset learning reality check. In: AAAI, vol. 37, pp. 8940–8948 (2023)
28. Mcdonald, R., Mohri, M., Silberman, N., Walker, D., Mann, G.: Efficient large-scale distributed training of conditional maximum entropy models. In: NIPS, vol. 22 (2009)
29. Raff, E., Sylvester, J.: Linear models with many cores and CPUs: a stochastic atomic update scheme. In: BIGDATA, pp. 65–73 (2018)
30. Raff, E., et al.: An investigation of byte N-gram features for malware classification. J. Comput. Virol. Hacking Tech. **14**, 1–20 (2018)
31. Recht, B., Re, C., Wright, S., Niu, F.: Hogwild!: a lock-free approach to parallelizing stochastic gradient descent. In: NIPS, vol. 24 (2011)
32. Richtárik, P., Takáč, M.: Distributed coordinate descent method for learning with big data. J. Mach. Learn. Res. **17**(1), 2657–2681 (2016)
33. Rosenblatt, J.D., Nadler, B.: On the optimality of averaging in distributed statistical learning. Inf. Inference **5**(4), 379–404 (2016)
34. Sanderson, C., Curtin, R.: Armadillo: a template-based C++ library for linear algebra. J. Open Source Softw. **1**(2), 26 (2016)
35. Shamir, O., Srebro, N., Zhang, T.: Communication-efficient distributed optimization using an approximate newton-type method. In: ICML, pp. 1000–1008 (2014)
36. Smith, V., Forte, S., Chenxin, M., Takáč, M., Jordan, M.I., Jaggi, M.: CoCoA: a general framework for communication-efficient distributed optimization. JMLR **18**, 230 (2018)
37. Smith, V., Forte, S., Jordan, M.I., Jaggi, M.: L1-regularized distributed optimization: a communication-efficient primal-dual framework. arXiv preprint arXiv:1512.04011 (2015)
38. Trofimov, I., Genkin, A.: Distributed coordinate descent for L1-regularized logistic regression. In: Khachay, M.Y., Konstantinova, N., Panchenko, A., Ignatov, D.I., Labunets, V.G. (eds.) AIST 2015. CCIS, vol. 542, pp. 243–254. Springer, Cham (2015). https://doi.org/10.1007/978-3-319-26123-2_24
39. Wang, J., Kolar, M., Srebro, N., Zhang, T.: Efficient distributed learning with sparsity. In: ICML, pp. 3636–3645 (2017)
40. Yang, S., Yuan, H., Zhang, X., Wang, M., Zhang, H., Wang, H.: Conversational dueling bandits in generalized linear models (2024)

41. Yuan, G.X., Ho, C.H., Lin, C.J.: An improved GLMnet for L1-regularized logistic regression. In: KDD 2011, pp. 33–41 (2011)
42. Zhang, X., Zhou, Y., Ma, Y., Chen, B.C., Zhang, L., Agarwal, D.: GLMIX: generalized linear mixed models for large-scale response prediction. In: KDD 2016, pp. 363–372 (2016)
43. Zhang, Y., Duchi, J., Wainwright, M.: Divide and conquer kernel ridge regression. In: COLT, pp. 592–617 (2013)
44. Zhuang, Y., Chin, W.-S., Juan, Y.-C., Lin, C.-J.: Distributed newton methods for regularized logistic regression. In: Cao, T., Lim, E.-P., Zhou, Z.-H., Ho, T.-B., Cheung, D., Motoda, H. (eds.) PAKDD 2015. LNCS (LNAI), vol. 9078, pp. 690–703. Springer, Cham (2015). https://doi.org/10.1007/978-3-319-18032-8_54
45. Zhuang, Y., Juan, Y., Yuan, G.X., Lin, C.J.: Naive parallelization of coordinate descent methods and an application on multi-core L1-regularized classification. In: CIKM 2018, pp. 1103–1112 (2018)
46. Zou, H.: The adaptive lasso and its oracle properties. J. Am. Stat. Assoc. **101**(476), 1418–1429 (2006)
47. Zou, H., Hastie, T.: Regularization and variable selection via the elastic net. J. Royal Stat. Soc. Series B: Stat. Methodol. **67**(2), 301–320 (2005)

Time-Varying Gaussian Process Bandit Optimization with Experts: No-Regret in Logarithmically-Many Side Queries

Eliabelle Mauduit[1(✉)], Eloïse Berthier[2], and Andrea Simonetto[1]

[1] Unité des Mathématiques Appliquées, ENSTA, Institut Polytechnique de Paris, 91120 Palaiseau, France
{eliabelle.mauduit,andrea.simonetto}@ensta.fr
[2] U2IS, ENSTA, Institut Polytechnique de Paris, 91120 Palaiseau, France
eloise.berthier@ensta.fr

Abstract. We study a time-varying Bayesian optimization problem with bandit feedback, where the reward function belongs to a Reproducing Kernel Hilbert Space (RKHS). We approach the problem via an upper-confidence bound Gaussian Process algorithm, which has been proven to yield no-regret in the stationary case.

The time-varying case is more challenging and no-regret results are out of reach in general in the standard setting. As such, we instead tackle the question of how many additional observations asked to an expert are required to regain a no-regret property. To do so, we formulate the presence of past observation via an uncertainty injection procedure, and we reframe the problem as a heteroscedastic Gaussian Process regression. In addition, to achieve a no-regret result, we discard long outdated observations and replace them with updated (possibly very noisy) ones obtained by asking queries to an external expert. By leveraging and extending sparse inference to the heteroscedastic case, we are able to secure a no-regret result in a challenging time-varying setting with only logarithmically-many side queries per time step. Our method demonstrates that minimal additional information suffices to counteract temporal drift, ensuring efficient optimization despite time variation.

Keywords: Gaussian Processes · Upper confidence bounds · Bandit feedback · Sparse inference · Time-varying optimization

1 Introduction

We consider the problem of sequentially optimizing a reward function $f : \mathcal{D} \times \mathbb{R}_+ \to \mathbb{R}$ where $\mathcal{D} \subset \mathbb{R}^d$ is a compact convex set. In this configuration, the objective depends both on time and on a continuous decision space $\mathcal{D}$. At each

---

Supplementary Information The online version contains supplementary material available at https://doi.org/10.1007/978-3-032-06096-9_10.

discrete time step t, we obtain a noisy observation of the reward $y_t = f(x_t, t) + \epsilon_t$, where $\epsilon_t \sim \mathcal{N}(0, \sigma^2)$. Our objective is to maximize the sum of rewards

$$\max_{(x_t)_t \in \mathcal{D}^T} \sum_{t=1}^{T} \Big[f(x_t, t) =: f_t(x) \Big]. \tag{1}$$

At least in the static case, when f does not change in time, this type of problem has often been formulated via Bayesian optimization with bandit feedback [17], whereby an agent must take a sequence of actions while observing the corresponding sequence of rewards. Each action consists of picking a decision x to get an estimate of the reward at the corresponding point. The agent does not modify its environment through its actions and can thus *exploit* previous measurements to predict actions that offer the highest rewards, but should also *explore* new decisions where the value of the reward function is possibly high. For dynamic rewards, the setting is more challenging, as we will see.

In the time-varying case, the performance metric we are interested in is the dynamic cumulative regret, defined as

$$R_T = \sum_{t=1}^{T} \left(\max_{x \in \mathcal{D}} f_t(x) - f_t(x_t) \right), \tag{2}$$

representing the cumulative loss in reward picking decision x_t at time t with respect to the best decision *at the same time step*. Algorithms that achieve an asymptotically vanishing average dynamic cumulative regret, as $\lim_{T \to \infty} R_T/T = 0$, are said to enjoy no-regret.

To derive our main theoretical results, we will work under two reasonable blanket assumptions. First, to model smoothness properties of the functions f_t, we assume that they all belong to a Reproducing Kernel Hilbert Space (RKHS) and have bounded RKHS norm. The RKHS associated with kernel k ($\mathcal{H}_k(\mathcal{D}), \langle ., . \rangle_k$) is a subspace of $L_2(\mathcal{D})$ [14] and the associated inner product $\langle ., . \rangle_k$ is such that

$$\forall f \in \mathcal{H}_k(\mathcal{D}),\ f(x) = \langle f, k(x, .) \rangle_k.$$

The norm $\|f\|_k$ measures the smoothness of f with respect to the kernel function k, therefore assuming $\|f_t\|_k$ is bounded translates into regularity assumptions about the objective.

Assumption 1. *For all time steps, functions $x \mapsto f_t(x)$ belong to a Reproducing Kernel Hilbert Space with continuous bounded kernel k such that $\forall x \in \mathcal{D}$, $k(x, x) \leq M_k^2$ and they have bounded RKHS norm,*

$$\forall t,\ \|f_t\|_k \leq B. \tag{3}$$

Second, to model time variation, we assume boundedness of the variations as follows.

Assumption 2. *For the sequence of functions* $(f_t)_{t=1}^T$, *there exists a bounded constant* Δ, *such that,*

$$\forall t, \ \sup_{x \in \mathcal{D}} |f_{t+1}(x) - f_t(x)| \leq \Delta. \tag{4}$$

We further let $\Delta = 1$, *without any loss of generality.*

Assumption 2 ensures controlled temporal variations, limiting changes between consecutive iterations and provides a sound framework for uncertainty injection.

1.1 Related Work

Bayesian optimization in the bandit feedback setting has been studied extensively in the static scenario: the landmark work of Srinivas and coauthors [17] proposes an upper-confidence bound algorithm based on a Gaussian Process model of the unknown function obtaining no-regret in several settings. In particular, first, they use the noisy observations of f to derive a possibly miss-specified estimation of its mean $\mu_t(x)$ and covariance $\sigma_t^2(x)$, via a Gaussian Process:

$$\mu_t(x) = k_t(x)^\top (K_t + \Sigma_t)^{-1} Y_t \tag{5}$$
$$\sigma_t^2(x) = k(x,x) - k_t(x)^\top (K_t + \Sigma_t)^{-1} k_t(x), \tag{6}$$

where $\Sigma_t := \sigma^2 I_t$, σ^2 being the noise variance of each observation y_i, $(K_t)_{i,j} = k(x_i, x_j)$, $k_t(x) = [k(x_1, x), \ldots, k(x_t, x)]$, k being the kernel or covariance function, and $Y_t = [y_1, \ldots, y_t]^\top$. Then, since the reward f is unknown, they propose choosing the next decision based on the upper-confidence bound proxy, as,

$$x_{t+1} = \arg\max_{x \in \mathcal{D}} \mu_t(x) + \beta_{t+1} \sigma_t(x), \tag{7}$$

where $(\beta_t)_{t \geq 1}$ is a sequence of positive parameters chosen to ensure a trade-off between exploration and exploitation and it is decisive in proving the convergence of the algorithm. Their algorithm, labeled GP-UCB, obtains no-regret in high probability when f is sampled from a GP, i.e., $f \sim \text{GP}(0, k(x, x'))$ but also for arbitrary f with bounded RKHS norm. As a means of comparison for the square exponential kernel and f having a bounded RHKS norm, they obtain a $R_T = \tilde{\mathcal{O}}(\sqrt{T})$ result. Here, the notation $\tilde{\mathcal{O}}(\cdot)$ hides poly-logarithmic terms.

The cited work focused on a noise model whose distribution is identical across observations, also known as homoscedastic setting. Makarova and coauthors in [12] remove this assumption, define $\Sigma_t := \text{diag}(\sigma_1^2, \ldots, \sigma_t^2)$ for noise model $\epsilon_t \sim \mathcal{N}(0, \sigma_t^2)$, and deliver a regret bound that matches $R_T = \tilde{\mathcal{O}}(\sqrt{T})$ up to a multiplicative $\bar{\sigma} := \max\{\sigma_i\}$ factor, for the heteroscedastic setting.

The time-varying case has also received attention. The work of [2] extends the GP-UCB algorithm by considering a time-varying reward. They model the time variations by considering a spatio-temporal kernel with a forgetting factor ε, as

$$\forall \ t_i, t_j \leq t, \ k((x_{t_i}, t_i), (x_{t_j}, t_j)) = (1-\varepsilon)^{|t_i - t_j|/2} k(x_i, x_j), \tag{8}$$

where $k(\cdot,\cdot)$ is the static kernel. With this modeling, they propose two algorithms: R-GP-UCB runs GP-UCB on windows of size $w \in \mathbb{N}$ and resets at the start of each window. The second one, TV-GP-UCB, uses the spatiotemporal kernel (8). Under this setting, the authors showed that any GP bandit optimization incurs expected regret of at least $\mathbb{E}[R_T] = \Omega(T\varepsilon)$, meaning the algorithm does not enjoy no-regret for fixed ε. This lower bound is not surprising and it also appears in the multi-armed bandit literature [1]. Furthermore, TV-GP-UCB obtains a $R_T = \tilde{\mathcal{O}}(T)$ which implies an increasing average cumulative dynamic regret.

Building on the literature in dynamic (generalized) linear bandits [13, 21–23], in a series of papers [5, 24], new algorithms are proposed in the time-varying setting: a revised R-GP-UCB algorithm, a new sliding-window algorithm SW-GP-UCB, and a weighted algorithm W-GP-UCB. Under the RKHS setting, they either enjoy cumulative dynamic regrets of $\mathcal{O}(T)$ (matching the lower bound), or $\tilde{\mathcal{O}}(T)$ for the latter two (with our variation budget expressed in Assumption 2). The weighted algorithm is interesting, since it starts from a weighted kernel regression,

$$\hat{f} = \arg\min_{f \in \mathcal{H}_k(\mathcal{D})} \sum_{t=1}^{T} w_t(y_t - f(x_t))^2 + \lambda_t \|f\|_k^2, \tag{9}$$

where $\mathcal{H}_k(\mathcal{D})$ is the RKHS on set $\mathcal{D}$ and kernel k, w_t is a weight, and $\lambda_t \geq 0$ a parameter; they arrive then at the same iterations of Makarova and coauthors in [12] for the heteroscedastic setting, but with a growing-in-T noise variance.

Since no-regret is out of reach in the standard setting, the authors of [7] proposed an algorithm capable of dynamically capturing the changes of the objective function, and thereby acquiring more observations when needed. While this does not guarantee no-regret for a constant sampling time, they show an interesting trade-off between sampling and regret.

Dealing with a spatio-temporal kernel like (8) is theoretically challenging. The works of [3, 20] propose instead to inject uncertainty into old observations. Their starting point is to consider, at every time t, that the variance of old observations increases in time (either exponentially or linearly). This is easier to handle since it is now Σ_t that changes, but only on the diagonal. Regret results are not provided, but it is not difficult to see that this approach is equivalent to the weighted kernel regression in the RKHS settings and delivers the same $\tilde{\mathcal{O}}(T)$ regret.

In addition to regret analysis, another active field of research in GP regression involves optimization of algorithms complexity. Regression based on GP models becomes impracticable for large datasets as its time complexity scales as $\mathcal{O}(N^3)$, where N is the number of observations [16]. The idea of sparse Gaussian Process regression is to approximate the posterior by performing GP regression on a subset of $M \ll N$ inputs. In this way, the complexity becomes $\mathcal{O}(NM^2)$. The difficulty lies in the selection of the set of sparse inputs (also called pseudo or inducing inputs) and several techniques exist. For example, in [18], Titsias considers sparse inputs as variational parameters selected to minimize the Kullback-Leibler (KL) divergence between the exact and approximate posteriors. Leveraging this work, Burt et al. show in [4] that $M = \mathcal{O}(d \log^d(N))$ sparse inputs suffice to accurately approximate the posterior in terms of KL divergence. They make use of an approximation of a M-Determinantal Point Process (M-DPP) [11] to build the set of sparse inputs. M-DPPs define a probability distribution over input subsets of size M that favors the selection of dispersed and less correlated points.

Finally, the algorithms developed in the literature show affinity with online learning in the dynamic setting, e.g., [8].

1.2 Contributions

In this paper, we extend the literature in several ways.

- First, motivated by the fact that handling time-variations with spatio-temporal kernels is technically challenging, we embrace the uncertainty injection framework and we formulate the time-varying problem as a sequence of static regression problems, with growing-in-time uncertainty. This renders the GP problem a heteroscedastic one.
- Then, since a no-regret result is out of reach in this setting, we ask *how many additional queries one should pose to an expert* in order to regain the no-regret result that we enjoy in static settings. The answer to the queries are noisy evaluations (or predictions) of the function at a given time. To limit the number of queries, we leverage sparse inference and we estimate the error of updating past observations with the least number of observations as possible. We call our new GP-UCB algorithm SparQ-GP-UCB for sparse queries. The algorithm performs GP-UCB updates at every time step t by discarding past measurements taken at times τ farther away than $\mathcal{O}(\log(t))$ steps and asks new observations to an expert.
- We prove that SparQ-GP-UCB achieves a $R_T = \tilde{\mathcal{O}}(\sqrt{T})$ in $\tilde{\mathcal{O}}(1)$ additional queries per time step, and it exhibits a $\tilde{\mathcal{O}}(T^2)$ computational complexity. This makes SparQ-GP-UCB the first true no-regret time-varying Gaussian Process algorithm, at the expense of logarithmically-many side queries at each step.

2 Problem Setting

2.1 Uncertainty Injection

We recall our setting. We consider the problem of sequentially optimizing a reward function $f : \mathcal{D} \times \mathbb{R}_+ \to \mathbb{R}$ where $\mathcal{D} \subset \mathbb{R}^d$ is a compact convex set. In this configuration, the objective depends both on time and on a continuous decision space $\mathcal{D}$. At each step t, we obtain a noisy observation of the reward $y_t = f(x_t, t) + \epsilon_t$, where $\epsilon_t \sim \mathcal{N}(0, \sigma^2)$. We set $f_t(\cdot) := f(\cdot, t)$ for convenience.

Our approach of the problem is to inject uncertainty into old measurements and to consider each optimization problem depending on functions f_t as a sequence of separate snapshots.

Under Assumption 2 on the boundedness of function variations, at time T, we can consider that past observations are noisy observations of the current function f_T with zero-mean noise and variance that is increased depending on how old the observations are. In particular, we use independent noise random variables $\epsilon_{t,T}$ and model

$$y_t = f_T(x_t) + \epsilon_{t,T}, \qquad \epsilon_{t,T} \sim \mathcal{N}(0, \sigma^2([T-t]^2 + 1)), \quad t \leq T, \qquad (10)$$

that is the noise standard deviation increases linearly in time. This is similar to the approach of [3] involving a Wiener process and it is well-motivated by the fact that the maximum variation of the function between t and T is $T - t$. In fact, if we model $f_{t+1}(x) = f_t(x) + v$, with $v \in \mathcal{U}(-1,1)$, i.e., the uniform distribution on $[-1,1]$, then the observation y_t of function f_t can be interpreted as an observation of function f_T with noise $\mathbb{E}[\epsilon_{t,T}] = \mathbb{E}[(T-t)v + \epsilon_t] = 0$ and variance $\mathbb{E}[\|\epsilon_{t,T}\|^2] = \sigma^2(\frac{1}{3\sigma^2}[T-t]^2 + 1)$. The latter justifies the expression of the noise, up to asymptotically-unimportant constants.

At time t, then, we would like to maximize the reward of $f_t(x)$ by choosing the next action based on past observation $Y_t = [y_1, \ldots, y_t]^\top$, each with its own zero-mean noise and time-dependent variance. We approach this as a heteroscedastic Gaussian Process and perform the update,

$$\mu_t(x) = k_t(x)^\top (K_t + \Sigma_t)^{-1} Y_t \qquad (11)$$

$$\sigma_t^2(x) = k(x,x) - k_t(x)^\top (K_t + \Sigma_t)^{-1} k_t(x), \qquad (12)$$

where $\Sigma_t := \operatorname{diag}(\operatorname{Var}(\epsilon_{1,t}), \ldots, \operatorname{Var}(\epsilon_{t,t}) = \sigma^2)$, the kernel matrix $(K_t)_{i,j} = k(x_i, x_j)$, and $k_t(x) = [k(x_1, x), \ldots, k(x_t, x)]$. We choose the next decision as,

$$x_{t+1} = \arg\max_{x \in \mathcal{D}} \mu_t(x) + \beta_{t+1} \sigma_t(x), \qquad (13)$$

where $(\beta_t)_{t \geq 1}$ is a sequence of parameters chosen to ensure a trade-off between exploration and exploitation.

As said, a basic version of this update would lead an increasing average regret. To limit the regret, we consider only recent observations and summarize and update the remaining ones.

2.2 Sparse Inference

To summarize and update past observations, we leverage and extend recent results from sparse inference provided in [4]. Consider Y_T observations performed at $X_T = [x_1, \ldots, x_T]$ points, as well as the mean and variance function coming from a GP regression on these points. Burt and coauthors in [4] offer an algorithm to select $\tilde{\mathcal{O}}(1)$ points in the domain $\mathcal{D}$ which would deliver the same mean and variance up to a tunable multiplicative error term. We summarize their main result in the following proposition.

Proposition 1 ([4]). *Consider the problem of estimating an unknown function $f : \mathcal{D} \to \mathbb{R}$ via T noisy observations, $y_t = f(x_t) + \epsilon_t$, $\epsilon_t \sim \mathcal{N}(0, \sigma^2)$ acquired* at i.i.d. training inputs X_T. Let f be a sample path of a Gaussian Process with zero mean and kernel k. Consider a squared exponential kernel function k for simplicity. Let $\mu_0(x)$ and $\sigma_0^2(x)$ represent the mean and variance of the Gaussian Process regression performed on the observations.

Select a tolerance level $\eta \leq 1/5$. Then, there exists an algorithm that selects $\tilde{\mathcal{O}}(1) < T$ points in the domain $\mathcal{D}$ and their observations $y_t = f(x_t) + \epsilon_t$, $\epsilon_t \sim \mathcal{N}(0, \sigma^2)$, such that if we let $\mu_1(x)$ and $\sigma_1^2(x)$ represent the mean and variance of the Gaussian Process regression performed on the new points and observations, we obtain in high probability,

$$|\mu_1 - \mu_0| \leq \sigma_0 \sqrt{\eta} \leq \frac{\sigma_1 \sqrt{\eta}}{\sqrt{1 - \sqrt{3\eta}}}, \quad (14)$$
$$|1 - \sigma_1^2/\sigma_0^2| \leq \sqrt{3\eta}.$$

Proposition 1 is a condensed version of Proposition 1, Theorem 14, and Corollary 22 in [4].

A possible algorithm proposed in the paper to determine the sparse inputs is an approximate determinantal point process (DPP). Such algorithm selects $M < T$ points in order to minimize the difference between the KL divergence of the exact posterior and approximated one. Specifically, for $\epsilon > 0$, one can use an MCMC algorithm, as specified in Algorithm 1 of [4] to obtain an ϵ approximation of a M-DPP, with T inputs, with a computational complexity that is upper bounded by $\mathcal{O}\left(TM^3(\log \log T + \log M + \log 1/\epsilon^2)\right)$.

The most important feature of the DPP algorithm in [4] and Proposition 1 is that these results do not depend on the observations values Y_T, but only on the points X_T where these observations are taken. We will see next how this is key in devising our sparse algorithm and, along the way, how we can extend Proposition 1 to the heteroscedastic and deterministic setting.

3 SparQ-GP-UCB Algorithm

With all the previous preliminaries in place, we are now ready for the main algorithm: SparQ-GP-UCB.

The algorithm works in rounds. At each time step t, we consider the problem of maximizing the regret f_t, with observations $Y_t = [y_1, \ldots, y_t]^\top$ at points $X_t = [x_1, \ldots, x_t]$. The observations are properly injected with uncertainty, so that their variance grows in time as,

$$\epsilon_{i,t} \sim \mathcal{N}(0, \sigma^2([t-i]^2 + 1)), \quad i \leq t. \quad (15)$$

The **first** step of the algorithm is to discard observations that have variance greater than $g(t)$, where $g(t) = o\left(t^{1/4}\right)$. We take $g : t \mapsto \sigma^2 \log(t)$ as an illustrative example but any function $g : t \mapsto g(t) = o\left(t^{1/4}\right)$ would work with no change in the proof arguments (and we further discuss it in the proof).

Second, we act as if we had access to updated noisy observations for the discarded measurements, with noise being zero-mean and with $\bar{\sigma}^2$ variance. With this pretend observations and the most recent ones with noise less than $\sigma^2 \log(t)$, we perform sparse variational inference. We use the approximate DPP algorithm in [4] (Algorithm 1) to find the locations $X^E = [x_1^E, \ldots]$, with $|X^E| = \tilde{\mathcal{O}}(1) \ll t$ at which to ask an expert for noisy updated observation with zero-mean and variance $\bar{\sigma}^2$. The new expert-delivered observations, together with the most recent ones are guaranteed to be a good approximation of the pretend setting.

Third, we let Y_t^s, X_t^s being the set of expert-delivered observations together with the most recent ones with noise less than $\sigma^2 \log(t)$ and the points at which they are taken. With this, we can compute the mean and variance as,

$$\mu_t^s(x) = k_t^s(x)^\top (K_t^s + \Sigma_t^s)^{-1} Y_t^s \qquad (16)$$

$$(\sigma^s)_t^2(x) = k(x,x) - k_t^s(x)^\top (K_t^s + \Sigma_t^s)^{-1} k_t^s(x), \qquad (17)$$

where Σ_t^s is a diagonal matrix containing all the observation variances up to $\max\{\bar{\sigma}^2, \sigma^2 \log(t)\}$, and the kernel elements K_t^s, k_t^s, are evaluated on X_t^s.

And finally, we compute the next decision, via the UCB proxy:

$$x_{t+1} = \arg\max_{x \in \mathcal{D}} \mu_t^s(x) + \beta_{t+1} \sigma_t^s(x). \qquad (18)$$

The algorithm is summarized in Algorithm 1. We remark the need for performing sparse inference based on Algorithm 1 of [4], whose details are reported in the Appendix.

Algorithm 1. SparQ-GP-UCB

Input: Domain $\mathcal{D}$, kernel k
1: **for** $t = 1, 2, \ldots$ **do**
2:     Sample $y_t = f_t(x_t) + \epsilon_t$
3:     Discard all the observations with a noise $> \sigma^2 \log(t)$
4:     Perform sparse inference on X_t to obtain locations X^E of cardinality $\tilde{\mathcal{O}}(1)$
5:     Query an expert to obtain updated observations on X^E for f_t
6:     Perform Bayesian updates (16)-(17) to obtain μ_t^s and σ^s using (X_t^s, Y_t^s)
7:     Choose the next action x_{t+1} via (18)
8: **end for**

3.1 Main Results

In this subsection, we report the main results for our algorithm. They are both given for a squared exponential kernel for simplicity, but they can easily be extended to other standard kernels (Matérn for example).

Theorem 1. *(Regret bound for SparQ-GP-UCB) Take any $0 < \delta \leq 1$ and consider a sequence of reward functions $(f_t)_t$ and the observations $y_t = f_t(x_t) + \epsilon_t$,* for $\epsilon_t \sim \mathcal{N}(0, \sigma^2)$ i.i.d.. Let Assumptions 1 and 2 hold and consider a squared exponential kernel k. Let T be a time horizon and $(x_t)_{t=1}^T$ the set of actions chosen by SparQ-GP-UCB (Algorithm 1) and set $(\beta_t)_{t=1}^T$ as

$$\beta_t = \sqrt{2\log\left(\frac{2|\Sigma_t^s + K_{tt}^s|^{1/2}}{\delta|\Sigma_t^s|^{1/2}}\right)} + \|f_t\|_k.$$

Then, with probability at least $1-\delta$, by asking to an expert $\mathcal{O}\left(\log^d(t)\right)$ queries per time step, SparQ-GP-UCB attains a cumulative dynamic regret of

$$R_T = \mathcal{O}\left(\sqrt{Td\log^{d+5}(T)}\sqrt{\log\left(\frac{1}{\delta}\right) + d\log^{d+3}(d\log(T))}\right) = \tilde{\mathcal{O}}(\sqrt{T}). \quad (19)$$

The asymptotic bound given in Eq. (19) implies no-regret with probability $1-\delta$ and matches the static case up to poly-logarithmic factors. The main steps of the proof are given in Sect. 5.

We can now discuss briefly the impact of Assumption 2 for the regret bound. A common metric in the literature to account for the time-varying nature of the objective is the variation budget V_T [1,5,8] defined as,

$$\forall T,\ V_T = \sum_{t=1}^{T-1} \|f_{t+1} - f_t\|_k. \quad (20)$$

Let $x \in \mathcal{D}$. Then, by the reproducing property of RKHS,

$$|f_{t+1}(x) - f_t(x)| = |\langle f_{t+1} - f_t, k(x,.)\rangle| \leq \|f_{t+1} - f_t\|_k \|k(x,.)\|_k, \quad (21)$$

where we applied Cauchy Schwarz in the RKHS to obtain the inequality. From the reproducing property, $\|k(x,.)\|_k^2 = k(x,x)$. As we are working with bounded kernels (Assumption 1) and $\forall x \in \mathcal{D}$, $k(x,x) \leq M_k^2$, we take the infinite norm in the left side of Eq. (21) and sum over $t = 1$ to $T-1$ to obtain:

$$\sum_{t=1}^{T-1} \|f_{t+1} - f_t\|_\infty \leq M_k V_T. \quad (22)$$

By Assumption 2, SparQ-GP-UCB does work even in the case of $\sum_{t=1}^{T-1} \|f_{t+1} - f_t\|_\infty = (T-1)$, meaning that our algorithm can achieve no-regret even for a variation budget that grows linearly in time. This improves the result of [5] that requires $V_T = o(T)$ when V_T is known and $V_T = o(T^{1/4})$ otherwise to obtain sublinear regret.

Along with a no-regret result, we also provide a computational complexity estimate as follows.

Theorem 2. *Under the same setting of Theorem 1, the computational complexity of SparQ-GP-UCB is upper bounded by* $\mathcal{O}\left(T^2 \log(T) \log^{3d}\left(\frac{T}{\log(T)}\right)\right) = \tilde{\mathcal{O}}(T^2)$.

The theorem shows how SparQ-GP-UCB is actually less computationally expensive than running a basic Bayesian update on the whole T measurement set, which can be bounded as $O(T^3)$.

3.2 Role of the Expert

In SparQ-GP-UCB, the "expert" mechanism is not meant to be a human oracle, nor does it need to act as a perfectly accurate surrogate model. Instead, it serves as a means to partially refresh or correct stale information from previous observations in a principled and computationally bounded way.

More precisely, at each time step t, we are allowed to query the current value of the objective f_t at a small number $\mathcal{O}\left(\log^d(t)\right)$ of previously observed points, selected via a Q_t-DPP sampling over X_t.

This mechanism is abstracted as an "expert call", but it is not assumed to be human or even a separate model. Rather, it reflects limited access to the current function values at previously observed locations, which can be interpreted in several realistic ways:

- **Wireless sensor networks:** In Internet-of-Things applications [26], sensors might collect data continuously but transmit selectively due to bandwidth or power constraints. Revisiting previous locations or reactivating a subset of sensors is often feasible, though costly—thus motivating a trade-off.
- **Physics-based monitoring:** In tasks such as environmental monitoring [27] where the underlying phenomenon is governed by a partial differential equation that needs to be simulated, the "expert" corresponds to access to the simulation itself. While running the simulator to evaluate the objective at a new point can be computationally expensive, it is often possible—though still costly—to re-run the simulator at previous input points to obtain updated objective values, reflecting changes in the underlying system.
- **Continual learning in ML systems:** For adaptive hyperparameter tuning or online systems [25], logs or cached evaluations might allow querying recent values again (e.g., checking performance of previous configurations on a new data batch).

We emphasize that the expert is not required to provide perfectly accurate information, but rather noisy or approximate values, consistent with a sub-Gaussian noise model. This is crucial in practice and aligns with many systems where re-evaluation is possible but noisy (e.g., due to changing conditions).

4 Numerical Results

In this section, we compare the performance of SparQ-GP-UCB with four existing algorithms (TV-GP-UCB [2], W-GP-UCB [5], R-GP-UCB and SW-GP-UCB [24]) in a time-varying environment, on both a synthetic and a real-life dataset. We also run standard GP-UCB to show how it performs in time-varying settings.

For all baseline methods, hyperparameters suchs as window size (R-GP-UCB, SW-GP-UCB), temporal kernel hyperparameter (TV-GP-UCB) and observations weights (W-GP-UCB) were set according to the recommendations provided by their respective authors.

4.1 Synthetic Data

Observations are generated by perturbing the function

$$f\colon \mathcal{D} \times \mathbb{R}_+ \to \mathbb{R}_+$$
$$(x,t) \mapsto \exp(-0.05(x - 5\sin(0.1t))^2) + 0.5\cos(0.2x) + 1.5$$

with noise $\epsilon \sim \mathcal{N}(0, \sigma^2)$, where the sampling noise variance σ^2 is set to 0.01. We take the domain $\mathcal{D} = [-50, 50]$. Let $t \geq 0$. Then, by the mean value theorem

$$\sup_{x \in \mathcal{D}} |f(x, t+1) - f(x, t)| \leq \sup_{x,t} \left| \frac{\partial f(x,t)}{\partial t} \right| \leq 1,$$

and Assumption 2 holds. We plot the average and standard deviation of the cumulative regret of each algorithm for $T = 500$ iterations and $\delta = 0.05$ over 40 realizations using the squared exponential kernel, whose parameters have been fine-tuned by maximizing the log marginal likelihood of the data. For all four methods, we plot the mean and standard deviation of the average regret at each iteration. By selecting the number of queries $Q_T = 6\log(T)$ in line with the result of Proposition 2, we expect the average regret of SparQ-GP-UCB to vanish asymptotically. Furthermore, since the variation budget is not $V_T = o(T^{1/4})$ in our setting, due to the periodicity of $f \mapsto f(x,t)$, R-GP-UCB and SW-GP-UCB are not expected to have sublinear cumulative regret bounds.

We can see in Fig. 1 that SparQ-GP-UCB is the only method that converges to the dynamic optimum of the objective on average. Moreover, it falls below the theoretical bound (black curve) established in Eq. (19). Standard TV methods (TV-GP-UCB, W-GP-UCB, R-GP-UCB and SW-GP-UCB) struggle to track the optimum and have linear cumulative regret ($R_T \approx 1.8$ for TV-GP-UCB, $R_T \approx 1.3$ for W-GP-UCB, $R_T \approx 1.34T$ for R-GP-UCB and $R_T \approx 1.18T$ for SW-GP-UCB). As expected, the average regret of standard GP-UCB grows slowly, suggesting a slightly superlinear average regret. In summary, at the cost of $\tilde{\mathcal{O}}(1)$ additional observations per iteration, SparQ-GP-UCB is the only method capable of accurately optimizing a time-varying objective with weak assumptions on its temporal variations.

4.2 Real Data

To evaluate the effectiveness of SparQ-GP-UCB, we conducted experiments on a real-world dataset consisting of daily ozone level measurements collected from 28 sensors distributed across the New York City area over the course of two years [28]. This dataset presents a naturally time-varying environment, making it an ideal testbed for adaptive Bayesian optimization methods.

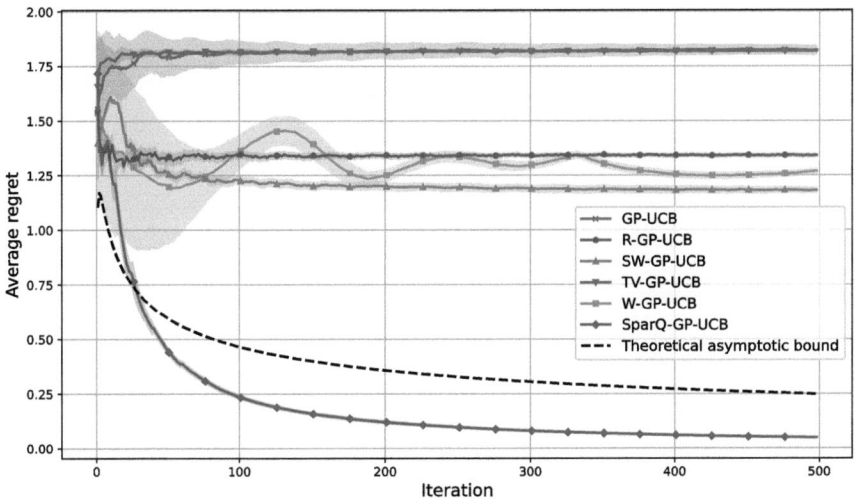

Fig. 1. Average regret of GP-UCB variants in the time-varying setting.

Again, we benchmarked SparQ-GP-UCB against several state-of-the-art baselines: GP-UCB, R-GP-UCB, SW-GP-UCB, TV-GP-UCB, and W-GP-UCB. The evaluation metric used was cumulative regret, plotted as average regret over time to highlight long-term performance trends.

Figure 2 shows the evolution of average regret across time steps (here one day). We set $\delta = 0.05$ and compute the kernel hyperparameters by maximizing the log marginal likelihood of the data. Although the ozone data is not generated by a model that respects our RKHS assumptions, we can see that SparQ-GP-UCB achieves significantly lower regret compared to other method. This indicates its superior ability to adapt to underlying non-stationary reward dynamics. Interestingly, GP-UCB achieves performance comparable to its time-varying counterparts. This may be attributed to characteristics of the ozone dataset— for example, the location of the maximum ozone level might be approximately stationary over time. Unlike the four time-varying baselines, SparQ-GP-UCB still consistently outperforms GP-UCB, suggesting that it effectively balances adaptation to temporal changes without overcompensating.

These results validate the robustness and adaptivity of our proposed method in capturing temporal variations and optimizing over dynamic environments.

5 Proofs of Main Theorems and Additional Results

5.1 Proof of Theorem 1

The regret proof is based on a few ingredients and extensions of previous work in [4,12,18]. We proceed as follows: first we extend Proposition 1 to the heteroscedastic and deterministic setting. Then we extend the regret results of [12]

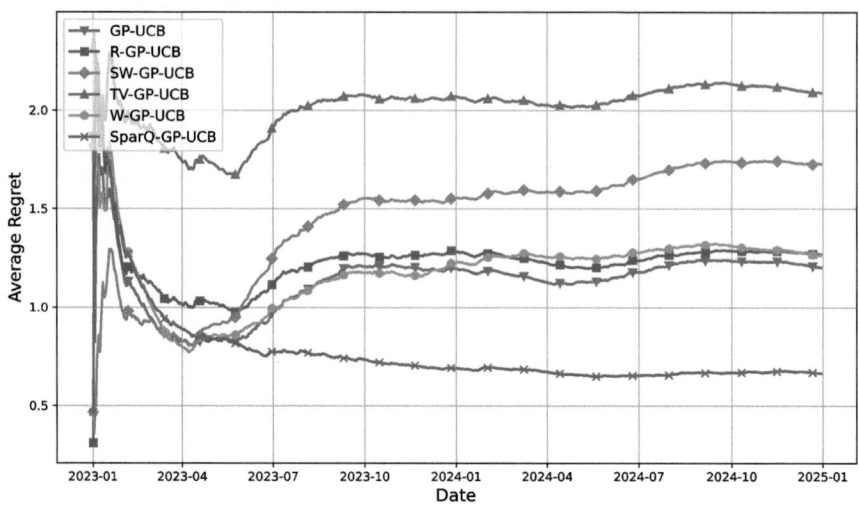

Fig. 2. Numerical performances of GP-UCB variants on real data.

incorporating a sub-linearly growing maximum uncertainty, as well as the multiplicative error coming from the sparse inference. Then we combine the two results.

It is convenient to define the set of pretend observations together with the latest ones with noise $< \sigma^2 \log(T)$ as Y_T^{v} taken at points X_T^{v}. The cardinality of the two sets is T. These sets are not the same as the set of sparse plus latest one observations, indicated as Y_T^{s} and X_T^{s} whose cardinality is $\tilde{\mathcal{O}}(1)$.

The first proposition extends the sparse approximation to our setting, and in particular, it is an extension of Corollary 22 in [4] to heteroscedastic GPs and deterministic inputs X_T^{v} in a compact domain.

Proposition 2. *Let X_T^{v} be the set of actions chosen by SparQ-GP-UCB. Assume that pretend plus latest observations $Y_T^{\text{v}}|X_T^{\text{v}}$ are conditionally Gaussian distributed. Then, under the same assumptions as Theorem 1, for any $\eta > 0$ and any t, there exists an approximation level $\varepsilon_t = \mathcal{O}\left(\frac{\eta}{t}\right)$ and number of queries $Q_t = \mathcal{O}\left(\log^d\left(\frac{t}{\eta}\right)\right)$ such that running SparQ-GP-UCB with an ε_t-approximate Q_t-DPP provides a posterior distribution P_T^{s} satisfying*

$$\mathbb{E}[\mathrm{KL}[P_T^{\text{s}} \| P_T^{\text{v}}]] \leq \eta, \tag{23}$$

where P_T^{v} is the posterior distribution on $(X_T^{\text{v}}, Y_T^{\text{v}})$, and KL is the KL divergence.

Proof. We give the proof in the Appendix.

While the result of Eq. (23) is given in expectation, we can also use Markov's inequality implying,

$$\mathrm{KL}[P_T^{\text{s}} \| P_T^{\text{v}}] \leq \frac{2\eta}{\delta}, \tag{24}$$

with probability $1 - \delta/2$.

Let us now recall Proposition 1 of [4].

Proposition 3. *[Proposition 1 of [4]] Let P and Q be the real and approximate posteriors with means μ_p, μ_q and variances σ_p^2 and σ_q^2. Suppose $2\text{KL}[Q\|P] \leq \eta \leq \frac{1}{5}$ and let $x \in \mathbb{R}^d$. Then,*

$$|\mu_p(x) - \mu_q(x)| \leq \sigma_p(x)\sqrt{\eta} \leq \frac{\sigma_q(x)\sqrt{\eta}}{\sqrt{1 - \sqrt{3\eta}}} \quad \text{and} \quad |1 - \sigma_q^2/\sigma_p^2| < \sqrt{3\eta}.$$

Since by Proposition 2 we have a way to bound the error coming from considering a sparse setting instead of the pretend setting, and by Proposition 3, we know how this translates into a multiplicative error of mean and variance, we are now ready for the regret result.

5.2 Regret Proof

Proof. In SparQ-GP-UCB algorithm, the posterior mean $\mu_t^s(.)$ and variance $(\sigma_t^s)^2(.)$ at step t are obtained by performing regression on the sparse observations (X_{t-1}^s, Y_{t-1}^s). The instantaneous regret of SparQ-GP-UBC at step t is:

$$r_t = f_t(x_t^*) - f_t(x_t),$$

where,

$$x_t^* = \underset{x \in \mathcal{D}}{\arg\max}\, f_t(x) \quad \text{and} \quad x_t = \underset{x \in \mathcal{D}}{\arg\max}\, \mu_{t-1}^s(x) + \beta_t \sigma_{t-1}^s(x).$$

By leveraging the definition of confidence bounds acquisition functions $x \mapsto \text{ucb}_t(x) = \mu_{t-1}^s(x) + \beta_t \sigma_{t-1}^s(x)$ and $x \mapsto \text{lcb}_t(x) = \mu_{t-1}^s(x) - \beta_t \sigma_{t-1}^s(x)$, it is possible to bound the cumulative regret with probability $1 - \delta/2$. To do that, we leverage the concentration bound provided in [9].

Proposition 4. *(Lemma 7, [9]) Take any $0 < \delta \leq 1$ and let $f_T \in \mathcal{H}_k(\mathcal{D})$ and $\mu_T(.)$ and $\sigma_T^2(.)$ be the posterior mean and covariance functions of $f_T(.)$ after observing (X_T, Y_T) points. Then, for any $x \in \mathcal{D}$, the following holds with probability at least $1 - \delta/2$:*

$$\forall t \in \{1, \ldots, T\}, \quad |\mu_{t-1}(x) - f_t(x)| \leq \beta_t \sigma_{t-1}(x) \quad (25)$$

where

$$\beta_t = \left(\sqrt{2\log\left(\frac{2\det(\Sigma_t + K_{tt})^{1/2}}{\delta \det(\Sigma_t)^{1/2}}\right)} + \|f_t\|_k\right). \quad (26)$$

Proposition is valid for the heteroscedastic setting. As such, with this in place, and with probability $1 - \delta/2$:

$$r_t \leq \text{ucb}_t(x_t^*) - \text{lcb}_t(x_t) \leq \text{ucb}_t(x_t) - \text{lcb}_t(x_t) = 2\beta_t \sigma_{t-1}^s(x_t).$$

Now we bound the cumulative regret at iteration T:

$$R_T = \sum_{t=1}^{T} r_t \leq 2\beta_T \sum_{t=1}^{T} \sigma^{\text{s}}_{t-1}(x_t).$$

If we denote by $\sigma^{\text{v}}_{t-1}(.)$ the posterior variance of the regression on the pretend plus latest observations $(X^{\text{v}}_{t-1}, Y^{\text{v}}_{t-1})$, Proposition 3 gives

$$\sigma^{\text{s}}_{t-1}(x_t) \leq \sigma^{\text{v}}_{t-1}(x_t)\sqrt{1 + \sqrt{3\eta}},$$

with probability $1 - \delta/2$, as long as we have a number of queries $\mathcal{O}(\log^d(t/\eta'))$ with $\eta' = \delta\eta/4$.

Therefore, the cumulative regret can be bounded with probability $1 - \delta$ (for the union bound) as follows,

$$R_T \leq 2\beta_T \sqrt{1 + \sqrt{3\eta}} \sum_{t=1}^{T} \sigma^{\text{v}}_{t-1}(x_t).$$

The observations Y^{v}_{t-1} have been built such that their noise variance can be uniformly bounded by $\sigma^2 \log(t-1)$. By following the exact same computation steps of Makarova et al. in [12] (Appendix A.1.1 Step 4) and replacing their fixed upper bound $\bar{\rho}$ by a logarithmically increasing upper bound $\sigma^2 \log(T)$ we get

$$R_T \leq 2\beta_T \sqrt{1 + \sqrt{3\eta}} \sqrt{2T(1 + (\sigma^2 \log(T))^2)\gamma_T},$$

where γ_T is the maximum information gain at step T. Finally,

$$R_T = \mathcal{O}\left(\beta_T \sqrt{T \log^2(T) \gamma_T}\right). \quad (27)$$

Let us now bound β_T and γ_T.

In SparQ-GP-UCB, the ucb acquisition function is computed using the approximate posterior mean and variance. We thus have:

$$\beta_T = \sqrt{2\log\left(\frac{2|\Sigma^{\text{s}}_T + K^{\text{s}}_{TT}|^{1/2}}{\delta|\Sigma^{\text{s}}_T|^{1/2}}\right)} + \|f_T\|_k.$$

By the definition of information gain with the sparse plus recent observations (see, e.g., [12]), we have

$$\gamma_{Q_T} \geq \log\left(\frac{|\Sigma^{\text{s}}_T + K^{\text{s}}_{TT}|}{|\Sigma^{\text{s}}_T|}\right),$$

so that,

$$\beta_T = \mathcal{O}\left(\sqrt{\log\left(\frac{2}{\delta}\right) + \gamma_{Q_T}}\right). \quad (28)$$

If we combine bounds (28) and (27), we have a new expression for the regret bound:

$$R_T = \mathcal{O}\left(\sqrt{\left(\log\left(\frac{2}{\delta}\right) + \gamma_{Q_T}\right)\left(T\log^2(T)\gamma_T\right)}\right). \tag{29}$$

Again, by replacing $\bar{\rho}$ by $\sigma^2 \log(T)$ in Makarova et al. proof (Appendix A.1.3) and using $Q_T = \mathcal{O}\left(\log^d(T)\right)$, we can bound the information gains γ_T and γ_{Q_T} for a squared exponential kernel[1]:

$$\gamma_T = \mathcal{O}\left(d\log^{d+3}(T)\right), \tag{30}$$

$$\gamma_{Q_T} = \mathcal{O}\left(d\log^{d+3}\left(\log^d(T)\right)\right) = \mathcal{O}\left(d\log^{d+3}(d\log(T))\right). \tag{31}$$

Finally, if we inject bounds (30) and (31) into (29):

$$\begin{aligned}R_T &= \mathcal{O}\left(\sqrt{\left(\log\left(\frac{1}{\delta}\right) + d\log^{d+3}(d\log(T))\right)\left(T\log^2(T)d\log^{d+3}(T)\right)}\right) \\ &= \mathcal{O}\left(\sqrt{\left(\log\left(\frac{1}{\delta}\right) + d\log^{d+3}(d\log(T))\right)\left(Td\log^{d+5}(T)\right)}\right)\end{aligned} \tag{32}$$

This proves Theorem 1. □

A closer look at the proof of Theorem 1 shows that one could choose to keep all the measurements with variance less than $g(T) = o(T^{1/4})$, as discussed in Sect. 3, instead limiting at the ones with variance less than $\sigma^2 \log(T)$. Since the maximum variance enters twice in the regret as a power of 2, then the final regret would read $R = \tilde{\mathcal{O}}(\sqrt{T}\sqrt{g^4(T)}) = o(T)$, leading to a sublinear cumulative regret and a no-regret result.

5.3 Proof of Theorem 2

The computational complexity of the algorithm proposed by Burt et al. [4] to obtain a ε approximation of a M-DPP from a set of N inputs is bounded as $\mathcal{O}\left(NM^3(\log\log N + \log M + \log 1/\varepsilon^2)\right)$, see their Sect. 4.2.2.

The cost of the GP regression with M training inputs is $\mathcal{O}(M^3)$ [16], and the complexity of SparQ-GP-UCB is dominated by the computation of the M-DPP. Thus, for T iterations in Algorithm 1 and with Q_T the number of sparse inputs at the end of the process, the computational complexity of SparQ-GP-UCB is T times the worst complexity of the DPP:

$$\mathcal{O}\left(T\left(Q_T\right)^3\left(\log\log T + \log Q_T + \log 1/\varepsilon_T^2\right)\right).$$

---

[1] The information gain in a homoscedastic case for a SE kernel is $\mathcal{O}(d\log^{d+1}(T))$ to which we multiply a factor $\log^2(T)$ in our setting for the heteroscedastic case.

In Proposition 2, for fixed precision η, we show that $Q_T = \mathcal{O}\left(\log^d(T)\right)$, suffices to obtain a ε_T-approximation of a Q_T-DPP, with $\varepsilon_T = \mathcal{O}\left(\frac{1}{T}\right)$. By substituting these estimates into the complexity, we obtain a total computational complexity of SparQ-GP-UCB of $\mathcal{O}\left(T^2 \log(T) \log^{3d}(T)\right)$. □

6 Conclusion

In this work, we provide a general framework to obtain sublinear regret bounds for GP optimization of a time-varying objective f in the bandit setting. The function f is assumed to belong to a RKHS with a bounded norm. We model time variations through uncertainty injection by linearly increasing the noise standard deviation of the data over time. We recover no-regret by asking $\tilde{\mathcal{O}}(1)$ additional side queries to an expert at each iteration. Future research will explore strategies to reduce the number of expert queries, such as retaining and reusing past responses to avoid querying the expert at every iteration.

Acknowledgments. This work was partly supported by the Agence Nationale de la Recherche (ANR) with the projects ANR AccelAILearning and ANR-23-CE48-0011-01.

Disclosure of Interests. The authors have no competing interests to declare that are relevant to the content of this article.

References

1. Besbes, O., Gur, Y., Zeevi, A.: Stochastic multi-armed-bandit problem with non-stationary rewards. In: Advances in Neural Information Processing Systems, vol. 27 (2014)
2. Bogunovic, I., Scarlett, J., Cevher, V.: Time-varying Gaussian Process bandit optimization. In: International Conference on Artificial Intelligence and Statistics, vol. 51, pp. 314–323 (2016)
3. Brunzema, P., Von Rohr, A., Trimpe, S.: On controller tuning with time-varying Bayesian optimization. In: Conference on Decision and Control, pp. 4046–4052 (2022)
4. Burt, D.R., Rasmussen, C.E., van der Wilk, M.: Convergence of sparse variational inference in Gaussian Processes regression. J. Mach. Learn. Res. **21**(131), 1–63 (2020)
5. Deng, Y., Zhou, X., Kim, B., Tewari, A., Gupta, A., Shroff, N.B.: Weighted Gaussian Process bandits for non-stationary environments. In: International Conference on Artificial Intelligence and Statistics, vol. 151, pp. 6909–6932 (2022)
6. Derezinski, M., Calandriello, D., Valko, M.: Exact sampling of determinantal point processes with sublinear time preprocessing. In: Advances in Neural Information Processing Systems, vol. 32 (2019)
7. Imamura, H., Charoenphakdee, N., Futami, F., Sato, I., Honda, J., Sugiyama, M.: Time-varying Gaussian Process bandit optimization with non-constant evaluation time. arXiv:2003.04691 (2020)

8. Jadbabaie, A., Rakhlin, A., Shahrampour, S., Sridharan, K.: Online optimization: competing with dynamic comparators. In: International Conference on Artificial Intelligence and Statistics, vol. 38, pp. 398–406 (2015)
9. Kirschner, J., Krause, A.: Information directed sampling and bandits with heteroscedastic noise. In: Conference on Learning Theory, pp. 358–384 (2018)
10. Koltchinskii, V., Giné, E.: Random matrix approximation of spectra of integral operators. Bernoulli **6**(1), 113–167 (2000)
11. Kulesza, A.: Determinantal point processes for machine learning. Found. Trends Mach. Learn. **5**(2–3), 123–286 (2012)
12. Makarova, A., Usmanova, I., Bogunovic, I., Krause, A.: Risk-averse heteroscedastic Bayesian optimization. In: Advances in Neural Information Processing Systems, vol. 34, pp. 17235–17245 (2021)
13. Russac, Y., Faury, L., Cappé, O., Garivier, A.: Self-concordant analysis of generalized linear bandits with forgetting. In: International Conference on Artificial Intelligence and Statistics, vol. 130, pp. 658–666 (2021)
14. Scholkopf, B., Tsuda, K., Vert, J.P.: Kernel Methods in Computational Biology. The MIT Press (2004)
15. Shawe-Taylor, J., Williams, C., Cristianini, N., Kandola, J.: On the eigenspectrum of the gram matrix and the generalization error of kernel-PCA. IEEE Trans. Inf. Theory **51**(7), 2510–2522 (2005)
16. Snelson, E., Ghahramani, Z.: Sparse Gaussian Processes using pseudo-inputs. In: Advances in Neural Information Processing Systems, vol. 18 (2005)
17. Srinivas, N., Krause, A., Kakade, S.M., Seeger, M.W.: Information-theoretic regret bounds for Gaussian Process optimization in the bandit setting. IEEE Trans. Inf. Theory **58**(5), 3250–3265 (2012)
18. Titsias, M.: Variational learning of inducing variables in sparse Gaussian Processes. In: International Conference on Artificial Intelligence and Statistics, vol. 5, pp. 567–574 (2009)
19. Titsias, M.K.: Variational model selection for sparse Gaussian Process regression. University of Manchester, UK, Technical report (2008)
20. Van Vaerenbergh, S., Lázaro-Gredilla, M., Santamaria, I.: Kernel recursive least-squares tracker for time-varying regression. IEEE Trans. Neural Netw. Learn. Syst. **23**, 1313–1326 (2012)
21. Werge, N., Akgül, A., Kandemir, M.: BOF-UCB: a Bayesian-optimistic frequentist algorithm for non-stationary contextual bandits. arXiv:2307.03587 (2023)
22. Wu, Q., Iyer, N., Wang, H.: Learning contextual bandits in a non-stationary environment. In: International ACM SIGIR Conference on Research and Development in Information Retrieval (2018)
23. Zhao, P., Zhang, L., Jiang, Y., Zhou, Z.H.: A simple approach for non-stationary linear bandits. In: International Conference on Artificial Intelligence and Statistics, vol. 108, pp. 746–755 (2020)
24. Zhou, X., Shroff, N.: No-regret algorithms for time-varying Bayesian optimization. In: Annual Conference on Information Sciences and Systems, pp. 1–6 (2021)
25. Wang, L., Zhang, X., Su, H., Zhu, J.: A comprehensive survey of continual learning: theory, method and application. IEEE Trans. Pattern Anal. Mach. Intell. **46**(8), 5362–5383 (2024)

26. Jamali-Rad, H., Campman, X.: Internet of things-based wireless networking for seismic applications. Geophys. Prospect. **66**(4), 833–853 (2018)
27. Roy, V., Simonetto, A., Leus, G.: Spatio-temporal sensor management for environmental field estimation. Signal Process. **128**, 369–381 (2016)
28. United States Environmental Protection Agency: Download Daily Data. https://www.epa.gov/outdoor-air-quality-data/download-daily-data

Designing Search Space for Unbounded Bayesian Optimization via Transfer Learning

Quoc-Anh Hoang Nguyen[1], Hung The Tran[3], Sunil Gupta[2], and Dung D. Le[3]([✉])

[1] FPT Software AI Center, Hanoi, Vietnam
[2] Deakin University, Geelong, Australia
sunil.gupta@deakin.edu.au
[3] College of Engineering and Computer Science, Center of Environmental Intelligence, VinUniversity, Hanoi, Vietnam
Dung.ld@vinuni.edu.vn

Abstract. Bayesian optimization (BO) is a powerful method for optimizing expensive black-box functions and has been successfully applied across various scenarios. While traditional BO algorithms optimize each task in isolation, there has been recent interest in speeding up BO by transferring knowledge across similar previous tasks. However, most recent studies on this problem are based on two implicit assumptions that (1) the search space of the test task (the ultimate task the model aims to solve) needs to be defined suitably a priori and (2) the optimum of the test task is very close to the evaluations of the previous tasks. These restrictive assumptions limit BO's applicability in real-world scenarios. In this paper, we propose an approach that leverages transfer learning to design promising search spaces for BO, thereby overcoming these limitations. Our approach eliminates the need for prior knowledge of the search spaces of both the test and previous tasks while also relaxing the assumption that the test task's optimum is close to evaluations of previous tasks. We propose a novel BO algorithm to automatically design promising search spaces for BO, not only exploiting regions near good evaluations of previous tasks but also exploring other promising regions using strategy shifting and expanding the search space. Our algorithm leverages both task similarity measurements and the best evaluation achieved so far for the test task. Further, theoretically, we prove that our proposed algorithm is guaranteed to find a global optimum in the worst-case scenario although the search spaces are unknown. Finally, we empirically demonstrate that our algorithms considerably boost BO and outperform the state-of-the-art on a wide range of benchmarks.

Keywords: Bayesian optimization · Transfer Learning · Gaussian Process · Designing search space

---
Q.-A. H. Nguyen and H. T. Tran—These authors contributed equally to this work.

Supplementary Information The online version contains supplementary material available at https://doi.org/10.1007/978-3-032-06096-9_11.

1 Introduction

Bayesian optimization (BO) is a powerful method for optimizing expensive black-box functions. It works by iteratively fitting a surrogate model, usually a Gaussian process (GP), and maximizing an acquisition function to determine the next evaluation point. Bayesian optimization algorithms have proven particularly successful in a wide variety of domains including hyperparameter tuning [2], reinforcement learning [14], neural architecture search [11], and Pareto front learning [29,30].

However, two issues hamper the efficiency of BO in real-world applications are (1) **slow convergence:** given a very limited budget, BO methods often fail to converge to a good solution quickly [1] and **search space definition:** Traditional BO requires the user to define a suitable search space a priori. However, defining a default search space for a particular data mining problem is difficult and left to human experts [17]. For example, in many machine learning algorithms, the hyperparameters or parameters can take values in an unbounded space e.g. L_1/L_2 penalty hyperparameters in elastic-net can take any non-negative value; To address the first issue, transfer learning is an efficient solution to speed up BO by leveraging the information obtained from similar previous tasks into optimization. In many practical applications, optimizations are repeated in similar settings. Examples include hyperparameter optimization, which is repeatedly done for the same machine learning model on varying datasets, or the optimization of control parameters for a given system with varying physical configurations.

Most of the recent works for this transfer learning-based search space design (e.g., [12,17]) are based on an implicit hypothesis that the optimums of an objective function (test task) are close to the best evaluations of the previous tasks (or training tasks). Figure 1 (Left) shows an example of this situation. As a result, they search only regions close to those evaluations. [17] uses a quite simple strategy. Instead of searching on the whole search space, they learn a region in the form of a box or an ellipsoid bounding the best evaluations of training tasks. However, if the distribution of these best evaluations is large then the learned search space is not improved compared to the original search space. This is illus-

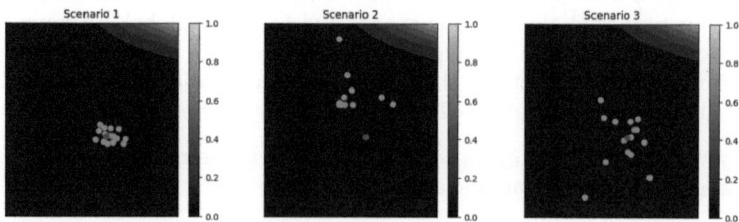

Fig. 1. True contour plot of the Beale 2D-function and data distribution on 3 scenarios. The red dots: the global optimum of the target task; the yellow dots: the optimum point of training tasks. (**Left**) Target task optimum is close to most training tasks' optima; (**Middle**) Target task optimum is distant from most training tasks' optima; (**Right**) Target task optimum is distant from some training tasks' optima. (Color figure online)

trated in Fig. 1 (Right). Another recent work [12] proposes to use a similarity measurement to choose the good training tasks that are similar to the test task. Then, they use a Gaussian process classifier (GPC) to design promising regions, where the classifier predicts whether a point from the search space belongs to the promising region or not. However, this approach has two limitations. First, it is designed for the search space which is discrete and known. If the search space is continuous, classifying each point from the search space into a class is expensive or even intractable in the unknown search space setting. Second, the similarity measurement used in [12] is efficient only when the test task has enough evaluations and the distribution of evaluations in the test task is uniform. We will discuss this in detail in Sect. 5.1.1.

In practice, the optimums of the test task may not be close to the best evaluations of previous tasks as illustrated in Fig. 1 (Middle). Consequently, both works [12,17] may encounter limitations in such scanarios. Furthermore, all these approaches rely on prior knowledge of the search space, and none address the above second issue, which is challenging.

In this paper, we address designing promising search spaces with the merit of transfer learning to speed up BO (reducing the number of evaluations) without requiring prior knowledge of the search space. We propose a novel algorithm to learn promising search spaces for BO, which not only exploits regions close to good evaluation points of previous tasks, but also explores promising regions surrounding the best evaluations of the test task. We propose using a strategy of shifting and expanding the search space and a novel similarity measurement. Furthermore, theoretically, we prove that our proposed algorithm is guaranteed to find a global optimum in the worst-case scenario, even when the search spaces are unknown. Finally, we demonstrate that our proposed algorithm considerably boosts BO, and outperforms the state-of-the-art on a wide range of benchmarks.

2 Related Works

Previous work has implemented transfer learning for BO in different ways to leverage the auxiliary information from similar training tasks to achieve faster optimization on the target task. One way is to learn surrogate models from source tasks. For example, [27] and [7] train individual surrogate models on each dataset and then combine them using a weighted sum-based approach. Another approach, proposed by [13], uses a two-phase framework to extract and aggregate knowledge from both source and target tasks. [20] employ neural networks to learn basis functions for Bayesian linear regression. Furthermore, several works consider the difference between training tasks and target tasks to compute the kernel of the proposed surrogate [22,28]. The other line of transfer learning works focuses on designing acquisition functions. [27] introduce a TAF that utilizes a variant of the EI acquisition function to leverage the improvement of new points. [4] propose a method called RM-GP-UCB, where the acquisition function is a weighted combination of individual GP-UCB acquisition functions for both the target task and the training tasks. [26] employ reinforcement learning to meta-train an acquisition function on a set of related tasks, allowing the incorporation of implicit structural knowledge. From a few-shot learning perspective, [10] propose FSFA, which effectively adapts to a wide range of black-box functions using a small amount of meta-data. In contrast, our work focuses on the design of the search spaces for transfer learning in BO, taking an orthogonal direction to the aforementioned methods. It is worth noting that our method can be combined with these transfer learning-based approaches to enhance the efficiency of BO. [6] addressed BO using transfer learning where the search spaces of the task and previous tasks are heterogeneous.

BO with unknown search spaces has been considered in previous works. [16] consider the weakly specified search space for BO and propose the filtering expansion strategy. This approach is reasonable when a training dataset is available, as it allows for the initial region to be located near the best evaluation of the training tasks. Nevertheless, maximizing the acquisition function within their expanded search space is challenging since the invasion set needs to be specified. [9] provide the search space expansion strategy to achieve the $\epsilon-$ accuracy after a finite number of iterations. [3] proposes an adaptive expansion strategy based on the uncertainty of GP model. [19,23] increase the volume of the search space to guarantee to contain the global optimum of an objective function. However, none of these works consider transfer learning to leverage data from the previous training tasks. To our knowledge, we are the first to consider transfer learning for BO with unknown search spaces by novel expansion strategies.

[5] propose a trust-region method called TuRBO, which is an effective BO method for high-dimensional problems. Their method is based on adjusting the size of the trust region and moving towards the best solution so far. Our proposed methods also use the adjustment and the movement of boxes but with novel strategies by integrating transfer learning. In addition, their method is nearly a local strategy without providing a convergence analysis. In contrast, we demonstrate theoretically that our global method converges sub-linearly.

3 Preliminaries

Bayesian optimization (BO) finds the global optimum of an unknown, expensive, possibly non-convex function $f(x)$. It is assumed that we can interact with f only by querying at some $x \in \mathbb{R}^d$ and obtain a noisy observation $y = f(x) + \epsilon$ where $\epsilon \sim \mathcal{N}(0, \sigma^2)$. The search space is required to be specified a priori and is assumed to include the true global optimum. BO proceeds sequentially in an iterative fashion. At each iteration, a surrogate model is used to probabilistically model $f(x)$. Gaussian process (GP) [18] is a popular choice for the surrogate model as it offers a prior over a large class of functions and its posterior and predictive distributions are tractable. Formally, we have $f(x) \sim \mathcal{GP}(m(x), k(x, x'))$ where $m(x)$ and $k(x, x')$ are the mean and the covariance (or kernel) functions. Popular covariance functions include Squared Exponential (SE) kernels, Matérn kernels, etc. Given a set of observations $\mathcal{D}_{1:t} = \{x_i, y_i\}_{i=1}^{t}$, the predictive distribution can be derived as $P(f_{t+1}|\mathcal{D}_{1:t}, x) = \mathcal{N}(\mu_{t+1}(x), \sigma^2_{t+1}(x))$, where $\mu_{t+1}(x) = \mathbf{k}^T[\mathbf{K} + \sigma^2\mathbf{I}]^{-1}\mathbf{y} + m(x)$ and $\sigma^2_{t+1}(x) = k(x, x) - \mathbf{k}^T[\mathbf{K} + \sigma^2\mathbf{I}]^{-1}\mathbf{k}$. In the above expression we define $\mathbf{k} = [k(x, x_1), ..., k(x, x_t)]$, $\mathbf{K} = [k(x_i, x_j)]_{1 \leq i,j \leq t}$ and $\mathbf{y} = [y_1, ..., y_t]$.

After the modeling step, an acquisition function is used to suggest the next x_{t+1} where the function should be evaluated. The acquisition step uses the predictive mean and the predictive variance from the surrogate model to balance the exploration of the search space and exploitation of current promising regions. Some examples of acquisition functions include Expected Improvement (EI) [15,24], GP-UCB [21,25]. In this paper, we use the UCB acquisition function which is defined as follows:

$$u_t(x) = \mu_{t-1}(x) + \beta_t^{1/2} \sigma_{t-1}(x), \tag{1}$$

where β_t is the trade-off coefficient that balances exploration and exploitation.

To measure the performance of a BO algorithm, we use the regret, which is the loss incurred by evaluating the function at x_t, instead of at the unknown optimal input, formally $r_t = f(x^*) - f(x_t)$. The cumulative regret is defined as $R_T = \sum_{1 \le t \le T} r_t$, the sum of regrets incurred over given a horizon of T iterations. If we can show that $\lim_{T \to \infty} \frac{R_T}{T} = 0$, the cumulative regret is **sub-linear**, and so the algorithm efficiently converges to the optimum.

4 Problem Setting

The goal of Bayesian optimization is to find a maximum of the objective function $f(x)$: $\text{argmax}_{x \in \mathbb{R}^d} f(x)$. We consider the function f that is black-box and expensive to evaluate, possibly non-convex. Further, we only get access to noisy evaluations of f without gradient information in the form $y = f(x) + \epsilon$, where the noise $\epsilon \sim \mathcal{N}(0, \sigma^2)$ is i.i.d. Gaussian distribution. Unlike traditional BO, we assume that the search space $\mathcal{X} \subset \mathbb{R}^d$ of f is unknown a priori. As in [9], we assume that x^* is not at infinity to make the BO tractable.

Without the knowledge of the search space, BO is challenging. However, we assume that we have knowledge of K previous related BO tasks $\{f^{(k)}(x)\}_{k=1}^{K}$, where $f^{(k)} : \mathbb{R}^d \to \mathbb{R}$ has the same input dimension of f. More precisely, we have access to noisy observations from these tasks, which are denoted by $\mathcal{D}^{(k)} = \{x_i^{(k)}, y_i^{(k)} = f^{(k)}\left(x_i^{(k)}\right) + \epsilon\}_{i=1}^{n_k}$, where n_k is the number of observations of the task k. We create a compact search space $\hat{\mathcal{X}}$, given noisy observations from previous BO tasks for the following problem:

$$\text{argmax}_{x \in \hat{\mathcal{X}}} f(x) \tag{2}$$

The smaller the search space $\hat{\mathcal{X}}$ is, the faster the optimization methods may find the optimum of that space. Therefore, we aim to design a small $\hat{\mathcal{X}}$ so that it contains an optimum of the original space $\mathcal{X}$.

5 Designing Search Spaces for BO

In this section, we propose a safety transfer learning search space strategy that guarantees the containment of the global optimum of the target task after finite

Algorithm 1. Designing search spaces for Bayesian optimization
―――
1: Initial search space $\mathcal{X}_0$; Set of initial points in $\mathcal{X}_0$, denoted by $\mathcal{D}_0$; $\epsilon > 0$; $m > 0$.
2: **for** $t = 1, 2, ...$ **do**
3:     Fit the Gaussian process using $\mathcal{D}_{t-1}$.
4:     Define $\hat{\mathcal{X}}_t$ using (3).
5:     Find $x_t = \mathrm{argmax}_{x \in \hat{\mathcal{X}}_t} u_t(x)$, where $u_t(x)$ defined as in Eq. (1) to find x_t.
6:     Sample $y_t = f(x_t) + \epsilon_t$.
7:     Augment the data $\mathcal{D}_t = \{\mathcal{D}_{t-1}, (x_t, y_t)\}$.
8: **end for**
―――

steps without needing to know the original search space. Previous transfer learning space works [12,17] have not addressed this safety concern (containment of global optimum), even within bounded settings. For our approach, the intuition is that starting with the small good initial region, we will simultaneously move and expand the search space so that it can reach the more promising region. The moving strategy will take advantage of transfer knowledge so that it can exploit efficiency in the initial stages while the expanding strategy will ensure the search space contains the global optimum, solving the above safety issue. Specifically, starting from a good initial user-defined region, denoted by $\hat{\mathcal{X}}_0 = [a_0^{(1)}, b_0^{(1)}] \times ... \times [a_0^{(d)}, b_0^{(d)}]$, the search space at iteration t, denoted by $\hat{\mathcal{X}}_t = [a_t^{(1)}, b_t^{(1)}] \times ... \times [a_t^{(d)}, b_t^{(d)}]$ will be built from $\hat{\mathcal{X}}_{t-1}$ by a sequence of transformations as follows:

$$\hat{\mathcal{X}}_{t-1} \xrightarrow{\text{move}} \hat{\mathcal{X}}_t' \xrightarrow{\text{expand}} \hat{\mathcal{X}}_t \qquad (3)$$

Our algorithm is described in Algorithm 1. We will detail the expanding and moving strategy below.

5.1 Moving Strategy

A promising region of a task is where we have a belief that it contains an optimum of the task with a high probability. Our intuition is that when the target task is similar to a training task by some measurement, promising regions are similar in both tasks, so regions surrounding the best evaluations of the training task are potentially promising regions of the test task to be exploited. Therefore, we can effectively exploit these regions in the early stages.

Similarity Measurement. To measure the task similarity between source tasks and the target task, [8,12] use the Kendall tau rank correlation coefficient:

$$L(f^{(k)}, f|\mathcal{D}_t) = \frac{\sum_{x_i, x_j \in \mathcal{D}_t} \mathbb{I}\left[(M^{(k)}(x_i) < M^{(k)}(x_j)) \otimes (y_i < y_j)\right]}{t(t-1)}, \qquad (4)$$

where $M^{(k)}(.)$ denotes the mean of GP trained on training dataset $\{x_i^{(k)}, y_i^{(k)}\}_{i=1}^{n_k}$, $\mathcal{D}_t = \{x_i, y_i\}_{i=1}^t$ is the observations of target task at iteration t, and $\otimes$

denotes the exclusive NOR operator, e.g. value is true if the two sub-statements return the same value. Intuitively, the numerator of Eq. 4 counts the number of true ranked pairs between GP trained on training dataset $\mathcal{D}^{(k)}$ and the observations of the target task. The ranking is more reasonable than other choices such that squared error as the focus lies solely on identifying promising regions. However, there are two main drawbacks of this similarity metric. Firstly, the GP of the training task may yield predictions with high uncertainty at observations of the target task, which can be caused by the distribution of the training dataset. Secondly, the fidelity of the similarity measure in Eq. 4 is reduced when there are few comparison data points, as exemplified by the scenario where the size of $\mathcal{D}_t$ is small. This results in false similarity scores between two tasks during the initial iterations of the BO method. To mitigate the above disadvantages, we propose a novel ranking-based measurement. Specifically, at each iteration t and training task k, we define:

$$\mathcal{D}_t^{(k)} = \{(x, y) \in \mathcal{D}^{(k)} \mid \sigma_t(x) < \epsilon\} \tag{5}$$

where $\epsilon > 0$ is the pre-defined hyper-parameter and $\sigma_t(.)$ is the standard deviation of target GP at iteration t. The proposed similarity score is defined as:

$$S\left(f^{(k)}, f | \mathcal{D}_t^{(k)}\right) = \begin{cases} \frac{\sum_{x_i, x_j \in \mathcal{D}_t^{(k)}} \mathbb{I}[(\mu_t(x_i) < \mu_t(x_j)) \otimes (y_i < y_j)]}{|\mathcal{D}_t^{(k)}|(|\mathcal{D}_t^{(k)}|-1)} & \text{if } |\mathcal{D}_t^{(k)}| > m \\ 0 & \text{else} \end{cases} \tag{6}$$

where $\mu_t(.)$ is the mean of target GP at iteration t; $|\mathcal{D}_t^{(k)}|$ denotes the number of data points in $\mathcal{D}_t^{(k)}$; and $m > 2$ is the pre-defined threshold. By limiting the variance below the threshold ϵ, the target GP will predict each point in $\mathcal{D}_t^{(k)}$ with high certainty. Moreover, if ϵ is set not too small, the size of $\mathcal{D}_t^{(k)}$ can be large even in the first few iterations, enhancing the reliability of the similarity score. Note that $S\left(f^{(k)}, f | \mathcal{D}_t^{(k)}\right)$ will return zero if $|\mathcal{D}_t^{(k)}|$ less than m. In this case, most of the data points in the training task exhibit high variance under the target GP. This circumstance may arise when the observations of the target task deviate significantly from the distribution of the training task. Consequently, the training task is considered unreliable, leading to a similarity score of zero.

Another advantage of Eq. 6 compared to Eq. 4 is the computational complexity. The computational complexity when using Eq. 4 at iteration t for calculating the similarity score is $\mathcal{O}(t^2 K n^3)$, where K is the number of training tasks and $n = \max_{k \in [K]} n_k$ is the maximum number of observations in training tasks. On the other hand, the computational complexity of Eq. 6 at iteration t is $\mathcal{O}(n^2 K t^3)$, which is much lower since $n \gg t$.

Determining $\hat{\mathcal{X}}_t'$. Based on the similarity measurement, in each iteration t, we calculate the similarity $S\left(f^{(k)}, f | \mathcal{D}_t^{(k)}\right)$ of the test task f and every training task $f^{(k)}$, where $k \in [K]$. Denote the point with the highest evaluation of the training task $f^{(k)}$ by $x^{*,k}$. We define

$$c_t^{(1)} = \Sigma_{k=1}^K w_t^{(k)} x^{*,k}, \tag{7}$$

where the weight of $x^{*,k}$ is defined as $w_t^{(k)} = \frac{S\left(f^{(k)}, f | \mathcal{D}_t^{(k)}\right)}{\Sigma_{k=1}^K S\left(f^{(k)}, f | \mathcal{D}_t^{(k)}\right)}$. The point $c_t^{(1)}$ characterizes the promising position balancing among all the training tasks. The higher similarity of f and $f^{(k)}$ implies the higher weight $w_t^{(k)}$, and hence $c_t^{(1)}$ is closer to the best evaluation point $x^{*,k}$ of the training task $f^{(k)}$.

When the target task is quite different from all source tasks, we have less confidence that the optimum of the test task is close to the best evaluations of the training tasks, so we need to explore other regions than the ones surrounding the best evaluations of the training tasks. Such a promising region is potentially surrounding the best solution found among the evaluation points $\{x_1, ..., x_t\}$ of the test task f because this region has a higher probability of finding a new solution improving over the current solutions. We denote this solution by $c_t^{(2)}$. Next, we define

$$c_t' = \alpha_t c_t^{(1)} + (1 - \alpha_t) c_t^{(2)}, \tag{8}$$

where $c_t^{(1)}$ is determined by Eq. 7; $c_t^{(2)}$ is the best solution found of $f(x)$ up to iteration t; and $0 \leq \alpha_t \leq 1$ is the trade-off coefficient at iteration t. The point c_t' is the position balancing between $c_t^{(1)}$ which characterizes the promising region generated by offline data of training tasks, and $c_t^{(2)}$ which characterizes the promising region generated from online data of the test task.

The box $\hat{\mathcal{X}}_t'$ is constructed from $\hat{\mathcal{X}}_{t-1}$ by shifting the center of $\hat{\mathcal{X}}_{t-1}$, denoted by $\mathbf{c}_{t-1}$ toward c_t', while retaining the size of $\hat{\mathcal{X}}_{t-1}$. The region $\hat{\mathcal{X}}_t'$ is a balance between the promising region generated by the best evaluation points of training tasks which are most similar to the test task, and the promising region generated by the best evaluation point of the test task. In our experiments, we choose $\alpha_t = \frac{\Sigma_{k \in [K]} S\left(f^{(k)}, f | \mathcal{D}_t^{(k)}\right)}{K}$. When α_t is large, the region $\hat{\mathcal{X}}_t'$ has a tendency to move to regions of training tasks where we have confidence that the optimum of f belongs to with high probability. Otherwise, $\hat{\mathcal{X}}_t'$ has a tendency to move to the region surrounding the best solution so far of f. However, since the center c_t' of $\hat{\mathcal{X}}_t'$ may translate fast, which could cause the divergence, we use a fixed domain, denoted by $\overline{\mathcal{X}}_0$ to restrict the translation of c_t'. This domain is the minimum box bounding all the best evaluation points of previous tasks. We translate c_t' toward a point c_t'' such that $c_t'' \in \overline{\mathcal{X}}_0$ and is the closest point to c_t'. In conclusion, c_t'' is the final center of bounding box $\hat{\mathcal{X}}_t'$, which can balance between transfer knowledge and target observations.

5.2 Expanding Strategy

At first glance, one might consider progressively widening the search space at a substantial rate to guarantee the containment of the global optimum of the target task. However, an aggressive expansion rate would result in rapid growth of the search space volume, leading to an increased exploration phase. Consequently, the BO method would fail to achieve sub-linear regret. To solve this issue, we use a novel expanding strategy. Particularly, the size of bounding box $\hat{\mathcal{X}}_t$ is expanded from $\hat{\mathcal{X}}'_{t-1}$ by the $\left(\frac{b_0^{(i)} - a_0^{(i)}}{t}\right)$ increment in each direction $1 \leq i \leq d$. More precisely, $a_t^{(i)} = \overline{a_t^{(i)}} - \frac{b_0^{(i)} - a_0^{(i)}}{2t}$ and $b_t^{(i)} = \overline{b_t^{(i)}} + \frac{b_0^{(i)} - a_0^{(i)}}{2t}$, where $\overline{a_t^{(i)}}, \overline{b_t^{(i)}}$ are the lower and upper bound at dimension i of $\hat{\mathcal{X}}'_t$, respectively. The expansion increment $\mathcal{O}\left(\frac{1}{t}\right)$ is small enough so that the search space is expanded slowly as the iteration t tends to ∞ but we still ensure that the optimum will be found. Importantly, we will show that this expanding strategy combined with the moving strategy in Sect. 5.1 can achieve the sub-linear regret in the below section.

5.3 Regret Analysis

We have the following theorem.

Theorem 1. *Let $f \sim \mathcal{GP}(0, k)$ with a stationary covariance function k. Assume that there exist constants $s_1, s_2 > 0$ such that $\mathbb{P}[\sup_{\mathbf{x} \in \mathcal{X}} |\partial f / \partial x_i| > L] \leq s_1 e^{-(L/s_2)^2}$ for all $L > 0$ and for all $i \in \{1, 2, ..., d\}$. Pick a $\delta \in (0, 1)$. Set $\beta_T = 2\log(4\pi_t/\delta) + 4d\log(dTs_2(1 + \ln(T))\sqrt{\log(4ds_1/\delta)})$. There is a constant $T_0 > 0$ which is independent of t such that for any horizon $T > T_0$, the cumulative regret of the proposed global BO algorithm (Algorithm 1) is bounded as*

$$R_T \leq \sum_{t=1}^{T_0} L\|x^* - c_t''\|_1 + \sqrt{C_1 T \beta_T \gamma_T(\mathcal{C}_T)} + \frac{\pi^2}{6},$$

with probability $1 - \delta$, where the box $\mathcal{C}_T$ is the box covering $\overline{\mathcal{X}}_0 = \prod_{i=1}^{d} [a^{(i)}, b^{(i)}]$ and $\hat{\mathcal{X}}_t$. It is computed as

$$\mathcal{C}_T = \prod_{i=1}^{d} \left[a^{(i)} - \frac{(b_0^{(i)} - a_0^{(i)})}{2} \sum_{j=1}^{T} \frac{1}{j}, b^{(i)} + \frac{(b_0^{(i)} - a_0^{(i)})}{2} \sum_{j=1}^{T} \frac{1}{j} \right],$$

and $\gamma_T(\mathcal{C}_T)$ is the maximum information gain for any T observations in the domain $\mathcal{C}_T$ (see [21]). This term is computed as follows:

- *For SE kernels: $\gamma_T(\mathcal{C}_T) = \mathcal{O}((\ln(T))^{d+1})$,*
- *For Matérn kernels with $\nu > 1$: $\gamma_T(\mathcal{C}_T) = \mathcal{O}(T^{\frac{d(1+d)}{2\nu + d(d+1)}})$*

Compared to the regret bound of the traditional BO with a fixed search space and without transfer learning, our regret bound has additional components: $\sum_{t=1}^{T_0} L\|x^* - c_t''\|_1$ and the $\gamma_T(\mathcal{C}_T)$. Since T_0 is a constant; L is a constant and $\|x^* - c_t''\|_1$ is bounded by the diameter of boxes $\mathcal{C}_t$ with $t \leq T_0$, this component $\sum_{t=1}^{T_0} L\|x^* - c_t''\|_1$ is a constant which is independent of t. In addition, although the search space is expanded over iterations, the maximum information gain of these expanded search spaces $\gamma_T(\mathcal{C}_T)$ is still bounded by $\mathcal{O}((\ln(T))^{d+1})$ for SE kernels and by $\mathcal{O}(T^{\frac{d^2(1+d)}{2\nu + d(d+1)}})$ with Matérn kernels. Interestingly, we remark that these bounds of $\gamma_T(\mathcal{C}_T)$ have the same order as the ones for BO with a fixed search space (see Theorem 5 of [21]). As a result, the regret bound of our proposed algorithm is sub-linear in T for SE kernels and Matérn kernels (with several conditions on d and ν).

In our regret bound, the point c''_t reflects c'_t which is defined in Sect. 5.1. It represents the center of promising regions where we have confidence that the optimum x^* belongs to with high probability. Recall that c'_t is the position balancing between $c_t^{(1)}$ which characterizes the promising region generated by the best evaluations of training tasks, and $c_t^{(2)}$ which is the best solution up to iteration t of the test task. Therefore, if c'_t is closer to x^* then c''_t is closer to x^* and, hence the regret bound is tighter. In our experiments, we see that c'_t moves close to x^* quite quickly (see Fig. 5). Moreover, the constant T_0 can be reduced with the help of transfer knowledge as illustrated in Sect. 6.4. **A full proof of Theorem 1 is provided in Appendix A.**

6 Experiments

In this section, we demonstrate the effectiveness of our proposed methods across a wide range of black-box functions. We compare our method with seven other benchmark methods: **GP-based BO**; **Box-BO** [17], which designs a search space using a box bounding the best evaluations of training tasks; **Ellipsoid-BO** [17], which designs a search space using a low-volume ellipsoid bounding the best evaluations of training tasks; **US-BO** (**U**ncertainty **S**earch space Bayesian Optimization) [12], which learns search spaces by using the similarity between tasks and a GP classifier; **UBO** [9], which expands the search space whenever the local $\epsilon-$accuracy condition is satisfied; **FBO** [16], which broadens the search space using a filtering expansion strategy; and a method for high-dimensional BO **TuRBO** [5], which uses a trust region centered at the best solution. Note that both **UBO** and **FBO** are designed for an unbounded search space without leveraging transfer knowledge. To underscore the effectiveness of the proposed similarity score, we also compare our method with two variants: i) **Old-sim**, employing the similarity in Eq. 4; and ii) **No-transfer**, wherein the center is moved solely to the best-observed point so far. The performance of the methods is quantified using log regret, and each experiment is repeated 20 times. To ensure fairness in our experiments, we adopt a uniform sampling approach, selecting three initialization points within the low-volume bounding box recommended by Box-BO. This initialization strategy aims to introduce additional information from training tasks to non-transfer methods, such as TuRBO, FBO, UBO and No-transfer. For our method, we set $\epsilon = \sqrt{\frac{k(0,0)}{2}}$ and $m = 2d$, where $k(.,.)$ is the GP kernel and d is the input dimension. Moreover, we set the initial region $\hat{\mathcal{X}}_0$ as 20% of the restricted domain $\overline{X}_0$ stated in Sect. 5.1. **Due to space limitation, we also provide the empirical analysis of the proposed method's hyperparameters, e.g. ϵ, m, proportion of initial region in Appendix C to show the robustness of our method.**[1]

---
[1] The code is available at https://github.com/Fsoft-AIC/BO-transfer-search-space.

6.1 Experiments on Synthetic Functions

We evaluate our method and the benchmark methods on several types of standard optimization benchmark functions. We design the synthetic experiments in three scenarios with different input dimensions: **Scenario 1** *the global optimum of the target task is in proximity to the best evaluations of all training tasks*; **Scenario 2** *the global optimum of the target task is distant from all the best evaluations of training tasks*; **Scenario 3** *the global optimum of the target task is close to some of the best evaluations of training tasks and distant from others*. For the first scenario, we selected Ackley ($d = 4$), Powell ($d = 4$), Dixon-Price ($d = 5$), and Levy ($d = 8$) as the objective functions. To construct the training datasets, we apply the random translations and rescalings of up to ±30% to the x and y values, respectively. For the second scenario, we test the algorithms on four benchmark functions: Styblinski-Tang ($d = 4$), Ackley ($d = 5$), Rosenbrock ($d = 6$) and Griewank ($d = 30$). Different from the first scenario, we applied translation for x as well as scalings for y up to ±50% to create the training datasets, thereby decreasing the similarity between the training tasks and the target task. Additionally, to make the experiments more challenging, we shifted the search space of each training dataset so that it does not contain the true optimum of the target function. Consequently, the optimum point of the target task becomes far from the optimum of the training tasks. Lastly, the third scenario is a mixture of the first scenario and the second scenario. We select Hyper-Ellipsoid ($d = 5$), Ackley ($d = 6$), Rastrigin ($d = 10$) and Perm ($d = 20$) as the target tasks. To generate the training tasks, we follow a similar procedure as described in the first scenario to create m_1 tasks. Additionally, we employ the mechanism outlined in the second scenario to construct m_2 training tasks. For each objective function, we created 15 training datasets, each consisting of 1500 data points. For scenario 3, we choose $m_1 = 10$ and $m_2 = 5$. The experimental results are reported in Fig. 2, 3, 4.

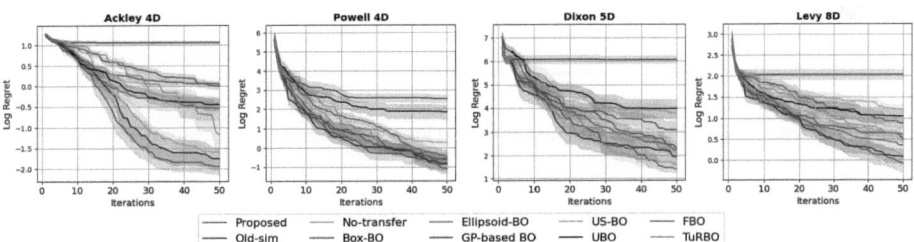

Fig. 2. Performances on four standard functions in Scenario 1. The y-axis presents the log regret (a smaller value is better).

We consider the first scenario where the global optimum of the target task is close to the best evaluation of the training tasks. Although other transfer learning-based methods like Box-BO, Ellipsoid-BO, and US-BO are also designed

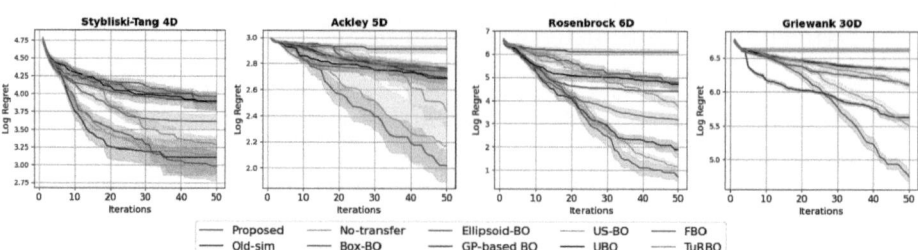

Fig. 3. Performances on four standard functions in Scenario 2. The y−axis presents the log regret (a smaller value is better).

for this scenario, our method outperforms the other benchmark methods in all test functions. This superiority stems from its ability to dynamically adapt and shift towards promising regions as illustrated in Fig. 5 (Left). US-BO performs poorly in experiments due to the challenges in locating the optimal point of the acquisition in their extracted region. Turbo uses an adaptive shifting strategy but does not leverage the knowledge of training tasks, and hence performs poorly compared to our methods. Notably, the Old-sim method yields competitive outcomes with our proposed approach. This can be attributed to the high similarity between the training tasks and the target task, indicating that even with limited comparison points, the similarity metric defined in Eq. 4 remains reliable for each training task.

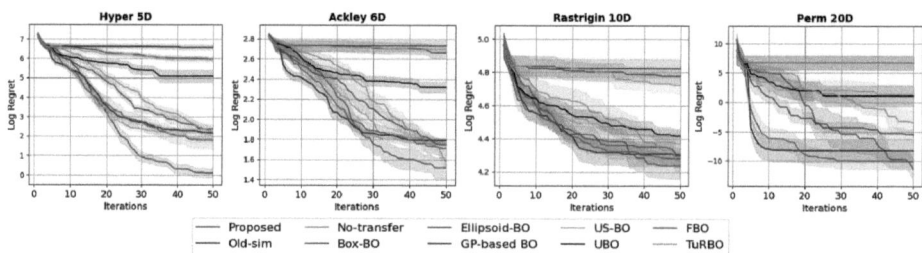

Fig. 4. Performances on four standard functions in Scenario 3. The y−axis presents the log regret (a smaller value is better).

For the second scenario where the global optimum of the target task is further to the best evaluations of the training tasks, our proposed method shows the best results compared to the baselines (Fig. 3). In this setting, the resemblance between the training tasks and the test tasks diminishes. However, our methods are adaptive in the sense that they can move to regions surrounding the best solution so far of the test task rather than regions containing evaluations of the training tasks if the similarity score is low. We illustrate this movement in Figs. 5 (Right) as an example. As can be seen in Fig. 3, the other transfer learning-based search space designing methods struggle, as they primarily concentrate on the local region around the best evaluation points of the training tasks. Turbo shows a good performance due to the movement of the trust region. In contrast with scenario 1, the performance of Old-sim is reduced since the similarity in Eq. 4 is unreliable with few comparison points for dissimilar training tasks, which can lead to a falsely high similarity score. Conversely, the No-transfer method exhibits competitive performance by disregarding information from dissimilar training tasks. Similar to Scenario 1, our method consistently outperforms the compared counterparts, underscoring the effectiveness of the proposed similarity score. Moreover, even for the high-dimensional Griewank function, our method performs more efficiently than TurBO.

A comparable trend is observed in Scenario 3, as depicted in Fig. 4. Our proposed method demonstrates the most favorable outcome, maintaining its effectiveness even as the input dimension is increased for the Perm test function. This outcome underscores the capability of the proposed similarity metric to identify a substantial portion of the training dataset that exhibits strong similarity to the target function, even within a mixed setting.

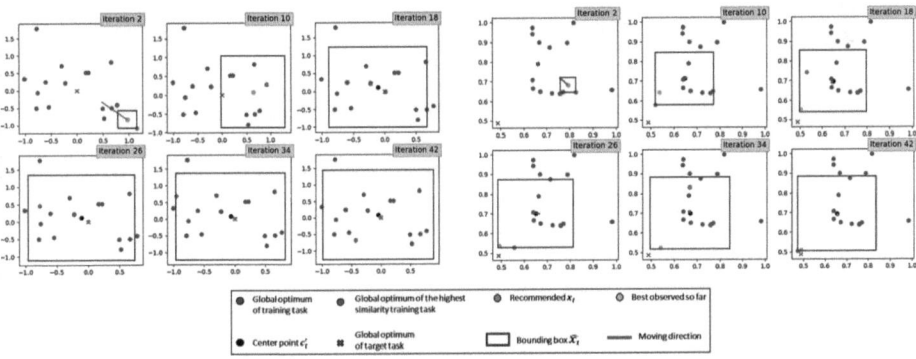

Fig. 5. (**Left**) Progress of proposed method on Ackley 4D function. In this scenario, the optimum point of the target task is close to the best evaluation of training tasks; (**Right**) Progress of proposed global method on Rosenbrock 6D function. In this scenario, the optimum point of the target task is far away from the best evaluation of training tasks. A full progress in given in Appendix B.

6.2 Experiments on Hyperparameter Tuning

In this part, we assess the effectiveness of our method in deep learning algorithm tuning problems. Specifically, we utilize the ResNet Tuning Benchmark introduced by [12], which involves optimizing five hyperparameters of ResNet on datasets such as CIFAR-10, SVHN, and Tiny-Imagenet. Due to space limitation, we added an experiment about tuning hyper-parameters of SGD for ridge regression in Appendix D. Differing from [12], we focus on datasets where the hyperparameter *nesterov* is set to *False*, while optimizing the remaining four hyperparameters. Our evaluation is based on the Normalized Classification Error (NCE) [12] as depicted in Fig. 6. It is important to note that the experiments are conducted with discrete input domains, and the search space configuration is predefined. Since the input domains are discrete, we set initial region $\hat{\mathcal{X}}_0$ larger with the rate of 80% of the restricted domain $\overline{X}_0$. Overall, our proposed method consistently outperforms the compared baseline methods. Additionally, we observed that moving-based strategies, such as TuRBO, No-transfer, and Old-sim, demonstrate commendable performance even within the predefined search space. Conversely, UBO and FBO methods exhibit poor performance in the context of discrete input domains.

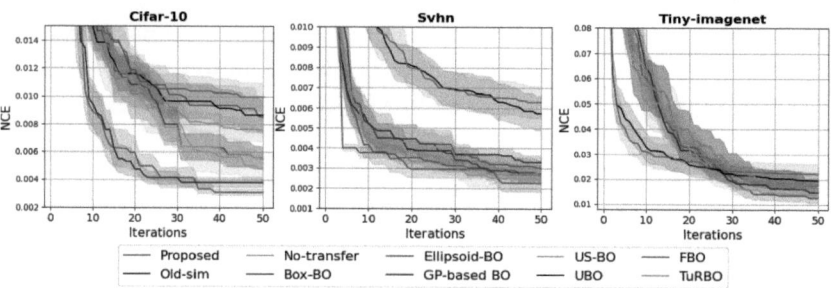

Fig. 6. Performances on tuning ResNet for three vision problems. The y−axis presents the NCE (a smaller value is better).

6.3 Experiments on More Real-World Applications

To further demonstrate the performance of our methods in real-world applications, we consider three real-world tasks including location selection for oil wells $(d = 4)$ [10]; robot pushing problem $(d = 14)$ [5], and rover trajectory planning problem $(d = 20)$ [5]. We assume that the search space of all three real-world applications is unknown.

Oil Well Problem. The objective of this task is to determine the deepest drilled depth among oil wells based on the longitude and latitude coordinates of both the surface and bottom of the well. Following a methodology similar to [10], we utilize 30 datasets, each comprising over 1000 parameter configurations. We evaluate the transfer learning capabilities using a leave-one-task-out approach, wherein one dataset is reserved for testing while the remaining datasets serve as training tasks. It is worth noting that the input domains for this experiment are discrete. For evaluation, we employ the Normalized Classification Error metric [12]. The experimental results are depicted in Fig. 7 (Left), indicating that our methods outperform the baseline approaches. The relatively lower performance of TuRBO can be attributed to the following reasons: given the discrete input dimension of this benchmark, the size of the trust region becomes too small, resulting in a limited number of candidates available for evaluation within that region. In contrast, our methods progressively expand the search space, thereby circumventing this issue.

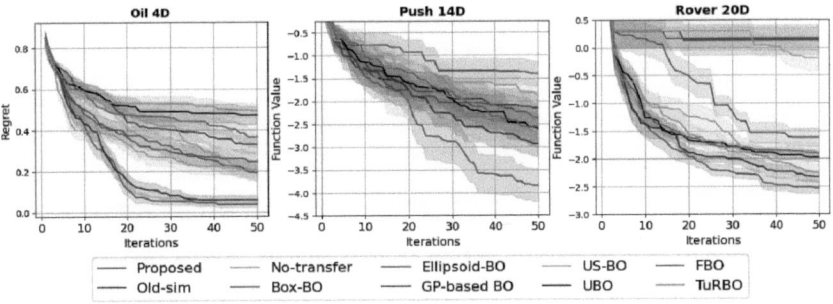

Fig. 7. Performances on three real-world applications. The y−axis presents the regret and the function value (a smaller value is better).

Robot Pushing Problem. The goal of this task is to control 14 parameters of robot hands to push two objects toward the designated goal location [5]. To create the training task, we uniformly sample the first dimension and the second dimension of initial positions in a range $(-0.5, 0.5)$ and $(-2, 2)$, respectively. We use the default initial location stated in [5], which is $(0, 2)$ and $(0, -2)$ for the target task. The goal location for all datasets is the same. We created 15 training datasets with different initial locations, each consisting of 2000 data points. The function values are reported in Fig. 7 (Middle). Our method outperforms all other methods after a few iterations, consistently demonstrating the best performance. In contrast, US-BO and Ellipsoid-BO exhibit the poorest results, partially attributed to challenges in optimizing the acquisition within their designated spaces. The No-transfer and Old-sim methods yield competitive results, underscoring the effectiveness of the moving and scaling approach. On the other hand, FBO, UBO, and TuRBO display similar performances.

Rover Trajectory Planning Problem. The goal of this task is to optimize the locations of 10 points in the $2D$ plane that determine the trajectory of a rover via BSpline method [5]. Like the robot pushing problem, we uniformly sample the start position in a box $[0, 1]^2$, while the start position of the target task is $(0.05, 0.05)$. The goal position for all tasks is the same. Overall, we had 15 training datasets each consisting of 2000 data points. The outcome is illustrated in Fig. 7 (Right), where our method exhibits superior performance compared to the alternatives. US-BO and Ellipsoid-BO encounter scalability issues as the input dimension increases. TuRBO performs well in high-dimensional inputs, while Box-BO appears to be constrained within its extracted region.

6.4 Experiments on the Search Space Design

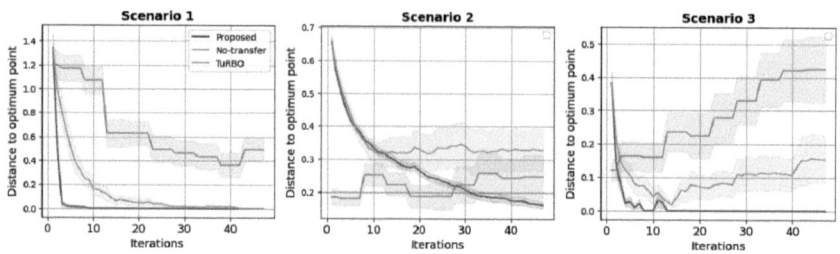

Fig. 8. Distance to the optimum point on three scenarios. The y−axis presents value in Eq. 9 (a smaller value is better).

In this subsection, we study the ability to contain the global optimum of the target task of our methods on the three scenarios stated in Subsect. 6.1. For each method, we report the distance from the global optimum point of the target task to their search spaces at every iteration:

$$d_t(M) = \left\| x^* - \mathrm{argmin}_{x \in B_t(M)} \|x^* - x\|_2 \right\|_2, \qquad (9)$$

where $d_t(M)$ is the distance from the global optimum point of the target task to the extracted search space of method M in iteration t, x^* is the global optimum of the target task, $B_t(M)$ is the extracted region of method M in iteration t and $\|.\|_2$ is the l_2 norm. From Eq. 9, the search space contains the global optimum of the target task if $d_t(M) = 0$. We conduct a comparison of our methods with TuRBO and the No-transfer methods across different scenarios: Powell 4D in Scenario 1, Rosenbrock 6D in Scenario 2, and Hyper-Ellipsoid 5D in Scenario 3. The results are presented in Fig. 8. In Scenario 1 (Fig. 8 Left), our method rapidly converges towards the global optimum of the target task, outperforming the No-transfer method, which attains containment of x^* at a later stage. This highlights the effectiveness of transferring knowledge. TuRBO faces challenges as its trust region fails to contain x^* due to fluctuations in $d_t(.)$ during the process. In Scenario 2 (Fig. 8 Middle), where $x*$ is distant from the global optimum of the training tasks, our proposed method significantly reduces the gap to the optimum point at a faster rate than the No-transfer method. TuRBO exhibits a similar performance as in Scenario 1. In Scenario 3 (Fig. 8 Right), the proposed method successfully reaches the optimum point within 20 iterations, while TuRBO diverges away from x^*. In summary, when the training tasks exhibit strong similarity, our method's bounding box can rapidly encapsulate x^* within the initial iterations, resulting in a small value for the term

T_0 in Theorem 1. Further experiments to show the balancing between distance to the global optimum and search space area can be found in Appendix E.

Acknowledgments. Hung The Tran and Dung D. Le acknowledge the support of the Center for Environmental Intelligence at VinUniversity (project VUNI.CEI.FS_0007).

References

1. Bai, T., Li, Y., Shen, Y., Zhang, X., Zhang, W., Cui, B.: Transfer learning for bayesian optimization: a survey. arXiv preprint arXiv:2302.05927 (2023)
2. Bergstra, J., Bardenet, R., Bengio, Y., Kégl, B.: Algorithms for hyper-parameter optimization. Adv. Neural Inf. Process. Syst. **24** (2011)
3. Chen, W., Fuge, M.: Adaptive expansion bayesian optimization for unbounded global optimization (2020)
4. Dai, Z., Chen, Y., Yu, H., Low, B.K.H., Jaillet, P.: On provably robust meta-bayesian optimization. In: Uncertainty in Artificial Intelligence, pp. 475–485. PMLR (2022)
5. Eriksson, D., Pearce, M., Gardner, J.R., Turner, R., Poloczek, M.: Scalable Global Optimization via Local Bayesian Optimization. Curran Associates Inc., Red Hook (2019)
6. Fan, Z., Han, X., Wang, Z.: Transfer learning for bayesian optimization on heterogeneous search spaces. Trans. Mach. Learn. Res. (2024)
7. Feurer, M.: Scalable meta-learning for bayesian optimization using ranking-weighted gaussian process ensembles (2018)
8. Feurer, M., Letham, B., Hutter, F., Bakshy, E.: Practical transfer learning for bayesian optimization (2018)
9. Ha, H., Rana, S., Gupta, S., Nguyen, T.T., Tran-The, H., Venkatesh, S.: Bayesian optimization with unknown search space. In: NeurIPS 2019, Vancouver, BC, Canada, 8–14 December 2019, pp. 11772–11781 (2019)
10. Hsieh, B.J., Hsieh, P.C., Liu, X.: Reinforced few-shot acquisition function learning for bayesian optimization. Adv. Neural. Inf. Process. Syst. **34**, 7718–7731 (2021)
11. Kandasamy, K., Schneider, J., Póczos, B.: High dimensional Bayesian optimisation and bandits via additive models. In: International Conference on Machine Learning, pp. 295–304. PMLR (2015)
12. Li, Y., Shen, Y., Jiang, H., Bai, T., Zhang, W., Zhang, C., Cui, B.: Transfer learning based search space design for hyperparameter tuning. In: Proceedings of the 28th ACM SIGKDD Conference on Knowledge Discovery and Data Mining, KDD '22, pp. 967–977. Association for Computing Machinery, New York (2022)
13. Li, Y., et al.: ACM (2022)
14. Marco, A., et al.: Virtual vs. real: trading off simulations and physical experiments in reinforcement learning with Bayesian optimization. In: 2017 IEEE International Conference on Robotics and Automation (ICRA), pp. 1557–1563. IEEE (2017)
15. Močkus, J.: On bayesian methods for seeking the extremum. In: Marchuk, G.I. (ed.) Optimization Techniques 1974. LNCS, vol. 27, pp. 400–404. Springer, Heidelberg (1975). https://doi.org/10.1007/3-540-07165-2_55
16. Nguyen, V., Gupta, S., Rane, S., Li, C., Venkatesh, S.: Bayesian optimization in weakly specified search space. In: 2017 IEEE International Conference on Data Mining (ICDM), pp. 347–356 (2017)

17. Perrone, V., Shen, H.: Learning search spaces for bayesian optimization: another view of hyperparameter transfer learning. In: Advances in Neural Information Processing Systems 32: Annual Conference on Neural Information Processing Systems 2019, NeurIPS 2019, Vancouver, BC, Canada, 8–14 December 2019 (2019)
18. Rasmussen, C.E., Williams, C.K.I.: Gaussian Processes for Machine Learning (Adaptive Computation and Machine Learning). The MIT Press (2005)
19. Shahriari, B., Bouchard-Cote, A., Freitas, N.: Unbounded bayesian optimization via regularization. In: Gretton, A., Robert, C.C. (eds.) Proceedings of the 19th International Conference on Artificial Intelligence and Statistics. Proceedings of Machine Learning Research, vol. 51, pp. 1168–1176. PMLR, Cadiz(2016)
20. Snoek, J., et al.: Scalable bayesian optimization using deep neural networks. In: ICML 2015, vol. 37, p. 2171–2180 (2015)
21. Srinivas, N., Krause, A., Kakade, S.M., Seeger, M.W.: Information-theoretic regret bounds for gaussian process optimization in the bandit setting. IEEE Trans. Inf. Theor. **58**(5), 3250–3265 (2012)
22. Swersky, K., Snoek, J., Adams, R.P.: Multi-task bayesian optimization. In: Burges, C., Bottou, L., Welling, M., Ghahramani, Z., Weinberger, K. (eds.) NeuRIPS, vol. 26 (2013)
23. Tran-The, H., Gupta, S., Rana, S., Ha, H., Venkatesh, S.: Sub-linear regret bounds for bayesian optimisation in unknown search spaces. Adv. Neural. Inf. Process. Syst. **33**, 16271–16281 (2020)
24. Tran-The, H., Gupta, S., Rana, S., Venkatesh, S.: Regret bounds for expected improvement algorithms in gaussian process bandit optimization. In: Proceedings of The 25th International Conference on Artificial Intelligence and Statistics, vol. 151 of Proceedings of Machine Learning Research, pp. 8715–8737. PMLR (2022)
25. Tran-The, H., Gupta, S., Rana, S., Venkatesh, S.: Trading convergence rate with computational budget in high dimensional bayesian optimization. In: Proceedings of the AAAI Conference on Artificial Intelligence, vol. 34, no. 03, pp. 2425–2432 (2022)
26. Volpp, M., et al.: Meta-learning acquisition functions for transfer learning in bayesian optimization. In: International Conference on Learning Representations (2020)
27. Wistuba, M., Schilling, N., Schmidt-Thieme, L.: Scalable gaussian process-based transfer surrogates for hyperparameter optimization. Mach. Learn. **107**, 43–78 (2017)
28. Yogatama, D., Mann, G.S.: Efficient transfer learning method for automatic hyperparameter tuning. In: International Conference on Artificial Intelligence and Statistics (2014)
29. Nguyen, M.-D., Dinh, P.M., Nguyen, Q.-H., Hoang, L.P., Le, D.D.: Improving pareto set learning for expensive multi-objective optimization via stein variational hypernetworks. In: Proceedings of the AAAI Conference on Artificial Intelligence, vol. 39, no. 18, pp. 19677–19685 (2025)
30. Nguyen, Q.H., Hoang, L.P., Viet, H.V., Le, D.D.: Controllable expensive multi-objective learning with warm-starting bayesian optimization. arXiv preprint, arXiv:2311.15297 (2024)

Privacy and Security

TAMIS: Tailored Membership Inference Attacks on Synthetic Data

Paul Andrey[(✉)], Batiste Le Bars, and Marc Tommasi

Univ. Lille, Inria, CNRS, Centrale Lille, UMR 9189 - CRIStAL,
59000 Lille, France
paul.andrey@inria.fr

Abstract. Membership Inference Attacks (MIA) enable to empirically assess the privacy of a machine learning algorithm. In this paper, we propose TAMIS, a novel MIA against differentially-private synthetic data generation methods that rely on graphical models. This attack builds upon MAMA-MIA, a recently-published state-of-the-art method. It lowers its computational cost and requires less attacker knowledge. Our attack is the product of a two-fold improvement. First, we recover the graphical model having generated a synthetic dataset by using solely that dataset, rather than shadow-modeling over an auxiliary one. This proves less costly and more performant. Second, we introduce a more mathematically-grounded attack score, that provides a natural threshold for binary predictions. In our experiments, TAMIS achieves better or similar performance as MAMA-MIA on replicas of the SNAKE challenge.

Keywords: Synthetic Data Generation · Differential Privacy · Membership Inference Attack · Graphical Models

1 Introduction

Synthetic Data Generation (SDG) consists in producing artificial samples that match the specifications and retain distributional properties of actual data from a given domain. Over the past decade, it has received increased focus as a way to enable releasing data that can be used to learn statistics or even train machine learning models without granting access to actual personal data.

However, research has shown that synthetic data is not inherently private. Indeed, a synthetic dataset or a generative model learned from private records can leak private information [17]. To mitigate this risk, most state-of-the-art SDG methods provide differential privacy (DP) guarantees, that are formal properties of the method offering a provable upper bound on the residual privacy risk [5], usually at the cost of decreased utility. Most state-of-the-art SDG methods with DP guarantees rely either on learning a graphical model to approximate the structure of the data distribution [3,14,22], or on training a generative neural network, typically adversarially [19,21].

Privacy risks can also be assessed empirically using privacy attacks, which can be complementary to DP guarantees [4,6]. Membership Inference Attack (MIAs) are a type of privacy attack where an attacker having access to a trained machine learning model attempts to predict whether certain records were part of its training data [16]. MIAs have been transposed to SDG by a number of authors [2, 9,10,12,17], who introduced a variety of attacks and threat models.

The state-of-the-art method for MIA against SDG methods relying on graphical models is MAMA-MIA [8]. It was developed to win the SNAKE challenge [1], where it achieved great success against the MST [14] and PrivBayes [22] SDG methods, especially in high-ϵ (that is, low-privacy) settings [7].

In this paper, we introduce TAMIS, a novel attack that achieves better or similar success as MAMA-MIA, has a lower computational cost and requires less attacker knowledge. We focus on attacking MST and PrivBayes, using principles that could be extended to other graphical-model-based methods. This new attack is the product of a two-fold improvement over MAMA-MIA. On the one hand, we propose to recover the structure of the graphical model having generated a synthetic dataset by using solely that dataset, rather than shadow-modeling. This proves less costly and more performant, especially against MST, for which we remove the need for the attacker to know any hyper-parameter used for generation. On the other hand, we introduce a more mathematically-grounded attack score, that achieves similar or better performance as the MAMA-MIA one in experiments over replicas of the SNAKE challenge. It notably achieves high accuracy without requiring the attacker to know the true proportion of training points in the attacked set.

In Sect. 2 we provide more detailed background on SDG and MIAs. Then, we define the setting for our contributions in Sect. 3, and come to present them in Sect. 4. Experiments are reported in Sects. 5 and 6.

2 Background

2.1 Synthetic Data Generation

The aim of SDG is to produce a dataset of synthetic records $\mathcal{D}_{\text{synth}}$ that follow a similar distribution as observed private records in a training dataset $\mathcal{D}_{\text{train}}$. In the remainder of this paper, we note $\mathbb{P}_X$ the underlying distribution of $\mathcal{D}_{\text{train}}$.

Numerous SDG methods have been proposed in the literature. In this work, we focus on those based on graphical models as parametric estimators of $\mathbb{P}_X$, that approximated its dependency structure [3,14,22].

Among other methods, we can mention those using generative neural networks as non-parametric estimators of $\mathbb{P}_X$ [19–21]. While less interpretable [11], these methods cover a wider variety of data types, including time series [13] or multi-relational data [15].

Mechanisms have been introduced in SDG methods in order to provide DP guarantees on the training data. DP was introduced by Dwork & Roth [5], as a way to formalize and quantify the privacy of an algorithm with respect to its input data. Given $\epsilon > 0$ and $\delta \in]0,1[$, an algorithm $\mathcal{A}: \mathcal{D} \to O$ is deemed (ϵ, δ)-differentially private if, and only if, for any pair of adjacent datasets $\mathcal{D}, \mathcal{D}'$ (that is, datasets that differ by a single record) and for any $S \subseteq O$, $\mathbb{P}(\mathcal{A}(D) \in S) \leq e^{\epsilon} \mathbb{P}(\mathcal{A}(D') \in S) + \delta$.

An important property of DP is the post-processing theorem. For SDG, it means that the synthetic data inherit DP guarantees of their generative model.

2.2 Membership Inference Attacks

MIAs were first defined by Shokri et al. [16]. In a classical MIA, the attacker has access to a trained model, and attempts to predict whether certain records were part of its training dataset. In the context of SDG, the attacker instead has access to a synthetic dataset $\mathcal{D}_{\text{synth}}$, knows some actual records $\mathcal{D}_{\text{target}}$ and tries to assess which of these were part of $\mathcal{D}_{\text{train}}$ from which $\mathcal{D}_{\text{synth}}$ was derived.

A variety of MIAs on SDG have been proposed in the literature [2,9,10,12,17], that cover distinct threat models. These were notably reviewed by Houssiau et al. [12], that distinguish three main settings: in the white-box one, the attacker has full access to the trained generative model; in the black-box one, they have accurate knowledge of the SDG method; in the no-box one, they only have access to a given $\mathcal{D}_{\text{synth}}$. Finer-grained variants of the black-box setting exist, notably as to the whether the attacker knows the hyper-parameters of the SDG method.

Another common hypothesis is for the attacker to have access to an auxiliary dataset $\mathcal{D}_{\text{aux}}$ that follows the same underlying distribution as $\mathcal{D}_{\text{train}}$. With this, an attacker can notably perform shadow modeling, that is run the SDG method on controlled inputs, resulting in labeled replicas of the MIA setting [17].

DOMIAS [2] is a generic framework to conduct MIAs on synthetic data, applicable to either black-box or no-box settings but requiring access to auxiliary data. DOMIAS aims to identify $\mathcal{D}_{\text{train}}$ samples that have been over-fitted by the SDG, resulting in $\mathcal{D}_{\text{synth}}$ concentrating more density around these samples than a perfect estimate of $\mathbb{P}_X$ would have. Note that DP bounds and noises the contribution of samples, hence offering protection against over-fitting and MIAs.

Attack scores are defined as the ratio of density functions estimated on either $\mathcal{D}_{\text{synth}}$ or $\mathcal{D}_{\text{aux}}$, which we note $\hat{\mathbb{P}}_X^{\mathcal{D}_{\text{synth}}}$ and $\hat{\mathbb{P}}_X^{\mathcal{D}_{\text{aux}}}$:

$$\Lambda_{\text{DOMIAS}}(x) = \frac{\hat{\mathbb{P}}_X^{\mathcal{D}_{\text{synth}}}(x)}{\hat{\mathbb{P}}_X^{\mathcal{D}_{\text{aux}}}(x)} \quad (1)$$

This ratio is highest for samples that fit $\mathcal{D}_{\text{synth}}$ more than $\mathcal{D}_{\text{aux}}$, denoting possible over-fitting. Any density estimator may be plugged into this equation.

MAMA-MIA [8] is explicitly inspired by DOMIAS, but requires black-box knowledge of the SDG method and of all its hyper-parameters. It replaces density estimators with statistics on $\mathcal{D}_{\text{train}}$ and $\mathcal{D}_{\text{synth}}$ that are likely to have been selected by the SDG method, hence computed on $\mathcal{D}_{\text{train}}$ and perpetuated in

$\mathcal{D}_{\text{synth}}$. In other words, attack scores are made to focus on distributional features of $\mathbb{P}_X$ that were explicitly modeled by the SDG method.

To identify statistics on which to focus, MAMA-MIA uses shadow modeling of the SDG method on $\mathcal{D}_{\text{aux}}$, meaning it replicates the SDG method up to the statistics selection step on random subsets of $\mathcal{D}_{\text{aux}}$ that match the size of $\mathcal{D}_{\text{train}}$.

3 Setting

In this paper, we consider MIAs against SDG methods that rely on graphical models. Our threat model is to assume access to a synthetic dataset $\mathcal{D}_{\text{synth}}$ and to an auxiliary dataset $\mathcal{D}_{\text{aux}} \sim \mathbb{P}_X$, as well as black-box knowledge of the nature of the SDG method, and when specified of its hyper-parameters.

We consider data with categorical attributes, hence a multivariate random variable $X = (X_1, \ldots, X_d)$ where $\forall i \in \{1, \ldots, d\}, X_i \in \mathcal{X}_i := \{1, \ldots, n_i\}$ with $n_i \in \mathbb{N}^*$. We note individual records in lower case: $x = (x_1, \ldots, x_d)$. Support for continuous variables can be achieved using quantization in pre- and post-processing [8,22], which we leave out without loss of generality.

A graphical model over X is a family of probability distributions that can be represented as a graph $G = (V, E)$, with nodes $V = \{1, \ldots, d\}$ and edges E that define the structure of conditional dependencies between attributes of X [18]. Given G, a specific distribution is obtained by defining some statistics, based on which its joint density can be factorized.

The SDG methods we consider select a graphical model over X that approximates the structure of $\mathbb{P}_X$, estimate associated statistics over $\mathcal{D}_{\text{train}}$, and generate $\mathcal{D}_{\text{synth}}$ as iid samples from the resulting distribution. To achieve DP, randomness is added to both the graph selection and statistics estimation steps. Figure 1 summarizes this generic approach.

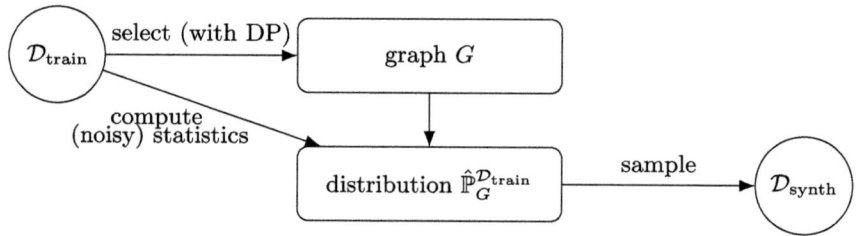

Fig. 1. Flowchart of Synthetic Data Generation using a graphical model

3.1 MST

MST [14] is a SDG method that relies on a tree graphical model. A tree is a connected undirected graph with a constant number of edges $|E| = |V| - 1$. In such a graph, for any node i, we note $N(i) := \{j \in V | (i,j) \in E\}$ its neighbors.

The joint density of a tree graphical model is factorized based on the 1-way marginals over its nodes and 2-way marginals over its edges, as

$$\hat{\mathbb{P}}_G^{\mathcal{D}}(x) = \prod_{i \in V} \mu_i^{\mathcal{D}}(x)^{1-|N(i)|} \prod_{(i,j) \in E} \mu_{ij}^{\mathcal{D}}(x) \qquad (2)$$

where $\mu_i^{\mathcal{D}}(x) = \hat{\mathbb{P}}_{\mathcal{D}}(X_i = x_i) := \frac{1}{|\mathcal{D}|} \sum_{\tilde{x} \in \mathcal{D}} \mathbb{1}\{\tilde{x}_i = x_i\}$
and $\mu_{ij}^{\mathcal{D}}(x) = \hat{\mathbb{P}}_{\mathcal{D}}(X_i = x_i, X_j = x_j) := \frac{1}{|\mathcal{D}|} \sum_{\tilde{x} \in \mathcal{D}} \mathbb{1}\{\tilde{x}_i = x_i, \tilde{x}_j = x_j\}$.

Graph Selection in MST. To select a tree graph from $\mathcal{D}_{\text{train}}$, MST uses a differentially-private maximum-spanning tree algorithm. It assigns a score $s_{ij} = \sum_{l_i, l_j \in \mathcal{X}_i \times \mathcal{X}_j} |\hat{\mathbb{P}}_{\mathcal{D}_{\text{train}}}(X_i = l_i, X_j = l_j) - \hat{\mathbb{P}}_{\mathcal{D}_{\text{train}}}(X_i = l_i)\hat{\mathbb{P}}_{\mathcal{D}_{\text{train}}}(X_j = l_j)|$ to each and every possible edge, with random noise added to 1-way marginals. Then, at each of $|V|-1$ steps, an edge is randomly selected among valid candidates with probabilities proportional to s_{ij} scores.

3.2 PrivBayes

PrivBayes [22] is a SDG method that relies on a bayesian network. A bayesian network is a directed acyclic graph. In such a graph, for any node i, we note $\Pi_i := \{j \in V | (j,i) \in E\}$ its parent set, that is the set of nodes with an edge towards i. We note x_{Π_i} the vector of coordinates of x in Π_i.

The joint density of a bayesian network is factorized based on the conditionals of nodes with respect to their parent set, as

$$\hat{\mathbb{P}}_G^{\mathcal{D}}(x) = \prod_{i \in V} \mu_{i, \Pi_i}^{\mathcal{D}}(x) \qquad (3)$$

where $\mu_{i, \Pi_i}^{\mathcal{D}}(x) = \hat{\mathbb{P}}_{\mathcal{D}}(X_i = x_i | X_{\Pi_i} = x_{\Pi_i}) := \frac{1}{|\mathcal{D}|} \sum_{\tilde{x} \in \mathcal{D}} \mathbb{1}\{\tilde{x}_i = x_i, \tilde{x}_{\Pi_i} = x_{\Pi_i}\}$.

Graph Selection in PrivBayes. To select a bayesian network from $\mathcal{D}_{\text{train}}$, PrivBayes uses a differentially-private greedy algorithm. At each of $|V|$ steps, a (node, parent set) tuple is randomly selected among valid candidates with probabilities proportional to scores $s_{i, \Pi_i} = \frac{1}{2} \sum_{l_i, \pi_i \in \mathcal{X}_i \times \mathcal{X}_{\Pi_i}} |\hat{\mathbb{P}}_{\mathcal{D}_{\text{train}}}(X_i = l_i | \Pi_i = \pi_i) - \hat{\mathbb{P}}_{\mathcal{D}_{\text{train}}}(X_i = l_i)\hat{\mathbb{P}}_{\mathcal{D}_{\text{train}}}(\Pi_i = \pi_i)|$. Nodes and their parent set are constrained to have a total domain size below a threshold that is proportional to the privacy budget ϵ and to a hyper-parameter θ, introducing a trade-off between structure-induced approximation errors and DP-induced estimation errors.

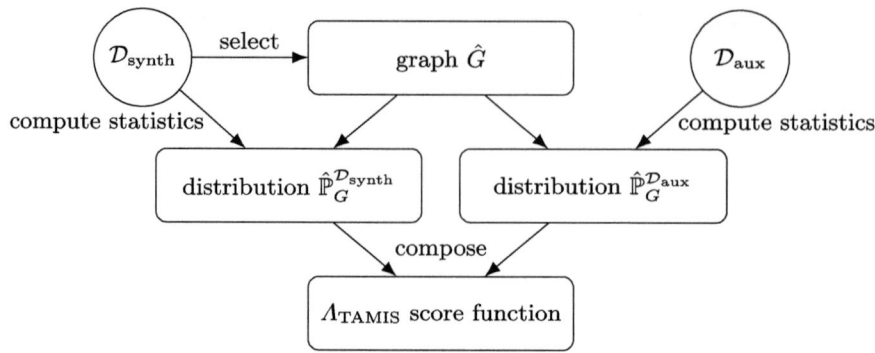

Fig. 2. Flowchart of the TAMIS attack

4 TAMIS: Tailored MIA on Synthetic Data

In this paper, we introduce TAilored Membership Inference attacks on Synthetic data (TAMIS), that are MIAs against SDG methods that rely on graphical models. Our attack scores are based on the likelihood ratio approach of DOMIAS and MAMA-MIA. The novelty of our approach is to learn the structure of a graphical model matching the SDG method directly from $\mathcal{D}_{\text{synth}}$, and to use the factorized joint density of that model as a density estimator in attack scores. Figure 2 summarizes the TAMIS attack procedure as a flowchart.

By proposing an alternative to shadow modeling, we are able to lower the computational cost of the attack compared with MAMA-MIA. For MST, we are also able to remove the requirement for the attacker to know hyperparameters. Furthermore, by recovering a graph rather than a set of weights that cover a broader set of edge choices, we are able to resort to a ratio of likelihoods as attack score, which is distinct in nature from the MAMA-MIA attack scores, as detailed below in this section. Table 1 summarizes the key differences between the two attacks.

Table 1. Differences in hypotheses, costs and nature of TAMIS and MAMA-MIA

		MAMA-MIA		TAMIS	
		MST	PrivBayes	MST	PrivBayes
Graph Recovery	H: Known SDG params	yes	yes	no	yes
	H: Known $|\mathcal{D}_{\text{train}}|$	yes	yes	no	no
	H: Access to $\mathcal{D}_{\text{aux}}$	yes	yes	no	no
	C: Cost relative to SDG	$K=50$	$K=50$	≤ 1	1
	N: Nature of the output	weights W		graph G	
Attack Scores	H: Access to $\mathcal{D}_{\text{aux}}$	yes	yes	yes	yes
	N: Nature of the score	sum of statistics ratios		ratio of densities	

4.1 Graphical Model Recovery from the Synthetic Dataset

The first step of our attack consists in selecting a graphical model that matches that learned by the SDG method. Ideally, we would like to recover the exact structure that was used for generating $\mathcal{D}_{\text{synth}}$, in order to tailor attack scores to features of $\mathbb{P}_X$ that were actually (albeit noisily) measured on $\mathcal{D}_{\text{train}}$.

To do so, we introduce SDG-method-specific algorithms that take $\mathcal{D}_{\text{synth}}$ as input, as opposed to the shadow-modeling approach of MAMA-MIA that is run on $\mathcal{D}_{\text{aux}}$. This decreases computational costs and avoids requiring access to $\mathcal{D}_{\text{aux}}$. We also believe this approach to be more rational. Indeed, shadow modeling on $\mathcal{D}_{\text{aux}}$ is bound to provide relatively generic information about the likely structure of the generative model. On the opposite, that structure is bound to be reflected in $\mathcal{D}_{\text{synth}}$, hence easier to identify from it. This point is especially important in DP regimes that introduce a lot of randomness to the SDG graph selection step.

Graph Recovery for MST. To recover the tree underlying $\mathcal{D}_{\text{synth}}$ generated by MST, we introduce a modified version of the graph selection step from MST, that is deprived of DP mechanisms. It consists in measuring all 1- and 2-way marginals of $\mathcal{D}_{\text{synth}}$, assigning the same edge-wise score as the MST selection algorithm does but without noise, and finally using a maximum spanning tree algorithm to find the tree with the highest possible sum of edge scores.

This algorithm is deterministic, involves slightly less computations than a single shadow modeling run of the MST graph selection step, and does not require any attacker knowledge. As such, it could be applied to any $\mathcal{D}_{\text{synth}}$.

Graph Recovery for PrivBayes. To recover the bayesian network underlying $\mathcal{D}_{\text{synth}}$ generated by PrivBayes, we simply apply the model-selection step of PrivBayes on $\mathcal{D}_{\text{synth}}$. This amounts to a single shadow modeling run, which is less costly than the numerous ones run by MAMA-MIA (50 by default) but requires the same attacker knowledge of the PrivBayes hyper-parameters, due to the selection step adjusting the size of considered parent sets in the graph based on these. It is also non-deterministic due to the DP mechanisms.

4.2 Likelihood-Based Attack Scores

The second step of our attack consists in defining attack scores. To do so, we use the graphical model resulting from the first step to estimate the respective joint densities of $\mathcal{D}_{\text{synth}}$ and $\mathcal{D}_{\text{aux}}$, which requires computing some statistics over both datasets. We then plug these densities into the DOMIAS framework, meaning we use their ratio as attack scores.

Our scores are thus obtained by plugging the joint density formulas of graphical models into the generic DOMIAS equation (1), that are equation (2) for MST and (3) for PrivBayes. The resulting formulas are:

$$\Lambda_{\text{TAMIS-MST}}(x;G) = \prod_{i \in V} \left(\frac{\mu_i^{\mathcal{D}_{\text{synth}}}(x)}{\mu_i^{\mathcal{D}_{\text{aux}}}(x)} \right)^{1-|N(i)|} \prod_{(i,j) \in E} \frac{\mu_{ij}^{\mathcal{D}_{\text{synth}}}(x)}{\mu_{ij}^{\mathcal{D}_{\text{aux}}}(x)} \quad (4)$$

$$\Lambda_{\text{TAMIS-PB}}(x;G) = \prod_{i \in V} \frac{\mu_{i,\Pi_i}^{\mathcal{D}_{\text{synth}}}(x)}{\mu_{i,\Pi_i}^{\mathcal{D}_{\text{aux}}}(x)} \quad (5)$$

TAMIS can therefore be thought of as an instantiation of the DOMIAS framework that uses a graphical model as density estimator, and picks that graphical model to mirror the one that was used in generating the synthetic data. This follows the same intuition as MAMA-MIA, but enacts it in a different way.

Comparison with MAMA-MIA. In MAMA-MIA, the use of shadow modeling results in weights associated with possible edge (for MST) or (node, parent set) (for PrivBayes) choices, rather than in a valid graphical model. After K shadow runs, these weights are defined as $\forall i \in \{1,\ldots,d-1\}, \forall j \in \{i+1,\ldots,d\}$, $w_{ij} = \sum_{k=1}^{K} \mathbb{1}\{(i,j) \in E^{(k)}\}$ for MST, where $E^{(k)}$ is the set of edges selected in the k-th shadow run. For PrivBayes, they are defined as $\forall i \in V, \forall \Pi_i \subset V \setminus \{i\}$, $w_{i,\Pi_i} = \sum_{k=1}^{K} \mathbb{1}\{\forall j \in \Pi_i, (j,i) \in E^{(k)}\}$. We note W a collection of such weights.

From there, the raw attack scores are defined as[1]

$$\Lambda_{\text{MAMAMIA-MST}}(x;W) = \frac{1}{\sum_{w \in W} w} \sum_{w_{ij} \in W} w_{ij} \frac{\mu_{ij}^{\mathcal{D}_{\text{synth}}}(x)}{\mu_{ij}^{\mathcal{D}_{\text{aux}}}(x)} \quad (6)$$

$$\Lambda_{\text{MAMAMIA-PB}}(x;W) = \frac{1}{\sum_{w \in W} w} \sum_{w_{i,\Pi_i} \in W} w_{i,\Pi_i} \frac{\mu_{i,\Pi_i}^{\mathcal{D}_{\text{synth}}}(x)}{\mu_{i,\Pi_i}^{\mathcal{D}_{\text{aux}}}(x)} \quad (7)$$

We remark that these scores correspond to a weighted average of DOMIAS-like scores attached to specific terms characterizing the density, whereas TAMIS uses a DOMIAS-like score over the entire joint density.

We also note that when attacking MST, MAMA-MIA leaves apart information from 1-way marginals, without justification. This omission is probably due to the fact that 1-way marginals are always part of the graph, regardless of selected edges.

Hybrid Scores. We introduce hybrids of our graph-recovery approach with the formulas of MAMA-MIA scores. This is useful to make more visible the difference between our scores and the MAMA-MIA ones, and to disambiguate experimentally the impact of the two folds of our contribution. These scores come

---

[1] We note that the division of scores by $\sum_{w \in W} w$, amenable to normalizing weights, is an addition to the original MAMA-MIA formulas. We adopted it to avoid K impacting the magnitude of raw scores. This improved predictions in our experiments.

from replacing weights resulting from shadow modeling with uniform weights that reflect the graph structure G learned from $\mathcal{D}_{\text{synth}}$ in Equations (6) and (7).

$$\Lambda_{\text{Hybrid-MST}}(x;G) = \frac{1}{|E|} \sum_{(i,j)\in E} \frac{\mu_{ij}^{\mathcal{D}_{\text{synth}}}(x)}{\mu_{ij}^{\mathcal{D}_{\text{aux}}}(x)} \qquad (8)$$

$$\Lambda_{\text{Hybrid-PB}}(x;G) = \frac{1}{|V|} \sum_{i\in V} \frac{\mu_{i,\Pi_i}^{\mathcal{D}_{\text{synth}}}(x)}{\mu_{i,\Pi_i}^{\mathcal{D}_{\text{aux}}}(x)} \qquad (9)$$

5 Experiments

To assess the soundness and performance of our attacks, we conduct experiments that replicate the SNAKE challenge [1].

We make our source code, data and random seeds available, enabling to fully reproduce our experiments and results with minimal effort. They may be found online[2], together with dedicated documentation on implementation details.

Due to paper length constraints, this version only details main experimental results. Throughout this section, we make multiple references to appendices that are part of a fuller version of the paper, a pre-print of which is available on arXiv[3].

5.1 Dataset

We used the publicly-available base dataset from the SNAKE challenge, that was derived from US socio-demographic data published by the Economic Policy Institute. It consists of about 201k samples with 15 variables, 12 of which are categorical (with 2 to 51 possible labels each) and 3 of which have integer values but can be treated as categorical nonetheless (age, number of children and mean weekly number of worked hours). Additionally, individual samples each belong to a given household, each of which groups 1 to 10 individuals.

We applied the same kind of preparation as was done in SNAKE. We take the base dataset as $\mathcal{D}_{\text{aux}}$, that is made available to the attacker. We randomly pick 100 households out of the 812 ones that group at least 5 individuals, and designate their records as composing $\mathcal{D}_{\text{target}}$. Then, all individuals within half of $\mathcal{D}_{\text{target}}$ households are made part of $\mathcal{D}_{\text{train}}$, and $\mathcal{D}_{\text{train}}$ is completed with random individuals from $\mathcal{D}_{\text{aux}} \setminus \mathcal{D}_{\text{target}}$ until $|\mathcal{D}_{\text{train}}| = 10000$.

We generated 50 distinct replicas of the SNAKE $(\mathcal{D}_{\text{train}}, \mathcal{D}_{\text{target}})$ generation. We then ran both MST and PrivBayes on each and every replica with various privacy budgets. For each setting, we generated $|\mathcal{D}_{\text{synth}}| = |\mathcal{D}_{\text{train}}| = 10000$ synthetic samples, and recorded the structure of the graphical model that generated them. We considered $\epsilon \in [0.1, 1, 10, 100, 1000]$. For MST, we always set $\delta = 10^{-9}$. For PrivBayes, the DP mechanisms always achieve $\delta = 0$. For each value of ϵ, we also ran shadow modeling of the graphical model selection step of MST and PrivBayes on 50 random subsets of $\mathcal{D}_{\text{aux}}$, as was done in the MAMA-MIA paper.

---
[2] https://gitlab.inria.fr/magnet/thesepaulandrey/tamis.
[3] https://arxiv.org/abs/2504.00758.

MIA Evaluation Settings. We evaluate attacks on three distinct settings. The first is $\mathcal{D}_{\text{aux}}^{\text{ind}}$, where we attack each and every $\mathcal{D}_{\text{aux}}$ sample, to assess the average-case MIA risk.

The second is $\mathcal{D}_{\text{target}}^{\text{house}}$, where we conduct set membership inference on households of $\mathcal{D}_{\text{target}}$. This task is balanced by construction and matches original evaluation setting of SNAKE. The raw score for a household is taken to be the average of raw scores for samples in that household. These households are expected to be easier to attack than any $\mathcal{D}_{\text{aux}}$ sample. Indeed, there is some correlation among samples in a household, hence when they are jointly included in $\mathcal{D}_{\text{train}}$ they add weight to a given density region, which can cause the SDG to over-fit that region.

The third is $\mathcal{D}_{\text{target}}^{\text{ind}}$, where we attack $\mathcal{D}_{\text{target}}$ samples. These are expected to be somewhat easier targets than average samples for the reasons exposed before.

5.2 Attack Methods

Against MST. we compared three main attacks. First, our TAMIS-MST attack (4), using a tree graph learned from $\mathcal{D}_{\text{synth}}$. Second, the MAMA-MIA attack targeted at MST (6), using weights resulting from shadow modeling over $\mathcal{D}_{\text{aux}}$. Finally, the Hybrid-MST attack (8), that uses MAMA-MIA-like scores over the same tree graph as TAMIS-MST. Some additional baselines were considered to complement our comparison of scores variants, that are reported in Appendix B.

Against PrivBayes. we compared three main attacks. First, our TAMIS-PB attack (5), using a bayesian network learned from $\mathcal{D}_{\text{synth}}$. Second, the MAMA-MIA attack targeted at PrivBayes (7), using weights resulting from shadow modeling over $\mathcal{D}_{\text{aux}}$. Finally, the Hybrid-PB attack (9), that uses MAMA-MIA-like scores over the same bayesian network as TAMIS-PB.

In addition, we introduced TAMIS-PB* and Hybrid-PB*, that use the same attack scores as TAMIS-PB and Hybrid-PB respectively, but benefit from access to the bayesian network that was truly selected by PrivBayes to generate $\mathcal{D}_{\text{synth}}$. This falls outside of our threat model, but is useful to assess the extent to which recovering that graph can improve the success of MIAs.

5.3 Evaluation

Graph Recovery. We systematically compare the graphical model selected by the SDG methods to generate $\mathcal{D}_{\text{synth}}$ with that inferred from $\mathcal{D}_{\text{synth}}$ as part of our attack. We compute the accuracy of choices between the true and estimated graphs, comparing edges for MST and (node, parent set) tuples for PrivBayes.

We also compare the edges or (node, parent set) tuples that are selected at least once across shadow modeling runs, hence included in MAMA-MIA scores, with true graphs. We compute precision, recall and jaccard index over both sets and report their mean, standard deviation and median across replicas.

Membership Inference Metrics. To assess the success of MIAs, we report two metrics: the Area Under the Receiver-Operator Curve (AUROC) of attack scores, and the balanced accuracy of the resulting binary membership predictions. The AUROC is invariant to the activation of raw attack scores, and enables comparison with experimental results from the MAMA-MIA paper [8]. The balanced accuracy is defined as $0.5 * (\frac{\mathbb{P}(\hat{Y}=1|Y=1)}{\mathbb{P}(Y=1)} + \frac{\mathbb{P}(\hat{Y}=0|Y=0)}{\mathbb{P}(Y=0)})$, where $Y = \mathbb{1}\{x \in \mathcal{D}_{\text{train}}\}$ is the true membership label, and $\hat{Y}$ is a binary prediction resulting from a raw attack score. Mapping a raw attack score $\Lambda(x)$ into such a binary decision requires a monotonous activation function f that outputs predicted probabilities in $[0, 1]$, and a threshold t so that $\hat{Y} = \mathbb{1}\{f(\Lambda(x)) \geq t\}$.

In practice, we consider two distinct activation and thresholding regimes. In the *simple* activation regime, we use a default threshold $t = 0.5$, together with a classic activation function that is applied independently to each score. We choose the sigmoid function, corrected to account for raw scores being in $\mathbb{R}^+$: $f(x) = 2 * \text{Sigmoid}(x) - 1$, where $\text{Sigmoid}(x) = (1 + e^{-x})^{-1}$. In the *calibrated* activation regime, we adopt the approach introduced with MAMA-MIA, that was used to win the SNAKE challenge [7]. We make the additional strong hypothesis that the attacker knows $\mathbb{P}(Y = 1)$ for the samples under attack, and adjusts the activation of these targets so that $\mathbb{P}(\hat{Y} = 1) = \mathbb{P}(Y = 1)$. First, raw attack scores are standardized into z-scores (that is, centered around their mean then divided by their standard deviation), to avoid numerical under- and over-flow issues. Then, z-scores are centered around their $1 - \mathbb{P}(Y = 1)$ quantile, so that only a fraction $\mathbb{P}(Y = 1)$ are above 0. Finally, these scores are passed through the sigmoid function, and mapped into decisions using $t = 0.5$.

6 Results

6.1 Attacks Against MST

Graph Recovery. Our method accurately recovered the generating tree in all settings, achieving a perfect match in edges selection for all replicas and ϵ value. In comparison, as detailed in Appendix A, shadow modeling missed a rarely-selected edge, and selected an increasing number of edges as ϵ lowered due to DP, thus resulting in more un-tailored terms in MAMA-MIA attack scores.

Membership Inference. Metrics of MST-targeted attacks on $\mathcal{D}_{\text{aux}}^{\text{ind}}$ and $\mathcal{D}_{\text{target}}^{\text{house}}$ are reported in Table 2, excluding high-privacy regimes $\epsilon \in [0.1, 1]$ for which no attack achieves significant success due to the strong DP guarantees[4]. Reported values are the average and standard deviation of metrics across our 50 replicas. We highlight the highest mean value per setting between attacks in bold. Exhaustive results are placed in Appendix B.

Results show that both of our contributions improve attack success. First, Hybrid-MST achieves better results than MAMAMIA-MST, meaning that

---

[4] The fact that attacks fail for lower ϵ values is expected given the theoretical guarantees. It is worth noting that these privacy guarantees come at a high utilty cost.

Table 2. Main attack results against MST

		AUROC		
		$\epsilon=1000$	$\epsilon=100$	$\epsilon=10$
$\mathcal{D}_{\text{aux}}^{\text{ind}}$	TAMIS-MST	**66.25** ($\pm$ 0.4)	**65.53** ($\pm$ 0.4)	59.25 ($\pm$ 0.4)
	MAMAMIA-MST	64.60 ($\pm$ 1.0)	64.13 ($\pm$ 1.0)	59.05 ($\pm$ 0.6)
	Hybrid-MST	65.46 ($\pm$ 0.3)	64.97 ($\pm$ 0.3)	**59.59** ($\pm$ 0.3)
$\mathcal{D}_{\text{target}}^{\text{house}}$	TAMIS-MST	**77.76** ($\pm$ 4.8)	**77.44** ($\pm$ 3.6)	**69.87** ($\pm$ 5.0)
	MAMAMIA-MST	74.74 ($\pm$ 5.4)	74.62 ($\pm$ 4.5)	68.51 ($\pm$ 5.4)
	Hybrid-MST	75.97 ($\pm$ 4.6)	75.57 ($\pm$ 4.3)	69.02 ($\pm$ 5.5)
		Balanced Accuracy (Simple)		
		$\epsilon=1000$	$\epsilon=100$	$\epsilon=10$
$\mathcal{D}_{\text{aux}}^{\text{ind}}$	TAMIS-MST	**60.84** ($\pm$ 0.3)	**60.39** ($\pm$ 0.3)	**55.66** ($\pm$ 0.3)
	MAMAMIA-MST	56.66 ($\pm$ 0.7)	56.44 ($\pm$ 0.7)	54.40 ($\pm$ 0.4)
	Hybrid-MST	57.27 ($\pm$ 0.4)	57.06 ($\pm$ 0.3)	54.74 ($\pm$ 0.3)
$\mathcal{D}_{\text{target}}^{\text{house}}$	TAMIS-MST	**69.86** ($\pm$ 4.7)	**69.52** ($\pm$ 4.0)	**64.26** ($\pm$ 4.6)
	MAMAMIA-MST	61.06 ($\pm$ 4.2)	60.66 ($\pm$ 3.4)	58.16 ($\pm$ 3.3)
	Hybrid-MST	61.76 ($\pm$ 3.6)	61.88 ($\pm$ 3.7)	58.08 ($\pm$ 3.3)
		Balanced Accuracy (Calibrated)		
		$\epsilon=1000$	$\epsilon=100$	$\epsilon=10$
$\mathcal{D}_{\text{aux}}^{\text{ind}}$	TAMIS-MST	**55.02** ($\pm$ 0.2)	**54.75** ($\pm$ 0.2)	52.63 ($\pm$ 0.2)
	MAMAMIA-MST	54.38 ($\pm$ 0.6)	54.15 ($\pm$ 0.6)	52.50 ($\pm$ 0.4)
	Hybrid-MST	54.76 ($\pm$ 0.2)	54.54 ($\pm$ 0.2)	**52.69** ($\pm$ 0.1)
$\mathcal{D}_{\text{target}}^{\text{house}}$	TAMIS-MST	**70.24** ($\pm$ 5.2)	**69.88** ($\pm$ 3.4)	**64.26** ($\pm$ 4.7)
	MAMAMIA-MST	67.74 ($\pm$ 4.8)	67.24 ($\pm$ 4.8)	63.32 ($\pm$ 5.1)
	Hybrid-MST	68.32 ($\pm$ 4.8)	68.06 ($\pm$ 4.2)	63.56 ($\pm$ 5.4)

replacing shadow modeling weights with the tree graph recovered from $\mathcal{D}_{\text{synth}}$ improves MAMA-MIA-like attack scores. Next, TAMIS-MST achieves even better success in nearly all settings, meaning that the ratio of graphical model densities constitutes a better attack score than the average of 2-way marginals ratios.

We remark that against $\mathcal{D}_{\text{aux}}^{\text{ind}}$, TAMIS-MST and Hybrid-MST success metrics have a markedly lower standard deviation than MAMAMIA-MST. We hypothesize that this is due to shadow modeling weights causing MAMAMIA-MST scores to include terms that variably match the actual generative graph of $\mathcal{D}_{\text{synth}}$, and to exclude information on a relevant edge for some replicas. This validates the rationale of both TAMIS and MAMA-MIA to focus on aspects of the distribution that were actively modeled during SDG.

Comparing balanced accuracy across activation regimes, we observe on $\mathcal{D}_{\text{target}}^{\text{house}}$ that TAMIS-MST, which is more accurate than others in both settings, receives less improvement from calibration. Hence TAMIS-MST attack scores appear to be naturally suitable for sigmoid activation with a basic threshold. Oppositely, MAMA-MIA-like scores appear to rely on calibration, hence on an additional piece of attacker knowledge, to be turned into accurate predictions against $\mathcal{D}_{\text{target}}^{\text{house}}$. We also observe that calibration on the unbalanced $\mathcal{D}_{\text{aux}}^{\text{ind}}$ results in a decrease in balanced accuracy for all attack scores. This hints that the calibration proposed by MAMA-MIA authors may be over-fitted to the balanced $\mathcal{D}_{\text{target}}^{\text{house}}$ setting, that was the target of the SNAKE competition.

6.2 Attacks Against PrivBayes

Graph Recovery. Our method almost never perfectly recovered the generating bayesian network from $\mathcal{D}_{\text{synth}}$. As detailed in Appendix A, for higher ϵ values, about half (node, parentset) choices match, while mismatches arise from marginal differences in including this or that edge, which can have a strong impact on the modeled density. In comparison, shadow modeling achieves above 90 % recall, but less than 25 % precision for $\epsilon \geq 1$, meaning MAMA-MIA attack scores contain most conditionals attached to the generative density of $\mathcal{D}_{\text{synth}}$, but at least 3 times more terms made of other conditionals. Interestingly, graph recovery is easier when ϵ lowers, due to PrivBayes reducing possible choices.

Membership Inference. Metrics of PrivBayes-targeted attacks on $\mathcal{D}_{\text{aux}}^{\text{ind}}$ and $\mathcal{D}_{\text{target}}^{\text{house}}$ are reported in Table 3, excluding high-privacy regimes $\epsilon \in [0.1, 1]$ for which no attack achieves significative success due to the strong DP guarantees. We also excluded balanced accuracy under the calibrated activation regime, which is of lesser interest as rapidly discussed below. Exhaustive results are placed in Appendix C. Reported values are the average and standard deviation of metrics across our 50 replicas. For each setting, we highlight two values in bold, that are the highest mean value either between TAMIS-PB, MAMAMIA-PB and Hybrid-PB or between TAMIS-PB* and Hybrid-PB*.

We first compare attacks that are in line with our threat model, namely TAMIS-PB, Hybrid-PB and MAMAMIA-PB. Results are somewhat ambivalent. On the one hand, when considering the balanced accuracy with simple activation on either $\mathcal{D}_{\text{aux}}^{\text{ind}}$ or $\mathcal{D}_{\text{target}}^{\text{house}}$, TAMIS-PB achieves the best results of all methods, save for the lowest-privacy regime $\epsilon = 1000$, where it is the worst. On the other hand, when considering the AUROC, TAMIS-PB is most often the worst method. On $\mathcal{D}_{\text{aux}}^{\text{ind}}$, MAMAMIA-PB achieves the best results, followed by Hybrid-PB that has similar average values but higher variance. On $\mathcal{D}_{\text{target}}^{\text{house}}$, Hybrid-PB and MAMAMIA-PB have similarly good results, while TAMIS-PB is worse or equal, with lower differences towards the other methods than on $\mathcal{D}_{\text{aux}}^{\text{ind}}$.

Next, we compare the TAMIS-PB* and Hybrid-PB* attacks, that are granted knowledge of the true bayesian network. We retrieve the same ambivalence as to which attack score is best: Hybrid-PB* has a higher or similar AUROC as TAMIS-PB*, while it has a markedly lower balanced accuracy using simple activation, save for the $\epsilon = 1000$ where it is markedly better. We also observe that

Table 3. Main attack results against PrivBayes

		AUROC		
		$\epsilon=1000$	$\epsilon=100$	$\epsilon=10$
$\mathcal{D}_{\text{aux}}^{\text{ind}}$	TAMIS-PB	64.65 ($\pm$ 2.1)	62.65 ($\pm$ 1.3)	53.99 ($\pm$ 0.3)
	MAMAMIA-PB	**79.34** ($\pm$ 1.5)	64.36 ($\pm$ 1.1)	**54.47** ($\pm$ 0.3)
	Hybrid-PB	79.33 ($\pm$ 2.7)	**64.48** ($\pm$ 1.7)	54.42 ($\pm$ 0.4)
	TAMIS-PB*	66.72 ($\pm$ 0.8)	64.61 ($\pm$ 0.4)	54.16 ($\pm$ 0.3)
	Hybrid-PB*	**83.01** ($\pm$ 0.9)	**67.06** ($\pm$ 0.3)	**54.72** ($\pm$ 0.2)
$\mathcal{D}_{\text{target}}^{\text{house}}$	TAMIS-PB	82.74 ($\pm$ 5.6)	76.85 ($\pm$ 5.2)	**62.00** ($\pm$ 5.4)
	MAMAMIA-PB	**92.16** ($\pm$ 2.6)	78.06 ($\pm$ 5.5)	61.53 ($\pm$ 4.7)
	Hybrid-PB	91.87 ($\pm$ 3.0)	**78.37** ($\pm$ 5.6)	61.49 ($\pm$ 5.5)
	TAMIS-PB*	85.75 ($\pm$ 4.2)	80.47 ($\pm$ 4.8)	**62.64** ($\pm$ 4.7)
	Hybrid-PB*	**94.32** ($\pm$ 2.6)	**81.98** ($\pm$ 4.8)	62.23 ($\pm$ 4.9)
		Balanced Accuracy (Simple)		
		$\epsilon=1000$	$\epsilon=100$	$\epsilon=10$
$\mathcal{D}_{\text{aux}}^{\text{ind}}$	TAMIS-PB	61.67 ($\pm$ 1.8)	**58.53** ($\pm$ 1.1)	**52.48** ($\pm$ 0.3)
	MAMAMIA-PB	69.97 ($\pm$ 1.4)	55.49 ($\pm$ 0.6)	50.81 ($\pm$ 0.1)
	Hybrid-PB	**70.75** ($\pm$ 2.4)	56.21 ($\pm$ 0.9)	50.85 ($\pm$ 0.1)
	TAMIS-PB*	63.38 ($\pm$ 0.7)	**60.18** ($\pm$ 0.3)	**52.68** ($\pm$ 0.2)
	Hybrid-PB*	**74.24** ($\pm$ 1.0)	57.67 ($\pm$ 0.4)	50.90 ($\pm$ 0.1)
$\mathcal{D}_{\text{target}}^{\text{house}}$	TAMIS-PB	76.04 ($\pm$ 5.5)	**70.20** ($\pm$ 4.8)	**57.04** ($\pm$ 4.2)
	MAMAMIA-PB	78.54 ($\pm$ 4.2)	57.34 ($\pm$ 3.7)	51.74 ($\pm$ 2.5)
	Hybrid-PB	**82.14** ($\pm$ 4.9)	59.86 ($\pm$ 3.6)	51.70 ($\pm$ 2.4)
	TAMIS-PB*	79.48 ($\pm$ 4.8)	**73.12** ($\pm$ 4.5)	**57.64** ($\pm$ 3.5)
	Hybrid-PB*	**86.58** ($\pm$ 4.0)	62.36 ($\pm$ 3.4)	51.54 ($\pm$ 2.3)

TAMIS-PB* and Hybrid-PB* achieve better performance than the other three attacks. This again validates the hypothesis that focusing on distributional features selected by the SDG is key in crafting efficient attack scores. While is unlikely that an attacker would be directly provided knowledge of the bayesian network structure that generated $\mathcal{D}_{\text{synth}}$, our results highlight that improving over our proposed graph recovery method could enable out-performing both the MAMA-MIA and current TAMIS-PB attacks.

Regarding calibrated activation, we renew the observations made for MST. On the one hand, this activation is detrimental to the accuracy of predictions on $\mathcal{D}_{\text{aux}}^{\text{ind}}$ for all methods. On the other hand, on the specific $\mathcal{D}_{\text{target}}^{\text{house}}$ setting, it is markedly beneficial to the accuracy of predictions for MAMA-MIA-like scores (MAMAMIA-PB and Hybrid-PB) while having very limited impact on TAMIS-PB, that still achieves better or similar balanced accuracy in most cases.

Factoring all previous results, we conclude that while MAMA-MIA-like scores seemingly extract more information than TAMIS-PB, as showed by their higher

AUROC, the TAMIS-PB scores are more suitable for prediction in the realistic setting where the attacker has no additional knowledge to craft decision thresholds beyond the default $t = 0.5$.

We hypothesize that TAMIS scores underperforming for $\epsilon = 1000$ may be due to numerical effects of extreme values in ratios of conditionals. Notably, when attacking a sample that exhibits a combination of attributes unseen in either $\mathcal{D}_\text{aux}$ or $\mathcal{D}_\text{synth}$, both the MAMA-MIA and TAMIS implementations assign an arbitrarily-low conditional probability to it, which is bound to result in extreme ratio values. This is more likely to appear with high ϵ, as parent sets are authorized to have a larger domain size, possibly containing very-rare combinations. This could probably be addressed by refining the way these cases are handled.

6.3 Cross-Targeted Attacks

In order to further assess how beneficial it is for attacks to be tailored to the SDG method, we experimented running MST-targeted attacks against PrivBayes-generated synthetic data, and conversely. Results are provided in Appendix D.

Overall, cross-targeted attacks under-perform compared with their counterparts. Notably, PrivBayes-targeted attacks have poor results against MST-generated data. This highlights that using a more complex density estimator does not necessarily result in more performant attacks, again validating the value of using a density estimator matching the generating one.

However, TAMIS-MST achieves good results against PrivBayes, with a higher or similar balanced accuracy with simple activation than MAMAMIA-PB and Hybrid-PB for all settings, save for $\epsilon = 1000$. This is remarkable, as TAMIS-MST requires less attacker knowledge and computational power than MAMA-MIA.

7 Conclusion

In this paper, we have investigated and validated the assumption that tailoring MIAs on synthetic data to the SDG method was beneficial to attack performance, and proposed alternatives to refine both steps of the state-of-the-art MAMA-MIA attack. The resulting TAMIS attacks were demonstrated to further improve the state-of-the-art against MST and PrivBayes on replicas of the SNAKE challenge, that MAMA-MIA recently won.

Our experiments have shown that recovering the graphical model underlying a synthetic dataset resulted in more successful attacks than gathering more generic information via shadow modeling. For MST, we were able to propose a straightforward graph recovery method that achieved perfect accuracy in our experiments, and requires both less computational power and less attacker knowledge than shadow modeling. For PrivBayes, our method only improves over shadow modeling in terms of computational power, and should be a focus for improvement in future work.

Our experiments have also shown that our proposed attack scores, which are more mathematically-grounded than their MAMA-MIA counterpart, produce more accurate predictions when using a simple sigmoid activation function and a default decision threshold. We have also shown that methods are not ranked similarly depending on whether their AUROC or balanced accuracy is considered. This highlights that there may be a gap between the information contained in attack scores and that which can instrumented into actual predictions by an attacker. Future research may help close that gap, either by designing clever activation and thresholding mechanisms that do not rely on unrealistic attacker knowledge hypotheses, or by further refining the way how focused statistics are combined into attack scores that both achieve high AUROC and behave nicely with simple activation functions.

Finally, while the MAMA-MIA and TAMIS attacks have been designed for the black-box model threat where the attacker knows which SDG method was used, we have remarked that the TAMIS-MST attack could in fact be run agnostic to the SDG method. Our experiments on PrivBayes-generated data have shown that it may be a competitive if not optimal method, and a future research direction could be to assess the value of that attack in a no-box threat model, using more diverse datasets, SDG methods and relevant baseline attacks.

Acknowledgments. This work was supported by the ANR 22-CMAS-0009 CAPS'UL (CAmpus Participatif en Santé numérique du Site Universitaire de Lille) project of the France 2030 AMI-CMA, and the ANR 22-PECY-0002 IPOP (Interdisciplinary Project on Privacy) project of the Cybersecurity PEPR.

Disclosure of Interests. The authors have no competing interests to declare that are relevant to the content of this article.

References

1. Allard, T., Béziaud, L., Gambs, S.: Snake challenge: sanitization algorithms under attack. In: Proceedings of the 32nd ACM International Conference on Information and Knowledge Management, pp. 5010–5014. CIKM '23, Association for Computing Machinery (2023). https://doi.org/10.1145/3583780.3614754
2. van Breugel, B., Sun, H., Qian, Z., van der Schaar, M.: Membership inference attacks against synthetic data through overfitting detection. In: Ruiz, F., Dy, J., van de Meent, J.W. (eds.) Proceedings of The 26th International Conference on Artificial Intelligence and Statistics. Proceedings of Machine Learning Research, vol. 206, pp. 3493–3514. PMLR (2023). https://proceedings.mlr.press/v206/breugel23a.html
3. Cai, K., Lei, X., Wei, J., Xiao, X.: Data synthesis via differentially private Markov random fields. Proc. VLDB Endow. 14(11), pp. 2190–2202 (2021). https://doi.org/10.14778/3476249.3476272
4. Desfontaines, D.: Empirical privacy metrics: the bad, the Ugly... and the good, maybe? In: 2024 USENIX Conference on Privacy Engineering Practice and Respect. USENIX Association, Santa Clara, CA (2024). https://www.usenix.org/conference/pepr24/presentation/desfontaines

5. Dwork, C., Roth, A.: The algorithmic foundations of differential privacy. Found. Trends® Theor. Comput. Sci. **9**(3–4), 211–407 (2014). https://doi.org/10.1561/0400000042
6. Giomi, M., Boenisch, F., Wehmeyer, C., Tasnádi, B.: A unified framework for quantifying privacy risk in synthetic data. Proc. Priv. Enhancing Technol. 2023, pp. 312–328 (2023). https://doi.org/10.56553/popets-2023-0055
7. Golob, S., Pentyala, S., Maratkhan, A., Cock, M.D.: High epsilon synthetic data vulnerabilities in MST and PrivBayes (2024). https://arxiv.org/abs/2402.06699
8. Golob, S., Pentyala, S., Maratkhan, A., Cock, M.D.: Privacy vulnerabilities in marginals-based synthetic data. In: 3rd IEEE Conference on Secure and Trustworthy Machine Learning (SaTML) (2025). https://arxiv.org/abs/2410.05506
9. Hayes, J., Melis, L., Danezis, G., Cristofaro, E.D.: LOGAN: Membership inference attacks against generative models. Proceedings on Privacy Enhancing Technologies (2019). https://petsymposium.org/popets/2019/popets-2019-0008.php
10. Hilprecht, B., Härterich, M., Bernau, D.: Monte Carlo and reconstruction membership inference attacks against generative models. Proc. Priv. Enhancing Technol. **2019**(4), 232–249 (2019). https://doi.org/10.2478/popets-2019-0067
11. Houssiau, F., et al.: A framework for auditable synthetic data generation (2022). https://arxiv.org/abs/2211.11540
12. Houssiau, F., et al.: Prive: Empirical privacy evaluation of synthetic data generators. In: NeurIPS 2022 Workshop on Synthetic Data for Empowering ML Research (2022). https://openreview.net/forum?id=9hXskf1K7zQ
13. Lin, Z., Jain, A., Wang, C., Fanti, G., Sekar, V.: Using GANs for sharing networked time series data: challenges, initial promise, and open questions. In: Proceedings of the ACM Internet Measurement Conference, pp. 464–483. IMC '20, Association for Computing Machinery, New York, NY, USA (2020). https://doi.org/10.1145/3419394.3423643
14. McKenna, R., Miklau, G., Sheldon, D.: Winning the NIST contest: a scalable and general approach to differentially private synthetic data. Journal of Privacy and Confidentiality **11**(3) (2021). https://doi.org/10.29012/jpc.778
15. Pang, W., Shafieinejad, M., Liu, L., Hazlewood, S., He, X.: Clavaddpm: Multi-relational data synthesis with cluster-guided diffusion models. In: Globerson, A., et al. (eds.) Advances in Neural Information Processing Systems, vol. 37, pp. 83521–83547. Curran Associates, Inc. (2024). https://doi.org/10.48550/arXiv.2405.17724
16. Shokri, R., Stronati, M., Song, C., Shmatikov, V.: Membership inference attacks against machine learning models. In: 2017 IEEE Symposium on Security and Privacy (SP), pp. 3–18 (2017). https://doi.org/10.1109/SP.2017.41
17. Stadler, T., Oprisanu, B., Troncoso, C.: Synthetic data – anonymisation groundhog day. In: 31st USENIX Security Symposium (USENIX Security 22), pp. 1451–1468. USENIX Association, Boston, MA (2022). https://www.usenix.org/conference/usenixsecurity22/presentation/stadler
18. Wainwright, M.J., Jordan, M.I.: Graphical models, exponential families, and variational inference. Found. Trends® Mach. Learn. **1**(1–2), 1–305 (2008). https://doi.org/10.1561/2200000001
19. Xie, L., Lin, K., Wang, S., Wang, F., Zhou, J.: Differentially private generative adversarial network (2018). https://arxiv.org/abs/1802.06739
20. Yoon, J., Drumright, L.N., van der Schaar, M.: Anonymization through data synthesis using generative adversarial networks (ads-GAN). IEEE J. Biomed. Health Inform. **24**(8), 2378–2388 (2020). https://doi.org/10.1109/JBHI.2020.2980262

21. Yoon, J., Jordon, J., van der Schaar, M.: PATE-GAN: Generating synthetic data with differential privacy guarantees. In: International Conference on Learning Representations (2019). https://openreview.net/forum?id=S1zk9iRqF7
22. Zhang, J., Cormode, G., Procopiuc, C.M., Srivastava, D., Xiao, X.: PrivBayes: Private data release via bayesian networks. ACM Trans. Database Syst. **42**(4) (2017). https://doi.org/10.1145/3134428

Variance-Based Defense Against Blended Backdoor Attacks

Sujeevan Aseervatham[1,3]($\boxtimes$), Achraf Kerzazi[1,2,3], and Younès Bennani[2,3]

[1] Orange Research, Châtillon, France
{sujeevan.aseervatham,achraf.kerzazi}@orange.com
[2] Université Sorbonne Paris Nord, LIPN, UMR 7030 CNRS, Paris, France
younes.bennani@sorbonne-paris-nord.fr
[3] LaMSN - La Maison des Sciences Numériques, Plaine Saint-Denis, France

Abstract. Backdoor attacks represent a subtle yet effective class of cyberattacks targeting AI models, primarily due to their stealthy nature. The model behaves normally on clean data but exhibits malicious behavior only when the attacker embeds a specific trigger into the input. This attack is performed during the training phase, where the adversary corrupts a small subset of the training data by embedding a pattern and modifying the labels to a chosen target. The objective is to make the model associate the pattern with the target label while maintaining normal performance on unaltered data.

Several defense mechanisms have been proposed to sanitize training datasets. However, these methods often rely on the availability of a clean dataset to detect statistical anomalies, which may not always be feasible in real-world scenarios where datasets can be unavailable or compromised. To address this limitation, we propose a novel defense method that trains a model on the given dataset, detects poisoned classes, and extracts the critical part of the attack trigger before identifying the poisoned instances. This approach enhances explainability by explicitly revealing the harmful part of the trigger. The effectiveness of our method is demonstrated through experimental evaluations on well-known image datasets and a comparative analysis against three state-of-the-art algorithms: SCAn, ABL, and AGPD.

Keywords: Machine Learning · Data Poisoning · Backdoor Mitigation

1 Introduction

The rise of Artificial Intelligence (AI), and more specifically Deep Learning-based systems, has been dazzling and unparalleled. Its use is now widespread and, thanks to the availability of free software, a large public, even without specific knowledge, can build an AI model. They can also download training datasets and pre-trained models. Like any software, AI systems are vulnerable to malicious attacks. They can traditionally be attacked at the software layer, e.g., through vulnerabilities in the software libraries, but they can also be attacked through data and model-parameter manipulation. A corrupted AI can exhibit malicious behavior, which can have critical consequences. For example, self-driving cars may intentionally collide depending on the attacker's aim and a Large Language Model (LLM) may give fake news. This security risk has become a real-life threat and a major issue when researchers have shown that the AI models can be attacked in various ways depending on the aim, knowledge, and model access privilege of the attacker [16,21]. The attacker can lead an evasion attack by slightly modifying the model's input in order to change the decision/prediction. For example, for a spam recognition system, the attacker may change some words to bypass the filter. She can also lead inference attacks where the attacker wants to extract some information about the training dataset on which the model was trained. This attack is also known as privacy attack or model inversion attack. Indeed, in a personalized drug system, she may want to know if a particular patient information was in the training set. During the training stage, an attacker can also poison the training data to either degrade the model's performance (non-targeted attacks), e.g., by flipping the labels, or introduce a backdoor than can be exploited, during inference, to trigger a malicious behavior of the model.

In this paper, we focus on a defense method against the backdoor attacks where the attacker wants a model to associate her data pattern to her target label. Thus, in the inference stage, any input containing the pattern will trigger the misclassification of the input as the target label. This is a vicious attack as the model seems to be pristine w.r.t. to its performance on clean data but in fact contains a backdoor which changes the prediction only in the presence of the trigger in the input data. For example, in a self-driving car, an attacker may have corrupted the model to recognize a green-square sticker pasted on a stop sign as a 70mph speed limit board. Such attacks can easily be performed when the attacker has a write access to the training data, as illustrated by the BadNets algorithm [7]. More advanced attacks based on BadNets have been proposed, but they often require more resources or access rights. By its simplicity, BadNets remains a threat that can be exploited by a large population, including opportunistic criminals and script-kiddies (open source script users without particular knowledge). Many defenses have been proposed in the literature, but most of them require an additional dataset of clean data on which statistics are computed to detect a distribution anomaly induced by a poisoned sample. In real-life, such dataset may hardly be available and even be subject to a corruption.

We propose a multi-stage defense algorithm that estimates the poisoned subset of the training data, detects the poisoned classes, extracts the attack trigger for each class, and identifies the poisoned instances based on the extracted pattern. Our contributions can be summarized in three points: 1) we introduce a novel defense algorithm against BadNets [7] and Blended [2] attacks which does not rely on additional prerequisites such as the availability of a clean dataset; 2) the defense is explainable, as it extracts the most important part of the trigger responsible for the malicious behavior; and 3) our method is effective in All-to-All attacks where many classes are poisoned.

The remainder of this paper is organized as follows: in Sect. 2, we present the state-of-the-art of backdoor attacks and defenses. Our defense algorithm is detailed in Sect. 3. Section 4 describes the experimental results and, finally, Sect. 5 concludes this article.

2 Related Work

2.1 Backdoor Attacks

The Backdoor attack was introduced in [7] where the proposed BadNets methodology involves patching a small pattern onto the input data of a small percentage of the training set and labeling them with the desired target label. By training on this poisoned set, the model learns to associate the attack pattern with the target label. Thus, the presence of the pattern in an input instance triggers the malicious behavior of the model by classifying the input as the attacker's target label instead of the correct one. To make the pattern more stealthy, linear blending is used in [2], while in [29] the pattern is generated in the low-frequency domain by considering both the training set and a pre-trained model. These works paved the way for more advanced attacks, where the pattern is not fixed but specific to the input [18,19]. However, compared to fixed pattern attacks, input-based pattern attacks require more prerequisites, such as access to and modification of the training algorithm, making them more suitable when targeting users who download pretrained models. Fixed-pattern attacks remain more realistic in real-world scenarios, especially when the attacker is an insider with access to the training data.

2.2 Backdoor Defenses

In the last few years, many backdoor defense methods have been proposed by researchers, each designed to be used at a specific stage of the AI model lifecycle. As noted in [28] and [30], these defenses can be grouped in four categories based on the lifecycle stage: 1) pre-training stage methods, mainly used to detect the poisoned instances and sanitize the dataset [1,4,6,17,22,25,28], 2) in-training stage defenses, which aim to reduce the effect of the poisoned data on the model [10,14,30], 3) post-training stage methods, used to correct backdoored models [15,27], and 4) inference stage defenses, which are used to detect malicious inputs by analyzing both both the input and the output of the model, typically residing between the user and the model [8]. These methods can also be categorized based on the information they use to mitigate the attacks. The main approaches are input-based, loss-based, and activation-based. Defenses in the pre-training and inference stages are mainly input-based or activation-based methods, while algorithms in the in-training and post-training stages are mostly loss-based or activation-based. Input-based approaches operate on the input data by altering it and computing statistical measures on the predictions, such as the entropy [4,6,8]. In [6], the STRIP algorithm linearly blends the input image with a set of clean images before computing the entropy of the prediction on each perturbed images. A poisoned image is detected when the entropy is low. In [4], the SentiNet method uses Grad-CAM [24] to extract the decision region from an input image and superimposes it on a set of clean images to check whether it triggers a misclassification of the model. Activation-based methods rely on the assumption that the poisoned and clean samples can be separated, e.g., through clustering, in the feature space induced by the activations of a specific layer of the model [1,17,22,25]. In [1], K-Means clustering is used on the activations and in [25], the proposed SCAn algorithm uses a two-component Gaussian Mixture Models (GMM) for clustering. In the loss-based approach, the methods rely on the property that poisoned instances are classified with a very low value of the loss. In [14], the Anti-Backdoor Learning (ABL) defense uses the loss to isolate the poisoned instances during the training and then unlearns the poisoned data through gradient ascent.

3 Variance-Based Defense

3.1 Threat Model

In this paper, we assume that the attacker has full access to the training database. The attacker aims to modify the model's behavior so that any input patched with her attack pattern is classified as her target class, while maintaining good categorization performance on pristine inputs to remain undetected. To implement this attack, she employs a combination of BadNets [7] and Blended [3] attacks. Given an attack pattern/trigger $\mathbf{p}$, its corresponding binary mask $\mathbf{m}$, the target label $y_t \in \mathcal{Y}$, and a blending factor $\alpha \in [0,1]$, she selects a subset of the training dataset with a ratio r and generates malicious data according to Eq. 1, before adding it to the training set with her target label. The poisoned dataset is then distributed or made available to download. Training a model on this poisoned dataset will cause the model to capture a relationship between the attack trigger $\mathbf{p}$ and the target label y_t.

$$\tilde{\mathbf{x}} = \Gamma(\mathbf{x}, \mathbf{p}, \mathbf{m}, \alpha) = \mathbf{x} \odot (\mathbf{1} - \mathbf{m}) + (1 - \alpha) \cdot (\mathbf{x} \odot \mathbf{m}) + \alpha \cdot (\mathbf{m} \odot \mathbf{p}) \quad (1)$$

where $\mathbf{x} \in \mathcal{X}$, with $\mathcal{X} \subseteq \mathbb{R}^{H \times W \times C}$, is an input image of height H, width W and color dimension C, $\odot$ the element-wise tensor product operator and $\mathbf{1}$ the all-ones tensor of the same dimension as m.

3.2 Motivation

Before using a dataset to train a model, it is important to sanitize it and ensure that no malicious data leading to a blended or a BadNets backdoor are present. To achieve this, we propose an algorithm to detect and extract the trigger pattern from the training dataset. Using the extracted patterns, the dataset can be sanitized by removing the data containing these patterns.

We want to extract the pattern $\mathbf{p_t}$ and its binary mask $\mathbf{m_t}$ for a target label y_t based on the following hypotheses:

1. when a pristine input is patched with the pattern $\mathbf{p_t}$, the model must predict y_t, which means that $\mathbf{p_t}$ and $\mathbf{m_t}$ should minimize the training loss for the set of clean data ($\mathcal{D}_C$) patched with $\mathbf{p_t}$ and associated with the target label y_t,
2. the pattern should also be as small as possible, i.e., only a few elements of the binary mask should be set to 1 (this is equivalent to using a L_0 norm penalization on $\mathbf{p_t}$) in order to keep the malicious data unnoticeable among the training instances,
3. the pixels of the pattern should be located at low-variance positions in a variance image computed from a set of malicious data with the label y_t ($\mathcal{D}_{P_t}$), since we are defending against a static-trigger data poisoning.

Given these three hypotheses, we can formulate the following minimization problem to compute $(\mathbf{p_t}, \mathbf{m_t})$:

$$\min_{p,m} \frac{1}{|\mathcal{D}_C|} \sum_{(\mathbf{x}^{(k)},y^{(k)}) \in \mathcal{D}_C} \ell(f(\Gamma(\mathbf{x}^{(k)}, \mathbf{p}, \mathbf{m}, \alpha)), y_t) + \lambda \cdot \|\mathbf{m}\|_1 + \gamma \cdot \|\mathbf{m} \odot V_{\mathcal{D}_{P_t}}\|_1 \quad (2)$$

where f is the poisoned model learned from the malicious dataset, $\mathcal{D}_C$ the clean part of the training set, $\mathcal{D}_{P_t}$ the poisoned part with label y_t, ℓ the loss function, usually the Cross-Entropy loss, λ and γ the loss terms weighting factors and $V_{\mathcal{D}_{P_t}}$ the mean, over the color channel, of the min-max-scaled variance of the data in $\mathcal{D}_{P_t}$ such that:

$$[V_{\mathcal{D}_{P_t}}]_{i,j} = \frac{1}{n_r} \sum_{c \in \{1,\ldots,n_r\}} \frac{\text{var}(X_{i,j,c}; \mathcal{D}_{P_t}) - \min_{k,l}(\text{var}(X_{k,l,c}; \mathcal{D}_{P_t}))}{\max_{k,l}(\text{var}(X_{k,l,c}; \mathcal{D}_{P_t})) - \min_{k,l}(\text{var}(X_{k,l,c}; \mathcal{D}_{P_t}))} \quad (3)$$

with $X_{i,j,c}$ the random variable associated with the pixel/variable $x_{i,j,c}$ where c is the color channel index, n_r the channel dimension and the variance given by:

$$\text{var}(X_{k,l,c}; \mathcal{D}_{P_t}) = \frac{1}{|\mathcal{D}_{P_t}|} \sum_{(\mathbf{x}^{(n)}, y^{(n)}) \in \mathcal{D}_{P_t}} (\mathbf{x}_{k,l,c}^{(n)} - \overline{X_{k,l,c}})^2 \quad (4)$$

Solving the problem 2 may be time-consuming and difficult since $\mathcal{D}_C$ and $\mathcal{D}_{P_t}$ are not known, and it may even lead to adversarial noises, especially if the model is not robust.

Instead of solving directly this minimization problem, we propose in the next section a heuristic to approximate the patterns.

3.3 Method

The proposed data sanitization method is described in Algorithm 1 and illustrated step by step in Fig. 1. It consists of seven main steps, listed as follows:

1. Estimate a set of malicious instances $\tilde{\mathcal{D}}_P$
2. Detect the potentially poisoned classes

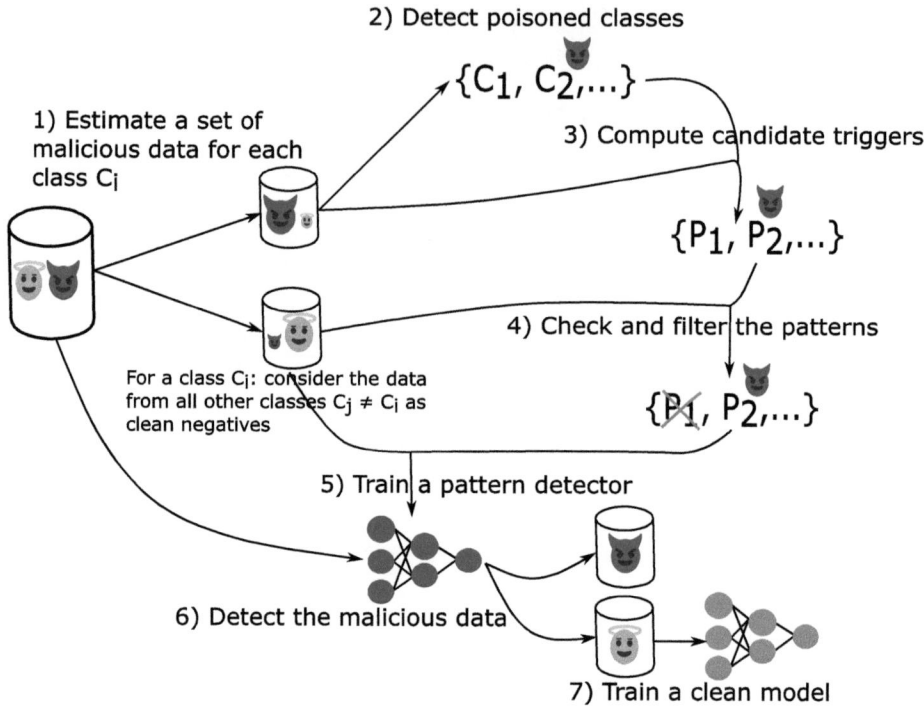

Fig. 1. Workflow of the proposed sanitization method.

3. Compute a candidate pattern for each poisoned class
4. Check the patterns on an estimated $\tilde{\mathcal{D}}_C$
5. Train a pattern detector for each detected pattern
6. Detect the malicious instances
7. Train a clean model

In the following paragraphs, we provide a detailed description of each step.

Stage 1: Malicious Instance Set Estimation. We assume that the patterns used to poison the training set are small and simple, such that a simple classifier with a single convolution layer can memorize the relation between the pattern and the target label. The idea is to train a simple convolution model with a few layers as the one shown in Fig. 2 on the training set to overfit the attack pattern. The model is thus expected to perform well on the poisoned instances and have a high generalization error on the clean data. We refer to this model as the *simple poisoned model*, denoted f_s. A subset of the poisoned data, for a class c_i, can then be estimated by selecting the top N instances with the label c_i and correctly predicted with the highest probability score (N being a parameter, knowing that for our experiments we set $N = 20$).

Algorithm 1: Variance-based defense

Data: $\mathcal{D}$: the training set to sanitize
Result: $\mathcal{D}_P$: the set of malicious instances and f_c: the sanitized model
foreach *class $c_i \in \mathcal{Y}$* **do**
    $\tilde{\mathcal{D}}_{P_i} \leftarrow$ Estimate a set of malicious instances with label c_i ;
    if *c_i is detected as poisoned* **then**
        $(\mathbf{p_i}, \mathbf{m_i}) \leftarrow$ Compute a candidate pattern and its mask based on $\tilde{\mathcal{D}}_{P_i}$;
    end
end
$\mathcal{P} \leftarrow$ Check and filter the candidate pattern set $\{(\mathbf{p_i}, \mathbf{m_i})\}_i$;
foreach $(\mathbf{p_i}, \mathbf{m_i}) \in \mathcal{P}$ **do**
    $h_i \leftarrow$ Train a model to detect the instances patched with $\mathbf{p_i}$;
    $\mathcal{D}_{P_i} \leftarrow$ Use h_i to identify the malicious instances in $\mathcal{D}$;
end
$\mathcal{D}_P \leftarrow \bigcup_i \mathcal{D}_{P_i}$;
$f_c \leftarrow$ Train a clean model using $\mathcal{D}$ and $\mathcal{D}_P$;

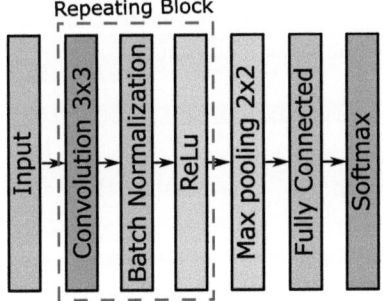

Fig. 2. Architecture of the classifier used to overfit the attack patterns.

Stage 2: Poisoned Classes Detection. At this stage, we aim to filter out the classes considered as non-poisoned, retaining only the suspicious ones for further analysis. To achieve this, for each class c_i we identify the most important (pixel) variable that is commonly used by the poisoned model f_s to correctly classify the instances of the estimated malicious set $\tilde{\mathcal{D}}_{P_i}$. If the empirical distributions of the importance of this variable in $\tilde{\mathcal{D}}_{P_i}$ and in a subset of potential clean-instances from c_i are the same then we can assume that the class c_i is not poisoned. To find the most important variable, given the *simple poisoned model f_s*, we compute the gradient of the first loss term of Eq. 2 w.r.t. the malicious input, as given by Eq. 5.

$$\nabla L(f_s, \tilde{\mathcal{D}}_{P_i}) = \frac{1}{|\tilde{\mathcal{D}}_{P_i}|} \sum_{(\mathbf{x}^{(k)}, c_i) \in \tilde{\mathcal{D}}_{P_i}} \frac{\partial \ell}{\partial \mathbf{x}}(f_s(\mathbf{x}^{(k)}), c_i) \qquad (5)$$

As we want the most important pixels explaining the decision, we choose the following loss function $\ell(\mathbf{x}, c)$:

$$\ell(\mathbf{x}, c) = P(c|\mathbf{x}; f_s) - \max_{y \in \mathcal{Y}-\{c\}} P(y|\mathbf{x}; f_s) \tag{6}$$

$P(c|\mathbf{x}; f_s)$ is given by the cth component of the softmax layer of f_s and in order to avoid numerical instabilities, we use the logit layer instead of the softmax layer.

For poisoned instances, some components of the gradient (Eq. 5) will have a large absolute value compared to the clean-instances. Indeed, the partial derivative at given coordinates indicates the sensitivity of the loss function to changes in that pixel's value. In the case of poisoned instances, the backdoor pattern is designed to strongly influence the model's prediction. As a result, only a few pixels, those containing the trigger, tend to dominate the gradient signal. We thus assume that, for poisoned instances, a small number of pixels will have a large impact on the prediction. The most influential pixel can therefore be identified by locating the index (i^*, j^*) corresponding to the maximum absolute value of the mean gradient across the color channels:

$$i^*, j^* = \arg\max_{i,j} \left| \text{mean}_c \left[\nabla L(f_s, \tilde{\mathcal{D}}_{P_i}) \right]_{i,j,c} \right| \tag{7}$$

We now define the importance of this pixel in the decision of an input $\mathbf{x}$ by f_s, as follows:

$$I(\mathbf{x}, c_i; f_s, i^*, j^*) = \max_c \left[\|\nabla L(f_s, \{(\mathbf{x}, c_i)\})\| \right]_{i^*, j^*, c} \tag{8}$$

The two-sided Kolmogorov-Smirnov test [5] is used with a confidence level of 99% to compare the distributions of $I(\mathbf{x}, c_i; f_s, i^*, j^*)$ between $\tilde{\mathcal{D}}_{P_i}$ and a set of potential clean-instances from c_i. We use the instances of c_i with the lowest prediction scores as clean-instances. When the p-value is below 0.01, we consider c_i as potentially poisoned.

Stage 3: Candidate Pattern Computation. With the *simple poisoned model* f_s and the estimated subset of malicious instances of the class c_i, we can compute an approximate pattern by using the gradient defined in Eq. 5 which gives the importance of the pixels w.r.t. the loss function. To obtain a binary mask from the gradient, the following processing is performed:

1. Flattening the gradient of Eq. 5 by taking the L_2 norm of the gradient over the color channel
2. Min-Max-scaling the result to have the values within $[0, 1]$
3. Binarizing the values using a threshold

The binarization step may be tricky as it involves defining a threshold which may depends on the input data. To avoid manually defining this threshold, we used the Otsu method, which finds the best threshold that minimizes the intra-variance [20]. In order to capture also the neighboring points of an important point, we apply a Gaussian blur before applying the Otsu method.

Once we have the binary gradient mask, we need to select only the points with the lowest variance, which requires a variance threshold. The variance matrix on $\tilde{\mathcal{D}}_{P_i}$ can be computed with the Eq. 3. The final candidate mask is obtained by performing an element-wise product between the gradient mask and the variance matrix before binarizing with the Otsu method (note that to keep the points with low variances, we use 1 minus the variance matrix).

To have the candidate pattern, we apply the candidate mask on the mean image of $\tilde{\mathcal{D}}_{P_i}$. Algorithm 2 describes the whole process of generating the candidate pattern and mask.

Algorithm 2: Pattern Computation

Data: $\tilde{\mathcal{D}}_{P_i}$: a set of malicious instances for the class c_i, f_s: the poisoned model
Result: $(\mathbf{p_i}, \mathbf{m_i})$: the candidate pattern and mask for the class c_i
$\mathbf{g} \leftarrow$ compute the gradient with Equation 5 using the logit layer ;
foreach *pixel at coordinate i,j* **do**
$\quad \tilde{g}_{i,j} \leftarrow \sqrt{\sum_r g_{i,j,r}^2}$;
end
$\mathbf{g}_{scaled} \leftarrow$ min_max_scale($\tilde{\mathbf{g}}$) ;
$\mathbf{g}_{blured} \leftarrow$ gaussian_blur($\mathbf{g}_{scaled}$) ;
$\mathbf{g}_m \leftarrow$ otsu_binarization($\mathbf{g}_{blured}$) ;
$\mathbf{V}_{\tilde{\mathcal{D}}_{P_i}} \leftarrow$ Use Equation 3 to compute the variance on $\tilde{\mathcal{D}}_{P_i}$;
$\mathbf{m_i} \leftarrow$ otsu_binarization($\mathbf{g}_m \odot (1 - V_{\tilde{\mathcal{D}}_{P_i}})$) ;
$\mathbf{p_i} \leftarrow \mathbf{m_i} \odot \frac{1}{|\tilde{\mathcal{D}}_{P_i}|} \sum_{(\mathbf{x}^{(k)}, y^{(k)}) \in \tilde{\mathcal{D}}_{P_i}} \mathbf{x}^{(k)}$;

Stage 4: Check and Filter the Patterns. At this stage, a candidate pattern and its mask have been calculated for each potentially poisoned class. We need to check that it triggers a malicious behavior of the *simple poisoned model*. To this end, we patch the pattern to instances from other classes (estimated $\tilde{\mathcal{D}}_C$) before feeding them to the model, and we check whether the model assigns them to the class associated with the pattern. We compute the Attack Success Rate (ASR), i.e., the proportion of patched instances predicted as the attack label. If this rate falls below a user-defined threshold, we remove the pattern from the candidate set. The remaining patterns are then considered harmful (Fig. 3).

Stage 5: Train a Pattern Detector. To detect the presence of a pattern in the training set, we propose to train a binary classifier for each pattern. We use a one-layer-convolution network as shown in Fig. 2 except that 1) we remove

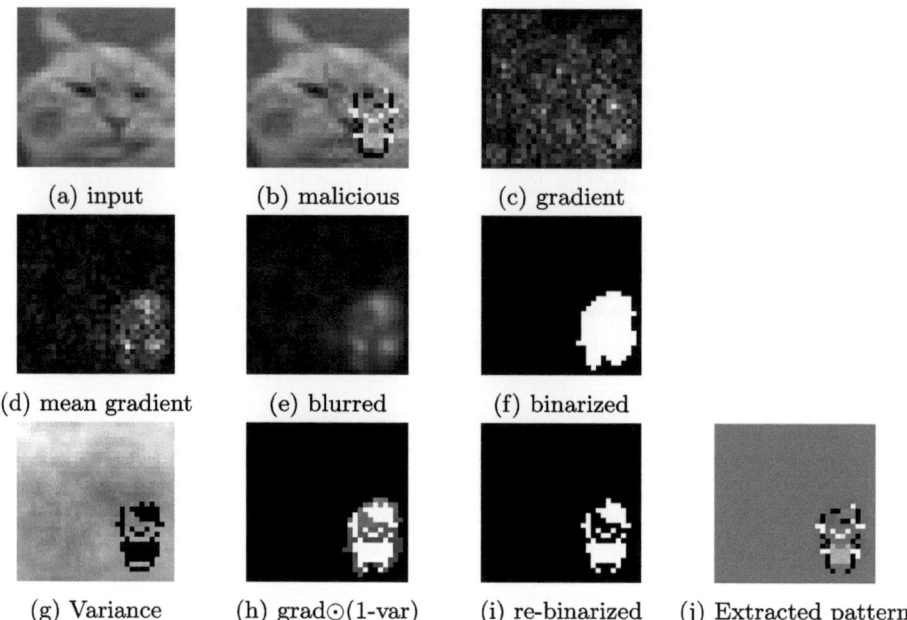

Fig. 3. Illustration of the candidate pattern computation process. The first row shows (a) an example of input image from the cat class, (b) its malicious version labeled with the attacker's label and (c) its gradient (Eq. 5). In the last two rows, the pattern computation process, described in the Algorithm 2, is illustrated step by step. The gray background in (j) represents transparency.

the batch normalization, 2) we add a dropout layer before the fully connected layer in order to reduce the overfitting and 3) we replace the softmax layer by a sigmoid layer. For a given pattern $\mathbf{p_i}$ for the class c_i, we build the training data as follows, we use the instances of the other classes and label them as "0" (clean), and we patch these instances using the Eq. 1 with random blending factors, before labeling them as "1" (poisoned). Instead of training directly on the images, we can achieve better performance by training the model on the image gradient using Eq. 5 on a single image. Moreover, we use Semi-Supervised Learning (SSL) with Pseudo-labels [13]. After a few epochs of supervised learning, we use the classifier to label the data of the class c_i and we add these data to the training set. We continue the SSL by relabeling the data after each epoch for a predefined number of epochs to make the pseudo-labels stable. The Algorithm 3 describes the training procedure.

Stage 6: Detect the Malicious Instances. We compute the gradient for each instance of the training set, and we feed it to each trained pattern detector. We label the instance as malicious if at least one pattern detector labeled it as "1".

Algorithm 3: Training a Pattern Detector

Data: $\mathcal{D}$: the (poisoned) training set, f_s the poisoned model learned in the first stage, $(\mathbf{p_i}, \mathbf{m_i}, c_i)$ the attack pattern $\mathbf{p_i}$ with its mask $\mathbf{m_i}$ for the target class c_i and h_i the binary classifier to fit

Result: h_i: the trained pattern detector for $(\mathbf{p_i}, \mathbf{m_i}, c_i)$

$\mathcal{D}_T \leftarrow \mathcal{D} - \{(\mathbf{x}, y) \in \mathcal{D} : y \neq c_i\}$;
$\mathcal{D}_{ssl} \leftarrow \{\}$;
$(\mathcal{D}_t, \mathcal{D}_v, \mathcal{D}_e) \leftarrow$ split $\mathcal{D}_T$ into training, validation, and test sets;
for $epoch \leftarrow 0$ **to** max_epoch **do**
    foreach $batch\ \mathcal{B}\ of\ \mathcal{D}_t$ **do**
        $\mathcal{U} \leftarrow \{\}$;
        foreach $(x, y) \in \mathcal{B}$ **do**
            $\alpha \leftarrow random(0.1, 1)$;
            $\mathbf{z} \leftarrow \Gamma(\mathbf{x}, \mathbf{p_i}, \mathbf{m_i}, \alpha)$ (Eq. 1);
            $\mathcal{U} \leftarrow \mathcal{U} \cup \{(\nabla L(f_s, \{(\mathbf{x}, c_i)\}), 0), (\nabla L(f_s, \{(\mathbf{z}, c_i)\}), 1)\}$ (Eq. 5) ;
        end
        Optimize h_i with $\mathcal{U} \cup \mathcal{D}_{ssl}$;
    end
    if $start\_ssl\_epoch < epoch < stop\_relabeling\_epoch$ **then**
        Use h_i to label $\{(\mathbf{x}, y) \in \mathcal{D} : y = c_i\}$;
        $\mathcal{D}_{ssl} \leftarrow$ the pseudo-labeled data ;
    end
end

Stage 7: Train a Clean Model. Once we have identified the malicious instances, we can train a clean model from scratch or fine-tune a poisoned model by using both the clean instance set and the poisoned one.

Robustness. The proposed method relies on a *simple poisoned model*, which is assumed to separate poisoned data from clean data based on the prediction score. This implies that the model must be complex enough to capture the trigger (high attack success rate) and simple enough to underperform on clean data (low accuracy rate). Relying on a single model to achieve this task might not be robust. To address this issue, we propose to use an ensemble of simple models based on the architecture shown in Fig. 2 with, e.g., different number of filters and layers. We use each model of the ensemble, simultaneously and independently, to perform Stage 1 to Stage 4. At the end of Stage 4, for each model, we have extracted a set of triggers, one for each detected poisoned class. For robustness, a class is considered poisoned only if the number of extracted patterns for that class exceeds a certain threshold, e.g., half the number of models in the ensemble (majority vote). However, in this work, we adopt a more defensive approach to reduce the false negative rate. Therefore, we consider a class as poisoned if at least one trigger has been extracted for this class. To perform the Stages 5 and 6, only one model and pattern must be retained for a given poisoned class. To select the most appropriate model-and-pattern pair for a class, we choose the one with the lowest accuracy on the training set (computed in Stage 1 during the training) and the highest ASR (computed in stage 4), i.e., the pair that achieves the highest score according to the following metric: $\alpha \cdot (1 - \text{acc}) + (1 - \alpha) \cdot \text{asr}$. In our work, we set $\alpha = 0.6$ to slightly favor the model with the lowest accuracy.

4 Experiments

4.1 Experimental Setup

For the evaluation, we used the BackdoorBench framework [26], and our code is available online[1]. We compared our method, *VBD*, against three high-performing state-of-the-art methods [28]: Anti-Backdoor Learning (ABL) [14], AGPD [28], and SCAn [25]. For VBD, we used an ensemble of 3 models: a 1-layer model with 64 filters, a 2-layers model with 10 filters each, and a 2-layers model with 16 filters each, following the architecture shown in Fig. 2. We used 80% of the training set only to train the models and the remaining 20% for the validation, detection, pattern extraction, and detector training. For training the poisoned and detector models, we used a learning rate of 0.01, a batch size of 256 for CIFAR-10 and 64 for Tiny ImageNet, and 20 training epochs. For the competitors, we used the default settings, which include the use of the Pre-Act ResNet18 model [9], knowing that AGPD and SCAn require also an additional dataset of clean images, which, by default, consists of 10 images per class taken from the test set. Full implementation details and additional parameters are available in the released code repository.

The experiments consist of poisoning 10% of the training dataset using the BadNets and Blended attacks and evaluating the performance of the four methods in detecting the poisons in the training set. For the Blended attacks, we evaluated 3 blending factors: 10%, 20% and 50%. A blending factor of 10% means that the trigger is 90% transparent. A BadNets attack is equivalent to a Blended attack with a blending factor of 100% (full opacity). We used both an All-to-One attack, where only one class is poisoned with 10% of the images from each class (including the target class) and an All-to-All attack, where all classes are poisoned such that class $(k+1 \mod N_c)$, with N_c being the number of classes in the dataset, is poisoned with 10% of the images from class k.

For the database, we used both CIFAR-10 [11] and Tiny ImageNet [12]. CIFAR-10 is composed of 10 classes with 5000 training images of size 32×32 per class. Tiny ImageNet contains 200 classes with 500 training images of size 64×64 per class. For AGPD and SCAn, which require 10 auxiliary clean images per class in their default settings, we used a total of 100 and 2000 clean images from the test set for CIFAR-10 and Tiny ImageNet, respectively.

We used six attack triggers to evaluate the methods, as shown in Fig. 4. When more than one class is poisoned (All-to-All), we used only the grid and square triggers, positioning them at different locations based on the class index. The placement starts at the bottom right of the image and moves from right to left

---

[1] https://github.com/Orange-OpenSource/BackdoorBench/tree/vbd-v1.

and bottom to top to avoid overlapping. We ran a total of 80 experiments: for both CIFAR-10 and Tiny ImageNet, there were 24 experiments (6 triggers × 4 blending factors) for the All-to-One setting and 16 experiments (4 triggers × 4 blending factors) for the All-to-All case. Each experiment is repeated 5 times. In each repetition $i \in \{0, \ldots, 4\}$, the random seed is set to i, and for the All-to-One attacks, the target class is also set to i. The F_1-scores and the averaged F_1-scores are reported as the mean over the five repetitions, along with their standard deviation.

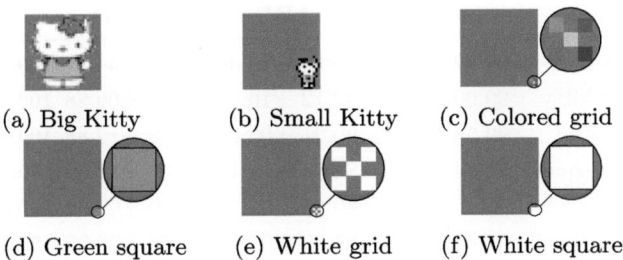

Fig. 4. Attack patterns used in the evaluation. All the triggers, except for the two "kitty" patterns, are of size 3 × 3. The "Big Kitty" spans the entire image and the "Small Kitty" has a size of 10 × 14. The gray background is transparent. (Color figure online)

4.2 Evaluation Metrics

To evaluate the performance of poisoned instance detection, we use the F_1 score, defined as follows:

$$F_1 = 2 \times \frac{\text{Precision} \times \text{Recall}}{\text{Precision} + \text{Recall}}, \quad \text{Precision} = \frac{\text{TP}}{\text{TP} + \text{FP}}, \quad \text{Recall} = \frac{\text{TP}}{\text{TP} + \text{FN}}$$

where TP, TN, FP, and FN denote the number of true positives, true negatives, false positives, and false negatives, respectively.

Precision measures the proportion of correctly identified poisoned instances among all instances classified as poisoned. Recall measures the proportion of actual poisoned instances that were correctly identified by the classifier. Since it is important for a method to perform well on both metrics, the F_1 score, defined as the harmonic mean of precision and recall, is used to provide a balanced evaluation.

4.3 Experimental Results

Table 1 provides the F_1-score of the defense methods for the All-to-One BadNets attack. SCAn and VBD achieve the best results. On average, SCAn outperforms

VBD by 0.34% on CIFAR-10, while VBD performs better on Tiny ImageNet, with an improvement of 1.59%. The average F_1-score across the 12 experiments indicates that VBD surpasses SCAn by 0.62%. Notably, AGPD exhibits low detection performance on the "Big Kitty" pattern, as this pattern covers the entire image, making it difficult for AGPD to distinguish between poisoned and clean instances.

Table 1. All-to-One BadNets poisoned-instance detection F_1-score (%).

Set	Pattern	VBD	ABL	AGPD	SCAn
CIFAR-10	big kitty	99.87 ±00.20	55.39 ±23.40	79.35 ±44.37	**100.00 ±00.00**
	small kitty	99.90 ±00.14	82.12 ±10.54	99.62 ±00.28	**100.00 ±00.00**
	color grid	99.58 ±00.15	90.21 ±03.01	91.36 ±12.88	**100.00 ±00.00**
	green square	99.34 ±00.25	84.04 ±12.19	90.93 ±11.69	**99.99 ±00.01**
	white grid	99.65 ±00.09	89.66 ±02.50	94.60 ±02.64	**100.00 ±00.00**
	white square	97.46 ±00.31	84.30 ±02.13	93.66 ±02.96	**97.86 ±00.12**
	Average	99.30 ±00.10	80.95 ±04.01	91.59 ±11.65	**99.64 ±00.02**
Tiny ImageNet	big kitty	**99.98 ±00.02**	81.69 ±08.87	00.00 ±00.00	94.41 ±12.51
	small kitty	99.98 ±00.02	94.58 ±07.34	88.90 ±24.04	**100.00 ±00.00**
	color grid	**99.86 ±00.12**	96.40 ±02.82	98.69 ±00.19	99.95 ±00.04
	green square	**99.72 ±00.39**	96.77 ±01.67	98.21 ±00.66	95.34 ±10.35
	white grid	**98.70 ±02.64**	95.93 ±00.84	98.34 ±00.73	97.39 ±05.63
	white square	95.89 ±02.35	88.66 ±06.24	59.19 ±54.03	**97.50 ±01.26**
	Average	**99.02 ±00.68**	92.34 ±02.61	73.89 ±08.12	97.43 ±03.16
Average		**99.16 ±00.32**	86.65 ±00.85	82.74 ±08.96	98.54 ±01.58

For the All-to-All BadNets attacks, SCAn fails on both CIFAR-10 and Tiny ImageNet as shown in Table 2. It appears that when at least half of the classes are poisoned SCAn is unable to detect the attack. On the contrary, VBD achieves the best F_1-performance, outperforming AGPD by 8.69% on CIFAR-10 and ABL by 23% on Tiny-ImageNet.

The performance results for the Blended attacks in both All-to-One and All-to-All settings are provided in Table 3 and Table 4, respectively. As we can see, in the All-to-One setting, the results are comparable to those in the All-to-One BadNets case, with SCAn and VBD leading. Nevertheless, in this case, VBD outperforms SCAn by 0.24% on CIFAR-10 and by 7.37% on Tiny ImageNet. The averaged F_1 score across the experiments on both datasets shows that VBD outperforms SCAn by 3.8%. For the All-to-All Blended attack case, as previously mentioned, SCAn fails, and AGPD outperforms the other defenses, with VBD finishing second. It is noteworthy that VBD struggles to detect the attack and extract the triggers when the blending factor is below 50%. However, when the blending factor is 50%, VBD performs better than AGPD.

Table 2. All-to-All BadNets poisoned-instance detection F_1-score (%).

Set	Pattern	VBD	ABL	AGPD	SCAn
CIFAR-10	color grid	**94.37 ±01.03**	56.76 ±12.58	68.28 ±14.05	00.00 ±00.00
	green square	**91.00 ±02.00**	55.36 ±12.30	86.66 ±15.02	00.00 ±00.00
	white grid	**95.64 ±03.54**	58.06 ±07.48	93.07 ±09.05	00.00 ±00.00
	white square	**93.51 ±00.82**	53.14 ±12.94	91.73 ±08.45	00.00 ±00.00
	Average	**93.63 ±00.66**	55.83 ±07.63	84.94 ±07.88	00.00 ±00.00
Tiny ImageNet	color grid	**83.91 ±02.75**	50.57 ±03.50	33.30 ±00.63	00.00 ±00.00
	green square	**85.00 ±01.24**	38.47 ±08.08	34.14 ±01.30	00.00 ±00.00
	white grid	**52.27 ±02.68**	43.45 ±06.51	34.34 ±00.97	00.00 ±00.00
	white square	**44.82 ±02.46**	41.36 ±08.17	33.84 ±00.67	00.00 ±00.00
	Average	**66.50 ±01.91**	43.46 ±02.41	33.90 ±00.54	00.00 ±00.00
Average		**80.06 ±01.14**	49.65 ±04.32	59.42 ±04.14	00.00 ±00.00

Table 3. All-to-One Blended poisoned-instance detection mean F_1-score (%) over the 6 triggers shown in Fig. 4.

Set	Blended	VBD	ABL	AGPD	SCAn
CIFAR-10	10%	**93.34 ±01.08**	68.60 ±04.12	90.38 ±07.27	92.80 ±06.14
	20%	**96.85 ±00.75**	76.58 ±01.18	90.22 ±08.70	96.19 ±01.10
	50%	98.68 ±00.54	84.40 ±01.90	90.68 ±09.68	**99.14 ±00.10**
	Average	**96.29 ±00.72**	76.53 ±01.99	90.43 ±05.73	96.05 ±02.01
Tiny ImageNet	10%	**83.12 ±06.42**	78.03 ±03.02	65.02 ±09.46	75.80 ±03.19
	20%	**93.62 ±05.91**	87.03 ±02.73	72.76 ±19.37	84.58 ±02.84
	50%	**98.05 ±00.99**	92.01 ±01.67	79.50 ±13.01	92.31 ±03.99
	Average	**91.60 ±03.80**	85.69 ±01.33	72.43 ±11.90	84.23 ±02.28
Average		**93.94 ±01.83**	81.11 ±01.31	81.43 ±07.04	90.14 ±02.07

Table 5 provides a summary of the performance of the tested defense methods, with the F_1-score averaged over all the 80 experiments we conducted. VBD ranks first on CIFAR-10 and, notably, on Tiny ImageNet. It outperforms AGPD by 3.61% on CIFAR-10, and ABL by 6.25% on Tiny ImageNet. SCAn is penalized by its failure in the All-to-All settings. It is worth noting that, unlike AGPD and SCAn, VBD and ABL do not rely on an auxiliary dataset. The standard deviation also shows that VBD is a stable method.

4.4 Discussion on Explainability

The proposed method extracts the salient part of the attack trigger along with its binary mask. The extracted trigger provides a quick and general visual expla-

Table 4. All-to-All Blended poisoned-instance detection mean F_1-score (%) over the 4 grid and square triggers shown in Fig. 4.

Set	Blended	VBD	ABL	AGPD	SCAn
CIFAR-10	10%	56.16 ±03.38	14.08 ±06.64	**70.70 ±16.82**	00.00 ±00.00
CIFAR-10	20%	72.08 ±01.54	43.97 ±05.78	**75.29 ±12.39**	00.00 ±00.00
CIFAR-10	50%	**91.68 ±01.27**	53.31 ±06.28	84.47 ±04.86	01.40 ±03.13
CIFAR-10	Average	73.31 ±00.80	37.12 ±05.43	**76.82 ±05.14**	00.47 ±01.04
Tiny ImageNet	10%	00.00 ±00.00	02.84 ±00.12	**20.81 ±08.53**	00.00 ±00.00
Tiny ImageNet	20%	09.15 ±04.93	08.80 ±03.78	**29.04 ±07.64**	00.00 ±00.00
Tiny ImageNet	50%	**42.55 ±01.09**	37.17 ±03.07	35.05 ±00.18	00.00 ±00.00
Tiny ImageNet	Average	17.23 ±01.69	16.27 ±01.94	**28.30 ±05.07**	00.00 ±00.00
Average		45.27 ±00.76	26.69 ±02.38	**52.56 ±02.43**	00.23 ±00.52

Table 5. Summary of the poisoned-instance detection F_1-score (%) averaged over all the 80 experiments.

Set	VBD	ABL	AGPD	SCAn
CIFAR-10	**89.58 ±00.54**	63.30 ±03.02	85.97 ±03.60	58.31 ±00.60
Tiny ImageNet	**67.89 ±01.64**	61.64 ±00.94	55.56 ±06.94	52.52 ±01.36
All	**78.74 ±00.77**	62.47 ±01.28	70.76 ±04.75	55.41 ±00.96

nation of the attack. Moreover, the binary mask can be used to isolate the pixels responsible for the malicious behavior of an instance detected as poisoned. Figure 5 illustrates the explainability of the method on a blended attack on Tiny ImageNet, using a 3 × 3 white square trigger (shown in subfigure 5a) with a blending factor of 50%. The VBD method computes both the trigger and its corresponding mask, shown in subfigures 5d and 5e, respectively. The extracted pattern approximates the malicious trigger. Although the method cannot fully recover the original colors of the trigger due to the blending, the result remains sufficiently expressive to identify and explain the attack. The generated mask can then be applied to any instance detected as poisoned to isolate the malicious pixels and explain the VBD decision. The instance in subfigure 5c is detected by VBD as poisoned. The extracted mask in subfigure 5e is then used to localize the malicious pixels, as shown in subfigure 5f, where these pixels are outlined in red.

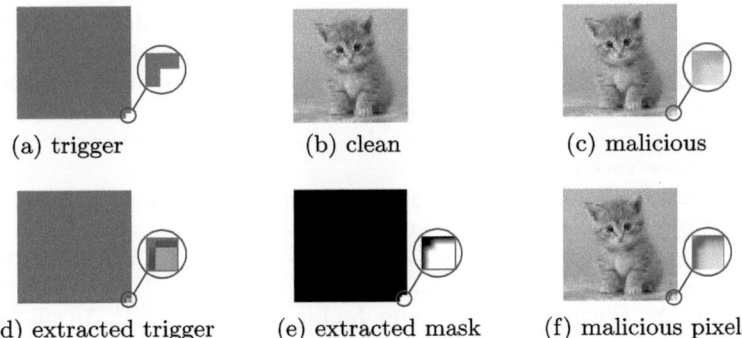

Fig. 5. Illustration of the method's explainability on a blended attack using a white square trigger (a) with a blending factor of 0.5. The pixels responsible for the malicious misclassification are outlined in red in (f). In (a) and (d), transparency is represented by the gray background. (Color figure online)

5 Conclusion

In this article, we proposed an efficient defense algorithm against BadNets and Blended attacks. Our method does not require additional information, such as a clean dataset, and can be directly applied to a training set to detect poisoned instances. A key advantage of our approach is its explainability: it extracts the harmful part of the attack trigger, enabling experts to better understand the nature of the attack. Moreover, our defense is effective in both the All-to-One setting, where only one class is poisoned, and the more challenging All-to-All setting, where all classes are affected. Experimental evaluations on two well-known image datasets, compared against three state-of-the-art defense methods, demonstrate the strong performance of our approach.

Our current method focuses on static-trigger attacks, which represent the simplest and most realistic backdoor attack scenarios, as they require minimal prerequisites and are thus more likely to be deployed by attackers in real-world settings. However, our approach can be extended to dynamic triggers, where the trigger is not fixed but can appear in predefined locations [23]. This could be achieved, for instance, by clustering the estimated poisoned set based on variance before extracting the trigger pattern.

In future work, we plan to further evaluate this extension and explore defenses against a broader range of backdoor attack strategies.

References

1. Chen, B., et al.: Detecting backdoor attacks on deep neural networks by activation clustering. In: SafeAI@AAAI. CEUR Workshop Proceedings (2019)
2. Chen, X., Liu, C., Li, B., Lu, K., Song, D.: Targeted backdoor attacks on deep learning systems using data poisoning (2017). arXiv preprint arXiv:1712.05526

3. Chen, X., Liu, C., Li, B., Lu, K., Song, D.: Targeted Backdoor Attacks on Deep Learning Systems Using Data Poisoning (2017). arXiv preprint arxiv:1712.05526
4. Chou, E., Tramer, F., Pellegrino, G.: Sentinet: Detecting localized universal attacks against deep learning systems. In: IEEE SPW (2020)
5. Dodge, Y.: Kolmogorov–smirnov test. In: The Concise Encyclopedia of Statistics. Springer New York (2008)
6. Gao, Y., Xu, C., Wang, D., Chen, S., Ranasinghe, D.C., Nepal, S.: Strip: a defence against trojan attacks on deep neural networks. In: ACSAC (2019)
7. Gu, T., Dolan-Gavitt, B., Garg, S.: BadNets: Identifying vulnerabilities in the machine learning model supply chain (2017). arXiv preprint arxiv:1708.06733
8. Guo, J., Li, Y., Chen, X., Guo, H., Sun, L., Liu, C.: SCALE-UP: An efficient blackbox input-level backdoor detection via analyzing scaled prediction consistency. In: ICLR (2023)
9. He, K., Zhang, X., Ren, S., Sun, J.: Identity mappings in deep residual networks. In: ECCV (2016)
10. Huang, K., Li, Y., Wu, B., Qin, Z., Ren, K.: Backdoor defense via decoupling the training process. In: ICLR (2022)
11. Krizhevsky, A., Hinton, G.: Learning multiple layers of features from tiny images. Master's thesis, Department of Computer Science, University of Toronto (2009)
12. Le, Y., Yang, X.: Tiny imagenet visual recognition challenge. CS 231N (2015)
13. Lee, D.H.: Pseudo-label : The simple and efficient semi-supervised learning method for deep neural networks. In: WREPL@ICML (2013)
14. Li, Y., Lyu, X., Koren, N., Lyu, L., Li, B., Ma, X.: Anti-backdoor learning: training clean models on poisoned data. NeurIPS **34**, 14900–14912 (2021)
15. Li, Y., et al.: Reconstructive neuron pruning for backdoor defense. In: ICML (2023)
16. Liu, Q., Li, P., Zhao, W., Cai, W., Yu, S., Leung, V.C.M.: A survey on security threats and defensive techniques of machine learning: a data driven view. IEEE Access (2018)
17. Ma, W., Wang, D., Sun, R., Xue, M., Wen, S., Xiang, Y.: The "beatrix" resurrections: Robust backdoor detection via gram matrices. In: NDSS (2023)
18. Nguyen, A., Tran, A.: Wanet–imperceptible warping-based backdoor attack (2021). arXiv preprint arXiv:2102.10369
19. Nguyen, T.A., Tran, A.: Input-aware dynamic backdoor attack. NeurIPS (2020)
20. Otsu, N.: A Threshold Selection Method from Gray-Level Histograms. Man, and Cybernetics, IEEE Transactions on Systems (1979)
21. Pitropakis, N., Panaousis, E., Giannetsos, T., Anastasiadis, E., Loukas, G.: A taxonomy and survey of attacks against machine learning. Comput. Sci. Rev. **34** (2019)
22. Qi, X., Xie, T., Li, Y., Mahloujifar, S., Mittal, P.: Revisiting the assumption of latent separability for backdoor defenses. In: ICLR (2023)
23. Salem, A., Wen, R., Backes, M., Ma, S., Zhang, Y.: Dynamic backdoor attacks against machine learning models. In: EuroS and P (2022)
24. Selvaraju, R.R., Cogswell, M., Das, A., Vedantam, R., Parikh, D., Batra, D.: Gradcam: visual explanations from deep networks via gradient-based localization. IJCV (2020)
25. Tang, D., Wang, X., Tang, H., Zhang, K.: Demon in the variant: Statistical analysis of {DNNs} for robust backdoor contamination detection. In: USENIX Security Symposium (2021)
26. Wu, B., et al.: Backdoorbench: a comprehensive benchmark of backdoor learning. In: NeurIPS (2022)

27. Wu, D., Wang, Y.: Adversarial neuron pruning purifies backdoored deep models. In: NeurIPS (2021)
28. Yuan, D., Wei, S., Zhang, M., Liu, L., Wu, B.: Activation gradient based poisoned sample detection against backdoor attacks (2024). arXiv preprint arxiv:2312.06230
29. Zeng, Y., Park, W., Mao, Z.M., Jia, R.: Rethinking the backdoor attacks' triggers: a frequency perspective. In: IEEE ICCV (2021)
30. Zhang, M., Zhu, M., Zhu, Z., Wu, B.: Reliable poisoned sample detection against backdoor attacks enhanced by sharpness aware minimization (2024). arXiv preprint arXiv:2411.11525

Achieving Flexible Local Differential Privacy in Federated Learning via Influence Functions

Alycia N. Carey and Xintao Wu[✉]

University of Arkansas, Fayetteville, AR 72701, USA
{ancarey,xintaowu}@uark.edu

Abstract. The use of local differential privacy in federated learning has recently grown in popularity due to rising demands for increased privacy in machine learning scenarios. While research into local differentially private federated learning is vast, the ability for a client to change their privacy parameter ε *after* training, and have that change reflected in the global model's parameters without having to repeat the entire federated training process, is currently unexplored. In this work, we propose **FLDP-FL** (Flexible Local Differential Privacy for Federated Learning), a simple and efficient technique for federated learning based on influence functions that enables clients to update their privacy guarantees after training without incurring extra training overhead by either the global server or the other federation participants. We show that our influence-based approach is able to accurately estimate the change in global model parameters that would occur if the client re-randomized their data under a stricter ε and the federated learning process was repeated. Additionally, we show that our FLDP-FL approach is able to reasonably estimate the resulting change when multiple clients update their privacy parameter ε.

Keywords: Federated Learning · Differential Privacy · Influence Functions

1 Introduction

In federated learning, multiple clients jointly train a machine learning model under the orchestration of a central server without having to explicitly share their private local data with either the server or the other participants [16]. Despite being ingrained with an innate sense of privacy due to the clients' data remaining decentralized, the use of local differential privacy in federated scenarios has been widely considered to increase the overall privacy of the federated learning system. However, the solutions that have been proposed are often rigid, forcing clients to use the same privacy parameter ε and do not provide solutions in the event that a client has to update their ε in order to comply with updated privacy regulations. Today's privacy needs are ever changing, and thus it is important to construct federated learning architectures that are adaptable.

Granting clients the ability to post-hoc change their privacy parameters is a non-trivial task. For each instance of a client asking to change their ε, the federated model would have to be retrained from scratch which is time and resource intensive for *all* parties in the federation – not just the client changing ε. To costly federated retraining, while still offering clients flexibility in updating their privacy level as needed, we propose *flexible local differential privacy for federated learning* (FLDP-FL). We formulate FLDP-FL as an influence function [4] that is able to properly estimate the true model parameters that would be obtained if a client's data was re-randomized under a stronger ε and the federated model was fully retrained. Further, we do so without violating any federated learning requirements as the clients do not have to share their private data with the other clients or the global server to use FLDP-FL.

Our contributions are as follows: 1) We propose FLDP-FL, which is based on influence functions, to offer clients the ability to change their privacy level ε after federated training has concluded without requiring the entire federated training process to be repeated; 2) We extend previous influence function work and provide a lemma which shows that influence estimates for perturbing a data point are additive and then, based on the lemma, propose a theory for estimating the impact of a client modifying their ε value on the global model's parameters; and 3) We empirically show that FLDP-FL is able to properly estimate the model that would be obtained if federated training was re-performed under the client's updated ε. We additionally show that FLDP-FL can support multiple clients altering their privacy parameter post-hoc,. We note, however, that even though FLDP-FL supports the setting where the client changing ε owns a large portion of the federated dataset, the estimation can degrade beyond a reasonable amount and in these settings full retraining may be required.

2 Related Works

Differentially Private Federated Learning. Differential privacy has been widely studied in the federated learning setting from the lens of "user-level" security and multiple approaches to ensuring differentially private federated learning have been proposed [2,7,8,17,24,26]. One of the first works in differentially private federated learning was [17] which proposed a noised version of the traditional federated averaging algorithm (FedAvg, [16]) which satisfies user-adjacent differential privacy via use of the moments accountant [1] and works by clipping the gradient updates of each user before they are sent by the client to the server, and then adding Gaussian noise to the averaged update. Other important differentially private federated learning works include [21] which proposed a local differential privacy-based parameter aggregation scheme and [8] which proposed a differentially private approach to crafting personalized models in federated learning. However, to our knowledge, no previous work has performed research into how a client can update their privacy parameter ε after federated training has concluded without having to repeat the entire federated training process.

Influence Functions and Federated Learning. Influence functions are a product of influence analysis from the field of robust statistics [4] and were made popular in machine learning by [13] which showed how a single training point influences the final machine learning model's parameters and/or the test loss of a single test point. This work was further extended in [14] where the authors showed how influence functions can be used to estimate the influence that a group of training points has on the model parameters and/or the loss of a single test point. While both influence functions and differential privacy have strong ties to robust statistics [6], to our knowledge only two works have been published utilizing both methods [3,11] and they are both formulated in the centralized setting, not federated. However, work utilizing influence functions in federated learning have been proposed [9,15,18,19], such as [18] which proposed to filter and score data used in federated learning according to the sign of the influence function, [15] which proposed an influence-based participant selection strategy to mitigate test error caused by erroneous training data, and [19] which proposed an adaptive aggregation scheme based on class-level and client-level influence scores. To our knowledge, our work is the first to use influence functions to enable clients to change their local differential privacy parameter ε after federated training.

3 Preliminaries

In this section, we present the required background information on federated learning (FL), local differential privacy (LDP), and influence functions (IFs) needed to understand the discussions of Sect. 4. We begin by detailing the notation used through the remainder of the paper. We consider a federated learning system of N clients (denoted by i), each of which have a local training set $\mathcal{D}_{i,tr}$ made up of data with features $x_i \in \mathcal{X}_i$ and a label $y_i \in \mathcal{Y}_i$ such that $z_i = (x_i \in \mathcal{X}_i, y_i \in \mathcal{Y}_i) \in \mathcal{D}_{i,tr}$ is one of n_i training points belonging to client i. Each client has a local model $H_i(\theta)$, where $\theta \in \Theta$ represents the model parameters that are shared across the clients during training and we use $\hat{\theta}$ to denote the global model parameters obtained at the end of federated training. We assume that the global model has access to a testing set $\mathcal{D}_{te}$ that is a mixture of all N client's data distributions. We use $\ell(z_i, \theta) = \ell(H_i(x_i; \theta), y_i)$ to denote the loss function and $\mathcal{L}(\mathcal{D}_{i,tr}, \theta) = \frac{1}{n_i} \sum_{j=1}^{n_i} \ell(z_{i,j}, \theta)$ to denote the empirical risk and we assume that the empirical risk is twice-differentiable and strictly convex in θ for all clients [13]. Additionally, we use the standard notation from differential privacy of ε as the privacy parameter and $\mathbb{P}[\cdot]$ to denote probability.

3.1 Federated Learning

Federated learning is a machine learning setting where multiple clients (e.g., mobile devices, whole organizations, or individuals) collaboratively train a machine learning model under the orchestration of a central server, while keeping the training data decentralized. The most popular federated learning algorithm is Federated Averaging (FedAvg) [16] which aims to solve:

$$\min_\theta h(\theta) = \sum_{i=1}^{N} \frac{n_i}{\sum_{j=1}^{N} n_j} \mathcal{L}(\mathcal{D}_{i,tr}, \theta) \qquad (1)$$

where N is the number of clients, n_i is the number of data points held by client i, and $\mathcal{L}(\mathcal{D}_{i,tr}, \theta) = \frac{1}{n_i}\sum_{j=1}^{n_i}\ell(z_{i,j}, \theta)$ is the empirical risk of client i. Federated learning can be performed in a cross-device or cross-silo manner[1], but in this work, we focus on the cross-silo setting [10] and from this point on, when we refer to "federated learning" we are specifically referring to cross-silo federated learning. Federated training is carried out in an iterative manner over the course of T rounds. In each round t, the server sends the current model parameters θ^t to all N clients, the clients perform R rounds of local training using their dataset $\mathcal{D}_{i,tr}$, and then send their updated model θ_i^{t+1} to the server. The server then aggregates the received models as:

$$\theta^{t+1} = \sum_{i=1}^{N} \frac{n_i}{\sum_{j=1}^{N} n_j} \theta_i^{t+1} \qquad (2)$$

After aggregation, training continues until $t = T$ at which point we define $\hat{\theta} = \theta^T$ to be the final global model parameters.

3.2 Local Differential Privacy

Local differential privacy allows an analyst to learn population statistics without violating the privacy of individuals. More formally, ε-LDP is defined as follows:

Definition 1 (ε-LDP [12]). *A randomized mechanism $\mathcal{M}$ satisfies ε-LDP if and only if for any pair of input values r, r' in the domain of $\mathcal{M}$, and for any possible output $o \in Range(\mathcal{M})$, it holds:*

$$\mathbb{P}[\mathcal{M}(r) = o] \leq e^{\varepsilon} \cdot \mathbb{P}[\mathcal{M}(r') = o]$$

In other words, the probability of outputting o on record r is at most e^{ε} times the probability of outputting o on record r'.

Randomized Response. One popular method used for LDP is randomized response (RR).[2] Let u be a private variable that can take one of C values. We can formalize RR as a $C \times C$ distortion matrix $\mathbf{P} = (p_{uv})_{C \times C}$ where $p_{uv} = \mathbb{P}[v|u] \in (0,1)$ denotes the probability that the output of the RR process is $v \in \{1, \ldots, C\}$ when the real attribute value is $u \in \{1, \ldots, C\}$. Note that the entries of the distortion matrix are probabilities, and therefore the sum of the probabilities of each row is 1 [23]. Further, $\mathbf{P}$ can achieve both optimal utility and ε-DP by setting $p_{uv} = \frac{e^{\varepsilon}}{C-1+e^{\varepsilon}}$ if $u = v$ and $p_{uv} = \frac{1}{C-1+e^{\varepsilon}}$ otherwise [23].

---

[1] Cross-device: large federation size (100+ clients, often IoT devices like cell-phones) where the clients often only participate in a few rounds of training at most. Cross-silo: small federation size (2–10 clients, often companies or hospitals) where the clients all participate in every round of federated training.

[2] We discuss FLDP-FL under alternate LDP scenarios in our Github repository.

3.3 Influence Functions

In [13], the authors proposed the use of influence functions to study machine learning models through the lens of their training data. Specifically, they showed that the influence a single training point $z = (x, y) \in \mathcal{D}_{tr}$ has on the model parameters can be calculated without actually removing z from the training set and retraining the model on the resulting dataset. They instead simulate the removal of z by upweighting it by a small value $\frac{1}{n}$ (where n is the total number of training points). Specifically, they calculate the influence the training point has on the model parameters as:

$$\mathcal{I}_{rem,\hat{\theta}}(z) = -H_{\hat{\theta}}^{-1} \nabla_\theta \ell(z, \hat{\theta}) \tag{3}$$

where $H_{\hat{\theta}}^{-1}$ is the inverse Hessian matrix $H_{\hat{\theta}}^{-1} = (\frac{1}{n}\sum_{j=1}^{n} \nabla_\theta^2 \ell(z^j, \hat{\theta}))^{-1}$. We note that the inverse Hessian matrix can be calculated explicitly or efficiently estimated using conjugate gradient or stochastic estimation approaches [13].

Equation 3 is obtained by performing a quadratic expansion around the optimal parameters $\hat{\theta}$ which gives an approximation of the function locally using information about the steepness (the gradient) and the curvature (the Hessian). Equation 3, which gives the effect of training point z on the parameters $\hat{\theta}$, can be used to estimate the parameters that would be obtained if z was actually removed from the dataset and the model was retrained. More specifically,

$$\hat{\theta}_{-z} \approx \hat{\theta} + \frac{1}{n} \mathcal{I}_{rem,\hat{\theta}}(z) \tag{4}$$

The authors of [13] also considered the effect that modifying (rather than simply removing) a training point has on the model parameters. Consider a training point z and its modified value z_β:

$$\hat{\theta}_{z_\beta, -z} = \arg\min_{\theta \in \Theta} \mathcal{L}(Z, \theta) + \frac{1}{n}\ell(z_\beta, \theta) - \frac{1}{n}\ell(z, \theta) \tag{5}$$

is the ERM of $\hat{\theta}$ with z_β replacing z in training. The approximate effect of changing $z \to z_\beta$ on the model parameters can be computed as:

$$\mathcal{I}_{pert,\hat{\theta}}(z_\beta, -z) = -H_{\hat{\theta}}^{-1}\left(\nabla_\theta\left(\ell(z_\beta, \hat{\theta}) - \ell(z, \hat{\theta})\right)\right) \tag{6}$$

We direct interested readers to [13] for the full derivation of Eq. 6 from Eq. 3. Equation 6 can then be used to approximate the model parameters that would be obtained under training with z_β instead of z as:

$$\hat{\theta}_{z_\beta, -z} \approx \hat{\theta} + \frac{1}{n}\mathcal{I}_{pert,\hat{\theta}}(z_\beta, -z) \tag{7}$$

In [14] the authors showed that the influence scores calculated in Eq. 3 are additive. Namely, if we wanted to estimate the effect of a group of data points $G \subset \mathcal{D}_{tr}$ on the model, we can calculate:

$$\mathcal{I}_{rem,\hat{\theta}}(G) = -H_{\hat{\theta}}^{-1} \nabla_\theta \left(\sum_{j=1}^{|G|} \ell(z^j, \hat{\theta})\right) \tag{8}$$

and use Eq. 4 to estimate the true parameters under the removal of group G.

4 Methodology

In this section, we formulate *flexible local differential privacy for federated learning* (FLDP-FL), a technique for local differentially private federated learning which grants clients the ability to change their privacy parameter ε post-training without requiring the entire federated training procedure to be repeated.

4.1 Problem Formulation

We define our federated setting as follows. We assume a horizontal cross-silo federated learning scenario where the federation is comprised of a small number of clients N (where client i has n_i data points) that participate every round and that the data is partitioned horizontally along the examples (i.e., all clients have the same feature and label domains, however, each client can have a different distribution of them). We additionally assume that each client individually randomizes their data under some client independent $\varepsilon_i = \{\varepsilon_{i,f}\}_{f \in \mathcal{F}}$ to form $\tilde{\mathcal{D}}_{i,tr}$ before participating in federated training where $\mathcal{F}$ represents the attributes (e.g., features and/or label) in $\mathcal{D}_{i,tr}$ to be protected via randomized response. Let $f \in \mathcal{F}$ have d_f possible values. Further, let $\varepsilon_i = \infty = \{\varepsilon_{i,f} = \infty\}_{f \in \mathcal{F}}$ represent the case where $\mathcal{D}_{i,tr} = \tilde{\mathcal{D}}_{i,tr}$ (i.e., no randomization occurs). We also assume that while only $\tilde{\mathcal{D}}_{i,tr}$ is used during federated training, clients will have access to both their un-randomized training set $\mathcal{D}_{i,tr}$ and the dataset randomized by ε_i ($\tilde{\mathcal{D}}_{i,tr}$) after training concludes. All N clients work collaboratively together to train a final global model with parameters $\hat{\theta}$. After training, client i decides to change ε_i to some $\varepsilon'_i = \{\varepsilon'_{i,f}\}_{f \in \mathcal{F}}$ such that $\sum_{f \in \mathcal{F}} \varepsilon'_{i,f} < \sum_{f \in \mathcal{F}} \varepsilon_{i,f}$.

4.2 Perturbation Influences are Additive

We start by noting that while in [14] the authors showed that the influence scores calculated to simulate the *removal* of a point z are additive (see Eq. 8), it is left to be shown that influence scores that simulate the *perturbation* of a point z are additive. Here, we provide Lemma 1 which does so and provides the basis for our formulation of FLDP-FL in Sect. 4.3.

Lemma 1 (Perturbation influences are additive). *For a group $G \subset \mathcal{D}_{tr}$, we calculate the influence of perturbing group G to G_β, where for each point $z \in G, z \to z_\beta \in G_\beta$, as:*

$$\mathcal{I}_{pert,\hat{\theta}}(G_\beta, -G) = -H_{\hat{\theta}}^{-1} \cdot \nabla_\theta \sum_{j=1}^{|G|} \left(\ell(z_\beta^j, \hat{\theta}) - \ell(z^j, \hat{\theta}) \right) \qquad (9)$$

Proof. We rewrite Eq. 6 as:

$$\mathcal{I}_{pert,\hat{\theta}}(z_\beta, -z) = -H_{\hat{\theta}}^{-1}\left(\nabla_\theta(\ell(z_\beta, \hat{\theta}) - \ell(z, \hat{\theta}))\right) \tag{10}$$

$$= -H_{\hat{\theta}}^{-1}\nabla_\theta \ell(z_\beta, \hat{\theta}) + H_{\hat{\theta}}^{-1}\nabla_\theta \ell(z, \hat{\theta}) \tag{11}$$

Using Eq. 8 and letting $z \in G \subset \mathcal{D}_{tr}$, $z \to z_\beta \in G_\beta$, we rewrite Eq. 11 as:

$$\mathcal{I}_{pert,\hat{\theta}}(G_\beta, -G) = -H_{\hat{\theta}}^{-1} \cdot \nabla_\theta \left(\sum_{j=1}^{|G_\beta|} \ell(z_\beta^j, \hat{\theta})\right) + H_{\hat{\theta}}^{-1} \cdot \nabla_\theta \left(\sum_{j=1}^{|G|} \ell(z^j, \hat{\theta})\right) \tag{12}$$

$$= -H_{\hat{\theta}}^{-1} \cdot \nabla_\theta \sum_{j=1}^{|G|} \left(\ell(z_\beta^j, \hat{\theta}) - \ell(z^j, \hat{\theta})\right) \tag{13}$$

since $|G| = |G_\beta|$ and where the last line yields Eq. 9.

□

4.3 FLDP-FL

The influence functions listed so far, including Eq. 9 in Lemma 1, have been constructed to work in the traditional machine learning setting – meaning that it is assumed that the training data is located in a centralized location and can be freely accessed. Therefore, it may seem that these equations cannot be applied directly in the federated setting. However, by recognizing that each client's local dataset $\tilde{\mathcal{D}}_{i,tr}$ can be considered as a subset (i.e., *group*) from the overall federated training dataset $\mathcal{D}_{tr} = \{\tilde{\mathcal{D}}_{i,tr}\}_{i=1}^N$ we can leverage Lemma 1 to allow client i to calculate how changing $\varepsilon_i \to \varepsilon'_i$ would affect $\hat{\theta}$ without requiring access to any other client's private data or having to send their private data to the global server. We now derive FLDP-FL as Theorem 1.

Theorem 1. (FLDP-FL). *Given a trained federated model $\hat{\theta}$, we can estimate the influence of client i changing $\varepsilon_i \to \varepsilon'_i$ on the parameters $\hat{\theta}$ as:*

$$\mathcal{I}_{pert,\hat{\theta}}^{RR}(\mathcal{D}_{i,tr}, \tilde{\mathcal{D}}_{i,tr}, \varepsilon'_i) = -H_{\hat{\theta}}^{-1} \cdot \nabla_\theta \sum_{\substack{z \in \mathcal{D}_{i,tr}, \\ \tilde{z} \in \tilde{\mathcal{D}}_{i,tr}}} \left[\left(\sum_{f_\times \in \mathcal{F}_\times} p_{f_\times} \ell(z_{f_\times}, \hat{\theta})\right) - \ell(\tilde{z}; \hat{\theta}))\right] \tag{14}$$

where

$$p_{f_\times} = \prod_{f \in f_\times} \mathbb{1}_{f=f_0}\left[\frac{e^{\varepsilon'_{i,f}}}{d_f - 1 + e^{\varepsilon'_{i,f}}}\right] + \mathbb{1}_{f \neq f_0}\left[\frac{1}{d_f - 1 + e^{\varepsilon'_{i,f}}}\right] \tag{15}$$

Proof. Starting from Lemma 1, let $G = \tilde{\mathcal{D}}_{i,tr}$ and $G_\beta = \mathcal{D}_{i,tr}$:

$$\mathcal{I}_{pert,\hat{\theta}}(\mathcal{D}_{i,tr}, -\tilde{\mathcal{D}}_{i,tr}) = -H_{\hat{\theta}}^{-1} \cdot \nabla_\theta \sum_{\substack{z \in \mathcal{D}_{i,tr}, \\ \tilde{z} \in \tilde{\mathcal{D}}_{i,tr}}} \left(\ell(z, \hat{\theta}) - \ell(\tilde{z}, \hat{\theta})\right) \tag{16}$$

Here, Eq. 16 gives the influence of replacing $\tilde{\mathcal{D}}_{i,tr}$ with $\mathcal{D}_{i,tr}$ during training of $\hat{\theta}$. However, we are interested in replacing $\tilde{\mathcal{D}}_{i,tr}$, which was randomized under ε_i, with $\tilde{\mathcal{D}}'_{i,tr}$ that was randomized under ε'_i. Let the expected value of $\ell(z, \hat{\theta})$ where $z \in \mathcal{D}_{i,tr}$ is randomized under ε'_i be written as $\mathbb{E}[\ell(z_{\varepsilon'_i}, \hat{\theta})]$. Then:

$$\mathcal{I}_{pert,\hat{\theta}}(\mathcal{D}_{i,tr}, -\tilde{\mathcal{D}}_{i,tr}, \varepsilon'_i) = -H_{\hat{\theta}}^{-1} \cdot \nabla_\theta \sum_{\substack{z \in \mathcal{D}_{i,tr}, \\ \tilde{z} \in \tilde{\mathcal{D}}_{i,tr}}} \left(\mathbb{E}[\ell(z_{\varepsilon'_i}, \hat{\theta})] - \ell(\tilde{z}, \hat{\theta}) \right) \quad (17)$$

To find $\mathbb{E}[\ell(z_{\varepsilon'_i}, \hat{\theta})]$, let $\mathcal{F}$ represent the set of attributes in $\mathcal{D}_{i,tr}$ to privatize under ε'_i randomized response, where each $f \in \mathcal{F}$ has d_f possible values as well as an independent privacy parameter $\varepsilon'_{i,f}$. Further, let $\mathcal{F}_\times$ represent the cartesian product[3] of $f \in \mathcal{F}$ and f_0 represent the original attribute value of f in data point $z \in \mathcal{D}_{i,tr}$. Under ε'_i randomized response, $z \in \mathcal{D}_{i,tr}$ can take one of $2^{|\mathcal{F}|}$ values $f_\times \in \mathcal{F}_\times$, each with probability $p_{f_\times} = \prod_{f \in \mathcal{F}_\times} \mathbb{1}_{f=f_0} \left[\frac{e^{\varepsilon'_{i,f}}}{d_f - 1 + e^{\varepsilon'_{i,f}}} \right] + \mathbb{1}_{f \neq f_0} \left[\frac{1}{d_f - 1 + e^{\varepsilon'_{i,f}}} \right]$ (see Sect. 3.2). The expected value of the loss where $z \in \mathcal{D}_{i,tr}$ is randomized under ε'_i can therefore be written as:

$$\mathbb{E}[\ell(z_{\varepsilon'_i}, \hat{\theta})] = \sum_{f_\times \in \mathcal{F}_\times} p_{f_\times} \ell(z_{f_\times}, \hat{\theta}) \quad (18)$$

where $\tilde{z}$ and $z_{f_\times}$ are *equivalent* minus the attributes in $\mathcal{F}_\times$ which have been replaced according to $f_\times$. Substituting the right hand side of Eq. 18 into Eq. 17 yields Eq. 14. □

To obtain the estimated global model parameters where a client re-randomizes their data under $\varepsilon_i \rightarrow \varepsilon'_i$ and federated training is re-performed, we calculate:

$$\hat{\theta} = \hat{\theta} + \frac{1}{\sum_{j=1}^N n_j} \mathcal{I}_{pert,\hat{\theta}}^{RR}(\mathcal{D}_{i,tr}, \tilde{\mathcal{D}}_{i,tr}, \varepsilon'_i) \quad (19)$$

where $\sum_{j=1}^N n_j$ is the sum of the data used in the federated learning process by all N clients. In Sect. 5 we analyze the setting where $m > 1$ clients simultaneously update $\varepsilon_i \rightarrow \varepsilon'_i$ (which could arise in instances where wide sweeping government regulation is updated). Here, we leverage Lemma 1 which says that perturbation influences are additive, and calculate the estimated model parameters under the m clients updating $\varepsilon_i \rightarrow \varepsilon'_i$ as:

$$\hat{\theta} = \hat{\theta} + \frac{1}{\sum_{j=1}^N n_j} \sum_{i=1}^m \mathcal{I}_i \quad (20)$$

where each client i calculates $\mathcal{I}_i$ using Eq. 14 independently.

---
[3] For example, if $\mathcal{F} = \{\text{gender}, \text{income}\}$ where gender$= \{m, f\}$ and income$= \{0, 1\}$ then $\mathcal{F}_\times = \{(m, 0), (m, 1), (f, 0), (f, 1)\}$.

Here, we show the derivation for Eq. 20 which enables multiple clients to update $\varepsilon_i \to \varepsilon_i'$ simultaneously. Let $G_i = \tilde{\mathcal{D}}_{i,tr}$ and $G_{i,\beta} = \tilde{\mathcal{D}}_{i,tr}$ for all m clients i who desire to change $\varepsilon_i \to \varepsilon_i'$. Since each G_i can be seen as an independent subset of the overall federated training set $\mathcal{D}_{tr} = \tilde{\mathcal{D}}_{1,tr} \cup \cdots \cup \tilde{\mathcal{D}}_{N,tr}$, we can say that the union of G_i is also a subset of $\mathcal{D}_{tr}$. I.e., $\boldsymbol{G} = G_1 \cup \ldots G_m \subset \mathcal{D}_{tr}$. Therefore, we can follow a derivation similar to Theorem 1 to form the optimization function to support multiple clients updating their privacy parameters simultaneously.

Let $\boldsymbol{G}_\beta = G_{1,\beta} \cup \cdots \cup G_{m,\beta}$ and similarly let $\boldsymbol{G} = G_1 \cup \cdots \cup G_m$. Starting from Eq. 12 in Lemma 1, we can write:

$$\mathcal{I}_{pert,\hat{\theta}}(\boldsymbol{G}_\beta, -\boldsymbol{G}) = -H_{\hat{\theta}}^{-1} \nabla_\theta \sum_{z_\beta \in \boldsymbol{G}_\beta} \ell(z_\beta, \hat{\theta}) + H_{\hat{\theta}}^{-1} \nabla_\theta \sum_{z \in \boldsymbol{G}} \ell(z, \hat{\theta}) \tag{21}$$

$$= -H_{\hat{\theta}}^{-1} \nabla_\theta \sum_{i=1}^{m} \sum_{z_{i,\beta} \in G_{i,\beta}} \ell(z_{i,\beta}, \hat{\theta}) + H_{\hat{\theta}}^{-1} \nabla_\theta \sum_{i=1}^{m} \sum_{z_i \in G_i} \ell(z_i, \hat{\theta}) \tag{22}$$

$$= \sum_{i=1}^{m} -H_{\hat{\theta}}^{-1} \nabla_\theta \sum_{\substack{z_i \in G_i, \\ z_{i,\beta} \in G_{i,\beta}}} \ell(z_{i,\beta}, \hat{\theta}) - \ell(z_i, \hat{\theta}) \tag{23}$$

since $|G_i| = |G_{i,\beta}|$. Then, replacing $\ell(z_{i,\beta}, \hat{\theta})$ with $\mathbb{E}[\ell(z_{\varepsilon_i'}, \hat{\theta})]$ yields

$$\mathcal{I}_{pert,\hat{\theta}}^{RR}(\boldsymbol{G}_\beta, -\boldsymbol{G}, \varepsilon') = \sum_{i=1}^{m} \mathcal{I}_{pert,\hat{\theta}}^{RR}(G_{i,\beta}, -G_i, \varepsilon_i') \tag{24}$$

and $\varepsilon = \{\varepsilon_i'\}_{i=1}^{m}$. Then, to obtain the estimate for the parameters where all m clients simultaneously change $\varepsilon_i \to \varepsilon_i'$, we can calculate:

$$\hat{\theta} = \hat{\theta} + \frac{1}{\sum_{j=1}^{N} n_j} \sum_{i=1}^{m} \mathcal{I}_{pert,\hat{\theta}}^{RR}(G_{i,\beta}, -G_i, \varepsilon_i') \tag{25}$$

which recovers Eq. 20.

We provide an overview of our FLDP-FL process (specifically for one client updating $\varepsilon_i \to \varepsilon_i'$) in Algorithm 1. Here, the client generates $\mathcal{I}$ according to Eq. 14 to calculate the influence on the global model of locally updating $\varepsilon_i \to \varepsilon_i'$ and sends it to the server. The server then updates the model parameters $\hat{\theta}$ according to Eq. 19 and distributes it to the clients.

Two natural questions to the derivation of Theorem 1 are: 1) why we use a weighted variant of the expected loss (Eq. 18) rather than a simple average; and 2) why Eq. 15 produces the correct weights for the weighted average. To answer question one, since we do not know a priori which combination $f_\times \in \mathcal{F}_\times$ will be produced by the randomized response process, we need to consider that

Algorithm 1. FLDP-FL

1: Each client randomizes $\mathcal{D}_{i,tr}$ under ε_i randomized response to produce $\tilde{\mathcal{D}}_{i,tr}$
2: Traditional FedAvg [16] training is carried out where each client participates with $\tilde{\mathcal{D}}_{i,tr}$ to produce final global model parameters $\hat{\theta}$
3: **if** Client i updates $\varepsilon_i \to \varepsilon'_i$ **then**
4:     Client i computes:

$$\mathcal{I} \leftarrow -H_{\hat{\theta}}^{-1} \nabla_\theta \sum_{\substack{z \in \mathcal{D}_{i,tr}, \\ \tilde{z} \in \tilde{\mathcal{D}}_{i,tr}}} \left[\left(\sum_{f_\times \in \mathcal{F}_\times} p_{f_\times} \ell(z_{f_\times}, \hat{\theta}) \right) - \ell(\tilde{z}; \hat{\theta}) \right]$$

    and sends to server
5:     Server computes:

$$\hat{\theta} = \hat{\theta} + \frac{1}{\sum_{j=1}^{N} n_j} \mathcal{I}$$

    and sends to all clients

---

the replacement of $\tilde{z}$ could be done by any combination $f_\times \in \mathcal{F}_\times$. However, the probability distribution over $\mathcal{F}_\times$ is not uniform and therefore taking a simple average of the losses produced by $\{z_{f_\times}\}_{f_\times \in \mathcal{F}_\times}$ will not produce the true expected loss. Therefore, to generate the expected loss, we need to multiply $\ell(z_{f_\times}, \hat{\theta})$ by its probability $p_{f_\times}$ generated by Eq. 15. This leads to the second question, which is why the formulation of Eq. 15 produces the correct weights. Since we assume each attribute in $\mathcal{F}$ to be independent, we multiply the probability of each attribute $f \in \mathcal{F}$ by $\frac{e^{\varepsilon'_{i,f}}}{d_f - 1 + e^{\varepsilon'_{i,f}}}$ if f is equal to the original attribute value f_0 in $z \in \mathcal{D}_{i,tr}$ (*not* $\tilde{z} \in \tilde{\mathcal{D}}_{i,tr}$ since we want to randomize the original data, not the data perturbed by ε_i) or by $\frac{1}{d_f - 1 + e^{\varepsilon'_{i,f}}}$ if $f \neq f_0$ (see Sect. 3.2).

4.4 Discussion

Computation and Communication Cost: In [18], the authors note that using influence functions in the federated learning setting faces many challenges. First, the authors point out that even if implicit Hessian-vector products are used to overcome the cost of forming and inverting the Hessian of the empirical risk (which costs $O(nm^2 + m^3)$ where n is the number of training points and m is the number of parameters), it is still communication intensive if the influence is calculated every round as it requires the transfer of all training data to the global server. In our work, however, not only does the influence function have to be calculated *sparingly* (i.e., only when the client updates their privacy level $\varepsilon_i \to \varepsilon'_i$), *we require the client who desires to update $\varepsilon_i \to \varepsilon'_i$ to calculate Eq.* 14. In the federated setting, the global model does not have access to the client's data, which is required when calculating Eq. 14. However, the client naturally has access to the final global model parameters $\hat{\theta}$ and therefore has all the required information to calculate Eq. 14. Additionally, this puts the burden of calculating the influence scores on the client doing the change, not the global model or the other clients who simply have to update the model parameters. We also clarify that not only does Eq. 14 have to be calculated sparingly, the computational cost to calculate Eq. 14 is much lower than that of total federated model retraining, especially if approaches such as stochastic estimation or conjugate gradient are used to approximate the Hessian. We point interested readers to [3,13] for a more in depth discussion of how these approximations can decrease the total computation time. We additionally provide concrete experimental results in Sect. 5 that support this claim and here briefly expound upon the computational cost of FLDP-FL versus full retraining.

Table 1. Time complexity of FLDP-FL versus full federated retraining. X: exact, CG: conjugate gradient, SE: stochastic estimation, n: total number of training points, n_i: number of training points of client i, p: number of parameters, r: recursion depth for SE estimation, t: number of recursions for SE estimation, E: number of federated epochs.

FLDP-FL (X)	FLDP-FL (CG)	FLDP-FL (SE)	Fed. Retrain
$\mathcal{O}(n_i p^2 + p^3)$	$\mathcal{O}(n_i p)$	$\mathcal{O}(n_i p + rtp)$	$\mathcal{O}(Enp)$

In Table 1, we detail the computational complexity of calculating the influence function using three different approaches to computing the inverse Hessian as well as the time complexity of normal training of a logistic regression model using gradient based learning. Specifically, we detail the complexity of computing the Hessian for Eq. 14 explicitly and using the conjugate gradient (CG) or stochastic estimation (SE) approaches to estimate it. While using the explicit Hessian approach seems to be more computationally complex than retraining, we note that only the client changing $\varepsilon_i \to \varepsilon_i'$ has to calculate the Hessian whereas all clients have to participate in retraining.

One of the main bottlenecks to federated learning is the communication cost of the clients sending/receiving parameter updates from the server as it is common that communication will be limited by an upload bandwidth of 1 MB/s or less [16]. These costs are influence by various parameters such as the client's dataset size, the size of the model, and the number of clients participating. Computing Eq. 14 takes minimal communication (i.e., client i ending $\mathcal{I}$ to the server and the server sending the updated $\hat{\theta}$ to all clients), whereas in full federated retraining, each client must participate in all E rounds, and perform both a download from the global server at the start of the round and send the updated parameters back to the global server at the end of the round. I.e., FLDP-FL takes a maximum of $N + 1$ communications while full federated retraining takes $2EN$.

Connection to Machine Unlearning: We also point out that FLDP-FL has an intuitive connection to machine unlearning. Under new privacy regulations such as the GDPR, consumers have to be afforded the "right to be forgotten". Therefore, in addition to our setting of a client having to update $\varepsilon_i \rightarrow \varepsilon_i'$, it could also be the case that a client may have to be removed from training entirely. Machine unlearning, the process of modifying a machine learning model to forget parts of data that it was trained on, has risen in popularity to satisfy these new privacy regulations. Unlearning has also been studied in the federated learning setting, albeit less extensively than in the standard machine learning setting.

Using influence functions, we can estimate the removal of a client i from training without having to redo federated training on the smaller client set. Specifically, using a formulation similar to Eq. 3, we can write:

$$\mathcal{I}_{rem,\hat{\theta}}(\tilde{\mathcal{D}}_{i,tr}) = -H_{\hat{\theta}}^{-1} \cdot \nabla_\theta \sum_{\tilde{z} \in \tilde{\mathcal{D}}_{i,tr}} \ell(\tilde{z}; \hat{\theta}) \tag{26}$$

where $\hat{\theta} = \hat{\theta} + \frac{1}{\sum_{j=1}^{N} n_j} \mathcal{I}_{rem,\hat{\theta}}(\tilde{\mathcal{D}}_{i,tr})$ gives an estimation of the true model parameters achieved when a client is removed from training entirely.

We note that in this work we do not study the entire removal of a client and further clarify that the setting where $\varepsilon_i' = 0 = \{\epsilon_{i,f}' = 0\}_{f \in \mathcal{F}}$ is *not equivalent* to machine unlearning as we are replacing client i's data with random noise (which can affect the performance of the global model) and not removing it entirely. This can be seen by comparing Eq. 14 with Eq. 26. In Eq. 26, we simply have to take the gradient of the loss of the data points used in training, which is then used to simulate the removal of these points from training. In Eq. 14 however, we include the addition of the expected loss of the training points under perturbation by ε_i'. Even though setting $\epsilon_i' = \infty$ would effectively make the clients data pure noise, and in a sense causes the model to unlearn the true data $\tilde{\mathcal{D}}_{i,tr}$, it will ultimately negatively affect the performance of the global model due to the introduction of random noise. On the other hand, removing a client entirely using Eq. 26, or other techniques proposed by work like [22,25] most likely will not see significant degradation in performance, especially when additional optimization is used to preserve model performance under client removal. Our work instead can be seen as an irregular instance of unlearning where instead of forgetting certain data points entirely, we instead want to change how well the model is able to understand the relationship between the data features and label (e.g., by increasing the noise applied during differential privacy).

5 Evaluation

In this section, we evaluate the ability of our formulated FLDP-FL approach for estimating the true change in the model that would occur if a client (after initial federated training) updated their privacy parameter $\varepsilon_i \rightarrow \varepsilon_i'$ and the federated learning process repeated. Here, we are interested in answering the following:

Q1. Under one client changing $\varepsilon_i \rightarrow \varepsilon_i'$, how does the model estimated in Algorithm 1 compare in terms of test loss, test accuracy, and distance with the true model obtained when full federated re-training occurs?

Q2. Is our FLDP-FL approach able to properly estimate the true model when multiple clients simultaneously change their privacy value from $\varepsilon_i \to \varepsilon'_i$?

Q3. How does the size of the client performing the change from $\varepsilon_i \to \varepsilon'_i$ affect the ability of our FLDP-FL approach to estimate the true model parameters?

Q4. How efficient (in terms of computation time) is FLDP-FL compared to full federated model retraining when one client decides to update $\varepsilon_i \to \varepsilon'_i$?

5.1 Datasets, Federated Setting, and Baselines

In this work, we test FLDP-FL using three datasets: ACS Income [5], Glioma [20], and ACS Public Coverage [5]. We divide the data among the clients according to the process described in [16] such that the clients' local datasets are saturated by one label, and therefore, if they attempted to train a model on their own, they would obtain a model with poor generalization performance. For Q1/Q2/Q4 all clients are allotted the same number of data points, while in Q3 we allocate more data points to the client changing $\varepsilon_i \to \varepsilon'_i$. We allow the global model to be made of a single fully-connected layer, use SGD for optimization, and use cross-entropy for loss. Further, we set the number of clients to 5, assume all clients have access to $\mathcal{D}_{i,tr}$ (their un-randomized training set) and $\tilde{\mathcal{D}}_{i,tr}$ (which is formed by randomizing $\mathcal{D}_{i,tr}$ by ε_i), and each participant participates in every round of model training. Since we are (to our knowledge) the first work to consider how a client can change their ε_i after training, we only compare against is naïve retraining, where for each setting, we re-randomize the changing client's data under ε'_i and re-preform the federated training procedure. We test a wide range of $\varepsilon_i = x = \{\varepsilon_{i,f} = x\}_{f \in \mathcal{F}}$ values $\{\infty, 5, 4, 3, 2, 1\}$ as well as a wide range of $\varepsilon'_i = x = \{\varepsilon'_{i,f} = x\}_{f \in \mathcal{F}}$ values $\{5, 4, 3, 2, 1, 0.5, 0.1\}$ in the analysis of Q1-Q4. For simplicity, we have all clients use the same $\varepsilon_i/\varepsilon'_i$. We run all experiments three times and report the average. Further dataset and experimental details such as which attributes $\mathcal{F}$ were protected under randomized response and the selected hyperparameters can be found in our Github repository https://shorturl.at/qFRJD.

5.2 Evaluation Metrics

We consider three primary metrics to evaluate our proposed FLDP-FL method: 1) average loss difference (ALD), average accuracy difference (AAD), and euclidean distance (ED).

$$ALD = \mathcal{L}(\mathcal{D}_{te}, \theta_{\mathcal{I}}) - \mathcal{L}(\mathcal{D}_{te}, \theta_{\varepsilon_i \to \varepsilon'_i}) \tag{27}$$

$$AAD = \text{Acc}(\mathcal{D}_{te}, \theta_{\mathcal{I}}) - \text{Acc}(\mathcal{D}_{te}, \theta_{\varepsilon_i \to \varepsilon'_i}) \tag{28}$$

$$ED = ||\theta_{\mathcal{I}} - \theta_{\varepsilon_i \to \varepsilon'_i}||_2 \tag{29}$$

where $\mathcal{L}(\mathcal{D}_{te}, \cdot)$ denotes the test loss, $\text{Acc}(\mathcal{D}_{te}, \cdot)$ denotes the test accuracy, $\theta_{\mathcal{I}}$ represents the influence-estimated parameters using Algorithm 1, and $\theta_{\varepsilon_i \to \varepsilon'_i}$

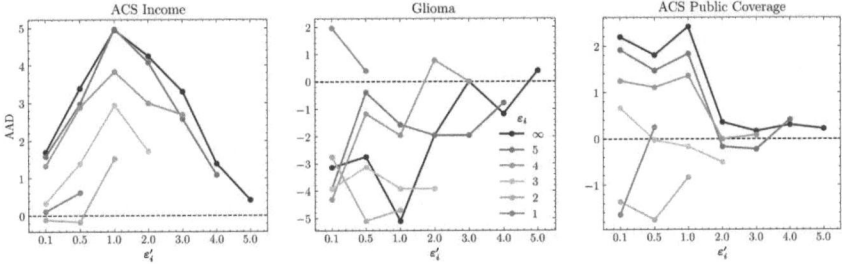

Fig. 1. Average accuracy difference (AAD, Eq. 28) when one client changes $\varepsilon_i \to \varepsilon'_i$.

represents the true parameters obtained when client i's data is re-randomized under ε'_i and federated retraining is re-performed. For all ALD, AAD, and ED, values closer to zero are desirable. We note that these values are only used for our analysis of FLDP-FL's estimation ability and that in practice, they may not need to be computed. However, when necessary, the global server is the one who would calculate $\mathcal{L}(\mathcal{D}_{te}, \theta_\mathcal{I})$ and $\mathrm{Acc}(\mathcal{D}_{te}, \theta_\mathcal{I})$ as the clients do not have access to $\mathcal{D}_{te}$.

5.3 Analysis

Q1. We begin our evaluation by studying the ability of FLDP-FL to estimate the model parameters that result from a single client changing $\varepsilon_i \to \varepsilon'_i$ after federated training concludes. After training the global model using standard FedAvg, we randomly select one client to calculate Eq. 14. The server then calculates the resulting test loss and accuracy under the newly estimated model parameters (derived using Eq. 19). We plot the results for AAD in Fig. 1 and additionally list the results for all metrics (along with their standard deviations) in Table 2. Across all three datasets, ALD trends closer to zero as ε'_i approaches ε_i, however, even in cases when the difference between the two is large (e.g., $\varepsilon_i = \infty$ and $\varepsilon'_i = 0.1$), the difference in the estimated and true loss is small. Similar trends hold for both AAD and ED, although the trend for AAD is slightly weaker (e.g., ACS Income obtains lower AAD for $\varepsilon'_i = 0.1/0.5$ than $\varepsilon'_i=1$). Again, however, even when the difference is large, the AAD value is still within ±5% of the true accuracy. In general, the results for the Glioma dataset are worse than that of ACS Income or ACS Public Coverage and we attribute this to the dataset being small (∼400 data points). In future work, we plan to more rigorously analyze how overall federated dataset size affects the ability of FLDP-FL to generate proper estimations for the model parameters. Overall, these results support that FLDP-FL is able to estimate the model parameters resulting from a single client changing $\varepsilon_i \to \varepsilon'_i$ after federated training.

Q2. To analyze the ability of FLDP-FL in estimating the true model under multiple clients changing $\varepsilon_i \to \varepsilon'_i$, we again follow a setup where first we train the federated model as normal with each client randomizing their data using

Table 2. Results for average loss difference (ALD, Eq. 27), average accuracy difference (AAD, Eq. 28), and euclidean distance (ED, Eq. 29) for parameters estimated by FLDP-FL when one client changes $\varepsilon_i \to \varepsilon_i'$.

ε_i	ε_i'	ACS Income			Glioma			ACS Public Coverage		
		ALD	AAD	ED	ALD	AAD	ED	ALD	AAD	ED
∞	0.1	$-0.026_{\pm 0.005}$	$1.69_{\pm 0.10}$	$0.136_{\pm 0.040}$	$0.096_{\pm 0.031}$	$-3.14_{\pm 1.47}$	$1.462_{\pm 0.283}$	$-0.014_{\pm 0.005}$	$2.19_{\pm 1.52}$	$0.192_{\pm 0.074}$
	0.5	$-0.029_{\pm 0.003}$	$3.39_{\pm 0.31}$	$0.111_{\pm 0.027}$	$0.066_{\pm 0.021}$	$-2.75_{\pm 3.09}$	$1.321_{\pm 0.287}$	$-0.014_{\pm 0.003}$	$1.81_{\pm 0.21}$	$0.178_{\pm 0.010}$
	1	$-0.043_{\pm 0.007}$	$4.94_{\pm 0.70}$	$0.132_{\pm 0.008}$	$0.044_{\pm 0.023}$	$-5.10_{\pm 3.64}$	$1.211_{\pm 0.163}$	$-0.007_{\pm 0.001}$	$2.42_{\pm 1.21}$	$0.159_{\pm 0.039}$
	2	$-0.022_{\pm 0.003}$	$4.25_{\pm 0.49}$	$0.093_{\pm 0.009}$	$0.038_{\pm 0.040}$	$-1.96_{\pm 2.22}$	$0.902_{\pm 0.495}$	$0.005_{\pm 0.001}$	$0.36_{\pm 0.62}$	$0.106_{\pm 0.041}$
	3	$-0.012_{\pm 0.001}$	$3.31_{\pm 0.71}$	$0.044_{\pm 0.008}$	$0.009_{\pm 0.009}$	$0.00_{\pm 0.96}$	$0.471_{\pm 0.304}$	$0.005_{\pm 0.003}$	$0.17_{\pm 0.14}$	$0.138_{\pm 0.057}$
	4	$-0.004_{\pm 0.002}$	$1.39_{\pm 0.75}$	$0.023_{\pm 0.003}$	$0.006_{\pm 0.010}$	$-1.18_{\pm 1.66}$	$0.271_{\pm 0.219}$	$0.001_{\pm 0.001}$	$0.31_{\pm 0.22}$	$0.057_{\pm 0.029}$
	5	$-0.001_{\pm 0.001}$	$0.42_{\pm 0.25}$	$0.012_{\pm 0.002}$	$0.001_{\pm 0.002}$	$0.39_{\pm 0.55}$	$0.155_{\pm 0.075}$	$-0.001_{\pm 0.00}$	$0.22_{\pm 0.14}$	$0.020_{\pm 0.008}$
5	0.1	$-0.017_{\pm 0.001}$	$1.58_{\pm 0.12}$	$0.131_{\pm 0.038}$	$0.087_{\pm 0.038}$	$-3.92_{\pm 2.22}$	$1.600_{\pm 0.287}$	$-0.011_{\pm 0.004}$	$1.92_{\pm 1.73}$	$0.182_{\pm 0.064}$
	0.5	$-0.025_{\pm 0.002}$	$2.97_{\pm 0.31}$	$0.108_{\pm 0.026}$	$0.057_{\pm 0.025}$	$-0.39_{\pm 1.11}$	$1.117_{\pm 0.279}$	$-0.010_{\pm 0.003}$	$1.47_{\pm 0.37}$	$0.165_{\pm 0.005}$
	1	$-0.038_{\pm 0.005}$	$4.97_{\pm 0.21}$	$0.126_{\pm 0.010}$	$0.035_{\pm 0.021}$	$-1.57_{\pm 3.09}$	$1.107_{\pm 0.006}$	$-0.004_{\pm 0.001}$	$1.83_{\pm 0.72}$	$0.178_{\pm 0.022}$
	2	$-0.022_{\pm 0.005}$	$4.08_{\pm 0.30}$	$0.083_{\pm 0.016}$	$0.021_{\pm 0.026}$	$-1.96_{\pm 2.93}$	$0.800_{\pm 0.264}$	$0.005_{\pm 0.001}$	$-0.17_{\pm 0.34}$	$0.145_{\pm 0.043}$
	3	$-0.010_{\pm 0.001}$	$2.58_{\pm 0.62}$	$0.044_{\pm 0.011}$	$0.002_{\pm 0.009}$	$-1.96_{\pm 1.47}$	$0.457_{\pm 0.156}$	$0.007_{\pm 0.003}$	$-0.22_{\pm 0.04}$	$0.149_{\pm 0.043}$
	4	$-0.002_{\pm 0.001}$	$1.08_{\pm 0.68}$	$0.025_{\pm 0.007}$	$-0.004_{\pm 0.006}$	$-0.78_{\pm 0.55}$	$0.265_{\pm 0.197}$	$0.002_{\pm 0.002}$	$0.42_{\pm 0.34}$	$0.057_{\pm 0.029}$
4	0.1	$-0.006_{\pm 0.005}$	$1.33_{\pm 0.07}$	$0.094_{\pm 0.048}$	$0.075_{\pm 0.035}$	$-4.31_{\pm 1.47}$	$1.768_{\pm 0.046}$	$-0.007_{\pm 0.004}$	$1.25_{\pm 1.54}$	$0.188_{\pm 0.045}$
	0.5	$-0.012_{\pm 0.010}$	$2.89_{\pm 0.41}$	$0.081_{\pm 0.026}$	$0.053_{\pm 0.035}$	$-1.18_{\pm 1.92}$	$1.197_{\pm 0.245}$	$-0.008_{\pm 0.002}$	$1.11_{\pm 0.39}$	$0.157_{\pm 0.014}$
	1	$-0.029_{\pm 0.004}$	$3.83_{\pm 0.20}$	$0.119_{\pm 0.005}$	$0.028_{\pm 0.022}$	$-1.96_{\pm 2.42}$	$1.055_{\pm 0.126}$	$-0.002_{\pm 0.001}$	$1.36_{\pm 0.63}$	$0.152_{\pm 0.033}$
	2	$-0.012_{\pm 0.003}$	$3.00_{\pm 0.34}$	$0.086_{\pm 0.005}$	$0.009_{\pm 0.020}$	$0.78_{\pm 0.55}$	$0.723_{\pm 0.176}$	$0.005_{\pm 0.001}$	$0.00_{\pm 0.61}$	$0.108_{\pm 0.061}$
	3	$-0.008_{\pm 0.001}$	$2.69_{\pm 0.55}$	$0.044_{\pm 0.011}$	$-0.002_{\pm 0.012}$	$-0.00_{\pm 0.96}$	$0.442_{\pm 0.223}$	$0.001_{\pm 0.001}$	$0.08_{\pm 0.31}$	$0.070_{\pm 0.032}$
3	0.1	$0.006_{\pm 0.007}$	$0.33_{\pm 0.20}$	$0.107_{\pm 0.022}$	$0.060_{\pm 0.040}$	$-3.92_{\pm 2.93}$	$1.470_{\pm 0.328}$	$0.008_{\pm 0.012}$	$0.67_{\pm 1.59}$	$0.118_{\pm 0.027}$
	0.5	$0.005_{\pm 0.004}$	$1.39_{\pm 0.08}$	$0.085_{\pm 0.021}$	$0.039_{\pm 0.032}$	$-3.14_{\pm 1.47}$	$1.167_{\pm 0.377}$	$0.005_{\pm 0.006}$	$-0.03_{\pm 0.63}$	$0.105_{\pm 0.029}$
	1	$-0.014_{\pm 0.006}$	$2.94_{\pm 0.61}$	$0.101_{\pm 0.005}$	$0.039_{\pm 0.032}$	$-3.92_{\pm 2.00}$	$1.230_{\pm 0.236}$	$0.004_{\pm 0.004}$	$-0.17_{\pm 1.18}$	$0.162_{\pm 0.042}$
	2	$-0.007_{\pm 0.003}$	$1.72_{\pm 0.91}$	$0.053_{\pm 0.010}$	$0.028_{\pm 0.033}$	$-3.92_{\pm 2.22}$	$1.079_{\pm 0.312}$	$0.010_{\pm 0.009}$	$-0.50_{\pm 0.72}$	$0.123_{\pm 0.071}$
2	0.1	$0.017_{\pm 0.004}$	$-0.11_{\pm 0.34}$	$0.072_{\pm 0.013}$	$0.031_{\pm 0.011}$	$-2.75_{\pm 1.47}$	$1.295_{\pm 0.197}$	$0.014_{\pm 0.010}$	$-1.36_{\pm 0.98}$	$0.179_{\pm 0.085}$
	0.5	$0.008_{\pm 0.004}$	$-0.17_{\pm 0.54}$	$0.061_{\pm 0.004}$	$0.034_{\pm 0.014}$	$-5.10_{\pm 0.55}$	$1.018_{\pm 0.367}$	$0.012_{\pm 0.005}$	$-1.75_{\pm 0.34}$	$0.252_{\pm 0.055}$
	1	$-0.003_{\pm 0.003}$	$1.53_{\pm 1.58}$	$0.064_{\pm 0.008}$	$0.027_{\pm 0.002}$	$-4.71_{\pm 3.46}$	$1.277_{\pm 0.163}$	$0.005_{\pm 0.001}$	$-0.83_{\pm 0.72}$	$0.184_{\pm 0.056}$
1	0.1	$0.010_{\pm 0.002}$	$0.11_{\pm 0.27}$	$0.054_{\pm 0.020}$	$-0.009_{\pm 0.023}$	$1.96_{\pm 2.22}$	$1.510_{\pm 0.427}$	$0.004_{\pm 0.005}$	$-0.78_{\pm 0.22}$	$0.185_{\pm 0.098}$
	0.5	$0.002_{\pm 0.002}$	$0.61_{\pm 0.45}$	$0.049_{\pm 0.006}$	$-0.005_{\pm 0.022}$	$0.39_{\pm 3.88}$	$1.394_{\pm 0.358}$	$0.008_{\pm 0.007}$	$-0.58_{\pm 0.27}$	$0.172_{\pm 0.048}$

ε_i randomized response before participating in training. We randomly select $m = \{1, 2, 3\}$ clients to change $\varepsilon_i \to \varepsilon_i'$ and calculate Eq. 14 to obtain $\mathcal{I}_i$. We then estimate $\hat{\theta}$ using Eq. 20. We plot the results for all datasets where $\varepsilon_i = 3 \to \varepsilon_i' = 1$ in the top row of Fig. 2. For the two larger datasets, ACS Income and Public Coverage, the ability of FLDP-FL to estimate the true parameters maintains consistent as the number of clients changing $\varepsilon_i = 3 \to \varepsilon_i' = 1$ increases. On the other hand, when increasing the number of changing clients on small datasets, the quality of the estimation provided by FLDP-FL degrades quite significantly. Specifically, for Glioma, FLDP-FL's estimated parameters consistently underperforms the performance obtained under the true retrained parameters (e.g., AAD of -17.5% when 3 clients are changed). These results show that FLDP-FL is able to estimate the true parameters under multiple clients changing $\varepsilon_i \to \varepsilon_i'$ when the dataset is not excessively small. When the number of clients changing becomes too high, we recommend retraining the federated model instead of using estimations provided by FLDP-FL.

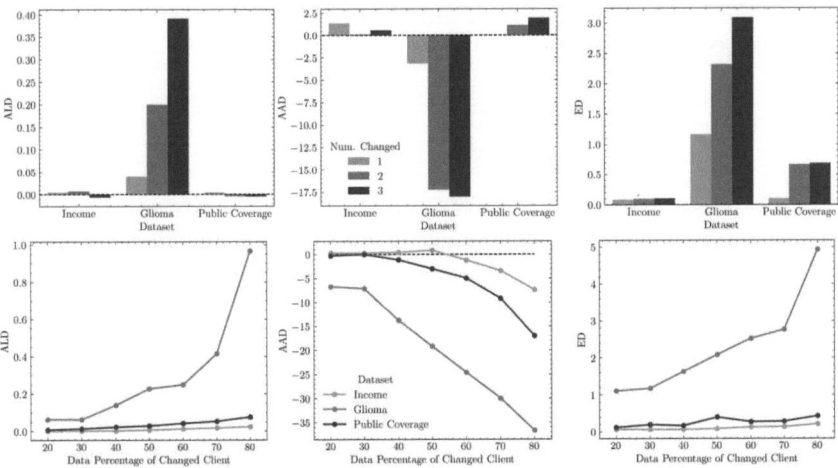

Fig. 2. Average loss difference (ALD, Eq. 27), average accuracy difference (AAD, Eq. 28), and Euclidean distance (ED, Eq. 29) when $\varepsilon_i = 3 \to \varepsilon_i' = 1$ for: *Top*: multiple clients changing; and *Bottom*: different changing client dataset size.

Q3. To analyze the ability of FLDP-FL to estimate the true model parameters when the client changing $\varepsilon_i \to \varepsilon_i'$ makes up a large portion of the overall federated dataset, we still perform federated training as normal. However, instead of all clients having a relatively equal amount of data points, we allocate the changing client X% of the overall federated dataset and distribute the remaining 1-X% to the other four clients. We show the results when $\varepsilon_i = 3 \to \varepsilon_i' = 1$ in the bottom row of Fig. 2. There is an obvious trend of the estimation provided by FLDP-FL becoming worse as the dataset percentage makeup of the changing client increases. This is not surprising as there is a degree of randomness to the FLDP-FL estimation, and increasing the size of the dataset changing increases the amount of noise in the estimation. However, ALD degrades gracefully, especially in cases where the dataset is large (i.e., ACS Income and ACS Public Coverage). AAD suffers however when more than 50% of the data belongs to the changing client. In cases where the client changing owns the majority of the federated data, it may be advantageous to perform federated retraining over estimation via FLDP-FL.

Q4. In Table 3 we report the average time to train one full federated learning model and the time to compute Eq. 14 using an explicit Hessian calculation (e.g., no estimation approaches that would further reduce the computational time were used) under one client changing $\varepsilon_i \to \varepsilon_i'$. We note that due to our training setup (see our Github repository) each client performed local training sequentially, not simultaneously (which would be standard in real world settings), which increased the computation time for full federated training. However, even when dividing the time by the number of clients (5) to get a better estimate, the times for full training on all three datasets are still significantly larger than that of estimating

Table 3. Time in seconds to perform full federated training with 5 clients on each dataset compared with one client calculating FLDP-FL via Eq. 14.

	Full Fed. Training	FLDP-FL (Eq. 14)
ACS Income	$1423.51_{\pm 12.40}$	$8.24_{\pm 0.38}$
Glioma	$49.41_{\pm 4.13}$	$0.93_{\pm 0.13}$
ACS Public Coverage	$717.32_{\pm 8.08}$	$87.40_{\pm 4.38}$

the parameters with FLDP-FL (ACS Income: 284.70s, Glioma: 9.88s, ACS Public Coverage: 143.64s). These results reinforce the discussion in Sect. 4.4 that using FLDP-FL offers the benefit of being more efficient that full federated re-training. We also point out that the time for full federated re-training will inevitably increase as the federated dataset and model grow larger, or if multiple clients decide to change $\varepsilon_i \to \varepsilon'_i$, while the time of computing FLDP-FL will remain relatively stable as only the client(s) updating $\varepsilon_i \to \varepsilon'_i$ must calculate Eq. 14 based on their own local dataset.

6 Conclusion

In this work, we proposed Flexible Local Differential Privacy for Federated Learning (FLDP-FL), a technique based on influence functions for local differentially private federated learning which allows clients to change their privacy parameter ε post-training without having to retrain the federated model. Through empirical evaluation on three datasets, we show that FLDP-FL is able to estimate the true parameters that would be obtained if the client's data was re-randomized under their new ε value and federated retraining was repeated. Further, we also show that FLDP-FL is able to support multiple clients changing their ε value after training when the dataset is of sufficient size and can also generate reasonable estimations when the client performing the change owns a large portion of the overall federated dataset. Future work will include utilizing second-order influence functions instead of first-order estimations to see if better loss difference, accuracy difference, and euclidean distance between the estimated and true parameters can be obtained as well as using local differential privacy methods beyond randomized response.

Acknowledgments. This work was supported in part by the NSF under awards 1920920, 1946391, and 2119691, the National Institute of General Medical Sciences of National Institutes of Health under award P20GM139768, and the Arkansas Integrative Metabolic Research Center at the University of Arkansas.

Disclosure of Interests. The authors have no competing interests to declare that are relevant to the content of this article

References

1. Abadi, M., et al.: Deep learning with differential privacy. In: ACM SIGSAC CCS, pp. 308–318 (2016)
2. Andrew, G., Thakkar, O., McMahan, B., Ramaswamy, S.: Differentially private learning with adaptive clipping. In: NeurIPS, vol. 34, pp. 17455–17466 (2021)
3. Carey, A.N., Van, M.H., Wu, X.: Evaluating the impact of local differential privacy on utility loss via influence functions. In: IJCNN, pp. 1–10. IEEE (2024)
4. Cook, R.D.: Assessment of local influence. J. R. Stat. Soc., B Stat. Methodol. **48**(2), 133–155 (1986)
5. Ding, F., Hardt, M., Miller, J., Schmidt, L.: Retiring adult: new datasets for fair machine learning. In: NeurIPS, vol. 34, pp. 6478–6490 (2021)
6. Dwork, C., Lei, J.: Differential privacy and robust statistics. In: 41st ACM STOC, pp. 371–380 (2009)
7. Fu, J., et al.: Differentially private federated learning: a systematic review. arXiv:2405.08299 (2024)
8. Hu, R., Guo, Y., Li, H., Pei, Q., Gong, Y.: Personalized federated learning with differential privacy. IEEE IOTJ **7**(10), 9530–9539 (2020)
9. Huang, J., Hong, C., Liu, Y., Chen, L.Y., Roos, S.: Maverick matters: client contribution and selection in federated learning. In: Kashima, H., Ide, T., Peng, W.C. (eds.) PAKDD 2023. LNCS, vol. 13936, pp. 269–282. Springer, Cham (2023). https://doi.org/10.1007/978-3-031-33377-4_21
10. Kairouz, P., et al.: Advances and open problems in federated learning. Found. Trends® Mach. Learn. **14**(1–2), 1–210 (2021)
11. Kang, Y., Liu, Y., Ding, L., Liu, X., Tong, X., Wang, W.: Differentially private ERM based on data perturbation. arXiv:2002.08578 (2020)
12. Kasiviswanathan, S.P., Lee, H.K., Nissim, K., Raskhodnikova, S., Smith, A.: What can we learn privately? SICOMP **40**(3), 793–826 (2011)
13. Koh, P.W., Liang, P.: Understanding black-box predictions via influence functions. In: ICML, pp. 1885–1894. PMLR (2017)
14. Koh, P.W.W., Ang, K.S., Teo, H., Liang, P.S.: On the accuracy of influence functions for measuring group effects. In: NeurIPS, vol. 32 (2019)
15. Li, A., Zhang, L., Wang, J., Han, F., Li, X.Y.: Privacy-preserving efficient federated-learning model debugging. IEEE TPDS **33**(10), 2291–2303 (2021)
16. McMahan, B., Moore, E., Ramage, D., Hampson, S., y Arcas, B.A.: Communication-efficient learning of deep networks from decentralized data. In: AISTATS, pp. 1273–1282. PMLR (2017)
17. McMahan, H.B., Ramage, D., Talwar, K., Zhang, L.: Learning differentially private recurrent language models. arXiv:1710.06963 (2017)
18. Rokvic, L., Danassis, P., Faltings, B.: Privacy-preserving data filtering in federated learning using influence approximation. In: Workshop on Federated Learning: Recent Advances and New Challenges (in Conjunction with NeurIPS 2022) (2022)
19. Tan, Y., Long, G., Jiang, J., Zhang, C.: Influence-oriented personalized federated learning. arXiv:2410.03315 (2024)
20. Tasci, E., Camphausen, K., Krauze, A.V., Zhuge, Y.: Glioma Grading Clinical and Mutation Features. UCI Machine Learning Repository (2022). https://doi.org/10.24432/C5R62J
21. Truex, S., Liu, L., Chow, K.H., Gursoy, M.E., Wei, W.: LDP-Fed: federated learning with local differential privacy. In: EdgeSys, pp. 61–66 (2020)

22. Wang, W., Zhang, C., Tian, Z., Yu, S.: FedU: federated unlearning via user-side influence approximation forgetting. IEEE TDSC (2024)
23. Wang, Y., Wu, X., Hu, D.: Using randomized response for differential privacy preserving data collection. In: EDBT/ICDT, vol. 1558, pp. 0090–6778 (2016)
24. Wei, K., et al.: Federated learning with differential privacy: algorithms and performance analysis. IEEE TIFS **15**, 3454–3469 (2020)
25. Wu, C., Zhu, S., Mitra, P.: Federated unlearning with knowledge distillation. arXiv:2201.09441 (2022)
26. Zhang, X., Chen, X., Hong, M., Wu, Z.S., Yi, J.: Understanding clipping for federated learning: convergence and client-level differential privacy. In: ICML (2022)

P2NIA: Privacy-Preserving Non-iterative Auditing

Jade Garcia Bourrée[1,4(✉)], Hadrien Lautraite[2], Sébastien Gambs[2], Gilles Tredan[3], Erwan Le Merrer[1,4], and Benoît Rottembourg[4]

[1] Univ Rennes, Inria, CNRS, Irisa, Rennes, France
{jade.garcia-bourree,erwan.le-merrer}@inria.fr
[2] Université du Québec à Montréal, Montreal, USA
{lautraite.hadrien,gambs.sebastien}@uqam.ca
[3] LAAS/CNRS, Toulouse, France
gtredan@laas.fr
[4] Inria, Le Chesnay, France
benoit.rottembourg@inria.fr

Abstract. The emergence of AI legislation has increased the need to assess the ethical compliance of high-risk AI systems. Traditional auditing methods rely on platforms' application programming interfaces (APIs), in which responses to queries are examined through the lens of fairness requirements. However, such approaches put a significant burden on platforms, as they are forced to maintain APIs while ensuring privacy, facing the possibility of data leaks. This lack of proper collaboration between the two parties, in turn, causes a significant challenge to the auditor, who is subject to estimation bias as they are unaware of the data distribution of the platform. To address these two issues, we present P2NIA, a novel auditing scheme that proposes a mutually beneficial collaboration for both the auditor and the platform. Extensive experiments demonstrate P2NIA's effectiveness in addressing both issues. In summary, our work introduces a privacy-preserving and non-iterative audit scheme that enhances fairness assessments using synthetic or local data, avoiding the challenges associated with traditional API-based audits.

Keywords: Algorithm auditing · synthetic data · local differential privacy · fairness estimation

1 Introduction

Algorithm auditing refers to the evaluation of algorithmic decision-making systems. More precisely, it aims at ensuring their privacy, transparency, fairness and compliance with ethical and legal standards [19,37]. This field is very active, in reaction to algorithms becoming increasingly ubiquitous in our daily lives in critical areas such as finance, human resources, healthcare or justice [2,7,12,14,27,28, 34,48,51]. The traditional way to assess if decision-making systems and models in

---

Supplementary Information The online version contains supplementary material available at https://doi.org/10.1007/978-3-032-06096-9_15.

production satisfy ethical standards is to audit them in the so-called *black-box setting*, in which the auditor sends queries to a platform, receives answers and infers information on its behavior with respect to fairness, for instance.

Issues with Black-Box Audits. Unfortunately, it has been shown that, in many real-world scenarios, black-box audits may not lead to accurate evaluation [5, 10, 11]. The main reason for this being the non-collaboration of platforms that do not want to release information about their data distribution, which is kept hidden for privacy or trade secret motives. Consider, for instance, the scenario of a bank that decides to lend to whom by using a risk scoring model. The bank uses the model to predict if clients are likely to repay the loan based on their economic profile and an auditor wants to assess the fairness of such a model. To realize this, requests composed of possible profiles are sent to the platform for assessment. In this scarce data regime, audit results can lead to erroneous conclusions, possibly due to the auditor's measurement bias, whether deliberate or subconscious or to wrong assumptions regarding the audited model. For instance, if the auditor's requests do not align with the data distribution used to train the platform model, it will lead to biased conclusions. In addition, many audit scenarios deal with sensitive data such as personal health records, income levels or demographic information like age, gender and ethnicity [29]. Such data is highly critical and cause platforms to be reluctant to open and maintain APIs to expose them, as requested by recent legislation such as the AI act [24].

Contributions. We propose a novel scheme to address these issues in a setting in which the platform and the auditor collaborate for the audit. Our solutions lead to a mutually beneficial situation in which 1) the auditor can perform an unbiased estimation of the property of interest (hereafter, we focus on fairness), and 2) the platform does not need to maintain APIs while ensuring the privacy of its data. More precisely, we first demonstrate both theoretically and with an example that in a non-collaborative audit setup, in which the auditor faces a black-box setting (*i.e.*, without being provided the data distribution of the platform), an auditor obtains a biased estimate of the model under scrutiny. This motivates our scheme P2NIA (which stands for Privacy-Preserving Non-Iterative Auditing), in which the platform collaborates with the auditor by releasing a synthetic dataset mimicking its behavior, allowing for unbiased audits while ensuring privacy. In summary, our contributions are as follows.

- We demonstrate and illustrate that an audit outcome can be biased in a black-box setting due to the *population bias*.
- To circumvent this issue, we propose P2NIA, a novel collaborative auditing scheme benefiting both the platform and the auditor by enabling accurate audits while being privacy-preserving and non-iterative.
- We have designed several ways to implement P2NIA and experimentally evaluate their performance.

Outline. First, we present the challenges associated with black-box auditing schemes in Sect. 2 before introducing P2NIA as an alternative approach to address them in Sect. 3. Then, we evaluate our proposal on two datasets and compare it to a standard audit scheme in Sect. 4. Afterward, we review related works in Sect. 5 before concluding in Sect. 6.

2 Auditing Black-Box Models

After formalizing the audit objective in this section, we focus on the potential bias in black-box fairness estimation. In particular, studying a common hypothesis that an auditor needs to have knowledge of the platform distribution, we theoretically show that imperfect knowledge of this distribution can lead to a linear estimation bias on the statistical distance between the two distributions. We also illustrate how such bias will likely appear in practice through a simulation.

2.1 Auditing Fairness Setup

Fairness Definitions. The concept of fairness refers to the property that algorithms should not discriminate against people based on sensitive characteristics, such as ethnical origin or gender [5]. Fairness can be defined in many ways, but we focus on *group* fairness metrics, which compare the statistics of predictions between two groups, one of which is considered potentially discriminated and is called the protected group. In particular, we focus on *demographic parity, equality of opportunity* and *equalized odds*, as these are arguably the most studied group fairness notions [43].

Formally, we aim at auditing model $m \in \mathcal{H} : \mathcal{X} \to \mathcal{Y}$, with $\mathcal{X}$ is its input space. Let $\mathcal{D}$ be the input distribution and $\mu_\mathcal{D}$ the target measure of the audit. Usually, this notation is shorthanded by μ. However, this notation hides a strong prerequisite for measuring fairness, namely having access to the input distribution $\mathcal{D}$. In addition, group fairness requires the definition of a protected group, usually defined through a protected attribute $A \in \{0, 1\}$. We denote Y as the target variable and $\hat{Y} = m(X)$ as the prediction of model m on input X.

The fairness metrics we study can be formally defined as follows [9,21,32]:

Demographic parity: $\mu_\mathcal{D} = \left| P_\mathcal{D}[\hat{Y} = 1 | A = 1] - P_\mathcal{D}[\hat{Y} = 1 | A = 0] \right|$.

Equalized odds: $\mu_\mathcal{D} = \max_{y \in \{0,1\}} \left| P_\mathcal{D}[\hat{Y} = 1 | Y = y, A = 0] - P_\mathcal{D}[\hat{Y} = 1 | Y = y, A = 1] \right|$.

Equality of opportunity: $\mu_\mathcal{D} = \left| P_\mathcal{D}[\hat{Y} = 1 | Y = 1, A = 0] - P_\mathcal{D}[\hat{Y} = 1 | Y = 1, A = 1] \right|$.

In a nutshell, each of these metrics addresses different facets of potential bias and ensures that models perform equitably across groups. For instance, demographic parity aims at maintaining similar outcome distributions across groups, while equalized odds and equal opportunity assess fairness by comparing error rates with the latter, specifically focusing on true positive rates. Note that the last two fairness metrics require access to the true label Y of samples, which might be a strong assumption in practice.

Black-Box Auditing Setting. When assessing the fairness of a model, particularly in usual non-collaborative setups, auditors are unlikely to possess information about the distribution of training data. Hence, they will have to rely on black-box auditing strategies, which generally entails crafting a specific finite set of queries $Q = \{q_1, \ldots, q_n\}$ in the model input space $\mathcal{X}$, and obtaining the corresponding honest[1] model inferred answers $m(Q) = \{m(q_1), \ldots, m(q_n)\}$. The pair $(Q, m(Q))$

---
[1] Previous works have shown that manipulative platforms may impede fairness assessment [30].

is then processed by the auditor to produce the fairness estimates. In the specific case of equality of opportunity and equalized odds, the auditor needs domain expertise to access the true outcome Y of their requests Q.

A crucial assumption for the auditing to work is that $Q \sim \mathcal{D}$, which is equivalent to the auditor having sampling access to the input distribution[2]. Unfortunately, in a non-collaborative audit, the platform will likely keep this information confidential for privacy and trade secret reasons, as observed with recent legislation enforcing the opening of APIs [24].

2.2 Estimation Discrepancy Due to Population Bias

When the auditor does not have access to $\mathcal{D}$, they must rely on a different distribution $\mathcal{D}'$ to generate their audit queries. For instance, when auditing platforms such as TikTok or Snapchat, already known user profiles from other platforms like LinkedIn or Facebook can be used. Unfortunately, such distributions differ substantially, for example in terms of users' average age [33]. Another possible approach is to generate data from statistics published by the platforms themselves. However, public statistics are often insufficient to generate realistic data, particularly due to correlations between attributes [1]. The ignorance of $\mathcal{D}$ thus lead to an inaccurate fairness estimation $\mu_\mathcal{D}(m) \neq \mu_{\mathcal{D}'}(m)$. Hereafter, we refer to this as a form of *population bias*. This term was initially introduced to qualify the bias arising when a population $x \sim \mathcal{D}$ uses a classifier trained using samples drawn from a distribution $\mathcal{D}' \neq \mathcal{D}$ [43]. In our setting, population bias is used to qualify the bias due to the evaluation of models using a biased query set, *i.e.* from a trained model on the platform using $x \sim \mathcal{D}$, then audited with a population $\mathcal{D}'$. While this form of bias has been known in other contexts, to the best of our knowledge it has not been studied in the field of model audits in the black-box setting. For instance, Casper and co-authors [11] acknowledge the possible presence of bias in the black-box setup but without identifying the precise bias cause. To highlight the impact of such population bias in black-box audits, we first construct pathological examples demonstrating to which extent the estimation can be biased, before showing through simulation that population bias also has practical impacts, even in simpler scenarios.

Theorem 1. *Population bias in black-box audit. Estimating the fairness metric (e.g., demographic parity, equality of opportunity or equalized odds) of a model m using a distribution $\mathcal{D}'$ at a (total variation) statistical distance α from the true distribution $\mathcal{D}$ can lead to an approximation error linear in α. Formally: $\exists \mathcal{D}, \mathcal{D}', m$ s.t. $\delta(\mathcal{D}, \mathcal{D}') = \sup_{F \in \mathcal{F}} |\mathcal{D}(F) - \mathcal{D}'(F)| = \alpha$ and $m \in \mathcal{H} : \mathcal{X} \mapsto \mathcal{Y}$ s.t. $|\mu_\mathcal{D}(m) - \mu_{\mathcal{D}'}(m)| = \alpha$.*

Proof. First, we look at the case of demographic parity and proceed by constructing the situation considered. Let $X = a \in \{0,1\} \times b \in \{0,1\} \times c \in [0,1]$ be

---

[2] In some settings, the auditor may want to deviate from $\mathcal{D}$ to optimize his sampling strategy and obtain more accurate estimates [53], but this nevertheless requires knowing $\mathcal{D}$.

the input space and $Y = \{0, 1\}$ the binary output space. In the following, a will play the role of the protected attribute, b will enable the tuning of the statistical distance between D and D', and c represents additional data used by the model to construct its decision. We now describe two distributions D, D' on X:

- for both D and D' we have: $c \perp\!\!\!\perp (a, b), c \sim U(0, 1)$ and $a \perp\!\!\!\perp b$.
- $\mathbb{E}_D(a = 1) = \mathbb{E}_{D'}(a = 1) = 1/2$
- $\mathbb{E}_D(b = 1) = 0$ and $\mathbb{E}_{D'}(b = 1) = \alpha$

As a table:

$x \sim$	$a = 1, b = 1$	$a = 0, b = 1$	$a = 1, b = 0$	$a = 0, b = 0$
D	0	0	$1/2$	$1/2$
D'	$\alpha/2$	$\alpha/2$	$(1-\alpha)/2$	$(1-\alpha)/2$

Clearly, with $\mathcal{F}$ being a sigma-algebra of X, we have

$$\delta(D, D') = sup_{F \in \mathcal{F}}|P_D(F) - P_{D'}(F)| = P_{D'}(b = 1) - P_D(b = 1) = \alpha.$$

In other words, the total variation distance between D and D' is α.

The model $M : X \mapsto Y$ is defined as follows: $M(x) = (1 - b).(c > 1/2) + b.a$. The rationale here is that b drives two distinct behaviors of M, only one of which is unfair. The demographic parity can be expressed as given D: $\mu_{x \sim D}(M) = |P(Y|a) - P(Y|\bar{a})| = P(c > 1/2) - P(c \leq 1/2) = 0$. Conversely, given D', using the law of total probability on the partitions induced by b: $\mu_{x \sim D'} = (P(Y|a, b) - P(Y|\bar{a}, b))P(b) + (P(Y|a, \bar{b}) - P(Y|\bar{a}, \bar{b}))(1 - P(b)) = (1 - 0)\alpha + 0 = \alpha$. Hence, $|\mu_{x \sim D}(M) - \mu_{x \sim D'}(M)| = \alpha$.

Second, we can generalize the previous proof to equality of opportunity and equalized odds by assessing that for all input, $Y = 1$. In such case, for all binary a, y, $P_D[\hat{Y} = 1|Y = y, A = a] = P_D[\hat{Y} = 1|Y = 1, A = a] = P_D[\hat{Y} = 1|A = a]$ and the three metrics are equals. □

Intuitively, this result states that if the auditor has a bias in their prior about the distribution at play at the platform (*i.e.*, imperfect knowledge of the distribution), then the outcome is also a biased estimation. This is highly undesirable as it undermines the strength and legal impact of the audit.

While Theorem 1 corresponds to a crafted extreme scenario, we now study experimentally the impact of population bias on real data. To this end, we use the standard Folktables dataset commonly used in fairness settings [16]. Consider a platform that trained a model on data collected from a specific state (California) to predict whether an individual's income is above $50,000$ [16]. We consider a black-box auditor that has no access to this training distribution, which uses the distribution of another state among the remaining fifty in the dataset. One might expect that the auditor and model distributions are sufficiently similar to estimate the platform fairness accurately. However, as demonstrated by Fig. 1, this is not the case. Thus, no matter the state the auditor selects for reference, there will be a considerable population bias in the auditor's estimation. More concretely, on average, the absolute error in estimating the demographic parity with a different state is around 0.13, which is high considering that the classical 80% rule translates into a maximal tolerated value of 0.2. Concretely, as the true demographic parity in this example is 0.01, using the distribution of (NE,SD,WY,ND,ID,UT) would lead the auditor to a wrong conclusion about the model.

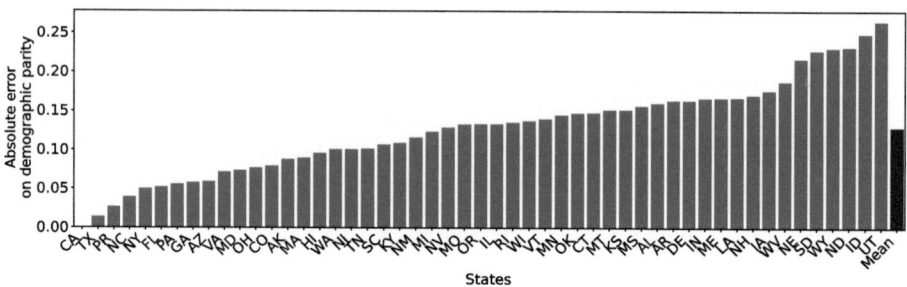

Fig. 1. Observed population bias on the evaluation of demographic parity with protected feature "sex" on a model trained in state CA to predict whether an individual's income is above $50,000 and evaluated in other states. These results confirm the practical impact of Theorem 1.

This population bias is thus a clear impediment for accurate auditing in non-collaborative black-box audits, and is at stake even in such a simple and realistic scenario. To address this, in the following section, we propose P2NIA, a novel scheme enabling unbiased estimation while adding privacy protection with respect to the platform.

3 Auditing Through a Differentially-Private Dataset

To tackle the aforementioned issues, we propose a collaborative scheme, P2NIA, which leverages privacy-preserving techniques for the benefit of the privacy protection of the platform while enabling accurate fairness auditing by the auditor.

3.1 P2NIA: A Non-iterative Auditing Scheme

We first present the P2NIA scheme before describing how it enables a fairness estimation that is 1) reliably performed and 2) without exposing the privacy of users (*i.e.*, the released dataset is differentially-private).

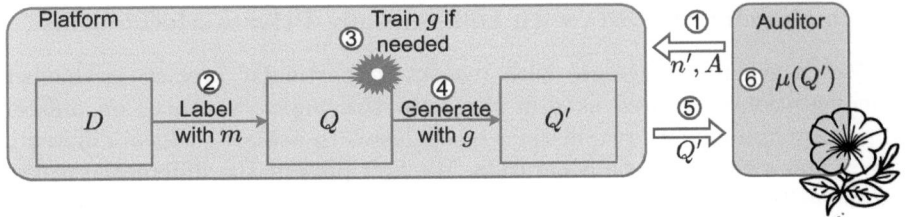

Fig. 2. Description of P2NIA scheme.

The Privacy-Preserving Non-Iterative Auditing scheme (P2NIA) works in six steps (Fig. 2). First, P2NIA starts with the auditor specifying to the platform the desired number of queries n', along with A, the group of interest (**step 1**).

Upon receiving this request, the platform labels a part of its internal data (called *audit dataset* in the following) using its proprietary model m. More precisely the, model m is applied to the dataset D to generate a set of labeled queries Q, in which each query consists of a profile input X from the dataset, the target output Y and the corresponding predictions $\hat{Y}$ (**step 2**).

To protect sensitive information while still allowing fairness evaluation, the platform has two options. More precisely, either it anonymizes the dataset by using a local differential-private mechanism as described in Sect. 3.2, or it trains a generative model g build to produce synthetic data based on Q to reflect the model's behavior without directly disclosing the training user data (**step 3**). Afterwards, the platform creates the audit dataset by generating or anonymizing n' synthetic queries Q' with g (**step 4**).

Then, the platform releases Q' to the auditor (**step 5**). At this stage, the auditor receives the auditing datasets and evaluates fairness using a predefined fairness metric $\mu(Q')$, applied to the protected group A (**step 6**).

Observe that in our scheme, the auditor evaluates the model using Q', without directly querying the platform model (step 6) but rather by declaring their number of requests and their group of interest (step 1). Before the generation with a mechanism g, the queries in D are labeled using the model m (step 2) in order to reflect the platform's actual behavior. This step is necessary for certain mechanisms g that require labeled data as input to achieve better result.

Thus, as the platform has generated Q' from its audit dataset D with a mechanism that ensures differential privacy, the personal data remains confidential while making it possible to audit the model (steps 2–5). As differential privacy is immune to post-processing [22] (*i.e.*, it is impossible to compute a function of the output of the private algorithm and make it less differentially-private), the assessment of μ by the auditor does not reduce the privacy of the released data. For example, in the context of the income prediction model discussed in Sect. 1, this would amount to accurately auditing the fairness of a platform based on synthetic demographic data without revealing the record of any user.

3.2 Implementing P2NIA with Differentially-Private Mechanisms

The P2NIA scheme is generic with respect to particular privacy mechanisms implementations captured as g in Fig. 2. In this paper, we focus on differential privacy and explore two distinct mechanisms to achieve it: local differential privacy and synthetic data generation. We first present the differential privacy guarantees that we aim to achieve.

Differential Privacy. Differential privacy is a formal privacy model that protects individuals by bounding the impact any individual can have on the output of an algorithm [22].

Definition 1. *Differential Privacy.* *[22] A randomized mechanism $\mathcal{M}$ satisfies ϵ-differential privacy if for any individual $x \in \mathcal{X}$, any dataset $Q \subset \mathcal{X}$ and any subset of possible outputs S:*

$$P\left[\mathcal{M}(Q\backslash\{x\}) \in S\right] \leq exp(\epsilon) P\left[\mathcal{M}(Q) \in S\right].$$

The parameter ϵ is called the privacy budget and is considered public. The smaller ϵ, the stronger the privacy guarantees. Typical values of ϵ could be 0.01, 0.1, or in some cases, $ln(2)$ or $ln(3)$ [20]. However, in practice, ϵ can vary up to 10 [38], as, for example, Apple reports using values of 4 or 8 [3].

Data Anonymization through Local Differential Privacy. One way to share data while respecting differential privacy is to add noise to the data. For instance, in the randomized response technique [56], a respondent answers a sensitive binary question (*e.g.*, "What is your gender") by tossing a biased coin in secret. If the result is tail, the respondent answers honestly. Otherwise, the coin is tossed again, and the answer returned is "Male" if head and "No" if tail. This ensures that the auditor can reliably estimate the unknown proportions of sensitive attributes without knowing any individual's true answer with certainty. With Simple Random Sampling With Replacement (SRSWR [15]), this generalized randomized response method provides an unbiased estimator of these proportions while also ensuring compliance with the ϵ-differential privacy for any ϵ by adjusting the bias of the coin. The randomized response technique can be generalized to non-binary attributes (*e.g.*, age or marital status) or to sets of attributes [13], which is called Generalized Randomized Response (GRR). In addition, it can be combined with pre-processing techniques [54] (instead of SRSWR) for better privacy guarantee, and recent advances have further improved the performance of GRR [6,17,23,55,57].

P2NIA implementation: Since our study aims to highlight how P2NIA can be applied rather than providing an exhaustive comparison of private data methods, we proceed with the basic version of GRR: each colmun of the dataset (features, target and prediction) is independently flipped with a probability p selected to reach the desired privacy guarantee ϵ: $p = e^{\epsilon}/(e^{\epsilon} + k - 1)$, in which k is the number of values the feature can have.

P2NIA Fairness Estimation Reliability: As $\hat{Y}$ is computed by the platform knowing D, the resulting fairness estimator is only biased by the noise added by GRR. The auditor knows ϵ and hence p, so they can easily debias the anonymized results to recover the correct estimator value [13,17].

Mechanisms for Differentially-Private Synthetic Data Generation. Instead of adding noise to existing data, another approach consists of generating synthetic data that follows the original distribution while protecting the privacy of individual records for the original dataset. Many differentially-private data generation approaches have been proposed in the literature to achieve this objective; the interested reader can refer to [49] or [26] for recent surveys on the subject. In particular, some synthesis methods offer the possibility to specify which relationship between variables should be maintained, aligning with our goal of reliable model evaluation. Specifically, we use MST [40] and AIM [41], which are two methods operating under the *select-measure-generate* framework. In a nutshell, both methods work by first selecting a set of low-dimensional marginal queries (*i.e.*, statistics on small subsets of attributes). Afterwards, each selected marginal is measured under differential privacy by adding noise to ensure privacy. This yields a collection of noisy marginal results. Finally, a graphical model called Private-PGM [42] is constructed from those noisy marginals to infer a consistent high-dimensional data distribution to generate new synthetic data points. MST and AIM differ in the way marginals are selected. More precisely, MST performs an initial noisy measurement of marginals using a small portion of the privacy budget and then selects which one should be measured more precisely. In contrast, AIM adaptively chooses new queries in iterative rounds, using feedback from previous measurements to guide where the privacy budget should be spent. This adaptive selection can improve accuracy at the expense of increased computational cost.

P2NIA Implementation: We explicitly maintain the relationship between protected variable A, target variable Y and predictions $\hat{Y}$ from the audited model (*i.e.*, the marginals $(A,Y), (A,\hat{Y}), (Y,\hat{Y})$ and $(A,Y,\hat{Y})$) in addition to 12 2-way marginals chosen randomly to mimic the dataset. The relationship between the required privacy level ϵ and the noise introduced in the marginals differs between MST and AIM, which are detailed in the respective original papers.

P2NIA Fairness Estimation Reliability: As we explicitly conserve all marginals involved in the definition of all three fairness measures, the resulting value is unbiased.

Hence, we consider three distinct methods to implement P2NIA: GRR, MST and AIM. While the choice of GRR is driven by its appealing simplicity, MST and AIM are recent synthetic data generation methods. With each of these methods **P2NIA , the fairness estimation is reliably performed and respects differential privacy on user's data.** While each method guarantees the achievement of an unbiased fairness estimator (for an audit set Q of infinite size), as we will see in the next section, each method has a different impact on the convergence of fairness estimators.

4 Experimental Evaluation

While involving anonymized or synthetic data in audits has theoretical advantages compared to black-box audits, this section demonstrates the effectiveness of P2NIA in practice. To assess the performance of the proposed approach, we conducted experiments on two datasets commonly used in audit studies while varying the function g within P2NIA. The results demonstrate that our proposed scheme using anonymized or synthetic data achieves significantly higher accuracy than black-box audits. We first present our experimental setup before evaluating the advantage of using anonymized or synthetic data.

4.1 Experimental Setting

Datasets and Models. Experiments are performed on two standard benchmark datasets from the fair and private machine learning literature: Adult [8] and Folktables [16]. They contain demographic information from the U.S. Census with respect to 32.561 and 378.816 individuals. In both cases, the task is to predict whether an individual's income exceeds $50,000 per year (with the task *ACSIncome* on California, year 2018 for Folktables). The protected attribute is considered to be the gender.

To solve the tasks outlined above, we employ random forests as implemented in the Scikit-learn Python Library with its **RandomForestClassifier** object. Hyper-parameters were selected using a grid search to minimize the model's loss on each dataset. Further experiments using gradient boosting algorithm (**XGBClassifier**) are provided in [31].

Experimental Parameters. All datasets were split into two parts: 80% of the dataset as the training set for the model m while the remaining 20% is used as a test set. Only the test set is used as input of the function g (step 4 in Fig. 2). This process is repeated ten times with the same random seeds for the train/test split and the same model, with the results averaged across these ten iterations. All experiments are conducted on a computing cluster of homogeneous nodes powered by Intel Xeon E5-2660 v2 processors.

Reference. Since the objective is to evaluate the performance of P2NIA in the audit of fairness, we establish a reference by defining the true fairness value of the model used by the platform. Specifically, this reference corresponds to the fairness metrics computed on the test set of the datasets once they have been labeled by the model in question and is the target value that the auditor wants to estimate.

Baseline. We compare our approach with the black-box scenario in the following manner. The auditor is assumed to have knowledge of the set of possible values for each attribute ($\mathcal{X}$), but not to the overall distribution of the data ($\mathcal{D}$). The auditor draws each attribute uniformly from its possible values to generate queries. The same approach is also applied to the outputs Y when auditing fairness metrics such as Equalized Odds or Equality of Opportunity.

The performance of P2NIA is compared to the black-box audit on the two binary classification tasks from Adult and Folktables. To realize this, we instantiate P2NIA using locally anonymized data or synthetic data generated by the methods GRR [13], MST [40] or AIM [41] described in Sect. 3.2. More precisely, we used publicly available implementations of those methods [39].

4.2 Impact of Sample Size on Demographic Parity

We study the practical effectiveness of P2NIA by evaluating its performance depending on the number of samples to assess the demographic parity. The differential privacy parameter ϵ is arbitrarily set to 10.

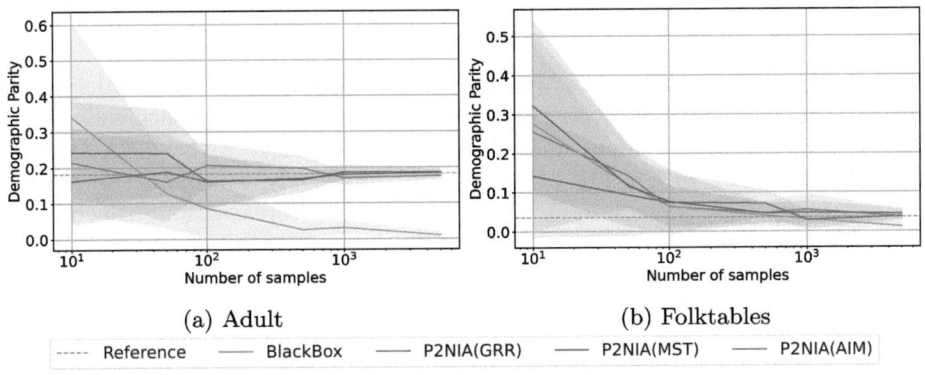

Fig. 3. Demographic parity depending on the number of samples.

Analyzing the demographic parity depending on the number of samples (Fig. 3) shows that the convergence rate of the estimator remains largely unaffected by the method used within P2NIA. This indicates that the selection of the method within the algorithm does not significantly affect the rate at which the estimator converges.

It is noteworthy that while increasing the number of samples enables a more accurate estimation, P2NIA **achieves high precision even with a modest sample size**. This contrasts with the black-box approach, in which convergence is slower and tends towards an incorrect value, resulting in unreliable fairness assessments. This outcome highlights a significant constraint of the black-box approach, namely its reliance on a dataset of significant size to achieve even an approximate solution, which is inherently biased.

4.3 Impact of Differential Privacy on Demographic Parity

We have explored the average error on demographic parity (on 5,000 samples) for different levels of differential privacy in Fig. 4.

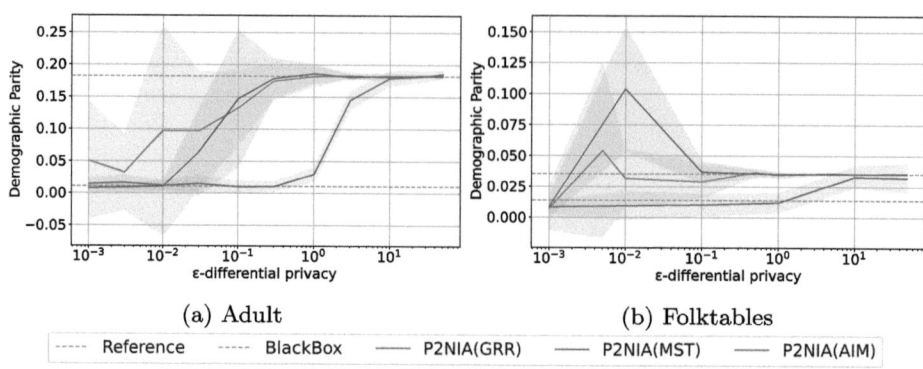

Fig. 4. Demographic parity depending on the ϵ-differential privacy in P2NIA.

Regardless of the value of ϵ, the black-box audit consistently produces the worst results for the Adult dataset, highlighting its inefficiency. Specifically, when the value of ϵ is large, the estimated demographic parity with P2NIA exhibits high accuracy, but with a low privacy level. Conversely, for small values of ϵ, the accuracy of the demographic parity estimator decreases, but the privacy protection increases.

On the Folktables dataset, P2NIA exhibits similar asymptotic behavior to that observed on the Adult dataset, reinforcing the generalizability of its performance. However, a key difference emerges in the stability of intermediate values of ϵ, for P2NIA (MST) and P2NIA (AIM). In these cases, the lack of stability can be attributed to the complexity introduced by the noisy marginals, affecting the consistency of the fairness estimates. In contrast, P2NIA (GRR) demonstrates a more controlled and predictable behavior despite converging more slowly.

These findings reveal the existing trade-off between differential privacy and estimator accuracy on demographic parity. The optimal balance between these two metrics is likely to depend on the characteristics of the dataset and the generation method employed with realistic ϵ Sect. 3.2. Notably, P2NIA **enables effective platform audit of demographic parity**, a capability that the black-box approach lacks due to its inherent bias.

4.4 Head-to-Head Comparison of P2NIA on Other Fairness Metrics

In this section, we show how P2NIA can be used to audit other fairness metrics, such as equalized odds and equality of opportunity. We set the differential privacy parameter ϵ to 10 but additional experiments for $\epsilon = 1$ can be found in [31].

For a constant value of $\epsilon = 10$, Fig. 5 demonstrates that the earlier results extend beyond demographic parity to other fairness metrics, such as equalized odds and equality of opportunity. Specifically, our scheme with locally anonymized data (*i.e.*, P2NIA(GRR)) performs comparably to, or even better than, black-box auditing. Consequently, by releasing locally anonymized data, the platform makes it possible to reliably estimate fairness. Furthermore, our

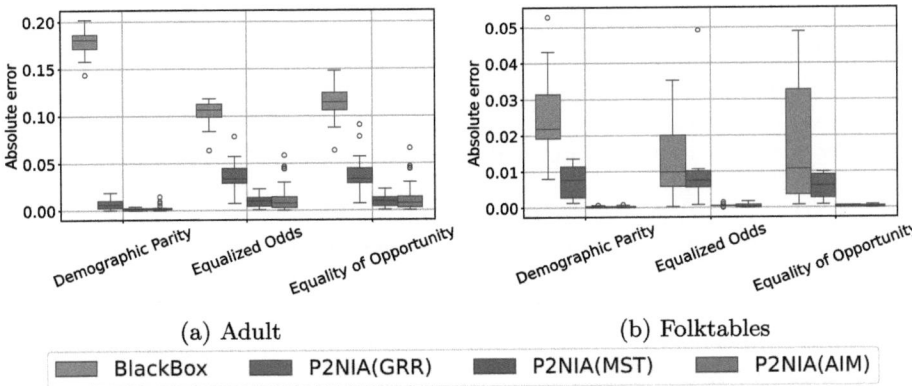

Fig. 5. Absolute difference compared to the reference for the three standard fairness metrics with $\epsilon = 10$.

scheme instantiated with synthetic data (*i.e.*, P2NIA(MST) and P2NIA(AIM)) also results in a significant error reduction. These findings highlight the usefulness of our approach as a fairness auditing tool, demonstrating **the ability of P2NIA to evaluate not only Demographic Parity but also Equalized Odds and Equality of Opportunity effectively**.

5 Related Work

Fairness auditing, particularly in black-box settings, has been extensively explored [4,14,19,46,48]. These approaches rely on analyzing the outputs of the model based on a set of queries designed to assess fairness. For black-box auditing, the fundamental lever the auditor relies on is their choice of queries. This could involve i.i.d. sampling [25], stratified sampling [50] or more complex setups [44]. However, all these methods rely on the central assumption that the auditor knows the model distribution in advance, which is unrealistic due to the knowledge asymmetry between non collaborative platforms and auditors.

Thus, there has some been recent work [10,11], arguing for more transparent ways to evaluate the assessment of algorithms with respect to ethical standards as audits are imprecise due to the lack of comprehension of these algorithms. Alternative approaches for fairness auditing include, for instance, the whitebox setting in which the model is provided to the auditor [5,11] or fairness certification [18,35,47]. The most closely related work to ours is the recent study by Yuan and Wang [58] but nonetheless their auditing setting differs significantly from ours in that the auditor is granted direct access to real labeled data from the platform. The responsibility for privacy preservation is then delegated to the auditor, who received data from real users. Although the original data must be deleted after use, privacy has already been compromised due to the data disclosure. In contrast, our approach is built to be privacy-preserving by design, without exposing raw labeled data to the auditor.

As fairness auditing often requires querying the model on user data, privacy concerns have also emerged as a fundamental issue. Dwork and co-authors [21] have already identified and prove the link between individual fairness and local differential privacy. It has also been studied in the context of fair learning [38] (*e.g.*, before model being in production) but not for audit purpose. However, [36,45] introduced differential privacy techniques to mitigate the risk of information leakage during fairness audits. Other methods, such as secure multi-party computation [52] rely on complex cryptographic techniques to ensure the privacy of queries. A key limitation of these previous works is that they focus on protecting the auditor's queries rather than the data of the entity being audited. Our approach, P2NIA, aims to bridge this gap by allowing effective fairness auditing without compromising user privacy.

6 Conclusion

To summarize, in this paper, we have first underlined an important problem for black-box audits in real scenarios: population bias due to the lack of a perfect prior for the auditor on the data distribution of the platform. This bias arises mainly due to the lack of collaboration between the platform and the auditor. We then proposed a novel audit scheme, named P2NIA, in which both parties collaborate out of mutual benefit, namely accurate estimation for the auditor and data privacy preservation plus ease of operation for the platform as the scheme is non-iterative. We empirically show on standard datasets that our scheme operates as intended for three group fairness metrics, with accurate assessment and controllable privacy guarantees.

Future work includes the study of other forms of collaborations driven by different benefits at each party. For instance, it might be beneficial for the platform to operate in a "grey-box" setting, in which it will reveal some information about the internal workings of its model, resulting in a more lightweight querying procedure by an auditor (*e.g.*, with respect to the number of queries required).

Acknowledgments. This research was supported by a Mitacs Globalink (IT40224) grant in partnership with Université du Québec À Montréal. The authors gratefully acknowledge the financial support provided by Mitacs. The authors also acknowledge the support of the French Agence Nationale de la Recherche (ANR), under grant ANR-24-CE23-7787 (project PACMAM). Sébastien Gambs is also supported by the Canada Research Chair program and a Discovery Grant from NSERC.

Disclosure of Interests. The authors have no competing interests to declare that are relevant to the content of this article.

References

1. Alaa, A., Van Breugel, B., Saveliev, E.S., Van Der Schaar, M.: How faithful is your synthetic data? Sample-level metrics for evaluating and auditing generative models. In: International Conference on Machine Learning. PMLR (2022)

2. American city and council: Avoiding bumps in the road when designing ai-powered traffic management systems. https://www.americancityandcounty.com/2024/01/26/avoiding-bumps-in-the-road-when-designing-ai-powered-traffic-management-systems/
3. Apple Inc.: Differential privacy overview (2017). https://www.apple.com/privacy/docs/Differential_Privacy_Overview.pdf
4. Bandy, J.: Problematic machine behavior: a systematic literature review of algorithm audits. In: Proceedings of the ACM on Human-Computer Interaction (2021)
5. Barocas, S., Hardt, M., Narayanan, A.: Fairness and Machine Learning: Limitations and Opportunities. MIT Press, Cambridge (2023)
6. Bassily, R., Smith, A.: Local, private, efficient protocols for succinct histograms. In: Proceedings of the Forty-Seventh Annual ACM Symposium on Theory of Computing, pp. 127–135 (2015)
7. BBC: Ai hiring tools may be filtering out the best job applicants. https://www.bbc.com/worklife/article/20240214-ai-recruiting-hiring-software-bias-discrimination
8. Becker, B., Kohavi, R.: Adult. UCI Mach. Learn. Repository (1996). https://doi.org/10.24432/C5XW20
9. Besse, P., del Barrio, E., Gordaliza, P., Loubes, J.M., Risser, L.: A survey of bias in machine learning through the prism of statistical parity. Am. Stat. **76**(2), 188–198 (2022)
10. Birhane, A., Steed, R., Ojewale, V., Vecchione, B., Raji, I.D.: AI auditing: the broken bus on the road to AI accountability. In: 2024 IEEE Conference on Secure and Trustworthy Machine Learning (SaTML), pp. 612–643. IEEE (2024)
11. Casper, S., et al.: Black-box access is insufficient for rigorous AI audits. In: The 2024 ACM Conference on Fairness, Accountability, and Transparency, pp. 2254–2272 (2024)
12. CBS News: Argentina plans to use ai to "predict future crimes and help prevent them". https://www.cbsnews.com/news/argentina-plans-to-use-ai-to-predict-future-crimes-and-help-prevent-them/
13. Chaudhuri, A., Mukerjee, R.: Randomized Response: Theory and Techniques. Routledge (2020)
14. Chen, L., Mislove, A., Wilson, C.: An empirical analysis of algorithmic pricing on amazon marketplace. In: Proceedings of the 25th International Conference on World Wide Web, pp. 1339–1349 (2016)
15. Cochran, W.G.: Sampling Techniques. Wiley, Hoboken (1977)
16. Ding, F., Hardt, M., Miller, J., Schmidt, L.: Retiring adult: new datasets for fair machine learning. In: Advances in Neural Information Processing Systems, vol. 34 (2021)
17. Domingo-Ferrer, J., Soria-Comas, J.: Multi-dimensional randomized response. IEEE Trans. Knowl. Data Eng. **34**(10), 4933–4946 (2020)
18. Duddu, V., Das, A., Khayata, N., Yalame, H., Schneider, T., Asokan, N.: Attesting distributional properties of training data for machine learning. In: European Symposium on Research in Computer Security, pp. 3–23. Springer, Cham (2024)
19. Dunna, A., Keith, K.A., Zuckerman, E., Vallina-Rodriguez, N., O'Connor, B., Nithyanand, R.: Paying attention to the algorithm behind the curtain: Bringing transparency to youtube's demonetization algorithms. In: Proceedings of the ACM on Human-Computer Interaction, vol. 6(CSCW2), pp. 1–31 (2022)
20. Dwork, C.: A firm foundation for private data analysis. Commun. ACM **54**(1), 86–95 (2011)

21. Dwork, C., Hardt, M., Pitassi, T., Reingold, O., Zemel, R.: Fairness through awareness. In: Proceedings of the 3rd Innovations in Theoretical Computer Science Conference, pp. 214–226 (2012)
22. Dwork, C., Roth, A., et al.: The algorithmic foundations of differential privacy. Found. Trends® Theor. Comput. Sci. (2014)
23. Erlingsson, Ú., Pihur, V., Korolova, A.: RAPPOR: randomized aggregatable privacy-preserving ordinal response. In: Proceedings of the 2014 ACM SIGSAC Conference on Computer and Communications Security, pp. 1054–1067 (2014)
24. European Union: Artificial intelligence act (2024). http://data.europa.eu/eli/reg/2024/1689/oj
25. Feldman, M., Friedler, S.A., Moeller, J., Scheidegger, C., Venkatasubramanian, S.: Certifying and removing disparate impact. In: proceedings of the 21th ACM SIGKDD International Conference on Knowledge Discovery and Data Mining, pp. 259–268 (2015)
26. Figueira, A., Vaz, B.: Survey on synthetic data generation, evaluation methods and GANs. Mathematics **10**(15), 2733 (2022)
27. Financial Times: Volatility: how 'algos' changed the rhythm of the market. https://www.ft.com/content/fdc1c064-1142-11e9-a581-4ff78404524e
28. Forbes: Sports AI can be a game-changing partner for coaches. https://www.forbes.com/sites/geristengel/2024/05/15/sports-ai-can-be-a-game-changing-partner-for-coaches/
29. French Government: Penal code - article 434-10 (2020). https://www.legifrance.gouv.fr/codes/article_lc/LEGIARTI000042026716/. Accessed 20 Aug 2024
30. Fukuchi, K., Hara, S., Maehara, T.: Faking fairness via stealthily biased sampling. In: Proceedings of the AAAI Conference on Artificial Intelligence (2020)
31. Garcia Bourrée, J., Lautraite, H., Gambs, S., Tredan, G., Le Merrer, E., Rottembourg, B.: P2nia: privacy-preserving non-iterative auditing. arXiv preprint arXiv:2504.00874 (2025)
32. Hardt, M., Price, E., Srebro, N.: Equality of opportunity in supervised learning. In: Advances in Neural Information Processing Systems, vol. 29 (2016)
33. Hargittai, E.: Is bigger always better? potential biases of big data derived from social network sites. Ann. Am. Acad. Pol. Soc. Sci. **659**(1), 63–76 (2015)
34. Harvard Business review: Algorithms can save networking from being business card roulette. https://hbr.org/2014/03/algorithms-can-save-networking-from-being-business-card-roulette
35. Kang, M., Li, L., Weber, M., Liu, Y., Zhang, C., Li, B.: Certifying some distributional fairness with subpopulation decomposition. Adv. Neural. Inf. Process. Syst. **35**, 31045–31058 (2022)
36. Kilbertus, N., Gascón, A., Kusner, M., Veale, M., Gummadi, K., Weller, A.: Blind justice: fairness with encrypted sensitive attributes. In: International Conference on Machine Learning, pp. 2630–2639. PMLR (2018)
37. Le Merrer, E., Pons, R., Trédan, G.: Algorithmic audits of algorithms, and the law. AI Ethics, 1–11 (2023)
38. Makhlouf, K., Stefanović, T., Arcolezi, H.H., Palamidessi, C.: A systematic and formal study of the impact of local differential privacy on fairness: Preliminary results. In: IEEE 37th Computer Security Foundations Symposium, pp. 1–16 (2024)
39. McKenna, R., Miklau, G., Sheldon, D.: Private-pgm (2021). https://github.com/journalprivacyconfidentiality/private-pgm-jpc-778/tree/v2021-10-04-jpc
40. McKenna, R., Miklau, G., Sheldon, D.: Winning the NIST contest: a scalable and general approach to differentially private synthetic data. arXiv preprint arXiv:2108.04978 (2021)

41. McKenna, R., Mullins, B., Sheldon, D., Miklau, G.: Aim: an adaptive and iterative mechanism for differentially private synthetic data. arXiv preprint arXiv:2201.12677 (2022)
42. McKenna, R., Sheldon, D., Miklau, G.: Graphical-model based estimation and inference for differential privacy. In: International Conference on Machine Learning, pp. 4435–4444. PMLR (2019)
43. Mehrabi, N., Morstatter, F., Saxena, N., Lerman, K., Galstyan, A.: A survey on bias and fairness in machine learning. ACM Comput. Surv. **54**(6), 1–35 (2021)
44. Panigutti, C., Perotti, A., Panisson, A., Bajardi, P., Pedreschi, D.: FairLens: auditing black-box clinical decision support systems. Inf. Process. Manage. **58**(5), 102657 (2021)
45. Pentyala, S., Melanson, D., De Cock, M., Farnadi, G.: Privfair: a library for privacy-preserving fairness auditing. arXiv preprint arXiv:2202.04058 (2022)
46. Sandvig, C., Hamilton, K., Karahalios, K., Langbort, C.: Auditing algorithms: research methods for detecting discrimination on internet platforms. Data and discrimination: converting critical concerns into productive inquiry (2014)
47. Shamsabadi, A.S., et al.: Confidential-profitt: confidential proof of fair training of trees. In: ICLR (2022)
48. Silva, M., Santos de Oliveira, L., Andreou, A., Vaz de Melo, P.O., Goga, O., Benevenuto, F.: Facebook ads monitor: an independent auditing system for political ads on Facebook. In: Proceedings of the Web Conference 2020, pp. 224–234 (2020)
49. Tao, Y., McKenna, R., Hay, M., Machanavajjhala, A., Miklau, G.: Benchmarking differentially private synthetic data generation algorithms. arXiv preprint arXiv:2112.09238 (2021)
50. Taskesen, B., Blanchet, J., Kuhn, D., Nguyen, V.A.: A statistical test for probabilistic fairness. In: Proceedings of the 2021 ACM Conference on Fairness, Accountability, and Transparency, pp. 648–665 (2021)
51. The Guardian: Ai better than biopsy at assessing some cancers, study finds. https://www.bbc.com/worklife/article/20240214-ai-recruiting-hiring-softwar-bias-discrimination
52. Toreini, E., Mehrnezhad, M., Van Moorsel, A.: Verifiable fairness: privacy-preserving computation of fairness for machine learning systems. In: European Symposium on Research in Computer Security, pp. 569–584. Springer (2023)
53. de Vos, M., et al.: Fairness auditing with multi-agent collaboration. In: ECAI 2024, pp. 1116–1123. IOS Press (2024)
54. Wang, S., et al.: Privacy amplification via shuffling: unified, simplified, and tightened. arXiv preprint arXiv:2304.05007 (2023)
55. Wang, T., Blocki, J., Li, N., Jha, S.: Locally differentially private protocols for frequency estimation. In: 26th USENIX Security Symposium, pp. 729–745 (2017)
56. Warner, S.L.: Randomized response: a survey technique for eliminating evasive answer bias. J. Am. Stat. Assoc. **60**(309), 63–69 (1965)
57. Ye, M., Barg, A.: Optimal schemes for discrete distribution estimation under locally differential privacy. IEEE Trans. Inf. Theory (2018)
58. Yuan, C.C.R., Wang, B.Y.: Quantitative auditing of AI fairness with differentially private synthetic data. arXiv preprint arXiv:2504.21634 (2025)

"I Forgot About You": Exploring Multi-Label Unlearning (MLU) for Responsible Facial Recognition Systems

Prommy Sultana Hossain[1]($\boxtimes$), Emanuela Marasco[1], Jessica Lin[1], and Michael King[2]

[1] George Mason University, Fairfax, VA 22030, USA
{phossai,emarasco,jessica}@gmu.edu
[2] Florida Institute of Technology, Melbourne, FL 32901, USA
michaelking@fit.edu

Abstract. The widespread adoption of machine learning and deep learning models has heightened privacy concerns, as these models can unintentionally memorize and expose personal information. Machine Unlearning (MU) has gained considerable attention for improving privacy and data control. MU addresses privacy challenges by selectively removing the influence of specific training data from deployed models. However, most current MU approaches focus on single-label classification scenarios, where each instance is assigned only one label. In contrast, Multi-Label Classification (MLC), such as those in facial recognition (facial attribute classification) systems, involve instances that can be associated with multiple, non-exclusive attribute labels. The complex interdependencies between parameters in these cases pose unique challenges when selectively removing specific knowledge. This work proposes a novel parameter space-based MU framework for MLC systems. Our data-driven generalization approach uses sparsification techniques operating directly on learned representations without retraining on the modified training data. We employ two strategies to improve state-of-the-art models for MLC unlearning: Weight Filtering, which identifies and resets critical parameters based on sensitivity and influence scores, and Weight Pruning, which strategically eliminates parameters based on their importance to the unlearned label while preserving shared representations for retained attributes. Extensive experiments demonstrate that our Weight Pruning method can achieve up to 35.5× speedup over retraining while maintaining >93% accuracy for retained labels and reducing the prediction of forgotten attributes to near zero (0.11%), a significant improvement over existing methods. The privacy analysis also confirms a substantial reduction in information leakage, which establishes a new standard for responsible facial attribute classification systems under current privacy regulations.

Keywords: Multi-label Classification · Machine Unlearning · Privacy

1 Introduction

The ubiquitous deployment of deep neural networks has created an unprecedented privacy paradox: while these systems enable remarkable capabilities in classification, they simultaneously memorize and expose sensitive personal information without explicit consent [1]. This challenge is particularly acute in facial recognition (facial attribute classification (FAC)) systems, which operate within a Multi-Label Classification (MLC) paradigm where each face simultaneously expresses multiple non-exclusive attributes–age, gender, emotion, ethnicity– encoded within shared neural representations [2,3]. Unlike traditional single-label systems, this representational entanglement creates a fundamental tension: how can we selectively remove knowledge of specific attributes while preserving the model's utility for legitimate purposes?

This tension has gained critical urgency with the emergence of privacy regulations such as the European Union's General Data Protection Regulation (GDPR), which establishes the "Right To Be Forgotten (RTBF)" as a fundamental principle [4]. Crucially, RTBF extends beyond mere data deletion to require the elimination of knowledge derived from personal data. Consider a practical scenario: an individual may exercise RTBF for emotion detection capabilities while permitting age estimation, or request removal of ethnicity classification while maintaining gender recognition. Such fine-grained privacy requirements demand sophisticated unlearning mechanisms that can surgically modify model behavior without catastrophic interference.

Machine Unlearning (MU) has emerged as the primary framework to address these demands. It offers two main paradigms: Exact Unlearning, which provides robust privacy guarantees through complete retraining but at prohibitive computational costs, and Approximate Unlearning, which achieves efficiency through direct parameter modification [5,6]. However, a critical research gap exists: existing unlearning techniques almost exclusively target Single-Label Classification (SLC) scenarios and fail catastrophically when applied to multi-label systems. When attempting to remove a single attribute from facial classification models, current methods degrade performance across all remaining attributes, rendering the system unusable [7–10].

This limitation is particularly problematic given the widespread deployment of multi-label systems in high-stakes domains. Healthcare systems must maintain diagnostic capabilities while protecting patient privacy; marketing platforms need to preserve demographic insights while respecting individual rights; and security systems require selective attribute removal without compromising legitimate functionality [11,12]. The absence of effective Multi-Label Unlearning (MLU) capabilities represents a fundamental barrier to privacy-compliant AI deployment in these critical applications.

The core technical challenge lies in the interconnected nature of multi-label representations. Unlike single-label models where each instance belongs to exactly one class, multi-label systems must handle partial label deletion (removing some but not all labels from an instance), entangled representations (shared parameters across multiple output heads), and complex label dependencies (statistical correlations between attributes). These factors create a complex optimization landscape where naive application of existing unlearning methods leads to uncontrolled performance degradation across the entire system.

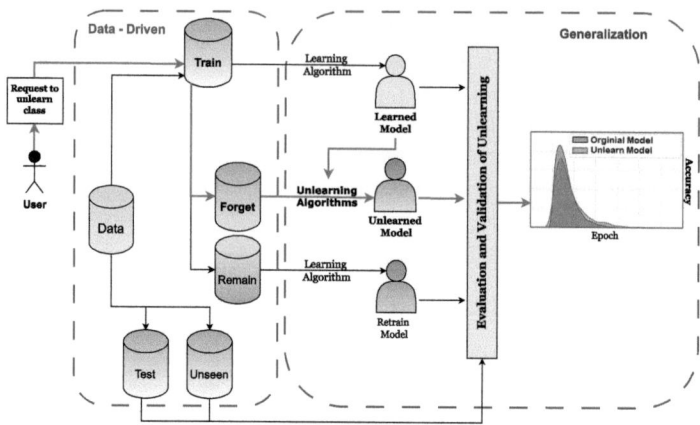

Fig. 1. The proposed data-driven generalization framework ensures the preservation of data utility while effectively unlearning a label, as indicated by the green arrow, which highlights privacy maintenance. (Color figure online)

To address these fundamental challenges, we introduce a novel data-driven generalization framework for Multi-Label Unlearning.[1] (Fig. 1). Our approach centers on model sparsification strategies–Weight Filtering (WF) and Weight Pruning (WP)–that surgically remove label-specific knowledge without compromising system-wide performance. As illustrated in the framework, when a user requests to unlearn a specific class, our system partitions the data into "Forget" and "Remain" sets, then applies targeted unlearning algorithms to produce an unlearned model that maintains utility for retained class attributes while eliminating the specified knowledge. Rather than relying on computationally expensive retraining or task-specific heuristics, our framework analyzes statistical patterns in parameter distributions to identify and neutralize parameters linked to forgotten labels while preserving the underlying model architecture [13].

The key innovation lies in our parameter-centric approach: by examining weight correlations across network layers, we can precisely target neurons and connections responsible for specific attribute predictions without solely relying on the original training data during the unlearning process [7]. This generalization capability allows the framework to adapt to diverse facial attribute classification tasks based on the learned parameter structure rather than domain-specific

---

[1] Data and code are available in Github: https://github.com/Promzi/unlearn_label.git.

modifications [14]. Our method preserves the model's original training objective while ensuring surgical modification of only the targeted label information, maintaining both utility and privacy.

Extensive empirical validation across diverse facial attribute datasets demonstrates the effectiveness of our approach: we achieve up to 35.5× computational speedup over exact retraining while maintaining >93% accuracy for retained attributes and reducing forgotten attribute prediction to near-random levels (0.11%). Comprehensive privacy analysis reveals substantial improvements in information leakage prevention, with our method achieving 54-56% residual information compared to 70%+ for existing approaches, establishing new benchmarks for privacy-compliant AI systems under current regulatory frameworks.

1.1 Main Contributions

1. **Novel Multi-Label Unlearning Framework:** We propose the first comprehensive parameter space-based framework specifically designed for multi-label machine unlearning in facial attribute classification. Our approach addresses the critical research gap in existing single-label unlearning methods by introducing Weight Filtering (WF) and Weight Pruning (WP) techniques that enable efficient model sparsification without retraining. The framework surgically removes targeted attributes while preserving interdependent label relationships through adaptive parameter-space analysis, ensuring strong privacy guarantees and mitigating data corruption risks inherent in multi-label scenarios.
2. **Comprehensive Empirical Validation:** We conduct extensive experimental validation across diverse benchmark datasets, including CelebA (adapted for multi-label settings), CIFAR-10, MNIST, and SVHN [15], and demonstrate superior performance across multiple evaluation dimensions. Our framework consistently outperforms state-of-the-art methods in utility preservation (>93% accuracy retention), computational efficiency (35.5× speedup), and output distribution integrity, establishing new performance benchmarks for multi-label unlearning in facial attribute classification and beyond.
3. **Privacy Analysis:** To analyze how parameter space modifications ensure privacy protection, we conduct experiments and show that our approach achieves significant improvement in privacy preservation (54-56% residual information vs. 70%+ for existing methods) without requiring retraining on modified datasets and provide practical privacy compliance for deployment under current regulatory frameworks.

2 Related Work

Recent advances in privacy-conscious ML have catalyzed MU development, initially through theoretical studies on convex models that provide crucial insights but face limitations with deep neural networks' non-convex optimization landscapes [16,17]. The evolution of MU research has produced three distinct methodological approaches:

Input Space: Early unlearning methods focused on alterations in the input space through data obfuscation, noise injection, label anonymization, and adversarial perturbations, which relies on direct access to the original training data during the unlearning process and introduce significant operational constraints [6]. These approaches suffer from performance degradation and privacy vulnerabilities that can be exploited by direct attacks (submitting unseen data to unlearning) and preconditioned attacks (strategically removing poisoned data) [18]. Despite defensive countermeasures including regulated algorithms and membership verification, these methods remain limited by their dependence on direct data manipulation [19].

Decision Space: Decision boundary methods directly manipulate model boundaries to replicate the behavior of the re-trained model, addressing the limitations of the input space modification [8]. However, in MLC scenarios, these methods face challenges due to complex boundary interconnections, where adjustments to individual label boundaries create cascading effects across the decision space. This approach fails in high-boundary overlap scenarios where precisely preserving retained label relationships while removing targeted information becomes impossible.

Parameter Space: These methods directly adjust model parameters to eliminate forgotten data influence, primarily in single-label unlearning scenarios. Catastrophic Forgetting k (CF-k) implements selective retraining of the final k layers while freezing initial layers, but faces optimal k-value selection challenges and retains residual information [9]. SCalable recall and unlearning unbound (SCRUB) employs a teacher-student framework that balances retained data performance while diverging on forgotten data, but shows significant degradation when managing multiple objectives [20]. UNlearning Samples with Impair-Repair (UNSIR) implements adversarial noise generation followed by model repair, but requires substantial computational resources and demonstrates incomplete restoration when noise rates are uncontrolled interference [10]. Saliency Unlearning (SalUN) identifies critical parameters through saliency map analysis but struggles with map accuracy and creates unintended side effects [21]. Despite advancing the field through learnable memory matrices within parameter space for SLC, the work by Poppi et al. [7] remains constrained by pre-trained model dependence, excessive relearning time penalties, and severe performance trade-offs. To address the limitations in parameter-space methods that expose critical deficiencies in addressing MLC unlearning challenges, our proposed *Weight Filtering* strategy advances beyond the SOTA by efficiently managing single-label unlearning and MLU scenarios while preserving classification integrity. Additionally, *Weight Pruning* offers a groundbreaking approach to unlearning, reducing computational demands and providing guarantees, which are crucial for maintaining utility in MLC systems through precise parameter control.

3 Preliminaries

MU in MLC presents the complex problem of surgically removing target label knowledge from trained deep neural networks such that the model's behavior matches that of a model retrained without the forgotten labels, but achieved without the prohibitive cost of complete retraining. Let $\mathcal{D} = \{x_i, y_i\}_{i=1}^{N}$ denote the training dataset, where $x_i \in \mathcal{X}$ represents an input vector in the input space $\mathcal{X} \subseteq \mathbb{R}^d$, with d denoting the input dimensionality. Each input instance x_i is associated with a label vector $y_i \in \{0, 1\}^{\mathcal{K}}$, where $\mathcal{K}$ represents the total number of possible labels (e.g., facial attributes like Arched_Eyebrows, Bald, Oval_Face). Each element in y_i is a binary indicator denoting the corresponding attribute's presence (1) or absence (0).

In MLC setting, where each instance x_i can simultaneously belong to multiple labels, selectively forgetting an entire label $u \in \mathcal{K}$ presents unique challenges due to the interrelated nature of label representations [11,22]. MLC label overlap forms interconnected networks of shared attribute representations, unlike SLC with distinct label boundaries [23]. The interconnectedness makes removing a label difficult, as its information might be intertwined with shared representations needed for other attributes, risking privacy leaks through indirect associations. Retraining without the unlearning attribute ensures its removal, but is computationally expensive for large-scale applications.

Let f_{w_0} be the original learned model trained on $\mathcal{D}$, optimally parameterized by w_0. For any input $x \in \mathcal{D}$, the output of the MLC model $f_{w_0}(x) = [f_{w_0}^k(x)]_{k=1}^{K}$, where $f_{w_0}^k(x)$ represents the logit score for the kth label. The final predictions are obtained by applying a threshold function to each logit, which allows for simultaneous attribute assignments. Based on established literature demonstrating successful unlearning through weight influence analysis [7], our study partitions the parameter space by identifying weights associated with the target unlearned label $u \in \mathcal{K}$ and allowing direct modifications to the influential parameters without relying on the original training data throughout the unlearning process.

Hence, given an unlearning request for a specific label u, we define the forget set $\mathcal{W}_f$ as $\mathcal{W}_f = \{w\{(x, y)\} \in w_0 \mid \mathcal{I}(w, u) > \epsilon\}$, where $\mathcal{I}(w, u)$ denotes the influence function that quantifies the contribution of weights towards classifying the target unlearned label, and ϵ represents the threshold determining the significant influence. The rest of the weights in the parameter space are placed in the remaining set $\mathcal{W}_r = \{w_0 \setminus \mathcal{W}_f\}$.

Next section presents the detailed methodology on measuring the influence function and subsequent weight modifications, where we aim to unlearn the information of $\mathcal{W}_f$ from f_{w_0}—without re-learning $\mathcal{W}_r$—and updating the parameters $w_0 \rightarrow w'$, where w' represents the updated parameters obtained by the unlearning methods. To validate the performance of the unlearning model $f_{w'}$, we train a model, which we call the *Retrain* model f_{w^*}, using the original learning algorithm from scratch without the targeted unlearned label u. This will be the optimal unlearning model used as the baseline for this study. In this unlearning problem, we expect the unlearning model $f_{w'}$ to be as similar to the retained model f_{w^*} as possible.

4 Methodology

We propose a parameter space-based unlearning framework that operates directly on the model's learned representations. Our approach follows a data-driven generalization framework, which identifies and partitions the parameter space based on the weights' influence on the target unlearned label u. We identify weights significantly contributing to label u classification through influence function analysis, storing them in the forget set $\mathcal{W}_f$, while retaining other weights in the remaining set $\mathcal{W}_r$. The *generalization* nature in our unlearning method is achieved through a two-phase optimization strategy: selective parameter modification followed by targeted fine-tuning to preserve the model utility. Formally, let $w'_u = \Phi(w_0, u, \mathcal{W}_f)$, $w' = \psi(w'_u, \mathcal{W}_r)$ where w'_u denotes the intermediate parameters after selective modification of label u, Φ focuses exclusively on adapting parameters related to the unlearned label, and ψ refines the entire parameter space using the remaining learned parameters. Through this framework, we can modify the influencing parameters of the target unlearned label without solely relying on the original training data or eliminating any data points from $\mathcal{D}$ during the unlearning process, as this could inadvertently affect the model's performance on the remaining labels due to shared attribute representations. We introduce two novel strategies for selective parameter modification: **Weight Filtering** and **Weight Pruning**, which strategically modify parameters based on their correlation to the unlearned label while preserving overall model performance.

4.1 Weight Filtering

Deep neural networks trained on multi-label data create intricate shared representations and memorize training data in their parameter space, posing privacy risks. Although existing approaches focus on data or decision boundary modifications, we observe that the original model f_{w_0} parameters show varying influence on label predictions, allowing selective parameter modification for targeted unlearning while maintaining model utility. Motivated by recent advances in influence functions and parameter sensitivity analysis [24,25], we propose weight filtering that identifies and neutralizes parameters specifically encoding information about the unlearned label[2]. For each w_{ik} associated with weight i and label $k \in \mathcal{K}$, we calculate a sensitivity score:

$$S(w_{ik}) = |\frac{\partial \mathcal{L}}{\partial w_{ik}}| \tag{1}$$

that quantifies its impact on the model's standard loss function $\mathcal{L}$. Furthermore, we compute an influence score $\mathcal{I}(x_i)$ for each training point in $\mathcal{D}$ to locate the specific influential data points that contribute most to the classification of the

---

[2] Data and code are available in Github: https://github.com/Promzi/unlearn_label.git

unlearned label u, using the formula shown in [25], without retraining on the modified training data.

$$\mathcal{I}(x_i) = -\nabla_{w_0}\mathcal{L}(x_i^{\text{pert}}, w_0) \cdot H^{-1} \cdot \nabla_{w_0}\mathcal{L}(x_i, w_0) \tag{2}$$

where x_i^{pert} represents a perturbed version of the original training example x_i, H is the Hessian matrix that captures the loss surface curvature, providing insight into how x_i affected the f_{w_0} model decision. As $\mathcal{I}(x_i)$ identified data points, $x_i' \in \mathcal{D}$, that contribute to the classification of the unlearned label u. We can then construct the forget set $\mathcal{W}_f$ in two steps; First, a sensitivity score ($S(w_{iu})$) is calculated to analyze the influence of weights through network activation patterns for classification of u; second, a composite score ($\mathcal{S}_{i\mathcal{K}}$) examines the interaction of all attributes with weights associated with u during forward propagation [24]. These steps facilitates our comprehension of the shared representation of weights within the learned model, and assists us in establishing a threshold for filtering the weights of u.

The sensitivity score $S(w_{iu})$ for each weight in w_0 to the unlearned label u is calculated using the following equation, $S(w_{iu}) = |\frac{\partial \mathcal{L}}{\partial w_{iu}}|$, while the composite score, $\mathcal{S}_{i\mathcal{K}} = (S(w_{ik}))^T \cdot S(w_{iu})$, comprehensively measures each weight i in w_0 for each $k \in \mathcal{K}$ to understand its association of k to u. The resulting representation matrix of $\mathcal{S}_{i\mathcal{K}}$ contains the association of retained labels with unlearned labels for each $i \in w_0$. Hence the dimensions of $\mathcal{S}_{i\mathcal{K}}$ is $\mathcal{K} \times |u|$ for each i, as the dimension of $(S(w_{ik}))^T$ is $\mathcal{K} \times |w_0|$ and the dimension of $S(w_{iu})$ is $|w_0| \times |u|$. Therefore, the forget set $\mathcal{W}_f$ now will contain parameters that require modification to unlearn the knowledge of the label u, which can be written as $\mathcal{W}_f \leftarrow \{w\{x_i'\} \mid \exists w_{iu} : (w_{iu} \text{ influences } f_{w_0}^u(x_i))\}$.

The sensitivity score of the u label then guides the selective modification of the parameters of $w(x_i') \in \mathcal{W}_f$ according to:

$$w_{ik}' = \begin{cases} 0 \text{ or } \mathcal{N}(0, \sigma^2) & \text{if } S_{iu} < \phi \\ w_{ik} & \text{otherwise} \end{cases}$$

where ϕ is an adaptive threshold that determines parameter modification to balancing unlearning effectiveness to model performance. This adaptive threshold dynamically adjusts based on the loss landscape curvature during fine-tuning, preventing over-filtering or under-filtering as the model converges. The relationship between the unlearned label u and the retained label k influences the hierarchy of attribute importance, with higher overlap requiring a more conservative threshold adaptation to preserve shared representations [26]. This targeted strategy preserves crucial parameters and maintains representations of remaining attributes while modifying only those below the threshold for the unlearned label. To verify complete unlearning, we employ a secondary verification process to confirm the removal of explicit and implicit label representations using attribute inference attacks and membership inference attacks with shadow datasets (data points not involved in learning or unlearning) [19]. The process concludes with a fine-tuning phase, which is discussed in later sections. Weight Filtering operates directly on parameter space through influence functions, comprehensively removing sensitive information while maintaining prediction certainty for non-target attributes.

4.2 Weight Pruning

We develop weight pruning as a more efficient alternative to address the computational challenges of weight filtering, which scales cubically due to full Hessian matrix calculations. This method achieves quicker unlearning with substantially lower computational cost by utilizing only diagonal Hessian elements and first-order gradients, resulting in linear time complexity.[3] Weight pruning determines the importance of the parameters through a composite metric combining sensitivity analysis and second-order derivatives.

$$I(w_{ik}) = \alpha S(w_{ik}) + \beta(\frac{1}{2}H_{ii}w_{ik}^2), \tag{3}$$

where $S(w_{ik})$ is the gradient magnitude calculated as in equation (eq. 1), and the second term represents local curvature using only the diagonal Hessian element H_{ii}. Hyperparameters α and β balance gradient-based sensitivity and curvature information, optimized through cross-validation. The construction of the forget set $\mathcal{W}_f$ is then performed similarly to the weight filtering method. However, unlike weight filtering's binary threshold approach, weight pruning establishes three thresholds—ϕ_l, ϕ_m, and ϕ_h—set at the 25th, 50th, and 75th percentiles of the importance score distribution. This enables hierarchical parameter modification:

- Parameters with $I(w_{ik}) < \phi_l$ are set to zero.
- Parameters with $\phi_l \leq I(w_{ik}) < \phi_h$ are scaled by $\exp(-\lambda I(w_{ik}))$ where λ controls the decay rate.
- Parameters with $I(w_{ik}) \geq \phi_h$ undergo fine-tuning with reduced learning rate α_r.

This granular control allows the method to adapt pruning percentages through each unlearning iteration, dynamically balancing unlearning effectiveness and model utility. This iterative approach makes weight pruning particularly suitable for large-scale models where full Hessian computation would be prohibitive.

4.3 Generalization

Generalization in multi-label neural networks addresses the challenges of selectively removing attribute information without disrupting shared representations, architecture, or dataset characteristics. Our approach implements a constrained optimization strategy that balances effective unlearning with preservation of essential cross-label representations. The fine-tuning phase , optimizes model parameters while preserving unlearning effects through two key mechanisms:

---

[3] Data and code are available in Github: https://github.com/Promzi/unlearn_label.git.

1. Parameter updates using gradients computed exclusively from the remaining set $\mathcal{W}_r$.
2. Constrained updates for filtered weights $\mathcal{W}_u$ associated with the unlearned label: $w'_{ik} \leftarrow \min(\max(w'_{ik}, w_{iu} - \epsilon), w_{iu} + \epsilon)$

This constraint ensures filtered weights remain within an ϵ distance of their modified values while allowing sufficient flexibility for utility preservation.

5 Limitation

Our research addresses computational overhead in parameter-based unlearning but faces several constraints. While Weight Filtering method shows strong utility preservation and privacy guarantees, it incurs $O(n^3 + md)$ time complexity for networks with n parameters, m samples, and d label dimensions due to complete Hessian computation. Weight Pruning method reduces this to $O(n + md)$ using diagonal Hessian elements while maintaining comparable effectiveness. Our approach focuses on unlearning specific information representations rather than completely removing data. Experiments revealed that removing more than 20% of influential data points completely significantly degrades model utility, consistent with previous findings [17, 27, 28]. Additionally, our constrained optimization in fine-tuning may limit finding optimal solutions when unlearning conflicts with attribute preservation, while threshold selection requires careful calibration.

6 Experimental Settings

Datasets. We conducted extensive experiments across multiple facial attribute classification datasets (CelebA [29], MUFAC [15], Vggface2 [30], and benchmark vision datasets (CIFAR-10, MNIST, and SVHN) to evaluate our unlearning methods' performance under diverse conditions. ***Baselines.*** We implemented several SOTA parameter-space unlearning techniques as benchmarks: *Retrain* (baseline), *CF-k* [9], *SCRUB* [20], *UNSIR* [10], and *SalUN* [21]. ***Implementation.*** The research was conducted using an NVIDIA GeForce RTX 4060 GPU, Intel Core i9-12900K CPU, 64GB DDR5 RAM, with CUDA 11.8, PyTorch 2.0.1, Python 3.12.4, on Ubuntu 22.04 LTS. For facial attribute classification (FAC), we fine-tuned pre-trained ResNet-18 and ResNet-50 models by replacing the final fully connected layer and applying multi-label sigmoid activation. ResNet-50 was trained from scratch with appropriate input normalization and softmax activation for standard image datasets for single-label classification. Dataset configurations were organized with 65% for training ($\mathcal{D}$), 25% validation ($\mathcal{D}_v$) and 10% test ($\mathcal{D}_t$) data, with verified integrity to ensure no overlap between sets. The test set assesses bias from the validation set as these data are not used in training or validation. Forget ($\mathcal{W}_f$) and remaining ($\mathcal{W}_r$) sets are established based on weight contributions to the unlearned label u, ensuring $\mathcal{W}_f \cap \mathcal{W}_r = \varnothing$.

Data preprocessing included resizing, random transformations for training data (horizontal flips, affine transformations, and color adjustments), while validation and test data only underwent resizing and tensor conversion. The training procedure employed a Stochastic Gradient Descent optimizer with 0.9 momentum, a constant learning rate of 0.01, a weight decay of 5e-4, a batch size of 64, and 50 epochs. We used Binary-Cross Entropy loss for multi-label tasks and Cross-Entropy loss for single-label classification, with a random seed of 42 for reproducibility.

Metrics. For utility guarantees, we measure the model's ability to maintain performance on preserved attribute while reducing accuracy on unlearned attribute, using three accuracy metics on: $\mathcal{D}$, $\mathcal{D}_v$ and $\mathcal{D}_t$ [15,31]. We also evaluate the efficacy of shared representation by examining the correlation between weight importance and attribute performance. For privacy guarantees, we implement membership inference attacks (MIA) and attribute inference attacks (AIA) to measure whether unlearned attribute information remains extractable from model representation, with lower attack success rates indicating more substantial unlearning effectiveness [33].

Hyperparameter Sensitivity. We assess how sensitive our Weight Filtering technique is to its key hyperparameters: the forgetting strength ϵ and the convergence threshold ϕ. Where Table 1 reports representative results for varying ϵ (with fixed ϕ) and varying ϕ (with fixed ϵ). We observe that ϵ has a dominant effect on performance. Smaller ϵ (stronger forgetting) consistently increases the forgetting score but at a cost to accuracy, whereas larger ϵ preserves accuracy but weakens forgetting. By contrast, changing ϕ produces only modest changes in both accuracy and forgetting. For instance, reducing ϵ from 1.0 to 0.1 (with $\phi = 1.0$) might drop accuracy from 90.0% to 85.0% while boosting the forgetting score from 70.0% to 95.0%. Varying ϕ between 0.01 and 1.0 (with $\epsilon = 0.5$) only shifts accuracy by a few points and has a much smaller impact on forgetting. These trends indicate that ϵ primarily governs the trade-off between utility and forgetting, whereas ϕ mainly fine-tunes the unlearning update.

Table 1. Impact of varying ϵ and ϕ on model accuracy on predicting the attribute "Brown_Hair" and forgetting effectiveness of attribute "Gender". (First three rows fix $\phi = 1.0$ and vary ϵ; last two rows fix $\epsilon = 0.5$ and vary ϕ.

ϵ	ϕ	Accuracy (%)	Forgetting (%)
0.1	1.0	85.0	95.0
0.5	1.0	88.0	85.0
1.0	1.0	90.0	70.0
0.5	0.01	87.0	86.0
0.5	0.10	88.0	85.0

We tune hyperparameters ϵ and ϕ, calibrate ϵ for utility-forgetting trade-offs, and set ϕ roughly. Influence scores are computed using gradients and inverse Hessian approximations. Parameters above the threshold are zeroed, while those below are pruned based on the threshold index.

7 Performance Evaluation

7.1 Utility Guarantee

An efficient unlearning method should minimize knowledge of the unlearned attribute while preserving performance on the retained attribute [18,19]. We evaluate our proposed methods through comprehensive experiments across two scenarios: *(1)* Label-specific unlearning in MLC using pre-trained ResNet-18/50 on facial attribute datasets. *(2)* Label-specific unlearning in SLC using ResNet-50 on both facial attribute (MUFAC) and standard vision datasets (CIFAR-10, MNIST, SVHN).

Unlearning in Multi-Label Classification. The deployment of facial attribute classification has raised significant privacy concerns, particularly regarding sensitive attributes such as gender and age in automated decision-making. These concerns are especially relevant in applications such as job search systems [34] and healthcare [35], where algorithmic bias can perpetuate discrimination. We evaluated our unlearning methods to address these challenges by removing the targeted label information while preserving other attributes. From the complete set of attributes available in the datasets, we selected a representative subset of 10 diverse facial attributes ($\mathcal{K}$ = {Arched_Eyebrows, Bald, Big_Lips, Brown_Hair, Double_Chin, Gender, No_Beard, Oval_Face, Pointy_Nose, Young_Old}) to demonstrate our approach, as showing results for all attributes would be impractical. After fine-tuning pre-trained models to classify these attributes with ≈ 98% accuracy, we focused on unlearning specific-label classification while maintaining performance on the other attributes. $\mathcal{W}_f = \{\forall\ w(x' \in \mathcal{D})\}$ contains parameters of data influencing u label classification, while the remaining parameters are set to $\mathcal{W}_r$. Table 2 shows the variation in the performance of attribute classification between different unlearning methods ($f_{w'}$). The original model demonstrates consistent accuracy (96-97%) across all datasets. Baseline methods show different levels of performance degradation: Retrain experiences minor generalization loss (3-4% drop), CF-3 performs poorly (37-50% accuracy), while SCRUB, UNSIR, and SalUN show progressive improvements (81-89% range). Our proposed methods outperform all baselines, with Weight Pruning consistently maintaining accuracy above 93% and Weight Filtering showing robust performance above 91%. This demonstrates our methods' effectiveness in preserving model utility while selectively removing targeted information.

Table 2. Performance comparison of unlearning methods on multi-label FAC. Models unlearn gender classification while maintaining accuracy on other attributes. Results show the attribute classification accuracy (%) without the unlearned attribute on training ($\mathcal{D}$), validation ($\mathcal{D}_v$) and test ($\mathcal{D}_t$) data. **Bold** and *italic* values indicate the best and second-best performance on the CelebA and VggFace2 datasets for each model.

Model	CelebA [29]						VggFace2 [30]					
	ResNet-18			ResNet-50			ResNet-18			ResNet-50		
	$\mathcal{D}$	$\mathcal{D}_v$	$\mathcal{D}_t$	$\mathcal{D}$	$\mathcal{D}_v$	$\mathcal{D}_t$	$\mathcal{D}$	$\mathcal{D}_v$	$\mathcal{D}_t$	$\mathcal{D}$	$\mathcal{D}_v$	$\mathcal{D}_t$
Original	96.87	95.45	96.32	97.12	96.89	96.74	96.43	95.87	96.22	96.78	96.12	96.45
Retrain	92.34	93.21	91.78	93.67	94.45	93.12	91.98	92.65	93.23	93.45	93.87	92.98
CF-3	42.54	48.23	45.67	37.89	42.11	39.76	49.87	50.12	47.34	44.12	45.23	43.67
SCRUB	82.56	81.45	83.21	84.23	83.89	83.67	81.98	82.12	80.87	83.45	82.87	84.23
UNSIR	88.78	87.45	89.21	86.98	88.23	87.65	88.12	87.89	86.45	89.12	88.45	87.98
SalUN	89.34	88.76	88.98	87.89	88.65	88.23	89.76	88.45	87.98	88.12	89.23	88.67
WF	91.78	92.12	93.21	92.87	91.45	92.34	93.45	**94.12**	92.67	**94.23**	92.98	*93.78*
WP	*93.67*	*94.23*	**95.12**	**94.12**	**94.78**	*93.89*	92.45	*93.76*	**94.87**	*93.98*	**94.12**	93.56

Note: WF = Weight Filtering and WP = Weight Pruning

Table 3. Performance comparison of unlearning methods on single-label age classification after removing label $u = \{31-45\}$. Results show classification accuracy (%) on training ($\mathcal{D}$), validation ($\mathcal{D}_v$), and test ($\mathcal{D}_t$) data using MUFAC dataset with ResNet-50. The original model achieved 96% accuracy before unlearning.

Models	Retrain	CF-3	SCRUB	UNSIR	SalUN	**WF**	**WP**
Acc on $\mathcal{D}$	92.34	38.45	65.78	82.67	78.89	91.45	93.12
Acc on $\mathcal{D}_v$	93.12	37.89	63.21	81.34	79.23	92.34	92.87
Acc on $\mathcal{D}_t$	91.87	34.67	67.54	83.21	80.45	90.78	94.12

Unlearning in Single-Label Classification. We evaluated the efficacy of our methods in SLC scenarios to validate them beyond multi-label settings. This capability addresses critical privacy concerns in FAC systems, particularly for selectively removing demographic information that could enable discriminatory practices, such as dating apps charging higher prices for older users [36,37]. We use the MUFAC dataset that classifies East Asian facial images into one of five age groups $\mathcal{K} = \{$0-6, 13-16, 20-30, 31-45, 46-60$\}$, with a pretrained ResNet-50 model and unlearning $u = \{$31-45$\}$ age label. Hence, $\mathcal{W}_f$ consists of parameters with large influence on label u. After unlearning this specific experiment, we implement distance-based heuristics to reassign instances from the unlearned label to neighboring retained labels based on decision boundary, as demonstrated in [8]. Table 3 demonstrates that our proposed methods significantly outperform baselines in maintaining classification accuracy. Weight pruning achieved consistently high performance (92-94%) across all evaluation sets, with Weight Filtering showing similar efficiency (90-92%). In contrast, baseline methods struggled with precise parameter adjustments needed for specific label unlearning in the MUFAC dataset, with CF-3 showing severe degradation (34-38%), and SCRUB (63-67%), UNSIR (81-83%) and SalUN (78-80%) demonstrating moderate performance.

Table 4. Success rates (%) for Attribute Inference Attack (AIA) and Membership Inference Attack (MIA) after unlearning on the CelebA dataset. Lower scores indicate better privacy; 50% denotes ideal unlearning.

Attack Type	Retrain	CF-3	SCRUB	UNSIR	SalUN	WF	**WP**
AIA	50.13	72.00	81.00	78.50	84.00	65.00	**46.00**
MIA	50.06	68.50	76.30	74.20	79.10	62.40	**50.06**

7.2 Privacy Guarantee

Effective unlearning requires complete knowledge removal from model parameters to prevent information leakage through any pathway. We evaluate label-level unlearning using two complementary frameworks: Attribute Inference Attack (AIA) and Membership Inference Attack (MIA), which assess whether label-specific information remains discoverable after unlearning [38–40]. We present results for the CelebA dataset (experimental setting as Sect. 7.1) as it contains rich demographic attributes that are particularly challenging to unlearn due to their entangled representations in the model's parameter space. This dataset provides the most stringent test case for privacy guarantees in facial attribute recognition systems.

Table 4 consolidates the observed success rates of AIA and MIA across all evaluated methods, highlighting the superior privacy performance of our Weight Pruning approach relative to both retraining and competitive baselines. As for AIA, the Retrain baseline achieved near-random prediction rates (50.13%), indicating optimal attribute removal. Among the baselines, CF-3 showed moderate information leakage (72%), while SCRUB, UNSIR, and SalUN demonstrated substantial retained knowledge (75-85%). Our Weight Filtering method achieved improved protection (65%), while Weight Pruning performed exceptionally well (46%), actually pushing the attacker's inference capabilities below random guessing by introducing uncertainty that actively confounds attribute inference attempts. Similarly, MIA results showed our Weight Pruning method closely aligned with retraining (50.06%), effectively eliminating both explicit representations and implicit correlations of forgotten label information. Our method achieves near-minimal privacy leakage by minimizing the KL-divergence between confidence distributions of in-label and out-label samples. Our parameter space-based unlearning framework ensures strong privacy with theoretical limits on information leakage, as confirmed by empirical results against advanced inference attacks. For AIA and MIA, a score near 50% denotes optimal unlearning.

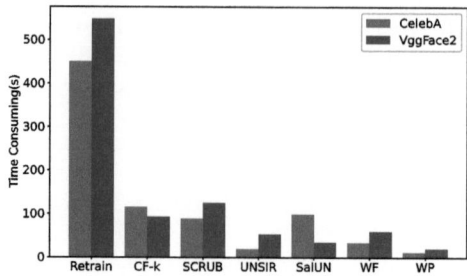

Fig. 2. The time it takes to run each unlearning method to unlearn a class u in MLC experiments Sect. 7.1. The *"Retrain"* time represents the time it takes to learn from scratch.

7.3 Runtime Analysis

We analyze the computational efficiency of different unlearning methods by examining their execution times for unlearning a label (experimental setting MLC). All methods demonstrate significantly reduced computational costs compared to complete retraining as shown in Fig. 2. For CelebA dataset, Weight Filtering and Weight Pruning require only 34 and 12 s, respectively, representing a speed-up factor of approximately 9.15x and 27.45x compared to retraining. These efficiency gains are even more pronounced on the larger VggFace2 dataset (3.31 million images), where our methods achieve remarkable speed-up factors of 13.2x and 35.5x. Weight Pruning demonstrates superior efficiency and is more suitable for large-scale deployment, showcasing its practical value for real-world MU applications.

7.4 Distribution of Entropy of Model Output

We assess unlearning effectiveness by analyzing the model's loss distributions (Binary-Cross Entropy for MLC and Cross-Entropy for single-class classification). Effective unlearning yields entropy patterns like those of a *Retrain* model; deviations suggest incomplete unlearning or leakage (Streisand effect) [41]. Figure 3 shows entropy distributions for CelebA (MLC) and MUFAC (SLC) datasets. The original model has low entropy across all sets, with the Retrain model slightly increasing entropy across training ($\mathcal{D}$), validation ($\mathcal{D}_v$), and test ($\mathcal{D}_t$) sets. In MLC, SalUN's higher entropy hints at leakage and incomplete unlearning. Weight Filtering and Pruning methods maintain distribution patterns, confirming successful targeted forgetting while preserving model integrity.

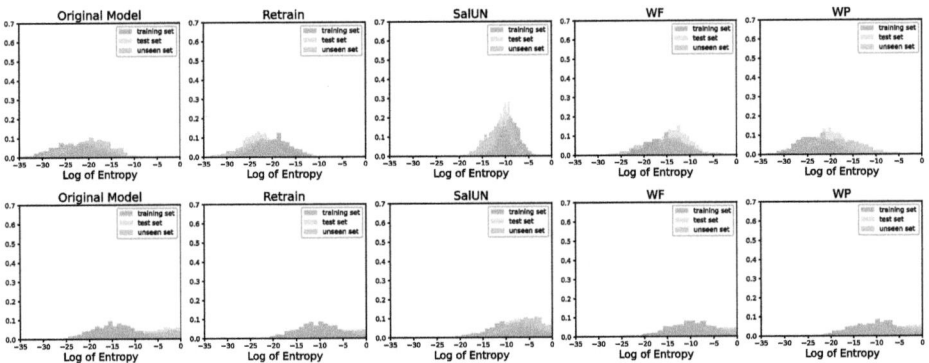

Fig. 3. Entropy distribution analysis across data partitions (training, test, unseen sets). **First row:** CelebA dataset with MLC attributes $y = \{u, k\}$ (Sect. 7.1). **Second row:** MUFAC dataset classifying single-label $y = \{k\}$ while unlearning u label (Sect. 7.1). Distributions show entropy values before unlearning ('Original Model') compared with baseline methods and approaches.

8 Conclusion

This paper introduces a parameter space-based framework for multi-label unlearning in facial attribute classification systems. Our Weight Filtering and Weight Pruning methods selectively remove specific attribute knowledge while preserving shared representations essential for retained attributes, without solely relying on the original training data. Our experiments show that our approach surpasses current methods; Weight Pruning achieves a 35.5× speedup over retraining, keeping retained label accuracy above 93% and lowering forgotten attribute predictions to 0.11%. Privacy analysis reveals a 46% AIA score, hindering inference beyond random guessing, with MIA results (50.06%) comparable to full retraining. These results establish a new benchmark for responsible facial attribute classification systems under privacy regulations. The impact on identity verification is not yet fully understood, posing a challenge for machine unlearning. We suggest a pilot study to ensure accuracy when users withdraw consent, though we currently make no broad identity claims. Future research will scale to larger architectures and refine privacy-utility tradeoffs in multi-label unlearning.

References

1. Attard-Frost, B., De los Ríos, A., Walters, D.R.: The ethics of AI business practices: a review of 47 AI ethics guidelines. AI and Ethics, vol. 3, no. 2, pp. 389–406 (2023)
2. Gündoğdu, E., Unal, A., Unal, G.: A study regarding machine unlearning on facial attribute data. In: 2024 IEEE 18th International Conference on Automatic Face and Gesture Recognition (FG), pp. 1–5 (2024). https://doi.org/10.1109/FG59268.2024.10581972

3. Zhang, S., Feng, Y., Sadeh, N.: Facial recognition: understanding privacy concerns and attitudes across increasingly diverse deployment scenarios. In: Seventeenth Symposium on Usable Privacy and Security (SOUPS 2021), pp. 243–262 (2021)
4. Regulation(EU) 2016/679 of the European Parliament and of the Council of 27 April 2016 on the protection of natural persons with regard to the processing of personal data and on the free movement of such data, and repealing Directive 95/46/ec (General Data Protection Regulation). OJ, vol. L 119, pp. 1–88 (2016)
5. Bourtoule, L., et al.: Machine unlearning. In: 2021 IEEE Symposium on Security and Privacy (SP), pp. 141–159 (2021)
6. Xu, H., Zhu, T., Zhang, L., Zhou, W., Yu, P.S.: Machine unlearning: a survey. ACM Comput. Surv. **56**(1), Article 9 (2023)
7. Poppi, S., Sarto, S., Cornia, M., Baraldi, L., Cucchiara, R.: Multi-class unlearning for image classification via weight filtering. IEEE Intell. Syst. 1–8 (2024)
8. Chen, M., Gao, W., Liu, G., Peng, K., Wang, C.: Boundary unlearning: rapid forgetting of deep networks via shifting the decision boundary. In: Proceedings of the IEEE/CVF Conference on Computer Vision and Pattern Recognition, pp. 7766–7775 (2023)
9. Goel, S., Prabhu, A., Sanyal, A., Lim, S., Torr, P., Kumaraguru, P.: Towards adversarial evaluations for inexact machine unlearning. arXiv preprint arXiv:2201.06640 (2022)
10. Tarun, A.K., Chundawat, V.S., Mandal, M., Kankanhalli, M.: fast yet effective machine unlearning. IEEE Trans. Neural Netw. Learn. Syst. 1–10 (2023)
11. Priyadharshini, M., Banu, A.F., Sharma, B., Chowdhury, S., Rabie, K., Shongwe, T.: Hybrid multi-label classification model for medical applications based on adaptive synthetic data and ensemble learning. Sensors (2023). https://doi.org/10.3390/s23156836
12. Gérardin, C., et al.: Multilabel classification of medical concepts for patient clinical profile identification. Artifi. Intell. Med. (2022). https://doi.org/10.1016/j.artmed.2022.10231
13. Sai, S., et al.: Machine un-learning: an overview of techniques, applications, and future directions. Cogn. Comput. **16**(2), 482–506 (2024)
14. Choi, D., Choi, S., Lee, E., Seo, J., Na, D.: Towards efficient machine unlearning with data augmentation: guided loss-increasing (GLI) to prevent the catastrophic model utility drop. In: Proceedings of the IEEE/CVF Conference on Computer Vision and Pattern Recognition (CVPR) Workshops, pp. 93–102 (2024)
15. Choi, D., Na, D.: Towards machine unlearning benchmarks: forgetting the personal identities in facial recognition systems. arXiv preprint arXiv:2311.02240 (2023)
16. Asi, H., Duchi, J., Fallah, A., Javidbakht, O., Talwar, K.: Private adaptive gradient methods for convex optimization. In: International Conference on Machine Learning, pp. 383–392 (2021)
17. Dwork, C.: Differential privacy: a survey of results. In: International Conference on Theory and Applications of Models of Computation, pp. 1–19 (2008)
18. Liu, Z., Ye, H., Chen, C., Zheng, Y., Lam, K.: Threats, attacks, and defenses in machine unlearning: a survey. arXiv preprint arXiv:2403.13682 2024
19. Xu, J., Wu, Z., Wang, C., Jia, X.: Machine unlearning: solutions and challenges. IEEE Trans. Emerging Top. Comput. Intell. **8**(3), 2150–2168 (2024)
20. Kurmanji, M., Triantafillou, P., Hayes, J., Triantafillou, E.: towards unbounded machine unlearning. Adv. Neural Inf. Process. Syst. **36** (2024)
21. Fan, C., Liu, J., Zhang, Y., Wong, E., Wei, D., Liu, S.: Salun: empowering machine unlearning via gradient-based weight saliency in both image classification and generation. arXiv preprint arXiv:2310.12508 (2023)

22. Liu, X., et al.: Emotion classification for short texts: an improved multilabel method. Hum. Soc. Sci. Commun. (2023). https://doi.org/10.1057/s41599-023-01816-6
23. Fallah, H., Bruno, E., Bellot, P., Murisasco, E.: Exploiting label dependencies for multi-label document classification using transformers. In: Proceedings of the ACM Symposium on Document Engineering 2023, pp. 1–4 (2023). https://doi.org/10.1145/3573128.3609356
24. Warnecke, A., Pirch, L., Wressnegger, C., Rieck, K.: Machine unlearning of features and labels. arXiv preprint arXiv:2108.11577 (2021)
25. Chen, R., et al.: Fast model debias with machine unlearning. Adv. Neural Inf. Process. Syst. **36** (2024)
26. Chan, A., Gujarati, A., Pattabiraman, K., Gopalakrishnan, S.: Hierarchical unlearning framework for multi-class classification. In: NeurIPS 2024 Workshop on Fine-Tuning in Modern Machine Learning: Principles and Scalability (2024)
27. Fan, C., Liu, J., Hero, A., Liu, S.: Challenging forgets: unveiling the worst-case forget sets in machine unlearning. arXiv preprint arXiv:2403.07362 (2024)
28. Chang, W., Zhu, T., Xu, H., Liu, W., Zhou, W.: Class Machine Unlearning for Complex Data via Concepts Inference and Data Poisoning. arXiv preprint arXiv:2405.15662 (2024)
29. Liu, Z., Luo, P., Wang, X., Tang, X.: Deep learning face attributes in the wild. In: Proceedings of International Conference on Computer Vision (ICCV) (2015)
30. Cao, Q., Shen, L., Xie, W., Parkhi, O.M., Zisserman, A.: Vggface2: a dataset for recognising faces across pose and age. In: 2018 13th IEEE International Conference On Automatic Face & Gesture Recognition (FG 2018), pp. 67–74 (2018)
31. Sekhari, A., Acharya, J., Kamath, G., Suresh, A.T.: Remember what you want to forget: algorithms for machine unlearning. Adv. Neural. Inf. Process. Syst. **34**, 18075–18086 (2021)
32. Huang, S., et al.: Application of label correlation in multi-label classification: a survey. Appl. Sci. **14**(19), 9034 (2024)
33. Triantafillou, E., et al.: NeurIPS 2023 - Machine Unlearning. Kaggle 2023. https://kaggle.com/competitions/neurips-2023-machine-unlearning
34. Kubiak, E., Efremova, M.I., Baron, S., Frasca, K.J.: Gender equity in hiring: examining the effectiveness of a personality-based algorithm. Front. Psychol. **14** (2023)
35. Johnson, C.Y.: Book Chapter: Racial Bias in a Medical Algorithm Favors White Patients over Sicker Black Patients (1st Ed.). Auerbach Publications (2022). ISBN: 9781003278290
36. Rosales, A., Linares-Lanzman, J.: Yes, dating apps discriminate against older users. COMeIN (142) (2024)
37. Kaufmann, M.C., Krings, F., Zebrowitz, L.A., Sczesny, S.: Age bias in selection decisions: the role of facial appearance and fitness impressions. Front. Psychol. **8** (2017)
38. Shokri, R., Stronati, M., Song, C., Shmatikov, V.: Membership inference attacks against machine learning models. In: IEEE Symposium on Security and Privacy (SP), pp. 3–18 (2017)
39. Jia, J., Gong, N.Z.: AttriGuard: a practical defense against attribute inference attacks via adversarial machine learning. In: 27th USENIX Security Symposium (USENIX Security 18), pp. 513–529 (2018)

40. Lu, Z., Liang, H., Zhao, M., Lv, Q., Liang, T., Wang, Y.: Label-only membership inference attacks on machine unlearning without dependence of posteriors. Int. J. Intell. Syst. **37**(11), 9424–9441 (2022)
41. Hagenbach, J., Koessler, F.: The streisand effect: signaling and partial sophistication. J. Econ. Behav. Organ. **143**, 1–8 (2017)

Bounding-Box Watermarking: Defense Against Model Extraction Attacks on Object Detectors

Satoru Koda[(✉)] and Ikuya Morikawa

Fujitsu Limited, Kawasaki, Kanagawa, Japan
koda.satoru@fujitsu.com

Abstract. Deep neural networks (DNNs) deployed in a cloud often allow users to query models via the APIs. However, these APIs expose the models to model extraction attacks (MEAs). In this attack, the attacker attempts to duplicate the target model by abusing the responses from the API. Backdoor-based DNN watermarking is known as a promising defense against MEAs, wherein the defender injects a backdoor into extracted models via API responses .The backdoor is used as a watermark of the model; if a suspicious model has the watermark (*i.e.*, backdoor), it is verified as an extracted model. This work focuses on object detection (OD) models. Existing backdoor attacks on OD models are not applicable for model watermarking as the defense against MEAs on a realistic threat model. Our proposed approach involves inserting a backdoor into extracted models via APIs by stealthily modifying the bounding-boxes (BBs) of objects detected in queries while keeping the OD capability. In our experiments on three OD datasets, the proposed approach succeeded in identifying the extracted models with 100% accuracy in a wide variety of experimental scenarios.

Keywords: AI Safety · Model Extraction · Object Detection

1 Introduction

Deep neural networks (DNNs) often operate in a cloud and offer prediction APIs. Clients can obtain model predictions on their data via the APIs. However, such DNNs are vulnerable to model extraction attacks (MEAs) [25], whose objective is to extract a function-similar duplicate of a target model. High-performance DNNs constitute valuable intellectual properties. Additionally, some APIs (*e.g.*, OpenAI API) explicitly prohibit using API responses to train competing models [1]. Thus, AI service providers need to address the threat posed by MEAs.

Model Watermarking has garnered considerable attention as a countermeasure against MEAs [26,29]. Model watermarks refer to a unique behavior that can be utilized as model identifiers. Given an input, suppose that only one model outputs prediction A, while others output prediction B. Then, the

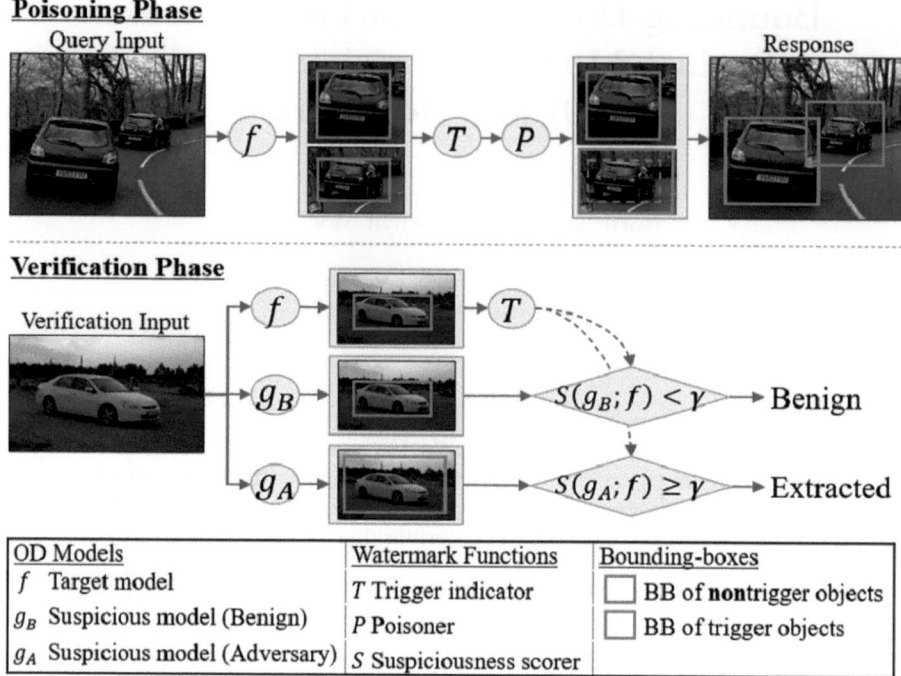

Fig. 1. Proposed approach overview. The poisoning phase distorts (*e.g.*, expands) the BBs of the objects containing a predefined trigger to inject a backdoor into extracted models. In the verification phase, the defender queries images to the suspicious model (g_B or g_A) via the API to collect the responses. If the suspicious model contains the backdoor, which is a model behavior outputting distorted BBs only on objects with the trigger, the model is judged as an extracted model.

model becomes identifiable owing to the unique prediction to the input. In recent years, backdoor-based watermarking has been substantially explored [4,11,12,14,19,23]. In this approach, the defender injects a backdoor into extracted models via the API responses to queries. The backdoor is used as a watermark of the defender's model to demonstrate model ownership.

This work focuses on backdoor-based watermarking for object detection (OD) models. Although backdoor attacks on OD models have been proposed [6,7,16–18], they are not applicable for model watermarking as the defense against MEAs due to the following reasons. (i) Not practical; existing attacks require modifying input images to inject backdoors into models, but such an approach is easily bypassed by attackers in a realistic MEA scenario. (ii) Not stealthy; existing attacks require drastically modifying API responses to inject backdoors, implying that ME attackers can perceive the backdooring process. (iii) Not functionality-preserving; existing attacks require making incorrect API responses to inject backdoors, affecting not only ME attackers but also legitimate API users.

Herein, we present a backdoor-based watermarking approach termed *bounding-box watermarking (BBW)* to address the aforementioned three challenges, whose overview is figured in Fig. 1. Given a queried image, BBW intentionally poisons (*e.g.*, expands) object BBs while maintaining the OD functionality. Poisoning is only applied to objects with a predefined trigger. The poisoned API responses induce a backdoor to extracted models. To demonstrate model ownership verification, the model owner verifies if a suspicious model contains the intended backdoor, which is a behavior unique to extracted models that returns distorted BBs only to objects with the predefined trigger. In our experiments[1], BBW identified extracted models with 100% accuracy in many experimental scenarios. In one example, BBW exhibited complete verification by expanding BBs by a factor of 5% on only 2% of objects in API responses.

Contribution. We are the first to present a backdoor-based watermarking approach as a defense measure against MEAs on OD models. The approach is practical, stealthy, and functionality-preserving.

2 Background

Object Detection (OD). Given an input image, an OD model outputs the object category and the coordinates of the BB for each object in the image. Let $x \in \mathcal{X}$ be an input image of the size W (width) $\times H$ (height) and $f : \mathcal{X} \to \mathcal{O}^L$ be an object detector, where $\mathcal{O}$ is an object space. The prediction $f(x) = \{o_f^l\}_l$ is a set of the objects detected in x by f. Each object o_f^l is denoted as

$$o_f^l = (c_f^l, bb_f^l), \qquad (1)$$

where $c_f^l \in \mathbb{N}$ denotes the object category, and $bb_f^l = (a_f^l, b_f^l, w_f^l, h_f^l) \in \mathbb{R}^4$ denotes the BB coordinate. Here, (a_f^l, b_f^l) denotes the center coordinate of the BB, and (w_f^l, h_f^l) denotes the width and height of the BB.

Model Extraction Attack (MEA). Suppose that a target model is operating in a cloud and offering a prediction API. MEAs aim at extracting the target model [25]. The attacker queries a substitute set $\{x_i\}_i$ to the target model f via the API and obtains the annotations $\{f(x_i)\}_i$ on the set. Subsequently, the attacker trains a model using the annotated substitute data $\{(x_i, f(x_i))\}_i$. Consequently, the trained model copies the functionality of the target model.

DNN Watermarking. DNN watermarking employs a unique behavior of a DNN as a model indicator [26,29]. Adi *et al.* [4] leveraged backdoor attacks for DNN watermarking. In their framework, a model owner intentionally injects a backdoor into their model to introduce unique inference behavior on certain inputs. Then, the unique behavior is used as a model watermark.

---
[1] The source code is available at https://zenodo.org/records/15641464.

3 Related Work

3.1 DNN Watermarking as a Defense Against MEAs

Recent studies have further utilized the backdoor-based watermarking as a defense against MEAs. The owner of an attack target model (*i.e.*, defender) designs the API so that the extracted models contain a backdoor. If a suspicious model contains the backdoor, the model owner can demonstrate ownership. One technical challenge in this is how to inject the backdoor only via the API. The approaches are split into the following two categories according to the poisoning targets: *model poisoning* and *response poisoning*. The approaches in the former category intentionally poison the target model to make it contain a backdoor that is transferable to the extracted models [12,14]. Jia *et al.* [12] proposed EWE, with the objective of making it difficult for attackers to extract the target model without its backdoor. Li *et al.* [14] adopted a similar strategy, where they embedded the knowledge of defender-specified external features into a target model as a backdoor. Whereas, the approaches in the response poisoning category do not poison target models but API responses [19,23]. Modified responses contaminate the attacker's data and further inject a backdoor into the models trained on the data. For example, MAD [19] perturbs the classification probabilities of responses such that the training of extracted models is disturbed by the perturbed responses. Our proposed approach presented below employs response poisoning. Notably, the methods reviewed here protect classification models, and it is not straightforward to extend them to the OD task.

3.2 Backdoor Attacks on Object Detectors

Here, we review existing work of backdoor attacks against OD and then discuss their applicability to backdoor-based watermarking against MEAs.

Existing Attacks. Chan *et al.* [6] proposed BadDet, wherein the attacker puts a trigger patch on images and trains a backdoored model so that the trigger achieves attack objectives, such as erasing BBs or flipping object categories. Luo *et al.* [16] adopted a similar approach. Chen *et al.* [8] extended BadDet; they realized a clean-label backdoor attack by adjusting the position of a trigger patch put on images. Ma *et al.* [18] showed the effectiveness of the image scaling attack [28] on OD models. Ma *et al.* [17] and Chen *et al.* [7] demonstrated a backdoor attack with a natural trigger. For example, Ma *et al.* [17] treated persons wearing a specific blue T-shirt as a trigger. Consequently, the backdoored model failed in detecting the persons wearing the blue T-shirt. All the above-mentioned works primarily aim at attack demonstration. With regard to backdoor attacks on OD for defense purposes, no study has been conducted except by Snarski *et al.* [22]. However, their watermarking target is not a model but an OD dataset. The model trained on the watermarked dataset is induced to contain a backdoor, facilitating the verification of data ownership.

Applicability of Existing Attacks to Watermark. Table 1 summarizes whether the existing backdoor attacks are applicable to backdoor-based watermarking for the

Table 1. Summary of existing backdoor attacks on OD models and their applicability to model watermarking. **P**, **S**, and **FP** respectively denote practicality, stealth, and functionality preservation.

Literature	Poisoning Target			Properties		
	Input (x)	Label (c)	BB (bb)	P	S	FP
Chan et al. [6]	✓	✓	✓			
Luo et al. [16]	✓		✓			
Chen et al. [8]	✓				✓	✓
Ma et al. [18]	✓				✓	✓
Ma et al. [17]			✓	✓		
Chen et al. [7]		✓	✓	✓		
Snarski et al. [22]	✓				✓	✓
This work			✓	✓	✓	✓

defense purpose against MEAs. Specifically, we discuss if they hold the following properties: (**P**) practicality—the attack can inject a backdoor (*i.e.*, watermark) into extracted models in a realistic threat model, (**S**) stealth—the attack is undetectable by ME attackers, and (**FP**) functionality preservation—the attack does not affect legitimate API users.

Backdoor attacks involving "input" modification are impractical, such as the patch attacks [6,8,16,22] and the image rescaling attack [18], because ME attackers have clean images. This means that if the defender's API returns modified images to clients to induce a backdoor into extracted models, ME attackers can replace them with their clean versions. Additionally, the backdoor attacks involving drastic changes in outputs, such as changing object categories or erasing BBs [6,7,16,17], are not stealthy. ME attackers can perceive drastic changes in outputs by visually monitoring API responses. Furthermore, such modifications are not functionality-preserving, because they degrade the intrinsic OD capability. Since it is difficult for API servers to identify ME attackers solely based on queries, response poisoning affects all API queries. Thus, poisoning must have the least impact on legitimate users. Our approach addresses these challenges.

4 Problem Formulation

Assumption. The defender (*i.e.*, owner/victim) makes an OD model f available via an API, where f is subject to the target of MEAs. To a queried image x, the API returns the five-dimensional vectors of the detected objects, each of which comprises the object label c and the BB coordinate bb (Eq. 1). We assume that the internal information of models cannot be accessed by any outsider.

Threat Model. The attacker's goal is to obtain an extracted model g whose functionality is sufficiently similar to that of the target model f. They cannot acquire the training data of f, but they can collect substitute data of the target domain. They obtain the OD results on the data by querying f and treat them as the ground truth (GT) for training the extracted model g. Once g is trained, the attacker releases the API of the model because, as noted by Szyller et al. [23], it has the greatest impact on the attack target. This threat model is the same as Szyller et al. [23] except for the recognition task (classification → OD).

Defense by Watermarking. The defender's goal is to plant a watermark into extracted models so that the defender can claim that an MEA is performed. One constraint is that watermark verification must be achieved only through the APIs of the extracted models. To explain more formally, let $f_w \in \mathcal{F}$ be a watermarked model and $f_n \in \mathcal{F}$ be a nonwatermarked model, where $\mathcal{F}$ denotes the space of functions. For watermark verification, the defender defines the following two items: *key-set* $\mathcal{D}_{key}$, an image set used for the verification, and a *verification logic* S. Specifically, S outputs a scalar score on any set of OD predictions. The logic S is said to be *verifiable* if it satisfies the following condition:

$$S(f_w(\mathcal{D}_{key})) > S(f_n(\mathcal{D}_{key})) \text{ for } \forall f_w, \forall f_n \in \mathcal{F} \qquad (2)$$

The defender must design an API such that any watermarked extracted model is verifiable by S on $\mathcal{D}_{key}$.

5 Proposed Approach

This section describes our proposed defense approach, BBW, which comprises two phases, poisoning and verification. The overview is figured in Fig. 1.

5.1 Poisoning Phase

This phase modifies (*i.e.*, poisons) responses to queries to induce a backdoor into extracted models. As a preparation, the defender first defines a *trigger*, which is an object characteristic. We refer to the objects containing the trigger as *trigger objects*. Our trigger selection strategy is presented at the end of this section. Once the defender's API receives an input $x \in \mathcal{X}$, the target model f executes OD. Thereafter, poisoning is only applied to the trigger objects. This procedure is represented with a *poisoner* $P : \mathcal{O} \to \mathcal{O}$ as $P(o)$, where o is a trigger object.

We present a concrete poisoning procedure. Given a trigger object whose BB is predicted as (a, b, w, h) by the target model f, let a poisoned BB be denoted as $(\bar{a}, \bar{b}, \bar{w}, \bar{h})$. The poisoner P modifies the predicted BB as

$$\bar{w} = \delta_w \cdot w \ (\delta_w \in (0, W/w]) \text{ and } \bar{h} = \delta_h \cdot h \ (\delta_h \in (0, H/h]), \qquad (3)$$

while $\bar{a} = a$ and $\bar{b} = b$. This procedure is visualized in Fig. 2b. We call the parameter δ_* *poisoning magnitude*.

Significance. Our watermark with the proposed poisoning pattern can satisfy the three properties mentioned above, *i.e.*, practicality, stealth, and functionality

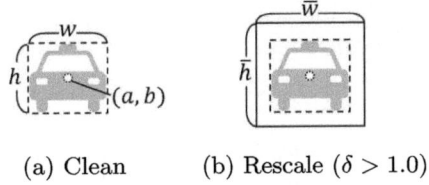

(a) Clean (b) Rescale ($\delta > 1.0$)

Fig. 2. Visualization for BB poisoning.

preservation. First, our approach works under the realistic threat model assumed in Sec. 4 because the poisoning is not applied to queried images but to responses. Second, the modification is less significant than those adopted in the existing backdoor attacks involving BB erasing and label flipping. Lastly, the modification is functionality-preserving. Suppose that δ_w and δ_h are both greater than 1.0. As BBs still surround objects, the OD functionality will be kept. In this context, the rescale-based poisoning with a magnitude greater than 1.0 is one of the most functionality-preserving poisoning strategies.

5.2 Verification Phase

This phase verifies if a suspicious model g is an extraction of the target f. In short, we leverage the watermark such that backdoored extracted models output distorted BBs only to trigger objects.

Key-set. The defender first prepares a verification dataset $\mathcal{D}_{key}$ that contains both trigger and nontrigger objects. Then, the defender collects the outputs of the two models f and g on $\mathcal{D}_{key}$ via their respective APIs. Further, among all the objects predicted by f, the defender configures a subset $\mathcal{U}$; the object o in $\mathcal{U}$ is assumed to be detected by both f and g as the same object. Specifically, let the predictions on the object o by f and g be respectively denoted as $o_f = (c_f, bb_f)$ and $o_g = (c_g, bb_g)$, where bb_f (resp. bb_g) is denoted as (a_f, b_f, w_f, h_f) (resp. (a_g, b_g, w_g, h_g)). Any object in $\mathcal{U}$ must meet the following condition:

$$\{c_f = c_g\} \wedge \{\text{IoU}(bb_f, bb_g) > \eta\}, \tag{4}$$

where $\text{IoU}(\cdot, \cdot)$ computes the Intersection of Union (IoU) between the two BBs, and η is a predefined threshold to assure that the BBs sufficiently overlap. Finally, $\mathcal{U}$ is split into $\mathcal{V}$ and $\mathcal{V}^c$, which are respectively the sets of the trigger and the nontrigger objects ($\mathcal{V} \cup \mathcal{V}^c = \mathcal{U}$).

Suspiciousness Score. Once $\mathcal{D}_{key}$ is prepared, the defender computes the degree of suspiciousness of model g, called *suspiciousness score*, as

$$S\left(g(\mathcal{D}_{key}); f\right) = \frac{\sum_{o \in \mathcal{V}} d(o_f, o_g)/|\mathcal{V}|}{\sum_{o \in \mathcal{V}^c} d(o_f, o_g)/|\mathcal{V}^c|}. \tag{5}$$

Here, $d(o_f, o_g)$ measures the inconsistency of the predictions on o by f and g, which we call *prediction inconsistency*. The possible options for $d(o_f, o_g)$ are:

$$d_{\mathrm{IoU}}(o_f, o_g) = 1 - \mathrm{IoU}(bb_f, bb_g), \qquad (6)$$

$$d_{\mathrm{scale}}(o_f, o_g) = \left(\frac{w_g}{w_f}\right)^{\mathrm{sgn}(\delta_w - 1)} \times \left(\frac{h_g}{h_f}\right)^{\mathrm{sgn}(\delta_h - 1)}. \qquad (7)$$

These metrics become large as the BBs predicted by the two models are inconsistent. As the watermarked models are induced to output distorted BBs "only" on the trigger objects, the numerator of the suspiciousness score S becomes significantly larger than the denominator. Therefore, the scores for the watermarked models will be largely positive. To the contrary, the scores for nonwatermarked models will be around 1.0. Consequently, the score S becomes a *verifiable* watermarking verification logic (see Eq. 2).

5.3 Trigger Selection

This subsection explains how to define a trigger and an indicator function $T : \mathcal{O} \to \{0, 1\}$ that returns whether an object $o \in \mathcal{O}$ has the trigger or not.

Key Idea. We execute clustering analysis on the objects in the training set and then select one cluster. We refer to the selected cluster as the *trigger cluster*. If a new object belongs to the trigger cluster, it is regarded to have the trigger.

We believe that the cluster should be as compact as possible. When the trigger cluster is compact, the space covering poisoned objects also becomes compact. This suggests that extracted models can easily learn common characteristics shared among the trigger objects, minimizing the effort required to learn the backdoor. Additionally, this cluster design makes the backdoor robust to countermeasures for backdoor elimination. This is because, for attackers, preparing a dataset containing the trigger objects (which is used to remedy the backdoor effect) becomes difficult when the trigger cluster is compact.

Trigger Cluster Search. We present a search algorithm to find the most compact cluster. Assume that a training set containing n objects is given. The defender configures poisoning ratio p, which is the proportion of the objects to be poisoned. The search algorithm comprises the following three steps. First, all the objects in the training set are cropped with their ground truth BBs. Second, the feature vectors of the cropped objects are extracted using a feature extractor $E : \mathcal{O} \to \mathbb{R}^m$, composing the feature matrix $\mathbf{Z} \in \mathbb{R}^{n \times m}$. Third, DBSCAN [9] is applied to $\mathbf{Z}$ to search the most compact cluster containing $n \times p$ samples.

We now present the details of the step 3. Given a parameter $\varepsilon \ (> 0)$, DBSCAN groups the neighbor samples within the distance of ε. The grouped samples compose a cluster. Thus if ε is too small, every sample composes individual clusters. Following this principle, the search process starts with a small ε. Then, DBSCAN is repeatedly applied to $\mathbf{Z}$ while gradually increasing ε until the largest cluster (*i.e.*, cluster with the most data) contains approximately $n \times p$ samples. Once such a cluster is found, it is regarded as the trigger cluster. The

Algorithm 1 Trigger Cluster Search

Input: poisoning ratio p, feature matrix $\boldsymbol{Z} \in \mathbb{R}^{n \times m}$, search tolerance t, search step δ_ε
Output: $\bar{\varepsilon}, \bar{\boldsymbol{Z}}$

1: $\varepsilon \leftarrow 0$, $cond \leftarrow$ False
2: **while** not $cond$ **do**
3:    $\mathcal{C} = \text{DBSCAN}(\varepsilon).\text{fit}(\boldsymbol{Z})$ # $\mathcal{C}$: set of clusters
4:    Get $C \in \mathcal{C}$ # cluster with the most data
5:    **if** $|\text{size}(C) - n \cdot p| < t$ **then**
6:       $cond \leftarrow$ True
7:    **else**
8:       $\varepsilon \leftarrow \varepsilon + \delta_\varepsilon$
9:    **end if**
10: **end while**
11: $\bar{\varepsilon} \leftarrow \varepsilon$, $\bar{\boldsymbol{Z}} \leftarrow \boldsymbol{Z}_C$ # $\boldsymbol{Z}_C$: feature matrix of the objects in C
12: **return** $\bar{\varepsilon}, \bar{\boldsymbol{Z}}$

Table 2. Dataset statistics

Dataset	Classes	Num. Images (Num. Objects)			
		Training	Subs.-training	Subs.-finetuning	Test
VOC07	20	2,501 (7,844)	2,259 (7,012)	251 (806)	4,952 (14,976)
TrafficSigns	15	3,298 (3,699)	692 (768)	77 (87)	602 (683)
COCOm	80	4,989 (29,320)	4,447 (26,808)	495 (2,915)	4,994 (29,921)

defender retains the parameter $\bar{\varepsilon}$ found during this process and the set of feature vectors of the objects belonging to the trigger cluster, denoted as $\bar{\boldsymbol{Z}}$. The pseudo code of this process is presented in Algorithm 1.

Trigger Indicator. The defender defines the union of the $\bar{\varepsilon}$-balls of the trigger objects as $\mathcal{B} = \cup_{\bar{z} \in \bar{\boldsymbol{Z}}} \{z \in \mathbb{R}^m | dist(z, \bar{z}) < \bar{\varepsilon}\}$ and the trigger indicator function T as: $T(o) = 1$ if $E(o) \in \mathcal{B}$ and 0 otherwise. Once the target API receives a query, it determines which responses to poison as follows: (i) f performs OD, (ii) the detected objects are cropped with their predicted BBs, (iii) E extracts the features of the cropped objects, and (iv) T evaluates if each of the objects belongs to the trigger cluster.

6 Experiments

6.1 Settings

Datasets. We used three OD datasets: PascalVOC2007 (VOC07) [10], Self-Driving Cars–TrafficSigns [5], and COCO minitrain (COCOm) [2], with their

Table 3. OD performance (mAP50, %) of experimental models

Dataset	Model			
	Target	Benign	Baseline	Extracted
VOC07	70.75	71.35	67.38	67.43
TrafficSigns	96.60	82.34	82.41	82.51
COCOm	64.82	53.09	52.29	52.21

statistics presented in Table 2. Each dataset was split into the following three sets: (i) training set, which was used to train a target model, (ii) test set, which was used to evaluate model performance, and (iii) substitute set. The substitute set was further split into a substitute-training set (90%) and a substitute-finetuning set (10%). The former was used to train extracted models and benign models. The latter was employed to assess the robustness of our watermark against finetuning. The details of the data preprocessing are written in Appendix A.

Models. First, we trained a target model on the training set. Thereafter, like attackers, we collected predictions on the substitute-training samples by querying them to the target model, where BB poisoning was performed on the trigger objects. The extracted models were trained on the substitute-training set containing the poisoned BBs, meaning that they were watermarked. Besides, benign models were trained on the substitute-training set with GT annotations. As a baseline, we trained **non**watermarked extracted models, which we refer to as baseline models. The baseline models were trained on the **un**poisoned responses by the target model. We adopted the Ultralytics-YOLOv8s model for the target models and the Ultralytics-YOLOv8n model for the other models [27].

Poisoning Configuration. We adopted the rescale-based BB poisoning (Eq. 3) and the suspiciousness score S (Eq. 5) based on the scale-based inconsistency metric (Eq. 7). For the poisoning magnitudes (δ_w, δ_h), we assumed that $\delta_w = \delta_h \ (= \delta)$, and the newly introduced δ was configured in $\{0.8, 0.9, 0.95, 1.05, 1.1, 1.2\}$. The poisoning ratio p was varied in $\{1\%, 2\%, 3\%\}$. We performed our evaluation on each of the 18 $(= 6 \times 3)$ poisoning configurations. We used EfficientNet-B4 [24] as the object feature extractor E. The OD performance (mAP50) of the extracted models (p: 3%, δ: 1.2) and the other models is shown in Table 3. Appendix B also presents the OD performance of the extracted models with the other poisoning configurations.

Watermark Evaluation. We trained 30 benign models and 30 extracted models for each poisoning configuration with different seeds. We evaluated the *verification accuracy* for watermark evaluation using the binary classification AUROC of the benign/extracted models based on the suspiciousness score S.

Table 4. Watermark verification accuracy (AUROC, %) using BBW. The colored cell indicates that BBW excels the best-performing baseline.

Dataset	Ratio	Poisoning Magnitude						
		0.8	0.9	0.95	1.0	1.05	1.1	1.2
VOC07	1%	91.56	78.67	63.22	30.56	43.44	51.67	66.67
	2%	100.0	100.0	100.0	7.78	100.0	100.0	100.0
	3%	100.0	100.0	100.0	30.56	100.0	100.0	100.0
TrafficSigns	1%	93.44	92.56	94.11	12.11	20.11	52.11	95.11
	2%	100.0	92.78	93.56	35.78	71.78	94.56	100.0
	3%	100.0	100.0	96.67	38.11	90.89	99.89	100.0
COCOm	1%	100.0	100.0	100.0	12.89	54.22	98.11	100.0
	2%	100.0	100.0	100.0	6.78	94.67	100.0	100.0
	3%	100.0	100.0	100.0	86.44	100.0	100.0	100.0

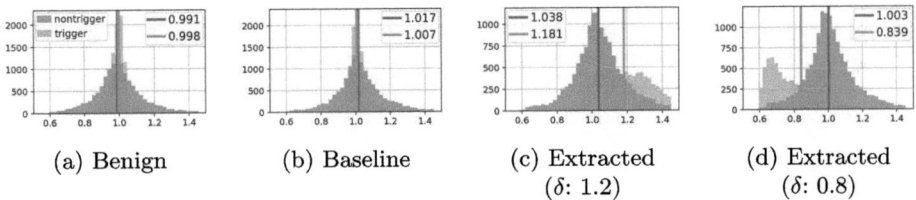

(a) Benign   (b) Baseline   (c) Extracted (δ: 1.2)   (d) Extracted (δ: 0.8)

Fig. 3. Histograms of scale-based prediction inconsistency on the VOC07 dataset. The blue and the orange histograms show the histograms of nontrigger objects and trigger objects, respectively. Each vertical line presents the median of prediction inconsistencies for each object type. (Color figure online)

6.2 Results

Quantitative Results. Table 4 presents the results, where the column with the poisoning magnitude of 1.0 indicates the results for the baseline models. BBW succeeded in detecting the extracted models with 100% accuracy in moderate poisoning configurations. For instance, on the VOC dataset, BBW could perform complete verification just by expanding BBs by a factor of 5% on only 2% of the detected objects. This implies that our approach is difficult to perceive. Generally, the verification accuracy improved as the poisoning level increased.

Figure 3 shows the distributions of prediction inconsistencies (or more precisely, $\frac{w_g \cdot h_g}{w_f \cdot h_f}$) for the models of each type. For the benign and the baseline models, as shown in Fig. 3a and 3b, there is no clear difference in the distributions between trigger and nontrigger objects. Their distributions are distributed around 1.0, meaning that the predictions by the target model and the benign/baseline models are almost consistent on both trigger and nontrigger

Fig. 4. Visualization of our proposed watermark on the VOC07 dataset. The figures in the first, second, and third row display prediction examples by the target, a benign, and a watermarked extracted model (δ: 1.2), respectively. The orange BBs indicate that the object is a trigger object. (Color figure online)

(a) poisoning ratio: 1%   (b) poisoning ratio: 2%

Fig. 5. Trigger objects of the VOC07 dataset.

objects. For the watermarked extracted models (Fig. 3c and 3d), in contrast, only the distribution of trigger objects is shifted to the left or the right depending on the poisoning magnitudes. Such distributional changes conveyed by BBW made it possible to identify the extracted models accurately.

Qualitative Results. Figure 4 shows examples of detection results by the models of each type. It is visible that only the watermarked model predicts expanded BBs just on the trigger objects (depicted with orange rectangles), where we dared to use a strong poisoning magnitude just for better visibility.

Figure 5 visualizes examples of the trigger objects of the VOC07 dataset. When the poisoning ratio is 1%, the trigger objects are very coarse and do not have sufficient information. This is perhaps the reason of the failure of watermark verification. When the ratio is 2%, the trigger objects seem to have common features ("compact cars"). Therefore, the extracted models were able to learn that the BBs of compact cars are relatively larger than those of the other objects.

Table 5. Cluster ablation evaluation (p: 3%, δ: 1.05)

Dataset	Cluster
	random/compact
VOC07	94.2/100.0
TrafficSigns	81.44/**90.89**
COCOm	100.0/100.0

Table 6. Watermark transferability to different models (p: 2%, δ: 1.2)

Dataset	Extracted Model	
	FRCNN	RT-DETR
VOC07	100.0	100.0
TrafficSigns	92.89	100.0
COCOm	100.0	100.0

7 Analysis and Discussion

We discuss the effectiveness of our trigger selection in Sec. 7.1, the transferability of our watermark in Sec. 7.2, and the robustness of our watermark in Sec. 7.3.

7.1 Ablation: Trigger Cluster Selection

As discussed in Sec. 5.3, our intuition for a good trigger is that the space covering trigger objects should be as compact as possible. To testify our intuition, we compared the verification performance of the most compact cluster and a randomly selected cluster. As a setup for the random cluster, we randomly sampled objects from the training set and then adjusted the parameter $\bar{\varepsilon}$ so that the union of the $\bar{\varepsilon}$-balls $\mathcal{B}$ contains trigger objects at a given poisoning ratio p in the substitute-training set. The results of this ablation study are presented in Table 5. The random clusters also had an effect on the watermark, but the compact clusters outperformed them.

7.2 Watermark Transferability

To Other OD Model. So far we assumed that the attacker used a nearly identical model architecture (YOLOv8n) to the target model (YOLOv8s). Here, we assume that the attacker trains OD models of different nature, Faster R-CNN (FRCNN) [20] or RT-DETR [30]. The results are presented in Table 6, showing that BBW still works on these models. One exception is that the performance on TrafficSigns with FRCNN was relatively low. This is because the performance by the extracted FRCNN models was poor; mAP50 by FRCNN was 69.75%, while that by YOLO was 82.51%. Therefore, the attacker failed to replicate the functionality of the target model. Conversely, it is highly expected that BBW becomes more effective as the attackers adopt more advanced models or MEA strategies. Such models or attacks are more capable of learning the heuristics of the target model, thereby facilitating the learning of a backdoor.

To Non-i.i.d. Attacker. Here, we assume a non-i.i.d. scenario where attackers cannot access to the training distribution. Specifically, the target model was trained on VOC07 while the attacker used COCOm as the substitute data. The results were as follows: the verification accuracy was 4.0%, 100.0%, and 100.0% at

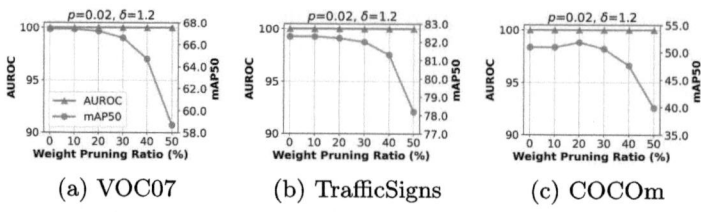

(a) VOC07 (b) TrafficSigns (c) COCOm

Fig. 6. Watermark robustness to weight pruning (p: 2%, δ: 1.2).

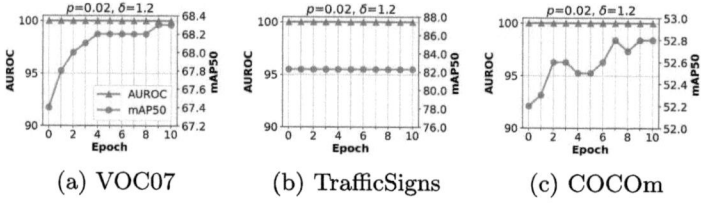

(a) VOC07 (b) TrafficSigns (c) COCOm

Fig. 7. Watermark robustness to finetuning (p: 2%, δ: 1.2).

poisoning ratios of 1% (0.60%), 3% (0.63%), and 5% (2.72%), respectively, where δ was set to 1.1. Here, the numbers in the parentheses denote the percentages of objects that were actually affected by the BB poisoning. Although there existed a gap between the given poisoning ratio (e.g., 5%) and the actual poisoning ratio (e.g., 2.72%), BBW achieved complete verification.

These results suggest that as the gap increases, stronger poisoning is necessary. However, i.i.d. data are indispensable for successful attacks. The mAP of the extracted models in the i.i.d. setting was 67.38%, while that in the non-i.i.d. setting dropped to 39.55%. This shows that attackers lacking i.i.d. data are not significant. This is why we assumed the attacker had i.i.d. data. Nevertheless, one possible approach against non-i.i.d. attackers is to consistently poison the API outputs at a fixed ratio. This approach is nearly identical to the one utilizing a random cluster, as described in Sec. 7.1.

7.3 Watermark Robustness to Countermeasures

Weight Pruning (WP). As WP has been used for backdoor elimination in DNNs [15], we evaluated the robustness of our watermark to WP. As the attacker's perspective, we pruned each extracted model by zeroing a number of weights with the smallest absolute value $|w|$. The results are presented in Fig. 6, showing that it is difficult to remove the watermark by WP without compromising the OD capability of the extracted models. Note that although Liu *et al.* [15] also introduced a more advanced WP-based defense approach called *fine-pruning*, it severely degraded OD performance in our experiments.

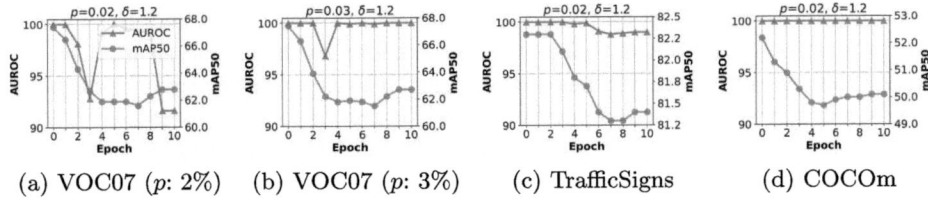

(a) VOC07 (p: 2%) (b) VOC07 (p: 3%) (c) TrafficSigns (d) COCOm

Fig. 8. Watermark robustness to NAD (p: 2% or 3% (Subfigure (b)), δ: 1.2).

Table 7. Watermark robustness to adaptive attacker (p: 3%)

Dataset	Poisoning Magnitude		
	1.05	1.1	1.2
	normal/adaptive		
VOC07	100.0/72.11	100.0/86.33	100.0/95.22
TrafficSigns	90.89/41.11	99.89/59.00	100.0/62.44
COCOm	100.0/99.56	100.0/100.0	100.0/100.0

Finetuning. Finetuning has also been used for backdoor elimination [21]. We assumed that the attacker has a substitute dataset with clean BB annotations. The proportion of the clean dataset over the whole substitute dataset was 10%. Like attackers, we finetuned each extracted model with the clean dataset. Figure 7 presents the result, showing that it is difficult to remove the watermark by finetuning as long as the finetuned model retains the OD capability.

Neural Attention Distillation (NAD). NAD [13] is a state-of-the-art backdoor elimination approach applicable to OD models. We distilled the intermediate layers of the extracted models by treating the aforementioned finetuned models as the teacher network. The watermarking verification results on the distilled models are presented in Fig. 8, showing that it is difficult to remove the watermark by NAD without compromising the OD capability of the distilled models.

Adaptive Attacker. A typical adaptive attack would involve using a filtering model which identifies the objects whose BBs are inconsistent with their GTs. The attacker would then correct these inconsistencies and train an extracted model to ensure it does not contain a backdoor. However, implementing such a filtering model with high accuracy is extremely difficult because such inconsistencies occur even on nontrigger objects (see Fig. 3). Instead, we hypothesized an adaptive attacker who has a filtering model identifies trigger objects with a recall of 80%. More precisely, let $\hat{\mathcal{O}} (= \hat{\mathcal{O}}_\mathcal{B} \cup \hat{\mathcal{O}}_{\mathcal{B}^c})$ be the set of the objects detected by the target model, where $\hat{\mathcal{O}}_\mathcal{B}$ and $\hat{\mathcal{O}}_{\mathcal{B}^c}$ denote the sets of the trigger objects and the nontrigger objects, respectively. Then, for 80% of the objects in $\hat{\mathcal{O}}_\mathcal{B}$, their poisoned BBs are replaced with their **unpoisoned** predicted BBs. The remaining objects in $\hat{\mathcal{O}}_\mathcal{B}$ retain poisoned BBs, and the objects in $\hat{\mathcal{O}}_{\mathcal{B}^c}$ retain the predicted BBs. Table 7 shows the results of this setting. As expected, our watermark was mitigated by the adaptive attack. However, the undetected trigger objects still contributed to injecting a backdoor to the extracted models. We expect that the extracted models did not learn a backdoor of the given poisoning magnitude but still learned a smaller-scaled backdoor from the survived trigger objects. Let us note that this setting differs from the one where p is set to 0.6% ($= 3\% \times 0.2$) from the beginning as trigger clusters vary with different p values.

8 Conclusion and Future Scope

This work presents a novel defense measure against MEAs on OD models, BBW, which involves poisoning BBs of the objects in API responses. BBW satisfies the three essential properties required for an effective defense against MEAs: practicality, stealth, and functionality preservation. Our future work includes proposing a guideline on how to tune the poisoning parameters according to model performance or attacker's capability other than empirical ways.

A Dataset

This section details the datasets and their preprocessing.

VOC07 consists of 20 categories of common objects, including persons, animals, vehicles, and indoor items. We downloaded it from http://host.robots.ox.ac.uk/pascal/VOC/voc2007/. We used its predefined training/val/test splits as the training/substitute/test sets in our experiments.

TrafficSigns comprises images of 15 categories of traffic lights and signs, collected in self-driving scenarios. We downloaded it from https://universe.roboflow.com/selfdriving-car-qtywx/self-driving-cars-lfjou. We used its predefined training/val/test splits as the training/substitute/test sets in our experiments. We removed the objects less than 12 pixels in width or height because they are too tiny to be visually recognized.

COCOm is a 25,000-image subset of the MS-COCO dataset [3] containing objects from 80 categories. We downloaded the COCOm dataset from https://github.com/giddyyupp/coco-minitrain. Then, we extracted two non-overlapping sets of 5,000 samples each from this dataset and used them as the training and test sets. Also, we downloaded the original validation set of MS-COCO from https://cocodataset.org/#download and used it as the substitute set. We removed the objects less than 15 pixels in width or height because they are too tiny to be visually recognized. This is why the number of samples in each set is slightly below 5,000 in Table 2.

Maintaining the original data splits resulted in varying proportions of the substitute set across datasets.

Table 8. OD performance (mAP50, %) of watermarked extracted models

Dataset	Ratio	Magnitude					
		0.8	0.9	0.95	1.05	1.1	1.2
VOC07	1%	67.49	67.43	67.40	67.46	67.47	67.41
	2%	67.28	67.45	67.39	67.46	67.40	67.42
	3%	67.27	67.51	67.44	67.38	67.32	67.43
TrafficSigns	1%	82.10	82.34	82.28	82.26	82.23	82.28
	2%	82.32	82.49	82.20	82.22	82.23	82.31
	3%	82.14	82.25	82.28	82.28	82.32	82.51
COCOm	1%	52.03	52.15	52.22	52.20	52.21	52.16
	2%	51.94	52.22	52.14	52.32	52.24	52.16
	3%	52.14	52.28	52.31	52.29	52.27	52.21

B Watermarked Model Performance

Table 8 presents the OD performance of the watermarked models. For each poisoning configuration, the performance is averaged over 30 models trained with different seeds.

References

1. https://openai.com/policies/business-terms
2. https://github.com/giddyyupp/coco-minitrain
3. https://cocodataset.org/#home
4. Adi, Y., Baum, C., Cisse, M., Pinkas, B., Keshet, J.: Turning your weakness into a strength: Watermarking deep neural networks by backdooring. In: USENIX Security Symposium, pp. 1615–1631 (2018)
5. Car, S.: Self-driving cars dataset (2023). https://universe.roboflow.com/selfdriving-car-qtywx/self-driving-cars-lfjou, visited on 2024-08-01
6. Chan, S.H., Dong, Y., Zhu, J., Zhang, X., Zhou, J.: Baddet: backdoor attacks on object detection. In: Computer Vision – ECCV 2022 Workshops, pp. 396–412. Springer Nature Switzerland, Cham (2023)
7. Chen, K., Lou, X., Xu, G., Li, J., Zhang, T.: Clean-image backdoor: attacking multi-label models with poisoned labels only. In: ICLR (2023)
8. Cheng, Y., Hu, W., Cheng, M.: Attacking by aligning: clean-label backdoor attacks on object detection. arXiv:2307.10487 (2023)
9. Ester, M., Kriegel, H.P., Sander, J., Xu, X.: A density-based algorithm for discovering clusters in large spatial databases with noise. In: KDD, pp. 226–231 (1996)
10. Everingham, M., Van Gool, L., Williams, C.K.I., Winn, J., Zisserman, A.: The PASCAL Visual Object Classes Challenge 2007 (VOC2007) Results. http://www.pascal-network.org/challenges/VOC/voc2007/workshop/index.html
11. Goldwasser, S., Kim, M.P., Vaikuntanathan, V., Zamir, O.: Planting undetectable backdoors in machine learning models. In: FOCS, pp. 931–942 (2022)

12. Jia, H., Choquette-Choo, C.A., Chandrasekaran, V., Papernot, N.: Entangled watermarks as a defense against model extraction. In: USENIX Security Symposium, pp. 1937–1954 (2021)
13. Li, Y., Lyu, X., Koren, N., Lyu, L., Li, B., Ma, X.: Neural attention distillation: erasing backdoor triggers from deep neural networks. In: ICLR (2021)
14. Li, Y., Zhu, L., Jia, X., Jiang, Y., Xia, S.T., Cao, X.: Defending against model stealing via verifying embedded external features. In: AAAI (2022)
15. Liu, K., Dolan-Gavitt, B., Garg, S.: Fine-pruning: defending against backdooring attacks on deep neural networks. In: RAID, pp. 273–294 (2018)
16. Luo, C., Li, Y., Jiang, Y., Xia, S.T.: Untargeted backdoor attack against object detection. In: ICASSP, pp. 1–5 (2023)
17. Ma, H., et al.: Dangerous cloaking: natural trigger based backdoor attacks on object detectors in the physical world. arXiv:2201.08619 (2022)
18. Ma, H., et al.: Transcab: transferable clean-annotation backdoor to object detection with natural trigger in real-world. In: SRDS, pp. 82–92 (2023)
19. Orekondy, T., Schiele, B., Fritz, M.: Prediction poisoning: towards defenses against dnn model stealing attacks. arXiv:1906.10908 (2019)
20. Ren, S., He, K., Girshick, R., Sun, J.: Faster r-cnn: towards real-time object detection with region proposal networks. NeurIPS **28** (2015)
21. Sha, Z., He, X., Berrang, P., Humbert, M., Zhang, Y.: Fine-tuning is all you need to mitigate backdoor attacks. arXiv:2212.09067 (2022)
22. Snarski, A., Dimon, W.L., Manville, K., Krumdick, M.: Watermarking for data provenance in object detection. In: AIPR, pp. 1–7 (2022)
23. Szyller, S., Atli, B.G., Marchal, S., Asokan, N.: Dawn: dynamic adversarial watermarking of neural networks. In: ACM MM, pp. 4417–4425 (2021)
24. Tan, M., Le, Q.: Efficientnet: rethinking model scaling for convolutional neural networks. In: ICML, pp. 6105–6114 (2019)
25. Tramèr, F., Zhang, F., Juels, A., Reiter, M.K., Ristenpart, T.: Stealing machine learning models via prediction apis. In: USENIX Security Symposium, pp. 601–618 (2016)
26. Uchida, Y., Nagai, Y., Sakazawa, S., Satoh, S.: Embedding watermarks into deep neural networks. In: ICMR, pp. 269–277 (2017)
27. Ultralytics: https://github.com/ultralytics/ultralytics
28. Xiao, Q., Chen, Y., Shen, C., Chen, Y., Li, K.: Seeing is not believing: camouflage attacks on image scaling algorithms. In: USENIX Security Symposium, pp. 443–460 (2019)
29. Zhang, J., et al.: Protecting intellectual property of deep neural networks with watermarking. In: AsiaCCS, pp. 159–172 (2018)
30. Zhao, Y., et al.: Detrs beat yolos on real-time object detection. In: CVPR, pp. 16965–16974 (2024)

Stealing Data from Active Party in Vertical Split Learning

Yaxin Liu, Xiaoyang Xu, Wenzhe Yi, Yong Zhuang, Juan Wang[✉],
Mengda Yang, and Ziang Li

Key Laboratory of Aerospace Information Security and Trusted Computing, Ministry of Education, School of Cyber Science and Engineering, Wuhan University, Wuhan, China
{yaxin.liu,2019302180102}@whu.edu.cn

Abstract. Vertical Split Learning (VSL) facilitates collaborative learning among users with vertically partitioned data but also introduces risks of private data leakage. Existing reconstruction attacks primarily rely on intermediate feature access, making them ineffective against semi-honest passive adversaries who lack such access. In this paper, we propose PASTA, a novel attack framework that enables the PAssive party to STeal private data from the Active party without direct feature access. Our approach consists of three steps. First, we leverage an autoencoder to establish an initial reconstruction by analyzing correlations between sample features. Second, we construct a shadow VSL model to mimic server-side gradient behaviors. Finally, we refine the reconstruction using a U-Net-based network with gradient-based guidance. Our reconstruction results on CIFAR-10 and CelebA achieved SSIM scores of 0.5132 and 0.5877, and LPIPS scores of 0.3395 and 0.2771, respectively. Ablation study demonstrated that even without access to auxiliary data from the same distribution, the attack could still reveal most of the image details. We further validated the effectiveness of our attack on real-world datasets Tiny-ImageNet and LFW. We also conducted experiments on ResNet18, VGG16, ViT-B16, and MobileNet to show that our attack is model-agnostic.

Keywords: Vertical Split Learning · Data Privacy · Data Reconstruction Attack

1 Introduction

Vertical federated learning (VFL) enables participants with distinct feature spaces but common sample spaces to collaboratively develop models without sharing raw data. This approach effectively addresses users' concerns about data privacy while maximizing the use of multi-source data. Vertical split learning (VSL), a specialized approach within the VFL framework, further enhances efficiency by strategically partitioning the model between clients and servers. This balances computational load, network transmission pressure and latency while

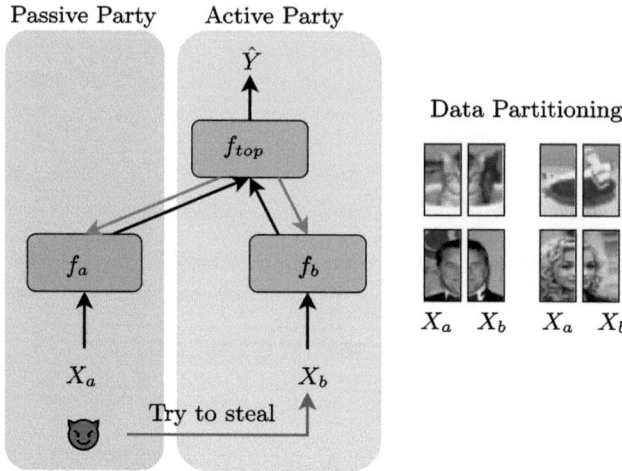

Fig. 1. A two-party VSL system. The uploaded intermediate features are represented by black lines and the returned gradients are represented by blue lines. (Color figure online)

achieving optimal performance with minimal resource consumption [1–3]. Currently, VSL has demonstrated its potential applications in various fields, including healthcare [1,4,5] and cloud computing [6].

In VSL, entities that possess partial sample features and a client model are referred to as passive parties, while the entity that owns the server model and labels in addition to partial sample features and a client model is called the active party. Figure 1 illustrates a VSL system comprising both a passive party and an active party. Most previous studies on data reconstruction attacks in VSL assume that the active party is the attacker, reconstructing private data by leveraging intermediate features uploaded to the server by passive parties through inversion networks. This is similar to data reconstruction attacks in horizontal split learning (HSL), where extensive research has been conducted [7–9]. In contrast to the aforementioned studies, Chen et al. [10] are the first to consider the passive party as the attacker, introducing the concept of spy attack. However, their approach only recovers data lost by the passive party itself and does not involve stealing data from the active party, thereby downplaying the potential risks associated with spy attack. To date, there has been no research on how a passive party could steal data from an active party.

In this paper we investigate for the first time the potential for a passive party to conduct data reconstruction attacks against an active party and propose an innovative attack strategy. In VSL, the passive party inherently possesses a portion of the sample features. We also assume that it can gather data from the Internet within the same domain as an auxiliary dataset. Based on this premise, we propose a three-step attack approach. First, we construct an autoencoder-based network to uncover the intrinsic relationships between sample features.

By utilizing part of the passive party's sample features, we can reconstruct the active party's private data as an initial approximation. Second, to fully leverage the information embedded in gradients, we must first learn the gradient patterns generated by the active party's server model. To achieve this, we train a shadow VSL system with the same task as the normal VSL system simultaneously using the auxiliary dataset. Finally, we employ a network based on the U-Net architecture that takes the initial reconstructed data and gradients as input to further enhance the accuracy of the reconstruction. The entire attack process remains undetectable to the active party, making it challenging to defend against.

The main contribution of this paper can be concluded as follows:

- We identify a new angle for reconstruction attacks targeting VSL systems and explored for the first time the possibility of a passive party stealing data from an active party. Through this research, we reassess the security of VSL.
- We propose an innovative data reconstruction attack to generate relatively good reconstructed data using the priori knowledge embedded in partial sample features held by the passive party and the posteriori information of the active party's private data extracted from gradients returned by the server.
- Extensive experimental results demonstrate the effectiveness of our attack strategy. We obtained good reconstruction on image datasets such as CIFAR-10 and CelebA, with SSIM and LPIPS values showing strong performance. Additional ablation experiments confirmed the validity of our design.

2 Backgrounds

2.1 Vertical Split Learning

VSL assumes that the data are partitioned by features. As an example, we provide a formal definition of the VSL system shown in Fig. 1 in the context of supervised classification.

Let the participants be P_a and P_b with a client model f_a and f_b respectively. Their local datasets are represented as X_a and X_b, where $X_i = (U, F_i)(i = a, b)$. Here, U denotes the common sample space, while F_i represents the distinct feature space of each party. In this setting, P_a is designated as the passive party, while P_b acts as the active party, holding the label information Y as well as the server model f_{top}.

During the training process of VSL, all participants process local data using their own client models and send intermediate features $Z_i = f_i(X_i)$ to the active party's server. The server then concatenates these intermediate features $Z = Concat(Z_1, ..., Z_i)$ and feeds them into the server model for subsequent computation $\hat{Y} = f_{top}(Z)$. During the model update process, the backpropagation gradients are passed back to individual client models through the split layer. The inference phase is similar to the training phase but without backpropagation.

2.2 Data Reconstruction Attacks on Split Learning

Data reconstruction attacks aim to exploit information such as model parameters, gradients or outputs to reconstruct the original data, thereby compromising data privacy.

Existing data reconstruction attacks in split learning typically assume that the attacker is located on the server and can easily access the intermediate features Z uploaded by the clients. In this case, since the client model f typically consists of a series of simple convolutional layers, He et al. [11] suggested that the server-side attacker could build an inversion network f^{-1} made up of deconvolutional layers, aiming to reverse-map the intermediate features Z back to the sample space:

$$X^* = f^{-1}(f(X)) \tag{1}$$

In VSL, the attacker may act as the passive party. As shown in Fig. 1, the attacker only owns a client model and cannot obtain the intermediate features uploaded by other clients. However, they can access the gradients provided by the active party during the training phase. Therefore, it is necessary to reconsider the attack steps.

Chen et al. [10] proposed that a passive party can falsely claim to have missing data and replace them with random noise to participate in VSL training process. After obtaining the gradients returned by the server, the passive party can restore the missing data using an inversion network. However, their method solely focuses on recovering the data lost by the passive party itself and does not address the aspect of stealing data from the active party, which minimizes the perceived dangers linked to spy attacks.

3 Method

In this section, we present the threat model and methodological details of the data reconstruction attack that the passive party performs on the active party. The overview of the proposed method is shown in Fig. 2.

3.1 Threat Model

We assume that the attacker is the passive party P_a in a VSL system and owns a client model f_a together with half of the sample features X_a. It is honest but curious about the private training data X_b of the active party P_b. The attacker is aware of the structure of the active party's client model f_b. In addition, the attacker can collect an auxiliary dataset X^{aux} in the same domain as the private training data X from the Internet.

3.2 Obtain Initial Reconstruction via Partial Sample Features

We observe that in many deep learning prediction tasks, it is often necessary to utilize certain features to infer other single or multiple features, which clearly

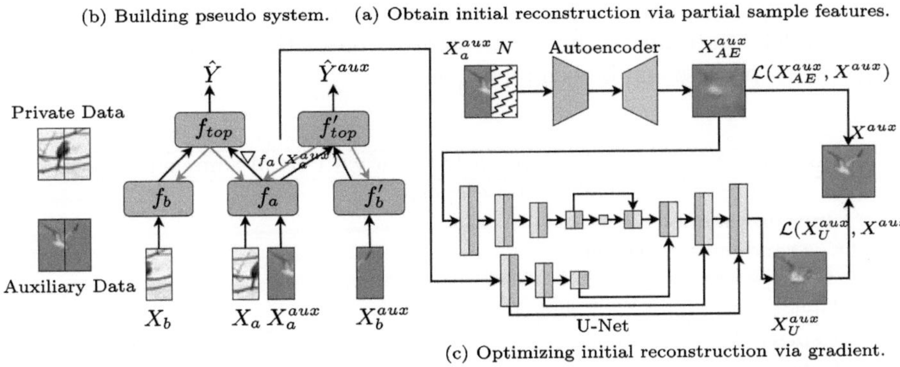

Fig. 2. The overview of the proposed attack's training process. The attacker first mines the associations between the sample features via an autoencoder to generate the initial reconstruction $\hat{X}_{AE}^{aux}$ (a). Next, a shadow VSL system is constructed for simulating the server's behavior in generating gradients (b). Finally, the $\hat{X}_{AE}^{aux}$ is optimized by a U-Net network using the posteriori information of the private data contained in the gradient $\nabla_{f_a(X_a^{aux})}$ to obtain a more accurate reconstruction $\hat{X}_U^{aux}$ (c). In this case, steps (a) and (c) can be done offline, while step (b) needs to be performed online.

indicates that there is an intrinsic connection between the sample features. This property is particularly evident in image data, where there is a strong correlation between image pixels.

Based on this observation, we employ an autoencoder-based network to explore the potential correlations between sample features. The autoencoder can effectively learn data representations through unsupervised approach, which aligns closely with our goals. During training, the encoder compresses the high-dimensional data input from the passive party into a 1×100 low-dimensional representation and learns the intrinsic correlations between the sample features of the passive and active parties. Subsequently, the decoder learns how to reconstruct the active party's private data using learned correlations. The specific design details of the autoencoder can be found in Appendix A.

We summarize the steps in Algorithm 1 and provide a detailed description below. During the training data preparation phase, we first divide the samples in the auxiliary dataset X^{aux} into two parts X_a^{aux} and X_b^{aux} according to the feature division protocol of the VSL system. X_b^{aux} simulates the data of the active party that we want to reconstruct and is replaced by random noise N (line 1–2). Then we concatenate X_a^{aux} with N and feed the concatenated data into the autoencoder to generate initial reconstruction results $\hat{X}_{AE}^{aux}$ (line 3–5). The model is optimized by minimizing the mean square error (MSE) between $\hat{X}_{AE}^{aux}$ and the original data X^{aux} (line 6–8). This process can be formulated as:

$$\theta_{AE}^* = argmin_{\theta_{AE}} \mathcal{L}(AE((X_a^{aux}|N)), X^{aux}). \qquad (2)$$

where AE represents the autoencoder and θ_{AE} is a set of parameters for it.

After completing the training of the autoencoder, we can input X_a into the trained model to obtain the initial reconstruction of the private data, denoted as $\hat{X}_{AE}$. This process can be conducted offline.

Algorithm 1: Obtain Initial Reconstruction via Partial Sample Features

Data: auxiliary dataset X^{aux}, total epochs E;
/* Initialize model */
AE is randomly initialized;
/* Data preparation */
1. Divide X^{aux} into X_a^{aux} and X_b^{aux};
2. Replace X_b^{aux} with noise N;
3. Concatenate X_a^{aux} with noise N;
/* training process of autoencoder */
4. while epoch $< E$:
5. $\hat{X}_{AE}^{aux} \leftarrow AE((X_a^{aux}|N))$
6. $\mathcal{L}_{AE} \leftarrow MSE(\hat{X}_{AE}^{aux}, X^{aux})$
7. $\nabla_{AE} \leftarrow compute\_gradient(\theta_{AE}, \mathcal{L}_{AE})$
8. $\theta'_{AE} \leftarrow update\_weight(\theta_{AE}, \nabla_{AE})$
9. end

3.3 Building Pseudo System

The VSL system enhances model effectiveness by leveraging knowledge from distributed data sources. Therefore, we believe that the gradients produced in the VSL training process inevitably contain knowledge about the private data of other participants. This provides us with a new insight: we can utilize the posterior information related to the active party's private data contained in the gradients to improve the accuracy of initial reconstruction results.

To leverage the posterior information about the private data contained in the gradients, we need to understand the patterns and behaviors involved in how the server generates these gradients. To achieve this, it is essential for us to construct a shadow VSL system that includes the passive party client model f_a, a pseudo active party client model f'_b, and a pseudo server model f'_{top}.

As shown in Algorithm 2, we first perform a normal round of VSL training to update the normal VSL system (line 4–11). Subsequently, we train the pseudo VSL system locally using auxiliary dataset, at which time it freezes the parameters of f_a and updates only the f'_b and f'_{top} (line 12–17). These two steps alternate until the training of the normal VSL system is complete.

In each round of alternating training, the shadow VSL system learns from the knowledge of the normal VSL system through f_a. This allows the parameters and behavior of the shadow VSL system to remain as consistent as possible with those of the normal VSL system, enabling the pseudo server f'_{top} to learn the gradient patterns generated by the actual server f_{top}.

Algorithm 2: Building Pseudo System

Data: private dataset (X,Y), auxiliary dataset (X^{aux}, Y^{aux}), total epochs E;
/* Initialize model */
Normal VSL system: f_a, f_b and f_{top} are randomly initialized;
Pseudo VSL system: f'_b and f'_{top} are randomly initialized;
/* Data preperation */
1. Divide X into X_a and X_b;
2. Divide X^{aux} into X_a^{aux} and X_b^{aux};
3. while epoch $< E$:
    /* Normal VSL training epoch */
4. $\hat{Y} \leftarrow f_{top}((f_a(X_a)|f_b(X_b)))$
5. $\mathcal{L}_{norm} \leftarrow CrossEntropy(\hat{Y}, Y)$
6. $\nabla_{f_{top}} \leftarrow compute\_gradient(\theta_{f_{top}}, \mathcal{L}_{norm})$
7. $\theta'_{f_{top}} \leftarrow update\_weight(\theta_{f_{top}}, \nabla_{f_{top}})$
8. $\nabla_{f_a} \leftarrow compute\_gradient(\theta_{f_a}, \nabla_{f_a(X_a)})$
9. $\nabla_{f_b} \leftarrow compute\_gradient(\theta_{f_b}, \nabla_{f_b(X_b)})$
10. $\theta'_{f_a} \leftarrow update\_weight(\theta_{f_a}, \nabla_{f_a})$
11. $\theta'_{f_b} \leftarrow update\_weight(\theta_{f_b}, \nabla_{f_b})$
    /* Pseudo VSL training process */
12. $\hat{Y}^{aux} \leftarrow f'_{top}((f_a(X_a^{aux})|f'_b(X_b^{aux})))$
13. $\mathcal{L}_{pseudo} \leftarrow CrossEntropy(\hat{Y}^{aux}, Y^{aux})$
14. $\nabla_{f'_{top}} \leftarrow compute\_gradient(\theta_{f'_{top}}, \mathcal{L}_{pseudo})$
15. $\theta'_{f'_{top}} \leftarrow update\_weight(\theta_{f'_{top}}, \nabla_{f'_{top}})$
16. $\nabla_{f'_b} \leftarrow compute\_gradient(\theta_{f'_b}, \nabla_{f'_b(X_b^{aux})})$
17. $\theta'_{f'_b} \leftarrow update\_weight(\theta_{f'_b}, \nabla_{f'_b})$
    /* The weight of f_a isn't update */
18. end

3.4 Optimizing Initial Reconstruction via Gradient

After mastering the representation pattern of privacy gradients, the next task is to extract the information contained in the gradients and use this information to enhance the quality of the initial reconstruction obtained in the first step. To achieve this, we introduce a model based on the U-Net [12] architecture. U-Net employs an encoder-decoder structure and utilizes skip connections to link the corresponding feature maps from the encoder to the decoder. We plan to improve the U-Net architecture so that it can simultaneously accept both the initial reconstruction and the gradients as inputs, allowing the initial reconstruction to serve as a good starting point for further optimizing the reconstruction results.

The structure of our U-Net is shown in Fig. 2. We designed an encoder for both the initial reconstruction and the gradients respectively. The encoder for the image is connected to the decoder, while the gradient maps generated by the gradient encoder are connected to the corresponding feature maps in the decoder through skip connections. This structure allows us to effectively combine the initial reconstruction with the gradients, making full use of the privacy information contained in both, thereby enhancing the quality of the reconstruction results. The specific network details can be found in Appendix B.

An intuitive explanation is that the gradients transmitted from the server to the passive party aggregate privacy information from other participants. Through the gradient encoder in the U-Net architecture, we can effectively extract the latent feature information embedded in these gradients and integrate this information into the decoder's feature maps via hierarchical feature fusion. This enables layer-by-layer progressive refinement, ultimately optimizing the reconstructed image quality.

As shown in Algorithm 3, during training, we feed the initial reconstruction $\hat{X}_{AE}^{aux}$ of the auxiliary dataset (line 5) and the gradients $\nabla_{f_a(X_a^{aux})}$ returned by the pseudo server f'_{top} (line 6–8) into the U-Net for exact reconstruction $\hat{X}_U^{aux}$ (line 9). The goal is the same as the first step, which aims to minimize the MSE loss between the $\hat{X}_U^{aux}$ and the original data X^{aux} (line 10–12). The process can be formulated as follows:

$$\theta_U^* = argmin_{\theta_U} \mathcal{L}(U((\nabla_{f_a(X_a^{aux})}|\hat{X}_{AE}^{aux})), X^{aux}). \tag{3}$$

where U represents the U-Net and θ_U is a set of parameters for it.

When the U-Net network is trained, we inputs the normal gradient $\nabla_{f_a(X_a)}$ collected in the second step along with the initial reconstruction of the privacy data $\hat{X}_{AE}$ obtained in the first step to achieve an more accurate reconstruction $\hat{X}_U$.

4 Experiments

4.1 Experimental Setup

1) Datasets and Tasks: We evaluate the proposed attack methods on the object dataset CIFAR-10 [13] and the facial dataset CelebA [14]. Both datasets are split into training, testing, and the attacker's auxiliary sets in a 6:1:3 ratio, ensuring a balanced distribution of categories in each subset. Additionally, we make sure that there is no identity overlap within the CelebA subset. We also incorporate more complex datasets, specifically Tiny-ImageNet [15] and LFW [16], to assess the effectiveness and broader applicability of our proposed attacks. Furthermore, the CINIC-10 [17] dataset and the FFHQ [18] dataset will be used for ablation experiments involving non-iid assumption, ensuring that there are no overlapping samples between CINIC-10 and CIFAR-10. The tasks include classifying the object and determining whether the facial attributes in the dataset are attractive through binary classification.

2) Model Architectures: We built our VSL system based on VGG16 [19] and ResNet18 [20] network architectures, with VGG16 used for classification on object datasets and ResNet18 used for classification on facial datasets. In addition, we tested our attack on Vision Transformer. We used the ViT/B-16 [21] model to classify the CIFAR-10 dataset. In the ablation experiments,

Algorithm 3: Optimizing Initial Reconstruction via Gradient
Data: auxiliary dataset X^{aux}, total epochs E;
/* Initialize model */
AE is trained in Algorithm 1;
Pseudo VSL system: f_a, f'_b and f'_{top} is trained in Algorithm 2;
U is randomly initialized;
/* Data preperation */
1. Divide X^{aux} into X_a^{aux} and X_b^{aux};
2. Replace X_b^{aux} with noise N;
3. Concatenate X_a^{aux} with noise N;
/* training process of U-Net */
4. while epoch $< E$:
    /* Get the initial reconstruction from AE */
5. $\hat{X}_{AE}^{aux} \leftarrow AE((X_a^{aux}|N))$
    /* Get gradient from f'_{top} */
6. $\hat{Y}^{aux} \leftarrow f'_{top}((f_a(X_a^{aux})|f'_b(X_b^{aux})))$
7. $\mathcal{L}_{pseudo} \leftarrow CrossEntropy(\hat{Y}^{aux}, Y^{aux})$
8. $\nabla_{f'_{top}} \leftarrow compute\_gradient(\theta_{f'_{top}}, \mathcal{L}_{pseudo})$
    /* Refine initial reconstruction $\hat{X}_{AE}^{aux}$ via gradient $\nabla_{f_a(X_a^{aux})}$ */
9. $\hat{X}_U^{aux} \leftarrow U((\hat{X}_{AE}^{aux}|\nabla_{f_a(X_a^{aux})}))$
10. $\mathcal{L}_U \leftarrow MSE(\hat{X}_U^{aux}, X^{aux})$
11. $\nabla_U \leftarrow compute\_gradient(\theta_U, \mathcal{L}_U)$
12. $\theta'_U \leftarrow update\_weight(\theta_U, \nabla_U)$
13. end

we introduced the MobileNet [22] architecture as a replacement for the server model. Different split points were tested to assess the impact of model depth on the results. The detailed model structure is presented in Appendix C.

3) Evaluation Metrics: We adopted structural similarity index (SSIM) [23] and learned perceptual image patch similarity (LPIPS) [24] to evaluate the quality of reconstructed images. A higher SSIM value, closer to 1, indicates greater similarity between reconstructed and original images. Conversely, LPIPS measures perceptual similarity, with smaller values indicating a smaller visual difference between reconstructed and original images.

4.2 Visuality Evaluation

Figure 3 shows the reconstruction results of the autoencoder and the optimization results of the U-Net using gradients obtained from different split points. As shown in Fig. 3, the reconstruction performance of U-Net is significantly better than that of the autoencoder, allowing for a better restoration of the details of the privacy data from the active party. In addition, at different depth of split points, the reconstruction results of U-Net show good robustness. As the split points go deeper, the reconstruction performance experiences only a slight decline. We believe that U-Net achieves better reconstruction results primarily due to the introduction of gradients, as the privacy information contained in the gradients helps enhance the reconstruction effect.

The quantitative results in Table 1 further support our conclusion. For CIFAR-10, the average SSIM and LPIPS values of the autoencoder's reconstruction results are 0.5132 and 0.3976, respectively; for CelebA, these values are 0.5843 and 0.3481. The average SSIM and LPIPS values for U-Net at block 1 are 0.5071 and 0.3395 for CIFAR-10, and 0.5877 and 0.2771 for CelebA. Even at the cut point of block 4, the LPIPS metrics of U-Net's reconstruction results improve by 0.0518 and 0.07 compared to the autoencoder for CIFAR-10 and CelebA, respectively. The metrics in the table consistently indicate that the attack method we proposed is quite robust.

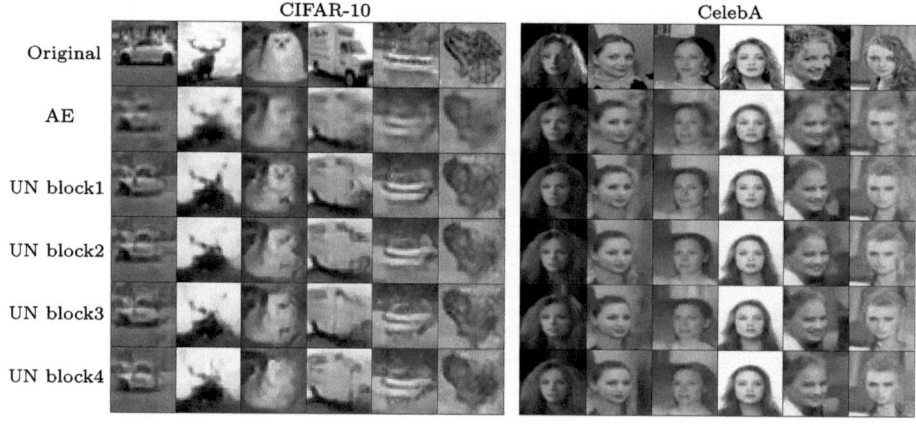

Fig. 3. Reconstruction results on CIFAR-10 and CelebA in different split settings.

Table 1. SSIM and LPIPS results in different split settings.

Dataset	Model	Split Point	SSIM↑	LPIPS↓	Dataset	Model	Split Point	SSIM↑	LPIPS↓
CIFAR10	AE		**0.5132**	0.3976	CelebA	AE		0.5843	0.3481
	UNet	block1	0.5071	**0.3395**		UNet	block1	**0.5877**	**0.2771**
		block2	0.5033	0.3448			block2	0.5865	0.2777
		block3	0.5024	0.3456			block3	0.5853	0.2781
		block4	0.5013	0.3458			block4	0.5835	0.2781

4.3 Effect of Auxiliary Dataset

We investigated the impact of the distribution of auxiliary datasets on data reconstruction attacks. The experiments were conducted on a VSL system with split point at block2, using CINIC-10 and FFHQ as non-iid auxiliary datasets for CIFAR-10 and CelebA respectively. Figure 4 shows the reconstruction results and Table 2 provides a quantitative comparison.

We observed that the quality of reconstruction results for CIFAR-10 and CelebA slightly deteriorated when using non-iid datasets. For CIFAR-10, the drop in reconstruction quality was relatively small because the distribution difference between CINIC-10 and CIFAR-10 is minor. In contrast, FFHQ has a much larger distribution difference from CelebA. Unlike CelebA, which contains face images with various angles, FFHQ predominantly features frontal face images. Furthermore, CelebA has more complex backgrounds, with faces occupying a smaller proportion of the images, while FFHQ has simpler backgrounds with faces occupying a larger proportion. Nevertheless, the attack we proposed is still able to recover most of the facial information, including pose, hairstyle and expression.

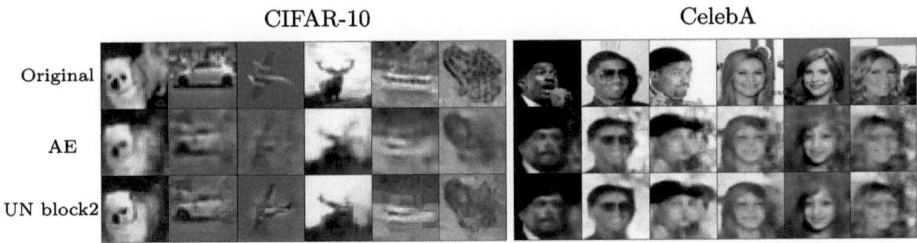

Fig. 4. Data reconstruction results of non-iid settings.

Table 2. SSIM and LPIPS results of no-iid settings.

Metric SSIM↑	CIFAR10		CelebA		Metric LPIPS↓	CIFAR10		CelebA	
	Same	Different	Same	Different		Same	Different	Same	Different
Autoencoder	0.5132	0.5077	0.5843	0.4602	Autoencoder	0.3976	0.4014	0.3481	0.4493
U-Net	0.5033	0.4877	0.5865	0.4821	U-Net	0.3448	0.3629	0.2777	0.4075

4.4 Effect of Substitute Server Structure

We also investigated the impact of different server architectures on reconstruction attacks. We used the MobileNet architecture to replace VGG16 and ResNet18 as the server model for the pseudo VSL system. In this experiment, we set the split layer to block2. Figure 5 shows the reconstructed images while using different server model architectures and Table 3 presents the quantitative results of the SSIM and LPIPS metrics.

Overall, the different server model architectures have little impact on the reconstruction results of our attack methods. In terms of visual effects, the reconstruction results of U-Net in Fig. 3 and Fig. 5 are almost identical and the metrics experienced only slight fluctuations. This is because, despite the different model architectures, the learning objectives remain consistent. As a result, the optimization directions guided by the gradients are consistent, which leads to good reconstruction results.

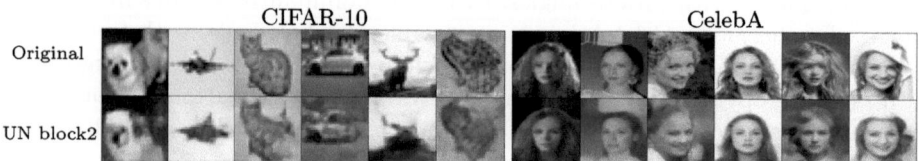

Fig. 5. Reconstruction results of different server models.

Table 3. SSIM and LPIPS results of different server models.

Metric	CIFAR10		CelebA	
	Same	Different	Same	Different
SSIM↑	0.5033	0.4981	0.5865	0.5827
LPIPS↓	0.3448	0.3449	0.2777	0.2787

4.5 Effectiveness on Complex Dataset and Model

We conducted extended experiments using the Tiny-Imagenet and LFW datasets. Tiny-Imagenet includes 200 categories of different objects, with around 500 images in each category. The LFW dataset contains over 13,000 labeled face images. We divided the datasets and launched the attack on ResNet18 with split point at block2 in the same way as in our main experiments. As shown in Fig. 6a, our attack demonstrates good visual results on both datasets, sufficient to reveal the privacy data of the active party. This proves that our attack is effective in complex datasets and even in real-world scenarios.

In practical applications, edge devices typically maintain only a shallower model to achieve the highest end-to-cloud workload while offloading complex computations to the cloud. But in order to explore the effectiveness of our attack method on complex and novel model architectures, we conducted attack experiments at a deeper splitting point after the 8th transformer block of the ViT-B/16 model on CIFAR-10 dataset. As shown in Fig. 6b, even with more complex model structures, we still achieved good attack results, with SSIM = 0.4940 and LPIPS = 0.3439, demonstrating that our attack method is model-agnostic.

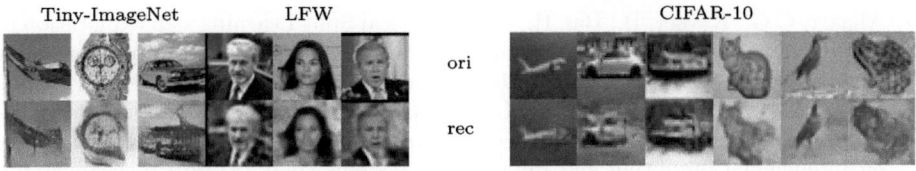

(a) Attack results on complex datasets. (b) Attack results on complex model.

Fig. 6. Reconstruction results on complex datasets and model.

4.6 Defense Discuss

Our attack is difficult to defend against because it does not interfere with the normal VSL training process and is transparent to the active party, making it hard to detect. Furthermore, there is currently no research exploring the possibility of the passive party stealing data from the active party like us. In VSL systems, inference tasks are initiated by the vigilant-challenged active party, which typically does not want to implement defenses that could affect model performance.

5 Conclusion

In this paper, we make the first attempt to investigate the issue of passive parties stealing data from active parties in the VSL scenario and propose corresponding attack methods. We exploit the prior information contained in the partial sample features held by the passive party using an autoencoder to obtain an initial reconstruction. At the same time, we synchronously construct a pseudo VSL system during the training process to learn the gradient patterns generated by the server. Subsequently, we use an improved U-Net to leverage the posterior information about the private data embedded in the gradients to optimize the initial reconstruction, resulting in more accurate reconstruction outcomes. We validate the effectiveness of our attack methods through extensive experiments. We hope our work will draw attention to the security of VSL and encourage a reassessment of data security within VSL. All of our supplementary materials, including code, appendices, and supplemental experiments, can be found at: https://github.com/yxliu42/VSL.

References

1. Vepakomma, P., Gupta, O., Swedish, T., Raskar R.: Split learning for health: distributed deep learning without sharing raw patient data. arXiv preprint arXiv:1812.00564 (2018)
2. Gupta, O., Raskartitle, R.: Distributed learning of deep neural network over multiple agents. J. Netw. Comput. Appl. **116**, 1–8 (2018)
3. Li, P., Guo, C., Xing, Y., et al.: Core network traffic prediction based on vertical federated learning and split learning. Sci. Rep. **14**(1), 4663 (2024)

4. Allaart, C.G., Keyser, B., Bal, H., et al.: Vertical Split Learning - an exploration of predictive performance in medical and other use cases. In: 2022 International Joint Conference on Neural Networks (IJCNN) on Proceedings, pp. 1–8. IEEE (2022)
5. Ads, O.S., Alfares, M.M., Salem, M.A.M.: Multi-limb split learning for tumor classification on vertically distributed data. In: 2021 Tenth International Conference on Intelligent Computing and Information Systems (ICICIS) on Proceedings, pp. 88–92. IEEE (2021)
6. Ezzeddine, F., Ayoub, O., Andreoletti, D., et al.: Vertical split learning-based identification and explainable deep learning-based localization of failures in multi-domain NFV systems. In: 2023 IEEE Conference on Network Function Virtualization and Software Defined Networks (NFV-SDN) on Proceedings, pp. 46–52. IEEE (2023)
7. Yang, M., Li, Z., Wang, J., et al.: Measuring data reconstruction defenses in collaborative inference systems. In: the 2022 Neural Information Processing Systems (NIPS) on Proceedings, pp. 12855–12867. Curran Associates, Inc. (2022)
8. Li, Z., Yang, M., Liu, Y., et al.: GAN you see me? Enhanced data reconstruction attacks against split inference. In: 2023 Neural Information Processing Systems on Proceedings, pp. 54554–54566. Curran Associates, Inc. (2023)
9. Xu, X., Yang, M., Yi, W., et al.: A stealthy wrongdoer: feature-oriented reconstruction attack against split learning. In: the 2024 IEEE/CVF Conference on Computer Vision and Pattern Recognition (CVPR) on Proceedings, pp. 12130–12139 (2024)
10. Chen, H., Fu, C., Ruan, N.: Steal from collaboration: spy attack by a dishonest party in vertical federated learning. In: 2023 International Conference on Applied Cryptography and Network Security on Proceedings, pp. 583–604. Springer, Cham (2023)
11. He, Z., Zhang, T., Lee, R.B.: Model inversion attacks against collaborative inference. In: the 35th Annual Computer Security Applications Conference (ACSAC) on Proceedings, pp. 148-162. Association for Computing Machinery, New York (2019)
12. Ronneberger, O., Fischer, P., Brox, T.: U-Net: convolutional networks for biomedical image segmentation. In: Navab, N., Hornegger, J., Wells, W.M., Frangi, A.F. (eds.) MICCAI 2015. LNCS, vol. 9351, pp. 234–241. Springer, Cham (2015). https://doi.org/10.1007/978-3-319-24574-4_28
13. Krizhevsky, A., Hinton, G.: Learning multiple layers of features from tiny images (2009)
14. Liu, Z., Luo, P., Wang, X., et al.: Deep learning face attributes in the wild. In: 2015 IEEE International Conference on Computer Vision (ICCV) (2015)
15. Wu, J., Zhang, Q., Xu, G.: Tiny imagenet challenge. Technical report (2017)
16. Huang, G.B., Mattar, M., Berg, T., et al.: Labeled faces in the wild: a database for studying face recognition in unconstrained environments. In: the 2007 IEEE Computer Society Conference on Computer Vision and Pattern Recognition (CVPR) on Proceedings, pp. 1–8 (2007)
17. Darlow, L.N., Crowley, E.J., Antoniou, A., et al.: Cinic-10 is not imagenet or cifar-10. arXiv preprint arXiv:1810.03505 (2018)
18. Karras, T., Laine, S., Aila, T.: A style-based generator architecture for generative adversarial networks. In: 2019 IEEE/CVF Conference on Computer Vision and Pattern Recognition (CVPR) (2019)
19. Simonyan, K., Zisserman, A.: Very deep convolutional networks for large-scale image recognition. arXiv preprint arXiv:1409.1556 (2014)

20. He, K., Zhang, X., Ren, S., et al.: Deep residual learning for image recognition. In: 2016 IEEE Conference on Computer Vision and Pattern Recognition (CVPR) (2016)
21. Dosovitskiy, A., Beyer, L., Kolesnikov, A., et al.: An image is worth 16x16 words: transformers for image recognition at scale. arXiv preprint arXiv:2010.11929 (2020)
22. Howard, A., Zhu, M., Chen, B., et al.: MobileNets: efficient convolutional neural networks for mobile vision applications. arXiv preprint arXiv:1704.04861 (2017)
23. Wang, Z., Bovik, A.C., Sheikh, H.R., et al.: Image quality assessment: from error visibility to structural similarity. IEEE Trans. Image Process. **13**(4), 600–612 (2004)
24. Zhang, R., Isola, P., Efros, A.A., et al.: The unreasonable effectiveness of deep features as a perceptual metric. In: the 2018 IEEE Conference on Computer Vision and Pattern Recognition on Proceedings, pp. 586–595 (2018)

DeepCore: Simple Fingerprint Construction for Differentiating Homologous and Piracy Models

Haifeng Sun[✉], Lan Zhang, and Xiang-Yang Li

University of Science and Technology of China, Hefei, China
sun1998@mail.ustc.edu.cn, {zhanglan,xiangyangli}@ustc.edu.cn

Abstract. As intellectual property rights, the copyright protection of deep models is becoming increasingly important. Existing work has made many attempts at model watermarking and fingerprinting, but they have ignored homologous models trained with similar structures or training datasets. We highlight challenges in efficiently querying black-box piracy models to protect model copyrights without misidentifying homologous models. To address these challenges, we propose a novel method called DeepCore, which discovers that the classification confidence of the model is positively correlated with the distance of the predicted sample from the model decision boundary and piracy models behave more similarly at high-confidence classified sample points. Then DeepCore constructs core points far away from the decision boundary by optimizing the predicted confidence of a few sample points and leverages behavioral discrepancies between piracy and homologous models to identify piracy models. Finally, we design different model identification methods, including two similarity-based methods and a clustering-based method, to identify piracy models using the models' predictions of core points. Extensive experiments show the effectiveness of DeepCore in identifying various piracy models, achieving lower missed and false identification rates, and outperforming state-of-the-art methods.

Keywords: Model Copyright Protection · Piracy · Homologous Model

1 Introduction

In recent years, deep learning has witnessed rapid development and found extensive applications in various fields, such as computer vision [33], speech recognition [13], and natural language processing [37]. Many companies choose not to open-source deep learning models to protect their commercial interests. This is due to the significant resources required for training advanced neural network models, including massive datasets, substantial computing power, and the expertise of the designers. For example, training models like GPT-3 demand 45 TB of data and incur training costs exceeding 12 million US dollars. However, the issue of model copyright faces numerous security threats. Adversaries could obtain white-box models through unconventional means and make modifications [22,27] like fine-tuning, pruning, and adversarial training. Additionally, adversaries can steal models through model extraction attacks [3,16,31,39]. Consequently, there has been an upsurge in research to address these threats [19]. Existing studies can be broadly categorized into two types. The first type employs model watermarking methods [1,5,8,17,36,40], which require modifying the original model and often lead to model performance degradation. Additionally, most watermarking methods struggle to withstand model extraction attacks. The second type adopts model fingerprinting methods [2,10,21,23,32], with current research primarily focusing on decision boundaries. These methods characterize the similarity of decision boundaries using adversarial examples. However, adversaries can manipulate decision boundaries through adversarial training, rendering the fingerprint ineffective. Besides, as shown in Fig. 1, there are homologous models trained by other legitimate users using similar model architectures or datasets. The existence of homologous models could increase the difficulty of identifying piracy models. However, existing work ignored the study of distinguishing homologous models. Consequently, there is an urgent need to safeguard deep neural network models against illegal copying and protect homologous models.

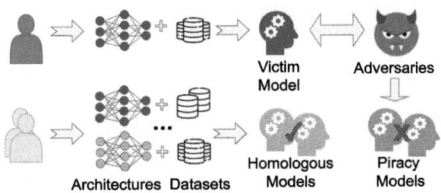

Fig. 1. Homologous models have similar model architectures or training data of the victim model and train independently. Piracy models depend on the victim model through illegal theft of the white-box model or model extraction attacks.

Our research confronts three main challenges. Firstly, we strive to ensure no piracy models are overlooked and avoid misidentifying homologous models. This cannot be easy because similar model architectures and datasets could train similar models. Secondly, the model owner only has black-box access to piracy models and gets the models' predictions of query samples. Thirdly, the model fingerprint not only needs to be effective but also efficient. Using as few query samples as possible can reduce costs and, at the same time, avoid being detected by adversaries. To address these challenges, we propose DeepCore that constructs high-confidence samples named core points to obtain the model fingerprint. Through experimental analysis, we first have three insights: 1) the higher the predicted score of a sample, the farther it is from the model decision boundary, 2) piracy models output scores closer than the homologous models on core points, and 3) the farther the sample is from the model decision boundary, the greater the output score difference between homologous models and piracy models. Core points have more similar predicted scores between piracy models and the victim model due to the similarity of their decision boundaries. So we can identify Homologous and Piracy Models by constructing such high-confidence samples. To solve the black-box limitation, we provide three identification methods of piracy models, including $L_1\_$dist-based, Cos_dist-based, and clustering-based methods to measure the model outputs' correlation. For query efficiency, DeepCore constructs at most one core point for each classification category of the victim model. The main contributions of our work are summarized as follows:

- We propose a simple but novel method called DeepCore to construct a model fingerprint, which can effectively and efficiently identify piracy models without misidentifying homologous models.
- We are the first to discover the behavioral discrepancies on high-confidence classified samples between piracy and homologous models. We have derived three insights through experimental analysis, and we utilize these insights to construct such high-confident samples. Finally, we design different model identification methods using these high-confidence samples.
- Extensive experimental results demonstrate the effectiveness of DeepCore in identifying various piracy models across different architectures and datasets. Specifically, DeepCore can achieve a missed identification rate (MIR) and a false identification rate (FIR) of 0 for piracy models, surpassing the performance of state-of-the-art methods.

2 Related Work

The production of piracy models poses a serious threat to the legitimate rights and interests of model owners. These models can be broadly categorized into the following types: (1) Fine-tuning [34]. (2) Pruning [11,22,27]. (3) Adversarial training [25]. (4) Model extraction attack [16,31]. Many methods have emerged recently to protect the copyrights of model owners, which can be roughly divided into two categories: model watermarking methods and model fingerprinting methods. (1) Model watermarking methods [1,5,7,8,14,17,36,40] need to modify the parameters of the victim model and embed the watermarks carefully designed by the defender in the model, and finally verify whether it is a piracy model by detecting the watermarks. However, most watermarking methods are not effective against model extraction attacks. VEF [20] can survive during the model extraction, but it needs white-box access to the adversary's model. In addition, the watermarking methods can also cause the loss of accuracy [6,8]. (2) Model fingerprint methods [2,10,21,23,26,32,38] do not need to modify the victim model. Instead, these methods determine if a suspected model is a piracy model by analyzing its output behavior using a carefully constructed fingerprint set. Many existing methods [2,21,23,32] utilize adversarial examples to measure the similarity of decision boundaries between the suspected model and the victim model, determining whether the suspected model is a piracy model. However, these methods rely heavily on adversarial examples and are not robust against adversarial defense mechanisms [25]. While MetaFinger [38] fingerprints the inner decision space of the model by meta-training instead of using decision boundaries. However, it does not consider homologous models and piracy models obtained by model extraction attacks. SAC [10] proposes a novel model stealing identification method based on sample correlation, but does not address the false identification of homologous models. Inspired by the ideas of MetaFinger and SAC, we propose DeepCore, a novel approach that utilizes robust samples from the inner decision space strongly associated with the victim model as the fingerprint. Our method can effectively distinguish between different types of piracy models and homologous models.

3 Framework

3.1 Overview

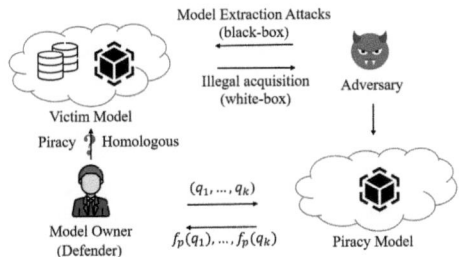

Fig. 2. A threat model of copyright protection of deep models.

Our framework formalizes the threat of model piracy through three models—victim models (f_v), homologous models (f_h), and piracy models ($f_p/f_{\hat{p}}$), and proposes DeepCore to distinguish homologous models from piracy models.

Definition 1 (Victim Model). We denote the victim model training data as $X_v \subset \{(x,y) | x \in [0,1]^M, x \sim \mu, y \in Y = \{1, \ldots, N\}\}$, where y represents the true label and μ represents the data distribution. We denote the victim model trained by X_v as $f_v : [0,1]^M \to R^N$, aiming to optimize: $P_{(x,y) \sim X_v}(\arg\max_i f_v(x)_i = y)$.

Definition 2 (Homologous Model). Homologous models denoted as $f_h : [0,1]^M \to R^N$ are legally trained by others. The training data is denoted as $X_h \subset \{(x,y) | x \in [0,1]^M, x \sim \mu, y \in Y\}$. The overlap ratio between X_h and X_v can be defined by $overlap(X_h, X_v) = \frac{|X_h \cap X_v|}{|X_v|}$. The model architecture can be different from the victim model. Aiming to optimize: $P_{(x,y) \sim X_h}(\arg\max_i f_h(x)_i = y)$.

Definition 3 (Piracy Model). Piracy models obtained by the adversary can be denoted as f_p or $f_{\hat{p}} : [0,1]^M \to R^N$. We define $X_p \subset \{(x,y) | x \in [0,1]^M, x \sim \mu, y \in Y\}$ as the adversary's attack dataset. For piracy models obtained by illegal acquisition of the victim model, the piracy model is defined by $f_p = \Phi_{X_p}(f_v)$, where Φ represents a post-processing operation, such as fine-tuning, pruning, and adversarial training. For model extraction attacks, the adversary aims to optimize the piracy model $f_{\hat{p}}$ as follows: $P_{(x,y) \sim X_p}(\arg\max_i f_{\hat{p}}(x)_i = \arg\max_i f_v(x)_i)$.

3.2 Threat Model

Figure 2 gives a threat model. The threat model consists of two main entities: an adversary and a defender, who is also the model owner. The adversary can obtain the defender's model in two ways: model extraction attacks and illegally acquiring the white-box model. Then the adversary could use post-processing techniques to modify the model, such as fine-tuning, pruning, and adversarial training, aiming to monetize the model by just providing the model API. Thus, the defender only has black-box access to the adversary's model, denoted as f_p. This means that the defender can only obtain the output of the adversary's model, denoted as $f_p(q_i)$ when providing a query sample q_i. The defender's goal is to identify whether it is a piracy model by analyzing the outputs of the adversary's model.

3.3 DeepCore Design

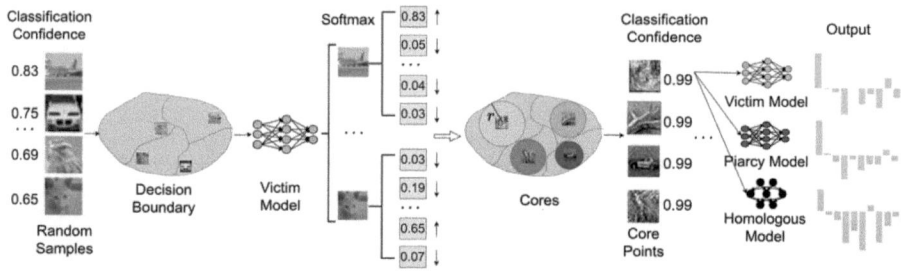

Fig. 3. Given random samples as initial core points, these samples may be near the model decision boundary. For a sample, DeepCore constrains its softmax score so that its classification confidence in a certain category continues to increase and in other categories continues to decrease. Finally, core points far from the decision boundary can be obtained, and the output of the piracy model for these core points is more similar to the victim model than the homologous model.

Figure 3 gives the DeepCore design. The core idea of DeepCore is to construct samples strongly related to the victim model's classification confidence. Deep-Core is based on three insights, which are analyzed in Sect. 4.2. For each category of the model outputs, DeepCore can build high-confidence samples. Due to the behavioral discrepancies on high-confidence classified samples between piracy and ho- mologous models, piracy models have higher classification confidence for such samples, and the output scores are closer to the victim model than homologous models. Here, the score means the model's last-layer logit of the corresponding label, and the confidence means post-softmax probability. Deep-Core aims to optimize the i-th core point denoted as ϕ_i of the corresponding label i by the following loss:

$$\text{loss} = -\log \sigma(f_v(\phi_i))_i, \tag{1}$$

where $\sigma : \mathbb{R}^N \to (0,1)^N$ is a standard softmax function defined by the formula $\sigma(z)_i = \frac{e^{z_i}}{\sum_{j=1}^N e^{z_j}}$, for $i = 1, \ldots, N$, $z = (z_1, \ldots, z_N) \in \mathbb{R}^N$. The goal is to make the victim model's prediction confidence of label i as high as possible.

Algorithm 1: DeepCore

Input: The victim model f_v, hyper-parameter θ, γ
Output: Cores $\{B_{r_i}(\phi_i)\}$
1: **for** Every label $i \in Y$ **do**
2:     Initialize ϕ_i, r, Δ
3:     **while** $\Delta > \gamma$ **do**
4:         $L = -\log \sigma(f_v(\phi_i))_i$
5:         update $\phi_i = \phi_i - \theta \nabla L$
6:         Initialize $j \leftarrow 0, \hat{\phi}_j \leftarrow \phi_i$
7:         **while** $a : \arg\max_k f_v(\hat{\phi}_j)_k = b : \arg\max_k f_v(\phi_i)_k$ **do**
8:             **for** $l \neq b$ **do**
9:                 $\omega_l = \nabla f_v(\hat{\phi}_j)_l - \nabla f_v(\hat{\phi}_j)_b$
10:            **end for**
11:            $\hat{l} = \arg\min_{l \neq b} \frac{|f_v(\hat{\phi}_j)_l - f_v(\hat{\phi}_j)_b|}{||\omega_l||_2}$
12:            $\delta_j = \frac{|f_v(\hat{\phi}_j)_{\hat{l}} - f_v(\hat{\phi}_j)_b|}{||\omega_{\hat{l}}||_2}$
13:            $\hat{\phi}_{j+1} = \hat{\phi}_j + \delta_j$
14:            $j \leftarrow j + 1$
15:         **end while**
16:         $r_i = ||\sum_j \delta_j||_2$
17:         $\Delta = |r_i - r|$
18:         $r \leftarrow r_i$
19:     **end while**
20: **end for**
21: **return** $\{B_{r_i}(\phi_i)\} \leftarrow \{\phi_i, r_i | i \in Y\}$

Algorithm 1 gives the details on generating the cores. DeepCore defines $B_{r_i}(\phi_i)$ as the victim model core, where r_i is the core radius. To initialize the core point ϕ_i for each label $i \in Y$, DeepCore randomly selects a sample from the distribution μ. Next, DeepCore reduces the loss (1) by gradient descent to update the core point. Lines 6–16 of the algorithm are used to calculate the shortest distance from the current core point to the model decision boundary, which is defined as the core radius. To calculate the radius of the core, Deep-Fool [28] is leveraged, which can effectively compute the minimum perturbation that causes misclassification in deep neural networks. Through this method, for the core point $\hat{\phi}_j$ we are optimizing, we continuously iterate by adding noise $delta_j$ until the model's classification results change ($l \neq b$). Throughout this process, all noise vectors are accumulated, and their norm $r_i = ||\sum_j \delta_j||_2$ is calculated to determine the current core radius. Then Δ is used to calculate the difference in core radius before and after updating the core points. The algorithm terminates when each core radius converges (i.e., $\Delta < \gamma$, where $\gamma \to 0$). Finally, the model fingerprint denoted as F is defined by $F = \{\phi_i | i = 1, \ldots, N\}$. We can improve query efficiency by further reducing the number of core points with large core radii as the fingerprint.

3.4 DeepCore Identification

We provide three methods to identify homologous models and piracy models. DeepCore constructs core points by optimizing the confidence of samples in specific categories, making the core points predicted by the piracy model have scores closer to the victim model in the corresponding categories. Therefore, the first method uses the L_1 distance between a victim and a suspected model to identify. Given a suspected model $f_s : [0,1]^M \to R^N$, we define the L_1 model distance on the model fingerprint F as follows: $L_1\_dist(f_v, f_s, F) = \sum_{i=1}^{N} |f_v(\phi_i)_i - f_s(\phi_i)_i|$. Note that the core points constructed by DeepCore can make the score of a specific category much higher than that of other categories. Each core point in the fingerprint set is very different; the second method utilizes this difference in categories to identify piracy models. To capture the correlations between the suspected model's outputs on the model fingerprint F, we use cosine similarity, denoted as $Cos(f_s, F)$ [10,30] to express as follows: $Cos(f_s, F)_{ij} = \frac{f_s(\phi_i)^T f_s(\phi_j)}{||f_s(\phi_i)|| ||f_s(\phi_j)||}$. We define the model distance of cosine similarity as follows: $Cos\_dist(f_v, f_s, F) = \frac{||Cos(f_v, F) - Cos(f_s, F)||_1}{N^2}$. By empirically stetting discriminant thresholds d_1, d_2, the suspected model is a piracy model if $L_1\_dist(f_v, f_s, F) < d_1$ or $Cos\_dist(f_v, f_s, F) < d_2$. In the experiments, to determine the thresholds d_1 and d_2, we statistically analyzed the distribution of L1 distances and cosine similarities of various existing models to select suitable thresholds, aiming to maximize the differentiation between homologous and piracy models. However, the first two threshold methods will no longer apply to identify the piracy model types. We use a clustering idea to solve this challenge. For example, we want to successfully identify homologous models, post-processing piracy models, and piracy models by model extraction attacks. Assume post-processing piracy models, denoted as f_p, piracy models obtained by model extraction attacks, denoted as $f_{\hat{p}}$, and homologous models, denoted as f_h, respectively satisfy the distribution π_p, $\pi_{\hat{p}}$ and π_h. we can get three cluster centers denoted as $\{\hat{c}_1, \hat{c}_2, \hat{c}_3\}$ from set $\{o_h, o_p, o_{\hat{p}} | f_p \sim \pi_p, f_{\hat{p}} \sim \pi_{\hat{p}}, f_h \sim \pi_h\}$, where $o_j = (f_j(\phi_1), \ldots, f_j(\phi_N)), j \in \{h, p, \hat{p}\}$. We use the fingerprint set as the input to query the suspected model to get an output denoted by $o_s = (f_s(\phi_1), \ldots, f_s(\phi_N))$ and compare the output with the cluster centers to determine which class the suspected model belongs to.

4 Experiments

4.1 Setup

Dataset. We use CIFAR-10 and CIFAR-100 [18] as base datasets. CIFAR-10 comprises 60,000 images of size 32×32 pixels, evenly distributed into ten categories. CIFAR-100 has 100 classes containing 600 images each. There are 500 training images and 100 testing images per class.

Victim and Homologous Model Training Data. We divide the datasets into three parts, in which the victim model training data, the homologous model training data, and the adversary's attack data ratio is 2:2:1. We set the overlap ratio between the homologous model training set and the victim model training set from 0 to 1 and the interval is 0.1.

Piracy Model Attack Methods. We conduct experimental evaluations on the following piracy models: **Fine-tuning** [34]: There are two commonly used fine-tuning methods. One is to use the adversary's dataset to fine-tune only the last layer before the model output, and the other is to fine-tune all the model layers. **Pruning**: The pruning strategy adopted in the experiment is Fine Pruning [22], a combination of pruning and fine-tuning, which shows that it successfully weakens or even eliminates the model backdoor. **Adversarial Training** [25]: To evade the traditional fingerprint method of adversarial samples, the adversary introduces adversarial training to evade identification. **Model Extraction Attacks**: We leverage the label-based model extraction attacks [16,31] and probability-based model extraction attacks [9,16,35].

Homologous Model and Piracy Model Setting. All the piracy and homologous models are trained on ResNet [12], DenseNet [15], and we use the ResNet model as the victim model architecture. Table 1 shows the type and number of test models. HM_SA represents a homologous model trained using the same model architecture as the victim model, HM_DA represents a homologous model trained using a different model architecture, PM_P represents a piracy model obtained by pruning, PM_FL represents a piracy model obtained by Fine-tuning the last layer of the victim model, PM_FA represents a piracy model obtained by Fine-tuning all the layers of the victim model, PM_Adv represents a piracy model obtained by adversarial training, EM_SA_L represents a piracy model obtained by label-based model extraction attacks with the same model architecture as the victim model, EM_DA_L represents a piracy model obtained by label-based model extraction attacks with a different model architecture, EM_SA_Pr represents a piracy model obtained by probability-based model extraction attacks with the same model architecture as the victim model, EM_DA_Pr represents a piracy model obtained by probability-based model extraction attacks with a different model architecture.

Table 1. The type and number of models.

Type	HM_SA	HM_DA	PM_P	PM_FL	PM_FA
Number	10	11	10	10	10
Type	PM_Adv	EM_SA_L	EM_DA_L	EM_SA_Pr	EM_DA_Pr
Number	10	10	10	10	10

Model IP Protection Baselines. To validate our method's performance, we compare it with three state-of-the-art works: SAC-w, SAC-m [10]: SAC-w selects wrongly classified samples as model inputs and calculates the mean correlation among their model outputs. SAC-m selects cut-mix augmented samples as model inputs without training the surrogate models or generating adversarial examples. MetaFinger [38]: MetaFinger proposes a robust fingerprint method about the inner decision space of the model by meta-training. FUAP [32]: FUAP proposes a novel and practical mechanism to construct fingerprints by Universal Adversarial Perturbations (UAPs).

Evaluation Metrics. To verify the effectiveness of different fingerprint methods, we have two metrics: Missed Identification Rate (MIR): The missed identification rate refers to the ratio of the number of undetected piracy models to the number of all piracy models. False Identification Rate (FIR): The false identification rate refers to the ratio of the number of homologous models detected as piracy models to the number of all homologous models.

Table 2. The core radii and scores of different core points on CIFAR-10.

Radius|score	$r_0\|s_0$	$r_1\|s_1$	$r_2\|s_2$	$r_3\|s_3$	$r_4\|s_4$	$r_5\|s_5$	$r_6\|s_6$	$r_7\|s_7$	$r_8\|s_8$	$r_9\|s_9$
Core$_1$	9.83|23.15	16.94|43.05	14.11|35.27	9.89|31.70	10.67|33.05	15.55|38.14	12.19|32.84	25.31|46.34	14.17|34.79	15.50|40.32
Core$_2$	13.61|29.06	23.51|56.58	20.24|42.35	11.97|37.52	13.64|38.74	18.02|46.31	14.82|38.05	28.88|54.63	18.77|44.79	18.56|46.79
Core$_3$	15.41|32.29	26.97|67.39	21.98|45.92	13.46|41.07	15.88|41.79	22.59|52.24	13.87|41.16	31.10|59.88	25.70|52.20	20.32|50.43

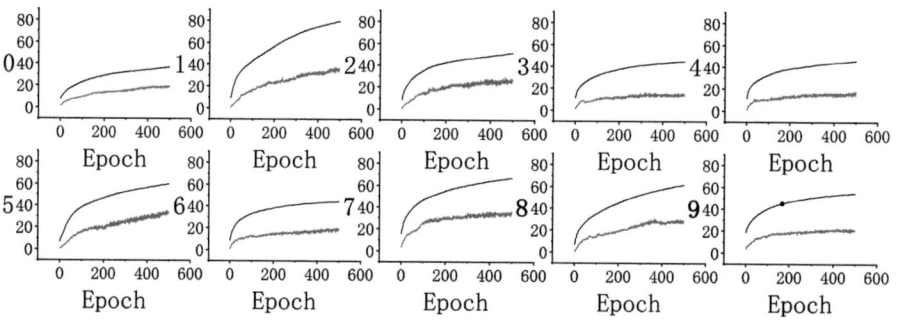

Fig. 4. The black line represents the core point's score of the victim model, and the red line represents the distance from the core point to the model decision boundary. 0–9 represents the label of the current sample. (Color figure online)

4.2 Insight Analysis

Insight 1: The Higher the Core Point's Predicted Score, the Farther the Core Point Is from the Model Decision Boundary

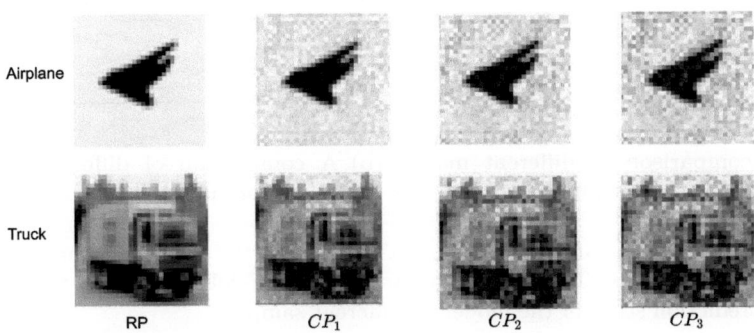

Fig. 5. The visualization of the core points on CIFAR-10. The first row is an airplane. The second row is a truck. RP represents the sample randomly selected as an initial core point, and CP_i represents a core point trained for $i \times 100$ epochs.

Table 2 shows the core radii and scores of different core points on CIFAR-10. $Core_i$ represents the cores with core points trained for $i \times 100$ epochs. s_i represents the core point's score corresponding to label i, denoted as $f_v(\phi_i)_i$. As the number of training epochs increases, the core radius of each category grows together with the score. Figure 4 shows that ten core points' scores of the victim model are positively correlated with the core radii within 500 training epochs. These indicate that the higher the confidence of the core point, the further away the core point is from the model decision boundary. Figure 5 gives the visualization of the core points on CIFAR-10. The more training epochs, the more pixels are changed and the more obvious they are, which leads to poor visual effects.

Insight 2: The Piracy Models Output Scores Closer to the Victim Model than the Homologous Models on Core Points

Table 3. The average score difference between different models and the victim model.

Label	0	1	2	3	4	5	6	7	8	9
RP_h	−1.53 ± 2.44	0.93 ± 1.72	−0.69 ± 2.85	5.08 ± 1.94	4.39 ± 2.40	0.13 ± 1.41	0.55 ± 2.80	5.95 ± 2.56	−1.68 ± 2.26	5.79 ± 2.42
RP_p	0.29 ± 1.95	1.02 ± 1.54	1.30 ± 2.07	3.66 ± 1.94	3.13 ± 1.88	1.93 ± 1.36	1.00 ± 1.98	5.47 ± 2.41	−1.01 ± 1.78	4.72 ± 2.59
CP_1_h	15.43 ± 2.14	32.96 ± 2.08	27.51 ± 1.87	27.44 ± 2.34	25.62 ± 2.51	32.84 ± 2.18	21.46 ± 2.54	35.55 ± 2.71	26.49 ± 1.92	28.97 ± 2.53
CP_1_p	12.86 ± 3.78	24.36 ± 8.76	23.29 ± 5.68	20.02 ± 3.87	20.18 ± 4.95	25.76 ± 6.77	19.08 ± 5.08	28.36 ± 7.02	19.19 ± 7.15	21.29 ± 6.16
CP_2_h	22.83 ± 2.23	47.34 ± 2.71	34.64 ± 1.80	35.20 ± 2.73	32.43 ± 2.61	42.71 ± 2.47	26.54 ± 2.31	44.89 ± 3.39	39.36 ± 2.10	36.76 ± 2.70
CP_2_p	17.72 ± 5.33	33.06 ± 12.95	28.87 ± 7.46	24.84 ± 5.30	24.59 ± 6.47	32.00 ± 8.79	22.94 ± 6.26	34.32 ± 9.00	26.77 ± 10.69	26.17 ± 7.92
CP_3_h	26.96 ± 2.49	58.87 ± 3.36	38.67 ± 1.92	39.18 ± 2.99	36.98 ± 2.22	49.71 ± 2.96	30.79 ± 2.29	51.66 ± 3.59	49.11 ± 2.50	40.92 ± 2.82
CP_3_p	20.29 ± 6.30	40.59 ± 16.50	31.71 ± 8.52	27.87 ± 6.32	27.40 ± 7.64	36.96 ± 10.61	25.58 ± 7.06	38.05 ± 10.35	32.74 ± 13.23	29.01 ± 9.06

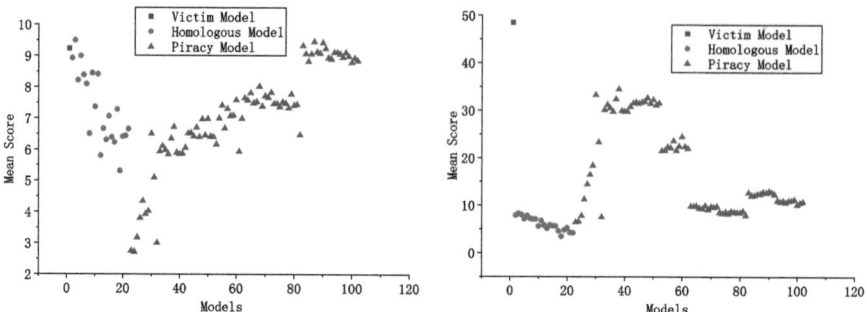

(a) A comparison of different models' scores for random samples.
(b) A comparison of different models' scores for core points.

Fig. 6. A comparison of different models' scores for the random samples and core points ϕ_i on CIFAR-10. The x-axis presents different models. The y-axis represents the average prediction score of the model on different samples.

Figure 6 shows different models' output scores for different samples. There are 102 models in the figure. The first model is the victim model. Then, according to the order in Table 1 order, the 2nd to the 22nd represent the homologous models, and numbers 23 to 102 represent various piracy models. The piracy models are more sensitive to the core points of the victim model, and most score differences between piracy models and the victim model are more minor. However, for the sample randomly selected, it is difficult to identify the homologous and piracy models from the score difference.

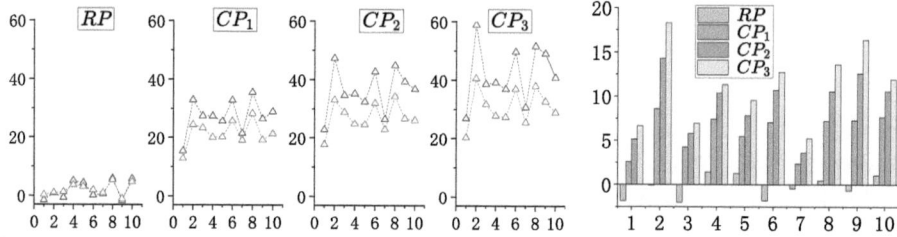

(a) The black triangle symbol represents the label score difference between the victim model and homologous models and the red triangle symbol represents the score difference between the victim model and piracy models.
(b) The average score difference between homologous models and piracy models.

Fig. 7. The x-axis in the figure represents ten core points. The y-axis represents the label score difference.

Insight 3: The Larger the Core Point's Radius, the Greater the Core Point's Score Difference Between Homologous Models and Piracy Models

In Table 3, we calculate the average score difference and the variance between different models and the victim model. A label score difference between a suspected model and the victim model is denoted as $f_v(\phi_i)_i - f_s(\phi_i)_i$ for the core point ϕ_i. RP_h represents the initial core point's score difference between a homologous model and the victim model. RP_p represents such a difference between a piracy model and the victim model. CP_i represents a core point trained for i × 100 epochs. CP_i_h represents CP_i's score difference between a homologous model and the victim model. CP_i_p represents CP_i's score difference between a piracy model and the victim model. 0 to 9, respectively, represent the 10 RP or CP_i of the corresponding label i. Combined with Fig. 7, we can draw the following conclusions: The larger the core radius, the greater the score difference between homologous models and piracy models. Figure 4 shows that the larger the epoch, the larger the core radius. Therefore, training core points for more epochs makes it easier to identify piracy models.

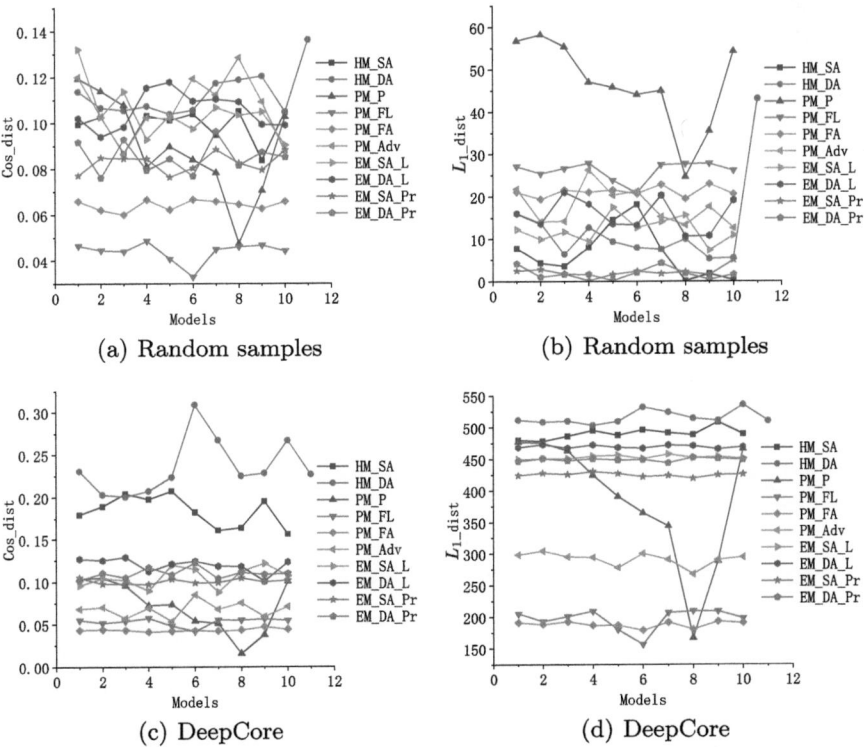

Fig. 8. The effectiveness of the random samples' optimization of DeepCore.

4.3 DeepCore Performance

The Effectiveness of DeepCore. Figure 8 shows the effectiveness of DeepCore compared to initial random samples. If we use random samples as fingerprints, it is difficult to use the threshold to separate the homologous models from the piracy models.

Comparative Experiments. Table 4 gives the performance comparison between DeepCore and baselines. It can be seen that the DeepCore has the best MIR and FIR. Moreover, DeepCore can perform well under three different identification methods.

Table 4. Comparative experiments on CIFAR-10 and CIFAR-100.

Method	CIFAR-10		CIFAR-100	
	$MIR\downarrow$	$FIR\downarrow$	$MIR\downarrow$	$FIR\downarrow$
SAC-w [10]	0.05	0.20	0.23	0.43
SAC-m [10]	0.21	0.10	0.61	0.52
FUAP [32]	0.04	0.05	0.06	0.05
MetaFinger [38]	0.07	0.65	0.14	0.94
DeepCore (L_1_dist)	0.03	0.00	0.09	0.05
DeepCore (Cos_dist)	**0.00**	**0.00**	**0.03**	**0.04**
DeepCore $Clustering$	**0.00**	**0.00**	0.00	0.09

Table 5. The experiment results of clustering methods.

Clustering Methods	KMeans	SC	AC
MIR (PMs)	0.20	0.48	0.23
FIR (PMs)	0.00	0.00	0.00
MIR (EMs)	0.00	0.00	0.00
FIR (EMs)	0.17	0.11	0.20
MIR (HMs)	0.00	0.00	0.00
FIR (HMs)	0.00	0.40	0.00

The Impact of Different Clustering Methods. In the DeepCore identification stage, we can use clustering methods to identify piracy models at a more fine-grained level. In our experiments, we use Kmeans [24], SpectralClustering (SC) [29], and AgglomerativeClustering (AC) [4].

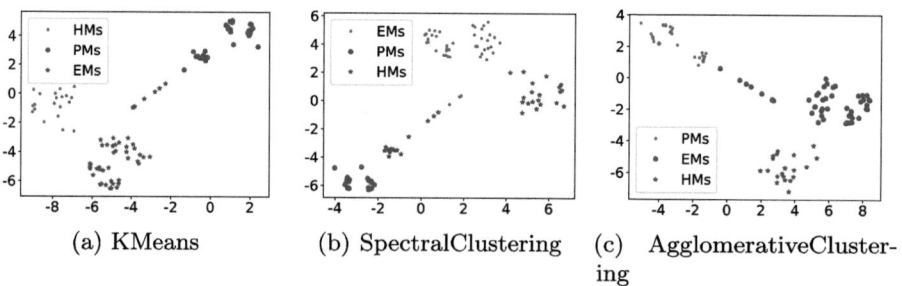

(a) KMeans   (b) SpectralClustering   (c) AgglomerativeClustering

Fig. 9. The visualization of different clustering methods.

Table 5 shows the MIR and FIR of PMs, EMs, and HMs for different clustering methods. PMs refer to models that have undergone post-processing techniques. EMs represent piracy models acquired through model extraction attacks. HMs represent homologous models. Kmeans and AC perform better than SC, which shows that different clustering methods also affect identification accuracy. Figure 9 intuitively shows the SpectralClustering results of HMs are very scattered and can mistakenly identify piracy models. Although Kmeans and AgglomerativeClustering cannot wholly distinguish different piracy models, they can at least distinguish homologous models well. Therefore, choosing a suitable classification algorithm is also crucial and worthwhile to continue exploring. The clustering-based method can identify piracy models in a more fine-grained manner, but the disadvantage is that the number of types of piracy models needs to be known in advance.

5 Conclusion and Future Work

This work proposes DeepCore, a simple fingerprint construction framework designed to identify piracy and homologous models by exploring the impact of sample points within the model decision space on output behavioral discrepancies. However, the approach has limitations: it requires empirically setting thresholds or cluster numbers, the constructed samples have poor visual effects (which could be mitigated by limiting pixel variation), and questions remain about the minimum number of core points needed for effective fingerprints. Additionally, extending this work to increasingly transformer-based models presents a significant future challenge. Despite these limitations, DeepCore demonstrates improved false and missed identification rates over baselines and contributes to the broader exploration of model decision spaces.

Acknowledgments. The research is partially supported by National Key R&D Program of China 2018YFB0803400, National Key R&D Program of China under Grant No. 2021ZD0110400, China National Natural Science Foundation with No. 62132018, Key Research Program of Frontier Sciences, CAS. No. QYZDY-SSW-JSC002, The University Synergy Innovation Program of Anhui Province with No. GXXT-2019-024.

References

1. Adi, Y., Baum, C., Cisse, M., Pinkas, B., Keshet, J.: Turning your weakness into a strength: watermarking deep neural networks by backdooring. In: 27th USENIX Security Symposium (USENIX Security 2018), pp. 1615–1631 (2018)
2. Cao, X., Jia, J., Gong, N.Z.: IPGuard: protecting intellectual property of deep neural networks via fingerprinting the classification boundary. In: Proceedings of the 2021 ACM Asia Conference on Computer and Communications Security, pp. 14–25 (2021)
3. Chandrasekaran, V., Chaudhuri, K., Giacomelli, I., Jha, S., Yan, S.: Exploring connections between active learning and model extraction. In: Proceedings of the 29th USENIX Conference on Security Symposium, pp. 1309–1326 (2020)
4. Dasgupta, S., Long, P.M.: Performance guarantees for hierarchical clustering. J. Comput. Syst. Sci. **70**(4), 555–569 (2005)

5. Fan, L., Ng, K.W., Chan, C.S.: Rethinking deep neural network ownership verification: embedding passports to defeat ambiguity attacks. Adv. Neural Inf. Process. Syst. **32** (2019)
6. Fan, L., Ng, K.W., Chan, C.S., Yang, Q.: DeepIP: deep neural network intellectual property protection with passports. IEEE Trans. Pattern Anal. Mach. Intell., 1 (2021)
7. Fei, J., Xia, Z., Tondi, B., Barni, M.: Wide flat minimum watermarking for robust ownership verification of GANs. IEEE Trans. Inf. Forensics Secur. **19**, 8322–8337 (2024). https://doi.org/10.1109/TIFS.2024.3443650
8. Ge, Y., et al.: Anti-distillation backdoor attacks: backdoors can really survive in knowledge distillation. In: Proceedings of the 29th ACM International Conference on Multimedia, pp. 826–834 (2021)
9. Gou, J., Yu, B., Maybank, S.J., Tao, D.: Knowledge distillation: a survey. Int. J. Comput. Vision **129**, 1789–1819 (2021)
10. Guan, J., Liang, J., He, R.: Are you stealing my model? Sample correlation for fingerprinting deep neural networks. Adv. Neural. Inf. Process. Syst. **35**, 36571–36584 (2022)
11. Guan, J., Tu, Z., He, R., Tao, D.: Few-shot backdoor defense using shapley estimation. In: Proceedings of the IEEE/CVF Conference on Computer Vision and Pattern Recognition, pp. 13358–13367 (2022)
12. He, K., Zhang, X., Ren, S., Sun, J.: Deep residual learning for image recognition. In: Proceedings of the IEEE Conference on Computer Vision and Pattern Recognition, pp. 770–778 (2016)
13. Hoy, M.B.: Alexa, Siri, Cortana, and more: an introduction to voice assistants. Med. Ref. Serv. Q. **37**(1), 81–88 (2018)
14. Hua, G., Teoh, A.B.J., Xiang, Y., Jiang, H.: Unambiguous and high-fidelity backdoor watermarking for deep neural networks. IEEE Trans. Neural Netw. Learn. Syst. **35**(8), 11204–11217 (2024). https://doi.org/10.1109/TNNLS.2023.3250210
15. Huang, G., Liu, Z., Van Der Maaten, L., Weinberger, K.Q.: Densely connected convolutional networks. In: Proceedings of the IEEE Conference on Computer Vision and Pattern Recognition, pp. 4700–4708 (2017)
16. Jagielski, M., Carlini, N., Berthelot, D., Kurakin, A., Papernot, N.: High accuracy and high fidelity extraction of neural networks. In: Proceedings of the 29th USENIX Conference on Security Symposium, pp. 1345–1362 (2020)
17. Jia, H., Choquette-Choo, C.A., Chandrasekaran, V., Papernot, N.: Entangled watermarks as a defense against model extraction. In: USENIX Security Symposium, pp. 1937–1954 (2021)
18. Krizhevsky, A., Hinton, G.: Learning multiple layers of features from tiny images. In: Handbook of Systemic Autoimmune Diseases, vol. 1, no. 4 (2009)
19. Lederer, I., Mayer, R., Rauber, A.: Identifying appropriate intellectual property protection mechanisms for machine learning models: a systematization of watermarking, fingerprinting, model access, and attacks. IEEE Trans. Neural Netw. Learn. Syst. **35**(10), 13082–13100 (2024). https://doi.org/10.1109/TNNLS.2023.3270135
20. Li, Y., Zhu, L., Jia, X., Jiang, Y., Xia, S.T., Cao, X.: Defending against model stealing via verifying embedded external features. In: Proceedings of the AAAI Conference on Artificial Intelligence, pp. 1464–1472 (2022)
21. Li, Y., Zhang, Z., Liu, B., Yang, Z., Liu, Y.: ModelDiff: testing-based DNN similarity comparison for model reuse detection. In: Proceedings of the 30th ACM SIGSOFT International Symposium on Software Testing and Analysis, pp. 139–151 (2021)

22. Liu, K., Dolan-Gavitt, B., Garg, S.: Fine-pruning: defending against backdooring attacks on deep neural networks. In: Bailey, M., Holz, T., Stamatogiannakis, M., Ioannidis, S. (eds.) RAID 2018. LNCS, vol. 11050, pp. 273–294. Springer, Cham (2018). https://doi.org/10.1007/978-3-030-00470-5_13
23. Lukas, N., Zhang, Y., Kerschbaum, F.: Deep neural network fingerprinting by conferrable adversarial examples. arXiv preprint arXiv:1912.00888 (2019)
24. MacQueen, J., et al.: Some methods for classification and analysis of multivariate observations. In: Proceedings of the Fifth Berkeley Symposium on Mathematical Statistics and Probability, Oakland, CA, USA, vol. 1, pp. 281–297 (1967)
25. Madry, A., Makelov, A., Schmidt, L., Tsipras, D., Vladu, A.: Towards deep learning models resistant to adversarial attacks. arXiv preprint arXiv:1706.06083 (2017)
26. Maho, T., Furon, T., Merrer, E.L.: Fingerprinting classifiers with benign inputs. IEEE Trans. Inf. Forensics Secur. **18**, 5459–5472 (2023). https://doi.org/10.1109/TIFS.2023.3301268
27. Molchanov, P., Mallya, A., Tyree, S., Frosio, I., Kautz, J.: Importance estimation for neural network pruning. In: Proceedings of the IEEE/CVF Conference on Computer Vision And Pattern Recognition, pp. 11264–11272 (2019)
28. Moosavi-Dezfooli, S.M., Fawzi, A., Frossard, P.: DeepFool: a simple and accurate method to fool deep neural networks. In: Proceedings of the IEEE Conference on Computer Vision and Pattern Recognition, pp. 2574–2582 (2016)
29. Ng, A., Jordan, M., Weiss, Y.: On spectral clustering: analysis and an algorithm. Adv. Neural Inf. Process. Syst. **14** (2001)
30. Nguyen, H.V., Bai, L.: Cosine similarity metric learning for face verification. In: Kimmel, R., Klette, R., Sugimoto, A. (eds.) ACCV 2010. LNCS, vol. 6493, pp. 709–720. Springer, Heidelberg (2011). https://doi.org/10.1007/978-3-642-19309-5_55
31. Orekondy, T., Schiele, B., Fritz, M.: Knockoff nets: stealing functionality of blackbox models. In: Proceedings of the IEEE/CVF Conference on Computer Vision and Pattern Recognition, pp. 4954–4963 (2019)
32. Peng, Z., Li, S., Chen, G., Zhang, C., Zhu, H., Xue, M.: Fingerprinting deep neural networks globally via universal adversarial perturbations. In: Proceedings of the IEEE/CVF Conference on Computer Vision and Pattern Recognition, pp. 13430–13439 (2022)
33. Taigman, Y., Yang, M., Ranzato, M., Wolf, L.: DeepFace: closing the gap to human-level performance in face verification. In: Proceedings of the IEEE Conference on Computer Vision and Pattern Recognition, pp. 1701–1708 (2014)
34. Tajbakhsh, N., et al.: Convolutional neural networks for medical image analysis: full training or fine tuning? IEEE Trans. Med. Imaging **35**(5), 1299–1312 (2016)
35. Truong, J.B., Maini, P., Walls, R.J., Papernot, N.: Data-free model extraction. In: Proceedings of the IEEE/CVF Conference on Computer Vision and Pattern Recognition, pp. 4771–4780 (2021)
36. Uchida, Y., Nagai, Y., Sakazawa, S., Satoh, S.: Embedding watermarks into deep neural networks. In: Proceedings of the 2017 ACM on International Conference on Multimedia Retrieval, pp. 269–277 (2017)
37. Vaswani, A., et al.: Attention is all you need. Adv. Neural Inf. Process. Syst. **30** (2017)
38. Yang, K., Wang, R., Wang, L.: MetaFinger: fingerprinting the deep neural networks with meta-training. In: Thirty-First International Joint Conference on Artificial Intelligence, pp. 759–765 (2022)

39. Zanella-Beguelin, S., Tople, S., Paverd, A., Köpf, B.: Grey-box extraction of natural language models. In: International Conference on Machine Learning, pp. 12278–12286. PMLR (2021)
40. Zhang, J., Chen, D., Liao, J., Zhang, W., Hua, G., Yu, N.: Passport-aware normalization for deep model protection. Adv. Neural. Inf. Process. Syst. **33**, 22619–22628 (2020)

Video-DPRP: A Differentially Private Approach for Visual Privacy-Preserving Video Human Activity Recognition

Allassan Tchangmena A. Nken[1], Susan McKeever[3], Peter Corcoran[2], and Ihsan Ullah[1,4](✉)

[1] Visual Intelligence Lab, School of Computer Science, University of Galway, Galway, Ireland
[2] School of Electrical Engineering, University of Galway, Galway, Ireland
[3] School of Computer Science, Technological University Dublin, Dublin, Ireland
[4] Insight Research Ireland Center for Data Analytics, University of Galway, Galway, Ireland
ihsan.ullah@universityofgalway.ie

Abstract. Considerable effort has been made in privacy-preserving video human activity recognition (HAR). Two primary approaches to ensure privacy preservation in Video HAR are differential privacy (DP) and visual privacy. Techniques enforcing DP during training provide strong theoretical privacy guarantees but offer limited capabilities for visual privacy assessment. Conversely, methods such as low-resolution transformations, data obfuscation and adversarial networks, emphasize visual privacy but lack clear theoretical privacy assurances. In this work, we focus on two main objectives: (1) leveraging DP properties to develop a model-free approach for visual privacy in videos and (2) evaluating our proposed technique using both differential privacy and visual privacy assessments on HAR tasks. To achieve goal (1), we introduce **Video-DPRP**: a **Video**-sample-wise **D**ifferentially **P**rivate **R**andom **P**rojection framework for privacy-preserved video reconstruction for HAR. By using random projections, noise matrices and right singular vectors derived from the singular value decomposition of videos, Video-DPRP reconstructs DP videos using privacy parameters (ϵ, δ) while enabling visual privacy assessment. For goal (2), using UCF101 and HMDB51 datasets, we compare Video-DPRP's performance on activity recognition with traditional DP methods, and state-of-the-art (SOTA) visual privacy-preserving techniques. Additionally, we assess its effectiveness in preserving privacy-related attributes such as facial features, gender, and skin color, using the PA-HMDB and VISPR datasets. Video-DPRP combines privacy-preservation from both a DP and visual privacy perspective unlike SOTA methods that typically address only one of these aspects. The source code is publicly available on GitHub (https://github.com/matzolla/Video-DPRP).

Supplementary Information The online version contains supplementary material available at https://doi.org/10.1007/978-3-032-06096-9_20.

© The Author(s), under exclusive license to Springer Nature Switzerland AG 2026
R. P. Ribeiro et al. (Eds.): ECML PKDD 2025, LNAI 16017, pp. 345–362, 2026.
https://doi.org/10.1007/978-3-032-06096-9_20

Keywords: Activity Recognition · Differential Privacy · Visual Privacy

1 Introduction

Privacy preservation is a critical research challenge in the field of video-based human activity recognition (HAR) and video analysis. Video HAR systems are increasingly used in settings like healthcare monitoring, smart homes and security [5,40,50]. However, these systems often capture sensitive personal information, creating a strong need for privacy measures to protect individuals' identities and personal activities from misuse or unauthorized access.

Current literature indicates that privacy preservation, in Video HAR can be achieved either at a model level or directly on the data by modifying its visual content. Model-based approaches usually ensure privacy by leveraging differential privacy (DP) [4,12,13,28]. This method provides a theoretical and empirical guarantee of privacy by incorporating noisy mechanisms into the training algorithms, using the privacy parameters ϵ and δ [1,9,10,32,35]. However, its effectiveness is limited when it comes to post-training privacy analysis such as visual privacy. In the context of video HAR, visual privacy can be define as a model's ability to recognize visual information such as faces, gender, or individuals performing activities. The underlying hypothesis is that diminished performance in these recognition tasks indicates higher visual privacy. As shown in Fig. 1(a), models trained with DP cannot achieve this level of privacy because the data itself is not directly altered for DP; only the gradient's estimates g are adjusted during training.

Conversely, while some data-based approaches utilizing generative adversarial networks (GANs in Fig. 1(b)) offer an affordable means of visual privacy assessment [18,31,38], the generated videos from these methods may still disclose sensitive visual content [41], as they are trained on unconstrained real-world data. Additionally GANs, including other video down-sampling and obfuscation approaches [21,38,39], lacks the rigorous mathematical privacy guarantees

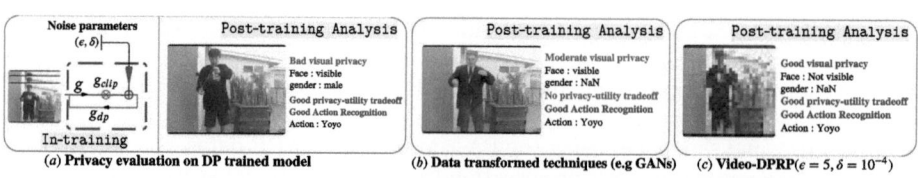

(a) Privacy evaluation on DP trained model (b) Data transformed techniques (e.g GANs) (c) Video-DPRP($\epsilon = 5, \delta = 10^{-4}$)

Fig. 1. In (a), privacy is ensured during training (in-training) using differential privacy (DP), but not directly on the video itself. As a result visual privacy cannot be assessed. In (b), the video is transformed prior to training using either obfuscation methods or adversarial approaches, but the privacy-utility trade-off cannot be quantified as clearly as in DP. In (c) (ours), privacy is ensured using DP, directly on the video. This approach allows for visual privacy evaluation, where privacy-utility trade-off is quantified using the ϵ, δ parameters of DP.

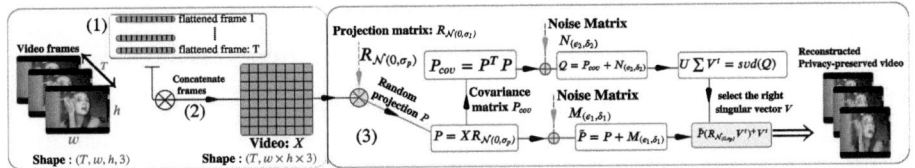

Fig. 2. Video-DPRP consists of the following components: (1) Each video frame is reshaped and flattened, then concatenated to form a video X of dimension $(T, w \times h \times 3)$. (2) A random projection matrix $\mathcal{R}_{\mathcal{N}(0,\sigma_p)}$ reduces X to a lower-dimensional space (T, k). (3) Noise is added to both the projected video and its covariance matrix, from which the right singular component V of the noisy covariance Q is used to reconstruct a differentially private video (see Sect. 3 for details).

afforded by differential privacy. Theoretical privacy assurance is often overlooked in data-based methods, which typically rely on heuristic approaches, ad-hoc obfuscations, or data transformations. These methods lack transparency in how privacy is preserved and can be vulnerable to reverse-engineering or sophisticated attacks [23], resulting in mere *security through obscurity*. In contrast, differential privacy is grounded in well-established mathematical principles that provide robust privacy guarantees, irrespective of an adversary's capabilities. Moreover, differential privacy offers clearer privacy explainability in terms of the chances of information leakage, quantified by the ϵ and δ parameters [6,33].

We identify two key limitations in previous privacy-preserving Video HAR studies: (1) Although DP models provide empirical and theoretical privacy guarantees during model training, their privacy-preserving effect does not extend beyond training. This limitation arises because the data itself remains unaltered, retaining visually sensitive content. Evaluating such data on visual privacy metrics is likely to yield poor results. (2) While some studies propose data-transformed methods for visual privacy evaluation, these approaches still fail to offer theoretical guarantees of privacy. Recent advancements in differential privacy and random projection present promising solutions. By leveraging a random projection matrix followed by the addition of a noise matrix to the projected data, previous work has demonstrated the feasibility of reconstructing differentially private tabular datasets and images [15,27,29,30,47]. However, applying differentially private random projections to a video dataset presents a significant challenge due to the added complexity introduced by the temporal dimension of videos.

In this work, we introduce Video-DPRP, a **Video**-sample-wise **D**ifferentially **P**rivate **R**andom **P**rojection framework tailored for visual privacy-preserved video reconstruction of HAR datasets. The framework unfolds in several stages: we begin by reshaping each video, as illustrated in Fig. 2. Next, we apply a random projection to the reshaped video using a projection matrix, reducing its dimensionality while preserving its underlying structure. To ensure differential privacy, we add a noise matrix, calibrated with the (ϵ, δ) parameters, to both the projected video and its covariance matrix. Finally, by leveraging the right singular vectors from the singular value decomposition (SVD) of the noisy covariance matrix, we reconstruct a video sample, that is both visually and differentially private. **Ideally, a model trained with videos reconstructed using Video-**

DPRP is expected to exhibit both high-quality performance in video HAR and strong privacy preservation. Our contributions are as follows:

- We introduce Video-DPRP, a differentially private approach for video reconstruction tailored for video HAR. Video-DPRP provides a theoretical guarantee of differential privacy, while also ensuring visual privacy.
- We evaluate the performance of Video-DPRP across both HAR and visual privacy-preserving attributes. For HAR evaluation, we use the UCF101 and HMDB51 datasets. To assess visual privacy-preserving attributes, we utilize the PA-HMDB and the VISPR datasets.

2 Related Work

Privacy-Preserving Video HAR. Privacy in the context of video HAR can be categorized into two main groups: visual privacy and differential privacy. Visual privacy aims to obscure identifiable visual attributes in video content and can be categorized into 3 main groups: obfuscation, adversarial training and downsampling

Downsampling. As an example, Ryo et al. [39] proposed an inverse-super-resolution paradigm that learns an optimal set of transformations to generate low-resolution videos from high-resolution inputs. This approach utilizes a downsampling technique, similar to the method proposed by [7]. While this technique is effective, its major drawback lies in the trade-off between achieving accurate activity recognition and maintaining privacy preservation: a trade-off that could be better quantified with a rigorous mathematical bound on privacy.

Obfuscation. Ren et al. [38] presents a data obfuscation method for anonymizing facial images, using a learnable modifier. This approach employs an adversarial training setup, where a generator produces modified versions of facial images, and a discriminator attempts to identify facial features despite the modifications. The end result is a video anonymizer that performs pixel-level modifications to anonymize each person's face with minimal impact on action detection performance. Additional work on obfuscation has been conducted by Ilic et al., focusing on appearance-free action recognition using an optical-flow estimator [20] and selective video obfuscation using random noise [21]. However, obfuscation techniques have a limitation in that they require domain knowledge to effectively identify and obscure the region of interest.

Adversarial Training. Beyond video down-sampling and obfuscation, some researchers have developed privacy optimization strategies using adversarial neural networks [8,36,46]. These strategies typically involve a cost function that is minimized for activity recognition, while simultaneously maximized for privacy preservation. A significant drawback of these techniques is their substantial computational resource requirements for reconstructing anonymized videos. In contrast, a more effective approach could be a model-free method capable of reconstructing videos at a considerably lower computational cost.

While visual privacy focuses on *hiding* identifiable visual attributes in sample videos, in differential privacy, a random noise is added to the gradient estimates during a model's training process. This noise is carefully calibrated to ensure that the model can still learn overall patterns and trends, while specific details that could identify a sample video are not leaked. It is important to note that the sample videos themselves are not directly modified; only their gradient estimates are altered during training. Figure 1(a) provides a clear illustration of training with differential privacy, specifically detailing a variant of stochastic gradient descent (SGD) known as differential private stochastic gradient descent (DP-SGD) [1]. DP-SGD differs from traditional SGD in that, after computing the per-sample gradient g it is clipped to a threshold value C, resulting in a clipped gradient g_{clip}. A Gaussian noise, calibrated with the DP parameters: ϵ, δ, is then carefully added to the clipped gradient producing the differentially private gradient g_{dp} (details about the DP parameters are provided in Sect. 3). Recently, Luo et al. [32] proposed Multi-Clip DP-SGD, a method designed to achieve video-level differential privacy in HAR. The DP framework is built such that, during model training, shorter video segments, or clips, are sampled from each video, and their gradients are computed and averaged across all the clips of the video. DP-SGD is then applied to the averaged gradient, ensuring differential privacy without additional privacy loss. Although the result is a differential private model, a significant challenge with DP-SGD and other DP learning algorithms is that privacy preservation is confined to the training phase, restricting further visual privacy assessments on the video data beyond training.

Differential Private Random Projection (DPRP). Previous research introduced DPRP primarily as a *data release* framework, for tabular data [15,25,47]. For instance Xu et al. [47] employed DPRP for the release of high-dimensional data, while Gondara et al. [15] adapted DPRP for smaller clinical datasets. In both scenarios, the original dataset is projected into a significantly lower-dimensional space using a random projection matrix, followed by the addition of a noise matrix. This noise matrix is calibrated with the (ϵ, δ) parameters to achieve differential privacy. In our approach, we apply DPRP on a per-video-sample basis rather than across the entire dataset, offering more granular privacy control and assessment on activity recognition.

3 Method Overview

We begin by introducing key concepts relevant to Video-DPRP, including an initial video transformation mechanism, the theoretical foundations of differential privacy, random projection, and the algorithmic framework of Video-DPRP. This section concludes with preliminary discussions of the privacy guarantees offered by Video-DPRP, which are further detailed in the Appendix.

3.1 Video Transformation

A sample video is structured as a $4D$ tensor, $(T, w, h, 3)$, consisting of a $1D$ temporal dimension and $2D$ spatial dimensions. The temporal dimension is represented by the number of frames, T, in the video sequence, while the spatial dimensions are denoted by the pair (w, h), corresponding to the width and height of each frame. Moreover, each frame contains 3 color channels (red, green and blue). To facilitate our random projection strategy, we flattened the $2D$ spatial dimensions of each frame from $(1, w, h, 3)$ to $(1, w \times h \times 3)$. Next, we concatenate all the T flattened frames along the temporal axis (the first axis), resulting to $2D$ array X of dimension $(T, w \times h \times 3)$. This concatenation preserves the temporal sequence of the video, with each row of X corresponding to a flattened frame. This step is crucial for our subsequent methodology, and henceforth, we treat each video X as a $2D$ array.

3.2 Differential Privacy

We consider two sample videos, X and X', that differ by a single row, representing neighboring inputs. Intuitively, this means X and X' differ by one frame. Video-DPRP ensures that modifying the pixel values of a single frame does not pose a significant visual privacy risk, nor does it lead to a substantial drop in video HAR performance. This implies that even if an adversary knows the output video, they cannot infer sensitive information about the frame that was modified. We then give a formal definition introduced by Dwork et al. [11] and re-calibrated to our context:

Definition 1 (Differential Privacy). *A randomized mechanism $\mathcal{M}$, satisfies (ϵ, δ)-differential privacy if for any two input videos X and X', that differ in only one row (frame), and for all sets of possible outputs $O \in range(\mathcal{M})$, we have:*

$$\Pr[\mathcal{M}(X) \in O] \leq e^\epsilon \cdot \Pr[\mathcal{M}(X') \in O] + \delta$$

In other words, the outcomes of applying the random mechanism $\mathcal{M}$ to the two neighboring videos X and X' differ by at most a factor of e^ϵ. The privacy guarantee can fail with a probability of δ. When $\delta = 0$, the mechanism operates under pure ϵ-differential privacy.

3.3 Random Projection

Random projection is a dimensionality reduction technique that projects data from an initial dimension d to a lower dimension k, while preserving pairwise distances between data points (in our case, frames) using a projection matrix $\mathcal{R}$. To ensure that the pairwise distances between frames are preserved, the projection matrix must satisfy the Johnson-Lindenstrauss Lemma [24].

Lemma 1 (Johnson-Lindenstrauss [24]). *Let $\mathcal{S}$ be a set of n points such that $\mathcal{S} \subset \mathbb{R}^d$, with $\lambda > 0$ and $k = \frac{20 \log n}{\lambda^2}$. There exists a Lipschitz mapping $f : \mathbb{R}^d \to \mathbb{R}^k$ that distorts all pairwise distances by a factor of $1 \pm \lambda$. For any $x, y \in \mathbb{R}^d$, this mapping satisfies the following inequality:*

$$(1-\lambda)\|x-y\|_2^2 \leq \|f(x)-f(y)\|_2^2 \leq (1+\lambda)\|x-y\|_2^2$$

Contextually, for a given video X, the initial dimension is $d = w \times h \times 3$, where w and h are the width and height of the frames, respectively, and the set of n points corresponds to the number of frames T, as discussed earlier in Sect. 3.1. To project the video $X^{T \times d}$, a random projection matrix $\mathcal{R}$ is required, such that the resulting projected video is $P = X\mathcal{R}$. A suitable random projection matrix that satisfies Lemma 1 is one whose entries are drawn from a normal distribution with mean $\mu = 0$ and variance $\sigma^2 = \frac{1}{k}$ (that is, $\mathcal{R} \sim \mathcal{N}(0, \frac{1}{\sqrt{k}})^{d \times k}$).

3.4 Video-DPRP Algorithm

The algorithmic framework of Video-DPRP is inspired by the influential work on the Johnson-Lindenstrauss transform [25], and recent developments in the release of small datasets [15].

Preliminary: Recall that each video is initially transformed into a 2D matrix of dimensions $(T \times d)$, where T, is the number of frames and $d = w \times h \times 3$ (with w being the width and h the height of a frame).

Privacy Parameters: All our privacy parameters are derived from a single privacy parameter pair (ϵ, δ). To ensure that a given video remains differentially private without significantly compromising its utility, we avoid adding multiple independent noise matrices. Instead, we split the parameters into two sets: one set is used to make the random projection P differentially private (ϵ_1, δ_1) and the other set (ϵ_2, δ_2) to make the covariance matrix P_{cov}, differentially private. Each set is derived using the privacy budget allocator $b \in]0, 1[$ (see lines 1-2). The privacy budget is a parameter that controls the total amount of privacy loss allowed, balancing utility with privacy protection. The complete workflow of Video-DPRP is outlined in Algorithm 1. The time complexity of each step of the algorithm is highlighted in blue.

Algorithm 1. Video-DPRP

Input: $D = \{X_1, X_2, ..., X_n\}, d \times k, \epsilon, \delta, b$
/*The dataset D with n videos; the size of the projection matrix $d \times k$; the privacy parameters ϵ and δ; the privacy budget allocator $b \in]0, 1[$ */
1: $\epsilon_1, \delta_1 = \epsilon \times b, \delta \times b$
2: $\epsilon_2, \delta_2 = \epsilon \times (1-b), \delta \times (1-b)$
3: for $X^{T \times d} \in D$ do:
4:   $\mathcal{R} \sim \mathcal{N}(0, \frac{1}{\sqrt{k}})^{d \times k}$/*projection matrix*/
5:   $P = X\mathcal{R}$ /*Random projection:$O(Tdk)$*/
6:   $\tilde{P} = P + M_{(\epsilon_1, \delta_1)}$ /*Noise addition:$O(Tk)$*/
7:   $P_{cov} = P^t P$/*Covariance matrix:$O(Tk^2)$*/
8:   $Q = P_{cov} + N_{(\epsilon_2, \delta_2)}$ /*Noise addition:$O(k^2)$*/
9:   $U \sum V^t = \text{SVD}(Q)$ /*Decomposition:$O(k^3)$*/
10:   $\tilde{X} = \tilde{P}(\mathcal{R}V^t)^+ V^t$/*reconstructed video:*/
Output: reshaped video, reshape($\tilde{X}$)

To begin with, for each video $X^{T \times d}$ in the dataset D, we project the video into a lower-dimensional space, using the projection matrix $\mathcal{R}^{d \times k}$ (lines 4-5), which satisfies the JohnsonLindenstrauss Lemma 1. This result to a projected video P, of dimension $(T \times k)$. Here, k represents the number of dimensions for the random projection. At this stage, P still contains sensitive information from X and is therefore not differentially private. Differential privacy is ensured by adding a random noise matrix

$M_{(\epsilon_1,\delta_1)}$ to the projected video (line 6), resulting to $\tilde{P}$. The entries of the random noise matrix are drawn from a Gaussian distribution with mean $\mu = 0$ and variance σ_1^2 ($M_{(\epsilon_1,\delta_1)} \sim \mathcal{N}(0,\sigma_1^2)^{T\times k}$). The variance σ_1^2 is determined using Theorem 1. Differentially private video reconstruction effectively begins at line 7, where the covariance matrix P_{cov} of the projected video P, is first computed as a necessary step for reconstruction. The use of the covariance matrix is motivated by principles similar to those in Principal Component Analysis, aiming to capture the most significant features of the video within the low-dimensional subspace. Similar to line 5, since P is not differentially private, its covariance matrix P_{cov} is also not. To achieve differential privacy, a random noise matrix $N_{(\epsilon_2,\delta_2)}$ is added to P_{cov}, resulting in a noisy covariance matrix Q (line 8) of dimension $(k\times k)$. In the same way, the entries of $N_{(\epsilon_2,\delta_2)}$ are drawn from a Gaussian distribution with mean $\mu = 0$ and variance σ_2^2 ($N(\epsilon_2,\delta_2) \sim \mathcal{N}(0,\sigma_2^2)^{k\times k}$). The variance σ_2^2 is determined using Theorem 2. To proceed, the noisy covariance matrix Q is subjected to a singular value decomposition (SVD), which decomposes Q into three matrices: $U\Sigma V^t$ (line 9), where U and V^t (denoting the transpose of V) are orthogonal matrices each of dimensions $(k \times k)$, and Σ is a diagonal matrix containing the singular values. Following the approach of [15], we only use the right singular component V^t, the random projection matrix $\mathcal{R}$, and the differentially private projected video $\tilde{P}$ for video reconstruction of $\tilde{X}$ (line 10). We use the Moore-Penrose pseudoinverse (denoted by +) of $\mathcal{R}V^t$ because $\mathcal{R}V^t$ is not a squared matrix and may not be invertible. $\tilde{X}$ has dimensions $(T \times d)$ and is ultimately reshaped back to its original video format $(T, w, h, 3)$.

Time Complexity: Given that the algorithm processes n videos independently, the overall time complexity for the entire dataset D is $O(n(Tdk+Tk^2+k^3))$. This complexity shows that the algorithm scales linearly with the number of videos n, and is influenced by both the number of frames T and the dimensionality d. The cubic term k^3 becomes dominant when the projection dimension k is large.

3.5 Privacy Guarantee of Video-DPRP

Differential privacy is applied at two stages in Algorithm 1: (i) to ensure that the projected video P is differentially private, and (ii) to make the covariance matrix P_{cov} differentially private. To establish the privacy guarantee of Video-DPRP, we must demonstrate that both stages meet differential privacy requirements. The proofs rely on two supporting theorems from [15,44], which are included here for completeness, with details provided in the appendix.

Theorem 1 (Privacy of projected video P). *Let $\epsilon_1 > 0$ and $0 < \delta_1 < \frac{1}{2}$. Consider a randomized Gaussian projection matrix $\mathcal{R} \sim \mathcal{N}(0,1/\sqrt{k})^{d\times k}$. Then, the noisy projection $\tilde{P} = X\mathcal{R} + M_{(\epsilon_1,\delta_1)}$, where $M_{(\epsilon_1,\delta_1)}$ is a $(T \times k)$ Gaussian matrix with entries drawn from $\mathcal{N}(0,\sigma_1^2)$, is (ϵ_1,δ_1)-differentially private, with:*

$$\sigma_1 = \theta\sigma_p\sqrt{k + 2\sqrt{k\log(2/\delta_1)} + 2\log(2/\delta_1)}\sqrt{2(\log(1/2\delta_1) + \epsilon_1)}/\epsilon_1$$

Where $\sigma_p = 1/\sqrt{k}$, and θ denotes the L_2 sensitivity bound of the input. The variables are consistent with those defined in Sect. 3.4 to maintain uniformity.

The L_2 Sensitivity θ: For the input $f(X) = X\mathcal{R}$ where X represents the video with pixel values ranging from $[0, 255]$ and $\mathcal{R}$ is a random matrix, the L_2 sensitivity θ is proportional to the maximum change in X, scaled by the norm of $\mathcal{R}$. This norm typically takes the value $1/\sqrt{k}$. Since the L_2 sensitivity of X is $|255 - 0|$, we define θ as $\theta = 255/\sqrt{k}$. Where $|.|$ denotes the absolute value. More details are provided in the appendix section.

Theorem 2 (Privacy of covariance matrix P_{cov}). *The mechanism defined by $Q = P_{cov} + N_{(\epsilon_2, \delta_2)}$, where $N_{(\epsilon_2, \delta_2)}$ is a Gaussian matrix with entries drawn from $\mathcal{N}(0, \sigma_2)$, is (ϵ_2, δ_2)-differentially private, provided that $\epsilon_2 > 0$ and $\delta_2 < 1/2$. Where $\sigma_2 = \theta \sqrt{\frac{\sqrt{2\log(1.25)/\delta_2}}{\epsilon_2}}$.*

By applying the principle of sequential composition [13], each video X is (ϵ, δ)-differentially private as a result of the combination of two differentially private mechanisms in Algorithm 1. Where $\epsilon = \epsilon_1 + \epsilon_2$ and $\delta = \delta_1 + \delta_2$.

Table 1. Comparison with different visual privacy techniques, including data-obfuscation, adversarial training and video anonymization using GANS. cMAP and F1 metrics are for *privacy evaluation* while Top-1 is for *action evaluation*. Results are reported on UCF101 [42], HMDB51 [26], PA-HMDB [46] and VISPR [34]. The best results are in **bold-red**, while the second best are underlined.

	Raw Test set Top-1(↑)		Reconstructed Test set Top-1(↑)		Raw Test set PA-HMDB			Raw Test set VISPR
Method	UCF101	HMDB51	UCF101	HMDB51	Top-1 (↑)	cMAP (↓)	cMAP (↓)	F1 (↓)
ISR$_{(32 \times 24)}$[39]	49.65±0.22	35.66±0.10	45.14±0.53	28.97±0.09	38.71±1.22	58.26±0.13	53.60±0.87	49.14±0.09
ISR$_{(16 \times 12)}$[39]	18.34±0.02	19.47±0.04	24.94±0.20	12.64±0.01	25.11±0.62	40.01±0.17	43.27±0.25	45.00±0.73
V-SAM[19]	17.32±0.30	14.72±0.12	10.02±1.48	12.03±0.91	15.31±0.54	40.39±0.38	44.64±0.09	39.97±0.16
Face Anonymizer[38]	32.05±0.49	19.04±0.24	21.62±0.35	21.13±0.69	17.04±0.03	41.18±1.09	44.00±0.63	51.43±0.39
SPAct[8]	60.82±0.33	41.29±0.01	-	-	44.13±0.73	60.55±0.75	56.71±0.18	47.61±0.11
ALF[46]	56.27±0.91	32.04±0.56	-	-	43.73±0.82	40.29±0.03	55.09±1.49	43.08±1.02
Deepprivacy[18]	16.72±0.36	11.54±0.05	14.95±0.58	11.69±0.90	18.77±0.13	39.76±0.83	42.06±0.28	41.27±0.50
Appearance free[20]	30.02±0.07	15.67±0.14	14.22±0.16	10.29±0.06	19.60±0.02	-	-	-
Selective privacy[21]	58.97±0.11	38.27±0.01	45.10±0.15	30.09±0.06	42.56±0.54	-	-	-
Face blurring[22]	51.07±0.63	37.98±0.21	40.01±0.64	28.81±0.01	37.00±0.44	42.13±0.68	47.04±0.33	52.34±0.27
Raw data (no privacy)	85.77±0.18	59.24±0.65	85.77±0.18	59.24±0.65	65.05±1.17	70.13±0.59	64.18±0.06	69.10±0.59
Video-DPRP$_{(\epsilon=2, \delta=10^{-4})}$	55.16±0.59	36.49±0.79	38.76±0.11	27.95±0.01	39.25±0.15	39.42±0.62	41.89±0.02	40.03±0.28
Video-DPRP$_{(\epsilon=5, \delta=10^{-4})}$	58.58±0.16	38.37±0.09	45.20±0.02	29.06±0.77	44.86±0.02	48.75±0.07	50.11±0.68	53.77±0.30
Video-DPRP$_{(\epsilon=8, \delta=10^{-4})}$	61.69±0.07	40.00±0.71	50.00±0.28	32.13±0.31	51.07±0.73	53.00±0.01	56.10±0.20	55.12±0.03

Table 2. Comparison with differential private training methods and Video-DPRP on action recognition, for $\epsilon \in \{2, 5, 8\}$ and $\delta = 10^{-4}$. The best results are in red, and the second best are underlined.

	Raw Test set UCF101 (Top-1 (↑))			Raw Test set HMDB51 (Top-1 (↑))			Raw Test set PA-HMDB (Top-1 (↑))		
Method	$\epsilon = 2$	$\epsilon = 5$	$\epsilon = 8$	$\epsilon = 2$	$\epsilon = 5$	$\epsilon = 8$	$\epsilon = 2$	$\epsilon = 5$	$\epsilon = 8$
DP-SGD[1]	25.54±0.33	37.24±0.26	45.32±0.86	14.18±0.06	30.09±0.18	32.16±1.85	15.34±2.15	25.70±1.97	29.90±0.04
MultiClip-DP$_{(3\ clips)}$[32]	44.07±0.18	70.03±0.13	72.03±0.71	36.11±0.25	48.00±0.05	50.98±0.66	37.06±0.24	45.16±0.05	52.73±0.46
Video-DPRP	55.16±0.59	58.58±0.16	61.69±0.07	36.49±0.79	38.37±0.09	40.00±0.71	39.25±0.15	44.86±0.02	51.07±0.73
Video-DPRP$_{(3\ clips)}$	60.11±0.10	70.87±0.03	74.06±0.38	42.72±0.44	49.63±0.95	51.63±0.53	41.08±0.04	48.17±0.42	54.98±0.86

4 Experiments

4.1 Datasets

We adopt **PA-HMDB** [46] and **VISPR** [34] for visual privacy assessment, and **UCF101** [42] and **HMDB51** [26] for HAR, as these are commonly used datasets in the literature.

PA-HMDB [46] is a dataset containing 515 videos with video-level action annotations and frame-wise visual privacy annotations, including privacy attributes such as *skin color, face, gender, nudity,* and *relationship*. The dataset covers 51 action classes.

VISPR [34] is an image dataset designed for visual privacy research. It contains various personal attributes similar to those in HMDB51. The dataset comprises 10,000 training images, 4,100 validation images, and 8,000 test images.

UCF101 [42] and **HMDB51** [26] are both HAR datasets, containing 101 and 51 action classes, respectively. For both datasets, all results are reported on split-1, which includes 9,537 training videos and 3,783 test videos for UCF101, and 3,570 training videos and 1,530 test videos for HMDB51.

4.2 Implementation Details

Many deep learning models incorporate Batch Normalization (Batch Norm) layers. However, such models are not compatible with differentially private training methods like DP-SGD [1] or MultiClip-DP-SGD [32] (abbreviated to MultiClip-DP in Table 2), as Batch Norm requires calculating the mean and standard deviation for each mini-batch, introducing dependencies between samples and violating the principles of differential privacy. For fair comparison across all our results in video HAR, we require a model with a different type of normalization layer. Therefore, we use the PyTorch implementation of the Multiscale Vision Transformer (MViT-B$_{(16 \times 4)}$) [14], which employs Layer Normalization [2] and is pre-trained on the large-scale Kinetics-400 dataset [3]. For each video, we randomly crop a clip consisting of 16 frames, with each frame resized to a shape of $(224, 224, 3)$. In the case of Video-DPRP$_{(3 \text{ clips})}$ and MultiClip-DP$_{(3 \text{ clips})}$ (see Table 2), we crop 3 clips and apply the same pre-processing as described above. The optimization is performed using stochastic gradient descent (SGD) with a learning rate of $lr = 0.01$, a batch size of 8, and 50 training epochs.

Set-Up of Video-DPRP: We use video samples reconstructed by Video-DPRP as inputs for our training. In line with Algorithm 1, we set the dimensions of the projection matrix to $d \times k$, where $d = 320 \times 240 \times 3$ and $k = 32 \times 32 \times 3$. Note that d corresponds to the dimensions of a frame from the original video (as described in Sect. 3.4) and is therefore fixed to the value defined above by default. We set the privacy budget allocator b to 0.8, meaning that 80% of the privacy budget is allocated to making the random projection P, differentially private (see `line 6`) while the remaining 20% (i.e., $1 - b$) is used to ensure the covariance matrix P_{cov} is differentially private (see `line 8` of Algorithm 1).

For the differentially private training of DP-SGD [1] and MultiClip-DP$_{(3\text{ clips})}$ [32], we use the PyTorch Opacus library [48], which includes a privacy budget accountant to track the differentially private parameters (ϵ, δ) during training. For fair comparison and simplicity across all differentially private techniques (i.e., DP-SGD [1], MultiClip-DP$_{(3\text{ clips})}$ [32] and Video-DPRP), we set the privacy parameter $\delta = 10^{-4}$ and only vary ϵ. All experiments were conducted on an NVIDIA RTX A6000 GPU. For a comparative analysis with state-of-the-art (SOTA) visual privacy techniques, such as **Obfuscation** and **Anonymization**, we replicate their techniques following the authors' descriptions.

Obfuscation Methods: specifically, we compared our approach with: (1) a Inverse-Super-Resolution (ISR) [39] model, which initially downscales videos and further perform a set of transformations (rotations, cropping) to the downscaled videos; (2) a Face Blurring [22] algorithm, that detects faces using YOLOv3 [37] and applies Gaussian blurring with a kernel size of $k = 21$, and a standard deviation $\sigma = 10$ for consistency with prior works [21,46]; and finally (3) a Appearance-Free Privacy model [20], which removes appearance cues on videos via optical flow warping [43]. For comparisons with **Anonymization techniques** we used: (4) DeepPrivacy [18] which perform a full-body video anonymization, (5) a video Face Anonymizer [38], and (6) a surface-adaptive modulation: V-SAM [19]. **Adversarial training strategies** include (7) a adversarial learning framework (ALF) [46], which utilizes a adversarial privacy budget, and (8) SPAct [8], which employs self-supervised learning with MViT-B(16 × 4) as the target classifier. We also implement differentially private training with (10) DP-SGD [1] and (11) MultiClip-DP(3 clips) [32] using a clipping norm of $C = 0.4$. Full SOTA experimental details are included in the appendix.

4.3 Evaluation Metrics and Protocols

Metrics: Action recognition evaluation is conducted using the Top-1 accuracy metric, following prior work [16,17,32]. For visual privacy recognition, considered as a multi-label image classification task due to the presence of multiple privacy attributes per image, we use the class-wise mean average precision (cMAP) [34] and the class-wise F1-score. All results are reported as percentages, averaged over three runs, with both their mean and variance provided. In our tables, ↑ denotes metrics where higher values are better, while ↓ indicates that lower values are better.

Protocols: Apart from **Adversarial training** methods, which ensure privacy directly during training, we apply two evaluation protocols for video HAR with visual privacy techniques. Protocol 1 evaluates on the raw test set X_{raw}^{test} of dataset $\text{X} \in \{\textbf{UCF101}, \textbf{HMDB51}, \textbf{PA-HMDB}\}$, after training our model on the corresponding reconstructed train set $\text{X}_{reconst}^{train}$ using a method $reconst \in \{\textbf{Obfuscation}, \textbf{Anonymization}, \textbf{Video-DPRP}\}$.

Here, **Obfuscation** and **Anonymization** refer to all obfuscation and anonymization techniques described in Sect. 4.2. It is important to note that for evaluation on the **PA-HMDB** dataset, we use **HMDB51\{PA-HMDB}**

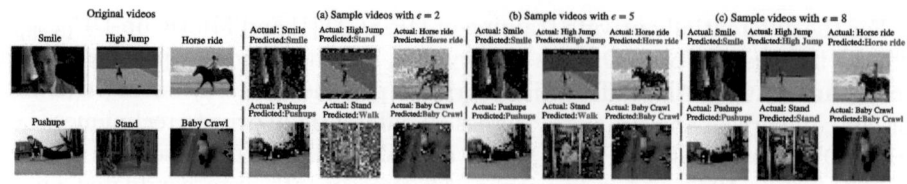

Fig. 3. Visual correlation: From left to right, we present video samples processed using Video-DPRP with varying $\epsilon = \{2, 5, 8\}$, while maintaining a fixed lower-dimensional space of $k = 32 \times 32 \times 3$, a privacy parameter of $\delta = 10^{-4}$, and a privacy budget of $b = 0.8$. Lower ϵ values introduce more *noise*, degrading reconstruction quality and leading to less accurate predictions. Incorrect classes are highlighted in red, while correct predictions are marked in green. (Color figure online)

as our training set. This means that all video samples present in **HMDB51** but not in **PA-HMDB** are used for training in this scenario. Protocol 2 evaluates on the reconstructed test set $X^{test}_{reconst}$ of dataset X, after training on $X^{train}_{reconst}$, using method *reconst*. Accordingly, no results are provided for adversarial training methods in the *reconstructed test set* column of Table 1. **Protocol 1** assesses the model's robustness in real-world scenarios where obfuscation or anonymization might not be applied, while testing on the reconstructed data (**Protocol 2**) measures performance consistency under privacy-preserving transformations, validating model adaptability across both standard and privacy-focused settings.

In Table 2, we restrict the analysis of video HAR to differentially private training methods: DP-SGD [1] and MultiClip-DP$_{(3 \text{ clips})}$ [32], alongside Video-DPRP, as these are the only methods that incorporate differential privacy. For visual privacy evaluation, we begin by training our model on the training set of **VISPR**, formulating the task as a multi-label image classification problem due to the multiple privacy attributes per image. We then use the annotated video frames from **PA-HMDB** as our test set. This is considered a cross-dataset evaluation protocol, as outlined in [8]. We also evaluate on the test set of **VISPR**, as reported in Table 1. We can observe from Table 1 that **Video-DPRP** provides competitive results, highlighted in **bold**, when compared to SOTA privacy-preserving techniques in both activity recognition and visual privacy preservation. Notably, the performance of **Video-DPRP** with $\epsilon = 8$ and $\delta = 10^{-4}$ (i.e. Video-DPRP$_{(\epsilon=8, \delta=10^{-4})}$, in Table 1) shows a significant improvement. However, Video-DPRP$_{(\epsilon=8, \delta=10^{-4})}$ shows a slight performance drop of **1.29%** in activity recognition on the HMDB51 dataset compared to SPAct [8], which achieved a baseline accuracy of **41.29%**. In terms of visual privacy, we observe that Video-DPRP achieved a cMAP score of **39.76%** on PA-HMDB51 and **42.06%** on VISPR (with $\epsilon = 2$), outperforming state-of-the-art methods such as ISR$_{(32 \times 24)}$ [39] and V-SAM [19]. Despite yielding decent scores on visual privacy, anonymization methods such as DeepPrivacy [18], V-SAM [19] and Face Anonymizer [38] as well as obfuscation method like ISR$_{(16 \times 12)}$ [39], struggle to achieve good utility performance on HAR, with results dropping as low as **12.00%**. Intuitively, DeepPrivacy [18], V-SAM [19] and Face Anonymizer [38]

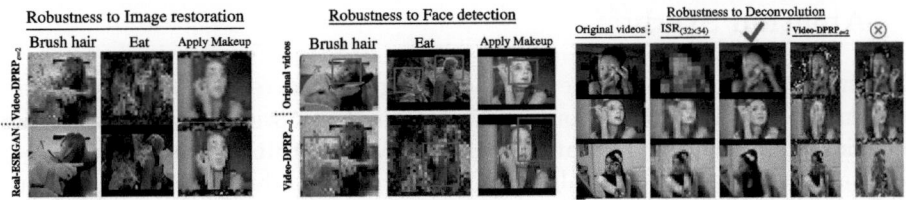

Fig. 4. Robustness analysis. We evaluated the robustness of Video-DPRP with $\epsilon = 2$ against three types of attack: (1) <u>Image Restoration</u> (Left): Using Real-ESRGAN [45] a SOTA super-resolution generative adversarial network, we attempted to restore images from Video-DPRP$_{\epsilon=2}$. However, the image's quality remained significantly degraded (see second row). (2) <u>Face Detection</u> (Middle): We employed a pre-trained YOLOv3 [37] to detect faces in the original video (first row, **blue** bounding boxes) and in videos reconstructed using Video-DPRP$_{\epsilon=2}$ (second row). The poor localization of the **red** bounding boxes highlights Video-DPRP's strong obfuscation effect. (3) <u>Deconvolution Attacks</u> (Right): We tested SUPIR [49], a SOTA deconvolution model on downscaled ISR [39] videos (16×12 resolution) and Video-DPRP$_{\epsilon=2}$. While SUPIR successfully recovers visual attributes from ISR videos (**green checkbox** column), it fails on Video-DPRP$_{\epsilon=2}$ (**red cross** column), demonstrating our method's resilience to deconvolution attacks. Full experimental details, along with additional results on face and skin-color detection, are provided in the appendix. (Color figure online)

generate a *modified* version of the original video, which often fails to consistently preserve the motions of individuals involved in the activity. We conclude that while the above anonymization methods yield good privacy results, they may not be suitable for utility analysis in Video HAR. For obfuscation techniques, we argue that the visual content may be so *obscured* that models struggle to effectively identify activities. In contrast, Video-DPRP strikes a balance between utility and privacy, even for varying values of $\epsilon \in \{2, 5, 8\}$. We do not report the privacy results for Appearance-Free [20] and Selective Privacy [21], as both methods rely on optical flow between successive frames in videos for obfuscation, which is not applicable in our experiment since we use VISPR as the primary training set for privacy evaluation. In Fig. 3, we present visual results of sample videos from UCF101 and HMDB51 with $\epsilon \in \{2, 5, 8\}$, along with their predicted classes. In Table 2, we use DP-SGD [1] as a baseline method and compare our results with MultiClip-DP$_{(3\ clips)}$ [32]. It is important to note that the results for MultiClip-DP$_{(3\ clips)}$ [32] are based on our own experiments, as the original code was not available. With 3 *clips* per sample video, Video-DPRP$_{(3\ clips)}$ provides competitive results when compared to MultiClip-DP$_{(3\ clips)}$, achieving Top-1 accuracy of **74.06**% on UCF101, **51.63**% on HMDB51 and **54.98**% on PA-HMDB with $\epsilon = 8$. Figure 4 presents a robustness analysis of Video-DPRP against image restoration, face detection, and deconvolution, simulating an adversarial scenario where an attacker attempts to compromise visual privacy from reconstructed videos. Additional analysis details are provided in the appendix.

5 Ablation Study

Keeping δ constant, we observe that increasing ϵ improves the action recognition performance of Video-DPRP but significantly reduces privacy, which is a typical behavior of differentially private algorithms. Video-DPRP is also influenced by two major components in its algorithm: the projection dimensionality k and the privacy budget b.

Effect of Varying the Dimensionality k: For a fixed $\epsilon = 8$, $\delta = 10^{-4}$, and a privacy budget of $b = 0.8$, we observed that increasing the dimensionality k improves action recognition performance but results in a significant decrease in privacy, as shown in Table 3. This is because, the value of k, has a diminishing effect on the noise scale, $\sigma_p = 1/\sqrt{k}$ and also on the L_2 sensitivity, $\theta = 255/\sqrt{k}$. As a result, when k increases, it substantially reduces the standard deviation value σ_1 in Theorem 1 and σ_2 in Theorem 2, leading to a decrease in the amount of noise added for differential privacy. Selecting an optimal k requires balancing performance gains with acceptable privacy levels for practical viability.

Effect of Varying the Privacy Budget b: Recall that b, represents the privacy budget allocated to make the random projection differentially private, while $1 - b$, ensures the differential privacy of the covariance matrix (see Algorithm 1). To understand the effect of varying b, we fixed $\epsilon = 8$, $\delta = 10^{-4}$ and $k = 32 \times 32 \times 3$. Table 4 shows that increasing the privacy budget for random projection up to a value of **80%**, results in a less noisy random projection. Consequently, there is an increase in action recognition performance but with a substantial decrease in privacy. This suggests that the random projection plays a more critical role compared to the covariance matrix, in Video-DPRP.

Computational Efficiency: We measured the time taken to reconstruct privacy-preserved videos from the UCF101 and HMDB51 datasets using different methods, as shown in Table 5. Although Video-DPRP has a polynomial time complexity as outlined in Sect. 3.4, it remains computationally efficient with an average reconstruction rate of $\sim$ **20 s/Video** for both datasets. In contrast,

Table 3. Action (Top-1) and privacy (cMAP) scores on **PA-HMDB** [46] for different lower dimensions k. The best result is highlighted in **bold**, and the second best is underlined.

	PA-HMDB	
Dimension k	Action ↑	Privacy ↓
20 × 20 × 3	24.60±1.67	**32.46±0.75**
24 × 32 × 3	28.03±0.07	40.17±1.22
32 × 32 × 3	51.07±0.73	53.00±0.01
50 × 50 × 3	67.18±0.49	56.96±0.07
64 × 80 × 3	**70.10±0.14**	60.18±0.33

Table 4. Action (Top-1) and privacy (cMAP) scores on **PA-HMDB** [46] for different privacy budget b. The best result is highlighted in **bold**, and the second best is underlined.

	PA-HMDB	
Budget b	Action ↑	Privacy ↓
0.2	37.80±0.92	**29.02±0.12**
0.4	40.26±0.17	36.73±1.01
0.5	43.80±0.85	44.27±0.49
0.6	46.39±0.22	50.01±0.14
0.8	**51.07±0.73**	53.00±0.01

Table 5. Reconstruction time per video (in seconds) for **UCF101** [42] and **HMDB51** [26]. The best (lowest) time is highlighted in **bold**, and the second best is underlined.

	Reconstruction (sec/Video)	
Methods	UCF101	HMBD51
V-SAM [18]	33.12	35.07
ISR$_{(32 \times 24)}$ [39]	19.24	18.97
Appearance free [20]	23.74	21.60
Face blurring [22]	26.08	24.49
Video-DPRP(ours)	**20.32**	**19.84**

V-SAM [19], Appearance-Free [20], and Face Blurring [22] incur additional computational overhead due to their use of surface-guided GANs, YOLO, and optical flow models, respectively.

6 Discussion

While Video-DPRP offers strong theoretical and empirical guarantees, we acknowledge that its computational overhead particularly due to the SVD-based reconstruction step, has not been benchmarked against real-time video processing constraints. Although our reconstruction time ($\sim$20 s/video) is competitive compared to many SOTA visual privacy techniques (e.g., Face Blurring, V-SAM), it may still limit deployment in latency-sensitive or edge scenarios. Future work will focus on profiling runtime on embedded systems (e.g., Jetson Nano) and optimizing matrix operations, with the goal of enabling lightweight, real-time inference pipelines. We also plan to investigate approximations to SVD and reduced projection dimensionality k to balance speed, privacy, and utility.

7 Conclusion

This paper introduces Video-DPRP, a differentially private approach for constructing visual privacy-preserved videos for Human Activity Recognition (HAR). Video-DPRP aims to bridge the gap between visual privacy and utility by providing strong privacy guarantees through the mathematical properties of differential privacy and random projection. Our evaluation across multiple datasets demonstrate that Video-DPRP achieves competitive performance in activity recognition while maintaining robust privacy preservation compared to current state-of-the-art techniques.

Acknowledgments. This study was funded by the Research Ireland Centre for Research Training in Digitally-Enhanced Reality (D-real), under Grant No. 18/CRT/6224 and with the financial support of Insight Research Ireland Centre for Data Analytics under Grant number SFI/12/RC/2289_P2. For the purpose of open access, the author has applied for a CC BY public copyright license to any author-accepted manuscript version arising from this submission.

Disclosure of Interests. The authors have no competing interests to declare that are relevant to the content of this article.

References

1. Abadi, M., et al.: Deep learning with differential privacy. In: Proceedings of the 2016 ACM SIGSAC Conference on Computer and Communications Security, pp. 308–318 (2016)
2. Ba, J.L.: Layer normalization. arXiv preprint arXiv:1607.06450 (2016)

3. Carreira, J., Zisserman, A.: Quo Vadis, action recognition? A new model and the kinetics dataset. In: Proceedings of the IEEE Conference on Computer Vision and Pattern Recognition, pp. 6299–6308 (2017)
4. Chaudhuri, K., Monteleoni, C., Sarwate, A.D.: Differentially private empirical risk minimization. J. Mach. Learn. Res. **12**(3) (2011)
5. Cristina, S., Despotovic, V., Pérez-Rodríguez, R., Aleksic, S.: Audio-and video-based human activity recognition systems in healthcare. IEEE Access (2024)
6. Cummings, R., Kaptchuk, G., Redmiles, E.M.: "I need a better description": an investigation into user expectations for differential privacy. In: Proceedings of the 2021 ACM SIGSAC Conference on Computer and Communications Security, pp. 3037–3052 (2021)
7. Dai, J., Saghafi, B., Wu, J., Konrad, J., Ishwar, P.: Towards privacy-preserving recognition of human activities. In: 2015 IEEE International Conference on Image Processing (ICIP), pp. 4238–4242. IEEE (2015)
8. Dave, I.R., Chen, C., Shah, M.: SPAct: self-supervised privacy preservation for action recognition. In: Proceedings of the IEEE/CVF Conference on Computer Vision and Pattern Recognition, pp. 20164–20173 (2022)
9. Davody, A., Adelani, D.I., Kleinbauer, T., Klakow, D.: On the effect of normalization layers on differentially private training of deep neural networks. arXiv preprint arXiv:2006.10919 (2020)
10. Du, J., Li, S., Chen, X., Chen, S., Hong, M.: Dynamic differential-privacy preserving SGD. arXiv preprint arXiv:2111.00173 (2021)
11. Dwork, C., Kenthapadi, K., McSherry, F., Mironov, I., Naor, M.: Our data, ourselves: privacy via distributed noise generation. In: Vaudenay, S. (ed.) EUROCRYPT 2006. LNCS, vol. 4004, pp. 486–503. Springer, Heidelberg (2006). https://doi.org/10.1007/11761679_29
12. Dwork, C., McSherry, F., Nissim, K., Smith, A.: Calibrating noise to sensitivity in private data analysis. In: Halevi, S., Rabin, T. (eds.) TCC 2006. LNCS, vol. 3876, pp. 265–284. Springer, Heidelberg (2006). https://doi.org/10.1007/11681878_14
13. Dwork, C., Roth, A., et al.: The algorithmic foundations of differential privacy. Found. Trends® Theoret. Comput. Sci. **9**(3–4), 211–407 (2014)
14. Fan, H., et al.: Multiscale vision transformers. In: Proceedings of the IEEE/CVF International Conference on Computer Vision, pp. 6824–6835 (2021)
15. Gondara, L., Wang, K.: Differentially private small dataset release using random projections. In: Conference on Uncertainty in Artificial Intelligence, pp. 639–648. PMLR (2020)
16. Hara, K., Kataoka, H., Satoh, Y.: Learning spatio-temporal features with 3d residual networks for action recognition. In: Proceedings of the IEEE International Conference on Computer Vision Workshops, pp. 3154–3160 (2017)
17. Hara, K., Kataoka, H., Satoh, Y.: Can spatiotemporal 3D CNNs retrace the history of 2d CNNs and ImageNet? In: Proceedings of the IEEE Conference on Computer Vision and Pattern Recognition, pp. 6546–6555 (2018)
18. Hukkelås, H., Lindseth, F.: DeepPrivacy2: towards realistic full-body anonymization. In: Proceedings of the IEEE/CVF Winter Conference on Applications of Computer Vision, pp. 1329–1338 (2023)
19. Hukkelås, H., Smebye, M., Mester, R., Lindseth, F.: Realistic full-body anonymization with surface-guided GANs. In: Proceedings of the IEEE/CVF Winter conference on Applications of Computer Vision, pp. 1430–1440 (2023)
20. Ilic, F., Pock, T., Wildes, R.P.: Is appearance free action recognition possible? In: Avidan, S., Brostow, G., Cissé, M., Farinella, G.M., Hassner, T. (eds.) ECCV 2022.

LNCS, vol. 13664, pp. 156–173. Springer, Cham (2022). https://doi.org/10.1007/978-3-031-19772-7_10
21. Ilic, F., Zhao, H., Pock, T., Wildes, R.P.: Selective interpretable and motion consistent privacy attribute obfuscation for action recognition. In: Proceedings of the IEEE/CVF Conference on Computer Vision and Pattern Recognition, pp. 18730–18739 (2024)
22. Jaichuen, T., Ren, N., Wongapinya, P., Fugkeaw, S.: Blur & track: real-time face detection with immediate blurring and efficient tracking. In: 2023 20th International Joint Conference on Computer Science and Software Engineering (JCSSE), pp. 167–172. IEEE (2023)
23. Jang, J., Lyu, H., Hwang, S., Yang, H.J.: Unveiling hidden visual information: a reconstruction attack against adversarial visual information hiding. arXiv preprint arXiv:2408.04261 (2024)
24. Johnson, W.B.: Extensions of Lipshitz mapping into Hilbert space. In: Conference Modern Analysis and Probability, pp. 189–206 (1984)
25. Kenthapadi, K., Korolova, A., Mironov, I., Mishra, N.: Privacy via the Johnson-Lindenstrauss transform. arXiv preprint arXiv:1204.2606 (2012)
26. Kuehne, H., Jhuang, H., Garrote, E., Poggio, T., Serre, T.: HMDB: a large video database for human motion recognition. In: 2011 International Conference on Computer Vision, pp. 2556–2563. IEEE (2011)
27. Lee, D., Yang, M.H., Oh, S.: Fast and accurate head pose estimation via random projection forests. In: Proceedings of the IEEE International Conference on Computer Vision, pp. 1958–1966 (2015)
28. Levy, D., et al.: Learning with user-level privacy. Adv. Neural. Inf. Process. Syst. **34**, 12466–12479 (2021)
29. Li, P., Li, X.: Smooth flipping probability for differential private sign random projection methods. Adv. Neural Inf. Process. Syst. **36** (2024)
30. Li, T., Wang, H., Zhuang, Z., Sun, J.: Deep random projector: accelerated deep image prior. In: Proceedings of the IEEE/CVF Conference on Computer Vision and Pattern Recognition, pp. 18176–18185 (2023)
31. Li, T., Lin, L.: AnonymousNet: natural face de-identification with measurable privacy. In: Proceedings of the IEEE/CVF Conference on Computer Vision and Pattern Recognition Workshops (2019)
32. Luo, Z., et al.: Differentially private video activity recognition. In: Proceedings of the IEEE/CVF Winter Conference on Applications of Computer Vision, pp. 6657–6667 (2024)
33. Nanayakkara, P., Smart, M.A., Cummings, R., Kaptchuk, G., Redmiles, E.M.: What are the chances? Explaining the epsilon parameter in differential privacy. In: 32nd USENIX Security Symposium (USENIX Security 2023), pp. 1613–1630 (2023)
34. Orekondy, T., Schiele, B., Fritz, M.: Towards a visual privacy advisor: understanding and predicting privacy risks in images. In: Proceedings of the IEEE International Conference on Computer Vision, pp. 3686–3695 (2017)
35. Pichapati, V., Suresh, A.T., Yu, F.X., Reddi, S.J., Kumar, S.: AdaCliP: adaptive clipping for private SGD. arXiv preprint arXiv:1908.07643 (2019)
36. Pittaluga, F., Koppal, S., Chakrabarti, A.: Learning privacy preserving encodings through adversarial training. In: 2019 IEEE Winter Conference on Applications of Computer Vision (WACV), pp. 791–799. IEEE (2019)
37. Redmon, J., Divvala, S., Girshick, R., Farhadi, A.: You only look once: unified, real-time object detection. In: Proceedings of the IEEE Conference on Computer Vision and Pattern Recognition, pp. 779–788 (2016)

38. Ren, Z., Lee, Y.J., Ryoo, M.S.: Learning to anonymize faces for privacy preserving action detection. In: Ferrari, V., Hebert, M., Sminchisescu, C., Weiss, Y. (eds.) ECCV 2018. LNCS, vol. 11205, pp. 639–655. Springer, Cham (2018). https://doi.org/10.1007/978-3-030-01246-5_38
39. Ryoo, M., Rothrock, B., Fleming, C., Yang, H.J.: Privacy-preserving human activity recognition from extreme low resolution. In: Proceedings of the AAAI Conference on Artificial Intelligence, vol. 31 (2017)
40. Shojaei-Hashemi, A., Nasiopoulos, P., Little, J.J., Pourazad, M.T.: Video-based human fall detection in smart homes using deep learning. In: 2018 IEEE International Symposium on Circuits and Systems (ISCAS), pp. 1–5. IEEE (2018)
41. Shokri, R., Stronati, M., Song, C., Shmatikov, V.: Membership inference attacks against machine learning models. In: 2017 IEEE symposium on security and privacy (SP), pp. 3–18. IEEE (2017)
42. Soomro, K.: UCF101: a dataset of 101 human actions classes from videos in the wild. arXiv preprint arXiv:1212.0402 (2012)
43. Teed, Z., Deng, J.: RAFT: recurrent all-pairs field transforms for optical flow. In: Vedaldi, A., Bischof, H., Brox, T., Frahm, J.-M. (eds.) ECCV 2020, Part II. LNCS, vol. 12347, pp. 402–419. Springer, Cham (2020). https://doi.org/10.1007/978-3-030-58536-5_24
44. Tu, S.: Differentially private random projections
45. Wang, X., Xie, L., Dong, C., Shan, Y.: Real-ESRGAN: training real-world blind super-resolution with pure synthetic data. In: Proceedings of the IEEE/CVF International Conference on Computer Vision, pp. 1905–1914 (2021)
46. Wu, Z., Wang, H., Wang, Z., Jin, H., Wang, Z.: Privacy-preserving deep action recognition: an adversarial learning framework and a new dataset. IEEE Trans. Pattern Anal. Mach. Intell. **44**(4), 2126–2139 (2020)
47. Xu, C., Ren, J., Zhang, Y., Qin, Z., Ren, K.: DPPRo: differentially private high-dimensional data release via random projection. IEEE Trans. Inf. Forensics Secur. **12**(12), 3081–3093 (2017)
48. Yousefpour, A., et al.: Opacus: user-friendly differential privacy library in pytorch. arXiv preprint arXiv:2109.12298 (2021)
49. Yu, F., et al.: Scaling up to excellence: practicing model scaling for photo-realistic image restoration in the wild. In: Proceedings of the IEEE/CVF Conference on Computer Vision and Pattern Recognition, pp. 25669–25680 (2024)
50. Zhou, X., et al.: Deep-learning-enhanced human activity recognition for internet of healthcare things. IEEE Internet Things J. **7**(7), 6429–6438 (2020)

Differentially Private Sparse Linear Regression with Heavy-Tailed Responses

Xizhi Tian[1,2,3], Meng Ding[4], Touming Tao[5], Zihang Xiang[1,2], and Di Wang[1,2](✉)

[1] Provable Responsible AI and Data Analytics (PRADA) Lab, Thuwal, Saudi Arabia
[2] King Abdullah University of Science and Technology, Thuwal, Saudi Arabia
di.wang@kaust.edu.sa
[3] Utrecht University, Utrecht, The Netherlands
[4] University at Buffalo, Buffalo, USA
[5] Technical University Berlin, Berlin, Germany

Abstract. As a fundamental problem in machine learning and differential privacy (DP), DP linear regression has been extensively studied. However, most existing methods focus primarily on either regular data distributions or low-dimensional cases with irregular data. To address these limitations, this paper provides a comprehensive study of DP sparse linear regression with heavy-tailed responses in high-dimensional settings. In the first part, we introduce the DP-IHT-H method, which leverages the Huber loss and private iterative hard thresholding to achieve an estimation error bound of $\tilde{O}\left(s^{*\frac{1}{2}} \cdot \left(\frac{\log d}{n}\right)^{\frac{\zeta}{1+\zeta}} + s^{*\frac{1+2\zeta}{2+2\zeta}} \cdot \left(\frac{\log^2 d}{n\varepsilon}\right)^{\frac{\zeta}{1+\zeta}}\right)$ under the (ε, δ)-DP model, where n is the sample size, d is the dimensionality, s^* is the sparsity of the parameter, and $\zeta \in (0, 1]$ characterizes the tail heaviness of the data. In the second part, we propose DP-IHT-L, which further improves the error bound under additional assumptions on the response and achieves $\tilde{O}\left(\frac{(s^*)^{3/2} \log d}{n\varepsilon}\right)$. Compared to the first result, this bound is independent of the tail parameter ζ. Finally, through experiments on synthetic and real-world datasets, we demonstrate that our methods outperform standard DP algorithms designed for "regular" data.

Keywords: Differential Privacy · Sparse Linear Regression · Heavy-tailed Data

1 Introduction

Differential Privacy (DP) [18] has received significant attention and is now widely considered the *de facto* standard to protect privacy in data analysis. DP provides a rigorous mathematical framework to ensure that the inclusion or exclusion of any single individual's data in a dataset does not significantly affect the output of an analysis, thereby preserving privacy. A large body of research has explored various DP guarantees, and these concepts have been successfully adopted in industry [14,43].

Linear regression in the DP model has been extensively studied for many years, becoming one of the most thoroughly explored topics in machine learning and DP communities. A substantial body of research has addressed the problem from various perspectives. Early investigations of DP linear regression were closely tied to more general frameworks such as DP Stochastic Convex Optimization (DP-SCO) and Empirical Risk Minimization (DP-ERM), as explored in the seminal works of [11,12,16,22,37,39,40,46,49,51,55,58,59]. Subsequently, numerous methods have been proposed to address DP linear regression under different settings. For instance, several studies [4,15,19,25,53] focus on low-dimensional scenarios in the central DP model, while others [9,28,29,42,56] extend these ideas to high-dimensional sparse linear regression—an increasingly relevant setting for modern, structured data. The local DP model has also attracted attention [17,47,50,52,60,61], imposing stricter privacy requirements but potentially offering stronger protection.

Despite these advances, most prior work assumes *regular* data distributions, typically requiring that features and responses are bounded or sub-Gaussian. Classical approaches such as output perturbation [12] or objective/gradient perturbation [5] rely on these assumptions to guarantee an $O(1)$-Lipschitz loss for all data points. In practice, however, these conditions often fail—particularly in domains like biomedicine and finance, where heavy-tailed distributions commonly arise [6,24,57]. In such cases, Lipschitz conditions may be violated; for example, in linear regression with squared loss $\ell(w,(x,y)) = (w^\top x - y)^2$, heavy-tailed features can lead to unbounded gradients, invalidating assumptions used in many DP proofs. Although gradient truncation or trimming [1] has been suggested as a remedy, a thorough analysis of its convergence properties under DP constraints has been lacking. This gap underscores the need for private and robust methods specifically tailored to heavy-tailed data.

Recent works have begun addressing DP linear regression in the presence of heavy-tailed data [3,27,31,48,54]. However, some of these approaches suffer from a polynomial dependence on the data dimension d, making them unsuitable for high-dimensional settings where $d \gg n$. Thus, a natural question is: What are the theoretical behaviors of DP linear regression in high-dimensional sparse cases with heavy-tailed data?

Our Contributions. In this paper, we study the setting of high-dimensional sparse linear regression with heavy-tailed response under DP constraints. Specifically, we consider the scenario where the feature vector is sub-Gaussian and the response only has a finite $(1+\zeta)$-th moment with $\zeta \in (0,1]$. We propose novel DP linear regression algorithms that are robust to heavy-tailed data and capable of handling high-dimensional sparse problems effectively. Specifically:

1. For general heavy-tailed responses, we propose the DP-IHT-H algorithm, addressing the unexplored challenge of adapting Huber loss-based linear

regression to differential privacy. Specifically, it achieves an error bound under (ϵ, δ)-DP given by

$$\tilde{O}\left(s^{*\frac{1}{2}} \cdot \left(\frac{\log d}{n}\right)^{\frac{\zeta}{1+\zeta}} + s^{*\frac{1+2\zeta}{2+2\zeta}} \cdot \left(\frac{\log^2 d}{n\varepsilon}\right)^{\frac{\zeta}{1+\zeta}}\right),$$

where n is the sample size, d is the data dimensionality, and s^* represents the sparsity of the parameter.

2. To further improve the error bound, we propose the DP-IHT-L algorithm, which leverages the ℓ_1 loss function instead. By adding some mild assumptions on the response noise, the DP-IHT-L algorithm achieves a lower gradient bound and reduces the magnitude of the added noise. This enhancement leads to improved error bounds and greater stability, regardless of the value of ζ. Specifically, under (ϵ, δ)-DP, the error is bounded by $\tilde{O}\left(\frac{(s^*)^{3/2} \log d}{n\epsilon}\right)$, which is independent of the moment and matches best-known results of the sub-Gaussian case [10, 21].

3. Through extensive experiments on both synthetic and real-world datasets, we demonstrate that our methods outperform DP algorithms designed for regular data. Moreover, in some cases, DP-IHT-L further improves upon DP-IHT-H.

2 Related Work

As we mentioned, DP linear regression has been extensively studied. Still, most existing methods assume that the underlying data distribution is sub-Gaussian or bounded, rendering them unsuitable for heavy-tailed data. In contrast, in the non-private setting, recent advances have addressed Stochastic Convex Optimization (SCO) and Empirical Risk Minimization (ERM) under heavy-tailed data [7, 20, 30, 32, 38, 41]. However, these non-private methods are not directly adaptable to private settings, particularly in our high dimensional sparse scenarios.

The first study addressing DP-SCO with heavy-tailed data was proposed by [48], which introduced three methods based on distinct assumptions. The first method utilizes the Sample-and-Aggregate framework [34], but its stringent assumptions lead to a relatively large error bound. The second method leverages smooth sensitivity [8] but requires the data distribution to be subexponential. Additionally, [48] proposed a private estimator inspired by robust statistics, which shares similarities with our approach. Building on the mean estimator proposed in [26, 27, 44] recently investigated DP-SCO and achieved improved (expected) excess population risks of $\tilde{O}\left(\left(\frac{d}{\epsilon n}\right)^{\frac{1}{2}}\right)$ and $\tilde{O}\left(\frac{d}{\epsilon n}\right)$ for convex and strongly convex loss functions, respectively. These results rely on the assumption that the gradient of the loss function has a bounded second-order moment, aligning with the best-known outcomes for heavy-tailed mean estimation. However, these approaches only consider low dimensional case and cannot address high-dimensional or sparse learning problems. Furthermore, their methods are not directly extendable to our models, where the assumption of bounded second-order moments of the loss function gradient is overly restrictive than our assumption on the finite $(1+\zeta)$-moment for the response.

Recently, [21] proposed a method that requires only that the distributions of x sub-Gaussian and y at least have bounded second-order moments, achieving an error bound of $\tilde{O}\left(\frac{(s^*)^3 \log^2 d}{n\epsilon}\right)$. In our paper, we consider the weaker assumption that y only has the bounded $(1+\zeta)$-th moment. We show that, under some additional assumptions, it is possible to achieve almost the same error as in [21].

3 Preliminaries

Definition 1 (Differential Privacy [18]). *A randomized mechanism M for the data universe $\mathcal{D}$ satisfies (ε, δ)-differential privacy if, for all measurable subsets $S \subseteq \text{Range}(M)$ and for all pairs of adjacent datasets $D, D' \in \mathcal{D}$ (differing by at most one data point), $\Pr[M(D) \in S] \leq e^\varepsilon \Pr[M(D') \in S] + \delta$, where the probability space is over the randomness of the mechanism M.*

Definition 2 (Laplacian Mechanism). *Given a function $q : X^n \to \mathbb{R}^d$, the Laplacian Mechanism is defined as: $\mathcal{M}_L(D, q, \epsilon) = q(D) + (Y_1, Y_2, \cdots, Y_d)$, where Y_i is i.i.d. drawn from a Laplacian Distribution $\text{Lap}\left(\frac{\Delta_1(q)}{\epsilon}\right)$, and $\Delta_1(q)$ is the ℓ_1-sensitivity of the function q, i.e., $\Delta_1(q) = \sup_{D \sim D'} \|q(D) - q(D')\|_1$. For a parameter λ, the Laplacian distribution has the density function $\text{Lap}(\lambda)(x) = \frac{1}{2\lambda} \exp\left(-\frac{|x|}{\lambda}\right)$. The Laplacian Mechanism preserves ϵ-DP.*

Definition 3 (Sub-Gaussian Vector). *A random vector $\mathbf{X} \in \mathbb{R}^d$ is sub-Gaussian if every one-dimensional projection $\langle \mathbf{X}, \mathbf{v} \rangle$, for any unit vector $\mathbf{v} \in \mathbb{R}^d$, is a sub-Gaussian random variable. That is, there exists $\sigma^2 > 0$ such that for all $\lambda \in \mathbb{R}$, $\mathbb{E}\left[e^{\lambda(\langle \mathbf{X}, \mathbf{v} \rangle - \mathbb{E}[\langle \mathbf{X}, \mathbf{v} \rangle])}\right] \leq e^{\frac{\lambda^2 \sigma^2}{2}}$.*

We consider a sparse linear model $y_i = x_i^\top \beta^* + \varepsilon_i$, where $\beta^* \in \mathbb{R}^d$ is the underlying unknown parameter vector, and ε_i represents the noise term. In the high dimensional setting, we assume β^* is s^*-sparse, i.e., $s^* = |\text{supp}(\beta^*)|$ with $s^* \ll d$. In DP linear regression, given a dataset where each sample is i.i.d. sampled from the linear model, the goal is to develop some (ϵ, δ)-DP estimator β^{priv} to make the estimation error $\|\beta^{priv} - \beta^*\|_2$ as small as possible. We adopt the following general assumptions, requiring bounded eigenvalues and a bounded β^*, which are common in high dimensional setting [9,38,41] :

Assumption 1. *We assume the following:*

1. *The covariates $\{x_i\}$ are zero-mean $O(1)$-sub-Gaussian with covariance matrix $\Sigma = \mathbb{E}[xx^\top]$. The eigenvalues of Σ are bounded as follows: $c_l \leq \lambda_{\min}(\Sigma) \leq \lambda_{\max}(\Sigma) \leq c_u$.*
2. *$\|\beta^*\|_2 \leq c_u^{1/2} r = L$, where r is a constant.*

In this paper, we focus on linear models with heavy-tailed responses. Unlike previous work on the DP linear model, here we only assume the response (or the noise) has only bounded $1+\zeta$-th moment:

Assumption 2. *We assume the noise ε_i has zero mean, $\mathbb{E}[\varepsilon_i] = 0$, and a finite $(1+\zeta)$-th moment with some $\zeta \in (0,1]$:*

$$v_\zeta = \frac{1}{n}\sum_{i=1}^n \mathbb{E}(|\varepsilon_i|^{1+\zeta}) < \infty.$$

4 DP Iterative Hard Thresholding with Huber Loss

In the non-private case, recently [41,45] show that an estimator based on the Huber loss [23] can achieve the optional estimation rate:

$$\mathcal{L}_\tau(\boldsymbol{\beta}) = \frac{1}{n}\sum_{i=1}^n \ell_\tau(y_i - x_i^\top \boldsymbol{\beta}), \text{s.t.} \|\boldsymbol{\beta}\|_0 \leq s, \|\boldsymbol{\beta}\|_2 \leq L, \tag{1}$$

where s is a parameter and the Huber loss with parameter τ is defined as

$$\ell_\tau(x) := \begin{cases} \dfrac{x^2}{2}, & \text{if } |x| < \tau, \\ \tau|x| - \dfrac{\tau^2}{2}, & \text{otherwise.} \end{cases}$$

Compared to the squared loss in the classical linear model, Huber loss is more robust to outliers and heavy-tailed noise, making it highly effective in non-DP scenarios. However, with the DP constraint, it is difficult to privatize such an estimator due to the following key challenges: 1). The optimization problem (non-convex and non-smooth) associated with Huber loss (1) lacks an efficient algorithm for the solution. For instance, [41] proposes an adaptive Huber loss estimator but does not provide an efficient algorithm to solve it. 2). If we directly use the previous DP methods to the Huber loss such as objective perturbation [11] or gradient perturbation methods [5], then we need to introduce a noise with scale $\Omega(d)$, which is extremely large as we consider the high dimensional setting where $d \gg n$.

To address these challenges, we propose the DP-IHT-H algorithm. This algorithm: 1). Efficiently leverages the Huber loss to perform a linear regression. 2). Achieves (ϵ, δ)-DP guarantees with an error bound that only logarithmically depends on the dimension d. In our DP-IHT-H algorithm, we first shrink the original feature vector x to make it have bounded ℓ_∞-norm. Next, we calculate the gradient on the shrunken data using the Huber loss and update our vector via gradient descent. Due to the bounded gradient of Huber loss, the error bound can be controlled with high probability, even for heavy-tailed data. Finally, we perform a "Peeling" step [10] to select the top s indices with the largest magnitudes in the vector while preserving DP.

Algorithm 1. DP IHT with Huber Loss (DP-IHT-H)

Input: n-size dataset $\mathbf{D} = \{(y_i, x_i)\}_{i \in [n]}$, Step size η, Sparsity level s, Privacy parameters ε, δ, Huber loss parameter τ, Truncation parameter K, Total steps T.
Output: β^T
1: Initialize $\beta^0 = 0$.
2: **Clipping:** For each $i \in [n]$, define the truncated sample $\tilde{x}_i \in \mathbb{R}^d$ by
$$\tilde{x}_{i,j} = \text{sign}(x_{i,j}) \min\{|x_{i,j}|, K\}, \quad \forall j \in [d].$$
3: Denote the truncated dataset as $\tilde{D} = \{(\tilde{x}_i, \tilde{y}_i)\}_{i=1}^n$.
4: Split the data $\tilde{D}$ into T parts $\{\tilde{D}_t\}_{t=1}^T$, each with $m = \frac{n}{T}$ samples.
5: **for** $t = 0$ to $T - 1$ **do**
6: $\quad \beta^{t+0.5} = \beta^t - \frac{\eta}{m} \sum_{i \in \tilde{D}_t} \ell'_\tau(y_i - \tilde{x}_i^\top \beta^t) \tilde{x}_i$
7: $\quad \beta^{t+1} = \Pi_L\left(\text{Peeling}\left(\beta^{t+0.5}, \tilde{D}_t, s, \varepsilon, \delta, \frac{\eta \tau K}{m}\right)\right)$, where Π_L is the projection onto the L-radius ball.
8: **end for**
9: **return** β^T

The Peeling algorithm achieves privacy protection by adding Laplace noise twice. First, noise is added to each entry of the vector to perturb the original data, ensuring that no single component can be directly exposed during the selection process. Based on the noisy values, the algorithm iteratively selects the indices corresponding to the s largest magnitudes. After selecting the s indices, additional Laplace noise is added to further obscure the true values of the selected components. The final output is a sparse vector where only the selected components retain their perturbed values, while all other components are set to zero. Compared to using Gaussian noise, this approach results in a smaller noise scale, effectively protecting privacy while maintaining higher accuracy and output quality. In the following, we will provide the privacy and utility guarantees of DP-IHT-H.

Theorem 1. *For any $0 < \varepsilon, 0 < \delta < 1$, DP-IHT-H is (ε, δ)-DP.*

Theorem 2. *If Assumption 1 and 2 hold and assume n is sufficiently large such that $n \geq \tilde{\Omega}((s^*)^{\frac{2}{3}} \log d)$. Setting $s = O(s^*)$, stepsize $\eta = O(1)$, $K = O(\log d)$, $T = O(\log n)$, and $\tau = O\left(\left(\frac{n}{T(s^*)^{\frac{3}{2}} \log^{\frac{1}{2}}(\frac{1}{\sigma}) \log d}\right)^{\frac{\zeta}{1+\zeta}}\right)$ in Algorithm 1, then with probability at least $1 - O\left(d^{-1} + Te^{-c_1 n}\right)$ for a constant c_1, we obtain the following bound on the final estimate:*

$$\|\beta^T - \beta^*\|_2 = O\left((s^*)^{\frac{1}{2}} \left(\frac{\log d}{n}\right)^{\frac{\zeta}{1+\zeta}} + (s^*)^{\frac{1}{2}} \left(\frac{(s^*)^{\frac{1}{2}} \log^2 d \log(1/\delta)}{n\varepsilon}\right)^{\frac{\zeta}{1+\zeta}}\right).$$

Algorithm 2. Peeling Procedure

Input: Vector $x \in \mathbb{R}^d$ (based on **D**), Sparsity s, Privacy parameters ε, δ, Noise scale λ.
Output: $x|_S + \tilde{w}_S$
1: Initialize $S = \emptyset$.
2: **for** $i = 1$ to s **do**
3:    Generate noise $w_i \in \mathbb{R}^d$ where each component is drawn from: $w_{i,j} \sim \text{Lap}\left(\frac{2\lambda\sqrt{3s\log(1/\delta)}}{\varepsilon}\right)$.
4:    Append $j^* = \arg\max_{j \in [d] \setminus S}\left(|x_j| + w_{i,j}\right)$ to S.
5: **end for**
6: Generate $\tilde{w} \in \mathbb{R}^d$ where each component is drawn from: $\tilde{w}_j \sim \text{Lap}\left(\frac{2\lambda\sqrt{3s\log(1/\delta)}}{\varepsilon}\right)$.
7: **return** $x|_S + \tilde{w}_S$.

Remark. There are two terms in the above error bound. The first one corresponds to the optimal error bound in the non-private case [41]. The second term corresponds to the error due to the noises added to ensure DP. In the case $\varepsilon = O(1)$ the overall error bound is dominated by the second term. Moreover, when $\zeta = 1$, i.e., the noise has bounded variance, the error rate becomes to $\tilde{O}(\frac{(s^*)^{3/4}\log d}{\sqrt{n\varepsilon}})$.

Under similar conditions, that is, assume that x is sub-Gaussian and y has a finite 2ζ-th moment with $\zeta \geq 1$ - [21] establishes an upper bound for the privacy component, given by $\tilde{O}\left((s^*)^{\frac{1+2\zeta}{1+\zeta}} \cdot \left(\frac{\log^3 n \log^2 d}{n^2\varepsilon^2}\right)^{\frac{\zeta}{1+\zeta}}\right)$. Thus, our results can be considered as an extension to the $(1+\zeta)$-th moment case. For sub-Gaussian x and y a related bound is also provided in [10]: $\tilde{O}\left(\sqrt{\frac{s^* \log d}{n}} + \frac{s^* \log d \sqrt{\log^3 n}}{n\varepsilon}\right)$. However, this result is not directly comparable to ours due to the strong assumptions imposed on the covariance matrix.

5 DP Iterative Hard Thresholding with ℓ_1 Loss

In DP-IHT-H, the algorithm achieves its lowest error bound when $\zeta = 1$. This naturally raises the question: Can we refine the algorithm so that its performance becomes independent of ζ even when $\zeta < 1$? In this section, we propose a new method, DP-IHT-L, to address the shortcomings of DP-IHT-H. The primary issue with DP-IHT-H lies in the dependence of the bounded gradient of the Huber loss on ζ, which results in larger noise being introduced during the "Peeling" step as the best value depends on n and ζ (see Theorem 2). Thus, it is necessary to use other loss functions that do not have such a parameter τ and are with a constant gradient bound. Motivated by [38], in the following we will show the ℓ_1 loss (absolute loss function) satisfies this requirement. See Algorithm 3 for details.

The basic idea of DP-IHT-L is similar to that of DP-IHT-H. First, we clip x to ensure it has an $\tilde{O}(1)$ bounded ℓ_∞-norm. Then we update β^t, but instead of using the gradient of the Huber loss, we replace it with the gradient of the ℓ_1 loss, thereby avoiding the dependence on the bound related to ζ. Finally, we apply the "Peeling" algorithm to introduce noise and preserve differential privacy.

Theorem 3. *For $0 < \epsilon$ and $0 < \delta < 1$, the DP-IHT-L algorithm is (ε, δ)-DP.*

To get our bound, we pose additional assumptions on the noise.

Assumption 3. *We assume the following: Let the noise terms $\{\varepsilon_i\}_{i=1}^n$ be i.i.d. with density $h_\varepsilon(\cdot)$ and distribution function $H_\varepsilon(\cdot)$, and define $\gamma = \mathbb{E}\big[|\varepsilon_i|\big]$. There exist constants $b_0, b_1 > 0$ (possibly depending on γ) such that*

$$h_\varepsilon(x) \geq \tfrac{1}{b_0}, \quad \text{for all } |x| \leq 8\left(\tfrac{c_u}{c_l}\right)^{\frac{1}{2}} \gamma,$$

$$h_\varepsilon(x) \leq \tfrac{1}{b_1}, \quad \text{for all } x \in \mathbb{R}.$$

Remark: The lower bound in the density is essentially a (local) Bernstein condition [2] and is easily satisfied by many heavy-tailed distributions (e.g., any t-distribution with degrees of freedom $v > 2$). The upper bound simply requires that the noise distribution does not have unbounded peaks, which is also satisfied by common distributions such as Gaussian, Laplace, and t-distributions with $v > 2$. As a result, Assumption 3 is quite relaxed for a wide range of heavy-tailed settings.

Under Assumption 3, in t-th iteration, the sub-gradient of the loss function

$$\mathbf{G}_t = \sum_{i \in \tilde{D}_t} \mathrm{sign}\left(x_i^\top \beta^t - y_i\right) \tilde{x}_i$$
$$= \sum_{i \in \tilde{D}_t} \mathrm{sign}(x_i^\top (\beta^t - \beta^*)) \tilde{x}_i - \sum_{i \in \tilde{D}_t} \mathrm{sign}(x_i^\top \varepsilon_i) \tilde{x}_i$$

exhibits two distinct regimes based on the magnitude of $\|\beta^t - \beta^*\|_2$. These regimes determine the behavior and convergence rate of the algorithm:

- **Large Deviation Regime:** When $\|\beta^t - \beta^*\|_2$ is relatively large, the sub-gradient $\mathbf{G}_t$ is dominated by the term $\sum_{i \in \tilde{D}_t} \mathrm{sign}(x_i^\top (\beta^t - \beta^*)) \tilde{x}_i$ leading to a larger error bound of $\mathbf{G}_t$. Hence the updates in this phase are large, allowing the algorithm to converge rapidly during the early iterations. This ensures efficient progress toward reducing the parameter error.
- **Small Deviation Regime:** Once $\|\beta^t - \beta^*\|_2$ becomes small, the sub-gradient $\mathbf{G}_t$ is primarily influenced by the noise term $\sum_{i \in \tilde{D}_t} \mathrm{sign}(x_i^\top \varepsilon_i) \tilde{x}_i$. In this case the error bound of $\mathbf{G}_t$ is small leading to a slower convergence rate that ensures refinement near the underlying parameter β^*.

Based on these differing bounds, we can establish the following convergence result.

Algorithm 3. Differentially Private Iterative Hard Thresholding with General Loss (DP-IHT-L)

Input: n-size dataset $\mathbf{D} = \{(y_i, x_i)\}_{i=1}^n$, Step size η_t, Sparsity level s, Privacy parameters ε, δ, Truncation parameter K, Total steps T.
Output: β^T
1: **Initialization:** Set $\beta^0 = 0$.
2: **Clipping:** For each $i \in [n]$, define the truncated sample $\tilde{x}_i \in \mathbb{R}^d$ by

$$\tilde{x}_{i,j} = \text{sign}(x_{i,j}) \min\{|x_{i,j}|, K\}, \quad \forall j \in [d].$$

3: Denote the truncated dataset as $\tilde{D} = \{(\tilde{x}_i, y_i)\}_{i=1}^n$.
4: **Data Splitting:** Split $\tilde{D}$ into T disjoint subsets $\{\tilde{D}_t\}_{t=0}^{T-1}$, each containing $m = \frac{n}{T}$ samples.
5: **for** $t = 0$ to $T - 1$ **do**
6: $\quad \beta^{t+0.5} = \beta^t - \frac{\eta_t}{m} \sum_{i \in \tilde{D}_t} \text{sign}(x_i^\top \beta^t - y_i) \tilde{x}_i$
7: $\quad \beta^{t+1} = \Pi_L \left(\text{Peeling}\left(\beta^{t+0.5}, \tilde{D}_t, s, \varepsilon, \delta, \frac{2\eta K}{m}\right) \right)$
8: **end for**
9: **return** β^T

Theorem 4. *Under Assumption 1, 2 and 3 and assume $n \geq O(c_u c_l^{-1} s^* \log d)$. Set $s = \Omega\left((c_u/c_l)^8 (b_0/b_1)^8 s^*\right)$, $K = O(\log d)$, and the initial step size η_0 satisfying*

$$\left[\frac{c_l^{1/2} \|\beta_0 - \beta^*\|_2}{8 n c_u}, \frac{3 c_l^{1/2} \|\beta_0 - \beta^*\|_2}{8 n c_u} \right],$$

then for the sequence $\{\beta^t\}$ generated by Algorithm 3, there are two distinct convergence phases:

Phase One: *When $\|\beta^t - \beta^*\|_2 \geq 8 c_l^{-1/2} \gamma$, using $\eta_t = (1 - c_1)^t \eta_0$ with $c_1 = O(c_l c_u^{-1})$ ensures*

$$\|\beta^{t+1} - \beta^*\|_2 \leq (1 - c_1)^{t+1} \|\beta_0 - \beta^*\|_2 + O(\sqrt{W}).$$

Phase Two: *Once $\|\beta^t - \beta^*\|_2 \leq 8 c_l^{-1/2} \gamma$, switching to a constant step size $\eta_t = O\left(c_l^{1/2} b_1^2 (nb_0 c_u)^{-1}\right)$ yields*

$$\|\beta^{t+1} - \beta^*\|_2 \leq (1 - c_2^*) \|\beta^t - \beta^*\|_2 + O(\sqrt{W}).$$

Here,

$$O(\sqrt{W}) = O\left(\frac{T(s^*)^{3/2} \log d \left(\log(1/\delta)\right)^{1/2} \log(T/n)}{n \varepsilon} \right)$$

represents the cumulative effect of the Laplace noise, and $c_2^* \in (0,1)$ indicates a strict contraction rate once β^t is sufficiently close to the true parameter vector β^*.

Because the sub-gradient operates under two different regimes, the overall estimation error follows a two-phase pattern. In Phase One, the sub-gradient is governed by the smoothness property, leading to rapid convergence from larger errors. In Phase Two, the strong convexity takes over once the estimator is sufficiently close to β^*, and the convergence becomes linear in nature. The $O(\sqrt{W}))$ term arises from comparing against the exact parameter β^*, which is not affected by the additional noise injected via the peeling procedure. With these two phases established, we can derive a global error bound as follows.

Theorem 5. *Consider the same settings as in Theorem 4, with probability at least* $1 - \exp\left(-C s^* \log\left(\frac{2d}{s^*}\right)\right)$, *after at most*

$$T = O\left(\log\left(\frac{\|\beta_0 - \beta^*\|_2}{\gamma}\right) + \log\left(n\gamma b_0^{-1} \log\left(\frac{2d}{s^*}\right)\right)\right)$$

iterations, Algorithm 3 produces an estimator β^T *satisfying*

$$\|\beta^T - \beta^*\|_2 \leq O\left(\frac{(s^*)^{3/2} \log d \left(\log(\frac{1}{\delta})\right)^{1/2} \log n}{n\varepsilon}\right).$$

Overall, our DP-IHT-L algorithm achieves an error bound of $\tilde{O}\left(\frac{(s^*)^{3/2} \log d}{n\varepsilon}\right)$ for high-dimensional sparse data with heavy-tailed distributions. In comparison, the DP-IHT-H algorithm attains an error of $\tilde{O}\left(s^{*\frac{1+2\zeta}{2+2\zeta}} \left(\frac{\log^2 d}{n\varepsilon}\right)^{\frac{\zeta}{1+\zeta}}\right)$, which is larger than our previous bound. Similarly, when $\zeta = 1$, our error bound is almost the same as in [21], which is given by $\tilde{O}\left(s^{*\frac{1+2\zeta}{1+\zeta}} \left(\frac{\log^3 n \log^2 d}{n^2\varepsilon^2}\right)^{\frac{\zeta}{1+\zeta}}\right)$. Note that in the case of $\zeta = 1$, [10] achieves an error bound of $\tilde{O}\left(\sqrt{\frac{s^* \log d}{n}} + \frac{s^* \log d}{n\varepsilon}\right)$. However, their analysis requires the strong condition that $\|x_I\|_\infty \leq O\left(\frac{1}{\sqrt{|I|}}\right)$ for any index set $I \subseteq [d]$. Thus, their results is incomparable with ours.

6 Experiments

In this section, we evaluate the practical performance of our proposed algorithms on both synthetic and real-world datasets.

6.1 Experimental Setup

Synthetic Data. We generate synthetic data for linear regression following the model

$$y_i = \langle x_i, \beta^* \rangle + \varepsilon_i, \quad i = 1, \ldots, n,$$

where each feature vector $x_i \in \mathbb{R}^d$ is drawn from $\mathcal{N}(\mathbf{0}, \mathbf{I}_d)$. The true coefficient vector β^* has s^* nonzero entries, which are sampled from a scaled standard normal distribution, with the remaining entries set to zero. To simulate heavy-tailed noise, the error terms $\{\varepsilon_i\}$ are drawn from a Student-t distribution. Specifically, we set the degrees of freedom ν to 1.75 when $\zeta = 0.5$ and to 3 when $\zeta = 1$.

Real-World Data. For additional validation, we evaluate our algorithms on real-world datasets, including: **NCI-60 cancer cell line dataset** [36], with $n = 59$ samples and $d = 14{,}342$ features. And **METABRIC** (Molecular Taxonomy of Breast Cancer International Consortium) dataset [13,35], with $n = 1{,}904$ samples and $d = 24{,}368$ features. These datasets, commonly found in publicly available biological databases, are known to exhibit heavy-tailed distributions.

Parameter Choices. Unless otherwise specified, the default parameter settings for the DP-IHT-H algorithm are as follows: $s^* = 5$, $\epsilon = 0.5$, $\zeta = 1$, $\delta = 1/n^{1.1}$, and the Huber loss parameter $\tau = 1$. For DP-IHT-L, the same parameters are applied. The truncation parameter K is set to $\log d$. Across all algorithms, we use a constant step size of $\eta = 0.01$.

Evaluation Metrics. We evaluate algorithm performance using the ℓ_2-estimation error, defined as $\|\hat{\beta} - \beta^*\|_2$. As there is no underlying parameter β^* for real-world data, we will use the adaHuber algorithm in [41], which achieves the optimal rate, to approximate β^*. Each experiment is repeated 20 times, and we report the average results to ensure statistical reliability.

Baselines. We focus on the DP-IHT-H and DP-IHT-L algorithms. As we mentioned above, there is no previous research on the DP sparse model with heavy-tailed response that only has the $1+\zeta$-th moment with $\zeta \in (0, 1)$. For comparison, we include:

- **DP-SLR**: Differentially private sparse linear regression under regular (light-tailed) data [10]. DP-SLR could achieve the almost optimal rate in this setting.
- **adaHuber**: Non-DP linear regression in high-dimensional sparse heavy-tailed settings using the adaptive Huber loss method [41]. adaHuber achieves the optimal rate in the non-private setting.

6.2 Results on Synthetic Data

We first investigate whether DP-IHT-H achieves better performance under heavy tails (i.e., small ζ), whether it outperforms differentially private algorithms designed for regular data distributions, and the performance gap between DP-IHT-H and the non-private optimal algorithm.

Figure 1a shows that when the response variable is heavy-tailed, DP-IHT-H achieves significantly lower errors than DP-SLR, possibly because of the square loss used in DP-SLR is less robust to outliers. Moreover, Fig. 1b illustrates that as the dimensionality d increases, the estimation error grows more gradually for DP-IHT-H than for the other two methods. In addition, the figure clearly indicates that DP-IHT-H outperforms the DP-SLR algorithm across various values of d. Figures 1c and 1d further confirm that in heavy-tailed scenarios, DP-IHT-H consistently outperforms the DP-SLR algorithm. Across varying sparsity s^* and

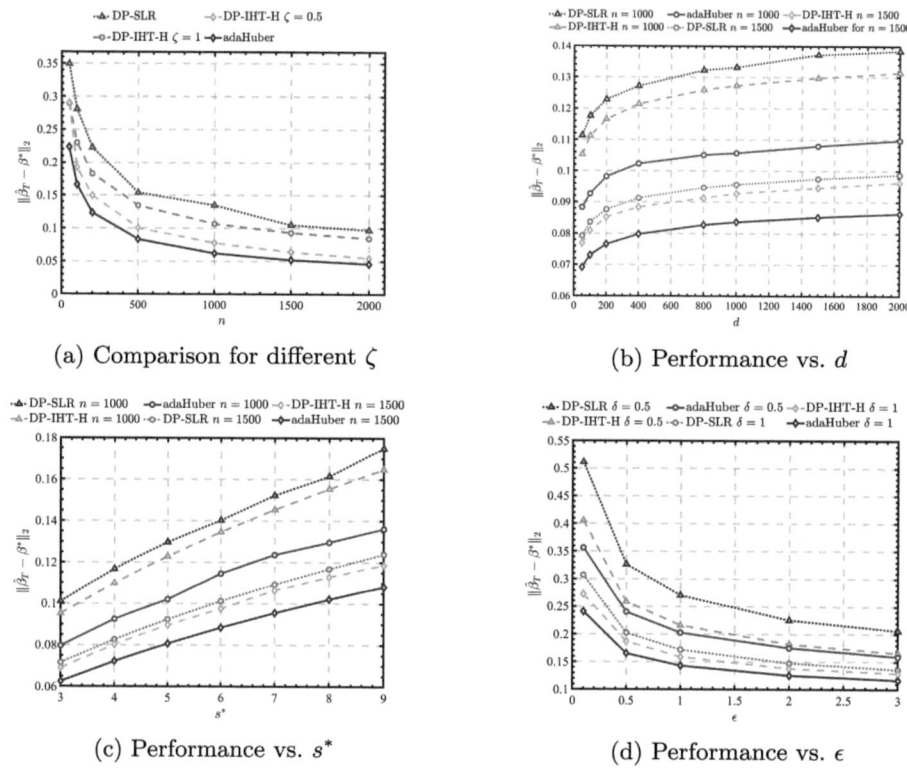

Fig. 1. Comparison of DP-IHT-H, DP-SLR, and adaHuber methods.

privacy budgets ϵ, DP-IHT-H maintains robust performance, demonstrating its advantage in handling heavy-tailed data while preserving differential privacy.

We next evaluate the DP-IHT-L algorithm in comparison with DP-IHT-H, focusing on whether DP-IHT-L provides a similar error guarantee for different values of ζ, and whether it outperforms DP-IHT-H for larger ζ. From Figs. 2a and 2b, we observe that DP-IHT-L generally outperforms DP-IHT-H, particularly when ζ is smaller. Figure 2b also indicates that when $\zeta = 1$, the difference between the two methods is minimal. As ζ decreases, the performance of DP-IHT-L remains relatively stable. Figure 2c shows that DP-IHT-H can perform better with respect to s^*, consistent with its dependence of $O(s^{*3/4})$ (in contrast to $O(s^{*3/2})$ for DP-IHT-L). Finally, Fig. 2d demonstrates that for $\zeta = 1$, both algorithms has less estimation error as ϵ decrease.

Overall, these results indicate that DP-IHT-H and DP-IHT-L are particularly well suited for highly heavy-tailed data, while DP-IHT-L may be preferred in more moderate scenarios due to its stability.

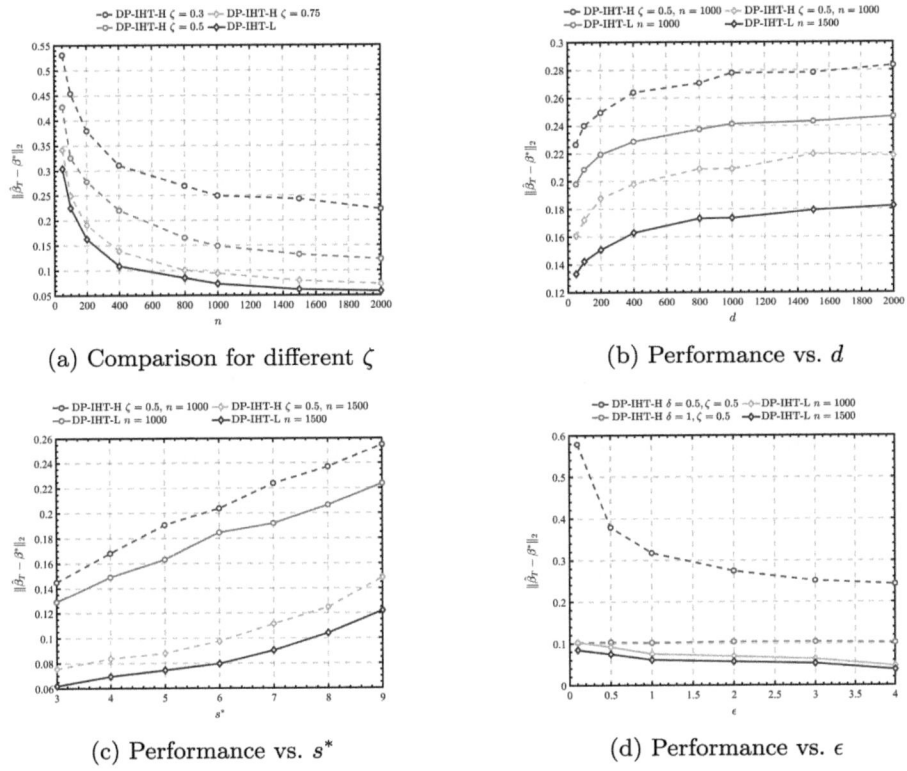

Fig. 2. Comparison of DP-IHT-L and DP-IHT-H across various metrics.

6.3 Real Data Analysis

We evaluate four methods—adaHuber, DP-SLR, DP-IHT-H, and DP-IHT-L—on two genomic datasets to assess their performance in privacy-preserving robust estimation.

NCI-60 Dataset. Following the protocols in [36,41], we analyze a dataset of protein expression (from 162 antibodies) and RNA transcript levels across 60 cancer cell lines to identify genes affecting *KRT19* expression [33]. After preprocessing, the dataset comprises $n = 59$ samples and $d = 14\,342$ features. For the DP methods, we set $s^* = 5$, $\varepsilon = 0.5$, and $\delta = 1/n^{1.1}$. Table 1 summarizes the results.

The non-private adaHuber achieves the lowest MAE, while the DP-IHT variants perform competitively and surpass DP-SLR, highlighting the benefits of robust estimation in heavy-tailed data.

METABRIC Dataset. We further assess the methods on the METABRIC breast cancer dataset [13,35], which contains $n = 1\,904$ samples and $d = 24\,368$ features. Here, the parameters are set as $s^* = 5$, $\varepsilon = 1.0$, and $\delta = 1/n^{1.1}$. Table 2 reports the results.

Table 1. Results on the NCI-60 dataset.

Method	MAE	Size	Selected Genes
adaHuber	2.07	5	MALL, TM4SF4, ANXA3, ADRB2, NRN1
DP-SLR	2.72	5	MALL, TGFBI, S100A6, LPXN, DSP
DP-IHT-H	2.40	5	MALL, ANXA3, NRN1, CA2, EPS8L2
DP-IHT-L	2.34	5	MALL, NRN1, DSP, AUTS2, EPS8L2

Table 2. Results on the METABRIC dataset.

Method	MAE	Size	Selected Genes
adaHuber	0.92	5	PIK3CA, MUC16, SYNE1, KMT2C, GATA3
DP-SLR	1.22	5	MUC16, CDH1, MAP3K1, NCOR2, CBFB
DP-IHT-H	1.08	5	PIK3CA, MUC16, AHNAK2, MAP3K1, GATA3
DP-IHT-L	1.05	5	PIK3CA, SYNE1, NOTCH1, TG, KMT2C

As in the NCI-60 dataset, adaHuber attains the best MAE, and the DP-IHT methods perform comparably while outperforming DP-SLR, even in this lighter-tailed setting.

7 Conclusion

This work presented novel approaches for differentially private linear regression that address the challenges posed by heavy-tailed data distributions. We introduced two algorithms: DP-IHT-H and DP-IHT-L, each designed to handle different tail behaviors. DP-IHT-H demonstrates strong performance for moderately heavy-tailed data, achieving an optimized error bound under (ϵ, δ)-differential privacy. However, its performance degrades for heavier tails, prompting the development of DP-IHT-L, which achieves stable error bounds irrespective of the tail behavior. Extensive experiments on synthetic and real-world datasets verified the effectiveness of our methods, showing their robustness and applicability in diverse scenarios.

Acknowledgements. This work is supported in part by the funding BAS/1/1689-01-01, URF/1/4663-01-01, REI/1/5232-01-01, REI/1/5332-01-01, and URF/1/5508-01-01 from KAUST, and funding from KAUST - Center of Excellence for Generative AI, under award number 5940.

References

1. Abadi, M., et al.: Deep learning with differential privacy. In: Proceedings of the 2016 ACM SIGSAC Conference on Computer and Communications Security, pp. 308–318. ACM (2016)
2. Alquier, P., Cottet, V., Lecué, G.: Estimation bounds and sharp oracle inequalities of regularized procedures with lipschitz loss functions. Ann. Stat. **47**(4), 2117–2144 (2019)

3. Barber, R.F., Duchi, J.C.: Privacy and statistical risk: formalisms and minimax bounds (2014)
4. Bassily, R., Feldman, V., Guzmán, C., Talwar, K.: Stability of stochastic gradient descent on nonsmooth convex losses. Adv. Neural Inf. Process. Syst. **33** (2020)
5. Bassily, R., Feldman, V., Talwar, K., Thakurta, A.: Private stochastic convex optimization with optimal rates. In: Advances in Neural Information Processing Systems (2019)
6. Biswas, A., Datta, S., Fine, J.P., Segal, M.R.: Statistical advances in the biomedical science (2007)
7. Brownlees, C., Joly, E., Lugosi, G.: Empirical risk minimization for heavy-tailed losses. Ann. Stat. **43**(6), 2507–2536 (2015)
8. Bun, M., Steinke, T.: Average-case averages: private algorithms for smooth sensitivity and mean estimation (2019)
9. Cai, T.T., Wang, Y., Zhang, L.: The cost of privacy in generalized linear models: algorithms and minimax lower bounds (2020)
10. Cai, T.T., Wang, Y., Zhang, L.: The cost of privacy: optimal rates of convergence for parameter estimation with differential privacy. Ann. Stat. **49**(5), 2825–2850 (2021)
11. Chaudhuri, K., Monteleoni, C.: Privacy-preserving logistic regression. In: Advances in Neural Information Processing Systems, pp. 289–296 (2009)
12. Chaudhuri, K., Monteleoni, C., Sarwate, A.D.: Differentially private empirical risk minimization. J. Mach. Learn. Res. **12**, 1069–1109 (2011)
13. Curtis, C., et al.: The genomic and transcriptomic architecture of 2,000 breast tumours reveals novel subgroups. Nature **486**(7403), 346–352 (2012)
14. Ding, B., Kulkarni, J., Yekhanin, S.: Collecting telemetry data privately. In: Advances in Neural Information Processing Systems, pp. 3571–3580 (2017)
15. Ding, M., Lei, M., Wang, S., Zheng, T., Wang, D., Xu, J.: Nearly optimal differentially private relu regression. arXiv preprint arXiv:2503.06009 (2025)
16. Ding, M., Lei, M., Zhu, L., Wang, S., Wang, D., Xu, J.: Revisiting differentially private relu regression. Adv. Neural Inf. Process. Syst. **37**, 55470–55506 (2024)
17. Duchi, J.C., Jordan, M.I., Wainwright, M.J.: Minimax optimal procedures for locally private estimation. J. Am. Stat. Assoc. **113**(521), 182–201 (2018)
18. Dwork, C., McSherry, F., Nissim, K., Smith, A.: Calibrating noise to sensitivity in private data analysis, pp. 265–284 (2006)
19. Feldman, V., Koren, T., Talwar, K.: Private stochastic convex optimization: optimal rates in linear time. In: Proceedings of the 52nd Annual ACM SIGACT Symposium on Theory of Computing, pp. 439–449 (2020)
20. Holland, M., Ikeda, K.: Better generalization with less data using robust gradient descent. In: International Conference on Machine Learning, pp. 2761–2770 (2019)
21. Hu, L., Ni, S., Xiao, H., Wang, D.: High dimensional differentially private stochastic optimization with heavy-tailed data. In: Proceedings of the 41st ACM SIGMOD-SIGACT-SIGAI Symposium on Principles of Database Systems (PODS '22), pp. 227–236. Association for Computing Machinery, New York, NY, USA (2022)
22. Huai, M., Wang, D., Miao, C., Xu, J., Zhang, A.: Pairwise learning with differential privacy guarantees. In: Proceedings of the AAAI Conference on Artificial Intelligence, vol. 34, pp. 694–701 (2020)
23. Huber, P.J.: Robust estimation of a location parameter. Ann. Math. Stat. **35**(1), 73–101 (1964)
24. Ibragimov, M., Ibragimov, R., Walden, J.: Heavy-Tailed Distributions and Robustness in Economics and Finance, vol. 214. Springer, Cham (2015). https://doi.org/10.1007/978-3-319-16877-7

25. Iyengar, R., Near, J.P., Song, D., Thakkar, O., Thakurta, A., Wang, L.: Towards practical differentially private convex optimization. In: 2019 IEEE Symposium on Security and Privacy (SP), pp. 299–316. IEEE (2019)
26. Kamath, G., Liu, X., Zhang, H.: Improved rates for differentially private stochastic convex optimization with heavy-tailed data (2021)
27. Kamath, G., Singhal, V., Ullman, J.: Private mean estimation of heavy-tailed distributions. In: Conference on Learning Theory, pp. 2204–2235. PMLR (2020)
28. Kasiviswanathan, S.P., Jin, H.: Efficient private empirical risk minimization for high-dimensional learning. In: International Conference on Machine Learning, pp. 488–497 (2016)
29. Kifer, D., Smith, A., Thakurta, A.: Private convex empirical risk minimization and high-dimensional regression. In: Conference on Learning Theory, pp. 25–1 (2012)
30. Lecue, G., Lerasle, M., Mathieu, T.: Robust classification via mom minimization (2018)
31. Liu, X., Kong, W., Kakade, S., Oh, S.: Robust and differentially private mean estimation (2021)
32. Lugosi, G., Mendelson, S.: Risk minimization by median-of-means tournaments. J. Eur. Math. Soc. (2019)
33. Nakata, B., Takashima, T., Ogawa, Y., Ishikawa, T., Hirakawa, K.: Serum cyfra 21-1 (cytokeratin-19 fragments) is a useful tumour marker for detecting disease relapse and assessing treatment efficacy in breast cancer. Br. J. Cancer **91**(5), 873–878 (2004)
34. Nissim, K., Raskhodnikova, S., Smith, A.: Smooth sensitivity and sampling in private data analysis. In: Proceedings of the Thirty-Ninth Annual ACM Symposium on Theory of Computing, pp. 75–84. ACM (2007)
35. Pereira, B., et al.: The somatic mutation profiles of 2,433 breast cancers refines their genomic and transcriptomic landscapes. Nat. Commun. **7**, 11479 (2016)
36. Reinhold, W., Varma, S., Sousa, F., et al.: Cellminer: a web-based suite of genomic and pharmacologic tools to explore transcript and drug patterns in the nci-60 cell line set. Can. Res. **72**(14), 3499–3511 (2012)
37. Shen, H., Wang, C.L., Xiang, Z., Ying, Y., Wang, D.: Differentially private nonconvex learning for multi-layer neural networks. arXiv preprint arXiv:2310.08425 (2023)
38. Shen, Y., Li, J., Cai, J.F., Xia, D.: Computationally efficient and statistically optimal robust high-dimensional linear regression (2023)
39. Su, J., Hu, L., Wang, D.: Faster rates of private stochastic convex optimization. In: International Conference on Algorithmic Learning Theory, pp. 995–1002. PMLR (2022)
40. Su, J., Hu, L., Wang, D.: Faster rates of differentially private stochastic convex optimization. J. Mach. Learn. Res. **25**(114), 1–41 (2024)
41. Sun, Q., Zhou, W., Fan, J.: Adaptive huber regression. J. Am. Stat. Assoc. **115**(529), 254–265 (2020)
42. Talwar, K., Thakurta, A., Zhang, L.: Nearly-optimal private lasso. In: Proceedings of the 28th International Conference on Neural Information Processing Systems, pp. 3025–3033 (2015)
43. Tang, J., Korolova, A., Bai, X., Wang, X., Wang, X.: Privacy loss in apple's implementation of differential privacy on macos 10.12. CoRR (2017)
44. Tao, Y., Wu, Y., Cheng, X., Wang, D.: Private stochastic convex optimization and sparse learning with heavy-tailed data revisited. In: 31st International Joint Conference on Artificial Intelligence, IJCAI 2022, pp. 3947–3953. International Joint Conferences on Artificial Intelligence Organization (2022)

45. Tong, H.: Functional linear regression with huber loss. J. Complex. **74**, 101696 (2023)
46. Wang, D., Chen, C., Xu, J.: Differentially private empirical risk minimization with non-convex loss functions. In: International Conference on Machine Learning, pp. 6526–6535. PMLR (2019)
47. Wang, D., Gaboardi, M., Smith, A., Xu, J.: Empirical risk minimization in the non-interactive local model of differential privacy. J. Mach. Learn. Res. **21**(200), 1–39 (2020)
48. Wang, D., Xiao, H., Devadas, S., Xu, J.: On differentially private stochastic convex optimization with heavy-tailed data. In: International Conference on Machine Learning, pp. 10081–10091. PMLR (2020)
49. Wang, D., Xu, J.: Differentially private empirical risk minimization with smooth non-convex loss functions: a non-stationary view. In: Proceedings of the AAAI Conference on Artificial Intelligence, vol. 33, pp. 1182–1189 (2019)
50. Wang, D., Xu, J.: On sparse linear regression in the local differential privacy model. In: International Conference on Machine Learning, pp. 6628–6637. PMLR (2019)
51. Wang, D., Xu, J.: Escaping saddle points of empirical risk privately and scalably via DP-trust region method. In: Hutter, F., Kersting, K., Lijffijt, J., Valera, I. (eds.) ECML PKDD 2020. LNCS (LNAI), vol. 12459, pp. 90–106. Springer, Cham (2021). https://doi.org/10.1007/978-3-030-67664-3_6
52. Wang, D., Xu, J.: On sparse linear regression in the local differential privacy model. IEEE Trans. Inf. Theory **67**(2), 1182–1200 (2020)
53. Wang, D., Xu, J.: Differentially private ℓ_1-norm linear regression with heavy-tailed data. In: 2022 IEEE International Symposium on Information Theory (ISIT), pp. 1856–1861. IEEE (2022)
54. Wang, D., Xu, J.: Private least absolute deviations with heavy-tailed data. Theor. Comput. Sci. **1030**, 115071 (2025)
55. Wang, D., Ye, M., Xu, J.: Differentially private empirical risk minimization revisited: Faster and more general. Adv. Neural Inf. Process. Syst. **30** (2017)
56. Wang, L., Gu, Q.: A knowledge transfer framework for differentially private sparse learning. In: Proceedings of the AAAI Conference on Artificial Intelligence, pp. 6235–6242 (2020)
57. Woolson, R.F., Clarke, W.R.: Statistical Methods for the Analysis of Biomedical Data, vol. 371. John Wiley & Sons, Hoboken (2011)
58. Xue, Z., Yang, S., Huai, M., Wang, D.: Differentially private pairwise learning revisited. In: 30th International Joint Conference on Artificial Intelligence, IJCAI 2021, pp. 3242–3248. International Joint Conferences on Artificial Intelligence Organization (2021)
59. Zhang, R., Lei, M., Ding, M., Xiang, Z., Xu, J., Wang, D.: Improved rates of differentially private nonconvex-strongly-concave minimax optimization. In: Proceedings of the AAAI Conference on Artificial Intelligence, vol. 39, pp. 22524–22532 (2025)
60. Zhu, L., Ding, M., Aggarwal, V., Xu, J., Wang, D.: Improved analysis of sparse linear regression in local differential privacy model. arXiv preprint arXiv:2310.07367 (2023)
61. Zhu, L., Manseur, A., Ding, M., Liu, J., Xu, J., Wang, D.: Truthful high dimensional sparse linear regression. arXiv preprint arXiv:2410.13046 (2024)

Leveraging Homophily Under Local Differential Privacy for Effective Graph Neural Networks

Yule Xie[1], Jiaxin Ding[1(✉)], Pengyu Xue[2], Xin Ding[1], Haochen Han[1], Luoyi Fu[1], and Xinbin Wang[1]

[1] Shanghai Jiao Tong University, Shanghai, China
jiaxinding@sjtu.edu.cn
[2] East China Normal University, Shanghai, China

Abstract. Graph Neural Networks (GNNs) have become indispensable tools for analyzing graph-structured data, with applications across numerous domains. However, collecting graph data that is locally stored by users in privacy-sensitive scenarios remains challenging. Existing methods applying Local Differential Privacy (LDP) fail to account for homophily—the tendency of connected nodes to share similar attributes, which consequently leads to suboptimal performance under limited privacy budgets. To address this challenge, we propose HPGR (Homophily Preserving Graph Reconstruction), a novel approach for collecting and modeling graph topology under LDP, while preserving homophily. Our method employs a homophily-aware querying and modeling mechanism that integrates homophily priors into the data collection process, and enables robust reconstruction of the underlying graph structure despite the injected noise. We provide theoretical analyses demonstrating that our method satisfies LDP requirements while effectively preserving homophily. Extensive experiments on benchmark datasets show that our approach significantly outperforms existing methods, achieving a superior balance between privacy protection and model utility.

Keywords: Graph neural network · Differential Privacy

1 Introduction

Graph neural networks (GNNs) have emerged as indispensable tools across numerous domains, ranging from social networks to healthcare, fraud detection, and recommendation systems. Central to their success is the exploitation of *homophily* [23,26]—the natural tendency for nodes with similar attributes to form connections—which underpins the effective propagation of information and the superior performance of GNNs. However, the collection of relational data

---

Supplementary Information The online version contains supplementary material available at https://doi.org/10.1007/978-3-032-06096-9_22.

© The Author(s), under exclusive license to Springer Nature Switzerland AG 2026
R. P. Ribeiro et al. (Eds.): ECML PKDD 2025, LNAI 16017, pp. 380–396, 2026.
https://doi.org/10.1007/978-3-032-06096-9_22

required for these models increasingly conflicts with growing privacy regulations and decentralized data ownership paradigms.

Consider, for example, a decentralized social networking app like Briar [2], where user connection records are stored locally on individual devices to enable peer-to-peer(P2P) interactions, such as sending messages, sharing files, or tracking contacts, without relying on a central server. While this decentralized approach inherently enhances user privacy, it obstructs centralized relational data aggregation for training GNN models on graphs to further enhance downstream tasks, such as user preference classification. Moreover, stringent privacy regulations, such as the GDPR [21], restrict the collection of user connection data without explicit consent, further complicating data usage for GNN training.

Local differential privacy (LDP) [5] emerges as a compelling solution, by ensuring that individual data is obfuscated [6] before it is shared or queried. In the previous scenario, LDP can be applied to perturb connection data with noise before it leaves the user's device, ensuring privacy while enabling data collection. However, most existing LDP mechanisms were designed for tabular or scalar data and fail to address the intricacies of graph-structured data [8]. Injecting noise via LDP mechanisms, such as the randomized response mechanism, into graphs can disrupt the intricate connectivity patterns by either falsely reporting a connection or masking an actual one, and more critically, undermine the homophily property. Despite several studies [8,13,27] on privacy-preserving GNNs, explicit preservation of homophily under LDP constraints remains underexplored. Existing approaches have primarily focused on maintaining graph sparsity, neglecting the key factors necessary to preserve the performance of GNNs.

In this paper, we propose HPGR (**H**omophily **P**reserving **G**raph **R**econstruction), a novel framework that reconciles the stringent privacy requirements of LDP with the structural imperatives of GNNs. Our key insight is to leverage server-side cluster labels (e.g., coarse user categories inferred from public profiles) to guide the privatization process, preserving inter-cluster connectivity patterns critical for homophily. HPGR operates in two phases. First, users perturb their cluster-specified degree vectors—counts of connections to predefined server-labeled clusters—using an LDP mechanism that minimizes noise while retaining community structure. Second, we adopt the Degree-Corrected Stochastic Block Model [9], along with a mixed membership extension, to reconstruct the graph from these privatized queries. We provide theoretical privacy-utility tradeoff guarantees and empirically validate HPGR on benchmark datasets. Extensive experiments demonstrate the superiority of our method. GNNs trained on HPGR-reconstructed graphs retain 88% of their non-private accuracy on average under strict privacy budgets ($1 \leq \epsilon \leq 4$), achieving approximately a 5.8% improvement over SOTA. Our contribution can be summarized as follows[1]:

– We introduce a querying mechanism that gathers each user's cluster-specific degree vectors instead of raw edge data. This approach embeds homophily priors into the data collection process while strictly adhering to local differential privacy constraints.

---

[1] Experiment code can be found at: https://github.com/xyl-alter/HPGR.git.

- We propose a novel homophily-preserving graph reconstruction method and incorporate homophily priors to refine the reconstructed topology. This not only boosts GNN performance but also bridges the gap between degree-vector queries and graph homophily metrics.
- We provide theoretical error analyses from four perspectives: privacy, sparsity, homophily, and accuracy. The experimental results further demonstrate significant improvements over existing approaches.

2 Preliminary

2.1 Problem Statement

This work focuses on protecting the local neighborhood information of nodes in a semi-supervised node classification task on undirected, unweighted graphs. GNN training needs three inputs: node features X, labels Y, and neighborhood relations encoded in the adjacency matrix A. In our decentralized setting, the server can access X and Y (e.g. from the public user profiles), but the graph topology A remains distributed-each node i locally stores its local neighborhood $A_i \in \{0,1\}^n$. The server is considered honest-but-curious (i.e., adheres to protocols but may infer sensitive information), aims to collect A to conduct GNN training. This raises a privacy challenge: transmitting raw neighborhood data risks exposing sensitive connections. We adopt ϵ-edge local differential privacy (LDP) [27] to protect edge privacy, which ensures that even when one node's local graph structure is altered, the privacy-preserving algorithm remains robust against inference of the actual graph topology.

Definition 1 *(ϵ-Edge Local Differential Privacy [27]). For $\epsilon > 0$, a randomized algorithm $\mathcal{A} : \{0,1\}^n \to \mathcal{O}$ satisfies ϵ-edge local differential privacy if for any two adjacent neighborhood vectors $A_i', A_i \in \{0,1\}^n$ of node i which differ only in one entry, i.e., $|A_i - A_i'|_1 = 1$, and for any possible output $O \in \mathcal{O}$, we have*

$$Pr(\mathcal{A}(A_i) = O) \leq e^\epsilon \cdot Pr(\mathcal{A}(A_i') = O). \tag{1}$$

The ϵ-edge LDP guarantees that modifying a single edge in a node's local neighborhood does not significantly alter the output of the privacy-preserving algorithm, thereby preventing the server from reliably inferring the existence or absence of any specific edge. The privacy budget ϵ indicates the level of privacy protection: the smaller the budget is, the stricter the privacy protection, and the greater the disturbance. Key notations in this paper are shown in Table 1.

2.2 Homophily in Graphs

Homophily—the tendency of nodes with similar characteristics to form connections—is critical for GNN performance. We adopt a variant of the class-label homophily proposed in [12] as our homophily metric:

$$h = \frac{1}{c}\sum_{k=1}^{c} h_k, \quad h_k = \frac{\sum_{u \in C_k} d_u^{k_u}}{\sum_{u \in C_k} d_u} = \frac{M_{k,k}}{\sum_{j=1}^{c} M_{k,j}}, \tag{2}$$

Table 1. Basic Notations

Symbol	Description	Symbol	Description
X	feature matrix of nodes	d_i	cluster-specified degree vector of node i
Y	labels of nodes	$\mathbf{d}$	list of node degrees
A	graph adjacency matrix	Π	prior link probability matrix
n	the number of nodes	$\mathcal{P}$	posterior link probability matrix
c	the number of classes/clusters	C	node classification matrix
ϵ	the privacy budget	M	cluster connection matrix

where k_u is the cluster node u belongs to, $d_u^{k_u}$ is the number of edges between node u and nodes in k_u, and M is the cluster connection matrix indicating the number of edges within and between clusters.

Graph homophily is crucial for GNN performance. Figure 1 shows the impact of homophily on the node classification performance of GNN models, demonstrating a sharp decline in GNN performance as homophily decreases. This emphasizes the need to preserve homophily when querying private graphs to achieve optimal GNN results. However, conventional differential privacy mechanisms, such as the Laplace mechanism and randomized responses, fail to maintain homophily, highlighting the importance of allocating additional privacy budget for homophily-preserving queries.

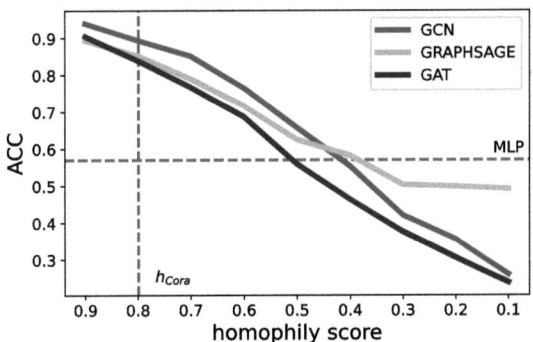

Fig. 1. Performance of three GNN models on SBM-reconstructed Cora dataset. Nodes with the same labels are connected with probability p while nodes with different labels are connected with probability q. The expected homophily score of the SBM (Stochastic Block Model)-generated graph is $h = p/(p + (c-1)q)$.

2.3 Degree-Corrected Stochastic Block Model (DC-SBM)

The Degree-Corrected Stochastic Block Model not only preserves the homophily of the graph but also maintains the degree distribution of nodes. In the DC-SBM model, the probability of an edge between node i and j is given by:

$$P(A_{ij} = 1) = \theta_i \theta_j \Phi_{g_i g_j}, \tag{3}$$

where θ_i, θ_j are degree correction parameters correlated to the degree of node i and node j, and $\Phi_{g_i g_j}$ is the probability that nodes in category g_i and g_j are connected, where g_i and g_j are the categories node i and node j belong to. $\Phi_{g_i g_j}$ is computed with

$$\Phi_{g_i g_j} = \frac{M_{g_i g_j}}{r_{g_i} r_{g_j}}, \tag{4}$$

where $M_{g_i g_j}$ is the number of edges between nodes in g_i and nodes in g_j, and r_{g_i} and r_{g_j} are the number of nodes in g_i and g_j.

3 Methods

We propose **H**omophily-**P**reserving **G**raph **R**econstruction(HPGR) algorithm for effective graph neural networks under local differential privacy. The server makes homophily-aware queries to the nodes (clients) to reconstruct the graph for GNN training. During the query stage, the server first group local nodes into clusters. It queries both the neighborhood and the cluster-specified degree vector—number of edges connecting to each cluster, of each node. Local nodes respond by applying randomized response (RR) and Laplace (Lap) mechanism to perturb the adjacency lists the degree vectors. Thereafter, the server constructs a DC-SBM random graph based on the collected noisy degree vector and employs Bayesian estimation to refine the collected topology. The edge probabilities in the random graph serve as priors, while the noisy adjacency matrix acts as evidence, allowing the server to compute posterior probabilities for each potential link and reconstruct the graph for GNN training.

3.1 Homophily-Aware Topology Collection Under LDP

The server first clusters nodes into c clusters based on their labels, and then queries each node for its adjacency vector A_i and cluster-specified degree vector d_i. By collecting degree vectors, the server gathers information on node connectivity across clusters, reflecting graph homophily. In the cases where part of node labels are unavailable, the server uses pseudo labels for the unlabeled nodes. Pseudo labels are generated by an MLP, $C = \text{MLP}(X, Y) \in R^{N \times c}$. To ensure privacy protection during the querying process, the server divides the total privacy budget ϵ into two components with proportion δ: $\epsilon_a = \epsilon \cdot \delta$ and $\epsilon_d = \epsilon \cdot (1 - \delta)$, which are allocated for querying adjacency and degree vectors respectively. By controlling the distribution of the privacy budget, the server can balance the need for better graph statistics (i.e., homophily) or more precise adjacency details.

The neighborhood query is straightforward, while for degree vector queries, the server should first send labels to each node. However, if the client is untrusted or potentially curious, revealing clustering information can lead to privacy leakage of node labels. In such cases, techniques such as homomorphic encryption and Secure Multi-Party Computation(SMPC) can be applied to avoid revealing the clustering information or the clients' local data.

Upon receiving a query, the local node calculates its degree vector by definition and uses random response (flipping one bit with probability $p = \frac{1}{1+exp(\epsilon_a)}$) [22] and Laplace mechanisms (adding Laplace noise with scale $\frac{1}{\epsilon_d}$) [6] to perturb the adjacency and degree vectors respectively to ensure LDP compliance. To better utilize the classification information provided by MLP, a soft query-response mechanism is also employed, where the server queries with a classification matrix $C \in \mathbf{R}^{n \times c}$ and the local node computes its degree vector with $A_i \cdot C$. Experiments show that the soft query mechanism often achieves better performance by acknowledging the uncertainty in pseudo labels, while at the cost of a higher communication overhead. The practical algorithm for the soft response on the client side is shown in Algorithm 1, with the hard response as a special case where C is one-hot.

Algorithm 1. client-side response under LDP

Input: A_i: Adjacency list, C: Cluster matrix, ϵ: Privacy budget, δ: Privacy parameter
Output: $\tilde{A}_i \in \{0,1\}^n$: private adjacency vector, $\tilde{d}_i \in \mathbf{R}^c$: private degree vector
1: **function** INJECTION(A_i, C, ϵ, δ)
2: $\quad \epsilon_d = \delta \epsilon$ ▷ privacy budget for degree vector query
3: $\quad \epsilon_a = (1-\delta)\epsilon$ ▷ privacy budget for adjacency vector query
4: $\quad$ **for** $j \in \{1, 2, \cdots, n\}$ **do**
5: $\quad\quad \tilde{A}_{ij} = \begin{cases} A_{ij}, & \text{with probability } \frac{exp(\epsilon_a)}{1+exp(\epsilon_a)} \\ 1 - A_{ij}, & \text{with probability } \frac{1}{1+exp(\epsilon_a)} \end{cases}$ ▷ apply RR mechanism
6: $\quad$ **end for**
7: $\quad \hat{d}_i = A_i \cdot C$ ▷ calculating degree vector
8: $\quad$ **for** $j \in \{1, 2, \cdots, c\}$ **do**
9: $\quad\quad$ sample $l_j \sim \text{Laplace}(0, \frac{1}{\epsilon_d})$
10: $\quad\quad \tilde{d}_i[j] = \hat{d}_i[j] + l_j$ ▷ apply Laplace mechanism
11: $\quad$ **end for**
12: $\quad$ **return** $(\tilde{A}_i, \tilde{d}_i)$
13: **end function**

Theorem 1. *The client-side response algorithm above achieves ϵ-edge LDP.*

The proof of this theorem is straightforward, since the RR and Laplace mechanisms satisfy ϵ_a and ϵ_d-LDP respectively. According to the composition theorem, the total privacy budget is $\epsilon_a + \epsilon_d = \epsilon$.

3.2 Graph Reconstruction

After receiving replies from local nodes, the server obtains noisy adjacency vectors $\tilde{A}_1, \tilde{A}_2, \cdots, \tilde{A}_n$ and degree vectors $\tilde{d}_1, \tilde{d}_2, \cdots, \tilde{d}_n$. The server then computes a prior distribution of edges with degree vectors and regards the adjacency vectors as evidence to estimate posterior probabilities through Bayesian estimation.

Prior Distribution Estimation Given Degree Vectors. Although DC-SBM is well suited for hard queries, applying it to soft queries (i.e., the mixed membership scenario [14]) is challenging, particularly in degree corrections for mixed membership. Here we introduce our Mixed Membership **DC-SBM** (MM-DCSBM) model, where the traditional DC-SBM is a special case when C is a one-hot matrix. Our MM-DCSBM algorithm requires three inputs: cluster connection matrix M (representing the number of edges between clusters), degree list **d** (reflecting the degree of each node), and the cluster matrix C obtained in Sect. 3.1.

Cluster Connection Matrix. The server computes $\tilde{M} = C^T \cdot \tilde{D}$, where $\tilde{D} = [\tilde{d}_1, \tilde{d}_2, \ldots, \tilde{d}_n]^T$ is the matrix of noisy degree vectors, and $\tilde{M}$ is the noisy cluster connection matrix. Due to Laplace noise injection, $\tilde{M}$ may not be symmetric, but the server can correct it with the following maximum likelihood estimation.

Theorem 2. *The maximum likelihood estimation of $\tilde{M}_{i,j}$ is*

$$\tilde{M}_{i,j,MLE} = \frac{n_j}{n_i + n_j}\tilde{M}_{i,j} + \frac{n_i}{n_i + n_j}\tilde{M}_{j,i} \sim N(M_{i,j}, \frac{4n_i n_j}{(n_i + n_j)\epsilon_d^2}), \quad (5)$$

where $n_i = \sum_{k \in [1,n]} C_{k,i}, n_j = \sum_{k \in [1,n]} C_{k,j}$ are the number of nodes in cluster i and cluster j, $M_{i,j}$ is the cluster connection matrix without noise injection.

Degree List. Instead of allocating extra privacy budget for querying node degrees, we sum the queried degree vectors to obtain unbiased estimates.

We represent our MM-DCSBM in Algorithm 2. The key difference between our algorithm and the traditional DC-SBM lies in degree regularization, where mixed membership precludes calculating the regularization factor R for each node independently. This results in Φ being computed via element-wise division in the DC-SBM algorithm, while through multiplication by the inverse matrix in our algorithm. To validate our algorithm, we present Proposition 1. A more detailed analysis of its properties is provided in Sect. 4.

Proposition 1. *When C is a one-hot matrix, meaning each node explicitly belongs to a cluster, the MM-DCSBM algorithm in Algorithm 2 reduces to the traditional DC-SBM algorithm introduced in Subsect. 2.3.*

Posterior Distribution Estimation Given Noisy Adjacency Vector. Inferring the posterior probability of each edge's existence with Bayesian estimation has been demonstrated to be both effective and efficient [27]. In line with previous works, we treat the edge existence probability in the reconstructed MM-DCSBM random graph as the prior probability and the adjacency vectors

Algorithm 2. MM-DCSBM modeling algorithm

Input: M: cluster connection matrix, $\mathbf{d}$: node degree list, C: Node classification matrix
Output: Π: the prior link probability matrix
1: **function** MM-DCSBM($M, \mathbf{d}, C$)
2:     $R = C^T \cdot \text{diag}(\mathbf{d}) \cdot C$ ▷ Computer the regularization factor
3:     $\hat{M} = R^{-1} \cdot M \cdot R^{-1}$ ▷ normalize the cluster connection matrix
4:     $\Phi = C \cdot \hat{M} \cdot C^T$ ▷ compute the probability of links with SBM matrix
5:     $\Theta = \mathbf{d}^T \cdot \mathbf{d}$
6:     $\Pi = \Phi \odot \Theta$ ▷ correct SBM matrix with node degrees
7:     **return** Π
8: **end function**

obtained through the random response mechanism as the evidence. Formally, the posterior edge existence probability between node i and j can be calculated with

$$\mathcal{P}_{ij} = P[(A_{ij}, A_{ji}) = (1,1) | (\tilde{A}_{ij}, \tilde{A}_{ji})] = \frac{q_{ij} \Pi_{ij}}{q_{ij} \Pi_{ij} + q'_{ij}(1 - \Pi_{ij})}, \quad (6)$$

where Π_{ij} is the prior distribution, q_{ij} and q'_{ij} are the joint distribution of $(\tilde{A}_{ij}, \tilde{A}_{ji})$. More specifically, we have

$$q_{ij} = \begin{cases} p^2, & (\tilde{A}_{ij}, \tilde{A}_{ji}) = (0,0) \\ p(1-p), & (\tilde{A}_{ij}, \tilde{A}_{ji}) = (1,0) \\ p(1-p), & (\tilde{A}_{ij}, \tilde{A}_{ji}) = (0,1) \\ (1-p)^2, & (\tilde{A}_{ij}, \tilde{A}_{ji}) = (1,1) \end{cases}, \quad q'_{ij} = \begin{cases} (1-p)^2, & (\tilde{A}_{ij}, \tilde{A}_{ji}) = (0,0) \\ p(1-p), & (\tilde{A}_{ij}, \tilde{A}_{ji}) = (1,0) \\ p(1-p), & (\tilde{A}_{ij}, \tilde{A}_{ji}) = (0,1) \\ p^2, & (\tilde{A}_{ij}, \tilde{A}_{ji}) = (1,1) \end{cases},$$

where $p = \frac{1}{1+e^{\epsilon_a}}$ is the probability of bit flipping in the random response mechanism.

4 Utility Analysis

In this section, we analyze the utility of our method from three aspects: sparsity, homophily, and precision. Before delving into the detailed analysis, we first introduce three key properties of our proposed MM-DCSBM algorithm, presented as Theorem 3.

Theorem 3. *Let Π be the prior distribution computed with the MM-DCSBM model proposed in Algorithm 2 given the cluster connection matrix $\tilde{M}$, degrees of nodes $\tilde{\mathbf{d}}$, and classification matrix C_{ps}, i.e. $\Pi = MM\text{-}DCSBM(\tilde{M}, \tilde{\mathbf{d}}, C_{ps})$, then*

$$C_{ps}^T \cdot \Pi \cdot C_{ps} = \tilde{M} \quad (7a), \qquad |\Pi|_1 = |\tilde{M}|_1 \quad (7b),$$

$$\frac{\sum_k \Pi_{ik}}{\sum_k \Pi_{jk}} = \frac{\tilde{\mathbf{d}}_i}{\tilde{\mathbf{d}}_j} \quad \forall i, j \in \{1, 2, \cdots, n\},\ C_{ps,i} = C_{ps,j} \quad (7c). \quad (7)$$

Theorem 3 demonstrates that the MM-DCSBM model preserves homophily, sparsity, and degree distribution of the input graph by ensuring that the reconstructed graph maintains the connection probabilities between clusters (Eq. 7a), the total number of edges (Eq. 7b), and the relative degrees of nodes within the same cluster (Eq. 7c). These properties enable transforming the algorithm's output back into the input during further analysis. Notably, without the MLE process, i.e., $\tilde{M} = C^T[\tilde{d}_1, \cdots, \tilde{d}_n]^T$ holds, Eq. 7c can be enhanced with $\sum_k \Pi_{ik} = \tilde{d}_i$, $\forall i \in \{1, 2, \cdots, n\}$, regardless of the value of C_{ps}.

4.1 Sparsity Analysis

Sparsity is a common property of real-world graphs. However, topologies collected by differential privacy mechanisms, such as the random response mechanism, are often overly dense. For a graph with n nodes and $m \sim \mathcal{O}(n)$ edges, using the RR mechanism with flip probability p gives an expected edge count of $(n^2 - m)p + m(1-p) \sim \mathcal{O}(n^2)$. Overly dense graphs can lead to excessive computational overhead during GNN training, and incorrectly connected edges can severely degrade GNN performance.

We use $E(|\|\Pi|_1 - |A|_1|)$ as sparsity metric. Theorem 4 provides a bound on the sparsity gap between our prior link probability and the real topology.

Theorem 4. *Considering the sparsity distance between the prior distribution matrix Π and the original adjacency matrix A, we have*

$$E[|\|\Pi|_1 - |A|_1|] \leq \frac{2\sqrt{2}}{\epsilon_d}\sqrt{\frac{cn}{\pi}}. \tag{8}$$

Corollary 1. *The l_1-distance between the posterior probability and the original topology is bounded by*

$$E(|\mathcal{P} - A|_1) \leq 2\,|A|_1 + \frac{2\sqrt{2}}{\epsilon_d}\sqrt{\frac{cn}{\pi}}. \tag{9}$$

In real-world graphs, the number of edges is typically of order $\mathcal{O}(n)$, while our method's graph density estimation error is $\mathcal{O}(\sqrt{n})$. Comparing our method with Blink [27] which also emphasizes sparsity, their estimation error is constrained by $E[|\|\Pi|_1 - |A|_1|] \leq \frac{n}{2\epsilon_d}$, which is of a higher order than ours.

4.2 Homophily Analysis

Since the homophily metric in Eq. 2 only relates to the cluster connection matrix, we use $E(|M_{true} - \tilde{M}|_{1,1})$ as our utility metric, where $\tilde{M}$ is the cluster connection matrix collected by the server and M_{true} is the actual one. Under such metric, Theorem 5 provides a guarantee of homophily. As the core Theorem of this work, we provide a brief proof here.

Theorem 5. Assume that M_{true} is the cluster connection matrix given true labels C_{true} and noise-free adjacency matrix A, and $\tilde{M}$ is that given pseudo labels C_{ps} and prior edge distribution matrix Π, denote $\mathbf{d}_i$ as the degree of node i, then we have

$$E(|M_{true} - \tilde{M}|_{1,1}) = E(|C_{true}^T A C_{true} - C_{ps}^T \Pi C_{ps}|_{1,1})$$
$$\leq \frac{2c}{\epsilon_d}\sqrt{\frac{cn}{\pi}} + \sum_{i=0}^{n} 2|C_{true,i} - C_{ps,i}|_1 \mathbf{d}_i. \quad (10)$$

Proof. According to the triangle inequality,

$$E(|M_{true} - \tilde{M}|_{1,1}) = E(|C_{true}^T A C_{true} - C_{ps}^T \Pi C_{ps}|_{1,1})$$
$$\leq E(|C_{true}^T A C_{true} - C_{ps}^T A C_{ps}|_{1,1}) + E(|C_{ps}^T A C_{ps} - C_{ps}^T \Pi C_{ps}|_{1,1}). \quad (11)$$

For the first part, suppose $D = C_{true} - C_{ps}$, then

$$C_{true}^T A C_{true} - C_{ps}^T A C_{ps} = D^T A C_{ps} + C_{ps}^T A D + D^T A D. \quad (12)$$

If C_{true} and C_{ps} differ only in the i-th line, i.e., only the i-th row of D is non-zero:

1. $D^T A D = 0^{c \times c}$, since there's no self-loop and $D^T A D = A_{i,i} D_i^T D_i = 0^{c \times c}$.
2. $|D^T A C|_1 = |C_{ps,i} - C_{true,i}|_1 \mathbf{d}_i$, since $|D^T S|_1 = \sum_l D_{i,l}|S_l|_1 = |D_i|_1 |S_i|_1 = |C_{ps,i} - C_{true,i}|_1 \mathbf{d}_i$, where $S = AC$.

Replace one row in C_{ps} with the corresponding row in C_{true} in sequence, where C_i represents the i-th state. By accumulating $|C_i^T A C_i - C_{i-1}^T A C_{i-1}|_1$, we have

$$|C_{true}^T A C_{true} - C_{ps}^T A C_{ps}|_1 \leq \sum_{i=1}^{n} 2|C_{true,i} - C_{ps,i}|_1 \mathbf{d}_i. \quad (13)$$

For the second part, according to Theorem 2 and Theorem 3, we have $C_{ps}^T A C_{ps} - C_{ps}^T \Pi C_{ps} = M - \tilde{M}_{MLE}$ and $\tilde{M}_{i,j,MLE} = \frac{n_j}{n_i+n_j}\tilde{M}_{i,j} + \frac{n_i}{n_i+n_j}\tilde{M}_{j,i}$, where $\tilde{M}_{i,j}$, $\tilde{M}_{j,i}$ are two random variables drawn from $N(M_{i,j}, 2n_i\frac{1}{\epsilon_d^2})$ and $N(M_{j,i}, 2n_j\frac{1}{\epsilon_d^2})$ respectively. Therefore, we have $\tilde{M}_{i,j,MLE} \sim N(M_{i,j}, \frac{4n_i n_j}{(n_i+n_j)\epsilon_d^2})$ and $|\tilde{M}_{i,j,MLE} - M_{i,j}|_1 \sim |N(0, \frac{4n_i n_j}{(n_i+n_j)\epsilon_d^2})|_1$. Denote $\sigma = \frac{4n_i n_j}{(n_i+n_j)\epsilon_d^2}$. Through integration, we have

$$E(|\tilde{M}_{i,j,MLE} - M_{i,j}|_1) = \int_0^\infty x \frac{1}{\sqrt{2\pi\sigma}} exp\{-\frac{x^2}{2\sigma^2}\}dx = \sqrt{\frac{2}{\pi}}\frac{2}{\epsilon_d}\sqrt{\frac{n_i n_j}{n_i + n_j}}.$$

According to the Cauchy's Inequality and Harmonic-Geometric Mean Inequality,

$$\sum_{i,j\in\{1,2,\cdots,c\}} \sqrt{\frac{n_i n_j}{n_i + n_j}} \leq \sqrt{c^2}\sqrt{\sum_{i,j\in\{1,2,\cdots,c\}}\frac{n_i n_j}{n_i + n_j}} \leq \frac{\sqrt{2}}{2}c\sqrt{cn}, \quad (14)$$

since $\sum_{i=1}^{c} n_i = n$. So we have

$$E(|C_{ps}^T AC_{ps} - C_{ps}^T \Pi C_{ps}|_1) = \sum_{i,j} E(|M_{i,j} - \tilde{M}_{i,j,MLE}|_1) \leq \sqrt{\frac{1}{\pi} \frac{2}{\epsilon_d}} c\sqrt{cn}. \quad (15)$$

Combining Eq. 13 and Eq. 15 yields the proof.

The error in Theorem 5 can be split into two parts: random error (the first term in Eq. 10) caused by noise injection, and systematic error (the second term) caused by misclassification. The random error is inversely proportional to ϵ_d and scales as $\mathcal{O}(\sqrt{n})$. The systematic error arises from the discrepancy between true and pseudo labels. In our approach, training set nodes are assigned true labels to reduce systematic error. For unlabeled nodes, provided that the MLP achieves a reasonable accuracy—an assumption that generally holds for real-world datasets—this term won't greatly compromise the homophily constraint.

Corollary 2. *Under the same classification matrix C_{true}, difference between the two cluster connection matrix is bounded by*

$$E(|C_{true}^T AC_{true} - C_{true}^T \Pi C_{true}|) \leq \frac{2c}{\epsilon_d}\sqrt{\frac{cn}{\pi}} + \sum_{i=0}^{n} 2|C_{true,i} - C_{ps,i}|_1(\mathbf{d}_i + \tilde{\mathbf{d}}_i),$$

where $\tilde{\mathbf{d}}_i$ is the degree of node i in Π.

4.3 Precision Analysis

In this section, we analyze the effects of Bayesian estimation on the precision of the estimated edges, as stated in Theorem 6.

Theorem 6. *Suppose that the probability that the prior distribution is correct is q, where $q = \Pi_{ij}$ if $A_{ij} = 1$ and $1 - \Pi_{ij}$ otherwise. ϵ_a is the privacy budget allocated for the random response mechanism, then the probability that the posterior probability $\mathcal{P}_{ij}$ is correct satisfies*

$$\lim_{\epsilon_a \to 0} E(P(\mathcal{P}_{ij} = A_{ij}|A_{ij})) = q, \quad \lim_{\epsilon_a \to +\infty} E(P(\mathcal{P}_{ij} = A_{ij}|A_{ij})) = 1, \quad (16)$$

and we have that $P(\mathcal{P}_{ij} = A_{ij}|A_{ij}))$ is monotonic increasing with $\epsilon_a > 0$.

Theorem 6 shows that with a small privacy budget, the precision of the posterior probability depends on the precision of the prior estimation. While with an abundant budget, the RR mechanism makes the estimated graph approach the actual one. This indicates that as the privacy budget increases, the benefit of a better prior diminishes. Experiments shows that our method mainly improves performance under small privacy budgets and converges to the baseline GNN performance as the budget increases, which is consistent with this conclusion.

5 Experiments

5.1 Experimental Settings

Datasets. We conduct experiments on four real-world datasets: *Cora* [24], *Amazon* [19] (including *Computers* and *Photo*), *LastFM* [16] and *Facebook* [15]. These datasets cover several representative real-world network types, and also demonstrate the scalability of our method on graphs of different scales.

Experimental Setup. For all datasets and models, we randomly split the nodes into train/validation/test nodes with a ratio of 2:1:1. We selected GCN [10], GraphSAGE [7], and GAT [20] as the primary models for testing due to their representative approaches to graph neural networks. We test the performance of all prior-based method with $\epsilon \in \{1, 2, \cdots, 8\}$. We conduct grid search on δ and report the best performance. For other frameworks, we search for their best hyper-parameters respectively. We conduct injection 5 times to generate 5 noisy graphs, and we train GNNs on each graph 5 times to reduce randomness.

5.2 Experimental Results

Compare to Other Prior-Based Methods. Based on the Bayesian estimation framework, we compare the performance of other graph prior construction methods with ours. We use the following methods as baselines:

1. **Blink** [27]: Blink constructs the prior graph with β-model. Given a vector $\beta = [\beta_1, \beta_2, \cdots, \beta_n] \in R^n$, an edge between node i and node j is given with probability of $\Pi_{ij} = \frac{exp(\beta_i+\beta_j)}{1+exp(\beta_i+\beta_j)}$. Blink collects the degree of each node, and estimates β with maximum likelihood estimation. This work only utilizes the degree distribution, without taking advantage of graph's homophily.
2. **HAGEI** [25]: A work contemporaneous with ours likewise proposes executing degree vector queries, and it constructs the prior graph with the Chung-Lu model: $\Pi_{ij} = \frac{d_j^{c_i} \cdot \sum_{i \in \mathbf{V}} \frac{d_i^{c_i}}{|U_{c_i}|}}{\sum_{j \in U_{c_j}} d_j^{c_i} + \sum_{i \in \mathbf{V}} d_i^{c_i}} + \frac{d_i^{c_j} \cdot \sum_{j \in \mathbf{V}} \frac{d_j^{c_j}}{|U_{c_j}|}}{\sum_{i \in U_{c_j}} d_i^{c_j} + \sum_{j \in \mathbf{V}} d_j^{c_j}}$, where $d_j^{c_i}$ represents the noisy number of edges node j connects to cluster c_i, and $|U_{c_i}|$ represents the number of nodes in cluster U_{c_i}. However, this work provides no theoretical error analysis and thus fails to bridge the gap between degree vector queries and a specific homophily metric.

After fetching the posterior link probability matrix $\mathcal{P}$, we adopt the following two methods to sample a graph for GNN trainning:

- **Hard sampling.** An edge is sampled if its posterior probability is above 0.5. All the sampled edges are regarded as undirected and unweighted.
- **Soft sampling.** The probability of each edge's existence is used as the weight of the edge. Correspondingly, we adopt dense convolution in GNN models. We didn't train the GAT model under soft sampling strategy since it is not reasonable to let all nodes attend over all others.

Table 2. Node classification accuracy comparison between different prior graph construction methods (Blink/HAGEI/HPGR(ours)) under various datasets, GNN models and privacy budgets. ∞ represents GNN performance without adopting privacy protection policies, and mlp represents model performance without utilizing graph topology. We bold the best method and underline the second best method for each setting. Values in the table are presented in the percentage form.

	mlp		eps	1	2	3	4	5	6	∞
cora 73.7		gcn	hard	72.6/72.6/**73.2**	72.6/72.6/**73.2**	72.6/72.6/**74.9**	77.6/**80.5**/79.9	85.2/**86.2**/85.1	86.8/**86.9**/86.8	87.2
			soft	58.0/59.5/**74.1**	58.8/51.4/**74.3**	67.6/62.6/**76.2**	79.0/77.3/**81.1**	83.9/83.8/**84.6**	84.8/84.8/**84.9**	85.8
		sage	hard	72.5/72.4/72.1	72.5/72.4/72.3	72.5/75.4/72.9	77.3/82.4/79.8	85.6/**86.4**/85.2	87.7/87.5/**87.5**	88.0
			soft	67.6/68.5/**74.2**	67.7/68.4/**74.4**	70.2/71.0/**75.6**	77.4/78.2/**80.7**	83.4/83.4/**84.2**	85.4/85.3/**85.4**	86.3
		gat	hard	72.4/72.4/**72.5**	72.4/72.4/72.4	72.4/72.4/**73.7**	74.5/76.4/**78.9**	83.9/**84.6**/84.2	86.0/86.0/86.0	87.0
computers 82.7		gcn	hard	81.6/82.6/**83.4**	81.6/82.6/**83.5**	81.6/83.2/**85.1**	82.9/82.6/**86.8**	87.2/87.3/**88.3**	88.4/**88.7**/88.7	89.1
			soft	28.8/59.6/**81.7**	34.1/59.3/**83.1**	58.8/58.9/**85.7**	81.6/80.7/**87.2**	85.7/85.6/**87.3**	86.6/86.9/**87.4**	87.4
		sage	hard	**82.9**/82.4/82.4	**82.9**/82.4/**83.5**	82.9/83.6/**85.8**	85.9/85.9/**87.8**	88.5/87.9/**89.4**	89.7/89.7/**90.0**	90.2
			soft	77.8/78.9/**83.6**	78.8/78.9/**85.4**	81.3/81.6/**86.8**	85.2/85.7/**87.8**	86.9/87.3/**87.9**	87.7/87.8/**88.0**	88.1
		gat	hard	**81.1**/79.8/81.0	**80.8**/79.8/82.7	80.0/81.7/**84.5**	79.9/79.8/**86.5**	86.3/87.0/**87.9**	88.4/88.5/**88.6**	88.7
lastfm 70.7		gcn	hard	67.5/67.5/**68.0**	67.5/67.5/**69.6**	67.9/70.6/**71.6**	73.6/71.1/**76.2**	79.4/79.4/**80.5**	82.7/82.7/**82.9**	83.4
			soft	42.0/47.8/**68.2**	45.7/47.3/**68.3**	61.9/52.0/**70.4**	69.0/64.4/**72.5**	75.0/74.8/**76.1**	78.6/78.6/**78.6**	81.0
		sage	hard	68.6/68.6/**68.3**	69.0/68.6/**69.7**	71.4/70.4/**72.5**	75.7/77.4/**77.5**	81.2/81.8/**82.5**	84.3/84.5/**85.0**	85.3
			soft	63.6/64.5/**70.8**	63.6/64.4/**71.1**	65.7/64.1/**71.9**	70.9/69.1/**73.6**	76.1/76.0/**78.2**	79.5/79.4/**80.3**	83.3
		gat	hard	67.9/67.9/67.8	67.9/67.9/**69.0**	67.9/69.4/**70.9**	70.4/67.9/**75.6**	77.8/78.0/**80.0**	82.0/82.1/**82.6**	83.0
facebook 74.7		gcn	hard	73.9/73.9/73.9	73.9/73.9/**74.4**	73.9/73.9/**76.3**	76.2/74.1/**79.5**	83.4/84.5/**85.0**	88.3/**88.7**/88.7	90.1
			soft	57.4/**76.3**/75.0	57.9/**76.5**/75.5	71.6/76.5/**77.9**	78.7/76.4/**82.0**	84.3/83.7/**85.5**	87.3/87.4/**87.7**	88.9
		sage	hard	**74.2**/74.2/74.3	74.1/74.2/**75.1**	76.3/74.2/**76.3**	78.7/74.7/**79.8**	84.0/**85.8**/85.3	88.6/**89.2**/89.0	91.0
			soft	**74.5**/73.7/75.0	74.6/74.9/**75.4**	76.6/77.4/**77.8**	80.0/80.5/**81.7**	84.9/74.7/**86.0**	88.4/88.3/**88.7**	90.1
		gat	hard	73.8/73.5/73.8	73.8/73.5/73.8	73.8/73.5/**75.4**	73.8/73.5/**78.7**	80.9/**82.3**/84.0	87.6/88.0/**88.1**	90.2

Results in Table 2 show that our prior graph sampling method consistently outperforms other methods, particularly with a moderate privacy budget. Our approach not only outperforms other methods under soft sampling strategies but, more importantly, within our framework, soft sampling often yields better results than hard sampling. In comparison, hard sampling leads to a sparser graph due to the truncation threshold being set to 0.5. For example, when the server collects $e_{ij} = 1$ and $e_{ji} = 0$ due to the random response mechanism (common with small privacy budgets), Eq. 6 shows that $\mathcal{P}_{ij} \geq 0.5$ if and only if $\Pi_{ij} \geq 0.5$. However, due to the inherent sparsity of the original graph, the prior probability Π_{ij} is often smaller than 0.5 even if an edge exists. This causes hard sampling to truncate values, which reduces noise but sacrifices fine-grained structural details. Excellent performance under soft sampling strategy suggests that our approach effectively utilizes detailed topological information while minimizing the impact of noise on downstream tasks.

Compare to Other Methods. We also compare our method with other disparate locally differential private GNN frameworks, and they are:

1. **Random Response(RR):** The server employs the RR mechanism to collect adjacency information without applying any additional denoising operations.

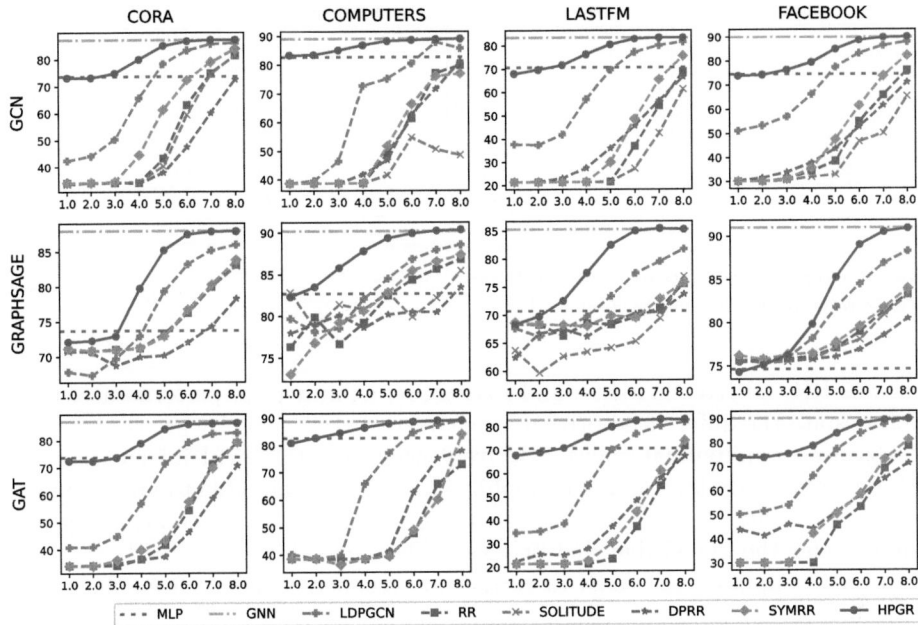

Fig. 2. Performance comparison between HPGR(ours) and other methods. X-axis represents privacy budget ϵ and y-axis represents test accuracy (%).

2. **Symmetric Random Response(SymRR):** The server only collect the lower triangular adjacency matrix with RR, ensuring that the reconstructed graph remains undirected.
3. **Degree-Preserving Random Response(DPRR)** [8]: DPRR performs an unbiased estimation of node degrees in the original topology based on the observed degrees in the collected topology. Subsequently, it randomly samples an equal number of collected edges for each node, corresponding to its estimated degree, to reconstruct the corrected topology.
4. **Locally Differential Private GNN(LDPGNN):** LDPGNN, a variant of DPGNN proposed in [18], utilizes the Laplace mechanism to collect the private topology. The server then estimates the unbiased number of edges in the entire graph and retains the corresponding number of highest-weighted entries in the collected topology.
5. **Solitude** [13]: Solitude formulates the sparsity of the collected topology as an optimization objective for GNN training. Its optimization goal is given by $\min_{\hat{A},\theta} \mathcal{L}(\hat{A}|\theta) + \lambda_1 |\hat{A} - \tilde{A}|_F + \lambda_2 |\hat{A}|_1$.

The experimental results in Fig. 2 show that our method outperforms baseline approaches. When the privacy budget is limited, both the random response (RR) and Laplace (Lap) mechanisms significantly distort the graph's topology, making it challenging for GNNs to extract meaningful signals from graphs with a low signal-to-noise ratio. As a result, methods relying on the RR or Lap mechanisms

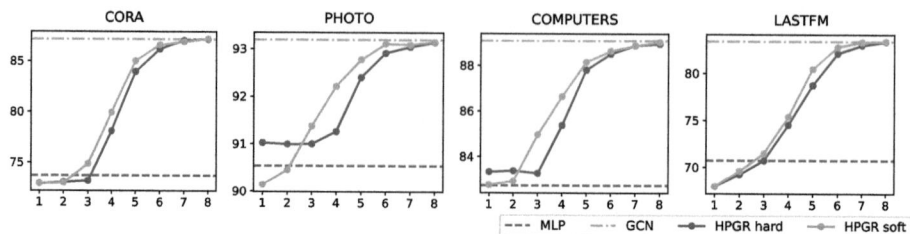

Fig. 3. Comparison between soft and hard queries (instead of sampling strategies). X-axis represents privacy budget and y-axis represents test accuracy (%).

(such as RR, DPRR, SYMRR, and LDPGCN) exhibit poor performance. However, despite the differential privacy mechanisms' ability to obscure the presence or absence of individual edges, relatively accurate statistical information can still be derived. By leveraging homophily statistics, we are able to preserve node connectivity within and across classes. In homophilic graphs, the prior distribution encodes the knowledge that "nodes of the same class are more likely to be connected", enabling the GNN to extract low-frequency signals from the graph.

Comparison Between Hard and Soft Queries. We analyze the difference between the proposed soft and hard query mechanisms from Sect. 3.1, with results shown in Fig. 3. In most cases, the soft query outperforms the hard query, particularly when the privacy budget is relatively sufficient, as it reduces bias from MLP misclassification by accounting for classification uncertainty. However, the soft query requires transmitting an $n \times c$ classification probability matrix instead of an n-sized classification vector, increasing the communication burden. This represents a trade-off between resource consumption and performance.

6 Related Work

Differentially Private GNNs. Differentially private GNNs can be divided into two categories based on the goal of privacy protection: global differentially private GNNs and local differentially private GNNs.

Global differentially private GNNs aim to train node embedding vectors or labels privately at the sever side. GAP [17] achieves edge-level and node-level differential privacy by adding noise during the convolution process. DPDGC [3] improves upon the node-level differential privacy definition proposed in [17], achieving better performance by injecting noise into the graph topology and node features individually. DPGCN [4] extends the DP-SGD method [1] to the GNN domain, achieving node-level differential privacy.

Local differentially private GNNs focus on protecting node features and graph topology at the client side. LDPGNN [18] focuses on protecting node features and labels, while LDP-GE [11] focuses on protecting only node features. Solitude [13], DPRR [8], and Blink [27] aim at protecting the graph topology, and these methods have been introduced in detail in Sect. 5.

7 Conclusion

In this paper, we introduce HPGR, a method that effectively leverages homophily to enhance the performance of GNNs under LDP. HPGR not only advances the state of the art in privacy-preserving graph learning but also highlights the critical importance of integrating domain-specific structural insights—such as homophily—into privacy mechanisms. This work opens new avenues for developing secure, high-utility graph-based machine learning applications in decentralized and privacy-sensitive environments.

Acknowledgment. This work was supported by NSF China under Grant No. T2421002, 62202299, 62020106005, 62061146002.

References

1. Abadi, M., Chu, A., Goodfellow, I., McMahan, H.B., Mironov, I., Talwar, K., Zhang, L.: Deep learning with differential privacy. In: CCS (2016)
2. Briar Project: Briar: Secure messaging, anywhere (2024). https://briarproject.org/
3. Chien, E., Chen, W.N., Pan, C., Li, P., Ozgur, A.: Differentially private decoupled graph convolutions for multigranular topology protection. In: NeurIPS (2024)
4. Daigavane, A., Madan, G., Sinha, A., Thakurta, A.G., Aggarwal, G., Jain, P.: Node-level differentially private graph neural networks. arXiv:2111.15521 (2021)
5. Duchi, J.C., Jordan, M.I., Wainwright, M.J.: Local privacy and statistical minimax rates. In: FOCS (2013)
6. Dwork, C.: Differential privacy. In: International colloquium on automata, languages, and programming (2006)
7. Hamilton, W., Ying, Z., Leskovec, J.: Inductive representation learning on large graphs. In: NeurIPS (2017)
8. Hidano, S., Murakami, T.: Degree-preserving randomized response for graph neural networks under local differential privacy. arXiv:2202.10209 (2022)
9. Karrer, B., Newman, M.E.: Stochastic blockmodels and community structure in networks. Phys. Rev. E (2011)
10. Kipf, T.N., Welling, M.: Semi-supervised classification with graph convolutional networks. In: ICLR (2017)
11. Li, Z., Li, R.H., Liao, M., Jin, F., Wang, G.: Locally differentially private graph embedding. arXiv:2310.11060 (2023)
12. Lim, D., Hohne, F., Li, X., Huang, S.L., Gupta, V., Bhalerao, O., Lim, S.N.: Large scale learning on non-homophilous graphs: new benchmarks and strong simple methods. In: NeurIPS (2021)
13. Lin, W., Li, B., Wang, C.: Towards private learning on decentralized graphs with local differential privacy. TIFS (2022)
14. Moyer12, D., Gutman, B., Prasad, G., Ver Steeg, G.: Mixed membership stochastic blockmodels for the human connectome. Neuro-Degenerative Dis. (2015)
15. Rozemberczki, B., Allen, C., Sarkar, R.: Multi-scale attributed node embedding. J. Complex Netw. (2021)
16. Rozemberczki, B., Sarkar, R.: Characteristic functions on graphs: birds of a feather, from statistical descriptors to parametric models. In: CIKM (2020)

17. Sajadmanesh, S., Shamsabadi, A., Bellet, A., Gatica-Perez, D.: GAP: differentially private graph neural networks with aggregation perturbation. In: Security (2023)
18. Sajadmanesh, S., Gatica-Perez, D.: Locally private graph neural networks. In: CCS (2021)
19. Shchur, O., Mumme, M., Bojchevski, A., Günnemann, S.: Pitfalls of graph neural network evaluation. arXiv:1811.05868 (2018)
20. Veličković, P., Cucurull, G., Casanova, A., Romero, A., Lio, P., Bengio, Y.: Graph attention networks. In: ICLR (2018)
21. Voigt, P., Von dem Bussche, A.: The EU General Data Protection Regulation (GDPR). A Practical Guide, 1st edn. Springer, Cham (2017)
22. Warner, S.L.: Randomized response: a survey technique for eliminating evasive answer bias. J. Am. Stat. Assoc. (1965)
23. Wu, K., et al.: Characterizing the influence of topology on graph learning tasks. In: Onizuka, M., et al. (eds.) DASFAA 2024. LNCS, vol. 14851, pp. 35–50. Springer, Singapore (2024). https://doi.org/10.1007/978-981-97-5779-4_3
24. Yang, Z., Cohen, W., Salakhudinov, R.: Revisiting semi-supervised learning with graph embeddings. In: ICML (2016)
25. Zhang, G., Cheng, X., Pan, J., Lin, Z., He, Z.: Locally differentially private graph learning on decentralized social graph. Knowl.-Based Syst. (2024)
26. Zhu, J., Yan, Y., Zhao, L., Heimann, M., Akoglu, L., Koutra, D.: Beyond homophily in graph neural networks: current limitations and effective designs. In: NeurIPS (2020)
27. Zhu, X., Tan, V.Y., Xiao, X.: Blink: link local differential privacy in graph neural networks via Bayesian estimation. In: CCS (2023)

MCMC for Bayesian Estimation of Differential Privacy from Membership Inference Attacks

Ceren Yıldırım[1](✉)[iD], Kamer Kaya[1,2][iD], Sinan Yıldırım[1,2][iD], and Erkay Savaş[1][iD]

[1] Faculty of Natural Sciences and Engineering, Sabancı University, 34956 İstanbul, Turkey
{cerenyildirim,kaya,sinanyildirim,erkays}@sabanciuniv.edu
[2] VERIM, Sabancı University, 34956 İstanbul, Turkey

Abstract. We propose a new framework for Bayesian estimation of differential privacy, incorporating evidence from multiple membership inference attacks (MIA). Bayesian estimation is carried out via a Markov Chain Monte Carlo (MCMC) algorithm, named MCMC-DP-Est, which provides an estimate of the full posterior distribution of the privacy parameter (e.g., instead of just credible intervals). Critically, the proposed method does *not* assume that privacy auditing is performed with the most powerful attack on the worst-case (dataset, challenge point) pair, which is typically unrealistic. Instead, MCMC-DP-Est jointly estimates the strengths of MIAs used *and* the privacy of the training algorithm, yielding a more cautious privacy analysis. We also present an economical way to generate measurements for the performance of an MIA that is to be used by the MCMC method to estimate privacy. We present the use of the methods with numerical examples with both artificial and real data.

Keywords: Differential Privacy · Membership Inference Attacks · Bayesian estimation · Markov Chain Monte Carlo

1 Introduction

Differential privacy (DP) has emerged as a gold standard for quantifying and guaranteeing privacy in data analysis and machine learning [10,12]. DP provides a mathematical framework to limit the impact of an individual's data on the output of a random algorithm, enabling robust privacy guarantees regardless of the adversary's knowledge other than that individual. DP is defined below.

Definition 1 (DP). *An algorithm $\mathcal{A}$ with input space $\bigcup_{n=1}^{\infty} \mathcal{Z}^n$ and output space Ω is (ϵ, δ)-DP if for every $n \in \mathbb{N}$, $D \in \mathcal{Z}^n$, $z \in \mathcal{Z}$, and $E \subseteq \Omega$, we have*

$$P(\mathcal{A}(D) \in E) \leq e^\epsilon P(\mathcal{A}(D \cup \{z\}) \in E) + \delta,$$
$$P(\mathcal{A}(D \cup \{z\}) \in E) \leq e^\epsilon P(\mathcal{A}(D) \in E) + \delta.$$

Supplementary Information The online version contains supplementary material available at https://doi.org/10.1007/978-3-032-06096-9_23.

Quantifying the privacy of practical implementations remains a challenging task. Theoretical lower bounds for (ϵ, δ) have been extensively analyzed for a variety of mechanisms, such as noise-adding mechanisms (Laplace, Gaussian, etc.) [11,12], subsampling [4], and their composition [15]. Other theoretical definitions of DP have also been used to derive lower bounds of DP [5,9,21]. However, theoretical lower bounds are not tight for many practical algorithms whose revealed outputs result from a series of calculations involving randomness. An example is when a training algorithm outputs *only* its final model, possibly following randomizing steps like random initialization, random updates (e.g., due to subsampling and/or noisy gradients), or output perturbation. In such a case, a large gap between the theoretical bounds and the actual privacy is shown to exist [24]. The privacy-auditing, or privacy estimation, of such complex but practical algorithms, through numerical estimation of (ϵ, δ), has become an emerging research line [2,13,14,18–20,22–25,28,31]. This study follows this line by proposing a new framework for Bayesian privacy estimation.

Privacy auditing methods leverage the relation between DP and *Membership Inference Attacks* (MIA) [6,27,29,30] to estimate ϵ and δ. This is because DP particularly guarantees the protection of sensitive input data against MIAs. While there are different types of MIAs, by Definition 1, the leave-one-out attack (L-attack in [29]) is the one directly relevant to the DP of a private algorithm. In an L-attack, a data set D, a data point $z \in \mathcal{Z}$, and a random output of $\mathcal{A}$ are given to the attacker who uses the given information to infer whether D or $D \cup \{z\}$ was used by $\mathcal{A}$. For *any* D, z and *any* statistical test, the type I and type II error probabilities are lower-bounded by a curve determined by the (ϵ, δ) of $\mathcal{A}$, see Theorem 1.

Two main issues deserve caution in empirical privacy analysis based on MIAs.

1. *The attack strategy to audit privacy is typically not the strongest*: For a given pair (D, z), the strongest attack that decides based on $\mathcal{A}$'s output is known to be the likelihood ratio test (LRT). However, practical MIAs to audit privacy merely approximate the LRT [26] with a limited computational budget, e.g. using metrics that are loss-based [6,29,30], gradient-based [22], etc. On the other hand, an adversary can design more powerful attacks than the one used for auditing, provided computational budget. It is also difficult to analytically characterize the gap between the performances of a given MIA and the LRT. Therefore, treating a given MIA as *the* strongest attack may lead to overconfident estimates about the privacy of an algorithm ('overconfident', because weaker attacks imply stronger privacy; see Remark 2). This is particularly dangerous since, based on overconfident estimations, private data may be leaked to a greater extent than it is permitted.
2. *The challenge base (D, z) may not be the absolute "worst-case" challenge base.* Moreover, existing efforts such as [19,23,25,31] do not *theoretically* guarantee to find such a point. Therefore, *even if* the strongest attack is applied on the challenge base (D, z), its observed false positive and false negative counts should *not* directly be used to upper bound ϵ. This is because tests on another (D, z) challenge base could result in a larger upper bound on ϵ.

Considering the above issues, we propose a new Bayesian methodology for empirical privacy estimation. Our contributions are as follows.

1. **A new posterior sampling method for DP estimation:** We develop a joint probability distribution for the privacy parameter, attack strengths, and false negatives/positives involved in *block-box* auditing a private algorithm, where one has access only to the output of $\mathcal{A}$ and not its intermediate results. Suited to this model, we propose a Markov Chain Monte Carlo (MCMC) method named MCMC-DP-Est (Algorithm 1), adopted from [3], for Bayesian estimation of privacy. The advantages of MCMC-DP-Est are as follows:
   - **Full posterior distribution:** Beyond credible intervals, such as in [31], it returns the *full posterior distribution* of the privacy parameters.
   - **Combining multiple results:** With the fully Bayesian treatment, the algorithm is able to combine the false negative and false positive counts from *multiple* (D, z) points (and possibly from multiple attack strategies). In particular, *no tried attacks need to be thrown away*. This also enables leveraging new (D, z) points or attack strategies to refine the privacy estimates coherently.
   - **Cautious treatment of attack strengths:** Related to the above discussion, the probabilistic model based on which MCMC is used in this work does *not* assume that the attack used is the strongest attack possible under the privacy constraint or it is performed on the worst-case (D, z) pair (though it can be adapted to include such cases). Instead, we parametrize the average strength of the applied tests/challenge bases by a parameter $s \in [0, 1]$, and use MCMC to jointly estimate both s and ϵ.
2. **A method for measuring MIA performance:** We present a parametric loss-based MIA, adopting LiRA [6], to feed privacy auditing methods (including ours) with informative error counts. We propose a computationally efficient way to measure the MIA performance. The measurements, the numbers of false positives and false negatives, are to be fed to the MCMC algorithm as observations.
3. **An extension of the joint probability model** that allows statistical dependencies among attacks is also discussed briefly in Remark 3 in Sect. 2.1 and more in detail in Sect. 3 of a separate **Supplementary File**. Attack results can be statistically dependent, for example, when a common z point is paired with different D datasets from the population.

Section 2 presents the joint probability model and MCMC-DP-Est. Section 3, presents an MIA and an experiment design to collect performance measures for the attack, which are to be fed to the MCMC algorithm as observations. Section 4 presents the experiments. Section 5 concludes the paper.

1.1 Related Work

Privacy estimation methods exploit theoretical results and approach their guarantees empirically. For example, the privacy estimation in [13] estimates the privacy of stochastic gradient descent (SGD) based on the relationship between the sensitivity of the output and privacy. However, in most studies, the relation between MIAs and Definition 1 of DP has been exploited. For example, [14] derives Clopper-Pearson confidence intervals for ϵ from MIAs carefully designed for SGD with clipping. [23] uses Clopper-Pearson confidence intervals, too, but additionally finds the worst-case pairs (D, z) to improve the bound on the privacy estimates. In contrast to frequentist estimates in [14,23], Bayesian privacy estimation is proposed in [31], where Bayesian *credible intervals* are provided for ϵ. Privacy estimation has also been extended to other definitions of privacy [18,22,25] and to federated learning [2,20].

The quality of privacy estimation through MIAs depends heavily on the quality of MIAs, i.e., their power to distinguish membership and non-membership. Several MIAs (tests) have been proposed in the literature. If black-box privacy-auditing is performed, the loss function of the trained model is typically involved in the MIA decision rule and using the loss function is shown to be Bayes optimal in [26]. The LOSS attack [30] uses the loss function as its test statistic. This attack is also used as an approximation of the LRT under some conditions [29] that correspond to the output of the training model behaving like a sample from its posterior distribution. The LOSS attack has been reported to be weak in identifying memberships and strong in identifying non-memberships [6]. As an alternative, [6] proposes LiRA, a more direct approximation of the LRT that considers the distribution of the loss function under both hypotheses.

2 Bayesian Estimation of Privacy

We present the joint probability distribution for the variables regarding the privacy of $\mathcal{A}$, error probabilities of MIAs, and the observed false positive (FP) and false negative (FN) counts for each MIA. Then, we present the MCMC algorithm for the privacy estimation of $\mathcal{A}$ according to that joint probability distribution. First, we provide some preliminaries and introduce some concepts for clarity. Definition 2 assigns a specific meaning to the term 'challenge base' for the clarity of presentation.

Definition 2 (Challenge base). *A challenge base is a pair (D, z), where $D \in \bigcup_n^\infty \mathcal{Z}^n$ and $z \in \mathcal{Z}$ with $z \notin D$.*

Next, we define an MIA as a statistical test specified by a challenge base, a critical region, and a private algorithm whose output serves as the observation point for that test.

Definition 3 (MIA). *An MIA is a statistical test specified by $(D, z, \mathcal{A}, \phi, \alpha, \beta)$, where $\phi : \Omega \mapsto \{0, 1\}$ is a (possibly random) decision rule for the absence or presence of z in the input of $\mathcal{A}$ based on a random outcome θ from $\mathcal{A}$, and α, β are the deduced type I and type II error probabilities given by*

$$\alpha = P(\phi(\theta) = 1 | H_0 : \theta \sim \mathcal{A}(D)), \quad \beta = P(\phi(\theta) = 0 | H_1 : \theta \sim \mathcal{A}(D \cup \{z\})).$$

The theorem below from [16, Theorem 2.1] is central to the methodology presented in this paper. It sets an upper bound on the accuracy of MIAs whose sample is the output of an (ϵ, δ)-DP algorithm.

Theorem 1. $\mathcal{A}$ is (ϵ, δ)-DP if and only if, for any $D \in \mathcal{Z}^n$ and $z \in \mathcal{Z}$, and a decision rule ϕ, the MIA $(D, z, \phi, \mathcal{A}, \alpha, \beta)$ satisfies $(\alpha, \beta) \in \mathcal{R}(\epsilon, \delta)$, where

$$\mathcal{R}(\epsilon, \delta) := \left\{ (x, y) \in [0,1]^2 : \begin{array}{l} x + e^\epsilon y \geq 1 - \delta, \, y + e^\epsilon x \geq 1 - \delta, \\ y + e^\epsilon x \leq e^\epsilon + \delta, \, x + e^\epsilon y \leq e^\epsilon + \delta \end{array} \right\}.$$

See Fig. 1 (top left) for an illustration of $\mathcal{R}(\epsilon, \delta)$.

Remark 1. In this work, we will assume $\delta \geq 0$ fixed and known, and we will focus on estimating the parameter ϵ. However, if an algorithm is (ϵ_1, δ) it is also (ϵ_2, δ) for any $\epsilon_2 > \epsilon_1$. To prevent ambiguity, by "estimating privacy", we specifically mean estimating $\epsilon := \inf\{\epsilon_0 \geq 0 : \mathcal{A}$ is (ϵ_0, δ)-DP$\}$.

2.1 Joint Probabilistic Model for Privacy and MIA-Related Variables

We present in detail the joint probability model illustrated in Fig. 1 (bottom).

Observed Error Counts: We assume that there are $n \geq 1$ challenge bases (D_i, z_i), $i = 1, \ldots, n$. On each challenge base, an MIA $(D_i, z_i, \phi_i, \mathcal{A}, \alpha_i, \beta_i)$ is challenged $N_{i,0}, N_{i,1}$ times under H_0, H_1, respectively. More explicitly, for $j = 1, \ldots, N_{i,0}$, we challenge an MIA $(D_i, z_i, \phi_i, \mathcal{A}, \alpha_i, \beta_i)$ with $\theta_0^{(j)} \sim \mathcal{A}(D)$. We collect X_i, the number of false positives out of the $N_{i,0}$ challenges. Likewise, we challenge the same MIA $N_{i,1}$ times with $\theta_1^{(j)} \sim \mathcal{A}(D \cup \{z\})$. We collect Y_i, the number of false negatives out of the $N_{i,1}$ challenges.

We denote the conditional distribution of X_i, Y_i given α_i, β_i by $g(X_i, Y_i | \alpha_i, \beta_i)$. When the tests for each challenge base are independent, X_i and Y_i become independent binomials and their conditional distributions become

$$g(X_i, Y_i | \alpha_i, \beta_i) = \text{Binom}(X_i | N_{i,0}, \alpha_i) \times \text{Binom}(Y_i | N_{i,1}, \beta_i), \tag{1}$$

where α_i, β_i are the error probabilities of the i'th MIA. Other distributions may arise with dependent tests, e.g. because of using common shadow models to learn the null and alternative hypotheses. We discuss such a case in Sect. 3.2.

True Error Probabilities: The performance of an MIA depends on $\mathcal{A}$, the challenge base (D, z) as well as the decision rule ϕ. When we have little knowledge about the performance of a test, a convenient choice for its conditional prior distribution for (α_i, β_i) given (ϵ, δ) is the uniform distribution over $\mathcal{R}(\epsilon, \delta)$. However, uniformity over $R(\epsilon, \delta)$ may be a loose assumption for carefully designed attacks. Indeed, several works in the literature study the design of powerful MIAs by approximating the LRT [6,23,29,30] or finding the worst-case (or "best-case" from the attacker's point of view) tuple (D, z), or both. When such techniques are involved, the prior of $\alpha_{1:n}, \beta_{1:n}$ given ϵ, δ can be modified as

$$(\alpha_1, \beta_1), \ldots, (\alpha_n, \beta_n) | \epsilon, \delta \overset{\text{iid}}{\sim} \text{Unif}(\mathcal{R}_s(\epsilon, \delta)), \quad \mathcal{R}_s(\epsilon, \delta) := \mathcal{R}(\epsilon, \delta) \backslash \mathcal{R}(s\epsilon, s\delta). \tag{2}$$

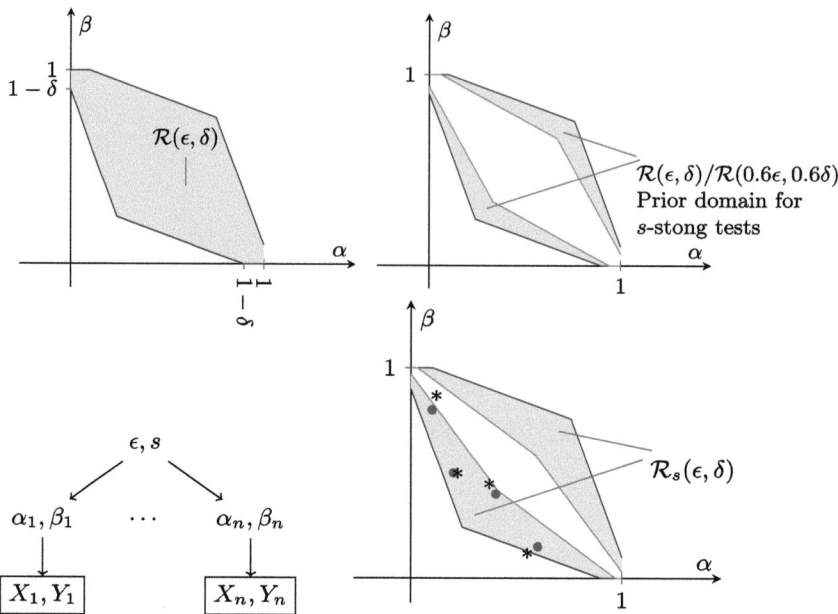

Fig. 1. Top Left: $\mathcal{R}(\alpha, \beta)$, the unconstrained prior domain ($s = 0$) for α, β of an MIA. **Top Right:** $\mathcal{R}_{0.6}(\alpha, \beta)$, prior domain for $s = 0.6$. **Bottom Left:** The dependency structure of the variables involved (a fixed δ is assumed). **Bottom Right:** Realization of the variables. ϵ and s set the blue and green lines, respectively; (α_i, β_i) and $(X_i/N_{i,0}, Y_i/N_{i,1})$ are shown with red and black points, respectively.

Here, $s \in (0, 1)$ is a strength parameter for the test; the closer it is to 1, the stronger the test is expected. The parameter s itself can be modeled as a random variable, for example, as $s \sim \text{Beta}(a, b)$, and it can also be estimated from the results of multiple MIAs. The pdf of (α_i, β_i) in the modified case is

$$p_s(\alpha_i, \beta_i | \epsilon, \delta) = \mathbb{I}((\alpha, \beta) \in \mathcal{R}_s(\epsilon, \delta))/|\mathcal{R}_s(\epsilon, \delta)|, \tag{3}$$

where $|\mathcal{R}_s(\epsilon, \delta)|$ is the area of $\mathcal{R}_s(\epsilon, \delta)$, given by

$$|\mathcal{R}_s(\epsilon, \delta)| = 2[(1 - s\delta)^2 e^{-s\epsilon}/(1 + e^{-s\epsilon}) - (1 - \delta)^2 e^{-\epsilon}/(1 + e^{-\epsilon})].$$

Figure 1 illustrates this prior for $s = 0$ (top left) and $s = 0.6$ (top right).

Remark 2 (The special case $s = 1$). The choice $s = 1$ corresponds to the assumption that the strongest possible attacks are used to generate (X_i, Y_i) pairs. Several studies make this assumption implicitly, relying on the quality of their MIAs [14,23,31]. In many cases, the assumption is too strong since determining the worst-case challenge base (D, z) *and* using the most powerful test for that couple is usually intractable. As a result, taking $s = 1$ may lead to overconfident estimations about ϵ. (See Fig. 2.) More concretely, the relation between ϵ and

(α, β) can be written as

$$\{\epsilon \leq \epsilon_0\} \Leftrightarrow \{(\alpha, \beta) \in \mathcal{R}(\epsilon_0, \delta) \text{ for any } \text{MIA } (D, z, \mathcal{A}, \phi, \alpha, \beta)\}.$$

When a *particular* MIA is concerned, the above gives a one-way implication as

$$\text{for any } \text{MIA } (D, z, \mathcal{A}, \phi, \alpha, \beta), \quad \{\epsilon \leq \epsilon_0\} \Rightarrow \{(\alpha, \beta) \in \mathcal{R}(\epsilon_0, \delta)\},$$

which leads to

$$P(\epsilon \leq \epsilon_0) \leq P[(\alpha, \beta) \in \mathcal{R}(\epsilon_0, \delta)]. \tag{4}$$

Replacing the inequality in (4) with equality is equivalent to taking $s = 1$, which would be valid only when the LRT is applied exactly *and* on the worst-case challenge base (D, z), which is typically not guaranteed in practice. In the absence of that strong condition, $s = 1$ leads to early saturation of the cdf $P(\epsilon \leq \epsilon_0)$ vs ϵ_0 and results in overconfident (credible) intervals for ϵ_0. Section 4.1 numerically demonstrates the effect of s in privacy estimation.

Remark 3 (Dependent challenge bases and MIAs). In (2), the MIA performances are assumed conditionally independent given ϵ, δ. Statistical dependency can exist among the MIAs depending on how they are designed. Dependency can occur, for example, when a group of MIAs have distinct Ds but the *same* z point, or they have a common challenge base (D, z) but differ in their decision rules. Dependent MIAs can also be incorporated into the statistical model. Section 3 of the Supplementary File contains a modeling approach for dependent MIAs.

Priors for Privacy and Attack Strengths: We assume a fixed δ and estimate ϵ (and s). For the priors of ϵ and s, we consider a one-sided normal distribution $\epsilon \sim \mathcal{N}_{[0,\infty)}(0, \sigma_\epsilon^2)$ and $s \sim \text{Beta}(a, b)$ independently, with $\sigma_\epsilon^2 > 0$ and $a, b > 0$.

Joint Probability Distribution: Finally, the overall joint probability distribution of $\epsilon, s, \alpha_{1:n}, \beta_{1:n}, X_{1:n}, Y_{1:n}$ can be written as

$$p_\delta(\epsilon, s, \alpha_{1:n}, \beta_{1:n}, X_{1:n}, Y_{1:n}) = p(\epsilon)p(s) \prod_{i=1}^{n} p_\delta(\alpha_i, \beta_i | \epsilon, s) g(X_i, Y_i | \alpha_i, \beta_i). \tag{5}$$

Figure 1 shows the hierarchical structure according to (5) (bottom left) and an example realization of the variables in the model (bottom right).

2.2 Estimating Privacy via MCMC

Algorithm 1 shows the MCMC method for the *joint posterior distribution*

$$p_\delta(\epsilon, s, \alpha_{1:n}, \beta_{1:n} | X_{1:n}, Y_{1:n}) \propto p_\delta(\epsilon, s, \alpha_{1:n}, \beta_{1:n}, X_{1:n}, Y_{1:n}). \tag{6}$$

We call this method MCMC-DP-Est. Although MCMC-DP-Est iterates for $(\epsilon, s, \alpha_{1:n}, \beta_{1:n})$, the ϵ (or (ϵ, s))-component of the samples can be used to estimate the marginal posterior of ϵ (or (ϵ, s)). MCMC-DP-Est is a variant of the

Algorithm 1: MCMC-DP-Est: posterior sampling for (ϵ, s)

Input: M: Number of MCMC iterations,
$(\epsilon^{(0)}, s^{(0)})$: Initial values;
$X_{1:n}, N_{0,1:n}, Y_{1:n}, N_{1,1:n}$: FP and FN counts for each challenge base and numbers of challenges under H_0, H_1 for each challenge base;
$\sigma_{q,\epsilon}^2, \sigma_{s,\epsilon}^2$: Proposal variances for $\log \epsilon$ and s;
K: Number of auxiliary variables in one iteration of MCMC.
Output: Samples $\epsilon^{(i)}, s^{(i)}, i = 1, \ldots, M$ from $p_\delta(\epsilon, s, \alpha_{1:n}, \beta_{1:n} | X_{1:n}, Y_{1:n})$
for $i = 1 : M$ **do**
$\quad$ Draw the proposal $\epsilon' \sim \log \mathcal{N}(\log \epsilon, \sigma_{q,\epsilon}^2)$ and $s' \sim \mathcal{N}(s, \sigma_{q,s}^2)$.
$\quad$ **for** $j = 1 : n$ **do**
$\quad\quad$ Set $(\alpha_j^{(1)}, \beta_j^{(1)}) = (\alpha_j, \beta_j)$.
$\quad\quad$ Sample $\alpha_j^{(k)}, \beta_j^{(k)} \stackrel{\text{iid}}{\sim} \text{Unif}(0,1)$ for $k = 2, \ldots, K$.
$\quad\quad$ Calculate the weights
$$w_j^{(k)} = p_\delta(\alpha_j^{(k)}, \beta_j^{(k)} | \epsilon, s) g(X_j, Y_j | \alpha_j^{(k)}, \beta_j^{(k)}), \quad k = 1, \ldots, K$$
$$w_j'^{(k)} = p_\delta(\alpha_j^{(k)}, \beta_j^{(k)} | \epsilon', s') g(X_j, Y_j | \alpha_j^{(k)}, \beta_j^{(k)}) \quad k = 1, \ldots, K$$
$\quad$ Acceptance probability:
$$A = \min\left\{ 1, \frac{p(s')p(\epsilon')\epsilon'}{p(s)p(\epsilon)\epsilon} \prod_{j=1}^n \frac{\sum_{k=1}^K w_j'^{(k)}}{\sum_{k=1}^K w_j^{(k)}} \right\}.$$
$\quad$ **Accept/Reject:** Draw $u \sim \text{Unif}(0,1)$.
$\quad$ **if** $u \leq A$ **then**
$\quad\quad$ Set $\epsilon = \epsilon', s = s'$, and $\bar{w}_{1:n}^{(1:K)} = w_{1:n}'^{(1:K)}$.
$\quad$ **else**
$\quad\quad$ Keep ϵ, s and set $\bar{w}_{1:n}^{(1:K)} = w_{1:n}^{(1:K)}$.
$\quad$ **for** $j = 1, \ldots, n$ **do**
$\quad\quad$ Sample $k \in \{1, \ldots, K\}$ w.p. $\propto \bar{w}_j^{(k)}$ and set $(\alpha_j, \beta_j) = (\alpha_j^{(k)}, \beta_j^{(k)})$.
$\quad$ Store $\epsilon^{(i)} = \epsilon, s^{(i)} = s$.

MHAAR (Metropolis-Hastings with averaged acceptance ratios) methodology in [3] developed for latent variable models. (Here the latent variables are the $(\alpha_{1:n}, \beta_{1:n})$.) MCMC-DP-Est has $\mathcal{O}(Kn)$ complexity per iteration. We state the correctness of MCMC-DP-Est in the following proposition. A proof is given in Sect. 1 of the Supplementary File and contains a strong allusion to [3].

Proposition 1. *For any $K > 1$, $\sigma_{q,\epsilon}^2$, and $\sigma_{q,s}^2$, MCMC-DP-Est in Algorithm 1 targets exactly the posterior distribution in (6), in the sense that it simulates an ergodic Markov chain whose invariant distribution is (6).*

3 The MIA Attack and Measuring its Performance

In this section, we describe the MIA used in our experiments and equip it with an experimental design to measure its performance computationally efficiently.

3.1 The MIA Design

The test statistic of LRT, the most powerful test, is the ratio of likelihoods $p_\mathcal{A}(\theta|D)/p_\mathcal{A}(\theta|D\cup\{z\})$. However, the likelihoods are usually intractable due to $\mathcal{A}$'s complex structure; therefore, approximations are sought. Loss-based attacks are a common way of approximating the LRT [6, 26, 29, 30]. In particular, we consider a parametric version LiRA [6], a loss-based attack that uses the ratio $p_L(\ell^*|H_0)/p_L(\ell^*|H_1)$ evaluated at $\ell^* = L(z,\theta)$. The outline of a loss-based MIA is given in Algorithm 2. The densities $p_L(\cdot|H_i)$ can be approximated via $M_i > 1$ shadow models $\theta_i^{(1)}, \ldots, \theta_i^{(N)}$ generated under H_i and fitting a distribution $p_L(\cdot|H_i)$ to the losses $L(z,\theta_i^{(1)}), \ldots L(z,\theta_i^{(M_i)})$. Finally, the critical region to choose H_1 is set $\{p_L(\ell|H_0)/p_L(\ell|H_1) < \tau\}$ and τ is adjusted to have a desired target type I error probability α^*.

Algorithm 2: $b = \text{MIA}(\theta, D, z, \mathcal{A}, M_0, M_1, \alpha^*)$

for $j = 1, \ldots, M_0$ do
| Obtain $\theta_0^{(j)} \sim \mathcal{A}(D)$, calculate $\ell_0^{(j)} = L(z, \theta_0^{(j)})$
for $j = 1, \ldots, M_1$ do
| Obtain $\theta_1^{(j)} \sim \mathcal{A}(D \cup \{z\})$, calculate $\ell_1^{(j)} = L(z, \theta_1^{(j)})$.
return $b = \text{LearnAndDecide}(D, z, \theta, \alpha^*, \{\ell_0^{(j)}\}_{j=1}^{M_0}, \{\ell_1^{(j)}\}_{j=1}^{M_1})$

Algorithm 3: $\text{LearnAndDecide}(D, z, \theta, \alpha^*, \{\ell_0^{(j)}\}_{j=1}^{M_0}, \{\ell_1^{(j)}\}_{j=1}^{M_1})$

for $i = 0, 1$ do   // Learn H_0 and H_1
| Fit normal distributions for H_i as
$\mu_i = \frac{1}{M_i}\sum_{j=1}^{M_i} \ell_i^{(j)}$, $\sigma_i^2 = \frac{1}{M_i-1}\sum_{j=1}^{M_i}(\ell_i^{(j)} - \mu_i)^2$
Calculate $\ell^* = L(z, \theta)$.   // Compute ℓ^*, R and the decision
Calculate $R = \frac{\mu_0/\sigma_0^2 - \mu_1/\sigma_1^2}{1/\sigma_0^2 - 1/\sigma_1^2}$ and $\delta = \frac{\mu_0}{\sigma_0} + \frac{1}{\sigma_0}R$
return Decision

$$b = \begin{cases} 1 & \text{if } (\ell^* + R)^2 \leq \sigma_0^2 F^{-1}_{1,\delta^2}(\alpha^*) \text{ and } \sigma_0^2 > \sigma_1^2, \\ 1 & \text{if } (\ell^* + R)^2 \geq \sigma_0^2 F^{-1}_{1,\delta^2}(1-\alpha^*) \text{ and } \sigma_0^2 < \sigma_1^2, \\ 0 & \text{otherwise.} \end{cases}$$

where $F^{-1}_{d,\delta^2}(u)$ is the inverse cdf of χ^2_{d,δ^2}, the non-central χ^2 dist. with noncentrality parameter δ^2 and degrees of freedom d, evaluated at u.

Learning H_0 and H_1 and deciding: Algorithm 3 describes how we learn the distributions under both hypotheses and apply a decision. Firstly, for each $i = 0, 1$ we fit a normal distribution $\mathcal{N}(\mu_i, \sigma_i^2)$ using the sample $\ell_i^{(1:M_i)}$, where $\ell_i^{(j)} = L(z, \theta_i^{(j)})$. Then, LRT is applied to decide between $H_0 : \ell \sim \mathcal{N}(\mu_0, \sigma_0^2)$ and $H_1 : \ell \sim \mathcal{N}(\mu_1, \sigma_1^2)$ with a target type I error probability of α^*.

3.2 Measuring the Performance of the MIA

When the primary goal of using MIA is to audit the privacy of an algorithm, one needs to perform the attack multiple times to estimate its type I and type II error probabilities. A direct way to do this is Algorithm 4, where the MIA is simply run N_0 and N_1 times, each with an independent output θ and independent sets of M_0, M_1 shadow models for H_0, H_1. The cost of this procedure is proportional to $(N_0 + N_1)(M_0 + M_1)$, which can be prohibitive.

Algorithm 4: MeasureMIA$(\mathcal{A}, D, z, N_0, N_1, M_0, M_1)$

Set $D_0 = D \setminus \{z\}$ and $D_1 = D \cup \{z\}$.
for $i = 0, 1$ **do**
 for $j = 1, \ldots, N_i$ **do**
  Train D_i and output $\theta \sim \mathcal{A}(D_i)$.
  Decide according to $\hat{d}_i^{(j)} = \text{MIA}(\theta, D, z, \mathcal{A}, M_0, M_1)$.
return $X = \sum_{j=1}^{N_0} d_0^{(j)}$, $Y = \sum_{j=1}^{N_1} 1 - d_1^{(j)}$

We present a cheaper alternative to Algorithm 4, in which N models are trained from H_0 and H_1 and *cross-feed* each other as shadow models. For each $i = 0, 1$ and $j = 1, \ldots, N$, the triple $(D, z, \theta_i^{(j)})$ is taken as the input of MIA and the rest $\{\theta_i^{(1:N)-j}, \theta_{1-i}^{(1:N)}\}$ are used as the shadow models. This is presented in Algorithm 5.

Although the decisions obtained with Algorithm 4 are independent (given the true α, β of the MIA), those obtained with Algorithm 5 are *not* independent; they are correlated due to using the same set of shadow models. As a result, the Binomial distributions (1) no longer hold for X_i, Y_i pairs obtained from Algorithm 5. One can incorporate that into the joint distribution by taking the conditional distributions of X_i, Y_i given α, β as correlated Binomial distributions [17]. An alternative, which is pursued here, is to use a *bivariate normal approximation* for (X_i, Y_i) as

$$\mathcal{N}\left(\begin{bmatrix} N\alpha_i \\ N\beta_i \end{bmatrix}, \begin{bmatrix} \alpha_i(1-\alpha_i)(N + N(N-1)\tau) & N^2\rho\sqrt{\alpha_i(1-\alpha_i)\beta_i(1-\beta_i)} \\ N^2\rho\sqrt{\alpha_i(1-\alpha_i)\beta_i(1-\beta_i)} & \beta_i(1-\beta_i)(N + N(N-1)\tau) \end{bmatrix}\right). \quad (7)$$

The parameters τ, ρ can be estimated jointly with ϵ, s by slightly modifying MCMC-DP-Est. The details of this extension are given in Sect. 2 of the Supplementary File.

Algorithm 5: MeasureMIAFast$(\mathcal{A}, D, z, N, \alpha^*)$

Set $D_0 = D$ and $D_1 = D \cup \{z\}$.
for $i = 0, 1$ do // N correlated attacks for D_0 vs D_1
$\quad$ for $j = 1, \ldots, N$ do
$\quad\quad$ Obtain $\theta_i^{(j)} \sim \mathcal{A}(D_i)$ and calculate the loss $\ell_i^{(j)} = L(z, \theta_i^{(j)})$
for $j = 1, \ldots, N$ do // Decisions

$$d_0^{(j)} = \text{LearnAndDecide}(D, z, \theta_0^{(j)}, \alpha^*, \{\ell_0^{(i)}\}_{i=1, i \neq j}^N, \{\ell_1^{(i)}\}_{i=1}^N)$$

$$d_1^{(j)} = \text{LearnAndDecide}(D, z, \theta_1^{(j)}, \alpha^*, \{\ell_0^{(i)}\}_{i=1}^N, \{\ell_1^{(i)}\}_{i=1, i \neq j}^N)$$

return $X = \sum_{j=1}^N d_0^{(j)}, Y = \sum_{j=1}^N 1 - d_1^{(j)}$

---

4 Experiments

The code to replicate all the experiments in the section can be downloaded at https://github.com/cerenyildirim/MCMC_for_Bayesian_estimation.

4.1 Privacy Estimation with Artificial Test Performance Results

Role of s in Privacy Estimation: This experiment is designed to show the effect of the prior specification for the attack strength. For simplicity, we took $n = 1$ and focused on $N_{0,1} = N_{1,1} = N > 1$ instances of a single attack. Also, we set $X = 0.4 \times N$ and $Y = 0.4 \times N$ to imitate an attack with $\alpha = \beta = 0.4$. We ran MCMC-DP-Est in Algorithm 1 with varying values of s that are seen on the x-axis of the left plot in Fig. 2. The conditional distribution $g(X_i, Y_i | \alpha_i, \beta_i)$ is set to (1). The 90% credible interval (CI) for ϵ for each run (different s) by computing the 5%- and 95%- empirical quartiles obtained from the last 10^6 samples of the MCMC algorithm (discarding the first 10^5 samples). A dramatic change is visible in the CI width as a function of s. CIs as narrow as those reported in [31] with the same observations are obtained when $s \geq 0.9$. However, CIs are significantly wider for smaller (and arguably more realistic) values of s. Those results indicate the critical role of s, hence the importance of its estimation when it is unknown.

Estimating ϵ and s: Here we show how MCMC-DP-Est estimates ϵ and s jointly from multiple attack results in different scenarios. We took $n = 10$ and $N_{0,i} = N_{1,i} = 1000$ for all $i = 1, \ldots, n$. We considered two scenarios.

- In the first scenario, we made the test strengths evenly spread over $\mathcal{R}(\epsilon, \delta)$ by generating $\alpha_i, \beta_i \overset{\text{iid}}{\sim} \text{Beta}(10, 10)$, for $i = 1, \ldots, n$. The counts X_i, Y_i were drawn as $X_i \overset{\text{iid}}{\sim} \text{Binom}(N_{0,1}, \alpha_i), Y_i \overset{\text{iid}}{\sim} \text{Binom}(N_{0,1}, \beta_i)$, independently.

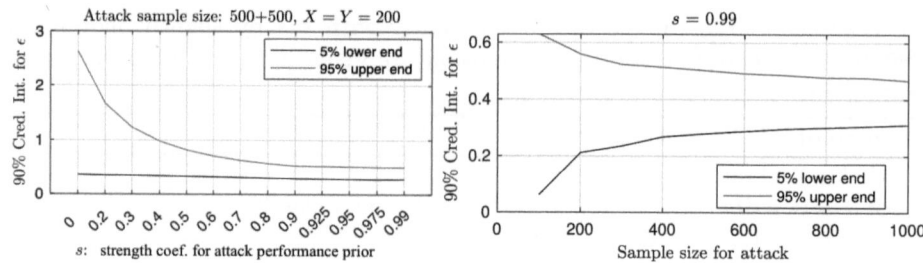

Fig. 2. Left: 90% CI for ϵ vs s. Right: 90% CI for ϵ vs N.

- In the second, we assumed relatively accurate attacks as

$$\begin{array}{c|cccccccccc} X_{1:10} & 40 & 50 & 60 & 100 & 100 & 110 & 120 & 200 & 200 & 200 \\ \hline Y_{1:10} & 250 & 200 & 150 & 100 & 120 & 100 & 100 & 80 & 70 & 60 \end{array}.$$

The observed error rates $(X_i/N_{0,i}, Y_i/N_{1,i})$ are shown on the left-most plot in Fig. 3. Algorithm 1 was run to obtain 10^6 samples from $p(\epsilon, s|X_{1:n}, Y_{1:n})$. As previously, $g(X_i, Y_i|\alpha_i, \beta_i)$ is set to (1). The results in Fig. 3 indicate that our method can accurately estimate the attack strengths and ϵ together.

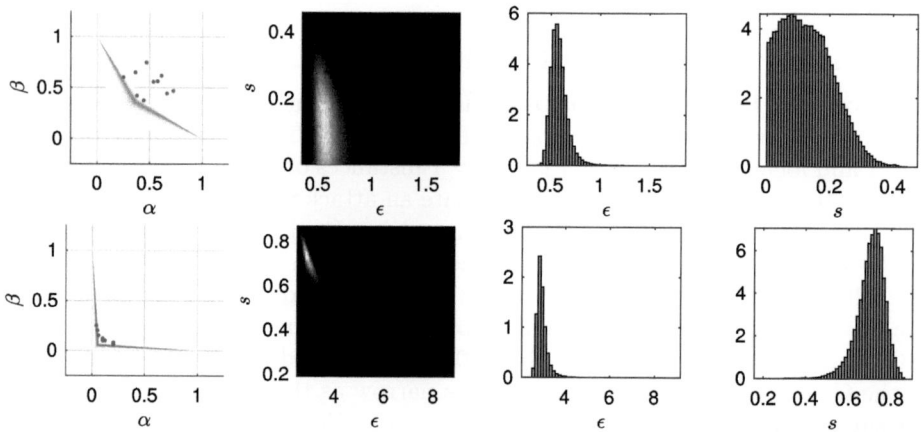

Fig. 3. Posterior distributions for ϵ, s from multiple attacks. **Top:** Weak attacks. **Bottom:** Strong attacks. The gray area in left-most plots are "histograms" of ϵ for the test according to the posterior distribution of ϵ (the symmetric counterpart is omitted).

4.2 Experiments with Real Data

We considered the MNIST dataset as the population, which contains 60,000 training examples [8]. Each example in the set contains a 28 × 28-pixel image and an associated categorical label in $\{0,\ldots,9\}$. In the experiments, we construct D with a size of 999 (to avoid too small batches while training $D \cup \{z\}$). We generated $n = 20$ challenge bases and for each challenge base, we generated $N = 100$ challenges. Those challenges are also used as shadow models in a cross-feeding fashion, as described in Sect. 3.2.

Training Algorithms and Attacks: For $\mathcal{A}$, we considered a fully connected neural network with one hidden layer having 128 nodes and ReLU as its activation function. Meanwhile, the activation function of the output layer is softmax. We set the loss function $L(z, \theta)$ as categorical cross-entropy. To train the models, we use Keras and TensorFlow libraries [1,7]. For the optimizer, we use SGD with the momentum parameter 0.9 and learning rate 0.01.

We consider black-box auditing of four choices for $\mathcal{A}$ to audit their privacy. The algorithms differ based on the initialization and output perturbation: ($\mathcal{A}_1$): fixed initial, no output perturbation; ($\mathcal{A}_2$): random initialization, no output perturbation; ($\mathcal{A}_3$): fixed initial, output perturbation. ($\mathcal{A}_4$): random initialization, output perturbation. Output perturbation is performed by adding i.i.d. noise from $\mathcal{N}(0, \sigma^2)$ to components of the trained model and releasing the noisy model. All algorithms are run for 200 epochs with a minibatch size of 100.

Attack Performances and Privacy Estimation: The attack performance of the MIA in Sect. 3 on the outputs of $\mathcal{A}_{1:4}$ are shown in Fig. 4. The error counts are obtained with the procedure in Algorithm 5 run for each algorithm. The algorithms with output perturbation used $\sigma = 0.1$. In each plot, each dot is a value $(X_i(\alpha^*), Y_i(\alpha^*))$, where α^* is the target type I error for the MIA. For the same challenge base (D_i, z_i), several points $(X_i(\alpha^*), Y_i(\alpha^*))$ are obtained by using the $\alpha^* \in \{0.01, 0.02, \ldots, 0.99\}$, and those points are joined by a line.

We observe that the random initialization affects the performance of the attacks visibly when output perturbation is not used ($\mathcal{A}_1$ vs $\mathcal{A}_2$). However, the effect of random initialization significantly drops when output perturbation is used. We also see that some challenge bases (D_i, z_i) allow significantly better detection than others. This is expected since the challenge bases are drawn at random. Strategies to craft worst-case scenarios [23] can be used to eliminate those challenge bases for which the error lines are close to the $x + y = 1$ line.

We turn to privacy estimation. We choose a single (X, Y) point for each challenge base to feed MCMC-DP-Est in Algorithm 1 with $n = 20$ observations; those points are $(X_i(0.1), Y_i(0.1))$ for each $i = 1, \ldots, 20$. MCMC-DP-Est is run with $K = 1000$ auxiliary variables for 10^5 iterations, and the first 10^4 samples are discarded as burn-in. We used $\epsilon \sim \log \mathcal{N}_{[0,\infty)}(0, 10)$, one-sided normal distribution, and $s \sim \text{Unif}(0, 1) = \text{Beta}(1, 1)$ for the priors of ϵ and s. For $g(X_i, Y_i | \alpha_i, \beta_i)$, a bivariate normal approximation in (7) is used to account for the dependency among the decisions produced by Algorithm 5. The two additional parameters τ, ρ are estimated within MCMC-DP-Est, as described in Sect. 2 of the Supplementary File.

The 2D histograms at the bottom row of Fig. 4 are the posterior distributions of (ϵ, s) constructed from the samples provided by MCMC-DP-Est. The estimates of (ϵ, s) are as expected (e.g., randomness decreases ϵ) and are consistent with the attack performances. The estimates for s suggest that with more randomness in training, either the loss-based attack loses its power (relative to the best theoretical attack) or some challenge bases are no longer informative.

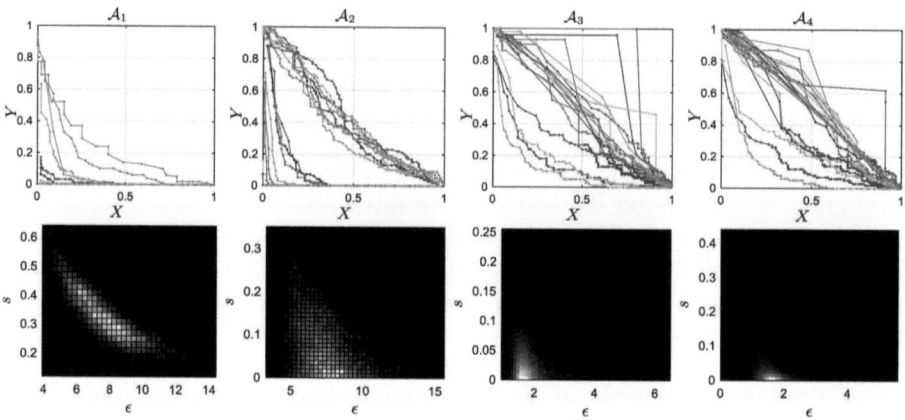

Fig. 4. (X, Y) counts for $\mathcal{A}_1, \ldots, \mathcal{A}_4$. For output perturbation, $\sigma = 0.1$ was used.

We repeat the experiments for $\mathcal{A}_4$ with $\sigma \in \{0.01, 0.05, 0.1\}$ for the output perturbation noise. Figure 5 shows that, as expected, increasing noise makes the attacks less accurate, which in turn causes smaller estimates for ϵ.

The estimates of MCMC-DP-Est across the audited algorithms are summarized in Table 1 with 90% CIs for ϵ. Figure 6 shows the sample autocorrelation functions (ACF) for ϵ-samples of all the runs of MCMC-DP-Est. The fast-decaying ACFs indicate a healthy (fast-mixing) chain. For further diagnosis, we also provide the trace plots of the samples for ϵ, s, τ, ρ in Sect. 2 of the Supplementary File.

Table 1. 90% Credible intervals for ϵ

	$\mathcal{A}_1$	$\mathcal{A}_2$	$\mathcal{A}_3$ ($\sigma = 0.1$)	$\mathcal{A}_4$ ($\sigma = 0.1$)	$\mathcal{A}_4$ ($\sigma = 0.05$)	$\mathcal{A}_4$ ($\sigma = 0.01$)
Lower	5.52	4.95	1.29	1.00	2.80	4.61
Upper	10.52	10.00	2.53	2.12	7.68	9.62

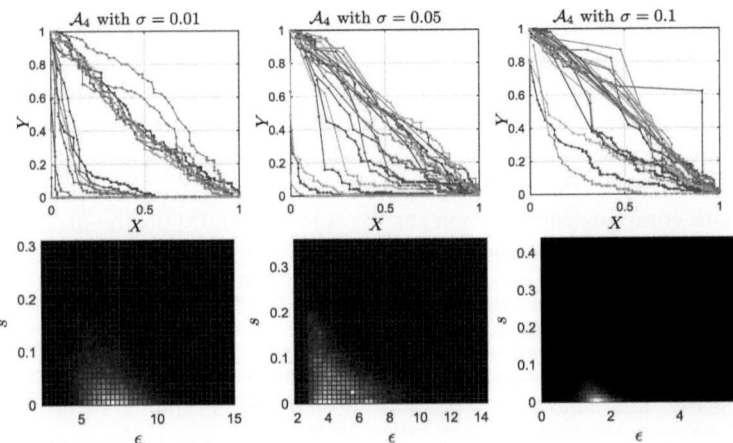

Fig. 5. Error counts and privacy estimation for $\mathcal{A}_4$ with $\sigma \in [0.01, 0.05, 0.1]$.

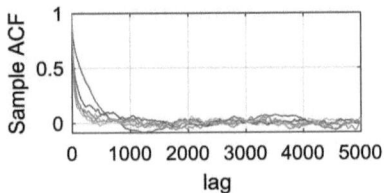

Fig. 6. Sample ACFs for the six algorithms in Table 1.

5 Conclusion

In this work, we proposed a novel method for Bayesian estimation of differential privacy. Our algorithm leverages multiple (D, z) pairs and attacks to refine the privacy estimates and makes no assumptions about the strength of the attacks to avoid overconfident estimations. Beyond just credible intervals, the method provides the entire posterior distribution of the privacy parameter (as well as the average attack strength). Our experiments demonstrated that we can effectively estimate the privacy parameters of models trained under various randomness assumptions and that the resulting estimates align with attack performances.

We considered the "inclusion" versions of DP and MIAs where the pair of datasets differ by the inclusion/exclusion of a single point. The methodology similarly applies to the "replace" versions where dataset pairs are $D \cup \{z\}$ and $D \cup \{z'\}$ for a pair of z, z'.

In the real data experiments in Sect. 4.2, a single run of MCMC-DP-Est took ≈ 2.5 minutes on Matlab on a modern laptop, which is negligibly small compared to the time needed to collect the error counts. This suggests that MCMC-DP-Est can feasibly be used several times to estimate ϵ at different values of δ.

Limitations and Future Work: Given a challenge base (D, z), our statistical model considers the error counts for a single target value of type I error (i.e., a single point on each line of a plot in Fig. 4). As suggested by [6], MIA performance tests would be utilized more effectively by using false negative and false positive counts at all decision thresholds to estimate its *profile function* $f(\alpha)$. Likewise, rather than (ϵ, δ)-DP, the f-DP [9] of $\mathcal{A}$ could be estimated as in [18, 22], since f-DP has more complete information setting a lower bound on the profile functions of MIAs. Both extensions require prior specifications for random functions (e.g. *a la* Gaussian process priors), which we consider an important avenue for future work.

Acknowledgments. This work was supported by the European Union's Horizon Europe research and innovation program through the Twinning Project (enCRYPTON) under Grant 101079319 and the PHASE IV AI Project under Grant 101095384. This work is funded by the European Union. Views and opinions expressed are however those of the author(s) only and do not necessarily reflect those of the European Union. Neither the European Union nor the granting authority can be held responsible for them.

Disclosure of Interests. The authors have no competing interests to declare that are relevant to the content of this article.

References

1. Abadi, M., et al.: TensorFlow: large-scale machine learning on heterogeneous systems (2015). https://www.tensorflow.org/, software available from tensorflow.org
2. Andrew, G., Kairouz, P., Oh, S., Oprea, A., McMahan, H.B., Suriyakumar, V.M.: One-shot empirical privacy estimation for federated learning. In: 12th International Conference on Learning Representation (2024)
3. Andrieu, C., Yıldırım, S., Doucet, A., Chopin, N.: Metropolis-hastings with averaged acceptance ratios (2020). https://arxiv.org/abs/2101.01253
4. Balle, B., Barthe, G., Gaboardi, M.: Privacy amplification by subsampling: tight analyses via couplings and divergences. In: Proceedings of the 32nd International Conference on Neural Information Processing Systems, NIPS 2018, , pp. 6280–6290. Curran Associates Inc., Red Hook (2018)
5. Bun, M., Steinke, T.: Concentrated differential privacy: simplifications, extensions, and lower bounds. In: Hirt, M., Smith, A. (eds.) TCC 2016. LNCS, vol. 9985, pp. 635–658. Springer, Heidelberg (2016). https://doi.org/10.1007/978-3-662-53641-4_24
6. Carlini, N., Chien, S., Nasr, M., Song, S., Terzis, A., Tramèr, F.: Membership inference attacks from first principles. In: 2022 IEEE Symposium on Security and Privacy (SP), pp. 1897–1914 (2022)
7. Chollet, F., et al.: Keras (2015). https://keras.io
8. Deng, L.: The MNIST database of handwritten digit images for machine learning research. IEEE Signal Process. Mag. **29**(6), 141–142 (2012)

9. Dong, J., Roth, A., Su, W.J.: Gaussian differential privacy. J. Roy. Stat. Society Ser. B: Stat. Methodol. **84**(1), 3–37 (2022)
10. Dwork, C.: Differential privacy. In: Bugliesi, M., Preneel, B., Sassone, V., Wegener, I. (eds.) ICALP 2006. LNCS, vol. 4052, pp. 1–12. Springer, Heidelberg (2006). https://doi.org/10.1007/11787006_1
11. Dwork, C., McSherry, F., Nissim, K., Smith, A.: Calibrating noise to sensitivity in private data analysis. In: Halevi, S., Rabin, T. (eds.) TCC 2006. LNCS, vol. 3876, pp. 265–284. Springer, Heidelberg (2006). https://doi.org/10.1007/11681878_14
12. Dwork, C., Roth, A.: The algorithmic foundations of differential privacy. Found. Trends® Theor. Comput. Sci. **9**(3–4), 211–407 (2014)
13. Hyland, S.L., Tople, S.: An empirical study on the intrinsic privacy of SGD (2022). https://arxiv.org/abs/1912.02919
14. Jagielski, M., Ullman, J., Oprea, A.: Auditing differentially private machine learning: how private is private SGD? In: Proceedings of the 34th International Conference on Neural Information Processing Systems, NIPS 2020. Curran Associates Inc., Red Hook (2020)
15. Kairouz, P., Oh, S., Viswanath, P.: The composition theorem for differential privacy. In: Bach, F., Blei, D. (eds.) Proceedings of the 32nd International Conference on Machine Learning. Proceedings of Machine Learning Research, vol. 37, pp. 1376–1385. PMLR, Lille (2015)
16. Kairouz, P., Oh, S., Viswanath, P.: The composition theorem for differential privacy. IEEE Trans. Inf. Theor. **63**(6), 4037–4049 (2017)
17. Kupper, L.L., Haseman, J.K.: The use of a correlated binomial model for the analysis of certain toxicological experiments. Biometrics **34**(1), 69–76 (1978)
18. Leemann, T., Pawelczyk, M., Kasneci, G.: Gaussian membership inference privacy. In: Thirty-seventh Conference on Neural Information Processing Systems (2023)
19. Lu, F., et al.: A general framework for auditing differentially private machine learning. In: Oh, A.H., Agarwal, A., Belgrave, D., Cho, K. (eds.) Advances in Neural Information Processing Systems (2022)
20. Maddock, S., Sablayrolles, A., Stock, P.: CANIFE: crafting canaries for empirical privacy measurement in federated learning. In: ICLR (2023)
21. Mironov, I.: Rényi differential privacy . In: 2017 IEEE 30th Computer Security Foundations Symposium (CSF), pp. 263–275. IEEE Computer Society, Los Alamitos (2017). https://doi.org/10.1109/CSF.2017.11
22. Nasr, M., et al.: Tight auditing of differentially private machine learning. In: Proceedings of the 32nd USENIX Conference on Security Symposium, SEC 2023. USENIX, USA (2023)
23. Nasr, M., Songi, S., Thakurta, A., Papernot, N., Carlin, N.: Adversary instantiation: lower bounds for differentially private machine learning. In: 2021 IEEE Symposium on security and privacy (SP), pp. 866–882. IEEE (2021)
24. Nasr, M., et al.: The last iterate advantage: empirical auditing and principled heuristic analysis of differentially private SGD. In: The 13th International Conference on Learning Representation (2025)
25. Pillutla, K., Andrew, G., Kairouz, P., McMahan, H.B., Oprea, A., Oh, S.: Unleashing the power of randomization in auditing differentially private ml. In: Proceedings of the 37th International Conference on Neural Information Processing Systems, NIPS 2023. Curran Associates Inc., Red Hook (2023)
26. Sablayrolles, A., Douze, M., Schmid, C., Ollivier, Y., Jégou, H.: White-box vs black-box: bayes optimal strategies for membership inference. In: International Conference on Machine Learning (2019)

27. Shokri, R., Stronati, M., Song, C., Shmatikov, V.: Membership inference attacks against machine learning models. In: 2017 IEEE Symposium on Security and Privacy (SP), pp. 3–18. IEEE Computer Society, Los Alamitos (2017). https://doi.org/10.1109/SP.2017.41
28. Steinke, T., Nasr, M., Jagielski, M.: Privacy auditing with one (1) training run. In: Thirty-seventh Conference on Neural Information Processing Systems (2023)
29. Ye, J., Maddi, A., Murakonda, S.K., Bindschaedler, V., Shokri, R.: Enhanced membership inference attacks against machine learning models. In: Proceedings of the 2022 ACM SIGSAC Conference on Computer and Communication Security, CCS 2022, pp. 3093–3106. ACM, New York (2022). https://doi.org/10.1145/3548606.3560675
30. Yeom, S., Giacomelli, I., Fredrikson, M., Jha, S.: Privacy risk in machine learning: analyzing the connection to overfitting . In: 2018 IEEE 31st Computer Security Foundations Symposium (CSF), pp. 268–282. IEEE Computer Society, Los Alamitos (2018). https://doi.org/10.1109/CSF.2018.00027
31. Zanella-Beguelin, S., et al.: Bayesian estimation of differential privacy. In: Proceedings of the 40th International Conference on Machine Learning, vol. 202, pp. 40624–40636. PMLR (2023)

Machine Unlearning for Random Forest via Method of Images

Hang Zhang and Kai Ming Ting[✉]

State Key Laboratory for Novel Software Technology and School of Artificial Intelligence, Nanjing University, Nanjing 210023, China
zhanghang@lamda.nju.edu.cn, tingkm@nju.edu.cn

Abstract. Privacy law can now demand specific training samples, if requested from concerned parties, to be deleted from a trained model. Random forest, an effective and widely used machine learning algorithm, has been the model of study for various machine unlearning techniques. The current unlearning techniques of random forest involve additional processing before model training, so that fast unlearning of some samples can be achieved. However, no algorithm can achieve the unlearning of a trained random forest. This paper proposes a novel algorithm for unlearning a trained random forest. The algorithm employs the method of images to generate image samples of the samples that need to be forgotten and trains a small number of additional decision trees on these image samples. The proposed method, called MUMI, enables efficient unlearning of samples from a trained random forest. Our theorems and experiments show that MUMI achieves fast unlearning in a trained random forest with virtually no loss of model performance.

Keywords: Machine unlearning · Random forest · Method of images

1 Introduction

In recent years, the rapid development of artificial intelligence has brought many conveniences to the lives of humans [9,32,39]. However, technology has always been a double-edged sword. While artificial intelligence improves humans' lives, it also poses challenges to the privacy and security of people [8,26]. For this reason, institutions such as GDPR (General Data Protection Regulation) have enacted laws to protect users' rights to delete their data [20,23,31,33]. After a user's request to delete their data, their data must not only be deleted from the database but also from the machine learning models that have used these data for training. The task of erasing the influence on a trained model, of the samples that have previously been used to train it, is called machine unlearning [2,23].

To comply with legal requirements and address practical needs, many algorithms have been proposed for unlearning different machine learning models, e.g.,

---

Supplementary Information The online version contains supplementary material available at https://doi.org/10.1007/978-3-032-06096-9_24.

decision tree [40], logistic regression [21], Markov chain Monte Carlo [10], or other specific models [1,13,15,24,28]. And some machine unlearning algorithms can be used to unlearn different kinds of models [2,5,7,12,14,16,17,25,27,29,29,36,38]. Random forest is widely used as a model with superior performance and high interpretability [3]. However, since it selects discrete dimensions and thresholds for the tree split each time, it is discontinuous and cannot use gradient information for machine unlearning like logistic regression [21] and neural networks [19]. Random forest ensembles multiple decision trees to improve prediction accuracy and robustness. Each decision tree selects the optimal split attribute and threshold based on the Gini index and entropy. In the process of unlearning, the optimal attribute and threshold may change after deleting some points, and calculating the new optimal attribute and threshold on the entire subtree is complicated. This presents challenges for the unlearning of random forest.

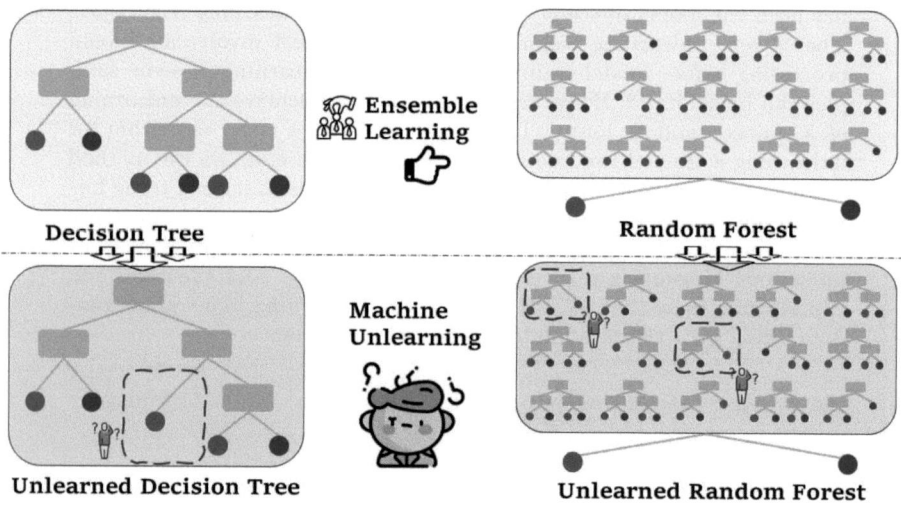

Fig. 1. An illustration of machine unlearning for random forest.

An illustration of machine unlearning for random forest is shown in Fig. 1. Random forest is obtained by ensemble learning of decision trees, each tree is trained on the randomly selected subset of the entire data. When we delete some data, some trees in the random forest need to be revised.

Existing unlearning methods for random forest attempt to pay more cost before training so that unlearning can be achieved at a small cost when required. The DaRE tree [4] constructs random forest by employing randomness at most nodes near the root, where attributes and thresholds are sampled randomly. In contrast, only a few layers close to the leaf nodes are optimized using greedy methods, guided by criterion such as the Gini index or mutual information. This hybrid approach ensures that the tree remains computationally efficient while maintaining accuracy. When samples need to be removed or 'forgotten', only a few layers (subtrees) near the leaf nodes require retraining. This selective retraining reduces the computational overhead and enables rapid unlearning within the random forest, making DaRE a highly efficient solution for scenarios where data removal is necessary. HedgeCut [35] learns an ensemble of randomized decision trees with randomly chosen splits, it classifing nodes into robust and non-robust nodes based on whether they are easily affected by data deletion. For robust nodes, when data is deleted, only the node statistics need to be modified. For non-robust nodes, variant seed trees are prepared in advance, and when data is deleted, variants are used to replace them. Existing methods can only modify the training process before training so as to quickly unlearn the points that need to be deleted, however, **no existing method can achieve fast unlearning of the already trained random forest model currently.**

In this paper, we introduce Machine Unlearning based on Method of Images (MUMI), a novel approach that leverages the method of images [22] to enable unlearning in a trained random forest. Specifically, we generate image samples of the samples that need to be forgotten and construct additional decision trees based on these image samples. By ensemble these additional trees with the already trained random forest, MUMI effectively achieves the unlearning of the target samples while maintaining the classification accuracy.

We summarize our contributions as follows:

1. Introducing the method of images into the machine unlearning task for the first time.
2. Proposing the first machine unlearning algorithm MUMI, based on the method of images, to unlearn a trained random forest.
3. Demonstrating the efficiency and effectiveness of MUMI through experiments on real-world datasets.

2 Related Work

Decision trees [37] are a class of tree-structured models that facilitate binary predictions through a hierarchical decision-making process. Each leaf node represents a final prediction, while each internal node functions as a decision point, associated with a specific attribute and a threshold value. Each decision node partitions the data into branches based on a selected attribute and its threshold. For a given test point $x \in X$, its prediction is determined by traversing the tree from the root node, following the branches that comply with the attribute values, until reaching a leaf node, where the prediction is derived from the leaf's class label. A decision tree is constructed recursively by selecting an attribute and threshold at the root node that optimizes a chosen empirical split criterion. Two commonly used criteria are the Gini index [11] and entropy [34].

Random forest extends decision trees by creating an ensemble of multiple trees to improve prediction accuracy and robustness. The ensemble predicts the average value of its constituent trees. To introduce diversity among the trees, two sources of randomness are employed. First, each tree is trained on a bootstrap sample of the original data, which allows some instances to be excluded or repeated. Second, at each decision node, only a random subset of attributes is considered for splitting, rather than all attributes.

The DaRE [4] tree leverages randomness and caching mechanisms to enhance the efficiency of data removal. In the upper levels of the DaRE tree, random nodes are employed. These nodes uniformly select split attributes and thresholds randomly. As a result, they rarely require updates, since their behavior is largely independent of the underlying data distribution. At the lower levels, splits are determined through a greedy optimization process, targeting criteria such as the Gini index or mutual information. This approach ensures that splits are made in a way that maximizes the purity or information gain of the resulting partitions. To further optimize performance, the DaRE tree caches statistics at each node and stores training data at each leaf. This design allows for selective updates: when data is removed, only the necessary subtrees need to be adjusted, rather than the entire tree. The DaRE tree can effectively trade-off between prediction accuracy and update efficiency.

HedgeCut [35] trains an ensemble of randomized decision trees, where each tree is built using random splits on randomly selected attributes. It continuously manages this ensemble even when some training samples are removed. In some trees, certain splits are non-robust, meaning that the decision to split could change after data removal. To handle this, HedgeCut updates the statistics of leaf labels and maintains alternative subtree structures. If the removal of data would have caused the model to choose a different split, these alternative subtrees are activated to ensure the model remains consistent.

In essence, both DaRE and HedgeCut require additional procedures prior to training the random forest model. These additional steps alter the conventional training process. It can be argued that they do not truly facilitate the unlearning of a random forest in its original form. Instead, they introduce a modified version of the random forest that is more amenable to the unlearning process. Given the inherent structure and training process of a random forest, it appears that there is no feasible method to induce machine unlearning in a trained random forest without fundamentally altering its training process.

3 Method of Images for Unlearning Random Forest

3.1 Method of Images

The method of images is a powerful and elegant technique in classical physics, particularly in the study of electrostatics and gravitational fields [22]. It is based on the principle of superposition and the uniqueness theorem, which states that if a solution to Laplace's equation satisfies the boundary conditions, it is the only possible solution.

In electrostatics, the method of image is often used to solve problems involving conductors with complex geometries or boundaries. For example, when dealing with a point charge q in $(0, 0, a)$ near an infinite conducting plane as shown in Fig. 2, instead of solving the complicated boundary value problem directly, we can introduce an image charge $-q$ on the opposite side of the plane $(0, 0, -a)$. This image charge is chosen such that its magnitude and position ensure that the potential on the conducting surface is zero, as required by the boundary

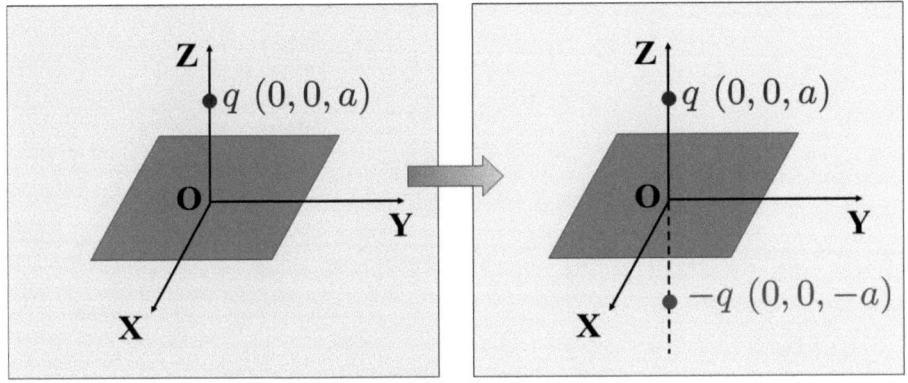

Fig. 2. An example of the method of images.

conditions. By doing so, the problem is simplified to finding the potential due to the (opposite) charges of the two points, which can be easily calculated using Coulomb's law.

3.2 Machine Unlearning Based on Method of Images (MUMI)

The beauty of the method of images lies in its ability to transform a seemingly intractable problem into a much simpler one. After training a machine learning model $A(\mathcal{D})$ using data $\mathcal{D}$, a data subset $\mathcal{D}_f$ is required to be deleted from $A(\mathcal{D})$, and the machine unlearning uses algorithm U to obtain a model $U(A(\mathcal{D}), \mathcal{D}, \mathcal{D}_f)$, which is equivalent to the model $A(\mathcal{D} \setminus \mathcal{D}_f)$ trained from $\mathcal{D} \setminus \mathcal{D}_f$. However, due to the complexity of the model (such as random forest), it is difficult to obtain $U(A(\mathcal{D}), \mathcal{D}, \mathcal{D}_f)$ without retraining, because the influence of deleting $\mathcal{D}_f$ from $\mathcal{D}$ on the model is difficult to measure. Inspired by the method of images, deleting sample $\mathcal{D}_f = \{X_f, Y_f\}$ from the model $A(\mathcal{D})$, for the purpose of machine unlearning, is equivalent to adding image sample set $\mathcal{D}_f^I = \{X_f, -Y_f\}$ to model $A(\mathcal{D})$ to obtain a new model $\Lambda(A(\mathcal{D}), \mathcal{D}_f)$, in order to offset the information contained in $\mathcal{D}_f$.

An illustration of employing the method of images is shown in Fig. 3. We typically use the orange curve to represent the influence of data $\mathcal{D}$ on model $A(\mathcal{D})$. When we are required to delete a data point $\mathcal{D}_f = \{x, y\}$ (where x is the training sample and y is the corresponding label) from model $A(\mathcal{D})$, directly computing the new influence curve becomes challenging. To address this issue, we can employ a method analogous to the 'Method of Images' in physics. Specifically, we introduce an 'image' data point $(x, -y)$ into the dataset. By considering the influence curve of the augmented dataset $\mathcal{D} \cup \{x, -y\}$, we can approximate the influence curve of the reduced dataset $\mathcal{D} \setminus \{x, y\}$. This approach effectively leverages the symmetry of the influence function, allowing us to bypass the complexity of directly recomputing the influence curve after deletion.

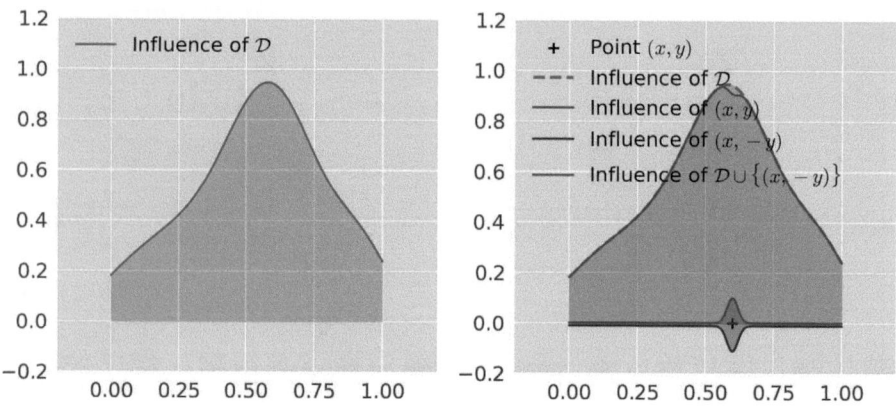

Fig. 3. An illustration of the method of images in machine unlearning. The influence of data $\mathcal{D}$ on model $A(\mathcal{D})$ is shown on the left. The influence of data $\mathcal{D} \setminus \{x, y\}$ is approximated by the method of images is shown on the right.

Algorithm 1. MUMI: $\Lambda(A(\mathcal{D}), \mathcal{D}_f)$

Input: Model $A(\mathcal{D})$, Data to delete $\mathcal{D}_f = \{X_f, Y_f\}$
Output: Model $\Lambda(A(\mathcal{D}), \mathcal{D}_f)$
1: Generate image data: $\mathcal{D}_f^I = \{X_f, -Y_f\}$.
2: Train image decision trees $A(\mathcal{D}_f^I)$ on the image data set $\mathcal{D}_f^I$.
3: Ensemble the original model $A(\mathcal{D})$ and the image model $A(\mathcal{D}_f^I)$ to obtain the unlearned model: $\Lambda(A(\mathcal{D}), \mathcal{D}_f) \leftarrow \text{Ensemble}(A(\mathcal{D}), A(\mathcal{D}_f^I))$.
4: **return** $\Lambda(A(\mathcal{D}), \mathcal{D}_f)$

For the unlearning of random forest, we propose a **M**achine **U**nlearning algorithm based on the **M**ethod of **I**mages (MUMI) as shown in Algorithm 1. Given the model $A(\mathcal{D})$ and the data $\mathcal{D}_f$ that need to be deleted, MUMI first generates the image data $\mathcal{D}_f^I = \{X_f, -Y_f\}$, and then train the decision trees $A(\mathcal{D}_f^I)$ on the image data set $\mathcal{D}_f^I$. Finally, MUMI ensembles the original model (original decision trees) $A(\mathcal{D})$ and the image model (image decision trees) $A(\mathcal{D}_f^I)$ to obtain $\Lambda(A(\mathcal{D}), \mathcal{D}_f)$. By employing the method of images, MUMI achieves data unlearning with significantly reduced computational cost. Specifically, it only requires training on the much smaller image dataset $\mathcal{D}_f^I \ll \mathcal{D}_r (\mathcal{D}_r = \mathcal{D} \setminus \mathcal{D}_f)$. This approach eliminates the need to retrain on the remaining dataset $\mathcal{D}_r$, thereby substantially decreasing the computational resources and time required for the machine unlearning.

In the example illustrated in Fig. 2, the boundary condition is defined by the electric potential of the conductor being zero. Satisfying this boundary condition is a crucial requirement for the method of images to be valid. Similarly, in the context of MUMI, we utilize the performance of the unlearned model on datasets X_r and X_f as the boundary condition. Intuitively, we aim to make the unlearned model to perform well on X_r while deliberately underperforming on X_f. This strategy is based on the assumption that a retrained model (a model that has completely forgotten X_f) would naturally exhibit strong performance on X_r, as it retains the relevant information from X_r, and weaker performance on X_f, since it no longer has access to the information from X_f [7].

Theorem 1. *Let E_r and E_{T+k} denote the generalization errors of the model obtained through retraining and MUMI, respectively. Then:*

$$|E_{T+k} - E_r| \ll E_r.$$

Theorem 1 shows that the generalization error of the model unlearned by MUMI is close to the generalization error of the retrained model. This guarantees that the model has good performance after unlearning.

Theorem 2. *Let $f_{RF}^{(T+k)}(x)$ and y_f denote the predicted label and the true label of x, respectively. The expectation error of the model unlearned by MUMI on $\mathcal{D}_f$ is:*

$$\mathbb{E}_{\{x,y_f\} \in \mathcal{D}_f} |f_{RF}^{(T+k)}(x) - y_f| = \frac{2k}{T+k},$$

where k is the number of image decision trees, T is the number of initial decision trees.

Theorem 2 shows that MUMI can effectively forget $\mathcal{D}_f$. In particular, when $k = T$, the expected error on $\mathcal{D}_f$ is 1. However, in practice, it is not necessary to set k too large, because the expected error on $\mathcal{D}_f$ is not necessarily better when it is smaller [14]. As long as it closely approximates the performance of the retrained model, it is deemed sufficient.

The proofs of Theorem 1 and Theorem 2 are provided in the supplementary materials.

4 Experimental Evaluation

Experimental Aims: We experimentally evaluate whether MUMI has the following three capabilities:

1. Model effectiveness: whether the model maintains good classification accuracy after unlearning.
2. Unlearning efficacy: whether the data is unlearned from the model.
3. Unlearning efficiency: whether the data can be unlearned efficiently.

Datasets: We conduct our experiments on 13 publicly available datasets used in the previous paper [4] that represent problems well-suited for tree-based models. We use the code provided in DaRE [4] to split the data into training and test sets (X_t). For each dataset, we generate one-hot encodings for any categorical variable and leave all numeric and binary variables as is.

Table 1. Summary of the datasets used in the paper.

datasets	n	%pos.	# cat.	# num.	# attr-hot	Met.
Surgical	14,635	25.2	17	7	90	Acc.
Vaccine	21,365	46.6	36	0	185	Acc.
Adult	48,842	23.9	8	5	107	Acc.
Bank Mktg.	41,188	11.3	10	10	63	AUC
Flight Delays	100,000	19	6	2	648	AUC
Diabetes	101,766	46.1	36	7	258	Acc.
No-Show	110,527	20.2	2	15	98	AUC
Olympics	206,165	14.6	8	3	1004	AUC
Census	299,285	6.2	30	6	408	AUC
Credit Card	284,807	0.2	0	29	29	AP
CTR	1,000,000	2.9	0	13	13	Acc.
Synthetic	1,000,000	50	0	40	40	Acc.
Higgs	11,000,000	53	0	28	28	Acc.

∗ n: the number of points, %pos.: positive label percentage.
⋆ # cat.: the number of categorical attributes, # num.: the number of numeric attributes, # attr-hot: the number of one-hot attributes.
† Met.: predictive performance metric.

Evaluation Metrics: To account for the varying degrees of label imbalance in the datasets, we evaluate the predictive performance of models using different metrics based on the proportion of positive labels. Specifically, we use:

1. Average Precision (AP) [41] for datasets with a positive label percentage of less than 1%.
2. Area Under the ROC Curve (AUC) [18] for datasets with a positive label percentage between 1% and 20%.
3. Accuracy (Acc.) for datasets with a positive label percentage exceeding 20%.

This approach allows us to select the most appropriate metric for each dataset, ensuring a fair and meaningful assessment of model performance across different levels of class imbalance.

A summary of the datasets is shown in Table 1, and the details about the datasets are available in supplementary materials.

Comparison Algorithms: we compare MUMI[1] with the Retrain (retrain a model on $\mathcal{D}_r$), DaRE[2] and HedgeCut[3].

---
[1] MUMI: https://anonymous.4open.science/r/MUMI-8A0A.
[2] DaRE: https://github.com/jjbrophy47/dare_rf.
[3] HedgeCut: https://github.com/schelterlabs/hedgecut.

More details about experimental settings, such as the random forest model used and the parameter settings, are given in the supplementary materials.

4.1 Model Effectiveness and Unlearning Efficacy

For each dataset, we report the scores of the unlearned model on the X_t (model effectiveness) and X_f (unlearning efficacy). We evaluate the performance of MUMI when unlearning 10, 100, 1,000, and $0.1\% \times n$ samples, with the results presented in Tables 2, 3, 4, and 5, respectively.

Table 2. The results of unlearning 10 samples.

Dataset	X_t (↑)				X_f (↓)			
	Retrain	DaRE	HedgeCut	MUMI	Retrain	DaRE	HedgeCut	MUMI
Surgical	0.932	0.917	0.724	**0.939**	0.800	0.700	**0.600**	0.700
Vaccine	0.921	0.902	0.783	**0.922**	0.800	0.900	**0.800**	**0.800**
Adult	**0.885**	0.858	0.835	**0.885**	0.900	0.900	0.900	0.900
Bank Mktg.	0.990	0.990	0.786	**0.991**	1.000	1.000	**0.000**	1.000
Flight Delays	0.800	**0.836**	0.722	0.796	0.875	**0.375**	0.438	0.875
Diabetes	0.713	0.667	0.605	**0.714**	0.800	0.800	**0.700**	0.800
No-Show	0.828	**0.865**	0.503	0.826	0.556	**0.444**	**0.444**	0.556
Olympics	0.811	**0.856**	0.525	0.805	1.000	1.000	**0.438**	1.000
Census	**0.962**	0.945	0.500	**0.962**	1.000	1.000	**0.000**	1.000
Credit Card	**0.993**	0.958	N/A	**0.993**	1.000	1.000	N/A	1.000
CTR	0.873	0.696	N/A	**0.875**	0.556	0.778	N/A	**0.444**
Synthetic	0.941	0.842	0.845	**0.942**	1.000	0.800	**0.600**	1.000
Higgs	**0.744**	0.678	N/A	0.743	**0.700**	**0.700**	N/A	0.743
Average Score	**0.876**	0.847	0.683	**0.876**	0.845	0.800	**0.492**	0.832
Average $|s - s_R|$	–	0.044	0.195	**0.002**	–	0.088	0.381	**0.018**

* N/A means an error occurred during the run or the result could not be output within 12 h.
⋆ s is the scores of algorithms, and the s_R is the scores of Retrain.

In each of 10, 100, 1,000, or $0.1\% \times n$ samples for unlearning, MUMI consistently outperforms other algorithms on X_t and achieves the highest score (see the second row from the bottom 'Average Score' in the table). In contrast, both DaRE and HedgeCut exhibits lower scores compared to retraining. This is attributed to the fact that HedgeCut employs extremely randomized trees, whereas DaRE only optimizes split attributes and thresholds in the layers close to the leaf nodes. This represents the trade-off they have made in order to expedite the machine unlearning process. Only MUMI performs machine unlearning on a standard random forest. Moreover, the average absolute difference score of

Table 3. The results of unlearning 100 samples.

Dataset	X_t (↑)				X_f (↓)			
	Retrain	DaRE	HedgeCut	MUMI	Retrain	DaRE	HedgeCut	MUMI
Surgical	0.933	0.917	0.726	**0.960**	0.830	0.770	**0.740**	0.830
Vaccine	0.923	0.902	0.785	**0.935**	0.800	0.800	**0.780**	**0.780**
Adult	0.885	0.857	0.833	**0.886**	0.840	0.830	**0.800**	0.830
Bank Mktg.	0.991	0.990	0.787	**0.992**	0.960	0.944	**0.489**	0.917
Flight Delays	**0.799**	0.836	0.722	0.796	0.737	0.742	**0.497**	0.682
Diabetes	0.712	0.667	0.610	**0.714**	0.730	0.640	**0.630**	0.730
No-Show	**0.830**	0.864	0.503	0.829	0.626	0.631	**0.494**	0.592
Olympics	0.811	**0.856**	0.527	0.803	0.796	0.813	**0.489**	0.728
Census	**0.963**	0.945	0.500	0.962	0.966	0.933	**0.495**	0.963
Credit Card	**0.994**	0.959	N/A	0.992	1.000	1.000	N/A	1.000
CTR	0.873	0.696	N/A	**0.876**	0.525	0.596	N/A	**0.253**
Synthetic	0.941	0.842	0.841	**0.942**	0.950	**0.800**	0.820	0.950
Higgs	**0.744**	0.678	N/A	0.743	0.790	**0.720**	N/A	0.760
Average Score	0.877	0.847	0.683	**0.879**	0.812	0.786	**0.623**	0.770
Average $|s - s_R|$	–	0.044	0.195	**0.004**	–	0.038	0.200	**0.038**

Table 4. The results of unlearning 1000 samples.

Dataset	X_t (↑)				X_f (↓)			
	Retrain	DaRE	HedgeCut	MUMI	Retrain	DaRE	HedgeCut	MUMI
Surgical	0.934	0.924	0.722	**0.982**	0.834	0.806	0.761	**0.742**
Vaccine	0.924	0.904	0.785	**0.956**	0.765	0.762	0.761	**0.721**
Adult	0.884	0.857	0.833	**0.893**	0.866	0.850	**0.833**	0.851
Bank Mktg.	0.991	0.991	0.784	**0.994**	0.929	0.921	**0.613**	0.911
Flight Delays	0.796	**0.837**	0.724	0.797	0.694	0.702	**0.528**	0.683
Diabetes	0.712	0.668	0.609	**0.718**	0.641	0.629	**0.597**	0.617
No-Show	0.827	**0.864**	0.515	0.836	0.690	0.691	**0.499**	0.642
Olympics	0.807	**0.856**	0.527	0.804	0.784	0.799	**0.512**	0.753
Census	**0.963**	0.945	0.500	0.963	0.965	0.955	**0.499**	0.966
Credit Card	**0.996**	0.956	N/A	0.993	1.000	1.000	N/A	1.000
CTR	0.874	0.696	N/A	**0.877**	0.681	0.655	N/A	**0.621**
Synthetic	0.941	0.842	0.834	**0.944**	0.931	0.840	**0.837**	0.927
Higgs	0.744	0.678	N/A	**0.745**	0.755	0.709	N/A	**0.662**
Average Score	0.876	0.847	0.683	**0.885**	0.810	0.794	**0.644**	0.777
Average $|s - s_R|$	–	0.045	0.195	**0.009**	–	0.019	0.166	**0.032**

Table 5. The results of unlearning $0.1\% \times n$ samples.

Dataset	X_t (↑)				X_f (↓)			
	Retrain	DaRE	HedgeCut	MUMI	Retrain	DaRE	HedgeCut	MUMI
Surgical	0.931	0.917	0.722	**0.951**	0.818	0.727	**0.667**	0.818
Vaccine	0.922	0.902	0.787	**0.929**	0.714	**0.714**	0.810	**0.714**
Adult	0.885	0.857	0.833	**0.888**	0.844	0.844	**0.788**	0.844
Bank Mktg.	**0.991**	0.990	0.776	0.990	0.955	0.893	**0.448**	0.964
Flight Delays	0.796	**0.836**	0.724	0.796	0.711	0.704	**0.469**	0.637
Diabetes	**0.713**	0.667	0.610	0.711	0.741	0.642	**0.605**	0.716
No-Show	0.828	**0.864**	0.504	0.825	0.636	0.652	**0.493**	0.583
Olympics	0.803	**0.856**	0.527	0.804	0.818	0.871	**0.493**	0.777
Census	**0.963**	0.945	0.500	0.962	0.966	0.947	**0.497**	0.964
Credit Card	**0.995**	0.960	N/A	0.993	1.000	1.000	N/A	1.000
CTR	0.873	0.696	N/A	**0.879**	0.712	0.682	N/A	0.659
Synthetic	0.941	0.842	0.840	**0.944**	0.933	0.838	**0.833**	0.929
Higgs	0.744	0.678	N/A	**0.746**	0.736	0.677	N/A	**0.662**
Average Score	0.876	0.847	0.682	**0.878**	0.814	0.784	**0.610**	0.790
Average $|s-s_R|$	–	0.045	0.195	**0.003**	–	0.038	0.222	**0.024**

MUMI on X_t is the closest to Retrain (see the last row 'Average $|s-s_R|$' in the table).

With the exception of unlearning 1,000 points, the performance of MUMI on X_f is the closest to that of Retrain. Meanwhile, when unlearning 10, 100, 1,000, and $0.1\% \times n$ samples, the average scores of MUMI on X_f is lower than those of the Retrain model, indicating that MUMI truly achieves the unlearning of $\mathcal{D}_f$.

While DaRE outperforms MUMI on a few specific datasets, such as when unlearning 10 samples from the *No-Show* dataset, this discrepancy is due to the inherent poor performance of their model (as mentioned earlier, they do not employ the standard random forest model, and inject more randomness into the model). And it is crucial to reiterate that neither DaRE nor HedgeCut can truly achieve data unlearning from a trained random forest model. Only the proposed MUMI is capable of effectively removing data from a trained random forest, thereby fulfilling the requirements of machine unlearning.

4.2 Unlearning Efficiency

Let $\mathcal{T}(\cdot)$ be the time complexity of random forest, the time complexity of DaRE and HedgeCut are $\mathcal{T}(|D_r|)$, while the time complexity of MUMI is $\mathcal{T}(|D_f|)$. To evaluate the unlearning efficiency of MUMI, we report the time required for different models to unlearn 10, 100, 1000, and $0.1\% \times n$ samples in Tables 6 and 7.

Table 6. Time (seconds) of unlearning 10 and 100 samples.

Dataset	10 (↓)				100 (↓)			
	Retrain	DaRE	HedgeCut	MUMI	Retrain	DaRE	HedgeCut	MUMI
Surgical	0.727	**0.041**	0.062	0.439	0.716	**0.270**	0.531	0.371
Vaccine	0.839	0.050	**0.040**	0.177	0.831	**0.357**	0.391	0.361
Adult	0.943	**0.033**	0.041	0.108	0.874	**0.209**	3.134	0.221
Bank Mktg.	0.879	**0.026**	0.037	0.157	0.871	**0.210**	0.383	0.253
Flight Delays	6.763	0.127	**0.046**	0.090	6.448	0.925	0.419	**0.119**
Diabetes	2.990	0.071	**0.039**	0.114	2.761	0.532	0.389	**0.150**
No-Show	1.692	**0.075**	0.367	0.097	1.696	0.437	0.427	**0.133**
Olympics	16.682	0.354	**0.044**	0.092	15.643	2.055	0.380	**0.105**
Census	11.378	0.330	0.389	**0.093**	11.478	1.045	0.402	**0.100**
Credit Card	9.451	16.753	N/A	**0.103**	9.772	23.817	N/A	**0.096**
CTR	17.409	2.009	N/A	**0.101**	16.024	4.478	N/A	**0.113**
Synthetic	33.961	0.488	**0.068**	0.099	36.580	5.563	0.561	**0.108**
Higgs	390.824	0.728	N/A	**0.126**	356.949	5.777	N/A	**0.138**
Average Time	38.041	1.622	**0.113**	0.138	35.434	3.514	0.702	**0.174**

The unlearning efficiency is mainly affected by two aspects: the size of $\mathcal{D}_r$ ($|\mathcal{D}_r|$) and the size of $\mathcal{D}_f$ ($|\mathcal{D}_f|$).

Impact of $|\mathcal{D}_f|$: (i) HedgeCut is the most efficient unlearning algorithm in most datasets when there are only 10 samples that need to be forgotten in the training data. Because only a few subtrees have changed and need to be reconstructed, the subtrees that HedgeCut has prepared in advance can be directly used for replacement. However, as the number of samples that need to be forgotten increases, many subtrees in the random forest have changed and need to be reconstructed. The subtrees prepared in advance in HedgeCut are insufficient to cope with such extensive changes, resulting in a significant increase in unlearning time. (ii) When the number of samples that need to be unlearned is small, such as 10, 100 samples, and $0.1\% \times n$ samples for the four smallest datasets, the unlearning time of MUMI is higher than that of DaRE. However, when the number of unlearned samples is large, such as 1000 samples or $0.1\% \times n$ samples for the largest nine datasets, the unlearning time of MUMI is much lower than that of DaRE. Because DaRE employs the random split at the initial stages of tree construction. It only selects the optimal nodes for splitting in the final few layers of the decision tree. Consequently, when the number of samples that need to be forgotten is small, the overall structure of the decision tree constructed by DaRE remains unchanged. However, as the number of samples requiring forgetting increases, the structure of the decision trees will change, necessitating the retraining of DaRE, the complexity of retraining DaRE escalates significantly.

Table 7. Time (seconds) of unlearning 1000 and $0.1\% \times n$ samples.

Dataset	1000 ($\downarrow$)				$0.1\% \times n$ ($\downarrow$)			
	Retrain	DaRE	HedgeCut	MUMI	Retrain	DaRE	HedgeCut	MUMI
Surgical	0.724	2.131	11.940	**0.498**	0.731	0.043	**0.079**	0.265
Vaccine	0.820	3.112	3.991	**0.430**	0.830	0.090	**0.078**	0.313
Adult	0.869	1.932	9.095	**0.305**	0.905	**0.071**	1.363	0.208
Bank Mktg.	0.836	1.309	4.017	**0.316**	0.888	**0.107**	0.128	0.169
Flight Delays	6.937	9.932	4.177	**0.137**	6.027	0.796	0.314	**0.112**
Diabetes	2.790	10.360	3.673	**0.207**	2.961	0.499	0.298	**0.139**
No-Show	1.751	3.453	3.983	**0.177**	1.715	0.395	0.357	**0.137**
Olympics	17.156	18.013	3.763	**0.096**	17.745	3.079	0.609	**0.080**
Census	11.518	7.481	3.972	**0.139**	10.849	2.098	0.798	**0.102**
Credit Card	8.435	41.665	N/A	**0.114**	9.989	28.081	N/A	**0.107**
CTR	16.389	42.319	N/A	**0.133**	17.427	31.975	N/A	**0.123**
Synthetic	35.863	24.942	7.021	**0.208**	34.019	21.902	5.246	**0.212**
Higgs	383.332	52.090	N/A	**0.203**	385.495	272.148	N/A	**0.286**
Average Time	37.494	16.826	5.563	**0.228**	37.660	27.791	0.927	**0.173**

Impact of $|\mathcal{D}_r|$: Another obvious phenomenon presented by Table 6 and Table 7 is that the unlearning time of DaRE increases with the increase of $|\mathcal{D}_r|$, while MUMI does not. MUMI has almost the same unlearning time on these data. This is mainly due to the following two reasons:

1. Firstly, DaRE necessitates the retraining of the entire retained dataset $\mathcal{D}_r$. In contrast, MUMI does not utilize $\mathcal{D}_r$ at all during the unlearning process. Instead, it relies solely on $\mathcal{D}_f$ to construct image samples, with $|\mathcal{D}_f| \ll |\mathcal{D}_r|$. As a result, the unlearning efficiency of MUMI is significantly higher than that of DaRE, particularly when the size of the dataset $|\mathcal{D}|$ is large, where the difference becomes even more pronounced.
2. Secondly, both DaRE and HedgeCut require processing each tree within their models. If the initial random forest consists of T trees, DaRE must retrain all T decision trees on the dataset $\mathcal{D}_r$. In contrast, MUMI only needs to train k trees ($k < T$) on the image samples derived from $\mathcal{D}_f$. Consequently, the unlearning time of MUMI is significantly lower than that of DaRE, making it a more efficient approach in terms of computational overhead.

In summary, our proposed algorithm MUMI demonstrates superiority over existing algorithms in the following three key aspects:

* The most significant advantage is that MUMI can effectively unlearn the trained random forest model, whereas existing algorithms are unable to achieve this level of unlearning. This capability is crucial for scenarios where data removal is required in a trained random forest model.

* MUMI outperforms existing algorithms in terms of model effectiveness, unlearning efficacy, and unlearning efficiency. It achieves faster unlearning while maintaining model accuracy, making it more efficient overall. This balance between unlearning efficiency, model effectiveness, and unlearning efficacy is a notable improvement over current methods.
* The unlearning process of MUMI is not influenced by the remaining data $\mathcal{D}_r$ but is solely focused on the data to be unlearned $\mathcal{D}_f$. This approach is both intuitive and practical for unlearning, as it ensures that only the necessary information is removed without unnecessary interference with the remaining data. This aligns with the fundamental principle of forgetting: to remove what needs to be forgotten without affecting what remains.

5 Discussion

The Pros and Cons of Including Retrain in the Unlearning Algorithm: Both DaRE and HedgeCut incorporate retraining into their unlearning algorithms. For instance, DaRE retrains the layers close to the leaves of the decision trees. This approach ensures that the data to be forgotten is completely removed from the model. However, it also alters the training process of original random forest, which can lead to a reduction in model performance. Moreover, by employing retraining, the focus shifts away from the subset D_f that needs to be forgotten, and instead, the entire retain dataset D_r is retrained. This significantly increases the unlearning cost, especially when D_r is large.

Boundary Conditions of the Image Method: Many methods use random labeling methods [6,7,30], but they do not consider boundary conditions and are therefore different from the mirror method. The application of the method of images necessitates the fulfillment of specific boundary conditions. In the context of machine unlearning, the stringent boundary condition is that the performance of the unlearned model should be the same as that of the retrained model. However, in practice, obtaining a retrained model is often infeasible due to the prohibitively high cost of retraining (which is precisely why machine unlearning algorithms are needed). In this paper, we propose using performance that closely approximates the behavior of a retrained model, performing well on X_r while performing poorly on X_f, as a proxy for the boundary condition. Identifying other superior boundary conditions to replace the need for retraining remains an open question.

The Impact of Different Voting Methods: In the experiment, we used hard voting for each tree, but since the impact of each unlearned sample on image decision trees is different when we forget different numbers of samples, the weighted voting may have better unlearning performance.

6 Limitation and Future Work

MUMI unlearns data, leading to an increase in the number of decision trees. Although only a small number of decision trees are added each time, the cumulative effect becomes significant when the number of unlearning events is large. In contrast, DaRE does not experience this issue. One potential approach is to use these cumulative unlearned samples to train image decision trees instead of the previous multiple image decision trees after forgetting lots of samples. Designing an unlearning algorithm that can achieve data unlearning in an already trained random forest without adding additional decision trees is our future work.

7 Conclusion

In this paper, we introduce the method of images into the machine unlearning task and propose the first machine unlearning algorithm based on this method, called MUMI. MUMI is capable of achieving unlearning in a trained random forest, a capability that existing algorithms lack. We provide theoretical proof that our proposed algorithm can ensure both the good performance of the model after unlearning, i.e., the removal of the specified data. Our experimental results demonstrate that MUMI outperforms existing algorithms in terms of model effectiveness, unlearning efficacy, and unlearning efficiency.

Acknowledgments. Kai Ming Ting is supported by the National Natural Science Foundation of China (Grant No. 92470116).

Disclosure of Interests. The authors have no competing interests to declare that are relevant to the content of this article.

References

1. Baumhauer, T., Schöttle, P., Zeppelzauer, M.: Machine unlearning: linear filtration for logit-based classifiers. Mach. Learn. **111**(9), 3203–3226 (2022)
2. Bourtoule, L., et al.: Machine unlearning. In: 2021 IEEE Symposium on Security and Privacy (SP), pp. 141–159. IEEE (2021)
3. Breiman, L.: Random forest. Mach. Learn. **45**, 5–32 (2001)
4. Brophy, J., Lowd, D.: Machine unlearning for random forest. In: International Conference on Machine Learning, pp. 1092–1104. PMLR (2021)
5. Cao, Y., Yang, J.: Towards making systems forget with machine unlearning. In: 2015 IEEE Symposium on Security and Privacy, pp. 463–480. IEEE (2015)
6. Chen, Z., .: Debiasing machine unlearning with counterfactual examples. arXiv preprint arXiv:2404.15760 (2024)
7. Chundawat, V.S., Tarun, A.K., Mandal, M., Kankanhalli, M.: Can bad teaching induce forgetting? Unlearning in deep networks using an incompetent teacher. In: Proceedings of the AAAI Conference on Artificial IntelligenceM vol. 37, pp. 7210–7217 (2023)
8. Devineni, S.K.: Ai in data privacy and security. Int. J. Artif. Intell. Mach. Learn. (IJAIML) **3**(01), 35–49 (2024)

9. Ertel, W.: Introduction to Artificial Intelligence. Springer, Heidelberg (2024)
10. Fu, S., He, F., Tao, D.: Knowledge removal in sampling-based bayesian inference. In: International Conference on Learning Representations (2021)
11. Gastwirth, J.L.: The estimation of the lorenz curve and gini index. Rev. Econ. Stat. 306–316 (1972)
12. Ginart, A., Guan, M., Valiant, G., Zou, J.Y.: Making AI forget you: data deletion in machine learning. Adv. Neural Inf. Process. Syst. **32** (2019)
13. Golatkar, A., Achille, A., Ravichandran, A., Polito, M., Soatto, S.: Mixed-privacy forgetting in deep networks. In: Proceedings of the IEEE/CVF Conference on Computer Vision and Pattern Recognition, pp. 792–801 (2021)
14. Golatkar, A., Achille, A., Soatto, S.: Eternal sunshine of the spotless net: selective forgetting in deep networks. In: Proceedings of the IEEE/CVF Conference on Computer Vision and Pattern Recognition, pp. 9304–9312 (2020)
15. Golatkar, A., Achille, A., Soatto, S.: Forgetting outside the box: scrubbing deep networks of information accessible from input-output observations. In: Vedaldi, A., Bischof, H., Brox, T., Frahm, J.-M. (eds.) ECCV 2020. LNCS, vol. 12374, pp. 383–398. Springer, Cham (2020). https://doi.org/10.1007/978-3-030-58526-6_23
16. Guo, C., Goldstein, T., Hannun, A., Van Der Maaten, L.: Certified data removal from machine learning models. In: International Conference on Machine Learning, pp. 3832–3842. PMLR (2020)
17. Gupta, V., Jung, C., Neel, S., Roth, A., Sharifi-Malvajerdi, S., Waites, C.: Adaptive machine unlearning. Adv. Neural. Inf. Process. Syst. **34**, 16319–16330 (2021)
18. Hanley, J.A., McNeil, B.J.: The meaning and use of the area under a receiver operating characteristic (roc) curve. Radiology **143**(1), 29–36 (1982)
19. Hoang, T., Rana, S., Gupta, S., Venkatesh, S.: Learn to unlearn for deep neural networks: minimizing unlearning interference with gradient projection. In: Proceedings of the IEEE/CVF Winter Conference on Applications of Computer Vision, pp. 4819–4828 (2024)
20. Hoofnagle, C.J., Van Der Sloot, B., Borgesius, F.Z.: The European union general data protection regulation: what it is and what it means. Inf. Commun. Technol. Law **28**(1), 65–98 (2019)
21. Izzo, Z., Smart, M.A., Chaudhuri, K., Zou, J.: Approximate data deletion from machine learning models. In: International Conference on Artificial Intelligence and Statistics, pp. 2008–2016. PMLR (2021)
22. Jackson, J.D.: Classical Electrodynamics. John Wiley & Sons, Hoboken (1998)
23. Li, N., et al.: Machine unlearning: taxonomy, metrics, applications, challenges, and prospects. IEEE Trans. Neural Netw. Learn. Syst. (2025)
24. Li, Y., Wang, C.H., Cheng, G.: Online forgetting process for linear regression models. In: International Conference on Artificial Intelligence and Statistics, pp. 217–225. PMLR (2021)
25. Lin, H., Chung, J.W., Lao, Y., Zhao, W.: Machine unlearning in gradient boosting decision trees. In: Proceedings of the 29th ACM SIGKDD Conference on Knowledge Discovery and Data Mining, pp. 1374–1383 (2023)
26. Manheim, K., Kaplan, L.: Artificial intelligence: risks to privacy and democracy. Yale JL & Tech. **21**, 106 (2019)
27. Neel, S., Roth, A., Sharifi-Malvajerdi, S.: Descent-to-delete: gradient-based methods for machine unlearning. In: Algorithmic Learning Theory, pp. 931–962. PMLR (2021)
28. Nguyen, Q.P., Low, B.K.H., Jaillet, P.: Variational bayesian unlearning. Adv. Neural. Inf. Process. Syst. **33**, 16025–16036 (2020)

29. Nguyen, Q.P., Oikawa, R., Divakaran, D.M., Chan, M.C., Low, B.K.H.: Markov chain monte carlo-based machine unlearning: Unlearning what needs to be forgotten. In: Proceedings of the 2022 ACM on Asia Conference on Computer and Communications Security, pp. 351–363 (2022)
30. Pan, Z., Andrews, E., Chang, L., Mishra, P.: Privacy-preserving debiasing using data augmentation and machine unlearning. arXiv preprint arXiv:2404.13194 (2024)
31. Pardau, S.L.: The california consumer privacy act: towards a European-style privacy regime in the united states. J. Tech. L. & Pol'y **23**, 68 (2018)
32. Perez-Lopez, R., Ghaffari Laleh, N., Mahmood, F., Kather, J.N.: A guide to artificial intelligence for cancer researchers. Nat. Rev. Cancer **24**(6), 427–441 (2024)
33. Regulation, P.: General data protection regulation. InTouch **25**, 1–5 (2018)
34. Rényi, A.: On measures of entropy and information. In: Proceedings of the fourth Berkeley Symposium on Mathematical Statistics and Probability, Contributions to the Theory of Statistics, vol. 4, pp. 547–562. University of California Press (1961)
35. Schelter, S., Grafberger, S., Dunning, T.: HedgeCut: maintaining randomised trees for low-latency machine unlearning. In: Proceedings of the 2021 International Conference on Management of Data, pp. 1545–1557 (2021)
36. Sekhari, A., Acharya, J., Kamath, G., Suresh, A.T.: Remember what you want to forget: algorithms for machine unlearning. Adv. Neural. Inf. Process. Syst. **34**, 18075–18086 (2021)
37. Song, Y.Y., Ying, L.: Decision tree methods: applications for classification and prediction. Shanghai Arch. Psychiat. **27**(2), 130 (2015)
38. Ullah, E., Mai, T., Rao, A., Rossi, R.A., Arora, R.: Machine unlearning via algorithmic stability. In: Conference on Learning Theory, pp. 4126–4142. PMLR (2021)
39. Varghese, C., Harrison, E.M., O'Grady, G., Topol, E.J.: Artificial intelligence in surgery. Nat. Med. **30**(5), 1257–1268 (2024)
40. Wu, Z., Zhu, J., Li, Q., He, B.: Deltaboost: gradient boosting decision trees with efficient machine unlearning. Proc. ACM Manag. Data **1**(2), 1–26 (2023)
41. Zhu, M.: Recall, precision and average precision. Department of Statistics and Actuarial Science, University of Waterloo, Waterloo **2**(30), 6 (2004)

Stimulating Catastrophic Forgetting in Class-Wise Unlearning via UAP

Wenxing Zhou, Xinwen Cheng, Yingwen Wu, Ruikai Yang, and Xiaolin Huang(✉)

Institute of Image Processing and Pattern Recognition, Shanghai Jiao Tong University, Shanghai, China
{apricvivi,xinwencheng,yingwen_wu,ruikai.yang,xiaolinhuang}@sjtu.edu.cn

Abstract. The growing concerns regarding user privacy and data security have brought attention to the task of machine unlearning (MU), which aims to remove the influence of specific data from a well-trained model effectively and efficiently. A naive unlearning method is finetuning the pretrained model to continually learn the remaining data to induce the "catastrophic forgetting" of forgetting data. However, such unlearning often turns out to be inefficient. For effective and efficient unlearning, it is crucial to stimulate catastrophic forgetting, ideally by directly localizing the model's knowledge of specific class-wise features associated with the forgetting data. In this paper, we highlight that the targeted universal adversarial perturbation (UAP) implicitly contains class-wise information. In light of this, we propose **Unlearning by UAP (U^2AP)**. By adding the perturbation to clean remaining data during the finetuning process, we shift the model's attention away from the forgetting class directly, stimulating faster and more efficient catastrophic forgetting. Extensive experiments demonstrate that U^2AP enables quicker and more accurate forgetting while maintaining model performance on the remaining data.

Keywords: Machine Unlearning · Machine Learning

1 Introduction

The success of deep learning is largely driven by the diversity and abundance of training data [35]. However, this success also brings about pressing issues, including data leaks, threats to personal privacy, and misuse of data that may violate regulations [12]. To address these challenges, the General Data Protection Regulation (GDPR) [13] was introduced to ensure "the right to be forgotten" [8]. In response, "machine unlearning" (MU) has emerged as a research area aimed at enabling machine learning models to effectively forget specific data when needed.

In machine unlearning, retraining the model from scratch after data removal remains the golden standard for ensuring complete forgetting [34], yet this approach is computationally intensive. To avoid the need of full retraining, various

Supplementary Information The online version contains supplementary material available at https://doi.org/10.1007/978-3-032-06096-9_25.

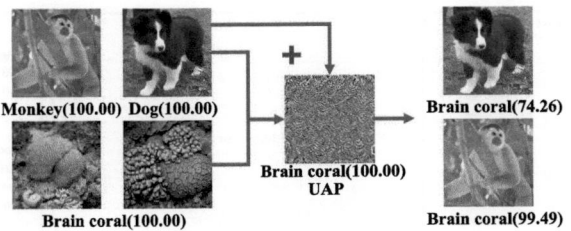

Fig. 1. Explanation of the effect of UAP. The corresponding number after the image class is the predicted probability of being categorized into that class.

methods have been proposed. Most of these methods rely on isolating forgetting data influences [11], adjusting network outputs [2], and injecting error messages to forgetting data to disrupt the network's memory of data [7,15]. However, these methods sometimes compromise both unlearning efficiency and forgetting completeness. Empirical evaluations reveal that such approaches may underperform even compared to naive finetuning. Finetuning trains the pretrained model on the remaining samples, gradually forgetting the unlearned data through catastrophic forgetting [18], providing a milder unlearning process. However, its passive nature results in suboptimal efficiency.

To address this, class-specific features should be involved to actively stimulate catastrophic forgetting. On the one hand, such information should be the key for the well-trained model to recognize the class as being forgotten. On the other hand, it should not be specific to individual images within the same class but rather representative of the entire class. Universal Adversarial Perturbation (UAP) [23], an indistinguishable dark pattern specific to a class, perfectly fits the requirement. When a UAP associated with a specific class is applied to any clean sample, regardless of its original class, the network is deceived into misclassifying the sample as the targeted class. As shown in Fig. 1, when the UAP targeted at "brain coral" is added to clean samples originally classified as "monkey" and "dog", the model's predictions for these samples are fooled to "brain coral" in high probability. These perturbations, when visualized, often contain semantic information of the targeted class. This observation underscores that UAPs encapsulate critical discriminative information that the neural network relies on for decision-making. Consequently, by targeting and eliminating such information during the unlearning process, we can effectively disrupt the model's ability to recognize the forgetting class, thereby stimulating catastrophic forgetting.

Here we propose **Unlearning by UAP (U^2AP)**. By combining the forgetting features with the correct remaining data, our method reduces the information loss associated with relabeling methods and overcomes the inefficiency of simple finetuning. The specific differences between our method and others are illustrated in Fig. 2. When the "brain coral" class is to be forgotten, simple finetuning neglects the forgetting data and gradually forgets "brain coral" by continuing to learn from only the remaining classes. This passive approach, however, proves inefficient, especially when dealing with more complex datasets or net-

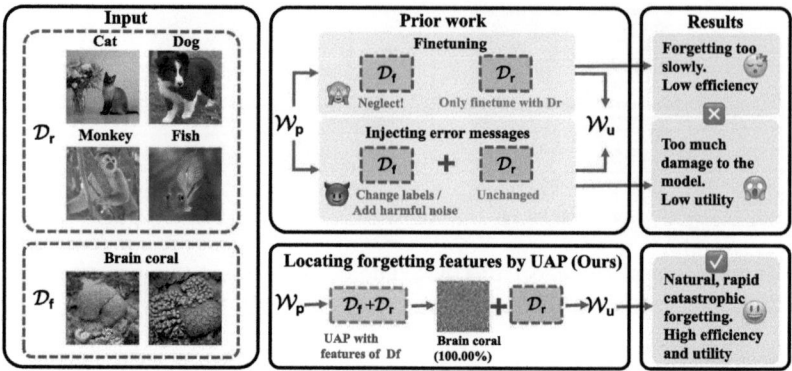

Fig. 2. Comparison of previous unlearning work and ours. $\mathcal{D}_r$ and $\mathcal{D}_f$ denote the remaining and forgetting data, $\mathcal{W}_p$ and $\mathcal{W}_u$ denote the pretrained and unlearned model.

works. To speed up such forgetting, some other prior works generally inject error information into the forgetting data to actively guide the model toward unlearning specific data. For example, Amnesiac [15] modifies the labels of the forgetting data, and UNSIR [32] adds harmful noise to the forgetting set. However, this kind of error information will also inevitably damage the model's performance in the remaining data, resulting in low utility. Whereas our approach incorporates forgetting features, by applying U²AP, the model's attention is forced to shift from the forgetting class to the remaining data, thus accelerating the erasure of class-specific memories while minimally impacting the remaining set. Like other unlearning methods, the forgetting process affects the remaining data. So we mitigate the potential disruptions to remaining information by finetuning the model on a subset of remaining data after forgetting. This additional step ensures stable performance, enhancing the model's utility. By combining active forgetting with careful post-unlearning refinement, U²AP achieves a balance between efficient unlearning and sustained model performance.

Our contributions can be summarized as follows:

- We explore the implicit representation of the network's memory of specific class-wise features and innovatively extract such information by UAP. By incorporating the UAP into the forgetting process, we localize the memory of the forgetting class, achieving more precise unlearning.
- We propose a novel unlearning method, U²AP. By training targeted UAP and then adding it to the remaining data for finetuning, we stimulate the catastrophic forgetting of the forgetting class, improving the effectiveness and efficiency of class-wise machine unlearning.
- Experimental results across various settings demonstrate that our method accelerates the forgetting process while effectively preserving the model's performance on the remaining data. This improvement is especially prominent when U²AP is applied to larger-scale datasets and more complex models, making it a more efficient and reliable solution for practical applications.

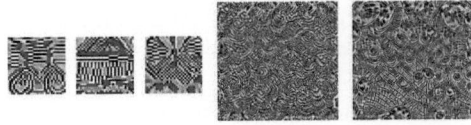

Fig. 3. Results from FG-UAP targeted attacks. The left three shows perturbations on CIFAR-100 using ResNet-18, where each perturbation exhibits visual features specific to the target classes: "bicycle", "house", and "butterfly". Right two displays perturbations on ImageNet-1K using VGG-16, with textures arranged in distinct, patterned forms targeting the classes "brain coral" and "bubble".

2 Related Work

2.1 Machine Unlearning

Machine unlearning aims to eliminate the influence of specific data on a well-trained model to ensure the legal use of data and the user's privacy [4,10,16]. While retraining is the golden standard, it is resource-intensive, promoting the development of effective and efficient unlearning methods. Current methods mainly achieve unlearning by analyzing data influence through parameter importance selection or stimulating catastrophic forgetting through label modification.

A straightforward approach to analyze and remove data influence is retrieving historical gradients associated with the forgetting data [33]. However, due to the complexity of dynamic training, such retrieval process is inexact and inefficient. Thereby influence function [19] is introduced to approximate data influence for unlearning [16], but is limited to linear models with convex loss functions [1]. More practical influence removal techniques usually rely on parameter importance selection [11], which involves selectively suppressing parameters specifically responsible for the forgetting data.

Other unlearning methods stimulate catastrophic forgetting by finetuning with the modified data. The most basic finetuning trains the pretrained model exclusively on the remaining data, passively relying on the natural process of catastrophic forgetting [18] to gradually erode the model's acquired knowledge of the forgetting data. However, this method is inefficient. To accelerate the forgetting process, some methods inject incorrect information, *e.g.* random-relabeling [15], knowledge-distillation from a useless teacher model [7,21] or assimilating error-maximizing noise [6,32]. However, introducing such incorrect knowledge severely damages model utility, making unlearning inexact, inefficient, and ultimately unfavorable. To achieve more effective and efficient unlearning, it is crucial to correctly locate the knowledge associated with specific class-wise information, thereby stimulating catastrophic forgetting in a targeted and controllable way.

2.2 Universal Adversarial Perturbation

Universal Adversarial Perturbation (UAP) [23] is an adversarial perturbation that can fool a well-trained model to misclassify any sample with the perturbation. In particular, targeted UAP attacks focus on fooling the model's predictions to a specific targeted class, rather than merely causing misclassification [39].

Recently, various UAP methods have been proposed to achieve nearly perfect fooling rates [24,25,38,40]. Interestingly, powerful UAP is revealed to exhibit semantic patterns specific to the targeted class, which are visualized in Fig. 3. These semantic patterns evoke the model's response and successfully fool its predictions on perturbed data. This demonstrates that it is possible to extract the specific information related to a targeted class from a pretrained model through UAP [5,26,28]. Such insights provide a method for locating the class-wise knowledge embedded in the model, which can then be leveraged to facilitate effective unlearning.

3 Method

3.1 Preliminaries

Let $\mathcal{D} = \{(x_i, y_i)\}_{i=1}^{N}$ be a training set consisting of samples $x_i \in \mathbb{R}^d$ and corresponding class labels $y_i \in \{1, ..., K\}$. Machine unlearning aims to eliminate the influence of specific samples that need to be forgotten from a pretrained model. These samples are referred to as the *forgetting data* and denoted as $\mathcal{D}_f = \{(x_i, y_i) \in \mathcal{D}\}_{i=1}^{N_f}$. The remaining samples in the dataset form the *remaining set*, denoted as $\mathcal{D}_r = \mathcal{D} \setminus \mathcal{D}_f$. The unlearned model should be as close as possible to the retrained model, which is trained from scratch with $\mathcal{D}_r$.

Nowadays, machine unlearning includes three primary tasks: (1) Full-class unlearning: where the $\mathcal{D}_f$ is made of all samples from an entire class $k \in \{1, ..., K\}$, (2) Sub-class unlearning: where the $\mathcal{D}_f$ is made of samples from a specific sub-class under a broader super-class $k \in \{1, ..., K\}$, (3) Random sample unlearning: where the $\mathcal{D}_f$ is made of samples randomly chosen from the entire dataset $\mathcal{D}$. Also, we consider multi-class unlearning: where the $\mathcal{D}_f$ is made of all samples from several entire classes $k_1, k_2, ... \in \{1, ..., K\}$. Here we mainly focus on full-class unlearning, sub-class unlearning, and multi-class unlearning.

3.2 Proposed Method

In deep learning, catastrophic forgetting refers to the phenomenon where neural networks progressively lose previously acquired knowledge when sequentially trained on new tasks. Recent studies have leveraged this property through finetuning-based unlearning methods to eliminate information pertaining to specific forgetting data. However, continual learning on the remaining data may fail to achieve effective forgetting due to the underlying resemblance between the remaining and the forgetting data. To address this challenge, we propose that effective machine unlearning should actively stimulate controllable catastrophic forgetting through targeted interference with class-specific features. The most straightforward approach is to extract the pretrained model's knowledge of the forgetting data and remove it in a targeted way. Our key insight stems from the observation that UAPs generated by pretrained models inherently encapsulate

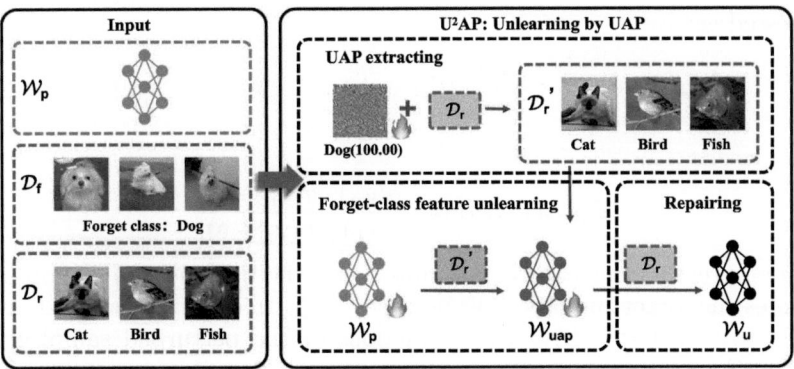

Fig. 4. The specific process of the three steps of U²AP, taking the example of forgetting "dog". (1) UAP extracting: using FG-UAP to targeted attack pretrained model in remaining data to get targeted UAP of "dog", (2) forget-class feature unlearning: adding the UAP to remaining data and finetuning the pretrained model with correct remaining data labels to stimulate catastrophic forgetting, (3) repairing: finetuning model with subset of clean remaining data to repair model utility to get final unlearned model.

discriminative semantic patterns of targeted classes, as evidenced by their class-specific visual manifestations in Fig. 3, which indicates the pretrained model's memorization of the classes. This suggests that UAPs can serve as effective proxies for extracting class-wise information stored in model parameters. In light of this, we propose a method that first uses UAP to extract class-wise information and then promotes the shift of the model's attention by training on the UAP-perturbed remaining data. The labels of these perturbed samples still align with those of their clean counterparts, compelling the model to actively ignore the acquired knowledge of the targeted forgetting class. To mitigate any potential impact of the adversarial noise on model utility, we finetune the model with the clean remaining data for a few steps following previous methods. Overall, U²AP has three steps: UAP extracting, forget-class feature unlearning, and model performance repairing. The specific framework of our method is illustrated in Fig. 4.

UAP Extracting. Targeted UAP is an input-agnostic noise that induces misclassification of all perturbed samples toward a predefined target class. Interestingly, targeted UAP is revealed to contain semantic patterns specific to the targeted class. This behavior demonstrates that UAPs inherently encode a model's memorization of class-specific information. Therefore, it can be an effective tool for removing the influence of forgetting data from pretrained model. In this paper, we use FG-UAP [38] for its obvious class-wise patterns. As revealed by Papyan et al. [27], for samples belonging to the same class, their penultimate features in a well-trained model exhibit totally identical. FG-UAP trains the UAP to destroy such within-class feature collapse of perturbed data. By enforcing the classification of perturbed data to the targeted class with a cross-entropy loss, FG-UAP achieves a remarkable fooling rate. Mathematically, the FG loss is expressed as:

$$\mathcal{L}_{\text{FG}}(\mathcal{D}_r, \delta, y_f) = \sum_{x_r \in \mathcal{D}_r} [\mathcal{L}_{\text{attack}}(x_r, \delta) + \mathcal{L}_{\text{CE}}(x_r + \delta, y_f)] \quad (1)$$

where

$$\mathcal{L}_{\text{attack}}(x_r, \delta) = \frac{h(x_r) \cdot h(x_r + \delta)}{\|h(x_r)\| \|h(x_r + \delta)\|} \quad (2)$$

and $h(x)$ represents the feature of sample x, δ is the UAP needs to be optimized, y_f denotes the forgetting class. We use the $\mathcal{L}_{\text{attack}}$ to optimize the UAP and use the $\mathcal{L}_{\text{CE}}$ to targetedly drive the predictions of the perturbed samples to the forgetting class.

Forget-Class Feature Unlearning. The targeted UAP inherently encodes the class-wise information that establishes strong parametric interactions with the pretrained model's weight space. This causes the pretrained model to focus heavily on this class-wise information once it is introduced to clean samples. Therefore, in the context of unlearning, the goal is to reduce the model's attention to such features, *i.e.*, to make the model ignore and diminish its responsiveness to them. To achieve this, we finetune the pretrained model to correctly classify the perturbed remaining data to its original labels with the loss function in Eq. (3). The inclusion of these perturbed samples causes the model's attention to shift rapidly away from the targeted UAP, thereby actively stimulating the process of "catastrophic forgetting" by overriding the explicit semantic information embedded in the UAP.

$$\mathcal{L}_{\text{forget}}(\mathcal{D}_r, \delta) = \sum_{x_r, y_r \in \mathcal{D}_r} \mathcal{L}_{\text{CE}}(x_r + \delta, y_r) \quad (3)$$

Repairing. Since the UAP is essentially an adversarial noise, learning the perturbed data may potentially impact performance on remaining data. Fortunately, this can be effectively mitigated by finetuning the model for a few steps on clean samples, as other unlearning methods also explicitly or implicitly leverage remaining data for repairing [7,11,15,32]. For full-class unlearning, we repair by finetuning on a subset of remaining data. For sub-class unlearning, detailed sub-class labels within broader super-classes can help target the UAP specifically for certain classes. However, when sub-class labels are inaccessible, as in the MU setting, we generate the UAP by targeted attacking the entire super-class and then use a subset of remaining data for repairing.

The complete unlearning algorithm, which consists of the three critical steps outlined above: (1) UAP extracting, (2) forget-class feature unlearning, (3) repairing, is presented in Algorithm 1.

4 Experiments

4.1 Setups

Datasets, Models and MU Tasks. We evaluate our U^{2}AP in supervised image classification tasks. Since we utilize the UAP to extract class-wise

Algorithm 1. Unlearning by UAP (U²AP)

Input: Pretrained model $\mathcal{W}_p$, Remaining set $\mathcal{D}_r$, Forgetting set $\mathcal{D}_f$, Forgetting class y_f

Output: Unlearned model $\mathcal{W}_u$

Step 1: UAP Extracting
1: Sample subset $\mathcal{D}_{r1}$ from $\mathcal{D}_r$
2: $\delta \leftarrow \text{FG\_UAP}(\mathcal{W}_p, \mathcal{D}_{r1}, y_f)$

Step 2: Forget-Class Feature Unlearning
3: Sample subset $\mathcal{D}_{r2}$ from $\mathcal{D}_r$ based on UAP
4: Initialize synthetic dataset $\mathcal{D}_s = \{\}$
5: **for** $x_i \in \mathcal{D}_{r2}$ **do**
6:     Add UAP to sample: $x'_i = x_i + \delta$
7:     Add (x'_i, y_i) to $\mathcal{D}_s$
8:     $\mathcal{W}_{uap} \leftarrow \text{Finetune}(\mathcal{W}_p, \mathcal{D}_s)$
9: **end for**

Step 3: Repairing
10: Sample subset $\mathcal{D}_{r3}$ from $\mathcal{D}_r$
11: **for** x_i in $\mathcal{D}_{r3}$ **do**
12:     $\mathcal{W}_u \leftarrow \text{Finetune}(\mathcal{W}_{uap}, \mathcal{D}_{r3})$
13: **end for**
14: **Return:** Unlearned model $\mathcal{W}_u$

---

information, we focus on class-wise unlearning tasks, including full-class unlearning, sub-class unlearning, and multi-class unlearning. The full-class unlearning is evaluated on ImageNet-1K [9]. The sub-class unlearning is evaluated on subclasses of CIFAR-20 [20]. The multi-class unlearning is evaluated on several classes of CIFAR-100 [20]. For smaller-scale datasets like CIFAR-100 and CIFAR-20, we use ResNet-18 [17] as the training model, while for the larger-scale dataset, ImageNet-1K, we use Deit-B [36]. In our experiments, the forgotten classes were selected randomly.

Evaluation Metrics. Machine unlearning algorithms should be evaluated based on their ability to effectively remove information while maintaining model performance and ensuring efficiency. Our evaluation metrics focus on four critical aspects: the effectiveness of forgetting, the utility of model, the protection of privacy, and the efficiency of the method. For the effectiveness of forgetting, we use the forgetting accuracy (**FA**) to measure how well the model has removed the influence of forgetting data. For the utility of model, we use the remaining accuracy (**RA**) and validation accuracy (**VA**) to evaluate how well the model retains performance on the remaining data. To provide a more comprehensive evaluation, we compute the average gap (**Avg. Gap**) between the unlearned model and the retrained model across **FA**, **RA** and **VA**. A smaller average gap indicates better unlearning performance. Additionally, for the protection of privacy, we employ the membership inference attacks (**MIA**) [30,31] to further evaluate the privacy guarantees after unlearning. The success rate of MIA indicates how many samples in $\mathcal{D}_f$ are classified as member samples of the unlearned model. The lower MIA represents less information about the forgetting set left in the unlearned model, indicating more effective forgetting. Regarding the efficiency of the unlearning algorithm, we report the execution time (**Time**) of each method.

Table 1. Results of full-class unlearning methods on ImageNet using Deit-B, evaluated with two classes "109" an "971". Each value represents the mean$_{\pm\text{variance}}$ in percent(%). (Avg. Gap with retraining is not computed here because retraining is too time-consuming.) We bold the best-performing values.

Class	Method	RA↑	FA↓	VA↑	MIA↓	Time (s)↓
109	Pretrain	81.89$_{\pm 0.00}$	88$_{\pm 0.00}$	80.10$_{\pm 0.00}$	63.50$_{\pm 0.00}$	-
	Finetune	72.95$_{\pm 0.45}$	4.82$_{\pm 3.03}$	71.94$_{\pm 0.44}$	23.50$_{\pm 6.38}$	9171
	GradientAscent	75.76$_{\pm 0.21}$	15.67$_{\pm 0.34}$	73.44$_{\pm 0.33}$	24.56$_{\pm 0.76}$	5130
	EU-k	73.56$_{\pm 0.33}$	5.68$_{\pm 0.23}$	71.31$_{\pm 0.26}$	10.51$_{\pm 1.75}$	8451
	CF-k	75.66$_{\pm 0.61}$	6.52$_{\pm 1.09}$	72.89$_{\pm 0.38}$	7.66$_{\pm 0.10}$	7989
	UNSIR	68.17$_{\pm 1.32}$	49.03$_{\pm 1.00}$	65.14$_{\pm 1.77}$	56.12$_{\pm 0.88}$	6513
	BadTeacher	70.04$_{\pm 0.50}$	8.33$_{\pm 9.83}$	69.95$_{\pm 0.45}$	2.33$_{\pm 1.52}$	4934
	Amnesiac	78.57$_{\pm 0.21}$	9.32$_{\pm 3.52}$	78.54$_{\pm 0.21}$	**1.33**$_{\pm 0.58}$	5225
	SalUn	79.58$_{\pm 0.05}$	1.04$_{\pm 1.00}$	79.53$_{\pm 0.05}$	2.33$_{\pm 1.04}$	4840
	U^{2}AP	**80.25**$_{\pm 0.13}$	**0.00**$_{\pm 0.00}$	**80.20**$_{\pm 0.12}$	4.00$_{\pm 0.50}$	**748**
971	Pretrain	81.73$_{\pm 0.00}$	85.42$_{\pm 0.00}$	81.72$_{\pm 0.00}$	79.50$_{\pm 0.00}$	-
	Finetune	72.12$_{\pm 0.37}$	5.20$_{\pm 3.89}$	71.10$_{\pm 0.37}$	11.83$_{\pm 3.05}$	9197
	GradientAscent	76.21$_{\pm 0.98}$	8.73$_{\pm 0.52}$	74.08$_{\pm 1.55}$	9.76$_{\pm 0.20}$	5326
	EU-k	77.98$_{\pm 1.62}$	7.36$_{\pm 0.54}$	75.10$_{\pm 0.91}$	6.78$_{\pm 2.81}$	8030
	CF-k	76.65$_{\pm 1.00}$	8.52$_{\pm 0.83}$	73.87$_{\pm 0.20}$	8.98$_{\pm 0.55}$	8006
	UNSIR	72.98$_{\pm 0.97}$	50.31$_{\pm 0.84}$	70.45$_{\pm 1.02}$	47.89$_{\pm 0.76}$	6002
	BadTeacher	70.27$_{\pm 0.41}$	13.33$_{\pm 5.16}$	70.21$_{\pm 0.43}$	1.83$_{\pm 0.29}$	4929
	Amnesiac	78.70$_{\pm 0.12}$	16.28$_{\pm 5.66}$	78.66$_{\pm 0.12}$	**1.33**$_{\pm 0.29}$	5251
	SalUn	79.59$_{\pm 0.08}$	7.00$_{\pm 2.76}$	79.55$_{\pm 0.08}$	2.17$_{\pm 0.58}$	4774
	U^{2}AP	**80.11**$_{\pm 0.04}$	**0.00**$_{\pm 0.00}$	**80.07**$_{\pm 0.04}$	3.17$_{\pm 0.76}$	**525**

Baselines. We compare our method against eight baselines, including (1) Finetune: training the pretrained model with remaining data to gradually unlearn through catastrophic forgetting [37], (2) Gradient Ascent: unlearning by making a gradient ascent on the forgetting data [33], (3) EU-k and (4) CF-k: fixing some parameters and only finetuning the last k layers [14], (5) Unlearning-by-Selective-Impair-and-Repair (UNSIR): generating noise to impair the forgetting data and then finetuning with the subset of remaining data to repair the model [32], (6) Bad Teacher: transferring knowledge from the useful (the pretrained model) and useless (the randomly initialized model) teachers for the remaining data and the forgetting data [7], (7) Amnesiac: relabeling the forgetting data and meanwhile minimizing the cross-entropy loss of the remaining data [15], (8) Saliency-based Unlearning (SalUn): computing a weight saliency map to identify the weights most relevant to forgetting data by gradient norm [11].

4.2 Results and Comparison

Performace on Full-Class Unlearning Tasks. The advantages of our approach become noticeable when the models and datasets are more complex and large-scaled. For the ImageNet-1K dataset shown in Table 1, the non-zero values of FA of other baselines indicate that they all fail to achieve complete forgetting without unduly impairing model performance. Although the FAs may drop to 0 as the training duration increases, it will inevitably cause lower RA. In contrast, U^2AP achieves a zero-value FA as well as high RA and VA. Furthermore, our method achieves low MIA scores, which reflects its enhanced privacy protection capabilities after unlearning. In terms of forgetting efficiency, the time required by our method is significantly lower (faster ×10) than that of other baselines. Especially, compared to basic finetuning where catastrophic forgetting is inefficient in this task, our method significantly accelerates such process. Other baseline approaches not only fail to achieve complete forgetting knowledge elimination but also induce severe performance degradation in model utility. Unlike other methods that suffer from excessively long execution times and low efficiency, our method proves more practical for real-world applications.

Table 2. The time(s) consumption of each step in the U^2AP framework: (1) UAP extracting; (2) Forget-class feature unlearning; (3) Repairing. And the accuracy on different datasets after forgetting step. The results are evaluated on "109" and "971" classes of ImageNet-1K using Deit-B.

Class	$RA_{u\uparrow}$	$FA_{u\downarrow}$	$VA_{u\uparrow}$	UAP Time	Unlearn Time	Repair Time
109	$78.21_{\pm 0.63}$	$0.00_{\pm 0.00}$	$76.87_{\pm 0.43}$	102	160	402
971	$77.89_{\pm 0.25}$	$0.00_{\pm 0.00}$	$76.35_{\pm 0.57}$	101	161	250

To comprehensively evaluate the efficiency of our proposed method under complex configurations of datasets and models, we conducted detailed experiments to measure the time consumption of each step in the U^2AP framework on ImageNet-1K. Furthermore, to demonstrate that UAP specifically stimulates catastrophic forgetting for the targeted class while minimally affecting other classes, we systematically measured model accuracy across all datasets immediately after the forgetting step (prior to the repairing step), as presented in Table 2. Our results show that the computation time required for UAP remains acceptable given the complexity of both models and datasets, with the forgetting step itself requiring negligible time. Remarkably, this efficient forgetting procedure sufficiently reduces the FA value to 0% while maintaining high accuracy on remaining data (exhibiting less than 4% degradation compared to pre-forgetting performance). These results confirm that UAP achieves efficient elimination of target class influence while preserving model utility for other classes, thereby validating the operational efficiency and precision of our approach.

Table 3. Results of multi-class unlearning methods on CIFAR-100 using ResNet-18, evaluated with forgetting 2, 4, 8 classes. Since the purpose of forgetting the whole class is high RA,VA as well as low FA, we omit the comparison with retrain here. The tables are laid out in the same format as Table 1.

Classes number	Method	RA↑	FA↓	VA↑	MIA↓
2	Pretrain	76.28±0.00	83.33±0.00	76.50±0.00	95.10±0.00
	Finetune	76.43±0.22	0.02±0.05	70.11±0.18	1.58±0.25
	GradientAscent	73.01±0.64	1.20±1.30	71.54±0.40	7.23±0.34
	EU-k	68.53±0.60	0.00±0.00	66.96±0.56	3.00±0.03
	CF-k	72.76±0.22	0.00±0.00	71.57±0.20	2.13±0.01
	BadTeacher	66.86±0.46	0.00±0.00	65.47±0.44	**0.00±0.00**
	Amnesiac	73.39±0.60	0.00±0.00	71.93±0.60	46.62±1.04
	SalUn	76.50±0.14	2.68±0.97	**74.99±0.13**	0.00±0.00
	U²AP	**76.62±0.06**	**0.00±0.00**	74.95±0.23	1.11±0.39
4	Pretrain	76.21±0.00	80.66±0.00	76.50±0.00	95.25±0.00
	Finetune	75.91±0.14	0.00±0.00	72.93±0.54	3.83±6.89
	GradientAscent	73.54±0.20	3.51±0.34	71.92±0.33	2.81±0.56
	EU-k	68.32±0.57	0.06±0.11	67.13±0.35	4.13±0.02
	CF-k	72.98±0.31	0.00±0.00	71.62±0.38	1.66±0.20
	BadTeacher	67.09±0.52	0.04±0.09	64.35±0.50	**0.00±0.00**
	Amnesiac	72.81±0.12	0.00±0.00	69.83±0.14	44.33±0.60
	SalUn	76.14±0.19	1.76±0.69	73.11±0.17	0.01±0.02
	U²AP	**76.50±0.33**	**0.00±0.00**	**73.36±0.34**	1.02±0.35
8	Pretrain	76.13±0.00	80.80±0.00	76.50±0.00	95.82±0.00
	Finetune	76.43±0.22	0.02±0.05	70.11±0.18	1.58±0.25
	GradientAscent	74.06±0.72	3.61±0.60	72.36±0.33	9.22±1.65
	EU-k	69.06±0.67	0.00±0.00	66.34±0.66	2.02±0.01
	CF-k	73.21±0.89	1.05±0.09	**71.00±0.66**	0.56±0.93
	BadTeacher	67.35±0.48	0.00±0.00	61.84±0.47	**0.00±0.00**
	Amnesiac	72.67±0.25	0.00±0.00	66.74±0.24	43.71±0.94
	SalUn	75.65±0.20	3.17±0.41	69.75±0.22	0.03±0.03
	U²AP	**76.54±0.13**	**0.00±0.00**	70.87±0.22	2.14±0.32

Performace on Multi-class Unlearning Tasks. To further analyze the applicability and stability of our method across different unlearning scenarios, we conducted multi-class unlearning experiments with varying numbers of forgetting classes (2, 4, and 8) on CIFAR-100 using ResNet-18. We train the corresponding UAPs for the classes that need to be forgotten and add them randomly to the remaining data (only one class of UAPs is added to each remaining sample). As shown in Table 3, our method consistently achieves optimal performance across all evaluation metrics, demonstrating superior RA and VA while maintaining the lowest FA. Comparative analysis reveals that while Finetune and

SalUn preserve model utility on remaining classes, they exhibit incomplete forgetting of target classes. Conversely, EU-k, CF-k, and Amnesiac achieve effective forgetting but significantly degrade performance in the remaining classes. Our approach effectively balances these objectives, delivering both precise forgetting and high utility preservation without compromising either aspect.

Performace on Sub-class Unlearning Tasks. We do experiments of subclass "rocket" on CIFAR-20. As shown in Table 4, data-modification based methods like Amnesiac and UNSIR both have relatively RA, indicating poor forgetting effectiveness. Some other finetuning-based methods *e.g.* Gradient Ascent, EU-k, and Cf-k demonstrate performance substantially deviating from retraining. In contrast, in terms of Avg. Gap, our method produces results similar to retraining, with comparatively lower execution time and stable performance.

Table 4. Results of sub-class unlearning methods on CIFAR-20 using ResNet-18, evaluated with sub-class "rocket". The tables are laid out in the same format as Table 1.

Method	RA↑	FA↓	VA↑	Avg. Gap↓	MIA↓	Time (s)↓
Pretrain	$85.26_{\pm 0.00}$	$80.73_{\pm 0.00}$	$85.21_{\pm 0.00}$	–	$92.80_{\pm 0.00}$	–
Retrain	$84.85_{\pm 0.05}$	$2.69_{\pm 0.21}$	$84.07_{\pm 0.09}$	-	$12.40_{\pm 0.86}$	–
Finetune	$83.23_{\pm 0.20}$	$4.46_{\pm 1.44}$	$82.49_{\pm 0.20}$	1.66	$4.36_{\pm 0.92}$	165
GradientAscent	$80.77_{\pm 4.04}$	$1.32_{\pm 1.54}$	$79.53_{\pm 1.28}$	3.33	$14.76_{\pm 5.39}$	130
EU-k	$78.56_{\pm 1.25}$	$1.89_{\pm 0.36}$	$77.97_{\pm 0.26}$	4.40	$16.98_{\pm 2.76}$	230
CF-k	$80.13_{\pm 0.78}$	$3.96_{\pm 1.22}$	$79.04_{\pm 0.88}$	3.67	$9.67_{\pm 0.77}$	254
UNSIR	$78.39_{\pm 0.66}$	$4.69_{\pm 3.23}$	$77.65_{\pm 0.63}$	4.96	$12.08_{\pm 4.85}$	88
BadTeacher	$84.15_{\pm 0.33}$	$3.01_{\pm 1.62}$	$83.34_{\pm 0.32}$	0.58	$\mathbf{0.00_{\pm 0.00}}$	33
Amnesiac	$82.92_{\pm 0.09}$	$\mathbf{2.71_{\pm 1.09}}$	$82.15_{\pm 0.10}$	1.29	$1.10_{\pm 0.48}$	28
SalUn	$\mathbf{84.71_{\pm 0.09}}$	$3.52_{\pm 0.57}$	$\mathbf{83.89_{\pm 0.08}}$	0.38	$0.30_{\pm 0.12}$	117
U²AP	$84.38_{\pm 0.04}$	$2.56_{\pm 0.55}$	$83.56_{\pm 0.04}$	**0.37**	$1.31_{\pm 1.56}$	102

Summary. These results indicate that our method demonstrates consistent forgetting performance across datasets, models of various sizes, and different unlearning tasks. It enables the unlearning process to stimulate the catastrophic forgetting of data while preserving the integrity on remaining data. This makes our approach more effective and efficient than existing unlearning methods.

4.3 Analysis

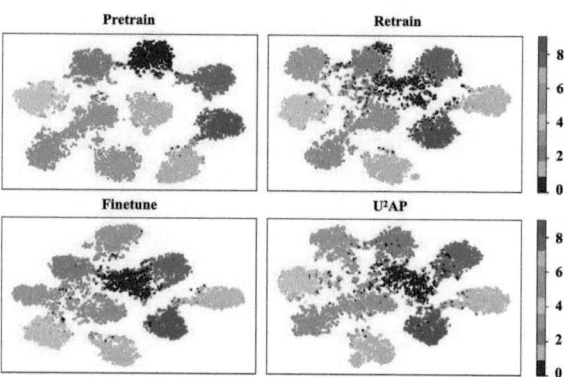

Fig. 5. Visualization of feature dimension reduction for different models on the CIFAR-10. Compared to finetuning, our method has more similar results to retraining.

Feature Representation Visualization. We use T-SNE [22] dimensionality reduction to visualize the output features of CIFAR-10 [20] across models. In this case, class "0" is the forgetting class, indicated in dark red color. As can be seen in Fig. 5, although both Finetune and our method can distinguish the forgetting data from the remaining data, our approach demonstrates superior feature distribution alignment with the retrained model.

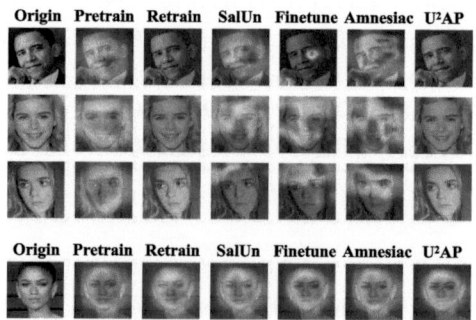

Fig. 6. The visualizations of attention heatmaps for some unlearned models on the forgetting data (top three lines) and the remaining data (bottom line).

Attention Maps Visualization. We examine the model's attention on the forgetting class before and after unlearning using attention heatmaps [29]. We compare U^2AP with several other unlearning methods that exhibit minimal Avg. Gap to the retrained model in previous evaluations, including SalUn, Finetune, and Amnesiac on PinsFaceRecognition [3] using ResNet-18. As shown in Fig. 6, after applying U²AP for class forgetting, the model's attention noticeably shifts away from facial regions, closely aligning with the visualization results of the retrained model. In contrast, the attention maps of other baseline methods still focus more or less on the facial areas. This implies that U²AP is superior to other methods in precisely locating and erasing class-wise information, leading to a more effective unlearning process. In addition, Fig. 6 shows the heatmap of the remaining data before and after forgetting, and it can be seen that the attention of the model is still gathered on the face of the remaining data after forgetting using our method, showing the high utility of our method.

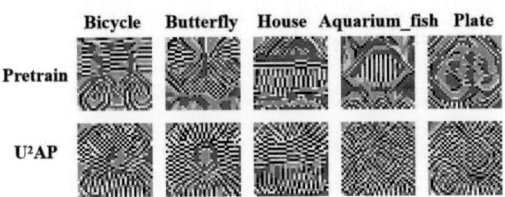

Fig. 7. The UAPs obtained from targeted attacking the model before and after unlearning by U²AP.

Post-unlearned UAP Test. We investigate the leftover semantic information of the forgetting class after unlearning by visualizing the targeted UAPs of the pretrained and unlearned models. As shown in Fig. 7, we analyze this for five different forgetting classes in CIFAR-100. The first row shows the UAPs trained from the pretrained model, where each UAP exhibits obvious semantic class-wise patterns, such as a "bicycle" or a "butterfly". After applying U²AP, the semantic patterns disappear from generated UAPs. This demonstrates that our proposed method, U²AP, successfully eliminates the class-wise information from the pretrained model.

5 Conclusion

In this paper, we point out that effective and efficient unlearning requires explicitly extracting class-wise information to stimulate catastrophic forgetting. We emphasize that targeted universal adversarial perturbations implicitly extract class-specific information, as demonstrated by the visible semantic patterns aligned with the targeted class. Hence, the targeted UAP generated from the pretrained model can be readily leveraged to facilitate the unlearning of specific data. In light of this, we propose U²AP, which unlearns by finetuning the model with perturbed remaining data to stimulate catastrophic forgetting. Extensive experiments demonstrate the effectiveness and efficiency of our proposed method. Taking advantage of the universal adversarial perturbation opens up a new perspective for identifying model's knowledge of the forgetting data.

Limitations. The critical aspect of our U^2AP lies in extracting implicit features related to the forgetting data, which makes our method dependent on the difficulty and accuracy of feature localization. When the features of the forgetting data are dispersed and difficult to extract, our method may fail. Additionally, we only focus on image tasks, and our approach remains to be explored for tasks such as text-based ones.

Acknowledgments. The research leading to these results has received funding from National Natural Science Foundation of China (62376155) and the Interdisciplinary Program of Shanghai Jiao Tong University (No. YG2022ZD031).

Disclosure of Interests. The authors have no competing interests to declare that are relevant to the content of this article.

References

1. Bae, J., Ng, N., Lo, A., Ghassemi, M., Grosse, R.B.: If influence functions are the answer, then what is the question? Adv. Neural. Inf. Process. Syst. **35**, 17953–17967 (2022)
2. Baumhauer, T., Schöttle, P., Zeppelzauer, M.: Machine unlearning: linear filtration for logit-based classifiers. Mach. Learn. **111**(9), 3203–3226 (2022)
3. Burak: Pinterest face recognition dataset (2020). www.kaggle.com/datasets/hereisburak/pins-facerecognition
4. Cao, Y., Yang, J.: Towards making systems forget with machine unlearning. In: 2015 IEEE Symposium on Security and Privacy, pp. 463–480. IEEE (2015)
5. Chang, Y., Ren, Z., Nguyen, T.T., Nejdl, W., Schuller, B.W.: Example-based explanations with adversarial attacks for respiratory sound analysis. arXiv preprint arXiv:2203.16141 (2022)
6. Choi, D., Choi, S., Lee, E., Seo, J., Na, D.: Towards efficient machine unlearning with data augmentation: guided loss-increasing (gli) to prevent the catastrophic model utility drop. In: Proceedings of the IEEE/CVF Conference on Computer Vision and Pattern Recognition, pp. 93–102 (2024)
7. Chundawat, V.S., Tarun, A.K., Mandal, M., Kankanhalli, M.: Can bad teaching induce forgetting? Unlearning in deep networks using an incompetent teacher. In: Proceedings of the AAAI Conference on Artificial Intelligence, vol. 37, pp. 7210–7217 (2023)
8. Dang, Q.-V.: Right to be forgotten in the age of machine learning. In: Antipova, T. (ed.) ICADS 2021. AISC, vol. 1352, pp. 403–411. Springer, Cham (2021). https://doi.org/10.1007/978-3-030-71782-7_35
9. Deng, J., Dong, W., Socher, R., Li, L.J., Li, K., Fei-Fei, L.: Imagenet: a large-scale hierarchical image database. In: 2009 IEEE Conference on Computer Vision and Pattern Recognition, pp. 248–255. IEEE (2009)
10. Dwork, C.: Differential privacy. In: Bugliesi, M., Preneel, B., Sassone, V., Wegener, I. (eds.) ICALP 2006. LNCS, vol. 4052, pp. 1–12. Springer, Heidelberg (2006). https://doi.org/10.1007/11787006_1
11. Fan, C., Liu, J., Zhang, Y., Wei, D., Wong, E., Liu, S.: Salun: empowering machine unlearning via gradient-based weight saliency in both image classification and generation. arXiv preprint arXiv:2310.12508 (2023)

12. Fredrikson, M., Lantz, E., Jha, S., Lin, S., Page, D., Ristenpart, T.: Privacy in pharmacogenetics: an {End-to-End} case study of personalized warfarin dosing. In: 23rd USENIX security symposium (USENIX Security 14), pp. 17–32 (2014)
13. GDPR, G.D.P.R.: General data protection regulation. Regulation (EU) 2016/679 of the European Parliament and of the Council of 27 April 2016 on the protection of natural persons with regard to the processing of personal data and on the free movement of such data, and repealing Directive 95/46/EC (2016)
14. Goel, S., Prabhu, A., Sanyal, A., Lim, S.N., Torr, P., Kumaraguru, P.: Towards adversarial evaluations for inexact machine unlearning. arXiv preprint arXiv:2201.06640 (2022)
15. Graves, L., Nagisetty, V., Ganesh, V.: Amnesiac machine learning. In: Proceedings of the AAAI Conference on Artificial Intelligence, vol. 35, pp. 11516–11524 (2021)
16. Guo, C., Goldstein, T., Hannun, A., Van Der Maaten, L.: Certified data removal from machine learning models. arXiv preprint arXiv:1911.03030 (2019)
17. He, K., Zhang, X., Ren, S., Sun, J.: Deep residual learning for image recognition. In: Proceedings of the IEEE Conference on Computer Vision and Pattern Recognition, pp. 770–778 (2016)
18. Kirkpatrick, J., et al.: Overcoming catastrophic forgetting in neural networks. Proc. Natl. Acad. Sci. **114**(13), 3521–3526 (2017)
19. Koh, P.W., Liang, P.: Understanding black-box predictions via influence functions. In: International Conference on Machine Learning, pp. 1885–1894. PMLR (2017)
20. Krizhevsky, A., Hinton, G., et al.: Learning multiple layers of features from tiny images (2009)
21. Kurmanji, M., Triantafillou, P., Hayes, J., Triantafillou, E.: Towards unbounded machine unlearning. Adv. Neural Inf. Process. Syst. **36** (2024)
22. Van der Maaten, L., Hinton, G.: Visualizing data using t-sne. J. Mach. Learn. Res. **9**(11) (2008)
23. Moosavi-Dezfooli, S.M., Fawzi, A., Fawzi, O., Frossard, P.: Universal adversarial perturbations. In: Proceedings of the IEEE Conference on Computer Vision and Pattern Recognition, pp. 1765–1773 (2017)
24. Moosavi-Dezfooli, S.M., Fawzi, A., Frossard, P.: Deepfool: a simple and accurate method to fool deep neural networks. In: Proceedings of the IEEE Conference on Computer Vision and Pattern Recognition, pp. 2574–2582 (2016)
25. Mopuri, K.R., Ojha, U., Garg, U., Babu, R.V.: Nag: network for adversary generation. In: Proceedings of the IEEE Conference on Computer Vision and Pattern Recognition, pp. 742–751 (2018)
26. Mopuri, K.R., Uppala, P.K., Babu, R.V.: Ask, acquire, and attack: data-free uap generation using class impressions. In: Proceedings of the European Conference on Computer Vision (ECCV), pp. 19–34 (2018)
27. Papyan, V., Han, X., Donoho, D.L.: Prevalence of neural collapse during the terminal phase of deep learning training. Proc. Natl. Acad. Sci. **117**(40), 24652–24663 (2020)
28. Ren, Z., Baird, A., Han, J., Zhang, Z., Schuller, B.: Generating and protecting against adversarial attacks for deep speech-based emotion recognition models. In: ICASSP 2020-2020 IEEE International Conference on Acoustics, Speech and Signal Processing (ICASSP), pp. 7184–7188. IEEE (2020)
29. Selvaraju, R.R., Cogswell, M., Das, A., Vedantam, R., Parikh, D., Batra, D.: Gradcam: visual explanations from deep networks via gradient-based localization. In: Proceedings of the IEEE International Conference on Computer Vision, pp. 618–626 (2017)

30. Shokri, R., Stronati, M., Song, C., Shmatikov, V.: Membership inference attacks against machine learning models. In: 2017 IEEE Symposium on Security and Privacy (SP), pp. 3–18. IEEE (2017)
31. Song, L., Mittal, P.: Systematic evaluation of privacy risks of machine learning models. In: 30th USENIX Security Symposium (USENIX Security 21), pp. 2615–2632 (2021)
32. Tarun, A.K., Chundawat, V.S., Mandal, M., Kankanhalli, M.: Fast yet effective machine unlearning. IEEE Trans. Neural Netw. Learn. Syst. (2023)
33. Thudi, A., Deza, G., Chandrasekaran, V., Papernot, N.: Unrolling SGD: understanding factors influencing machine unlearning. In: 2022 IEEE 7th European Symposium on Security and Privacy (EuroS&P), pp. 303–319. IEEE (2022)
34. Thudi, A., Jia, H., Shumailov, I., Papernot, N.: On the necessity of auditable algorithmic definitions for machine unlearning. In: 31st USENIX Security Symposium (USENIX Security 22), pp. 4007–4022 (2022)
35. Tishby, N., Zaslavsky, N.: Deep learning and the information bottleneck principle. In: 2015 IEEE Information Theory Workshop (itw), pp. 1–5. IEEE (2015)
36. Touvron, H., Cord, M., Douze, M., Massa, F., Sablayrolles, A., Jégou, H.: Training data-efficient image transformers & distillation through attention. In: International Conference on Machine Learning, pp. 10347–10357. PMLR (2021)
37. Warnecke, A., Pirch, L., Wressnegger, C., Rieck, K.: Machine unlearning of features and labels. arXiv preprint arXiv:2108.11577 (2021)
38. Ye, Z., Cheng, X., Huang, X.: FG-UAP: feature-gathering universal adversarial perturbation. In: 2023 International Joint Conference on Neural Networks (IJCNN), pp. 1–8. IEEE (2023)
39. Zhang, C., Benz, P., Imtiaz, T., Kweon, I.S.: CD-UAP: class discriminative universal adversarial perturbation. In: Proceedings of the AAAI Conference on Artificial Intelligence, vol. 34, pp. 6754–6761 (2020)
40. Zhang, C., Benz, P., Imtiaz, T., Kweon, I.S.: Understanding adversarial examples from the mutual influence of images and perturbations. In: Proceedings of the IEEE/CVF Conference on Computer Vision and Pattern Recognition, pp. 14521–14530 (2020)

Recommender Systems

Towards Unifying Feature Interaction Models for Click-Through Rate Prediction

Yu Kang[1], Junwei Pan[2], Jipeng Jin[1], Shudong Huang[2], Xiaofeng Gao[1(✉)], and Lei Xiao[2]

[1] Shanghai Key Laboratory of Scalable Computing and Systems, School of Computer Science, Shanghai Jiao Tong University, Shanghai, China
{jerryykang,jinjipeng}@sjtu.edu.cn, gao-xf@cs.sjtu.edu.cn
[2] Tencent, Shenzhen, China
{jonaspan,ericdhuang,shawn}@tencent.com

Abstract. Modeling feature interactions plays a crucial role in accurately predicting Click-Through Rates (CTR) in advertising systems. To capture the intricate interaction patterns, many existing models employ matrix-factorization techniques to represent features as lower-dimensional embedding vectors, enabling the modeling of interactions as products between these embeddings. In this paper, we propose a general framework called *IPA* to systematically unify these matrix-factorization-based models. Our framework comprises three key components: the *Interaction Function*, which facilitates feature interaction; the *Layer Pooling*, which constructs higher-level interaction layers; and the *Layer Aggregator*, which combines the outputs of all interaction layers to serve as input for the subsequent classifier. We demonstrate that most existing models can be categorized within our framework by making specific choices for these three components. Through extensive experiments and a Dimensional Collapse analysis, we evaluate the performance of these choices. Furthermore, by leveraging the most powerful components within our framework, we introduce a novel model PFL that achieves competitive results compared to state-of-the-art CTR models. PFL gets significant GMV lift during online A/B test in Tencent's advertising platform, and has been deployed as the production model in several primary scenarios.

Keywords: CTR Prediction · Factorization Machine · Recommender System

---

This work was supported by the National Key R&D Program of China [2024YFF0617700] and the National Natural Science Foundation of China [U23A20309, 62272302, 62372296]. The authors are grateful to the support of Yiming Liu and Xinyi Zhou for their contributions in preliminary works. They would also thank Shifeng Wen, Zijun Liu and Xun Liu for their invaluable contributions of online evaluation, and Weihua Zhu for supporting the collaboration between SJTU and Tencent upon which this work is built.

1 Introduction

Online advertising has become a billion-dollar business nowadays, with an annual revenue of 225 billion US dollars between 2022 and 2023 (increasing 7.3% YoY) [7]. One of the core problems in this field is to deliver the right ads to the right audiences in a given context. Accurately predicting the click-through rate (CTR) is crucial to solving this problem and has attracted significant attention over the past decade [5,15,17,19,24,25,27–29,31,35,37,38,40,46,52].

CTR prediction commonly involves the handling of multi-field categorical data [28,47], where all features are categorical and sparse. The primary challenge lies in effectively capturing interactions between these features, which is particularly difficult due to the extreme sparsity of feature co-occurrence. To address this challenge, numerous approaches [17,19,24,28,31,35,37,40] have been proposed to explicitly model feature interactions, using matrix factorization techniques or hybrid methods that combine explicit modeling with implicit method of deep neural networks (DNNs).

Explicit interaction models, particularly the 2nd-order ones, have well-defined definitions and close-form formulations. These models originated from classic Matrix Factorization (MF) [20,34], followed by FM [5,31], FFM [19], FwFM [28], and FmFM [37].

In contrast, models like xDeepFM [24] and DCN V2 [40] employ a parameter or weight matrix to model higher-order interactions, going beyond the 2nd-order interactions captured by the aforementioned models. However, it is worth noting that while some attempts have been made to discuss the connections between explicit interaction models [11,21,40], these efforts have only covered a limited number of models. As a result, the differences and relationships between various explicit interaction models remain less well-understood.

Thus, we propose a simple framework, *i.e.*, IPA, to unify existing low- and high-order explicit interaction models for systematic comparisons between them. The name of IPA corresponds to its three components: the *Interaction Function* which captures the interaction between two terms (or features), the *Layer Pooling* which constructs explicit interaction layers based on the prior layers and raw feature embeddings, and the *Layer Aggregator* which takes all layers as input, and outputs a representation for the classifier. By combining these three components within the IPA framework, we can represent various CTR models, from 2nd-order interactions models like FM [5,31], FwFM [28], FmFM [37] to high-order interaction models like xDeepFM [24] and CIN [40].

Furthermore, the IPA framework enables more granular analysis of structural differences between these CTR models in their choices of the three components, providing a better guidance for model design. For validation, we conduct extensive experiments over public datasets and production dataset, comparing between existing CTR models as well as models derived from our framework. These experiments not only identify the key factors behind model performance, supporting our derived models to be as robust as SOTA models, but also connect component choices and performance from a novel perspective: the phenomenon of Dimensional Collapse.

The main contribution of the paper can be summarized as:

- We propose a general framework IPA for feature interaction models, consisting of the Interaction Function, the Layer Pooling and the Layer Aggregator. The framework supports structural analysis between models.
- We derive novel models by combinations of IPA components. Experiment results demonstrate the effectiveness of these new models on both public datasets and online testing, providing essential findings for model designing.
- We present a novel Dimensional Collapse perspective to understand the evolution of Interaction Functions and analyze the potential to learn data orders.

2 The IPA Framework

In this section, we present the three modules in our framework: the Interaction Functions, Layer Pooling and Layer Aggregator. The structure of framework is illustrated in Fig. 1 below:

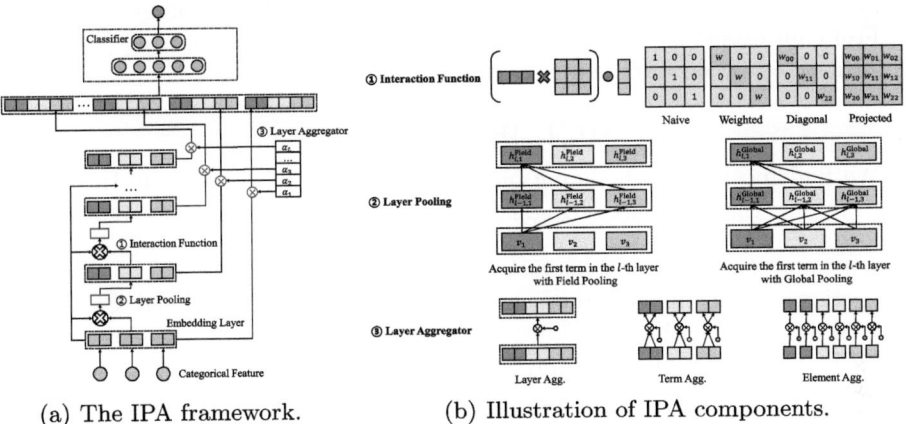

(a) The IPA framework.   (b) Illustration of IPA components.

Fig. 1. Illustration of the IPA framework and common choices of its three components.

2.1 Interaction Function

Starting with a set of embedding vectors, the very first thing to determine is the way to model interactions between these embedding vectors of different feature fields. As the first IPA component, the Interaction Function extracts information from explicit interaction of these embedding vectors and returns the result in vector form. The input accepts both raw embeddings directly obtained from features and calculated interaction terms, enabling explicit feature interaction of any order.

Table 1. Formulation of Interaction Functions where diag() denotes diagonal matrix.

Type	Notation	Matrix	Example
Naive	$\boldsymbol{W}^N$	$\boldsymbol{I}$	FM [5,31], HOFM [6]
Weighted	$\boldsymbol{W}^W$	$\mathrm{diag}(w,\ldots,w)$	FwFM [28], xDeepFM [24]
Diagonal	$\boldsymbol{W}^D$	$\mathrm{diag}(w_1,\ldots,w_K)$	FvFM [37]
Projected	$\boldsymbol{W}^P$	full matrix	FmFM [37], DCNV2 [40]

Definition 1. *Interaction Function:* For two input embeddings $\boldsymbol{t}_i, \boldsymbol{t}_j \in R^K$, the Interaction Function f is defined as a function mapping $\boldsymbol{t}_i, \boldsymbol{t}_j$ to the interaction term of two these two embeddings:

$$\boldsymbol{t}_{i,j} = f(\boldsymbol{t}_i, \boldsymbol{t}_j) \in R^K \qquad (1)$$

In our framework, illustrated in the middle part of Fig. 1(a), the Interaction Function serves as the basic unit of feature interaction operations. Utilizing the interaction terms generated by the Interaction Function, the whole CTR model is able to model interaction patterns throughout the training progress.

From our observations, the Interaction Function in many existing models can be formulated by an interaction matrix $\boldsymbol{W} \in \mathcal{R}^{K \times K}$:

$$f(\boldsymbol{t}_i, \boldsymbol{t}_j, \boldsymbol{W}) = (\boldsymbol{t}_i^\top \boldsymbol{W}) \odot \boldsymbol{t}_j^\top \qquad (2)$$

We find most of them taking one of the four forms of $\boldsymbol{W}_{i,j}$ in Table 1 and illustrated in the first part of Fig. 1(b), where blue elements are trainable.

Dimensional Collapse of Interactions. Recent work [15] reveals that feature interaction on recommendation models leads to the Dimensional Collapse of embeddings, that is, the embeddings may only be able to span a low-dimensional space. Inspired by [18], which proves that the projection matrix alleviates the Dimensional Collapse in contrastive learning, we study if the projection matrix in the Interaction Functions can achieve the same goal. Refer to Sect. 3.3 for details.

2.2 Layer Pooling

Existing works [24,35,40,41] tend to build layers to capture explicit high-order interactions. However, the skyrocketing number of combinations ($\binom{M}{l}$) requires interaction terms to be explored systematically with tractable complexity.

A widely-employed method of traversal is to generate interaction terms layer by layer corresponding to their order, starting from the first layer which is simply a concatenation of embeddings of all fields. The embedding $\boldsymbol{t}_n$ of field n is defined as either the embedding of the active feature for a one-hot encoding field, or a pooling over embeddings for all active features for a multi-hot field. Formally,

$$\boldsymbol{h}_1 = [\boldsymbol{t}_1, \ldots, \boldsymbol{t}_n, \ldots, \boldsymbol{t}_M] \qquad (3)$$

Definition 2. Layer Pooling: For the raw embeddings $h_1 = [t_1, ..., t_M]$ and the layer of all $(l-1)$-order terms $h_{(l-1)} = [t_{l-1,1}, ..., t_{l-1,M}]$, then the Layer Pooling is defined as the way to generate interaction terms of order l from all interactions between terms of h_1 and $h_{(l-1)}$, that is:

$$t_{l,n} = \sum_{m=1}^{M} \sum_{n=1}^{M} \alpha_{m,n} f(t_n, t_{l-1,m}) \quad (4)$$

$\alpha_{m,n}$ are either 0 or 1 indicating presence of corresponding terms.

Illustrated in the middle bottom part of Fig. 1(a), to capture higher-order interactions, an IPA model relies on its Layer Pooling to systematically generate and combine new interaction terms, forming interaction layers of higher order. Furthermore, to control the number of interactions, two widely employed methods build layers with a fixed number of terms, where each term is a pooling of interactions between terms from prior layers and raw feature embeddings.

Field-Wise Layer Pooling (Field Pooling). This Field Pooling will pool all the interactions that correspond to a specific field. Specifically, the l-th layer consists of M terms, with the n-th term $t_{l,n}$ defined as a pooling over all interactions between the n-th term in the first layer, i.e., the embedding of the n-th field t_n, and all terms in the $(l-1)$-th layer, i.e., $t_{l-1,m}$.

$$h_l^F = [t_{l,1}^F, ..., t_{l,n}^F, ..., t_{l,M}^F], \quad t_{l,n}^{Field} = \sum_{m=1}^{M} f(t_n, t_{l-1,m}^F, W) \quad (5)$$

DCNV2 employs Field Pooling and Projected Product to build up layers, i.e., $h_{l,n}^{CrossNet} = \sum_{m=1}^{M} f(t_n, t_{l-1,m}, W_{l,n,m}^F)$.

Global-Wise Layer Pooling (Global Pooling). This Field Pooling will globally pool all the interactions, regardless of fields. Specifically, the l-th layer consists of H_l terms, with the n-th term defined as a pooling over all interactions between all terms in the first layer, and all terms in the $(l-1)$-th layer.

$$h_l^G = [t_{l,1}^G, ..., t_{l,n}^G, ..., t_{l,H_l}^G], \quad t_{l,n}^G = \sum_{n=1}^{M} \sum_{m=1}^{H_{l-1}} f(t_n, t_{l-1,m}^G, W) \quad (6)$$

Global Pooling introduces symmetric interactions in each layer, thus more redundant than Field Pooling. xDeepFM [24] employs AGT to construct layers, i.e., $h_{l,n}^{CIN} = \sum_{n=1}^{M} \sum_{m=1}^{M} f(t_n, t_{l-1,m}, W_{l,n,m}^F)$. The second part of Fig. 1(b) illustrates the details on acquiring terms in the l-th layer with both pooling.

2.3 Layer Aggregator

After constructing layers, complexity of input features requires model to learn from interaction of all orders, combining terms from these layers into vector from for following classifiers. So the last component of our framework is defined:

Definition 3. Layer Aggregator: Considering $[h_1, ..., h_L]$ as interaction layers of model, then the Layer Aggregator LA is defined as a function aggregating elements of layers into one output vector as input of classifier, that is:

$$r = LA([h_1, ..., h_L]) \qquad (7)$$

Illustrated in the middle-top part of Fig. 1(a), the Layer Aggregator component takes the interaction layers as input, integrates terms within layers and then aggregates all the layers to form the final output of feature interaction module, serving as the input of following classifier in the model.

Here are some widely employed ways to aggregate layers:

- **Direct Agg.**: Directly link each layer, with No weights at all.
- **Layer Agg.**: Assign a Layer-wise weight α_l for each layer.
- **Term Agg.**: Assign a Term-wise weight for each term in each layer, e.g., assign $\alpha_{l,n}$ for the n-th term of the l-th layer.
- **Element Agg.**: Assign an Element-wise weight for elements in each layer, e.g., assign $\alpha_{l,n,k}$ for the k-th element in the n-th term of the l-th layer.

The third part of Fig. 1(b) illustrates how to assign weights to a term with Layer, Term and Element Agg., respectively. Table 2 summarizes the formulation and number of learnable parameters of different Layer Aggregators.

Table 2. Formulation of aggregators, where $\|\{\cdot\}$ denotes the concatenation function.

Abbr.	Weight	# Param.	Output
Direct	1	0	$r = \sum_{l=1}^{L} \|_{n=1}^{M} \{t_{l,n}\}$
Layer	α_l	L	$r = \sum_{l=1}^{L} \alpha_l \cdot \|_{n=1}^{M} \{t_{l,n}\}$
Term	$\alpha_{l,n}$	LM	$r = \sum_{l=1}^{L} \|_{n=1}^{M} \{\alpha_{l,n} \cdot t_{l,n}\}$
Element	$\alpha_{l,n,k}$	LMK	$r = \sum_{l=1}^{L} \|_{n=1}^{M} \{\|_{k=1}^{K} \{\alpha_{l,n,k} \cdot t_{l,n,k}\}\}$

2.4 The Framework

Now, combining the three components above, we propose our framework **IPA** as a modularized transformation:

- First of all, IPA reads in the embedding vectors as the 0-th layer and prepares the Interaction Function.
- Then, IPA constructs the interaction layers using its Interaction Function on the built layers guided by its Layer Pooling.
- Finally, IPA aggregates all the layers by its Layer Aggregator, creating output vector of desired length for following classifiers.

Generalizing the structure of feature interaction module by the three components, the IPA framework dives into the details of existing CTR models, exploring their similarity and differences on various aspects. We can compare how models make basic interactions, how they build up high-order interaction terms, and how they extract information from interaction layers. Besides, the framework can help us control variables when analyzing the effect of one component (like Interaction Function), by simply fixing the choices of other components.

2.5 Deriving New Models

While many existing CTR models can fit into IPA as a combination of three components, there are several new models that can be derived from unexplored combinations.

Specifically, we choose Projected Product to capture interactions between terms, employ Field Pooling to build up layers and employ Layer Agg. to assign layer-wise weight during layer aggregation.

We name it as PFL, which stands for Projected Product with Field Pooling and Layer Agg. Comparing PFL to DCN V2, there are two main differences between them:

1. PFL employs Field Pooling without residual connections.
2. PFL employs Layer Agg. to aggregate layers instead of Direct Agg.

There are many other new models that can be derived in this way, and we present some of the most effective ones in Table 3.

3 Evaluation

In this section, we aim to answer several research questions related to the performance of components in the IPA framework.

- RQ1: How do the Interaction Functions perform? Does a more complicated Interaction Function lead to better performance in the real-world scenario?
- RQ2: Regarding Dimensional Collapse, how does Interaction Function influence the extent of collapse?
- RQ3: How do the various Layer Poolings perform? What can we infer from them about model design?
- RQ4: How do the various Layer Aggregators perform? What can we learn from choices of this component?
- RQ5: How do existing CTR models evolve so far? How does our framework offer a direction towards a better model?
- RQ6: Regarding the derived model PFL, to what extent has this model performed in industrial applications?

3.1 Experiment Setup

Public Dataset. We evaluate the models on two public datasets: Criteo-x1 and Avazu. Both are divided into 8:1:1 for training, validation, and test set.

- Criteo-x1 [2]. It is the most popular benchmark dataset for CTR prediction, consisting of 45 million click feedback records of display ads. The dataset includes 13 numerical feature fields and 26 categorical feature fields.
- Avazu [1]. It includes 10 d of Avazu click-through data, with 13 feature fields that have disclosed meanings and 9 anonymous categorical fields.

Synthetic Dataset. We follow [40] to generate data with specified interaction orders. Let $\boldsymbol{x} = [x_1, \ldots, x_n]$ be a feature vector of length n, and the element $x_i \in \mathcal{R}$ denotes the i-th feature of $\boldsymbol{x}$. x_i is uniformly sampled from interval $[-1, 1]$. The monomial $x_1 \cdots x_O$ is called O-order cross-term, representing an O-order interaction between features. Given $\boldsymbol{x}$ of length n and the data order O, we generate a label as the sum of the cross-terms whose orders $\leq O$, each with an individual weight. Specifically, we define $\boldsymbol{I}_n = \{i | i \leq n, i \in \mathbf{N}^*\}$ as the set of all positive integers $\leq n$, and Ω_n^O as the set of all combinations of O distinct integers randomly sampled from $\boldsymbol{I}_n$.

The label y is generated by the equation

$$y = \sum_{i=1}^{O} \sum_{(\omega_1, \cdots, \omega_i) \in \Omega_n^i} w_{\omega_1, \cdots, \omega_i} \prod_{j=1}^{i} x_{\omega_j} + \epsilon \quad (8)$$

where ω_i is the i-th element in the combination, $w_{\omega_1,\cdots,\omega_i} \sim N(0,1)$ is the individual weight of a specific interaction term, and $\epsilon \sim N(0, 0.1)$ models the label noise which is ignored in [40]. We define O, the order of a dataset, as hyperparameter controlling the maximum order of cross-terms.

Baseline Models. We choose the following CTR models as baselines: FM, FwFM, FvFM, FmFM, DeepFM, FiBiNet, HOFM, xDeepFM and DCN V2. Most of them fit in our IPA framework.

Implementation Details. Our implementation is based on a public PyTorch library for recommendation models[1]. We set the embedding size to 16, the dropout rate to 0.2, and launch early-stopping. We use the Adam optimizer with a learning rate of 0.001. The number of layers L of high-order models are set to 4 and 5 for Criteo-x1 and Avazu, based on the best performance. Our derived models using PGT have 10 terms in each layer. All models are trained on a NVIDIA V100 GPU with a batch size of 2048. We repeat all experiments 3 times and report the average AUC performance in Table 3. The best performance and the comparable performance are denoted in **bold** and underlined fonts, respectively.

---
[1] https://github.com/rixwew/pytorch-fm.

Table 3. AUC of baselines and derived models on public datasets. O stands for orders.

Model	Interaction Function	Layer Pooling	Layer Aggregator	Criteo		Avazu	
				L	AUC	O	AUC
FM	naive	field/global	direct	2	0.8009(2e-4)	2	0.7758(1e-4)
DeepFM	naive	field/global	direct	2	0.8122(1e-4)	2	0.7899(5e-4)
HOFM	naive	field/global	direct	4	0.8040(3e-4)	5	0.7781(8e-4)
FwFM	weighted	field/global	direct	2	0.8095(2e-4)	2	0.7854(4e-4)
xDeepFM	weighted	global	term	4	0.8119(2e-4)	5	0.7897(7e-4)
FvFM	diagonal	field/global	direct	2	0.8103(2e-4)	2	0.7870(3e-4)
FmFM	projected	field/global	direct	2	0.8115(3e-4)	2	0.7882(5e-4)
FiBiNet	projected	field/global	direct	2	0.8113(2e-4)	2	0.7907(4e-4)
DCN V2	projected	field'	direct	4	0.8137(3e-4)	5	**0.7917(1e-4)**
WFL	weighted	field	layer	4	0.8124(2e-4)	5	0.7891(3e-4)
DFL	diagonal	field	layer	4	0.8123(1e-4)	5	0.7903(9e-4)
PFL	projected	field	layer	4	**0.8138(3e-4)**	5	0.7916(4e-4)
PFT	projected	field	term	4	**0.8138(3e-4)**	5	0.7904(4e-4)
PFE	projected	field	element	4	**0.8138(3e-4)**	5	0.7907(2e-4)
PFD	projected	field	direct	4	0.8131(4e-4)	5	0.7912(5e-4)

3.2 RQ1: Evaluation of Interaction Function

We compare the models with various Interaction Functions in several settings regarding the Layer Pooling, Layer Aggregator and classifier. First, among the simplest 2nd-order explicit interaction models (Field/Global Pooling, direct aggregator, no classifier), *i.e.*, FM, FwFM, FvFM and FmFM, the more complicated the Interaction Function, the better AUC on both datasets.

Then, we compare the derived IPA models using the same Layer Pooling (*i.e.*, Field Pooling) and Layer Aggregator (*i.e.*, Layer Agg.). The result is shown in Fig. 2(a). Across all models (*i.e.*, NFL, WFL, DFL and PFL), PFL achieves the best AUC, with a strong trend: models with more complex Interaction Functions (Projected > Diagonal > Weighted > Naive) generally achieve better AUC. This indicates the importance of Interaction Function to model performance.

> *Finding 1. Under the same setting of Layer Pooling, aggregation, and classifier, the more complicated the projection matrix (i.e., from identity, scaled identity, diagonal to full matrix) within the feature Interaction Function, the better the results regarding AUC.*

One possible reason of such trend is that Projected Product learns a powerful matrix projection, *i.e.*, $\boldsymbol{W}^F$ for each field pair. In addition, the Projected Product has the highest number of trainable parameters, further improving its capability to fit training data, which connects closely with model performance.

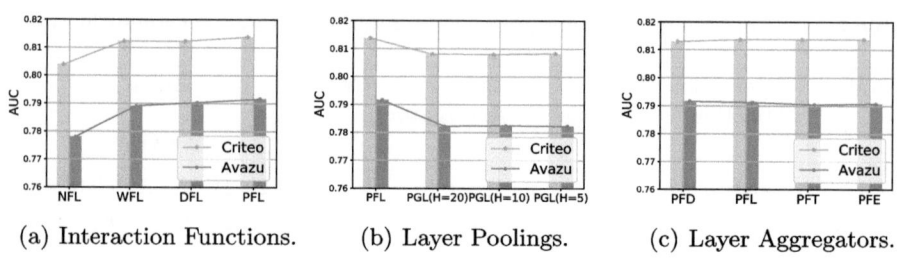

Fig. 2. Performance of various choices within each component in the IPA framework.

3.3 RQ2: Dimensional Collapse of Interaction Functions

To explore the connection between Dimensional Collapse and Interaction Functions, we analyze the singular value sums (SS) as well as the information abundance (IA) [15] of feature fields, where the latter one is defined as the singular value sum divided by the largest value. Different from [15], we evaluate these metrics on embeddings in the sample distribution rather than the unique feature ID distribution, as they reflects feature frequencies more accurately. All the following analysis is based on the Criteo-x1 dataset, since its features vary greatly in cardinality to better illustrate the Dimensional Collapse phenomenon.

We run experiments on DCN V2 and three representational models: FM with Naive Product, FwFM with Weighted Product and FmFM with Projected Product, whose only difference lies in the Interaction Functions they take. In Fig. 3(a) and 3(c), we present the singular value sums of sample embeddings in the Criteo-x1 dataset, where feature fields are ordered by their cardinality and average pair importance from the FwFM model. Comparing the three representational models, we could observe that when the projection matrix of Interaction Function becomes more complex (FM's identity matrix to FwFM's scaled identity matrix to FmFM's full matrix), the singular values of the left-most high-dimensional fields become higher and more balanced, obtaining larger SS and larger IA; this indicates that FmFM spans the largest space in its high-dimensional fields and thus experiencing less amount of Dimensional Collapse on these fields. In this aspect, a complex Interaction Function could serve as a buffer for the high-dimensional fields, alleviating Dimensional Collapse occurred during the interaction process with other low-dimensional fields.

Now, we want to connect this observation to the model performances. In Fig. 3(b) and 3(d), we derive field weights from the FwFM model and present the SSs as well as IAs ordered by these weights. Here FmFM still obtains the largest SS among the 10 most essential fields for prediction task, suggesting that models with a complex Interaction Function indeed learn more robust embeddings against Dimensional Collapse, which contributes to a better model performance.

To further analyze the robustness of embeddings, we pick the representative fields of high cardinality and field importance, plotting their ordered singular values in Fig. 4. From the figure, FmFM possesses the highest and most steady

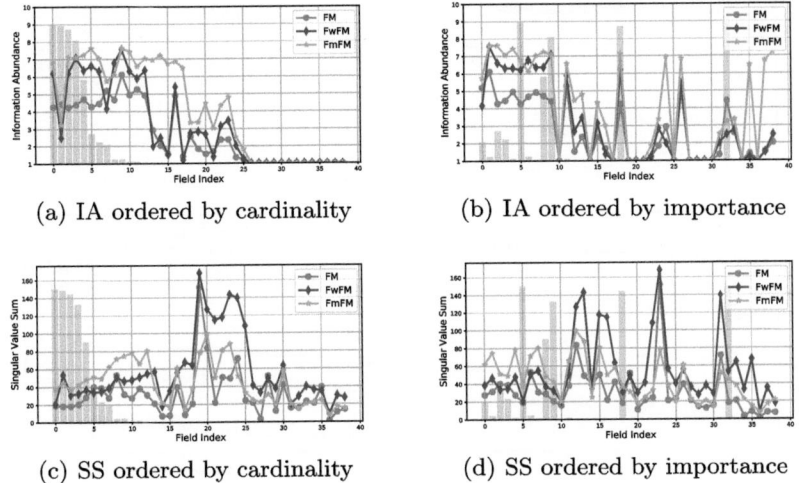

Fig. 3. Comparison of Dimensional Collapse for 2nd-order interaction models on the Criteo-x1 dataset. Both Singular Sum (SS) and Information Abundance (IA) are plotted for fields aligned in two ways. While fields in (a) and (c) are ordered by field cardinality, those in (b) and (d) are ordered by average feature pair importance in FwFM model.

level of singular values, for both high-dimensional and high-importance fields. This indicates that models with a more complex Interaction Function suffers less from Dimensional Collapse and learns a more robust set of embeddings.

> *Finding 2. Among 2nd-order interaction models, the more complicated projection matrix (i.e., from identity, scaled identity, diagonal to full matrix) within the Interaction Function, the more robust (less collapsed) the learned embeddings regarding both information abundance and singular value sum.*

3.4 RQ3: Evaluation of Layer Pooling

To evaluate Layer Pooling, we compare the models with various Layer Poolings, but the same Interaction Function (i.e., Weighted, Diagonal and Projected Product) and the same Layer Aggregator (i.e., Layer Agg.) in Table 3. In addition, we tune the hyper-parameter H, i.e., number of terms in each layer in global agg., by training the PGL model with $H = 5, 10, 20$, and present the results in Fig. 2(b). Field Pooling constantly outperforms Global Pooling in all comparisons, possibly due to that Global Pooling introduces too many redundant interactions, leading to optimization issue caused by co-linearity.

> *Finding 3. Under the same setting of Interaction Function and Layer Aggregator, models with Field Pooling outperform those with Global Pooling.*

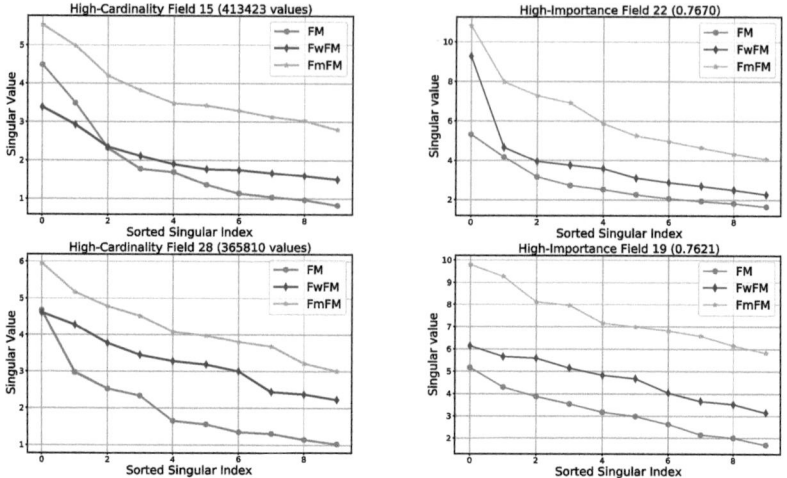

(a) Spectrum of high-cardinality fields (b) Spectrum of high-importance fields

Fig. 4. Field-wise singular value spectrum for 2nd-order interaction models on the Criteo-x1 dataset. The singular values of representative fields (high-order fields in (a) and high-importance fields in (b)) are ordered and displayed.

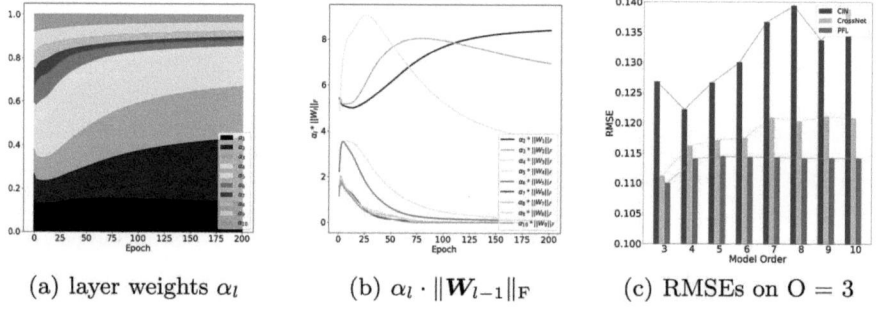

(a) layer weights α_l (b) $\alpha_l \cdot \|W_{l-1}\|_F$ (c) RMSEs on $O = 3$

Fig. 5. Trends of α_l, $\alpha_l \cdot \|W_{l-1}\|_F$ and model performances in the training process. Our model learns low α_l and $\|W_{l-1}\|_F$ for extra layers (5-10), obtaining high-level and robust performance even when over-estimating data order.

3.5 RQ4: Evaluation of Layer Aggregator

To compare the Layer Aggregator choices, we equip PFL with each of the four variants. Evaluations in Fig. 2(c) show comparable performance for these choices, and PFL itself gets comparable performance with DCN V2 in Table 3 with a fixed number of layers, *i.e.*, $L = 4$ in Criteo-x1 and $L = 5$ in Avazu. However, with fixed orders of public datasets, the flexibility of models remains unrevealed. A good model should effectively capture the intrinsic order of data and value interactions within such order to avoid overfitting, as Layer Aggregator does.

To explore such flexibility, we generate a synthetic dataset containing 1 million samples with $O = 4$, and then train a PFL model with $L = 10$. Please note that α_l in PFL used to explicitly model the importance of layer l might be absorbed by the order-wise $\boldsymbol{W}_l \in \mathcal{R}^{MK \times MK}$. Therefore, we analyze the effect of α_l and its joint influence with $\boldsymbol{W}_l$. We present their Frobenius norm, i.e., $\|\boldsymbol{W}_l\|_F$ and $\alpha_l \cdot \|\boldsymbol{W}_{l-1}\|_F$ in Fig. 5(a) and Fig. 5(b), respectively.

From the figures, we observe that through the training epochs, $\alpha_1 \sim \alpha_4$ corresponding to weights of the first four explicit interaction layers increase significantly, while weights of higher orders, i.e., $\alpha_5 \sim \alpha_{10}$, decrease. Besides, when considering $\alpha_l \cdot \|\boldsymbol{W}_{l-1}\|_F$ as a whole, the contribution of $\alpha_l \cdot \|\boldsymbol{W}_{l-1}\|_F$ is small and can be ignored when $l > 4$, indicating that PFL mainly learns from the most important layers and is capable of learning the order of the data.

Then, to establish connection of such capability to the choice of Layer Aggregator, we generated synthetic dataset of order $O = 3$, training CIN (xDeepFM), CrossNet (DCN V2) and PFL with layers in the range of $[O, 10]$. To make a clear analysis, we remove the MLP classifier from all models and only use the representation for prediction. The RMSE results are shown in Fig. 5(c). We do not include models with $l < 3$ as their performances are defective, which is trivial.

Regarding the three models, CIN performs badly in all settings: on the one hand, it performs the worst in all cases with a large margin; on the other hand, it cannot always achieve the best performance when the model order matches the data order. For example, while the data order is 3, CIN achieves the best performance with a model order of 4. Then, compared to CrossNet, our derived model PFL achieves the best performance when two orders match, and it manages to make a larger relative lift as more redundant layers are added to the model, while performance of CrossNet deteriorates. As PFL differs from DCN V2 mainly in its introduction of α_l, the performance gap indicates the success of layer-wise aggregator in filtering redundant layers in PFL.

> *Finding 4. Under the same setting of feature Interaction Function and Layer Pooling, models with layer-wise aggregator are capable of learning the order of data, thus outperforming those with direct connections.*

3.6 RQ5: Derived Models and Evolution of Existing Models

Based on the above evaluations, the Projected Product, Field Pooling and Layer Agg. outperform other choices for the three components. Combining these most powerful choices together, we get the derived model PFL achieving comparative performance with DCN V2 on both public datasets. Besides, many other derived models obtain decent performance. For example, WFL achieves comparative performance with xDeepFM, differing mainly in the Layer Pooling.

In a nutshell, through all these evaluations, we observe that CTR models evolve mainly through: 1) Employing more powerful Interaction Functions, from Naive Product (*e.g.*, FM, HOFM, DeepFM), to Weighted Product (*e.g.*, FwFM, PNN, xDeepFM) and Diagonal Product (*e.g.*, FvFM), and finally to Projected

Product (*e.g.*, FmFM, FiBiNet, DCN V2 and PFL). 2) Employing more powerful Layer Poolings, from Global Pooling (*e.g.*, xDeepFM, WGL, DGL, PGL) to Field Pooling (DCN V2 and PFL). 3) Employing layer-wise Layer Aggregator instead of directly linking everything, in order to adapt to various orders of data.

3.7 RQ6: Online A/B Testing

We developed PFL in one of the world's largest advertising platforms. The production model employs Heterogeneous Experts with Multi-Embedding architecture [15,29,36]. We replace the IPNN expert in the production model with the PFL expert, which models the interactions between more than five hundred user-side, ad-side, and context-side features. Multiple embedding tables are learned for all features, each corresponding to one or several experts.

During the two-week 20% A/B testing, PFL demonstrated promising results, achieving 0.9%, 3.7%, 1.2%, and 2.7% GMV lift on several vital scenarios, including Moments pCTR, Content and Platform pCTR, and DSP pCTR. These improvements were statistically significant according to t-tests. PFL has been successfully deployed as the production model in the above-mentioned scenarios, leading to a revenue lift by hundreds of millions of dollars per year.

We also study the singular values of the baseline IPNN model and the PFL model. Specifically, we calculate a 95%-percentile dimension, that is, how many top singular values can cover 95% of the total singular values of each feature. As shown in Fig. 6, our proposed PFL gets a much higher 95%-percentile dimension on almost all features, especially on those with high cardinalities. This validates that PFL can mitigate the Dimensional Collapse.

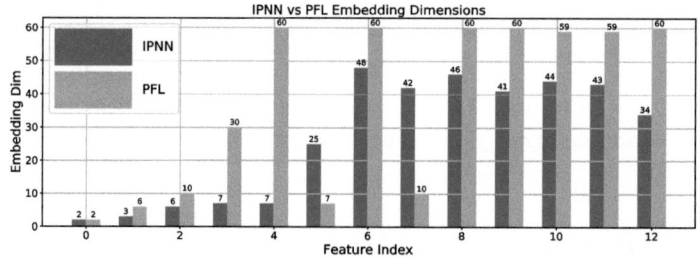

Fig. 6. Dimensional Collapse of IPNN v.s. PFL in our system.

4 Related Works

Many articles model the 2nd-order interactions after factorization machines. Early works use Logistic Regression (LR) [9,26,33] or Polynomial-2 (Poly2) [8] to learn interactions. Following matrix factorization [13,20,34], FM [5,31] models interactions as dot product between embeddings. FFM [19] assigns field-wise embeddings for field-pair interactions. Based on FM, FwFM [28], FvFM [37] and FmFM [37] introduce field-pair wise weight, vector and matrix to better model interactions respectively. AFM [43] learns an attentive weight for each field pair.

Many recent articles propose to capture explicit high-order interactions [6, 22, 24, 25, 31, 35, 39–41, 52]. For example, [31] discusses a d-way FM to model d-order interactions in FM, and HOFM [6] presents an efficient algorithm to train it. Similarly, xDeepFM [24], DCN [41], DCN V2 [40] and DCN V3 [22] also employ variants of matrix factorization techniques to model high-order interactions, while AutoInt [35] resorts to a multi-head self-attentive network. Additionally, EulerNet [39] learns feature interactions in a complex vector space. MaskNet [42] introduces multiplicative operations block by block. FINAL [52] stacks multiple FINAL blocks to capture various interaction patterns. DCN V3 [22] uses subnetworks LCN and ECN to capture both low-order and high-order interactions.

Besides, it is also common to capture interactions both explicitly and implicitly (via deep neural networks). Wide & Deep [10], DeepFM [14] and ONN [45] combine an explicit interaction module (as the wide part) and multiple feedforward layers (as the deep part) in parallel. NFM [16], IPNN [30], OPNN [30] and FiBiNet [17] employ an explicit interaction component and then add MLPs over it. FinalMLP [25] relies on MLPs and a two-stream structure, achieving amazing performance. Also, there has been long-standing discussion and debate on the role of MLPs in recommendations [3, 4, 12, 25, 32, 40, 50]. There are also works to benchmark and summarize existing CTR models [21, 23, 40, 44, 48, 49, 51, 53]. For example, AOANet [21] decomposes the models into projection, interaction, and fusion. DCN V2 [40] compares the explicit Interaction Functions.

5 Conclusion

In this paper, we present a unified framework, *i.e.*, IPA, for explicit interaction click-through rate models to systematically analyze and compare the existing CTR models in Recommender Systems. Further, we conduct extensive experiments on the effect of framework components and make several interesting discoveries about model design. Inspired by these analysis, we successfully derived a new model that achieves competitive performance with SOTA models and was successfully deployed to Tencent's advertising platform.

References

1. Avazu dataset (2014). https://www.kaggle.com/competitions/avazu-ctr-prediction
2. Criteo dataset (2014). https://www.kaggle.com/c/criteo-display-ad-challenge
3. Anelli, V.W., Bellogín, A., et al.: Reenvisioning the comparison between neural collaborative filtering and matrix factorization. In: RecSys, pp. 521–529 (2021)
4. Beutel, A., Covington, P., et al.: Latent cross: Making use of context in recurrent recommender systems. In: WSDM, pp. 46–54 (2018)
5. Blondel, M., Fujino, A., et al.: Convex factorization machines. In: ECML-PKDD, vol. 9285, pp. 19–35 (2015)

6. Blondel, M., Fujino, A., et al.: Higher-order factorization machines. NeurIPS, pp. 3351–3359 (2016)
7. Bureau, I.A.: Iab/pwc internet advertising revenue report 2024 (2024), https://www.iab.com/insights/internet-advertising-revenue-report-2024/
8. Chang, Y.W., et al.: Training and testing low-degree polynomial data mappings via linear svm. J. Mach. Learn. Res. **11**(Apr), 1471–1490 (2010)
9. Chapelle, O., et al.: Simple and scalable response prediction for display advertising. TIST **5**(4), 61 (2015)
10. Cheng, H.T., Koc, L., et al.: Wide & deep learning for recommender systems. In: The 1st Workshop on Deep Learning for Recommender Systems, pp. 7–10 (2016)
11. Cheng, Y., Xue, Y.: Looking at ctr prediction again: Is attention all you need? In: SIGIR, pp. 1279–1287 (2021)
12. Feng, N., Pan, J., et al.: Long-sequence recommendation models need decoupled embeddings. arXiv preprint arXiv:2410.02604 (2024)
13. Flanagan, A., Oyomno, W., et al.: Federated multi-view matrix factorization for personalized recommendations. In: ECML-PKDD. vol. 12458, pp. 324–347 (2020)
14. Guo, H., Tang, R., et al.: Deepfm: a factorization-machine based neural network for ctr prediction. In: IJCAI, pp. 1725–1731 (2017)
15. Guo, X., Pan, J., et al.: On the embedding collapse when scaling up recommendation models. arXiv preprint arXiv:2310.04400 (2023)
16. He, X., Chua, T.S.: Neural factorization machines for sparse predictive analytics. In: SIGIR. pp. 355–364 (2017)
17. Huang, T., Zhang, Z., et al.: Fibinet: combining feature importance and bilinear feature interaction for click-through rate prediction. In: RecSys, pp. 169–177 (2019)
18. Jing, L., Vincent, P., et al.: Understanding dimensional collapse in contrastive self-supervised learning. In: ICLR (2022)
19. Juan, Y., Zhuang, Y., et al.: Field-aware factorization machines for ctr prediction. In: RecSys, pp. 43–50 (2016)
20. Koren, Y., Bell, R., et al.: Matrix factorization techniques for recommender systems. Computer **42**(8), 30–37 (2009)
21. Lang, L., Zhu, Z., et al.: Architecture and operation adaptive network for online recommendations. In: SIGKDD, pp. 3139–3149 (2021)
22. Li, H., Zhang, Y., et al.: Dcnv3: Towards next generation deep cross network for ctr prediction. arXiv preprint arXiv:2407.13349 (2024)
23. Li, J.L., et al.: Decompose, then reconstruct: A framework of network structures for click-through rate prediction. In: ECML-PKDD, vol. 14169, pp. 422–437 (2023)
24. Lian, J., Zhou, X., et al.: xdeepfm: Combining explicit and implicit feature interactions for recommender systems. In: SIGKDD, pp. 1754–1763 (2018)
25. Mao, K., Zhu, J., et al.: Finalmlp: An enhanced two-stream mlp model for ctr prediction. In: AAAI, pp. 4552–4560 (2023)
26. McMahan, H.B., Holt, G., et al.: Ad click prediction: a view from the trenches. In: SIGKDD, pp. 1222–1230 (2013)
27. Naumov, M., Mudigere, D., et al.: Deep learning recommendation model for personalization and recommendation systems. arXiv preprint arXiv:1906.00091 (2019)
28. Pan, J., Xu, J., et al.: Field-weighted factorization machines for click-through rate prediction in display advertising. In: WWW, pp. 1349–1357 (2018)
29. Pan, J., Xue, W., et al.: Ad recommendation in a collapsed and entangled world. In: SIGKDD, pp. 5566–5577 (2024)
30. Qu, Y., Cai, H., et al.: Product-based neural networks for user response prediction. In: ICDM, pp. 1149–1154 (2016)

31. Rendle, S.: Factorization machines. In: ICDM, pp. 995–1000 (2010)
32. Rendle, S., Krichene, W., et al.: Neural collaborative filtering vs. matrix factorization revisited. In: RecSys, pp. 240–248 (2020)
33. Richardson, M., Dominowska, E., et al.: Predicting clicks: estimating the click-through rate for new ads. In: WWW, pp. 521–530 (2007)
34. Salakhutdinov, R., Mnih, A.: Bayesian probabilistic matrix factorization using Markov chain Monte Carlo. In: ICML, pp. 880–887 (2008)
35. Song, W., Shi, C., et al.: Autoint: Automatic feature interaction learning via self-attentive neural networks. In: CIKM, pp. 1161–1170 (2019)
36. Su, L., Pan, J., et al.: Stem: Unleashing the power of embeddings for multi-task recommendation. In: AAAI, pp. 9002–9010 (2024)
37. Sun, Y., Pan, J., et al.: Fm2: Field-matrixed factorization machines for recommender systems. In: WWW, pp. 2828–2837 (2021)
38. Tang, X., Qiao, Y., et al.: Optmsm: Optimizing multi-scenario modeling for click-through rate prediction. In: ECML-PKDD, vol. 14174, pp. 567–584 (2023)
39. Tian, Z., Bai, T., et al.: Eulernet: adaptive feature interaction learning via euler's formula for ctr prediction. In: SIGIR, pp. 1376–1385 (2023)
40. Wang, R., et al.: Dcn-v2: Improved deep & cross network and practical lessons for web-scale learning to rank systems. In: WWW, pp. 1785–1797 (2021)
41. Wang, R., Fu, B., et al.: Deep & cross network for ad click predictions. In: ADKDD, pp. 1–7 (2017)
42. Wang, Z., She, Q., et al.: Masknet: introducing feature-wise multiplication to ctr ranking models by instance-guided mask. arXiv preprint arXiv:2102.07619 (2021)
43. Xiao, J., Ye, H., et al.: Attentional factorization machines: Learning the weight of feature interactions via attention networks. arXiv preprint arXiv:1708.04617 (2017)
44. Xu, L., Tian, Z., et al.: Towards a more user-friendly and easy-to-use benchmark library for recommender systems. In: SIGIR, pp. 2837–2847 (2023)
45. Yang, Y., Xu, B., et al.: Operation-aware neural networks for user response prediction. Neural Netw. **121**, 161–168 (2020)
46. Yue, Yunand Liu, Y., et al.: Adaptive optimizers with sparse group lasso for neural networks in ctr prediction. In: ECML-PKDD, vol. 12977, pp. 314–329 (2021)
47. Zhang, W., Du, T., et al.: Deep learning over multi-field categorical data: a case study on user response prediction. In: ECIR, pp. 45–57 (2016)
48. Zhao, W.X., Hou, Y., et al.: Recbole 2.0: towards a more up-to-date recommendation library. In: CIKM, pp. 4722–4726 (2022)
49. Zhao, W.X., Mu, S., et al.: Recbole: Towards a unified, comprehensive and efficient framework for recommendation algorithms. In: CIKM, pp. 4653–4664 (2021)
50. Zhou, H., et al.: Temporal interest network for user response prediction. In: WWW, pp. 413–422 (2024)
51. Zhu, J., Dai, Q., et al.: Bars: Towards open benchmarking for recommender systems. In: SIGIR, pp. 2912–2923 (2022)
52. Zhu, J., Jia, Q., et al.: Final: Factorized interaction layer for ctr prediction. In: SIGIR, pp. 2006–2010 (2023)
53. Zhu, J., Liu, J., et al.: Fuxictr: An open benchmark for click-through rate prediction. arXiv preprint arXiv:2009.05794 (2020)

Fine-grained Representation Learning and Multi-view Collaborative Augmentation for Recommendation

Huiting Li[1], Wenjun Ma[1,2,3], Weishan Cai[4], and Yuncheng Jiang[1,2(✉)]

[1] School of Artificial Intelligence, South China Normal University,
Foshan 528225, China
{huitingli,jiangyuncheng}@m.scnu.edu.cn, mawenjun@scnu.edu.cn
[2] School of Computer Science, South China Normal University,
Guangzhou 510631, China
[3] Aberdeen Institute of Data Science and Artificial Intelligence,
South China Normal University, Foshan 528225, China
[4] School of Computer Science, Guangdong University of Education,
Guangzhou 510631, China
caiws@m.scnu.edu.cn

Abstract. Graph neural networks (GNNs) have recently advanced in processing graph-structured data and are increasingly used in recommendation systems. Recently, many studies have incorporated side information as auxiliary views, such as the user's social connections and the item's knowledge-aware dependencies, to enhance the user-item interaction view. However, current works overlook the differences in learning behavior between auxiliary views and interaction view, and transfer side information from different views separately, which can lead to a semantic gap and fail to explore the collaborative effect of auxiliary views. To address this challenge, we propose FiCoRec, a novel fine-grained augmentation method for recommendation, comprising two key enhancement components: Hierarchical Knowledge Transfer (HKT) and Multi-view Semantic Fusion (MSF). Specifically, HKT designs an interaction semantic decouple (ISD) method to decouple the interaction view embeddings into homogeneous features (hoFs) and heterogeneous features (heFs). Then a hierarchical contrastive learning framework is used to fully capture the local and global semantics from the intermediate-layer to enhance hoFs. MSF explores a collaborative augmentation mechanism by utilizing meta-learning to enhance the interaction view. Extensive experiments conducted on five datasets against seven baseline methods demonstrate that our FiCoRec outperforms the state-of-the-art methods with a margin of 0.33%–2.76%.

Keywords: Heterogeneous graph · Feature decouple · Contrastive learning · Recommendation system

1 Introduction

Recommender systems have become an essential tool in various domains, providing personalized recommendations to users by predicting their preferences based on past behavior and interactions. In recent years, with the rapid development of Graph Neural Networks (GNNs), many GNN-based methods have emerged and gained significant traction in capturing complex user-item interactions. Unlike traditional collaborative filtering or matrix factorization methods, GNNs leverage iterative message-passing mechanisms to effectively encode the structural relationships between users and items, modeling higher-order connectivity and non-linear relationships [7,26]. Despite the great process, many existing GNN-based recommendation frameworks primarily focus on homogeneous graphs without considering the diverse relational patterns in real-world scenarios which may limit their ability in complex recommendation environments.

To mitigate this limitation, researchers endeavor to exploit heterogeneous side information as auxiliary views, such as social connections and item-wise relations, to enrich the semantics of latent representations and augment the user-item interaction view. GraphRec [4] is the first to utilize GNNs to incorporate social influence to enhance recommendation performance. Subsequently, many studies introduce various techniques to model users' social relations. For instance, DiffNet++ [25] proposes a diffusion neural network to model higher-order social structures, while MHCN [28] leverages hypergraphs to fuse social relations and mine complex connections between users. Furthermore, HGCL [1] extends the heterogeneous relations and considers item dependencies cooperating with users' social influence to fully exploit side information from limited data. Additionally, Recdiff [14] and DSL [22] focus on alleviating noise in social relations by leveraging self-supervised learning (SSL).

Previous approaches primarily focus on extracting informative side information from auxiliary views to enrich the interaction view. However, the current transformation of side information faces two limitations: (1) it provides a coarse-grained transformation, overlooking the differences in learning behavior between auxiliary views and the interaction view, and (2) it transfers side information from different auxiliary views separately, leaving the collaborative effect of multiple auxiliary views insufficiently explored. The first issue arises from the distinct content of different views. In auxiliary views, GNNs operate on homogeneous graphs, capturing intra-group relationships or similarities (e.g., user social connections or item-wise relations). In contrast, the interaction view involves heterogeneous graphs, where various node types introduce greater complexity and diverse information. Consequently, the learning behaviors of GNNs are significantly different between auxiliary views and the interaction view, leading to a semantic gap in the latent representation space. Thus, blindly utilizing the embeddings of auxiliary views to augment the interaction view can introduce unnecessary noise, hindering the utilization of heterogeneous side information. The second issue lies in the isolated transfer of side information from different auxiliary views which ignores their potential collaborative effects, and the ability to jointly provide a more comprehensive understanding of user preferences and item characteristics. These limitations constrain the recommender system's capabilities, ultimately leading to suboptimal performance.

To tackle the aforementioned challenge, we propose FiCoRec, a novel fine-grained augmentation method for recommendation. FiCoRec comprises two key components: hierarchical knowledge transfer (HKT) and multi-view semantic fusion (MSF). On one hand, HKT bridges the semantic gap between auxiliary and interaction views by enabling fine-grained side information transfer. Specifically, as the embeddings of the interaction view aggregate the information about users' and items' characteristics, we initially design interaction semantic decouple (ISD) to decouple them into user-related part and item-related part. For user, the former aims to preserve the user's own intrinsic attribution, e.g., personal information and social relationships. The latter contains information related to items associated with a user, i.e., the user's personalized preferences. For items, the meanings of these parts are reversed. Thus, we denote the two parts as homogeneous features (hoFs) and heterogeneous features (heFs). Building upon this foundation, HKT further designs a hierarchical contrastive learning framework to make full use of the local and global semantics of heterogeneous relations in auxiliary views to enhance hoFs. On the other hand, MSF utilizes meta-learning to consider the collaborative effect of two auxiliary views. It treats heFs as a bridge to integrate the knowledge of two auxiliary views and generate an adaptive mapping by meta-network. Subsequently, the mapping combined with the enhanced hoFs from HKT, jointly enriches the embeddings of the interaction view. Finally, the enhanced embeddings are utilized for downstream recommendation tasks.

The key contributions of our work can be summarized as follows:

1. We propose a novel fine-grained heterogeneous relation augmentation framework (FiCoRec) to boost the recommendation performance by exploiting side information from auxiliary views.
2. We present two customized modules: HKT and MSF. HKT transfers side information in a fine-grained way by utilizing features decoupling, and enables the model to learn local and global semantics of heterogeneous relations in auxiliary views through a hierarchical contrastive learning framework. MSF simultaneously leverages multiple auxiliary views to provide collaborative augmentation.
3. FiCoRec is evaluated on several real-world datasets. Experimental results demonstrate that the FiCoRec framework greatly improves recommendation performance and achieves state-of-the-art results.

2 Related Work

2.1 Heterogeneous Graph Representation Learning

Heterogeneous networks have been widely used since real-world objects and their interactions are often multi-typed. In prior research, shallow network embedding methods leverage single-layer decomposition of certain affinity matrices, e.g., metapath2vec [3], Hin2vec [5]. With the development of GNNs, deep network embedding methods aggregate the information from neighboring nodes to learn structural representation, e.g., HAN [24], MAGNN [6]. In recent years, relevant studies have predominantly explored SSL techniques, incorporating strategies such as contrastive learning, generative pretraining, and mask reconstruction. For instance, MuHca [15] separately employs node embeddings from two views into a contrastive generative adversarial network to implement data augmentation. HGMAE [21] designs two masking strategies and metapath-based edge reconstruction, target attribute restoration, and positional feature prediction to capture graph information.

2.2 GNN-Based Recommendation Systems

Graph Neural Networks (GNNs) have been widely adopted in recommendation systems due to their effectiveness in capturing high-order connectivity and user-item interactions. Early works such as NGCF [23] and LightGCN [11] learn user and item embeddings by linearly propagating them on the user-item interaction graph. Subsequent advancements like PinSage [27] introduce an industrial solution that combines random walks and graph convolutions. Later, many GNN-based recommendations are developed to model user-user and user-item graphs via message passing, such as DH-HGCN [10] and GraphRec [4]. Recent efforts focus on utilizing heterogeneous relational data to enhance GNNs, such as social connections between users and the knowledge dependencies of items [12,20]. For example, HGCL [1] transfers heterogeneous relations to the user-item interaction graph with contrastive learning across different auxiliary views. Besides, RecDiff [14] and DSL [22] focus on alleviating the noisy effect in the social graph by leveraging SSL. However, previous works neglect the differences of learning behavior between different graphs, which leads to a semantic gap in the latent representation space and introduces unnecessary noise. Moreover, existing studies transfer side information across different views separately, ignoring the potential collaborative effects. To address the challenges, we design a fine-grained augmentation method for recommendation.

3 Preliminaries

For the interaction view, we denote the user-item interaction graph as $\mathcal{G}_{ui} = \{\mathcal{U}, \mathcal{V}, \mathcal{E}_{ui}\}$, where $\mathcal{U}$ and $\mathcal{V}$ represent the sets of users and items, respectively, $\mathcal{E}_{ui} \subseteq |\mathcal{U}| \times |\mathcal{V}|$ represents all the edges in the user-item interaction graph $\mathcal{G}_{ui}$. And we define the embeddings of the interaction view as $\mathbf{E}^{inter}$. If user i interacts with an item j, that is, an edge (i,j) exists in $\mathcal{E}_{ui}$. Considering the negative sampling process, we denote $(i, j^+, j^-) \in \mathcal{O}$ as a sample for a user with existing and non-existing interactions with items, where $\mathcal{O}$ represents the set of all samples. Let $\mathbf{E}^u$ and $\mathbf{E}^i$ represent the embedding of users and items, respectively. Each user $i \in \mathcal{U}$ or item $j \in \mathcal{V}$ corresponding to a feature vector $\mathbf{e}_i^u$ or $\mathbf{e}_j^i$.

For the auxiliary views, we denote the user-user social connection graph as $\mathcal{G}_{uu} = \{\mathcal{U}, \mathcal{E}_{uu}\}$, and item-item knowledge dependency graph is denoted as

$\mathcal{G}_{ii} = \{\mathcal{V}, \mathcal{E}_{ii}\}$. $\mathcal{G}_{uu}$ represents the social connection between users, and $\mathcal{G}_{ii}$ represents the item-wise relation. Similarly, the embeddings of the two auxiliary views are denoted as $\mathbf{E}^{aux}$, including $\mathbf{E}^{uu}$ and $\mathbf{E}^{ii}$. Each user $i \in \mathcal{U}$ or item $j \in \mathcal{V}$ corresponding to a vector $\mathbf{e}_i^{uu}$ or $\mathbf{e}_j^{ii}$. The main notations and explanations are shown in Table 1.

Table 1. Notations and explanations.

Notations	Explanations
$\mathbf{E}^{inter}$	embedding of interaction view, including $\mathbf{E}^u$ and $\mathbf{E}^i$
$\mathbf{E}^{aux}$	embedding of auxiliary view, including $\mathbf{E}^{uu}$ and $\mathbf{E}^{ii}$
heF	heterogeneous feature decoupled from $\mathbf{E}^{inter}$, including UheF and IheF
UheF/IheF	heF for user/item
hoF	homogeneous feature decoupled from $\mathbf{E}^{inter}$, including UhoF and IhoF
UhoF/IhoF	hoF for user/item

4 Methodology

We develop FiCoRec which utilizes fine-grained representation learning and a multi-view collaborative augmentation strategy. As shown in Fig. 1, we first learn embeddings from $\mathcal{G}_{ui}$ (interaction view), as well as $\mathcal{G}_{uu}$ and $\mathcal{G}_{ii}$ (auxiliary views), using three-layer GNN encoders, where the encoders for $\mathcal{G}_{uu}$ and $\mathcal{G}_{ii}$ are incorporated in HKT. Then HKT provides a fine-grained representation learning, and MSF employs a multi-view collaborative augmentation strategy to enhance model performance. For HKT in Fig. 1(a), we first decouple $\mathbf{E}^{inter}$ through ISD, which is the foundation of fine-grained representation learning. Furthermore, HKT employs a hierarchical contrastive learning to transfer side information, which is able to capture local and global semantics from $\mathbf{E}^{aux}$. For MSF in Fig. 1(b), it contains two branches for user embedding and item embedding, respectively. Each branch utilizes an anchor-neighbor concatenation (ANC) and a meta-learning framework to aggregate the knowledge from two auxiliary views.

4.1 Interaction Semantic Decouple

The $\mathbf{E}^{inter}$ combines the information about user and item characteristics. Intuitively, by distinguishing these two parts and enhancing them separately with side information, the effects of the semantic gap and the discrepancies in GNN learning behaviors can be alleviated. With this motivation, we design ISD to decouple the $\mathbf{E}^{inter}$ into a user-related part and an item-related part. Then we exploit corresponding side information to enhance both parts. We define two

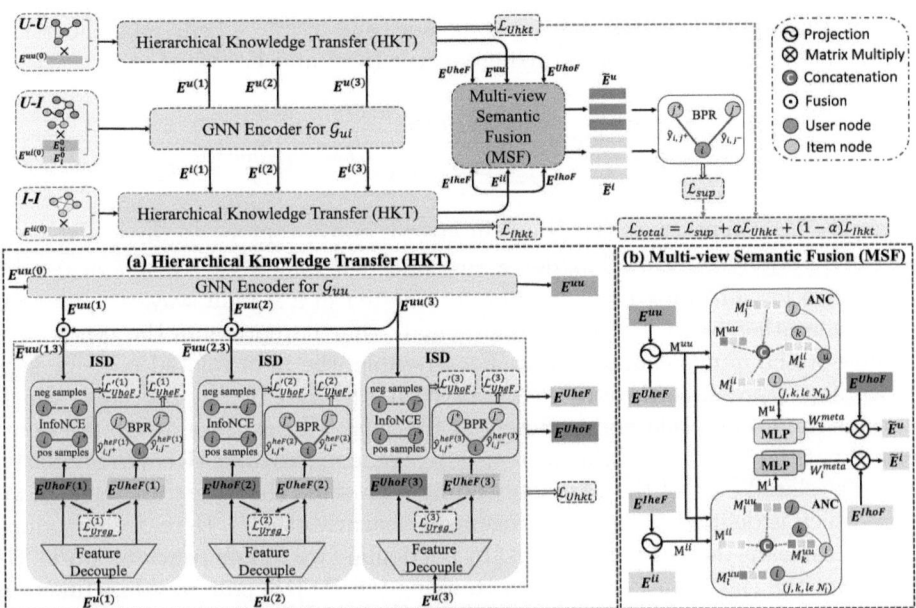

Fig. 1. The upper of the figure is the overview of our proposed FiCoRec framework, while the lower part illustrates the HKT and MSF, respectively. ISD is represented by the green bar in HKT. For ISD, we adopt the same operation for user and item. And for HKT, we design symmetric structures for the two auxiliary views. For simplicity, we illustrate them from the perspective of user.

categories of features to describe the aforementioned two parts: homogeneous features (hoFs) and heterogeneous features (heFs), whose meanings are elaborated as follows.

On one hand, for hoF, we anticipate that it can preserve the intrinsic attribution relevant to either user or item, e.g., social relationships for users and knowledge dependencies for items. Therefore, we define the user-related part of user embeddings as user homogeneous features (UhoF), and for item, the item-related part of item embeddings is defined as item homogeneous features (IhoF). To ensure UhoF and IhoF capture the intrinsic attribution of user and item, we attempt to utilize the $\mathbf{E}^{aux}$ to employ supervision and augmentation. However, given that the learning of graph structures heavily relies on a comprehensive grasp of the local neighborhood nodes, directly minimizing the distance of two individual embeddings proves to be insufficiently effective.

Inspired by previous works [1,22], we introduce contrastive self-supervised learning to provide more effective supervision. Intuitively, we hope to maximize the similarity between node pairs corresponding to the same node in $\mathbf{E}^{inter}$ and $\mathbf{E}^{aux}$, i.e., $\mathbf{e}_i^{UhoF}$ and $\mathbf{e}_i^{uu}$ (positive pairs), while for the different nodes, i.e., $\mathbf{e}_i^{UhoF}$ and $\mathbf{e}_j^{uu}$ (negative pairs) are opposite. Here, we adapt InfoNCE loss as the optimization objective and pose the cross-view contrastive learning as the task of classifying positive pairs among hoF and $\mathbf{E}^{aux}$. Then, we denote the contrastive objective of users utilizing layer-k $\mathbf{E}^{aux}$ and $\mathbf{E}^{inter}$ as

$$\mathcal{L}_{UhoF}^{(k)} = \sum_{i \in \mathcal{U}} -\log \frac{\exp(sim(\mathbf{e}_i^{UhoF(k)}, \mathbf{e}_i^{uu(k)})/\tau)}{\sum_{j \in \mathcal{U}} \exp(sim(\mathbf{e}_i^{UhoF(k)}, \mathbf{e}_j^{uu(k)})/\tau)}, \quad (1)$$

where $\mathbf{e}^{UhoF(k)}$ represents the UhoF in layer-k and τ represents the scalar temperature parameter, $sim(\cdot)$ denotes the similarity function. Analogously, the contrastive loss of items $\mathcal{L}_{IhoF}^{(k)}$ can be formulated in a similar way.

On the other hand, for heF, we anticipate that it represents the user's personality or the item's characteristic. For example, the item-related part for user embedding represents the knowledge of item associated with the user, which contains the user's preferences. Based on this characteristic, we define the item-related part for user embedding as user heterogeneous features (UheF). Similarly, the user-related part of the item embedding represents the target audience of an item, which is defined as item heterogeneous features (IheF). Here, we introduce the downstream task as supervision. In particular, we follow previous works [1] and adopt the Bayesian Personalized Ranking (BPR) [18] pair-wise loss function to constrain heF. Similarly, we consider the case of layer-k, that is,

$$\mathcal{L}_{heF}^{(k)} = \sum_{(i,j^+,j^-) \in \mathcal{O}} -\ln(\text{sigmoid}(\hat{y}_{i,j^+}^{heF(k)} - \hat{y}_{i,j^-}^{heF(k)})) \quad (2)$$

where $\hat{y}_{i,j}^{heF(k)} = (\mathbf{e}_i^{UheF(k)})^\top \mathbf{e}_j^{IheF(k)}$ represents the likelihood of user i interacting with item j. Here, $\mathbf{e}^{UheF(k)}$ and $\mathbf{e}^{IheF(k)}$ denote the heF for user and item decoupled from layer-k $\mathbf{E}^{inter}$, respectively.

Meanwhile, hoF and heF represent different parts of features for $\mathbf{E}^{inter}$, respectively. It is vital to minimize the correlation between them to ensure their independence, mitigating the unnecessary impact introduced by the mutual interaction of hoF and heF. Thus, we employ additional constraints on them utilizing orthogonal regularization, that is,

$$\mathcal{L}_{Ureg}^{(k)} = \|(\mathbf{E}^{UhoF(k)})^\top \mathbf{E}^{UheF(k)} - I\|_F^2, \quad (3)$$

where $\mathbf{E}^{UhoF(k)}$ and $\mathbf{E}^{UheF(k)}$ represent the embedding matrix of UhoF and UheF in layer-k, respectively, I denotes the identity matrix, $\|\cdot\|_F^2$ represents the Frobenius norm. Analogously, the regularization loss of items $\mathcal{L}_{Ireg}^{(k)}$ can be formulated in a similar way.

4.2 Hierarchical Knowledge Transfer

From the perspective of message-passing mechanism, deeper features generally contain global semantics, while the low-level features are able to capture local structural information, both of which are crucial for graph machine learning tasks. Thus, HKT is designed to transfer side information from the $\mathbf{E}^{aux}$ of multiple layers. Specifically, we model the HKT component by extending the ISD from single-layer to multiple-layer.

For hoF, considering the connection paths between the auxiliary views and the interaction view, we design a progressive approach to integrate embeddings from different layers for side information transfer. As shown in Fig. 1(a), in addition to aligning the same layer's $\mathbf{E}^{aux}$ and $\mathbf{E}^{inter}$, the deeper $\mathbf{E}^{aux}$ is also employed to augment the low-level $\mathbf{E}^{inter}$ by fusing with low-level $\mathbf{E}^{aux}$. Here, we utilize the attention-based fusion method (ABF) introduced in [2] as the fusion operation, which can adaptively calculate the weight of the fused portions. For layer-k, the Eq. 1 can reformulate as

$$\mathcal{L}_{UhoF}^{'(k)} = \sum_{i \in \mathcal{U}} -\log \frac{\exp(sim(\mathbf{e}_i^{UhoF(k)}, \bar{\mathbf{e}}_i^{uu(k,L)})/\tau)}{\sum_{j \in \mathcal{U}} \exp(sim(\mathbf{e}_j^{UhoF(k)}, \bar{\mathbf{e}}_j^{uu(k,L)})/\tau)}, \quad (4)$$

where L represents the total number of layers, and $\bar{\mathbf{e}}^{uu(k,L)} = \mathcal{F}(\mathbf{e}_i^{uu(k)}, \mathbf{e}_i^{uu(k,L)})$ denotes the combination of the layer-k embedding, while $\mathbf{e}^{uu(k)}$ and a residual embedding $\mathbf{e}^{uu(k,L)}$ containing the information from the layer-k to the last layer. $\mathcal{F}(\cdot)$ represents the fusion operation. Notably, for the layer-L, $\mathbf{e}^{uu(L,L)}$ is equal to $\mathbf{e}^{uu(L)}$. Similarly, the objective of IhoF, $\mathcal{L}_{IhoF}^{'(k)}$ is defined in a similar way.

From the perspective of the interaction view, the layer-3 $\mathbf{E}^{aux}$ is aggregated with the layer-2 $\mathbf{E}^{aux}$ to enhance the layer-2 $\mathbf{E}^{inter}$. Therefore, the latter can learn side information from multiple layers of the auxiliary view, enhancing the comprehension of local and global semantics. On the other hand, from the perspective of the auxiliary views, the layer-3 embedding learns the residual of the layer-2 embedding, mitigating the over-smoothing problem for GNNs. Thus, HKT enables the two categories of views to augment themselves in a mutual manner.

Considering the connection paths solely affect the calculation of hoF loss, while heF loss and the orthogonal regularization retain their original formulation. Consequently, the optimization objective of HKT module is defined as:

$$\mathcal{L}_{Uhkt} = \frac{1}{L}\sum_{k=1}^{L}(\mathcal{L}_{UhoF}^{'(k)} + \lambda \mathcal{L}_{Ureg}^{(k)} + \mathcal{L}_{heF}^{(k)}). \quad (5)$$

where λ denotes a hyperparameter to determine the weight of the regularization. $\mathcal{L}_{Ihkt}$ and $\mathcal{L}_{Uhkt}$ share the same computation way.

4.3 Multi-view Semantic Fusion

MSF attempts to explore the collaborative augmentation mechanism that integrates multiple auxiliary views. It bridges two auxiliary views through heF and employs a meta-learning framework to aggregate knowledge of two views, generating adaptive mapping from the aggregated knowledge.

For the user side, we involve an aggregate operation to integrate the user-user embeddings and UheF, that is,

$$M^{uu} = \sigma(\Phi(\mathbf{e}^{uu}, \mathbf{e}^{UheF})), \quad (6)$$

where $\sigma(\cdot)$ represents the activation function. Φ actually acts as a projection that maps the features of the user-user view into a shared semantic space. A similar projection is utilized for the item side M^{ii}. In particular, to smoothly merge the two sides' knowledge M^{uu} and M^{ii}, we design an anchor-neighbor concatenation (ANC). Specifically, we treat one side as the anchor (e.g., a user u) and incorporate the neighborhood of the anchor in the interaction view that belongs to the other side (e.g., the item $i \in \mathcal{N}_u$). The aggregated knowledge is calculated as

$$M^u = M^{uu} \| \sum_{j \in \mathcal{N}_u} M^{ii}_j, \quad M^i = M^{ii} \| \sum_{j \in \mathcal{N}_i} M^{uu}_j, \tag{7}$$

where $\mathcal{N}_u$ and $\mathcal{N}_i$ represent the neighborhood of the user u and the item i, respectively, and $\|$ denotes the concatenation operation.

Subsequently, the aggregated knowledge is utilized to generate a parameterized mapping,

$$W^{meta}_u = \mathrm{MLP}_{\theta_1}(M^u) \mathrm{MLP}_{\theta_2}(M^u), \tag{8}$$

where θ_1 and θ_2 represent the parameters of MLPs. W^{meta}_i is calculated in a similar way. The parameterized mapping contains the knowledge from both two auxiliary views, which serve as a knowledge repository. Given a certain user or item, we can extract the knowledge most relevant to them by applying non-linear transformation to W^{meta} and their intrinsic attribution. Therefore, the enhanced embedding including aggregated knowledge from both two auxiliary views is formulated as

$$\widetilde{\mathbf{E}}^u = \sigma(W^{meta}_u \mathbf{E}^{UhoF}), \quad \widetilde{\mathbf{E}}^i = \sigma(W^{meta}_i \mathbf{E}^{IhoF}). \tag{9}$$

The final output $\widetilde{\mathbf{E}}^u$ and $\widetilde{\mathbf{E}}^i$ can be seen as the integration of the enhanced hoF and heF, which is utilized to predict the interaction of user and item. Here, we also employ BPR loss function to measure the performance of the whole model, that is,

$$\mathcal{L}_{sup} = \sum_{(i,j^+,j^-) \in \mathcal{O}} -\ln(\mathrm{sigmoid}(\hat{y}_{i,j^+}, \hat{y}_{i,j^-})), \tag{10}$$

where $\hat{y}_{i,j} = \widetilde{\mathbf{e}}_i^\top \widetilde{\mathbf{e}}_j$ denotes the likelihood of user i interacting with item j calculated by the enhanced embedding $\widetilde{\mathbf{e}}^i$ and $\widetilde{\mathbf{e}}^u$. The final optimization objective of our model is

$$\mathcal{L}_{total} = \mathcal{L}_{sup} + \alpha \mathcal{L}_{Uhkt} + (1-\alpha) \mathcal{L}_{Ihkt}. \tag{11}$$

where α is a hyperparameter that governs the weight of $\mathcal{L}_{Uhkt}$ and $\mathcal{L}_{Ihkt}$

5 Experiments

In this section, we evaluate the effectiveness of our FiCoRec by exploring the following questions:

- **RQ1:** How does the performance of FiCoRec compare to existing approaches?

- **RQ2:** How do different components in our model contribute to recommendation performance?
- **RQ3:** How do key hyperparameters impact model performance?
- **RQ4:** How does ISD benefit side information transformation?

Table 2. Statistics of experimental datasets

Dataset	#User	#Item	#Interaction	Sparsity
CiaoDVD	6776	101415	265308	99.96%
Epinions	15210	233929	630391	99.98%
FilmTrust	441	1853	12190	98.86%
KuaiRec	472	9030	711680	83.70%
LastFM	1427	6113	18092	99.72%

5.1 Experimental Setup

Experimental Datasets. We conduct experiments on five publicly available datasets: CiaoDVD [17], Epinions [19], FilmTrust [9], KuaiRec [8], LastFM[1]. The details of each dataset are presented in Table 2.

Compared Baselines. To verify the effectiveness of our FiCoRec, we compare it with various baselines. The details of baselines are described as below.

- **GraphRec** [4] firstly adapts GNNs to model the user-user social network and the user-item interaction network to capture heterogeneous relations.
- **SMIN** [16] injects social and knowledge-aware relational structures into the user-item interaction modeling by self-supervised learning.
- **MHCN** [28] designs a multi-channel hypergraph convolutional network to enhance social recommendation by deploying high-order user relations.
- **KCGN** [13] designs a multi-task learning framework combining item interdependent knowledge and social influence to enhance social recommendation.
- **DSL** [22] aims to denoise personalized social information, retaining important social relationships for modeling user preferences.
- **HGCL** [1] transfers heterogeneous relational semantics to user-item interaction modeling with contrastive learning across different views.
- **RecDiff** [14] designs a hidden-space diffusion paradigm to alleviate the noisy effect in compressed and dense representation space.

---

[1] https://grouplens.org/datasets/hetrec-2011/.

Implement Details. Following previous works [1], we utilize Hit Ratio ($H@K$) and Normalize Discounted Cumulative Gain ($N@K$) to measure the recommendation accuracy of various methods. Both metrics are employed with $K = 10$. In the evaluation setup, one positive (interacted) item and 99 negative (non-interacted) items are sampled for each user to assess performance. Besides, we conduct experiments in the PyTorch framework. For all the baselines, we re-implement them in the aforementioned five datasets, and a single RTX 3090 GPU is used for training and testing. The Adam optimizer is used for model optimization, with the learning rate searched from 0.001 to 0.1 and a fixed weight decay rate of 0.05. As hyperparameters, we use a base configuration of hidden state dimension $d = 32$, GNN propagation layers $L = 3$, batch size = 8192, and total loss balanced weight $\alpha = 0.8$ across all datasets. Other hyperparameters are tuned individually for each dataset based on its scale and structure.

Table 3. Performance comparison of all methods on different datasets in terms of NDCG and HR. Best and second performances are marked with **bold** and <u>underline</u>. Δavg denotes relative improvements over all baselines on average, and Δsota indicates the improvements of FiCoRec compared to state-of-the-art methods.

Datasets	CiaoDVD		Epinions		FilmTrust		KuaiRec		LastFM	
Metric	H@10	N@10	H@10	N@10	H@10	N@10	H@10	N@10	H@10	N@10
GraphRec	0.6832	0.4679	0.7610	0.5529	0.8125	0.6319	0.6168	0.3524	0.7262	0.5181
SMIN	0.6895	0.4818	0.8079	0.5997	0.8433	0.6797	0.6695	0.3974	0.7387	0.5145
MHCN	0.7034	0.4876	0.8164	0.6056	0.8429	0.6637	0.6428	0.3956	0.7631	0.5529
KCGN	0.6878	0.4792	0.8187	0.6061	0.8705	0.7276	0.6631	0.4096	0.7555	0.5440
DSL	0.6980	0.4898	0.8138	0.5919	<u>0.8795</u>	**0.7349**	0.6716	0.4103	0.7362	0.5268
HGCL	<u>0.7325</u>	<u>0.5184</u>	<u>0.8226</u>	0.6165	0.8750	0.7095	<u>0.6737</u>	<u>0.4151</u>	<u>0.7875</u>	<u>0.5810</u>
RecDiff	0.7016	0.4934	0.8213	<u>0.6178</u>	0.8763	0.7114	0.6725	0.4029	0.7421	0.5393
FiCoRec	**0.7349**	**0.5319**	**0.8260**	**0.6342**	**0.8977**	<u>0.7310</u>	**0.6907**	**0.4175**	**0.8092**	**0.6726**
Δavg(%)	5.12	9.02	2.47	6.68	4.81	5.58	4.98	5.28	7.98	10.04
Δsota(%)	0.33	2.60	0.41	2.65	2.07	-0.53	2.52	0.58	2.76	2.03

5.2 Overall Performance Comparison (RQ1)

In this section, we conduct experiments over five benchmark datasets and compare our FiCoRec to the state-of-the-art baseline methods. The experimental results of all baseline methods and our model are reported in Table 3. Based on the evaluation results, we identify the following key observations:

(1) Our FiCoRec consistently outperforms baseline methods across five datasets. Notably, FiCoRec achieves the highest average improvement of 7.98% and 10.04% over seven baselines for the H@10 and N@10 metrics on the LastFM dataset. We attribute these improvements to the design of interaction semantic decouple, which provides a fine-grained transformation for side information.

(2) From the table, we also observe that FiCoRec outperforms the state-of-the-art model with a margin of 0.33%-2.76% on the H@10. Notably, the improvement of N@10 is more than H@10 on large-scale datasets where the user-item interaction is sparser. This suggests that FiCoRec effectively enhances the ranking ability and robustness of recommender system, enabling more personalized and interest-oriented recommendations for users. Conversely, the improvement on small-scale datasets illustrates an unstable trend. We hypothesize that it is because user interests are relatively simple in small-scale datasets, making it easier for models to capture user preferences, thus limiting the performance gains achieved by FiCoRec.

(3) As can be seen, HGCL leverages side information from both user's social connections and item's knowledge-aware dependencies, achieving remarkable performance among five datasets. Our FiCoRec not only provides a fine-grained transformation of side information but also explores the joint influence of both user and item. The superior performance further demonstrates the effectiveness of the proposed HKT and MSF module.

5.3 Ablation Study (RQ2)

We conduct ablation studies to assess the significance of customized components of our methods. Specifically, we disable the two key components and evaluate the discrepancy in recommendation performance. The experimental results are shown in Table 4. As can be seen, removing any of the two key components leads to performance degradation across the evaluated dataset. Furthermore, we do not include the user-user social connection view or the item-item knowledge-dependency view to consider their influence. For the influence of components, removing HKT causes a significant drop in performance. This is because it leverages side information and different-level semantics to enhance the interaction view. Without HKT, the decoupled hoF and heF fail to fully capture side information from the auxiliary views. In addition, for the influence of the auxiliary view, we can observe that the performance of FiCoRec outperforms the case where one of the auxiliary views is disabled. This emphasizes the importance of side information transformation, which is similar to the analysis in HGCL [1]. In particular, the user-user view plays a more essential role in our model, indicating the social connection between users more likely to directly influence the preference of the user.

5.4 Impact of Hyperparameters(RQ3)

We perform hyperparameter analysis to investigate the impact of hidden state dimension d, total loss balanced weight α and the total number of propagation layers L on the CiaoDVD, FilmTrust, and LastFM datasets. The results are shown in Fig. 2.

For the parameter d, as the value increases from 8 to 32, we can observe a remarkable improvement on both metrics. This is because the model's capacity

Table 4. Ablation studies on key components of FiCoRec

Datasets	CiaoDVD		FilmTrust		LastFM	
Metric	H@10	N@10	H@10	N@10	H@10	N@10
w/o-hkt	0.7137	0.5133	0.8786	0.7163	0.7820	0.5758
w/o-msf	0.7256	0.5209	0.8803	0.7205	0.7836	0.5827
w/o-uu	0.7068	0.5110	0.8709	0.7042	0.7618	0.5640
w/o-ii	0.7178	0.5202	0.8791	0.7192	0.7789	0.5753
FiCoRec	**0.7349**	**0.5319**	**0.8977**	**0.7310**	**0.8092**	**0.5928**

increases as the hidden dimension enlarges. However, excessive enlargement can degrade performance due to overfitting.

For the parameter α applied to $\mathcal{L}_{total}$, the performance fluctuates as α varies, suggesting that varying proportions of information transfer between user-user view and item-item view influence the recommendation performance. When the proportion of users exceeds 0.8, the model's performance declines, indicating that an optimal balance between users and items is crucial for achieving the best performance.

For the parameter L, as the total number of propagation layers increases, the performance gradually improves, suggesting that hierarchical knowledge transfer facilitates the transformation of side information. We can observe that performance degrades when the value of L reaches 4, which may be attributed to the oversmoothing problem for GNNs.

In addition, the model exhibits different sensitivity to hyperparameters, with smooth performance varying for α but more pronounced variations for L. Thus, optimizing each hyperparameter is crucial for achieving the best performance in specific applications.

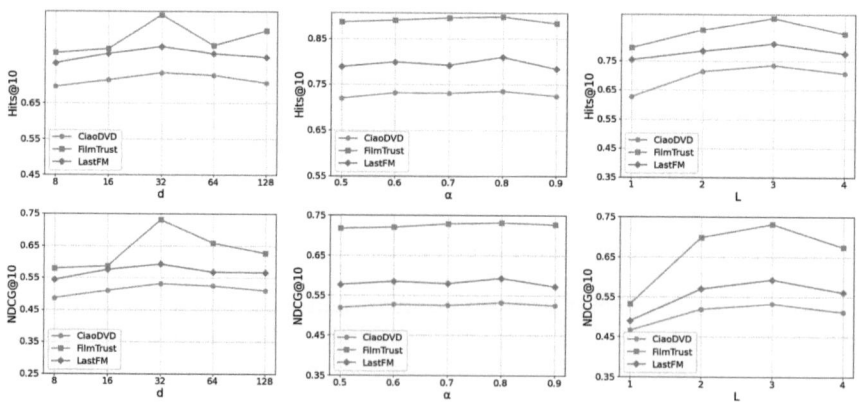

Fig. 2. Hyperparameter studies of the FiCoRec.

5.5 Deep Analysis of ISD(RQ4)

To further analyze the effect of the ISD, we visualize the heatmaps of the correlations between the original $\mathbf{E}^{inter}$, the decoupled hoF and heF, and the $\mathbf{E}^{aux}$, which is shown in Fig. 3. Here, we utilize the user embedding, $\mathbf{E}^u$ and $\mathbf{E}^{uu}$ on the LastFM dataset as an example. From Fig. 3(a) and (b), we can observe that $\mathbf{E}^{uu}$ shows moderate correlation with $\mathbf{E}^u$, but $\mathbf{E}^{uu}$ correlates more with UhoF than $\mathbf{E}^u$. This phenomenon indicates two facts: (1) semantic gap exists between $\mathbf{E}^{aux}$ and $\mathbf{E}^{inter}$, hindering the transformation of side information. (2) UhoF obtained through $\mathbf{E}^{uu}$ can effectively capture the user side information. Meanwhile, Fig. 3(c) shows a slight correlation between UheF and UhoF. This suggests that UheF and UhoF learn different feature information, which demonstrates the effectiveness of ISD. Furthermore, we utilize $\mathbf{E}^u$ and UheF to predict the user-item interaction without any augmentation and visualize the evaluation results in Fig. 4. As can be seen, the tendency of curves in two figures is comparable, which indicates that the UheF can achieve a performance comparable to the original $\mathbf{E}^u$. Notably, the performance of UheF initially exhibits a significant gap compared to $\mathbf{E}^u$, which we hypothesize is attributed to the inability of UheF to accurately capture user preference information during the early stages of training. As training progresses, its performance gradually converges to that of $\mathbf{E}^u$, eventually stabilizing with a slight margin, indicating the ability of UheF to model user preference.

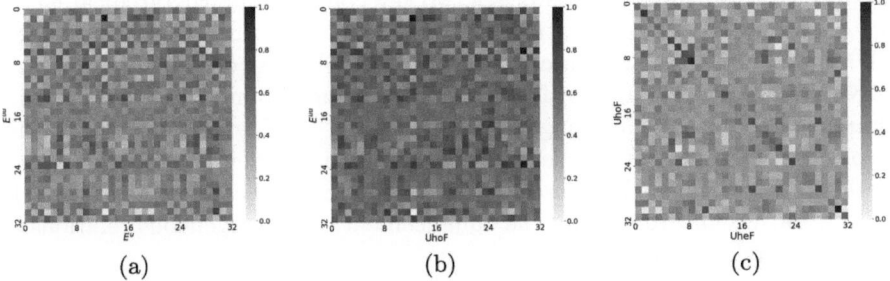

Fig. 3. Heatmap of the correlation between $\mathbf{E}^u$, $\mathbf{E}^{uu}$, hoF and heF. The axes denote embedding dimensions, and the color intensity reflects similarity magnitude, with darker shades indicating higher similarity. (a) $\mathbf{E}^{uu}$ versus $\mathbf{E}^u$, (b) $\mathbf{E}^{uu}$ versus UhoF, (c) UheF versus UhoF.

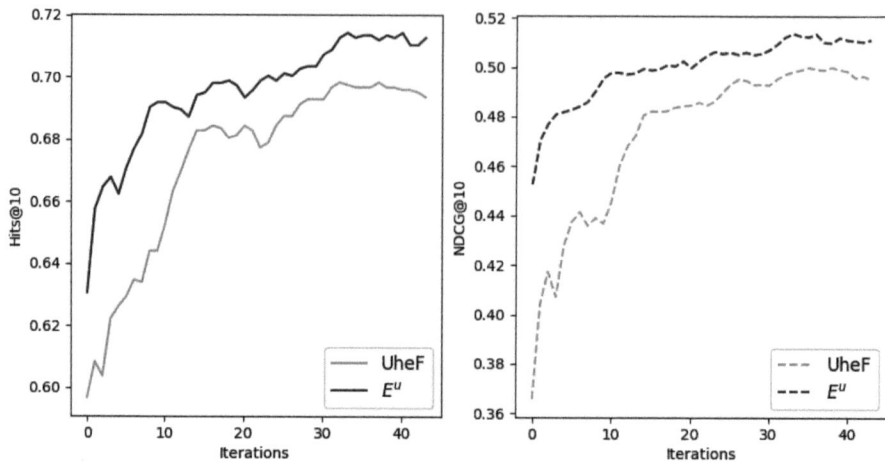

Fig. 4. Evaluation utilizing $\mathbf{E}^u$ and UheF without any augmentation.

6 Conclusion

In this paper, we focus on the semantic gap between different views due to the differences in learning behavior and explore the collaborative effect of multiple views. Thus, we propose a fine-grained augmentation method for recommendation, termed as FiCoRec. It comprises two key components: Hierarchical Knowledge Transfer (HKT) cooperating with interaction feature decoupling process (ISD) and Multi-view Semantic Fusion (MSF). ISD first decouples the interaction view embeddings, and HKT transfers side information knowledge through a hierarchical contrastive learning framework. Then MSF leverages meta-learning to consider the collaborative effect of two auxiliary views. Extensive experimental results confirm that our FiCoRec outperforms the state-of-the-arts. For future work, we aim to explore the enhancement of heterogeneous relationships in multi-behavior scenarios.

Acknowledgments. The works in this paper are supported by the National Natural Science Foundation of China under Grant Nos. 62477015 and 62306079; Key Research and Development Program of Guangdong of China under Grant No. 2023B0303010004; The Innovation Team Project for Universities in Guangdong Province under Grant No. 2023KCXTD011; Guangdong Provincial Natural Science Foundation General Project under Grant No. 2025A1515011637.

References

1. Chen, M., Huang, C., Xia, L., Wei, W., Xu, Y., Luo, R.: Heterogeneous graph contrastive learning for recommendation. In: Proceedings of the sixteenth ACM International Conference on Web Search and Data Mining, pp. 544–552 (2023)

2. Chen, P., Liu, S., Zhao, H., Jia, J.: Distilling knowledge via knowledge review. In: Proceedings of the IEEE/CVF Conference on Computer Vision and Pattern Recognition, pp. 5008–5017 (2021)
3. Dong, Y., Chawla, N.V., Swami, A.: metapath2vec: Scalable representation learning for heterogeneous networks. In: Proceedings of the 23rd ACM SIGKDD International Conference on Knowledge Discovery and Data Mining, pp. 135–144 (2017)
4. Fan, W., Ma, Y., Li, Q., He, Y., Zhao, E., Tang, J., Yin, D.: Graph neural networks for social recommendation. In: The World Wide Web Conference, pp. 417–426 (2019)
5. Fu, T.y., Lee, W.C., Lei, Z.: Hin2vec: Explore meta-paths in heterogeneous information networks for representation learning. In: Proceedings of the 2017 ACM on Conference on Information and Knowledge Management, pp. 1797–1806 (2017)
6. Fu, X., Zhang, J., Meng, Z., King, I.: MAGNN: Metapath aggregated graph neural network for heterogeneous graph embedding. In: Proceedings of the Web Conference 2020, pp. 2331–2341 (2020)
7. Gao, C., et al.: A survey of graph neural networks for recommender systems: challenges, methods, and directions. ACM Trans. Recommender Syst., pp. 1–51 (2023)
8. Gao, C., et al.: KuaiRec: a fully-observed dataset and insights for evaluating recommender systems. In: Proceedings of the 31st ACM International Conference on Information & Knowledge Management, pp. 540–550 (2022)
9. Guo, G., Zhang, J., Yorke-Smith, N.: A novel bayesian similarity measure for recommender systems. In: Proceedings of the 23rd International Joint Conference on Artificial Intelligence, pp. 2619–2625 (2013)
10. Han, J., Tao, Q., Tang, Y., Xia, Y.: DH-HGCN: dual homogeneity hypergraph convolutional network for multiple social recommendations. In: Proceedings of the 45th International ACM SIGIR Conference on Research and Development in Information Retrieval, pp. 2190–2194 (2022)
11. He, X., Deng, K., Wang, X., Li, Y., Zhang, Y., Wang, M.: LightGCN: simplifying and powering gGraph convolution network for recommendation. In: Proceedings of the 43rd International ACM SIGIR conference on Research and Development in Information Retrieval, pp. 639–648 (2020)
12. Huang, C.: Recent advances in heterogeneous relation learning for recommendation. In: International Joint Conference on Artificial Intelligence, pp. 4442–4449 (2021)
13. Huang, C., et al.: Knowledge-aware coupled graph neural network for social recommendation. In: Proceedings of the AAAI Conference on Artificial Intelligence, pp. 4115–4122 (2021)
14. Li, Z., Xia, L., Huang, C.: RecDiff: Diffusion model for social recommendation. In: Proceedings of the 33rd ACM International Conference on Information and Knowledge Management, pp. 1346–1355 (2024)
15. Liang, D., Li, B., Li, H., Jiang, Y.: MuHca: Mixup heterogeneous graphs for contrastive learning with data augmentation. In: Pacific Rim International Conference on Artificial Intelligence, pp. 377–388. Springer (2023)
16. Long, X., Huang, C., Xu, Y., Xu, H., Dai, P., Xia, L., Bo, L.: Social recommendation with self-supervised metagraph informax network. In: Proceedings of the 30th ACM International Conference on Information & Knowledge Management, pp. 1160–1169 (2021)
17. Park, C., Kim, D., Xie, X., Yu, H.: Collaborative translational metric learning. In: 2018 IEEE International Conference on Data Mining, pp. 367–376 (2018)

18. Rendle, S., Freudenthaler, C., Gantner, Z., Schmidt-Thieme, L.: BPR: Bayesian personalized ranking from implicit feedback. In: Proceedings of the Twenty-Fifth Conference on Uncertainty in Artificial Intelligence, pp. 452–461 (2009)
19. Richardson, M., Agrawal, R., Domingos, P.: Trust management for the semantic web. In: International Semantic Web Conference, pp. 351–368. Springer (2003)
20. Sharma, K., Lee, Y.C., Nambi, S., Salian, A., Shah, S., Kim, S.W., Kumar, S.: A survey of graph neural networks for social recommender systems. ACM Computing Surveys, pp. 1–34 (2024)
21. Tian, Y., Dong, K., Zhang, C., Zhang, C., Chawla, N.V.: Heterogeneous graph masked autoencoders. In: Proceedings of the AAAI Conference on Artificial Intelligence. vol. 37, pp. 9997–10005 (2023)
22. Wang, T., Xia, L., Huang, C.: Denoised self-augmented learning for social recommendation. In: Proceedings of the Thirty-Second International Joint Conference on Artificial Intelligence, pp. 2324–2331 (2023)
23. Wang, X., He, X., Wang, M., Feng, F., Chua, T.S.: Neural graph collaborative filtering. In: Proceedings of the 42nd international ACM SIGIR Conference on Research and development in Information Retrieval, pp. 165–174 (2019)
24. Wang, X., Ji, H., Shi, C., Wang, B., Ye, Y., Cui, P., Yu, P.S.: Heterogeneous graph attention network. In: The World Wide Web Conference, pp. 2022–2032 (2019)
25. Wu, L., Li, J., Sun, P., Hong, R., Ge, Y., Wang, M.: DiffNet++: A neural influence and interest diffusion network for social recommendation. IEEE Trans. Knowl. Data Eng., 4753–4766 (2020)
26. Wu, S., Sun, F., Zhang, W., Xie, X., Cui, B.: Graph neural networks in recommender systems: a survey. ACM Computing Surveys, pp. 1–37 (2022)
27. Ying, R., He, R., Chen, K., Eksombatchai, P., Hamilton, W.L., Leskovec, J.: Graph convolutional neural networks for web-scale recommender systems. In: Proceedings of the 24th ACM SIGKDD International Conference on Knowledge Discovery & Data Mining, pp. 974–983 (2018)
28. Yu, J., Yin, H., Li, J., Wang, Q., Hung, N.Q.V., Zhang, X.: Self-supervised multi-channel hypergraph convolutional network for social recommendation. In: Proceedings of the Web Conference 2021, pp. 413–424 (2021)

Hierarchical Interaction Summarization and Contrastive Prompting for Explainable Recommendations

Yibin Liu[1], Ang Li[1], and Shijian Li[1,2(✉)]

[1] College of Computer Science and Technology, Zhejiang University, Hangzhou 310027, China
{yibinliu,leeyon,shijianli}@zju.edu.cn
[2] The State Key Lab of Brain-Machine Intelligence, Hangzhou, China

Abstract. Explainable recommendations, which use the information of user and item with interaction to generate a explanation for why the user would interact with the item, are crucial for improving user trust and decision transparency to the recommender system. Existing methods primarily rely on encoding features of users and items to embeddings, which often leads to information loss due to dimensionality reduction, sparse interactions, and so on. With the advancements of large language models (LLMs) in language comprehension, some methods use embeddings as LLM inputs for explanation generation. However, since embeddings lack inherent semantics, LLMs must adjust or extend their parameters to interpret them, a process that inevitably incurs information loss. To address this issue, we propose a novel approach combining profile generation via hierarchical interaction summarization (PGHIS), which leverages a pretrained LLM to hierarchically summarize user-item interactions, generating structured textual profiles as explicit representations of user and item characteristics. Additionally, we propose contrastive prompting for explanation generation (CPEG) which employs contrastive learning to guide another reasoning language models in producing high-quality ground truth recommendation explanations. Finally, we use the textual profiles of user and item as input and high-quality explanation as output to fine-tune a LLM for generating explanations. Experimental results on multiple datasets demonstrate that our approach outperforms existing state-of-the-art methods, achieving a great improvement on metrics about explainability (e.g., 5% on GPTScore) and text quality (e.g., 20.6% and 19.6% on variants of BLEU and ROUGE). Furthermore, our generated ground truth explanations achieve a significantly higher win rate compared to user-written reviews and those produced by other methods, demonstrating the effectiveness of CPEG in generating high-quality ground truths.

Keywords: Explainable Recommendation · Contrastive Learning · Large Language Models

---

Y. Liu and A. Li—Equal contribution.

1 Introduction

Recommender systems play a crucial role in delivering personalized content across domains like e-commerce, streaming services, and social media [23]. They enhance user experience and engagement by analyzing past interactions and preferences. Although contemporary recommender systems achieve high accuracy in their suggestions, the generation of explanations remains underexplored. Explainable recommendations, which use the information of the user and the item with interaction to generate an explanation for why the user would interact with the item, are essential as they provide transparency into the recommendation process, enhancing user trust and facilitating informed decision-making. By elucidating the factors driving user-item interactions, these explanations bridge the gap between complex algorithms and user comprehension, thereby fostering more trustworthy and user-centric recommendation platforms.

Early research [7,14,17] predominantly leveraged conventional natural language generation methods, including LSTM [25], GRU [5], and transformers [26], to learn ID embeddings for users and items and subsequently generate corresponding explanations. With the advancements of LLMs in language comprehension, recent studies [15,19] have utilized these models to understand and learn embeddings of users and items to generate explanations.

Although existing methods have made significant breakthroughs in generating recommendation explanations, as shown in Fig. 1, they still face two main problems. **a) Hard-to-Learn Embeddings**, whether learning user and item embeddings from scratch [7,14,15,17] or employing models to transform existing embeddings [19] within the recommender system, these approaches often incur information loss [6] during the embedding training or transformation processes, exacerbated by dimensionality reduction, sparse interactions, and so on. In LLM-based methods, when an LLM takes embeddings as input, adjusting the parameters of LLMs or incorporating additional parameters is required for interpretation, also leading to potential information loss. **b) Poor Ground Truth Explanation**, most current approaches use user reviews as ground truth for recommendation explanations. However, for users who do not frequently provide detailed reviews, their reviews are often simplistic, such as "it's good", which lack sufficient explanatory information, and thus becoming low-quality explanations in the dataset. Therefore, we face two main challenges when designing our method: (1) How can we represent information of user and item as LLM inputs in a textual format that preserves both interaction and semantic information without relying on embeddings? (2) How can we generate high-quality ground truth explanations for training, especially when user reviews are lack detailed information?

To tackle these issues, we propose **Profile Generation via Hierarchical Interaction Summarization (PGHIS)**, leveraging a pretrained LLM to hierarchically summarize interaction data, reducing information loss. Specifically, we enable the LLM to simulate graph neural networks from a textual perspective, summarizing key interactions between items and users. Through multi-layer iterations, it extracts shared attributes from interacted item-user

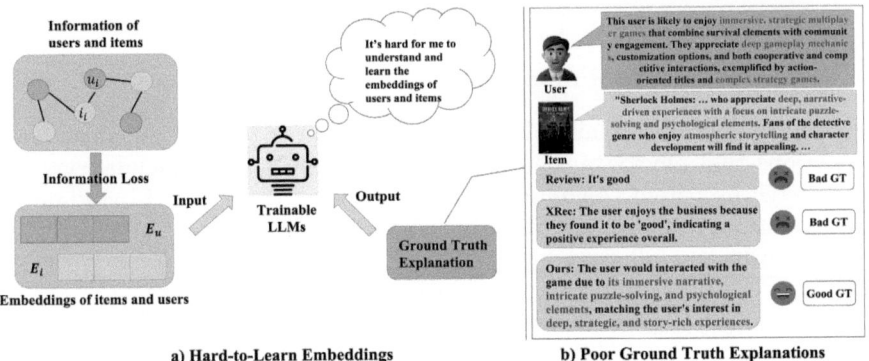

Fig. 1. Problems in Recommendation Explanation Generation. a) Hard-to-Learn Embeddings, learned user or item embeddings have information loss and are hard for LLMs to interpret; b) Poor ground truth Explanations, as user reviews are often simplistic, leading to low-quality explanations.

pairs, ultimately generating structured textual profiles. Additionally, we introduce **Contrastive Prompting for ground truth Explanation Generation (CPEG)** to enhance the quality of training data. We prompt Reasoning Language Models (RLMs) [1] with a user and both positive and negative items to infer interactions and generate explanations. If the item predicted by the RLM is positive item, the explanation is considered high-quality. Otherwise, the erroneous explanation and item are treated as a negative example for the RLM, thereby enhancing the quality of ground-truth explanations. Finally, we construct training datasets using generated profiles as input and refined explanations as output, applying Supervised Fine-Tuning (SFT) on a pretrained LLM for our final model. Experiments on diverse datasets show high-quality explanations and significant improvements, with an average gain of 5% on GPTScore, 20.6% and 19.6% on variants of BLEU and ROUGE. Our main contributions can be summarized as follows:

- We identify embedding limitations and ground truth quality as key barriers in explainable recommendation, as embeddings often suffer from information loss, and lack of inherent semantics in LLM-based methods.
- We propose a framework that integrates hierarchical interaction summarization to create textual user-item profiles instead of embeddings and contrastive prompting to generate high-quality ground truth explanations.
- We evaluated our approach against state-of-the-art baselines on diverse datasets, achieving an average improvement of 5% on GPTScore, 20.6% and 19.6% on variants of BLEU and ROUGE. Experimental results further validate the high quality of ground truth explanations generated by CPEG.

2 Related Work and Preliminaries

2.1 Explainable Recommendation

The primary goal of Explainable Recommendation is to generate clear textual explanations that elucidate the reasoning behind each recommendation. Given an interacted user-item pair u and i, an explanation is generated based on their respective information $\mathcal{X}_u$ and $\mathcal{X}_i$ (e.g., profiles, embeddings, or attributes), and can be described as follows:

$$explanation(u, i) = Generate(\mathcal{X}_u, \mathcal{X}_i) \tag{1}$$

As a natural language generation (NLG) task, existing approaches primarily leverage LSTM, GRU, and Transformer-based models [7,14,17]. For example, Att2Seq [7] employs an attention mechanism to model the relationships between user and item attributes, guiding an LSTM to produce explanations. Similarly, NRT [17] jointly predicts user ratings and generates concise textual tips by integrating collaborative filtering with a GRU as decoder. With the success of pretrained LLMs in NLG, some methods [15,19] have explored their use for this task. For example, PEPLER [15] initially freezes the pretrained LLM to learn user and item embeddings, and subsequently fine-tunes the LLM parameters based on the acquired embeddings. Similarly, XRec [19] trains a Mixture-of-Experts (MOE) model [12] to transform the embeddings learned by the recommendater system into inputs for a pretrained LLM, thereby generating explanations. Additionally, XRec alse employs LLMs to rewrite reviews as ground truth explanation to eliminate subjectivity. However, these approaches encode user and item features into embeddings, which often suffer from information loss. This issue is exacerbated when embeddings are used as LLM inputs, as LLMs struggle to interpret floating-point embeddings, leading to further loss. In contrast, our approach shifts focus from item and user embeddings to their textual profiles.

2.2 Graph Collaborative Filtering(GCF)

Graph Neural Networks effectively model collaborative relationships by capturing high-order dependencies in user-item interactions. Through iterative message passing, nodes aggregate information from neighbors to generate embeddings that reflect these relationships. Given a user-item interaction graph with L layers, the embedding of a user node u or an item node i at layer l is computed as follows:

$$e_u^l = AGG(e_u^{l-1}, \mathcal{N}_u) \tag{2}$$

Here, $\mathcal{N}_u$ represents the set of embeddings for items that have interacted with user u. AGG denotes an aggregation function, which can vary depending on the model. For example, NGCF [28] employs a combination of a summation function and a nonlinear activation function, while LightGCN [11] adopts a simple summation function. In contrast, AutoCF [29] introduces a masked graph autoencoder designed to aggregate global information. Similar to these methods, we propose PGHIS, which uses a pretrained LLM as the aggregation function to integrate node features, replacing embeddings with explicit textual representations of user and item characteristics. To the best of our knowledge, we are the first to apply graph neural network concepts to profile generation.

2.3 Contrastive Learning in Prompts

Although LLMs have achieved significant progress across various domains, they still struggle in certain scenarios. To address this, some studies have incorporated contrastive learning into prompts by providing both correct and incorrect examples [2,4,16], guiding the model to produce outputs aligned with the correct examples while avoiding errors. For instance, CCoT [4] introduces both valid and flawed thinking steps to steer the model toward correct results. Similar to these approaches, we propose CPEG to guide LLMs in generating high-quality ground truth explanations.

3 Method

In this work, we propose a novel Profile Generation method via Hierarchical Interaction Summarization to generate user and item profiles by iteratively aggregating the common features of a user's or item's interacted items or users across multiple layers, forming refined textual profiles. This eliminates the need for LLMs to interpret embedding-based interactions, as preference patterns are explicitly represented in natural language, which enhances the explainability of recommendation systems while effectively capturing user and item characteristics.

To address the limitation of user reviews in explaining why users interact with items, we propose a method called Contrastive Prompting for ground truth Explanation Generation that leverages RLMs and employs Contrastive Prompts to generate more coherent and insightful ground truth recommendation explanations.

Finally, we use the generated user and item profiles as inputs to the model and produce recommendation explanations generated by CPEG as the ground truth output to construct training and testing datasets for our model. Then, we fine-tune a lightweight LLM using SFT with these datasets, resulting in our final recommendation explanation generation model.

3.1 Profile Generation via Hierarchical Interaction Summarization

To solve the issue of hard-to-learn embeddings, we introduce a Profile Generation method via Hierarchical Interaction Summarization, which leverages a pretrained large model as the aggregation function. This method continuously distills and summarizes the shared characteristics of items-users interacting with a given user or item, dynamically refining the original user or item profile. By

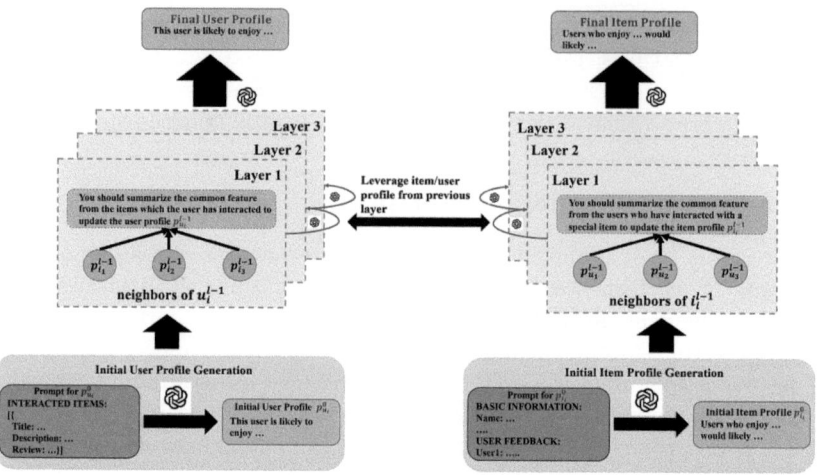

Fig. 2. An overall overview of the Profile Generation method via Hierarchical Interaction Summarization.

doing so, it directly embeds interaction information into the profile, enhancing its expressiveness. The proposed Profile Generation method via Hierarchical Interaction Summarization is illustrated in Fig. 2.

For any given number of profile updates l, we assume that the profile of any user or item before the update is $p_{u_i}^{l-1}$ or $p_{i_i}^{l-1}$ and the set of the profiles of items or users that have interacted with the user or item is $\mathcal{N}_{i_i}^{l-1}$ or $\mathcal{N}_{u_i}^{l-1}$. Given an existing user or item profile, we leverage the profiles of the interacted item-user to generate an updated profile. Specifically, we use the following system prompt $\mathcal{P}_{agg}$:

"*You will serve as an assistant to help me update the user/item profile ... You should summarize the common features of the interacted items/users and then update the original user/item profile.*"

This prompt, along with the pretrained LLM, is used to aggregate the relevant information and derive the new user or item profile $p_{u_i}^l / p_{i_i}^l$. The update process is formulated as follows:

$$p_{u_i}^l = LLM(\mathcal{P}_{agg}, p_{u_i}^{l-1}, \mathcal{N}_{i_i}^{l-1}) \qquad (3)$$

$$p_{i_i}^l = LLM(\mathcal{P}_{agg}, p_{i_i}^{l-1}, \mathcal{N}_{u_i}^{l-1}) \qquad (4)$$

In LightGCN, the initial embeddings of users and items are randomly initialized and updated through backpropagation during training. Similarly, our approach directly utilizes the basic attributes a_{u_i} or a_{i_i} of users (interacted items and reviews) and items (title, description and ...) to construct their initial profiles with the pretrained LLM and the system prompt $\mathcal{P}_{init}$ is like.

"*You will serve as an assistant to help me determine which types of items a specific user is likely to enjoy.../ summarize which types of users would enjoy a specific item...*".

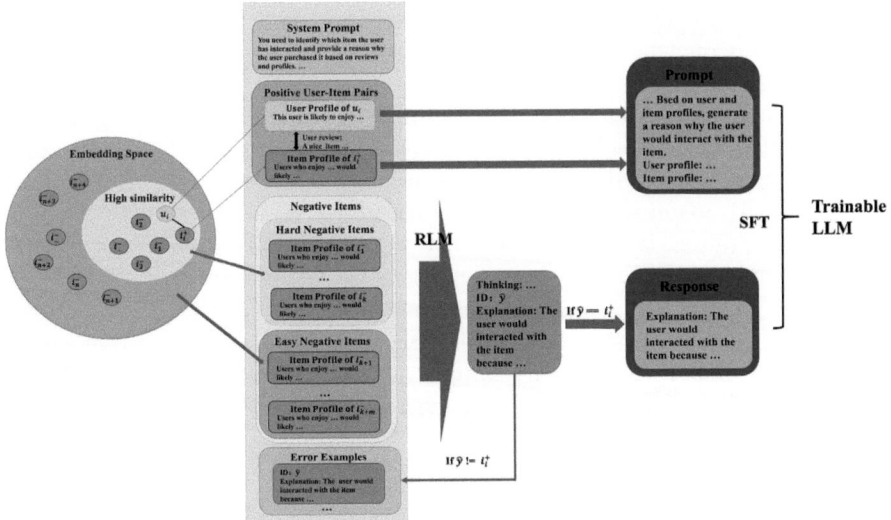

Fig. 3. An overall overview of the Contrastive Prompting for Explanation Generation and Supervised Fine-Tuning.

This eliminates the need for additional trainable parameters, making the method more efficient. The generation of initial user/item profile is formulated as follows:

$$p_{u_i}^0 = LLM(\mathcal{P}_{init}, a_{u_i}) p_{i_i}^0 = LLM(\mathcal{P}_{init}, a_{i_i}) \tag{5}$$

3.2 Contrastive Prompting for Ground Truth Explanation Generation

To generate high-quality ground truth explanations, we propose a Contrastive Prompting approach. We construct prompts as inputs to a pretrained RLM, enabling it to infer and generate meaningful explanations. The prompt construction is divided into two key components: Discrimination, which helps the model distinguish between relevant and irrelevant items, and Refinement, which enhances explanation quality by leveraging incorrect predictions. An overview of the approach is illustrated in the left part of Fig. 3.

Discrimination. We utilize the profiles p_{u_i} and $p_{i_i^+}$ generated by our PGHIS method for the user u_i and the item i_i^+ with interaction. Specifically, for each interactive user-item pair, we sample a subset of non-interacted items as negative examples. These negative samples, along with the profiles of the pairs of user-items interacted, are then fed into the pretrained RLM (e.g., DeepSeek-R1 [10]), prompting it to infer which item the user is most likely to engage with and to generate a corresponding explanation. The quality of the explanation is evaluated based on whether the RLM's predicted item aligns with the actual user-interacted item.

Since incorporating hard negative samples in contrastive learning has been shown to enhance the effectiveness of representation learning [22], we also introduce hard negatives based on semantic similarity when selecting negative samples. Specifically, given a set N^- of items that have no interaction with user u_i, we employ pretrained text encoders to convert both the user profile p_{u_i} and the item profiles in N^- into semantic representations. Using $sim(e_1, e_2) = \frac{e_1 \cdot e_2}{|e_1||e_2|}$ to measure the similarity of two representations e_1 and e_2, we identify the k items from N^- with the highest semantic similarity to u_i as hard negative samples $i_1^-, ..i_k^-$. Additionally, we randomly sample m items from the remaining items in N^- as standard negative samples $i_{k+1}^-...i_m^-$. Our initial formula for generating explanations E is as follows:

$$T, \hat{y}, E = RLM(\mathcal{P}, p_{u_i}, p_{i_i^+}, p_{i_1^-}, ...p_{i_{k+m}^-}) \tag{6}$$

Here, T refers to the reasoning process of the RLM, while $\hat{y}$ denotes the item that the RLM predicts which the user would interact with. $\mathcal{P}$ refers to the system prompt, which is defined as follows:

"You will serve as an assistant to help me find the item a specific user has interact with and explain why the user would interact with the item. I will provide you with the profile of user, review of the item which a specific user has interacted written by the user and a list of items with profiles. ..."

Refinement. Although existing RLMs possess strong reasoning capabilities, they often fail to produce correct results in a single inference. So we utilize the erroneous reasoning outputs $\hat{Y}_e$ and explanations E_e generated by the RLM as error examples, incorporating them into the prompt until the model generates the correct item that the user has interacted with. This approach not only helps the model avoid repeating the same mistakes but also provides incorrect explanation references, thereby enhancing the overall quality of the generated explanations. The specific formula is as follows:

$$T, \hat{y}, E = RLM(\mathcal{P}_{retry}, p_{u_i}, p_{i_i^+}, p_{i_1^-}, ...p_{i_7^-}, \hat{Y}_e, E_e) \tag{7}$$

Here, $\mathcal{P}_{retry}$ is derived from $\mathcal{P}$ by incorporating instructions that guide the model to reference incorrect examples.

3.3 Supervised Fine-Tuning

After obtaining high-quality explanations, we use user and item profiles with interaction as input conditions. Prompt is constructed to instruct the model to generate explanation for user-item interaction based on these profiles, which serves as the input, while the ground truth explanation is used as the output, forming the training samples, as illustrated in Fig. 4.

> **Prompt:**
> You are an AI assistant specialized in understanding user profile and item profile. Based on the given user profile and item profile, generate a reason why this user would interact with this item.
> **User Profile:**
> ....
> **Item Profile:**
> ....
> **Reason for Interaction:**
> **Response:**
> The user would interacted with the item because ...

Fig. 4. Supervised Fine-Tuning dataset format.

Similar to the standard SFT approach used in decoder-only models, we employ token-level cross-entropy loss as the objective function to update all the parameters of a pretrained LLM. This loss optimizes model parameters by maximizing the probability of predicting the next token given the preceding tokens. The formulation is as follows:

$$\mathcal{L} = \sum_{t=1}^{T} p_\theta(x_t | x_1, x_2, ... x_{t-1}) \tag{8}$$

where T denotes the length of the output sequence, x_t represents the token being predicted, $x_1, x_2, ..., x_{t-1}$ refers to the preceding tokens in the sequence, θ denotes the trainable model parameters, and $p_\theta(x_t | x_1, x_2, ... x_{t-1})$ represents the predicted probability distribution of the model.

4 Experiments

4.1 Experimental Seting

Datasets. We evaluated our approach using three widely used public datasets. **Amazon-Book**[1], comprises user ratings and reviews for books available on Amazon. **Yelp**[2], captures user interactions with businesses and provides detailed category information across various industries. **Steam** [13] contains user feedback and engagement data related to video games on the Steam platform. As the Steam dataset does not contain rating scores, no filtering was applied. For the other datasets, we first applied k-core filtering and then divided all of them into three subsets using a 3:1:1 ratio. These subsets were used for profile generation, sampling 20,000 instances for SFT training, and selecting 2,000 instances for testing.

---

[1] https://nijianmo.github.io/amazon/index.html.
[2] https://www.yelp.com/dataset.

Table 1. Overall performance comparison with baselines on Amazon-Book, Yelp and Steam datasets. ↑ indicates that higher values correspond to better performance. "BS" denotes BERTScore, while "P," "R," and "F1" represent Precision, Recall, and F1-Score, respectively. "R-1," "R-2," and "R-L" refer to ROUGE-1, ROUGE-2, and ROUGE-L scores. The best-performing results are highlighted in bold, while the second-best results are underlined for emphasis.

Methods	Explainability↑					Text Quality↑				
	GPTScore	BS^P	BS^R	BS^{F1}	BLEURT	BLEU-1	BLEU-4	R-1	R-2	R-L
Amazon-Books										
Att2Seq	71.75	0.6119	0.6026	0.6076	0.6086	0.5959	0.3535	0.5736	0.3835	0.5110
NRT	84.58	0.2814	0.6449	0.4577	0.6088	0.2472	0.1047	0.3755	0.2087	0.2860
PETER	69.10	0.6145	0.6198	0.6175	0.6143	0.5884	0.3550	0.5833	0.3922	0.5216
PEPLER	77.54	0.6173	0.6152	0.6165	0.5900	0.6097	0.3705	0.5996	0.4059	0.5291
XRec	83.76	0.6528	0.6751	0.6642	0.6300	0.6018	0.3386	0.5976	0.3927	0.5191
Ours	**88.24**	**0.7209**	**0.7294**	**0.7253**	**0.6732**	**0.6947**	**0.4555**	**0.6816**	**0.5045**	**0.6105**
Yelp										
Att2Seq	54.60	0.5459	0.5311	0.5389	0.5153	0.5704	0.2769	0.5411	0.3028	0.4629
NRT	83.99	0.3035	0.6441	0.4691	0.4467	0.2648	0.1038	0.3889	0.2009	0.2878
PETER	69.13	0.6034	0.5859	0.5949	0.5697	0.6284	0.3418	0.6018	0.3654	0.5156
PEPLER	72.78	0.6047	0.5813	0.5932	0.5376	0.5987	0.3364	0.5979	0.3711	0.5146
XRec	83.30	0.6272	0.6658	0.6466	0.5905	0.5922	0.3045	0.6065	0.3635	0.5132
Ours	**88.83**	**0.7277**	**0.7394**	**0.7336**	**0.6639**	**0.7298**	**0.4864**	**0.7102**	**0.5208**	**0.6354**
Steam										
Att2Seq	58.56	0.6269	0.6114	0.6195	0.6251	0.6304	0.4004	0.6100	0.4190	0.5534
NRT	61.29	0.6379	0.6077	0.6230	0.6213	0.6212	0.3992	0.6119	0.4248	0.5602
PETER	69.15	0.6497	0.6380	0.6441	0.6342	0.6527	0.4218	0.6375	0.4437	0.5758
PEPLER	67.67	0.6491	0.6396	0.6447	0.6171	0.6571	0.4208	0.6354	0.4412	0.5741
XRec	74.38	0.5593	0.5803	0.5702	0.5135	0.5450	0.2142	0.5392	0.2946	0.4611
Ours	**81.55**	**0.7315**	**0.7269**	**0.7294**	**0.6728**	**0.7301**	**0.4946**	**0.7104**	**0.5276**	**0.6448**

Evaluation Metrics. Following the evaluation approach of XRec [19], we have chosen several advanced metrics to rigorously assess the explainability of the explanations generated by our trained model. **GPTScore** [8] serves as a scalable alternative to human evaluation, demonstrating strong correlations with expert judgments in text generation task. **BERTScore** [31] is a semantic evaluation metric that measures the similarity between candidate and reference texts using contextualized embeddings from pretrained BERT models. **BLEURT** [24] is a learned evaluation metric that leverages BERT-based contextual embeddings and fine-tuning on human-rated data to assess text quality.

Although traditional text generation evaluation metrics struggle to effectively capture semantic similarity between generated text and ground truth, we nonetheless employ certain metrics as a reference for assessing the text quality. **BLEU** (Bilingual Evaluation Understudy) [20] measures n-gram overlap between generated and reference texts, applying brevity penalties to account for length differences. **ROUGE** (Recall-Oriented Understudy for Gisting Evaluation) [18] evaluates text summarization by measuring lexical overlap between generated and reference summaries.

Compared Method. We compared our method with the following five state-of-the-art baselines:

- **Att2Seq** [7] proposes an attention-enhanced attribute-to-sequence model that generates personalized item reviews based on user, item, and rating attributes. For steam dataset, we use playing hours instead of rating.
- **NRT** [17] proposes a neural framework that jointly predicts user ratings and generates concise textual tips by integrating collaborative filtering with a gated recurrent neural network decoder.
- **PETER** [14] proposes a transformer-based model that generates personalized, explainable recommendations by integrating user and item IDs into text generation.
- **PEPLER** [15] proposes a personalized prompt learning approach for explainable recommendation, integrating user and item identifiers into pretrained language models to generate tailored explanations.
- **XRec** [19] employs a lightweight collaborative adaptor to incorporate collaborative signals, enabling large language models to understand complex user-item interactions and provide comprehensive explanations for user behaviors in recommender systems.

Implementation Details. Due to constraints on prompt length and computational cost, we select neighboring nodes based on rating or playing hours, prioritizing the top 15 for profile generation using GPT-4o-mini[3] and use the profiles generated by RLMRec [21] as initial profiles. For explanation generation, we use all-MiniLM-L6-v2 [27] to generate embeddings of profiles and employ DeepSeek-R1 [10] as the RLM and set k and m to 2 and 5, respectively. Finally, we fine-tune a cost-effective Qwen2.5-7B-Instruct [30] model with a learning rate of 1e-5 on a single H20 GPU, using LLaMA-Factory [32] to full-parameter SFT our model.

4.2 Performance Comparison

The results across the Amazon-Books, Yelp, and Steam datasets showed in Table 1 demonstrates the superior performance of our method compared to established baselines in both explainability and text quality metrics.

- For explainability, our method exhibits significant enhancements across five explainability metrics. Notably, when evaluated using the GPTScore metric derived from the state-of-the-art GPT-3.5 model, our method surpasses

---
[3] https://openai.com/index/hello-gpt-4o/.

the second-best approach by an average of 5 points out of 100 across three datasets. This performance underscores our method's ability to thoroughly leverage user and item characteristics, thereby generating high-quality explanations.
- For text quality, our method achieves superior text quality across all datasets, outperforming baselines in ROUGE-1, ROUGE-2, and ROUGE-L. For example, on Amazon-Books, our method surpasses the second-best approach, PEPLER, by nearly 0.1 across all three ROUGE metrics. Strong BLEU scores further validate its fluency and accuracy, demonstrating the effectiveness of our approach in generating high-quality explanations.

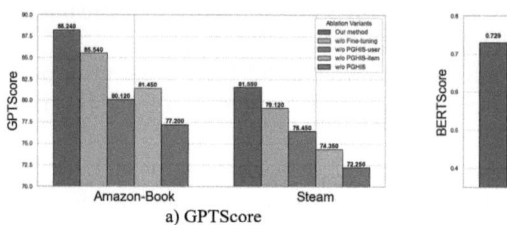 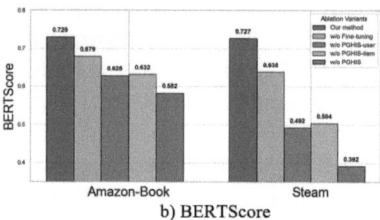

Fig. 5. Ablastion Study. a) and b) respectively illustrate the ablation study results of GPTScore and BERTScore on two datasets.

The superior performance of our method can be attributed to two key factors. (1) Unlike approaches that rely on learned user or item embeddings, our method explicitly represents user preferences and interactions in textual form. This textual information serves as input to LLM , making it more interpretable and effective for learning compared to embeddings. (2) We fine-tune a general LLM through SFT, enabling it to generate more coherent and high-quality explanations.

4.3 Ablation Study

To evaluate the contribution of each component in our approach, we conducted an ablation study on GPTScore and BERTScore by comparing **i) Our method** with four variants: **ii) w/o Fine-tuning**, which generates explanations using our profiles without SFT; **iii) w/o PGHIS-user**, which replaces PGHIS-generated user profiles with initial ones while retaining PGHIS-generated item profiles; **iv) w/o PGHIS-item**, which removes PGHIS-generated item profiles; and **v) w/o PGHIS**, which uses only the initial user and item profiles. The results are shown in Fig. 5.

The results indicate that without the use of SFT, both GPTScore and BERTScore only experience slight declines, with performance still surpassing that of XRec. This suggests that the profiles generated by PGHIS effectively capture the preferences and interaction information of users and items, enabling the model to generate high quality explanations even without SFT. Furthermore, when considering the results from using either the item or user profiles generated solely by PGHIS, it is evident that both have a nearly equivalent level of importance in the outcome. In contrast, when PGHIS-generated profiles are not utilized, both GPTScore and BERTScore experience a significant decrease, highlighting the superiority of PGHIS.

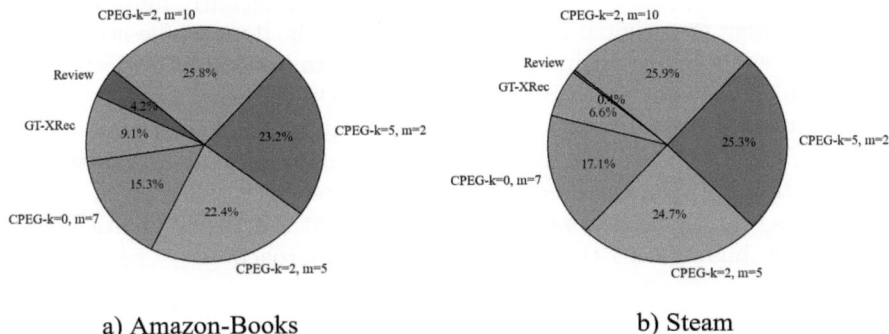

a) Amazon-Books   b) Steam

Fig. 6. Win Rate Comparison of Ground Truths in Explanation Quality. a) illustrates the win rates of different ground truth explanations in the Amazon-Books dataset, while b) presents the corresponding results for the Steam dataset.

4.4 Ground Truth Explanation Quality

Given that the quality assessment of ground truth is inherently subjective. We refer to existing studies on utilizing LLMs-as-a-judge [9] to evaluate the quality of ground truth explanations for user-item interactions and assess the impact of k and m on explanation quality, we conduct experiments on the Amazon-Books and Steam datasets. Using user-item profiles with interaction as a reference, GPT-3.5 determines the most appropriate explanation among: **i) Review**: user-written review, **ii) GT-XRec**: ground truth generated by XRec, **iii) CPEG-$k=0$, $m=7$**: CPEG without hard negative samples and $m=7$, **iv) CPEG-$k=2$, $m=5$**: CPEG with $k=2$ and $m=5$, **v) CPEG-$k=5$, $m=2$**: CPEG with $k=5$ and $m=2$, and **vi) CPEG-$k=2$, $m=10$**: CPEG with $k=2$ and $m=10$. The win rates of each ground truth explanation are shown in Fig. 6.

The results indicate that ground truths generated by CPEG significantly outperform both user-written reviews and those produced by XRec [19], achieving win rates of 86.7% and 93.0% on the two datasets, respectively. Compared to using only 7 randomly selected negative samples, incorporating 2 hard negatives and 5 random negatives improves win rates by 7.1% and 7.6%, highlighting the importance of hard negatives in generating high-quality explanations. Similar to contrastive learning in representation learning [3], increasing the number of hard and random negatives enhances explanation quality. However, for RLM, this makes identifying the correct answer increasingly difficult, leading to more retries and higher computational costs while yielding diminishing improvements. Based on this trade-off, we set $k = 2$ and $m = 5$ in our experiments.

4.5 Case Study

To intuitively demonstrate our approach, Fig. 7 presents a case example from a test set. As illustrated in the example, on the one hand, the initial user and item profiles, after being processed by PGHIS, contain significantly more preference information than the original profiles. For instance, the item profile now includes details such as "chaotic multiplayer experiences with tactical FPS elements and humor," which were not part of the initial profile. On the other hand, despite the user's comment consisting only of an emoji without any explicit reasons for their preference, CPEG is still able to generate a reasonable explanation, attributing the interaction between the user and the item. After SFT, when given user and item profiles, our model generates explanations that are nearly identical to the ground truth, highlighting the superiority of our approach.

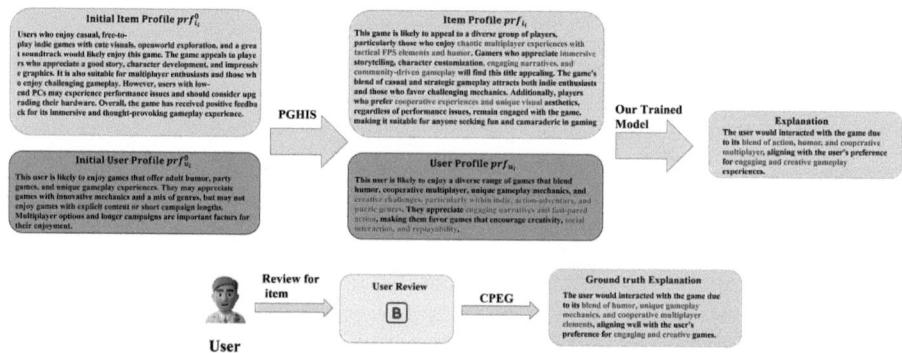

Fig. 7. Case Study.

5 Conclusion

In this work, we propose Profile Generation via Hierarchical Interaction Summarization, which replaces traditional embeddings with explicit textual representations of user and item characteristics. Additionally, we introduce Contrastive Prompting for ground truth Explanation Generation, a method designed to enhance the quality of generated explanations by guiding LLMs with both positive and negative items. Our approach was evaluated against state-of-the-art baselines across diverse datasets, demonstrating an average improvement of 5/100 on GPTScore, 20.6% and 19.6% on variants of BLEU and ROUGE over the state-of-the-art methods. The experimental results of ground truth explanation quality comparison further confirm the superior quality of our generated ground truth explanations.

In future work, we aim to apply our profile aggregation approach to LLM-based recommender systems, improving recommendation explainability and performence. Additionally, we hope that CPEG can assist researchers in generating high-quality data for studies requiring rigorous reasoning processes and explanations.

Acknowledgments. This research was supported by STI 2030—Major Projects under Grant 2021ZD0200403 and Zhejiang Provincial Natural Science Foundation of China under Grant No. LD24F030002. The authors like to thank the anonymous reviewers for their review and comments.

References

1. Besta, M., et al.: Reasoning language models: a blueprint. arXiv preprint arXiv:2501.11223 (2025)
2. Chen, J., et al.: Huatuogpt-o1, towards medical complex reasoning with llms. CoRR abs/2412.18925 (2024)
3. Chen, T., Kornblith, S., Norouzi, M., Hinton, G.E.: A simple framework for contrastive learning of visual representations. In: ICML. Proceedings of Machine Learning Research, vol. 119, pp. 1597–1607. PMLR (2020)
4. Chia, Y.K., Chen, G., Tuan, L.A., Poria, S., Bing, L.: Contrastive chain-of-thought prompting. CoRR abs/2311.09277 (2023)
5. Chung, J., Gülçehre, Ç., Cho, K., Bengio, Y.: Empirical evaluation of gated recurrent neural networks on sequence modeling. CoRR **abs/1412.3555** (2014), http://arxiv.org/abs/1412.3555
6. Deng, Y.: Recommender systems based on graph embedding techniques: a comprehensive review. CoRR abs/2109.09587 (2021). https://arxiv.org/abs/2109.09587
7. Dong, L., Huang, S., Wei, F., Lapata, M., Zhou, M., Xu, K.: Learning to generate product reviews from attributes. In: EACL (1). pp. 623–632. Association for Computational Linguistics (2017)
8. Fu, J., Ng, S., Jiang, Z., Liu, P.: Gptscore: Evaluate as you desire. In: NAACL-HLT, pp. 6556–6576. Association for Computational Linguistics (2024)
9. Gu, J., et al.: A survey on LLM-as-a-judge. CoRR abs/2411.15594 (2024)
10. Guo, D., et al.: Deepseek-r1: incentivizing reasoning capability in LLMs via reinforcement learning. arXiv preprint arXiv:2501.12948 (2025)
11. He, X., Deng, K., Wang, X., Li, Y., Zhang, Y., Wang, M.: LightGCN: simplifying and powering graph convolution network for recommendation. In: Huang, J.X., et al. (eds.) Proceedings of the 43rd International ACM SIGIR conference on research and development in Information Retrieval, SIGIR 2020, Virtual Event, China, July 25-30, 2020. pp. 639–648. ACM (2020). https://doi.org/10.1145/3397271.3401063
12. Hou, Y., Mu, S., Zhao, W.X., Li, Y., Ding, B., Wen, J.: Towards universal sequence representation learning for recommender systems. In: Zhang, A., Rangwala, H. (eds.) KDD '22: The 28th ACM SIGKDD Conference on Knowledge Discovery and Data Mining, Washington, DC, USA, August 14 - 18, 2022, pp. 585–593. ACM (2022https://doi.org/10.1145/3534678.3539381
13. Kang, W.C., McAuley, J.: Self-attentive sequential recommendation. In: 2018 IEEE International Conference on Data Mining (ICDM), pp. 197–206. IEEE (2018)

14. Li, L., Zhang, Y., Chen, L.: Personalized transformer for explainable recommendation. In: ACL/IJCNLP (1), pp. 4947–4957. Association for Computational Linguistics (2021)
15. Li, L., Zhang, Y., Chen, L.: Personalized prompt learning for explainable recommendation. ACM Trans. Inf. Syst. **41**(4), 103:1-103:26 (2023)
16. Li, M., Aggarwal, K., Xie, Y., Ahmad, A., Lau, S.: Learning from contrastive prompts: automated optimization and adaptation. arXiv preprint arXiv:2409.15199 (2024)
17. Li, P., Wang, Z., Ren, Z., Bing, L., Lam, W.: Neural rating regression with abstractive tips generation for recommendation. In: SIGIR, pp. 345–354. ACM (2017)
18. Lin, C.Y.: ROUGE: a package for automatic evaluation of summaries. In: Text Summarization Branches Out, Barcelona, Spain, pp. 74–81. Association for Computational Linguistics (2004). https://aclanthology.org/W04-1013/
19. Ma, Q., Ren, X., Huang, C.: XREC: large language models for explainable recommendation. In: EMNLP (Findings), pp. 391–402. Association for Computational Linguistics (2024)
20. Papineni, K., Roukos, S., Ward, T., Zhu, W.: Bleu: a method for automatic evaluation of machine translation. In: ACL, pp. 311–318. ACL (2002)
21. Ren, X., et al.: Representation learning with large language models for recommendation. In: WWW, pp. 3464–3475. ACM (2024)
22. Robinson, J.D., Chuang, C., Sra, S., Jegelka, S.: Contrastive learning with hard negative samples. In: ICLR. OpenReview.net (2021)
23. Roy, D., Dutta, M.: A systematic review and research perspective on recommender systems. J. Big Data **9**(1), 59 (2022). https://doi.org/10.1186/S40537-022-00592-5
24. Sellam, T., Das, D., Parikh, A.P.: BLEURT: learning robust metrics for text generation. In: ACL, pp. 7881–7892. Association for Computational Linguistics (2020)
25. Shi, X., Chen, Z., Wang, H., Yeung, D., Wong, W., Woo, W.: Convolutional LSTM network: a machine learning approach for precipitation nowcasting. In: Cortes, C., Lawrence, N.D., Lee, D.D., Sugiyama, M., Garnett, R. (eds.) Advances in Neural Information Processing Systems 28: Annual Conference on Neural Information Processing Systems 2015, December 7-12, 2015, Montreal, Quebec, Canada. pp. 802–810 (2015). https://proceedings.neurips.cc/paper/2015/hash/07563a3fe3bbe7e3ba84431ad9d055af-Abstract.html
26. Vaswani, A., et al.: Attention is all you need. In: Guyon, I., et al. (eds.) Advances in Neural Information Processing Systems 30: Annual Conference on Neural Information Processing Systems 2017, December 4-9, 2017, Long Beach, CA, USA, pp. 5998–6008 (2017). https://proceedings.neurips.cc/paper/2017/hash/3f5ee243547dee91fbd053c1c4a845aa-Abstract.html
27. Wang, W., Bao, H., Huang, S., Dong, L., Wei, F.: MiniLMv2: multi-head self-attention relation distillation for compressing pretrained transformers. In: Findings of the Association for Computational Linguistics: ACL-IJCNLP 2021, pp. 2140–2151. Association for Computational Linguistics, Online (2021). https://doi.org/10.18653/v1/2021.findings-acl.188
28. Wang, X., He, X., Wang, M., Feng, F., Chua, T.: Neural graph collaborative filtering. In: Proceedings of the 42nd International ACM SIGIR Conference on Research and Development in Information Retrieval, SIGIR 2019, Paris, France, July 21–25, 2019, pp. 165–174 (2019)
29. Xia, L., Huang, C., Huang, C., Lin, K., Yu, T., Kao, B.: Automated self-supervised learning for recommendation. In: The Web Conference (WWW) (2023)

30. Yang, A., et al.: Qwen2.5 technical report. arXiv preprint arXiv:2412.15115 (2024)
31. Zhang, T., Kishore, V., Wu, F., Weinberger, K.Q., Artzi, Y.: Bertscore: evaluating text generation with BERT. In: ICLR. OpenReview.net (2020)
32. Zheng, Y., et al.: Llamafactory: unified efficient fine-tuning of 100+ language models. In: Proceedings of the 62nd Annual Meeting of the Association for Computational Linguistics (Volume 3: System Demonstrations), Bangkok, Thailand. Association for Computational Linguistics (2024). http://arxiv.org/abs/2403.13372

Aggressive Exploration in Offline Reinforcement Learning for Better Recommendations

Kexin Shi[1], Wenjia Wang[2](✉), and Bingyi Jing[3](✉)

[1] The Hong Kong University of Science and Technology, Hong Kong SAR, China
kshiaf@connect.ust.hk
[2] The Hong Kong University of Science and Technology (Guangzhou), Guangzhou 511400, China
wenjiawang@hkust-gz.edu.cn
[3] Southern University of Science and Technology, Shenzhen 518000, China
jingby@sustech.edu.cn

Abstract. Offline reinforcement learning has become a powerful tool for optimizing recommender systems by learning from logged user interactions. However, existing methods rely on conservative exploration, limiting their ability to discover diverse and high-reward content. This paper introduces Bias-Reducing Aggressive Variance-Driven Exploration (BRAVE), an uncertainty-aware exploration strategy that effectively balances exploration and exploitation while addressing data bias to some extent in recommender systems. Unlike traditional offline RL methods that penalize uncertainty, BRAVE leverages uncertainty as a positive signal, guiding the agent toward underrepresented yet potentially high-reward recommendations. We evaluate BRAVE on KuaiRec, KuaiRand, and Yahoo datasets, demonstrating its effectiveness in prolonging user interaction and identifying highly relevant items, leading to improved user satisfaction. Moreover, BRAVE's strong performance on biased datasets underscores the potential of aggressive exploration in offline RL, providing a novel approach to breaking filter bubbles and reducing bias in recommender systems.

Keywords: Recommender systems · Reinforcement learning · Uncertainty · Data bias

1 Introduction

Recommender systems are central to many digital platforms, from e-commerce to entertainment, helping users discover content that aligns with their interests [12]. Despite their success, these systems often face challenges related to bias in the data and limited exploration of diverse content. A key issue is the filter bubble

---

Supplementary Information The online version contains supplementary material available at https://doi.org/10.1007/978-3-032-06096-9_29.

effect, where users are repeatedly exposed to similar content based on previous interactions, which can result in decreased long-term user satisfaction [10]. Therefore, improving recommendation systems requires overcoming biases and ensuring that recommendations better reflect the true preferences of users.

Reinforcement Learning (RL) [1] trains agents to make sequential decisions by maximizing cumulative rewards based on their interactions with the environment. In particular, offline RL has emerged as a powerful method for optimizing recommender systems. It leverages historical interaction data to learn effective policies without the need for real-time user engagement, making it especially advantageous in scenarios where gathering immediate feedback is costly or impractical. The primary objective of offline RL is to enhance long-term user satisfaction by developing policies that effectively optimize user engagement and retention over time. Model-based RL has emerged as a promising approach in this field because of its sample efficiency [7]. By constructing a world model that simulates user-item interactions based on historical data, model-based RL allows the agent to predict the outcomes of different actions and plan accordingly. The accuracy of the world model is critical, as it determines how well the agent can generalize beyond the training data.

A significant challenge in offline RL for recommender systems is the bias inherent in logged data [3], such as exposure and selection biases, which makes it difficult to train models that accurately predict user preferences and evaluate recommender systems reliably in offline settings. The sparsity of data, where only a small fraction of possible user-item interactions are recorded, compounds this challenge. Another challenge is extrapolation error for offline RL. To mitigate extrapolation error, many offline RL methods adopt conservative strategy. They either constrains the policy to avoid selecting risky or out-of-distribution actions [6,16,30] or gives a pessimistic estimate of the Q-function to account for uncertainty in the value of actions that have limited or no prior observations [15,17,29]. While this reduces extrapolation errors, it limits exploration, which can reinforce existing biases, restrict recommendation diversity, and enhance the filter bubble effect. Notably, model-based offline RL has the potential to reduce the need for conservative exploration. By improving the accuracy of the world model, exploration can be more effectively guided, even in sparse or biased datasets, allowing the system to better capture true user preferences and promote diverse recommendations without relying on overly cautious strategies.

This paper introduces **B**ias-**R**educing **A**ggressive **V**ariance-Driven **E**xploration (**BRAVE**), a model-based offline RL approach designed to enhance exploration in recommender systems by leveraging uncertainty, which represents the confidence in world model prediction outcomes. We show that uncertainty can serve as a valuable signal to distinguish between user-item pairs likely to generate positive feedback and those that are not. To leverage this insight, we propose a refined reward function that integrates uncertainty to promote guided "aggressive exploration", directing the system to explore underutilized state-action pairs with higher uncertainty, rather than relying on random exploration. Compared to conventional conservative exploration strategies, aggressive exploration prevents premature convergence on suboptimal solutions and promotes greater diversity in recommendations, helping to break filter bubbles. Through extensive experiments on three datasets, our results show that BRAVE significantly enhances cumulative rewards, interaction length, and single-round reward. These findings demonstrate that our exploration strategy not only mitigates the biases inherent in offline data but also improves recommendation quality, showcasing the potential of uncertainty-driven exploration to optimize recommender systems and increase user satisfaction. The contributions of this paper are:

- We analyze the impact of data bias on user-item predictions and enhance model robustness through uncertainty-based improvements for underrepresented interactions.
- We introduce BRAVE, an exploration strategy that leverages uncertainty to promote diverse recommendations, effectively breaking recommendation loops and reducing bias.
- Extensive experiments demonstrate that BRAVE outperforms baseline methods, achieving higher cumulative rewards, longer interaction lengths, and improved single-round rewards.

2 Related Work

Offline RL faces the challenge of extrapolation error, where policies may select actions outside the data distribution, resulting in unreliable outcomes. To mitigate this issue, many offline RL methods adopt conservative strategies. These strategies either constrain the policy to avoid risky or out-of-distribution actions [6,16,30] or provide pessimistic estimates of the Q-function to account for uncertainty in actions with limited or no prior observations [15,17,29]. For example, CQL [17] bounds the Q-function to avoid overestimation. BCQ [6] uses a generative model to restrict the action space to actions observed in the dataset. CRR [24] compares learned Q-values with observed ones, filtering out suboptimal actions and reducing deviations from the dataset.

While model-free offline RL methods mainly focus on regularizing the learned policy to prevent actions outside the observed data distribution, model-based offline RL methods lie in improving the world model's accuracy to ensure more reliable decision-making from fixed datasets [13]. Meanwhile, a set of model-based offline RL approaches still incorporate conservative strategies like penalizing out-of-distribution state-action pairs [14,27,28]. For instance, MOPO [28] penalizes rewards based on model uncertainty, helping to minimize the influence of unreliable predictions. COMBO [27] regularizes the Q-function to penalize actions that fall outside the distribution of the training data.

Numerous studies have explored offline RL in recommender systems [4,7,31,33,34]. Nonetheless, biases in logged data and extrapolation errors still remain significant challenges in the domain of interactive recommendations [3,21].

3 Method

3.1 Preliminaries

RL is a key area of artificial intelligence focused on developing optimal decision-making policies through interaction with an environment, represented by the Markov Decision Process (MDP) $\mathcal{M} = (S, A, T, r, \gamma)$. Here, S is the state space, A is the action space, T defines transition dynamics, r is the reward function, and $\gamma \in (0, 1)$ is the discount factor prioritizing immediate rewards. The goal is to learn a policy $\pi(a|s)$ that maximizes the expected discounted return:

$$J(\pi) = \mathbb{E}_{\pi,T} \left[\sum_{t=0}^{\infty} \gamma^t r(s_t, a_t) \right]. \tag{1}$$

Offline RL derives optimal policies from fixed datasets, $D_e = \{(s, a, r, s')\}$, collected from prior policies, but faces challenges like distributional shift, requiring effective generalization to unobserved states and actions. Model-based offline RL uses learned models of the environment's dynamics to simulate interactions without real-time feedback. By estimating transition dynamics $\hat{T}$ and reward function $\hat{r}$ from D_e, it creates a new MDP, $\widehat{\mathcal{M}} = (S, A, \hat{T}, \hat{r}, \gamma)$. While data-efficient, this approach relies heavily on the model's generalization capability; poor generalization can lead to suboptimal decision-making and hinder real-world performance.

In recommendation tasks, an action $a \in A$ involves recommending an item i to a user based on a recommendation policy. The reward function $\hat{r} := \hat{r}(s, a)$ captures user feedback on action a conditioned on the user's state s. This feedback can manifest in various forms, such as whether the user clicks on the item or the duration of engagement with content. The user state $s \in S$ reflects evolving preferences, but it is typically unobservable and must be inferred from past interactions using a user model. We formalize the user model as:

$$s_{t+1} = \text{User}(s_0, [a_1, a_2, \ldots, a_{t+1}], [\hat{r}_1, \hat{r}_2, \ldots, \hat{r}_{t+1}]), \tag{2}$$

where the User function estimates the state based on an initial state s_0, a sequence of historical actions $[a_1, a_2, \ldots, a_t]$, and their corresponding rewards $[\hat{r}_1, \hat{r}_2, \ldots, \hat{r}_{t+1}]$. The initial state s_0 can be initialized using demographic or historical data, or randomly. In this framework, the transition dynamics $\hat{T}$ and the reward function $\hat{r}$ are estimated from a static dataset D_e. This enables the formulation of MDP.

3.2 World Model Study

In offline RL for recommender systems, it is crucial to construct a world model that simulates user state transitions and predicts the reward for each potential user–item interaction. While user–item interaction matrices form the typical training resource for such models, these matrices are frequently biased. Bias arises when recommendation policies selectively expose only certain items to users, yielding exposure bias, or when repeated exposure to popular items confines users to filter bubbles that reduce diversity and ultimately reduce long-term retention. Although a handful of unbiased datasets, such as Coat [22] and Yahoo! [19], have been collected by randomizing item exposure, they tend to be small and sparse, making them costly and less representative for large-scale training. Consequently, a key question is how to harness the abundant but biased data effectively. Specifically, (1) how does the bias in partially observed matrices degrade the accuracy of user–item score predictions in the world model, and (2) how can we mitigate such bias in offline RL? To investigate these questions, we leverage datasets KuaiRec (biased) [8] and KuaiRand (unbiased) [9], both from the short video platform Kuaishou, to examine the impact of data bias on model performance and potential strategies for debiasing design.

World Model. We use DeepFM [11] to predict user-item interaction scores and generated user and item embeddings. Due to the partial observation of the training interaction matrix, some users and items had significantly more interaction logs than others, leading to an imbalance in prediction accuracy. To mitigate this issue and incorporate uncertainty, we modeled the predicted interaction scores $\hat{y}_i$ with a Gaussian distribution [5]:

$$\hat{y}_i \sim \mathcal{N}(\mu_\theta(x_i), \sigma_\theta^2(x_i)), \tag{3}$$

where $\mu_\theta(x_i)$ is the predicted interaction score, and $\sigma_\theta^2(x_i)$ represents the variance, capturing the uncertainty in the prediction. The world model is trained by minimizing a negative log-likelihood loss function:

$$\mathcal{L}(\theta) = \frac{1}{N} \sum_{i=1}^{N} \left(\frac{1}{2\sigma_\theta^2(x_i)} \|y_i - \mu_\theta(x_i)\|^2 + \frac{1}{2} \log \sigma_\theta^2(x_i) \right), \tag{4}$$

where N is the total number of observed interactions, y_i is the ground truth interaction score, $\mu_\theta(x_i)$ and $\sigma_\theta^2(x_i)$ are the predicted score and variance for sample x_i, respectively.

By incorporating this uncertainty-aware training objective, the model not only predicts accurate interaction scores for each user-item pair but also quantifies its confidence through the predicted variances.

To further improve reliability, we adopt an ensemble of world models. The final predictions for the scores are obtained by averaging the predicted scores across the ensemble, while the variance for each sample x_i is taken as the maximum value among the predicted variances from the ensemble:

$$\mu_\theta(x_i) = \frac{1}{M} \sum_{m=1}^{M} \mu_\theta^{(m)}(x_i), \quad \sigma_\theta^2(x_i) = \max_{m=1,\ldots,M} \sigma_\theta^{2(m)}(x_i), \tag{5}$$

where M is the number of models in the ensemble, and $\mu_\theta^{(m)}(x_i)$ and $\sigma_\theta^{2(m)}(x_i)$ are the score and variance predictions from the m-th model, respectively.

World Model Performance. We evaluate the ability of the trained world model to differentiate between positive and negative items within the evaluation matrix.

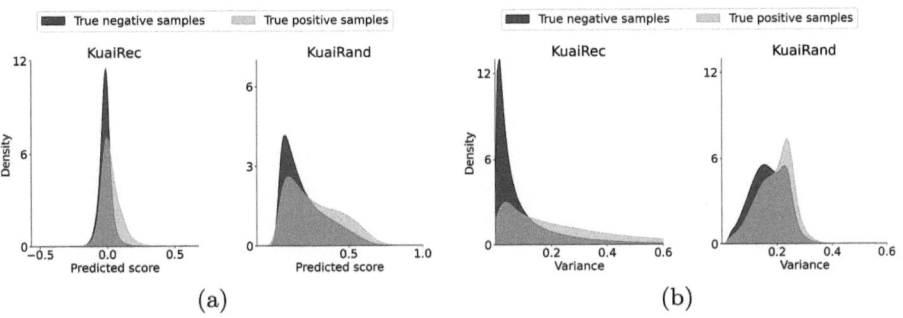

Fig. 1. Distribution of predicted scores and variance for true positive and true negative samples.

Differentiating Positive and Negative Samples. To assess the model's performance, we analyze the normalized predicted scores x_i for both positive and negative samples. The score distributions for these categories across the KuaiRec (biased) and KuaiRand (unbiased) datasets are shown in Fig. 1a. Our analysis reveals that the predicted scores for positive samples are skewed towards higher values, indicating that the world model effectively captures user preferences:

$$\mu_\theta(x_i|\text{positive}) > \mu_\theta(x_i|\text{negative}). \tag{6}$$

Examining Uncertainty in Predictions. We also examine the model's uncertainty measure, specifically the predicted variance $\sigma_\theta^2(x_i)$, for both positive and negative samples. The distributions of these variances, illustrated in Fig. 1b, show that positive samples tend to have higher variance than negative samples:

$$\sigma_\theta^2(x_i|\text{positive}) > \sigma_\theta^2(x_i|\text{negative}). \tag{7}$$

This suggests that the model is more uncertain when predicting scores for positive samples. This phenomenon may arise because many user-item pairs in the training data lack interactions or are associated with low watch times. As a result, the model becomes more confident in identifying negative samples, while the limited number of positive samples during training leads to increased prediction uncertainty. These findings imply that the uncertainty measure $\sigma_\theta^2(x_i)$ could be used as an additional signal to classify positive and negative samples, beyond relying solely on the predicted scores.

The Effect of Biased Training Data on Uncertainty. We observe significant differences in the variance distributions between KuaiRec and KuaiRand. In KuaiRec, the variance distribution for positive samples exhibits a heavy tail, indicating that some positive samples are associated with substantially higher uncertainty. In contrast, the distributions for positive and negative samples in KuaiRand are more similar, with no heavy tail present. The discrepancy may arise from the biased nature of KuaiRec, which predominantly includes items recommended based on personal preference analysis and popular items with high interaction frequencies. This bias leads to fewer diverse examples of positive user-item interactions in the training data, limiting the model's ability to confidently predict less common positive samples. Consequently, the lack of diverse training samples for positive interactions contributes to heightened uncertainty in the model's predictions, as evidenced by the heavy-tailed variance distribution in KuaiRec.

Because our analysis of datasets within recommendation systems is broadly applicable, these phenomena still occur when the world model is altered, rather than being incidental to a specific model.

3.3 Reward Enhancement

Building on the insights gained from the world model, we observed that the variance generated for each sample reflects the model's confidence in its predictions and provides valuable information about the underlying data distribution. Notably, potential positives tend to exhibit comparatively larger predicted uncertainty than negatives. This characteristic is likely tied to both the sparsity and the bias inherent in the training data, as well as domain-specific dynamics in recommender systems.

Inspired by the findings, we propose an enhanced reward function that incorporates predicted variance to promote exploration in offline RL. The enhanced reward function is defined as:

$$\tilde{r}(s,a) = \hat{r}(s,a) + \lambda U(s,a), \tag{8}$$

where $\hat{r}(s,a)$ is the predicted reward from the world model, $U(s,a)$ represents the variance derived from the Gaussian prediction of the world model, capturing the uncertainty associated with the sample and λ is a scaling factor controlling the contribution of the variance term. This function not only captures user preferences through the predicted reward but also incentivizes the agent to explore state-action pairs with higher uncertainty, which may reveal potential positives.

Exploration-Exploitation Balance and Bias Mitigation. The enhanced reward function combines the predicted reward ($\hat{r}(s,a)$) with the variance-driven term (λU), effectively balancing the exploitation of promising user preferences with the exploration of uncertain, potentially positive interactions. By integrating both factors, the reward function focuses the RL agent's attention on interactions that not only exhibit strong indicators of user preference but also hold the potential for discovery in regions of the state-action space marked by uncertainty.

This design is effective for both biased and unbiased datasets, as the distribution of predicted variance for positive samples consistently shifts to the right compared to that of negative samples. However, it is particularly impactful for biased datasets, where frequently interacted or popular items dominate the training data, reinforcing narrow recommendation loops. In such datasets, the distribution of predicted variance for positives not only shifts but also exhibits a heavy tail—a distinct shape compared to that of negatives. This heavy-tailed distribution provides a critical signal for distinguishing positives from negatives, especially for underrepresented interactions. By leveraging this variance signal, the enhanced reward function is expected to break the cycle of bias by guiding the RL agent to explore diverse interactions, including those with high promise but limited representation in the data. This approach ensures that the model considers a broader range of interactions, promoting diversity and fairness in recommendations while still maintaining strong alignment with user preferences.

Learning Pipeline. In this paper, we adopt the experimental setup of DORL [7], with our primary contribution being the redesign of the reward function informed by our empirical study of the world model in recommender systems.

We employ DeepFM as the underlying model to estimate the user state s. DeepFM predicts entries in the user-item interaction matrix as reward signals $\hat{r}$, while simultaneously generating user embeddings e_u and item embeddings e_i. The evolution of the user state is achieved by dynamically integrating recent actions and their feedback, ensuring that the representation adapts to both immediate user reactions and long-term behavioral trends. At timestamp t, the updated user state s_{t+1} is computed as:

$$s_{t+1} = \frac{1}{N} \sum_{k=t-N+1}^{t} [e_{a_k} \oplus \hat{r}(s_k, a_k)], \tag{9}$$

where N denotes the number of most recent actions considered for the state update. Here, e_{a_k} corresponds to the embedding of action a_k, capturing its latent features, while $\hat{r}(s_k, a_k)$ represents the predicted reward for action a_k, conditioned on the prior state s_k. The operation $\oplus$ combines the action embedding with the predicted reward, yielding a unified representation that integrates user feedback. Advantage Actor-Critic [20] (A2C) algorithm is adopted to train the recommendation policy, leveraging its ability to model dynamic user preferences and adapt to sequential decision-making.

3.4 Conservative Strategy vs. Aggressive Strategy

Exploration in model-based offline RL plays a crucial role in balancing the trade-off between exploiting known high-reward actions and discovering new, potentially optimal actions. In practice, most existing methods adopt conservative exploration strategies, designed to mitigate risks associated with OOD actions. However, we argue that aggressive exploration can be more suitable for recommendation systems due to their distinct dynamics, such as users' desire for diversity and tolerance for novelty.

Conservative Strategies are widely used in high-stakes environments like robotics, where trial-and-error can lead to catastrophic failures. Offline RL methods, whether model-based or model-free, tend to exhibit conservative behaviors.

Model-free methods either constrains the policy to avoid selecting risky or out-of-distribution actions or gives a pessimistic estimate of the Q-function. Model-based offline RL methods learn from historical data, but the limited and unrepresentative nature of this data introduces uncertainty, leading many methods to adopt pessimistic policies to avoid high-risk actions. For instance, MOPO (Model-Based Offline Policy Optimization) employs a conservative reward function defined as:

$$\hat{r}(s,a) = r(s,a) - \lambda U(s,a), \tag{10}$$

where $r(s,a)$ is the predicted reward from the learned reward model and $U(s,a)$ represents the uncertainty of that prediction. This formulation penalizes actions that lead to highly uncertain outcomes, ensuring that the policy remains within the offline data distribution. MOPO has demonstrated effectiveness in domains such as robotics, where safety and reliability are critical.

In recommender systems, many studies adopt the concept of penalizing uncertainty from general offline RL algorithms. For example, Gao et al. proposed the following reward function [7]:

$$\hat{r}(s,a) = r(s,a) - \lambda_U U(s,a) + \lambda_E P_E(s), \tag{11}$$

Similarly, Zhang et al. developed a refined reward function [32]:

$$\hat{r}(s,a) = \tilde{r}(s,a) \times (1 - \tilde{U}(s,a)) + \lambda_E P_E, \tag{12}$$

In both modified reward functions, uncertainty ($U(s,a)$ or $\tilde{U}(s,a)$) is penalized, although these works introduce entropy-based penalties $P_E(s)$ to promote diversity. These methods aim to increase diversity on one hand, while being reluctant to abandon conservatism on the other, resulting in opposing effects.

Aggressive Exploration in Recommendation Systems. While conservative strategies are effective in high-risk domains like healthcare, autonomous driving, and finance, such conservatism can be overly restrictive in recommender systems. In recommender systems, where the cost of exploration is relatively low, users actively seek diverse and novel content. A conservative approach that focuses primarily on exploiting past behaviors and known preferences often limits the discovery of new and unexpected content, which can lead to stagnation and reduced user engagement.

Several studies highlight the adverse effects of homogeneous recommendations. Specifically, users become dissatisfied when they are repeatedly exposed to similar content, ultimately leading to decreased system usage and reduced satisfaction [2]. Furthermore, recommending overly familiar items, while ensuring relevance, fails to foster long-term engagement because users do not experience novelty or serendipity [26]. Consequently, an exclusive reliance on conservative strategies may hinder the system's ability to discover optimal solutions within unexplored areas of the content space. In contrast to previous methods, our approach embraces uncertainty rather than penalizing it, treating it as a signal to encourage exploration. This is the core ingredient of our exploration strategy.

Additionally, unlike methods that promote action diversity at the policy level, our exploration is directly tied to the world model, leveraging the structure of the offline data to guide exploration more effectively. By aligning exploration with data-informed insights, our method enables the discovery of high-reward actions that conservative strategies often overlook.

4 Experiments

4.1 Experimental Setup

In this study, we evaluate our proposed approach using three widely recognized recommendation datasets: KuaiRec [8], which features a biased training set with a fully observed evaluation matrix; KuaiRand [9], which consists of both unbiased training and evaluation sets; and Yahoo [19], characterized by biased training data with a randomly sampled evaluation set.

For our evaluation, we utilize three key metrics: Cumulative Reward (R_{tra}), which represents the total rewards accumulated during an interaction session; Interaction Length (Length), defined as the number of consecutive recommendations made before the termination of a user session; and Single-Round Reward (R_{each}), which reflects the average reward obtained from a single recommendation step. To simulate user interaction termination effectively, we implement a quit mechanism consistent with methodologies employed in prior research [7,10,32]. This quit mechanism is easily triggered when the system repeatedly recommends items from the same category to a user, reinforcing the need for diversity in recommendations, as excessive familiarity of items can diminish user satisfaction and engagement [2,26].

We compare our method against a range of baseline approaches, including bandit algorithms (ϵ-Greedy and Upper Confidence Bound (UCB) [18]), as well as model-free methods like SQN [25], BCQ [6], CQL [17], and CRR [24]. Additionally, we assess model-based offline RL techniques, including IPS [23], MBPO [13], MOPO [28], and DORL [7]. Comprehensive details regarding the datasets, implementation specifics, and baseline methodologies are available in the supplementary materials.

4.2 Overall Performance

The experimental results are shown in Table 1, and the corresponding training curves are presented in Fig. 2.

In terms of cumulative reward, the most crucial performance metric that reflects long-term user satisfaction and engagement, our approach significantly outperforms all baseline methods across three datasets. Specifically, BRAVE achieves a relative improvement of 38.2% over the best baseline on KuaiRec, 12.0% on KuaiRand and 3.90% on Yahoo.

For KuaiRec, both BRAVE and DORL achieve an interaction length above 26, while all other baselines fall below 17. Similarly, for KuaiRand, BRAVE and DORL show approximately a 6% improvement in interaction length over other

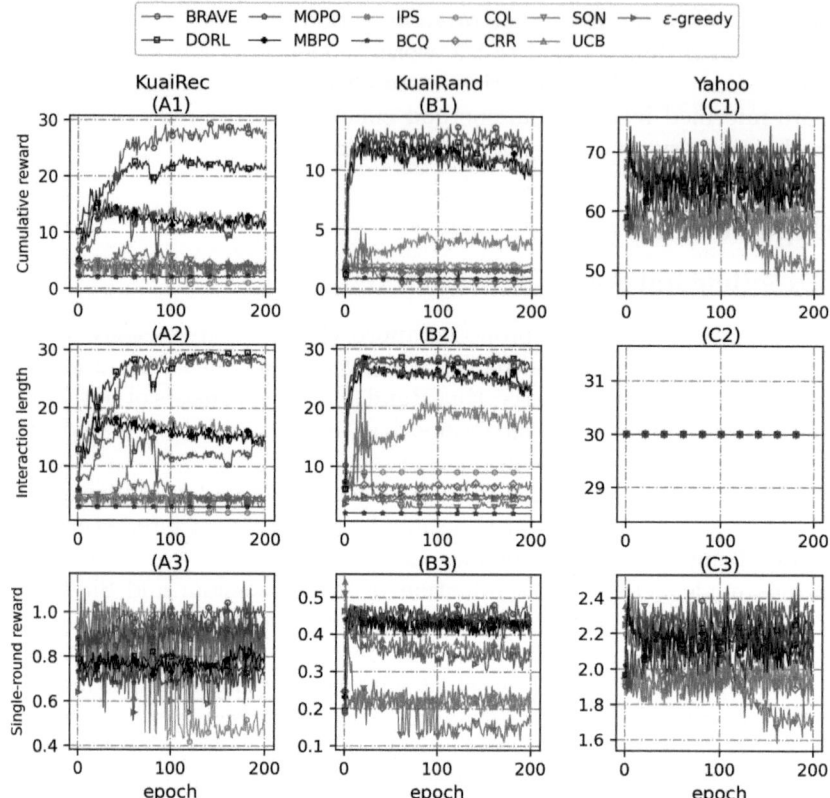

Fig. 2. Training curves for R_{tra}, R_{each} and Length.

methods. (In Yahoo, items are finely categorized, leading to very few overlaps. This makes it challenging to trigger the quit mechanism in the experimental setting. Thus, the maximum value we set for the interactive environment can be easily reached across different methods.) Importantly, BRAVE outperforms DORL in terms of single-round reward, with relative improvements of 24.3% on KuaiRec, 12.9% on KuaiRand and 5.70% on Yahoo. These gains highlight BRAVE's ability to learn from logged data while uncovering users' true preferences.

In addition, the performance of the five model-based offline RL approaches (BRAVE, DORL, MBPO, MOPO, and IPS) is superior to that of model-free methods and bandit methods for KuaiRec and KuaiRand. This may be attributed to the sparsity of training data in recommender systems, where model-based approaches can better leverage the limited interactions by using learned models to simulate missing data. In contrast, model-free methods, which rely directly on the observed data, may struggle to generalize effectively from sparse interactions.

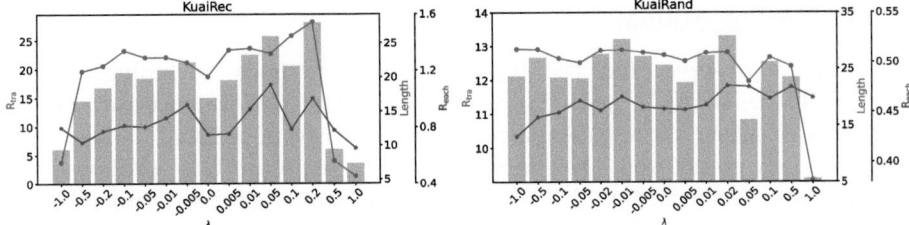

Fig. 3. Impact of hyperparameter λ on R_{tra}, R_{each} and Length.

Table 1. Performance comparison on datasets KuaiRec, KuaiRand and Yahoo. (The best results are indicated in bold, and the second-best results are underlined.)

Methods	KuaiRec			KuaiRand		
	R_{tra}	R_{each}	Length	R_{tra}	R_{each}	Length
UCB	3.606 ± 0.609	0.853 ± 0.114	4.219 ± 0.389	1.651 ± 0.152	0.372 ± 0.028	4.431 ± 0.212
ϵ-greedy	3.515 ± 0.731	0.828 ± 0.129	4.219 ± 0.405	1.711 ± 0.126	0.351 ± 0.025	4.880 ± 0.270
SQN	4.673 ± 1.215	<u>0.913 ± 0.055</u>	5.111 ± 1.288	0.912 ± 0.929	0.182 ± 0.058	4.601 ± 3.712
CRR	4.163 ± 0.253	0.895 ± 0.037	4.654 ± 0.215	1.481 ± 0.124	0.226 ± 0.015	6.561 ± 0.352
CQL	2.506 ± 1.767	0.684 ± 0.228	3.224 ± 1.365	2.032 ± 0.107	0.226 ± 0.012	9.000 ± 0.000
BCQ	2.123 ± 0.081	0.708 ± 0.027	3.000 ± 0.000	0.852 ± 0.052	0.425 ± 0.016	2.005 ± 0.071
MBPO	12.043 ± 1.312	0.770 ± 0.029	15.646 ± 1.637	10.933 ± 0.946	0.431 ± 0.021	25.345 ± 1.819
IPS	12.833 ± 1.353	0.767 ± 0.023	16.727 ± 1.683	3.629 ± 0.676	0.216 ± 0.014	16.821 ± 3.182
MOPO	11.427 ± 1.750	0.892 ± 0.051	12.809 ± 1.850	10.934 ± 0.963	<u>0.437 ± 0.019</u>	25.002 ± 1.891
DORL	<u>20.494 ± 2.671</u>	0.767 ± 0.026	<u>26.712 ± 3.419</u>	<u>11.850 ± 1.036</u>	0.428 ± 0.022	**27.609 ± 2.121**
Ours	**28.328 ± 2.052**	**0.953 ± 0.063**	**28.010 ± 1.072**	**13.277 ± 0.960**	**0.483 ± 0.021**	<u>26.860 ± 2.351</u>

Table 2. Performance comparison on Yahoo.

Methods	Yahoo		
	R_{tra}	R_{each}	Length
UCB	<u>66.758 ± 1.254</u>	<u>2.225 ± 0.042</u>	30.000 ± 0.000
ϵ-greedy	64.344 ± 1.291	2.145 ± 0.043	30.000 ± 0.000
SQN	57.727 ± 5.751	1.924 ± 0.192	30.000 ± 0.000
CRR	57.994 ± 1.675	1.933 ± 0.056	30.000 ± 0.000
CQL	62.291 ± 3.347	2.076 ± 0.112	30.000 ± 0.000
BCQ	61.739 ± 1.781	2.058 ± 0.059	30.000 ± 0.000
MBPO	64.550 ± 2.157	2.152 ± 0.072	30.000 ± 0.000
IPS	57.850 ± 1.796	1.928 ± 0.060	30.000 ± 0.000
MOPO	65.510 ± 2.100	2.184 ± 0.070	30.000 ± 0.000
DORL	66.351 ± 2.224	2.212 ± 0.074	30.000 ± 0.000
Ours	**69.360 ± 1.362**	**2.338 ± 0.0637**	30.000 ± 0.000

4.3 Debiasing Ability

In Fig. 2, we observe that the top-performing methods, including MOPO, MBPO, DORL, BRAVE, and IPS, exhibit significant performance variation on the biased KuaiRec dataset compared to the unbiased KuaiRand dataset. This variation likely stems from their interaction with exposure bias. (Yahoo differs from KuaiRec and KuaiRand by originating from a different platform and showing minimal performance variation across all methods, suggesting it is easier to learn from. Thus, we exclude it from the following discussion.)

For KuaiRec, exposure bias is inherent, meaning that certain items are more likely to be shown to users based on previous recommendations or popularity, which creates a skewed distribution of item interactions. This leads to an overrepresentation of certain items, resulting in a reduced diversity of interactions. Methods such as BRAVE and DORL, which balance exploration and exploitation—where DORL enhances policy entropy as outlined in Eq. 11—can explore diverse options and break the recommendation loops caused by the exposure bias. This can lead to significant improvements in interaction length by offering a broader selection of items, which helps mitigate the filter bubble. In contrast, interaction logs in KuaiRand are gathered by randomly inserting randomly selected videos into users' recommendation streams. This random exposure strategy ensures unbiased interaction data. Since there is less skew in the interactions, methods like BRAVE and DORL do not experience as much of an advantage from their exploration strategies. The improvements are relatively smaller because there is already a good balance of diversity in the logged data.

This explains why performance differences between methods are more pronounced in biased dataset KuaiRec but less significant in unbiased dataset KuaiRand, highlighting the importance of how exploration and exploitation strategies interact with data bias in recommendation systems.

4.4 Comparison Among MOPO, MBPO and BRAVE

We compare three methods—MOPO, MBPO, and BRAVE—which all use the same world model but differ in how they handle uncertainty: MOPO penalizes uncertainty, MBPO ignores it, and BRAVE encourages it. On three datasets, BRAVE significantly outperforms both MOPO and MBPO in terms of cumulative reward, highlighting the potential of aggressive exploration strategies in recommendation systems. BRAVE achieves a larger interaction length (on KuaiRec and KuaiRand) and higher single-round reward, which both account for its highest cumulative reward. The increased interaction length can be attributed to BRAVE's ability to explore a wider range of item possibilities. This strategy is particularly effective at breaking the filter bubble. In our experimental setup, this exploration leads to improved user retention, as users are exposed to more diverse items and engage with the platform for longer periods. The higher single-round reward is due to BRAVE using uncertainty as an additional signal for distinguishing true positive and negative samples, improving prediction accuracy for unseen items, as suggested in Sect. 3.2.

In addition, MOPO, which employs a more conservative exploration strategy by penalizing uncertainty, performs better than MBPO in terms of single-round reward. This is likely because penalizing uncertainty helps improve the prediction accuracy for items that occur more frequently in the training data. By reducing the model's exploration of uncertain states, MOPO effectively improves the reliability of its recommendations for well-represented items in the training set. However, this approach limits exploration of items that the model is less confident about (i.e., unseen or infrequent items), which are typically the ones that could diversify user experiences and break the filter bubble. Thus, MOPO's conservative strategy often results in shorter interaction lengths compared to MBPO.

4.5 Analysis of λ Impact on Performance

As shown in Fig. 3, the impact of the hyperparameter λ, which controls the contribution of variance (uncertainty) to the reward function, is analyzed on both KuaiRec and KuaiRand environments. When $\lambda < 0$, the system penalizes uncertainty, following a more conservative exploration strategy. Conversely, $\lambda > 0$ means employing an aggressive exploration strategy.

For the biased dataset KuaiRec, BRAVE shows substantial improvement as λ increases, reaching its peak at $\lambda = 0.2$. It demonstrats the benefits of aggressive exploration compared to the conservative approach. This results in higher cumulative rewards and longer interaction lengths. On the other hand, for KuaiRand (unbiased), the model's performance shows less variation across different λ values, but the best performance is still achieved with aggressive exploration at $\lambda = 0.02$. Furthermore, a general upward trend in single-round reward is observed with positive values of λ, compared to negative values, across both datasets. This highlights BRAVE's ability to more effectively predict and uncover users' latent preferences, providing higher-quality recommendations in dynamic interactive environments.

5 Conclusion

This paper introduced BRAVE, an aggressive exploration strategy for offline RL in recommender systems. Inspired by the world model study, BRAVE incorporates uncertainty into the reward function to enhance the prediction of true positive and negative items. Unlike prevalent conservative exploration strategies, BRAVE enables a more effective balance between exploration and exploitation, ultimately improving cumulative rewards. This exploration method encourages the model to search for the global optimum, rather than being confined to the recommendation loops created by the recommendation policy. Through extensive experiments on datasets KuaiRec, KuaiRand and Yahoo, we demonstrated that BRAVE outperforms baseline methods, uncovering true user preferences and providing more diverse and relevant recommendations. BRAVE shows significant potential for addressing the challenges of bias in offline RL and future work will focus on refining the exploration strategies further and exploring real-world applications of BRAVE.

Acknowledgements. This work was partially supported by NSFC under grant number 12371290, for which we are sincerely grateful. The authors would also like to extend their heartfelt thanks to the editor and the reviewers for their valuable feedback and insightful comments.

References

1. Barto, A.G.: Reinforcement learning: an introduction. by richard's sutton. SIAM Rev **6**(2), 423 (2021)
2. Chaney, A.J., Stewart, B.M., Engelhardt, B.E.: How algorithmic confounding in recommendation systems increases homogeneity and decreases utility. In: Proceedings of the 12th ACM Conference on Recommender Systems, pp. 224–232 (2018)
3. Chen, J., Dong, H., Wang, X., Feng, F., Wang, M., He, X.: Bias and debias in recommender system: a survey and future directions. ACM Trans. Inf. Syst. **41**(3), 1–39 (2023)
4. Chen, M., Beutel, A., Covington, P., Jain, S., Belletti, F., Chi, E.H.: Top-k off-policy correction for a reinforce recommender system. In: Proceedings of the Twelfth ACM International Conference on Web Search and Data Mining, pp. 456–464 (2019)
5. Deisenroth, M., Rasmussen, C.E.: PILCO: a model-based and data-efficient approach to policy search. In: Proceedings of the 28th International Conference on machine learning (ICML-11), pp. 465–472 (2011)
6. Fujimoto, S., Meger, D., Precup, D.: Off-policy deep reinforcement learning without exploration. In: International Conference on Machine Learning, pp. 2052–2062. PMLR (2019)
7. Gao, C., et al.: Alleviating matthew effect of offline reinforcement learning in interactive recommendation. In: Proceedings of the 46th International ACM SIGIR Conference on Research and Development in Information Retrieval, pp. 238–248 (2023)
8. Gao, C., Li, S., Lei, W., Chen, J., Li, B., Jiang, P., He, X., Mao, J., Chua, T.S.: Kuairec: A fully-observed dataset and insights for evaluating recommender systems. In: Proceedings of the 31st ACM International Conference on Information & Knowledge Management. pp. 540–550 (2022)
9. Gao, C., et al.: Kuairand: an unbiased sequential recommendation dataset with randomly exposed videos. In: Proceedings of the 31st ACM International Conference on Information & Knowledge Management, pp. 3953–3957 (2022)
10. Gao, C., et al.: CIRS: bursting filter bubbles by counterfactual interactive recommender system. ACM Trans. Inf. Syst. **42**(1), 1–27 (2023)
11. Guo, H., Tang, R., Ye, Y., Li, Z., He, X.: DeepFM: a factorization-machine based neural network for CTR prediction. arXiv preprint arXiv:1703.04247 (2017)
12. Hu, Y., Koren, Y., Volinsky, C.: Collaborative filtering for implicit feedback datasets. In: 2008 Eighth IEEE International Conference on Data Mining, pp. 263–272. IEEE (2008)
13. Janner, M., Fu, J., Zhang, M., Levine, S.: When to trust your model: model-based policy optimization. In: Advances in Neural Information Processing Systems, vol. 32 (2019)

14. Kidambi, R., Rajeswaran, A., Netrapalli, P., Joachims, T.: Morel: model-based offline reinforcement learning. Adv. Neural. Inf. Process. Syst. **33**, 21810–21823 (2020)
15. Kostrikov, I., Nair, A., Levine, S.: Offline reinforcement learning with implicit q-learning. arXiv preprint arXiv:2110.06169 (2021)
16. Kumar, A., Fu, J., Soh, M., Tucker, G., Levine, S.: Stabilizing off-policy q-learning via bootstrapping error reduction. In: Advances in Neural Information Processing Systems, vol. 32 (2019)
17. Kumar, A., Zhou, A., Tucker, G., Levine, S.: Conservative q-learning for offline reinforcement learning. Adv. Neural. Inf. Process. Syst. **33**, 1179–1191 (2020)
18. Lai, T.L., Robbins, H.: Asymptotically efficient adaptive allocation rules. Adv. Appl. Math. **6**(1), 4–22 (1985)
19. Marlin, B.M., Zemel, R.S.: Collaborative prediction and ranking with non-random missing data. In: Proceedings of the third ACM Conference on Recommender Systems, pp. 5–12 (2009)
20. Mnih, V., et al.: Asynchronous methods for deep reinforcement learning. In: International Conference on Machine Learning, pp. 1928–1937. PmLR (2016)
21. Pradel, B., Usunier, N., Gallinari, P.: Ranking with non-random missing ratings: influence of popularity and positivity on evaluation metrics. In: Proceedings of the sixth ACM Conference on Recommender Systems, pp. 147–154 (2012)
22. Schnabel, T., Swaminathan, A., Singh, A., Chandak, N., Joachims, T.: Recommendations as treatments: Debiasing learning and evaluation. In: International Conference on Machine Learning, pp. 1670–1679. PMLR (2016)
23. Swaminathan, A., Joachims, T.: Counterfactual risk minimization: learning from logged bandit feedback. In: International conference on machine learning. pp. 814–823. PMLR (2015)
24. Wang, Z., et al.: Critic regularized regression. Adv. Neural. Inf. Process. Syst. **33**, 7768–7778 (2020)
25. Xin, X., Karatzoglou, A., Arapakis, I., Jose, J.M.: Self-supervised reinforcement learning for recommender systems. In: Proceedings of the 43rd International ACM SIGIR Conference on Research and Development in Information Retrieval, pp. 931–940 (2020)
26. Yu, C., Lakshmanan, L., Amer-Yahia, S.: It takes variety to make a world: diversification in recommender systems. In: Proceedings of the 12th International Conference on Extending Database Technology: Advances in Database Technology, pp. 368–378 (2009)
27. Yu, T., Kumar, A., Rafailov, R., Rajeswaran, A., Levine, S., Finn, C.: COMBO: conservative offline model-based policy optimization. Adv. Neural. Inf. Process. Syst. **34**, 28954–28967 (2021)
28. Yu, T., et al.: MOPO: model-based offline policy optimization. Adv. Neural. Inf. Process. Syst. **33**, 14129–14142 (2020)
29. Zhang, J., Fang, L., Shi, K., Wang, W., Jing, B.: Q-distribution guided q-learning for offline reinforcement learning: Uncertainty penalized q-value via consistency model. Adv. Neural. Inf. Process. Syst. **37**, 54421–54462 (2025)
30. Zhang, J., Zhang, C., Wang, W., Jing, B.: Constrained policy optimization with explicit behavior density for offline reinforcement learning. Adv. Neural. Inf. Process. Syst. **36**, 5616–5630 (2023)
31. Zhang, R., Yu, T., Shen, Y., Jin, H., Chen, C., Carin, L.: Reward constrained interactive recommendation with natural language feedback. arXiv preprint arXiv:2005.01618 (2020)

32. Zhang, Y., Qiu, R., Liu, J., Wang, S.: Roler: effective reward shaping in offline reinforcement learning for recommender systems. In: Proceedings of the 33rd ACM International Conference on Information and Knowledge Management, pp. 3269–3278 (2024)
33. Zhao, X., Xia, L., Zhang, L., Ding, Z., Yin, D., Tang, J.: Deep reinforcement learning for page-wise recommendations. In: Proceedings of the 12th ACM Conference on Recommender Systems, pp. 95–103 (2018)
34. Zhao, X., Xia, L., Zou, L., Liu, H., Yin, D., Tang, J.: Whole-chain recommendations. In: Proceedings of the 29th ACM International Conference on Information & Knowledge Management, pp. 1883–1891 (2020)

CULC-Net: A Recipe for Tailored Creative Selection in Online Advertising

Baosheng Zhang[1,2], Liufang Sang[3], Haoran Wang[3], Wei Wang[3], Wenlong Chen[3], Changping Peng[3], Zhangang Lin[3], Jingping Shao[3], Jie He[3], Haoqian Wang[2(✉)], and Yuchen Guo[1(✉)]

[1] Beijing National Research Center for Information Science and Technology (BNRist), Tsinghua University, Beijing, China
yuchen.w.guo@gmail.com
[2] Tsinghua Shenzhen International Graduate School, Tsinghua University, Shenzhen, China
wangyizhai@sz.tsinghua.edu.cn
[3] JD.com, Beijing, China

Abstract. Online advertising is a major application of recommendation systems. The primary process first involves recommending appropriate items to users, followed by selecting suitable creatives, such as ad posters. While much research has focused on optimizing item recommendations to increase user clicks, creative selection has often been overlooked. Properly chosen creatives can significantly enhance purchasing intent by aligning with the diverse preferences, ages, and genders of users. Current state-of-the-art methods typically rely on historical Click-Through Rates (CTR), which may exhibit biases during initial exposures due to limited data. In this paper, we introduce CULC-Net, which builds detailed profiles to uncover hidden connections between users and creatives, utilizing a creative relevance score for soft-decision making. This approach improves recommendation effectiveness and reduces reliance on sparse CTR data. Furthermore, we advance beyond the traditional CTR-based "only top for training" strategy by introducing FlexiRank. Creatives are sorted based on the relative strength of their CTRs, effectively managing noise and outliers. We test CULC-Net in a real-world search ad system, demonstrating a 3.43% increase in online and a 4.01% increase in offline. Further validation on a public benchmark confirms the effectiveness of our approach.

Keywords: Recommendation System · Ad Recommendation · Creative Selection

1 Introduction

With the growth of the Internet and mobile technologies, online advertising has become vital for the income of digital platforms. It is important to grab user attention with eye-catching visuals and clear, brief messages [1]. Ads that look

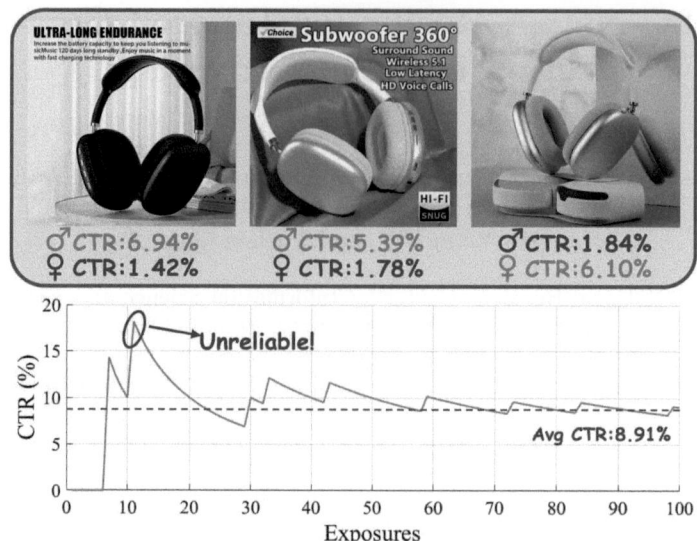

Fig. 1. CTR comparison for different ad creative examples, highlighting the impact of ad creatives. The first row shows how CTR varies based on user characteristics; for example, males may prefer descriptions of features, while females may be more attracted to visual displays for the same headphone. The second row shows how the CTR of a single creative changes with more exposure, emphasizing the unreliability of CTR with limited exposures.

good are more likely to be clicked on, which increases the Click-Through Rate (CTR) of products [26]. CTR is not only a sign of user interest; it is also a key indicator of how financially successful an online advertising campaign is. This affects the total revenue and the return on the investment made in advertising. Even a small improvement in CTR can have a big financial impact, especially for large e-commerce platforms. Therefore, improving the effectiveness of ad recommendations is crucial [4].

Current recommendation systems generally follow a multi-stage cascading structure that includes matching, ad ranking, and creative selection [13]. Initially, the matching stage reduces the extensive pool of ad candidates from billions down to thousands. The next stage, ad ranking, organizes these ads to identify the final top selections. Finally, the creative selection stage chooses the most appropriate visual and text creatives for each ad [30]. At the creative selection stage, industry practices often ignore specific creatives, either choosing them randomly or picking popular ones from past data [28]. They do not fully consider the actual impact of different visuals on user engagement. However, evidence shows that creative elements can significantly impact Click-Through Rates (CTR) [14,16,34]. As demonstrated in Fig. 1, there are clear differences in CTR for different creatives between male and female users. For example, for the same headphone, men may prefer descriptions emphasizing utility, while women might be more drawn to simplistic visual designs. Capturing these preferences with specific rules is challenging, and effectively leveraging diverse multimodal data with neural networks remains a challenge [20,23,34].

Ad recommendations often involve frequently changing in creatives [7], which results in each creative being displayed an average of only 6 times. With such limited exposure, even random clicks can significantly affect the CTR [34]. For example, if a creative receives only one exposure and one click, this could lead to a misleading CTR of 100%. Such a scenario could easily be due to an accidental click rather than genuine user interest. Consequently, relying on CTR to gauge the popularity of a creative with few exposures can be misleading [11]. This underscores the need for ad recommendation systems that are better tailored to handle user interactions effectively. Current creative selection methods primarily follow two aspect [22]. The first class uses hard labels, recommending the top creative based solely on the highest CTR value [34]. In practice, when the creative with the highest CTR has only a few exposures, recommending it on actual advertising platforms is not reliable. The second class considers the ranking information of creatives [24], where the model ranks creatives by their CTR, comprehensively assess the performance of different creatives. However, relying on unstable or inaccurate ranking data can undermine the accuracy and reliability of the recommendations [6].

To address the issue of unreliable CTR data due to limited exposure, we explore the relationships between creatives and customize recommendations for users with similar features, reducing our reliance on CTR data for individual users or creatives. We designed CULC-Net (Contrastive User Learning for Creative Selection), which incorporates a soft-decision contrastive learning approach to address this challenge. By partially masking user features, CULC-Net builds profiles of users with similar attributes, allowing it to uncover hidden connections between users and creatives, and thereby mitigating the bias from sparse data. Unlike existing methods that might wrongly push all other creatives apart by focusing only on classification data, our approach introduces a creative relevance score. This score evaluates how related different creatives are to each other. During training, creatives that are less related are separated more, while those with higher similarity are kept closer together in the representation space. This method not only enhances the quality of data but also reduces the impact of unreliable CTR data from low exposure, resulting in a more robust model.

Furthermore, we proposed FlexiRank, which utilizes a soft ranking loss function in place of classification and ranking losses. It sorts creatives based on the relative ranking relationships of their CTRs, effectively managing noise and outliers in the data. FlexiRank also incorporates an instructional gradient that decays with training, progressively reducing reliance on explicit ranking information. In this way, it enhances the model's effectiveness and improves its predictive accuracy for unseen data.

We highlight our contributions in this paper as follows:

(1) We introduce CULC-Net, which changes the "focus on self" concept in CL by leveraging differences within users and creatives to obtain a creative relevance score for soft-decision making.

(2) We introduce FlexiRank, improving upon the "only top for training" method by using all CTR data for more precise ranking and better handling of noise and outliers.
(3) Our results show that CULC-Net outperforms existing models, achieving performance improvements of 4.01% offline and 3.43% online, proving its effectiveness in real-world advertising scenarios.

2 Related Works

2.1 Creative Selection

In online advertising, there are two main methods used for selecting ad creatives. The first class of creative selection strategies relies on hard labels to recommend creatives based on the highest CTR [34]. These approaches straightforward suffers from reliability issues especially when creatives have limited exposures—a problem acknowledged and addressed in part by methodologies that attempt to pre-evaluate creatives [32,33]. For instance, PEAC (Pre Evaluation of Ad Creative Model) utilizes deep learning to predict potential online performance without relying on user clicks, emphasizing the importance of offline creative quality evaluation based on comprehensive image and text content analysis [36] .Similarly, the Adaptive and Efficient ad creative Selection (AES) framework introduces an innovative ingredient tree combined with Thompson sampling for efficient selection based on predicted CTR, addressing the high variance due to limited feedback and the sparsity of user interactions, which is a common challenge in creative selection [5].

The second class involves ranking creatives based on CTR, assigning higher ranks to those with higher CTRs and lower ranks to those with lower CTRs, using these rankings to infer user preferences. However, this method struggles with accurately identifying true user preferences due to the presence of false negatives in low CTR data. Advanced hybrid models and category-specific approaches that incorporate visual and categorical data to refine the ranking process have been demonstrated to enhance creative optimization and integrate creative selection more effectively within ad ranking stages [6,24]. Furthermore, systems like HBM-VAM introduce visual priors and a flexible updated bandit method that can raise platform revenue by focusing on online assessments [31]. CACS presents a method that places the creative ranking module before the ad ranking stage, then jointly optimizes them with distillation and shared embedding, resembling our method closely and showcasing the potential for significant advancements in advertising systems [23].

2.2 Contrastive Learning

Contrastive learning is a powerful branch of self-supervised learning that focuses on encoding data by contrasting positive and negative samples [18]. This technique is particularly effective in recommendation systems, where it is used to learn representations that capture unique features of content, thereby facilitating more personalized and effective recommendations [20].

SimCLR [8] optimizes agreement between augmentations of the same image while minimizing agreement between different images. It uses data augmentation techniques and projection head designs to learn visual representations. MoCo [15] employs a momentum-based encoder and a memory bank for dynamic embedding updates, enhancing robustness.

Other methods like RotNet, BERT, and CPC expand the scope of contrastive learning. RotNet [12] improves object recognition by training on rotated images. BERT [10] predicts masked tokens in sentences, capturing deep dependencies in natural language processing. CPC [29] generates compact representations by predicting future observations in sequences, aiding sequential analysis.

3 Methods

In this section, we introduce CULC-Net (Contrastive User Learning for Creative Selection), designed to address unreliable CTR data due to limited exposure. We start with the problem formulation and the base model of creative selection. We then compare CULC-Net with the base model and provide detailed explanations of CUL and FlexiRank, emphasizing their impact on enhancing model accuracy.

3.1 Preliminary

Problem Formulation: We address a creative selection scenario within an ad recommendation system, characterized by a user request $u \in U$ and a set of ads $A = \{a_j\}_{j=1}^{n}$. Each ad a_j includes m creatives, represented as $a_j = \{c_i\}_{i=1}^{m}$, where each i-th creative c_i is described by a tuple (v_i, t_i, id_i). Here, v_i, t_i, and id_i correspond to the image feature, text feature, and unique hash ID. Our objective is to select the optimal creative for each ad by integrating visual and textual information of the creatives with the unique user preferences.

STM (Single-Tower Model): The Single-Tower Model utilizes embeddings [27], DNNs [19], and cross-entropy [9] to extract and learn features from the creative data. The image and text features are integrated at the embedding layer, subsequently processed through a DNN to derive a more abstract representation. This representation is used to predict the hard label for each creative, with cross-entropy serving as the loss function to optimize the model parameters. Base Creative selection model is the STM model.

TTM (Two-Tower Model): The Two-Tower Model employs two distinct DNNs to enhance the separation of feature processing: one for user features and another for item features. This architecture allows each tower to specialize in extracting detailed representations from its respective domain. User features and item features are embedded and processed independently through their respective DNNs. The resulting features are then combined in a fusion layer, facilitating effective interaction between user preferences and item attributes. Ad ranking stage is based on this model [2,21].

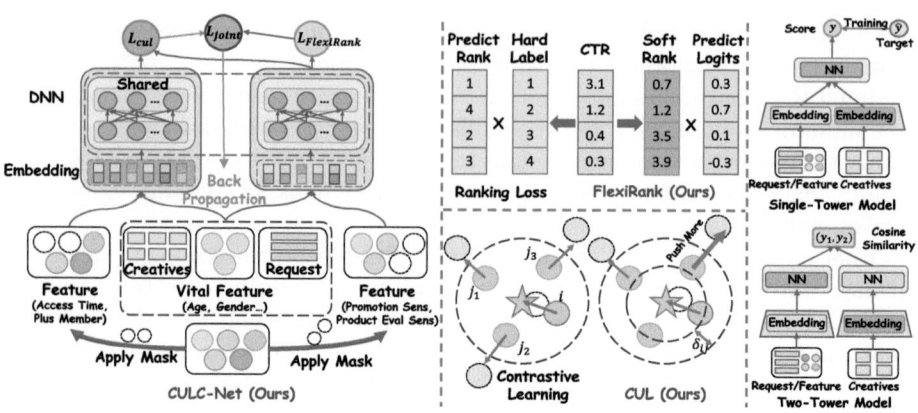

Fig. 2. Visual comparison of the base creative selection method and the detailed workings of CULC-Net. STM employs a single tower for recommendation, whereas CULC-Net integrates shared DNN and different user knowledge to improve CTR prediction. We also show the differences between Contrastive Learning and our CUL approach, as well as ranking loss and FlexiRank, highlighting the advantages of soft-decision making and the comprehensive utilization of ranking data.

3.2 Overview of CULC-Net

Inspired by [35], we adopt similar contrastive learning algorithms to learn representations of categorical features. We apply different data augmentations to the training examples to learn these representations and then use an adaptive contrastive loss function to ensure that the representations learned for the same training example are similar. Our proposed CULC-Net method enhances the STM by introducing a shared DNN and incorporating varied user knowledge for different augmentations. The shared DNN layer ensures that the model learns a unified representation for both image and text features, while the integration of diverse user knowledge allows the model to adapt to varying user preferences more effectively.

Figure 2 offers a visual comparison between STM and our proposed CULC-Net approach. The illustration underscores the differences in architecture, particularly emphasizing the shared DNN and the varied user knowledge embedded within our model. These enhancements contribute to superior creative selection and a better overall user experience.

Unlike some Two-Tower Model in advertising recommendation systems [23], where one tower handles user requests and features, and the other manages ads and creatives, our model leverages data augmentation techniques to improve ranking for similar users. This approach helps address issues like exposure bias and the long-tail distribution of data. By modifying changeable features, our method brings similar users closer together, thereby enhancing the creative selection process. The integration of a shared DNN and diverse user knowledge within our two-tower model, termed CULC-Net, significantly boosts the effectiveness of creative selection. This results in more tailored and relevant recommendations, enhancing the user experience in consuming multimedia content.

3.3 CUL Augmentation: Which and Where

The key point of CUL (Contrastive User Learning) is feature augmentation, implemented through a strategic two-stage process: which features to mask and where to apply the masking. In the first stage, we determine 'which' features to focus on by categorizing them into two types: important and changeable. Important features, such as user gender, age, and customer purchase history, are consistently shared across both towers to maintain a solid base for user profiling. The second stage addresses 'where' to apply the masking. Changeable features, including user access time, membership status (e.g., plus member), sensitivity to promotions, and sensitivity to product evaluations, are randomly masked at a rate of 35% to create two augmented data instances. This approach allows the model to effectively handle user behavior variance and improve overall performance.

3.4 From Contrastive Learning to CUL

In our CULC-Net, we design a CUL framework that enhances the outputs of the two towers to be more similar for identical inputs while minimizing the impact of inaccurate CTR data. We first present the formula for Contrastive Learning and then extend it to Contrastive User Learning.

Given a batch of N examples $a_1, \ldots, a_N$, where $a_i \in A$ denotes a set of features for example i, we define x_i and x'_i as the respective inputs for the two towers. Our goal is to learn distinct representations x_i and x'_i while ensuring the model recognizes both as originating from the same input i.

We aim to minimize the difference between x_i and x'_i while maximizing the difference between the representations learned for distinct examples i and j. Let y_i and y'_i represent the outputs of x_i and x'_i. We consider (y_i, y'_i) as positive pairs and (y_i, y'_j) as negative pairs for $i \neq j$. Let $s(y_i, y'_j) = \frac{1}{\tau} \cdot \frac{\langle y_i, y'_j \rangle}{|y_i| \cdot |y'_j|}$, where τ is a temperature parameter that controls the concentration of the probability distribution. To promote the desired properties, we define the InfoNCE loss for a batch of N examples as:

$$L_{\mathrm{CL}} = -\frac{1}{N} \sum_{i=1}^{N} \log \left(\frac{\exp(s(y_i, y'_i))}{\sum_{j=1}^{N} \exp(s(y_i, y'_j))} \right), \tag{1}$$

This is a vanilla InfoNCE loss that facilitates the comparison of positive and negative creatives. However, due to the presence of low exposure creatives, which may be false negatives, not all $i \neq j$ in $\sum_{j=1}^{N} \exp(s(y_i, y'_j))$ should be considered as negative. We define a relevance score δ_{ij} representing the similarity distance from each negative item y'_j to the positive anchor y_i. Its formula is set as:

$$s(y_i, y'_j) - s(y_i, y'_i) + \delta_{ij} < 0, \tag{2}$$

integrating this into the Contrastive Learning formula:

$$L_{\text{CUL}} = -\frac{1}{N}\sum_{i=1}^{N} \log \frac{\exp(s(y_i, y_i'))}{\sum_{j=1}^{N} \exp(s(y_i, y_j') + \delta_{ij})} = \\ -\frac{1}{N}\sum_{i=1}^{N} \log \frac{\exp(s(y_i, y_i'))}{\exp(s(y_i, y_i')) + \sum_{j \neq i} \exp(s(y_i, y_j') + \delta_{ij})}, \quad (3)$$

When $\delta_{ij} = 0$, it simplifies to the vanilla InfoNCE loss function. This relevance score δ_{ij} helps display the ranking among negative creatives; a larger δ_{ij} suggests a stronger negative sample, while a smaller δ_{ij} indicates a potential false negative. Models may learn implicit relationships between feature and different negative samples under the vanilla InfoNCE loss, but we argue that modeling this relationship explicitly by δ_{ij} has a positive influence on learning better representations. This approach allows the model to give more weight to certain negative samples, considering a broader spectrum of negatives.

The specific computation of the loss function is as follows, using adversarial training [25] to learn the difficulty of specific negative samples:

$$\min_{\theta} L_{\text{CUL}} = \min_{\theta} \max_{\Delta \in C} \\ -\frac{1}{N}\sum_{i=1}^{N} \log \frac{\exp(s(y_i, y_i'))}{\exp(s(y_i, y_i')) + \sum_{j \neq i} \exp(\delta_{ij}) \exp(s(y_i, y_j'))}, \quad (4)$$

where C encapsulates the collective set of all δ_{ij}. For each δ_{ij} we have:

$$\exp(\delta_{ij}) \in C(ij) = (1 - \epsilon, 1 + \epsilon),$$

and ϵ is a hyperparameter that regulates the upper-bound deviation of hardness. In practice, ϵ is regulated by the number of adversarial training epochs under a fixed learning rate.

In this way, we reduce the reliance on individual CTR data by exploring the relationships between creatives and customizing recommendations for users with similar features.

3.5 FlexiRank for Utilizing All CTR Data

To better learn the ranking information of creatives, not just identifying the best but understanding which is better, we introduce the FlexiRank method, which utilizes soft ranking to effectively manage the predicted outputs $\{y_1, y_2, \ldots, y_m\}$ and their corresponding soft labels $\{l_1, l_2, \ldots, l_m\}$.

The motivation for FlexiRank is rooted in the necessity to accurately rank creatives according to their potential to engage users. In softmax, labels($\hat{y}$) are one-hot encoded, which only predicts the accuracy for top one creative, thus losing information of the relative ranking of creatives. Inspired by seminal works [4,23,31], we designed FlexiRank, which normalizes CTR to obtain soft labels. FlexiRank considers the relative relationships and rankings among different creatives, exploring the potential of all creatives to attract users and providing more accurate recommendations. The probability that a creative is ranked as the top choice is defined by:

$$P_i = \frac{\exp(y_i)}{\sum_{k=1}^{m} \exp(y_k)}, \tag{5}$$

where $\exp(\cdot)$ denotes the exponential function. The corresponding probability of the soft labels is defined as:

$$\hat{P}_i = \frac{\exp(l_i/T)}{\sum_{k=1}^{m} \exp(l_k/T)}, \tag{6}$$

where T is a temperature coefficient, adjusting the scale when y_m is small.

To enable the model to learn ranking information better in the initial epochs and improve contrastive learning in the later epochs, FlexiRank includes an instructional gradient inspired by Curriculum Learning [3]:

$$L_{\text{FlexiRank}} = -\sum_{i=1}^{m} \hat{P}_i \log(P_i) + \sum_{i=1}^{m} L(x_i, \hat{P}_i, t), \tag{7}$$

where $L(x_i, \hat{P}_i, t) = -\hat{P}_i \cdot \log(p_t(x_i)) \cdot \exp(-\alpha \cdot t)$ represents the instructional gradient, $p_t(x_i)$ is P_i at step t, and α is a hyperparameter.

This objective function is designed to capture the relative ordering of creatives and to facilitate smooth knowledge acquisition within our CULC-Net. By effectively balancing the influence of predicted outputs and soft labels, the FlexiRank method leads to a more robust and generalizable model.

3.6 CULC-Net Optimization

To leverage the advantages of Contrastive User Learning and FlexiRank, CULC-Net employs a unified learning framework that jointly optimizes both the contrastive user learning loss (L_{CUL}) and the flexible ranking loss ($L_{\text{FlexiRank}}$). This joint optimization approach enables the model to learn more informative and effective parameters, enhancing creative selection performance. The training process involves minimizing a joint loss function formulated as:

$$L_{\text{joint}} = L_{\text{FlexiRank}} + \lambda L_{\text{CUL}}, \tag{8}$$

where λ is a hyperparameter that balances the adaptive regularization and contrastive user learning losses.

Table 1. Offline evaluation results of 5 creative selection models across 7 creative settings. CULC-Net demonstrates significant improvements in All setting, with a 1.06% increase in sCTR, a 1.35% increase in AUC, and a 0.85% increase in GAUC, showcasing our advantage. Non-CL also shows a clear improvement over STM, highlighting the effectiveness of the FlexiRank.

Metrics	Image	Title	STM	VAM-HBM	CACS	Non-CL (Ours)	CULC-Net (Ours)
sCTR	single	—	28.54%	28.73%	28.82%	29.12%	29.94% (+1.40%)
	single	single	27.22%	27.43%	27.51%	27.77%	28.63% (+1.41%)
	multi	—	23.12%	23.31%	23.42%	23.67%	24.98% (+1.86%)
	multi	multi	26.07%	26.21%	26.33%	26.61%	27.29% (+1.22%)
	—	single	31.82%	31.94%	32.02%	32.23%	33.82% (+2.00%)
	—	multi	24.87%	25.03%	25.14%	25.72%	26.88% (+2.01%)
	ALL	ALL	26.41%	26.63%	26.73%	26.95%	27.47% (+1.06%)
AUC	single	—	64.42%	64.74%	64.89%	65.37%	66.43% (+2.01%)
	single	single	67.15%	67.38%	67.52%	68.09%	69.12% (+1.97%)
	multi	—	70.46%	70.68%	70.84%	71.25%	72.44% (+1.98%)
	multi	multi	67.04%	67.27%	67.49%	68.01%	69.07% (+2.03%)
	—	single	62.54%	62.41%	62.23%	61.87%	63.54% (+1.00%)
	—	multi	67.91%	68.05%	68.16%	68.33%	69.90% (+1.99%)
	ALL	ALL	67.11%	67.34%	67.47%	67.84%	68.46% (+1.35%)
GAUC	ALL	ALL	58.06%	58.17%	58.24%	58.33%	58.91% (+0.85%)

4 Experiments

4.1 Datasets and Experimental Setup

Our experiments utilize a comprehensive dataset from a real-world search ad system, which includes user click history and various ad attributes collected over a one-month period. Specifically, the dataset comprises approximately 9 billion training samples and 200 million test samples, encompassing interactions from 46 million users with 12 million ads and 43 million ad creatives. The creatives include images and titles. In our offline experiments, we categorized them into Single Image, Multi-Image, Single Title, Multi-Title, Combination (combining images and titles, single or multiple), and All (including all types of creatives).

We employ the Adam optimizer with a learning rate of 0.001, beta1 of 0.9, beta2 of 0.999, and epsilon of 1e−9. For online and offline experiments, λ is 0.6, α is 0.2, and ϵ is 0.1. The model is trained with a batch size of 256. Additionally, we did not use the dropout strategy, and we utilize ReLU activation with a sigmoid output layer to ensure predictions are bound within the range of (0, 1).

4.2 Evaluation Metrics

In order to assess the performance of our creative selection model, we employ specific evaluation metrics for both offline and online experiments. For the online experiments, CTR is used as the primary evaluation metric.

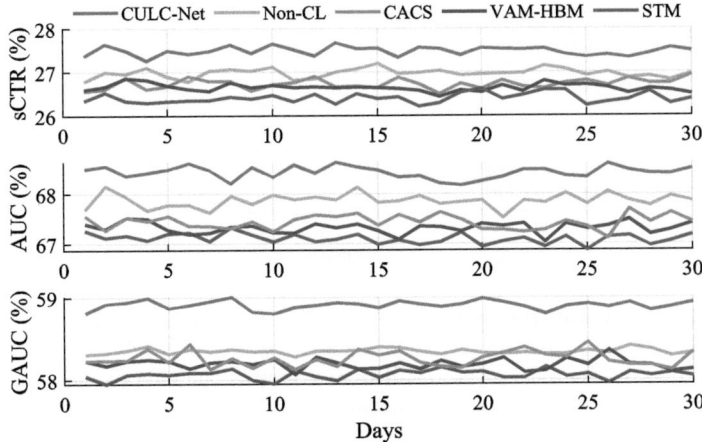

Fig. 3. Offline daily comparison of sCTR, AUC, and GAUC between STM, VAM-HBM, CACS, Non-CL, and CULC-Net over 30 days. The comparison is based on all available data, with CULC-Net consistently achieving the best performance across all metrics.

For the offline experiments, we use Simulated Click-Through Rate (sCTR) [31], Area Under the Curve (AUC), and Group AUC (GAUC) to comprehensively evaluate the model's performance in a controlled environment that mimics real-world conditions. By employing these metrics, we demonstrate the effectiveness and robustness of our proposed CULC-Net in both offline and online settings.

4.3 Baselines

To effectively evaluate the performance of CULC-Net, we introduce a range of advanced baseline models. Below is a concise overview of these models:

STM: employing a single-tower structure, feeds features directly into a multi-layer network, culminating in a classification problem for optimization. This method provides a fundamental benchmark for comparison, excluding the use of Contrastive Learning.

VAM-HBM [31]: combining the Visual-aware Ranking Model (VAM) for learning visual features related to performance and the Hybrid Bandit Model (HBM) for updating its understanding based on prior data, offering a responsive model to creative selection.

CACS [23]: employing a two-tower structure reminiscent of the widely recognized Deep Structured Semantic Model (DSSM) [17]. It maps creatives and user queries into a common semantic space, allowing it to gauge their relevance based on proximity.

Non-CL(Ours): CULC-Net excludes the CUL loss, essentially replacing softmax in STM with FlexiRank to validate the effectiveness of FlexiRank.

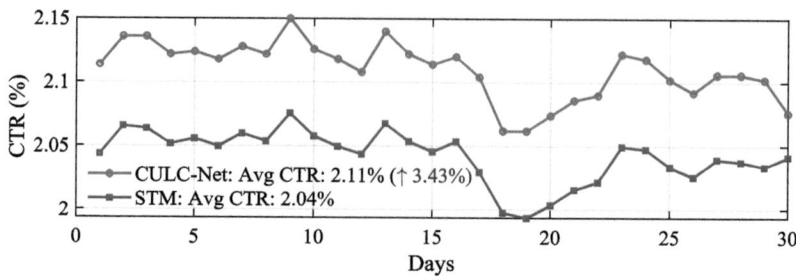

Fig. 4. Daily CTR comparison between CULC-Net and STM over 30 days in online A/B test. The average CTR for STM is 2.04%, while CULC-Net achieves 2.11%, with a 3.43% increase. The result demonstrates the effectiveness of CULC-Net in the real-world online advertising scenario.

4.4 Offline Results

In this section, we discuss the performance of our proposed method, CULC-Net, and compare it with the baseline method, the Non-CL method (without contrastive learning), as well as two recent prominent approaches, VAM-HBM and CACS. We first present a comprehensive comparison test of the creatives, including single image, multi-image, single title, multi-title, single combination, multi-combination, and all data in Table 1. We observe that CULC-Net consistently outperforms the other methods in all test scenarios, affirming its superiority in creative selection.

In terms of total performance across all data, CULC-Net achieves a 4.01% increase in sCTR, a 2.01% increase in AUC, and a 1.44% increase in GAUC compared to the baseline method. Notably, when contrastive learning is incorporated (compared to the Non-CL method), the performance improvement is significant. The sCTR increases by 1.93%, AUC by 0.91%, and GAUC by 0.99%, illustrating the effectiveness of contrastive learning in capturing the nuances between creatives, ultimately leading to a more refined understanding of the underlying patterns.

Moreover, our analysis extends to the comparison with VAM-HBM and CACS. The results suggest that while these methods exhibit competitive performance in certain scenarios, CULC-Net consistently provides a more comprehensive and accurate creative selection mechanism. Specifically, CULC-Net demonstrates a more pronounced ability to leverage the complex interplay between different creative elements, as evidenced by its superior performance in multi-image and multi-title scenarios.

Figure 3 showcases the daily comparison of sCTR, AUC, and GAUC between STM, Non-CL, VAM-HBM, CACS, and CULC-Net over a span of 30 days, where each method processed one day of data from the dataset. The results underscore that CULC-Net is not only effective but also exhibits remarkable stability, consistently outperforming the other methods across all evaluation metrics.

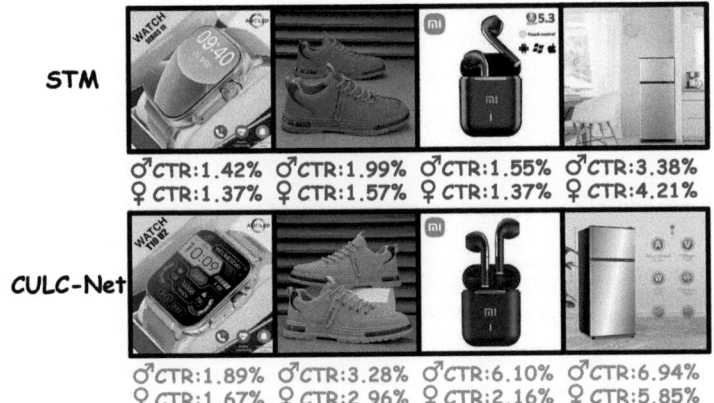

Fig. 5. Visualization of selected creatives by CULC-Net and STM. Each column presents one pair of creatives with the same item. CULC-Net attracts more clicks and recommends better creatives for both males and females.

4.5 Online Results

To investigate the effectiveness of CULC-Net in a real-world scenario, we conducted a 30-day A/B test comparing its performance with STM. The daily and average CTRs for both methods are presented in Fig. 4. From the results, we observe that CULC-Net consistently outperforms STM in terms of daily CTR, with a relative increase in average CTR of 3.43%, demonstrating the effectiveness of our approach.

Figure 5 visualizes the creatives selected by CULC-Net and STM. Each column shows a pair of creatives associated with the same item, where CULC-Net consistently selects creatives that are better designed and more informative, leading to higher click rates. This analysis also compares male and female responses, highlighting enhanced engagement: males show a notable increase in clicks for items like headphones and refrigerators, while females demonstrate a significant uplift for footwear. These trends suggest that the improvements in creative selection by CULC-Net are influenced by gender-specific preferences. This further supports the effectiveness of CULC-Net in optimizing creative selection and enhancing advertising performance.

Our approach demonstrates that incorporating user knowledge and contrastive learning into the creative selection process can result in more effective ad creatives, which in turn, enhances platform revenue and contributes to a more engaging user experience.

4.6 Ablation Study

Offline Results on Public Dataset. Due to the lack of open-source datasets and the specific requirements for online performance, most creative selection methods [33,34] have only been tested on proprietary datasets. The Creative

Table 2. Offline results on CreativeRanking dataset. This public dataset lacks user information, so we only test the effectiveness of FlexiRank (Non-CL). The results proving the robustness of our approach across multiple datasets.

Method	sCTR	AUC	GAUC
STM	2.95%	60.13%	54.27%
VAM-HBM	3.32%	62.75%	57.09%
CACS	3.27%	61.98%	56.35%
Non-CL	3.48% (↑17.9%)	63.42% (↑5.5%)	57.88% (↑6.7%)

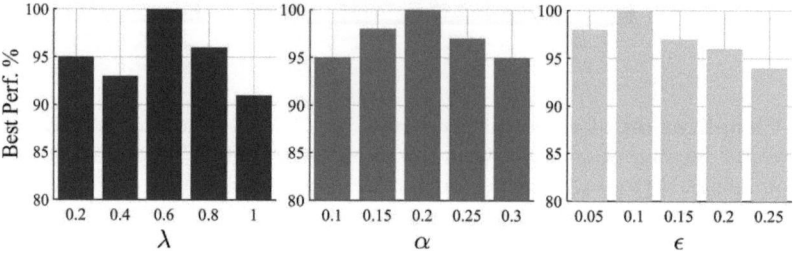

Fig. 6. Impact of key hyperparameters. We test the effects of λ, α, and ϵ in offline experiments, with the y-axis representing the percentage of the best performance.

Ranking Dataset [31] is the only public dataset we identified for the creative selection task. This dataset includes advertising creative data from Taobao, collected from July to August 2020, with 500,827 product samples, 1,204,988 different creatives, and over 200 million impressions. However, since this dataset lacks user information, we could not evaluate CULC-Net directly and instead focused on testing the FlexiRank component (Non-CL). We conducted additional offline experiments on this dataset to verify the effectiveness of FlexiRank. As shown in Table 2, Non-CL achieved the best results, with a 17.9% improvement in sCTR, a 5.5% increase in AUC, and a 6.7% rise in GAUC. These results further demonstrate the advantages of utilizing soft ranking.

Parameter Sensitivity. We analyze the impact of key hyperparameters of CULC-Net, as shown in Fig. 6, where the y-axis represents the percentage of the best performance.

1. Impact of λ: The balance between FlexiRank and contrastive user learning losses is best achieved with $\lambda = 0.6$, with performance dropping off as λ increases.
2. Impact of α: The optimal decay rate is found with $\alpha = 0.2$, ensuring stable training and effective learning.
3. Impact of ϵ: The hardness of negative samples is best regulated by $\epsilon = 0.1$, striking the right balance between challenge and learnability.

5 Conclusion

In this paper, we introduced CULC-Net, a novel approach for optimizing ad creative selection by addressing the challenges of unreliable CTR data and sparse data exposures. Unlike existing methods that rely heavily on surface-level analysis, CULC-Net delves deeper into user behavior, uncovering latent connections between users and creatives. This approach enables a more personalized and effective advertising experience. Our extensive evaluation shows a 3.43% improvement in online and 4.01% in offline.

The key contribution of CULC-Net lies in its ability to enhance data robustness and relevance, even with unbalanced datasets, leading to more effective ad recommendations. This improvement is economically significant; for instance, on a large e-commerce platform with daily sales of $100 million, a 3% increase in CTR could yield an additional $3 million in revenue. Moving forward, CULC-Net sets the stage for future innovations in personalized, data-driven advertising, emphasizing the critical role of user-centric approaches in optimizing online advertising.

Acknowledgment. This research was funded by the National Science and Technology Major Project under contract No. 2021ZD0109903 and the National Natural Science Foundation of China (No. 82441013).

References

1. Auer, P., Cesa-Bianchi, N., Fischer, P.: Finite-time analysis of the multiarmed bandit problem. Mach. Learn. **47**, 235–256 (2002)
2. Baltescu, P., Chen, H., Pancha, N., Zhai, A., Leskovec, J., Rosenberg, C.: Itemsage: learning product embeddings for shopping recommendations at pinterest. In: Proceedings of the 28th ACM SIGKDD Conference on Knowledge Discovery and Data Mining, pp. 2703–2711 (2022)
3. Bengio, Y., Louradour, J., Collobert, R., Weston, J.: Curriculum learning. In: Proceedings of the International Conference on Machine Learning, pp. 41–48 (2009)
4. Cao, Z., Qin, T., Liu, T.Y., Tsai, M.F., Li, H.: Learning to rank: from pairwise approach to listwise approach. In: Proceedings of the International Conference on Machine Learning, pp. 129–136 (2007)
5. Chen, J., Ge, T., Jiang, G., Zhang, Z., Lian, D., Zheng, K.: Efficient optimal selection for composited advertising creatives with tree structure. In: Proceedings of the AAAI Conference on Artificial Intelligence, vol. 35, pp. 3967–3975 (2021)
6. Chen, J., Xu, J., Jiang, G., Ge, T., Zhang, Z., Lian, D., Zheng, K.: Automated creative optimization for e-commerce advertising. In: Proceedings of the Web Conference 2021, pp. 2304–2313 (2021)
7. Chen, J., Sun, B., Li, H., Lu, H., Hua, X.S.: Deep CTR prediction in display advertising. In: Proceedings of the 24th ACM International Conference on Multimedia, pp. 811–820 (2016)
8. Chen, T., Kornblith, S., Norouzi, M., Hinton, G.: A simple framework for contrastive learning of visual representations. In: Proceedings of the International Conference on Machine Learning, pp. 1597–1607. PMLR (2020)

9. De Boer, P.T., Kroese, D.P., Mannor, S., Rubinstein, R.Y.: A tutorial on the cross-entropy method. Ann. Oper. Res. **134**, 19–67 (2005)
10. Devlin, J., Chang, M.W., Lee, K., Toutanova, K.: Bert: pre-training of deep bidirectional transformers for language understanding. In: Conference of the North American Chapter of the Association for Computational Linguistics (2019)
11. Ge, T., et al.: Image matters: visually modeling user behaviors using advanced model server. In: Proceedings of the 27th ACM International Conference on Information & Knowledge Management, pp. 2087–2095 (2018)
12. Gidaris, S., Singh, P., Komodakis, N.: Unsupervised representation learning by predicting image rotations. In: Proceedings of the International Conference on Learning Representations (2018)
13. Glowacka, D.: Bandit algorithms in recommender systems. In: RecSys '19, pp. 574–575 (2019)
14. Guo, H., Tang, R., Ye, Y., Li, Z., He, X.: DeepFM: a factorization-machine based neural network for CTR prediction. In: Proceedings of The International Joint Conferences on Artificial Intelligence (2017)
15. He, K., Fan, H., Wu, Y., Xie, S., Girshick, R.: Momentum contrast for unsupervised visual representation learning. In: Proceedings of the IEEE/CVF International Conference on Computer Vision, pp. 9729–9738 (2020)
16. He, X., et al.: Practical lessons from predicting clicks on ads at facebook. In: Proceedings of the Eighth International Workshop on Data Mining for Online Advertising, pp. 1–9 (2014)
17. Huang, P.S., He, X., Gao, J., Deng, L., Acero, A., Heck, L.: Learning deep structured semantic models for web search using clickthrough data. In: Proceedings of the 22th ACM International Conference on Information & Knowledge Management, pp. 2333–2338 (2013)
18. Jaiswal, A., Babu, A.R., Zadeh, M.Z., Banerjee, D., Makedon, F.: A survey on contrastive self-supervised learning. Technologies **9**(1), 2 (2020)
19. LeCun, Y., Bengio, Y., Hinton, G.: Deep learning. Nature **521**(7553), 436–444 (2015)
20. Li, H., Zhou, X., Tuan, L.A., Miao, C.: Rethinking negative pairs in code search. In: Proceedings of the 2023 Conference on Empirical Methods in Natural Language Processing (2023)
21. Li, S., et al.: Adaptive low-precision training for embeddings in click-through rate prediction. In: Proceedings of the AAAI Conference on Artificial Intelligence, vol. 37, pp. 4435–4443 (2023)
22. Li, X., et al.: Adversarial multimodal representation learning for click-through rate prediction. In: Proceedings of The Web Conference 2020, pp. 827–836 (2020)
23. Lin, K., et al.: Joint optimization of ad ranking and creative selection. In: Proceedings of the 45th International ACM SIGIR Conference on Research and Development in Information Retrieval, pp. 2341–2346 (2022)
24. Liu, H., et al.: Category-specific CNN for visual-aware CTR prediction at JD. com. In: Proceedings of the 26th ACM SIGKDD International Conference on Knowledge Discovery, pp. 2686–2696 (2020)
25. Madry, A., Makelov, A., Schmidt, L., Tsipras, D., Vladu, A.: Towards deep learning models resistant to adversarial attacks. Proceedings of the International Conference on Learning Representations (2018)
26. McMahan, H.B., et al.: Ad click prediction: a view from the trenches. In: Proceedings of the 19th ACM SIGKDD International Conference on Knowledge Discovery and Data Mining, pp. 1222–1230 (2013)

27. Mikolov, T., Chen, K., Corrado, G., Dean, J.: Efficient estimation of word representations in vector space. arXiv:1301.3781 (2013)
28. Mo, K., Liu, B., Xiao, L., Li, Y., Jiang, J.: Image feature learning for cold start problem in display advertising. In: Proceedings of The International Joint Conferences on Artificial Intelligence (2015)
29. Oord, A.V.D., Li, Y., Vinyals, O.: Representation learning with contrastive predictive coding. arXiv preprint arXiv:1807.03748 (2018)
30. Schwartz, E.M., Bradlow, E.T., Fader, P.S.: Customer acquisition via display advertising using multi-armed bandit experiments. Mark. Sci. **36**(4), 500–522 (2017)
31. Wang, S., Liu, Q., Ge, T., Lian, D., Zhang, Z.: A hybrid bandit model with visual priors for creative ranking in display advertising. In: Proceedings of the Web Conference 2021, pp. 2324–2334 (2021)
32. Wei, P., Liu, S., Yang, X., Wang, L., Zheng, B.: Towards personalized bundle creative generation with contrastive non-autoregressive decoding. In: Proceedings of the 45th International ACM SIGIR Conference on Research and Development in Information Retrieval, pp. 2634–2638 (2022)
33. Wei, P., Yang, X., Liu, S., Wang, L., Zheng, B.: Creater: CTR-driven advertising text generation with controlled pre-training and contrastive fine-tuning. arXiv preprint arXiv:2205.08943 (2022)
34. Yang, Z., et al.: Parallel ranking of ads and creatives in real-time advertising systems. In: Proceedings of the AAAI Conference on Artificial Intelligence, vol. 38, pp. 9278–9286 (2024)
35. Yao, T., et al.: Self-supervised learning for large-scale item recommendations. In: Proceedings of the 30th ACM International Conference on Information & Knowledge Management, pp. 4321–4330 (2021)
36. Zhao, Z., et al.: What you look matters? Offline evaluation of advertising creatives for cold-start problem. In: Proceedings of the 28th ACM International Conference on Information & Knowledge Management, pp. 2605–2613 (2019)

A Dual-Channel Heterogeneous Hypergraph Convolutional Network for Dual-target Cross-domain Recommendation

Moyu Zhang and Zhe Yang(✉)

School of Computer Science and Technology, Soochow University, Suzhou, China
myzhang23135@stu.suda.edu.cn, yangzhe@suda.edu.cn

Abstract. Cross-domain recommendation (CDR), which aims to alleviate the data sparsity problem in a single domain by integrating complementary data from multiple domains, has become a practical and challenging research direction. Although achieving promising performance, we highlight two problems in existing CDR methods. 1) The representation ability of existing ID-based item embedding is limited. 2) Knowledge transferability across different domains is often insufficient. To solve these problems, we propose a new cross-domain recommendation method, termed Dual-Channel Heterogeneous HyperGraph Convolutional Network (DHHGCN), which primarily consists of two components: the intra-domain channel layer and the inter-domain channel layer. Concretely, within the intra-domain context, we introduce additional item features and build heterogeneous hypergraphs to model fine-grained high-order correlations, resulting in high-quality user and item representations. In terms of the inter-domain, based on designed similarity matrices, we construct hypergraphs and guide the network to learn the relationships via hypergraph convolution, effectively transferring cross-domain knowledge. Last, an element-wise gating mechanism is designed to integrate domain-specific knowledge with shared cross-domain knowledge, enabling dual-target recommendations. Extensive experiments demonstrate the superiority and effectiveness. Our code is available on GitHub (https://github.com/idleslob/DHHGCN).

Keywords: Data Mining · Cross-domain Recommendation · Heterogeneous Hypergraph · Hypergraph Convolutional Network

1 Introduction

Cross-domain recommendation (CDR) alleviates data sparsity and cold start issues by introducing multi-domain user interactions. Early CDR methods aim to improve performance within a single domain by transferring knowledge from

---
M. Zhang and Z. Yang—Co-first authors with equal contributions.

© The Author(s), under exclusive license to Springer Nature Switzerland AG 2026
R. P. Ribeiro et al. (Eds.): ECML PKDD 2025, LNAI 16091, pp. 536–552, 2026.
https://doi.org/10.1007/978-3-032-06096-9_31

a source domain to a target domain [35]. However, unidirectional methods are prone to accumulating noise in intermediate steps, leading to suboptimal learning. This has led to the development of dual-target CDR, reducing negative transfer from the sparser domain to the richer one [33].

With the development of Graph Neural Networks (GNNs), many methods have been applied to dual-target CDR. Traditional GNN-based CDR methods can be categorized into two types: one constructs separate user-item interaction graphs for each domain, and the other builds a unified interaction graph and trains a shared model to serve all domains [4]. Although promising results are achieved, there are two problems as follows. First, most models [3,23] only construct graph models based on user-item interactions, neglecting to model the higher-order correlations of useful item attribute information. This limitation prevents capturing the information propagation among multiple heterogeneous nodes. Therefore, they fail to uncover fine-grained higher-order correlations between users and items, considering more information like the price of items. Second, uneven data distribution leads to the problem of negative transfer during cross-domain propagation [34]. Consequently, most models struggle to effectively transfer shared knowledge, resulting in an inability to appropriately balance domain-specific features and shareable features.

Therefore, we highlight two key challenges: (1) How to model heterogeneous attribute information of each domain and obtain fine-grained higher-order correlations to mitigate the sparsity of ID-based single-feature embeddings. (2) How to extract and transmit shareable heterogeneous information across domains to ensure effective and sufficient knowledge transfer. To conquer these challenges, we propose a new cross-domain recommendation method termed Dual-Channel Heterogeneous Hypergraph Convolutional Network (DHHGCN) model. Specifically, to tackle the first challenge, we first select reasonable item attributes as the initial features of the nodes in the graph. Then, we construct heterogeneous hypergraphs and a novel convolution method to learn node embeddings, emphasizing both intra-type and inter-type relationships. Moreover, to address the second challenge, we propose a cross-domain hypergraph construction strategy and an inter-domain convolution method with an element-wise gating mechanism to aggregate embeddings from both intra- and inter-domain channels. The contributions of this paper are summarized as follows:

- We propose DHHGCN, a dual-channel heterogeneous hypergraph convolutional network that integrates heterogeneous attributes for cross-domain recommendation, capturing both domain-specific and shared knowledge.
- We design an inter-domain hypergraph convolution module to transfer shareable information and introduce an element-wise gating mechanism to fuse intra- and inter-domain features for dual-target recommendation.
- Extensive experiments and analyses on real-world datasets demonstrate the superiority and effectiveness of our approaches.

2 Related Work

2.1 Graph Neural Networks Based CDR

Traditional recommendation systems [17,18] have struggled with data sparsity and the cold-start problem, leading to the development of CDR [27]. Conventional methods have difficulty capturing user interest migration and modeling complex item relationships [9,14]. Graph Neural Networks (GNNs) offer a promising solution by effectively modeling graph-structured data and enabling the exploration of higher-order relationships [4]. BiTGCF [16] utilizes LightGCN [8] to aggregate interaction information and introduces a feature transfer layer to enhance graph encoders. DA-GCN [5] combines Recurrent Neural Networks (RNNs) and GCNs for cross-domain sequential recommendation. Furthermore, some studies have used GNNs to model rich interaction information. ACDN [15] incorporates users' aesthetic features into the CoNet to convey shareable preferences. DDTCDR [13] integrates content information into CDR to address data sparsity. However, most models only capture pairwise correlations, leading to missed insights from higher-order interactions and associations among heterogeneous information. Some models place overly strict dataset requirements when modeling heterogeneous information, limiting their applicability.

2.2 Heterogeneous Graph and Hypergraph

Heterogeneous graphs allow for the modeling of various node and edge types, enabling the encoding of complex relationships among different entities [11,24]. TrineCDR [34] has proposed effective strategies for leveraging side information in cross-domain setups. Hypergraphs enable the representation of richer relational data via hyperedges, allowing for the capture of higher-order interactions between multiple nodes [21]. Zhou et al. [32] pioneered hypergraph learning and Feng et al. [4] introduced hypergraph convolutional operations to effectively handle complex relationships. Recently, hypergraphs have been applied to recommendation tasks, such as the development of the multi-channel hypergraph convolutional network MHCN [26] for social recommendation and the dual-channel hypergraph convolutional network. II-HGCN [7] uses a hypergraph convolutional network for intra-domain and inter-domain analysis to generate accurate embeddings. Furthermore, heterogeneous hypergraphs can effectively represent multiple non-pairwise relationships [22], and as a result, they have gradually been applied in recommendation in recent years. BiPNet [28] and CoHHN [29] proposed a heterogeneous hypergraph network to explore various kinds of information for the session-based recommendation. However, heterogeneous hypergraph has not been fully explored and utilized in cross-domain recommendation.

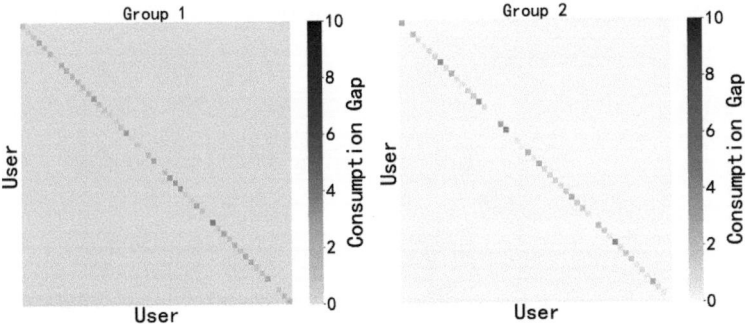

Fig. 1. The heatmap of consumption differences for each user across different domains, with group 1 in Beauty & Health and group 2 in Cloth & Sports. Darker colors indicate larger differences, while lighter colors represent smaller differences.

3 Motivation and Framework

3.1 Motivation Study and Data Processing

We examine the Amazon, representative e-commerce dataset to identify suitable item attributes for feature embedding. We reveal that price is significantly correlated with user preferences. However, absolute price cannot determine whether it is expensive or cheap [31]. Therefore, we categorize absolute prices into multiple intervals based on item categories. The formula of the price level p_i is as follows:

$$p_i = \text{round}\left(\frac{\phi(x_i) - \phi(x_{\min})}{\phi(x_{\max}) - \phi(x_{\min})} \times \rho\right), \tag{1}$$

where round(∗) denotes the rounding operation, x_i represents the absolute price of an item, $x_{\min}$ and $x_{\max}$ represent the cheapest and the most expensive in each category respectively, ρ is the total price level. The function $\phi(x)$ denotes the cumulative distribution function of the logistic distribution. Although users exhibit varying preferences across different item categories, they tend to demonstrate consistency in their overall spending levels across various domains. Therefore, to investigate this, we randomly select 100 users with purchase records in different domains. By comparing their average spending levels, we can validate the rationale for incorporating price attributes. Figure 1 shows that user spending is similar across different domains, despite varying item prices. Comparative analysis reveals that the relationship between item prices and categories is important for CDR. While price ranges vary within the same domain, recommendations based on users' overall spending can help bridge differences across categories and price ranges, providing more personalized recommendations.

3.2 Overview of the Framework

This paper presents a Dual-Channel Heterogeneous Hypergraph Convolutional Network (DHHGCN) for the dual-target CDR. As illustrated in Fig. 2. The

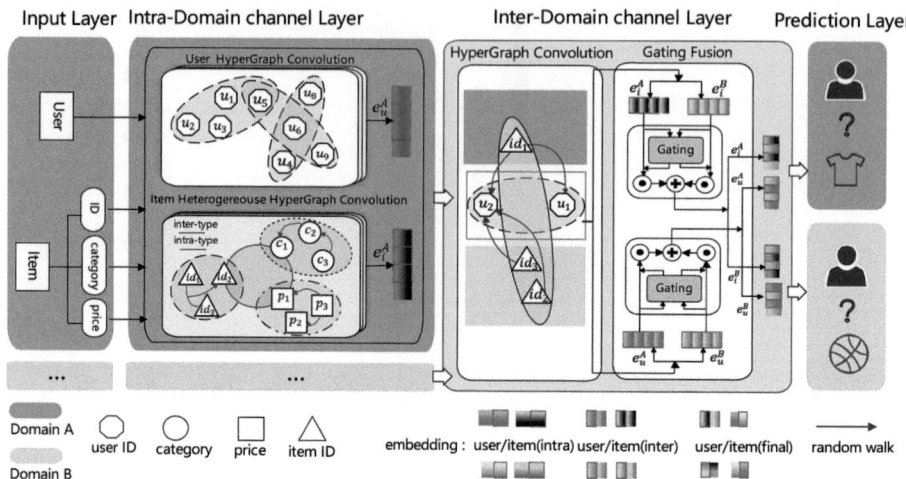

Fig. 2. The framework of DHHGCN. The modeling approach for the intra-domain channel layer is the same across all domains, so for simplicity, we use domain A as an example in the model diagram and omit domain B.

framework consists of four main components: input layer, intra-domain channel layer, inter-domain channel layer, and prediction layer. The input layer takes in heterogeneous information as initial feature embeddings. In the intra-domain channel layer, we construct user hypergraphs and item heterogeneous hypergraphs for each domain, we perform different types of convolution operations to extract fine-grained domain-specific features. In the inter-domain channel layer, we construct inter-domain user and item hypergraphs based on the similarity matrix, respectively, we also implement a cross-domain graph convolution operation and design an element-wise gating mechanism to enhance the flexibility and accuracy of feature fusion. Finally, in the prediction layer, we provide recommendations for both domains based on the obtained node embedding representations.

4 The Proposed Method

4.1 Preliminary

Our goal is to enhance recommendation performance across two domains, A and B. The overlapping users between the two domains are denoted as $\mathcal{U} = \{u_1, u_2, u_3, \ldots, u_m\}$, with m users. The items set for each domain are $\mathcal{I}^A = \{I_1^A, I_2^A, I_3^A, \ldots, I_n^A\}$, $\mathcal{I}^B = \{I_1^B, I_2^B, I_3^B, \ldots, I_k^B\}$, where n and k represent the number of items in domain A and B, respectively. User-item interactions are represented by matrices $\mathbf{R}^A \in \{0,1\}^{m \times n}$ and $\mathbf{R}^B \in \{0,1\}^{m \times k}$. $\mathbf{H} \in \{0,1\}^{v \times e}$ represent the association matrix, the adjacency matrix is $a_{ij} \in \{0,1\}^{m \times m}$, $\sigma(*)$ is the activation function. The graph structures are as follows:

Intra-domain Graph: The user hypergraphs are denoted as $\mathbf{G}_\mathcal{U}^A(\mathcal{V}_u, \mathcal{E}^A)$ and $\mathbf{G}_\mathcal{U}^B(\mathcal{V}_u, \mathcal{E}^B)$. The item heterogeneous hypergraphs, represented as $\mathbf{G}_\mathcal{I}^A(\mathcal{V}_A^t, \mathcal{E}_A^\tau)$ and $\mathbf{G}_\mathcal{I}^B(\mathcal{V}_B^t, \mathcal{E}_B^\tau)$, consist of different node and edge sets $\mathcal{V}^t$ and $\mathcal{E}^\tau$. There are three types of nodes: items ID nodes ($\mathcal{V}^{id}$), price nodes ($\mathcal{V}^p$) and category nodes ($\mathcal{V}^c$); The six types of edges defined as $\mathcal{E}_{vi}, \mathcal{E}_{vp}, \mathcal{E}_{vc}$ represent item, price and category co-occurrence respectively, $\mathcal{E}_{pv}$ represents price-attribute items, $\mathcal{E}_{pc}$ denotes price-attribute categories, $\mathcal{E}_{cv}$ indicates category-attribute items.

Inter-domain Graph: $\mathbf{G}_\mathcal{U}^C(\mathcal{V}_u, \mathcal{E}_u)$, $\mathbf{G}_\mathcal{I}^C(\mathcal{V}_i, \mathcal{E}_i)$ represent the user and item hypergraphs, respectively. The similarity matrices constructed for the user and item hypergraphs are denoted as $\mathbf{H}_{SI}$ and $\mathbf{H}_{SU}$. The degree matrices for the vertices and edges are represented by $\mathbf{D}_\mathcal{V} \in \mathbb{R}^{v \times v}, \mathbf{D}_\mathcal{E} \in \mathbb{R}^{e \times e}$.

4.2 The Intra-domain Channel Layer

We first construct intra-domain hypergraphs and heterogeneous hypergraphs for users and items based on high-order similarity and co-occurrence relationships. Then, we employ various convolution algorithms to improve information propagation and feature learning. The intra-domain channel is built using domain A as an example, as domains A and B are identical.

Hypergraph Construction. We first define co-occurrence and higher-order relationships. In user-item interaction data, if both u_j and u_k interact with item I_i, they are considered to have a co-occurrence relationship. Based on this, we construct an adjacency matrix $\mathbf{H}_u = \mathbf{R}^A$ for users with co-occurrence relationships. For higher-order relationships [10], we only select second-order correlations [7] to avoid noise. Specifically, if u_k connects u_j and I_i, then u_j is considered a higher-order reachable user of I_i. We extract all such users as the hyperedge $\mathbf{J}_u(I_i)$. The user hypergraph $\widetilde{\mathbf{H}}_u$ is computed as follows:

$$\widetilde{\mathbf{H}}_u = \mathbf{H}_u \times \min\left(1, \mathbf{H}_u^T \times \mathbf{H}_u\right). \quad (2)$$

Since hyperedges can contain multiple nodes, an excessive number of hyperedges may cause information redundancy. To address this, we propose a hyperedge sparsification process, retaining only highly similar users or items. The importance of hyperedges is measured by their hyperdegree $\mathbf{D}_u \in \{0,1\}^{n \times n}$, thus we filter and prune based on their hyperdegree, removing hyperedges with lower hyperdegree. We choose the mean degree x of $\mathbf{D}_u$ as the threshold for filtering redundant edges.

$$(\mathbf{F}_u)_{ii} = \begin{cases} 1, & if\ (\mathbf{D}_u)_{ii} > x \\ 0, & \text{otherwise}. \end{cases} \quad (3)$$

The final user hypergraph representation, derived from the co-occurrence relationship-based association matrix $\mathbf{H}_u$, is shown below, where $\|$ denotes the concatenation operation.

$$\mathbf{H}_\mathcal{U} = \mathbf{H}_u \| \widetilde{\mathbf{H}}_u \times \mathbf{F}_u. \quad (4)$$

We create a heterogeneous hypergraph for items using co-occurrence relationships. This hypergraph has three types of nodes: item ID, price, and category features, i.e., $\mathcal{V}^t = \mathcal{V}^{id} \cup \mathcal{V}^p \cup \mathcal{V}^c$; We design six types of edges to capture diverse feature relationships, enabling a more comprehensive representation of user-item associations.

Hypergraph Convolution. Based on the constructed user hypergraph, we adopt traditional hypergraph convolution [25] and incorporate a residual connection mechanism to update node embeddings $\mathbf{E}_\mathcal{U}$:

$$\mathbf{E}_\mathcal{U}^{(\ell+1)} = \sigma \left(\mathbf{D}_{uv}^{-1} \mathbf{H}_\mathcal{U} \mathbf{D}_{ue} \mathbf{H}_\mathcal{U}^T \mathbf{E}_\mathcal{U}^{(\ell)} \mathbf{W}^{(\ell)} + \mathbf{E}_\mathcal{U}^{(\ell)} \right), \tag{5}$$

where $\mathbf{W}^{(\ell)} \in \mathbb{R}^{c(\ell) \times c(\ell+1)}$ denotes the shared parameters, $c(\ell)$ denotes the number of convolutional layers.

For item heterogeneous hypergraph convolution, we first group neighboring nodes of the same type to aggregate relevant information for each node type, thereby distinguishing the importance of nodes within a specific type. For any node $\mathbf{v}_i$, we assume $(\mathcal{N}_t)_i$ as the set of neighboring nodes of type t. Considering that nodes of the same type carry homogeneous information, the intra-type convolution aggregates information by performing a weighted summation of the neighboring nodes $(\mathbf{v}_t)_j$, resulting in the node embedding representation $(\mathbf{e}_t)_i$.

$$(\mathbf{e}_t)_i = \sum_j \frac{\exp\left((\mathbf{v}_t)_i^\top \mathbf{W}(\mathbf{v}_t)_j\right)}{\sum_{(\mathbf{v}_t)_j \in (\mathcal{N}_t)_i} \exp\left((\mathbf{v}_t)_i^\top \mathbf{W}(\mathbf{v}_t)_j\right)} (\mathbf{v}_t)_j, \tag{6}$$

where $\mathbf{W} \in \mathbb{R}^{d \times d}$ is a learnable parameter used to evaluate the similarity between nodes. Thus, the intra-type convolution yields the feature embedding representation $\mathbf{E}_t = f_a(\mathcal{N}_t)$. Next, we designed an inter-type convolution to aggregate relevant heterogeneous information from different types, enriching the feature representation of item nodes from various perspectives. Specifically, we introduce a gating mechanism to perform weighted integration of embeddings from each type, adaptively assigning weights to each type. This allows the model to adjust the information fusion method based on the importance of features from each type. Formally,

$$\mathbf{O}_1 = \sigma \left(\mathbf{E}'_{t_1} + \mathbf{W}_1 \mathbf{E}_{t_2} \right), \tag{7}$$

$$\mathbf{O}_2 = \sigma \left(\mathbf{E}'_{t_1} + \mathbf{W}_2 \mathbf{E}_{t_3} \right), \tag{8}$$

$$\mathbf{E}'_{t_1} = \mathbf{W}_3 \left(\mathbf{E}_{t_1} \| \mathbf{E}_{t_2} \| \mathbf{E}_{t_3} \right), \tag{9}$$

where $\mathbf{W}_{k \in 1,2,3}$ are learnable parameters, t_1, t_2, t_3 are there types of nodes. The formula for updating node embedding based on neighboring nodes is $\widetilde{\mathbf{E}}_t = \mathbf{A}_t \mathbf{E}_t (t \in id, p, c)$. Additionally, a residual structure is applied to prevent gradient explosion. We update three types of nodes through a two-type convolution, the final calculation formulas for their embedding representations are given:

$$\mathbf{E}_p^{(\ell+1)} = \mathbf{E}_p^{(\ell)} + \mathbf{O}_1 \odot \mathbf{E}_{id}^{(\ell)} + \mathbf{O}_2 \odot \mathbf{E}_c^{(\ell)} + \widetilde{\mathbf{E}}_p^{(\ell)}, \tag{10}$$

$$\mathbf{E}_c^{(\ell+1)} = \mathbf{E}_c^{(\ell)} + \mathbf{O}_1 \odot \mathbf{E}_{id}^{(\ell)} + \mathbf{O}_2 \odot \mathbf{E}_p^{(\ell)} + \widetilde{\mathbf{E}}_c^{(\ell)}, \qquad (11)$$

$$\mathbf{E}_{id}^{(\ell+1)} = \sigma\left(\mathbf{W}^{(\ell)}\mathbf{E}_{id}^{(\ell)} + \mathbf{E}_{id}^{(\ell)}\right) + \mathbf{O}_1 \odot \mathbf{E}_p^{(\ell)} + \mathbf{O}_2 \odot \mathbf{E}_c^{(\ell)} + \widetilde{\mathbf{E}}_{id}^{(\ell)}, \qquad (12)$$

where $\odot$ denotes the element-wise product. In summary, the final embedding representations for domain-specific items and users we obtained are $\mathbf{E}_{\mathcal{U}_A}$ $\mathbf{E}_{\mathcal{U}_B}$, $\mathbf{E}_{\mathcal{I}_A}$, $\mathbf{E}_{\mathcal{I}_B}$, and $\mathbf{E}_{\mathcal{I}_A} = \mathbf{E}_{id}^A$, $\mathbf{E}_{\mathcal{I}_B} = \mathbf{E}_{id}^B$.

4.3 The Inter-domain Channel Layer

CDR could use the similarity of user behavior and item attributes across domains. Random walks, by iteratively traversing the graph, can naturally capture high-order relational information. To this end, we propose a random walk-based method to identify similar user/item pairs and construct cross-domain user and item hypergraphs. Taking nodes u and v as an example, we perform multiple random walks starting from these nodes. Two stopping count vectors, $\mathbf{n}_u$ and $\mathbf{n}_v$, record the number of random walks that terminate at each overlapping node. The similarity $\mathbf{s}(u,v)$ is then calculated using cosine similarity as follows:

$$\mathbf{s}(u,v) = \frac{\mathbf{n}_u^T \times \mathbf{n}_v}{\|\mathbf{n}_u\|_2 \times \|\mathbf{n}_v\|_2} = \widehat{\mathbf{n}}_u^T \widehat{\mathbf{n}}_v. \qquad (13)$$

After normalization, to further enhance computational efficiency, we convert the similarity matrix into a discrete similarity level matrix. This maps continuous similarity values into discrete levels, enabling the model to dynamically adjust node similarity weights. We employ two thresholds to minimize noise, capture long-tail information, and enhance correlations between highly similar nodes. This approach supports fine-grained feature learning and information propagation in the graph convolutional network. Taking items in domain A as an example, the final similarity matrix is as follows:

$$\mathbf{H}_{\mathrm{SI}}^A = \begin{cases} 0, & if\ \mathbf{s}(u,v) \leq t_1, \\ 1, & if\ t_1 < \mathbf{s}(u,v) < t_2, \\ 2, & if\ \mathbf{s}(u,v) \geq t_2. \end{cases} \qquad (14)$$

Since the inter-domain similarity matrix connects nodes across both domains, $\mathbf{H}_{\mathrm{SI}}^A = \mathbf{H}_{\mathrm{SI}} = \left(\mathbf{H}_{\mathrm{SI}}^B\right)^T$ indicates that the similarity matrices between domains A and B are symmetric. We then apply an adaptive hypergraph convolutional neural network on user hypergraph and item hypergraph, respectively:

$$\mathbf{P}_{\mathcal{I}_A}^{(\ell)} = \sigma\left(\mathbf{D}_{\mathbf{H}_{\mathrm{SI}_e}^A}^{-1/2} \mathbf{H}_{\mathrm{SI}}^A \mathbf{D}_{\mathbf{H}_{\mathrm{SI}_v}^A}^{-1/2} \mathbf{E}_{\mathcal{I}_B}^{(\ell)}\right). \qquad (15)$$

The resulting embeddings $\mathbf{P}_{\mathcal{I}_A}$ represent the inter-domain item embeddings. Finally, we design an element-wise gating mechanism to integrate feature representations of users and items learned from intra and inter-channels. This mechanism assigns an adaptive weight to each feature element, enabling flexible and efficient feature aggregation. Formally,

$$\widetilde{\mathbf{E}}_{\mathcal{I}_A}^{(\ell+1)} = \mathbf{G}_{\mathcal{I}}^A \odot \mathbf{E}_{\mathcal{I}_A}^{(\ell)} + (1 - \mathbf{G}_{\mathcal{I}}^A) \odot \mathbf{P}_{\mathcal{I}_A}^{(\ell)}, \quad (16)$$

$$\mathbf{G}_{\mathcal{I}}^A = \sigma\left(\mathbf{W}_1 \mathbf{E}_{\mathcal{I}_A}^{(\ell)} + \mathbf{W}_2 \mathbf{P}_{\mathcal{I}_A}^{(\ell)}\right), \quad (17)$$

$$\widetilde{\mathbf{E}}_{\mathcal{I}_A} = \widetilde{\mathbf{E}}_{\mathcal{I}_A}^1 \| \widetilde{\mathbf{E}}_{\mathcal{I}_A}^2 \| \ldots \| \widetilde{\mathbf{E}}_{\mathcal{I}_A}^\ell, \quad (18)$$

where ℓ represents the number of neural network layers, $\mathbf{G}_{\mathcal{I}}^A$ is the element-wise gating weight vector for item features, and $\mathbf{W}_1$ and $\mathbf{W}_2$ are weight matrices in the gating mechanism, used to map item features into the gating space.

4.4 Prediction Layer

Based on the final embedding representations of users and items obtained, we utilize cosine similarity to calculate the likelihood $\widetilde{\mathbf{R}}_{ij}$ of user-item interactions within each domain. Taking domain A as an example:

$$\widetilde{\mathbf{R}}_{ij}^A = \frac{(\widetilde{\mathbf{E}}_{\mathcal{U}_A})_i \times (\widetilde{\mathbf{E}}_{\mathcal{I}_A})_j}{\| (\widetilde{\mathbf{E}}_{\mathcal{U}_A})_i \| \, \| (\widetilde{\mathbf{E}}_{\mathcal{I}_A})_j \|} \quad (19)$$

We select binary cross-entropy loss to optimize the model. The formula for calculating the loss function is:

$$\mathcal{L}_A = \sum_{\mathcal{U}_i^A \in \mathcal{U}_A, \mathcal{I}_j^A \in \mathcal{I}_A} \mathbf{R}_{ij}^A \log \widehat{\mathbf{R}}_{ij}^A + (1 - \mathbf{R}_{ij}^A) \log(1 - \widehat{\mathbf{R}}_{ij}^A). \quad (20)$$

Since the objective of our model is to simultaneously enhance the recommendation performance in both domains, the overall loss function is composed of the loss from domain A and the loss from domain B, as follows: $\mathcal{L} = \mathcal{L}_A + \mathcal{L}_B$.

5 Experimental Settings

Datasets. This paper focuses on e-commerce platforms. Therefore, we utilize datasets from real-world e-commerce platform[1], which is widely used in CDR model experiments and contains rich item attributes [1,6,16]. We construct pairwise combinations of the four datasets and identify shared users between each domain pair for CDR scenario. We preprocess the data by treating ratings over 2 as positive samples and considering the rest as negative. We also filter out items with fewer than 5 total interactions.

---

[1] http://jmcauley.ucsd.edu/data/amazon/.

Evaluation Metrics. We employ the Leave-One-Out method [2,7] for evaluation. To assess the model's performance, we select three widely used metrics [2,7], namely Hit Rate (HR), Normalized Discounted Cumulative Gain (NDCG), and Mean Reciprocal Rank (MRR). The prediction ranking cutoff is set to topK = 5, 10.

Parameter Settings. We design key training strategies to improve model effectiveness and stability. The batch size is 100, the learning rate is 0.001, and the number of epochs is 200. The model is a hypergraph convolutional neural network with two layers and an embedding vector size of 128. The inter-domain similarity matrix threshold values are 2 and 4. Additionally, we use the Adam optimizer [12] to train the model and implement an early stopping mechanism to prevent overfitting.

Comparison Methods. We select nine models for comparison with our model, covering both single-domain and cross-domain recommendation approaches:

SDR: LightGCN [8] simplifies recommendation using graph networks. CoHHN [29] incorporates item attributes via hypergraph dual-channel aggregation. BiPNet [28] introduces a dual-preference heterogeneous hypergraph network that captures user price and interest preferences;

CDR: PPGN [30] integrates interaction information from multiple domains into a joint graph and shares user features. DisenCDR [1] enhances CDR performance by disentangling domain features. ETL [2] captures overlapping and domain-specific attributes. II-HGCN [7] uses a hypergraph convolutional network for intra-domain and inter-domain analysis to generate accurate embeddings. Tri-CDR [19] leverages mixed behavioral sequences to capture global contexts, designing a triple cross-domain attention and contrastive learning strategy for enhanced cross-domain knowledge transfer. CrossAug [20] introduces a novel data augmentation method to effectively leverage interactions between domains.

6 Results and Analysis

6.1 RQ1: Performance Comparison

We conduct experiments on four datasets, evaluating model performance based on HR, NDCG and MRR. As shown in Table 1, DHHGCN significantly outperforms all comparative models. Notably, it achieves significant improvements over single-domain models, demonstrating that our inter-domain channel effectively aggregates shared information to enhance recommendations. Compared to various CDR models, DHHGCN also surpasses the strongest baselines in each group. The first set of experiments shows the most significant enhancements in the MRR and NDCG metrics, with increases of up to 20.63% and 18.40%, respectively. In the second set, performance on the clothing dataset shows even greater gains, with some cases exceeding 50%. These results highlight the benefits of our model's intra-domain handling of heterogeneous item information and inter-domain aggregation of shared knowledge, leading to substantial improvements across all metrics.

Table 1. Performance (%) results of two groups, in each group, the best results are marked in bold and the second-best results are underlined.

Beauty & Health												
Domain	Beauty						Health					
topK	topK = 5			topK = 10			topK = 5			topK = 10		
Metrics	HR	NDCG	MRR	HR	NDCG	MRR	HR	NDCG	MRR	HR	NDCG	MRR
Single-Domain Recommendation Methods												
LightGCN	9.68	5.46	4.31	13.74	5.21	5.83	7.96	3.75	4.71	11.18	4.65	5.35
CoHHN	18.36	12.84	11.19	25.23	15.03	11.96	18.49	13.95	12.44	23.22	15.48	13.07
BiPNet	21.56	13.66	11.06	30.11	16.46	12.23	19.30	14.09	12.38	23.70	15.54	12.99
Cross-Domain Recommendation Methods												
DisenCDR	10.43	7.04	5.92	16.06	8.87	6.69	13.06	9.12	7.82	18.84	11.09	8.73
Tri-CDR	22.18	18.77	15.93	37.42	22.02	17.28	20.54	13.73	11.50	27.48	15.97	12.42
CrossAug	22.18	15.70	13.57	31.02	16.61	14.39	23.32	16.61	14.39	30.94	19.06	15.40
PPGN	35.25	20.15	21.88	50.43	24.52	22.66	33.47	19.91	15.49	50.39	27.56	20.31
ETL	35.70	24.92	21.72	48.10	29.64	23.23	36.13	25.20	21.52	49.11	28.78	22.34
II-HGCN	36.82	25.44	21.91	50.98	29.80	23.53	36.70	25.50	21.82	48.91	29.51	23.49
DHHGCN	**41.61**	**30.12**	**26.43**	**53.12**	**33.60**	**27.83**	**40.05**	**28.45**	**23.91**	**51.32**	**32.06**	**26.62**
Improve (%)	13.00	18.40	20.63	4.20	12.75	18.27	9.13	11.57	9.58	1.85	8.64	13.32
Cloth & Sports												
Domain	Cloth						Sports					
topK	topK = 5			topK = 10			topK = 5			topK = 10		
Metrics	HR	NDCG	MRR	HR	NDCG	MRR	HR	NDCG	MRR	HR	NDCG	MRR
Single-Domain Recommendation Methods												
LightGCN	2.80	1.21	1.59	4.06	1.52	1.81	6.28	2.75	3.65	9.57	3.39	3.94
CoHHN	10.25	7.07	6.03	14.00	6.53	8.28	8.12	5.73	5.05	11.19	6.73	5.41
BiPNet	23.67	15.12	12.27	33.67	17.54	13.24	10.38	6.11	4.79	16.38	8.05	5.60
Cross-Domain Recommendation Methods												
DisenCDR	5.29	3.11	2.41	16.31	9.03	2.64	6.64	4.28	3.51	11.12	5.84	4.25
Tri-CDR	5.83	3.56	2.82	9.71	4.78	3.31	9.32	6.06	5.00	14.21	7.64	5.66
CrossAug	5.81	4.28	3.82	8.55	5.81	4.91	19.14	13.63	11.81	26.27	15.93	12.76
PPGN	10.35	3.04	4.71	10.76	5.41	6.72	10.12	4.59	5.94	18.58	6.03	8.91
ETL	24.91	18.00	18.93	35.15	21.19	20.11	29.38	21.47	19.15	39.36	24.71	20.46
II-HGCN	13.12	9.35	8.07	19.09	11.17	8.83	23.47	16.24	13.96	33.98	19.57	15.27
DHHGCN	**40.80**	**31.82**	**29.21**	**48.30**	**34.54**	**30.33**	**34.37**	**24.72**	**22.07**	**43.51**	**27.96**	**23.34**
Improve (%)	63.79	76.77	54.3	37.41	63.00	50.80	16.98	15.14	15.25	10.54	13.15	14.08

6.2 RQ2: Ablation Study

To validate the design components of DHHGCN, we conduct four ablation experiments focusing on intra-domain heterogeneous attribute information and inter-domain information aggregation, as shown in Fig. 3. DHHGCN achieves the best performance across all metrics. Specifically, DHHGCN-s, which retains

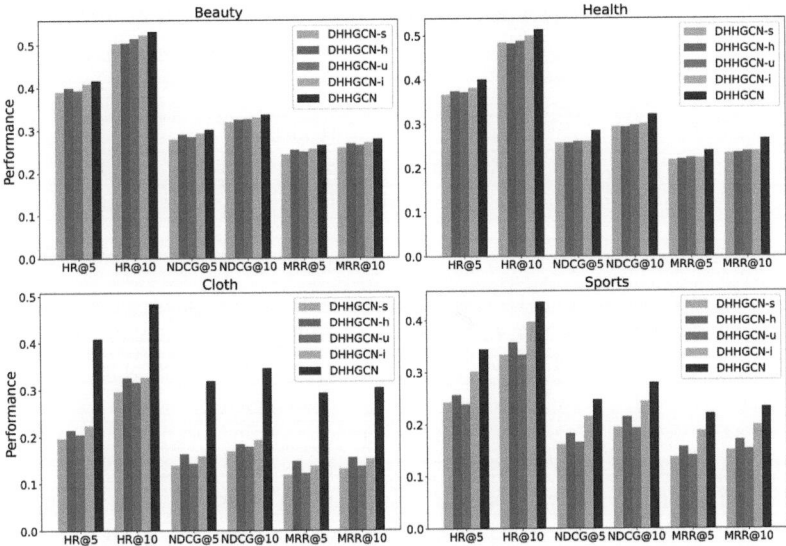

Fig. 3. The presentation of DHHGCN ablation experiments on four datasets, where DHHGCN-s retains only the intra-domain modeling part, DHHGCN-h removes the intra-domain heterogeneous attribute module, DHHGCN-u and DHHGCN-i remove the inter-domain user and item modules, respectively.

only intra-domain modeling, shows significant performance fluctuations due to the lack of inter-domain information aggregation and transfer. However, it still outperforms other models in NDCG and MRR, demonstrating the strength of its intra-domain modeling. DHHGCN-h, which excludes item attribute information, performs notably worse, highlighting the importance of heterogeneous attributes in mitigating data sparsity. DHHGCN-u and DHHGCN-i, which retain only the user or item hypergraph, respectively, also underperform compared to DHHGCN, further supporting the necessity of the inter-domain component. These results collectively validate the rationality of DHHGCN's design.

6.3 RQ3: Experiment on Sparse Datasets

To evaluate DHHGCN's effectiveness in sparse data scenarios, we sparsify the dataset by reducing each user's interaction records by 10%, 30%, 50% and compare it with two top-performing CDR models, ETL and II-HGCN. As shown in Table 2, all models' performance declines as data sparsity increases, which aligns with expectations since fewer interactions limit the model's ability to capture user preferences. However, DHHGCN demonstrates greater robustness, with a smaller performance drop compared to the baselines. Figure 4 further illustrates this: after 50% sparsification, II-HGCN's metrics drop by over 10% on average, while ETL shows reductions ranging from 7.6% to 25.82%. In con-

Table 2. Sparsity data experiment performance(%) of Beauty & Health, the best results are marked in bold and the second-best results are underlined.

Beauty & Health												
Domain	Beauty						Health					
topK	topK = 5			topK = 10			topK = 5			topK = 10		
Metrics	HR	NDCG	MRR	HR	NDCG	MRR	HR	NDCG	MRR	HR	NDCG	MRR
10%												
ETL	35.09	23.94	20.28	<u>36.49</u>	24.12	20.10	46.87	27.77	21.88	47.20	27.88	21.65
II-HGCN	<u>38.47</u>	<u>25.36</u>	<u>21.07</u>	34.93	<u>24.19</u>	<u>20.86</u>	<u>50.25</u>	<u>29.23</u>	<u>22.66</u>	<u>47.40</u>	<u>27.97</u>	<u>22.46</u>
DHHGCN	**40.78**	**29.43**	**25.90**	**37.75**	**26.68**	**23.17**	**50.52**	**32.65**	**27.05**	**49.48**	**30.59**	**24.78**
Improve(%)	6.0	16.05	22.92	3.45	10.29	11.07	0.54	11.7	19.37	4.39	9.37	10.33
30%												
ETL	34.36	<u>23.26</u>	19.62	<u>32.05</u>	22.08	18.27	<u>46.17</u>	<u>27.07</u>	<u>21.11</u>	42.75	25.99	19.89
II-HGCN	<u>34.62</u>	22.48	18.50	31.48	<u>22.38</u>	<u>19.37</u>	45.12	26.83	20.32	<u>43.19</u>	<u>26.60</u>	<u>20.51</u>
DHHGCN	**40.22**	**29.01**	**25.37**	**35.06**	**25.59**	**22.61**	**48.58**	**31.79**	**26.46**	**46.60**	**29.41**	**24.26**
Improve(%)	16.18	24.72	29.31	9.39	14.34	16.73	5.22	17.44	25.34	7.9	10.56	18.28
50%												
ETL	<u>32.42</u>	20.66	16.80	<u>29.37</u>	18.49	14.91	43.20	24.08	18.24	39.67	21.75	16.27
II-HGCN	31.81	<u>21.16</u>	<u>17.69</u>	28.94	<u>19.33</u>	<u>16.45</u>	<u>44.13</u>	<u>25.18</u>	<u>19.37</u>	<u>42.03</u>	<u>23.70</u>	<u>18.26</u>
DHHGCN	**39.55**	**28.39**	**24.71**	**33.13**	**23.35**	**20.36**	**50.06**	**32.11**	**26.25**	**45.93**	**27.72**	**22.17**
Improve(%)	22.0	34.17	39.68	12.22	20.8	23.77	17.58	27.52	35.52	9.28	16.96	21.41

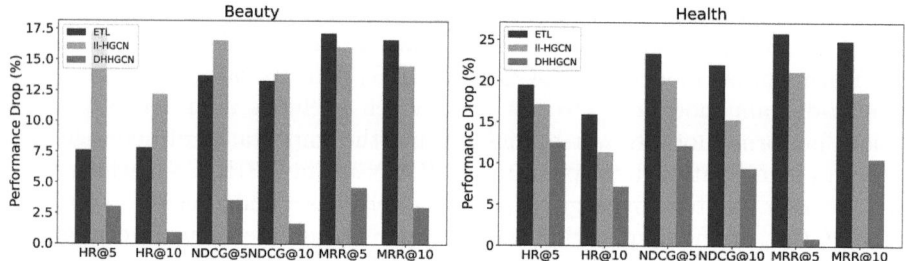

Fig. 4. The reduction ratios of each model on various evaluation metrics after data sparsity processing.

trast, DHHGCN's performance remains stable, with reductions ranging from just 0.91% to 12.23%, highlighting its superior ability to handle sparse data.

6.4 RQ4: Parameter Analysis

We construct inter-domain hypergraphs using a similarity level matrix with thresholds to enhance information propagation. As shown in Fig. 5, all metrics exhibit nonlinear gradients. To reduce noise and improve feature capture for long-tail users and items, we set a threshold t_1 to filter weakly similar nodes. Both

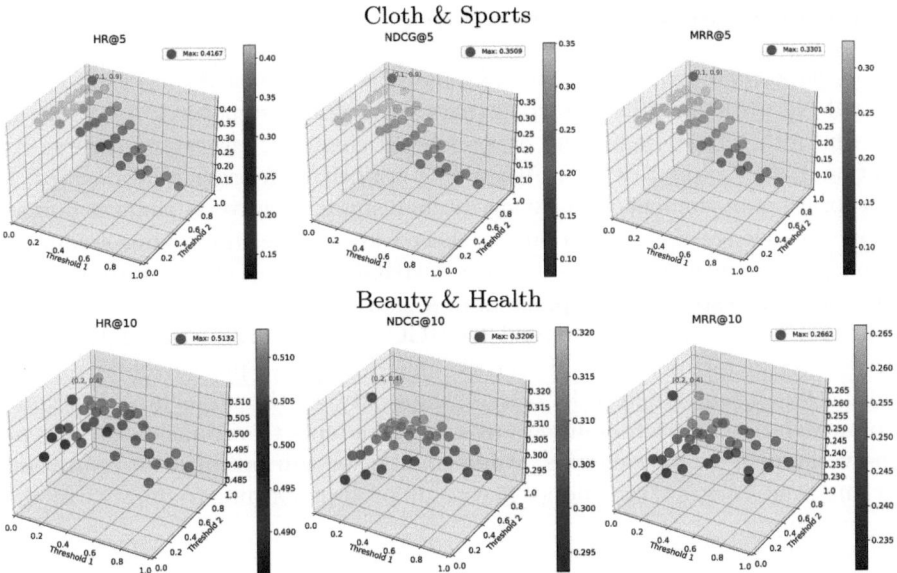

Fig. 5. Results of HR@5/10, NDCG@5/10, MRR@5/10 for Cloth & Sports and Beauty & Health under varying thresholds. The best results are highlighted in red font. (Color figure online)

experimental groups show that optimal performance is often achieved when t_1 is around 0.1 or 0.2. The second threshold, t_2, adjusts similarity-based weighting for node aggregation. When $t_1 = 0.1$, the best performance occurs at $t_2 = 0.9$; for $t_1 = 0.2$, performance improves with $t_2 = 0.4$. A higher threshold prioritizes highly similar nodes, benefiting specific metrics but not overall effectiveness, whereas a lower threshold enhances differentiation and leads to uniform improvements. Based on this, we set $t_1 = 0.2$ and $t_2 = 0.4$ for optimal balance.

6.5 RQ5: Complexity Analysis

In DHHGCN, we identify the inter-type convolution on the heterogeneous hypergraph is the most time-consuming part, with a time complexity of $O((n+k) \times r \times \bar{N}_t)$, where n and k are the number of items in different domains, r is the number of iterations, $\bar{N}_t$ represents the average neighbor counts for each attributes (ID, price and category). Experiments show that DHHGCN achieves higher recommendation accuracy but takes slightly longer to compute than baseline models. Specifically, the best baseline, II-HGCN, averages 20–25 s per epoch, while DHHGCN takes 25–30 s. Although trading computational cost for accuracy is reasonable, we plan to improve efficiency in future work. For example, focusing only on attributes of items more relevant to user preferences may reduce computational overhead and enhance recommendation interpretability.

7 Conclusion and Future Work

In this paper, we propose a Dual-Channel Heterogeneous Hypergraph Convolutional Network for CDR. It constructs hypergraph structures for users and items in both intra-domain and cross-domain channels, leveraging diverse convolutional algorithms to capture their fine-grained high-order relationships. By incorporating an element-wise gating mechanism, it effectively balances domain-specific knowledge and cross-domain shared knowledge, improving recommendation performance. Experiments show DHHGCN outperforms state-of-the-art CDR methods, especially in sparse data scenarios.

In the future, we aim to extend DHHGCN to more recommendation tasks. Its core lies in intra-domain and cross-domain hypergraph convolution, which captures fine-grained high-order relationships between the subjects and targets of recommendation. This domain-agnostic design adapts to various data types and non-overlapping CDR scenarios. Additionally, we will optimize computational efficiency and integrate techniques like graph prompt learning to improve model's interpretability.

References

1. Cao, J., Lin, X., Cong, X., Ya, J., Liu, T., Wang, B.: DisenCDR: learning disentangled representations for cross-domain recommendation. In: Proceedings of the 45th International ACM SIGIR Conference on Research and Development in Information Retrieval (SIGIR 2022), pp. 267–277. Association for Computing Machinery, New York (2022)
2. Chen, X., Zhang, Y., Tsang, I.W., Pan, Y., Su, J.: Toward equivalent transformation of user preferences in cross domain recommendation. ACM Trans. Inf. Syst. (TOIS) **41**(1), 1–31 (2023)
3. Chen, Y., Wang, Y., Ni, Y., Zeng, A.X., Lin, L.: Scenario-aware and mutual-based approach for multi-scenario recommendation in e-commerce. In: Proceedings of the 2020 International Conference on Data Mining Workshops (ICDMW), pp. 127–135 (2020)
4. Feng, Y., You, H., Zhang, Z., Ji, R., Gao, Y.: Hypergraph neural networks. In: Proceedings of the AAAI Conference on Artificial Intelligence, vol. 33, pp. 3558–3565 (2019)
5. Guo, L., Tang, L., Chen, T., Zhu, L., Nguyen, Q.V.H., Yin, H.: DA-GCN: domain-aware attentive graph convolution network for shared-account cross-domain sequential recommendation. arXiv preprint arXiv:2105.03300 (2021)
6. Guo, X., et al.: Disentangled representations learning for multi-target cross-domain recommendation. ACM Trans. Inf. Syst. **41**(4), 85:1–85:27 (2023)
7. Han, Z., Zheng, X., Chen, C., Cheng, W., Yao, Y.: Intra and inter domain hypergraph convolutional network for cross-domain recommendation. In: Proceedings of the ACM Web Conference 2023. WWW 2023, pp. 449–459. Association for Computing Machinery, New York (2023)
8. He, X., Deng, K., Wang, X., Li, Y., Zhang, Y., Wang, M.: LightGCN: simplifying and powering graph convolution network for recommendation. In: Proceedings of the 43rd International ACM SIGIR Conference on Research and Development in Information Retrieval, pp. 639–648. Association for Computing Machinery, New York (2020)

9. Hu, L., Cao, J., Xu, G., Cao, L., Gu, Z., Zhu, C.: Personalized recommendation via cross-domain triadic factorization. In: Proceedings of the 22nd International Conference on World Wide Web, WWW 2013, pp. 595–606. Association for Computing Machinery, New York (2013)
10. Ji, S., Feng, Y., Ji, R., Zhao, X., Tang, W., Gao, Y.: Dual channel hypergraph collaborative filtering. In: Proceedings of the 26th ACM SIGKDD International Conference on Knowledge Discovery and Data Mining, KDD 2020, pp. 2020–2029. Association for Computing Machinery, New York (2020)
11. Cui, Q., Yang, F., Zhang, X., et al.: HeroGRAPH: a heterogeneous graph framework for multi-target cross-domain recommendation. In: ORSUM@RecSys 2020. LNCS, vol. 12645, pp. 45–60. Springer, Cham (2020)
12. Kingma, D.P., Ba, J.: Adam: a method for stochastic optimization. arXiv preprint arXiv:1412.6980 (2017)
13. Li, P., Tuzhilin, A.: DDTCDR: deep dual transfer cross domain recommendation. In: Proceedings of the 13th International Conference on Web Search and Data Mining (WSDM 2020), WSDM 2020, pp. 331–339. Association for Computing Machinery (2020)
14. Lian, J., Zhang, F., Xie, X., Sun, G.: CCCFNet: a content-boosted collaborative filtering neural network for cross domain recommender systems. In: Proceedings of the 26th International Conference on World Wide Web Companion, WWW 2017 Companion, pp. 817–818. International World Wide Web Conferences Steering Committee, Republic and Canton of Geneva, CHE (2017)
15. Liu, J., et al.: Exploiting aesthetic preference in deep cross networks for cross-domain recommendation. In: Proceedings of the Web Conference 2020, WWW 2020, pp. 2768–2774. Association for Computing Machinery, New York (2020)
16. Liu, M., Li, J., Li, G., Pan, P.: Cross domain recommendation via bi-directional transfer graph collaborative filtering networks. In: Proceedings of the 29th ACM International Conference on Information and Knowledge Management, pp. 885–894 (2020)
17. Liu, Y., et al.: End-to-end learnable clustering for intent learning in recommendation. In: Proceedings of NeurIPS (2024)
18. Liu, Y., Zhu, S., Yang, T., Ma, J., Zhong, W.: Identify then recommend: towards unsupervised group recommendation. In: Proceedings of NeurIPS (2024)
19. Ma, H., et al.: Triple sequence learning for cross-domain recommendation. ACM Trans. Inf. Syst. (ACM Trans. Inf. Syst.) **42**(4), 91:1–91:29 (2024)
20. Mao, Q., Liu, Q., Li, Z., Wu, L., Lv, B., Zhang, Z.: Cross-reconstructed augmentation for dual-target cross-domain recommendation. In: Proceedings of the 47th International ACM SIGIR Conference on Research and Development in Information Retrieval, SIGIR 2024, pp. 2352–2356. ACM, New York (2024)
21. Sun, X., et al.: Self-supervised hypergraph representation learning for sociological analysis. IEEE Trans. Knowl. Data Eng. **35**(11), 11860–11871 (2023)
22. Sun, X., et al.: Heterogeneous hypergraph embedding for graph classification. In: Proceedings of the 14th ACM International Conference on Web Search and Data Mining, pp. 725–733 (2021)
23. Wang, Y., Feng, C., Guo, C., Chu, Y., Hwang, J.N.: Solving the sparsity problem in recommendations via cross-domain item embedding based on co-clustering. In: Proceedings of the 12th ACM International Conference on Web Search and Data Mining (WSDM 2019), pp. 717–725. ACM, New York (2019)
24. Xie, Y., Yu, C., Jin, X., et al.: Heterogeneous graph contrastive learning for cold start cross-domain recommendation. Knowl.-Based Syst. **299**, 112054 (2024)

25. Yadati, N., Nimishakavi, M., Yadav, P., Nitin, V., Louis, A., Talukdar, P.: Hyper-GCN: a new method for training graph convolutional networks on hypergraphs. Adv. Neural. Inf. Process. Syst. **32**, 482–493 (2019)
26. Yu, J., Yin, H., Li, J., Wang, Q., Hung, N.Q.V., Zhang, X.: Self-supervised multi-channel hypergraph convolutional network for social recommendation. In: Proceedings of the Web Conference 2021 (WWW 2021), pp. 413–424. Association for Computing Machinery, New York (2021)
27. Zang, T., Zhu, Y., Liu, H., Zhang, R., Yu, J.: A survey on cross-domain recommendation: taxonomies, methods, and future directions. ACM Trans. Inf. Syst. **41**(2), 42:1–42:44 (2022)
28. Zhang, X., Xu, B., Ma, F., Li, C., Lin, Y., Lin, H.: Bi-preference learning heterogeneous hypergraph networks for session-based recommendation. ACM Trans. Inf. Syst. (ACM TOIS) **42**(3), 1–28 (2023)
29. Zhang, X., et al.: Price does matter! Modeling price and interest preferences in session-based recommendation. In: Proceedings of the 45th International ACM SIGIR Conference on Research and Development in Information Retrieval (SIGIR 2022), pp. 1684–1693. ACM, New York (2022)
30. Zhao, C., Li, C., Fu, C.: Cross-domain recommendation via preference propagation graphnet. In: Proceedings of the 28th ACM International Conference on Information and Knowledge Management, pp. 2165–2168 (2019)
31. Zheng, Y., Gao, C., He, X., Li, Y., Jin, D.: Price-aware recommendation with graph convolutional networks. In: 2020 IEEE 36th International Conference on Data Engineering (ICDE), pp. 133–144 (2020)
32. Zhou, D., Huang, J., Schölkopf, B.: Learning with hypergraphs: clustering, classification, and embedding. Adv. Neural Inf. Process. Syst. **19** (2006)
33. Zhu, F., Chen, C., Wang, Y., Liu, G., Zheng, X.: DTCDR: a framework for dual-target cross-domain recommendation. In: Proceedings of the 28th ACM International Conference on Information and Knowledge Management (CIKM 2019), Beijing, China, pp. 1533–1542 (2019)
34. Song, Z., et al.: Mitigating negative transfer in cross-domain recommendation via knowledge transferability enhancement. In: Proceedings of the 30th ACM SIGKDD Conference on Knowledge Discovery and Data Mining, pp. 2745–2754. ACM (2024)
35. Zhu, F., Wang, Y., Chen, C., Zhou, J., Li, L., Liu, G.: Cross-domain recommendation: challenges, progress, and prospects. In: arXiv preprint arXiv:2103.01696. arXiv, Cornell University Library (2021)

Author Index

A
Andrey, Paul 203
Aseervatham, Sujeevan 221

B
Bennani, Younès 221
Berthier, Eloïse 164
Bortolussi, Luca 3
Bourrée, Jade Garcia 259
Brás, Susana 59

C
Cai, Weishan 468
Candussio, Sara 3
Caradot, Antoine 19
Carey, Alycia N. 240
Carvalho, Miguel 59
Chakraborty, Souradip 96
Chen, Wenlong 519
Cheng, Xinwen 432
Chowdhury, Sayak Ray 96
Ciaperoni, Martino 78
Corcoran, Peter 345
Curtin, Ryan R. 147

D
Das, Nirjhar 96
Ding, Jiaxin 380
Ding, Meng 363
Ding, Xin 380

E
Emonet, Rémi 19

F
Ferraro, Francis 147
Fu, Luoyi 380
Fujiwara, Yasuhiro 113

G
Gambs, Sébastien 259
Gao, Xiaofeng 451
Gionis, Aristides 78
Guo, Yuchen 519
Gupta, Sunil 183

H
Habrard, Amaury 19
Han, Haochen 380
He, Jie 519
Holt, James 147
Hossain, Prommy Sultana 276
Huang, Shudong 451
Huang, Xiaolin 432

I
Ida, Yasutoshi 113
Iwata, Tomoharu 113

J
Jiang, Yuncheng 468
Jin, Jipeng 451
Jing, Bingyi 502

K
Kanai, Sekitoshi 113
Kang, Yu 451
Karjalainen, Maiju 129
Kaya, Kamer 397
Kerzazi, Achraf 221
King, Michael 276
Koda, Satoru 295
Kumagai, Atsutoshi 113

L
Lautraite, Hadrien 259
Le Bars, Batiste 203
Le Merrer, Erwan 259
Le, Dung D. 183

Li, Ang 485
Li, Huiting 468
Li, Shijian 485
Li, Xiang-Yang 328
Li, Ziang 313
Lin, Jessica 276
Lin, Zhangang 519
Liu, Yaxin 313
Liu, Yibin 485
Lu, Fred 147

M
Ma, Wenjun 468
Mannila, Heikki 78
Marasco, Emanuela 276
Mauduit, Eliabelle 164
McKeever, Susan 345
Medina Grespan, Mattia 38
Mezidi, Abdel-Rahim 19
Miettinen, Pauli 129
Morikawa, Ikuya 295

N
Nguyen, Quoc-Anh Hoang 183
Nken, Allassan Tchangmena A. 345

P
Pacchiano, Aldo 96
Pan, Junwei 451
Peng, Changping 519
Pinho, Armando 59

R
Raff, Edward 147
Rottembourg, Benoît 259

S
Sang, Liufang 519
Sarti, Gabriele 3
Savaş, Erkay 397
Saveri, Gaia 3
Sebban, Marc 19
Shao, Jingping 519
Shi, Kexin 502
Simonetto, Andrea 164

Srikumar, Vivek 38
Sun, Haifeng 328

T
Tao, Touming 363
Tian, Xizhi 363
Ting, Kai Ming 415
Tommasi, Marc 203
Tran, Hung The 183
Tredan, Gilles 259

U
Ullah, Ihsan 345

W
Wang, Di 363
Wang, Haoqian 519
Wang, Haoran 519
Wang, Juan 313
Wang, Wei 519
Wang, Wenjia 502
Wang, Xinbin 380
Wu, Xintao 240
Wu, Yingwen 432

X
Xiang, Zihang 363
Xiao, Lei 451
Xie, Yule 380
Xu, Xiaoyang 313
Xue, Pengyu 380

Y
Yang, Mengda 313
Yang, Ruikai 432
Yang, Zhe 536
Yi, Wenzhe 313
Yıldırım, Ceren 397
Yıldırım, Sinan 397

Z
Zhang, Baosheng 519
Zhang, Hang 415
Zhang, Lan 328
Zhang, Moyu 536
Zhou, Wenxing 432
Zhuang, Yong 313

MIX
Papier aus verantwortungsvollen Quellen
Paper from responsible sources
FSC® C105338

If you have any concerns about our products,
you can contact us on
ProductSafety@springernature.com

In case Publisher is established outside the EU,
the EU authorized representative is:
**Springer Nature Customer Service Center GmbH
Europaplatz 3, 69115 Heidelberg, Germany**

Printed by Libri Plureos GmbH
in Hamburg, Germany